D1399099

# BASC™3

## Behavior Assessment System for Children
Third Edition
**MANUAL**

Cecil R. Reynolds, PhD
Randy W. Kamphaus, PhD

# About the Authors

**Cecil R. Reynolds, PhD,** is emeritus professor of educational psychology, professor of neuroscience, and Distinguished Research Scholar at Texas A&M University. Well known for his work in psychological testing and assessment and in neuropsychology, he is author or editor of more than 50 books, including *The Handbook of School Psychology,* the *Encyclopedia of Special Education,* and the two-volume *Handbook of Psychological and Educational Assessment of Children.* He also authored or coauthored more than 30 tests, including the BASC–3 Parenting Relationship Questionnaire (BASC–3 PRQ), BASC–3 Behavioral and Emotional Screening System (BASC–3 BESS), the Revised Children's Manifest Anxiety Scale: Second Edition (RCMAS-2), and the Reynolds Intellectual Assessment Scales–Second Edition (RIAS–2), and has published more than 300 scholarly works.

Dr. Reynolds has received a number of national awards for his work, including the Lightner Witmer Award from the American Psychological Association (APA) and Early Career Awards from two APA divisions (15, Educational Psychology; and 5, Measurement and Statistics). He is a recipient of the APA Division 16 Senior Scientist Award, the APA Division of Clinical Psychology Distinguished Assessment Psychologist Award, the APA Division 5 Messick Award for Lifetime Distinguished Contributions to Measurement Science, the National Academy of Neuropsychology's Distinguished Clinical Neuropsychologist Award, and several other national awards for his research on testing and assessment. Dr. Reynolds is the current editor-in-chief of two APA journals, *Psychological Assessment* and *Archives of Scientific Psychology;* former editor-in-chief of *Archives of Clinical Neuropsychology* and of *Applied Neuropsychology;* and has served as associate editor of the *Journal of School Psychology.* Active in professional affairs, he has served as president of the National Academy of Neuropsychology, a member of APA's Committee on Psychological Testing and Assessment, president of three APA divisions (5, 16, and 40), and on the executive committee of the National Association of School Psychologists. He is currently president of the American Academy of Pediatric Neuropsychology. Dr. Reynolds now practices forensic neuroscience in Austin, TX.

**Randy W. Kamphaus, PhD,** is professor and dean of the College of Education at the University of Oregon. He has received the Senior Scientist Award from the Division of School Psychology of the American Psychological Association (APA) and the Russell H. Yeany Jr. Research and Alumni Lifetime Achievement Awards from the College of Education at the University of Georgia, where he has twice received college-wide teaching awards. Dr. Kamphaus is best known for his research in classification methods, differential diagnosis, test development, and learning disability and attention-deficit/ hyperactivity disorder (ADHD) assessment. Dr. Kamphaus, coauthor of the BASC–3 Parenting Relationship Questionnaire (BASC–3 PRQ) and BASC–3 Behavioral and Emotional Screening System (BASC–3 BESS), has served as principal investigator, co-investigator, and consultant on Institute of Education Sciences and other agency-funded research projects dealing with mental health screening, early intervention and prevention, child classification methods, prevalence of ADHD and conduct disorder in Latin America, and aggression reduction in schools. Dr. Kamphaus has authored or coauthored numerous books, psychological and educational tests, scientific journal articles, test reviews, and book chapters on these topics. As a licensed psychologist and a fellow of the APA, he has contributed extensively to his profession, having served as president of APA's Division of School Psychology and as a member of the APA Council of Representatives. He also participates in scholarship in the field through service as past-editor of *School Psychology Quarterly* and ad hoc reviewer for several other scientific journals.

Individuals using the Behavior Assessment System for Children, Third Edition (BASC–3) interpret its various components and use them in the evaluation, diagnosis, and treatment of developmental, learning, and behavioral disorders. Users are expected to have completed a recognized graduate training program in psychology; received formal academic training in the administration, scoring, and interpretation of behavior rating scales and personality scales; and received supervised experience with such instruments. Most clinical, school, pediatric, counseling, neuro-, and applied developmental psychologists have received such training. Administration and scoring of the various BASC–3 components may, with appropriate training and supervision, be completed by clerical staff. Individuals who use the BASC–3 with specialized populations (e.g., sensory impaired or recent immigrants from nonwestern cultures) are expected to have specialized training and experience in the use of such assessment devices and intervention materials with these populations.

Because of the wide variability across jurisdictions in certification requirements and the use of professional titles, it is not possible to determine solely by title, licensure, or certification who is qualified to use the BASC–3. Consistent with the principles presented in the *Standards for Educational and Psychological Testing* (American Educational Research Association [AERA], American Psychological Association [APA], & National Council on Measurement in Education [NCME], 2014), each individual practitioner must decide whether his or her formal academic training and supervised experience provide the necessary background and knowledge to use and interpret the BASC–3 appropriately. A variety of other professionally trained or certified staff (e.g., psychometrists, educational diagnosticians, clinical social workers, psychiatrists, pediatricians) might have received the necessary formal academic training and supervised experience to use instruments like the BASC–3.

# Preface

When we conceptualized the Behavior Assessment System for Children (BASC) in 1985, the need for services for children with emotional and behavioral difficulties had skyrocketed, and the tools for assessing children's emotions and behavior were less numerous and less developed technically than now. There was a need for an integrated assessment of child and adolescent personality, history, and behavior at home and at school. This need for a diverse choice of instrumentation, and the technological challenge its creation would pose, led us to develop the original BASC. We felt strongly that appropriate diagnostic tools should be made available. As practicing psychologists and trainers of psychologists, we knew firsthand of the need for personality construct and behavior measures that aspired to meet high psychometric standards.

We were also keenly aware of clinicians' diverse needs in such settings as the school, clinic, or hospital. We believed that most instruments were tailored to particular settings or informants and were inappropriate for others. Consequently, we set out to design a system that was coordinated but not redundant.

Following a period of initial resistance (change in clinical and educational settings being at times quite slow), we were surprised at the growth in use and adoption of the BASC throughout the United States. We were also gratified that our efforts had been rewarded and that so many agreed with us that an integrated system such as the BASC had the potential to help a range of clinicians improve children's lives.

The BASC was published in 1992 after approximately seven years of development, standardization, and validation. By the late 1990s, it had become the dominant set of behavior rating scales in the public schools. Within its first decade, more than 125 independent research articles and dissertations were completed using the BASC. By the time of the BASC–2 release in 2004, it was being used annually in the evaluation of more than one million children and adolescents in the United States alone, and its popularity had expanded to include Latin America. The BASC–2 family of products became even more widely accepted, making the BASC–2 one of the most widely-used scales of its type in the English-speaking world, with expansion into many other countries and cultures as well. Given all of the success of the BASC editions and the positive commentary received from our colleagues, students, and clinicians worldwide, we approached a BASC–2 revision with both excitement and trepidation—as with the original BASC. Even though the BASC and BASC–2 instruments were successful, we still felt there was room for improvement, especially in computing and software design. We also believed the original BASC model and our approach to behavior evaluation—which involved a triangulation of behavior ratings and observation, self-report of behavior, emotion, and affect, and history or clinical context—remained valid. As our guide in revision, we adopted the old, oft-ignored adage, "If it ain't broke, don't fix it." With this in mind, and in partnership with Pearson Clinical Assessment and thousands of BASC–2 users who provided feedback over the years, we set out to improve and expand the BASC–2 family of instruments.

While the core elements of the BASC–3 retain those of the original BASC and the improvements implemented in the BASC–2, we have added the Flex Monitor to the cadres of BASC products, enhanced user options for digital administration and scoring, improved the interpretive reporting to add support to actuarial models of diagnosis, and enhanced our links to evidence-based interventions. With Dr. Kimberly Vannest in the lead, we have revised the BASC–3 Behavior Intervention Guide to make it even more practical for clinical and school use and also integrated it more fully into aspects of the interpretive reporting systems. All of the BASC–3 components are tailored to setting and informant and have relevance to diagnosis, evaluation, and/or treatment. The Self-Report of Personality (SRP) items are statements of children's and adolescents' own feelings, attitudes, and beliefs, rather than reworded items from a behavior-problem checklist filled out by parents or teachers. Similarly, the Teacher Rating Scales (TRS) is specifically designed for teachers and includes scales (such as Study Skills) that are uniquely relevant to the school setting. The Parent Rating Scales (PRS) likewise provides items designed specifically for parents and addresses behavior about which parents have special knowledge. The Student Observation System (SOS) defines behaviors commonly seen in structured educational and daycare settings, providing traditional tallies of behavior occurrences. While the BASC–3 SOS remains available as a paper-and-pencil form, there is a digital version available through Q-global. The Structured Developmental History (SDH) provides history of and context for the child's behavior and is designed for completion by a knowledgeable caregiver in either a questionnaire or interview format. The SDH now has a digital format that allows the integration of much of this information into the automated reporting system.

The BASC–3 is sensitive to both obvious and subtle behavioral and emotional disorders as expressed in school and clinical settings, and to academic and familial demands on child and adolescent development. We believe it provides a sophisticated approach to the evaluation of behavioral and emotional disorders among children and adolescents. We await your comments about BASC–3 and believe it is indeed an improvement of the previous editions that continues to support objective, accurate diagnosis and linkages to effective interventions.

# Acknowledgments

Many individuals contributed to both the original BASC and BASC–2 efforts. Without their enthusiastic involvement and assistance, the BASC and BASC–2 would have remained ideas. More than anyone else, our students made the most substantial contributions at critical points in the original BASC test development process. Early in the original BASC project, Joan Kappus proved particularly helpful in reviewing literature and test items. Elaine Fletcher-Janzen asked excellent questions and freely discussed the conceptualization of the BASC and later stimulated our thinking about changes for BASC–2. Drs. Mary Peery, Rebecca LeBlanc, Gloria Maccow, and Ron Palomares, all of whom completed dissertations at Texas A&M University using BASC data, were instrumental in helping us conceptualize the BASC–2.

At the University of Georgia and elsewhere, the BASC has been used in numerous dissertation studies, the results of which have clarified our thinking about the BASC, child psychopathology, and socioemotional development. We are grateful to all researchers who helped us advance our thinking.

Dr. Gail Matazow and Dr. Allison Hynd's numerous contributions to the original BASC project are greatly appreciated. They contributed tireless effort and keen insight throughout development.

The authors owe a very special debt to Dr. Harrison C. Stanton. Initially, as a research assistant at Texas A&M University on the BASC project, and later as a colleague and lead author of the original BASC Plus interpretive software, Harrison made monumental contributions to the first BASC effort. At every stage of development, from initial item-writing through the preparation of the final manuals, Harrison's contributions were untiring and insightful. His thoughts and insights remain evident in our thinking about revisions to the BASC model and the content of the BASC–2 and BASC–3.

We especially find invaluable the hard work, dedication, and technical and conceptual contributions of Rob Altmann, the Pearson Clinical Assessment BASC–2 and BASC–3 project director. Rob put forth a Herculean effort in organizing and carrying out both BASC revisions, without which completion of the BASC–3 would have been years in the future. We are certain that his leadership and hard work have made the BASC–3 a better set of instruments.

Dr. Kimberly Vannest's contributions to the links to intervention in all things BASC–3 and her leadership in the development of the BASC–3 Behavior Intervention Guide and its various components was invaluable and continues to influence our thinking as well. We also would like to acknowledge Dr. Mauricio Garcia-Barrera's work on the executive functioning indexes that are available for the TRS and PRS; we firmly believe these new indexes will prove invaluable to BASC–3 users.

We also are grateful for the assistance of the numerous staff members at Pearson Clinical Assessment. A project of this size requires the coordination and teamwork of many people across a variety of areas. We thank all of those members from the Content Development, Design, Editorial, Field Research, Procurement, Psychometric, and Software Development departments. Thank you for all of your work on this project. We hope that you share our pride in the BASC–3 family of products and know that each of you played an important role in making it second to none.

To our common mentor, Dr. Alan S. Kaufman, we owe far too many debts to acknowledge. He continues to inspire and to be an exemplary model of applied scholarship and teaching to which we both aspire. At the same time, his friendship and continued collegiality and mentorship continue to foster our personal and intellectual growth.

We also owe a debt of thanks to the many BASC and BASC–2 users who have attended our workshops over the years and to our students, all of whom have shared their insights, criticisms, and kudos concerning these instruments. From this pooled wisdom we drew many of our ideas for improving and expanding each subsequent BASC edition. We hope you will all continue to converse with us as we collectively seek to improve how we diagnose, evaluate, and treat disorders of development, learning, and behavior.

CRR owes his greatest debt, however, to Dr. Julia Hickman, not only for her work on the original BASC, but also for her loving, nurturing companionship and emotional support. Her faith in him and his efforts is simply indispensable and is too seldom acknowledged. He would also like to acknowledge his appreciation and admiration for his colleague and coauthor, Dr. Randy Kamphaus, on this and numerous other projects. Test development in particular is a team effort, and a better colleague and team member is difficult to imagine.

RWK acknowledges the sacrifices and hard work of his parents, Richard and Nancy Kamphaus, who instilled in him the work ethic and high aspirations necessary to achieve his career and personal objectives. He also acknowledges the good fortune of having married well to Norma Lea Ehrhardt, his wife of more than 30 years. Most recently, he is indebted to his children Ashley and Natalie, two of the most genial, wise, and principled individuals whom he has ever known.

Cecil R. Reynolds

Randy W. Kamphaus

# Table of Contents

## Chapter 3: Using and Interpreting the Structured Developmental History

## Chapter 4: Using and Interpreting the Student Observation System

## Chapter 5: Interpreting the Teacher and Parent Rating Scales: The Primary Scales and Validity Indicators

# Chapter 8: Standardization and Norms Development . . . . . . . . . . . . . . . . . . . . . . . 105

# Chapter 9: Teacher Rating Scales: Reliability and Validity . . . . . . . . . . . . . . . . . . . 117

# Chapter 10: Parent Rating Scales: Reliability and Validity . . . . . . . . . . . . . . . . . . . 169

## Figures

## Tables

The Behavior Assessment System for Children, Third Edition (BASC™–3) is a multimethod, multidimensional system used to evaluate the behavior and self-perceptions of children and young adults ages 2 through 25 years. The BASC–3 system includes the following components:

- Behavioral and Emotional Screening System (BESS)

- Teacher Rating Scales (TRS)

- Parent Rating Scales (PRS)

- Self-Report of Personality (SRP)

- Structured Developmental History (SDH)

- Student Observation System (SOS)

- Behavior Intervention Guide

- Behavioral and Emotional Skill Building Guide - part of the BASC–3 family of products

- Flex Monitor

- Parenting Relationship Questionnaire (PRQ™)

Typically, emotional and behavioral difficulties have various facets. Consequently, these difficulties need to be assessed from a number of different viewpoints. Clinicians tend to obtain such views in a fairly ad hoc manner, using a variety of measures, observations, or other data that may prove difficult to integrate into a total picture. This is why the integrated assessment approach of the BASC–3 components is so desirable. Together, the BASC–3 components offer a comprehensive system for identifying, evaluating, monitoring, and remediating behavioral and emotional problems in children and adolescents. Each component can be used individually or in whatever combination is best suited to the situation at hand.

This manual provides an in-depth discussion about the TRS, PRS, SRP, SDH, and SOS, including information about their administration, interpretation, development, and technical properties. Other BASC–3 components (listed above) include their own manuals. This chapter presents a brief description of all of the BASC–3 components, as well as a summary of the features and uses of the TRS, PRS, SRP, SDH, and SOS.

## Description of the BASC–3 Components

The BASC–3 components are used by a variety of educational and clinical professionals who work with children, adolescents, and young adults who are either experiencing or at the risk of experiencing behavioral and/or emotional problems. While not all professionals have the required qualifications to use all of the components, the information obtained across professionals can be easily integrated to inform the evaluation, intervention/treatment planning, or diagnostic process. A description of each component is provided below.

## BASC–3 BEHAVIORAL AND EMOTIONAL SCREENING SYSTEM

The BASC–3 Behavioral and Emotional Screening System (BESS) is a brief screening tool designed to identify behavioral and emotional strengths and weaknesses in children and adolescents in preschool through high school. It includes Teacher, Parent, and Student Forms that are short (20, 29, and 28 items, respectively) and easy to complete, usually within 5 minutes or less for the Teacher and Parent Forms, and 5 to 15 minutes for the Student Form. Spanish forms are available for the Parent and Student Forms; both English and Spanish forms can be completed digitally or on paper. On each form, a Behavioral and Emotional Risk Index provides an overall indication for risk of having or developing a behavioral or emotional problem; additional scores are also provided that are used to identify specific risk for more specific problem areas.

## BASC–3 TEACHER RATING SCALES

The BASC–3 Teacher Rating Scales (TRS) is a comprehensive measure of both adaptive and problem behaviors in the school setting. It is designed for use by teachers or others who fill a similar role, such as teacher assistants or preschool caregivers. The TRS has three forms, with items targeted at three age levels: preschool (ages 2 through 5), child (ages 6 through 11), and adolescent (ages 12 through 21). The forms contain descriptors of behaviors that the respondent rates on a four-point scale of frequency, ranging from *Never* to *Almost always*. The TRS takes 10 to 15 minutes to complete for teachers with experience completing rating scales.

## BASC–3 PARENT RATING SCALES

The BASC–3 Parent Rating Scales (PRS), available in English or Spanish, is a comprehensive measure of a child's adaptive and problem behaviors in community and home settings. The PRS uses the same four-choice response format as the TRS and takes 10 to 20 minutes to complete. Like the TRS, the PRS has three age-level forms: preschool, child, and adolescent.

## BASC–3 SELF-REPORT OF PERSONALITY

The BASC–3 Self-Report of Personality (SRP), available in English and Spanish, is an omnibus personality inventory consisting of statements that respondents answer in one of two ways. Some of the items (presented first on the record form) require a *True* or *False* response, while others use the four-point scale of frequency, ranging from *Never* to *Almost always*. The SRP takes 20 to 30 minutes to complete. It has three age-level forms: child (ages 8 through 11), adolescent (ages 12 through 21), and young adults attending a postsecondary school (ages 18 through 25).

A fourth level of the SRP is the interview version (SRP–I), designed for children ages 6 through 7 years. The SRP–I contains a series of 14 questions asked by an interviewer, who then records the child's *Yes* or *No* responses, along with responses given to follow-up questions that are asked when a child provides an item response that indicates a possible behavioral or emotional problem.

## BASC–3 STRUCTURED DEVELOPMENTAL HISTORY

The BASC–3 Structured Developmental History (SDH) provides a thorough review of social, psychological, developmental, educational, and medical information about a child that may influence diagnosis and treatment decisions. It is designed to be useful in numerous settings, including clinics, schools, and hospitals. The SDH is used either as a structured interview with a parent (or someone who fills a similar role) or as a questionnaire that can be filled out in a clinician's office, school, or at home. The SDH is available as an electronic/digital form and a paper form, in both English and Spanish. When used in conjunction with the BASC–3 PRS, the digitally administered version of the SDH can deliver supplemental items based on PRS scale scores that provide additional information for making accurate classification or diagnostic decisions.

## BASC–3 STUDENT OBSERVATION SYSTEM

The BASC–3 Student Observation System (SOS) is a 15-minute observation procedure designed to enable the clinician to record and evaluate a student's behavior in a classroom environment. The SOS is available digitally using a smartphone, tablet, or laptop computer, and is also available on paper.

## BASC–3 BEHAVIOR INTERVENTION GUIDE

The BASC–3 Behavior Intervention Guide provides a collection of evidence-based interventions designed to help remediate emotional and behavioral problems experienced by children and adolescents from preschool through high school. The comprehensive how-to content is organized around some of the most common problem behaviors seen by teachers and parents and reported by children themselves. It is designed for use by psychologists and other professionals who help children and adolescents experiencing behavioral and emotional problems. In addition, Parent Tip Sheets are available for a number of behavioral and emotional problems. These tip sheets enable parents to work more effectively with behavioral professionals to become an active part of their child's success by providing information to help them learn more about their child's problem. The Parent Tip Sheets also offer several different strategies to be used at home to help address the identified problem or concern.

## BEHAVIORAL AND EMOTIONAL SKILL BUILDING GUIDE - PART OF THE BASC–3 FAMILY OF PRODUCTS

The Behavioral and Emotional Skill Building Guide - part of the BASC–3 family of products provides activities and small-group or classroom-based lessons that promote and develop a number of core behavioral and emotional skills, such as communicating, problem solving, listening effectively, and relaxation strategies. This guide is used by teachers, behavior coaches, counselors, social workers, or others who work in a school or similar setting. When used in conjunction with the BASC–3 BESS, this guide can also be used by school administrators to enhance the skills of the student community and promote behaviors that lead to school-wide success.

## BASC–3 FLEX MONITOR

The BASC–3 Flex Monitor is used to monitor and track the effect of a behavioral intervention implemented by a psychologist or other professional in a school or clinical environment. An Internet-based tool, the BASC–3 Flex Monitor provides a bank of behaviorally or emotionally based items that can be selected to create a customized monitoring form that enables score comparisons to a nationally representative population sample. While creating forms, users can calculate reliability estimates based on a normative sample. In addition, existing forms can simply be selected and used to measure behavioral performance across a variety of common behavioral areas (e.g., hyperactivity, attention). Behavioral performance is measured and displayed over a period of time, thereby helping to establish the effectiveness of an intervention strategy.

## BASC–3 PARENTING RELATIONSHIP QUESTIONNAIRE

The BASC–3 Parenting Relationship Questionnaire (PRQ) is designed to capture a parent's perspective of the parent–child relationship (or the perspective of a person serving a similar role). It assesses traditional parent–child dimensions such as attachment and involvement and also provides information on parenting style, parenting confidence, stress, and satisfaction with the child's school. The BASC–3 PRQ is used in clinical, pediatric, counseling, school, and other settings where there is a need to understand the nature of the parent–child relationship. It is particularly important when implementing home-based intervention strategies and/or treatment monitoring. The BASC–3 PRQ can be completed in approximately 15 minutes and is available in English and Spanish. It should be administered to mothers and fathers (or caregivers) of children ages 2 through 18 years.

# Features of the TRS, PRS, SRP, SDH, and SOS

The BASC and BASC–2 TRS, PRS, SRP, SDH, and SOS (Reynolds & Kamphaus, 1992, 2004) have become well-established tools used in school and clinical settings for assessing behavioral and emotional problems in children and adolescents. Used individually, the BASC–3 components provide a view of behavior in a particular setting and/or from a particular view or context. Used together, they provide a comprehensive picture of behavioral and emotional functioning that informs clinical diagnosis (e.g., using the *Diagnostic and Statistical Manual of Mental Disorders,* 5th ed. [*DSM-5*™; American Psychiatric Association (APA), 2013]) or the need for additional educational supports and services (e.g., those addressed by the Individuals with Disabilities Education Act [IDEA, 2004]). These BASC–3 components offer several features that maximize their utility and efficiency in use, including:

- Comprehensiveness of behavioral and emotional domains: The TRS, PRS, and SRP assess a wide variety of dimensions that are supported both theoretically and empirically, and that are easily interpretable. Often, this reduces the need to use more specialized or narrow-band instruments, helping to make evaluations more efficient and minimizing their costs.

- Identification of behavioral and emotional strengths and deficiencies: The BASC–3 components continue their tradition of measuring both maladaptive and adaptive behavior, allowing clinicians to better understand existing strengths to leverage when developing individualized intervention or treatment plans.

- Developmental sensitivity: The BASC–3 TRS, PRS, and SRP cover the full age range of students from preschool through high school while maintaining differences in behaviors that occur across age levels consistent with the manifestation of behavioral problems through childhood and adolescence. In addition, a college version of the SRP is available for use in technical schools, colleges, and universities to identify behavioral and emotional problems that can interfere with academic performance.

- Multiple sources of information: Gathering multiple perspectives that describe behavior in a variety of general and specific settings serves to provide a comprehensive view of behavioral and emotional functioning critical for the proper identification and remediation of problems.

- Strong scientific rigor: The BASC–3 TRS, PRS, and SRP were developed using a balanced approach of theory and statistics that resulted in tools with strong psychometric properties and clinical utility. There are also hundreds of research studies of these instruments available. In addition, norms were developed on large, demographically representative samples that enhance the interpretability of scores.

- Multiple languages: The BASC–3 PRS, SRP, and SDH are available in the United States in both English and Spanish. As the BASC–3 is adapted for use in other countries, additional languages will be offered.

- Ease of administration and scoring: The BASC–3 components are offered primarily through Q-global™, a secure Internet-based administration, scoring, and reporting platform. Paper administration and hand scoring are also available.

- Detection of threats to response validity: The BASC–3 TRS, PRS, and SRP offer a number of scales that help to detect threats to the validity of the obtained responses, such as dissimulation, inattentiveness, positive or negative response sets, or a lack of understanding of the items.

# Detailed Descriptions of the TRS, PRS, SRP, SDH, and SOS

## TEACHER RATING SCALES AND PARENT RATING SCALES

Rating scales are particularly well suited to the recording of specific and observable behaviors. Teachers and parents usually observe children in different social and activity settings. The TRS and PRS assess both broad- and narrow-based behavioral and emotional domains across these settings, as well as both maladaptive and adaptive behavior. Three levels are provided for each: preschool (ages 2 through 5), child (ages 6 through 11), and adolescent (ages 12 through 21). Table 1.1 shows the composites, scales, and indexes for all TRS and PRS levels. The slight differences between levels are due to developmental changes in the behavioral manifestations of children's potential problems. Nevertheless, scales and composites with the same name contain similar content at all age levels.

In addition to scale and composite scores, the TRS and PRS provide a broad composite, the Behavioral Symptoms Index (BSI), which assesses the overall level of problem behaviors. The BSI is composed of scales that best measure a general problem factor underlying the TRS or PRS.

Both the TRS and PRS also offer content scales that are more specific or syndrome-oriented than the primary scales; examples include Anger Control, Bullying, and Executive Functioning (see Table 1.1). Initially developed based on theory and expert review, they have since been used in a number of research studies, supporting their overall utility (e.g., see chapter 5). These scales aid in interpreting the clinical and adaptive scales and also serve to broaden content coverage.

In addition to content scales, a variety of index scores are offered. These indexes are empirically derived and composed of items from other scales that were selected based on their ability to differentiate those children with and without a behavioral or emotional functioning diagnosis or classification. The Executive Functioning Index scores (only available in Q-global reports) are designed to identify specific executive functioning skills a child might possess.

The TRS and PRS can be completed online or on paper in about 10 to 20 minutes. In addition, PRS forms are available in Spanish.

**Table 1.1** TRS and PRS Scales and Indexes

| Scale | TRS | | | PRS | | |
|---|---|---|---|---|---|---|
| | P | C | A | P | C | A |
| **Composite** | | | | | | |
| Adaptive Skills | • | • | • | • | • | • |
| Behavioral Symptoms Index | • | • | • | • | • | • |
| Externalizing Problems | • | • | • | • | • | • |
| Internalizing Problems | • | • | • | • | • | • |
| School Problems | | • | • | | | |
| **Clinical and adaptive scales** | | | | | | |
| Activities of Daily Living | | | | • | • | • |
| Adaptability | • | • | • | • | • | • |
| Aggression | • | • | • | • | • | • |
| Anxiety | • | • | • | • | • | • |
| Attention Problems | • | • | • | • | • | • |
| Atypicality | • | • | • | • | • | • |
| Conduct Problems | | • | • | | • | • |
| Depression | • | • | • | • | • | • |
| Functional Communication | • | • | • | • | • | • |
| Hyperactivity | • | • | • | • | • | • |
| Leadership | | • | • | | • | • |
| Learning Problems | | • | • | | | |
| Social Skills | • | • | • | • | • | • |
| Somatization | • | • | • | • | • | • |
| Study Skills | | • | • | | | |
| Withdrawal | • | • | • | • | • | • |
| **Content scale** | | | | | | |
| Anger Control | • | • | • | • | • | • |
| Bullying | • | • | • | • | • | • |
| Developmental Social Disorders | • | • | • | • | • | • |
| Emotional Self-Control | • | • | • | • | • | • |
| Executive Functioning | • | • | • | • | • | • |
| Negative Emotionality | • | • | • | • | • | • |
| Resiliency | • | • | • | • | • | • |
| **Clinical index** | | | | | | |
| ADHD Probability Index | | • | • | | • | • |
| Autism Probability Index | | • | • | | • | • |
| Clinical Probability Index | • | | | • | | |

**Table 1.1** TRS and PRS Scales and Indexes *(continued)*

| Scale | TRS | | | PRS | | |
|---|---|---|---|---|---|---|
| | P | C | A | P | C | A |
| EBD Probability Index | | • | • | | • | • |
| Functional Impairment Index | • | • | • | • | • | • |
| **Executive Functioning Index** | | | | | | |
| Attentional Control Index | • | • | • | • | • | • |
| Behavioral Control Index | • | • | • | • | • | • |
| Emotional Control Index | • | • | • | • | • | • |
| Overall Executive Functioning Index | • | • | • | • | • | • |
| Problem Solving Index | | • | • | | • | • |

# SELF-REPORT OF PERSONALITY

In contrast to rating scales, self-report scales lend themselves well to recording what goes on in the inner world of the child; they are best suited to report thoughts, feelings, attitudes, and internal reactions to people and events, which give information on the respondent's position on various personality dimensions. The SRP is an omnibus personality inventory consisting of statements that respondents answer in one of two ways. Four levels are provided: interview (SRP–I; ages 6 through 7), child (SRP–C; ages 8 through 11), adolescent (SRP–A; ages 12 through 21), and college (SRP–COL; ages 18 through 25).

The interview version consists of 14 items that the child responds to by answering *Yes* or *No.* The interviewer may follow up those responses with additional items to which the child responds in an open-ended format. On the SRP–C, –A, and –COL levels, the first set of items requires a *True* or *False* response, while the second set uses a four-point scale of frequency, ranging from *Never* to *Almost always.* Some item stems lend themselves naturally to a frequency rating while others are intrinsically true/false statements (see the BASC–2 Manual, Reynolds & Kamphaus, 2004, for a detailed discussion). The transition from one response format to the other was found to be an easy one for respondents to make.

The SRP–C, –A, and –COL forms take about 20 to 30 minutes to complete and can be completed online (in a supervised setting) or on paper. These levels overlap considerably in scales and structure, and contain similar items. The SRP–I form offers a single Total Score that indicates a general measure of overall behavioral and emotional functioning. The child and adolescent levels have identical composite scores: School Problems, Internalizing Problems, Inattention/Hyperactivity, Personal Adjustment, and an overall composite score—the Emotional Symptoms Index (ESI). The college level has all of these composite scores except the School Problems composite. Unlike the BSI of the rating scales, the ESI is composed of both negative (clinical) scales and positive (adaptive) scales; like the BSI, the ESI includes scales that measure a general problem factor underlying the SRP. See Table 1.2 for a list of the SRP scales.

The SRP–A and SRP–COL forms offer additional content scales (e.g., Anger Control, Ego Strength; see Table 1.2) that are more specific or syndrome-oriented than the other scales. In addition, the SRP–C and SRP–A offer a Functional Impairment Index, which was empirically derived and is composed of items from other scales that were selected based on their ability to differentiate those with and without a behavioral or emotional functioning diagnosis or classification.

**Table 1.2** SRP Scales and Indexes

| Scale | I | C | A | COL |
|---|---|---|---|---|
| **Composite** | | | | |
| Emotional Symptoms | | • | • | • |
| Inattention/Hyperactivity | | • | • | • |
| Internalizing Problems | | • | • | • |
| Personal Adjustment | | • | • | • |
| School Problems | | • | • | |
| Total Score | • | | | |
| **Clinical and adaptive scales** | | | | |
| Alcohol Abuse | | | | • |
| Anxiety | | • | • | • |
| Attention Problems | | • | • | • |
| Attitude to School | | • | • | |
| Attitude to Teachers | | • | • | |
| Atypicality | | • | • | • |
| Depression | | • | • | • |
| Hyperactivity | | • | • | • |
| Interpersonal Relations | | • | • | • |
| Locus of Control | | • | • | • |
| Relations With Parents | | • | • | • |
| School Maladjustment | | | | • |
| Self-Esteem | | • | • | • |
| Self-Reliance | | • | • | • |
| Sensation Seeking | | | • | • |
| Sense of Inadequacy | | • | • | • |
| Social Stress | | • | • | • |
| Somatization | | | • | • |
| **Content scale** | | | | |
| Anger Control | | | • | • |
| Ego Strength | | | • | • |
| Mania | | | • | • |
| Test Anxiety | | | • | • |
| **Clinical index** | | | | |
| Functional Impairment Index | | • | • | |

# STRUCTURED DEVELOPMENTAL HISTORY

The SDH, available in English and Spanish, is an extensive history and background survey that is completed via an interview with a parent or guardian or as a questionnaire. It can be administered using Q-global or can be completed using a paper form. When completed using Q-global with a corresponding PRS form, the SDH administration includes additional questions that are relevant to corresponding scale elevations from the administration of the PRS.

A clinician uses the SDH to systematically gather information that is crucial to the diagnostic and treatment process. Many developmental milestones and medical or related problems in the family may have an impact on a child's current behavior. The SDH is a structured way to gather child and family history, both social and medical. Because it is comprehensive, the SDH is an asset to any evaluation of a child, whether or not other BASC–3 components are used. Gathering a developmental history using tools such as the SDH provides the clinician with information about the context of the child's or adolescent's behavior.

## STUDENT OBSERVATION SYSTEM
Behavior rating scales are based on impressions formed over time and are not used to record actual numbers of occurrences of behaviors as they happen. To do that, a direct observation scale such as the SOS is needed. The SOS form is used to conduct a direct observation of the classroom behavior of a child. It can be completed using Q-global or a paper form (along with a timing device).

The SOS uses the technique of momentary time sampling (i.e., systematic coding during 3-second intervals spaced 30 seconds apart over a 15-minute period) to record a wide range of children's behaviors, including positive behaviors (such as teacher–student interaction) as well as negative behaviors (such as inappropriate movement or inattention). It also includes a 71-item observer rating scale that is completed after the time-sampling procedure and gives in-depth information about student behaviors that may impede or promote learning and adjustment in the classroom. The SOS is used in regular- and special-education classes as part of the diagnostic process in the initial assessment and/or it can be used repetitively to evaluate the effectiveness of educational, behavioral, psychopharmacological, or other treatments.

# Description of Materials
## MANUAL
This manual provides instructions for administering and scoring the TRS, PRS, and SRP; gives guidance in using the SDH and SOS; and includes general norm tables (clinical norm tables are provided in the Q-global resource section). It also provides information on the development, appropriate uses, validity, reliability, and interpretation of the TRS, PRS, SRP, SDH, and SOS. Users should be familiar with this manual before attempting to use the BASC–3 components.

## FORMS AND HAND-SCORING WORKSHEETS
The TRS, PRS, and SRP can be administered using Q-global or with a paper form. Each form can be scored online for either administration method or by using corresponding hand-scoring worksheets. The hand-scoring worksheets include a graph that is used to plot scale *T* scores. Note that using the hand-scoring worksheets requires the use of this manual.

## Q-GLOBAL
Q-global is a secure, online web-based system used to administer and score the TRS, PRS, SRP, SDH, and SOS forms. Administration of the TRS, PRS, and the SDH can be done remotely by sending an email to the respondent containing a weblink needed to complete the form (Internet access is required to complete the forms). The TRS, PRS, SRP, SDH, and SOS can also be administered via an on-screen assessment that is initiated while in the Q-global system (e.g., at a school, in a clinician's office). When completed remotely, the person sending the email to the rater will receive an email indicating the form is complete. All completed forms are available for immediate scoring and reporting. Responses from paper forms can be entered into Q-global for online scoring and reporting.

# Uses of the BASC–3 TRS, PRS, SRP, SDH, and SOS
The BASC–3 TRS, PRS, SRP, SDH, and SOS are designed to provide information important to differential diagnosis and educational classification of a variety of children's emotional and behavioral disorders and to aid in the design of treatment plans. They can be used in a variety of settings and applications.

## CLINICAL DIAGNOSIS
As previously mentioned, the BASC–3 components aid in the clinical diagnosis of disorders that usually first appear in childhood or adolescence. They assess a variety of symptoms that are noted in the *DSM-5.* Because each component can be used separately or in combination, they are easily used in residential settings, in clinics, or by private practitioners. The PRS and SDH can be completed by a parent while the child is being evaluated by the practitioner, which reduces the practitioner's time in the data collection process. The TRS, PRS, SRP, and SOS can be repeated on a regular basis to monitor a child's progress and response to treatment.

It is highly desirable that a diagnosis be linked clearly to intervention. The BASC–3 Behavior Intervention Guide and corresponding Parent Tip Sheets are easily used with results from the TRS, PRS, and/or SRP. Q-global reports containing intervention strategy recommendations based on the TRS, PRS, and/or SRP results can be automatically generated. Additional strategies are also provided in the guide.

## EDUCATIONAL CLASSIFICATION

Differential diagnosis is an important issue in school settings. This is partly because the complexity of many children's problems requires an array of interventions that must be tailored to the individual child's needs. Consequently, the BASC–3 components are designed to be sensitive to numerous presenting problems in the classroom, including deficiencies in social skills, study skills, or other adaptive skills.

Academic difficulties are frequently linked to behavior problems. Syndromes such as ADHD and depression have known academic consequences, and learning disabilities and intellectual disabilities are often associated with adjustment problems such as low self-concept or anxiety. It is strongly suggested that every child experiencing academic difficulties receive a behavioral assessment. Additionally, research demonstrates that good behavioral assessment of constructs like those on the scales Attitude to School, Attitude to Teachers, Study Skills, Attention Problems, and Adaptability, in tandem with cognitive assessment, improves the prediction of both school performance and response to intervention (Yen, Konold, & McDermott, 2004).

The BASC–3 components are also useful for assessing severe emotional disturbance. The rating scales help distinguish between children with conduct disorders or social maladjustment on the one hand and those with severe emotional/behavioral disturbance on the other, as called for by IDEA (2004). The BASC–3 components help assess all aspects of the federal definition of severe emotional disturbance. In addition, the BASC–3 components may be particularly useful in designing individual educational plans (IEPs). These components allow the selection of target behaviors as well as clusters of behaviors to delineate syndromes that are an important focus of the IEP.

The BASC–3 rating scales were also designed for use at the preschool level to help develop family service plans (FSPs) and/or IEPs for children ages 2 through 5. The SDH is well suited for identifying the service needs of families in such settings.

## MANIFESTATION DETERMINATION

Manifestation determination refers to a process for determining the origin of behavior. The procedure is commonly encountered in special education and in 504 proceedings related to disciplinary actions or conduct problems (IDEA, 2004; Section 504 [Rehabilitation Act, 1973]). Prior to the application of any adverse action against a student with a disability, a multidisciplinary team must determine that the behavior in question was not a direct result of the student's disability. This method is based on the premise that students with a disability should not be punished for behavior that is considered to be a manifestation of the disability. For example, suppose a child with schizophrenia is experiencing auditory hallucinations at school and tells a teacher that another child is threatening to commit a violent act. Because these auditory experiences were a manifestation of the child's disability, he or she should not be punished for reporting them as actual threats.

In most cases, the information obtained from the BASC–3 forms is helpful in the manifestation determination process. The original BASC forms have a long history of effectiveness in differentiating social maladjustment and conduct disorder from behavior associated with an emotional disturbance as defined in IDEA (2004; see Reynolds & Kamphaus, 2002). The BASC–3 content scales enhance the forms' utility for such purposes.

## ASSESSMENT OF INDIVIDUALS WITH LIMITATIONS OF VISION AND HEARING

The BASC–3 scales are used to evaluate the behavioral and emotional status of children and adolescents with sensory impairments. The interpretation of BASC–3 test scores for these individuals requires specialized training, expertise, and supervised experience in working with groups with sensory impairment. BASC–3 TRS, PRS, and SRP score profiles based on a small number of children identified with a hearing impairment are found in the reliability and validity chapters for each form.

## PROGRAM EVALUATION

Repeated use of the BASC–3 TRS, PRS, SRP, and SOS aids in identifying a child's progress in specific programs. Improvement in designated areas of behavior and in affective states may be noted and strengths and weaknesses of programs identified. A number of evaluation studies showed the original BASC to be sensitive to the effects of various intervention programs for young children (including the evaluation component of Head Start's Project Mastery) and adolescents (e.g., the evaluation by the Civilian Health and Medical Program of the Uniformed Services [CHAMPUS] of the effectiveness of residential treatment for adolescents). These and other applications of the BASC in program evaluation are reviewed in Reynolds and Kamphaus (2002). With the acceptable score reliabilities and broad content coverage in both clinical and adaptive domains, the BASC–3 components can be used in the evaluation of programs and of interventions at both the individual and program levels.

## FORENSIC EVALUATION

The BASC–3 is appropriate for use in legal or forensic settings. According to several U.S. Supreme Court rulings of the 1990s (e.g., Daubert v. Merrell Dow Pharmaceuticals, 1993; also see Reynolds, 2001a, 2001b), evidence of the psychometric properties of tests used in a forensic setting is crucial for determining the admissibility of expert testimony based on test results. Reynolds and Kamphaus (2002) provide examples of uses of the original BASC in forensic situations such as child custody evaluations, personal injury litigation, and juvenile certification. This manual contains considerable information on the reliability of BASC–3 scores and associated standard errors of measurement, on the normative samples, and on validation studies, all of which are considered by judges in determining admissibility of testimony based partially or wholly on test data. Also presented are additional crucial data on the ability of the BASC–3 scale scores to measure child and adolescent psychopathology and to discriminate, among various diagnostic groups, capabilities that also are included in the consideration of admissible evidence. The BASC–3 tools are well established in clinical environments such as schools, child guidance centers, university clinics, and private practice settings in the United States and abroad. The use of tests in a wide variety of settings is important in establishing credibility and admissibility in various legal proceedings.

When choosing instruments for forensic evaluations, it also is important for clinicians to evaluate the instruments' ability to detect dissimulation (Reynolds, 1997). In court proceedings, individuals may have much to gain by appearing to have more or fewer problems than actually exist. Because nearly any behavioral or emotional problem or disorder can be minimized or exaggerated, objective methods are needed to determine whether dissimulation has occurred. The BASC–3 validity scales identify exaggerated responding, minimization of problem reporting, inconsistencies, random answering patterns, and other response methods that lead to inaccurate depictions of the child's or adolescent's behavior.

## RESEARCH

The BASC–3 is well suited to research on childhood psychopathology and behavior disorders. The interpretive chapters in this manual provide several examples of this research. The overlapping norm samples for the TRS, PRS, and SRP, along with the common scales across form and age, provide a level of score comparability that facilitates both decision making and inference about profiles across scales. The previous BASC editions have been used in hundreds of research studies conducted in a variety of settings, countries, and languages, and with various clinical populations.

# Chapter 2

# Administering and Scoring the Rating Scales and Self-Report of Personality

This chapter discusses the general issues that apply to the administration and scoring of the BASC–3 Teacher Rating Scales (TRS), the Parent Rating Scales (PRS), and the Self-Report of Personality (SRP). Having a good understanding of the administration and scoring will enable examiners to maximize the information obtained from these instruments. Although this manual focuses on paper-and-pencil administration and hand scoring of the TRS, PRS, and SRP, most of the topics discussed in this chapter apply equally to Q-global computer administration and scoring.

## General Administration Information

### FORMS

The BASC–3 record forms and hand-scoring worksheets allow the instruments to be administered and scored when digital scoring is not a viable option. The record form captures rater responses, while the hand-scoring worksheet summarizes results for the examiner's interpretation. The hand-scoring worksheet features a Summary Table, an Adaptive Profile, and a Clinical Profile for interpreting scores. A pen with a hard tip or a sharp pencil will make the clearest impression on the scoring page.

### Selecting Teacher Raters

The TRS is designed to be completed by any adult who has had an extended opportunity to observe the child in a school, preschool, or similar setting, including a teacher, teacher aide, daycare worker, or other person who fills a similar role. For school-age children, it is preferable, when possible, to obtain the ratings from a teacher who supervises students in an organized class setting. Such a setting would require seat work, perhaps group or computer work, and teacher–student interaction. Ratings from multiple teachers who observe the child or adolescent in different classes can be useful to show how he or she responds to various teaching styles, academic demands, and disciplinary standards.

To give a valid rating, the teacher should have had a considerable amount of contact with the child. A month of daily contact or 6 to 8 weeks of several-days-a-week observation is typically sufficient. In some cases it is appropriate, when a child must be evaluated during the summer or near the beginning of the school year, to have ratings completed by the previous year's teacher(s) who knew the child best.

### Selecting Parent Raters

The PRS is designed to be completed by the child's parent, guardian, foster parent, or custodial caregiver (i.e., the informant). Obtain ratings from two parents or two caretakers when possible. Two ratings provide more information about the child's behavior and also can reveal areas of disagreement that may be important in diagnosis and in designing a treatment plan. If it is not possible to obtain two ratings, the person with the most recent and frequent contact with the child should complete the rating form.

### RAPPORT

Good rapport between the examiner and the respondent motivates the respondents to fill out the BASC–3 forms truthfully, completely, and in a timely fashion. How each examiner establishes rapport will vary with the age of the informant and the reasons for assessment, among other factors. Consider the informant's previous experience, if any, with the assessment process. Communicate appropriate information about the nature of the instruments and emphasize the value of honest responses. Informed consent can lessen some of the impediments to establishing trust.

Be forthcoming and honest regarding the intended uses of the results, reasons for the evaluation, limits of confidentiality, and legal issues such as local laws regarding privileged communication. When you adequately inform respondents about the testing process and request their consent, they are more likely to be comfortable and forthcoming when responding to the questionnaire items.

The assessment of children and adolescents with the SRP may present particular complexities for rapport building. Some children and adolescents may lack motivation for many reasons, including: (1) they are not seeking help of their own volition, (2) they are referred for behavior difficulties and feel they are being punished, (3) the assessment situation might be a new experience, and (4) the various developmental stages of childhood and adolescence make rapport building challenging. Anticipating such motivational differences is a good start to effectively dealing with them. A one-size-fits-all approach to establishing rapport with children and adolescents will likely be unsuccessful. Anastasi and Urbina (1997) and Frick, Burns, & Kamphaus (2009) offer guidance on establishing rapport.

# Completing the TRS, PRS, and SRP

## TRS FORM
When administering the TRS form, emphasize to teachers the importance of responding to all items on the form, even if the teacher is not absolutely certain how to answer a given item. Explain that a *Never* response means that the teacher has not personally observed the behavior, not that the behavior does not occur in any setting.

Instructions may be given this way: "I am evaluating Suzanne and would appreciate your assistance. I would like to know how Suzanne behaves in your class in order to help her. This form takes 10 to 20 minutes to complete. Please read the instructions on the form and respond to all of the items, even if you do not have direct knowledge about Suzanne's behavior related to a particular item. A response of *Never* indicates that you personally have never observed that behavior or emotion. It does not mean that the behavior or emotion has never occurred. Contact me if you have any questions. I appreciate you helping me better understand Suzanne."

Teachers can complete the TRS in 10 to 20 minutes using a digital or paper record form. Ideally, the teacher will complete it in a single sitting free of distractions. Forms can be completed in a clinician's office (or similar setting) or mailed/emailed to the teacher. The TRS form provides instructions for completing the form. When using a paper record form, the clinician should fill in the student information (i.e., name, birth date, gender, and age). When using a digital record form, the student information can be provided in the email to the teacher that details how to launch the digital form.

The TRS form also requires some background information about the child and teacher. Information about the type of class in which the teacher observes the child is requested on the form because it may be important when interpreting scores. For example, a special-education class may be organized differently from other classes, resulting in different teacher perceptions. Or, a child may behave differently in a class with a teacher assistant, parent volunteer, or student teacher versus a class with only one teacher. Teachers are also given an opportunity to record any concerns about a child's vision and hearing, because vision or hearing problems can contribute to learning, behavioral, or emotional problems. Finally, at the end of the administration, teachers may record behavioral and emotional strengths of the child and may note specific behavioral and emotional concerns he or she may have about the child. These observations from teachers might convey insights that parents or the children themselves do not possess, and can provide helpful context to the overall evaluation process.

## PRS FORM
When administering PRS forms, emphasize the importance of responding to all items on the form, even if the parent is not absolutely certain how to answer a given item. Instructions may be given this way: "Parents know their children's behavior better than anyone. In evaluating the difficulties Aiden has encountered, I need your help in many ways. One way is to gather information from you about his behavior as you see it. You will be presented with a series of statements that describe how a child might act. Please read the instructions and rate Aiden on all of the statements, even if some are difficult to answer or do not seem to apply. Respond to all items even if you do not have direct knowledge about Aiden's behavior related to a particular item. A response of *Never* indicates that you personally have never observed that behavior

or emotion. It does not mean that the behavior or emotion has never occurred outside the home or in another setting where you were not present. If you have any questions or come across anything you don't understand, please ask for my help."

Parents can complete the PRS in 10 to 20 minutes using a digital or paper record form. Ideally, the parent will complete the form in a single sitting free of distractions. Forms can be completed in a clinician's office (or similar setting) or mailed/emailed to the parent or guardian. The PRS form provides instructions for completing the form and requires some background information about the child (e.g., birth date, age, etc.) and parent.

Like the TRS, the PRS provides an opportunity to note any concerns about a child's vision or hearing. The PRS also allows parents to record concerns about a child's eating habits. At the end of the PRS form, parents may record information about a child's behavioral and emotional strengths and share specific behavioral or emotional concerns about a child. These observations can provide helpful context to the overall evaluation process and can also serve as a starting point for talking to the parent about his or her child.

## SRP FORM

### Interview
The Self-Report of Personality–Interview (SRP–I) form is used with children ages 6 and 7, and requires the interviewer to ask the child a series of yes/no and open-ended questions. Most children will complete the interview in 25 minutes or less, although assessment times can vary depending on the answers that are provided. Clinicians unfamiliar with the SRP–I form must carefully review it prior to beginning an assessment session. Listed below are some guidelines for administration.

1. Establishing rapport: Examiners should have experience administering tests to and establishing rapport with young children. General guidelines for establishing rapport were provided previously. Some additional guidelines for the SRP–I include (a) providing a comfortable physical environment; (b) spending some relaxed time in play or conversation prior to the assessment; (c) stating the purpose of the assessment; and (d) showing sincerity, enthusiasm, support, respect, and a nonjudgmental attitude toward the child during the administration.

2. Introducing the SRP–I: Reinforce to the child that you are interested in hearing what he or she has to say, and that you want to learn a little bit more about him or her. Present the survey in a positive light. For example, you might use the following introduction: "I would like to take a few minutes to get to know you better. I am going to ask you some questions today that describe how some children think, feel, or act. Some of the questions can be answered by saying 'Yes' or 'No.' Other questions will ask you to tell me a little bit more about yourself. Let's get started with the first question." Remain flexible, as each child may require a slightly different approach before becoming comfortable answering questions.

3. Administering the questions: When reading the questions, be sure to speak clearly and in a manner the child can easily hear and understand. The SRP–I form uses a step-by-step approach for administration. Rules for each of these steps are provided below. Some questions require you to circle a *Yes* or *No* response. Other questions require you to record the child's response. You are not required to write verbatim responses. Rather, capture enough of the response to provide examples for the question being asked. It is permissible to repeat questions to the child as needed; however, do not supply alternative meanings for words or phrases used in the items.

   Step A: Administer questions 1 through 4 together. Encourage the child to provide a *Yes* or *No* answer to each item. If the child responds both "Yes" and "No" to a question, prompt the child to provide only one answer. Do not spend too much time on a single item. If the child cannot answer the item, move on to the next item.

   Step B: Administer the follow-up questions in this step based on the response to Question 1. If the child answers "Yes" to Question 1, use Question 1a to elicit more information about things the child likes about school. If the child answers "No" to Question 1, use Question 1d to elicit more information about things the child does not like about school. Additional prompts are provided for Questions 1a and 1d, and should only be used when the initial question was not answered (or when the answer provided is "I don't know"). If the child is unable to provide an answer after additional prompting, proceed to Step C.

Step C: Administer the follow-up questions in this step only if the child answers "Yes" to Question 2, 3, or 4. For example, administer Question 2a if the child answers "Yes" to Question 2. Similarly, administer Question 3a if the child answers "Yes" to Question 3, and administer Question 4a if the child answers "Yes" to Question 4. Prompts are provided for each of the questions in Step C and should be used if the child does not respond or says "I don't know" to the follow-up question. If the child does not respond to the prompt, then proceed to the next appropriate question, as indicated on the SRP–I form.

Step D: Administer questions 5 through 8 together. As with Step A, encourage the child to provide a *Yes* or *No* answer to each item, but do not spend too much time on a single item. If the child cannot answer an item, move on to the next item.

Step E: Administer the follow-up questions in this step based on the response to Question 5. If the child answers "Yes" to Question 5, use Question 5a to elicit more information about reasons the child is liked by other children. If the child answers "No" to Question 5, use Question 5d to elicit more information about reasons the child is not liked by other children. Additional prompts are provided for Questions 5a and 5d, and should only be used when the initial question was not answered (or when the answer provided is "I don't know"). If the child is unable to provide an answer after additional prompting, proceed to Step F.

Step F: Administer the follow-up questions in this step only if the child answers "No" to Question 6, or if the child answers "Yes" to Question 7 or 8. For example, administer Question 6a if the child answers "No" to Question 6. Similarly, administer Question 7a if the child answers "Yes" to Question 7, and administer Question 8a if the child answers "Yes" to Question 8. Prompts are provided for each of the questions in Step F and should be used if the child does not respond or says "I don't know" to the follow-up question. If the child does not respond to the prompt, then proceed to the next appropriate question, as indicated on the SRP–I form.

Step G: Administer questions 9 through 14 together. Encourage the child to provide a *Yes* or *No* answer to each item, but do not spend too much time on a single item. If the child cannot answer an item, move on to the next item.

Step H: Administer the follow-up questions in this step only if the child answers "Yes" to the corresponding question in Step G (Question 9, 10, 11, 12, 13, or 14). For example, administer Question 9a only if the child answers "Yes" to Question 9, administer Question 10a only if the child answers "Yes" to Question 10, and so on. Prompts are provided for each of the questions in Step H and should be used if the child does not respond or says "I don't know" to the follow-up question. If the child does not respond to the prompt, then proceed to the next appropriate question or to the end of the interview if the child does not respond to Question 14a. Otherwise, read the final statement at the bottom of page 4 to the child.

## Child, Adolescent, and College

Because the SRP forms span a wide age range (ages 8 through 25), you may want to use a different approach to introduce the form to children, adolescents, and young adults. For younger children, introduce the SRP by saying something like, "Part of my job today is to learn a little bit more about you. I am going to give you a paper that will ask you some questions that will help me get to know you better. I need you to do your best when answering the questions." For adolescents or young adults, you can introduce the SRP by saying something like, "Part of my job today is to learn a little bit more about you. I am going to give you a questionnaire that asks about your thoughts, behaviors, and emotions. I need you to answer the questions as honestly as you can and to do your best." Use your best judgment when introducing the forms and modify the introduction as needed based on the setting and the characteristics of the child, adolescent, or young adult. In juvenile detention and other forensic settings, you may encounter special problems of rapport and response styles; handle these situations the same way as other assessment challenges in such settings.

Your instructions for completing the SRP should describe basic expectations of completing the test. Emphasize the importance of responding to *all items on the form,* even if the respondent is not absolutely certain how to answer a given item.

For example, you might say, "You will read a number of sentences that may or may not describe how you think, feel, or act. Please answer all of the sentences as truthfully as you can. You may think some sentences do not apply to you, but answer them as best as you can. If you come across something you don't understand, please ask me to help you. First, read the instructions, and then read and respond to the sentences."

Most respondents can complete the SRP in 20 to 30 minutes using a digital or paper record form. Ideally, the respondent should complete the SRP in a controlled setting with supervision, such as an office, a clinic or hospital waiting room, or a testing or examination room. A controlled setting is desirable *both to enhance the quality of the data obtained and to prevent unauthorized release of test materials. The SRP forms should not be sent home or otherwise allowed outside the clinician's control.* Supervision of those completing the SRP is recommended. Administrations in uncontrolled settings or unsupervised might result in lost SRP forms or in respondents answering questions in random fashion simply to rid themselves of the task. (Random or patterned responding is readily detected when the tests are given or scored using the computer-generated reports.) In this context, supervision refers to someone being in the same room while maintaining the individual's privacy when responding to the items.

The SRP form provides instructions for completing the form and requires background information about the respondent (e.g., name, school name, age). Depending on the age and capability of the respondent, you might decide to fill in this information prior to distributing the SRP form.

## TEST SECURITY

Professional practice dictates maintaining the security of both unused and completed BASC–3 materials (see *Standards for Educational and Psychological Testing;* American Educational Research Association [AERA], American Psychological Association [APA], & National Council on Measurement in Education [NCME], 2014). Maintain control of unused BASC–3 materials by not allowing them to be distributed without authorization. Similarly, do not share BASC–3 results with individuals who have no need to know them. Ultimately, the professional using the testing materials is responsible for their confidentiality and copyright protection.

# General Scoring Information

## COMMUNICATING RESULTS

Communicate BASC–3 results in a manner that minimizes the potential for misuse. When communicating BASC–3 results to a teacher or parent, accompany the scores with interpretations and warnings about their limitations. The American Psychological Association, other professional organizations, and, in some cases, state and federal laws have established guidelines for the appropriate use and communication of test information.

It is important to share results with both adult and child respondents. This courtesy builds trust so that you can return to a respondent for BASC–3 or other information in the future.

## USABILITY OF FORMS

To obtain accurate results, forms must be completed with few, if any, omissions or multiple responses to a single item. Digital administrations require raters/examinees to complete all test items before allowing the submission of a completed form. When using a paper form, check each completed form for omitted or multiple responses. If any items were skipped, ask the respondent to try to answer those items. Likewise, ask the respondent to choose only one response if he or she marked multiple responses to an item.

Too many omitted items or items marked with more than one answer will undermine the validity of the scale and composite scores. The BASC–3 forms permit a maximum of two unscorable (omitted or multiply-marked) items per scale; three or more unscorable items render the scale itself unscorable (and any composite scale the unscorable scale is included in), although other scales on the form may be scored.

The hand-scoring worksheet for each form provides spaces to record the number of unscorable items on each scale. If there are one or two such items, an estimate of the scale's raw score is made by adding a constant for each unscorable item to the sum of scores for the other items. The constant represents the average score on that scale's items in the general norm sample, rounded to the nearest whole number. On the clinical scales, unscorable items are treated as if they have scores of 0 or 1. On the adaptive scales, where the typical responses are *Often, Almost always,* or *True,* the unscorable items are treated as if they have a score of 2.

The tendency to skip items may have clinical significance, as may the content of the skipped items. You may wish to examine these omissions further.

## TYPES OF NORMATIVE SCORES

There are two types of normative scores for each scale: *T* scores and percentile ranks. *T* scores indicate the distance of scores from the norm-group mean. They are standard scores with a mean of 50 and a standard deviation of 10. Thus, a *T* score of 80 indicates that the person's score is three standard deviations above the norm-group mean, and a *T* score of 30 is two standard deviations below the mean. The BASC–3 *T* scores are not normalized; they are linear transformations of raw scores, so they preserve the shape of the raw-score distributions, some of which are significantly skewed.

A percentile rank indicates the percentage of the norm sample scoring at or below a given raw score. For example, a percentile rank of 96 means that the person's score is in the top 4% of the norm sample.

*T* scores and percentile ranks provide different kinds of information. BASC–3 *T* scores describe the extremeness of a score (i.e., the distance of the score from the mean), while percentile ranks describe the frequency (or infrequency) of a score. Extreme scores are more unusual for some behaviors than others. Because of this, the relationship between *T* scores and percentile ranks varies somewhat across scales. For example, on a scale such as Social Skills, which has an approximately normal distribution, a *T* score of 70 corresponds to a percentile rank of about 97 or 98. In contrast, on the extremely skewed Aggression scale of the TRS, a *T* score of 70 has a percentile rank of about 94—that is, about 6% percent of people obtain *T* scores of 70 or higher on this scale. For this reason, the norm tables for each scale provide both the *T* score and the percentile rank corresponding to each raw score. Both types of scores are important for interpretation.

## CHOICE OF NORM SAMPLE

Each of the BASC–3 rating scale and self-report forms offers a choice of either general or clinical norm samples. Combined-gender (i.e., both females and males) and separate-gender (i.e., females only or males only) norms are available for each norm sample. In addition to a combined clinical norm sample that includes children who have been identified with a variety of behavioral and emotional disorders, an attention-deficit/hyperactivity disorder (ADHD) norm sample for ages 6 through 18 is also provided. A clinical norm group based on a sample of young adults ages 19 through 21 who are still attending high school is also available. Table 2.1 presents a summary of BASC–3 norm groups. Each norm set has certain advantages, as discussed in the following paragraphs.

**Table 2.1** BASC–3 TRS, PRS, and SRP General and Clinical Norm Samples

| General | | Clinical | | ADHD | |
|---|---|---|---|---|---|
| Ages | Norm group | Ages | Norm group | Ages | Norm group |
| 2–3 | • | 4–5 | • | 4–5 | |
| 4–5 | • | | | | |
| 6–7 | • | 6–11[a] | • | 6–11[a] | • |
| 8–11 | • | | | | |
| 12–14 | • | 12–18 | • | 12–18 | • |
| 15–18 | • | | | | |
| 18–25 | • | 19–21 | • | | |

*Note.* Combined- and separate-gender norms available for all norm groups except ages 19–21. The ages 18–25 norm group is for the SRP–COL form only.

[a]For SRP–C norm groups, the age range for the Clinical and ADHD samples is 8–11.

## General Norms

The general norms are based on a large national sample that is representative of the general population of children in the United States with regard to gender, race/ethnicity, parent education, and clinical or special-education classification. These norms are subdivided by age and, therefore, indicate how the child compares with the general population of children that age. For many applications, the general combined-gender norms are preferred and recommended for general use. General combined-gender norms are superior in establishing an accurate diagnosis in most instances (e.g., see Reynolds, 2014).

Several scales of the TRS, PRS, and SRP show gender differences. Males tend to obtain higher raw scores than females on the Hyperactivity, Aggression, Conduct Problems, Attention Problems, and Learning Problems scales of the TRS and PRS and on the Attitude to School, Attitude to Teachers, Sensation Seeking, and Self-Esteem scales of the SRP. Females tend to score higher than males on the Social Skills, Leadership, Study Skills, and Functional Communication scales of the TRS and PRS and on the Anxiety and Somatization scales of the SRP. These differences in scores likely reflect real differences between males and females in the incidence of the indicated behavioral or emotional problems or the suggested strengths in adaptive skills.

For these gender differences to be reflected in the normative scores, a common set of norms must be used for both males and females. The general combined-gender norms serve this purpose. General combined-gender norms answer the question "How commonly does this level of rated or self-reported behavior occur in the general population at this age?" When combined-gender norms are used, more males than females will show high *T* scores on Aggression, for example, and more females than males will have high *T* scores on Social Skills. This result is desirable if you consider it appropriate for differences to exist between the genders in the proportions of children receiving particular diagnoses, types of special school services, or treatments such as medications. However, you may prefer to use the separate-gender norms (see the next section) if you believe such raw-score differences between the genders are due simply to psychometric artifacts.

## Female Norms and Male Norms

The female norms and male norms are based on subsets of the general norm samples; each is representative of the general population of children of that age and gender. The effect of using separate-gender norms is to eliminate *T*-score differences between females and males, thereby equating the behavior of males and females on all scales. For example, although raw-score ratings on the Aggression scale tend to be higher for males than females, use of separate-gender norms removes this difference, resulting in an overall average *T* score that is the same for both genders.

In contrast to combined-gender norms, which are well suited to the identification of individuals in need of services, separate-gender norms may be particularly helpful for clinical diagnosis because they identify children with ratings or self-reports that are rare for their age and gender. For example, you might be interested in the fact that a female's Aggression rating is extremely high when compared with other females, even though the aggressive behavior score is not especially high when compared with a combined male and female norm sample.

In summary, the decision whether to use combined-gender or separate-gender norms can be guided by whether it is appropriate for gender differences to exist in the outcome of the particular type of assessment. If you are interested in identifying children who have a behavioral or emotional problem that is believed to occur more often in one gender than the other, use the combined-gender norms. On the other hand, if you consider the extremity of the child's score relative to others of the child's own gender to be of primary importance, use separate-gender norms. There may also be times when it is appropriate to look at both sets of norms.

## Clinical Norms

Clinical norms are most helpful when a child's problems are extreme in comparison with the general youth population. Behavior ratings of children who have significant problems are often so much higher than the ratings of nonreferred children that ceiling effects are encountered when the general norms are used. Such effects may make differential diagnosis of behavior problems quite difficult. The use of clinical norms helps to relieve this problem. For many scales, the score distributions of behavior ratings for seriously emotionally disturbed children differ from those for the general population not only in elevation, but also in shape and dispersion; raw-score means, standard deviations, kurtosis, and skewness also might differ. Although general norms are useful for evaluating the overall level of behavior problems of such individuals, determining subcategories of the problem—such as ADHD, depression, or even social maladjustment—might best be accomplished using the clinical norms.

Figure 2.1 illustrates this concept. The profile, as plotted using general norms, is relatively flat and near the extreme score range (roughly four or more standard deviations) on the externalizing problem scales. With the clinical norms, however, clear peaks and valleys are visible in the profile, showing in more detail this young person's serious externalizing problems.

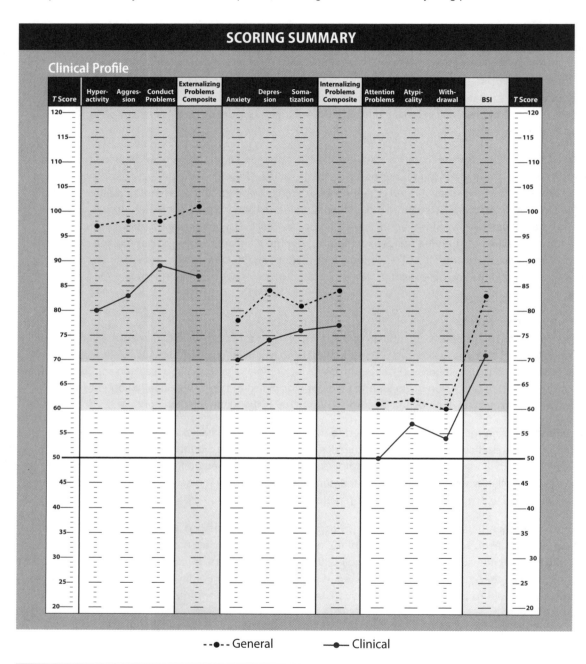

**Figure 2.1** Comparison of general norms and clinical norms on a PRS–A profile

Scores on the SRP tend to differ less between clinical and nonclinical groups than do scores on the parent and teacher rating forms. However, it still may be useful to compare a child's scores against both sets of norms for the reasons just given.

## Multiple Norms

When using the hand-scoring worksheets or generating a digital report, you can record or report more than one group of norms for a particular case. It is expected that scores will sometimes be reported in terms of both general and clinical norms. On the hand-scoring worksheets, you may record a second set of T scores and percentile ranks in the shaded area next to the initial set of scores. It is helpful to use different ink colors or symbols to clarify the differences and mark the boxes for norm sets used (above the Summary Table on TRS and PRS forms; to the right of the Summary Table on SRP forms) with the applicable colors or symbols.

## CONFIDENCE INTERVALS

Because test scores are not perfectly reliable, it is helpful to think of a confidence interval or score range within which the person's true score is likely to lie. The width of this confidence interval will be proportional to the average amount of measurement error associated with that particular scale or composite: less-reliable scales (that is, those with larger average error) will have wider intervals than more-reliable scales.

There are several different approaches to constructing confidence intervals for T scores. The simplest, and the one that has been used the longest, is to add and subtract a constant to the observed T score, forming what Gulliksen (1950) refers to as "reasonable limits" for the true score. This constant is a multiple of the standard error of measurement (SEM). Adding and subtracting 1 SEM yields a 68% confidence interval, resulting in a score range that will include the true T score 68% of the time. When the constant is 2 SEMs, a 95% confidence interval is formed.

To facilitate use of this type of confidence interval, a constant is printed at the bottom of each column of the norm tables. This constant is the SEM multiplied by 1.64, which, when added to and subtracted from the observed T score, yields a 90% confidence interval. (The SEMs themselves are reported in chapters 9 through 11.) The Summary Table of the hand-scoring worksheet for each form provides a column for recording these T-score confidence intervals; plotting the intervals on the profile gives a clear display of the reasonable limits for each score.

## SCORE CLASSIFICATION

As an aid to report writing and other professional communication, a descriptive label may be applied to each scale and composite score using the classification system shown in Table 2.2.

**Table 2.2** Scale and Composite Score Classification

| Classification | | T-score range |
|---|---|---|
| Adaptive scales | Clinical scales | T-score range |
| Very High | Clinically Significant | 70 and above |
| High | At-Risk | 60–69 |
| Average | Average | 41–59 |
| At-Risk | Low | 31–40 |
| Clinically Significant | Very Low | 30 and below |

On all of the scales, the Average T-score range (within which about two-thirds of the general population will score) is 41 through 59. Scale scores in the At-Risk range are between one and two standard deviations from the mean. On the clinical scales, this corresponds to T scores from 60 through 69. On the adaptive scales, the At-Risk range is from 31 through 40. Psychologists and other diagnosticians often use the term at-risk to indicate the presence of significant problems that, while requiring treatment, may not be severe enough to warrant a formal diagnosis. Alternatively, scores in the At-Risk range may signify potential or developing problems that need to be monitored carefully. Finally, scores in the Clinically Significant range denote a high level of maladaptive behavior or absence of adaptive behavior. This range corresponds to scores two standard deviations or more from the mean.

## INDEXES OF VALIDITY AND RESPONSE SET

Several indexes are provided to help BASC–3 users judge the quality of a completed form. Several factors can threaten validity, including failure to pay attention to item content, carelessness, an attempt to portray the child in a highly negative or positive light, lack of motivation to respond truthfully, or poor comprehension of the items. Chapter 7 includes information on the development of these indexes and setting cutoff scores.

### F Index

The F Index, included on all of the TRS, PRS, and SRP hand-scoring worksheets, is a measure of the respondent's tendency to be excessively negative about the child's behaviors, self-perceptions, or emotions.

On the PRS and TRS, the F Index is scored by counting the number of times the respondent answered *Almost always* to a description of negative behavior or *Never* to a description of positive behavior. On the SRP, the F Index is scored by counting the number of times the child answered *True* or *Almost always* to a description of a negative behavior or attitude and *Never* or *False* to a description of a positive behavior or attitude. The TRS, PRS, and SRP hand-scoring worksheets show what levels of F-Index scores are high enough to be of concern.

### L Index

The L Index on the SRP measures the child's tendency to give an extremely positive picture of himself or herself—what might be called "faking good." The index consists of items that are unrealistically positive statements (such as "I tell the truth every single time.") or are mildly self-critical statements that most people would endorse (such as "I have some bad habits."). The SRP hand-scoring worksheets show which L scores should be of concern.

### V Index

Each level of the SRP includes a V Index made up of three or four nonsensical or highly implausible statements (such as "I drink 50 glasses of milk every day."). The V Index serves as a basic check on the validity of the SRP scores. If a respondent agrees (i.e., answers *True, Often,* or *Almost always*) with several of these statements, the SRP may be invalid.

### Indexes of Validity Available With BASC–3 Digital Scoring

Reports generated using Q-global offer additional indexes of validity not available to users of the hand-scoring worksheets. The Consistency Index flags cases in which the respondent has given different responses to items that usually are answered similarly. The Response Pattern Index detects two types of response patterning: repeated and cyclical. Both the Consistency Index and Response Pattern Index are available for the TRS, PRS, and SRP forms. Chapters 5 and 6 include full information on the use and interpretation of these indexes.

## Scoring Instructions for Hand-Scoring Worksheets

Scoring instructions are consistent across the TRS, PRS, and SRP hand-scoring worksheets, although there are some differences among forms and among levels. Scoring for the SRP–I is described at the end of this section.

### STEP 1: TRANSFERRING AND SUMMING THE RESPONSES

Select the hand-scoring worksheet that corresponds to the completed TRS, PRS, or SRP record form (note that corresponding English and Spanish forms use the same worksheet). Open the hand-scoring worksheet to find the Scoring Tables (see Figure 2.2). There is one Scoring Table for every scale on the assessment; the scale names are at the top of each table. The numbers in the Item # column refer to the item numbers on the BASC–3 record form, while the numbers in the N, S, O, and A columns represent the scoring values associated with the item responses. (*Note:* On the Spanish record form, N, A, F, and S correspond to N, S, O and A, respectively.) Transfer the item responses from the record form by circling the scoring values in the appropriate columns of the Scoring Tables. (*Note:* Some item responses, such as critical items not associated with scale scoring, will not be transferred to the Scoring Tables.) When all responses have been transferred to the Scoring Tables, sum the scoring values and record the result in the Sum area at the bottom of each table. Make sure this number does not exceed the maximum value that appears beneath the line. Next, record the total number of omitted items in the designated area at the bottom of each table. (*Note:* If there are three or more item omissions for any scale, do not score that scale.)

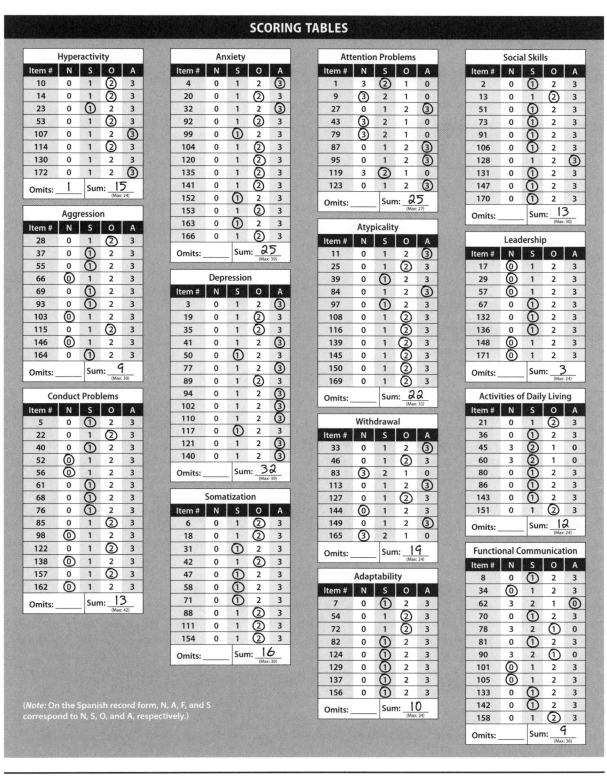

**Figure 2.2** Scoring tables on a PRS–A hand-scoring worksheet

## STEP 2: CHECKING THE *F* INDEX

The BASC–3 hand-scoring worksheet provides an *F* Index designed to detect excessively negative responses. The *F*-Index table appears after the Summary Table. Many of the *F*-Index items also appear in the Scoring Tables for other scales and therefore are scored twice—once for the main scale the item belongs to and once for the *F* Index.

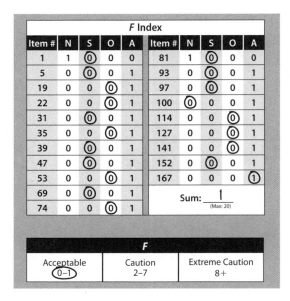

**Figure 2.3** Completed *F*-Index table

To compute the *F*-Index score, transfer the item responses from the record form by circling the scoring values in the appropriate columns in the *F*-Index table (see Figure 2.3). (*Note:* All values for the *F* Index will be 1 or 0, and values of 1 appear only in the N or A columns.) When all responses have been transferred to the *F*-Index table, sum the item scores and record the result in the Sum area at the bottom of the table. Next, circle the corresponding number or numeric range for this raw score in the *F*-Index area (or Validity Indexes area for SRP forms). If the *F*-Index score falls in the Caution or Extreme Caution area, examine the responses that contributed to the total score. Consider whether it is more likely that there are severe behavior problems or that the respondent provided excessively negative responses. In the latter case, refer to chapter 5 or 6 for interpretive guidelines.

### Checking the *L* Index

The *L* Index on the SRP forms are scored in a similar way as the *F* Index. To compute the *L*-Index score, use the *L*-Index table below the *F*- and *V*-Index tables. Transfer the item responses from the record form by circling the scoring values in the appropriate columns in the *L*-Index table. When all responses have been transferred to the *L*-Index table, sum the items and record the results in the Sum area at the bottom of the table. Next, circle the corresponding number or numeric range for this raw score in the Validity Indexes area. If the *L*-Index score falls in the Caution or Extreme Caution area, determine whether the child is trying to present an overly positive self-description or if other factors might be present. Refer to chapter 6 for interpretive guidelines.

### Checking the *V* Index

The *V* Index on the SRP forms are scored in a similar way as the *F* and *L* Indexes. To compute the *V*-Index score, use the *V* Index table below the *F*-Index table. Transfer the item responses from the record form by circling the scoring values in the appropriate columns in the *V*-Index table. When all responses have been transferred to the *V*-Index table, sum the items and record the results in the Sum area at the bottom of the table. Next, circle the corresponding number or numeric range for this raw score in the Validity Indexes area. If the *V*-Index score falls in the Caution or Extreme Caution area, examine the responses that contributed to the score. Subsequent discussion with the child might clarify the reason for those responses. Refer to chapter 6 for interpretive guidelines.

# STEP 3: COMPUTING RAW SCORES FOR SCALES

Transfer the sum for each scale from the Scoring Tables to the Sum column in the Summary Table on the Scoring Summary page (see **a** in Figure 2.4). To compute the raw score for each scale, multiply the number of "omits" (if any) by the constant printed in the Summary Table and add this product to the sum. The scoring of the Hyperactivity scale illustrates this procedure (see **b** in Figure 2.4). If there are three or more omits, do not score the scale. Record the total in the Raw Score column (see **c** in Figure 2.4).

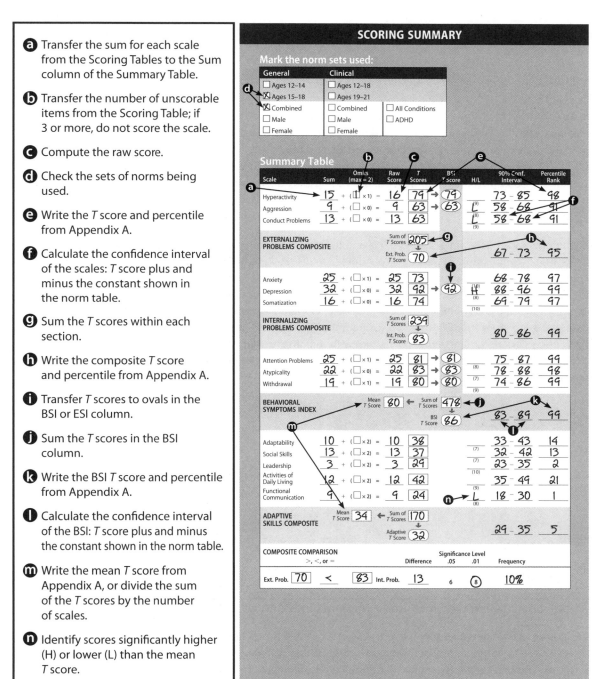

**a** Transfer the sum for each scale from the Scoring Tables to the Sum column of the Summary Table.

**b** Transfer the number of unscorable items from the Scoring Table; if 3 or more, do not score the scale.

**c** Compute the raw score.

**d** Check the sets of norms being used.

**e** Write the *T* score and percentile from Appendix A.

**f** Calculate the confidence interval of the scales: *T* score plus and minus the constant shown in the norm table.

**g** Sum the *T* scores within each section.

**h** Write the composite *T* score and percentile from Appendix A.

**i** Transfer *T* scores to ovals in the BSI or ESI column.

**j** Sum the *T* scores in the BSI column.

**k** Write the BSI *T* score and percentile from Appendix A.

**l** Calculate the confidence interval of the BSI: *T* score plus and minus the constant shown in the norm table.

**m** Write the mean *T* score from Appendix A, or divide the sum of the *T* scores by the number of scales.

**n** Identify scores significantly higher (H) or lower (L) than the mean *T* score.

**Figure 2.4** Completed portion of the Summary Table of a PRS–A hand-scoring worksheet

After choosing the general or clinical norm set, indicate the desired age level (e.g., 15–18) and norm type (e.g., combined) by marking the applicable boxes (see **d** in Figure 2.4).

The general norm tables for the BASC–3 TRS, PRS, and SRP are located in Appendix A. To find the applicable table, first locate the section corresponding to the form used (TRS, PRS, or SRP). Within that section, locate the table for the normative sample desired (e.g., general combined) and for the child's age. To use the norm table, find the raw score in the far-left or far-right column and read across that row to find the T score and percentile rank in the two columns (labeled "T" and "%ile") for the scale being scored. Enter these numbers in the appropriate columns in the Summary Table on the Scoring Summary page (see **e** in Figure 2.4).

Compute the 90% confidence interval for the T score, using the constant printed at the bottom of the scale columns in the norm table, by adding this number to (and subtracting it from) the T score. Enter these values, if desired, in the Summary Table (see **f** in Figure 2.4).

## STEP 4: SCORING TRS AND PRS COMPOSITES AND THE BEHAVIORAL SYMPTOMS INDEX

The Summary Table is divided into horizontal sections corresponding to the composites: Externalizing Problems, Internalizing Problems, Adaptive Skills, and, at the child and adolescent levels of the TRS, School Problems. (Some scales shown in the Summary Table are not part of composites and may be ignored at this point.) To score each composite, sum the T scores of the scales within each section (see **g** in Figure 2.4). Convert the sum of T scores for each composite to a composite scale T score and percentile rank using the norm table that immediately follows the applicable scale-level norm table in Appendix A. Record these normative scores in the Summary Table (see **k** in Figure 2.4). Note that there is a single table of composite norms for the general combined, general female, and general male norm groups.

The Behavioral Symptoms Index (BSI; on TRS and PRS) and Emotional Symptoms Index (ESI; on the Self-Report of Personality–Child [SRP–C], Self-Report of Personality–Adolescent [SRP–A], and Self-Report of Personality–College [SRP–COL]) are scored in the same way as the composites. For the six scales contributing to the BSI or ESI, transfer their T scores to the ovals in the BSI or ESI T-Score column (see **i** in Figure 2.4). For the BSI, write the sum of these T scores in the indicated rectangle toward the bottom of that column (see **j** in Figure 2.4), and convert this number to a BSI T score and percentile rank (see **k** in Figure 2.4). For the ESI, subtract the Self-Esteem and Self-Reliance T scores from 100 in order to make the scoring direction of the scale consistent with the other scales included in the index (see **a** in Figure 2.5). Then, sum those difference scores with the T scores from the other four ESI scales. The BSI and ESI norm tables are presented on the same pages as the composite norm tables.

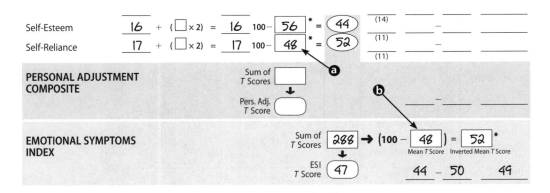

**Figure 2.5** Method of calculating the Emotional Symptoms Index on an SRP–A hand-scoring worksheet

If one of the scales is unscorable because too many items were omitted or multiple responses were given for the same items, it will not be possible to compute any composites (or the BSI or ESI) to which that scale normally contributes. Therefore, it is extremely important to ensure that respondents answer all of the TRS, PRS, and SRP items.

You may construct 90% confidence intervals for the composites the BSI and ESI in the same way as for the scales, using the constant printed at the bottom of the columns of the composite and BSI norm tables. If desired, add this constant to (and subtract it from) the T score, and write the interval in the Summary Table (see **l** in Figure 2.4).

At this point, scoring is completed.

## STEP 5: CALCULATING AND COMPARING MEAN *T* SCORES

### TRS and PRS

You may calculate the mean *T* scores by hand by dividing the sum of *T* scores by the number of scales contributing to the composite (six for the BSI, and three to five for the Adaptive Skills composite) and rounding to a whole number. Alternatively, you may look up the mean *T* scores in Table B.3 of Appendix B. Write these numbers in the indicated boxes in the Summary Table (see **μ** in Figure 2.4). You can then compare each clinical scale *T* score with the mean of the *T* scores making up the BSI, and each adaptive scale *T* score with the mean of the *T* scores forming the Adaptive Skills composite.

### SRP

You may directly compare the clinical scales (those in the School Problems, Internalizing Problems, and Inattention/Hyperactivity composites) with the mean ESI *T* score. However, because the adaptive scales (those in the Personal Adjustment composite) are scored in the positive direction, they cannot be compared with the ESI mean, which is scored in the negative direction. You must first invert the ESI mean *T* score (subtracted from 100) using the indicated box in the Summary Table (see **b** in Figure 2.5). You may then compare each adaptive scale *T* score with the inverted mean ESI *T* score. **Note that, for this comparison, you must use the original (noninverted) *T* scores for the Self-Esteem and Self-Reliance scales.**

## STEP 6: IDENTIFYING HIGH AND LOW SCALE SCORES

The Summary Table includes an H/L column that may be used to identify scale scores that are significantly above or significantly below the respondent's own average. Compute the difference between each scale's *T* score and the applicable mean. If the difference is as large as or larger than the number printed in the H/L column, the difference is statistically significant at the .05 level after adjusting for multiple comparisons. You may have confidence that the child is higher (or lower) on this scale than on the average of the other scales. As with **μ** in Figure 2.4, note any such significant differences by writing an "H" (for higher) or an "L" (for lower) in the H/L column.

If a scale's *T* score is significantly above or significantly below the person's average, it is important to know how rare that discrepancy is in the general population. Tables B.7 and B.8 in Appendix B provide this information for TRS and PRS scores based on the general norm sample. Table B.9 in Appendix B provides this information for SRP scores based on the general norm sample.

## STEP 7: GRAPHING THE *T* SCORES

You may plot the *T* scores and, if desired, their confidence intervals on the Adaptive and Clinical profiles (on the Scoring Summary pages of the hand-scoring worksheet) to provide a graphical display of the pattern of scores. See Figure 2.6 for an example of how to plot these scores.

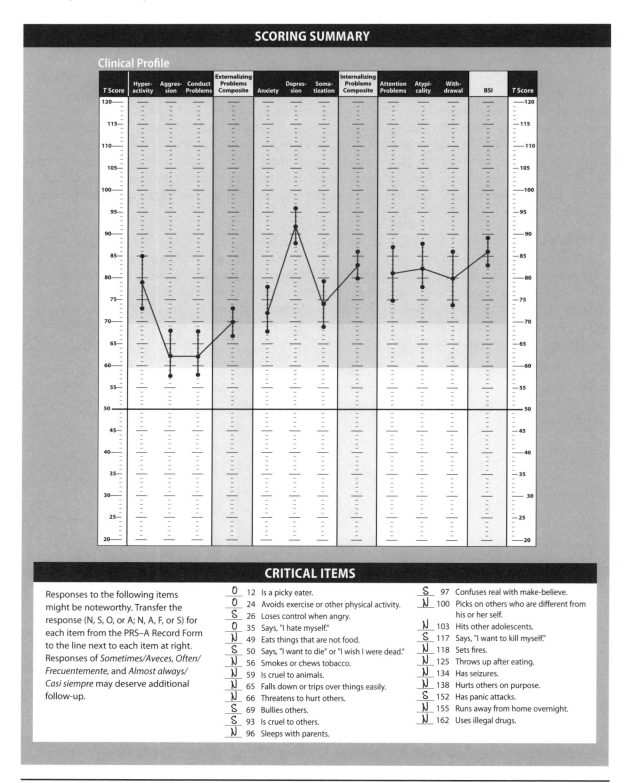

**SCORING SUMMARY**

**Clinical Profile**

**CRITICAL ITEMS**

Responses to the following items might be noteworthy. Transfer the response (N, S, O, or A; N, A, F, or S) for each item from the PRS-A Record Form to the line next to each item at right. Responses of *Sometimes/Aveces, Often/ Frecuentemente,* and *Almost always/ Casi siempre* may deserve additional follow-up.

| | | |
|---|---|---|
| O | 12 | Is a picky eater. |
| O | 24 | Avoids exercise or other physical activity. |
| S | 26 | Loses control when angry. |
| O | 35 | Says, "I hate myself." |
| N | 49 | Eats things that are not food. |
| S | 50 | Says, "I want to die" or "I wish I were dead." |
| N | 56 | Smokes or chews tobacco. |
| N | 59 | Is cruel to animals. |
| N | 65 | Falls down or trips over things easily. |
| N | 66 | Threatens to hurt others. |
| S | 69 | Bullies others. |
| S | 93 | Is cruel to others. |
| N | 96 | Sleeps with parents. |

| | | |
|---|---|---|
| S | 97 | Confuses real with make-believe. |
| N | 100 | Picks on others who are different from his or her self. |
| N | 103 | Hits other adolescents. |
| S | 117 | Says, "I want to kill myself." |
| N | 118 | Sets fires. |
| N | 125 | Throws up after eating. |
| N | 134 | Has seizures. |
| N | 138 | Hurts others on purpose. |
| S | 152 | Has panic attacks. |
| N | 155 | Runs away from home overnight. |
| N | 162 | Uses illegal drugs. |

**Figure 2.6** Clinical Profile and Critical Items

## STEP 8: COMPARING COMPOSITE SCORES

You may use the final section of the Summary Table to identify statistically significant differences among the clinical composites. These clinical composites for TRS and PRS are Externalizing Problems, Internalizing Problems, and, for the Teacher Rating Scales–Child (TRS–C) and Teacher Rating Scales–Adolescent (TRS–A), School Problems. For the SRP–C, SRP–A, and SRP–COL, these clinical composites are School Problems, Internalizing Problems, and Inattention/ Hyperactivity. Transfer the composite *T* scores to the boxes in this section, and compute the difference between each pair, as illustrated in Figure 2.4. If a difference equals or exceeds one of the values printed to the right, it is statistically significant at the .05 or .01 level (adjusting for multiple comparisons), depending on its magnitude. Circle the larger value equaled or exceeded, and write a greater-than sign (>) or less-than sign (<) in the space between the two composites. You may have confidence that the child's rated level of problems is greater in one of these areas than in the other. If the difference is not statistically significant, write an equal sign (=) to indicate that the observed difference (if any) might be due to chance.

If the difference between two composites is statistically significant, it can be important for interpretation to know how frequently a difference of that size occurs in the general population. Table B.2 in Appendix B provides this information based on the general norm sample. Write this frequency in the space provided in the Composite Comparison area.

## STEP 9: ASSESSING CRITICAL ITEMS

Some individual items, listed in the Critical Items section of the hand-scoring worksheet, may have importance as single items. A few of these items are included in the BASC–3 solely for this singular attention and are not a part of any scale (for example, the BASC–3 PRS item "Falls down or trips over things easily."). Others are scale items that have special significance, such as the BASC–3 TRS item "Loses control when angry."

For each of these items, locate the corresponding letter response (N, S, O, or A, or N, A, F, or S for Spanish forms) that appears in the record form. Transfer this letter to the applicable item in the Critical Items section of the hand-scoring worksheet (see Figure 2.6 for a completed Critical Items section). Review the responses for items that require attention and follow up with the respondent as necessary.

## SCORING THE SRP–I

The SRP–I contains 11 items that are scored in Steps A, D, and G (items 2 through 12). To compute the SRP–I score, count the responses that contribute to the score (*No* responses for items 5 and 6; *Yes* responses for items 2 through 4 and 7 through 12). Obtain the score by scoring items according to the values provided in Table 2.3. To obtain the Total Score, sum the scored values of the items and transfer the score to the Total Score section on the cover of the BASC–3 SRP–I record form. Next, in the Total Score area, circle the corresponding number or numeric range for the Total Score (see Figure 2.7). If the score falls into the High or Very High area, refer to chapter 6 for interpretive guidelines.

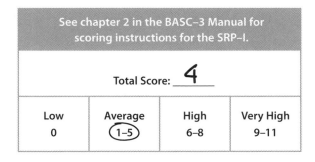

**Figure 2.7** SRP–I Total Score section

Note that items 1, 13, and 14 do not contribute to the Total Score. Item 1 is considered a transition item, allowing the examiner to build some momentum into the administration of scored items. Items 13 and 14 are considered general screening items that provide an opportunity for the child to identify vision or hearing issues that might adversely impact classroom behavior or academic performance.

**Table 2.3** SRP–I Total Score Table

| Item | Yes | No |
|:---:|:---:|:---:|
| 2 | 1 | 0 |
| 3 | 1 | 0 |
| 4 | 1 | 0 |
| 5 | 0 | 1 |
| 6 | 0 | 1 |
| 7 | 1 | 0 |
| 8 | 1 | 0 |
| 9 | 1 | 0 |
| 10 | 1 | 0 |
| 11 | 1 | 0 |
| 12 | 1 | 0 |

# Items Belonging to Each Scale

Appendix C presents a list of the numbers of the items belonging to each scale on each form. This list enables users to find the items belonging to a particular scale, which is especially important when investigating the reasons for an elevated or depressed scale score. BASC–3 Q-global reports provide a reporting option for listing items and responses by scale.

Chapter 3

# Using and Interpreting the Structured Developmental History

When evaluating behavioral and emotional functioning in children, it is critical to obtain information from a variety of sources, across several settings. While this information is considered primary in such an evaluation, it can be hard to interpret without some additional context. A key to conducting an appropriate evaluation is to obtain information about a child's developmental course and trajectory (Sattler, 2014). Such information often provides the additional context necessary to make an appropriate classification or diagnostic decision that best serves the child.

The Structured Developmental History (SDH) provides a thorough review of social, psychological, developmental, educational, and medical information about a child that may influence diagnosis and treatment. The information it provides may be essential for differential diagnosis and may be necessary for referrals to other professionals. Not all of the information obtained in the SDH is significant for every case, but some will always be significant. It is designed to be useful in numerous settings, including clinics, schools, and hospitals. The SDH may be used either as a structured interview with a parent (or someone who fills a similar role) or as a questionnaire to be filled out in the clinician's office, at school, or at home. When used as a questionnaire, the SDH should be reviewed carefully by the clinician in case clarification or elaboration is needed from the respondent.

The SDH is available as an electronic/digital form and a paper form, in both English and Spanish. When used in conjunction with the BASC–3 Parent Rating Scales (PRS), the digitally administered version of the SDH delivers supplemental items based on PRS scale scores, providing additional context that can be helpful for making accurate classification or diagnostic decisions. In addition, the digital form enables a more streamlined administration experience by suppressing unnecessary questions based on the response to a previous question. For example, if the parent indicates the child does not have any siblings, then no additional questions about the child's siblings will appear during the administration.

## Description of the SDH

The SDH represents a comprehensive view of a child's developmental history, gathering information across a wide range of developmental areas and milestones. The sections of the SDH are sequenced in the order they often occur in a report, facilitating report-writing by clinicians and other professionals. Each section has a prominent heading enabling the clinician to skip to sections of interest or cross out sections that may be omitted. Table 3.1 lists the sections included in the SDH; a general overview of the sections is provided next.

**Table 3.1** SDH Sections

| Person Answering Questions | Child's Residence | Friendships |
|---|---|---|
| Referral Information | Family Relations | Recreation/Interests |
| Parents | Pregnancy | Behavior/Temperament |
| Primary Caregivers | Birth | Educational History |
| Child Care | Development | Additional Comments |
| Family History | Medical History | |
| Brothers/Sisters | Family Health | |

The SDH begins by surveying fundamental information about the person answering the questions and the reasons for bringing the child for services. In a clinic or private office, this is crucial to formulating an assessment plan. In cases where someone other than the respondent or a primary caregiver refers a child (e.g., a teacher, counselor, pediatrician), it is important to ascertain the parent's or caregiver's understanding of the referral information.

Next, the SDH gathers demographic, educational, language, and vocational data about the parents. Because the child may live somewhere other than with parents (e.g., with grandparents or foster parents) and a substantial portion of the child's day may be spent with yet another caregiver, the SDH includes additional sections for information describing primary caregivers and child care.

The next sections focus on family history, brothers and sisters, the child's residence, and family relations, including general activities, educational goals, and disciplinary practices. Knowledge of parental expectations and philosophy regarding education and discipline is useful in devising interventions and communicating with parents.

The history of the pregnancy and birth may uncover problems of etiological significance. The relative difficulty and complexity of these events may affect the family's interactions with the child and thus influence behavior. Subtle problems such as prolonged emotional distress during pregnancy, often overlooked, may also have implications for understanding current referral questions.

The SDH asks the respondent about milestones in development. Age of acquisition of basic motor and language skills varies considerably. A consistent delay in overall skill development or a serious gap between motor and language development is noteworthy because such uneven maturation may persist. (See Ramsay, Reynolds, and Kamphaus [2002] for information on evaluating age of acquisition of developmental milestones.)

Parents often have difficulty recalling early developmental events, particularly if they have two or more children. It may be helpful for parents to bring along the child's Baby Book or request pediatrician's records, which are useful when parents' records are incomplete, as they also provide a record of the child's illnesses.

The child's medical history may shed light on his or her current status, provide information relevant to etiology, influence treatment recommendations, or suggest the need for further assessments. For example, a child with a history of prolonged high fever, meningitis, encephalitis, head injury, febrile seizures, or chronic use of psychoactive medications probably should undergo a comprehensive neuropsychological examination in addition to psychological and behavioral assessment.

In addition to surveying past illnesses and injuries, the SDH asks about respiratory, cardiovascular, gastrointestinal, genitourinary, musculoskeletal, dermatological, neurological, and allergy problems. Such problems, if persistent, often have educational and psychological implications. Tarter, Butters, and Beers (2001) provide reviews of the impact of medical problems on psychological, neurological, and behavioral functioning.

The SDH also covers speech, hearing, and vision. Even minor problems in these areas can lead to learning and behavior disorders and often go undetected prior to school entrance.

The SDH also requests information on any history of medical and psychological care the individual has received, including any specialty care such as neurological, psychiatric, or psychological exams.

The family health history explores genetic, chromosomal, and high-risk health factors that may be relevant to diagnosis, referral, or treatment. Additional information about these factors can be found in Fletcher-Janzen and Reynolds (2003), Goldstein and Reynolds (1999), and Tarter et al. (2001). If a broad category such as Mental Illness, Physical Handicaps, Nervousness, Behavior Disorder, Emotional Disturbance, or Other Learning Problems is marked *Yes,* the clinician should ask follow-up questions.

Information on friendships and recreational interests is gathered next, followed by information about behavior, temperament, and fundamental adaptive skills. A quick screen of behavioral disposition can often highlight areas that need more thorough assessment.

Educational history is the last content section in the SDH. Schooling, the major structured component of a child's life, greatly influences socialization and psychological development. Changing schools often may have a substantial impact on a child.

## Uses of the SDH

The collection of a developmental and psychosocial history provides important qualitative information to the diagnostic and treatment process. For a number of types of childhood psychopathology, the antecedents and etiologies are extremely important for diagnosis. A good history is essential to making informed judgments about additional referrals, particularly to other specialists in psychology (e.g., neuropsychologists) or to specialty physicians. Furthermore, information from a thorough history can lead to an earlier diagnosis of many disorders than when diagnosis relies solely on a child's current status.

A history is often the only way to determine whether a disorder is acute or chronic. And for disorders having clear developmental progressions, the history may be essential for diagnosis. The difference between functional and organic disturbance may be revealed by the history. Fixation of development as well as deteriorations in functioning are crucial and typically can be detected only through the process of history-gathering and careful evaluation.

The diagnosis of childhood depression, for example, requires careful analysis of onset, course, and chronicity (persistence) of symptoms. Both psychiatric (*DSM-5* [APA, 2013]) and educational (IDEA, 2004) diagnostic systems specify that depressive symptomatology must have existed for a certain minimum time period to make the diagnosis. Information on date of onset and chronicity is not documented by the rating scales but is easily obtained from the SDH in conjunction with follow-up questioning. If the parent acknowledges that the child is "unhappy most of the time," the clinician can easily question the parent regarding the onset, duration, and severity of the symptoms to help make the proper diagnosis.

Differentiating among clinical disorders also may require a careful history. Consider attention-deficit/hyperactivity disorder (ADHD), generalized anxiety disorder (GAD), and posttraumatic stress disorder (PTSD). These disparate-sounding disorders share some of their most prominent symptoms. However, differential diagnosis of these disorders is imperative because treatments differ dramatically.

The National Institute of Neurological Disorders and Stroke, part of the National Institutes of Health, lists well over 400 neurodegenerative diseases on its website; most are known or suspected to have a genetic or chromosomal basis. Some, such as Huntington's disease, are generally considered to be disorders of adulthood but may have their first manifestations in childhood. Often, the first symptoms may be considered psychological or neuropsychological rather than physical; without a good history these disorders might be misdiagnosed. Although the SDH does not list every genetic disorder, it does highlight several relatively high-frequency conditions and asks about their occurrence in family members.

Disorders that may or may not be genetic, such as schizophrenia, bipolar disorder, and depression, may be more clearly diagnosed if there is a family history of their occurrence. Disorders that are not specifically listed in the SDH may be noted by the respondent in more general categories such as Mental Illness. Follow-up questioning by the clinician is necessary to pinpoint the disorder.

If a child is undergoing psychopharmacological intervention, a careful history is useful in detecting undesirable effects of medication. For example, tics and habit spasms, which may be a problem for many children, can occur in conjunction with stimulant or antidepressant therapy for ADHD. A family history can help in differentiating among related clinical disorders, the onset of a new disorder, and undesirable effects of a treatment regimen.

Medical and psychosocial aspects of a family both have great potential to influence a child's presentation when seen for psychological or educational testing. Without a careful structured history, such as obtained with the SDH, many disorders may be overlooked by the clinician as diagnostic possibilities.

# Administering the SDH

The SDH is administered digitally or via paper forms. While both options provide a comprehensive picture of a child's developmental history, digital administration can enhance the administration for both the parent and clinician. Similar to the PRS, it is important to establish good rapport with the parent or guardian completing the form (see chapter 2). Collecting information about a child's developmental history may initially seem overwhelming to a parent, so it can be helpful to reassure the parent of the importance of gathering such information in the evaluation process. If both parents are available, encourage them to complete the form together. Encourage parents to gather and refer to any documentation they have to assist them in completing the SDH (e.g., a Baby Book containing already-reached developmental milestones).

## DIGITAL FORM

The SDH is administered digitally via Q-global, a secure online administration, scoring, and reporting system. Forms are completed via an on-screen assessment in a school or clinical setting. Alternatively, an e-mail is sent to a parent containing a link to a website to complete the SDH digitally at home, if necessary.

When coupled with a BASC–3 PRS administration, the digital SDH uses PRS results to include additional questions in the SDH administration. These questions are presented based on PRS scale elevations. The questions are designed to capture more information about a specific problem area. This information is useful for establishing the presence or absence of a specific behavioral or emotional disorder or for making an educational classification decision.

Linking PRS and SDH administrations in Q-global is easily done when setting up an on-screen or remote on-screen assessment. Administer the PRS form first and, after the completed PRS form is submitted, administer the SDH form. The rater can complete the SDH form immediately after submitting the PRS form or can do so at a later time. Once both forms have been completed, results will be available for immediate reporting and review.

## PAPER FORM

The paper form is completed at home or in a school or clinical setting. Completion time varies widely, depending on the amount of noteworthy information recorded by parents or guardians. It might be helpful to tell parents to plan for at least 30 minutes to complete the form and longer if the family size is large or if the family has a history of medical- and health-related problems.

The paper form may also be administered by the clinician via a structured interview format with a parent or guardian. The clinician can simply read the items aloud and record the answers. On each page, there is a space for recording notes. This space can be used to record any noteworthy comment that may be useful in understanding the responses provided by the parent or to record additional information that is useful to the overall evaluation of the child or adolescent.

# Development of Additional SDH Items

The complete list of additional SDH questions triggered by elevated scale scores can be viewed in the Q-global resource library. Items were selected based on their relevance to a diagnostic/classification category. Items were written based on the authors' clinical judgment and a review of various reference materials (e.g., *DSM-5*) and published research.

# Chapter 4

## Using and Interpreting the Student Observation System

The BASC–3 Student Observation System (SOS) guides a 15-minute observation procedure that enables the clinician to evaluate a student's behavior in a classroom environment. The SOS is available on the Q-global platform in a digital format that allows the observer to record behavior observations using a smartphone, tablet, or laptop computer. The SOS also is available as a paper form to record children's behaviors; the results can be entered into the Q-global platform for scoring and reporting.

Among the BASC–3 components, the SOS is unique in being the only structured assessment instrument that is used directly by the clinician. Because the SOS is a direct observation procedure, it is likely to be less vulnerable to the biases of a particular respondent than are rating scales. Therefore, the SOS, as an additional source of data, complements the Teacher Rating Scales (TRS), the Parent Rating Scales (PRS), and the Self-Report of Personality (SRP). Unlike many other direct observation systems that were developed for laboratory or research use, the SOS does not require extensive training or equipment. In fact, behavior specialists, special-education consultants, school psychologists, principals, or others involved in evaluating student behavior in the school setting can use the SOS.

In keeping with the philosophy that it is important to identify positive behaviors, not just problems, the SOS assesses a broad spectrum of behaviors, both adaptive and maladaptive. Specifically, the observation form lists 13 positive behaviors and 58 problem behaviors. In contrast, many other observation systems focus attention on narrowly defined clinical syndromes. The SOS includes four adaptive behavior domains: Response to Teacher/Lesson, Peer Interaction, Work on School Subjects, and Transition Movement.

## Purpose of the SOS

The SOS may be used as an aid in diagnosis, treatment planning, and monitoring the effects of treatment. The types of questions that may be addressed by the SOS include the following:

- What types of appropriate and inappropriate behavior is Chris exhibiting in the classroom?

- Does Mariah respond better to direction from her math teacher or her language arts teacher?

- In which type of classroom or under which style of teaching management is James more attentive?

- Does José exhibit more problem behavior in the classroom this year than he did last year?

- How has Ashley responded to her medication?

- What classroom organization schemes (contingencies) discourage Paul's aggression?

- How does Desmond's behavior compare with that of other boys his age in the same classroom?

Many regulations regarding educational assessment require a regimen of direct behavior observation such as the one the SOS provides. The SOS was designed specifically for use with children whose emotional or behavioral problems are significant enough to impede academic progress.

## AID IN DIAGNOSIS

To facilitate diagnosis, information from the SOS may be compared with information from the TRS, PRS, and SRP. The SOS also may be used to validate another respondent's description of the child.

Comparison of SOS data from several different classes (e.g., language arts, math, and science) may be especially useful in making diagnostic decisions concerning children who may have a learning disability or emotional disturbance. Classroom observations have been viewed as particularly helpful for the diagnosis of ADHD.

The SOS may be used to compare the target child's behavior to that of a peer group. Although the SOS is not norm-referenced, the clinician may collect some "rough" normative data by completing the SOS while observing two or three other randomly selected students of the same gender in the same classroom.

## TREATMENT PLANNING

The SOS can be used for treatment planning, and the form contains three parts to help implement this purpose. The three parts—the Behavior Key and Checklist (Part A), the Time Sampling of Behavior (Part B), and the Teacher's Interaction With Student (Part C)—address different treatment-planning needs. The Behavior Key and Checklist enables the observer to specify those behaviors that warrant intervention by indicating which behaviors are most frequent and which are most disruptive. The Time Sampling of Behavior gathers reliable information about deviant or adaptive behavior in the classroom setting. The Teacher's Interaction With Student defines contingencies—that is, discriminative stimuli and reinforcing events—that may influence the child's behavior in the classroom setting. Essentially, Part C of the SOS suggests that interventions be developed within the framework of applied behavior analysis.

## TREATMENT MONITORING

The SOS is also designed to measure changes in the target child's or group's behavior across settings or after intervention. Following intervention, changes in behavior can be evaluated by another administration of the SOS.

## RESEARCH

For research purposes, standardized observational instruments such as the SOS may be useful in comparing groups of individuals. Other research uses of the SOS include validation of assessment instruments (where the SOS serves as a criterion variable) and comparison of treatment methods.

# Using the SOS

The SOS can be completed digitally via Q-global or using a paper observation form, which requires a stopwatch or other device that tracks seconds. Observations may be taken in regular, special-education, or subject-specific classroom settings. The SOS can be administered as often as the situation requires. Multiple administrations can provide insight into the consistency of a student's behavior over time and across settings, thereby providing important information for making treatment decisions and maximizing outcomes. Before using the SOS, the clinician must become familiar with the definitions of the categories and behaviors given in the SOS Time-Sampling Recording Guide at the end of this chapter (see Table 4.1). The word *teacher* is used generically throughout the SOS and may refer to a teacher aide, assistant, parent volunteer, or other person in a similar capacity.

## THE OBSERVER

The observer should make arrangements for the observation with the classroom teacher before class begins. Explaining the nature of the SOS (e.g., its use for consultation, evaluation, and designing pre-referral interventions) is helpful to the teacher.

Children and adolescents often adapt quickly to the presence of an observer in the classroom because of the frequency of such situations. By addressing the reason for the observer's presence, an introduction by the teacher can help focus students' attention on the teacher rather than on the observer.

It is vital that the observer avoid giving the impression of focusing attention on one particular child. It is important to choose a location from which all or most of the students can be viewed simultaneously. The observer should be careful not to react too quickly to the target student's behaviors.

# THE SOS FORM

## Part A–Behavior Key and Checklist

Part A (see Figure 4.1) is a categorized list of specific behaviors that can be used in two ways: first as a reference during the 15-minute observation period and second as a checklist to be completed at the end of the observation period. Part A is positioned before Part B on the form to enable the observer to refer to the listed behaviors when checking categories of behavior during the momentary time sampling.

The 71 specific behaviors listed in Part A are grouped into 14 categories. The four categories of positive behaviors are listed first, followed by ten categories of problem behaviors. For convenience, the problem-behavior categories are listed in an approximate descending order of frequency. New to the BASC–3 SOS form is the Inappropriate Interactions category, which captures behaviors associated with unsuccessful interactions with others and distracting others from the task at hand. The blank spaces in category 15 (Other) can be used to record noteworthy behaviors that do not seem to fit in one of the other behavior categories.

After the 15-minute observation period, Part A is used to indicate how frequently each behavior was observed during the *entire* period (not just during the 3-second intervals). The observer marks the column that best reflects the frequency of each behavior: NO (not observed), SO (sometimes observed), or FO (frequently observed). Notes recorded in Part B can be used to inform Part A ratings. When an observed behavior was disruptive to the class, a check mark can be placed in the corresponding Dis (Disruptive) column. A behavior is considered disruptive when it gains the attention of the teacher and other students, forces the teacher to stop class or the students to stop their work to interact, or causes other students to imitate the behavior. Such behaviors are usually noteworthy when preparing a formal evaluation of a student.

For each behavior category on the checklist, an *Other* row has been included to record any behaviors that are not listed in the category but that fit the general definition of the category. The *Other* item is to be used only in exceptional cases. See Table 4.1 at the end of this chapter for examples of such behavior.

## Part B–Time Sampling of Behavior

Part B is used to document the behaviors that occur during the 15-minute observation period. This period is divided into 30 observations, each includes a 3-second interval to observe the student and a 27-second interval to record the behaviors viewed during the previous three seconds.

During a digital SOS administration, Part B appears first, followed by Part A and then Part C. The digital administration provides prompts for when to observe the student and when to record the behaviors observed. Paper administration will require a stopwatch or a watch/clock with a second hand.

During each 30-second observation interval, more than one behavior category can be marked to indicate each of the behaviors observed during the 3-second interval. However, it is not necessary to have a check mark for each 30-second interval. Use the Comments section to record overall behavior impressions and other general observations. Use the Total column on the paper form to record the sum of the total number of occurrences for each behavior category.

## Part C–Teacher's Interaction With Student

Part C can be used to document information that might prove relevant to understand behaviors that occur during class and to remediate those that are undesirable. Describing the teacher's positioning during the classroom session and the teacher's techniques used to respond to student behaviors can reveal existing practices that are effective or ineffective. Such descriptions can also help to identify techniques that need to be modified or replaced. Part C includes an area to record additional observations deemed noteworthy during the observation session.

## PART A–BEHAVIOR KEY AND CHECKLIST

**Directions:** Use the following list of behaviors as a reference during the 15-minute observation period of Part B. At the end of the period, mark the frequency of each behavior. If the behavior occurred, indicate if it was disruptive.

CHECK ONE:
**NO** = NOT OBSERVED
**SO** = SOMETIMES OBSERVED
**FO** = FREQUENTLY OBSERVED
IF BEHAVIOR IS DISRUPTIVE, CHECK **DIS**.

**NO SO FO — 1. Response to Teacher/Lesson**
Listening to teacher/classmate or following directions
Interacting with teacher in class/group
Working with teacher one-on-one
Standing at teacher's desk
Other _____

**NO SO FO — 2. Peer Interaction**
Playing/working with other student(s)
Talking with other student(s)
Touching another student appropriately
Other _____

**NO SO FO — 3. Work on School Subjects**
Doing seat work
Working at a computer or workstation
Other _____

**NO SO FO — 4. Transition Movement**
Putting on/taking off coat
Moving around room (appropriately)
Preparing materials for beginning/end of lesson
Being out of the room
Other _____

**NO SO FO Dis — 5. Inappropriate Interactions**
Preventing others from working
Ignoring appropriate requests from others
Distracting others by:
  Intruding into others' personal space
  Touching (nonsexual)
  Making noises
  Moving around
Other _____

**NO SO FO Dis — 6. Inappropriate Movement**
Fidgeting in seat
Walking around classroom
Using electronic device (e.g., smartphone) at inappropriate time
Being removed from the classroom
Using work materials inappropriately
Passing notes
Copying answers
Jumping out of seat
Running around classroom
Sitting/standing **beside** desk (on floor)
Sitting/standing **on** desk
Clinging to teacher
Other _____

**NO SO FO Dis — 7. Inattention**
Staring blankly/daydreaming
Doodling
Looking around
Looking at hands
Fiddling with object(s)/fingers
Other _____

**NO SO FO Dis — 8. Inappropriate Vocalization**
Laughing inappropriately
Tattling
Teasing
Making disruptive noises
Arguing/talking back to teacher
Arguing with student
Talking out
Crying
Other _____

**NO SO FO Dis — 9. Somatization**
Sleeping/head down
Complaining of not feeling well
Other _____

**NO SO FO Dis — 10. Repetitive Motor Movements**
Finger/pencil tapping
Foot tapping/swinging
Spinning an object
Rocking
Hand flapping/waving
Pacing
Talking/humming/singing to self
Other self-stimulatory behavior
_____

**NO SO FO Dis — 11. Aggression**
Kicking others
Hitting others with hand
Throwing object(s) at others
Destroying property
Pushing others
Stealing
Other _____

**NO SO FO Dis — 12. Self-Injurious Behavior**
Pulling own hair
Hitting self
Head-banging
Eye-gouging
Biting self
Eating or chewing nonfood items (pica)
Other self-mutilation _____

**NO SO FO Dis — 13. Inappropriate Sexual Behavior**
Engaging in sexual or imitative sexual behavior with a partner
Engaging in sexual or imitative sexual behavior without a partner
Touching others inappropriately
Masturbating
Other _____

**NO SO FO Dis — 14. Bowel/Bladder Problems**
Enuresis
Encopresis
Other _____

**NO SO FO Dis — 15. Other**
_____
_____
_____
_____

2

**Figure 4.1** Part A of the SOS form

# Interpreting the SOS

Before using the SOS, the clinician needs to consider the primary reason for its use, such as intervention planning and evaluation, special-education eligibility, or differential diagnosis. The interpretation is, in part, a function of the purpose of the observation. Part A is intended to give information not only on the types of behaviors exhibited but also on the frequency and disruptiveness of those behaviors. This information is most useful for diagnostic purposes because specific behaviors are identified. These behaviors can be compared to diagnostic criteria from the *DSM-5* (APA, 2013) or another classification system to aid in differential diagnosis. Part A is also useful for targeting specific behavior problems for intervention. This section provides information to be used when writing behavior change objectives.

Part B provides space to record tallies of the frequency of a child's behaviors in broad descriptive terms. Interpretation of frequency requires considerable clinical acumen and is more powerful with baseline data. For example, whether or not a child's displays of aggression are significant can be determined only by applying clinical judgment or collecting additional data. Comparison data can be obtained in a number of ways: (1) randomly select two or three other students of the same gender and observe them as well as the target child, (2) repeat the SOS after intervention has been implemented, or (3) administer the SOS for the same child in different situations.

Comparisons also may be made between categories such as adaptive and maladaptive behaviors. For example, the clinician could evaluate the proportion of time a child spends engaged in adaptive versus maladaptive classroom behaviors.

Part C supports intervention planning by enabling the clinician to record possible factors in the classroom that may be influencing a child's behavior. The additional observations area may be used to record other contingencies (e.g., the influence of peer behavior and the subject matter of the class) deemed important by the clinician.

# Development of the SOS

The SOS was designed to be clinically useful but not dependent on the extensive observer training or special equipment associated with many observation systems. However, to enhance the quality and usability of the results, some structure was required. The momentary time-sampling procedure meets the dual objectives of simplicity and reliability.

The SOS was developed as part of the BASC system to assess a broad spectrum of adaptive and maladaptive classroom behaviors. Behaviors were included on the form based on expert judgment and analyses used to identify underlying behavioral themes (see the BASC–2 Manual [Reynolds & Kamphaus, 2004] for a detailed discussion of this procedure). As part of the BASC–3 standardization project, a group of psychologists participating in the reliability study (discussed below) reviewed the items for both comprehensiveness and relevance of behaviors in today's classrooms. Their recommendations resulted in the addition of the Inappropriate Interactions behavior category and some minor modifications to a few of the existing behaviors.

# Reliability

During the BASC–3 standardization project, school psychologists were recruited to participate in a study designed to provide support for the reliability of the scores derived from the SOS form (i.e., the sums of occurrence for the observed behavior categories). Due to logistical constraints and the inherent uncertainty in conducting a live observation, this study centered on taping a mock third-grade classroom in which a male student was identified as the target of the observation. The simulated classroom session included two brief student transition movements, a spelling quiz, a teacher–group interaction session (i.e., discussion of current events), and a brief math lesson followed by some student seat work. The target student's behaviors during the classroom session consisted mainly of naturally occurring behaviors, although a few off-camera prompts were given to the student to ensure an adequate number of observable behaviors for the study.

Nineteen school psychologists agreed to participate in the study. All participants had experience using the BASC–2 instruments, with more than half reporting 5 or more years of experience, although eight participants had not used the SOS in the previous 12 months. Seventeen participants reported conducting direct observations on a monthly basis, while the remaining two participants (who were university faculty) reported training students how to conduct direct observations.

Study participants were mailed an instructional packet, an SOS form, and a DVD of the classroom session. The target student was identified in the instructional materials. After becoming familiar with the SOS form, participants completed the SOS form while observing the target student during the classroom session. After returning the completed materials, participants were paid a nominal amount for completing the study.

To demonstrate the level of consistency in ratings made in Part A and Part B, Fleiss Kappa estimates were computed. On Part A, across each of the 13 behavior categories on the BASC–2 form, the mean level of agreement was 81%, ranging from 44% to 100%. (Note that there were several categories in which no behaviors were exhibited [e.g., Self-Injurious Behavior], resulting in perfect agreement.) On Part B, the mean level of agreement across all behavior categories was 89%, ranging from 62% to 100%. Overall, the amount of agreement between raters was considered to be strong. Not surprisingly, behavior categories with the lowest levels of agreement were Work on School Subjects and Inattention. These behavior categories can be difficult to determine in a limited context such as watching a DVD; the actual environment will likely offer rich contextual information that makes it easier for the rater to determine the full extent of the nature of a behavior.

**Table 4.1** SOS Time-Sampling Recording Guide

| Category/definition | Specific behavior examples |
|---|---|
| **1. Response to Teacher/Lesson:** This category describes the student's *appropriate* academic behaviors involving the teacher or class. This category does not include working on school subjects (see Category 3). | Raising hand to ask/answer a question; contributing to class discussion; waiting for help or for an assignment or task |
| **2. Peer Interaction:** This category assesses positive or appropriate interactions with other students. | Conversing with others in small group or class discussion; lightly touching another student in a friendly or encouraging manner; giving a pat on the back or shaking hands |
| **3. Work on School Subjects:** This category includes *appropriate* academic behaviors that the student engages in alone, without interacting with others. | Working on a school subject either at the student's own desk or in a learning center |
| **4. Transition Movement:** This category is for appropriate and nondisruptive behaviors of children while moving from one activity or place to another. Most are out-of-seat behaviors and may be infrequent during a classroom observation period. | Walking to the front of the class; getting a book; sharpening a pencil; lining up; taking a water/bathroom break; performing an errand; following others in line |
| **5. Inappropriate Interactions:** This category includes interactions with others that can be distracting or perceived by others negatively. | Preventing others from working; ignoring appropriate requests from others; distracting others by intruding into others' personal space; touching (nonsexual); making noises; moving around |
| **6. Inappropriate Movement:** This category is intended for inappropriate motor behaviors that are unrelated to classroom work. | Being asked to leave the room or being physically removed from the room; hitting others with a classroom-related object (e.g., a musical instrument); refusing to leave a teacher's side to participate in school activities |
| **7. Inattention:** This category includes inattentive behaviors that are not disruptive. | Scribbling on paper or desks; looking at objects unrelated to classroom activity while not paying attention |
| **8. Inappropriate Vocalization:** This category includes disruptive vocal behaviors. Only vocal behavior should be checked. | Criticizing another harshly; picking on another student; making disruptive noises such as screaming, belching, moaning, grinding teeth, or "shhh" sounds; refusing to do schoolwork or participate in an activity; talking out of turn, during a quiet time, or without permission |
| **9. Somatization:** This category includes behaviors regardless of inferred reason (e.g., a student may be sleeping because of medication, boredom, or poor achievement motivation). | Complaining that stomach hurts; complaining that head hurts |
| **10. Repetitive Motor Movement:** This category includes repetitive behaviors (both disruptive and nondisruptive) that appear to have no external reward. Generally, the behaviors should be of 15-second duration or longer to be checked and may be more likely to be checked on Part A than on Part B because of their repetitive nature. They may, however, be checked during either part. | Rapping finger(s)/pencil on desk; tapping foot on floor; swinging foot in the air; twirling or spinning a pencil or toy; moving body back and forth or from side to side while sitting; walking back and forth or in a circle in one area; sucking on back of hand; staring fixedly at moving hand; twisting hair |

**Table 4.1** SOS Time-Sampling Recording Guide *(continued)*

| Category/definition | Specific behavior examples |
|---|---|
| **11. Aggression:** This category includes harmful behaviors directed at another student, the teacher, or property. The student must attempt to hurt another or destroy property for the behavior to be checked in this category. Aggressive play would not be included here. | Intentionally tearing, ripping, or breaking own or another's work, belongings, or property |
| **12. Self-Injurious Behavior:** This category includes severe behaviors that attempt to injure oneself. These behaviors should not be confused with self-stimulatory behaviors. This category is intended to capture behaviors of children with severe disabilities who are being served in special classes in schools and institutions. | Pulling own hair with enough force to pull it out; slapping or punching self with enough force to cause a bruise or laceration; banging head on a wall, floor, or object with enough force to bruise or injure; scratching or poking at own eyes with enough force to cause injury; placing paper, dirt, or grass in mouth and attempting to ingest it |
| **13. Inappropriate Sexual Behavior:** This category includes behaviors that are explicitly sexual in nature. The student could be seeking sexual gratification. Behaviors that are not flagrant and specifically sexual (e.g., hitting others) are not included here. | "Petting" self or others |
| **14. Bowel/Bladder Problems:** This category includes urination and defecation. | Urinating in his or her pants; having a bowel movement outside the toilet; soiling or smearing in pants |
| **15. Other:** This category includes behaviors that do not seem to fit in any other categories. It should be used infrequently. | |

Chapter **5**

# Interpreting the Teacher and Parent Rating Scales: The Primary Scales and Validity Indicators

The BASC–3 Teacher Rating Scales (TRS) and Parent Rating Scales (PRS) are complementary measures of child behavior in school, home, and community settings. The TRS and PRS share many common scales that are derived from both a theoretical and an empirical basis, facilitating comparison across multiple settings. Although several items are shared, overall a significant number of items differ between the TRS and PRS. The item similarities promote comparison of behaviors across settings, whereas the item differences allow the detection of important differences in behaviors that are unique to specific settings. The TRS has two scales (Learning Problems and Study Skills) that are relevant only to the school setting; the PRS includes one scale (Activities of Daily Living) most appropriately rated by a parent or caregiver.

This chapter presents information on interpreting the TRS and PRS. Detailed descriptions of the instruments are provided at the item, scale, and composite levels. The discussions include interpretive suggestions based on research with the previous editions of the BASC, validation evidence gathered on the BASC–3 scale scores, clinical group BASC–3 score profiles, and clinical expertise gained by the authors and other users of the BASC editions. Once the TRS and PRS are firmly understood, the interpretive guidelines presented in this chapter may be used to identify significant features of a child's scale score pattern.

A clinician's ability to achieve an adequate understanding of the scores provided by any instrument, such as the BASC–3 TRS or PRS, is often a function of the instrument's quality. Clearly conceptualized a priori scales have long been recognized as important to the process of producing meaningful conceptual behavior models (Loevinger, 1957). By analogy, clearly defined a priori scales are just as crucial for developing meaningful interpretations of a set of scores. Such scales will be clear conceptually and also will be more likely to possess content, predictive, and other types of validity. Schaefer (1971) describes the following process of developing scales using a priori methods:

> In the development of a priori scales, the investigator attempts to assemble a set of homogeneous items to define a more general concept. If a number of items are assembled for each concept, it is usually possible to refine and shorten the scales from analyses of empirical data on item and scale characteristics (p. 135).

During the BASC–3 development, clearly conceptualized scales that incorporate a balance between theory and empiricism—a hallmark of the BASC and BASC–2 editions (Ostrander, Weinfurt, Yarnold, & August, 1998; Sandoval & Echandia, 1994)—remained a primary goal of the revision. In addition, consideration was also given to symptomatology associated with popular diagnostic references such as the ICD-10, *DSM-5* (APA, 2013), and regulatory schemes including IDEA (2004), the Americans With Disabilities Act (ADA, 1990), and Section 504 (Rehabilitation Act, 1973). Clinicians can therefore interpret the scales confidently in the multidimensional environments where children with disabilities receive services.

## Assessing Validity

Results from the TRS and PRS should be interpreted cautiously if there is serious reason to question whether the respondent has given accurate information. The validity of TRS and PRS results may be compromised for a variety of reasons, including positive and negative response sets, intentional dishonesty, emotional difficulties, stress on the part of the teacher or parent, or the inadequate familiarity of the respondent with the child being evaluated. Positively and negatively worded items are included on the rating scales to guard against positive and negative response sets (Comrey, 1988). However, when evaluating TRS and PRS results, it remains important to apply available methods of detecting invalid results such as those described in the following paragraphs.

## *F* INDEX

The *F* ("faking bad") Index assesses the possibility that a teacher or parent rated a child in an inordinately negative fashion. This classic validity scale consists of items that represent maladaptive behaviors to which the respondent answered *Almost always* (A) and adaptive behaviors to which the respondent answered *Never* (N). Hence, high scores on this index would either indicate that extraordinarily maladaptive behavior is present or suggest that the teacher or parent rated the child's performance more severely than is warranted. Table 5.1 presents the items that are included in the *F* Index.

**Table 5.1** TRS and PRS: *F*-Index Items

| TRS–P | TRS–C | TRS–A | PRS–P | PRS–C | PRS–A | Item |
|-------|-------|-------|-------|-------|-------|------|
|  |  | 123 |  | 166 | 53 | Acts out of control. (A) |
|  |  |  | 118 |  |  | Acts strangely. (A) |
|  |  |  |  | 31 | 141 | Appears tense. (A) |
| 18 | 123 |  |  |  |  | Avoids making friends. (A) |
| 37 |  | 91 | 82 | 96 | 127 | Avoids other children/adolescents. (A) |
|  | 132 |  |  | 157 |  | Babbles to self. (A) |
|  |  |  | 58 |  |  | Bangs head. (A) |
| 59 |  |  |  |  |  | Breaks other children's things.  (A) |
| 92 |  | 86 | 96 | 117 | 69 | Bullies others. (A) |
|  | 149 |  |  |  |  | Cheats in school. (A) |
|  |  |  | 18 |  |  | Complains about health. (A) |
|  |  | 33 | 122 |  | 47 | Complains of pain. (A) |
|  |  | 94 |  |  |  | Complains that lessons go too fast. (A) |
|  |  |  |  |  | 97 | Confuses real with make-believe. (A) |
|  | 35 |  |  | 43 |  | Deceives others. (A) |
|  | 82 |  |  |  |  | Defies teachers.  (A) |
|  |  |  |  |  | 114 | Disrupts other adolescents' activities.  (A) |
|  |  |  | 20 |  |  | Disrupts the play of other children. (A) |
|  |  |  | 145 |  |  | Does strange things. (A) |
|  | 66 |  |  |  |  | Engages in repetitive movements. (A) |
|  |  |  | 63 |  |  | Expresses fear of getting sick. (A) |
|  |  |  |  |  | 5 | Gets into trouble. (A) |
|  | 80 |  |  |  | 31 | Gets sick. (A) |
| 23 |  |  |  |  |  | Has fevers. (A) |
| 76 |  | 47 |  |  |  | Has headaches. (A) |
|  | 26 | 22 |  | 136 | 152 | Has panic attacks. (A) |
| 88 |  |  |  |  |  | Has sore throats. (A) |
|  | 73 | 70 |  |  |  | Hits other children/adolescents.  (A) |
|  |  | 157 |  | 55 |  | Hurts others on purpose. (A) |

**Table 5.1** TRS and PRS: *F*-Index Items *(continued)*

| TRS–P | TRS–C | TRS–A | PRS–P | PRS–C | PRS–A | Item |
|---|---|---|---|---|---|---|
| | | | | | 93 | Is cruel to others. (A) |
| | 8 | 10 | | | | Is fearful. (A) |
| 13 | | | 49 | | | Is mean. (A) |
| 74 | | | 90 | | | Is negative about things. (A) |
| 95 | | | 138 | | | Is nervous. (A) |
| 41 | | 149 | 14 | | 19 | Is sad. (A) |
| | | | 40 | | | Is shy with other children. (A) |
| | | 80 | | | | Is suspicious of others. (A) |
| 103 | | | | | | Isolates self from others. (A) |
| | | | | | 22 | Lies. (A) |
| | | | 38 | 28 | | Listens to directions. (N) |
| 1 | | | 16 | 1 | 1 | Pays attention. (N) |
| | 109 | 109 | | 108 | 100 | Picks on others who are different from his or her self. (A) |
| | 57 | 55 | | 94 | | Puts others down. (A) |
| 44 | 78 | | 69 | 79 | 74 | Reacts negatively. (A) |
| | 20 | 46 | | | | Refuses advice. (A) |
| | 37 | 3 | | | | Refuses to talk. (A) |
| | | | | 5 | 81 | Responds appropriately when asked a question. (N) |
| | 156 | | | | | Says, "I don't have any friends." (A) |
| | 97 | | | | 35 | Says, "I hate myself." (A) |
| | | 153 | | 52 | | Says, "I want to die" or "I wish I were dead." (A) |
| | | | | 124 | | Says, "I want to kill myself." (A) |
| 65 | | | 129 | | | Says, "I'm afraid I will make a mistake." (A) |
| 29 | 12 | | 105 | | | Says, "Nobody likes me." (A) |
| | | | | 14 | | Says, "please" and "thank you." (N) |
| | 128 | | | | | Says things that make no sense. (A) |
| | | | 34 | | | Seems odd. (A) |
| 8 | 50 | | | | 39 | Seems out of touch with reality. (A) |
| | | 136 | | | | Seems unaware of others. (A) |
| | | | 32 | | | Shares toys or possessions with other children. (N) |
| 83 | | | | | | Shows feelings that do not fit the situation. (A) |
| | | | | | 167 | Tells lies about others. (A) |
| 55 | 61 | | | 35 | | Threatens to hurt others. (A) |
| | | 113 | | | | Uses others' things without permission. (A) |
| | | | 7 | | | Will seek help when he or she needs it. (N) |
| 69 | | | | | | Worries about things that cannot be changed. (A) |

Table 5.2 provides an interpretation summary for the TRS and PRS *F*-Index scores. If the *F*-Index score for a child is in either the Caution or Extreme Caution range, the examiner should consider the possibility that a negative response set has skewed the TRS or PRS results (as discussed in the next section).

**Table 5.2** *F*-Index Raw-Score Interpretation Summary

|  | Acceptable | Caution | Extreme Caution |
|---|---|---|---|
| TRS–P | 0–1 | 2 | 3–20 |
| TRS–C | 0–1 | 2 | 3–20 |
| TRS–A | 0–1 | 2 | 3–20 |
| PRS–P | 0–1 | 2–3 | 4–20 |
| PRS–C | 0–1 | 2 | 3–20 |
| PRS–A | 0–1 | 2–7 | 8–20 |

Based on the BASC–3 general norm sample, the number of completed cases in which the *F*-Index score was in either the Caution or Extreme Caution range was very small (approximately 3% or less in the Caution range and 1% or less in the Extreme Caution range). Additional information on the development and validation of this index can be found in chapter 7.

## INCONSISTENCY WITH OTHER RESULTS

One way to explore the possibility of invalid test results is to compare the ratings to other BASC–3 results. For example, if one teacher's ratings are strongly negative (perhaps indicated by a high *F*-Index score) but the results on the PRS, SRP, or a TRS from another of the child's teachers are less adverse, then the first teacher's ratings may have resulted in a negative response set. On the other hand, if the results from one or more other raters show similarly maladaptive tendencies, then it is likely the respondent is accurately reporting the child's extensive behavior problems. It is important to consider, however, that a child might simply behave differently in the presence of one respondent as compared to another or in one setting versus another. It is not unusual for a child or adolescent to behave differently with a mother, father, or stepparent, just as it is not unusual for a student to behave quite differently with teachers who teach different subject matter areas and/or who have different classroom management approaches. When discrepancies across raters occur, it can be the result of unreliable ratings. However, an alternative view is that these differences can be informative, providing evidence regarding the pervasiveness of some behaviors and the episodic nature of others as well as the contextual determinants of behavior, all very valuable information in both diagnosis and in planning interventions. When discrepancies are present, using the Student Observation System (SOS) may help clarify the reason for the different ratings, as will a comprehensive clinical interview with the child or adolescent and a detailed history assisted by the Structured Developmental History (SDH).

The clinician may also become suspicious of TRS or PRS results for a child referred for behavior problems if the ratings do not indicate any problems. The respondent may have attempted to make the child "look good." If the previous example were reversed, and only one of the child's TRS forms suggested no difficulties but other sources indicated the presence of problems, then the clinician should consider the possibility of a positive response set. An alternative explanation of results that are inconsistent with those from other sources might be that the child's behaviors are situation-specific.

The BASC–3 Q-global scoring reports allow comparisons between different ratings of the child on the TRS and/or PRS. This information is useful for determining how similar or divergent the results are from two or more ratings.

## OMITTED ITEMS

When using the TRS or PRS paper forms, an excessive number of omitted items may compromise the interpretability of BASC–3 scores. (Administrations completed with Q-global require responses to each item, thereby negating the impact of omitted items.) Whenever possible, the clinician should encourage the respondent to answer all items. The layout of the TRS and PRS record forms makes it easy to count the total number of omitted items. In some cases, the respondent may omit items simply because he or she is unclear of their meaning and may be able to complete them with some assistance. On the other hand, the respondent may have been unwilling to answer items on certain topics. The clinician may want to examine the content of omitted items to explore this possibility.

On all TRS and PRS record forms, a maximum of two unscorable (i.e., omitted or multiply-marked) items is allowed per scale. Three or more unscorable items on a single scale will invalidate that scale and any subsequent composite scale score(s) to which the unscorable scale contributes. When one or two items are unscorable, raw scores are adjusted using adjustment factor values that were derived based on the average item responses for each scale obtained in the general norm sample. The purpose of the adjustment is to present a more accurate scaled score estimation. Without the adjustment, clinical scale scores would estimate the child being closer to "average" than he or she may really be; scores on the adaptive scales would suggest the child has more problems than is actually the case. When scoring paper TRS or PRS record forms with Q-global, it is important to note that too many total missing items will prevent a report from being generated.

Table 5.3 provides a summary of the adjustment factors used on each TRS and PRS record form. To adjust the raw score of the Withdrawal scale, for example, locate the adjustment factor ("1") in the table. If the respondent omitted two Withdrawal scale items from a PRS record form, the number of unscorable items is multiplied by the adjustment factor as follows: 2 x 1 = 2. Thus, 2 points would be added to the Withdrawal raw score prior to its conversion to a *T* score.

**Table 5.3** TRS and PRS Adjustment Factors for Unscorable Item Responses

| Scale | TRS | | | PRS | | |
|---|---|---|---|---|---|---|
| | P | C | A | P | C | A |
| Hyperactivity | 1 | 1 | 0 | 1 | 1 | 1 |
| Aggression | 0 | 0 | 0 | 0 | 0 | 0 |
| Conduct Problems | — | 0 | 0 | — | 1 | 0 |
| Anxiety | 0 | 0 | 0 | 1 | 1 | 1 |
| Depression | 1 | 0 | 0 | 1 | 0 | 0 |
| Somatization | 0 | 0 | 0 | 0 | 0 | 0 |
| Attention Problems | 1 | 1 | 1 | 1 | 1 | 1 |
| Learning Problems | — | 1 | 1 | — | — | — |
| Atypicality | 0 | 0 | 0 | 0 | 0 | 0 |
| Withdrawal | 0 | 0 | 0 | 1 | 1 | 1 |
| Adaptability | 2 | 2 | 2 | 2 | 2 | 2 |
| Social Skills | 2 | 2 | 2 | 2 | 2 | 2 |
| Leadership | — | 2 | 2 | — | 2 | 2 |
| Study Skills | — | 2 | 2 | — | — | — |
| Activities of Daily Living | — | — | — | 2 | 2 | 2 |
| Functional Communication | 2 | 2 | 2 | 2 | 2 | 2 |
| Anger Control | 0 | 0 | 0 | 1 | 1 | 1 |
| Bullying | 1 | 0 | 0 | 0 | 0 | 0 |
| Developmental Social Disorders | 1 | 1 | 1 | 1 | 1 | 1 |
| Emotional Self-Control | 1 | 1 | 0 | 1 | 1 | 1 |
| Executive Functioning | 1 | 1 | 1 | 1 | 1 | 1 |
| Negative Emotionality | 1 | 0 | 0 | 1 | 1 | 1 |
| Resiliency | 2 | 2 | 2 | 2 | 2 | 2 |

## PATTERNED RESPONDING

Examiners should review responses on the record forms carefully for patterned responding. For example, if a respondent marks all *N*s (or only *N*s and *A*s) or alternates responses by giving all *N*s in one column and all *S*s in the next, the validity of the rating scales should be questioned.

The Response Pattern Index, available in the BASC–3 Q-global reports, is designed to identify forms that may be invalid because the respondent was inattentive to the item content. The first pattern is characterized by the identical response to many items in succession (e.g., N-N-N-N . . .). The second pattern detected by the Response Pattern Index is an alternating or cyclical pattern (e.g., N-S-O-A-N- S-O-A . . .). A respondent who pays little attention to the items might find it easy to answer using one of these patterns.

The Response Pattern Index is a tally of the number of times an item response differs from the response to the previous item. A very low tally indicates the respondent tended to choose the same response option repeatedly when completing the form. A very high tally suggests the respondent might have completed the form in a cyclical pattern. Valid TRS and PRS record forms will tend to have a Response Pattern Index score that falls somewhere between these extremes. Scores in the Caution-Low and Caution-High ranges are intended to identify the extreme 0.5% of each end of the Response Pattern Index score distribution, based on the general norm sample for that record form.

Table 5.4 provides an interpretation summary for the Response Pattern Index. A Caution-Low score indicates there were very few changes in item responses. A Caution-High score shows considerable variation in item responses. A score in either cautionary range would warrant a review of the record form (or the item responses) to see whether obvious patterns exist that would suggest the respondent disregarded the item content. The Consistency Index (described next) may provide supporting evidence. If a Caution-High or Caution-Low score is obtained on the Response Pattern Index, it may be necessary to question the respondent directly.

**Table 5.4** Response Pattern Index Raw-Score Interpretation Summary

|       | Caution-Low | Acceptable | Caution-High |
|-------|-------------|------------|--------------|
| TRS–P | 0–23        | 24–82      | 83–104       |
| TRS–C | 0–45        | 46–123     | 124–155      |
| TRS–A | 0–38        | 39–128     | 129–164      |
| PRS–P | 0–23        | 24–108     | 109–138      |
| PRS–C | 0–45        | 46–135     | 136–174      |
| PRS–A | 0–42        | 43–130     | 131–172      |

## CONSISTENCY INDEX

The Consistency Index, available in the BASC–3 Q-global reports, identifies cases where the respondent has given differing responses to items that usually are answered similarly. Like the Response Pattern Index, the Consistency Index is designed to identify BASC–3 forms with results that may be invalid because the respondent disregarded the item content. More generally, the Consistency Index detects BASC–3 record forms with responses that are not internally consistent (i.e., where the respondent frequently answered very similar items differently). Inconsistency can occur for a variety of reasons, including:

- A respondent changing his or her perspective when completing a form

- Different respondents completing different parts of a form (e.g., the mother completing the first half of the form and the father completing the second)

- A respondent misunderstanding the items because of poor reading ability or language comprehension

The Consistency Index was created by pairing items for each form that are highly correlated (either positively or negatively) and then summing the absolute values of the score differences between the items in each pair. The directionality of the scoring of each item in a pair was considered to ensure that the difference would be meaningful.

The cutoff values for each form are set at a point that effectively separates the distribution of Consistency Index values in a large sample of general and clinical norm cases from the distribution of values in a set of randomly generated scores. Table 5.5 presents the cutoff values and interpretation categories for each record form. Because the sum of score differences is actually a direct measure of inconsistency, a high score on the Consistency Index signifies that the results should be interpreted cautiously, and the possibility that the form is invalid should be explored. When the Consistency Index is in the Caution or Extreme Caution score range, the computer reports list the item pairs contributing to the high score. This information is helpful for determining, case by case, whether the response disagreements are plausible or implausible. Additional information on the distribution properties and validity evidence of the Consistency Index can be found in chapter 7.

**Table 5.5** Consistency Index Raw-Score Interpretation Summary

|  | Acceptable | Caution | Extreme Caution |
|---|---|---|---|
| TRS–P | 0–12 | 13–17 | 18 or higher |
| TRS–C | 0–11 | 12–13 | 14 or higher |
| TRS–A | 0–11 | 12–14 | 15 or higher |
| PRS–P | 0–14 | 15–17 | 18 or higher |
| PRS–C | 0–12 | 13–14 | 15 or higher |
| PRS–A | 0–10 | 11–14 | 15 or higher |

## READING DIFFICULTIES

Parents may produce invalid responses on the PRS if they lack English or Spanish reading proficiency, perhaps as a result of linguistic differences, reading disability, or lack of education. Check this hypothesis by carefully reviewing parental background information, observing nervousness or unease by a parent who is asked to complete a form, or noting that a parent has asked for clarification of the meaning of several individual items. See chapter 7 for a summary on the reading levels for the PRS forms.

# Interpreting TRS and PRS Scale Scores

The BASC–3 TRS and PRS record forms offer several types of scales: clinical, adaptive, composite, content, and a variety of indexes. Each scale type is defined in its corresponding section below. An overview of each scale is also provided, including a description of its content and interpretive guidelines. Table 5.6 briefly describes each of the scale types.

**Table 5.6** BASC–3 Scale Types

| Scale type | Description |
|---|---|
| Clinical | Measure maladaptive behaviors, where high scores indicate problematic levels of functioning. Items are unique to a clinical or adaptive scale. |
| Adaptive | Measure adaptive behaviors or behavioral strengths, where low scores indicate possible problem areas. Items are unique to a clinical or adaptive scale. |
| Content | Measure maladaptive or adaptive behaviors; are composed of a few unique items along with items from other clinical or adaptive scales. |
| Composite | Composed of scale groupings that are based on theory and factor-analytic results. |
| Indexes | Empirically derived scales composed of items from other scales that were selected based on their ability to differentiate those with and without behavioral or emotional functioning diagnosis or classification. |

## CLINICAL SCALES

The clinical scales measure maladaptive behavior and consist of items written for each corresponding scale (in contrast to content scales or indexes, which consist of items from a variety of scales; see scale type discussions for additional information). High scores on the clinical scales represent negative or undesirable characteristics that are generally problematic and cause impaired functioning in home, school, peer relationships, or community settings. As mentioned in chapter 2 (see Table 2.2), clinical scale scores in the 60 through 69 range are considered at-risk, and scores 70 or higher are considered clinically significant. Table 5.7 provides brief descriptions of each clinical scale.

**Table 5.7** TRS and PRS Clinical Scale Descriptions

| Clinical scale | Description |
|---|---|
| Aggression | The tendency to act in a hostile manner (either verbal or physical) that is threatening to others |
| Anxiety | The tendency to be nervous, fearful, or worried about real or imagined problems |
| Attention Problems | The tendency to be easily distracted and unable to concentrate more than momentarily |
| Atypicality | The tendency to behave in ways that are considered odd or commonly associated with psychosis |
| Conduct Problems | The tendency to engage in antisocial and rule-breaking behavior, including destroying property |
| Depression | Feelings of unhappiness, sadness, and stress that may result in an inability to carry out everyday activities or may bring on thoughts of suicide |
| Hyperactivity | The tendency to be overly active, rush through work or activities, and act without thinking |
| Learning Problems | The presence of academic difficulties, particularly understanding or completing homework |
| Somatization | The tendency to be overly sensitive to and complain about relatively minor physical problems and discomforts |
| Withdrawal | The tendency to evade others to avoid social contact |

## Aggression

Aggression centers on behavior that can result in physical or emotional harm to others or their property. It is associated with a variety of disorders (e.g., conduct disorder; Patterson, DeBaryshe, & Ramsey, 1989). Symptoms of aggression are among the leading causes of children's referrals to pediatric mental health providers, and if not treated early, aggression can contribute to delinquency at older ages (Bassarath, 2003; Broidy et al., 2003). The Aggression scale assesses both verbal and physical aggression. Items measuring verbal aggression refer to such behaviors as arguing, teasing, and verbally threatening others. Items assessing physical aggression include breaking others' possessions and hitting others. The remaining items refer to more general aggressive behaviors, such as getting back at others, being overly aggressive, or bullying others. Aggression scale scores in the Clinically Significant range signify highly disruptive behavior that often is of great concern to teachers, parents, and other caregivers. Additional follow-up on such scores is recommended to determine if there is a risk to self or others.

The Aggression scale correlates with other BASC–3 scales in a predictable fashion. It correlates highly with other measures of Externalizing Problems, and it tends to be elevated for children with disruptive behavior disorders, such as conduct disorder (CD) and attention-deficit/hyperactivity disorder (ADHD). In the BASC–3 clinical samples, Aggression scale scores are generally elevated on both the TRS and PRS for children classified as having an emotional/behavioral disturbance (EBD), and on the PRS for the ADHD sample (see chapters 9 and 10 for additional information).

## Anxiety

Anxiety disorders are common in children and adolescents, and they are often comorbid with other conditions (e.g., depression; Cummings, Caporino, & Kendall, 2014). According to the *DSM-5* diagnostic criteria, anxiety disorders are marked by a number of behaviors, many of which are included on the Anxiety scale. Excessive worry is a central characteristic of anxiety disorders (Strauss, 1990). Other symptomatic behaviors measured by the Anxiety scale include fears and phobias, self-deprecation (e.g., "I'm not very good at this"), and nervousness.

By itself, an elevated Anxiety scale score typically is not sufficient to support the diagnosis of an anxiety disorder, which usually is accompanied by other symptoms such as somatic complaints or depression. For example, a combination of elevated Anxiety and Somatization scale scores may be a more appropriate basis than the Anxiety score alone for determining whether a child meets the *DSM-5* diagnostic criteria for separation anxiety disorder or panic disorder. Or, a Somatization scale score might indicate the presence of an anxiety disorder, such as separation anxiety, in the absence of a deviant score on the Anxiety scale. In such cases, the possibility of an anxiety disorder should be considered, even when an accompanying Anxiety scale score is not within the Clinically Significant range. A careful history-gathering and examination of related symptoms is typically required to determine whether an elevated Anxiety scale score is associated with an anxiety-related disorder or if it is the manifestation of another disorder.

The Anxiety scale correlates the highest with the other BASC–3 Internalizing Problems scales (i.e., Depression and Somatization); correlations with other BASC–3 scales are low. In the BASC–3 clinical samples, Anxiety scale scores were elevated for the EBD clinical groups (see chapters 9 and 10 for additional information). Anxiety issues can be comorbid with a variety of mental health conditions and are associated with a variety of pathological behaviors that can result in functional impairment (APA, 2013).

## Attention Problems

The Attention Problems scale measures an inability to maintain attention and the tendency to be easily distracted from tasks requiring attention. It was designed to be useful for identifying a subset of core ADHD symptoms (i.e., hyperactivity, impulsivity, and inattention; Henker & Whalen, 1989).

When coupled with the Hyperactivity scale, the Attention Problems scale has been shown to accurately distinguish between the three presentations of ADHD: combined, predominantly inattentive, and predominantly hyperactive/impulsive (Vaughn, Riccio, Hynd, & Hall, 1997). Research has also shown that attention problems have particular relevance for those in educational settings because inattention is more highly correlated with academic problems than is hyperactivity (Hartley, 1999). These problems can persist into adolescence and adulthood, resulting in a variety of personal, social, or occupational problems (Miranda, Berenguer, Colomer, & Roselló, 2014; Schwanz, Palm, & Brallier, 2007). These results suggest it is important to treat attention problems effectively through behavioral and/or medical interventions to prevent long-term effects associated with poor academic performance and social relationships.

The Attention Problems scale is moderately correlated with a number of other BASC–3 scales. Correlations with the Hyperactivity and Study Skills scales are strongest, which is consistent with BASC–2 results (Reynolds & Kamphaus, 2004). Factor-analytic information in chapters 9 and 10 provide support for distinguishing between attention problems and externalizing-behavior constructs such as hyperactivity, upholding the notion that children may be inattentive without displaying externalizing-behavior problems.

## Atypicality

The Atypicality scale measures a child's tendency to behave in ways that are considered odd or strange. Many of the Atypicality items center on a child's disconnection from or unawareness of his or her normal surroundings (e.g., being unaware of others, saying things that make no sense, acting like others aren't there). Other items represent specific unusual behaviors (e.g., picking at things, banging head, babbling to self).

Over the last decade, research has shown the Atypicality scale to be markedly elevated in children diagnosed with an autism spectrum disorder (Hass, Brown, Brady, & Johnson, 2012; Volker et al., 2010). Those results are consistent with the BASC–3 validity evidence provided in chapters 9 and 10 that reports mean scale scores for a variety of clinical groups. In addition to the autism samples, children classified as having an emotional/behavioral disturbance (EBD) also show elevated Atypicality scale scores, as do children identified with ADHD (when reviewing PRS results). Thus, elevated Atypicality scale scores can be interpreted in the context of a developmental delay or a disruptive behavior disorder. Clinical acumen is crucial when interpreting elevated Atypicality scale scores; a careful study of item responses can be helpful in this regard, as can looking at other scale scores and comparing them to the clinical profiles presented in this manual. In addition, a thorough clinical interview with the child might provide helpful information for interpreting an elevated Atypicality scale score.

## Conduct Problems

The Conduct Problems scale (similar to delinquency or antisocial behavior scales from other instruments) measures socially deviant and disruptive behaviors that are characteristic of such *DSM-5* disorders as oppositional defiant disorder (ODD) and conduct disorder (CD). These behaviors include general rule-breaking, cheating in school, stealing, lying, and deception. It can be helpful to understand that the Conduct Problems and Aggression scales are closely related but measure distinct dimensions. The former focuses on antisocial and rule-breaking behaviors, whereas the latter measures behaviors (particularly verbal ones) that are directed against others and/or their property.

The Conduct Problems scale is not included at the preschool level of the TRS and PRS because its behaviors rarely occur at those ages. Conduct disorder worsens with age, exacerbated by such factors as ineffective parenting practices, academic failure, and peer rejection (Patterson et al., 1989). Because these factors can also lead to depressed mood, elevated scores may co-occur with high scores on other scales, including Learning Problems and Depression. Such relationships should not be overlooked in treatment planning. In addition, it is important to note that disorders such as ODD and CD tend to be more common in males than females (APA, 2013); males also tend to score higher on the Conduct Problems scale than females (see chapter 8 for male and female scale score differences).

## Depression

The Depression scale measures a variety of common symptoms associated with depression, including sudden changes in mood, negativity, and sadness. Items consist of a mix between behavioral statements that teachers or parents rate and quoted statements that assess the presence of maladaptive child cognitions about oneself (e.g., "Says, 'I hate myself.'"). Depression is a prevalent disorder with symptoms occurring in as much as 15% of the child and adolescent population (Bhatia & Bhatia, 2007). The disorder is often not diagnosed correctly in young people, and its effects can alter social relationships and academic achievement.

Depressive problems frequently occur with other disorders such as anxiety (Cummings et al., 2014; Semrud-Clikeman, Bennett, & Guli, 2003) and conduct disorder (Patterson et al., 1989). In addition, research has shown that 15 to 25% or more of children with ADHD have a comorbid mood disorder (Neul, Applegate, & Drabman, 2003). In clinical samples, BASC–3 Depression scale scores are elevated in children classified as having EBD (see chapters 9 and 10). In addition, the Depression scale has moderate correlations with the Anxiety and Conduct Problems scales, along with other scales across the various TRS and PRS levels.

## Hyperactivity

The Hyperactivity scale assesses the hyperactivity and impulsivity aspects of ADHD. Item behaviors focusing on hyperactivity include fiddling with things, interrupting others, being overactive, and having poor self-control. Items related to impulsivity include acting without thinking and being unable to wait for one's turn in a group activity. As discussed with regard to the Attention Problems scale, confirmatory factor analyses indicated that hyperactivity is distinguishable from the attention-problem aspect of ADHD.

In addition to exhibiting hyperactivity and attention problems, children diagnosed with ADHD have been shown to have problems with aggression, learning, conduct disorders, depression, and social skills (Henker & Whalen, 1989; Neul et al., 2003). A similar pattern is evident in the ADHD scale score profiles presented in chapters 9 and 10, particularly in the PRS profiles.

## Learning Problems

The Learning Problems scale (available on the TRS–C and TRS–A) was developed to gather information from teachers that may be valuable in screening for academic problems or determining the presence of learning disabilities. The Learning Problems scale samples a variety of academic domains, including reading, mathematics, and spelling as well as more general examples of school performance (e.g., failing grades, lessons going too fast, critical thinking skills). Scores in the At-Risk range or higher on this scale indicate a need for careful investigation of academic skills. The Learning Problems scale has been shown to be a significant correlate of academic achievement outcomes for children in elementary school (Hartley, 1999; Oehler-Stinnett & Boykin, 2001). In addition, it has been shown to be sensitive to differences between a sample of children who experienced traumatic brain injury and a control sample (Thaler, Mayfield, Reynolds, Hadland, & Allen, 2012).

Learning Problems scale scores are elevated in a number of clinical samples shown in chapter 9; they also are strongly related to other BASC–3 scales, including Study Skills, Attention Problems, Leadership, and Functional Communication (see chapter 10).

## Somatization

The Somatization scale assesses the tendency to be overly sensitive and complain about relatively minor physical problems or ailments, and to over-report the occurrence of various physical complaints. Consistent with somatic symptom disorder, as characterized in the *DSM-5,* such complaints typically cannot be attributed to a physical cause or to generally poor physical health. Often these complaints have persisted for extended time periods (for months or years). Somatization scale items are a sampling of behaviors that include fears about being sick and complaints about symptoms and health. Many of the items center on the child's complaints, encouraging the rater to attend to the child's verbal report rather than interpret the child's behavior.

There is considerable evidence of the occurrence of somatization in children (Garber, Walker, & Zeman, 1991; Gledhill & Garralda, 2006). Somatization problems are associated with other internalizing problems (Abelkop, 2001; see also BASC–3 scale score intercorrelations presented in chapters 9 and 10) and have been shown to be associated with children experiencing trauma (Kugler, Bloom, Kaercher, Truax, & Storch, 2012) and weaker school performance (Hughes, Lourea-Waddell, & Kendall, 2008). When interpreting elevated Somatization scale scores, it is important to thoroughly assess anxiety or other mood-related disorders. In addition, it is important to consider elevations that might be attributable to underlying medical disorders (Martin et al., 2012).

## Withdrawal

The Withdrawal scale measures a child's tendency to avoid social contact and to lack interest in making contact in social settings. Items on the Withdrawal scale include behaviors associated with shyness, initiating friendships, and preferring to be alone. In mild form, withdrawal may represent a symptom of depression. An elevated Withdrawal scale score could suggest the need for sociometric assessment to differentiate between neglected and rejected status. Rejected children are more often plagued by loneliness (Asher & Wheeler, 1985) and tend to respond poorly to social-skills training (Tiffen & Spence, 1986).

Similar to Atypicality scale scores, high Withdrawal scale scores have been associated with children diagnosed with an autism spectrum disorder (Hass et al., 2012; Volker et al., 2010); this is also supported by the clinical group profiles provided in chapters 9 and 10. A propensity to be withdrawn from peers has also been shown to inhibit social learning, resulting in poor social skills (Booth-LaForce & Oxford, 2008). Children with elevated Withdrawal scale scores are likely to have difficulty bonding with both peers and adults. Interpretation of the underlying cause of the withdrawal pattern is facilitated by knowing to what extent the withdrawal is consistent with a child's personality; withdrawal that is inconsistent can be a sign of an environmental cause for the symptoms.

# ADAPTIVE SCALES

The adaptive scales included on the TRS and PRS measure constructs that are often considered behavioral strengths. High scores on the adaptive scales represent positive or desirable characteristics and low scores represent possible problem areas. As mentioned in chapter 2 (see Table 2.2), adaptive scales scores in the 31 through 40 range are considered at-risk and scores 30 or lower are considered clinically significant. Table 5.8 provides brief descriptions of each adaptive scale.

**Table 5.8** TRS and PRS Adaptive Scale Descriptions

| Adaptive scale | Description |
| --- | --- |
| Activities of Daily Living | The skills associated with performing basic, everyday tasks in an acceptable and safe manner |
| Adaptability | The ability to adapt readily to changes in the environment |
| Functional Communication | The ability to express ideas and communicate in a way others can easily understand |
| Leadership | The skills associated with accomplishing academic, social, or community goals, including the ability to work with others |
| Social Skills | The skills necessary for interacting successfully with peers and adults in home, school, and community settings |
| Study Skills | The skills that are conducive to strong academic performance, including organizational skills and good study habits |

## Activities of Daily Living

The Activities of Daily Living scale is available only on the PRS. It is intended to screen for adaptive-behavior deficits and to alert the examiner to additional differential diagnostic considerations associated with lower levels of cognitive functioning. It is also useful in determining the least restrictive environment in which a child may be placed for intervention for various behavioral and emotional disorders. The more skilled a child is in daily-living activities, the less restrictive a placement may need to be. Items included on this scale assess behaviors related to acting in a safe manner, performing simple daily tasks, and organizing tasks (Kamphaus, 2003). Behaviors necessary to promote functional daily living have long been considered to be core competencies of child and adult functioning in communities and at home (Doll, 1953; Kamphaus, 1987). This scale was developed to be consistent with this well-established view. It is important to note that the list of behaviors included on this scale, however, is not exhaustive for purposes of treatment planning. Scores in the At-Risk range or lower may suggest evidence of adaptive-behavior deficits associated with intellectual disability and other severe disorders such as lower-functioning autism. Follow-up assessment with a more diagnostic measure may be needed for making a definitive diagnosis and for treatment planning.

The Activities of Daily Living scale tends to have moderate correlations with other BASC–3 scales, providing some support that lower functioning is associated with other behavioral and emotional problems. BASC–3 clinical group scores presented in chapter 10 indicate low Activities of Daily Living scale scores for several groups, including ADHD, autism, and EBD.

## Adaptability

The Adaptability scale was developed based on temperament research (Frick et al., 2009). Adaptability is one of a number of temperament variables (which also include attention or distractibility and activity level) that correlate with early school achievement. Items on this scale assess the ability to adjust to changes in routine or plans, transition, and recover after a setback.

Research shows that Adaptability scale scores tend to be low in many samples of children with disabilities and poor behavioral and academic adjustment at school. Results from this research indicate that low Adaptability scale scores (40 or less) should trigger further psychological and educational evaluation due to the presence of significant risk (DiStefano, Kamphaus, Horne, & Winsor, 2003). Low Adaptability scale scores may also indicate a child's tendency toward negative emotionality and poor emotional self-control (Thorpe, 2004). This finding further strengthens the recommendation that children with low Adaptability scale scores should be evaluated because of their increased risk for poor outcomes. BASC–3 clinical group scores presented in chapters 9 and 10 indicate low Adaptability scale scores for several groups, including autism and EBD.

## Functional Communication

Functional Communication assesses the child's ability to express ideas and communicate in ways that others can easily understand. This scale further strengthens the adaptive-behavior assessment capabilities of the TRS and PRS, especially when used with the Social Skills and Activities of Daily Living scales. Like activities of daily living, functional communication is considered a core aspect of adaptive-behavior functioning (Doll, 1953; Kamphaus, 1987). Behaviors assessed on this scale include both rudimentary and advanced expressive-communication skills (e.g., giving one's full name when asked, communicating clearly), receptive-communication skills (e.g., responding appropriately to a question), and written skills (e.g., accurately taking down messages). Scores in the At-Risk range or lower should be used to initiate follow-up assessment to definitively rule out an adaptive-behavior deficit.

The Functional Communication scale has moderate to high correlations with other scales, including Adaptability, Social Skills, and Leadership. Functional Communication scale scores are generally lower than average across most clinical groups presented in chapters 9 and 10, most notably for the autism group, where scores are well over one standard deviation under the general population mean. Similar results were obtained by Hass et al. (2012), Lopata et al. (2013), and Volker et al. (2010).

## Leadership

The Leadership scale assesses additional competencies related to good community and school adaptation. This scale was developed to assess behaviors that may be associated with leadership potential (Morgan, 1989). Items on this scale include behaviors associated with decision making, getting others to work together, creativity, and working well under pressure.

As shown in chapters 9 and 10, BASC–3 clinical groups typically score lower on the Leadership scale. Leadership has moderate to high correlations with other adaptive scales.

## Social Skills

Social skills have long been recognized as important for adequate adaptation. In his pioneering work, Edgar Doll (1953) recognized the importance of social-skills development in children. In addition, social skills have always been a part of the Vineland Adaptive Behavior Scales (Sparrow, Balla, & Cicchetti, 1984). The Social Skills scale emphasizes the interpersonal aspects of social adaptation. Examples of such behaviors include complimenting others, encouraging others, offering assistance, and saying "please" and "thank you."

Scores on the Social Skills scale may have a variety of important diagnostic and treatment implications. A score in the At-Risk range or lower may indicate the need for social-skills training. Individual items may focus on the specific behaviors that need work. The Social Skills scale tends to have moderate to high correlations with other adaptive scales and is markedly lower in samples of children identified with autism-related disorders (see chapters 9 and 10).

## Study Skills

The Study Skills scale (available on the TRS–C and TRS–A) is relevant to a number of behaviors that are important for academic success. Items for the Study Skills scale were derived from a variety of sources, but they rely heavily on metamemory research (Kreutzer, Leonard, & Flavell, 1975) and research on learning strategies (Weinstein & Macdonald, 1986). The influence of metacognitive research is shown in items concerning analyzing a problem before solving it and note-taking. Other items assess aspects of motivation to achieve and organizational skills (e.g., completing homework, trying to do well, turning in work on time).

Scores in the At-Risk range or lower may serve as early warnings of more substantial behavior problems to come. For example, failure to complete assignments may be a first step in the deterioration of school performance that is associated with developing depression or conduct disorder (Patterson et al., 1989). Not surprisingly, Study Skills scale scores for clinical group populations are generally lower compared to the general norm group (see chapter 9).

# CONTENT SCALES

The content scales included on the TRS and PRS were introduced in the BASC–2 (Reynolds & Kamphaus, 2004) as theoretically derived scales that were wholly made up of items from other BASC–2 scales and were available only in a limited number of BASC–2 software reports. However, due to their widespread acceptance by practitioners and researchers, the content scales are now available in standard BASC–3 Q-global reports. Each content scale now contains some unique items written specifically for the scale, in addition to items shared from other clinical and adaptive scales. All content scales except Resiliency are interpreted using the same criteria as clinical scales (scores 60 through 69 are considered at-risk, and scores 70 or higher are considered clinically significant). The Resiliency scale is interpreted in the same way as the adaptive scales (scores 31 through 40 are considered at-risk, and scores 30 or lower are considered clinically significant). Table 5.9 provides brief descriptions of each content scale.

**Table 5.9** Content Scale Descriptions

| Content scale | Description |
|---|---|
| Anger Control | The tendency to become irritated and/or angry quickly and impulsively, coupled with an inability to regulate affect and self-control |
| Bullying | The tendency to be intrusive, cruel, threatening, or forceful to get what is wanted through manipulation or coercion |
| Developmental Social Disorders | The tendency to display behaviors characterized by deficits in social skills, communication, interests, and activities; such behaviors may include self-stimulation, withdrawal, and inappropriate socialization |
| Emotional Self-Control | The ability to regulate one's affect and emotions in response to environmental changes |
| Executive Functioning | The ability to control behavior by planning, anticipating, inhibiting, or maintaining goal-directed activity, and by reacting appropriately to environmental feedback in a purposeful, meaningful way |
| Negative Emotionality | The tendency to react in an overly negative way to any changes in everyday activities or routines |
| Resiliency | The ability to access both internal and external support systems to alleviate stress and overcome adversity |

## Anger Control

The Anger Control content scale is intended to assess how well a child or adolescent can keep his or her anger-related emotions under control. Individuals with high Anger Control scale scores tend to exhibit a quick escalation of emotions, poor conflict-management skills, an inability to control anger, and general unhappiness. Such individuals may appear docile and, under some circumstances, well regulated. When irritated, however, they can quickly become angry and unable to exercise control over their actions. Specific, targeted behavioral interventions are recommended when working with children or young adults with elevated Anger Control scale scores.

As shown in the clinical group scores presented in chapters 9 and 10, Anger Control scores are much higher for the ADHD and EBD groups compared to the general population. It is possible that anger-control problems are associated with disturbances of executive functioning and self-regulation. However, anger-control problems may also occur as a specific emotional response to unpleasant circumstances that the individual does not understand. Such reactions may occur when the individual is unfamiliar with proper adaptive coping skills.

## Bullying

The Bullying content scale provides an indication of whether a child or adolescent engages in behaviors that are perceived as threatening or intimidating by others. Specific behaviors on the Bullying scale include teasing, making threats toward others, manipulating others, and minimizing others. In the last decade or so, bullying has increasingly become a social and legislative issue, with most states passing some legislation applicable to public schools (Maag & Katsiyannis, 2012). Bullying behaviors appear to be a high-frequency occurrence in schools; more than one-fourth of students ages 12 through 18 report being bullied at school (Robers, Kemp, Rathbun, & Morgan, 2014). For perpetrators of bullying there can be long-term effects that extend into adolescence and adulthood (Farrington & Ttofi, 2011; Kim, Catalano, Haggerty, & Abbott, 2011).

Most often, high scores on the Bullying scale reflect a persistent pattern of social maladjustment and can be comorbid with a variety of other developmental psychopathologies, including hyperactivity and depression. Bullying can be viewed as a facet of overall aggression, one that is characterized by a manipulative and possibly pleasurable intent. As is the case with aggression or conduct problems, bullying behavior is usefully differentiated from behavior that is distinctly related to a qualified severe emotional disturbance (considered a disability) in a manifestation determination.

## Developmental Social Disorders

The Developmental Social Disorders content scale provides a global indication of deficits in social skills, communication, interests, and activities. Behaviors included on this scale center on one's ability to adjust to change, awareness of others and the present situation, ability to communicate and express emotions clearly, and unusual or repetitive movements or actions. High scores on this scale may indicate symptoms of autism spectrum disorders (as evidenced by the clinical group scores provided in chapters 9 and 10, Hass et al. [2012], and Volker et al. [2010]) or simply may reflect poor socialization.

An autism spectrum disorder might be more likely when the Developmental Social Disorders content scale score is elevated but the Conduct Problems and Aggression scale scores are not. Additionally, an autism spectrum disorder could be indicated when this scale score is elevated along with the Withdrawal, Atypicality, and Attention Problems scale scores. As with many such conclusions, however, a detailed history-gathering and a thorough clinical interview of the respondent are necessary before an interpretive decision can be made.

## Emotional Self-Control

The Emotional Self-Control content scale measures the ability to regulate one's affect and emotions in response to environmental changes. Similar to the Anger Control scale, this scale evaluates a subset of self-regulation or executive functioning. High scores on the Emotional Self-Control scale may reflect the influence of a variety of negative emotions, including sadness, frustration, and stress or fear. Scores on this scale tend to be elevated in children identified with an EBD (see clinical group scores presented in chapters 9 and 10).

Specific problems with regulation of affect, in the absence of more pervasive executive- functioning difficulties, is likely to represent an emotional problem related to disturbances of the temporal lobes, the limbic system, or the interactions within the temporolimbic system. Such disturbances can stem from emotional or physical trauma and a variety of neurodevelopmental problems. Most often, elevations on the Emotional Self-Control content scale are associated with more pervasive self-regulation and executive-functioning problems (Reynolds & French, 2003).

## Executive Functioning

The Executive Functioning content scale provides an overall indication of one's ability to exercise control over his or her behavior. Items on this scale assess a variety of behaviors associated with organization and planning, using a step-by-step approach to solving problems, attentional focus, remaining under control, and overall decision-making ability. High scores on this content scale may identify individuals who experience nearly all types of self-regulation difficulties. Individuals with elevated Executive Functioning scale scores may also present with ADHD symptoms, because frontal-lobe arousal and functionality deficits have been suggested as a root cause of ADHD-related behaviors. Depression is also often comorbid in such individuals because of associations with the dopaminergic system and frontal-lobe dysfunction. Two complicating factors displayed by an individual with frontal-lobe injuries are low motivation (sometimes referred to as amotivational syndrome) and anosognosia (low awareness of behavioral changes or deficits). As scientific advances in the relationship between organic causes and behavioral problems continue and as school psychological services are expanded to support children with problems such as traumatic brain injury, the assessment of constructs such as executive functioning will continue to gain prominence.

Clinical group scores indicate elevated Executive Functioning scale scores for several clinical groups (see chapters 9 and 10), particularly EBD and ADHD. This is consistent with other research that has shown clinical populations to have higher Executive Functioning scale scores (Sullivan & Riccio, 2006).

## Negative Emotionality

The Negative Emotionality content scale describes a child or adolescent's propensity to react in an overly negative way to changes in everyday activities or routines. Items on this scale capture behaviors associated with becoming quickly upset or frustrated, being overly negative or pessimistic, and being argumentative. Children and adolescents with elevated scores on this scale may have few friends and may be described as rigid and easily irritated. The Negative Emotionality content scale was derived from temperament literature, which gives considerable evidence to suggest that such problems can be chronic and are identifiable within weeks after childbirth by mothers of children with this condition (Thorpe, 2004). Negative emotionality during infancy may lay the groundwork for the development of anger-control or emotional self-regulation problems later in life. Because such problems are related to temperament, cases with extreme scores may require comprehensive, multimodal, and longstanding treatment. Clinical group scores indicate elevated Negative Emotionality scale scores for children identified with EBD (see chapters 9 and 10).

## Resiliency

The Resiliency content scale measures an ability to overcome adversity and is interpreted in the same manner as the adaptive scales. Behaviors included on this scale highlight adjusting or coping with change, quickly recovering from setbacks, and demonstrating problem-solving ability. Individuals with high Resiliency scale scores tend to do well in short-term, focused therapeutic approaches and to generally possess positive mental health.

Clinical group mean scores presented in chapters 9 and 10 indicate low levels of resiliency across several clinical groups. Individuals with low Resiliency scale scores are often described as having difficulties with environmental or social changes. When implementing behavioral or emotional interventions, it is important to consider the Resiliency scale score, particularly when designing treatment or behavior modification plans that may significantly interrupt the person's normal routine. The Resiliency scale has been used in a similar way in medical settings; the preexisting mental health status of adolescents was determined prior to orthopedic surgery in an attempt to identify and remediate any existing mental health problems (Podeszwa, Richard, Nguyen, De La Rocha, & Shapiro, 2015).

## COMPOSITE SCALES

Although lacking the precision of individual scales for pinpointing specific syndromes or behavioral strengths, the composite scales scores of the TRS and PRS are helpful for summarizing performance and for drawing broad conclusions regarding different types of adaptive and maladaptive behavior. The composite scores represent behavior dimensions that are distinct but not independent; problem behaviors often occur in concert rather than individually. Chapters 9 and 10 provide evidence for the TRS and PRS factor structure. All composite scales except Adaptive Skills are interpreted using the same criteria as presented for the clinical scales (scores 60 through 69 are considered at-risk, and scores 70 or higher are considered clinically significant); low scores for the Adaptive Skills scale are interpreted as problematic (scores 31 through 40 are considered at-risk, and scores 30 or lower are considered clinically significant). Table 5.10 provides a list of the scales that comprise each composite scale.

**Table 5.10** Summary of TRS and PRS Composite Scales

| | Externalizing Problems | Internalizing Problems | School Problems | Adaptive Skills | Behavioral Symptoms Index |
|---|---|---|---|---|---|
| TRS–P | Hyperactivity Aggression | Anxiety Depression Somatization | | Adaptability Social Skills Functional Communication | Hyperactivity Aggression Depression Attention Problems Atypicality Withdrawal |
| TRS–C, TRS–A | Hyperactivity Aggression Conduct Problems | Anxiety Depression Somatization | Learning Problems Attention Problems | Adaptability Social Skills Functional Communication Leadership Study Skills | Hyperactivity Aggression Depression Attention Problems Atypicality Withdrawal |
| PRS–P | Hyperactivity Aggression | Anxiety Depression Somatization | | Adaptability Social Skills Functional Communication Activities of Daily Living | Hyperactivity Aggression Depression Attention Problems Atypicality Withdrawal |
| PRS–C, PRS–A | Hyperactivity Aggression Conduct Problems | Anxiety Depression Somatization | | Adaptability Social Skills Functional Communication Leadership Activities of Daily Living | Hyperactivity Aggression Depression Attention Problems Atypicality Withdrawal |

## Externalizing Problems

The scales on the Externalizing Problems composite include Hyperactivity, Aggression, and, at the child and adolescent levels, Conduct Problems. A central characteristic of the Externalizing Problems composite is the disruptive nature of the child's behavior. Such children readily come to the attention of teachers and health care professionals because they disrupt the activities of both peers and adults, they often are unresponsive to adult direction, and they have more problematic relationships with peers.

## Internalizing Problems

The Internalizing Problems composite consists of the Anxiety, Depression, and Somatization scales. Behaviors associated with these scales are typically not disruptive. Children with internalizing problems tend to monitor their own actions to excess and to be compliant, and their problems may easily go unnoticed. Although such behaviors are not disruptive, research suggests that peer relationships could be adversely affected by the presence of internalizing symptomatology (Kamphaus, DiStefano, & Lease, 2003).

## School Problems

The School Problems composite (on the TRS–C and TRS–A) consists of the Attention Problems and Learning Problems scales. This composite reflects academic difficulties, including problems of motivation, attention, and learning and cognition. A high score on this composite scale is a sign that the teacher perceives behaviors that are very likely to interfere with academic achievement.

## Adaptive Skills

The scales on the Adaptive Skills composite include Adaptability, Activities of Daily Living (on the PRS only), Functional Communication, Social Skills, Leadership (at the child and adolescent levels only), and Study Skills (on TRS–C and TRS–A only). This composite summarizes appropriate emotional expression and control, daily-living skills inside and outside the home, and communication skills, as well as prosocial, organizational, study, and other adaptive skills. These skills assess core characteristics of adaptive behavior that are important for functioning at home and school, with peers, and in the community. They may also be indicative of risk and poor prognosis, as well as the presence of intellectual disability, autism spectrum disorder, or other disorders.

## Behavioral Symptoms Index

The Behavioral Symptoms Index (BSI) consists of the Hyperactivity, Aggression, Depression, Attention Problems, Atypicality, and Withdrawal scales and reflects the overall level of problem behavior. The BSI appears to reasonably estimate the general level of functioning or presence of impairment for an individual with a disability or diagnosed condition.

# PROBABILITY, IMPAIRMENT, AND EXECUTIVE FUNCTIONING INDEXES

The final types of scores provided on the TRS and PRS are the probability indexes, the Functional Impairment Index, and the executive functioning indexes. In this application, *probability* is used to refer to the degree to which a score is indicative of a child or adolescent that might be classified into a general clinical, ADHD, autism, or EBD group.

Index *T* scores that fall within the range of 60 through 69 are considered at-risk, while *T* scores 70 or above are considered clinically significant; such scores indicate a stronger possibility that a child or adolescent has behavioral problems that meet the level of a clinical classification. *T* scores less than 60 are considered to indicate a relatively low likelihood that a child or adolescent exhibits a pattern of problems similar to those who have been classified or diagnosed with a behavioral or emotional problem, or a relatively low likelihood that a child or adolescent experiences a significant level of functional impairment. Appendix C lists the item numbers belonging to each index described below.

## Clinical Probability Index

The Clinical Probability Index, available at the preschool level of the TRS and PRS, provides an overall indication of the similarity between the obtained behavioral ratings and the ratings of similarly aged children known to have a behavioral or emotional problem or classification. This index is based on items from a broad range of TRS and PRS scales across each of the composite scale groupings. A broad-based approach for item selection was used at the preschool level due to the difficulty differentiating between various disorders among children in this age range. Children with elevated scores on this index likely present with a variety of behavioral challenges that may include an inability to adjust well to change and pay attention, a propensity to do or say unusual things, problems with behavioral and/or emotional regulation, and difficulty maintaining appropriate social relationships.

## EBD Probability Index
The EBD Probability Index, available at the child and adolescent levels of the TRS and PRS, provides an indication of the similarity between the obtained behavioral ratings and the ratings of children identified as having an emotional or behavioral disturbance or disability (a classification typically given in educational settings when making placement decisions). This index consists of items primarily from the TRS and PRS Externalizing Problems and Adaptive Skills scales, as well as a number of items from the Attention Problems, Depression, and Withdrawal scales. Children who present with elevated scores on this index likely exhibit a variety of behaviors that are disruptive, unusual, or antisocial, resulting in strained relationships with both adults and peers. In addition, they may display a range of negative emotions including anger, pessimism, and sadness.

## Autism Probability Index
The Autism Probability Index, available at the child and adolescent levels of the TRS and PRS, provides an indication of the similarity between the obtained behavioral ratings and the ratings of children identified as having an autism spectrum disorder. This index consists of items primarily from the Atypicality, Functional Communication, Leadership, Social Skills, and Withdrawal scales. Children who present with elevated scores on this index likely exhibit a variety of behaviors that are unusual and experience problems with developing and maintaining social relationships.

## ADHD Probability Index
The ADHD Probability Index, available at the child and adolescent levels of the TRS and PRS, provides an indication of the similarity between the obtained behavioral ratings and the ratings of children identified as having attention-deficit/hyperactivity disorder. In addition to items from the Hyperactivity and Attention Problems scales, this index includes items from a variety of other scales. Children who present with elevated scores on this index likely experience problems that will adversely affect their academic performance, such as difficulty focusing or maintaining attention, inability to organize tasks effectively, difficulty making decisions, or difficulty moderating their own activity level.

## Functional Impairment Index
The Functional Impairment Index, available at all levels of the TRS and PRS, provides an indication of the level of difficulty a child has engaging in successful or appropriate behavior across a variety of situations including interactions with others, performing age-appropriate tasks, regulating mood, and performing school-related tasks. This index consists of items from a heterogeneous mix of other scales across each of the TRS and PRS composite scales.

Children who present with elevated scores on this index likely experience problems that adversely impact their ability to respond appropriately to everyday settings and situations. Most mental health and EBD diagnoses require that the disorder evident in the individual's symptoms have some adverse impact or create impairment in some functional aspect of the person's life prior to assigning a diagnosis. The BASC–3 Functional Impairment Index provides a quantitative indication of disturbances in function in important areas of the child or adolescent's life and is related to initiating a diagnosis. Changes in the Functional Impairment Index over time can be used to monitor the impact of intervention programs on how weak a person functions across many domains of important behavior and are easily plotted and viewed on most BASC–3 Q-global scoring reports.

## Executive Functioning Indexes
New to the BASC–3 TRS and PRS forms are the executive functioning indexes, which include the Problem-Solving Index, Attentional Control Index, Behavioral Control Index, Emotional Control Index, and Overall Executive Functioning Index. These indexes are available only via Q-global software reports. They were developed in conjunction with Dr. Mauricio Garcia-Barrera and are based on a series of studies conducted with the BASC–2 TRS and PRS (Garcia-Barrera, Kamphaus, & Bandalos, 2011; Garcia-Barrera, Karr, & Kamphaus, 2013). Additional information about the development of the BASC–3 executive functioning indexes can be found in chapter 7. For each index, only a raw score is provided, which can be interpreted based on the classification ranges provided in Table 5.11. Higher scores reflect deficiencies in functioning within each domain.

**Table 5.11** Raw-Score Classification Categories for the Executive Functioning Indexes

| | Problem-Solving Index | Attentional Control Index | Behavioral Control Index | Emotional Control Index | Overall Executive Functioning Index |
|---|---|---|---|---|---|
| **TRS–P** | | | | | |
| Not elevated | | 0–9 | 0–7 | 0–11 | 0–25 |
| Elevated | | 10–12 | 8–10 | 12–15 | 26–35 |
| Extremely elevated | | 13–15 | 11–15 | 16–24 | 36–54 |
| **TRS–C** | | | | | |
| Not elevated | 0–19 | 0–15 | 0–9 | 0–7 | 0–48 |
| Elevated | 20–24 | 16–19 | 10–13 | 8–12 | 49–61 |
| Extremely elevated | 25–27 | 20–24 | 14–21 | 13–21 | 62–93 |
| **TRS–A** | | | | | |
| Not elevated | 0–22 | 0–17 | 0–5 | 0–5 | 0–46 |
| Elevated | 23–27 | 18–21 | 6–9 | 6–8 | 47–61 |
| Extremely elevated | 28–30 | 22–30 | 10–18 | 9–18 | 62–96 |
| **PRS–P** | | | | | |
| Not elevated | | 0–12 | 0–9 | 0–9 | 0–29 |
| Elevated | | 13–15 | 10–12 | 10–15 | 30–38 |
| Extremely elevated | | 16–21 | 13–18 | 16–21 | 39–60 |
| **PRS–C** | | | | | |
| Not elevated | 0–16 | 0–12 | 0–8 | 0–6 | 0–40 |
| Elevated | 17–20 | 13–15 | 9–12 | 7–9 | 41–51 |
| Extremely elevated | 21–24 | 16–21 | 13–18 | 10–12 | 52–75 |
| **PRS–A** | | | | | |
| Not elevated | 0–17 | 0–14 | 0–8 | 0–5 | 0–42 |
| Elevated | 18–21 | 15–19 | 9–12 | 6–8 | 43–54 |
| Extremely elevated | 22–27 | 20–27 | 13–21 | 9–12 | 55–87 |

## Problem-Solving Index

This index measures one's ability to demonstrate planfulness and to make decisions and solve problems effectively in everyday life; this is often different from the problem-solving required on abstract tasks such as on an intelligence test. People with elevated scores on this scale are often disorganized or scattered in their approach to life's problems and even in carrying out daily activities. For such students with academic problems, the School Motivation and Learning Strategies Inventory (SMALSI; Stroud & Reynolds, 2006) is often a useful addition to the assessment process and will provide comprehensive information on students' skills in developing and applying systematic learning strategies to academic issues.

## Attentional Control Index

This index measures one's ability to sustain attention and attend to the current task. High scorers are likely to be easily distracted, unable to focus attention on any one task for a viable period of time, and frequently move unpredictably from task to task unproductively.

## Behavioral Control Index

This index measures one's ability to maintain self-control and avoid distracting or interrupting others. People who score high on this scale often expend considerable effort not to engage in a variety of behavior, such as interrupting, speaking out, and acting impulsively, but are still unable to control such behaviors in most circumstances. They are often mistakenly seen as attention-seeking, when in fact they lack the control of ordinary inhibitory mechanisms used by others of the same age and development.

### Emotional Control Index

This index measures one's ability to maintain control over emotions in challenging situations. High scores are indicative of individuals who very often overreact and may be seen as histrionic as well as being difficult to console. They often recognize the intrusiveness of such emotions later and may be regretful, but they continue to have difficulty controlling their emotions and regulating not so much the type but the level of emotional response they produce.

### Overall Executive Functioning Index

This index is composed of all of the items from each of the executive functioning indexes just described, providing an overall indication of executive functioning. High scores indicate pervasive problems with self-regulation in the multiple domains of what is considered executive functioning. These individuals often have issues with many ADHD-like symptoms and are often diagnosed with ADHD and other disorders of the self-regulation of behavior. Traumatic brain injury patients are likely to have high scores on this scale. High scorers fail to integrate the necessary components of executive functioning successfully to engage in age-appropriate levels of day-to-day planning, problem-solving, and organization necessary for success in most learning environments.

## Systematic Approach to Interpretation

An approach for interpreting the BASC–3 TRS and PRS scales is described in the following paragraphs. Note that a careful review of the validity indexes available for the BASC–3 instruments is recommended before any test profiles are interpreted.

### STEP 1: INTERPRETING COMPOSITE SCORES

The clinical scales composite scores are useful indicators of a child's overall degree of behavioral psychopathology and functional impairment. Psychopathology refers to the existence of a mental health disorder, whereas functional impairment indicates that an individual's current behavior impairs his or her adjustment to an important developmental environment (e.g., school, peer circles, home, or community for a child and place of employment for a young adult). Children with a mental health disorder also experience functional impairment (DSM-5), but a child without a mental health disorder can experience functional impairment as well. For example, Scahill et al. (1999) demonstrated how an individual with attention problems below the DSM diagnostic threshold (or At-Risk range in BASC–3 terms) nevertheless experiences significant functional impairment in school. Moreover, Cantwell (1996) uses the label subsyndromal psychopathology for cases in which functional impairment is evident but symptoms fall short of a diagnosis. Both clinically significant and at-risk T scores should be noted, as such scores will become the focus of further interpretation.

The overall composite—the Behavioral Symptoms Index (BSI) for the TRS and PRS, or the Emotional Symptoms Index (ESI) for the Self-Report of Personality (SRP)—should be examined first. Scores in the Clinically Significant range will generally indicate pervasive and serious behavioral or emotional problems. It is important to note that such a finding can occur even when none of the scale scores that compose the index is significantly elevated. For example, scale T scores consistently in the high 50s and low 60s can result in a BSI or ESI in the upper 60s or low 70s. This is because it is more unusual for a person to be above the mean on all of the scale scores than it is to be above the mean on only some. The global composite scores are thus most useful when only some scale T scores are elevated.

Next, the remaining composite scales should be reviewed to determine if they are consistent with the overall index score and with one another. If the BSI or ESI is significantly elevated, the clinician should determine whether this is caused by only a few high scale scores or by a smaller group of moderate scale elevations. When composite scales scores are consistently elevated, a pervasive form of behavioral or emotional disturbance is likely. Additional evaluation methods (including use of other BASC–3 components, structured interviews, observation, etc.) would be required to obtain a specific diagnosis.

When composite scores are not consistent, more specific disorders might be present. An analysis of individual scales may prove useful in such cases. Statistical comparisons can be made among the composites to help determine consistency of the composite scores. Such comparisons provide an ipsative, or within-person, analysis of the relationship between scale scores. Table B.1 in Appendix B presents the critical values for identifying a statistically significant difference between each clinical composite in a pair. (Comparisons of clinical with adaptive composites are not included in this manual because these composites are scored in opposite directions and the interpretation of such differences is conceptually complex. The interpretation of individual composite scores is more important for profile interpretation than the frequency and statistical significance of differences between clinical and adaptive scales scores.)

Table B.2 in Appendix B indicates the frequency of various sizes of composite-score difference in the general norm sample. Whereas statistical significance determines whether or not a difference between scores is reliable, the frequency information gauges the rarity of such a score difference. In other words, differences that are statistically significant may nevertheless be common in the general population.

Discrepancies among the clinical scales composite scores will usually suggest interpretive hypotheses and will help identify primary problem areas warranting further investigation. For example, an elevated Externalizing Problems $T$ score suggests a general area of investigation—namely, the presence of a disruptive-behavior disorder.

## STEP 2: INTERPRETING SCALE SCORES

The individual scales are highly interpretable because of the manner in which they were conceived. During development, a particular emphasis was placed on creating scales with high content validity and relevance to behavioral and emotional problems. The highly recognizable content of most of the scales will help make their interpretation intuitive.

When reviewing individual scale scores, both clinically significant and at-risk $T$ scores should be noted. For each scale, the examiner should determine whether the score is consistent with the score on the composite to which the scale belongs. If it is, this gives strong credence to a broad interpretation at the composite level. However, if the scale score is quite different from the composite score, a stronger focus on the scale and its meaning is necessary. For example, if the Depression score is in the Clinically Significant range while the other internalizing scales scores are in the Average range, the Depression scale warrants further investigation.

When clinical scales scores are unusually high (or adaptive scales scores are unusually low), it may be necessary to evaluate the individual scale items. When doing so, certain patterns stemming from items on an individual scale might become evident. For example, an elevated score on Depression could be the result of items (e.g., "Says, 'I don't have any friends,'" "Seems lonely," or "Says, 'Nobody likes me'") that might be related to other problem scales such as Social Skills or Withdrawal. Such information can be particularly useful when creating and implementing intervention plans. The BASC–3 Q-global reports offer the option of printing the items by scale and the item responses.

The normative analysis of the scales and the inspection of the critical items provide a strong basis for interpretation. However, normative information does not capture all of the useful information in a child's profile. For example, a child whose clinical scales $T$ scores are all above 60 and whose adaptive scales scores are all below 40 clearly is having extraordinary difficulties, but some of the problems may be considerably worse than others.

The BASC–3 offers a method for determining which clinical scales are significantly high or significantly low in comparison with the child's or young adult's overall level of problems as indexed by the mean score on the scales in the BSI or ESI. Adaptive rating scales may also be compared with the overall level of adaptive functioning. This ipsative comparison of scores can aid in describing the details of the respondent's behavior, personality, and feelings and emotions, adding to the information already available about his or her broad level of problems. Comparisons between individual scale scores and the BSI or ESI mean-score values are provided in the Score Summary table of the Q-global reports and in the H/L column in the Summary Table of the hand-scoring worksheets. Information on calculating these scores using the hand-scoring worksheets can be found in chapter 2. Note that these comparisons are available only when using the general norms.

High and low scores identified through ipsative analysis can supplement decisions regarding differential diagnosis and treatment. Although less helpful in cases of only one or two scale elevations, ipsative scores are especially useful for understanding the greatest area of concern within psychopathological domains for a respondent with multiple scale elevations. Such scores can also aid in the description of normal variation in personality and behavior. However, normative comparisons should generally be the overall focus of interpretation.

## STEP 3: INTERPRETING ITEMS

Individual items are narrow samples of behavior and, as such, are often unreliable indicators of broad behavior dimensions. Furthermore, a certain amount of error accompanies any single item response. However, item responses can be extremely valuable in the assessment of behavioral and emotional problems, if approached cautiously and combined with follow-up interview and assessment. Many TRS and PRS items assess specific behaviors or self-reports that will sometimes warrant interpretation. For reasons of reliability, item interpretation requires clinical acumen and corroboration across assessment methods and raters; careful consideration of the respondent's history and the referral context is needed.

The critical items presented in the Q-global reports and the hand-scoring worksheets were selected because they frequently suggest danger to the well-being of the child or others. If a teacher or parent indicates that a child often says "I want to die" or "I wish I were dead," the seriousness of the child's statements should be investigated.

Other items, not denoted as critical, may also demand special attention. If, for instance, a parent indicates that a child almost always "Complains of pain," this information requires further inquiry. Checking the record form for all items marked *Never* or *Almost always* could uncover deviant items that may require individual interpretation.

Item responses can form the basis for identifying target behaviors for intervention. Individual item scores can also be used to rank items in priority for intervention. Clinical scales items ranked by parents or teachers as occurring *Almost always* may be the highest priority for intervention, while behaviors that occur only *Sometimes* may be of lower priority. (Some behaviors, of course, require immediate attention even if they occur only sometimes; an example is "Has seizures.")

Targeting behaviors for intervention depends on the setting. For example, although the item "Refuses to talk" may be rated as occurring *Almost always* by both teachers and parents, remediating this behavior may be a higher priority for the teacher than for the parent. The child's lack of verbal interaction may be merely a hindrance at home, but it may stand in the way of academic progress in a school setting.

## COMPARING BASC–2 AND BASC–3 SCALE SCORES

Users of the BASC–2 may need to compare BASC–2 and BASC–3 scale scores in certain situations such as triennial evaluations. During BASC–3 development, all items from the BASC–2 TRS and PRS forms were included on the BASC–3 TRS and PRS standardization forms. As a result, both BASC–2 and BASC–3 scale scores can be computed for each child included in the BASC–3 norm samples. The average differences (in *T*-score units, using the general combined norms) between BASC–3 and BASC–2 scale scores are presented in Tables 5.12 (TRS) and 5.13 (PRS). These tables reflect the values that would be added to (or, for negative values, subtracted from) BASC–2 scale scores to derive an estimated BASC–3 scale score. The values in the tables should be viewed as estimates and may not represent true differences between BASC–2 and BASC–3 scale scores. Information on correlations between these scores can be found in chapters 9 (TRS) and 10 (PRS).

**Table 5.12** TRS: *T*-Score Mean Differences Between the BASC–3 and BASC–2 Scales for General Combined Norms

| | Age | | | | | |
| | Preschool | | Child | | Adolescent | |
| | 2–3 | 4–5 | 6–7 | 8–11 | 12–14 | 15–18 |
|---|---|---|---|---|---|---|
| **Composite** | | | | | | |
| Externalizing Problems | –2 | –1 | 0 | 1 | 0 | –1 |
| Internalizing Problems | –2 | –1 | 0 | –1 | 0 | 0 |
| School Problems | — | — | 0 | 1 | 0 | 0 |
| Adaptive Skills | –1 | –1 | –1 | –2 | –1 | –3 |
| Behavioral Symptoms Index | 0 | 0 | 1 | 1 | 0 | 0 |
| **Clinical scale** | | | | | | |
| Hyperactivity | –2 | –2 | 0 | 0 | 0 | –2 |
| Aggression | –2 | 0 | 1 | 1 | 0 | 0 |
| Conduct Problems | — | — | 1 | 2 | 1 | –1 |
| Anxiety | –1 | 1 | 0 | –2 | –1 | 0 |
| Depression | –1 | 1 | 1 | 0 | 0 | 1 |
| Somatization | –3 | –3 | 1 | –2 | 0 | 1 |
| Attention Problems | 0 | 0 | 0 | 1 | 0 | –1 |
| Learning Problems | — | — | 1 | 1 | 0 | 1 |
| Atypicality | 1 | 0 | 1 | 1 | 1 | 0 |
| Withdrawal | 2 | 1 | 2 | 1 | 1 | 1 |
| **Adaptive scale** | | | | | | |
| Adaptability | 2 | 0 | –1 | –1 | 0 | –2 |
| Social Skills | –4 | –4 | –1 | –3 | –2 | –3 |
| Leadership | — | — | –1 | –3 | –2 | –4 |
| Study Skills | — | — | 0 | –1 | 0 | –2 |
| Functional Communication | 0 | 0 | 0 | 0 | –2 | –3 |
| **Content scale** | | | | | | |
| Anger Control | –1 | –1 | 0 | 0 | 0 | 1 |
| Bullying | 0 | 0 | 1 | 1 | 1 | 0 |
| Developmental Social Disorders | 2 | 1 | 1 | 1 | 1 | 2 |
| Emotional Self-Control | –1 | 0 | 1 | 1 | 0 | 1 |
| Executive Functioning | –2 | –2 | 0 | 0 | 0 | –2 |
| Negative Emotionality | –2 | –2 | 1 | 2 | 0 | 0 |
| Resiliency | 1 | 0 | –1 | –1 | –1 | –3 |

**Table 5.13** PRS: *T*-Score Mean Differences Between the BASC–3 and BASC–2 Scales for General Combined Norms

| | Age | | | | | |
|---|---|---|---|---|---|---|
| | Preschool | | Child | | Adolescent | |
| | 2–3 | 4–5 | 6–7 | 8–11 | 12–14 | 15–18 |
| **Composite** | | | | | | |
| Externalizing Problems | 2 | 0 | 0 | 2 | 2 | 0 |
| Internalizing Problems | 1 | 0 | 1 | 0 | −1 | −3 |
| Adaptive Skills | −1 | 0 | 2 | 1 | −1 | 1 |
| Behavioral Symptoms Index | 1 | −1 | 0 | 1 | 2 | −2 |
| **Clinical scale** | | | | | | |
| Hyperactivity | 1 | −1 | 0 | 1 | 2 | −1 |
| Aggression | 3 | 1 | 2 | 3 | 3 | 2 |
| Conduct Problems | — | — | −1 | 0 | 0 | −1 |
| Anxiety | −1 | 0 | 1 | 0 | −2 | −2 |
| Depression | 0 | 0 | 0 | 1 | 1 | −2 |
| Somatization | 2 | 1 | 1 | 0 | −1 | −2 |
| Attention Problems | 0 | −1 | −1 | 0 | 1 | −1 |
| Atypicality | 0 | −3 | −2 | 0 | 0 | −3 |
| Withdrawal | 1 | 0 | −1 | −1 | 1 | −2 |
| **Adaptive scale** | | | | | | |
| Adaptability | 0 | 1 | 2 | 0 | 0 | 1 |
| Social Skills | −3 | −2 | −1 | −3 | −3 | −1 |
| Leadership | — | — | 0 | −1 | −3 | −1 |
| Activities of Daily Living | 0 | 0 | 6 | 7 | 1 | 4 |
| Functional Communication | 0 | 2 | 2 | 0 | −1 | 2 |
| **Content scale** | | | | | | |
| Anger Control | 2 | 0 | −1 | 1 | 2 | −1 |
| Bullying | 2 | 0 | 1 | 2 | 3 | 0 |
| Developmental Social Disorders | 1 | 0 | 0 | 2 | 2 | −1 |
| Emotional Self-Control | 1 | 0 | −1 | 1 | 1 | 0 |
| Executive Functioning | 1 | 0 | −1 | 1 | 2 | −1 |
| Negative Emotionality | 1 | 0 | −1 | 1 | 1 | 0 |
| Resiliency | −1 | 1 | 1 | 0 | −1 | 1 |

Chapter **6**

# Interpreting the Self-Report of Personality

The Self-Report of Personality (SRP) is designed to evaluate the personality, affect, and self-perceptions of children and young adults. Four levels of the SRP are offered: Interview (SRP–I, ages 6 and 7); Child (SRP–C, ages 8 through 11), Adolescent (SRP–A, ages 12 through 21), and College (SRP–COL, ages 18 through 25).

Although the age ranges of the SRP–A and SRP–COL overlap at age 18 for general norms and from ages 19 to 21 for clinical norms, selection of one form over another will depend on the setting in which it will be used. The SRP–A is intended for use with students ages 12 through 18 or with students ages 19 through 21 who are still in high school. The SRP–COL is designed for use with students ages 18 through 25 who are no longer in high school and presently attending a college, university, or technical or trade school. The SRP–A includes two clinical scales (Somatization and Sensation Seeking) that do not appear on the SRP–C form and two clinical scales (Attitude to School and Attitude to Teachers) that do not appear on the SRP–COL form. The SRP–COL includes two clinical scales (Alcohol Abuse and School Maladjustment) that are not a part of the SRP–A. Across all SRP levels, the item content differs somewhat to reflect developmental changes in how various disorders manifest and in how children and young adults tend to think about themselves and their behavior. Despite these minor differences, the SRP levels have the same structure and may be interpreted in the same way.

Like the Teacher Rating Scales (TRS) and Parent Rating Scales (PRS), the SRP scales were developed to measure clearly defined a priori constructs. In addition, they sample the symptomatology associated with popular diagnostic references such as the ICD-10, *DSM-5* (APA, 2013), and regulatory schemes including IDEA (2004), the Americans With Disabilities Act (ADA, 1990), and Section 504 (Rehabilitation Act, 1973). Clinicians can therefore interpret the scales confidently in the multidimensional environments where children with disabilities receive services.

This chapter presents detailed descriptions of the SRP scales and composites, along with information on how to interpret their scores. SRP results should be interpreted cautiously if there is serious reason to question whether the respondent has given accurate information. Therefore, before discussing the scales and composites, guidelines on using the SRP validity indexes are presented. As is the case with the use of any test or set of scales, the interpretive process begins with an assessment of the validity of the obtained responses.

## Assessing Validity

The validity of SRP results may be compromised for a variety of reasons, including positive or negative response sets, noncooperation, intentional dishonesty, and reading problems. Positively and negatively worded items are included on the rating scales to guard against positive or negative response sets (Comrey, 1988). Nevertheless, it is important to apply available methods of detecting invalid results such as those described in the following paragraphs. Additionally, the use of two types of response options—*True* or *False* and *Never, Sometimes, Often,* or *Almost always*—may make purposeful distortion somewhat more difficult and certain response sets more easily detectable.

### *F* INDEX

The *F* Index assesses the possibility that a child rated him- or herself in an inordinately negative fashion or, in fact, has severe diverse problems requiring immediate attention. This classic validity scale consists of maladaptive behavior items to which the respondent answered *True* (T) or *Almost always* (A) or adaptive behavior items to which the respondent answered *False* (F) or *Never* (N). *F*-Index items are presented in Table 6.1.

**Table 6.1** SRP: *F*-Index Items and Item Numbers

| SRP–C | SRP–A | SRP–COL | Item |
|---|---|---|---|
| 64 | | | I am good at schoolwork. (N) |
| 95 | | 120 | I am liked by others. (N) |
| 135 | | | I am proud of my parents. (N) |
| | | 107 | I am reliable. (N) |
| | 171 | | I am someone you can rely on. (N) |
| | | 79 | I drink alcohol when I am by myself. (A) |
| 81 | | | I feel depressed. (A) |
| | 111 | | I feel dizzy. (A) |
| | 124 | 116 | I feel life isn't worth living. (A) |
| | 68 | | I feel like people are out to get me. (A) |
| 112 | | | I feel out of place around people. (A) |
| | | 128 | I feel that nobody likes me. (A) |
| 43 | | 157 | I get along well with others. (N) |
| 110 | | | I get along with my teacher. (N) |
| | 100 | 136 | I get so nervous I can't breathe. (A) |
| | 78 | | I have trouble breathing. (A) |
| | | 73 | I hear things that others cannot hear. (A) |
| | | 150 | I hear voices in my head that no one else can hear. (A) |
| 74 | | | I like going places with my parents. (N) |
| 50 | 137 | | I like my parents. (N) |
| 67 | | | I like my teacher. (N) |
| 33 | | | I like who I am. (F) |
| | | 192 | I miss classes because of drinking or having a hangover. (A) |
| | | 149 | I need alcoholic beverages to have a good time. (A) |
| | 60 | | I quit easily. (A) |
| | 154 | | I'm a good person. (N) |
| 101 | | | I'm happy with who I am. (N) |
| 123 | | | My looks bother me. (A) |
| 105 | | | My parents like to be with me. (N) |
| | 130 | | My teacher gets mad at me for no good reason. (A) |
| | | 22 | Nothing about me is right. (T) |
| | | 34 | Nothing feels good to me. (T) |
| 57 | 93 | | Other kids hate to be with me. (A) |
| | 116 | | Other people are against me. (A) |
| | 88 | 132 | People act as if they don't hear me. (A) |
| | 189 | | People think I am fun to be with. (N) |
| | 164 | 92 | Someone wants to hurt me. (A) |

Measures of this type are often referred to as infrequency indexes. Individuals may have elevated *F*-Index scores for many reasons, including reading difficulties, a failure to follow directions, or random responding. Clinicians must exercise judgment to discern the reason for a high *F*-Index score.

The *F* Index also may be considered a "faking bad" index because individuals, in an effort to look severely disturbed, may choose items that reflect an abnormally high number of symptoms. Such patterns of symptoms may not correspond to any known disorder. However, individuals who present in acute psychological distress also may score highly on this scale, and for them the *F*-Index item responses may signal that they recognize a need for help. A clinical interview with the examinee, especially in conjunction with information gathered from the Structured Developmental History (SDH), often will clarify the meaning of a high *F*-Index score. Table 6.2 presents the interpretation summary of SRP *F*-Index raw scores.

**Table 6.2** *F*-Index Raw-Score Interpretation Summary

|  | Acceptable | Caution | Extreme Caution |
|---|---|---|---|
| SRP–C | 0–2 | 3–4 | 5–15 |
| SRP–A | 0–1 | 2–3 | 4–15 |
| SRP–COL | 0–1 | 2 | 3–15 |

## *L* INDEX

The *L* Index is designed to detect a response set that may be characterized as one of social desirability or "faking good," and consists of items written specifically for the *L*-Index scale. A point is added to the *L* Index when the respondent answers *True* (T) to positive behaviors or *False* (F) or *Never* (N) to negative behaviors. *L*-Index items are presented in Table 6.3.

Several possible reasons can explain an elevated *L*-Index score. A high score may simply reflect a high degree of psychological naïveté and below-average insight into one's own behavior and feelings. Alternatively, a high score may indicate that the individual is defensive or unwilling to share information about him or herself. Random responding or an inability to read and comprehend the items may also elevate this index.

The *L* Index may also detect responses that tend to present an idealized view of the self. Some people may choose item responses that correspond to the image they wish others had of them and not to how they really are. Unless the individual obviously is functioning well (a rare occurrence in referred populations), a high *L*-Index score suggests that SRP scale scores may be overly positive. Table 6.4 presents the interpretation summary of *L*-Index scores.

**Table 6.3** SRP: *L*-Index Items and Item Numbers

| SRP–C | SRP–A | SRP–COL | Item |
|---|---|---|---|
|  | 51 |  | I always do homework on time. (T) |
| 36 | 49 |  | I always do what my parents tell me. (T) |
| 19 | 13 |  | I always go to bed on time. (T) |
|  | 98 | 86 | I am jealous of others. (N) |
| 11 | 17 | 36 | I get mad at my parents sometimes. (F) |
| 100 | 106 | 154 | I get mad at others. (N) |
| 32 | 42 | 41 | I have never been mean to anyone. (T) |
| 39 | 59 | 57 | I have some bad habits. (F) |
| 2 | 2 | 12 | I like everyone I meet. (T) |
| 107 | 113 | 181 | I make mistakes. (N) |
| 29 | 38 | 5 | I never break the rules. (T) |
| 6 | 7 | 17 | I never get into trouble. (T) |
| 24 | 54 | 45 | I tell my parents everything. (T) |
| 15 | 21 | 25 | I tell the truth every single time. (T) |
| 22 | 30 |  | My parents are always right. (T) |

**Table 6.4** *L*-Index Raw-Score Interpretation Summary

|         | Acceptable | Caution | Extreme Caution |
|---------|------------|---------|-----------------|
| SRP–C   | 0–9        | 10–11   | 12–13           |
| SRP–A   | 0–9        | 10–12   | 13–15           |
| SRP–COL | 0–5        | 6–7     | 8–11            |

## *V* INDEX

The *V* Index consists of nonsensical items that may be marked because of carelessness or a failure to understand the questions due to limited reading skills or cooperation with the assessment process. *V*-Index items are listed in Table 6.5, and an interpretation summary is presented in Table 6.6. Scores in the Caution or Extreme Caution range suggest a highly questionable response protocol and typically indicate a child or youth who is uncooperative.

**Table 6.5** SRP: *V*-Index Items and Item Numbers

| SRP–C | SRP–A | SRP–COL | Item |
|-------|-------|---------|------|
| 126   |       |         | I drink 50 glasses of milk every day. |
|       | 186   |         | I get phone calls from popular movie actors. |
|       | 47    | 32      | I have just returned from a 9-month trip on an ocean liner. |
| 41    |       |         | I have never been in a car. |
| 17    |       |         | I have never been to sleep. |
| 30    |       |         | I have no teeth. |
|       | 15    | 56      | I have not seen a car in at least 6 months. |
|       | 33    |         | I take a plane trip from New York to Chicago at least twice a week. |
|       |       | 186     | I take a plane trip from New York to Tokyo at least twice a week. |

**Table 6.6** *V*-Index Raw-Score Interpretation Summary

|         | Acceptable | Caution | Extreme Caution |
|---------|------------|---------|-----------------|
| SRP–C   | 0–1        | 2       | 3–9             |
| SRP–A   | 0–1        | 2       | 3–9             |
| SRP–COL | 0          | 1       | 2–7             |

## INCONSISTENCY WITH OTHER RESULTS

The clinician may also become suspicious of SRP results from a referred child if the responses do not indicate any problems. If other sources suggest problems are present, then the clinician should consider the possibility of a positive, or faking good, response set. This type of dissimulation will often be detected by the *L* Index, but there are exceptions. In some cases, the respondent might infer the intended purpose of the *L*-Index items and thereby choose not to endorse them. Further interview and follow-up might be needed to determine the presence of a positive response set.

## OMITTED ITEMS

When using paper forms, an excessive number of omitted items may also compromise validity. (Administrations completed on Q-global require responses to each item, thereby negating the impact of omitted items.) Whenever possible, the clinician should encourage the respondent to answer all items. The layout of the SRP record form makes it easy to count the total number of omitted items. In some cases, the respondent may omit items simply because he or she is unclear of their meaning and may be able to complete them with some assistance. On the other hand, the respondent may have been unwilling to answer items on certain topics. An examination of the content of omitted items may help explore this possibility. To facilitate this process, the BASC–3 Q-global reports provide a listing of the item content for all omitted and multiply-marked items.

On the SRP, a maximum of two unscorable (i.e., omitted or multiply-marked) items are allowed per scale. Three or more unscorable items on a single scale will invalidate that scale and any subsequent composite scale score(s) to which the unscorable scale contributes. When one or two items are unscorable, raw scores are adjusted using values based on the average item responses for each scale obtained in the general norm sample. The purpose of the adjustment is to present a more accurate scaled score estimation. Without the adjustment, clinical scale scores would estimate the child as being closer to "average" than he or she may really be; scores on the adaptive scales would estimate the child as having more problems than is actually the case.

Table 6.7 summarizes the adjustment factors used on each SRP form. To adjust the raw score of the Anxiety scale, for example, locate the adjustment factor ("1") in the table. If the respondent omitted two Anxiety scale items, the number of unscorable items is multiplied by the adjustment factor as follows: 2 x 1 = 2. Thus, 2 points would be added to the Anxiety scale raw score prior to its conversion to a *T* score.

**Table 6.7** SRP Adjustment Factors for Unscorable Item Responses (Maximum 2 per Scale)

| Scale | SRP | | |
|---|---|---|---|
| | C | A | COL |
| Attitude to School | 1 | 1 | — |
| Attitude to Teachers | 1 | 1 | — |
| Sensation Seeking | — | 1 | 1 |
| Atypicality | 1 | 0 | 0 |
| Locus of Control | 1 | 1 | 0 |
| Social Stress | 1 | 1 | 1 |
| Anxiety | 1 | 1 | 1 |
| Depression | 0 | 0 | 0 |
| Sense of Inadequacy | 1 | 1 | 1 |
| Somatization | — | 0 | 0 |
| Attention Problems | 1 | 1 | 1 |
| Hyperactivity | 1 | 1 | 1 |
| Alcohol Abuse | — | — | 0 |
| School Maladjustment | — | — | 1 |
| Relations With Parents | 2 | 2 | 2 |
| Interpersonal Relations | 2 | 2 | 2 |
| Self-Esteem | 2 | 2 | 2 |
| Self-Reliance | 2 | 2 | 2 |
| Anger Control | — | 1 | 1 |
| Ego Strength | — | 2 | 2 |
| Mania | — | 1 | 1 |
| Test Anxiety | — | 1 | 1 |

# PATTERNED RESPONDING

Examiners should review responses on the record forms carefully for patterned responding. For example, if a respondent marks all *N*s (or only *N*s and *A*s) or alternates responses by giving all *N*s in one column and all *S*s in the next, the validity of the rating scales should be questioned.

The Response Pattern Index, available in the BASC–3 Q-global reports, is designed to identify forms that may be invalid because the respondent was inattentive to the item content. The first pattern is characterized by the identical response to many items in succession (e.g., *N-N-N-N. . .*). The second pattern detected by the Response Pattern Index is an alternating or cyclical pattern (e.g., *T-F-T-F-T-F . . .* or *N-S-O-A-N-S-O-A . . .*). A respondent who pays little attention to the items might find it easy to answer using one of these patterns.

The Response Pattern Index is a tally of the number of times an item response differs from the response to the previous item. (Note the transition between the last *T-F* item and the first *N-S-O-A* item is not counted in this index.) A very low tally indicates the respondent tended to choose the same response option repeatedly when completing the form. A very high tally suggests the respondent might have completed the form in a cyclical pattern. Valid SRP forms will tend to have a Response Pattern Index score that falls somewhere between these extremes. Scores in the Caution-Low and Caution-High ranges are intended to identify the extreme 0.5% of each end of the Response Pattern Index score distribution in the general and clinical norm samples for that form.

Table 6.8 provides an interpretation summary for the Response Pattern Index. A Caution-Low score indicates that there were very few changes in item responses. A Caution-High score shows considerable variation in item responses. A score in either cautionary range would warrant a review of the record form (or the item responses) to see whether obvious patterns exist that would suggest the respondent disregarded the item content. The Consistency Index (described next) may provide supporting evidence. If necessary, it may be helpful to question the respondent directly.

**Table 6.8** Patterned Responding Score Interpretation Summary

|  | Caution-Low | Acceptable | Caution-High |
|---|---|---|---|
| SRP–C | 0–45 | 46–102 | 103–135 |
| SRP–A | 0–55 | 56–138 | 139–187 |
| SRP–COL | 0–80 | 81–137 | 138–190 |

## CONSISTENCY INDEX

The Consistency Index, available in the BASC–3 Q-global reports, identifies cases where the respondent has given differing responses to items that usually are answered similarly. Like the Response Pattern Index, it is designed to identify forms with results that may be invalid because the respondent disregarded the item content. More generally, the Consistency Index detects BASC–3 forms with responses that are not internally consistent (i.e., where the respondent frequently answered very similar items differently). Inconsistency also can occur for reasons other than ignored item content. For example, a respondent might change his or her perspective during the completion of a form or might misunderstand the items because of poor reading ability or language comprehension.

The Consistency Index was created by pairing items for each form that are highly correlated (either positively or negatively) and then summing the absolute values of the score differences between the items in each pair. The cutoff values for each form are set at a point that effectively separates the distribution of Consistency Index values in a large sample of general and clinical norm cases from the distribution of values in a set of randomly generated scores. Table 6.9 presents the cutoff values for each form. Because the sum of score differences is actually a direct measure of inconsistency, a high score on the Consistency Index signifies that the results should be interpreted cautiously, and the possibility that the form is invalid should be explored. When the Consistency Index is in the Caution or Extreme Caution score range, the Q-global reports will list the item pairs contributing to the high score. This information can be helpful for determining, case by case, whether the response disagreements are plausible or implausible. Additional information on the distribution properties and validity evidence of the Consistency Index can be found in chapter 7.

**Table 6.9** Consistency Index Score Interpretation Summary

|  | Acceptable | Caution | Extreme Caution |
|---|---|---|---|
| SRP–C | 0–17 | 18–21 | 22 or higher |
| SRP–A | 0–14 | 15–19 | 20 or higher |
| SRP–COL | 0–12 | 13–15 | 16 or higher |

## READING DIFFICULTIES

Children or young adults may produce invalid responses on the SRP if they lack English or Spanish reading proficiency, perhaps as a result of linguistic differences, reading disability, or lack of education. This hypothesis may be checked by observing trepidation by a child or young adult who is asked to complete a form or by noting that the child or young adult has asked for clarification of the meaning of several individual items. See chapter 7 for a summary of the minimum reading levels of the SRP forms.

# SRP–I Form

The BASC–3 SRP–I offers a standardized procedure for interviewing young children ages 6 through 7 about some basic behavioral and emotional concerns. As discussed in chapter 2, a single Total Score is derived that provides an overall indication of behavioral or emotional concerns being experienced by a child. Interpretive classifications for the Total Score are provided in Table 6.10.

**Table 6.10** SRP–I Total Score Interpretation Summary

|  | Low | Average | High | Very High |
| --- | --- | --- | --- | --- |
| Total Score | 0 | 1–5 | 6–8 | 9–11 |

The classification of the Total Score can provide a useful gauge for understanding the level of problems being experienced by a child since the categories are based on scores obtained in a representative normative sample. Scores in the Low range indicate one or more standard deviations below the mean. A classification of High indicates scores one or more standard deviations above the mean, while Very High indicates two or more standard deviations above the mean.

The responses obtained to follow-up questions may yield the most clinically useful information gained from the SRP–I. These qualitative responses can be particularly useful when creating a final report for a comprehensive evaluation on a child. They can also serve as a basis for helping to understand the BASC–3 results obtained from teachers or parents. For example, responses to items 5 ("Do you think other kids like you?") and 6 ("Do other kids play with you?") could provide additional context for interpreting a problematic TRS Social Skills scale score. In addition, the information obtained on the SRP–I can provide direct insight into the types of problems a child is experiencing, enabling the clinician to deal directly with these concerns. Finally, because of their open-ended nature, responses to these items may provide information about unanticipated problems or challenges. A child may, for example, report that her parent's deteriorating relationship causes her to worry and do worse in school. This unanticipated insight has direct implications for treatment planning.

Table 6.11 provides some summary information that can be helpful when evaluating SRP–I scores. The first column presents the endorsement percentages for items 2 through 14. (Item 1 is not shown since it serves as a "warm-up" item for children being interviewed and is not scored.) The second column presents the response category for the responses obtained from the corresponding follow-up questions asked during the interview, along with the percentage of children providing a response in that category; note that the percentage is based only on those children endorsing the initial question. The third column lists general examples of the types of responses children provided when the follow-up question was asked.

**Table 6.11** SRP–I Item Endorsements and Response Categories and Examples

| Item | General category (Percentage of responses) | Examples |
|---|---|---|
| 2. Do you ever get bored at school? (Yes=49%) | Activities/classwork/homework (56%) | Art, music, reading, math, writing |
| | Waiting/quiet time/time out (35%) | When tired; when have to be quiet; when have to finish work; losing recess |
| 3. Do you ever get into trouble at school? (Yes=39%) | Disrespect/aggression/blaming others (24%) | Throw things; push others; talking back; being loud |
| | Social/emotional aspects (48%) | Talking when shouldn't; being mean; calling others' names |
| | Disorganization/inattention (13%) | Not listening; being distracted; not following directions |
| 4. Does your teacher ever make you feel bad? (Yes=15%) | Punishment/withholding reinforcement (58%) | Can't go to recess if work not done; get yelled at; can't be line leader |
| | Corrective feedback (23%) | Tells child to make good choices; tells child to sit down; changes status of tracking tool (e.g., moves picture to another color) |
| 5. Do you think other kids like you? (No=12%) | Physical attributes (31%) | Glasses; face/teeth/eye color; clothing/ shoes; backpack |
| | Personality and behaviors (19%) | Child is not fun; child is annoying; child is mean to others |
| | Social situations/activities (17%) | Don't like to play with child; child does not have same group of friends |
| 6. Do other kids play with you? (No=6%) | Activities/academics (32%) | Child likes to play things others don't |
| | Negative behaviors (26%) | Child is mean to others; others don't like the child |
| | Social situations (21%) | Prefer to play with children other than the child; no friends in class; new to school |
| 7. Do other kids say bad things to you? (Yes=31%) | Social rejection/personal attributes (60%) | Don't like child; call child ugly/fat/mean/ liar; make fun of appearance |
| 8. Do other kids make fun of you? (Yes 24%) | Social rejection/personal attributes (49%) | Make fun of laugh/appearance/name/ being different |
| | Activities/academics (27%) | Can't do something (draw, kick, ride bike); types of books child reads; not being smart |
| 9. Are you afraid of things? (Yes=57%) | Animals/insects/natural events or things (45%) | Bugs/spiders; Tigers/snakes/big dogs; fire/storms; blood |
| | Isolation (35%) | The dark/bedtime/night; getting lost or being alone; first day of school |
| | Imaginary themes (27%) | Scary stories/movies; bad dreams; monsters |

**Table 6.11** SRP–I Item Endorsements and Response Categories and Examples *(continued)*

| Item | General category (Percentage of responses) | Examples |
|---|---|---|
| 10. Do you feel sad? (Yes=34%) | Problems with others (40%) | When people are mean; getting bullied; fights with siblings |
| | Loneliness/grief (38%) | Missing others; when someone dies; when dad is gone in army; when pet dies/runs away |
| 11. Do you feel like you are all alone? (Yes=25%) | Recreation/free time (52%) | At recess; during free time |
| | Home/family (38%) | In room; when doesn't know where family members are; when goes places without parents |
| 12. Do you feel like you are always doing things wrong? (18%) | Academics (52%) | Math/reading/art; homework; during tests |
| | Behavior (Yes=33%) | Not listening; when chart gets moved to different color; when doesn't clean room |
| 13. Do you have a hard time hearing what your teacher says? (Yes=33%) | Classroom arrangement (58%) | Too far away |
| 14. Do you have a hard time seeing things on a page, screen, or on the board? (Yes=27%) | Physical issues (74%) | At the screen; small words when teacher writes; when child is in back row |

The SRP–I should not be used as the sole basis for determining the presence or absence of a behavioral or emotional problem. The information obtained from the SRP–I should supplement other information obtained during a comprehensive assessment.

# Interpreting Scale Scores on the SRP–C, SRP–A, and SRP–COL Forms

## SRP SCALES

This section provides an overview of each scale, including a description of its content and interpretation and a discussion of the scale's relationship to diagnostic, prevention, intervention planning, and evaluation processes. Several of the discussions refer to the clinical group score profiles, which are documented in chapter 11. Table 6.12 briefly summarizes the content of each scale.

### Clinical Scales

The clinical scales measure maladjustment. High scores on these scales represent negative or undesirable characteristics that cause impaired functioning in home, school, peer relationships, or community contexts. As mentioned in chapter 2, clinical scale scores in the 60 through 69 range are considered at-risk, and scores of 70 or higher are considered clinically significant. For the adaptive scales, scores in the 31 through 40 range are considered at-risk, and scores of 30 or lower are considered to be clinically significant.

**Table 6.12** SRP Scale Definitions

| Scale | Definition |
|---|---|
| Alcohol Abuse | The tendency to use alcohol to feel better or to calm down and to experience adverse outcomes as a result of alcohol use |
| Anxiety | Feelings of nervousness, worry, and fear; the tendency to be overwhelmed by problems |
| Attention Problems | The tendency to report being easily distracted and unable to concentrate more than momentarily |
| Attitude to School | Feelings of alienation, hostility, and dissatisfaction regarding school |
| Attitude to Teachers | Feelings of resentment and dislike of teachers; beliefs that teachers are unfair, uncaring, or overly demanding |
| Atypicality | The tendency toward bizarre thoughts or other thoughts and behaviors considered "odd" |
| Depression | Feelings of unhappiness, sadness, and dejection; a belief that nothing goes right |
| Hyperactivity | The tendency to report being overly active, rushing through work or activities, and acting without thinking |
| Interpersonal Relations | The perception of having good social relationships and friendships with peers |
| Locus of Control | The belief that rewards and punishments are controlled by external events or people |
| Relations With Parents | A positive regard toward parents and a feeling of being esteemed by them |
| School Maladjustment | Perceived difficulties associated with attending postsecondary institutions, including feeling overwhelmed, unmotivated, and forced to attend school |
| Self-Esteem | Feelings of self-esteem, self-respect, and self-acceptance |
| Self-Reliance | Confidence in one's ability to solve problems; a belief in one's personal dependability and decisiveness |
| Sensation Seeking | The tendency to take risks and to seek excitement |
| Sense of Inadequacy | Perceptions of being unsuccessful in school, unable to achieve one's goals, and generally inadequate |
| Social Stress | Feelings of stress and tension in personal relationships; a feeling of being excluded from social activities |
| Somatization | The tendency to be overly sensitive to, to experience, or to complain about relatively minor physical problems and discomforts |

## Alcohol Abuse

This scale, available only on the SRP–COL form, assesses the tendency to use alcohol in ways that could lead to alcohol abuse. Alcohol abuse can manifest itself in failing major responsibilities at work, school, or home, drinking in dangerous situations such as when driving, continued drinking despite problems created by or worsened by drinking, and can turn into a dependence on alcohol (U.S. Department of Health and Human Services, Centers for Disease Control and Prevention [CDC], 2014). This problem can become significant, especially for males. For example, drinking heavily during the first year of college has been associated with an increased chance of dropout prior to the second year of college (Liguori & Lonbaken, 2015).

Items on the SRP–COL are used to discover tendencies that include using alcohol to feel better or calm down, drinking alcohol when alone, and being overcome by thoughts of future opportunities to drink alcohol. This scale also assesses outcomes associated with drinking alcohol, which include reports that others suspect excessive alcohol use by the respondent and reports of getting into trouble because of alcohol use. High scores on this scale warrant further inquiry and, possibly, additional evaluation for alcohol-abuse problems.

## Anxiety

The Anxiety scale assesses generalized fears, nervousness, and worries that typically are irrational and poorly defined in the mind of the individual. Among young people, anxiety disorders are relatively common and often co-occur with depression (Cummings et al., 2014). High scorers on this scale may feel a sense of dread and may be troubled by obsessive, intrusive, and bothersome thoughts. At clinically significant score levels, these thoughts may produce confusion in the decision-making process. Additional obsessive-compulsive features, such as ritualistic or perseverative behavior, may be present.

*T* scores below 41 may reflect an inflated sense of well-being and, when coupled with high scores on the Sensation Seeking scale, may suggest the beginnings of a conduct disorder. The absence of anxiety over the harmful effects of one's behavior is one of the most widely accepted indications of sociopathy, often presenting in childhood and adolescence as conduct disorder. Anxiety scale scores in the At-Risk range denote levels of distress that may be chronic or acute. Individuals with chronic anxiety may feel overburdened by the minor mishaps of life and may be prone to stress reactions. Clinically significant *T* scores indicate a clear presence of emotional or psychological distress and a tendency to respond negatively to one's environment. Persons with high anxiety levels may become extremely rigid in their thought processes or, in extreme cases, confused and disoriented. Small slights are likely to be taken as major disappointments, and the person may be hypersensitive to criticism.

The Anxiety scale has moderate correlations (generally .50s to .60s) with several of the scales comprising the Internalizing Problems composite scale. When looking at the BASC–3 clinical samples, the Anxiety scale score is highest (albeit below the At-Risk level) among the conditions for children classified as having an emotional/behavioral disturbance (EBD).

## Attention Problems

The Attention Problems scale was designed for use in diagnosing the presence or absence of the core symptoms of attention-deficit/hyperactivity disorder (ADHD). The Attention Problems scale measures the inability to maintain attention and the tendency to be easily distracted from tasks requiring attention.

The Attention Problems scale, when used in conjunction with the Hyperactivity scale, may help distinguish the three presentations of ADHD: combined, predominantly inattentive, and predominantly hyperactive/impulsive. Inattention has been shown to be negatively related to academic success. For example, a longitudinal study showed that inattention symptoms could independently predict failure to graduate from secondary school and lower academic performance (Galéra, Melchior, Chastang, Bouvard, & Fombonne, 2009). Moreover, inattention has been shown to be more predictive than hyperactivity of later problems with substance abuse (Molina & Pelham, 2003), although childhood ADHD combined with delinquency has also been found to predict substance abuse problems (Harty, Galanopoulos, Newcorn, & Halperin, 2013).

Attention Problems scale scores in the Clinically Significant range denote attentional deficits that interfere with activities, especially tasks (such as learning) that require close attention and concentration. While ADHD is the most likely cause of such problems, anxiety disorders, including posttraumatic stress disorder (PTSD), may also elevate the Attention Problems scale score. Proper differential diagnosis and interpretation of such scales routinely require a clinical interview and history-gathering.

The Attention Problems scale has the highest correlation with the Hyperactivity scale on each of the SRP levels. In the BASC–3 clinical samples, the Attention Problems scale score is the highest among scales for children classified as having ADHD, although the score is slightly below the At-Risk range.

## Attitude to School

The Attitude to School scale (available on the SRP–C and SRP–A) surveys the respondent's general opinion of the utility of school, along with his or her level of comfort with school-related matters. Scores below 41 demonstrate relative satisfaction and comfort with school. Individuals with elevated Attitude to School scale scores are unlikely to find anything, beyond peer relationships, satisfying about their school experience. Scores in the At-Risk range indicate a pervasive discomfort with school. Clinically significant *T* scores may suggest an increased risk of dropping out, especially if the individual has high scores on the Sensation Seeking and Sense of Inadequacy scales and a low score on the Interpersonal Relations scale.

Because school is so prominent in the lives of children and young adults, high scorers on the Attitude to School scale often have other problems. Younger children and females may tend to internalize problems and show somatic symptoms, while adolescent males are more likely to show externalizing behavior problems and, at times, antisocial behavior. When coupled with learning problems, poor attitudes toward schooling may lead to a poor prognosis for success in many life tasks.

## Attitude to Teachers

The Attitude to Teachers scale (included on the SRP–C and SRP–A) assesses the individual's perception of teachers as being uncaring, unfair, or unmotivated to help their students. As on the Attitude to School scale, scores may fluctuate in reaction to recent occurrences of conflict with (or special assistance from) a teacher or school administrator.

A low score indicates that teachers are held in high regard. Scores in the At-Risk range, on the other hand, indicate a general dissatisfaction with teachers, and clinically significant T scores suggest that such dissatisfaction is pervasive. Such scores, when accompanied by high scores on the Attitude to School, Sensation Seeking, and Sense of Inadequacy scales and a low score on the Interpersonal Relations scale, may suggest an increased risk of quitting school. If none of these other scales are elevated and if the Attitude to School scale score is within the typical range, the presence of personality conflicts with particular teachers should be explored.

## Atypicality

The Atypicality scale evaluates unusual thoughts and perceptions (e.g., seeing or hearing things that are not there, feeling that one is being watched or targeted) that are commonly associated with severe forms of psychopathology such as schizophrenia. Boys identified by their peers as behaving in atypical ways have reported experiences of rejection, victimization, and loneliness at school. Both genders who were identified as behaving in atypical ways have reported social anxiety in connection to rejection and victimization (DeRosier & Mercer, 2009).

Elevated Atypicality scale scores could point to a variety of problems. Scores in the At-Risk range or above may indicate confused thought and, possibly, a decompensation process. Scores in the Clinically Significant range may be an indicator of severe emotional disturbance and may be associated with serious thought disorders, a developing (or developed) schizophrenic process, and poor ego strength. Social alienation or the highly individualistic lifestyle of a family might also be interpretations to consider for scores at this level. Whenever an extreme Atypicality scale score is obtained, particular emphasis should be placed on evaluating the SRP validity indexes to help rule out the possibility of an invalid rating scale profile.

The Atypicality scale generally has the highest correlation coefficient with the Social Stress scale across the SRP levels. In the BASC–3 clinical samples, the Atypicality scale has the highest score in the group of children diagnosed with an emotional/behavioral disturbance.

## Depression

The Depression scale assesses traditional symptoms of depression, including feelings of loneliness, sadness, and an inability to enjoy life. A sense of hopelessness, pessimism, and dread underlies many of the items. Scores in the At-Risk range may represent significant levels of depression. Scores in the Clinically Significant range are associated with broad problems of adjustment that may be overlooked by others because such children and adolescents are notably unobtrusive. Depression is an important construct to measure on a self-report instrument. For example, self-reporting has been shown to be a better method of detecting suicidal thoughts among adolescents than parent reporting (Lewis et al., 2014).

Children and young adults with high scores on the Depression scale are often seen as reserved or introverted but with evidence of anxiety and emotional lability. They seldom take chances, but they may appear agitated at times. Mild to moderate problems in relating to other people and in emotional expression are often present at home, at school, and with peers. High scores on the Depression scale should therefore be compared with Depression scale ratings on the TRS and PRS.

In general, the Depression scale scores correlate highest with the Anxiety, Social Stress, Locus of Control, Sense of Inadequacy, and Self-Esteem scales. In the BASC–3 clinical samples, the groups with the highest Depression scale scores include autism and EBD (although the scores are below the At-Risk range).

## Hyperactivity

The Hyperactivity scale focuses primarily on the excessive activity level associated with ADHD disorders. This scale assesses behaviors such as having trouble standing still, talking while others are talking, and being too noisy. Scores in the At-Risk and Clinically Significant ranges typically indicate that such behavior is pervasive and at a level that will result in significant behavior problems.

Some research suggests that adolescents are better able to describe hyperactivity symptoms than symptoms of either impulsivity or inattention (Smith, Pelham, Gnagy, Molina, & Evans, 2000). Other findings indicate that adolescents have difficulty reporting both inattention and hyperactivity problems (Hope et al., 1999). Thus, elevated Hyperactivity scale scores should always be interpreted jointly with TRS and PRS results and SDH information, and the Student Observation System (SOS) for younger children, to gauge the accuracy of the SRP results.

The Hyperactivity scale has the highest correlations with the Attention Problems and Functional Impairment scales, providing some evidence of the widespread impact that behavior-control deficits can have on overall behavioral and emotional adjustment. In the BASC–3 clinical samples, the Hyperactivity scale is the second highest scale score for children classified as having ADHD, second to the Attention Problems scale.

### Locus of Control

The Locus of Control scale assesses an individual's perception of his or her level of control over external events. Low scores on this scale indicate the perception of having internal control over events, whereas a high score indicates the belief of being controlled by others or by fate or some other abstract force. These external forces typically include authority figures such as parents or teachers. Overall, this scale assesses a major component of a child's attribution system.

Scores in the At-Risk or Clinically Significant ranges may indicate a sense of helplessness and may indicate a strong belief in luck. Children and young adults with such scores will tend to project blame for all of their problems onto others, including peers, parents, and teachers. They will also tend to believe that, even when behaving as expected, rewards will not be systematically or appropriately distributed.

Clinically significant *T* scores also may reveal a pathological view of external control that may destroy motivation and the sense of controlling one's destiny that seems to underlie much of general mental health. Such scores may be obtained by individuals who are mildly paranoid about the world that surrounds them. They may see a world without reason or responsibility. These views may induce anxiety or depression, robbing children and young adults of the feelings of safety and security that are so important to healthy development, particularly in childhood. Recent trauma victims may also have elevated scale scores, as well as individuals suffering from more extended PTSD. Pervasive mental health problems may be associated with clinically significant scores.

The Locus of Control scale scores correlate the highest with the Depression, Sense of Inadequacy, and Social Stress scales.

### School Maladjustment

This scale, available only on the SRP–COL form, assesses the perceived difficulties associated with attending postsecondary institutions. Such difficulties might include boredom, feeling overwhelmed by school demands, feeling pressured to go to school, and generally lacking motivation to attend classes and do well academically. For many students, making the transition from secondary to postsecondary school is quite challenging. This scale is designed to show the student's coping methods in making this transition. High scores indicate a general dissatisfaction toward school and significant difficulty with adapting to the demands of higher education. Further investigation into the sources of such difficulties via the use of a clinical interview is recommended.

### Sensation Seeking

Sensation seeking has been defined as "the seeking of varied, novel, complex, and intense sensations and experiences, and the willingness to take physical, social, legal, and financial risks for the sake of such experience" (Zuckerman, 1994, p. 27). The Sensation Seeking scale, which is included on the SRP–A and SRP–COL forms, assesses this trait by investigating both the desire to engage in thrilling or potentially hazardous activities and a preference for excitement associated with risk-taking.

Scores in the At-Risk and Clinically Significant ranges indicate a tendency to be bored easily, to have a high energy level, and to engage in risky and potentially delinquent behavior. School conduct problems may often be seen in individuals who receive high scores for the Sensation Seeking scale. The potential for alcohol and drug use or experimentation increases with high scores on this scale, which is not surprising since sensation seeking has been associated with smoking, binge drinking, alcohol consumption, and sexual risk-taking during early adolescence (Charnigo et al., 2013;

Doran et al., 2011; MacPherson, Magidson, Reynolds, Kahler, & Lejuez, 2010; Sargent, Tanski, Stoolmiller, & Hanewinkel, 2010). When accompanied by low Anxiety scale scores, high Sensation Seeking scale scores tend to be associated with the diagnosis of conduct disorder. High scores on the Sensation Seeking scale also may be seen with elevated Depression scale scores, especially in males. Such individuals may increasingly engage in risk-taking behaviors to overcome depressive feelings that are not understood and to surmount anhedonia, a common depression symptom. The use of self-reporting is important for identifying sensation-seeking tendencies; research has indicated that teachers are often unaware of a child's inclination to engage in risky activities (Rowe, 1999).

### Sense of Inadequacy

The Sense of Inadequacy scale assesses perceptions of low achievement expectations, a tendency not to persevere, and a perception of being unsuccessful (primarily in academic endeavors). The person may feel inadequate to meet expectations set either by him- or herself or by others. The scale is related to the concept of level of aspiration, in that a child who sets or accepts unrealistically high goals would be likely to score high on this scale.

Scores in the At-Risk range denote mildly to moderately depressed confidence. A clinically significant score typically indicates an individual who feels unable to compete in mainstream society, one who may have "given up" to go his or her own way and who chooses not to pursue traditional goals.

Individuals with high Sense of Inadequacy scale scores tend to lack persistence. Although high scorers may seem self-assured, they often will show some evidence of depression or anxiety (except in the case of those having blatant conduct disorders or antisocial personality disorders). Elevated Sense of Inadequacy scale scores may be found in cases of academic failure or underachievement, cognitive deficit secondary to neurological impairment, intellectual disability, learning disability (LD), and depression, among other problems.

The Sense of Inadequacy scale has the highest correlations with the Depression, Locus of Control, and Social Stress scales. In the BASC–3 clinical samples, Sense of Inadequacy scale scores are higher than average for several clinical groups; however the clinical group averages for the Sense of Inadequacy scale are below the At-Risk range.

### Social Stress

The Social Stress scale assesses the level of stress experienced by children in relation to their interactions with peers and others. Feelings of tension, pressure, and a lack of coping resources (especially outlets through close friends and social contact) are evident in social stress. As measured on the SRP, social stress is likely to be pervasive and chronic rather than acute and transient (as defined in some other conceptualizations of stress).

Scores in the At-Risk range or higher may show problems related to anxiety, confusion, and somatic complaints. Young children with clinically significant scores may turn inward in an unsuccessful attempt to cope with those tensions. They may appear shy and be prone to guilt, but they may also be emotionally labile and may display an unexplained edginess or hyperirritability.

### Somatization

The Somatization scale, available on the SRP–A and SRP–COL, assesses the tendency to complain about relatively minor physical problems as an expression of psychological difficulties. As noted in chapter 5, somatization has been shown to be linked with trauma (Kugler et al., 2012) and weaker school performance (Hughes et al., 2008). This scale evaluates the level and nature of a series of health-related problems, fears, and concerns. The various physical complaints noted may be experienced as real or imaginary but typically are psychogenic if more than a few items are marked. Young children are unreliable reporters of such phenomena, but adolescents and young adults respond clearly to such questions.

Scores in the At-Risk range or higher are associated with anxiety, internalization, and suppression of feelings, although chronic complaining may be evident. At clinically significant levels, more serious problems may develop, hysteria may occur, and histrionic displays may become more common. Clinically significant levels may also be associated with the development of serious physical ailments such as ulcers. Poor development of ego strength is common at such high levels and, if the Personal Adjustment composite is significantly low, a diagnosis of identity disorder might be considered if other criteria are met.

In the BASC–3 clinical samples, children classified as having EBD have the highest scale score (although the score is slightly below the At-Risk threshold).

## Adaptive Scales

The adaptive scales measure positive adjustment. Unlike scores on the clinical scales, high scores on the adaptive scales represent positive or desirable characteristics and low scores represent possible problem areas. As mentioned in chapter 2, adaptive scale scores of 31 through 40 are considered at-risk and scores 30 or lower are considered clinically significant. Overall, the adaptive scales tend to have the highest correlations with the BASC–3 Depression, Social Stress, and Sense of Inadequacy scales.

### Interpersonal Relations

The Interpersonal Relations scale assesses the individual's reports of success in relating to others and the degree of enjoyment derived from this interaction. Scores in the At-Risk range denote problems in relating to others and in developing social skills. Clinically significant scores signify the possibility of significant problems, particularly with peers but also with adults. This may hold especially true with elevated Attitude to Teachers scale scores or significantly low Relations With Parents scale scores. Individuals with problematic scores on the Interpersonal Relations scale may be withdrawn and lack the energy for social interaction, especially if the Depression scale score is high. However, such individuals may intrude into others' interactions, thereby prompting rebuke instead of social approval. Children with very low scores tend to be guilt-prone, blaming themselves for a lack of success. Most desire good interpersonal relations, but their efforts to seek them out are unsuccessful.

### Relations With Parents

The Relations With Parents scale surveys the individual's perception of being important in the family, the status of the child–parent relationship, and the child's perception of the degree of parental trust and concern. High scores on the Relations With Parents scale indicate positive adjustment.

Scores in the At-Risk range denote mildly to moderately disturbed relations with parents. Clinically significant scores indicate the possibility of severe family problems and perhaps outright alienation. Conduct disorder may be common among very low scorers. Adolescents with such scores may be quite active and prone to acting out. Younger children with very low scores often may appear reserved or as displaying inappropriate feelings. Emotional lability and a negative attitude may be common at scores of about 30 or below.

### Self-Esteem

The Self-Esteem scale assesses a child's and young adult's self-satisfaction, with reference to both physical and more global characteristics. High scores on this scale are indicative of positive self-esteem. Such individuals are often seen by others as warm, open, venturesome, and self-assured. They typically have good peer relations, a positive sense of their identity, and appropriate levels of ego strength.

Individuals with low self-esteem, particularly those with clinically significant *T* scores, tend to reveal a pervasive sense of dissatisfaction with the self. Shyness and a feeling of tension are often evident, and the possibility of anxiety and depression exists. Moreover, studies indicate a relationship between low self-esteem and eating disorders (Obeid, Buchholz, Boerner, Henderson, & Norris, 2013; Sassaroli & Ruggiero, 2005). Some adolescents possess low self-esteem in the absence of any other self-reported difficulties (Kamphaus et al., 2003). Heavily directive or confrontational approaches to intervention may exacerbate the presenting problems of such individuals. An atmosphere of acceptance and trust is crucial to the intervention process for children with poor self-esteem.

### Self-Reliance

The Self-Reliance scale assesses self-confidence and assurance in one's ability to make decisions. This scale is a strong measure of personal adjustment. High scores indicate a tendency to take on responsibility and to face life's challenges. Individuals with high scores tend not to be fearful of their emotions but to be well controlled by internal systems.

Scores in the At-Risk and Clinically Significant ranges may indicate a lack of self-confidence and difficulty in facing life's challenges (especially in school achievement). Younger people may show high levels of depression and separation anxiety. Children with depressed Self-Reliance scale scores may also be rated by their parents and teachers at half a standard deviation above the mean (indicative of mild symptoms) on the Attention Problems, Hyperactivity, and Learning Problems scales (Kamphaus et al., 2003).

## SRP Content Scales

The content scales included on the SRP were introduced in the BASC–2 as theoretically derived scales wholly made up of items from other BASC–2 scales and were available only in a limited number of BASC–2 software reports. However, due to their widespread acceptance by practitioners and researchers, they are now available in standard BASC–3 Q-global reports. Each content scale now contains some unique items written specifically for the scale, in addition to items shared from other clinical and adaptive scales. All content scales except Ego Strength are interpreted using the same criteria as the clinical scales (scores 60 through 69 are considered at-risk and scores 70 or higher are considered clinically significant). The Ego Strength scale is interpreted in the same way as the adaptive scales (scores 31 through 40 are considered at-risk and scores 30 or lower are considered clinically significant). Table 6.13 provides brief descriptions of each content scale.

**Table 6.13** SRP Content Scale Descriptions

| Content scale | Description |
| --- | --- |
| Anger Control | The tendency to become irritated and/or angry quickly and impulsively, coupled with an inability to regulate affect and self-control |
| Ego Strength | The expression of a strong self-identity and overall emotional competence, including feelings of self-awareness, self-acceptance, and positive perception of one's social support network |
| Mania | The tendency toward extended periods of heightened arousal, excessive activity (at times obsessive in focus), and rapid idea generation in the absence of normal fatigue |
| Test Anxiety | The propensity for irrational worry over and fear of taking routine school tests of aptitude or academic skills, regardless of one's degree of study preparation or confidence in knowledge of the test content |

These scales are designed to supplement interpretation of the primary scales of the TRS, PRS, and SRP. The following content scales are available for the SRP–A and SRP–COL levels in the BASC–3 Q-global reports.

### Anger Control

Although its application is specific to use with the self-report, the Anger Control content scale on the SRP is essentially the same construct as previously defined for the TRS and PRS. It is described as the tendency to become irritated quickly and impulsively coupled with the inability to regulate affect and self-control. Unique to the Anger Control scale on the SRP is that investigation of specific item responses on this scale might help to discern the underlying cause or motivation of angry outbursts. Examples of items with responses that might be of particular interest are "When I get angry, I want to break something," "I get angry easily," and "I threaten to hurt others when I get angry."

### Ego Strength

The Ego Strength content scale gauges the expression of a strong self-identity and overall emotional competence, including feelings of self-awareness, self-acceptance, and positive perception of one's social support network. This scale is a measure of an adaptive strength. Individuals with high scores on this content scale report self-confidence and high levels of self-awareness and self-acceptance. Such people tend to respond to intervention, and a high score on Ego Strength is a good indicator of a positive prognosis if treatment is provided. In exceptional cases, particularly where other interpersonal difficulties are seen, extremely high scores may reflect ego inflation used as a defense mechanism; classic narcissistic features might then be present. Such instances could suggest a developing personality disorder, but only where chronic interpersonal relationship problems are clearly indicated. Individuals with significantly low scores on this content scale are likely to have low self-esteem, a poor support network, and depression-like symptoms.

**Mania**

The Mania content scale measures the tendency toward extended periods of heightened arousal, excessive activity (at times obsessive in focus), and rapid idea generation in the absence of normal fatigue. High scores on this content scale will be associated with self-reported difficulty in slowing down and relaxing and in the ability to "turn off" one's mind. This content scale can help in discerning the common elements of a manic episode (see *DSM-5*) and might also be useful for differentiating ADHD from bipolar disorder in children and adolescents. In cases where such conditions are suspected, a definitive diagnosis requires a detailed history from a knowledgeable caregiver, coupled with a careful clinical interview of the respondent.

A variety of factors can influence the development of a manic episode, including substance abuse, toxic exposure, nutritional factors, acute stress, and anxiety (especially if trauma-induced). In addition, manic episodes may simply be characteristic of another behavioral problem such as ADHD. The clinician should explore such considerations when making an educational classification or clinical diagnosis.

**Test Anxiety**

The Test Anxiety content scale gauges the propensity for irrational worry over and fear of taking routine school tests of aptitude or academic skills, regardless of one's degree of study preparation or confidence in knowledge of the test content. High scores on this scale indicate a chronic condition where a respondent experiences higher anxiety during testing than is typical for his or her peers. Fears associated with a specific test for which the individual failed to prepare should not result in an elevated scale score. For some individuals, this heightened test anxiety will be specific to group tests and may well explain discrepancies encountered between classroom-based testing and testing of individuals by a psychologist or diagnostician.

## SRP Composites

Although lacking the precision of scale scores for pinpointing specific syndromes or strengths, scores from the SRP composite scales are helpful for summarizing responses and for making broad conclusions regarding different types of adaptive and maladaptive personality tendencies. The SRP–C and SRP–A yield five composite scale scores: School Problems, Internalizing Problems, Inattention/Hyperactivity, Personal Adjustment, and an overall composite, the Emotional Symptoms Index (ESI). The SRP–COL, which does not include the School Problems composite, yields four composite scale scores. The composites were derived through factor-analytic techniques and rational analysis of the scales, as described in chapter 7. The SRP composite scale scores provide good indications of global problems of personality and behavior. With the exception of the Personal Adjustment composite, scores 60 through 69 are in the At-Risk range and scores 70 or higher are in the Clinically Significant range. For the Personal Adjustment composite, scores 31 through 40 are in the At-Risk range and scores 30 or lower are in the Clinically Significant range. Table 6.14 summarizes the scales associated with each SRP composite.

**Table 6.14** Summary of SRP Composite Scales

|  | School Problems | Internalizing Problems | Inattention/ Hyperactivity | Emotional Symptoms Index | Personal Adjustment |
|---|---|---|---|---|---|
| SRP–C | Attitude to School<br>Attitude to Teachers | Atypicality<br>Locus of Control<br>Social Stress<br>Anxiety<br>Depression<br>Sense of Inadequacy | Attention Problems<br>Hyperactivity | Social Stress<br>Anxiety<br>Depression<br>Sense of Inadequacy<br>Self-Esteem<br>Self-Reliance | Relations With Parents<br>Interpersonal Relations<br>Self-Esteem<br>Self-Reliance |
| SRP–A | Attitude to School<br>Attitude to Teachers<br>Sensation Seeking | Atypicality<br>Locus of Control<br>Social Stress<br>Anxiety<br>Depression<br>Sense of Inadequacy<br>Somatization | Attention Problems<br>Hyperactivity | Social Stress<br>Anxiety<br>Depression<br>Sense of Inadequacy<br>Self-Esteem<br>Self-Reliance | Relations With Parents<br>Interpersonal Relations<br>Self-Esteem<br>Self-Reliance |
| SRP–COL | — | Atypicality<br>Locus of Control<br>Social Stress<br>Anxiety<br>Depression<br>Sense of Inadequacy<br>Somatization | Attention Problems<br>Hyperactivity | Social Stress<br>Anxiety<br>Depression<br>Sense of Inadequacy<br>Self-Esteem<br>Self-Reliance | Relations With Parents<br>Interpersonal Relations<br>Self-Esteem<br>Self-Reliance |

## School Problems

Scales on the School Problems composite include Attitude to School (SRP–C and SRP–A), Attitude to Teachers (SRP–C and SRP–A), and Sensation Seeking (SRP–A). This factor is a broad measure of adaptation to school. Regardless of the setting where a child is seen (e.g., private office, clinic, psychiatric hospital), it is important for the clinician to recognize that school and the child's relationships in the school setting are extremely salient in the child's life.

High scores on the School Problems composite indicate a pervasive pattern of dissatisfaction with schooling, school personnel, and the structure of the educational process. Scores in the At-Risk range should be noted and investigated. Individuals with such scores may be experiencing academic deficiencies, but this will not always be the case. Scores in the Clinically Significant range are usually associated with severe problems with schooling and within the school environment. Adolescents with such scores may be at risk of dropping out. Elevations on the School Problems composite represent more specific problems than elevations on the Internalizing Problems composite. Nevertheless, pervasive problems at school seldom occur in total isolation from other personal and emotional difficulties.

## Internalizing Problems

The Internalizing Problems composite consists of the Atypicality, Locus of Control, Social Stress, Anxiety, Depression, Sense of Inadequacy scales, as well as the Somatization scale on the SRP–A and SRP–COL. This factor's emergence on the SRP supports the notion that children and adolescents themselves may be particularly able to report on their own internalizing symptoms (Frick et al., 2009; Kamphaus et al., 2003).

The Internalizing Problems composite can be characterized as a broad index of inwardly directed distress that reflects internalizing problems a child may experience. Scores in the At-Risk range or above should be evaluated thoroughly in order to rule out a depressive, anxiety, or somatoform disorder.

A person who does not show a marked elevation on any individual SRP scale may nevertheless score highly on the Internalizing Problems composite from the cumulative effect of his or her emotional problems. Thus, this composite may be quite useful in identifying people who, while having average or moderately elevated scores on individual SRP scales, have problems that are more serious than was initially believed.

Scores in the At-Risk range or higher deserve careful consideration. Clinically significant T scores almost certainly indicate the presence of substantial problems. If the Internalizing Problems composite is elevated and the Personal Adjustment composite is low, the child may be somewhat emotionally fragile and have few coping resources. In such cases, a careful evaluation of the profile will be crucial, and intervention should not be delayed.

## Inattention/Hyperactivity

The Inattention/Hyperactivity composite scale represents an aggregated score containing scales most directly associated with ADHD symptomatology. When coupled with results from the TRS and/or PRS, Inattention/Hyperactivity composite scores in the At-Risk or Clinically Significant range may warrant further consideration of an ADHD diagnosis.

## Personal Adjustment

The Personal Adjustment composite consists of the Relations With Parents, Interpersonal Relations, Self-Esteem, and Self-Reliance scales. Unlike scores on the clinical scale composites, high scores on this composite indicate positive levels of adjustment, and low scores indicate problematic levels of adjustment. At-risk scores suggest problems with interpersonal relationships, self-acceptance, identity development, and ego strength. Scores in the Clinically Significant range often indicate deficiencies in one's support system and coping skills. Low scorers on this scale will tend to have disturbed peer relationships, to be prone to withdrawal and introversion, to repress uncomfortable feelings and thoughts, and to have few positive outlets for alleviating stress. An elevated score on the Internalizing Problems composite accompanied by a low score on the Personal Adjustment composite denotes the likelihood of serious problems and a lack of both support and effective coping strategies.

## Emotional Symptoms Index

The Emotional Symptoms Index (ESI) is the SRP's most global indicator of serious emotional disturbance, particularly internalized disorders. It is composed of four scales from the Internalizing Problems composite (Social Stress, Anxiety, Depression, and Sense of Inadequacy) and two scales from the Personal Adjustment composite (Self-Esteem and Self-Reliance). Note that scores on the Self-Esteem and Self-Reliance scales need to be inverted (making high scores on all scales indicative of more problems) prior to being added to the other scale scores to form the ESI.

Elevated scores on the ESI will almost always signal the presence of serious emotional disturbance that is broad-based in its impact on the thoughts and feelings of the individual. Like the Internalizing Problems composite, the ESI is sensitive to the cumulative effects of numerous emotional difficulties, none of which may be considered serious on its own. However, for most individuals with high ESI scores, high scores will also be observed on several of the component scales and on at least one other composite.

An elevated ESI score may also occur with elevations on the F-Index scale. In these cases, all of the SRP validity indexes and the presenting history should be examined closely. If the SRP form is deemed valid, then high ESI scores will denote clear, pervasive distress and the possibility of a serious emotional disturbance. A careful examination of the SRP scales that do not contribute to the ESI will be useful in evaluating the nature of the emotional disturbance. It will also be valuable to compare this information with the BASC–3 TRS and PRS scales and the information contained in the Structured Developmental History (SDH). In some cases, however, a referred person will have an ESI score in the Average range. Such instances may reflect denial of one's problems, outright faking of responses to present a socially desirable or idealized self, or psychological naïveté relative to one's peers.

## Functional Impairment Index

The final type of score provided on the SRP–C and SRP–A is the Functional Impairment Index. This index indicates the level of difficulty a child has engaging in successful or appropriate behavior across a variety of situations including interactions with others, performing age-appropriate tasks, regulating mood, and performing school-related tasks. This index consists of items from a heterogeneous mix of other SRP scales. Children who present with elevated scores on this index are likely experiencing problems that adversely impact their ability to respond appropriately to everyday settings and situations. Most mental health and EBD diagnoses require that the disorder evident in the individual's symptoms have some adverse impact or create impairment in some functional aspect of the person's life prior to assigning a diagnosis. The BASC–3 Functional Impairment Index provides a quantitative indication of disturbances in function in important areas of the child or adolescent's life and are related to initiating a diagnosis. Changes in the Functional Impairment Index over time is used to monitor the impact of intervention programs by signifying weakness across many domains of important behavior; these changes are easily plotted and viewed on most BASC–3 automated scoring reports.

Index $T$ scores that fall within the range of 60 to 69 are considered at-risk, while $T$ scores 70 or above are considered clinically significant; such scores indicate a stronger possibility that a child or adolescent has behavioral problems that meet the level of a clinical classification. $T$ scores less than 60 indicate a relatively low likelihood that a child or adolescent is exhibiting a pattern of problems similar to those who have been classified or diagnosed with a behavioral or emotional problem or a relatively low likelihood that a child or adolescent is experiencing a significant level of functional impairment.

## Comparing BASC–2 and BASC–3 Scale Scores

Users of the BASC–2 may need to compare BASC–3 and BASC–2 scale scores in certain situations such as triennial evaluations. During BASC–3 development, all items from the BASC–2 SRP forms were included on the BASC–3 SRP standardization forms. As a result, both BASC–3 and BASC–2 scale scores can be computed for each child included in the BASC–3 norm samples. The average differences (in $T$-score units, using the general combined norms) between BASC–3 and BASC–2 scale scores are presented in Table 6.15. This table reflects the values that would be added to (or, for negative values, subtracted from) BASC–2 scale scores to derive an estimated BASC–3 scale score. Most of these score differences are trivial at 0 to 1 $T$-score points. Values approach a half standard deviation at 4 points for some scales in the 12- through 14-year age group, revealing a general trend toward poorer adjustment for this age group on the BASC–3. The values in the table should be viewed as estimates and may not represent true differences between BASC–3 and BASC–2 scale scores. Information on correlations between these scores can be found in chapter 11.

**Table 6.15** SRP: *T*-Score Mean Differences Between the BASC–3 and BASC–2 Scales for General Combined Norms

| | Age | | |
| --- | --- | --- | --- |
| | Child | Adolescent | |
| | 8–11 | 12–14 | 15–18 |
| **Composite** | | | |
| School Problems | 1 | 4 | 3 |
| Internalizing Problems | 2 | 3 | 1 |
| Inattention/Hyperactivity | –1 | 1 | –1 |
| Emotional Symptoms | 2 | 4 | 1 |
| Personal Adjustment | –1 | –4 | –2 |
| **Clinical scale** | | | |
| Attitude to School | 1 | 3 | 2 |
| Attitude to Teachers | 1 | 4 | 3 |
| Sensation Seeking | — | 3 | 2 |
| Atypicality | 2 | 2 | 1 |
| Locus of Control | 1 | 3 | 1 |
| Social Stress | 2 | 3 | 2 |
| Anxiety | 0 | 1 | –1 |
| Depression | 3 | 4 | 2 |
| Sense of Inadequacy | 1 | 1 | –1 |
| Somatization | — | 3 | 1 |
| Attention Problems | 0 | 1 | 0 |
| Hyperactivity | –1 | 1 | –1 |
| **Adaptive scale** | | | |
| Relations With Parents | 1 | –2 | –1 |
| Interpersonal Relations | –3 | –3 | –1 |
| Self-Esteem | –1 | –3 | –1 |
| Self-Reliance | –1 | –4 | –2 |
| **Content scale** | | | |
| Anger Control | — | 4 | 2 |
| Ego Strength | — | –3 | 0 |
| Mania | — | 1 | 0 |
| Test Anxiety | — | 1 | 0 |

# Chapter 7

# Development of the Teacher Rating Scales, Parent Rating Scales, and Self-Report of Personality

The previous BASC editions relied on a development approach steeped in both theory and psychometric rigor; the development of the BASC–3 continues this approach. The primary development objective for the BASC–3 Teacher Rating Scales (TRS), Parent Rating Scales (PRS), and Self-Report of Personality (SRP) was to further enhance the utility of the information provided, while maintaining its ease of use. This chapter describes the development approach used for the BASC–3 TRS, PRS, and SRP forms.

## Item Development

During the development of the original BASC, teachers and students were surveyed about negative and positive behaviors they observed in their classrooms. These responses helped create the original BASC items (for a complete review, see Reynolds & Kamphaus, 2002), resulting in items that were highly relevant and easy for raters to answer.

At the start of the BASC–3 project, a similar survey was conducted. In addition to teachers and students, parents were also included in the survey in order to identify behaviors that might lead to new items. Over 120 teachers, 100 parents, and 400 students participated in the survey. Teachers and parents were asked several questions about student/ child behavior (e.g., What are some behaviors that are the most difficult to manage? What are behaviors that are most disruptive to you? What are some of the positive behaviors you observe?). Students were asked similar questions about behaviors they observed other students doing. Survey responses were reviewed and similar behaviors were consolidated. Approximately 90 negative behaviors and 50 positive behaviors were identified. These behaviors were compared to the existing BASC–2 item pool; most were already represented. However, the behaviors gathered in the surveys resulted in a total of approximately 10 to 15 newly written items for the BASC–3 TRS, PRS, and SRP standardization forms.

The BASC–2 forms, the newly written items, and items from the original BASC edition not included on the BASC–2 edition served as the basis of the standardized form items. The forms were carefully reviewed and additional items were written as needed to broaden the coverage of each domain. In addition, given the widespread acceptance of the content scales that were introduced on the BASC–2 forms, items specific to each scale were developed, increasing their depth and clinical utility.

The final step in the development of the BASC–3 standardization forms was a review by experts outside of the United States in preparation for the international adoption of the BASC–3 TRS, PRS, and SRP forms. Professionals from the Publisher's international offices in Australia, Canada, France, Germany, India, Netherlands, Sweden, Spain, and the United Kingdom reviewed all items and provided comments and edits to make the items more applicable in their respective countries. This resulted in approximately 20 items that were revised and/or dropped from further consideration.

## Spanish Item Development

The Spanish versions of the PRS, SRP, and SDH forms are designed for use with Spanish-speaking individuals residing in the United States. They were developed concurrently with the English versions of the BASC–3 PRS, SRP, and SDH. Bilingual members of the Publisher's development team who have extensive experience with translating and adapting English test items for use with Spanish speakers reviewed the translations of items from the BASC–2 forms (modifying items as needed for clarity and consistency), and provided translations and/or adaptations for newly written items. Newly translated items were back translated to help evaluate the quality of the translations. The BASC–3 Spanish items were then submitted to 10 bilingual professionals in various regions of the United States who represent the fields of psychology and education. Reviewers were asked to evaluate the accuracy of the translations/adaptations and to look for biases in regard to race or ethnicity. Each reviewer contributed a number of suggestions to clarify or improve item wording. The bilingual members of the Publisher's development team resolved the reviewers' suggestions, resulting in the final translations/adaptations used on the BASC–3 Spanish standardization forms.

# Final Item Selection and Scale Definition

The procedure used to collect the BASC–3 standardization data is described in detail in chapter 8. The samples used for item selection were larger than those reported for the general norm sample, and contained a higher percentage of clinical cases. The inclusion of many clinical cases helped ensure the sensitivity of the analyses to how the BASC–3 items and scales function at clinical score levels. Sample sizes for the TRS and PRS preschool levels were 800 and 1,022, respectively, with approximately 11% of the sample with a reported clinical classification/condition. At the child level, sample sizes for the TRS, PRS, and SRP forms ranged from 705 (SRP) to 1,330 (PRS), with approximately 30% of the sample with a reported clinical classification/condition. At the TRS, PRS, and SRP adolescent levels, sample sizes ranged from 956 (TRS) to 1,286 (PRS), with approximately 29% of the sample with a reported clinical classification/ condition. Finally, at the SRP-COL level, the sample size was 440, with approximately 15% of the sample with a reported classification/condition.

Items on the TRS and PRS were scored using a 0-1-2-3 point system. For the SRP, a 2 or 0 point rubric was used for *T-F* items, while a 0-1-2-3 point system was used for the *N-S-O-A* items. The 2-point weighting of the *T-F* items was to make the standard deviation more consistent with the standard deviations of the *N-S-O-A* items to ensure that the *T-F* items were not removed during item analyses due to a smaller standard deviation. The same approach was used for the BASC–2 SRP analyses.

## ITEM EVALUATION

The primary goal of the BASC–3 standardization analyses was to evaluate the reliability, distinctiveness, and interpretability of the scores from the various scales. Items should represent the construct of the scale to which they belong, should correlate highly with their own scale, and should correlate with other scales to the extent predicted from the correlations between the scales. The analyses were performed in two steps: scale-by-scale analysis and analysis of all scales simultaneously.

The first step was a separate item analysis for each scale, evaluating item-scale correlations in a series of coefficient alpha analyses. In general, items with the highest item-scale correlations were retained for further analysis. Consideration was also given to the unique contribution of an item's content to the overall scale in an effort to maximize the diversity and representativeness of behaviors measured in the scale. Finally, consideration was also given to the clinical utility of the item.

The second step of analysis included the items retained from step one as the basis for Covariance Structure Analysis (CSA; also known as confirmatory factor analysis) using the Amos™ 6.0 program (Arbuckle, 2005). CSA provides a number of advantages for scale development, which include (1) allowing theoretical considerations to guide (but not to determine) the scale structure, (2) using a relatively simple model of how underlying dimensions influence item scores, and (3) providing diagnostic information that pinpoints items unduly influenced by dimensions other than that measured by the items' scale (Hoyle, 1991). Each item was placed on one factor (scale), and all factors were allowed to intercorrelate. A good item should be a strong measure of the dimension assessed by the item's own scale, but should not correlate excessively highly with other scales. This evaluation of the relationship of items to scales not their own can be made using the modification indexes (MIs) produced by CSA programs. An item can have a high MI with a scale other than the one to which it belongs. In such a case, the item correlates differently (either higher or lower) with that other scale than would be predicted both from the item's loadings on its own scale and from the scale intercorrelations. Typically, this happens when the item has some content that strongly relates to the dimension measured by a scale other than its own.

As a result of this second step, some items were dropped, either because of high MIs that indicated excessive overlap with another behavior dimension or because of low loadings on these items' own dimension. Results of the MI analysis were quite consistent for the same item across levels or between the TRS and the PRS. The number of items dropped during this step was minimal.

The standardized factor loadings of each item on the BASC–3 scales are presented in Tables 7.1 (TRS and PRS) and 7.2 (SRP). Typically, items selected for the final forms functioned similarly across levels and across teacher and parent rating forms. Item and scale robustness contributes to the interpretation of data across ages and respondents and supports the validity of the CSA procedure used for these analyses.

**Table 7.1** TRS and PRS: Item Factor Loadings in the Final Amos Analysis

| | Item | Teacher Rating Scales | | | Parent Rating Scales | | |
|---|---|---|---|---|---|---|---|
| | | P | C | A | P | C | A |
| **Activities of Daily Living** | Acts in a safe manner. | — | — | — | — | .53 | .50 |
| | Cleans up after self. | — | — | — | — | .63 | .59 |
| | Has trouble eating with a fork. | — | — | — | .54 | — | — |
| | Has trouble fastening buttons on clothing. | — | — | — | .80 | .33 | — |
| | Has trouble following regular routines. | — | — | — | — | .57 | — |
| | Is able to keep to a schedule. | — | — | — | — | — | .78 |
| | Is careless with belongings. | — | — | — | — | .55 | .51 |
| | Makes healthy food choices. | — | — | — | — | .42 | .47 |
| | Needs help bathing self. | — | — | — | .67 | — | — |
| | Needs help putting on clothes. | — | — | — | .77 | — | — |
| | Needs help tying shoes. | — | — | — | .47 | — | — |
| | Needs help using zippers. | — | — | — | .75 | — | — |
| | Needs to be reminded to brush teeth. | — | — | — | .38 | .46 | .43 |
| | Organizes chores or other tasks well. | — | — | — | — | .71 | .76 |
| | Sets realistic goals. | — | — | — | — | .67 | .71 |
| **Adaptability** | Accepts things as they are. | — | .80 | .75 | — | .68 | .62 |
| | Adjusts easily to new surroundings. | — | — | — | .71 | — | — |
| | Adjusts well to changes in family plans. | — | — | — | .68 | .76 | .82 |
| | Adjusts well to changes in plans. | — | — | .81 | — | — | .83 |
| | Adjusts well to changes in routine. | .89 | .75 | .78 | .69 | .75 | .80 |
| | Adjusts well to new teachers (or caregivers). | .83 | .69 | .74 | .57 | .62 | .62 |
| | Handles winning and losing well. | — | .78 | — | — | .64 | .59 |
| | Is easily calmed when angry. | .79 | .63 | — | .57 | .64 | |
| | Is easy to please. | — | .80 | .74 | .62 | .57 | .59 |
| | Recovers quickly after a setback. | .79 | .76 | .77 | .71 | .73 | .62 |
| | Refuses advice. | — | .70 | .57 | — | — | — |
| | Seems to take setbacks in stride. | .61 | — | — | — | — | — |
| | Shares toys or possessions with other children. | .86 | — | — | .55 | — | — |
| | Transitions well. | .78 | .78 | .81 | — | — | — |
| | Tries new things. | — | — | — | .58 | — | — |

|  | Item | Teacher Rating Scales | | | Parent Rating Scales | | |
|---|---|---|---|---|---|---|---|
|  |  | P | C | A | P | C | A |
| **Aggression** | Annoys others on purpose. | .63 | .77 | .79 | — | — | — |
|  | Argues when denied own way. | .66 | .81 | .71 | .56 | .60 | .53 |
|  | Breaks other children's (adolescents') things. | .66 | — | — | .59 | — | — |
|  | Bullies others. | .69 | .73 | .75 | .51 | .50 | .70 |
|  | Defies teachers (or caregivers, people in authority). | .74 | .75 | .81 | — | — | — |
|  | Disrupts the play of other children. | .69 | — | — | .65 | — | — |
|  | Gets back at others. | — | .69 | .75 | — | .64 | .70 |
|  | Hits other children (adolescents). | .67 | .46 | .65 | .67 | .62 | .56 |
|  | Is cruel to others. | — | — | — | — | — | .71 |
|  | Is overly aggressive. | .57 | .67 | .59 | .67 | .59 | .69 |
|  | Loses temper too easily. | .72 | .74 | .70 | — | — | — |
|  | Manipulates others. | — | — | .74 | — | .52 | .65 |
|  | Teases others. | — | .77 | .76 | .46 | .55 | .59 |
|  | Threatens to hurt others. | .53 | .53 | .64 | .47 | .60 | .68 |
|  | Throws or breaks things when angry. | — | — | — | — | .64 | .60 |
| **Anxiety** | Appears tense. | .48 | .67 | — | — | .56 | .63 |
|  | Gets very upset when things are lost. | .44 | — | — | — | — | — |
|  | Has panic attacks. | — | .58 | .56 | — | .46 | .52 |
|  | Has trouble making decisions. | — | — | .61 | — | — | .54 |
|  | Is easily stressed. | .79 | .78 | .75 | .48 | .70 | .72 |
|  | Is fearful. | — | .70 | .71 | — | .61 | .64 |
|  | Is nervous around new people. | .60 | — | — | — | — | — |
|  | Is nervous. | .33 | .69 | .75 | .48 | .64 | .69 |
|  | Says, "I get nervous during tests" or "Tests make me nervous." | — | .54 | .59 | — | — | .51 |
|  | Says, "I'm afraid I will make a mistake." | .46 | .54 | .63 | .57 | .62 | .58 |
|  | Says, "I'm not very good at this." | — | — | — | .56 | .57 | .57 |
|  | Says, "It's all my fault." | — | — | — | — | .53 | — |
|  | Tries to be perfect. | — | — | — | .59 | — | — |
|  | Worries about making mistakes. | — | — | — | .77 | .57 | .59 |
|  | Worries about parents. | .25 | — | — | .54 | — | — |
|  | Worries about things that cannot be changed. | .53 | .72 | .66 | .58 | .74 | .68 |
|  | Worries about what other children (adolescents) think. | — | — | — | .60 | .55 | — |
|  | Worries about what parents think. | — | — | — | .66 | .34 | — |
|  | Worries about what teachers think. | — | — | — | — | .36 | .38 |
|  | Worries. | .76 | .77 | .80 | .63 | .74 | .68 |

| | Item | Teacher Rating Scales | | | Parent Rating Scales | | |
|---|---|---|---|---|---|---|---|
| | | P | C | A | P | C | A |
| **Attention Problems** | Has a short attention span. | .39 | .88 | .81 | .55 | .80 | .70 |
| | Has trouble concentrating. | .40 | .84 | .81 | .62 | .75 | .72 |
| | Is easily distracted from class work. | — | .88 | .83 | .63 | — | — |
| | Is easily distracted. | .39 | .88 | .81 | .80 | .76 | .74 |
| | Is organized. | — | — | .80 | — | — | .68 |
| | Listens attentively. | .94 | — | — | — | — | — |
| | Listens carefully. | .92 | .82 | .83 | .75 | .82 | .80 |
| | Listens to directions. | .89 | .81 | .81 | .72 | .78 | .78 |
| | Makes careless mistakes. | — | .71 | .69 | — | — | — |
| | Misses deadlines. | — | — | .72 | — | — | .66 |
| | Pays attention when being spoken to. | — | — | — | .74 | .76 | .74 |
| | Pays attention. | .50 | .82 | .83 | — | .75 | .71 |
| **Atypicality** | Acts as if other children are not there. | .66 | — | — | — | .56 | — |
| | Acts confused. | — | .69 | — | — | .47 | — |
| | Acts strangely. | .76 | .86 | .84 | .76 | .81 | .75 |
| | Babbles to self. | .57 | .62 | .62 | .49 | .41 | .61 |
| | Bangs head. | — | — | — | .21 | — | — |
| | Confuses real with make-believe. | — | — | — | — | .43 | .60 |
| | Does strange things. | .69 | .80 | — | .88 | .83 | — |
| | Does weird things. | — | — | — | .87 | .78 | .73 |
| | Has strange ideas. | — | — | .74 | — | — | .63 |
| | Is suspicious of others. | — | — | .46 | — | — | .45 |
| | Picks at things like own hair, nails, or clothing. | — | .48 | .48 | — | — | — |
| | Says things that make no sense. | .64 | .64 | .73 | .52 | .59 | .66 |
| | Seems odd. | .76 | .85 | .82 | .65 | .72 | .77 |
| | Seems out of touch with reality. | .64 | .71 | .73 | — | .56 | .69 |
| | Seems unaware of others. | — | — | .61 | .51 | .48 | .46 |
| | Shows feelings that do not fit the situation. | .62 | — | — | .52 | .51 | — |
| | Speech is confused or disorganized. | — | .57 | .57 | — | .43 | — |
| | Stares blankly. | — | — | — | .45 | .39 | .58 |

**Table 7.1** TRS and PRS: Item Factor Loadings in the Final Amos Analysis *(continued)*

| | Item | Teacher Rating Scales | | | Parent Rating Scales | | |
|---|---|---|---|---|---|---|---|
| | | P | C | A | P | C | A |
| **Conduct Problems** | Breaks the rules just to see what will happen. | — | — | — | — | .62 | .62 |
| | Breaks the rules. | — | .83 | .85 | — | .68 | .72 |
| | Cheats in school. | — | .45 | .60 | — | — | — |
| | Deceives others. | — | .67 | .74 | — | — | — |
| | Disobeys. | — | .84 | .84 | — | .76 | .72 |
| | Gets into trouble. | — | .81 | .84 | — | .67 | .65 |
| | Hurts others on purpose. | — | .67 | .65 | — | .51 | .60 |
| | Is in trouble with the police. | — | — | — | — | — | .26 |
| | Lies to get out of trouble. | — | — | — | — | .73 | .76 |
| | Lies. | — | .75 | .75 | — | .71 | .72 |
| | Smokes or chews tobacco. | — | — | — | — | — | .39 |
| | Sneaks around. | — | .67 | .74 | — | .58 | .66 |
| | Steals. | — | — | — | — | .52 | .47 |
| | Uses foul language. | — | — | .68 | — | — | .54 |
| | Uses illegal drugs. | — | — | — | — | — | .32 |
| | Uses others' things without permission. | — | .73 | .67 | — | — | — |
| **Depression** | Changes moods quickly. | — | — | — | .61 | .59 | .61 |
| | Cries easily. | .61 | .64 | .48 | .60 | .53 | .53 |
| | Holds a grudge. | — | — | — | .42 | — | — |
| | Is easily frustrated. | .79 | — | — | .71 | — | — |
| | Is easily upset. | .62 | .78 | .77 | .72 | .68 | .68 |
| | Is irritable. | .65 | .77 | .64 | .68 | .64 | .60 |
| | Is negative about things. | .49 | .79 | .69 | .57 | .69 | .65 |
| | Is pessimistic. | .45 | .73 | .70 | — | — | — |
| | Is sad. | .42 | .62 | .66 | .46 | .55 | .59 |
| | Pouts. | .47 | — | — | .56 | — | — |
| | Says, "I can't do anything right." | — | .44 | .57 | — | .59 | .67 |
| | Says, "I don't have any friends." | — | .38 | .61 | — | .58 | .61 |
| | Says, "I hate myself." | — | .37 | .54 | — | .58 | .68 |
| | Says, "I want to die" or "I wish I were dead." | — | — | .43 | — | .48 | .55 |
| | Says, "I want to kill myself." | — | — | — | — | .41 | .51 |
| | Says, "Nobody likes me." | .38 | .44 | .62 | .25 | .65 | .67 |
| | Seems lonely. | — | .53 | .62 | — | .60 | .67 |
| | Whines. | — | — | — | .53 | — | — |

**Table 7.1** TRS and PRS: Item Factor Loadings in the Final Amos Analysis *(continued)*

| | Item | Teacher Rating Scales | | | Parent Rating Scales | | |
|---|---|---|---|---|---|---|---|
| | | P | C | A | P | C | A |
| **Functional Communication** | Accurately takes down messages. | — | — | — | — | .58 | .62 |
| | Answers telephone properly. | — | — | — | .54 | .56 | — |
| | Communicates clearly. | .62 | .76 | .81 | .79 | .69 | .70 |
| | Has difficulty explaining rules of games to others. | — | .69 | .63 | — | .63 | .48 |
| | Has trouble getting information when needed. | — | .69 | .63 | — | .57 | .60 |
| | Is able to describe feelings accurately. | .82 | .73 | .74 | .76 | .59 | .65 |
| | Is clear when telling about personal experiences. | .84 | .80 | .79 | .82 | .74 | .70 |
| | Is effective when presenting information to a group. | — | — | — | — | — | .77 |
| | Is unclear when presenting ideas. | .39 | .66 | .66 | .56 | .65 | .50 |
| | Likes to talk about his or her day. | — | — | — | — | .50 | .35 |
| | Provides full name when asked. | .64 | — | — | .59 | — | — |
| | Provides home address when asked. | .36 | .51 | — | .41 | — | — |
| | Responds appropriately when asked a question. | .85 | .83 | .67 | .74 | .71 | .73 |
| | Says all letters of the alphabet when asked. | .59 | — | — | .57 | — | — |
| | Speaks in short phrases that are hard to understand. | — | — | — | .62 | — | — |
| | Starts conversations. | .71 | .49 | .55 | .63 | .49 | .43 |
| | Tracks down information when needed. | — | .79 | .80 | — | .66 | .70 |
| **Hyperactivity** | Acts out of control. | .74 | .72 | .67 | .75 | .72 | .67 |
| | Acts without thinking. | — | .82 | .76 | .62 | .69 | .63 |
| | Bothers other children when they are working. | .78 | — | — | — | — | — |
| | Cannot wait to take turn. | .73 | .67 | .64 | .60 | .54 | .55 |
| | Disrupts other children's (adolescents') activities. | — | .88 | .83 | — | .65 | .57 |
| | Disrupts the schoolwork of other children (adolescents). | — | .85 | .83 | — | — | — |
| | Fiddles with things while at meals. | — | — | — | .54 | .56 | |
| | Has poor self-control. | .78 | .77 | .75 | .73 | .79 | .72 |
| | Has trouble keeping hands or feet to self. | .84 | .71 | — | — | — | — |
| | Has trouble staying seated. | .80 | .80 | .76 | — | — | — |
| | Interrupts others when they are speaking. | — | — | — | .53 | .63 | .68 |
| | Interrupts parents when they are talking on the phone. | — | — | — | .52 | .55 | .55 |
| | Is in constant motion. | .39 | .66 | .63 | .49 | .48 | — |
| | Is overly active. | .41 | .70 | .67 | .63 | .60 | — |
| | Is unable to slow down. | — | — | — | .70 | .67 | — |
| | Needs too much supervision. | — | — | — | .59 | — | — |
| | Seeks attention while doing schoolwork. | — | — | .65 | — | — | — |
| | Speaks out of turn during class. | .69 | .77 | .81 | — | — | — |
| | Talks over others. | — | — | — | — | — | .61 |

**Table 7.1** TRS and PRS: Item Factor Loadings in the Final Amos Analysis *(continued)*

| | Item | Teacher Rating Scales | | | Parent Rating Scales | | |
|---|---|---|---|---|---|---|---|
| | | P | C | A | P | C | A |
| **Leadership** | Gives good suggestions for solving problems. | — | .81 | .80 | — | .71 | .77 |
| | Is a "self-starter." | — | — | — | — | .67 | .72 |
| | Is creative. | — | .70 | .65 | — | — | — |
| | Is good at getting people to work together. | — | .80 | .80 | — | .74 | .72 |
| | Is highly motivated to succeed. | — | .83 | .83 | — | .70 | .70 |
| | Is usually chosen as a leader. | — | .75 | .76 | — | .62 | .64 |
| | Makes decisions easily. | — | .70 | .73 | — | .66 | .63 |
| | Prefers to be a leader. | — | — | — | — | .60 | .55 |
| | Works well under pressure. | — | .80 | .80 | — | | .68 |
| **Learning Problems** | Complains that lessons go too fast. | — | — | .59 | — | — | — |
| | Demonstrates critical thinking skills. | — | .74 | .72 | — | — | — |
| | Does not complete tests. | — | .61 | .73 | — | — | — |
| | Gets failing school grades. | — | .75 | .75 | — | — | — |
| | Has problems with mathematics. | — | .77 | — | — | — | — |
| | Has reading problems. | — | .76 | .68 | — | — | — |
| | Has spelling problems. | — | .72 | .67 | — | — | — |
| | Has trouble keeping up in class. | — | .83 | .84 | — | — | — |
| | Performs poorly on school assignments. | — | .77 | .79 | — | — | — |
| **Social Skills** | Accepts people who are different from his or her self. | — | .58 | .65 | — | .50 | .51 |
| | Begins conversations appropriately. | — | — | — | .65 | — | — |
| | Compliments others. | .79 | .82 | .83 | .76 | .73 | .72 |
| | Congratulates others when good things happen to them. | .49 | .75 | .78 | .78 | .81 | .75 |
| | Encourages others to do their best. | .88 | .87 | .90 | .79 | .84 | .81 |
| | Makes others feel welcome. | — | .78 | .84 | — | .74 | .75 |
| | Makes positive comments about others. | — | .87 | .86 | — | .69 | .68 |
| | Offers help to other children (adolescents). | .81 | .82 | .85 | .73 | .78 | .74 |
| | Politely asks for help. | .74 | — | — | .63 | — | — |
| | Says, "please" and "thank you." | .65 | .67 | .64 | .51 | .54 | .54 |
| | Shows interest in others' ideas. | — | .78 | .81 | — | .64 | .62 |
| | Tries to help others be their best. | — | .86 | .87 | — | .82 | .80 |
| | Uses appropriate table manners. | — | — | — | .55 | — | — |
| | Volunteers to help with things. | — | — | — | .63 | — | — |

**Table 7.1** TRS and PRS: Item Factor Loadings in the Final Amos Analysis *(continued)*

| Item | Teacher Rating Scales | | | Parent Rating Scales | | |
|---|---|---|---|---|---|---|
| | P | C | A | P | C | A |
| **Somatization** | | | | | | |
| Complains about health. | .37 | .85 | .86 | .55 | .81 | .77 |
| Complains of being cold. | — | — | — | .43 | — | — |
| Complains of being sick when nothing is wrong. | — | — | — | — | .62 | .65 |
| Complains of pain. | .53 | .76 | .76 | .64 | .75 | .76 |
| Complains of physical problems. | .47 | .81 | .88 | .65 | .73 | .66 |
| Complains of stomach pain. | .48 | .72 | .80 | .60 | .62 | .68 |
| Expresses fear of getting sick. | — | — | — | — | .54 | .53 |
| Gets colds. | .53 | — | — | .41 | — | — |
| Gets sick. | .44 | .60 | .64 | .49 | .52 | .48 |
| Has fevers. | .49 | .34 | — | .53 | .31 | — |
| Has headaches. | .54 | .72 | .64 | .42 | .37 | .58 |
| Has sore throats. | .65 | — | — | .54 | — | — |
| Is afraid of getting sick. | — | .55 | .60 | — | .51 | .53 |
| Makes frequent visits to the doctor. | — | — | — | .47 | — | — |
| Misses school (or daycare) because of sickness. | .53 | — | — | .55 | — | — |
| Says, "I think I'm sick." | — | — | — | — | .72 | .72 |
| Vomits. | — | — | — | .45 | .32 | — |
| **Study Skills** | | | | | | |
| Analyzes the nature of a problem before starting to solve it. | — | .63 | .77 | — | — | — |
| Completes homework. | — | .72 | .81 | — | — | — |
| Forgets to bring learning materials to class. | — | — | .65 | — | — | — |
| Has good study habits. | — | .89 | .91 | — | — | — |
| Is well organized. | — | .77 | .89 | — | — | — |
| Knows how to study. | — | — | .87 | — | — | — |
| Reads assigned chapters. | — | — | .77 | — | — | — |
| Reads. | — | .66 | — | — | — | — |
| Stays on task. | — | .79 | .84 | — | — | — |
| Takes careful notes during lectures. | — | — | .79 | — | — | — |
| Tries to do well in school. | — | .81 | .78 | — | — | — |
| Turns in work on time. | — | .78 | .78 | — | — | — |
| **Withdrawal** | | | | | | |
| Avoids making friends. | .85 | .74 | .82 | .70 | .70 | .76 |
| Avoids other children (adolescents). | .80 | .71 | .78 | .72 | .69 | .71 |
| Clings to parent in strange surroundings. | — | — | — | .49 | — | — |
| Has trouble making new friends. | .71 | .77 | .77 | .67 | .76 | .75 |
| Is shy with adults. | — | — | — | .55 | .45 | — |
| Is shy with other children (adolescents). | — | — | — | .66 | .60 | .59 |
| Isolates self from others. | .57 | .82 | .85 | .53 | .64 | .66 |
| Makes friends easily. | — | .75 | .71 | .73 | .78 | .72 |
| Prefers to play alone. | .56 | .68 | .80 | .57 | .54 | .62 |
| Quickly joins group activities. | .47 | .70 | .65 | .66 | .67 | .59 |
| Readily starts up conversations with new people. | — | — | — | .53 | — | — |
| Refuses to talk. | .66 | .59 | .61 | — | — | — |
| Shows fear of strangers. | — | — | — | .46 | — | — |

## Table 7.2 SRP: Item Factor Loadings in the Final Amos Analysis

| | Item | Type | Self-Report of Personality C | A | COL |
|---|---|---|---|---|---|
| **Anxiety** | I am afraid I might do something bad. | MC | .60 | — | — |
| | I am afraid of a lot of things. | MC | .64 | — | — |
| | I am bothered by thoughts about death. | MC | .59 | — | — |
| | I can never seem to relax. | TF | — | .48 | .55 |
| | I feel anxious. | MC | — | .66 | .79 |
| | I feel guilty about things. | MC | — | .54 | .51 |
| | I feel stressed. | MC | .66 | .70 | .70 |
| | I get nervous when things do not go the right way for me. | MC | .56 | .66 | .68 |
| | I get nervous. | MC | .43 | .65 | .72 |
| | I get so nervous I can't breathe. | MC | — | .55 | .60 |
| | I often worry about something bad happening to me. | TF | .49 | .59 | .61 |
| | I worry a lot of the time. | TF | — | .63 | .64 |
| | I worry about what is going to happen. | MC | .68 | .71 | .77 |
| | I worry but I don't know why. | MC | .68 | .76 | .75 |
| | I worry when I go to bed at night. | MC | .62 | .69 | .69 |
| | Little things bother me. | MC | .55 | .58 | .66 |
| **Attention Problems** | I am a good listener. | MC | .63 | — | — |
| | I am easily distracted. | MC | — | .76 | .84 |
| | I forget to do things. | MC | .56 | .54 | .52 |
| | I get into trouble for not paying attention. | MC | .72 | — | .62 |
| | I have a hard time concentrating. | MC | — | .79 | .77 |
| | I have attention problems. | TF | .56 | .61 | .66 |
| | I have trouble paying attention to lectures. | MC | — | — | .69 |
| | I have trouble paying attention to the teacher. | MC | .74 | .72 | — |
| | I have trouble paying attention to what I am doing. | MC | .71 | .73 | .76 |
| | I listen when people are talking to me. | MC | .56 | — | — |
| | I think that I have a short attention span. | TF | .54 | .64 | .67 |
| | People tell me I should pay more attention. | TF | .55 | .57 | .49 |
| **Atypicality** | Even when alone, I feel like someone is watching me. | MC | .62 | .70 | .64 |
| | I do things over and over and can't stop. | MC | — | .57 | .53 |
| | I feel like people are out to get me. | MC | .52 | .61 | .56 |
| | I have trouble controlling my thoughts. | MC | .58 | .65 | .61 |
| | I hear things that others cannot hear. | MC | .72 | .63 | .61 |
| | I hear voices in my head that no one else can hear. | MC | .78 | .63 | .59 |
| | I see things that others cannot see. | MC | .74 | — | — |
| | I see weird things. | MC | .74 | .69 | .65 |
| | People think I'm strange. | MC | .57 | .56 | .61 |
| | Someone wants to hurt me. | MC | — | .55 | .47 |
| | Sometimes I want to hurt myself. | TF | .39 | — | — |
| | Sometimes, when alone, I hear my name. | TF | .43 | .51 | .51 |

| | Item | Type | Self-Report of Personality | | |
|---|---|---|---|---|---|
| | | | C | A | COL |
| **Attitude to School** | I can't wait for school to be over. | TF | .45 | — | — |
| | I don't care about school. | TF | .60 | .51 | — |
| | I don't like thinking about school. | TF | .55 | .54 | — |
| | I feel like I want to quit school. | MC | .79 | .67 | — |
| | I feel safe at school. | MC | .45 | .43 | — |
| | I get bored in school. | MC | — | .71 | — |
| | I hate school. | MC | .87 | .79 | — |
| | My school feels good to me. | MC | .54 | .56 | — |
| | School is boring. | MC | .78 | .73 | — |
| **Attitude to Teachers** | I get along with my teacher. | MC | .75 | .75 | — |
| | I like my teacher. | MC | .68 | .74 | — |
| | My teacher cares about me. | TF | — | .46 | — |
| | My teacher gets mad at me for no good reason. | MC | .59 | .49 | — |
| | My teacher is proud of me. | MC | .67 | .74 | — |
| | My teacher trusts me. | MC | .71 | .67 | — |
| | My teacher understands me. | TF | .55 | .49 | — |
| | Teachers are unfair. | MC | .59 | .50 | — |
| | Teachers look for the bad things that you do. | MC | — | .48 | — |
| **Depression** | I don't seem to do anything right. | TF | .44 | .60 | .60 |
| | I feel depressed. | MC | .60 | .78 | .73 |
| | I feel life isn't worth living. | MC | — | .66 | .65 |
| | I feel like I have no friends. | MC | .71 | .66 | .61 |
| | I feel like my life is getting worse and worse. | MC | .73 | .74 | .76 |
| | I feel lonely. | MC | .70 | .73 | .68 |
| | I feel sad. | MC | .61 | .68 | .61 |
| | I have too many problems. | TF | .50 | — | — |
| | I just don't care anymore. | TF | — | .54 | .55 |
| | I used to be happier. | TF | — | .59 | — |
| | No one understands me. | MC | .63 | .67 | .66 |
| | Nobody ever listens to me. | TF | .47 | — | — |
| | Nothing about me is right. | TF | — | .56 | .44 |
| | Nothing ever goes right for me. | TF | .50 | .53 | .47 |
| | Nothing feels good to me. | TF | — | — | .49 |

| | Item | Type | C | A | COL |
|---|---|---|---|---|---|
| | | | Self-Report of Personality | | |
| **Hyperactivity** | I feel like I have to get up and move around. | MC | — | .61 | .54 |
| | I have trouble sitting still. | MC | .65 | .76 | .79 |
| | I have trouble standing still in lines. | MC | .66 | .65 | .73 |
| | I often do things without thinking. | TF | .42 | — | — |
| | I talk while other people are talking. | MC | .65 | .49 | .46 |
| | I talk without waiting for others to say something. | MC | .63 | .47 | — |
| | People tell me that I am too noisy. | MC | .66 | .52 | .50 |
| | People tell me to be still. | MC | .71 | .72 | .72 |
| | People tell me to slow down. | MC | .61 | .65 | .50 |
| **Interpersonal Relations** | I am liked by others. | MC | .60 | .70 | .71 |
| | I enjoy meeting others. | MC | — | — | .60 |
| | I feel that nobody likes me. | MC | .72 | .70 | .68 |
| | I feel uncomfortable around others. | MC | — | .61 | — |
| | I get along well with others. | MC | .53 | .61 | .67 |
| | I have a hard time making friends. | TF | .57 | .54 | .58 |
| | My classmates don't like me. | TF | .53 | .51 | — |
| | Other children don't like to be with me. | TF | .53 | .53 | — |
| | Other kids hate to be with me. | MC | .72 | .65 | — |
| | Other people don't like me. | TF | — | — | .47 |
| | Other people make fun of me. | MC | .68 | — | — |
| | Others have respect for me. | MC | — | — | .66 |
| | People think I am fun to be with. | MC | — | .59 | .69 |
| **Locus of Control** | I am blamed for things I don't do. | MC | .67 | .68 | .52 |
| | I can never really do what I want to do. | TF | — | — | .54 |
| | I can't seem to control what happens to me. | TF | .48 | — | — |
| | I get blamed for things I can't help. | MC | .66 | .69 | .58 |
| | I never get my way. | TF | .42 | — | — |
| | I never really feel in control of my life. | TF | — | — | .69 |
| | My life seems out of my control. | MC | — | — | .67 |
| | My parents blame too many of their problems on me. | TF | .39 | .49 | — |
| | My parents expect too much from me. | MC | .57 | .59 | .51 |
| | My parents have too much control over my life. | TF | — | .45 | — |
| | People get mad at me, even when I don't do anything wrong. | MC | .68 | .70 | .55 |
| | Things go wrong for me, even when I try hard. | TF | .49 | .53 | .62 |
| | What I want never seems to matter. | TF | — | .48 | .48 |

| | Item | Type | Self-Report of Personality | | |
|---|---|---|---|---|---|
| | | | C | A | COL |
| **Relations With Parents** | I am proud of my parents. | MC | .67 | .73 | .77 |
| | I get along well with my parents. | TF | — | .48 | .54 |
| | I like going places with my parents. | MC | .52 | .60 | .64 |
| | I like my parents. | MC | .57 | .77 | .78 |
| | My mother and father help me if I ask them to. | MC | .64 | .74 | .70 |
| | My mother and father like my friends. | MC | .56 | .64 | .59 |
| | My parents are easy to talk to. | MC | .62 | .72 | .75 |
| | My parents are proud of me. | MC | .71 | .69 | .73 |
| | My parents like to be with me. | MC | .64 | .76 | .78 |
| | My parents listen to what I say. | MC | .66 | .68 | .76 |
| | My parents trust me. | MC | .69 | .74 | .65 |
| **School Maladjustment** | I am bored with school. | TF | — | — | .62 |
| | I am tired of going to school. | TF | — | — | .60 |
| | I enjoy doing schoolwork. | MC | — | — | .54 |
| | I feel like I belong at my school. | MC | — | — | .49 |
| | I feel like quitting school. | MC | — | — | .73 |
| | I feel overwhelmed by the demands of school. | MC | — | — | .47 |
| | I never seem to feel like working on school assignments. | TF | — | — | .62 |
| | I think that I am going to school for the wrong reasons. | TF | — | — | .51 |
| | I wonder why I am going to school. | MC | — | — | .66 |
| | I worry about being able to complete my school degree. | MC | — | — | .53 |
| | My parents are pressuring me to go to school. | TF | — | — | .52 |
| **Self-Esteem** | I feel good about myself. | TF | .47 | .65 | .68 |
| | I get upset about my looks. | MC | .53 | — | — |
| | I have confidence in myself. | MC | — | .71 | .80 |
| | I like the way I look. | MC | .64 | .75 | .72 |
| | I like who I am. | TF | .55 | .61 | .56 |
| | I wish I were different. | TF | .54 | .62 | .66 |
| | I'm happy with who I am. | MC | .72 | .80 | .84 |
| | My looks bother me. | MC | .57 | .66 | .76 |
| **Sensation Seeking** | I am more daring than my friends are. | TF | — | — | .62 |
| | I do things for the thrill of it. | MC | — | .66 | — |
| | I do things that my friends are afraid to do. | MC | — | .63 | .73 |
| | I find dangerous things exciting. | MC | — | .77 | .77 |
| | I like it when my friends dare me to do something. | MC | — | .73 | .63 |
| | I like to be the first one to try new things. | MC | — | .47 | .66 |
| | I like to dare others to do things. | MC | — | .65 | .54 |
| | I like to experiment with new things. | MC | — | — | .57 |
| | I like to ride in a car that is going fast. | MC | — | .55 | .59 |
| | I like to stretch the rules. | TF | — | — | .48 |
| | I like to take chances. | TF | — | .38 | .51 |
| | I like to take risks. | MC | — | .66 | .75 |

| | Item | Self-Report of Personality | | | |
| --- | --- | --- | --- | --- | --- |
| | | Type | C | A | COL |
| **Sense of Inadequacy** | Doing my best is never good enough. | TF | — | .55 | .62 |
| | Even when I try hard, I fail. | MC | .64 | .61 | .62 |
| | I am disappointed with my grades. | MC | .50 | .53 | .62 |
| | I fail at things. | MC | .58 | .52 | .57 |
| | I never quite reach my goal. | TF | — | .49 | .59 |
| | I never seem to get anything right. | TF | .43 | .57 | .61 |
| | I quit easily. | MC | — | .46 | .52 |
| | I want to do better, but I can't. | MC | .64 | .68 | .75 |
| | I'd rather quit than fail. | TF | — | .42 | — |
| | It is hard for me to keep my mind on schoolwork. | MC | .69 | — | — |
| | Most things are harder for me than for others. | TF | — | .55 | .51 |
| | People tell me to try harder. | MC | .56 | .51 | .52 |
| | When I take tests, I can't think. | MC | .59 | .49 | .57 |
| **Social Stress** | I am bothered by teasing from others. | MC | .42 | — | — |
| | I am left out of things. | MC | .63 | .67 | .67 |
| | I am lonely. | MC | .63 | .69 | .63 |
| | I don't feel comfortable around other people. | TF | — | — | .66 |
| | I don't know how to act around others. | TF | — | — | .64 |
| | I feel out of place around people. | MC | .66 | .71 | .79 |
| | I feel that others do not like the way I do things. | MC | — | .69 | .63 |
| | My friends have more fun than I do. | TF | .41 | .47 | .49 |
| | Other children are happier than I am. | TF | — | .49 | — |
| | Other people are against me. | MC | — | .63 | — |
| | Other people are happier than I am. | TF | — | — | .56 |
| | Other people find things wrong with me. | MC | .68 | .65 | .53 |
| | Other people seem to ignore me. | MC | .75 | .73 | .72 |
| | People act as if they don't hear me. | MC | .67 | .65 | .54 |
| | People say bad things to me. | MC | .65 | .60 | — |
| **Somatization** | I am in pain. | MC | — | .58 | .52 |
| | I feel dizzy. | MC | — | .55 | .44 |
| | I get sick more than others. | TF | — | .55 | .57 |
| | I have trouble breathing. | MC | — | .47 | .55 |
| | It seems like I'm always sick. | TF | — | .60 | .54 |
| | My stomach gets upset more than most people's. | TF | — | .69 | .69 |
| | Often I feel sick in my stomach. | TF | — | .70 | .72 |

| | Item | | Self-Report of Personality | | |
|---|---|---|---|---|---|
| | | Type | C | A | COL |
| Self-Reliance | I am a dependable friend. | MC | .65 | — | — |
| | I am dependable. | MC | .68 | .68 | .63 |
| | I am good at making decisions. | MC | .59 | .58 | .48 |
| | I am good at schoolwork. | MC | .52 | — | — |
| | I am reliable. | MC | — | .76 | .80 |
| | I am someone you can count on. | MC | .65 | — | — |
| | I am someone you can rely on. | MC | — | .73 | .81 |
| | I can solve difficult problems by myself. | MC | .36 | .50 | .44 |
| | I try to do things myself before asking for help. | MC | — | .36 | — |
| | If I have a problem, I can usually work it out. | TF | .40 | .32 | .43 |
| | My friends come to me for help. | MC | — | .57 | .47 |
| | Others ask me to help them. | MC | — | .62 | .46 |
| Alcohol Abuse | Drinking alcohol helps me cope with my problems. | MC | — | — | .79 |
| | I do embarrassing things when I drink too much alcohol. | MC | — | — | .60 |
| | I drink alcohol so I can be at ease around others or at a party. | MC | — | — | .71 |
| | I drink alcohol to calm down. | MC | — | — | .74 |
| | I drink alcohol to feel better. | MC | — | — | .79 |
| | I drink alcohol when I am bored. | MC | — | — | .72 |
| | I drink alcohol when I am by myself. | MC | — | — | .56 |
| | I drink more alcohol than I plan to drink. | MC | — | — | .75 |
| | I feel better after a couple of drinks of alcohol. | MC | — | — | .80 |
| | I get into trouble because of my drinking. | TF | — | — | .54 |
| | I miss classes because of drinking or having a hangover. | MC | — | — | .52 |
| | I need alcoholic beverages to have a good time. | MC | — | — | .76 |
| | I think about when I can go drinking again. | MC | — | — | .78 |
| | People tell me I drink alcohol too much. | MC | — | — | .70 |

## BIAS ANALYSES

The test items were arranged into scales based on the standardization data and were then evaluated to see whether items functioned in the same way for females and males and for African American, Hispanic, and white children.

This was done using two Differential Item Functioning (DIF) methods: Rasch-based and Mantel-Haenszel. The Rasch-based method is based on the work of Mellenbergh (1982); person ability is estimated first using all data and then person abilities are fixed at the values obtained before and item difficulty parameters for all groups are estimated separately and compared. If the difference between the estimates for the two groups is larger than .50 logits and t test is significant at the .01 level, the item is considered as being potentially biased (Draba, 1977). The Mantel-Haenszel DIF method was proposed by Holland and Thayer (1988) and Zwick, Thayer, and Mazzeo (1997). This method estimates DIF based on cross-tabulation of the classification using the measure of the trait. Absolute DIF size larger than .64 logits indicates moderate to large bias, which correspondents to delta unit 1.5, [i.e., the criteria proposed by Holland and Thayer (1988)]. Items were considered for removal when a consistent pattern emerged across forms and levels. Only a small number of items were removed based on these criteria.

## SCALE DIFFERENTIATION

The CSA and reliability analyses were also helpful in choosing whether to combine item sets whose content was distinct from one another or to keep the item sets separate. The Amos program estimates correlations between the actual underlying dimensions, controlling for scale unreliability. When two factors correlate highly, a statistical test may be applied to determine whether the distinction between the factors is statistically significant; if the distinction is not, the scales should be merged. The scale intercorrelations reported in chapters 9 through 11 demonstrate the degree of scale independence that was achieved. For example, although the Hyperactivity and Attention Problems scales are highly correlated behavioral dimensions, they are conceptually distinct, and retaining them as separate scales enables the clinician to integrate the two pieces of information to make a diagnosis. Combining both item sets into a single scale would sacrifice interpretability, because a high score on the composite scale could arise from high ratings either on the Attention Problems items or on Hyperactivity items.

## FORMATION OF COMPOSITE SCALES

Composite scales for the TRS, PRS, and SRP were established through a series of confirmatory and exploratory factor analyses. These analyses are described in detail in chapters 9 through 11.

## FORMATION OF THE PROBABILITY, IMPAIRMENT, AND EXECUTIVE FUNCTIONING INDEXES

The Clinical, ADHD, Autism, and Emotional or Behavioral Disturbance (EBD) probability indexes were empirically derived using samples of children identified with the corresponding disorder. At the TRS and PRS preschool level, an overall Clinical Probability Index was used instead of specific clinical disorders due to the imprecision in diagnosis that is often found in children of such young ages. Probability indexes for ADHD, autism, and EBD were developed for the TRS and PRS child and adolescent levels. The procedure to develop the indexes was the same across forms. For the TRS and PRS level, effect sizes were computed for each item, comparing children not identified with a clinical condition to those identified with a clinical condition (i.e., ADHD, autism, EBD, or the combined clinical group). Items were considered for inclusion onto an index based on the magnitude of the effect size, the pattern of effect sizes across clinical groups (items that had a high effect size relative to the other clinical groups were given preference over effect sizes that did not differentiate between groups), and the clinical importance of an item to each group. Reliability estimates for each index were evaluated, resulting in an iterative process of item reassignments until no additional scale improvements could be made.

The Functional Impairment indexes were created in a similar fashion. Mean item performance between nonclinical and clinical samples was evaluated to identify items that appeared to differentiate between groups. In addition, a careful review of the content of the items was conducted to identify items that indicated some level of impairment in everyday functioning (such as academic performance, developing/maintaining relationships, emotional regulation, etc.). Items meeting both criteria were included in the index.

The Executive Functioning indexes were developed in conjunction with Dr. Mauricio Garcia-Barrera and are based on a series of studies conducted with the BASC–2 TRS and PRS that indicate a multifactor model of executive functioning (Garcia-Barrera et al., 2011, 2013; Garcia-Barrera, Karr, Duran, Direnfeld, & Pineda, 2015). First, items identified as representing executive behavior were assigned to one of four executive components identified in the previous research (Problem Solving, Attentional Control, Behavioral Control, and Emotional Control). For Attentional Control, items belonging to the Attention Problems scale were primarily used, as the Attention Problems scale adequately indicates the construct of attention self-regulation. Other factors included item assignments from a variety of scales (e.g., Hyperactivity, Depression, Emotional Self-Control, etc.). Second, reliability estimates based on the initial item selections were evaluated; item reassignments were made until a minimum reliability coefficient of .80 or higher was achieved. Third, a series of first-order and second-order (i.e., all first-order factors loading on one higher-order factor) confirmatory factor analyses were conducted to evaluate the overall fit of the model. Notably, the preschool data did not fit well with four factors and the problem-solving factor was removed from this scale. Various metrics were utilized to assess the quality of model fit, including the Comparative Fit Index (CFI), the Tucker-Lewis Index (TLI), and the Root Mean Square Error of Approximation (RMSEA). CFI and TLI values for the TRS levels were all above .94, with RMSEA values .10 or lower. For the PRS preschool and child levels, CFI and TLI values were .90 or higher; for the adolescent level these values were .86 or higher. All PRS RMSEA values ranged from .10 to .11. Overall, these results were determined to support a multifactor model of executive functioning.

# Readability Analyses

Because reading ability varies widely among the parents and students who complete the PRS and SRP, it is important to keep the reading-difficulty level of the items as low as possible. The reading level of the PRS and SRP items was measured using the Flesch-Kincaid Reading Index, which is sensitive to sentence length and number of syllables per word. The Reading Index values, expressed in grade levels, range from 4.6 through 4.8 for the three levels of the PRS and from 1.9 through 2.1 for the child and adolescent levels of the SRP. Overall, this analysis suggests that the PRS items are written at about a Grade 4 level and the SRP items at about a Grade 2 level.

# Measures of Response Validity

The BASC–3 TRS, PRS, and SRP include a number of indexes designed to assess the veracity of item responses.

Validity indexes available on the TRS and PRS include the $F$ Index, Consistency Index, and Response Pattern Index. The SRP has these indexes but also offers an $L$ Index and $V$ Index. Information on the development of these validity scales is described in the next paragraphs. More on interpretation of these scales is provided in chapters 5 and 6.

## $F$ INDEX

The $F$-Index score is a tally of the number of times the respondent gave a very negative behavior rating or self-report. High scores can result when the respondent attempted to present problems as worse than they actually are; however, it is possible for high scores to represent a child's many serious behavioral or emotional problems. To help differentiate between these possibilities, the index was constructed from item responses that were chosen very infrequently in the item-development samples. Typically, the $F$-Index items were endorsed by less than 3% of the respondents in the item-development samples.

The $F$ Index (and the indexes to be discussed next) has a highly skewed frequency distribution. Such skewed distributions are desirable for validity indexes if it is assumed that most cases are valid and only a small number are invalid. Approximately 96% to 99% of the cases included in the general combined norm samples are in the Acceptable interpretive range across the TRS, PRS, and SRP forms and levels.

## CONSISTENCY INDEX

The Consistency Index, available in the BASC–3 Q-global reports, identifies cases where the respondent has given differing responses to items that usually are answered similarly. It is scored by summing the absolute values of the score differences between each set of item pairs in the index. It then serves conceptually as a check on the reliability of an individual rater much as coefficient alpha and like internal consistency statistics serve as reliability estimates of the aggregation of raters across all raters or responders in the standardization sample. That is, a rater with a high Consistency Index is not responding in the same way to highly correlated items with similar content and thus the reproducibility and dependability of this person's ratings is suspect.

To create the index, an item-correlation matrix for each test form was established. Each matrix was then reviewed to identify the item pairs with the highest correlations. If an item was included in an item pair, it was then excluded from consideration in subsequent item pairings so that all items contributed equally to the index. A total of 20 item pairs were selected from each test form. Table 7.3 presents the item pairs for each test form. Note that item numbers followed by an R are reverse coded.

**Table 7.3** Consistency Index Item Pairs

| Form | Item pairs |
|------|------------|
| TRS–P | (97,64) (77,24) (100,28) (7,81) (72,51) (38,11) (82,34) (99,60) (49,15) (56,19) (105,22) (13,92) (30,79) (103,37) (17R,32R) (57R,1R) (66,26) (44,74) (21,53) (3,40) |
| TRS–C | (70,23) (131,105) (135,82) (110,40) (9,63) (17,58) (75,111) (147,28) (107,53) (88,14) (102,155) (29,91) (16,96) (85,35) (64R,21R) (150,113) (44,117) (124,90) (116,141) (77,94) |
| TRS–A | (132,120) (122,44) (140,41) (83R,48R) (16,36) (76,110) (115,150) (105,53) (96,14) (165,31) (68,34) (124R,2R) (158,107) (21R,71R) (127,102) (90,63) (58,100) (147,98) (25,128) (7,130) |
| PRS–P | (45R,15R) (54R,39R) (8,88) (28,78) (59R,115R) (118,34) (135,94) (52,109) (85,30) (120,66) (73,2) (102,137) (121,13) (133,111) (123,11) (100,22) (6,48) (97,18) (75R,130R) (125,91) |
| PRS–C | (103,47) (70,26) (11,91) (28R,83R) (17,115) (171,145) (23,141) (3,68) (124,52) (129,80) (44,4) (32,151) (42,159) (166,73) (95,120) (8,92) (137,174) (113,154) (161,63) (111,163R) |
| PRS–A | (156,129) (69,138) (63,26) (123,87) (43R,79R) (169,108) (160,93) (22,122) (98,162) (117,50) (121,77) (110,35) (48,3) (15R,112R) (53,164) (23,172) (85,157) (106,147) (154,58) (149,113) |
| SRP–C | (70,119) (69,88) (78,103) (87,109) (92,116) (53,122) (55,99) (51,75) (3,33) (80R,110R) (96,130) (94,114) (58,93) (48R,123R) (66R,127R) (8,38) (89,106) (84,101) (60,135) (91,125) |
| SRP–A | (70,108) (101,150) (137,157) (139,174) (99,131) (3,37) (67,97) (96,134) (148,169) (120,171) (152R,175R) (11,56) (112,129) (124,167) (127,155) (23,50) (86,105) (109,145) (165,180) (61,103) |
| SRP–COL | (82,113) (175,135) (65,94) (161,107) (6,42) (188,60) (153,111) (81,127) (100,174R) (144,103) (177,156) (150,73) (24,53) (67,109) (16,35) (11,48) (118,149) (19,38) (158,116) (126,184) |

The Consistency Index can be viewed as a measure of random responding; its validity can be demonstrated by the accuracy with which it detects item responses that are randomly generated. To this end, a series of data sets based on item frequencies within the standardization data were electronically generated. Scores from item pairs in these randomly generated data sets agreed only to the extent determined by their response distributions. Cutoffs designed to identify approximately 5% or less of the cases in the general norm sample were used to analyze the random data sets. Across all random data sets, cutoff values based on the general norm samples achieved a median average detection level of 66% of the cases when the values from the Caution and Extreme Caution ranges were used. Thus, the Consistency Index appears to be effective in identifying randomly generated data.

Approximately 94% to 97% of the cases included in the general combined norm samples are in the Acceptable interpretive range across the TRS, PRS, and SRP forms and levels.

## RESPONSE PATTERN INDEX
The Response Pattern Index, available in the BASC–3 Q-global reports, is designed to identify forms that may be invalid because the respondent was inattentive to the item content. It is a tally of the number of times an item response differs from the response to the previous item. The Caution-Low and Caution-High ranges (see chapters 5 and 6 for interpretation) were constructed to identify the extreme half-percentage at each end of the distribution of the Response Pattern Index in the general and clinical combined norm samples.

## *L* INDEX
The *L* Index appears only on the SRP and is a tally of the number of times the student responded *True* or *Almost always* to an unrealistically positive self-description or *False* or *Never* to a mildly self-critical statement that most people endorsed. As with the *F*-Index items, the *L*-Index items are marked in the scored directions relatively infrequently. Approximately 95% of the cases included in the general combined norm samples are in the Acceptable interpretive range.

## *V* INDEX
The *V* Index also appears only on the SRP and consists of nonsensical items that are rarely endorsed if a student is paying close attention to and understands the item content. Among the initial SRP forms collected in standardization, approximately 1% of cases met or exceeded the Extreme Caution ranges presented in chapter 6.

# Chapter 8

## Standardization and Norms Development

Standardization of the BASC–3 Teacher Rating Scales (TRS), Parent Rating Scales (PRS), and Self-Report of Personality (SRP) took place from April 2013 through November 2014. A total of more than 9,000 forms from 311 examiners in 44 states were collected as part of the BASC–3 standardization project (see Figure 8.1).

SAS/GRAPH® Software                                                                                                    US Cities

**Figure 8.1** Testing sites

## Locating and Testing the Samples

The primary goal of standardization data collection was to collect and derive general and clinical norms and to provide evidence of reliability, validity, and clinical utility for the final forms. For the general norms, data were obtained from a large and representative sample of children across the United States. The sample was designed to resemble the population with respect to gender, socioeconomic status (as indicated by parental education), race/ethnicity, geographic region, and classification in special education or gifted/talented programs. Sample overlap among TRS, PRS, and SRP forms was maximized to make the interpretation of scores across forms more comparable.

The clinical norm sample is composed of children ages 4 through 18 identified with a diagnosis or classification of one or more emotional or behavioral problems. In many cases, these children were receiving special-education services at school, a community mental health clinic, or a university- or hospital-based mental health clinic. Children with a variety of emotional, behavioral, and physical problems were targeted for participation.

Trained recruiters and independent examiners identified children and young adults from daycare, school, and clinic settings for the general and clinical norm samples. Participants were selected who met the specified inclusion criteria of the standardization samples and fit the sampling plan matrix. Examiners and participants were paid an incentive for participating in the project.

Examiners were required to have a graduate degree in psychology or clinical social work to be certified as an educational diagnostician or to be supervised by a person with such a degree or certification. Parents/guardians received a parent letter describing the project and a consent form. The consent form requested basic demographic information about the child, the parents' education level, any emotional, behavioral, or physical problems identified for the child, and any special school services currently received. The consent form, once signed, permitted the child to complete a self-report, a teacher to rate the child's behavior, and indicated the parent's willingness to rate their child's behavior.

Except for parents included in the interrater reliability studies, only one parent was asked to complete a PRS for each child. Likewise, only one teacher was asked to complete a TRS for each child. Teachers, however, were allowed to participate in the project for more than one student (up to a maximum of 10). A limited number of teachers, parents, and students were invited to complete additional forms that were part of various reliability and validity studies. Assignment of cases continued until the demographic targets were met for the normative samples and reliability and validity studies.

Most of the BASC–3 forms were collected digitally using a secure Internet testing site; additional paper forms (approximately 30%) were collected when digital testing was not possible. Teachers, parents, and students were encouraged to respond to all items on a form. Forms with more than 10% unscorable items (unmarked or multiply-marked) were excluded from all analyses. In addition, any form missing responses to three or more items on a single scale (using the final scale configurations) was excluded from norm samples. For the purpose of norms construction, if one or two item responses were missing from a scale, the raw score for that scale was adjusted using the method described in the Omitted Items section in chapters 5 and 6.

During standardization, Spanish-speaking parents and students had the option of completing a Spanish version of the PRS or SRP. Some of these cases are included in the general norm sample so that the sample better represents how the BASC–3 will be used in educational and clinical practice.

# Description of the Samples

## GENERAL NORM SAMPLE

The data collection procedure succeeded in achieving a large amount of overlap for the TRS, PRS, and SRP forms in the general norm sample. The overlap is shown in Table 8.1.

**Table 8.1** Overlap of General Norm Samples Across Forms

| Form | N | Number also taking | | |
| | | TRS | PRS | SRP |
|------|---|-----|-----|-----|
| TRS–P | 500 | — | 218 | — |
| TRS–C | 600 | — | 238 | 120 |
| TRS–A | 600 | — | 230 | 315 |
| PRS–P | 600 | 218 | — | — |
| PRS–C | 600 | 238 | — | 170 |
| PRS–A | 600 | 230 | — | 302 |
| SRP–C | 300 | 120 | 170 | — |
| SRP–A | 600 | 315 | 302 | — |

An effort was made to include approximately equal numbers of examinees at each year of age. As shown in Table 8.2, this goal was largely achieved. Larger age bands (i.e., age groupings) were established for norming purposes because there is very little difference in score levels on BASC–3 scales at different years of age within age groupings.

**Table 8.2** Representation of the General Norm Samples, by Age

| Age | TRS N | PRS N | SRP N |
|-----|-------|-------|-------|
| 2 | 82 | 141 | — |
| 3 | 118 | 159 | — |
| Total | 200 | 300 | — |
| 4 | 143 | 148 | — |
| 5 | 157 | 152 | — |
| Total | 300 | 300 | — |
| 6 | 146 | 128 | — |
| 7 | 154 | 172 | — |
| Total | 300 | 300 | — |
| 8 | 78 | 72 | 65 |
| 9 | 70 | 78 | 66 |
| 10 | 76 | 78 | 79 |
| 11 | 76 | 72 | 90 |
| Total | 300 | 300 | 300 |
| 12 | 90 | 96 | 108 |
| 13 | 123 | 117 | 112 |
| 14 | 87 | 87 | 80 |
| Total | 300 | 300 | 300 |
| 15 | 82 | 82 | 84 |
| 16 | 86 | 92 | 101 |
| 17 | 60 | 56 | 63 |
| 18 | 72 | 70 | 52 |
| Total | 300 | 300 | 300 |
| Grand total | 1700 | 1800 | 900 |

Normative information is based on national samples that are representative of the U.S. population for children. The age groupings for children ages 2 through 18 are shown in Tables 8.3 through 8.5. For the TRS, PRS, and SRP, a stratified sampling plan ensured that the general norm sample included representative proportions of children according to selected demographic variables. An analysis of data gathered in 2013 by the U.S. Census Bureau American Community Survey (U.S. Census Bureau, 2013) provided the basis for stratification using the following variables within each age grouping:

- parent education level (i.e., the highest school grade completed by the child's mother or female guardian, or the child's father if the mother's education level was unavailable): grade 11 or less (1), high school graduate (2), 1 to 3 years of college or technical school (3), and 4 years of college or more (4)

- race/ethnicity (African American, Asian, Hispanic, white, and other racial/ethnic groups)

- geographic region (Northeast, Midwest, South, West)

The general norms consisted of an equal number of male and female children in each age grouping. In addition, attention was given to the presence of emotional, behavioral, or physical diagnoses or classifications reported for the child.

Tables 8.3 through 8.6 report the percentages of demographic characteristics of the BASC–3 general norm sample in comparison with these population estimates. These data indicate a close correspondence between the normative sample and the 2013 census proportions across most of the forms and age bands.

**Table 8.3** Demographic Characteristics of the Normative Sample by Parent Education Level, Race/Ethnicity, Geographic Region, and Gender, by Age Group: TRS

| Age | | Mother's education level | | | | Race/ethnicity | | | | | Region | | | |
|---|---|---|---|---|---|---|---|---|---|---|---|---|---|---|
| | | 1 | 2 | 3 | 4 | African American | Asian | Hispanic | Other | White | Midwest | Northeast | South | West |
| 2–3 | U.S. population | 14.4 | 22.7 | 31.8 | 31.1 | 13.9 | 4.4 | 25.8 | 6.0 | 49.8 | 20.9 | 16.1 | 38.5 | 24.5 |
| | Normative sample | 6.5 | 25.0 | 33.5 | 35.0 | 13.5 | 3.5 | 26.5 | 6.0 | 50.5 | 20.5 | 16.5 | 40.0 | 23.0 |
| 4–5 | U.S. population | 14.5 | 22.9 | 32.7 | 29.9 | 13.7 | 4.6 | 26.1 | 5.9 | 49.7 | 21.3 | 15.8 | 38.3 | 24.6 |
| | Normative sample | 13.0 | 23.7 | 32.7 | 30.7 | 13.7 | 4.3 | 26.3 | 6.3 | 49.3 | 22.3 | 15.0 | 40.0 | 22.7 |
| 6–7 | U.S. population | 14.0 | 22.4 | 33.0 | 30.7 | 13.5 | 4.7 | 25.0 | 5.7 | 51.2 | 21.4 | 15.8 | 38.4 | 24.5 |
| | Normative sample | 11.3 | 23.7 | 33.0 | 32.0 | 13.7 | 4.7 | 25.0 | 5.3 | 51.3 | 23.3 | 10.0 | 40.7 | 26.0 |
| 8–11 | U.S. population | 13.7 | 22.3 | 33.1 | 30.9 | 13.5 | 4.8 | 24.0 | 5.3 | 52.5 | 21.7 | 16.2 | 38.1 | 24.1 |
| | Normative sample | 14.0 | 22.3 | 33.0 | 30.7 | 13.3 | 5.0 | 24.0 | 5.3 | 52.3 | 22.0 | 16.0 | 38.0 | 24.0 |
| 12–14 | U.S. population | 14.0 | 23.0 | 33.5 | 29.5 | 13.9 | 4.6 | 22.8 | 4.9 | 53.8 | 21.5 | 16.6 | 37.9 | 24.0 |
| | Normative sample | 14.0 | 23.3 | 33.3 | 29.3 | 13.7 | 4.7 | 23.0 | 5.0 | 53.7 | 21.0 | 17.3 | 37.3 | 24.3 |
| 15–18 | U.S. population | 14.2 | 24.2 | 33.2 | 28.4 | 13.8 | 4.5 | 21.7 | 4.6 | 55.4 | 21.7 | 17.0 | 37.3 | 24.0 |
| | Normative sample | 14.3 | 24.0 | 32.7 | 29.0 | 13.7 | 4.3 | 22.7 | 4.3 | 55.0 | 24.0 | 11.7 | 38.3 | 26.0 |

**Table 8.4** Demographic Characteristics of the Normative Sample by Parent Education Level, Race/Ethnicity, Geographic Region, and Gender, by Age Group: PRS

| Age | | Mother's education level | | | | Race/ethnicity | | | | | Region | | | |
|---|---|---|---|---|---|---|---|---|---|---|---|---|---|---|
| | | 1 | 2 | 3 | 4 | African American | Asian | Hispanic | Other | White | Midwest | Northeast | South | West |
| 2–3 | U.S. population | 14.4 | 22.7 | 31.8 | 31.1 | 13.9 | 4.4 | 25.8 | 6.0 | 49.8 | 20.9 | 16.1 | 38.5 | 24.5 |
| | Normative sample | 14.3 | 22.7 | 31.7 | 31.3 | 13.7 | 3.3 | 25.7 | 6.0 | 51.3 | 20.3 | 16.3 | 38.7 | 24.7 |
| 4–5 | U.S. population | 14.5 | 22.9 | 32.7 | 29.9 | 13.7 | 4.6 | 26.1 | 5.9 | 49.7 | 21.3 | 15.8 | 38.3 | 24.6 |
| | Normative sample | 14.3 | 23.0 | 32.7 | 30.0 | 13.7 | 4.7 | 26.0 | 6.0 | 49.7 | 21.0 | 15.7 | 38.3 | 25.0 |
| 6–7 | U.S. population | 14.0 | 22.4 | 33.0 | 30.7 | 13.5 | 4.7 | 25.0 | 5.7 | 51.2 | 21.4 | 15.8 | 38.4 | 24.5 |
| | Normative sample | 14.0 | 22.3 | 33.0 | 30.7 | 13.7 | 4.7 | 24.7 | 4.7 | 52.3 | 21.3 | 15.7 | 38.3 | 24.7 |
| 8–11 | U.S. population | 13.7 | 22.3 | 33.1 | 30.9 | 13.5 | 4.8 | 24.0 | 5.3 | 52.5 | 21.7 | 16.2 | 38.1 | 24.1 |
| | Normative sample | 14.7 | 23.3 | 32.0 | 30.0 | 13.3 | 4.7 | 24.0 | 5.7 | 52.3 | 21.7 | 16.3 | 38.3 | 23.7 |
| 12–14 | U.S. population | 14.0 | 23.0 | 33.5 | 29.5 | 13.9 | 4.6 | 22.8 | 4.9 | 53.8 | 21.5 | 16.6 | 37.9 | 24.0 |
| | Normative sample | 14.3 | 23.3 | 33.3 | 29.0 | 14.3 | 4.7 | 22.7 | 4.7 | 53.7 | 21.7 | 16.3 | 37.7 | 24.3 |
| 15–18 | U.S. population | 14.2 | 24.2 | 33.2 | 28.4 | 13.8 | 4.5 | 21.7 | 4.6 | 55.4 | 21.7 | 17.0 | 37.3 | 24.0 |
| | Normative sample | 14.3 | 24.7 | 34.0 | 27.0 | 13.7 | 4.3 | 22.0 | 4.3 | 55.7 | 21.3 | 17.0 | 37.7 | 24.0 |

**Table 8.5** Demographic Characteristics of the Normative Sample by Parent Education Level, Race/Ethnicity, Geographic Region, and Gender, by Age Group: SRP

| Age | | Mother's education level | | | | Race/ethnicity | | | | | Region | | | |
|---|---|---|---|---|---|---|---|---|---|---|---|---|---|---|
| | | 1 | 2 | 3 | 4 | African American | Asian | Hispanic | Other | White | Midwest | Northeast | South | West |
| 6–7 | U.S. population | 13.9 | 22.4 | 32.8 | 31.0 | 13.3 | 4.7 | 24.9 | 5.6 | 51.5 | 21.4 | 15.8 | 38.3 | 24.4 |
| | Normative sample | 10.7 | 21.0 | 34.7 | 33.7 | 11.3 | 5.3 | 24.3 | 6.0 | 53.0 | 18.7 | 17.7 | 37.7 | 26.0 |
| 8–11 | U.S. population | 13.7 | 22.3 | 33.1 | 30.9 | 13.5 | 4.8 | 24.0 | 5.3 | 52.5 | 21.7 | 16.2 | 38.1 | 24.1 |
| | Normative sample | 14.0 | 22.0 | 33.0 | 31.0 | 13.7 | 4.7 | 23.7 | 5.0 | 53.0 | 21.3 | 16.3 | 38.7 | 23.7 |
| 12–14 | U.S. population | 14.0 | 23.0 | 33.5 | 29.5 | 13.9 | 4.6 | 22.8 | 4.9 | 53.8 | 21.5 | 16.6 | 37.9 | 24.0 |
| | Normative sample | 14.0 | 23.3 | 33.3 | 29.3 | 13.7 | 5.0 | 22.7 | 4.3 | 54.3 | 21.7 | 16.3 | 37.0 | 25.0 |
| 15–18 | U.S. population | 14.6 | 24.9 | 33.3 | 27.1 | 14.2 | 4.4 | 22.3 | 4.6 | 54.6 | 21.4 | 16.9 | 37.6 | 24.1 |
| | Normative sample | 14.3 | 25.3 | 33.3 | 27.0 | 12.7 | 4.3 | 23.0 | 4.3 | 55.7 | 23.0 | 16.3 | 36.0 | 24.7 |

A representative proportion of children from various special-education classifications was added to the normative sample to reflect the U.S. population as a whole. Approximately 14% to 16% of the general norm sample in each age grouping includes children from the classifications shown in Table 8.6. Overall, the BASC–3 percentages for these classifications are very similar to those found in the census data.

**Table 8.6** Representation of the General Norm Samples, by Special-Education Classification and Form Level

|  | TRS % | | PRS % | | SRP % | | | U.S. pop. % |
| --- | --- | --- | --- | --- | --- | --- | --- | --- |
|  | 6–11 | 12–18 | 6–11 | 12–18 | 6–7 | 8–11 | 12–18 |  |
| Attention-deficit/hyperactivity disorder | 5.8 | 6.2 | 5.5 | 6.0 | 4.7 | 6.7 | 5.8 | 6.0 |
| Emotional/behavioral disturbance | 0.7 | 1.0 | 1.2 | 1.0 | 2.0 | 1.0 | 1.5 | 0.8 |
| Autism spectrum disorder | 2.0 | 1.7 | 2.2 | 2.0 | 3.3 | 2.3 | 2.0 | 2.0 |
| Developmental delay/developmental disorders | 1.0 | 1.0 | 0.8 | 1.0 | 0.3 | 0.3 | 0.3 | 0.8 |
| Specific learning disorder | 5.3 | 4.8 | 5.2 | 4.7 | 1.7 | 5.7 | 5.3 | 4.9 |
| Other | 1.3 | 4.0 | 0.5 | 1.0 | 3.0 | 1.0 | 1.3 | — |

Data for the college level of the SRP (SRP–COL) were collected from 300 students ages 18 through 25 attending various colleges, universities, and technical schools throughout the United States. Information on the age and gender composition of this norm sample is presented in Table 8.7. An effort was made to include a variety of examinees with respect to year of age within the sample. As shown in Table 8.7, the predominant ages are traditional college-age adults (ages 18 through 21). The percentages are reported for enrollment in 2-year and 4-year degree programs, in another type of program (e.g., a 1-year certificate program), and for those enrolled but not seeking a degree.

**Table 8.7** Representation of the SRP–COL Norm Sample, by Gender, Age, and Degree Program

|  | Sample size | | |
| --- | --- | --- | --- |
| Age | Combined | Female | Male |
| 18 | 55 | 23 | 32 |
| 19 | 56 | 29 | 27 |
| 20 | 59 | 34 | 25 |
| 21 | 54 | 31 | 23 |
| 22 | 20 | 10 | 10 |
| 23 | 27 | 10 | 17 |
| 24 | 21 | 10 | 11 |
| 25 | 8 | 3 | 5 |
| **Degree sought/obtained** | | | |
| None | 35 | 21 | 14 |
| 2-year | 63 | 31 | 32 |
| 4-year | 189 | 91 | 98 |
| Other | 13 | 7 | 6 |

# CLINICAL NORM SAMPLE

For the clinical norm sample, a large amount of overlap across forms was achieved. The overlap is shown in Table 8.8.

**Table 8.8** Overlap of Clinical Norm Samples Across Forms

| Form | N | Number also taking | | |
|---|---|---|---|---|
| | | TRS | PRS | SRP |
| TRS–P | 65 | — | 44 | — |
| TRS–C | 280 | — | 198 | 144 |
| TRS–A | 266 | — | 144 | 184 |
| PRS–P | 83 | 44 | — | — |
| PRS–C | 356 | 198 | — | 189 |
| PRS–A | 316 | 144 | — | 183 |
| SRP–C | 237 | 144 | 189 | — |
| SRP–A | 282 | 184 | 183 | — |

Table 8.9 shows the percentages of the representation of diagnostic categories in the clinical norm sample. The preschool levels of the TRS and PRS are composed of mostly children with developmental delays/disorders or conditions falling into the Other category (which were predominantly children with speech and language problems), while the largest numbers of children from the child and adolescent clinical samples are diagnosed with attention-deficit/hyperactivity disorder (ADHD), emotional/behavioral disturbance (EBD), or autism spectrum disorder.

**Table 8.9** Representation of the Clinical Norm Samples, by Diagnosis and Form Level

| Diagnosis category | Percentage of sample | | | | | | | |
|---|---|---|---|---|---|---|---|---|
| | TRS | | | PRS | | | SRP | |
| | Preschool | Child | Adolescent | Preschool | Child | Adolescent | Child | Adolescent |
| Attention-deficit/hyperactivity disorder | 6.2 | 31.1 | 30.1 | 9.6 | 39.6 | 44.6 | 39.7 | 43.6 |
| Emotional/behavioral disturbance | 4.6 | 10.7 | 16.9 | 2.4 | 11.8 | 15.8 | 14.3 | 17.4 |
| Autism spectrum disorder | 15.4 | 16.4 | 16.2 | 19.3 | 13.8 | 13.6 | 16.0 | 13.5 |
| Developmental delay/ developmental disorders | 35.4 | 8.9 | 7.9 | 22.9 | 5.3 | 6.3 | 1.3 | 1.4 |
| Specific learning disorder | — | 15.0 | 16.5 | 2.4 | 13.8 | 9.5 | 13.9 | 15.6 |
| Other | 38.5 | 17.9 | 12.4 | 43.4 | 15.7 | 10.1 | 14.8 | 8.5 |

Because the clinical norm sample includes large numbers of students with ADHD at the child and adolescent levels, norms have been constructed for this subgroup in addition to the overall clinical norms. As reported in chapters 9 through 11 of this manual, the ADHD subgroup has distinct score profiles. These more specific norms should enhance the clinician's ability to make diagnostic decisions. Additional clinical norm groups were created for students ages 19 through 21 who are still in high school. The age in years for these samples is shown in Table 8.10.

**Table 8.10** TRS, PRS, and SRP: Representation of the Clinical Norm Sample for 19- Through 21-Year-Olds, by Age

| Age | TRS | | | PRS | | | SRP | | |
|---|---|---|---|---|---|---|---|---|---|
| | Combined | Female | Male | Combined | Female | Male | Combined | Female | Male |
| 19 | 28 | 9 | 19 | 75 | 35 | 40 | 22 | 11 | 11 |
| 20 | 9 | 5 | 4 | 20 | 9 | 11 | 15 | 9 | 6 |
| 21 | 4 | 2 | 2 | 19 | 11 | 8 | 10 | 7 | 3 |
| Total | 41 | 16 | 25 | 114 | 55 | 59 | 47 | 27 | 20 |

Unlike the general norm sample, the clinical norm sample is not demographically matched to the U.S. population. The number of children diagnosed with behavioral or emotional difficulties varies across conditions and gender, a finding that is consistent with known population differences. Table 8.11 presents the demographic characteristics of the overall clinical norm sample and the ADHD norm sample by age and gender. Table 8.12 shows the makeup of the overall clinical norm sample and the ADHD norm sample by age. Table 8.13 shows the makeup of the overall clinical norm sample and ADHD norm sample by age and race/ethnicity. Table 8.14 presents the distribution by age and geographic region for the overall clinical norm sample and the ADHD norm sample.

**Table 8.11** Representation of the Clinical Norm Samples, by Gender and Age

| Age | Gender | TRS | | PRS | | SRP | |
|---|---|---|---|---|---|---|---|
| | | All | ADHD | All | ADHD | All | ADHD |
| 4–5 | Female | 25 | — | 33 | — | — | — |
| | Male | 40 | — | 50 | — | — | — |
| | Combined | 65 | — | 83 | — | — | — |
| 6–11 | Female | 84 | 26 | 99 | 32 | 68 | 22 |
| | Male | 196 | 61 | 257 | 109 | 169 | 72 |
| | Combined | 280 | 87 | 356 | 141 | 237 | 94 |
| 12–18 | Female | 83 | 15 | 109 | 39 | 83 | 26 |
| | Male | 183 | 65 | 207 | 102 | 199 | 97 |
| | Combined | 266 | 80 | 316 | 141 | 282 | 123 |

**Table 8.12** Representation of the Clinical Norm Samples, by Age

| Age | TRS | | PRS | | SRP | |
|---|---|---|---|---|---|---|
| | All | ADHD | All | ADHD | All | ADHD |
| 4 | 38 | — | 44 | — | — | — |
| 5 | 27 | — | 39 | — | — | — |
| Total | 65 | — | 83 | — | — | — |
| 6 | 28 | 8 | 32 | 9 | — | — |
| 7 | 42 | 13 | 49 | 17 | — | — |
| Total | 70 | 21 | 81 | 26 | — | — |
| 8 | 51 | 15 | 64 | 25 | 55 | 21 |
| 9 | 55 | 19 | 72 | 35 | 57 | 25 |
| 10 | 62 | 17 | 76 | 32 | 70 | 30 |
| 11 | 42 | 15 | 63 | 23 | 55 | 18 |
| Total | 210 | 66 | 275 | 115 | 237 | 94 |
| 12 | 49 | 10 | 42 | 19 | 51 | 18 |
| 13 | 63 | 22 | 62 | 27 | 58 | 23 |
| 14 | 48 | 16 | 57 | 28 | 52 | 27 |
| Total | 160 | 48 | 161 | 74 | 161 | 68 |
| 15 | 21 | 2 | 35 | 10 | 26 | 6 |
| 16 | 35 | 13 | 51 | 25 | 36 | 19 |
| 17 | 23 | 7 | 37 | 14 | 28 | 15 |
| 18 | 27 | 10 | 32 | 18 | 31 | 15 |
| Total | 106 | 32 | 155 | 67 | 121 | 55 |
| Grand total | 611 | 167 | 755 | 282 | 519 | 217 |

**Table 8.13** Representation of the Clinical Norm Samples, by Race/Ethnicity and Age

| Age | Race/ethnicity | TRS All | TRS ADHD | PRS All | PRS ADHD | SRP All | SRP ADHD |
|---|---|---|---|---|---|---|---|
| 4–5 | African American | 3 | — | 6 | — | — | — |
| | Asian | 4 | — | 12 | — | — | — |
| | Hispanic | 13 | — | 19 | — | — | — |
| | Other | 6 | — | 6 | — | — | — |
| | White | 39 | — | 40 | — | — | — |
| | Total | 65 | — | 83 | — | — | — |
| 6–11 | African American | 42 | 8 | 42 | 12 | 30 | 10 |
| | Asian | 5 | 1 | 6 | 3 | 6 | 3 |
| | Hispanic | 42 | 8 | 55 | 21 | 23 | 5 |
| | Other | 11 | 3 | 19 | 8 | 10 | 4 |
| | White | 180 | 67 | 234 | 97 | 168 | 72 |
| | Total | 280 | 87 | 356 | 141 | 237 | 94 |
| 12–18 | African American | 24 | 7 | 28 | 10 | 27 | 9 |
| | Asian | 13 | 2 | 6 | 4 | 14 | 4 |
| | Hispanic | 34 | 5 | 43 | 17 | 30 | 11 |
| | Other | 19 | 4 | 24 | 9 | 25 | 6 |
| | White | 176 | 62 | 215 | 101 | 186 | 93 |
| | Total | 266 | 80 | 316 | 141 | 282 | 123 |

**Table 8.14** Representation of the Clinical Norm Samples, by Geographic Region and Age

| Age | Region | TRS All | TRS ADHD | PRS All | PRS ADHD | SRP All | SRP ADHD |
|---|---|---|---|---|---|---|---|
| 4–5 | Midwest | 16 | — | 20 | — | — | — |
| | Northeast | 5 | — | 5 | — | — | — |
| | South | 24 | — | 40 | — | — | — |
| | West | 20 | — | 18 | — | — | — |
| | Total | 65 | — | 83 | — | — | — |
| 6–11 | Midwest | 90 | 23 | 104 | 33 | 67 | 21 |
| | Northeast | 68 | 14 | 70 | 22 | 58 | 19 |
| | South | 87 | 40 | 120 | 61 | 73 | 38 |
| | West | 35 | 10 | 62 | 25 | 39 | 16 |
| | Total | 280 | 87 | 356 | 141 | 237 | 94 |
| 12–18 | Midwest | 65 | 26 | 87 | 48 | 85 | 43 |
| | Northeast | 42 | 8 | 59 | 17 | 50 | 12 |
| | South | 107 | 39 | 117 | 58 | 90 | 50 |
| | West | 52 | 7 | 53 | 18 | 57 | 18 |
| | Total | 266 | 80 | 316 | 141 | 282 | 123 |

# Norms Development

## AGE AND GENDER DIFFERENCES

The first step in developing general norms for the TRS, PRS, and SRP was to determine whether age or gender differences on the scales were sufficiently large enough to justify separate norms for subgroups. Similar analyses conducted during the development of the BASC–2 showed age and gender differences on a number of scales. Raw scores were computed for each age (i.e., 2, 3, 4, etc.), and these raw scores were used to form various age bands that are designed to preserve behavioral differences across the ages reflected in the normative data (see Reynolds & Kamphaus, 2004, for a more detailed discussion).

The general norm samples were divided into these normative age groupings: 2 through 3, 4 through 5, 6 through 7, 8 through 11, 12 through 14, and 15 through 18. (Normative age groupings for the SRP start at age 8.) Statistically significant differences were found on various scales between several of the age groupings across TRS, PRS, and SRP samples (e.g., Depression, Anxiety, Social Skills). This result is consistent with the previous BASC editions and demonstrates the need to offer norms across a variety of age bands.

Gender differences between scale scores were explored next. Means and standard deviations of raw scores for each age and gender group can be found in the scale norm tables presented in Appendix A. For each scale, comparisons between males and females resulted in difference patterns that were similar to those found in previous BASC editions. For example, males generally scored higher (i.e., exhibited more problems) on scales such as Aggression, Attention Problems, Hyperactivity, and Sensation Seeking, and on the composite scales of Externalizing Problems and the Behavioral Symptoms Index. Females generally scored higher (i.e., exhibited more problems) on the Anxiety scale at the adolescent and college (SRP) levels and also scored higher (i.e., exhibited behavioral strengths) on several adaptive scales, including Adaptability, Social Skills, and Study Skills, as well as the Adaptive Skills composite.

These gender differences are the primary reason for offering separate-gender norms in addition to the combined-gender norms. However, as discussed in chapter 2, the existence of gender differences does not imply that separate-gender norms should be used routinely for interpretation.

## CONSTRUCTION OF SCALE AND COMPOSITE NORMS

Both T scores and percentile scores were developed for each scale. Several different methods of constructing these types of norms were carefully considered; the rationale for the choices made is discussed next.

### T Scores

A T score measures in standard deviation units the distance of a raw score from the norm group's mean raw score. A linear transformation was used to create BASC–3 T scores based solely on the observed mean and standard deviation of raw scores. Measures of uncommon problem behaviors may show a skewed distribution of raw scores, with most of the sample bunched together at the nonproblem end of the scale and with a long "tail" stretching toward the other end. As such, the skewness of each normative distribution for the TRS, PRS, and SRP scale scores was evaluated. In general, over one half of the values were equal to or greater than 1.0, or equal to or less than -1.0. (A skewness value of 0 denotes a symmetrical distribution; positive and negative values, respectively, indicate that the distribution has a tail extending toward high or low scores.) Scales such as Atypicality, Bullying, and Somatization tended to have some of the highest skewness values, while scales such as Adaptability and Social Skills tended to have values closer to 0. Highly skewed distributions permit T scores that are relatively far from 50 in the direction of the tail; scales that are more symmetrical will result in lower T-score ranges.

Because linear T scores are used in the BASC–3, it is important to note that the resulting percentiles associated with the T scores will not necessarily result in the same percentiles associated with the normal distribution. The long tail in these skewed distributions includes more cases than predicted by the normal curve, as discussed in the following paragraphs.

### Percentiles

A percentile rank indicates the percentage of the norm sample scoring at or below a particular raw score. (Technically, the midinterval percentiles used in the BASC–3 norms are based on the number of cases scoring below the raw score plus half the number of cases scoring at the raw score.) The relationship between the linear T scores and percentile ranks varies with the shape of the score distribution. For example, if a scale is positively skewed so that its distribution has a long tail stretching toward the high end, a high T score is not as rare (and will not correspond to as high a percentile) as if the distribution were symmetrical or skewed in the opposite direction. For this reason, the BASC–3 norm tables present both T scores and percentile ranks for each scale. It is important to interpret the rarity of these T scores in terms of these percentiles.

The BASC–3 percentiles have been calculated using an algorithm developed by Hill (1976); Hill, Hill, and Holder (1976); and Roid (1989) that is based on systems of frequency curves described by Johnson (1949). The mean, standard deviation, skewness, and kurtosis of a scale's observed raw score and one of three possible Johnson curves were used to generate a theoretical distribution for each scale, yielding the smoothed midinterval percentile rank norms for each scale. These methods preserve the real underlying distributions of the constructs assessed by the BASC–3 scales within the population at large. These distributions are reflected in various prevalence estimates for many forms of emotional and behavioral disorders, prior research with thousands of cases from the BASC and the BASC–2, and distributions evident in the scaling of competing behavior rating scales. Thus, the distributions provide a more accurate basis for score interpretation than do nonlinear transformations that force these percentile distributions into the shape of the "normal" curve.

# Chapter 9

# Teacher Rating Scales: Reliability and Validity

This chapter presents technical information about the Teacher Rating Scales (TRS), including evidence of reliability (i.e., internal consistency, test–retest, interrater) and validity (i.e., factor structure of the scales, correlations with other instruments, score profiles of clinical groups). Technical information about the Parent Rating Scales (PRS) and Self-Report of Personality (SRP) is found in chapters 10 and 11, respectively. Technical information about the relationship between the TRS, PRS, and SRP components is presented in chapter 12.

## Evidence of Reliability

The reliability of a test score refers to its accuracy, consistency, and stability across situations (Anastasi & Urbina, 1997; Sattler, 2008). Reliability of scores can be measured in several ways, each taking into account particular sources of error. The following types of reliability evidence were analyzed for the BASC–3 TRS and are presented in this chapter.

- *Internal consistency:* shows the degree to which all of the items of a scale are measuring the same behavioral or emotional dimension

- *Test–retest reliability*: reflects the consistency of ratings from the same teacher over a brief time interval

- *Interrater reliability:* describes the level of agreement among independent teacher ratings of the same child

### EVIDENCE OF INTERNAL CONSISTENCY

Internal consistency addresses the question, How homogeneous is this set of items in measuring a particular behavioral dimension? High internal consistency (represented by the statistic coefficient alpha) suggests that all items in a scale largely reflect the same underlying dimension. Table 9.1 reports coefficient alpha for each TRS composite and scale score, based on all of the cases in each of the general norm groups with complete item data for the scale. Table 9.2 presents the same type of information for the clinical norm samples. Because reliability is affected by both the variability of scores in a sample and the quality of the items, each table shows separate reliability coefficients for the scores of the combined, female, and male samples, and for the ADHD and 19- through 21-year-old clinical subsamples.

**Table 9.1** TRS: Coefficient Alpha Reliabilities of Composites, Scales, and Indexes, by Gender and Age, General Norm Samples

| | Preschool | | | | | | Child | | | | | | Adolescent | | | | | |
| | Ages 2–3 | | | Ages 4–5 | | | Ages 6–7 | | | Ages 8–11 | | | Ages 12–14 | | | Ages 15–18 | | |
| | Combined | Female | Male | Combined | Female | Male | Combined | Female | Male | Combined | Female | Male | Combined | Female | Male | Combined | Female | Male |
|---|---|---|---|---|---|---|---|---|---|---|---|---|---|---|---|---|---|---|
| **Composite** | | | | | | | | | | | | | | | | | | |
| Externalizing Problems | .94 | .94 | .93 | .95 | .95 | .95 | .96 | .97 | .96 | .96 | .95 | .97 | .97 | .95 | .97 | .97 | .97 | .96 |
| Internalizing Problems | .89 | .90 | .86 | .92 | .93 | .92 | .93 | .93 | .93 | .92 | .92 | .93 | .93 | .94 | .92 | .95 | .96 | .94 |
| School Problems | — | — | — | — | — | — | .96 | .96 | .96 | .95 | .94 | .95 | .94 | .93 | .95 | .96 | .96 | .95 |
| Adaptive Skills | .95 | .94 | .95 | .95 | .95 | .95 | .97 | .98 | .97 | .97 | .97 | .97 | .98 | .97 | .98 | .98 | .98 | .98 |
| Behavioral Symptoms Index | .96 | .96 | .95 | .97 | .97 | .97 | .97 | .97 | .96 | .97 | .96 | .98 | .97 | .96 | .97 | .98 | .98 | .97 |
| **Clinical scale** | | | | | | | | | | | | | | | | | | |
| Hyperactivity | .89 | .89 | .88 | .90 | .89 | .89 | .94 | .94 | .94 | .93 | .90 | .94 | .93 | .89 | .94 | .92 | .92 | .91 |
| Aggression | .89 | .88 | .89 | .91 | .91 | .92 | .90 | .90 | .90 | .90 | .88 | .90 | .91 | .85 | .93 | .91 | .92 | .90 |
| Conduct Problems | — | — | — | — | — | — | .89 | .90 | .89 | .90 | .87 | .91 | .91 | .91 | .92 | .92 | .94 | .91 |
| Anxiety | .77 | .75 | .79 | .81 | .80 | .81 | .86 | .88 | .84 | .86 | .85 | .86 | .85 | .85 | .85 | .89 | .91 | .87 |
| Depression | .80 | .84 | .75 | .87 | .88 | .85 | .84 | .82 | .86 | .86 | .83 | .88 | .83 | .84 | .81 | .88 | .89 | .88 |
| Somatization | .78 | .80 | .75 | .85 | .86 | .85 | .88 | .87 | .89 | .87 | .88 | .84 | .90 | .91 | .88 | .85 | .86 | .85 |
| Attention Problems | .87 | .86 | .88 | .93 | .93 | .92 | .94 | .93 | .95 | .94 | .93 | .94 | .94 | .91 | .95 | .94 | .94 | .94 |
| Learning Problems | — | — | — | — | — | — | .92 | .92 | .93 | .89 | .88 | .90 | .86 | .84 | .88 | .90 | .90 | .89 |
| Atypicality | .87 | .90 | .84 | .90 | .91 | .89 | .85 | .85 | .84 | .87 | .73 | .90 | .86 | .83 | .88 | .89 | .89 | .89 |
| Withdrawal | .78 | .76 | .79 | .82 | .80 | .84 | .81 | .82 | .80 | .90 | .85 | .92 | .87 | .88 | .86 | .89 | .85 | .91 |
| **Adaptive scale** | | | | | | | | | | | | | | | | | | |
| Adaptability | .88 | .88 | .87 | .89 | .89 | .88 | .89 | .89 | .90 | .90 | .87 | .90 | .89 | .87 | .90 | .92 | .93 | .92 |
| Social Skills | .90 | .89 | .90 | .91 | .88 | .92 | .93 | .94 | .92 | .94 | .94 | .94 | .94 | .94 | .94 | .95 | .95 | .95 |
| Leadership | — | — | — | — | — | — | .90 | .92 | .88 | .88 | .89 | .87 | .90 | .89 | .90 | .92 | .92 | .91 |
| Study Skills | — | — | — | — | — | — | .91 | .92 | .90 | .90 | .89 | .90 | .95 | .92 | .95 | .96 | .95 | .95 |
| Functional Communication | .87 | .85 | .89 | .87 | .87 | .87 | .87 | .87 | .88 | .88 | .85 | .89 | .87 | .88 | .85 | .90 | .90 | .91 |
| **Content scale** | | | | | | | | | | | | | | | | | | |
| Anger Control | .87 | .87 | .86 | .90 | .90 | .90 | .87 | .89 | .85 | .90 | .87 | .91 | .88 | .83 | .91 | .86 | .88 | .85 |
| Bullying | .78 | .75 | .80 | .79 | .79 | .79 | .89 | .88 | .89 | .90 | .89 | .90 | .91 | .88 | .93 | .91 | .91 | .90 |
| Developmental Social Disorders | .87 | .87 | .87 | .90 | .90 | .90 | .87 | .88 | .86 | .90 | .85 | .91 | .88 | .87 | .90 | .91 | .89 | .92 |
| Emotional Self-Control | .90 | .92 | .87 | .92 | .93 | .92 | .88 | .88 | .89 | .91 | .89 | .92 | .90 | .88 | .92 | .90 | .92 | .86 |
| Executive Functioning | .90 | .90 | .90 | .91 | .92 | .90 | .94 | .94 | .93 | .94 | .93 | .94 | .96 | .95 | .96 | .96 | .96 | .96 |
| Negative Emotionality | .79 | .82 | .76 | .88 | .88 | .89 | .87 | .89 | .86 | .93 | .90 | .93 | .91 | .90 | .92 | .91 | .91 | .91 |
| Resiliency | .81 | .82 | .81 | .87 | .88 | .85 | .92 | .92 | .92 | .92 | .92 | .91 | .92 | .91 | .93 | .95 | .96 | .94 |
| **Clinical index** | | | | | | | | | | | | | | | | | | |
| Clinical Probability Index | .86 | .86 | .85 | .90 | .90 | .90 | — | — | — | — | — | — | — | — | — | — | — | — |
| ADHD Probability Index | — | — | — | — | — | — | .93 | .93 | .91 | .92 | .91 | .93 | .87 | .83 | .88 | .89 | .88 | .88 |
| EBD Probability Index | — | — | — | — | — | — | .91 | .91 | .91 | .93 | .89 | .94 | .94 | .92 | .95 | .94 | .95 | .90 |
| Autism Probability Index | — | — | — | — | — | — | .90 | .91 | .89 | .92 | .89 | .92 | .83 | .81 | .84 | .89 | .88 | .90 |
| Functional Impairment Index | .85 | .82 | .86 | .86 | .86 | .85 | .95 | .95 | .94 | .95 | .94 | .96 | .95 | .94 | .95 | .96 | .96 | .96 |

**Table 9.2** TRS: Coefficient Alpha Reliabilities of Composites, Scales, and Indexes, by Gender and Age, Clinical Norm Samples

| | Preschool | | | Child | | | | | | Adolescent | | | | | | Ages 19–21 |
| | All clinical | | | All clinical | | | ADHD | | | All clinical | | | ADHD | | | |
| | Combined | Female | Male | Combined | Female | Male | Combined | Female | Male | Combined | Female | Male | Combined | Female | Male | Combined |
|---|---|---|---|---|---|---|---|---|---|---|---|---|---|---|---|---|
| **Composite** | | | | | | | | | | | | | | | | |
| Externalizing Problems | .94 | .93 | .94 | .97 | .96 | .97 | .96 | .97 | .96 | .97 | .97 | .97 | .97 | .95 | .97 | .96 |
| Internalizing Problems | .94 | .93 | .95 | .94 | .94 | .94 | .95 | .96 | .94 | .95 | .96 | .94 | .93 | .95 | .92 | .96 |
| School Problems | – | – | – | .95 | .96 | .94 | .95 | .96 | .95 | .94 | .95 | .94 | .93 | .95 | .92 | .96 |
| Adaptive Skills | .93 | .94 | .93 | .97 | .98 | .97 | .96 | .97 | .96 | .97 | .98 | .97 | .97 | .98 | .97 | .98 |
| Behavioral Symptoms Index | .97 | .97 | .97 | .97 | .97 | .97 | .97 | .97 | .97 | .97 | .98 | .97 | .96 | .96 | .96 | .98 |
| **Clinical scale** | | | | | | | | | | | | | | | | |
| Hyperactivity | .89 | .90 | .88 | .94 | .93 | .94 | .93 | .94 | .93 | .93 | .92 | .93 | .94 | .94 | .94 | .90 |
| Aggression | .92 | .86 | .93 | .92 | .89 | .92 | .90 | .91 | .90 | .93 | .91 | .93 | .92 | .83 | .93 | .91 |
| Conduct Problems | – | – | – | .91 | .90 | .92 | .90 | .90 | .90 | .93 | .93 | .93 | .92 | .91 | .92 | .91 |
| Anxiety | .88 | .80 | .91 | .90 | .90 | .90 | .90 | .92 | .90 | .88 | .90 | .88 | .89 | .88 | .89 | .90 |
| Depression | .87 | .83 | .89 | .88 | .83 | .89 | .89 | .90 | .89 | .87 | .87 | .87 | .80 | .86 | .78 | .89 |
| Somatization | .89 | .90 | .89 | .89 | .92 | .86 | .91 | .93 | .88 | .92 | .94 | .90 | .93 | .96 | .90 | .92 |
| Attention Problems | .94 | .96 | .93 | .94 | .94 | .93 | .94 | .94 | .94 | .93 | .94 | .93 | .92 | .94 | .92 | .96 |
| Learning Problems | – | – | – | .90 | .92 | .89 | .91 | .93 | .89 | .86 | .88 | .86 | .83 | .88 | .82 | .91 |
| Atypicality | .91 | .92 | .91 | .86 | .79 | .87 | .80 | .80 | .80 | .88 | .89 | .87 | .85 | .86 | .85 | .89 |
| Withdrawal | .87 | .85 | .88 | .91 | .90 | .92 | .89 | .90 | .89 | .92 | .93 | .91 | .88 | .87 | .88 | .92 |
| **Adaptive scale** | | | | | | | | | | | | | | | | |
| Adaptability | .86 | .85 | .87 | .92 | .92 | .90 | .89 | .90 | .88 | .92 | .92 | .92 | .89 | .91 | .89 | .89 |
| Social Skills | .89 | .87 | .91 | .94 | .94 | .93 | .92 | .90 | .92 | .94 | .94 | .93 | .93 | .95 | .92 | .94 |
| Leadership | – | – | – | .86 | .88 | .85 | .84 | .84 | .84 | .87 | .90 | .86 | .88 | .94 | .85 | .92 |
| Study Skills | – | – | – | .89 | .91 | .88 | .88 | .88 | .88 | .94 | .93 | .93 | .93 | .92 | .93 | .97 |
| Functional Communication | .85 | .89 | .81 | .89 | .90 | .88 | .83 | .87 | .82 | .88 | .90 | .86 | .85 | .93 | .82 | .90 |
| **Content scale** | | | | | | | | | | | | | | | | |
| Anger Control | .91 | .90 | .92 | .91 | .92 | .90 | .88 | .86 | .88 | .92 | .89 | .92 | .89 | .88 | .89 | .91 |
| Bullying | .78 | .75 | .79 | .91 | .88 | .92 | .91 | .89 | .92 | .93 | .93 | .93 | .94 | .94 | .94 | .93 |
| Developmental Social Disorders | .90 | .91 | .90 | .92 | .92 | .92 | .88 | .92 | .86 | .91 | .92 | .91 | .89 | .89 | .89 | .92 |
| Emotional Self-Control | .94 | .93 | .95 | .92 | .92 | .92 | .91 | .91 | .90 | .91 | .91 | .91 | .88 | .92 | .87 | .92 |
| Executive Functioning | .92 | .93 | .91 | .94 | .95 | .93 | .91 | .93 | .91 | .95 | .96 | .95 | .95 | .97 | .95 | .96 |
| Negative Emotionality | .89 | .86 | .90 | .91 | .91 | .91 | .89 | .88 | .90 | .92 | .91 | .92 | .91 | .92 | .90 | .92 |
| Resiliency | .86 | .87 | .85 | .93 | .94 | .92 | .91 | .92 | .90 | .92 | .92 | .91 | .92 | .95 | .91 | .93 |
| **Clinical index** | | | | | | | | | | | | | | | | |
| Clinical Probability Index | .90 | .92 | .88 | – | – | – | – | – | – | – | – | – | – | – | – | – |
| ADHD Probability Index | – | – | – | .92 | .92 | .92 | .91 | .93 | .90 | .85 | .85 | .84 | .87 | .90 | .86 | .87 |
| EBD Probability Index | – | – | – | .92 | .91 | .92 | .91 | .92 | .90 | .95 | .95 | .95 | .94 | .95 | .94 | .95 |
| Autism Probability Index | – | – | – | .91 | .91 | .91 | .88 | .90 | .88 | .89 | .89 | .89 | .84 | .86 | .83 | .89 |
| Functional Impairment Index | .83 | .86 | .81 | .95 | .95 | .95 | .94 | .96 | .93 | .95 | .96 | .94 | .93 | .96 | .92 | .97 |

For the general norm samples, composite scale score reliability coefficients are excellent, largely ranging from the middle to upper .90s. Reliability coefficients of the scores from the individual clinical and adaptive scales are in the good to excellent range, with the large majority of values above .80. The scale scores with the highest reliability coefficients (ranging from the high .80s to middle .90s) are Hyperactivity, Aggression, Conduct Problems, Attention Problems, and Learning Problems—the scales that make up the Externalizing Problems and School Problems composites. Similarly, the Adaptive Skills composite scale scores exhibit high reliability coefficients ranging from the high .80s to middle .90s. Although slightly lower compared to other composites, the reliability coefficients of the scores from the Internalizing Problems scales range from adequate (.70s) to excellent (.90s).

Reliability coefficients for the scores from the content scales range from adequate to excellent; scores on the Developmental Social Disorders, Emotional Self-Control, and Executive Functioning scales have the highest reliability coefficients. Reliability coefficients for the clinical index scores range from good to excellent with most values from the middle .80s and higher.

Reliability coefficients for the clinical norm samples are generally similar to or higher than the reliability coefficients from the general norm sample. Most coefficients are above .80, with composite scale scores and clinical index scores typically in the .90s.

In summary, internal-consistency score reliability coefficients of the BASC–3 TRS composite and scale scores are high and are generally consistent between females and males, clinical and nonclinical groups, and different age levels. This indicates that the composite and scale scores are reliable estimates of their behavioral dimensions.

## EVIDENCE OF TEST–RETEST RELIABILITY

Another method of indicating the consistency of test scores is for a teacher to rate the same child twice over several weeks. In this brief period of time, the child's behavior is unlikely to change much and it should also be long enough to avoid bias from a teacher recalling his or her prior ratings. Therefore, high test–retest reliability indicates that scores are unlikely to change greatly at different times. However, one can expect a teacher's responses to differ somewhat from one occasion to another because the child's most recent behaviors will be uppermost in the teacher's mind, and because some children may actually have altered their behavior between ratings.

At each TRS level (Preschool, Child, and Adolescent), a sample of children was rated twice by the same teacher, with an interval of 7 to 70 days between ratings across the three samples. These samples include both children with clinical diagnoses and children from the general population. Demographic characteristics of the retest samples are shown in Table 9.3 (see chapter 8 for a more complete description of the demographic characteristics).

**Table 9.3** TRS: Demographic Characteristics of Test–Retest Reliability Study Samples

| Characteristic | Preschool | Child | Adolescent |
|---|---|---|---|
| *N* | 72 | 82 | 95 |
| **Age** | | | |
| Mean | 4.3 | 8.7 | 14.9 |
| *SD* | 0.9 | 1.5 | 1.7 |
| Range | 2–5 | 6–11 | 12–18 |
| **Test interval** | | | |
| Mean | 18.0 | 21.7 | 23.3 |
| Range | 7–56 | 7–69 | 7–70 |
| **Mother's education level** | | | |
| 1 | 5.6 | 6.1 | 4.2 |
| 2 | 15.3 | 13.4 | 10.5 |
| 3 | 19.4 | 28.0 | 27.4 |
| 4 | 59.7 | 52.4 | 57.9 |
| **Race/ethnicity** | | | |
| African American | 6.9 | 4.9 | 13.7 |
| Asian | 6.9 | 3.7 | 0 |
| Hispanic | 11.1 | 31.7 | 15.8 |
| Other | 11.1 | 1.2 | 2.1 |
| White | 63.9 | 58.5 | 68.4 |
| **Region** | | | |
| Midwest | 18.1 | 20.7 | 13.7 |
| Northeast | 27.8 | 8.5 | 11.6 |
| South | 38.9 | 35.4 | 54.7 |
| West | 15.3 | 35.4 | 20.0 |
| **Gender** | | | |
| Female | 55.6 | 46.3 | 54.7 |
| Male | 44.4 | 53.7 | 45.3 |

The TRS test–retest stability coefficients, both unadjusted and adjusted for restriction of range, are reported in Tables 9.4, 9.5, and 9.6 for the preschool, child, and adolescent levels, respectively. The general combined-gender norms were used in the analyses. Adjusted correlations remove the biasing effect that results from sampling differences in the variability of scale scores. The raw test–retest correlations were adjusted using the standard deviation at Time 1 relative to the norm-sample standard deviation of 10. The result is a correlation that better reflects what one would expect if the variability of scale scores from the obtained sample better matched that of the population. The tables also report the standard differences (i.e., effect sizes) between the first and second testing. The standard difference was calculated using the mean score difference between the two testing sessions, divided by the pooled standard deviation (Cohen, 1996).

**Table 9.4** TRS: Test–Retest Reliabilities of Composites, Scales, and Indexes, Preschool

| | Preschool | | | | | | |
| | First rating | | Second rating | | | Corrected | Standard |
| | Mean | SD | Mean | SD | r | r | difference |
|---|---|---|---|---|---|---|---|
| **Composite** | | | | | | | |
| Externalizing Problems | 48.0 | 8.0 | 47.6 | 8.2 | .90 | .94 | −0.05 |
| Internalizing Problems | 48.2 | 7.6 | 48.1 | 7.7 | .80 | .88 | −0.01 |
| Adaptive Skills | 54.3 | 9.8 | 54.8 | 11.0 | .91 | .91 | 0.05 |
| Behavioral Symptoms Index | 47.1 | 8.1 | 47.0 | 8.5 | .90 | .93 | −0.01 |
| **Clinical scale** | | | | | | | |
| Hyperactivity | 48.3 | 8.6 | 47.9 | 9.0 | .87 | .90 | −0.05 |
| Aggression | 48.1 | 7.7 | 47.8 | 7.3 | .88 | .93 | −0.04 |
| Anxiety | 49.4 | 7.9 | 48.6 | 7.1 | .71 | .82 | −0.11 |
| Depression | 48.5 | 7.6 | 47.6 | 8.2 | .77 | .87 | −0.11 |
| Somatization | 47.7 | 8.6 | 49.2 | 9.3 | .76 | .82 | 0.17 |
| Attention Problems | 45.4 | 9.2 | 46.0 | 9.2 | .83 | .86 | 0.07 |
| Atypicality | 47.7 | 6.9 | 48.1 | 7.3 | .82 | .91 | 0.06 |
| Withdrawal | 48.8 | 9.3 | 48.9 | 9.1 | .89 | .90 | 0.01 |
| **Adaptive scale** | | | | | | | |
| Adaptability | 54.5 | 9.5 | 55.4 | 10.0 | .77 | .79 | 0.09 |
| Social Skills | 53.6 | 9.8 | 53.6 | 10.7 | .87 | .88 | 0.00 |
| Functional Communication | 53.2 | 10.3 | 53.7 | 11.1 | .92 | .92 | 0.05 |
| **Content scale** | | | | | | | |
| Anger Control | 48.2 | 7.8 | 47.6 | 7.4 | .84 | .90 | −0.08 |
| Bullying | 47.1 | 7.9 | 47.0 | 8.4 | .80 | .88 | −0.01 |
| Developmental Social Disorders | 46.6 | 8.8 | 46.7 | 9.6 | .93 | .95 | 0.01 |
| Emotional Self-Control | 47.6 | 8.5 | 47.0 | 8.3 | .84 | .88 | −0.07 |
| Executive Functioning | 46.7 | 9.1 | 46.4 | 9.5 | .87 | .89 | −0.03 |
| Negative Emotionality | 48.6 | 8.9 | 47.5 | 8.2 | .78 | .83 | −0.13 |
| Resiliency | 54.4 | 9.4 | 54.3 | 9.6 | .81 | .83 | −0.01 |
| **Clinical index** | | | | | | | |
| Clinical Probability Index | 46.9 | 9.2 | 47.2 | 9.7 | .88 | .90 | 0.03 |
| Functional Impairment Index | 46.3 | 10.2 | 46.4 | 10.4 | .93 | .93 | 0.01 |

**Table 9.5** TRS: Test–Retest Reliabilities of Composites, Scales, and Indexes, Child

| | Child | | | | | | |
| --- | --- | --- | --- | --- | --- | --- | --- |
| | First rating | | Second rating | | | Corrected | Standard |
| | Mean | SD | Mean | SD | r | r | difference |
| **Composite** | | | | | | | |
| Externalizing Problems | 49.0 | 9.0 | 49.2 | 9.2 | .82 | .85 | 0.02 |
| Internalizing Problems | 50.5 | 10.9 | 50.6 | 11.2 | .81 | .77 | 0.01 |
| School Problems | 47.5 | 9.3 | 47.9 | 9.9 | .90 | .91 | 0.04 |
| Adaptive Skills | 51.7 | 9.6 | 51.4 | 10.9 | .86 | .87 | −0.03 |
| Behavioral Symptoms Index | 49.0 | 9.3 | 49.1 | 9.5 | .86 | .88 | 0.01 |
| **Clinical scale** | | | | | | | |
| Hyperactivity | 49.0 | 8.7 | 48.8 | 9.0 | .82 | .86 | −0.02 |
| Aggression | 48.8 | 8.9 | 48.9 | 8.5 | .81 | .85 | 0.01 |
| Conduct Problems | 48.8 | 9.2 | 49.6 | 10.2 | .82 | .85 | 0.08 |
| Anxiety | 51.8 | 13.0 | 51.1 | 10.8 | .86 | .76 | −0.06 |
| Depression | 49.3 | 7.9 | 49.8 | 8.8 | .77 | .86 | 0.06 |
| Somatization | 50.1 | 10.2 | 50.5 | 12.4 | .66 | .65 | 0.04 |
| Attention Problems | 47.8 | 10.0 | 48.4 | 10.3 | .90 | .90 | 0.06 |
| Learning Problems | 47.5 | 8.2 | 47.7 | 8.6 | .87 | .91 | 0.02 |
| Atypicality | 50.1 | 11.3 | 50.3 | 10.1 | .89 | .86 | 0.02 |
| Withdrawal | 49.8 | 9.1 | 49.1 | 9.4 | .75 | .79 | −0.08 |
| **Adaptive scale** | | | | | | | |
| Adaptability | 51.0 | 9.6 | 50.5 | 10.3 | .81 | .82 | −0.05 |
| Social Skills | 50.7 | 10.1 | 50.6 | 11.1 | .85 | .85 | −0.01 |
| Leadership | 51.7 | 9.5 | 51.4 | 11.0 | .79 | .81 | −0.03 |
| Study Skills | 51.8 | 9.6 | 52.1 | 10.9 | .83 | .84 | 0.03 |
| Functional Communication | 52.0 | 9.5 | 51.5 | 10.0 | .86 | .87 | −0.05 |
| **Content scale** | | | | | | | |
| Anger Control | 49.1 | 8.6 | 48.6 | 7.8 | .77 | .83 | −0.06 |
| Bullying | 48.7 | 9.2 | 49.3 | 9.2 | .76 | .80 | 0.07 |
| Developmental Social Disorders | 48.6 | 9.5 | 48.4 | 10.0 | .86 | .87 | −0.02 |
| Emotional Self-Control | 49.5 | 8.9 | 48.8 | 8.4 | .83 | .87 | −0.08 |
| Executive Functioning | 48.2 | 9.5 | 47.6 | 10.6 | .86 | .87 | −0.06 |
| Negative Emotionality | 49.8 | 8.4 | 49.8 | 9.4 | .83 | .88 | 0.00 |
| Resiliency | 51.8 | 10.0 | 51.6 | 10.5 | .84 | .84 | −0.02 |
| **Clinical index** | | | | | | | |
| ADHD Probability Index | 48.1 | 9.5 | 48.3 | 10.2 | .85 | .86 | 0.02 |
| EBD Probability Index | 48.5 | 8.6 | 49.0 | 9.2 | .81 | .86 | 0.06 |
| Autism Probability Index | 48.7 | 9.8 | 49.1 | 10.4 | .85 | .86 | 0.04 |
| Functional Impairment Index | 48.2 | 9.3 | 48.4 | 9.9 | .88 | .90 | 0.02 |

**Table 9.6** TRS: Test–Retest Reliabilities of Composites, Scales, and Indexes, Adolescent

| | Adolescent | | | | | | |
| | First rating | | Second rating | | | Corrected | Standard |
| | Mean | SD | Mean | SD | r | r | difference |
|---|---|---|---|---|---|---|---|
| **Composite** | | | | | | | |
| Externalizing Problems | 47.9 | 8.0 | 47.6 | 7.7 | .80 | .87 | −0.04 |
| Internalizing Problems | 48.0 | 7.7 | 47.5 | 7.3 | .76 | .86 | −0.07 |
| School Problems | 46.5 | 7.8 | 46.2 | 7.9 | .90 | .94 | −0.04 |
| Adaptive Skills | 53.8 | 9.2 | 54.5 | 9.4 | .90 | .92 | 0.08 |
| Behavioral Symptoms Index | 47.0 | 7.8 | 46.4 | 7.5 | .86 | .91 | −0.08 |
| **Clinical scale** | | | | | | | |
| Hyperactivity | 48.7 | 8.4 | 48.3 | 8.0 | .76 | .83 | −0.05 |
| Aggression | 47.6 | 7.1 | 47.9 | 7.3 | .77 | .88 | 0.04 |
| Conduct Problems | 47.8 | 8.1 | 47.4 | 7.5 | .76 | .84 | −0.05 |
| Anxiety | 48.1 | 7.4 | 47.8 | 7.3 | .66 | .81 | −0.04 |
| Depression | 47.1 | 6.6 | 46.7 | 6.5 | .75 | .89 | −0.06 |
| Somatization | 49.1 | 9.5 | 48.5 | 8.6 | .81 | .83 | −0.07 |
| Attention Problems | 46.7 | 8.5 | 46.5 | 8.8 | .89 | .92 | −0.02 |
| Learning Problems | 46.7 | 7.4 | 46.2 | 7.4 | .87 | .93 | −0.07 |
| Atypicality | 47.9 | 8.2 | 47.2 | 7.2 | .85 | .90 | −0.09 |
| Withdrawal | 47.1 | 7.5 | 46.8 | 7.9 | .85 | .92 | −0.04 |
| **Adaptive scale** | | | | | | | |
| Adaptability | 53.4 | 8.8 | 54.3 | 9.2 | .77 | .82 | 0.10 |
| Social Skills | 53.6 | 9.1 | 54.2 | 9.3 | .85 | .88 | 0.07 |
| Leadership | 53.8 | 8.9 | 54.4 | 9.5 | .86 | .89 | 0.07 |
| Study Skills | 53.3 | 9.4 | 54.2 | 9.6 | .88 | .89 | 0.09 |
| Functional Communication | 52.5 | 9.9 | 53.0 | 9.0 | .88 | .88 | 0.05 |
| **Content scale** | | | | | | | |
| Anger Control | 47.7 | 6.3 | 47.9 | 7.1 | .74 | .90 | 0.03 |
| Bullying | 48.3 | 7.6 | 47.9 | 7.0 | .75 | .86 | −0.05 |
| Developmental Social Disorders | 46.6 | 9.0 | 46.1 | 8.6 | .86 | .89 | −0.06 |
| Emotional Self-Control | 47.3 | 6.6 | 47.6 | 7.2 | .72 | .88 | 0.04 |
| Executive Functioning | 46.2 | 8.6 | 45.7 | 9.0 | .87 | .90 | −0.06 |
| Negative Emotionality | 47.7 | 7.4 | 47.3 | 7.5 | .78 | .88 | −0.05 |
| Resiliency | 53.8 | 8.8 | 54.1 | 9.2 | .84 | .88 | 0.03 |
| **Clinical index** | | | | | | | |
| ADHD Probability Index | 47.1 | 9.0 | 46.1 | 8.8 | .85 | .88 | −0.11 |
| EBD Probability Index | 46.8 | 7.2 | 46.4 | 6.9 | .81 | .90 | −0.06 |
| Autism Probability Index | 46.5 | 8.8 | 45.9 | 8.6 | .83 | .87 | −0.07 |
| Functional Impairment Index | 46.6 | 8.6 | 46.1 | 8.7 | .89 | .92 | −0.06 |

Test–retest stability coefficients for the various scale scores generally possess adequate stability across time for all scale types and levels, with most corrected stability coefficients in the middle .80s or higher. Mean scores between administrations are very similar, with most effect sizes under .10, indicating very stable performance across the testing interval.

# EVIDENCE OF INTERRATER RELIABILITY

The third type of reliability evaluated for the TRS is the agreement of scores obtained from different raters who provided ratings at about the same point in time. This type of reliability indicates the level of agreement in teachers' perceptions of a child's behavior and the degree to which they interpret TRS items similarly. At least three factors can cause the relationship between two teachers' ratings to be weaker than the relationship between ratings given by one teacher at two points in time. First, teachers may have different interpretations of items. Second, they may perceive the intensity of behaviors differently. Finally, the child's behavior may vary in different settings or in the presence of different teachers, just as behavior often varies when a child or adolescent is with one parent or the other.

An interrater reliability study was done at each age level of the TRS. Each child included in the study was rated by two different teachers. Table 9.7 presents the demographic characteristics of the TRS interrater reliability studies (see chapter 8 for a more complete description of the demographic characteristics). The period between teacher ratings ranged from 0 to 70 days across all three age levels.

**Table 9.7** TRS: Demographic Characteristics of Interrater Reliability Study Samples

| Characteristic | Preschool | Child | Adolescent |
|---|---|---|---|
| *N* | 71 | 116 | 80 |
| **Age** | | | |
| Mean | 4.2 | 9.1 | 14.9 |
| *SD* | 1.1 | 1.7 | 2.0 |
| Range | 2–5 | 6–11 | 12–18 |
| **Test interval** | | | |
| Mean | 12.3 | 17.2 | 14.5 |
| Range | 0–58 | 0–70 | 0–61 |
| **Mother's education level** | | | |
| 1 | 7.0 | 5.2 | 5.0 |
| 2 | 19.7 | 12.1 | 5.0 |
| 3 | 19.7 | 23.3 | 27.5 |
| 4 | 53.5 | 59.5 | 62.5 |
| **Race/ethnicity** | | | |
| African American | 12.7 | 10.3 | 12.5 |
| Asian | 4.2 | 0.9 | 5.0 |
| Hispanic | 16.9 | 23.3 | 12.5 |
| Other | 8.5 | 2.6 | 3.8 |
| White | 57.7 | 62.9 | 66.3 |
| **Region** | | | |
| Midwest | 16.9 | 11.2 | 15.0 |
| Northeast | 21.1 | 11.2 | 12.5 |
| South | 50.7 | 62.9 | 52.5 |
| West | 11.3 | 14.7 | 20.0 |
| **Gender** | | | |
| Female | 50.7 | 50.9 | 45.0 |
| Male | 49.3 | 49.1 | 55.0 |

Tables 9.8, 9.9, and 9.10 show the interrater reliabilities, corrected for restriction of range, for scale scores from the preschool, child, and adolescent levels. Both unadjusted and adjusted correlations are presented. In general, interrater correlations are lower than the estimates obtained in the coefficient alpha and test–retest reliability studies. The range of reliabilities among scale scores varies widely across all TRS levels, a result that is consistent with the findings in previous

BASC editions (Reynolds & Kamphaus, 1992, 2004). Most reliability coefficients are in the .60s or higher across the preschool, child, and adolescent levels, results that are higher than interrater reliability estimates found on other rating scale instruments (Youngstrom, Loeber, & Stouthamer-Loeber, 2000).

**Table 9.8** TRS: Interrater Reliabilities of Composites, Scales, and Indexes, Preschool

| | Preschool | | | | | | |
| | First teacher | | Second teacher | | | Corrected | Standard |
| | Mean | SD | Mean | SD | r | r | difference |
|---|---|---|---|---|---|---|---|
| **Composite** | | | | | | | |
| Externalizing Problems | 47.9 | 8.7 | 48.7 | 9.6 | .64 | .73 | 0.09 |
| Internalizing Problems | 49.8 | 8.6 | 51.0 | 11.7 | .41 | .56 | 0.12 |
| Adaptive Skills | 52.3 | 9.3 | 52.6 | 10.2 | .80 | .83 | 0.03 |
| Behavioral Symptoms Index | 48.1 | 8.2 | 49.1 | 10.1 | .57 | .71 | 0.11 |
| **Clinical scale** | | | | | | | |
| Hyperactivity | 48.0 | 8.4 | 49.5 | 9.9 | .58 | .70 | 0.16 |
| Aggression | 48.3 | 8.7 | 48.5 | 8.9 | .67 | .75 | 0.02 |
| Anxiety | 49.3 | 8.1 | 51.2 | 12.1 | .37 | .59 | 0.18 |
| Depression | 50.3 | 8.0 | 50.0 | 10.0 | .53 | .70 | −0.03 |
| Somatization | 49.5 | 9.5 | 51.4 | 11.7 | .36 | .42 | 0.18 |
| Attention Problems | 47.4 | 10.1 | 48.5 | 10.6 | .63 | .62 | 0.11 |
| Atypicality | 48.0 | 6.8 | 49.7 | 9.5 | .38 | .71 | 0.21 |
| Withdrawal | 49.2 | 8.6 | 50.2 | 10.4 | .59 | .70 | 0.10 |
| **Adaptive scale** | | | | | | | |
| Adaptability | 52.4 | 9.2 | 52.0 | 9.5 | .64 | .70 | −0.04 |
| Social Skills | 50.8 | 9.2 | 52.0 | 10.3 | .71 | .75 | 0.12 |
| Functional Communication | 52.8 | 9.3 | 52.7 | 10.5 | .80 | .83 | −0.01 |
| **Content scale** | | | | | | | |
| Anger Control | 48.8 | 8.5 | 49.2 | 9.1 | .58 | .70 | 0.05 |
| Bullying | 48.6 | 9.3 | 48.5 | 9.0 | .72 | .76 | −0.01 |
| Developmental Social Disorders | 47.4 | 8.3 | 48.5 | 9.4 | .63 | .75 | 0.12 |
| Emotional Self-Control | 48.7 | 8.2 | 49.3 | 9.4 | .58 | .72 | 0.07 |
| Executive Functioning | 48.0 | 9.1 | 48.8 | 10.0 | .66 | .72 | 0.08 |
| Negative Emotionality | 50.4 | 9.2 | 50.8 | 10.1 | .52 | .59 | 0.04 |
| Resiliency | 52.1 | 9.1 | 52.0 | 9.4 | .58 | .65 | −0.01 |
| **Clinical index** | | | | | | | |
| Clinical Probability Index | 47.8 | 8.8 | 48.8 | 9.6 | .66 | .74 | 0.11 |
| Functional Impairment Index | 47.0 | 9.6 | 47.5 | 10.5 | .77 | .79 | 0.05 |

**Table 9.9** TRS: Interrater Reliabilities of Composites, Scales, and Indexes, Child

| | Child | | | | | | |
| --- | --- | --- | --- | --- | --- | --- | --- |
| | First teacher | | Second teacher | | | Corrected | Standard |
| | Mean | SD | Mean | SD | r | r | difference |
| **Composite** | | | | | | | |
| Externalizing Problems | 48.4 | 8.1 | 48.3 | 8.3 | .59 | .73 | −0.01 |
| Internalizing Problems | 48.9 | 9.9 | 49.1 | 9.1 | .36 | .37 | 0.02 |
| School Problems | 47.0 | 9.9 | 47.1 | 10.0 | .69 | .70 | 0.01 |
| Adaptive Skills | 52.8 | 10.5 | 51.9 | 11.3 | .70 | .67 | −0.08 |
| Behavioral Symptoms Index | 48.1 | 9.8 | 48.5 | 9.2 | .67 | .68 | 0.04 |
| **Clinical scale** | | | | | | | |
| Hyperactivity | 48.9 | 8.5 | 48.5 | 8.0 | .56 | .68 | −0.05 |
| Aggression | 48.1 | 8.0 | 48.6 | 8.7 | .56 | .72 | 0.06 |
| Conduct Problems | 48.0 | 7.3 | 47.9 | 8.3 | .59 | .78 | −0.01 |
| Anxiety | 49.3 | 10.2 | 50.0 | 8.3 | .35 | .32 | 0.08 |
| Depression | 48.4 | 9.4 | 48.8 | 8.4 | .59 | .64 | 0.04 |
| Somatization | 49.6 | 8.1 | 48.5 | 7.9 | .23 | .49 | −0.14 |
| Attention Problems | 47.6 | 10.4 | 47.8 | 9.6 | .66 | .63 | 0.02 |
| Learning Problems | 46.9 | 8.7 | 47.0 | 10.0 | .63 | .72 | 0.01 |
| Atypicality | 49.5 | 10.4 | 49.8 | 10.2 | .69 | .66 | 0.03 |
| Withdrawal | 48.5 | 9.2 | 49.3 | 10.6 | .52 | .59 | 0.08 |
| **Adaptive scale** | | | | | | | |
| Adaptability | 52.4 | 10.4 | 51.7 | 10.5 | .57 | .53 | −0.07 |
| Social Skills | 51.1 | 10.6 | 51.3 | 10.9 | .56 | .51 | 0.02 |
| Leadership | 52.7 | 10.7 | 52.1 | 11.2 | .58 | .52 | −0.05 |
| Study Skills | 52.5 | 10.1 | 52.0 | 10.8 | .62 | .61 | −0.05 |
| Functional Communication | 52.6 | 10.3 | 51.6 | 10.3 | .64 | .62 | −0.10 |
| **Content scale** | | | | | | | |
| Anger Control | 48.3 | 8.4 | 49.0 | 9.0 | .62 | .73 | 0.08 |
| Bullying | 47.9 | 7.5 | 48.3 | 7.9 | .57 | .76 | 0.05 |
| Developmental Social Disorders | 48.0 | 10.3 | 49.0 | 11.0 | .68 | .66 | 0.09 |
| Emotional Self-Control | 48.5 | 9.4 | 49.2 | 9.6 | .66 | .70 | 0.07 |
| Executive Functioning | 47.5 | 10.4 | 47.8 | 10.5 | .67 | .64 | 0.03 |
| Negative Emotionality | 48.4 | 8.5 | 49.0 | 8.2 | .56 | .68 | 0.07 |
| Resiliency | 53.2 | 10.7 | 52.3 | 11.2 | .60 | .54 | −0.08 |
| **Clinical index** | | | | | | | |
| ADHD Probability Index | 47.7 | 10.6 | 47.9 | 10.0 | .67 | .63 | 0.02 |
| EBD Probability Index | 47.8 | 8.5 | 48.1 | 8.3 | .58 | .70 | 0.04 |
| Autism Probability Index | 48.3 | 11.1 | 48.7 | 11.3 | .69 | .62 | 0.04 |
| Functional Impairment Index | 47.5 | 10.6 | 48.0 | 10.5 | .73 | .70 | 0.05 |

**Table 9.10** TRS: Interrater Reliabilities of Composites, Scales, and Indexes, Adolescent

| | Adolescent | | | | | | |
| | First teacher | | Second teacher | | | Corrected | Standard |
| | Mean | SD | Mean | SD | r | r | difference |
|---|---|---|---|---|---|---|---|
| **Composite** | | | | | | | |
| Externalizing Problems | 47.1 | 7.4 | 47.3 | 6.6 | .46 | .70 | 0.03 |
| Internalizing Problems | 46.8 | 7.6 | 47.0 | 6.9 | .44 | .68 | 0.03 |
| School Problems | 45.3 | 7.6 | 46.3 | 8.6 | .60 | .77 | 0.12 |
| Adaptive Skills | 55.2 | 9.1 | 53.7 | 9.4 | .57 | .64 | −0.16 |
| Behavioral Symptoms Index | 46.2 | 7.6 | 46.6 | 7.5 | .46 | .69 | 0.05 |
| **Clinical scale** | | | | | | | |
| Hyperactivity | 47.9 | 7.7 | 48.5 | 7.3 | .29 | .58 | 0.08 |
| Aggression | 47.0 | 6.7 | 47.0 | 6.4 | .55 | .80 | 0.00 |
| Conduct Problems | 47.2 | 8.0 | 47.0 | 6.8 | .47 | .66 | −0.03 |
| Anxiety | 47.1 | 8.0 | 46.9 | 8.0 | .43 | .64 | −0.03 |
| Depression | 46.1 | 6.0 | 46.7 | 6.7 | .55 | .84 | 0.09 |
| Somatization | 46.9 | 5.2 | 48.1 | 7.0 | .41 | .84 | 0.19 |
| Attention Problems | 45.7 | 8.2 | 47.0 | 9.0 | .52 | .68 | 0.15 |
| Learning Problems | 45.3 | 7.1 | 46.0 | 8.1 | .65 | .82 | 0.09 |
| Atypicality | 47.7 | 8.2 | 47.8 | 8.4 | .32 | .54 | 0.01 |
| Withdrawal | 46.8 | 7.2 | 46.5 | 8.4 | .67 | .83 | −0.04 |
| **Adaptive scale** | | | | | | | |
| Adaptability | 54.6 | 8.9 | 52.8 | 9.0 | .49 | .60 | −0.20 |
| Social Skills | 54.6 | 9.2 | 53.6 | 9.4 | .57 | .64 | −0.11 |
| Leadership | 55.2 | 9.7 | 53.3 | 9.4 | .54 | .57 | −0.20 |
| Study Skills | 54.8 | 8.8 | 53.5 | 10.2 | .56 | .66 | −0.14 |
| Functional Communication | 53.9 | 8.8 | 53.3 | 8.9 | .53 | .64 | −0.07 |
| **Content scale** | | | | | | | |
| Anger Control | 47.2 | 7.8 | 47.5 | 7.3 | .57 | .74 | 0.04 |
| Bullying | 47.7 | 7.1 | 47.1 | 6.8 | .44 | .72 | −0.09 |
| Developmental Social Disorders | 45.8 | 8.6 | 46.3 | 8.8 | .50 | .63 | 0.06 |
| Emotional Self-Control | 46.6 | 7.4 | 47.2 | 7.1 | .43 | .69 | 0.08 |
| Executive Functioning | 44.7 | 9.1 | 46.5 | 9.3 | .56 | .64 | 0.20 |
| Negative Emotionality | 47.0 | 8.0 | 47.1 | 8.4 | .56 | .72 | 0.01 |
| Resiliency | 55.4 | 9.9 | 53.3 | 9.0 | .46 | .47 | −0.22 |
| **Clinical index** | | | | | | | |
| ADHD Probability Index | 46.0 | 8.6 | 47.6 | 9.2 | .52 | .64 | 0.18 |
| EBD Probability Index | 46.2 | 7.9 | 45.8 | 6.8 | .57 | .73 | −0.05 |
| Autism Probability Index | 45.8 | 8.7 | 46.9 | 9.6 | .46 | .59 | 0.12 |
| Functional Impairment Index | 45.1 | 8.3 | 45.9 | 8.5 | .61 | .73 | 0.10 |

## STANDARD ERRORS OF MEASUREMENT AND CONFIDENCE INTERVALS

The standard error of measurement *(SEM)* of a test score represents the average amount by which observed scores differ from true scores. The true score, which can never be known with certainty, is the score that would be obtained with a perfectly accurate measuring instrument. The *SEM,* therefore, helps the clinician understand how much error is associated with any observed score. The *SEM* in *T*-score units on each BASC–3 composite and scale (based on internal-consistency reliabilities) is presented in Table 9.11 for the general norm samples and in Table 9.12 for the clinical norm samples. Composite and scale scores with higher reliability coefficients have smaller *SEM*s; the pattern of *SEM*s replicates the pattern of reliability coefficients shown in Tables 9.1 and 9.2. *SEM*s for composite scores are generally 3 or less, while *SEM*s for the other scale scores are generally less than 4.

**Table 9.11** TRS: *T*-Score Standard Errors of Measurement of Composites, Scales, and Indexes, by Gender and Age, General Norm Samples

| | Preschool | | | | | | | Child | | | | | | |
| --- | --- | --- | --- | --- | --- | --- | --- | --- | --- | --- | --- | --- | --- | --- |
| | Ages 2–3 | | | Ages 4–5 | | | Ages 2–5 | Ages 6–7 | | | Ages 8–11 | | | Ages 6–11 |
| | Combined | Female | Male | Combined | Female | Male | Combined total | Combined | Female | Male | Combined | Female | Male | Combined total |
| **Composite** | | | | | | | | | | | | | | |
| Externalizing Problems | 2.45 | 2.45 | 2.65 | 2.24 | 2.24 | 2.24 | 2.35 | 2.00 | 1.73 | 2.00 | 2.00 | 2.24 | 1.73 | 2.00 |
| Internalizing Problems | 3.32 | 3.16 | 3.74 | 2.83 | 2.65 | 2.83 | 3.08 | 2.65 | 2.65 | 2.65 | 2.83 | 2.83 | 2.65 | 2.74 |
| School Problems | — | — | — | — | — | — | — | 2.00 | 2.00 | 2.00 | 2.24 | 2.45 | 2.24 | 2.12 |
| Adaptive Skills | 2.24 | 2.45 | 2.24 | 2.24 | 2.24 | 2.24 | 2.24 | 1.73 | 1.41 | 1.73 | 1.73 | 1.73 | 1.73 | 1.73 |
| Behavioral Symptoms Index | 2.00 | 2.00 | 2.24 | 1.73 | 1.73 | 1.73 | 1.87 | 1.73 | 1.73 | 2.00 | 1.73 | 2.00 | 1.41 | 1.73 |
| **Clinical scale** | | | | | | | | | | | | | | |
| Hyperactivity | 3.32 | 3.32 | 3.46 | 3.16 | 3.32 | 3.32 | 3.24 | 2.45 | 2.45 | 2.45 | 2.65 | 3.16 | 2.45 | 2.55 |
| Aggression | 3.32 | 3.46 | 3.32 | 3.00 | 3.00 | 2.83 | 3.16 | 3.16 | 3.16 | 3.16 | 3.16 | 3.46 | 3.16 | 3.16 |
| Conduct Problems | — | — | — | — | — | — | — | 3.32 | 3.16 | 3.32 | 3.16 | 3.61 | 3.00 | 3.24 |
| Anxiety | 4.80 | 5.00 | 4.58 | 4.36 | 4.47 | 4.36 | 4.59 | 3.74 | 3.46 | 4.00 | 3.74 | 3.87 | 3.74 | 3.74 |
| Depression | 4.47 | 4.00 | 5.00 | 3.61 | 3.46 | 3.87 | 4.06 | 4.00 | 4.24 | 3.74 | 3.74 | 4.12 | 3.46 | 3.87 |
| Somatization | 4.69 | 4.47 | 5.00 | 3.87 | 3.74 | 3.87 | 4.30 | 3.46 | 3.61 | 3.32 | 3.61 | 3.46 | 4.00 | 3.54 |
| Attention Problems | 3.61 | 3.74 | 3.46 | 2.65 | 2.65 | 2.83 | 3.17 | 2.45 | 2.65 | 2.24 | 2.45 | 2.65 | 2.45 | 2.45 |
| Learning Problems | — | — | — | — | — | — | — | 2.83 | 2.83 | 2.65 | 3.32 | 3.46 | 3.16 | 3.08 |
| Atypicality | 3.61 | 3.16 | 4.00 | 3.16 | 3.00 | 3.32 | 3.39 | 3.87 | 3.87 | 4.00 | 3.61 | 5.20 | 3.16 | 3.74 |
| Withdrawal | 4.69 | 4.90 | 4.58 | 4.24 | 4.47 | 4.00 | 4.47 | 4.36 | 4.24 | 4.47 | 3.16 | 3.87 | 2.83 | 3.81 |
| **Adaptive scale** | | | | | | | | | | | | | | |
| Adaptability | 3.46 | 3.46 | 3.61 | 3.32 | 3.32 | 3.46 | 3.39 | 3.32 | 3.32 | 3.16 | 3.16 | 3.61 | 3.16 | 3.24 |
| Social Skills | 3.16 | 3.32 | 3.16 | 3.00 | 3.46 | 2.83 | 3.08 | 2.65 | 2.45 | 2.83 | 2.45 | 2.45 | 2.45 | 2.55 |
| Leadership | — | — | — | — | — | — | — | 3.16 | 2.83 | 3.46 | 3.46 | 3.32 | 3.61 | 3.31 |
| Study Skills | — | — | — | — | — | — | — | 3.00 | 2.83 | 3.16 | 3.16 | 3.32 | 3.16 | 3.08 |
| Functional Communication | 3.61 | 3.87 | 3.32 | 3.61 | 3.61 | 3.61 | 3.61 | 3.61 | 3.61 | 3.46 | 3.46 | 3.87 | 3.32 | 3.54 |
| **Content scale** | | | | | | | | | | | | | | |
| Anger Control | 3.61 | 3.61 | 3.74 | 3.16 | 3.16 | 3.16 | 3.39 | 3.61 | 3.32 | 3.87 | 3.16 | 3.61 | 3.00 | 3.39 |
| Bullying | 4.69 | 5.00 | 4.47 | 4.58 | 4.58 | 4.58 | 4.64 | 3.32 | 3.46 | 3.32 | 3.16 | 3.32 | 3.16 | 3.24 |
| Developmental Social Disorders | 3.61 | 3.61 | 3.61 | 3.16 | 3.16 | 3.16 | 3.39 | 3.61 | 3.46 | 3.74 | 3.16 | 3.87 | 3.00 | 3.39 |
| Emotional Self-Control | 3.16 | 2.83 | 3.61 | 2.83 | 2.65 | 2.83 | 3.00 | 3.46 | 3.46 | 3.32 | 3.00 | 3.32 | 2.83 | 3.24 |
| Executive Functioning | 3.16 | 3.16 | 3.16 | 3.00 | 2.83 | 3.16 | 3.08 | 2.45 | 2.45 | 2.65 | 2.45 | 2.65 | 2.45 | 2.45 |
| Negative Emotionality | 4.58 | 4.24 | 4.90 | 3.46 | 3.46 | 3.32 | 4.06 | 3.61 | 3.32 | 3.74 | 2.65 | 3.16 | 2.65 | 3.17 |
| Resiliency | 4.36 | 4.24 | 4.36 | 3.61 | 3.46 | 3.87 | 4.00 | 2.83 | 2.83 | 2.83 | 2.83 | 2.83 | 3.00 | 2.83 |
| **Clinical index** | | | | | | | | | | | | | | |
| Clinical Probability Index | 3.74 | 3.74 | 3.87 | 3.16 | 3.16 | 3.16 | 3.46 | — | — | — | — | — | — | — |
| ADHD Probability Index | — | — | — | — | — | — | — | 2.65 | 2.65 | 3.00 | 2.83 | 3.00 | 2.65 | 2.74 |
| EBD Probability Index | — | — | — | — | — | — | — | 3.00 | 3.00 | 3.00 | 2.65 | 3.32 | 2.45 | 2.83 |
| Autism Probability Index | — | — | — | — | — | — | — | 3.16 | 3.00 | 3.32 | 2.83 | 3.32 | 2.83 | 3.00 |
| Functional Impairment Index | 3.87 | 4.24 | 3.74 | 3.74 | 3.74 | 3.87 | 3.81 | 2.24 | 2.24 | 2.45 | 2.24 | 2.45 | 2.00 | 2.24 |

**Table 9.11** TRS: *T*-Score Standard Errors of Measurement of Composites, Scales, and Indexes, by Gender and Age, General Norm Samples (*continued*)

| | Adolescent | | | | | | |
| | Ages 12–14 | | | Ages 15–18 | | | Ages 12–18 |
| | Combined | Female | Male | Combined | Female | Male | Combined total |
|---|---|---|---|---|---|---|---|
| **Composite** | | | | | | | |
| Externalizing Problems | 1.73 | 2.24 | 1.73 | 1.73 | 1.73 | 2.00 | 1.73 |
| Internalizing Problems | 2.65 | 2.45 | 2.83 | 2.24 | 2.00 | 2.45 | 2.45 |
| School Problems | 2.45 | 2.65 | 2.24 | 2.00 | 2.00 | 2.24 | 2.24 |
| Adaptive Skills | 1.41 | 1.73 | 1.41 | 1.41 | 1.41 | 1.41 | 1.41 |
| Behavioral Symptoms Index | 1.73 | 2.00 | 1.73 | 1.41 | 1.41 | 1.73 | 1.58 |
| **Clinical scale** | | | | | | | |
| Hyperactivity | 2.65 | 3.32 | 2.45 | 2.83 | 2.83 | 3.00 | 2.74 |
| Aggression | 3.00 | 3.87 | 2.65 | 3.00 | 2.83 | 3.16 | 3.00 |
| Conduct Problems | 3.00 | 3.00 | 2.83 | 2.83 | 2.45 | 3.00 | 2.92 |
| Anxiety | 3.87 | 3.87 | 3.87 | 3.32 | 3.00 | 3.61 | 3.61 |
| Depression | 4.12 | 4.00 | 4.36 | 3.46 | 3.32 | 3.46 | 3.80 |
| Somatization | 3.16 | 3.00 | 3.46 | 3.87 | 3.74 | 3.87 | 3.53 |
| Attention Problems | 2.45 | 3.00 | 2.24 | 2.45 | 2.45 | 2.45 | 2.45 |
| Learning Problems | 3.74 | 4.00 | 3.46 | 3.16 | 3.16 | 3.32 | 3.46 |
| Atypicality | 3.74 | 4.12 | 3.46 | 3.32 | 3.32 | 3.32 | 3.54 |
| Withdrawal | 3.61 | 3.46 | 3.74 | 3.32 | 3.87 | 3.00 | 3.47 |
| **Adaptive scale** | | | | | | | |
| Adaptability | 3.32 | 3.61 | 3.16 | 2.83 | 2.65 | 2.83 | 3.08 |
| Social Skills | 2.45 | 2.45 | 2.45 | 2.24 | 2.24 | 2.24 | 2.35 |
| Leadership | 3.16 | 3.32 | 3.16 | 2.83 | 2.83 | 3.00 | 3.00 |
| Study Skills | 2.24 | 2.83 | 2.24 | 2.00 | 2.24 | 2.24 | 2.12 |
| Functional Communication | 3.61 | 3.46 | 3.87 | 3.16 | 3.16 | 3.00 | 3.39 |
| **Content scale** | | | | | | | |
| Anger Control | 3.46 | 4.12 | 3.00 | 3.74 | 3.46 | 3.87 | 3.60 |
| Bullying | 3.00 | 3.46 | 2.65 | 3.00 | 3.00 | 3.16 | 3.00 |
| Developmental Social Disorders | 3.46 | 3.61 | 3.16 | 3.00 | 3.32 | 2.83 | 3.24 |
| Emotional Self-Control | 3.16 | 3.46 | 2.83 | 3.16 | 2.83 | 3.74 | 3.16 |
| Executive Functioning | 2.00 | 2.24 | 2.00 | 2.00 | 2.00 | 2.00 | 2.00 |
| Negative Emotionality | 3.00 | 3.16 | 2.83 | 3.00 | 3.00 | 3.00 | 3.00 |
| Resiliency | 2.83 | 3.00 | 2.65 | 2.24 | 2.00 | 2.45 | 2.55 |
| **Clinical index** | | | | | | | |
| Clinical Probability Index | — | — | — | — | — | — | — |
| ADHD Probability Index | 3.61 | 4.12 | 3.46 | 3.32 | 3.46 | 3.46 | 3.47 |
| EBD Probability Index | 2.45 | 2.83 | 2.24 | 2.45 | 2.24 | 2.45 | 2.45 |
| Autism Probability Index | 4.12 | 4.36 | 4.00 | 3.32 | 3.46 | 3.16 | 3.74 |
| Functional Impairment Index | 2.24 | 2.45 | 2.24 | 2.00 | 2.00 | 2.00 | 2.12 |

# Table 9.12 TRS: *T*-Score Standard Errors of Measurement of Composites, Scales, and Indexes, by Gender and Age, Clinical Norm Samples

| | Preschool | | | Child | | | | | | Adolescent | | | | | |
| | All clinical | | | All clinical | | | ADHD | | | All clinical | | | ADHD | | |
| | Combined | Female | Male | Combined | Female | Male | Combined | Female | Male | Combined | Female | Male | Combined | Female | Male |
|---|---|---|---|---|---|---|---|---|---|---|---|---|---|---|---|
| **Composite** | | | | | | | | | | | | | | | |
| Externalizing Problems | 2.45 | 2.65 | 2.45 | 1.73 | 2.00 | 1.73 | 2.00 | 1.73 | 2.00 | 1.73 | 1.73 | 1.73 | 1.73 | 2.24 | 1.73 |
| Internalizing Problems | 2.45 | 2.65 | 2.24 | 2.45 | 2.45 | 2.45 | 2.24 | 2.00 | 2.45 | 2.24 | 2.00 | 2.45 | 2.65 | 2.24 | 2.83 |
| School Problems | – | – | – | 2.24 | 2.00 | 2.45 | 2.24 | 2.00 | 2.24 | 2.45 | 2.24 | 2.45 | 2.65 | 2.24 | 2.83 |
| Adaptive Skills | 2.65 | 2.45 | 2.65 | 1.73 | 1.41 | 1.73 | 2.00 | 1.73 | 2.00 | 1.73 | 1.41 | 1.73 | 1.73 | 1.41 | 1.73 |
| Behavioral Symptoms Index | 1.73 | 1.73 | 1.73 | 1.73 | 1.73 | 1.73 | 1.73 | 1.73 | 1.73 | 1.73 | 1.41 | 1.73 | 2.00 | 2.00 | 2.00 |
| **Clinical scale** | | | | | | | | | | | | | | | |
| Hyperactivity | 3.32 | 3.16 | 3.46 | 2.45 | 2.65 | 2.45 | 2.65 | 2.45 | 2.65 | 2.65 | 2.83 | 2.65 | 2.45 | 2.45 | 2.45 |
| Aggression | 2.83 | 3.74 | 2.65 | 2.83 | 3.32 | 2.83 | 3.16 | 3.00 | 3.16 | 2.65 | 3.00 | 2.65 | 2.83 | 4.12 | 2.65 |
| Conduct Problems | – | – | – | 3.00 | 3.16 | 2.83 | 3.16 | 3.16 | 3.16 | 2.65 | 2.65 | 2.65 | 2.83 | 3.00 | 2.83 |
| Anxiety | 3.46 | 4.47 | 3.00 | 3.16 | 3.16 | 3.16 | 3.16 | 2.83 | 3.16 | 3.46 | 3.16 | 3.46 | 3.32 | 3.46 | 3.32 |
| Depression | 3.61 | 4.12 | 3.32 | 3.46 | 4.12 | 3.32 | 3.32 | 3.16 | 3.32 | 3.61 | 3.61 | 3.61 | 4.47 | 3.74 | 4.69 |
| Somatization | 3.32 | 3.16 | 3.32 | 3.32 | 2.83 | 3.74 | 3.00 | 2.65 | 3.46 | 2.83 | 2.45 | 3.16 | 2.65 | 2.00 | 3.16 |
| Attention Problems | 2.45 | 2.00 | 2.65 | 2.45 | 2.45 | 2.65 | 2.45 | 2.45 | 2.45 | 2.65 | 2.45 | 2.65 | 2.83 | 2.45 | 2.83 |
| Learning Problems | – | – | – | 3.16 | 2.83 | 3.32 | 3.00 | 2.65 | 3.32 | 3.74 | 3.46 | 3.74 | 4.12 | 3.46 | 4.24 |
| Atypicality | 3.00 | 2.83 | 3.00 | 3.74 | 4.58 | 3.61 | 4.47 | 4.47 | 4.47 | 3.46 | 3.32 | 3.61 | 3.87 | 3.74 | 3.87 |
| Withdrawal | 3.61 | 3.87 | 3.46 | 3.00 | 3.16 | 2.83 | 3.32 | 3.16 | 3.32 | 2.83 | 2.65 | 3.00 | 3.46 | 3.61 | 3.46 |
| **Adaptive scale** | | | | | | | | | | | | | | | |
| Adaptability | 3.74 | 3.87 | 2.83 | 2.83 | 2.83 | 3.00 | 3.32 | 3.16 | 3.46 | 2.83 | 2.83 | 2.83 | 3.32 | 3.00 | 3.32 |
| Social Skills | 3.32 | 3.61 | 3.00 | 2.45 | 2.45 | 2.65 | 2.83 | 3.16 | 2.83 | 2.45 | 2.45 | 2.65 | 2.65 | 2.24 | 2.83 |
| Leadership | – | – | – | 3.74 | 3.46 | 3.87 | 4.00 | 4.00 | 4.00 | 3.61 | 3.16 | 3.74 | 3.46 | 2.45 | 3.87 |
| Study Skills | – | – | – | 3.32 | 3.00 | 3.46 | 3.46 | 3.46 | 3.46 | 2.45 | 2.65 | 2.65 | 2.65 | 2.83 | 2.65 |
| Functional Communication | 3.87 | 3.32 | 4.36 | 3.32 | 3.16 | 3.46 | 4.12 | 3.61 | 4.24 | 3.46 | 3.16 | 3.74 | 3.87 | 2.65 | 4.24 |
| **Content scale** | | | | | | | | | | | | | | | |
| Anger Control | 3.00 | 3.87 | 2.83 | 3.00 | 2.83 | 3.00 | 3.46 | 3.46 | 3.46 | 2.83 | 3.32 | 2.83 | 3.32 | 3.46 | 3.32 |
| Bullying | 4.69 | 5.00 | 4.58 | 3.00 | 3.46 | 2.65 | 3.00 | 3.32 | 2.83 | 2.65 | 2.65 | 2.65 | 2.45 | 2.45 | 2.83 |
| Developmental Social Disorders | 3.16 | 3.00 | 3.16 | 2.83 | 2.83 | 2.83 | 3.46 | 2.83 | 3.74 | 3.00 | 2.83 | 3.00 | 3.32 | 3.32 | 3.32 |
| Emotional Self-Control | 2.45 | 2.65 | 2.24 | 2.83 | 2.83 | 2.83 | 3.00 | 3.00 | 3.16 | 3.00 | 3.00 | 3.00 | 3.46 | 2.83 | 3.61 |
| Executive Functioning | 2.83 | 2.65 | 3.00 | 2.45 | 2.24 | 2.65 | 3.00 | 2.65 | 3.00 | 2.24 | 2.00 | 2.24 | 2.24 | 1.73 | 2.24 |
| Negative Emotionality | 3.32 | 3.74 | 3.16 | 3.00 | 3.00 | 3.00 | 3.32 | 3.46 | 3.16 | 2.83 | 3.00 | 2.83 | 3.00 | 2.83 | 3.16 |
| Resiliency | 3.74 | 3.61 | 3.87 | 2.65 | 2.45 | 2.83 | 3.00 | 2.83 | 3.16 | 2.83 | 2.83 | 3.00 | 2.83 | 2.24 | 3.00 |
| **Clinical index** | | | | | | | | | | | | | | | |
| Clinical Probability Index | 3.16 | 2.83 | 3.46 | – | – | – | – | – | – | – | – | – | – | – | – |
| ADHD Probability Index | – | – | – | 2.83 | 2.83 | 2.83 | 3.00 | 2.65 | 3.16 | 3.87 | 3.87 | 4.00 | 3.61 | 3.16 | 3.74 |
| EBD Probability Index | – | – | – | 2.83 | 3.00 | 2.83 | 3.00 | 2.83 | 3.16 | 2.24 | 2.24 | 2.24 | 2.45 | 2.24 | 2.45 |
| Autism Probability Index | – | – | – | 3.00 | 3.00 | 3.00 | 3.46 | 3.16 | 3.46 | 3.32 | 3.32 | 3.32 | 4.00 | 3.74 | 4.12 |
| Functional Impairment Index | 4.12 | 3.74 | 4.36 | 2.24 | 2.24 | 2.24 | 2.45 | 2.00 | 2.65 | 2.24 | 2.00 | 2.45 | 2.65 | 2.00 | 2.83 |

As discussed in chapter 2, a confidence interval may be formed around the observed $T$ score to indicate, with a particular level of confidence (e.g., 90%), the range of $T$ scores within which the person's true score is likely to fall. This confidence interval is constructed using a multiple of the $SEM$. The resulting value is added to (and subtracted from) the observed $T$ score, forming 90% confidence intervals (see the bottom row of the norm tables presented in Appendix A).

# Evidence of Validity

Validity refers to the appropriateness and supporting evidence for the proposed interpretations given to test scores. Three types of evidence about the validity of the TRS as a measure of multiple behavioral constructs are discussed in this section. The first is the empirical support from scale intercorrelations and factor analysis for the grouping of scales into composites. The second is the pattern of correlations of TRS composite and scale scores with scores obtained on other behavior measures. The last consists of the TRS score profiles of groups of children with particular clinical diagnoses or educational classifications. Additional validity evidence related to test content (i.e., item development and selection) is presented in chapter 7.

## EVIDENCE BASED ON INTERNAL STRUCTURE

One way of evaluating how well a scale measures the dimension it is designed to measure is to see whether its correlations with other scale scores reflect the current scientific understanding of behavioral dimensions. Tables 9.13 through 9.15 show the intercorrelations of scale scores at each age level of the general and clinical norm samples. Within each TRS level, the pattern and magnitude of correlations are very similar between the two samples. As expected, correlations of scores within clinical scales and of scores within adaptive scales are positive, while correlations between scores from clinical and adaptive scales are negative.

**Table 9.13** TRS–P: Intercorrelations of Composites, Scales, and Indexes, General and Clinical Samples

| | Composite | | | | Clinical scale | | | | | | | |
|---|---|---|---|---|---|---|---|---|---|---|---|---|
| | Externalizing Problems | Internalizing Problems | Adaptive Skills | Behavioral Symptoms Index | Hyperactivity | Aggression | Anxiety | Depression | Somatization | Attention Problems | Atypicality | Withdrawal |
| **Composite** | | | | | | | | | | | | |
| Externalizing Problems | — | .50 | -.40 | .84 | .93 | .92 | .38 | .61 | .28 | .59 | .52 | .21 |
| Internalizing Problems | .48 | — | -.50 | .69 | .35 | .59 | .85 | .89 | .78 | .37 | .48 | .49 |
| Adaptive Skills | -.45 | -.31 | — | -.70 | -.33 | -.41 | -.38 | -.51 | -.33 | -.60 | -.63 | -.67 |
| Behavioral Symptoms Index | .87 | .66 | -.64 | — | .78 | .78 | .54 | .76 | .46 | .75 | .82 | .63 |
| **Clinical scale** | | | | | | | | | | | | |
| Hyperactivity | .94 | .37 | -.41 | .82 | — | .71 | .26 | .44 | .20 | .68 | .53 | .16 |
| Aggression | .94 | .54 | -.44 | .83 | .78 | — | .45 | .69 | .32 | .42 | .44 | .22 |
| Anxiety | .33 | .86 | -.27 | .52 | .24 | .38 | — | .72 | .43 | .28 | .29 | .43 |
| Depression | .67 | .84 | -.43 | .80 | .54 | .71 | .65 | — | .54 | .37 | .50 | .44 |
| Somatization | .20 | .76 | -.07 | .30 | .14 | .23 | .45 | .41 | — | .31 | .40 | .33 |
| Attention Problems | .64 | .29 | -.67 | .76 | .69 | .52 | .20 | .42 | .11 | — | .54 | .34 |
| Atypicality | .53 | .51 | -.50 | .78 | .50 | .49 | .46 | .51 | .28 | .50 | — | .71 |
| Withdrawal | .34 | .51 | -.56 | .68 | .28 | .36 | .49 | .53 | .24 | .39 | .62 | — |
| **Adaptive scale** | | | | | | | | | | | | |
| Adaptability | -.50 | -.43 | .85 | -.64 | -.42 | -.51 | -.41 | -.53 | -.13 | -.57 | -.47 | -.49 |
| Social Skills | -.35 | -.14 | .88 | -.49 | -.32 | -.34 | -.08 | -.28 | .02 | -.57 | -.35 | -.44 |
| Functional Communication | -.34 | -.23 | .89 | -.55 | -.34 | -.31 | -.20 | -.31 | -.06 | -.62 | -.49 | -.53 |
| **Content scale** | | | | | | | | | | | | |
| Anger Control | .86 | .56 | -.44 | .81 | .73 | .89 | .39 | .77 | .22 | .49 | .46 | .41 |
| Bullying | .88 | .47 | -.54 | .82 | .79 | .87 | .32 | .63 | .21 | .60 | .49 | .42 |
| Developmental Social Disorders | .50 | .49 | -.82 | .79 | .46 | .48 | .45 | .53 | .22 | .62 | .80 | .79 |
| Emotional Self-Control | .80 | .71 | -.54 | .85 | .69 | .82 | .57 | .89 | .29 | .54 | .52 | .47 |
| Executive Functioning | .87 | .51 | -.68 | .92 | .84 | .79 | .38 | .71 | .19 | .84 | .59 | .50 |
| Negative Emotionality | .73 | .78 | -.43 | .79 | .60 | .78 | .63 | .92 | .37 | .44 | .48 | .45 |
| Resiliency | -.54 | -.49 | .83 | -.71 | -.47 | -.54 | -.45 | -.61 | -.16 | -.66 | -.52 | -.51 |
| **Clinical index** | | | | | | | | | | | | |
| Clinical Probability Index | .69 | .44 | -.73 | .87 | .70 | .60 | .37 | .54 | .19 | .83 | .77 | .65 |
| Functional Impairment Index | .63 | .38 | -.85 | .79 | .62 | .57 | .31 | .51 | .12 | .81 | .59 | .61 |

**Table 9.13** TRS–P: Intercorrelations of Composites, Scales, and Indexes, General and Clinical Samples (continued)

| | Adaptive scale | | | Content scale | | | | | | | Clinical index | |
|---|---|---|---|---|---|---|---|---|---|---|---|---|
| | Adaptability | Social Skills | Functional Communication | Anger Control | Bullying | Developmental Social Disorders | Emotional Self-Control | Executive Functioning | Negative Emotionality | Resiliency | Clinical Probability Index | Functional Impairment Index |
| **Composite** | | | | | | | | | | | | |
| Externalizing Problems | −.58 | −.21 | −.19 | .84 | .88 | .48 | .74 | .84 | .71 | −.61 | .64 | .60 |
| Internalizing Problems | −.64 | −.34 | −.30 | .65 | .45 | .55 | .82 | .64 | .83 | −.67 | .52 | .52 |
| Adaptive Skills | .74 | .87 | .86 | −.44 | −.56 | −.82 | −.54 | −.70 | −.52 | .75 | −.78 | −.87 |
| Behavioral Symptoms Index | −.71 | −.54 | −.48 | .79 | .80 | .84 | .80 | .95 | .78 | −.77 | .89 | .82 |
| **Clinical scale** | | | | | | | | | | | | |
| Hyperactivity | −.44 | −.18 | −.21 | .63 | .79 | .44 | .56 | .80 | .51 | −.48 | .66 | .59 |
| Aggression | −.64 | −.22 | −.16 | .91 | .83 | .44 | .81 | .76 | .81 | −.65 | .52 | .52 |
| Anxiety | −.64 | −.16 | −.16 | .55 | .28 | .42 | .73 | .52 | .70 | −.64 | .37 | .40 |
| Depression | −.69 | −.32 | −.27 | .80 | .54 | .57 | .91 | .73 | .93 | −.73 | .54 | .56 |
| Somatization | −.30 | −.29 | −.25 | .31 | .29 | .39 | .43 | .40 | .46 | −.35 | .40 | .36 |
| Attention Problems | −.53 | −.44 | −.50 | .41 | .56 | .58 | .43 | .81 | .35 | −.61 | .80 | .77 |
| Atypicality | −.45 | −.59 | −.52 | .49 | .53 | .88 | .52 | .69 | .49 | −.51 | .85 | .68 |
| Withdrawal | −.43 | −.70 | −.53 | .32 | .36 | .87 | .38 | .49 | .42 | −.47 | .66 | .60 |
| **Adaptive scale** | | | | | | | | | | | | |
| Adaptability | — | .44 | .40 | −.69 | −.62 | −.63 | −.79 | −.74 | −.74 | .93 | −.59 | −.66 |
| Social Skills | .60 | — | .72 | −.28 | −.44 | −.72 | −.30 | −.49 | −.33 | .49 | −.66 | −.68 |
| Functional Communication | .62 | .71 | — | −.14 | −.32 | −.67 | −.26 | −.50 | −.24 | .44 | −.68 | −.80 |
| **Content scale** | | | | | | | | | | | | |
| Anger Control | −.51 | −.35 | −.30 | — | .75 | .51 | .90 | .81 | .89 | −.68 | .53 | .55 |
| Bullying | −.57 | −.46 | −.40 | .78 | — | .58 | .62 | .78 | .62 | −.62 | .68 | .65 |
| Developmental Social Disorders | −.74 | −.63 | −.79 | .48 | .55 | — | .55 | .74 | .56 | −.67 | .87 | .83 |
| Emotional Self-Control | −.66 | −.37 | −.39 | .88 | .72 | .57 | — | .82 | .96 | −.78 | .55 | .60 |
| Executive Functioning | −.66 | −.54 | −.59 | .82 | .80 | .69 | .85 | — | .77 | −.79 | .87 | .86 |
| Negative Emotionality | −.55 | −.28 | −.29 | .82 | .67 | .50 | .92 | .75 | — | −.75 | .52 | .58 |
| Resiliency | .91 | .63 | .65 | −.54 | −.57 | −.75 | −.69 | −.72 | −.60 | — | −.64 | −.69 |
| **Clinical index** | | | | | | | | | | | | |
| Clinical Probability Index | −.60 | −.59 | −.73 | .59 | .68 | .84 | .63 | .87 | .54 | −.66 | — | .91 |
| Functional Impairment Index | −.67 | −.69 | −.88 | .58 | .64 | .83 | .63 | .84 | .51 | −.72 | .91 | — |

**Table 9.14** TRS–C: Intercorrelations of Composites, Scales, and Indexes, General and Clinical Samples

| | Composite | | | | | Clinical scale | | | | | | | | | |
|---|---|---|---|---|---|---|---|---|---|---|---|---|---|---|---|
| | Externalizing Problems | Internalizing Problems | School Problems | Adaptive Skills | Behavioral Symptoms Index | Hyper-activity | Aggression | Conduct Problems | Anxiety | Depression | Soma-tization | Attention Problems | Learning Problems | Atypicality | Withdrawal |
| **Composite** | | | | | | | | | | | | | | | |
| Externalizing Problems | — | .36 | .47 | -.51 | .82 | .89 | .93 | .94 | .14 | .53 | .17 | .58 | .25 | .52 | .29 |
| Internalizing Problems | .44 | — | .33 | -.36 | .61 | .32 | .36 | .32 | .84 | .82 | .72 | .31 | .29 | .50 | .50 |
| School Problems | .57 | .39 | — | -.69 | .63 | .51 | .30 | .49 | .28 | .32 | .19 | .89 | .89 | .54 | .34 |
| Adaptive Skills | -.54 | -.35 | -.77 | — | -.75 | -.46 | -.46 | -.48 | -.23 | -.52 | -.11 | -.68 | -.54 | -.67 | -.64 |
| Behavioral Symptoms Index | .86 | .61 | .73 | -.73 | — | .78 | .75 | .73 | .42 | .78 | .26 | .72 | .41 | .83 | .69 |
| **Clinical scale** | | | | | | | | | | | | | | | |
| Hyperactivity | .89 | .32 | .57 | -.48 | .79 | — | .71 | .75 | .18 | .44 | .14 | .65 | .25 | .53 | .23 |
| Aggression | .93 | .44 | .44 | -.49 | .80 | .72 | — | .85 | .12 | .56 | .16 | .39 | .13 | .44 | .33 |
| Conduct Problems | .94 | .44 | .56 | -.51 | .78 | .75 | .84 | — | .09 | .47 | .18 | .55 | .31 | .47 | .23 |
| Anxiety | .20 | .82 | .33 | -.26 | .41 | .15 | .20 | .21 | — | .61 | .38 | .22 | .28 | .39 | .38 |
| Depression | .63 | .81 | .46 | -.50 | .79 | .49 | .65 | .60 | .56 | — | .35 | .35 | .23 | .60 | .61 |
| Somatization | .20 | .74 | .13 | -.06 | .24 | .13 | .20 | .23 | .39 | .37 | — | .16 | .17 | .19 | .20 |
| Attention Problems | .67 | .36 | .91 | -.75 | .79 | .72 | .52 | .61 | .27 | .46 | .11 | — | .58 | .57 | .32 |
| Learning Problems | .37 | .36 | .91 | -.65 | .54 | .32 | .29 | .40 | .33 | .39 | .12 | .67 | — | .38 | .28 |
| Atypicality | .56 | .47 | .58 | -.58 | .81 | .50 | .50 | .53 | .38 | .55 | .19 | .59 | .47 | — | .64 |
| Withdrawal | .35 | .43 | .43 | -.62 | .69 | .27 | .35 | .33 | .34 | .53 | .15 | .41 | .38 | .63 | — |
| **Adaptive scale** | | | | | | | | | | | | | | | |
| Adaptability | -.60 | -.43 | -.53 | .81 | -.71 | -.52 | -.60 | -.54 | -.31 | -.59 | -.12 | -.59 | -.38 | -.48 | -.53 |
| Social Skills | -.46 | -.18 | -.50 | .84 | -.58 | -.40 | -.44 | -.44 | -.09 | -.36 | .02 | -.53 | -.38 | -.43 | -.56 |
| Leadership | -.40 | -.30 | -.74 | .93 | -.61 | -.36 | -.35 | -.39 | -.26 | -.41 | -.05 | -.69 | -.66 | -.51 | -.56 |
| Study Skills | -.52 | -.26 | -.82 | .88 | -.67 | -.51 | -.43 | -.49 | -.17 | -.40 | -.04 | -.80 | -.70 | -.51 | -.45 |
| Functional Communication | -.36 | -.33 | -.73 | .87 | -.61 | -.31 | -.30 | -.37 | -.32 | -.40 | -.06 | -.64 | -.69 | -.61 | -.61 |
| **Content scale** | | | | | | | | | | | | | | | |
| Anger Control | .86 | .51 | .46 | -.51 | .82 | .72 | .90 | .75 | .27 | .74 | .20 | .54 | .30 | .51 | .40 |
| Bullying | .85 | .40 | .41 | -.42 | .69 | .61 | .88 | .86 | .17 | .56 | .21 | .46 | .30 | .44 | .28 |
| Developmental Social Disorders | .46 | .44 | .60 | -.83 | .77 | .39 | .44 | .45 | .36 | .57 | .11 | .60 | .50 | .76 | .84 |
| Emotional Self-Control | .77 | .66 | .49 | -.60 | .83 | .67 | .78 | .68 | .47 | .84 | .26 | .56 | .34 | .54 | .47 |
| Executive Functioning | .77 | .43 | .85 | -.88 | .87 | .76 | .67 | .69 | .29 | .60 | .13 | .89 | .65 | .62 | .50 |
| Negative Emotionality | .78 | .67 | .48 | -.52 | .80 | .61 | .81 | .72 | .42 | .87 | .30 | .52 | .35 | .49 | .44 |
| Resiliency | -.52 | -.39 | -.68 | .94 | -.70 | -.46 | -.49 | -.48 | -.31 | -.52 | -.09 | -.69 | -.55 | -.53 | -.57 |
| **Clinical index** | | | | | | | | | | | | | | | |
| ADHD Probability Index | .78 | .47 | .88 | -.84 | .90 | .77 | .67 | .72 | .34 | .62 | .16 | .93 | .68 | .69 | .53 |
| EBD Probability Index | .92 | .58 | .65 | -.65 | .91 | .74 | .90 | .88 | .34 | .79 | .24 | .68 | .51 | .64 | .51 |
| Autism Probability Index | .57 | .46 | .73 | -.91 | .82 | .51 | .53 | .54 | .37 | .60 | .12 | .71 | .62 | .76 | .73 |
| Functional Impairment Index | .66 | .57 | .88 | -.91 | .88 | .59 | .58 | .63 | .46 | .68 | .22 | .83 | .78 | .74 | .68 |

**Table 9.14** TRS–C: Intercorrelations of Composites, Scales, and Indexes, General and Clinical Samples *(continued)*

| | Adaptive scale | | | | | Content scale | | | | | | | Clinical index | | | |
|---|---|---|---|---|---|---|---|---|---|---|---|---|---|---|---|---|
| | Adaptability | Social Skills | Leadership | Study Skills | Functional Communication | Anger Control | Bullying | Developmental Social Disorders | Emotional Self-Control | Executive Functioning | Negative Emotionality | Resiliency | ADHD Probability Index | EBD Probability Index | Autism Probability Index | Functional Impairment Index |
| **Composite** | | | | | | | | | | | | | | | | |
| Externalizing Problems | -.60 | -.41 | -.37 | -.51 | -.29 | .84 | .85 | .40 | .72 | .76 | .73 | -.52 | .76 | .92 | .52 | .59 |
| Internalizing Problems | -.51 | -.21 | -.32 | -.26 | -.28 | .52 | .27 | .47 | .68 | .47 | .66 | -.44 | .49 | .57 | .50 | .61 |
| School Problems | -.41 | -.38 | -.70 | -.79 | -.68 | .36 | .29 | .50 | .39 | .77 | .39 | -.58 | .82 | .50 | .60 | .81 |
| Adaptive Skills | .81 | .85 | .93 | .86 | .86 | -.55 | -.37 | -.82 | -.62 | -.85 | -.59 | .93 | -.81 | -.64 | -.90 | -.90 |
| Behavioral Symptoms Index | -.76 | -.61 | -.63 | -.64 | -.59 | .83 | .63 | .78 | .85 | .89 | .82 | -.75 | .90 | .91 | .85 | .88 |
| **Clinical scale** | | | | | | | | | | | | | | | | |
| Hyperactivity | -.52 | -.33 | -.36 | -.50 | -.26 | .72 | .61 | .37 | .66 | .78 | .58 | -.48 | .77 | .76 | .49 | .56 |
| Aggression | -.62 | -.43 | -.31 | -.38 | -.24 | .87 | .88 | .39 | .73 | .64 | .77 | -.48 | .63 | .91 | .49 | .52 |
| Conduct Problems | -.53 | -.36 | -.37 | -.51 | -.30 | .72 | .86 | .35 | .59 | .69 | .66 | -.48 | .69 | .87 | .45 | .55 |
| Anxiety | -.36 | -.06 | -.23 | -.13 | -.22 | .33 | .02 | .36 | .53 | .32 | .45 | -.33 | .34 | .32 | .39 | .48 |
| Depression | -.68 | -.43 | -.40 | -.36 | -.38 | .72 | .43 | .61 | .83 | .59 | .85 | -.58 | .59 | .75 | .64 | .68 |
| Somatization | -.17 | -.01 | -.11 | -.13 | -.07 | .18 | .19 | .16 | .25 | .19 | .27 | -.14 | .23 | .28 | .16 | .30 |
| Attention Problems | -.49 | -.42 | -.66 | -.77 | -.58 | .46 | .36 | .51 | .47 | .85 | .43 | -.62 | .89 | .56 | .61 | .75 |
| Learning Problems | -.24 | -.25 | -.57 | -.64 | -.62 | .19 | .15 | .37 | .23 | .53 | .27 | -.41 | .57 | .33 | .44 | .69 |
| Atypicality | -.58 | -.53 | -.58 | -.55 | -.65 | .55 | .35 | .82 | .61 | .70 | .54 | -.63 | .73 | .63 | .84 | .78 |
| Withdrawal | -.59 | -.66 | -.56 | -.38 | -.59 | .48 | .21 | .87 | .58 | .51 | .55 | -.61 | .50 | .51 | .79 | .71 |
| **Adaptive scale** | | | | | | | | | | | | | | | | |
| Adaptability | — | .70 | .66 | .61 | .55 | -.74 | -.48 | -.71 | -.82 | -.77 | -.79 | .90 | -.70 | -.73 | -.75 | -.75 |
| Social Skills | .65 | — | .74 | .59 | .63 | -.48 | -.34 | -.73 | -.52 | -.63 | -.51 | .77 | -.56 | -.53 | -.82 | -.67 |
| Leadership | .66 | .76 | — | .79 | .80 | -.41 | -.25 | -.73 | -.49 | -.78 | -.45 | .87 | -.74 | -.50 | -.82 | -.82 |
| Study Skills | .64 | .63 | .81 | — | .71 | -.43 | -.36 | -.58 | -.46 | -.82 | -.44 | .76 | -.80 | -.55 | -.67 | -.79 |
| Functional Communication | .60 | .63 | .82 | .74 | — | -.32 | -.20 | -.80 | -.40 | -.66 | -.36 | .73 | -.68 | -.43 | -.80 | -.82 |
| **Content scale** | | | | | | | | | | | | | | | | |
| Anger Control | -.65 | -.42 | -.37 | -.44 | -.32 | — | .66 | .53 | .92 | .75 | .89 | -.61 | .71 | .88 | .63 | .66 |
| Bullying | -.50 | -.39 | -.30 | -.39 | -.28 | .72 | — | .27 | .51 | .52 | .60 | -.38 | .52 | .82 | .36 | .41 |
| Developmental Social Disorders | -.71 | -.70 | -.74 | -.65 | -.82 | .48 | .39 | — | .62 | .70 | .56 | -.78 | .69 | .59 | .92 | .84 |
| Emotional Self-Control | -.76 | -.46 | -.46 | -.49 | -.42 | .89 | .63 | .58 | — | .77 | .90 | -.71 | .74 | .83 | .71 | .74 |
| Executive Functioning | -.76 | -.67 | -.80 | -.86 | -.71 | .70 | .57 | .70 | .75 | — | .70 | -.84 | .96 | .80 | .82 | .89 |
| Negative Emotionality | -.68 | -.43 | -.40 | -.44 | -.34 | .88 | .68 | .50 | .89 | .67 | — | -.64 | .68 | .87 | .64 | .70 |
| Resiliency | .89 | .75 | .87 | .78 | .77 | -.53 | -.42 | -.79 | -.65 | -.84 | -.55 | — | -.77 | -.66 | -.85 | -.84 |
| **Clinical index** | | | | | | | | | | | | | | | | |
| ADHD Probability Index | -.71 | -.63 | -.77 | -.83 | -.73 | .69 | .57 | .72 | .73 | .96 | .67 | -.78 | — | .80 | .83 | .90 |
| EBD Probability Index | -.67 | -.53 | -.54 | -.60 | -.50 | .86 | .84 | .61 | .83 | .81 | .86 | -.63 | .83 | — | .68 | .75 |
| Autism Probability Index | -.71 | -.81 | -.86 | -.75 | -.83 | .56 | .45 | .88 | .64 | .85 | .57 | -.84 | .83 | .71 | — | .90 |
| Functional Impairment Index | -.73 | -.68 | -.83 | -.84 | -.85 | .62 | .52 | .84 | .71 | .91 | .65 | -.84 | .92 | .79 | .91 | — |

# Table 9.15 TRS–A: Intercorrelations of Composites, Scales, and Indexes, General and Clinical Samples

| | Composite | | | | | Clinical scale | | | | | | | | | |
|---|---|---|---|---|---|---|---|---|---|---|---|---|---|---|---|
| | Externalizing Problems | Internalizing Problems | School Problems | Adaptive Skills | Behavioral Symptoms Index | Hyperactivity | Aggression | Conduct Problems | Anxiety | Depression | Somatization | Attention Problems | Learning Problems | Atypicality | Withdrawal |
| **Composite** | | | | | | | | | | | | | | | |
| Externalizing Problems | — | .43 | .49 | -.51 | .79 | .87 | .94 | .93 | .21 | .58 | .29 | .58 | .32 | .40 | .17 |
| Internalizing Problems | .51 | — | .43 | -.47 | .72 | .36 | .42 | .40 | .82 | .87 | .81 | .39 | .40 | .63 | .56 |
| School Problems | .67 | .53 | — | -.73 | .69 | .49 | .39 | .45 | .35 | .47 | .27 | .91 | .91 | .49 | .34 |
| Adaptive Skills | -.58 | -.45 | -.81 | — | -.75 | -.44 | -.49 | -.49 | -.34 | -.56 | -.28 | -.71 | -.62 | -.57 | -.61 |
| Behavioral Symptoms Index | .85 | .74 | .78 | -.73 | — | .72 | .75 | .70 | .51 | .83 | .47 | .74 | .52 | .78 | .64 |
| **Clinical scale** | | | | | | | | | | | | | | | |
| Hyperactivity | .90 | .47 | .65 | -.51 | .81 | — | .71 | .68 | .24 | .45 | .20 | .62 | .28 | .39 | .06 |
| Aggression | .95 | .48 | .57 | -.53 | .80 | .77 | — | .88 | .16 | .60 | .29 | .46 | .26 | .36 | .22 |
| Conduct Problems | .94 | .47 | .65 | -.58 | .77 | .76 | .87 | — | .17 | .55 | .28 | .50 | .33 | .34 | .18 |
| Anxiety | .35 | .87 | .42 | -.32 | .56 | .35 | .31 | .31 | — | .61 | .56 | .28 | .36 | .53 | .45 |
| Depression | .62 | .88 | .55 | -.52 | .85 | .56 | .61 | .56 | .61 | — | .56 | .45 | .41 | .61 | .61 |
| Somatization | .35 | .84 | .40 | -.31 | .51 | .32 | .32 | .34 | .56 | .60 | — | .25 | .23 | .45 | .33 |
| Attention Problems | .72 | .47 | .94 | -.79 | .80 | .72 | .60 | .68 | .35 | .52 | .36 | — | .65 | .47 | .29 |
| Learning Problems | .54 | .52 | .94 | -.72 | .67 | .51 | .46 | .54 | .44 | .52 | .39 | .77 | — | .42 | .32 |
| Atypicality | .59 | .66 | .58 | -.54 | .84 | .59 | .53 | .53 | .54 | .70 | .47 | .56 | .53 | — | .67 |
| Withdrawal | .30 | .58 | .44 | -.61 | .68 | .24 | .31 | .30 | .46 | .66 | .38 | .40 | .43 | .64 | — |
| **Adaptive scale** | | | | | | | | | | | | | | | |
| Adaptability | -.60 | -.51 | -.67 | .88 | -.73 | -.52 | -.57 | -.58 | -.40 | -.60 | -.33 | -.69 | -.57 | -.55 | -.57 |
| Social Skills | -.49 | -.27 | -.59 | .89 | -.60 | -.38 | -.47 | -.51 | -.14 | -.40 | -.17 | -.61 | -.50 | -.42 | -.60 |
| Leadership | -.46 | -.38 | -.74 | .94 | -.62 | -.39 | -.42 | -.48 | -.29 | -.44 | -.27 | -.72 | -.69 | -.44 | -.55 |
| Study Skills | -.61 | -.37 | -.88 | .88 | -.69 | -.57 | -.52 | -.61 | -.25 | -.43 | -.29 | -.89 | -.78 | -.47 | -.42 |
| Functional Communication | -.45 | -.47 | -.74 | .88 | -.66 | -.42 | -.39 | -.44 | -.38 | -.50 | -.33 | -.66 | -.73 | -.58 | -.62 |
| **Content scale** | | | | | | | | | | | | | | | |
| Anger Control | .87 | .58 | .59 | -.54 | .82 | .75 | .90 | .79 | .43 | .71 | .37 | .61 | .49 | .57 | .39 |
| Bullying | .88 | .44 | .53 | -.51 | .73 | .69 | .92 | .86 | .29 | .54 | .31 | .56 | .44 | .49 | .28 |
| Developmental Social Disorders | .48 | .57 | .65 | -.85 | .78 | .42 | .45 | .47 | .44 | .65 | .38 | .61 | .61 | .73 | .85 |
| Emotional Self-Control | .79 | .76 | .58 | -.53 | .85 | .72 | .78 | .70 | .65 | .84 | .49 | .59 | .51 | .64 | .47 |
| Executive Functioning | .74 | .52 | .90 | -.92 | .83 | .70 | .67 | .70 | .39 | .59 | .38 | .91 | .78 | .59 | .50 |
| Negative Emotionality | .83 | .69 | .63 | -.60 | .86 | .71 | .84 | .78 | .51 | .83 | .46 | .64 | .53 | .61 | .49 |
| Resiliency | -.53 | -.45 | -.73 | .95 | -.68 | -.46 | -.50 | -.52 | -.35 | -.51 | -.31 | -.73 | -.66 | -.50 | -.56 |
| **Clinical index** | | | | | | | | | | | | | | | |
| ADHD Probability Index | .75 | .47 | .89 | -.82 | .81 | .78 | .64 | .69 | .34 | .53 | .35 | .93 | .74 | .57 | .42 |
| EBD Probability Index | .92 | .65 | .74 | -.72 | .91 | .77 | .91 | .89 | .49 | .76 | .45 | .75 | .64 | .66 | .50 |
| Autism Probability Index | .47 | .63 | .65 | -.84 | .78 | .42 | .43 | .45 | .55 | .66 | .41 | .62 | .61 | .74 | .83 |
| Functional Impairment Index | .68 | .68 | .89 | -.92 | .88 | .63 | .61 | .66 | .56 | .72 | .48 | .84 | .83 | .72 | .70 |

**Table 9.15** TRS-A: Intercorrelations of Composites, Scales, and Indexes, General and Clinical Samples *(continued)*

| | Adaptive scale | | | | | Content scale | | | | | | | Clinical index | | | |
|---|---|---|---|---|---|---|---|---|---|---|---|---|---|---|---|---|
| | Adapt-ability | Social Skills | Leader-ship | Study Skills | Functional Communication | Anger Control | Bullying | Develop-mental Social Disorders | Emotional Self-Control | Executive Functioning | Negative Emotionality | Resiliency | ADHD Probability Index | EBD Probability Index | Autism Probability Index | Functional Impairment Index |
| **Composite** | | | | | | | | | | | | | | | | |
| Externalizing Problems | -.58 | -.37 | -.37 | -.52 | -.29 | .87 | .87 | .35 | .76 | .72 | .81 | -.50 | .68 | .91 | .27 | .58 |
| Internalizing Problems | -.56 | -.25 | -.37 | -.33 | -.45 | .52 | .39 | .58 | .73 | .50 | .65 | -.53 | .37 | .62 | .61 | .69 |
| School Problems | -.54 | -.37 | -.68 | -.84 | -.64 | .41 | .34 | .50 | .43 | .82 | .46 | -.67 | .79 | .54 | .48 | .82 |
| Adaptive Skills | .82 | .81 | .91 | .81 | .83 | -.50 | -.43 | -.80 | -.54 | -.86 | -.56 | .94 | -.71 | -.64 | -.74 | -.91 |
| Behavioral Symptoms Index | -.76 | -.54 | -.61 | -.63 | -.61 | .77 | .67 | .76 | .81 | .83 | .82 | -.74 | .73 | .87 | .72 | .88 |
| **Clinical scale** | | | | | | | | | | | | | | | | |
| Hyperactivity | -.48 | -.23 | -.31 | -.49 | -.30 | .69 | .59 | .27 | .66 | .68 | .64 | -.43 | .76 | .70 | .25 | .53 |
| Aggression | -.59 | -.41 | -.35 | -.45 | -.24 | .90 | .92 | .34 | .76 | .65 | .83 | -.49 | .54 | .92 | .25 | .53 |
| Conduct Problems | -.54 | -.38 | -.35 | -.50 | -.26 | .80 | .87 | .33 | .67 | .63 | .75 | -.45 | .56 | .88 | .24 | .54 |
| Anxiety | -.40 | -.12 | -.30 | -.20 | -.41 | .25 | .16 | .47 | .54 | .33 | .38 | -.41 | .27 | .36 | .58 | .57 |
| Depression | -.67 | -.39 | -.43 | -.40 | -.43 | .70 | .53 | .62 | .83 | .60 | .83 | -.60 | .42 | .77 | .60 | .73 |
| Somatization | -.33 | -.11 | -.20 | -.23 | -.28 | .33 | .28 | .36 | .45 | .32 | .41 | -.31 | .24 | .41 | .34 | .43 |
| Attention Problems | -.58 | -.40 | -.63 | -.84 | -.53 | .47 | .38 | .46 | .48 | .85 | .51 | -.65 | .89 | .58 | .44 | .76 |
| Learning Problems | -.39 | -.29 | -.61 | -.68 | -.63 | .28 | .25 | .45 | .32 | .64 | .32 | -.56 | .55 | .41 | .43 | .74 |
| Atypicality | -.51 | -.36 | -.47 | -.37 | -.65 | .41 | .33 | .80 | .52 | .54 | .45 | -.53 | .43 | .51 | .82 | .73 |
| Withdrawal | -.56 | -.59 | -.54 | -.29 | -.58 | .27 | .21 | .88 | .39 | .39 | .40 | -.59 | .23 | .39 | .85 | .67 |
| **Adaptive scale** | | | | | | | | | | | | | | | | |
| Adaptability | — | .67 | .62 | .56 | .59 | -.64 | -.50 | -.72 | -.69 | -.72 | -.73 | .87 | -.56 | -.73 | -.62 | -.77 |
| Social Skills | .75 | — | .71 | .49 | .55 | -.40 | -.40 | -.67 | -.38 | -.57 | -.43 | .72 | -.41 | -.50 | -.62 | -.63 |
| Leadership | .77 | .83 | — | .75 | .73 | -.36 | -.30 | -.69 | -.38 | -.78 | -.39 | .87 | -.63 | -.50 | -.71 | -.79 |
| Study Skills | .71 | .70 | .82 | — | .59 | -.43 | -.38 | -.49 | -.41 | -.86 | -.45 | .73 | -.84 | -.56 | -.45 | -.76 |
| Functional Communication | .73 | .72 | .80 | .73 | — | -.28 | -.21 | -.80 | -.37 | -.65 | -.33 | .74 | -.53 | -.40 | -.73 | -.85 |
| **Content scale** | | | | | | | | | | | | | | | | |
| Anger Control | -.61 | -.45 | -.44 | -.51 | -.42 | — | .76 | .39 | .89 | .71 | .88 | -.53 | .52 | .90 | .31 | .58 |
| Bullying | -.53 | -.47 | -.42 | -.50 | -.38 | .78 | — | .31 | .62 | .54 | .72 | -.41 | .45 | .87 | .22 | .47 |
| Developmental Social Disorders | -.80 | -.76 | -.76 | -.67 | -.86 | .51 | .42 | — | .49 | .61 | .46 | -.77 | .45 | .52 | .92 | .84 |
| Emotional Self-Control | -.62 | -.39 | -.42 | -.47 | -.45 | .91 | .68 | .54 | — | .70 | .87 | -.58 | .51 | .84 | .47 | .68 |
| Executive Functioning | -.82 | -.74 | -.86 | -.91 | -.78 | .70 | .62 | .74 | .67 | — | .68 | -.83 | .87 | .76 | .56 | .87 |
| Negative Emotionality | -.68 | -.50 | -.49 | -.54 | -.48 | .88 | .74 | .57 | .88 | .70 | — | -.59 | .52 | .92 | .40 | .65 |
| Resiliency | .91 | .82 | .92 | .81 | .82 | -.53 | -.48 | -.81 | -.52 | -.88 | -.57 | — | -.64 | -.66 | -.71 | -.86 |
| **Clinical index** | | | | | | | | | | | | | | | | |
| ADHD Probability Index | -.69 | -.64 | -.74 | -.89 | -.70 | .63 | .58 | .65 | .59 | .92 | .64 | -.74 | — | .61 | .43 | .73 |
| EBD Probability Index | -.74 | -.60 | -.62 | -.68 | -.58 | .89 | .87 | .65 | .85 | .82 | .91 | -.68 | .75 | — | .44 | .72 |
| Autism Probability Index | -.75 | -.75 | -.81 | -.65 | -.80 | .50 | .41 | .92 | .57 | .74 | .57 | -.79 | .66 | .64 | — | .79 |
| Functional Impairment Index | -.81 | -.74 | -.83 | -.84 | -.89 | .67 | .57 | .88 | .71 | .92 | .72 | -.85 | .85 | .81 | .86 | — |

The TRS composites assess broader behavioral dimensions than those measured by the individual scales. These broad dimensions are evident in the correlations among the scale scores. When scores correlate relatively highly, they are measuring a common dimension that is represented by the composite. Factor analysis is the statistical technique used in identifying these broad dimensions. This technique is important not only for providing construct validation of the composites but also for validating the scales themselves. The correlations between a scale score and the broad dimensions it measures are shown in factor analysis by the scale's loadings on factors.

The TRS composites were based partly on factor analyses of the scale intercorrelations at the preschool, child, and adolescent levels. In this process, the correlations are derived from the entire item-development sample, which includes a greater proportion of clinical cases than those included in the general norm groups. The item-development sample was used for factor analysis instead of the norm samples because the former more closely represents the population with whom the TRS is used—that is, children who receive services or who have been referred for evaluation of various behavioral, emotional, or educational difficulties. In general, the item-development samples include cases that have a greater incidence of problems than those found in the general norm samples.

Two types of factor analysis were performed in developing the composites. The primary technique was covariance structure analysis (CSA; also known as confirmatory factor analysis) using the Amos 6.0 program (Arbuckle, 2005). CSA has three important advantages for analyzing an instrument such as the BASC–3 TRS. First, there is a large research base (derived from the previous BASC editions and similar instruments) that points to a starting factor structure that can be tested in the analysis. Second, CSA works well with instruments, such as the TRS, for which some factors are expected to correlate highly. Third, CSA identifies which aspects of a hypothesized factor-structure model are inconsistent with the data. It is important to note that CSA was used not to confirm a hypothesized model but rather to evaluate the model and modify it in appropriate ways according to the results of the analysis.

The second type of factor analysis, principal-axis analysis, is a purely exploratory method used to determine whether factor-structure models other than those evaluated with CSA could provide a good fit to the scale intercorrelation data. The results of principal-axis analysis can be more difficult to compare across samples (especially those with highly correlated factors) than those of CSA. However, if several principal-axis analyses point to an alternative structure, then that structure should be strongly considered. Thus, use of the principal-axis method complements CSA because it may reveal a substantially different factor structure not indicated by CSA.

## Covariance Structure Analyses

The starting CSA models were based on the final TRS factor structure models reported in the BASC–2 Manual (Reynolds & Kamphaus, 2004). For each level, scale modification indexes (MIs) were examined to see if possible changes might be evident that would substantially improve the model's overall fit to the data. Scales with high MI value loadings on other composite scales (relative to other modification indexes) were identified, and a new model fit was evaluated after adding a parameter between the scale and the composite. However, these changes to the model did not result in a substantial improvement in model fit. (Consistent with the BASC–2 analyses, fit was evaluated using the chi-square, Comparative Fit Index [CFI] and the Root Mean Squared Error of Approximation [RMSEA] fit indexes.) Therefore, the starting models for each level were retained. Fit indexes for each model are presented in Table 9.16, and standardized loadings and factor correlations for the models are presented in Table 9.17. The primary use of the fit indexes was to evaluate the potential model changes. The overall fit of the models is moderate, a finding that is consistent with analyses conducted on the previous BASC editions.

**Table 9.16** TRS: Fit of Various CSA Models (Item-Development Samples)

| Teacher Rating Scales | df | $x^2$ | CFI | RMSEA |
|---|---|---|---|---|
| Preschool | 41 | 1,383.9 | 0.76 | 0.20 |
| Child | 83 | 3,056.2 | 0.81 | 0.18 |
| Adolescent | 83 | 2,632.4 | 0.82 | 0.18 |

**Table 9.17** TRS: CSA Factor Loadings for the Final Models (Item-Development Samples)

| | TRS–P | | | TRS–C | | | | TRS–A | | | |
|---|---|---|---|---|---|---|---|---|---|---|---|
| | Externalizing Problems | Internalizing Problems | Adaptive Skills | Externalizing Problems | Internalizing Problems | School Problems | Adaptive Skills | Externalizing Problems | Internalizing Problems | School Problems | Adaptive Skills |
| Hyperactivity | .89 | — | — | .82 | — | — | — | .82 | — | — | — |
| Aggression | .87 | — | — | .89 | — | — | — | .94 | — | — | — |
| Conduct Problems | — | — | — | .94 | — | — | — | .93 | — | — | — |
| Anxiety | — | .72 | — | — | .59 | — | — | — | .72 | — | — |
| Depression | — | .88 | — | — | .81 | — | — | — | .90 | — | — |
| Somatization | — | .46 | — | — | .35 | — | — | — | .60 | — | — |
| Attention Problems | .71 | — | — | — | — | .90 | — | — | — | .94 | — |
| Learning Problems | — | — | — | — | — | .76 | — | — | — | .84 | — |
| Atypicality | — | .72 | — | — | .79 | — | — | — | .81 | — | — |
| Withdrawal | — | .66 | — | — | .78 | — | — | — | .75 | — | — |
| Adaptability | — | — | .79 | — | −.47 | — | .76 | — | −.32 | — | .82 |
| Social Skills | — | — | .79 | — | — | — | .76 | — | — | — | .82 |
| Leadership | — | — | — | — | — | — | .93 | — | — | — | .93 |
| Study Skills | — | — | — | — | — | — | .89 | — | — | — | .89 |
| Functional Communication | — | — | .80 | — | — | — | .87 | — | — | — | .86 |
| **Factor Correlations** | | | | | | | | | | | |
| Externalizing Problems | — | .75 | — | — | .63 | .68 | −.56 | — | .62 | .69 | −.59 |
| Adaptive Skills | −.59 | −.57 | — | — | −.73 | — | — | — | −.66 | — | — |
| School Problems | — | — | — | — | .71 | — | −.91 | — | .66 | — | −.90 |

## Principal-Axis Factor Analyses

Principal-axis analyses were carried out at each level of the TRS. Three- and four-factor (TRS–C and TRS–A only) solutions were obtained using oblique and orthogonal rotations; because the results were similar, only the orthogonal (Varimax) results are reported. Results of these analyses are reported for the preschool level in Table 9.18, for the child level in Table 9.19, and for the adolescent level in Table 9.20.

**Table 9.18** TRS–P: Principal-Axis Factor Matrix, Varimax Rotation

| | 3-factor | | |
|---|---|---|---|
| Scale | I | II | III |
| Hyperactivity | .21 | .18 | .93 |
| Aggression | .23 | .39 | .72 |
| Anxiety | .12 | .84 | .11 |
| Depression | .23 | .72 | .47 |
| Somatization | −.03 | .52 | .12 |
| Attention Problems | .59 | .11 | .54 |
| Atypicality | .43 | .49 | .37 |
| Withdrawal | .56 | .51 | .09 |
| Adaptability | −.63 | −.28 | −.34 |
| Social Skills | −.78 | .01 | −.18 |
| Functional Communication | −.86 | −.07 | −.11 |

**Table 9.19** TRS–C: Principal-Axis Factor Matrix, Varimax Rotation

| Scale | 3-factor | | | 4-factor | | | |
|---|---|---|---|---|---|---|---|
| | I | II | III | I | II | III | IV |
| Hyperactivity | −.31 | .77 | .12 | .33 | .78 | −.08 | .13 |
| Aggression | −.18 | .86 | .24 | .07 | .85 | −.29 | .18 |
| Conduct Problems | −.26 | .86 | .15 | .24 | .85 | −.16 | .14 |
| Anxiety | −.19 | .03 | .76 | .17 | .03 | −.15 | .78 |
| Depression | −.28 | .45 | .71 | .13 | .45 | −.41 | .64 |
| Somatization | −.02 | .10 | .47 | .06 | .11 | .02 | .50 |
| Attention Problems | −.69 | .48 | .15 | .75 | .49 | −.15 | .18 |
| Learning Problems | −.69 | .14 | .22 | .77 | .13 | −.12 | .28 |
| Atypicality | −.51 | .33 | .45 | .41 | .32 | −.35 | .42 |
| Withdrawal | −.55 | .17 | .49 | .29 | .13 | −.65 | .40 |
| Adaptability | .57 | −.48 | −.31 | −.34 | −.46 | .58 | −.22 |
| Social Skills | .66 | −.33 | −.10 | −.39 | −.30 | .72 | .05 |
| Leadership | .91 | −.18 | −.15 | −.73 | −.16 | .55 | −.10 |
| Study Skills | .84 | −.36 | −.04 | −.78 | −.35 | .33 | −.04 |
| Functional Communication | .87 | −.10 | −.24 | −.72 | −.09 | .50 | −.20 |

**Table 9.20** TRS–A: Principal-Axis Factor Matrix, Varimax Rotation

| Scale | 3-factor | | | 4-factor | | | |
|---|---|---|---|---|---|---|---|
| | I | II | III | I | II | III | IV |
| Hyperactivity | −.28 | .22 | .75 | .35 | .23 | .72 | −.06 |
| Aggression | −.22 | .23 | .86 | .12 | .21 | .91 | −.21 |
| Conduct Problems | −.29 | .19 | .85 | .26 | .18 | .83 | −.18 |
| Anxiety | −.18 | .71 | .12 | .21 | .74 | .08 | −.06 |
| Depression | −.26 | .81 | .39 | .15 | .78 | .39 | −.27 |
| Somatization | −.12 | .56 | .16 | .13 | .57 | .15 | −.07 |
| Attention Problems | −.70 | .24 | .49 | .76 | .26 | .43 | −.23 |
| Learning Problems | −.66 | .30 | .29 | .74 | .34 | .22 | −.19 |
| Atypicality | −.36 | .66 | .27 | .27 | .65 | .27 | −.28 |
| Withdrawal | −.49 | .66 | .00 | .15 | .62 | .03 | −.60 |
| Adaptability | .63 | −.40 | −.37 | −.37 | −.36 | −.38 | .56 |
| Social Skills | .74 | −.21 | −.22 | −.33 | −.09 | −.27 | .85 |
| Leadership | .89 | −.27 | −.17 | −.62 | −.24 | −.17 | .63 |
| Study Skills | .83 | −.14 | −.38 | −.80 | −.15 | −.32 | .37 |
| Functional Communication | .79 | −.40 | −.12 | −.59 | −.38 | −.11 | .54 |

The principal-axis analyses generally support the factor structures analyzed using CSA and reflect the pattern of results found in the previous BASC editions. The analyses point to an Externalizing Problems factor defined by the Aggression, Hyperactivity, and Conduct Problems scales, with smaller loadings for the Depression, Attention Problems, and Adaptability scales. An Internalizing Problems factor is also indicated that reflects primarily the Anxiety, Depression, and Somatization scales, with additional loadings for the Withdrawal and Atypicality scales. The factor corresponding to the Adaptive Skills composite has moderate to strong loadings for the Adaptability, Social Skills, Leadership, Study Skills, and Functional Communication scales. However, for the TRS–C and TRS–A scales, Leadership, Study Skills, and Functional Communication also have high loadings on the factor that includes the School Problems composite (i.e., the Attention Problems and Learning Problems scales). Results from the CSA analyses indicate strong correlations between the Adaptive Skills and School Problems factors. However, alternative CSA models that removed the School Problems factor and assigned the Attention Problems and Learning Problems scales to the Adaptive Skills factor proved to have significantly worse fit (i.e., significant change in chi-square and a change in CFI of .01 or higher) than models that retained the School Problems factor. This demonstrates the effectiveness of the CSA procedure in differentiating highly correlated factors often not identified using principal-axis or other exploratory procedures.

## CORRELATIONS WITH OTHER MEASURES OF BEHAVIOR

Several studies were carried out in which the TRS and another behavior-rating scale were completed by the same teacher at about the same time. The correlations between scores on the two instruments indicate the degree to which they measure the same behavioral dimensions. Correlations that have been adjusted for restriction of range are indicated for each study. The fact that scales on different instruments have the same or similar names does not ensure that those scales measure the same construct; the scales may define the behavioral dimension differently. Thus, in interpreting the results of correlation studies, it is important to consider the item content of the scales on both instruments.

Demographic information for the samples used for the correlational studies is presented in Table 9.21 (see chapter 8 for a more complete description of the demographic characteristics). In each study, the BASC–3 TRS cases were scored using either the general combined-gender or general separate-gender norms to match the type of scores available for the other instrument. Each sample was collected from several sites and composed primarily of children and adolescents from regular school settings.

**Table 9.21** TRS: Demographic Characteristics of BASC–3 and Validity Studies

| Characteristic | TRS-P | | | TRS-C | | | | | TRS-A | | |
|---|---|---|---|---|---|---|---|---|---|---|---|
| | ASEBA | ASRS | CARS-2 | ASEBA | ASRS | CARS-2 | Conners 3 | D-REF | ASEBA | Conners 3 | D-REF |
| N | 90 | 92 | 42 | 45 | 52 | 30 | 65 | 46 | 70 | 44 | 54 |
| **Age** | | | | | | | | | | | |
| Mean | 4.0 | 4.0 | 4.3 | 8.4 | 9.6 | 8.3 | 8.5 | 8.8 | 14.7 | 15.2 | 14.6 |
| SD | 1.1 | 1.2 | 1.0 | 1.7 | 1.5 | 1.5 | 1.5 | 1.8 | 1.8 | 1.9 | 2.1 |
| Range | 2–5 | 2–5 | 2–5 | 6–11 | 6–11 | 6–11 | 6–11 | 6–11 | 12–18 | 12–18 | 12–19 |
| **Test interval** | | | | | | | | | | | |
| Mean | 12.9 | 10.8 | 15.2 | 12.1 | 8.6 | 17.5 | 13.3 | 12.5 | 19.2 | 11.9 | 9.0 |
| Range | 0–60 | 0–56 | 0–56 | 0–56 | 0–32 | 4–48 | 0–51 | 0–60 | 0–68 | 0–68 | 0–61 |
| **Mother's education level** | | | | | | | | | | | |
| 1 | 2.2 | 7.6 | 7.1 | 2.2 | 3.8 | 3.3 | 7.7 | 13.0 | 4.3 | 11.4 | 7.4 |
| 2 | 11.1 | 21.7 | 19.0 | – | 48.1 | 10.0 | 18.5 | 15.2 | 8.6 | 18.2 | 27.8 |
| 3 | 22.2 | 21.7 | 16.7 | 28.9 | 30.8 | 26.7 | 10.8 | 34.8 | 24.3 | 29.5 | 38.9 |
| 4 | 64.4 | 48.9 | 57.1 | 68.9 | 17.3 | 60.0 | 63.1 | 37.0 | 62.9 | 40.9 | 25.9 |
| **Race/ethnicity** | | | | | | | | | | | |
| African American | 6.7 | 8.7 | 19.0 | 15.6 | 15.4 | 3.3 | 9.2 | 26.1 | 4.3 | 9.1 | 9.3 |
| Asian | 3.3 | 1.1 | – | – | – | – | – | 4.3 | – | 4.5 | 1.9 |
| Hispanic | 21.1 | 15.2 | 16.7 | 2.2 | 9.6 | 10.0 | 13.8 | 34.8 | 11.4 | 20.5 | 20.4 |
| Other | 5.6 | 7.6 | 4.8 | 6.7 | 1.9 | – | 6.2 | 2.2 | 2.9 | 2.3 | 14.8 |
| White | 63.3 | 67.4 | 59.5 | 75.6 | 73.1 | 86.7 | 70.8 | 32.6 | 81.4 | 63.6 | 53.7 |
| **Region** | | | | | | | | | | | |
| Midwest | 32.2 | 17.4 | 21.4 | 28.9 | 1.9 | 10.0 | 16.9 | 21.7 | 25.7 | 34.1 | 11.1 |
| Northeast | 13.3 | 16.3 | 23.8 | 8.9 | 13.5 | 16.7 | 16.9 | 4.3 | 7.1 | 20.5 | 18.5 |
| South | 38.9 | 57.6 | 35.7 | 51.1 | 80.8 | 30.0 | 35.4 | 56.5 | 54.3 | 34.1 | 38.9 |
| West | 15.6 | 8.7 | 19.0 | 11.1 | 3.8 | 43.3 | 30.8 | 17.4 | 12.9 | 11.4 | 31.5 |
| **Gender** | | | | | | | | | | | |
| Female | 52.2 | 51.1 | 47.6 | 51.1 | 51.9 | 30.0 | 38.5 | 60.9 | 51.4 | 54.5 | 59.3 |
| Male | 47.8 | 48.9 | 52.4 | 48.9 | 48.1 | 70.0 | 61.5 | 39.1 | 48.6 | 45.5 | 40.7 |

## Behavior Assessment System for Children, Second Edition

As discussed in chapter 7, the BASC–3 standardization forms contained all of the items found on the BASC–2 forms, as well as newly written BASC–3 items. As such, correlations between scores from the BASC–3 and BASC–2 scales can be derived using a large sample representative of the U.S. population (i.e., the BASC–3 general combined-gender norms); see Table 9.22 for the scales from each TRS level. As expected, correlations between the corresponding scale scores are extremely high. Overall, these results provide a sound basis for generalizing research done on the BASC–2 TRS to the BASC–3 TRS.

**Table 9.22** BASC–3 TRS: Correlations With the BASC–2 Teacher Rating Scales, General Combined Norm Samples

| BASC–3 | BASC–2 | | |
|---|---|---|---|
| | TRS–P | TRS–C | TRS–A |
| **Composite** | | | |
| Externalizing Problems | .98 | .99 | .99 |
| Internalizing Problems | .97 | .97 | .98 |
| School Problems | — | .98 | .98 |
| Adaptive Skills | .99 | .99 | .99 |
| Behavioral Symptoms Index | .99 | .99 | .99 |
| **Clinical scale** | | | |
| Hyperactivity | .95 | .98 | .98 |
| Aggression | .98 | .98 | .98 |
| Conduct Problems | — | .99 | .98 |
| Anxiety | .90 | .94 | .95 |
| Depression | .98 | .98 | .98 |
| Somatization | .98 | .96 | .96 |
| Attention Problems | .99 | .98 | .97 |
| Learning Problems | — | .97 | .96 |
| Atypicality | .97 | .97 | .97 |
| Withdrawal | .93 | .96 | .96 |
| **Adaptive scale** | | | |
| Adaptability | .96 | .93 | .95 |
| Social Skills | .99 | .97 | .98 |
| Leadership | — | .99 | .98 |
| Study Skills | — | .96 | .97 |
| Functional Communication | .98 | .98 | .99 |
| **Content scale** | | | |
| Anger Control | .77 | .75 | .75 |
| Bullying | .96 | .82 | .88 |
| Developmental Social Disorders | .90 | .89 | .93 |
| Emotional Self-Control | .94 | .91 | .88 |
| Executive Functioning | .88 | .82 | .76 |
| Negative Emotionality | .92 | .87 | .88 |
| Resiliency | .83 | .92 | .92 |

## Achenbach System of Empirically Based Assessment Caregiver-Teacher Report Form

The TRS and the Achenbach System of Empirically Based Assessment (ASEBA®) Caregiver-Teacher Report Form for Ages 1.5–5 (Achenbach & Rescorla, 2000) were completed for 90 children ages 2 through 5 years. The TRS and the ASEBA Teacher's Report Form for Ages 6–18 (Achenbach & Rescorla, 2001) also were completed for 45 children ages 6 through 11 years and for 70 adolescents ages 12 through 18 years. Correlations between the TRS and ASEBA composites and scales, adjusted for restriction of range, are shown in Tables 9.23 through 9.25.

# Table 9.23 TRS-P: Correlations With the ASEBA Caregiver-Teacher Report Form for Ages 1.5–5

| BASC-3 | Empirically based scales | | | | | | | | | DSM-oriented scales | | | | | BASC-3 | |
|---|---|---|---|---|---|---|---|---|---|---|---|---|---|---|---|---|
| | Emotionally Reactive | Anxious/ Depressed | Somatic Complaints | Withdrawn | Attention Problems | Aggressive Behavior | Internalizing Problems | Externalizing Problems | Total Problems | Affective Problems | Anxiety Problems | Pervasive Development Problems | ADHD | Oppositional Defiant Problems | Mean | SD |
| **Composite** | | | | | | | | | | | | | | | | |
| Externalizing Problems | .56 | .44 | .49 | .54 | .59 | .73 | .60 | .76 | .72 | .49 | .33 | .53 | .64 | .67 | 47.0 | 7.9 |
| Internalizing Problems | .53 | .55 | .33 | .40 | .25 | .39 | .57 | .42 | .54 | .44 | .47 | .43 | .32 | .38 | 48.3 | 9.7 |
| Adaptive Skills | -.16 | -.25 | -.12 | -.49 | -.40 | -.24 | -.34 | -.35 | -.37 | -.42 | -.19 | -.42 | -.37 | -.18 | 53.5 | 9.7 |
| Behavioral Symptoms Index | .59 | .63 | .47 | .76 | .64 | .65 | .73 | .74 | .77 | .69 | .51 | .72 | .67 | .60 | 47.1 | 8.1 |
| **Clinical scale** | | | | | | | | | | | | | | | | |
| Hyperactivity | .42 | .37 | .53 | .51 | .65 | .60 | .50 | .71 | .64 | .38 | .28 | .47 | .67 | .49 | 47.5 | 8.1 |
| Aggression | .61 | .46 | .40 | .52 | .46 | .78 | .63 | .73 | .72 | .55 | .35 | .52 | .54 | .77 | 47.1 | 7.7 |
| Anxiety | .58 | .55 | .38 | .40 | .29 | .41 | .60 | .43 | .56 | .40 | .53 | .48 | .32 | .43 | 48.5 | 9.5 |
| Depression | .65 | .65 | .38 | .61 | .33 | .54 | .70 | .59 | .69 | .66 | .54 | .60 | .41 | .54 | 47.7 | 8.4 |
| Somatization | .23 | .29 | .15 | .12 | .08 | .15 | .24 | .15 | .23 | .17 | .21 | .14 | .14 | .10 | 49.5 | 10.3 |
| Attention Problems | .21 | .30 | .26 | .56 | .61 | .32 | .42 | .52 | .50 | .42 | .24 | .44 | .58 | .26 | 47.3 | 9.2 |
| Atypicality | .46 | .49 | .38 | .72 | .56 | .45 | .59 | .56 | .61 | .54 | .45 | .65 | .55 | .39 | 48.1 | 7.9 |
| Withdrawal | .33 | .55 | .21 | .59 | .28 | .27 | .50 | .33 | .44 | .58 | .38 | .60 | .29 | .28 | 48.9 | 8.9 |
| **Adaptive scale** | | | | | | | | | | | | | | | | |
| Adaptability | -.36 | -.39 | -.24 | -.51 | -.41 | -.36 | -.49 | -.45 | -.50 | -.49 | -.33 | -.48 | -.40 | -.32 | 52.8 | 9.7 |
| Social Skills | -.08 | -.13 | -.05 | -.42 | -.36 | -.12 | -.20 | -.26 | -.25 | -.31 | -.13 | -.33 | -.31 | -.05 | 53.0 | 9.1 |
| Functional Communication | .01 | -.09 | -.02 | -.39 | -.34 | -.12 | -.19 | -.25 | -.24 | -.31 | -.02 | -.32 | -.29 | -.08 | 53.3 | 9.6 |
| **Content scale** | | | | | | | | | | | | | | | | |
| Anger Control | .70 | .56 | .51 | .57 | .34 | .74 | .69 | .69 | .73 | .62 | .48 | .57 | .46 | .71 | 46.8 | 7.2 |
| Bullying | .55 | .47 | .50 | .64 | .60 | .66 | .61 | .70 | .69 | .58 | .33 | .60 | .65 | .57 | 47.0 | 7.5 |
| Developmental Social Disorders | .34 | .46 | .28 | .73 | .54 | .35 | .54 | .50 | .54 | .59 | .36 | .66 | .52 | .28 | 47.3 | 8.5 |
| Emotional Self-Control | .68 | .64 | .48 | .63 | .47 | .68 | .76 | .69 | .77 | .65 | .57 | .62 | .54 | .66 | 47.1 | 8.0 |
| Executive Functioning | .52 | .51 | .43 | .69 | .66 | .61 | .66 | .73 | .74 | .59 | .42 | .62 | .69 | .53 | 46.7 | 8.3 |
| Negative Emotionality | .58 | .54 | .34 | .52 | .34 | .58 | .64 | .59 | .66 | .55 | .47 | .50 | .42 | .55 | 47.6 | 9.2 |
| Resiliency | -.39 | -.44 | -.27 | -.52 | -.45 | -.41 | -.55 | -.53 | -.56 | -.49 | -.35 | -.49 | -.45 | -.37 | 53.2 | 9.9 |
| **Clinical index** | | | | | | | | | | | | | | | | |
| Clinical Probability Index | .36 | .41 | .30 | .69 | .60 | .42 | .54 | .57 | .59 | .52 | .37 | .58 | .58 | .35 | 47.2 | 8.7 |
| Functional Impairment Index | .22 | .33 | .23 | .62 | .56 | .33 | .45 | .50 | .51 | .50 | .25 | .54 | .53 | .28 | 46.2 | 8.6 |
| **ASEBA mean** | 53.1 | 53.2 | 51.9 | 52.7 | 53.8 | 52.8 | 46.3 | 48.8 | 46.7 | 53.0 | 53.6 | 53.0 | 53.3 | 52.9 | — | — |
| **ASEBA SD** | 5.3 | 5.3 | 4.3 | 4.3 | 6.5 | 4.4 | 9.8 | 8.1 | 9.8 | 5.0 | 5.9 | 4.7 | 6.1 | 4.4 | — | — |

**Table 9.24** TRS-C: Correlations With the ASEBA Teacher's Report Form for Ages 6–18

| | Syndrome scales | | | | | | | | | | | | |
|---|---|---|---|---|---|---|---|---|---|---|---|---|---|
| BASC-3 | Anxious/ Depressed | Withdrawn/ Depressed | Somatic Complaints | Social Problems | Thought Problems | Inattention | Hyperactivity/ Impulsivity | Attention Problems Total | Rule-Breaking Behavior | Aggressive Behavior | Internalizing Problems | Externalizing Problems | Total Problems |
| **Composite** | | | | | | | | | | | | | |
| Externalizing Problems | −.06 | .52 | −.13 | .64 | .30 | .75 | .89 | .91 | .70 | .88 | .13 | .70 | .73 |
| Internalizing Problems | .65 | .40 | .28 | .22 | .43 | .09 | .04 | .00 | −.09 | .15 | .57 | .16 | .29 |
| School Problems | .26 | .31 | .02 | .46 | .42 | .80 | .73 | .71 | .46 | .58 | .23 | .61 | .77 |
| Adaptive Skills | −.17 | −.31 | −.10 | −.49 | −.40 | −.68 | −.67 | −.67 | −.60 | −.61 | −.31 | −.69 | −.70 |
| Behavioral Symptoms Index | .26 | .69 | −.04 | .73 | .55 | .88 | .91 | .93 | .78 | .91 | .34 | .83 | .90 |
| **Clinical scale** | | | | | | | | | | | | | |
| Hyperactivity | −.07 | .31 | −.20 | .61 | .27 | .77 | .93 | .82 | .56 | .69 | .00 | .54 | .73 |
| Aggression | −.08 | .57 | −.13 | .66 | .32 | .68 | .80 | .87 | .69 | .91 | .16 | .72 | .68 |
| Conduct Problems | −.02 | .54 | −.07 | .58 | .26 | .68 | .80 | .87 | .72 | .87 | .18 | .71 | .69 |
| Anxiety | .62 | .27 | .04 | −.06 | .34 | −.10 | −.12 | −.18 | −.21 | −.06 | .44 | −.03 | .07 |
| Depression | .36 | .78 | .04 | .68 | .55 | .61 | .70 | .75 | .74 | .85 | .47 | .82 | .75 |
| Somatization | .39 | .01 | .49 | .21 | .15 | .03 | −.09 | −.14 | −.23 | −.08 | .38 | −.07 | .13 |
| Attention Problems | .06 | .26 | −.04 | .40 | .31 | .82 | .77 | .74 | .48 | .56 | .06 | .56 | .75 |
| Learning Problems | .46 | .30 | .13 | .45 | .49 | .64 | .55 | .54 | .37 | .51 | .41 | .56 | .67 |
| Atypicality | .59 | .58 | .45 | .93 | .67 | .92 | .79 | .86 | .61 | .85 | .61 | .75 | .88 |
| Withdrawal | .42 | .76 | .04 | .23 | .59 | .42 | .42 | .50 | .59 | .60 | .52 | .65 | .62 |
| **Adaptive scale** | | | | | | | | | | | | | |
| Adaptability | −.20 | −.50 | −.08 | −.62 | −.47 | −.69 | −.66 | −.74 | −.60 | −.79 | −.38 | −.77 | −.70 |
| Social Skills | .04 | −.29 | .02 | −.24 | −.21 | −.45 | −.51 | −.54 | −.60 | −.46 | −.19 | −.60 | −.56 |
| Leadership | −.25 | −.29 | −.06 | −.39 | −.46 | −.64 | −.55 | −.57 | −.48 | −.47 | −.34 | −.57 | −.65 |
| Study Skills | −.02 | −.16 | −.08 | −.33 | −.23 | −.64 | −.66 | −.65 | −.53 | −.51 | −.13 | −.57 | −.61 |
| Functional Communication | −.37 | .03 | −.39 | −.57 | −.41 | −.49 | −.39 | −.35 | −.26 | −.30 | −.35 | −.47 | −.49 |
| **Content scale** | | | | | | | | | | | | | |
| Anger Control | −.17 | .57 | −.09 | .72 | .34 | .73 | .81 | .85 | .70 | .90 | .14 | .75 | .71 |
| Bullying | −.02 | .54 | −.07 | .55 | .27 | .62 | .69 | .84 | .67 | .89 | .17 | .67 | .62 |
| Developmental Social Disorders | .30 | .52 | .18 | .64 | .60 | .67 | .65 | .71 | .68 | .73 | .46 | .78 | .73 |
| Emotional Self-Control | .33 | .64 | .03 | .77 | .53 | .70 | .77 | .78 | .61 | .87 | .46 | .77 | .79 |
| Executive Functioning | .14 | .41 | −.01 | .62 | .43 | .84 | .86 | .83 | .65 | .74 | .25 | .72 | .85 |
| Negative Emotionality | .11 | .63 | −.10 | .58 | .30 | .62 | .69 | .76 | .64 | .85 | .27 | .72 | .66 |
| Resiliency | −.37 | −.44 | −.22 | −.58 | −.59 | −.68 | −.59 | −.64 | −.54 | −.64 | −.50 | −.71 | −.75 |
| **Clinical index** | | | | | | | | | | | | | |
| ADHD Probability Index | .14 | .44 | .01 | .63 | .44 | .86 | .87 | .85 | .65 | .78 | .22 | .74 | .85 |
| EBD Probability Index | .13 | .61 | −.11 | .65 | .34 | .70 | .81 | .86 | .71 | .90 | .24 | .74 | .74 |
| Autism Probability Index | .31 | .53 | .19 | .66 | .55 | .79 | .73 | .77 | .69 | .73 | .47 | .78 | .83 |
| Functional Impairment Index | .36 | .45 | .21 | .67 | .58 | .82 | .79 | .79 | .67 | .76 | .42 | .81 | .84 |
| **ASEBA mean** | 52.4 | 51.8 | 52.4 | 52.2 | 51.1 | 3.5 | 2.8 | 52.5 | 51.9 | 52.0 | 46.6 | 47.0 | 47.2 |
| **ASEBA SD** | 4.2 | 3.8 | 4.9 | 4.8 | 3.3 | 5.1 | 4.1 | 5.3 | 4.5 | 5.6 | 7.9 | 7.7 | 7.6 |

**Table 9.24** TRS–C: Correlations With the ASEBA Teacher's Report Form for Ages 6–18 (continued)

| BASC–3 | DSM-oriented scales | | | | | | BASC–3 | |
| --- | --- | --- | --- | --- | --- | --- | --- | --- |
| | Affective Problems | Anxiety Problems | Somatic Problems | ADHD | Oppositional Defiant Problems | Conduct Problems | Mean | SD |
| **Composite** | | | | | | | | |
| Externalizing Problems | .64 | −.08 | −.13 | .86 | .76 | .89 | 47.6 | 9.7 |
| Internalizing Problems | .16 | .63 | .32 | −.05 | .15 | .04 | 47.7 | 8.1 |
| School Problems | .54 | .14 | .02 | .73 | .51 | .46 | 46.4 | 8.6 |
| Adaptive Skills | −.54 | −.22 | −.07 | −.65 | −.53 | −.53 | 55.4 | 8.2 |
| Behavioral Symptoms Index | .79 | .13 | −.05 | .90 | .85 | .89 | 46.1 | 7.5 |
| **Clinical scale** | | | | | | | | |
| Hyperactivity | .56 | .00 | −.19 | .85 | .59 | .72 | 48.2 | 8.0 |
| Aggression | .65 | −.12 | −.14 | .79 | .83 | .89 | 47.8 | 9.7 |
| Conduct Problems | .62 | −.09 | −.07 | .80 | .73 | .90 | 47.4 | 10.8 |
| Anxiety | .03 | .58 | .05 | −.19 | −.04 | −.15 | 48.3 | 10.5 |
| Depression | .69 | .20 | .05 | .71 | .83 | .84 | 46.5 | 5.5 |
| Somatization | −.05 | .46 | .54 | −.17 | −.09 | −.16 | 49.8 | 8.7 |
| Attention Problems | .51 | .02 | −.04 | .80 | .51 | .51 | 47.0 | 9.3 |
| Learning Problems | .45 | .26 | .13 | .52 | .41 | .30 | 46.5 | 7.6 |
| Atypicality | .79 | .38 | .47 | .82 | .81 | .76 | 46.4 | 5.3 |
| Withdrawal | .66 | .49 | −.03 | .38 | .59 | .63 | 46.1 | 7.4 |
| **Adaptive scale** | | | | | | | | |
| Adaptability | −.67 | −.29 | −.03 | −.66 | −.77 | −.67 | 54.5 | 7.4 |
| Social Skills | −.35 | −.01 | .03 | −.47 | −.40 | −.51 | 54.7 | 9.1 |
| Leadership | −.47 | −.30 | −.06 | −.55 | −.39 | −.39 | 54.9 | 9.0 |
| Study Skills | −.49 | −.03 | −.03 | −.67 | −.43 | −.46 | 53.2 | 9.2 |
| Functional Communication | −.31 | −.38 | −.37 | −.29 | −.23 | −.15 | 55.9 | 6.8 |
| **Content scale** | | | | | | | | |
| Anger Control | .73 | −.12 | −.14 | .79 | .87 | .87 | 47.9 | 7.7 |
| Bullying | .56 | −.07 | −.07 | .70 | .76 | .90 | 47.8 | 12.2 |
| Developmental Social Disorders | .64 | .44 | .15 | .62 | .65 | .66 | 44.3 | 6.5 |
| Emotional Self-Control | .74 | .30 | .00 | .72 | .86 | .77 | 47.2 | 6.8 |
| Executive Functioning | .67 | .14 | −.02 | .85 | .66 | .68 | 45.9 | 8.4 |
| Negative Emotionality | .66 | −.06 | −.12 | .68 | .83 | .81 | 47.8 | 8.2 |
| Resiliency | −.59 | −.42 | −.19 | −.56 | −.61 | −.52 | 55.6 | 8.3 |
| **Clinical index** | | | | | | | | |
| ADHD Probability Index | .69 | .09 | −.01 | .86 | .71 | .71 | 46.3 | 8.1 |
| EBD Probability Index | .65 | −.01 | −.11 | .80 | .78 | .88 | 47.0 | 10.0 |
| Autism Probability Index | .67 | .29 | .17 | .72 | .66 | .71 | 44.9 | 7.5 |
| Functional Impairment Index | .69 | .31 | .18 | .76 | .69 | .66 | 45.2 | 7.0 |
| **ASEBA mean** | 51.6 | 52.9 | 52.4 | 52.7 | 51.9 | 52.0 | — | — |
| **ASEBA SD** | 3.6 | 4.8 | 5.2 | 4.8 | 5.0 | 6.5 | — | — |

**Table 9.25** TRS–A: Correlations With the ASEBA Teacher's Report Form for Ages 6–18

| BASC–3 | Anxious/ Depressed | Withdrawn/ Depressed | Somatic Complaints | Social Problems | Thought Problems | Inattention | Hyperactivity/ Impulsivity | Attention Problems Total | Rule-Breaking Behavior | Aggressive Behavior | Internalizing Problems | Externalizing Problems | Total Problems |
|---|---|---|---|---|---|---|---|---|---|---|---|---|---|
| **Composite** | | | | | | | | | | | | | |
| Externalizing Problems | .25 | .03 | .11 | .51 | .02 | .46 | .83 | .65 | .65 | .80 | .05 | .75 | .55 |
| Internalizing Problems | .74 | .59 | .78 | .83 | .39 | .71 | .64 | .71 | .70 | .71 | .72 | .74 | .76 |
| School Problems | .34 | .41 | .39 | .61 | .22 | .84 | .48 | .78 | .54 | .50 | .35 | .52 | .59 |
| Adaptive Skills | -.32 | -.44 | -.41 | -.55 | -.17 | -.65 | -.40 | -.62 | -.47 | -.49 | -.35 | -.49 | -.52 |
| Behavioral Symptoms Index | .46 | .47 | .34 | .77 | .22 | .78 | .79 | .81 | .74 | .80 | .38 | .75 | .72 |
| **Clinical scale** | | | | | | | | | | | | | |
| Hyperactivity | .25 | -.12 | -.05 | .35 | -.11 | .25 | .74 | .47 | .41 | .59 | -.03 | .50 | .36 |
| Aggression | .08 | .00 | .05 | .48 | .02 | .44 | .79 | .60 | .56 | .78 | -.08 | .73 | .48 |
| Conduct Problems | .30 | .20 | .30 | .57 | .13 | .53 | .81 | .69 | .76 | .84 | .20 | .80 | .61 |
| Anxiety | .69 | .35 | .21 | .61 | .16 | .59 | .54 | .65 | .47 | .52 | .57 | .56 | .63 |
| Depression | .61 | .63 | .70 | .83 | .35 | .75 | .80 | .81 | .82 | .88 | .65 | .85 | .80 |
| Somatization | .37 | .37 | .83 | .58 | .31 | .29 | .13 | .16 | .33 | .20 | .45 | .27 | .33 |
| Attention Problems | .30 | .28 | .25 | .58 | .09 | .71 | .55 | .68 | .50 | .55 | .23 | .52 | .55 |
| Learning Problems | .32 | .46 | .45 | .57 | .29 | .86 | .35 | .77 | .48 | .38 | .40 | .43 | .56 |
| Atypicality | .38 | .48 | .11 | .66 | .28 | .69 | .49 | .65 | .54 | .49 | .34 | .41 | .52 |
| Withdrawal | .37 | .68 | .43 | .65 | .36 | .68 | .29 | .62 | .59 | .44 | .55 | .43 | .59 |
| **Adaptive scale** | | | | | | | | | | | | | |
| Adaptability | -.28 | -.35 | -.34 | -.49 | -.14 | -.55 | -.38 | -.58 | -.46 | -.51 | -.27 | -.49 | -.43 |
| Social Skills | -.27 | -.41 | -.32 | -.49 | -.12 | -.56 | -.45 | -.52 | -.40 | -.47 | -.32 | -.44 | -.54 |
| Leadership | -.31 | -.39 | -.40 | -.53 | -.09 | -.58 | -.36 | -.55 | -.45 | -.46 | -.36 | -.50 | -.53 |
| Study Skills | -.31 | -.36 | -.44 | -.57 | -.18 | -.67 | -.41 | -.64 | -.53 | -.49 | -.29 | -.49 | -.49 |
| Functional Communication | -.31 | -.54 | -.40 | -.50 | -.20 | -.67 | -.23 | -.57 | -.36 | -.34 | -.40 | -.38 | -.46 |
| **Content scale** | | | | | | | | | | | | | |
| Anger Control | .25 | -.08 | .18 | .62 | -.06 | .44 | .87 | .73 | .80 | .89 | .10 | .85 | .68 |
| Bullying | .25 | .17 | .17 | .57 | .21 | .55 | .75 | .61 | .57 | .74 | .10 | .73 | .53 |
| Developmental Social Disorders | .43 | .58 | .37 | .61 | .28 | .71 | .33 | .64 | .50 | .46 | .48 | .47 | .57 |
| Emotional Self-Control | .72 | .21 | .47 | .78 | .28 | .60 | .86 | .80 | .87 | .91 | .58 | .89 | .80 |
| Executive Functioning | .33 | .35 | .34 | .60 | .09 | .66 | .53 | .70 | .54 | .59 | .30 | .57 | .56 |
| Negative Emotionality | .35 | .16 | .40 | .66 | .12 | .52 | .83 | .70 | .73 | .84 | .24 | .81 | .63 |
| Resiliency | -.26 | -.34 | -.34 | -.46 | -.11 | -.54 | -.31 | -.54 | -.40 | -.43 | -.28 | -.44 | -.43 |
| **Clinical index** | | | | | | | | | | | | | |
| ADHD Probability Index | .26 | .30 | .27 | .55 | .04 | .63 | .53 | .62 | .42 | .48 | .21 | .44 | .48 |
| EBD Probability Index | .47 | .35 | .41 | .73 | .26 | .72 | .84 | .81 | .78 | .88 | .36 | .86 | .73 |
| Autism Probability Index | .46 | .56 | .39 | .65 | .26 | .74 | .44 | .68 | .52 | .49 | .50 | .52 | .64 |
| Functional Impairment Index | .48 | .59 | .51 | .73 | .25 | .82 | .53 | .78 | .62 | .61 | .54 | .62 | .69 |
| **ASEBA mean** | 52.4 | 51.9 | 51.3 | 52.1 | 50.8 | 2.1 | 1.3 | 51.6 | 51.5 | 51.7 | 46.3 | 46.3 | 44.4 |
| **ASEBA SD** | 4.7 | 4.1 | 5.8 | 4.7 | 2.7 | 4.4 | 2.4 | 3.8 | 4.2 | 3.7 | 8.7 | 6.5 | 8.9 |

**Table 9.25** TRS–A: Correlations With the ASEBA Teacher's Report Form for Ages 6–18 *(continued)*

| BASC–3 | DSM-oriented scales | | | | | | BASC–3 | |
|---|---|---|---|---|---|---|---|---|
| | Affective Problems | Anxiety Problems | Somatic Problems | ADHD | Oppositional Defiant Problems | Conduct Problems | Mean | SD |
| **Composite** | | | | | | | | |
| Externalizing Problems | .50 | .16 | .00 | .71 | .81 | .69 | 46.5 | 6.3 |
| Internalizing Problems | .83 | .75 | .74 | .66 | .62 | .67 | 46.3 | 5.4 |
| School Problems | .63 | .34 | .24 | .69 | .35 | .61 | 45.2 | 7.7 |
| Adaptive Skills | -.53 | -.34 | -.33 | -.54 | -.35 | -.53 | 55.2 | 8.9 |
| Behavioral Symptoms Index | .66 | .37 | .19 | .83 | .75 | .79 | 45.4 | 5.7 |
| **Clinical scale** | | | | | | | | |
| Hyperactivity | .29 | .14 | -.11 | .60 | .66 | .41 | 46.9 | 6.4 |
| Aggression | .38 | .03 | -.08 | .65 | .77 | .67 | 46.6 | 6.1 |
| Conduct Problems | .63 | .20 | .19 | .71 | .84 | .77 | 46.8 | 6.8 |
| Anxiety | .55 | .69 | .10 | .58 | .43 | .45 | 47.0 | 7.0 |
| Depression | .85 | .54 | .63 | .82 | .80 | .83 | 45.5 | 4.4 |
| Somatization | .58 | .46 | .84 | .09 | .18 | .28 | 47.5 | 7.0 |
| Attention Problems | .51 | .27 | .13 | .68 | .45 | .56 | 45.6 | 7.6 |
| Learning Problems | .66 | .35 | .29 | .61 | .20 | .57 | 45.2 | 7.9 |
| Atypicality | .44 | .30 | -.02 | .62 | .43 | .62 | 46.8 | 6.2 |
| Withdrawal | .52 | .32 | .39 | .56 | .32 | .61 | 46.1 | 6.4 |
| **Adaptive scale** | | | | | | | | |
| Adaptability | -.46 | -.28 | -.27 | -.54 | -.39 | -.50 | 54.5 | 8.7 |
| Social Skills | -.45 | -.25 | -.27 | -.47 | -.40 | -.47 | 54.3 | 8.9 |
| Leadership | -.50 | -.37 | -.35 | -.49 | -.34 | -.49 | 55.3 | 9.0 |
| Study Skills | -.55 | -.34 | -.36 | -.59 | -.39 | -.57 | 55.2 | 8.5 |
| Functional Communication | -.53 | -.34 | -.31 | -.41 | -.14 | -.42 | 53.7 | 8.5 |
| **Content scale** | | | | | | | | |
| Anger Control | .50 | .14 | .12 | .83 | .89 | .80 | 46.3 | 5.0 |
| Bullying | .48 | .22 | .04 | .59 | .68 | .70 | 47.7 | 7.1 |
| Developmental Social Disorders | .52 | .44 | .31 | .54 | .28 | .56 | 45.2 | 7.3 |
| Emotional Self-Control | .69 | .65 | .44 | .86 | .90 | .83 | 46.1 | 5.2 |
| Executive Functioning | .52 | .34 | .26 | .70 | .50 | .58 | 44.3 | 8.1 |
| Negative Emotionality | .61 | .26 | .34 | .75 | .82 | .74 | 46.2 | 5.7 |
| Resiliency | -.42 | -.30 | -.28 | -.48 | -.30 | -.45 | 54.9 | 9.4 |
| **Clinical index** | | | | | | | | |
| ADHD Probability Index | .47 | .26 | .19 | .62 | .42 | .48 | 45.6 | 7.9 |
| EBD Probability Index | .69 | .41 | .30 | .81 | .83 | .83 | 45.9 | 6.4 |
| Autism Probability Index | .58 | .49 | .31 | .58 | .33 | .56 | 44.9 | 7.6 |
| Functional Impairment Index | .71 | .47 | .41 | .69 | .47 | .67 | 44.8 | 7.5 |
| **ASEBA mean** | 51.3 | 52.1 | 51.2 | 51.6 | 51.4 | 51.2 | — | — |
| **ASEBA SD** | 4.1 | 4.7 | 6.1 | 3.6 | 3.7 | 4.2 | — | — |

The mean TRS scores indicate that overall the samples appear to include somewhat smaller proportions of children with behavior problems than is true for the population as a whole. Relatedly, the variability in behavioral performance of the samples is generally smaller than that of the general population; the adjusted correlations presented in the tables correct for these differences in sampling variability. In addition, mean BASC–3 composite scale TRS scores tend to be at the same level of corresponding ASEBA scores; however, corresponding scale scores tend to be about one-third to one-half standard deviation lower for BASC–3 scale scores than ASEBA scale scores, a finding similar to that found in the BASC–2 standardization sample (Altmann & Reynolds, 2005).

Composite scale and clinical scale correlations between corresponding TRS and ASEBA scales that measure similar constructs are moderate to high. Low to moderate correlations were expected at times, particularly for scales between tests that are not directly comparable (e.g., BASC–3 Anxiety with ASEBA Anxiety/Depression). Scales measuring externalizing behaviors typically demonstrated higher correlations than did scales measuring internalizing behaviors, a finding consistent across the BASC editions and evident throughout the behavioral assessment literature.

## Conners 3 Teacher Form

The TRS child and adolescent forms were filled out along with the teacher form of the Conners 3™ (Conners 3rd Edition™; Conners, 2008) for 65 children ages 6 through 11 years and for 44 adolescents ages 12 through 18 years. Demographic characteristics of the samples are provided in Table 9.21. Tables 9.26 and 9.27 show correlations between TRS and Conners rating scale scores.

**Table 9.26** TRS–C: Correlations With the Conners 3 Teacher Form

| BASC–3 | Inattention | Hyper-activity/Impulsivity | Learning Problems/Executive Functioning | Learning Problems | Executive Functioning | Aggression | Peer Relations | ADHD: Inattentive | ADHD: Impulsive | Conduct Disorder | Oppositional Defiant Disorder | Conners 3 Global Index | Conners 3GI: Emotional Lability | Conners 3GI: Restless-Impulsive | BASC–3 Mean | BASC–3 SD |
|---|---|---|---|---|---|---|---|---|---|---|---|---|---|---|---|---|
| **Composite** | | | | | | | | | | | | | | | | |
| Externalizing Problems | .67 | .62 | .55 | .45 | .59 | .77 | .45 | .65 | .59 | .69 | .71 | .64 | .54 | .68 | 48.9 | 9.6 |
| Internalizing Problems | .49 | .54 | .40 | .26 | .42 | .54 | .48 | .46 | .50 | .40 | .59 | .64 | .70 | .60 | 49.0 | 7.5 |
| School Problems | .81 | .37 | .81 | .75 | .75 | .47 | .46 | .80 | .34 | .41 | .46 | .53 | .42 | .56 | 47.7 | 11.6 |
| Adaptive Skills | -.70 | -.30 | -.66 | -.58 | -.65 | -.45 | -.55 | -.66 | -.26 | -.38 | -.41 | -.45 | -.39 | -.47 | 53.6 | 11.2 |
| Behavioral Symptoms Index | .77 | .61 | .66 | .56 | .68 | .72 | .61 | .75 | .58 | .57 | .68 | .70 | .63 | .71 | 48.3 | 10.1 |
| **Clinical scale** | | | | | | | | | | | | | | | | |
| Hyperactivity | .59 | .70 | .45 | .37 | .47 | .59 | .33 | .56 | .67 | .39 | .60 | .64 | .50 | .66 | 49.2 | 9.9 |
| Aggression | .66 | .58 | .56 | .47 | .62 | .82 | .54 | .65 | .55 | .79 | .75 | .63 | .57 | .67 | 48.2 | 9.2 |
| Conduct Problems | .62 | .46 | .53 | .45 | .57 | .73 | .40 | .59 | .43 | .75 | .65 | .52 | .42 | .57 | 48.8 | 9.7 |
| Anxiety | .25 | .28 | .25 | .21 | .20 | .16 | .30 | .24 | .25 | .07 | .27 | .36 | .43 | .32 | 50.3 | 9.2 |
| Depression | .62 | .64 | .46 | .35 | .50 | .79 | .63 | .55 | .61 | .61 | .79 | .73 | .83 | .67 | 48.0 | 7.3 |
| Somatization | .17 | .24 | .11 | -.01 | .21 | .19 | .05 | .20 | .23 | .24 | .23 | .30 | .24 | .32 | 49.3 | 7.4 |
| Attention Problems | .81 | .44 | .75 | .66 | .71 | .46 | .46 | .79 | .41 | .35 | .46 | .57 | .44 | .60 | 47.8 | 11.5 |
| Learning Problems | .75 | .28 | .83 | .80 | .74 | .47 | .44 | .74 | .26 | .46 | .44 | .47 | .39 | .49 | 48.0 | 10.7 |
| Atypicality | .67 | .49 | .62 | .53 | .64 | .57 | .61 | .70 | .46 | .47 | .53 | .61 | .57 | .61 | 50.0 | 11.1 |
| Withdrawal | .48 | .26 | .40 | .34 | .39 | .49 | .62 | .45 | .24 | .41 | .42 | .36 | .31 | .36 | 48.5 | 8.5 |
| **Adaptive scale** | | | | | | | | | | | | | | | | |
| Adaptability | -.62 | -.44 | -.54 | -.43 | -.58 | -.57 | -.62 | -.59 | -.40 | -.46 | -.55 | -.58 | -.60 | -.56 | 53.5 | 10.0 |
| Social Skills | -.48 | -.23 | -.36 | -.29 | -.38 | -.43 | -.46 | -.40 | -.20 | -.36 | -.38 | -.30 | -.23 | -.32 | 52.5 | 11.0 |
| Leadership | -.62 | -.22 | -.61 | -.54 | -.58 | -.39 | -.54 | -.59 | -.19 | -.33 | -.39 | -.39 | -.33 | -.41 | 53.3 | 11.4 |
| Study Skills | -.73 | -.29 | -.75 | -.66 | -.74 | -.37 | -.42 | -.75 | -.26 | -.37 | -.31 | -.42 | -.30 | -.47 | 53.0 | 11.1 |
| Functional Communication | -.69 | -.21 | -.73 | -.68 | -.66 | -.31 | -.43 | -.66 | -.19 | -.29 | -.29 | -.39 | -.38 | -.40 | 53.1 | 10.8 |
| **Content scale** | | | | | | | | | | | | | | | | |
| Anger Control | .68 | .69 | .57 | .44 | .61 | .83 | .61 | .66 | .65 | .61 | .83 | .77 | .79 | .73 | 48.4 | 8.4 |
| Bullying | .59 | .48 | .52 | .42 | .58 | .80 | .51 | .58 | .46 | .84 | .68 | .53 | .45 | .59 | 48.6 | 9.7 |
| Developmental Social Disorders | .74 | .36 | .70 | .65 | .67 | .53 | .64 | .71 | .34 | .48 | .47 | .53 | .48 | .53 | 47.6 | 9.8 |
| Emotional Self-Control | .59 | .58 | .45 | .35 | .50 | .69 | .60 | .55 | .54 | .45 | .72 | .69 | .77 | .64 | 48.9 | 9.9 |
| Executive Functioning | .75 | .49 | .68 | .58 | .68 | .54 | .52 | .73 | .45 | .41 | .53 | .60 | .51 | .62 | 47.0 | 11.1 |
| Negative Emotionality | .71 | .68 | .56 | .41 | .62 | .82 | .67 | .66 | .66 | .62 | .80 | .78 | .80 | .75 | 48.4 | 8.2 |
| Resiliency | -.67 | -.37 | -.62 | -.54 | -.61 | -.47 | -.58 | -.64 | -.33 | -.39 | -.47 | -.52 | -.48 | -.52 | 54.0 | 11.1 |
| **Clinical index** | | | | | | | | | | | | | | | | |
| ADHD Probability Index | .77 | .47 | .70 | .60 | .70 | .55 | .52 | .75 | .43 | .40 | .54 | .60 | .52 | .61 | 47.3 | 11.7 |
| EBD Probability Index | .75 | .60 | .64 | .56 | .67 | .85 | .66 | .71 | .57 | .76 | .78 | .69 | .64 | .71 | 47.6 | 9.3 |
| Autism Probability Index | .67 | .37 | .61 | .53 | .61 | .53 | .65 | .64 | .34 | .42 | .50 | .52 | .50 | .53 | 47.3 | 10.8 |
| Functional Impairment Index | .79 | .41 | .76 | .67 | .72 | .56 | .59 | .77 | .38 | .46 | .53 | .58 | .54 | .59 | 47.5 | 10.8 |
| **Conners 3 mean** | 51.3 | 55.1 | 50.1 | 50.5 | 49.9 | 51.6 | 51.1 | 50.9 | 55.0 | 49.0 | 53.2 | 54.0 | 52.7 | 53.0 | — | — |
| **Conners 3 SD** | 11.9 | 16.2 | 11.7 | 11.8 | 11.4 | 12.9 | 12.3 | 12.1 | 16.6 | 9.4 | 15.5 | 15.2 | 15.5 | 13.8 | — | — |

**Table 9.27** TRS-A: Correlations With the Conners 3 Teacher Form

| BASC-3 | Inattention | Hyper-activity/ Impulsivity | Learning Problems/ Executive Functioning | Learning Problems | Executive Functioning | Aggression | Peer Relations | ADHD: Inattentive | ADHD: Impulsive | Conduct Disorder | Opposi-tional Defiant Disorder | Conners 3 Global Index | Conners 3Gi: Emotional Lability | Conners 3Gi: Restless-Impulsive | BASC-3 Mean | BASC-3 SD |
|---|---|---|---|---|---|---|---|---|---|---|---|---|---|---|---|---|
| **Composite** | | | | | | | | | | | | | | | | |
| Externalizing Problems | .84 | .83 | .70 | .48 | .75 | .84 | .53 | .78 | .87 | .72 | .84 | .89 | .78 | .86 | 47.7 | 7.5 |
| Internalizing Problems | .72 | .58 | .71 | .55 | .65 | .59 | .50 | .71 | .64 | .53 | .63 | .68 | .59 | .60 | 49.6 | 10.4 |
| School Problems | .83 | .58 | .86 | .72 | .85 | .58 | .60 | .82 | .62 | .55 | .57 | .74 | .49 | .71 | 48.3 | 9.4 |
| Adaptive Skills | -.67 | -.52 | -.63 | -.45 | -.68 | -.50 | -.48 | -.64 | -.55 | -.42 | -.53 | -.63 | -.42 | -.63 | 51.5 | 11.2 |
| Behavioral Symptoms Index | .85 | .68 | .77 | .58 | .79 | .73 | .65 | .82 | .73 | .62 | .74 | .80 | .62 | .75 | 48.1 | 8.8 |
| **Clinical scale** | | | | | | | | | | | | | | | | |
| Hyperactivity | .77 | .87 | .65 | .47 | .69 | .79 | .49 | .71 | .91 | .65 | .77 | .89 | .73 | .88 | 48.3 | 7.8 |
| Aggression | .81 | .74 | .66 | .41 | .72 | .89 | .61 | .74 | .80 | .63 | .89 | .81 | .75 | .75 | 47.3 | 6.7 |
| Conduct Problems | .78 | .72 | .65 | .44 | .70 | .70 | .40 | .72 | .75 | .71 | .69 | .81 | .68 | .78 | 48.0 | 8.3 |
| Anxiety | .71 | .55 | .79 | .68 | .72 | .42 | .56 | .72 | .59 | .56 | .46 | .65 | .57 | .60 | 48.2 | 8.6 |
| Depression | .82 | .62 | .71 | .53 | .72 | .73 | .52 | .77 | .68 | .55 | .73 | .74 | .65 | .68 | 49.0 | 8.8 |
| Somatization | .42 | .40 | .42 | .34 | .35 | .41 | .30 | .42 | .43 | .35 | .42 | .43 | .33 | .38 | 51.2 | 13.7 |
| Attention Problems | .80 | .60 | .79 | .58 | .83 | .58 | .60 | .78 | .65 | .53 | .58 | .73 | .46 | .73 | 47.7 | 9.5 |
| Learning Problems | .77 | .51 | .87 | .79 | .78 | .53 | .55 | .79 | .54 | .53 | .50 | .68 | .46 | .63 | 49.1 | 9.3 |
| Atypicality | .67 | .50 | .67 | .57 | .57 | .44 | .63 | .66 | .55 | .59 | .48 | .56 | .34 | .52 | 49.1 | 9.2 |
| Withdrawal | .50 | .17 | .45 | .30 | .49 | .32 | .42 | .50 | .20 | .23 | .35 | .34 | .17 | .30 | 49.6 | 9.8 |
| **Adaptive scale** | | | | | | | | | | | | | | | | |
| Adaptability | -.75 | -.60 | -.66 | -.44 | -.73 | -.59 | -.48 | -.70 | -.65 | -.48 | -.63 | -.72 | -.52 | -.70 | 52.4 | 10.4 |
| Social Skills | -.54 | -.43 | -.45 | -.31 | -.53 | -.40 | -.40 | -.50 | -.45 | -.35 | -.43 | -.49 | -.31 | -.50 | 51.2 | 10.8 |
| Leadership | -.59 | -.43 | -.61 | -.46 | -.64 | -.44 | -.50 | -.58 | -.46 | -.36 | -.47 | -.55 | -.39 | -.53 | 51.8 | 11.0 |
| Study Skills | -.69 | -.48 | -.68 | -.46 | -.76 | -.47 | -.43 | -.67 | -.52 | -.40 | -.47 | -.64 | -.37 | -.64 | 51.5 | 10.8 |
| Functional Communication | -.62 | -.54 | -.66 | -.56 | -.63 | -.47 | -.54 | -.62 | -.56 | -.47 | -.50 | -.64 | -.46 | -.62 | 50.0 | 10.3 |
| **Content scale** | | | | | | | | | | | | | | | | |
| Anger Control | .83 | .87 | .70 | .45 | .76 | .85 | .50 | .78 | .90 | .62 | .90 | .88 | .83 | .85 | 48.0 | 7.1 |
| Bullying | .86 | .79 | .76 | .57 | .78 | .88 | .63 | .81 | .84 | .74 | .89 | .86 | .81 | .81 | 48.4 | 6.8 |
| Developmental Social Disorders | .60 | .42 | .55 | .41 | .59 | .42 | .48 | .57 | .46 | .35 | .48 | .53 | .36 | .52 | 48.8 | 10.4 |
| Emotional Self-Control | .84 | .86 | .75 | .56 | .77 | .82 | .57 | .81 | .90 | .70 | .84 | .89 | .85 | .85 | 47.9 | 7.5 |
| Executive Functioning | .78 | .64 | .76 | .57 | .79 | .63 | .56 | .76 | .68 | .53 | .64 | .76 | .55 | .74 | 47.9 | 10.3 |
| Negative Emotionality | .82 | .72 | .67 | .45 | .72 | .77 | .48 | .74 | .77 | .58 | .81 | .79 | .69 | .75 | 48.6 | 9.4 |
| Resiliency | -.66 | -.54 | -.64 | -.48 | -.67 | -.52 | -.48 | -.63 | -.57 | -.42 | -.55 | -.64 | -.44 | -.63 | 51.5 | 10.9 |
| **Clinical index** | | | | | | | | | | | | | | | | |
| ADHD Probability Index | .77 | .65 | .74 | .57 | .76 | .63 | .58 | .74 | .69 | .57 | .62 | .76 | .51 | .74 | 48.5 | 9.3 |
| EBD Probability Index | .87 | .73 | .76 | .54 | .78 | .78 | .56 | .81 | .79 | .61 | .82 | .84 | .70 | .80 | 48.1 | 9.1 |
| Autism Probability Index | .61 | .38 | .59 | .45 | .60 | .39 | .49 | .59 | .40 | .38 | .42 | .50 | .38 | .46 | 48.7 | 11.1 |
| Functional Impairment Index | .78 | .59 | .77 | .58 | .77 | .57 | .57 | .77 | .64 | .52 | .59 | .74 | .53 | .70 | 48.6 | 10.4 |
| **Conners 3 mean** | 50.5 | 52.3 | 50.6 | 52.0 | 50.0 | 52.9 | 52.8 | 50.3 | 52.3 | 48.5 | 54.8 | 51.1 | 51.7 | 50.9 | — | — |
| **Conners 3 SD** | 11.7 | 13.3 | 11.9 | 13.1 | 11.9 | 15.0 | 13.1 | 11.5 | 13.4 | 9.0 | 16.0 | 12.6 | 11.3 | 12.9 | — | — |

The mean TRS scores indicate that overall the samples appear to include somewhat smaller proportions of children with behavior problems than is true for the population as a whole. Mean scale scores of the Conners teacher form tend to be somewhat higher than corresponding TRS scale scores by approximately one-fourth to one-half of a standard deviation.

Correlations between TRS and Conners teacher form scale scores that measure similar constructs are generally high across both TRS levels; the adolescent-level correlations are somewhat higher than the child level across several scales. The BASC–3 content scales and clinical indexes correlate moderately or higher across a number of Conners scales.

## Autism Spectrum Rating Scales Teacher Forms

As discussed in chapter 5, the BASC–2 has become increasingly used in evaluations involving children suspected of having an autism spectrum disorder. As such, two different measures of autism were included in the BASC–3 standardization project, the Autism Spectrum Rating Scales™ (ASRS®; Goldstein & Naglieri, 2010), and the Childhood Autism Rating Scale™, Second Edition (CARS™-2, Schopler & Van Bourgondien, 2010). The TRS–P and TRS–C were completed along with the ASRS teacher rating forms for 92 children ages 2 through 5 years and for 52 children ages 6 through 11 years. Demographic characteristics of the sample are presented in Table 9.21. Tables 9.28 and 9.29 show the correlations between the TRS and ASRS scores.

**Table 9.28** TRS-P: Correlations With the Autism Spectrum Rating Scales (2–5) Teacher Ratings

| BASC-3 | Social/ Communication | Unusual Behaviors | DSM–IV–TR | Peer Socialization | Adult Socialization | Social/ Emotional Reciprocity | Atypical Language | Stereotypy | Behavioral Rigidity | Sensory Sensitivity | Attention/ Self-Regulation | Total | BASC-3 Mean | BASC-3 SD |
|---|---|---|---|---|---|---|---|---|---|---|---|---|---|---|
| **Composite** | | | | | | | | | | | | | | |
| Externalizing Problems | .40 | .38 | .42 | .30 | .42 | .38 | .24 | .38 | .28 | .39 | .46 | .43 | 48.3 | 8.6 |
| Internalizing Problems | .29 | .46 | .40 | .27 | .31 | .19 | .37 | .45 | .38 | .43 | .34 | .45 | 49.1 | 8.4 |
| Adaptive Skills | –.55 | –.42 | –.57 | –.45 | –.44 | –.54 | –.38 | –.39 | –.34 | –.42 | –.38 | –.52 | 52.3 | 8.8 |
| Behavioral Symptoms Index | .52 | .48 | .55 | .43 | .47 | .48 | .34 | .49 | .36 | .49 | .49 | .55 | 48.2 | 9.0 |
| **Clinical scale** | | | | | | | | | | | | | | |
| Hyperactivity | .38 | .41 | .41 | .26 | .37 | .35 | .26 | .38 | .31 | .38 | .51 | .45 | 48.4 | 8.4 |
| Aggression | .37 | .31 | .39 | .30 | .43 | .36 | .19 | .34 | .23 | .34 | .37 | .38 | 48.6 | 8.7 |
| Anxiety | .16 | .41 | .30 | .13 | .30 | .12 | .29 | .30 | .36 | .39 | .17 | .34 | 50.1 | 9.3 |
| Depression | .26 | .35 | .32 | .28 | .34 | .19 | .27 | .31 | .31 | .31 | .24 | .35 | 48.3 | 8.5 |
| Somatization | .24 | .31 | .27 | .21 | .06 | .13 | .32 | .42 | .20 | .28 | .38 | .36 | 49.3 | 8.5 |
| Attention Problems | .53 | .46 | .54 | .35 | .46 | .51 | .41 | .41 | .36 | .46 | .59 | .54 | 47.5 | 8.7 |
| Atypicality | .52 | .45 | .53 | .46 | .39 | .44 | .39 | .49 | .29 | .44 | .50 | .54 | 49.3 | 8.9 |
| Withdrawal | .42 | .34 | .45 | .39 | .30 | .41 | .14 | .39 | .25 | .40 | .16 | .41 | 49.8 | 9.7 |
| **Adaptive scale** | | | | | | | | | | | | | | |
| Adaptability | –.46 | –.48 | –.53 | –.40 | –.41 | –.41 | –.37 | –.42 | –.44 | –.43 | –.41 | –.52 | 52.0 | 8.9 |
| Social Skills | –.37 | –.26 | –.40 | –.32 | –.27 | –.43 | –.27 | –.26 | –.18 | –.31 | –.17 | –.32 | 51.7 | 9.5 |
| Functional Communication | –.56 | –.33 | –.54 | –.43 | –.44 | –.55 | –.31 | –.31 | –.21 | –.33 | –.39 | –.47 | 52.3 | 8.8 |
| **Content scale** | | | | | | | | | | | | | | |
| Anger Control | .35 | .35 | .42 | .31 | .44 | .33 | .21 | .36 | .30 | .36 | .32 | .38 | 48.8 | 8.7 |
| Bullying | .43 | .31 | .43 | .34 | .37 | .45 | .16 | .34 | .23 | .34 | .37 | .40 | 48.2 | 9.4 |
| Developmental Social Disorders | .61 | .49 | .63 | .49 | .45 | .59 | .34 | .53 | .37 | .51 | .42 | .61 | 48.4 | 9.1 |
| Emotional Self-Control | .32 | .39 | .40 | .28 | .41 | .26 | .31 | .35 | .36 | .35 | .35 | .41 | 48.7 | 9.1 |
| Executive Functioning | .53 | .48 | .55 | .42 | .53 | .48 | .36 | .44 | .38 | .46 | .52 | .56 | 47.9 | 8.7 |
| Negative Emotionality | .23 | .31 | .29 | .23 | .31 | .16 | .18 | .28 | .31 | .26 | .23 | .33 | 49.3 | 9.2 |
| Resiliency | –.47 | –.46 | –.51 | –.40 | –.47 | –.41 | –.36 | –.43 | –.38 | –.42 | –.40 | –.51 | 52.1 | 9.5 |
| **Clinical index** | | | | | | | | | | | | | | |
| Clinical Probability Index | .59 | .51 | .62 | .45 | .49 | .55 | .42 | .51 | .39 | .50 | .57 | .61 | 48.4 | 8.9 |
| Functional Impairment Index | .57 | .45 | .58 | .42 | .52 | .55 | .38 | .44 | .34 | .45 | .49 | .55 | 48.0 | 8.9 |
| **ASRS mean** | 50.9 | 55.6 | 52.9 | 55.0 | 53.0 | 48.8 | 50.9 | 53.7 | 56.4 | 53.2 | 47.4 | 53.5 | — | — |
| **ASRS SD** | 9.5 | 11.8 | 10.4 | 10.7 | 10.5 | 9.3 | 11.7 | 11.7 | 10.8 | 12.5 | 9.9 | 10.4 | — | — |

**Table 9.29** TRS–C: Correlations With the Autism Spectrum Rating Scales

| BASC-3 | Social/ Communication | Unusual Behaviors | Self-Regulation | DSM–IV–TR | Peer Socialization | Adult Socialization | Social/ Emotional Reciprocity | Atypical Language | Stereotypy | Behavioral Rigidity | Sensory Sensitivity | Attention | Total | BASC-3 Mean | BASC-3 SD |
|---|---|---|---|---|---|---|---|---|---|---|---|---|---|---|---|
| **Composite** | | | | | | | | | | | | | | | |
| Externalizing Problems | .16 | .42 | .53 | .30 | .23 | .40 | .20 | .40 | .27 | .35 | .46 | .49 | .38 | 50.3 | 10.6 |
| Internalizing Problems | .37 | .39 | .32 | .40 | .45 | .39 | .39 | .34 | .25 | .34 | .42 | .23 | .39 | 50.1 | 14.5 |
| School Problems | .25 | .48 | .62 | .39 | .27 | .40 | .33 | .53 | .31 | .41 | .47 | .61 | .48 | 53.0 | 11.7 |
| Adaptive Skills | -.43 | -.61 | -.52 | -.54 | -.48 | -.44 | -.53 | -.52 | -.37 | -.59 | -.56 | -.55 | -.58 | 48.8 | 10.3 |
| Behavioral Symptoms Index | .35 | .56 | .53 | .46 | .42 | .48 | .39 | .50 | .35 | .48 | .57 | .48 | .52 | 50.8 | 12.3 |
| **Clinical scale** | | | | | | | | | | | | | | | |
| Hyperactivity | .11 | .40 | .51 | .26 | .17 | .36 | .15 | .45 | .26 | .29 | .41 | .53 | .36 | 49.8 | 10.3 |
| Aggression | .22 | .45 | .51 | .36 | .28 | .46 | .24 | .40 | .35 | .41 | .50 | .44 | .40 | 49.6 | 9.5 |
| Conduct Problems | .13 | .33 | .48 | .25 | .21 | .33 | .17 | .28 | .17 | .31 | .39 | .41 | .31 | 51.1 | 11.8 |
| Anxiety | .38 | .43 | .31 | .43 | .43 | .41 | .43 | .39 | .26 | .43 | .45 | .21 | .42 | 50.0 | 13.2 |
| Depression | .44 | .47 | .36 | .49 | .51 | .44 | .46 | .37 | .32 | .43 | .48 | .26 | .48 | 50.5 | 13.7 |
| Somatization | .19 | .15 | .19 | .19 | .29 | .22 | .18 | .14 | .10 | .06 | .23 | .13 | .18 | 49.8 | 12.1 |
| Attention Problems | .12 | .38 | .51 | .24 | .13 | .28 | .20 | .41 | .21 | .31 | .33 | .52 | .35 | 51.9 | 12.0 |
| Learning Problems | .34 | .49 | .58 | .45 | .35 | .42 | .39 | .52 | .35 | .43 | .50 | .55 | .51 | 53.6 | 11.8 |
| Atypicality | .26 | .41 | .38 | .33 | .33 | .33 | .28 | .39 | .23 | .35 | .46 | .36 | .38 | 51.5 | 14.8 |
| Withdrawal | .50 | .57 | .34 | .54 | .59 | .47 | .51 | .39 | .37 | .53 | .53 | .27 | .52 | 50.4 | 11.7 |
| **Adaptive scale** | | | | | | | | | | | | | | | |
| Adaptability | -.45 | -.58 | -.41 | -.53 | -.47 | -.44 | -.49 | -.42 | -.36 | -.61 | -.49 | -.40 | -.54 | 49.3 | 9.9 |
| Social Skills | -.35 | -.47 | -.37 | -.43 | -.39 | -.39 | -.45 | -.31 | -.25 | -.49 | -.46 | -.40 | -.45 | 49.9 | 10.7 |
| Leadership | -.31 | -.48 | -.46 | -.41 | -.35 | -.34 | -.45 | -.45 | -.24 | -.45 | -.47 | -.50 | -.47 | 48.7 | 10.3 |
| Study Skills | -.22 | -.44 | -.48 | -.36 | -.27 | -.31 | -.30 | -.49 | -.27 | -.39 | -.39 | -.55 | -.42 | 47.4 | 10.2 |
| Functional Communication | -.47 | -.59 | -.48 | -.54 | -.52 | -.40 | -.52 | -.54 | -.44 | -.55 | -.59 | -.48 | -.57 | 49.8 | 11.1 |
| **Content scale** | | | | | | | | | | | | | | | |
| Anger Control | .57 | .77 | .71 | .70 | .62 | .66 | .58 | .70 | .61 | .73 | .71 | .66 | .73 | 49.3 | 8.6 |
| Bullying | .08 | .25 | .37 | .18 | .14 | .26 | .13 | .21 | .16 | .21 | .34 | .33 | .24 | 51.0 | 11.1 |
| Developmental Social Disorders | .49 | .59 | .41 | .55 | .54 | .48 | .52 | .46 | .37 | .55 | .59 | .38 | .55 | 50.5 | 12.7 |
| Emotional Self-Control | .58 | .72 | .58 | .70 | .63 | .62 | .62 | .65 | .52 | .71 | .69 | .48 | .69 | 49.7 | 9.8 |
| Executive Functioning | .32 | .60 | .62 | .47 | .35 | .45 | .41 | .58 | .37 | .53 | .55 | .64 | .55 | 51.3 | 10.5 |
| Negative Emotionality | .52 | .65 | .58 | .62 | .57 | .59 | .55 | .51 | .45 | .65 | .64 | .45 | .63 | 50.1 | 10.5 |
| Resiliency | -.42 | -.56 | -.46 | -.51 | -.45 | -.42 | -.52 | -.47 | -.32 | -.58 | -.52 | -.48 | -.54 | 49.5 | 10.1 |
| **Clinical index** | | | | | | | | | | | | | | | |
| ADHD Probability Index | .26 | .55 | .60 | .42 | .32 | .44 | .34 | .56 | .33 | .46 | .53 | .60 | .50 | 51.4 | 11.3 |
| EBD Probability Index | .34 | .53 | .54 | .46 | .41 | .48 | .39 | .46 | .35 | .48 | .57 | .47 | .50 | 51.0 | 11.4 |
| Autism Probability Index | .45 | .61 | .49 | .53 | .51 | .49 | .51 | .50 | .36 | .55 | .62 | .48 | .56 | 51.1 | 12.5 |
| Functional Impairment Index | .45 | .63 | .57 | .55 | .50 | .49 | .50 | .57 | .40 | .57 | .59 | .53 | .61 | 51.4 | 12.2 |
| **ASRS mean** | 54.1 | 53.8 | 53.0 | 53.9 | 55.3 | 53.1 | 53.1 | 49.8 | 53.0 | 53.1 | 53.2 | 53.2 | 54.4 | — | — |
| **ASRS SD** | 11.8 | 10.1 | 9.6 | 11.5 | 10.9 | 11.0 | 11.3 | 9.6 | 11.6 | 10.2 | 10.9 | 9.6 | 10.6 | — | — |

The mean scores on most of the TRS composites indicate that these samples are about average with respect to their level of behavior problems, but the variability in scores is somewhat higher than the general population. TRS scores compared to corresponding ASRS scores are somewhat lower (approximately one-fourth of a standard deviation in several cases). Correlations between similar TRS and ASRS scales (e.g., TRS Developmental Social Disorders and Autism Probability Index scores with the ASRS Total Scores and the *DSM–IV–TR*™ [APA, 2000] scores) are moderate.

## Childhood Autism Rating Scale, Second Edition

The TRS–C and the CARS-2 High-Functioning Version form were completed for 30 children ages 6 through 11 years. Demographic characteristics of the sample are reported in Table 9.21. Table 9.30 shows the correlations between the TRS–C and CARS-2 scale scores.

The TRS–C scales' mean scores indicate that these samples are average to slightly below average in their levels of behavior problems and are slightly above average in adaptive skills; the variability in scores is a bit higher than the general population. As discussed in chapter 5, there are several BASC–3 scales that have been shown to be elevated in score profiles of children with autism-related disorders, including Atypicality, Developmental Social Disorders, Functional Communication, and Withdrawal. Correlations between these scale scores and the CARS-2 Total Score are generally high.

**Table 9.30** TRS–C: Correlations With the Childhood Autism Rating Scale 2 High-Functioning Version

| BASC–3 | CARS-2 Total Score | BASC–3 Mean | BASC–3 *SD* |
|---|---|---|---|
| **Composite** | | | |
| Externalizing Problems | .11 | 49.0 | 6.1 |
| Internalizing Problems | .32 | 47.4 | 6.4 |
| School Problems | .50 | 45.7 | 8.5 |
| Adaptive Skills | −.41 | 54.2 | 9.7 |
| Behavioral Symptoms Index | .63 | 48.4 | 7.6 |
| **Clinical scale** | | | |
| Hyperactivity | .12 | 50.8 | 9.2 |
| Aggression | .08 | 47.6 | 5.0 |
| Conduct Problems | .07 | 48.6 | 6.0 |
| Anxiety | −.07 | 48.1 | 7.2 |
| Depression | .70 | 47.6 | 6.7 |
| Somatization | .00 | 48.3 | 7.0 |
| Attention Problems | .37 | 47.6 | 10.3 |
| Learning Problems | .69 | 44.5 | 5.9 |
| Atypicality | .53 | 50.2 | 9.3 |
| Withdrawal | .58 | 48.5 | 9.2 |
| **Adaptive scale** | | | |
| Adaptability | −.39 | 53.5 | 9.0 |
| Social Skills | −.24 | 51.6 | 11.3 |
| Leadership | −.39 | 53.9 | 10.3 |
| Study Skills | −.30 | 53.6 | 9.6 |
| Functional Communication | −.56 | 55.3 | 7.6 |
| **Content scale** | | | |
| Anger Control | .33 | 48.7 | 6.8 |
| Bullying | −.33 | 47.2 | 5.2 |
| Developmental Social Disorders | .63 | 47.3 | 9.6 |
| Emotional Self-Control | .35 | 48.4 | 7.0 |
| Executive Functioning | .33 | 47.1 | 9.5 |
| Negative Emotionality | .32 | 48.0 | 6.1 |
| Resiliency | −.43 | 54.7 | 10.0 |
| **Clinical index** | | | |
| ADHD Probability Index | .41 | 47.2 | 9.2 |
| EBD Probability Index | .44 | 47.5 | 6.1 |
| Autism Probability Index | .44 | 47.3 | 9.1 |
| Functional Impairment Index | .64 | 45.8 | 7.5 |
| **CARS-2 mean** | 22.7 | — | — |
| **CARS-2 *SD*** | 5.9 | — | — |

## Delis Rating of Executive Functions Teacher Rating Form

The TRS–C and TRS–A forms were completed along with the Delis Rating of Executive Functions (D-REF; Delis, 2012) Teacher Rating Form for 46 children ages 6 through 11 years and for 54 children and adolescents ages 12 through 19 years. Demographic characteristics of the sample are provided in Table 9.21. Tables 9.31 and 9.32 present the correlations between the TRS and D-REF core index and clinical index scale scores.

The mean TRS scores indicate that the samples are generally average in their levels of behavior problems, although Internalizing Problems on the child level is slightly above average. The scale score variability is about average in the TRS–C sample but generally a bit lower than average in the TRS–A sample.

The correlations between the TRS scales that assess various aspects of executive functioning (e.g., Hyperactivity, Attention Problems, Anger Control, Executive Functioning, Emotional Self-Control) are consistently high across the various D-REF scales, particularly with the Total Composite scale.

Table 9.31 TRS–C: Correlations With the D-REF Teacher Rating Form

| BASC–3 | Behavioral Functioning Index | Emotional Functioning Index | Executive Functioning Index | Total Composite | Attention/ Working Memory Index | Activity Level/ Impulse Control Index | Compliance/ Anger Management Index | Abstract Thinking/Problem Solving Index | BASC–3 Mean | BASC–3 SD |
|---|---|---|---|---|---|---|---|---|---|---|
| **Composite** | | | | | | | | | | |
| Externalizing Problems | .78 | .67 | .61 | .72 | .64 | .75 | .78 | .57 | 50.2 | 10.2 |
| Internalizing Problems | .42 | .57 | .44 | .52 | .39 | .37 | .49 | .49 | 53.0 | 12.4 |
| School Problems | .63 | .57 | .84 | .77 | .84 | .59 | .56 | .77 | 48.7 | 9.8 |
| Adaptive Skills | -.54 | -.59 | -.75 | -.70 | -.74 | -.51 | -.54 | -.69 | 49.1 | 10.3 |
| Behavioral Symptoms Index | .70 | .70 | .73 | .76 | .74 | .67 | .72 | .69 | 51.0 | 10.7 |
| **Clinical scale** | | | | | | | | | | |
| Hyperactivity | .74 | .60 | .59 | .67 | .64 | .73 | .70 | .55 | 49.3 | 9.4 |
| Aggression | .72 | .70 | .58 | .69 | .60 | .71 | .78 | .54 | 50.2 | 10.4 |
| Conduct Problems | .71 | .56 | .54 | .66 | .57 | .67 | .70 | .50 | 50.8 | 10.9 |
| Anxiety | .41 | .58 | .41 | .49 | .41 | .38 | .50 | .45 | 52.9 | 10.9 |
| Depression | .46 | .62 | .43 | .55 | .39 | .41 | .55 | .47 | 52.1 | 11.2 |
| Somatization | .35 | .39 | .44 | .45 | .34 | .28 | .35 | .46 | 52.0 | 11.2 |
| Attention Problems | .73 | .59 | .82 | .80 | .87 | .70 | .62 | .72 | 48.3 | 9.9 |
| Learning Problems | .41 | .45 | .73 | .60 | .68 | .37 | .39 | .68 | 49.3 | 9.6 |
| Atypicality | .43 | .48 | .60 | .54 | .61 | .41 | .46 | .57 | 52.2 | 12.4 |
| Withdrawal | .28 | .39 | .53 | .44 | .48 | .25 | .35 | .51 | 51.9 | 9.1 |
| **Adaptive scale** | | | | | | | | | | |
| Adaptability | -.44 | -.59 | -.54 | -.56 | -.53 | -.43 | -.52 | -.53 | 48.1 | 11.0 |
| Social Skills | -.26 | -.34 | -.43 | -.35 | -.41 | -.26 | -.33 | -.38 | 49.1 | 9.8 |
| Leadership | -.50 | -.49 | -.70 | -.65 | -.69 | -.47 | -.46 | -.63 | 48.5 | 10.7 |
| Study Skills | -.71 | -.62 | -.86 | -.82 | -.87 | -.66 | -.62 | -.76 | 51.4 | 10.2 |
| Functional Communication | -.36 | -.43 | -.65 | -.56 | -.63 | -.32 | -.34 | -.62 | 49.1 | 10.5 |
| **Content scale** | | | | | | | | | | |
| Anger Control | .71 | .76 | .64 | .72 | .63 | .68 | .79 | .64 | 50.2 | 10.5 |
| Bullying | .64 | .49 | .38 | .52 | .39 | .62 | .62 | .33 | 50.4 | 11.5 |
| Developmental Social Disorders | .44 | .50 | .61 | .55 | .62 | .42 | .46 | .57 | 52.3 | 10.7 |
| Emotional Self-Control | .57 | .77 | .57 | .67 | .54 | .51 | .70 | .61 | 52.4 | 11.3 |
| Executive Functioning | .79 | .74 | .86 | .88 | .87 | .75 | .76 | .80 | 50.0 | 10.2 |
| Negative Emotionality | .70 | .73 | .61 | .73 | .59 | .68 | .76 | .61 | 50.7 | 9.7 |
| Resiliency | -.42 | -.57 | -.59 | -.57 | -.58 | -.40 | -.46 | -.57 | 48.2 | 10.9 |
| **Clinical index** | | | | | | | | | | |
| ADHD Probability Index | .71 | .67 | .82 | .83 | .84 | .66 | .68 | .78 | 50.1 | 10.5 |
| EBD Probability Index | .78 | .75 | .71 | .79 | .71 | .75 | .82 | .69 | 50.7 | 9.7 |
| Autism Probability Index | .50 | .56 | .70 | .63 | .69 | .47 | .54 | .67 | 52.3 | 10.7 |
| Functional Impairment Index | .66 | .71 | .85 | .82 | .84 | .60 | .67 | .81 | 50.7 | 10.5 |
| **D-REF mean** | 46.8 | 48.9 | 48.2 | 46.8 | 48.4 | 47.1 | 48.5 | 49.2 | — | — |
| **D-REF SD** | 11.0 | 10.8 | 12.4 | 12.5 | 11.7 | 10.7 | 10.7 | 10.9 | — | — |

**Table 9.32** TRS–A: Correlations With the D-REF Teacher Rating Form

| BASC–3 | Behavioral Functioning Index | Emotional Functioning Index | Executive Functioning Index | Total Composite | Attention/ Working Memory Index | Activity Level/ Impulse Control Index | Compliance/ Anger Management Index | Abstract Thinking/Problem Solving Index | BASC–3 Mean | BASC–3 SD |
|---|---|---|---|---|---|---|---|---|---|---|
| **Composite** | | | | | | | | | | |
| Externalizing Problems | .86 | .82 | .82 | .87 | .79 | .82 | .85 | .74 | 48.6 | 8.1 |
| Internalizing Problems | .67 | .67 | .67 | .71 | .58 | .64 | .54 | .71 | 49.4 | 8.2 |
| School Problems | .84 | .51 | .90 | .81 | .91 | .80 | .62 | .80 | 47.4 | 8.4 |
| Adaptive Skills | –.60 | –.54 | –.76 | –.66 | –.76 | –.59 | –.62 | –.71 | 51.8 | 7.4 |
| Behavioral Symptoms Index | .82 | .70 | .81 | .82 | .79 | .79 | .73 | .73 | 48.6 | 10.3 |
| **Clinical scale** | | | | | | | | | | |
| Hyperactivity | .81 | .59 | .76 | .75 | .76 | .79 | .67 | .66 | 49.1 | 10.1 |
| Aggression | .71 | .79 | .66 | .76 | .62 | .66 | .80 | .56 | 49.1 | 8.8 |
| Conduct Problems | .79 | .83 | .76 | .83 | .68 | .75 | .80 | .73 | 48.2 | 6.7 |
| Anxiety | .39 | .51 | .43 | .46 | .32 | .40 | .33 | .54 | 50.9 | 9.2 |
| Depression | .78 | .81 | .76 | .83 | .70 | .75 | .76 | .71 | 48.6 | 8.2 |
| Somatization | .47 | .28 | .49 | .45 | .38 | .40 | .22 | .54 | 48.5 | 8.1 |
| Attention Problems | .86 | .54 | .90 | .84 | .92 | .83 | .63 | .76 | 48.1 | 8.9 |
| Learning Problems | .73 | .43 | .84 | .72 | .84 | .70 | .53 | .80 | 46.8 | 7.7 |
| Atypicality | .62 | .49 | .64 | .60 | .62 | .60 | .51 | .63 | 49.9 | 12.1 |
| Withdrawal | .63 | .61 | .67 | .66 | .68 | .65 | .60 | .64 | 48.7 | 8.3 |
| **Adaptive scale** | | | | | | | | | | |
| Adaptability | –.62 | –.71 | –.66 | –.69 | –.68 | –.60 | –.70 | –.62 | 51.8 | 7.6 |
| Social Skills | –.37 | –.43 | –.48 | –.43 | –.49 | –.37 | –.49 | –.47 | 51.6 | 8.0 |
| Leadership | –.35 | –.45 | –.59 | –.46 | –.53 | –.32 | –.49 | –.60 | 51.2 | 8.2 |
| Study Skills | –.71 | –.36 | –.80 | –.68 | –.82 | –.67 | –.51 | –.63 | 52.7 | 8.2 |
| Functional Communication | –.44 | –.23 | –.62 | –.42 | –.65 | –.44 | –.31 | –.63 | 50.8 | 7.6 |
| **Content scale** | | | | | | | | | | |
| Anger Control | .75 | .77 | .65 | .77 | .64 | .70 | .78 | .53 | 49.8 | 9.0 |
| Bullying | .52 | .65 | .45 | .58 | .39 | .44 | .62 | .35 | 49.4 | 8.8 |
| Developmental Social Disorders | .60 | .54 | .67 | .61 | .68 | .61 | .54 | .65 | 48.7 | 8.5 |
| Emotional Self-Control | .78 | .81 | .70 | .80 | .67 | .73 | .78 | .63 | 49.0 | 8.2 |
| Executive Functioning | .79 | .67 | .86 | .80 | .85 | .76 | .73 | .80 | 48.1 | 7.7 |
| Negative Emotionality | .74 | .80 | .70 | .80 | .66 | .69 | .79 | .59 | 48.9 | 8.4 |
| Resiliency | –.47 | –.59 | –.65 | –.57 | –.62 | –.46 | –.62 | –.68 | 51.5 | 7.5 |
| **Clinical index** | | | | | | | | | | |
| ADHD Probability Index | .86 | .60 | .89 | .84 | .90 | .84 | .71 | .78 | 48.5 | 8.7 |
| EBD Probability Index | .80 | .84 | .78 | .84 | .73 | .75 | .83 | .71 | 48.4 | 8.2 |
| Autism Probability Index | .55 | .60 | .68 | .62 | .66 | .55 | .58 | .68 | 49.0 | 8.9 |
| Functional Impairment Index | .82 | .66 | .88 | .82 | .88 | .80 | .70 | .84 | 47.8 | 7.9 |
| **D-REF mean** | 49.0 | 49.3 | 47.2 | 48.6 | 47.7 | 50.6 | 48.3 | 47.8 | — | — |
| **D-REF SD** | 10.2 | 8.1 | 9.6 | 9.5 | 9.4 | 9.9 | 8.6 | 8.3 | — | — |

# PROFILES OF CLINICAL GROUPS

When interpreting BASC–3 results, it is helpful to know the profiles of mean scale scores of groups of children and adolescents who have been identified with behavioral or emotional problems. In general, such individuals tend to have various behavioral strengths along with higher than average deficits.

Often, these differences between the strengths and deficits are defining features of the problem area itself; for example, attention-deficit/hyperactivity disorder (ADHD) is defined by hyperactivity and attention problems. An understanding of these profiles is helpful when making complex differential diagnoses. The presentation of group score profiles gives added empirical support for the use of the BASC–3 in identifying behavioral and emotional problems.

As discussed in chapters 7 and 8, the clinical norm samples were created from groups of children and adolescents identified as having one or more behavioral, emotional, physical, or learning problems. There were sufficient cases of each of the following groups to calculate profiles:

- Attention-deficit/hyperactivity disorder (ADHD)

- Autism spectrum disorder

- Emotional/behavioral disturbance (EBD)

- Hearing impairment

- Specific learning disorder

- Speech or language disorder

The mean *T* scores for these groups on the TRS composites and scales appear in Table 9.33 and are displayed graphically in Figures 9.1 through 9.6. General combined-gender norms were used for all cases. The following points summarize the results for each group. For each diagnostic group, results are combined across the child and adolescent levels. Scores from the preschool level are not presented because of the imprecision of diagnoses at such a young age. Selected results of these profiles include:

- ADHD: highest scale scores on Attention Problems and Hyperactivity (although they are lower than the At-Risk range of scores)

- Autism: high scores on the Developmental Social Disorders, Atypicality, and Withdrawal scales, as well as markedly lower scores on several of the adaptive scales

- EBD: high scores for the Aggression, Anxiety, and Depression scales

**Table 9.33** Mean *T* Scores for Clinical Groups on the TRS Composites, Scales, and Indexes

| | All Clinical | | Attention-Deficit/ Hyperactivity Disorder | | Autism Spectrum Disorder and Pervasive Developmental Disorder | | Emotional/Behavioral Disturbance | | Hearing Impairment | | Learning Disability | | Speech/Language Disorder | |
| | Child/Adolescent | | Child/Adolescent | | Child/Adolescent | | Child/Adolescent | | Child/Adolescent | | Child/Adolescent | | Child/Adolescent | |
| | Mean | SD | Mean | SD | Mean | SD | Mean | SD | Mean | SD | Mean | SD | Mean | SD |
|---|---|---|---|---|---|---|---|---|---|---|---|---|---|---|
| **Composite** | | | | | | | | | | | | | | |
| Externalizing Problems | 54.6 | 12.6 | 54.6 | 11.8 | 55.7 | 12.6 | 59.6 | 15.2 | 55.9 | 11.6 | 51.7 | 11.4 | 49.6 | 11.2 |
| Internalizing Problems | 56.8 | 13.2 | 54.3 | 12.3 | 59.1 | 12.4 | 64.2 | 15.2 | 53.2 | 15.4 | 56.4 | 11.7 | 50.9 | 11.2 |
| School Problems | 58.7 | 10.7 | 58.4 | 10.2 | 62.0 | 10.0 | 57.1 | 10.9 | 56.8 | 11.5 | 60.6 | 9.8 | 52.0 | 10.7 |
| Adaptive Skills | 43.2 | 9.7 | 44.5 | 9.0 | 38.1 | 8.0 | 42.3 | 9.5 | 44.7 | 10.0 | 45.2 | 9.7 | 49.2 | 9.7 |
| Behavioral Symptoms Index | 57.9 | 12.2 | 56.4 | 10.7 | 63.2 | 12.1 | 62.7 | 13.7 | 56.0 | 12.3 | 54.3 | 10.6 | 49.6 | 8.2 |
| **Clinical scale** | | | | | | | | | | | | | | |
| Hyperactivity | 55.1 | 12.3 | 56.5 | 12.6 | 56.3 | 11.5 | 58.4 | 13.3 | 55.8 | 12.1 | 51.4 | 11.2 | 49.3 | 10.5 |
| Aggression | 53.9 | 13.3 | 52.7 | 12.1 | 55.1 | 13.4 | 60.3 | 17.2 | 55.3 | 11.2 | 51.3 | 11.1 | 50.3 | 11.4 |
| Conduct Problems | 53.7 | 12.6 | 53.5 | 11.8 | 54.2 | 12.8 | 58.1 | 15.0 | 55.3 | 11.5 | 52.0 | 11.8 | 49.2 | 11.5 |
| Anxiety | 56.9 | 13.4 | 53.6 | 12.8 | 59.4 | 13.2 | 62.5 | 14.2 | 51.5 | 14.8 | 58.8 | 12.1 | 52.6 | 12.6 |
| Depression | 56.4 | 13.4 | 53.8 | 11.8 | 60.2 | 14.1 | 63.9 | 15.0 | 53.3 | 13.2 | 54.8 | 12.0 | 48.9 | 8.5 |
| Somatization | 53.1 | 13.3 | 52.5 | 13.6 | 52.7 | 11.2 | 58.5 | 15.9 | 53.6 | 15.8 | 51.8 | 11.9 | 50.3 | 13.5 |
| Attention Problems | 57.7 | 10.3 | 59.3 | 9.9 | 59.9 | 9.3 | 57.6 | 10.9 | 55.6 | 10.6 | 56.5 | 9.9 | 50.8 | 10.3 |
| Learning Problems | 58.3 | 11.7 | 56.1 | 10.8 | 62.2 | 12.1 | 55.6 | 11.2 | 57.1 | 12.1 | 63.0 | 10.2 | 52.9 | 10.8 |
| Atypicality | 57.7 | 13.9 | 54.6 | 11.6 | 66.9 | 14.9 | 61.0 | 14.0 | 57.0 | 13.9 | 52.5 | 10.8 | 48.9 | 7.6 |
| Withdrawal | 56.5 | 13.4 | 53.0 | 11.3 | 64.6 | 14.4 | 59.3 | 13.2 | 51.7 | 11.3 | 54.0 | 11.3 | 49.6 | 10.7 |
| **Adaptive scale** | | | | | | | | | | | | | | |
| Adaptability | 44.7 | 11.1 | 46.6 | 10.1 | 40.7 | 10.4 | 40.0 | 11.1 | 46.3 | 10.9 | 47.2 | 11.5 | 50.6 | 9.7 |
| Social Skills | 45.7 | 9.9 | 46.4 | 9.3 | 41.4 | 9.2 | 44.6 | 9.4 | 46.3 | 10.2 | 49.0 | 10.6 | 49.9 | 9.1 |
| Leadership | 43.4 | 8.8 | 44.0 | 8.8 | 38.8 | 7.4 | 43.7 | 8.1 | 45.9 | 9.3 | 44.8 | 8.5 | 48.4 | 9.3 |
| Study Skills | 43.6 | 9.5 | 43.4 | 9.1 | 40.5 | 8.7 | 44.3 | 9.9 | 44.0 | 9.4 | 44.4 | 8.9 | 49.6 | 10.2 |
| Functional Communication | 42.9 | 10.7 | 45.6 | 9.5 | 36.3 | 9.8 | 43.4 | 10.1 | 44.0 | 12.0 | 43.9 | 10.2 | 47.8 | 10.3 |
| **Content scale** | | | | | | | | | | | | | | |
| Anger Control | 56.0 | 13.9 | 54.4 | 12.3 | 59.2 | 14.5 | 63.5 | 17.0 | 54.9 | 10.9 | 52.3 | 11.8 | 49.2 | 10.2 |
| Bullying | 52.8 | 12.9 | 51.9 | 12.1 | 52.6 | 11.9 | 58.6 | 16.3 | 55.3 | 12.3 | 50.8 | 10.9 | 50.8 | 13.9 |
| Developmental Social Disorders | 57.0 | 12.3 | 54.1 | 10.5 | 65.8 | 12.1 | 59.0 | 12.1 | 52.9 | 12.3 | 53.3 | 10.1 | 49.8 | 9.2 |
| Emotional Self-Control | 56.5 | 12.9 | 54.2 | 11.3 | 60.8 | 13.3 | 63.5 | 14.5 | 54.7 | 12.8 | 53.7 | 11.7 | 49.1 | 8.0 |
| Executive Functioning | 57.8 | 10.2 | 57.6 | 9.4 | 61.7 | 9.0 | 60.0 | 11.2 | 56.3 | 10.5 | 55.1 | 9.5 | 50.5 | 10.2 |
| Negative Emotionality | 55.6 | 12.6 | 53.6 | 11.6 | 58.3 | 13.1 | 62.7 | 14.5 | 55.1 | 9.6 | 53.9 | 11.2 | 48.1 | 8.4 |
| Resiliency | 43.6 | 9.6 | 44.9 | 9.3 | 39.0 | 7.8 | 40.9 | 9.0 | 45.3 | 9.7 | 45.9 | 9.5 | 49.6 | 9.8 |
| **Clinical index** | | | | | | | | | | | | | | |
| ADHD Probability Index | 57.8 | 10.4 | 58.8 | 10.3 | 60.6 | 9.2 | 58.5 | 11.5 | 56.3 | 10.7 | 55.5 | 9.5 | 50.9 | 10.0 |
| EBD Probability Index | 56.2 | 12.4 | 54.7 | 11.3 | 58.6 | 12.1 | 63.0 | 15.0 | 55.2 | 10.9 | 54.0 | 11.0 | 50.0 | 9.9 |
| Autism Probability Index | 58.0 | 11.9 | 55.6 | 10.0 | 66.7 | 11.7 | 59.3 | 11.1 | 55.0 | 12.7 | 54.1 | 10.0 | 50.6 | 8.6 |
| Functional Impairment Index | 58.9 | 10.9 | 56.9 | 9.9 | 64.8 | 9.5 | 60.9 | 11.7 | 56.4 | 12.1 | 57.9 | 10.0 | 51.5 | 9.5 |

## Clinical Profile

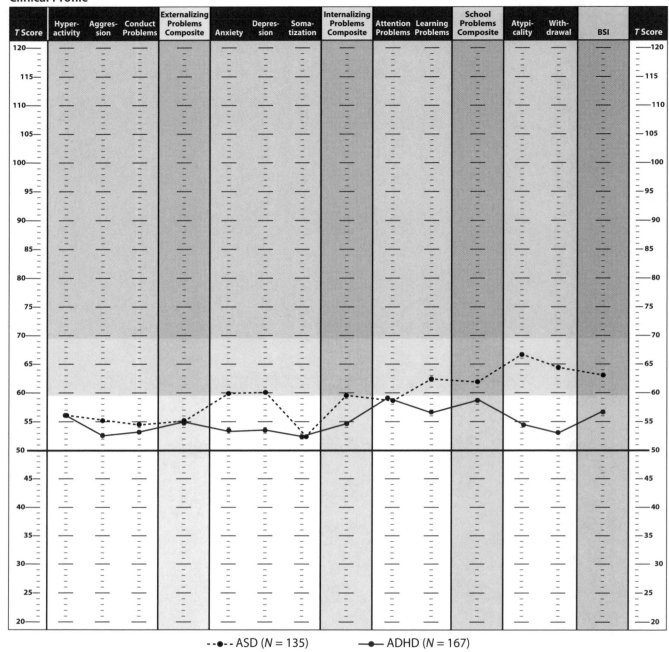

**Figure 9.1** TRS: Clinical group *T* scores for attention-deficit/hyperactivity disorder and autism spectrum disorder in the Clinical Profile

## Adaptive Profile

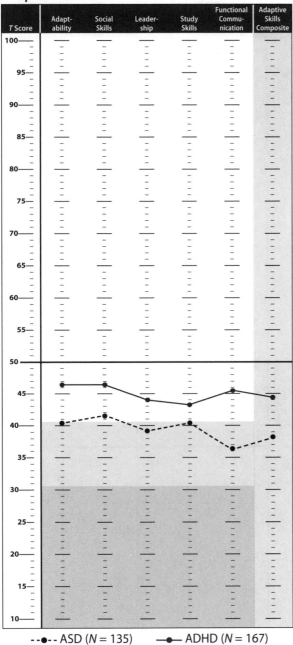

**Figure 9.2** TRS: Clinical group *T* scores for attention-deficit/hyperactivity disorder and autism spectrum disorder in the Adaptive Profile

## Clinical Profile

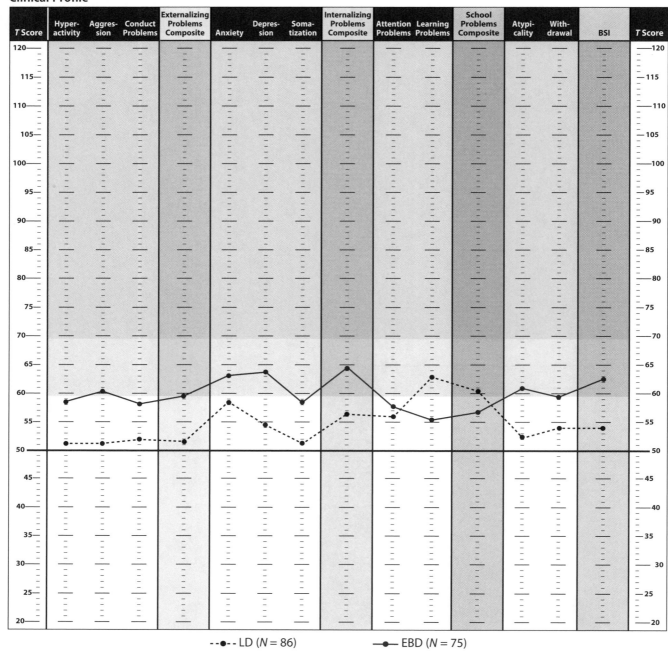

--●-- LD (N = 86)          —●— EBD (N = 75)

**Figure 9.3** TRS: Clinical group T scores for emotional/behavioral disturbance and specific learning disorder in the Clinical Profile

## Adaptive Profile

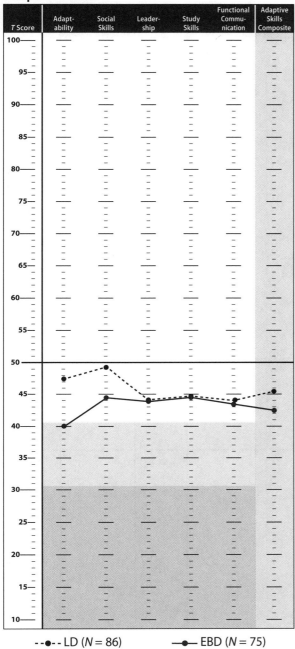

**Figure 9.4** TRS: Clinical group *T* scores for emotional/
behavioral disturbance and specific learning
disorder in the Adaptive Profile

## Clinical Profile

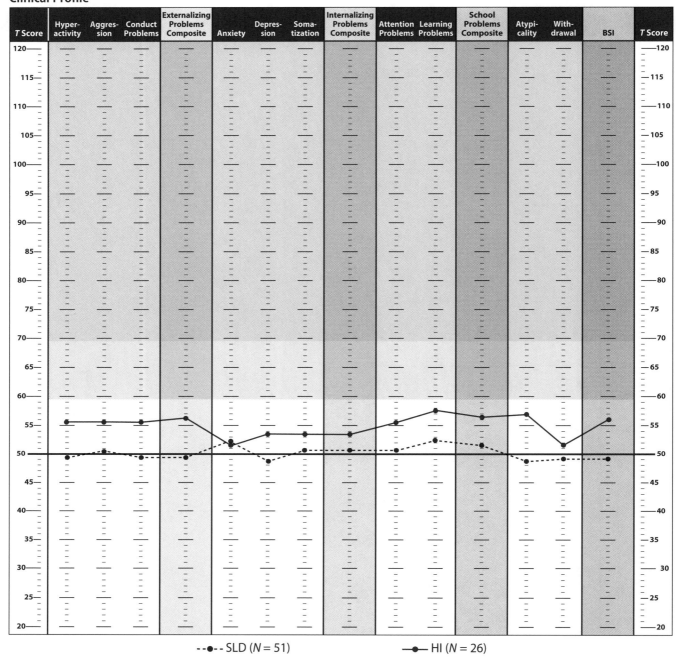

**Figure 9.5** TRS: Clinical group *T* scores for hearing impairment and speech or language disorder in the Clinical Profile

## Adaptive Profile

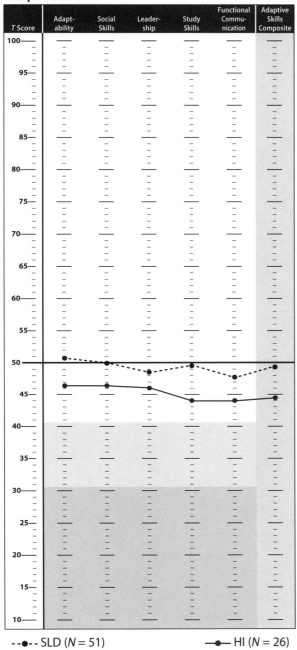

--•-- SLD (*N* = 51)          —•— HI (*N* = 26)

**Figure 9.6** TRS: Clinical group *T* scores for hearing
impairment and speech or language disorder
in the Adaptive Profile

# Chapter 10

## Parent Rating Scales: Reliability and Validity

This chapter presents technical information about the Parent Rating Scales (PRS), including evidence of reliability (i.e., internal consistency, test–retest, interrater) and validity (i.e., factor structure of the scales, correlations with other instruments, score profiles of clinical groups). Technical information about the Teacher Rating Scales (TRS) and Self-Report of Personality (SRP) is found in chapters 9 and 11, respectively. Technical information about the relationship between the TRS, PRS, and SRP components is presented in chapter 12.

## Evidence of Reliability

The following types of reliability evidence were analyzed for the BASC–3 PRS and are presented in this chapter.

- *Internal consistency:* shows the degree to which all of the items of a scale are measuring the same behavioral or emotional dimension

- *Test–retest reliability:* reflects the consistency of ratings from the same parent over a brief time interval

- *Interrater reliability:* describes the level of agreement among parents of the same child

### EVIDENCE OF INTERNAL CONSISTENCY

#### English Forms

For PRS scale and composite scores, internal-consistency reliabilities measured by coefficient alpha are presented in Table 10.1. These estimates are based on all of the English-form cases in each of the general norm groups with complete item data for the scale. Table 10.2 presents the same type of information for the clinical norm samples. Because reliability is affected by both the variability of scores in a sample and the quality of the items, each table shows separate reliability coefficients for the scores of the combined, female, and male samples, and for the ADHD and 19- through 21-year-old clinical subsamples.

# Table 10.1 PRS: Coefficient Alpha Reliabilities of Composites, Scales, and Indexes, by Gender and Age, General Norm Samples

| | Preschool | | | | | | Child | | | | | | Adolescent | | | | | |
| | Ages 2–3 | | | Ages 4–5 | | | Ages 6–7 | | | Ages 8–11 | | | Ages 12–14 | | | Ages 15–18 | | |
| | Combined | Female | Male | Combined | Female | Male | Combined | Female | Male | Combined | Female | Male | Combined | Female | Male | Combined | Female | Male |
|---|---|---|---|---|---|---|---|---|---|---|---|---|---|---|---|---|---|---|
| **Composite** | | | | | | | | | | | | | | | | | | |
| Externalizing Problems | .89 | .90 | .88 | .91 | .89 | .92 | .95 | .94 | .96 | .93 | .93 | .93 | .96 | .96 | .96 | .96 | .97 | .93 |
| Internalizing Problems | .93 | .94 | .92 | .92 | .91 | .92 | .92 | .92 | .92 | .93 | .94 | .93 | .95 | .95 | .95 | .96 | .97 | .94 |
| Adaptive Skills | .93 | .92 | .93 | .94 | .93 | .94 | .97 | .96 | .97 | .96 | .95 | .96 | .97 | .97 | .97 | .97 | .96 | .97 |
| Behavioral Symptoms Index | .95 | .95 | .94 | .96 | .96 | .97 | .96 | .96 | .97 | .95 | .95 | .95 | .97 | .97 | .97 | .97 | .98 | .97 |
| **Clinical scale** | | | | | | | | | | | | | | | | | | |
| Hyperactivity | .82 | .85 | .80 | .89 | .86 | .90 | .88 | .87 | .89 | .84 | .84 | .84 | .88 | .86 | .89 | .87 | .90 | .83 |
| Aggression | .81 | .83 | .78 | .82 | .80 | .83 | .87 | .84 | .88 | .79 | .80 | .78 | .89 | .91 | .88 | .90 | .93 | .83 |
| Conduct Problems | — | — | — | — | — | — | .88 | .84 | .90 | .87 | .85 | .89 | .91 | .93 | .88 | .92 | .95 | .85 |
| Anxiety | .83 | .83 | .84 | .81 | .78 | .82 | .83 | .82 | .84 | .87 | .87 | .87 | .89 | .89 | .89 | .89 | .89 | .87 |
| Depression | .85 | .87 | .83 | .86 | .85 | .87 | .86 | .86 | .86 | .87 | .86 | .87 | .90 | .90 | .90 | .93 | .95 | .88 |
| Somatization | .87 | .90 | .82 | .85 | .84 | .85 | .84 | .83 | .85 | .85 | .84 | .86 | .88 | .88 | .88 | .90 | .92 | .84 |
| Attention Problems | .81 | .78 | .84 | .90 | .87 | .91 | .90 | .91 | .88 | .89 | .88 | .88 | .90 | .88 | .91 | .88 | .88 | .89 |
| Atypicality | .85 | .87 | .82 | .89 | .87 | .91 | .88 | .88 | .89 | .86 | .83 | .87 | .92 | .93 | .90 | .92 | .93 | .88 |
| Withdrawal | .82 | .82 | .81 | .86 | .83 | .88 | .83 | .81 | .85 | .85 | .80 | .87 | .86 | .86 | .87 | .88 | .87 | .88 |
| **Adaptive scale** | | | | | | | | | | | | | | | | | | |
| Adaptability | .82 | .81 | .82 | .86 | .88 | .83 | .89 | .88 | .90 | .85 | .84 | .85 | .90 | .88 | .91 | .89 | .88 | .90 |
| Social Skills | .88 | .87 | .88 | .88 | .88 | .88 | .92 | .91 | .92 | .91 | .90 | .91 | .92 | .93 | .91 | .90 | .89 | .91 |
| Leadership | — | — | — | — | — | — | .85 | .85 | .86 | .85 | .81 | .85 | .89 | .88 | .89 | .88 | .88 | .88 |
| Activities of Daily Living | .76 | .71 | .79 | .78 | .71 | .82 | .80 | .82 | .78 | .80 | .79 | .80 | .82 | .79 | .82 | .82 | .79 | .83 |
| Functional Communication | .84 | .84 | .85 | .86 | .85 | .87 | .87 | .85 | .89 | .87 | .83 | .87 | .89 | .88 | .89 | .87 | .86 | .88 |
| **Content scale** | | | | | | | | | | | | | | | | | | |
| Anger Control | .83 | .83 | .83 | .85 | .83 | .86 | .89 | .89 | .89 | .84 | .84 | .84 | .89 | .89 | .89 | .88 | .90 | .86 |
| Bullying | .79 | .79 | .78 | .77 | .73 | .79 | .88 | .82 | .91 | .85 | .85 | .85 | .93 | .93 | .92 | .94 | .96 | .88 |
| Developmental Social Disorders | .80 | .79 | .81 | .89 | .86 | .90 | .89 | .87 | .91 | .88 | .86 | .88 | .91 | .91 | .89 | .89 | .89 | .90 |
| Emotional Self-Control | .88 | .87 | .88 | .89 | .88 | .90 | .88 | .89 | .87 | .87 | .85 | .87 | .90 | .91 | .90 | .90 | .90 | .90 |
| Executive Functioning | .89 | .88 | .89 | .93 | .92 | .93 | .92 | .92 | .93 | .91 | .91 | .90 | .92 | .92 | .93 | .92 | .92 | .92 |
| Negative Emotionality | .83 | .84 | .82 | .83 | .83 | .83 | .84 | .85 | .83 | .83 | .79 | .85 | .88 | .88 | .88 | .88 | .91 | .84 |
| Resiliency | .80 | .78 | .81 | .84 | .84 | .84 | .88 | .87 | .89 | .87 | .85 | .86 | .93 | .92 | .93 | .92 | .93 | .92 |
| **Clinical index** | | | | | | | | | | | | | | | | | | |
| Clinical Probability Index | .84 | .81 | .86 | .90 | .89 | .90 | — | — | — | — | — | — | — | — | — | — | — | — |
| ADHD Probability Index | — | — | — | — | — | — | .89 | .88 | .89 | .86 | .85 | .85 | .87 | .85 | .87 | .86 | .85 | .87 |
| EBD Probability Index | — | — | — | — | — | — | .92 | .90 | .93 | .89 | .90 | .88 | .92 | .92 | .92 | .90 | .91 | .90 |
| Autism Probability Index | — | — | — | — | — | — | .79 | .76 | .81 | .83 | .80 | .84 | .90 | .90 | .89 | .89 | .89 | .90 |
| Functional Impairment Index | .88 | .87 | .89 | .92 | .89 | .93 | .94 | .93 | .94 | .93 | .93 | .93 | .94 | .94 | .94 | .94 | .93 | .94 |

| | Preschool | | | Child | | | | | | Adolescent | | | | | | Ages 19–21 |
| | All clinical | | | All clinical | | | ADHD | | | All clinical | | | ADHD | | | |
| | Combined | Female | Male | Combined | Female | Male | Combined | Female | Male | Combined | Female | Male | Combined | Female | Male | Combined |
|---|---|---|---|---|---|---|---|---|---|---|---|---|---|---|---|---|
| **Composite** | | | | | | | | | | | | | | | | |
| Externalizing Problems | .93 | .90 | .94 | .96 | .96 | .96 | .95 | .96 | .95 | .96 | .97 | .95 | .94 | .95 | .94 | .98 |
| Internalizing Problems | .95 | .95 | .95 | .95 | .95 | .95 | .94 | .93 | .95 | .96 | .96 | .95 | .94 | .94 | .94 | .98 |
| Adaptive Skills | .95 | .93 | .95 | .96 | .95 | .96 | .95 | .94 | .95 | .95 | .97 | .96 | .95 | .95 | .96 | .95 |
| Behavioral Symptoms Index | .97 | .97 | .97 | .97 | .97 | .97 | .96 | .94 | .96 | .96 | .98 | .96 | .96 | .96 | .96 | .98 |
| **Clinical scale** | | | | | | | | | | | | | | | | |
| Hyperactivity | .90 | .90 | .90 | .91 | .92 | .91 | .89 | .89 | .89 | .89 | .90 | .89 | .86 | .84 | .87 | .92 |
| Aggression | .87 | .79 | .89 | .88 | .88 | .88 | .88 | .89 | .88 | .91 | .93 | .89 | .86 | .88 | .85 | .95 |
| Conduct Problems | — | — | — | .91 | .92 | .91 | .92 | .92 | .92 | .91 | .94 | .89 | .88 | .92 | .85 | .96 |
| Anxiety | .87 | .88 | .87 | .88 | .89 | .88 | .88 | .85 | .88 | .90 | .91 | .89 | .89 | .86 | .90 | .93 |
| Depression | .91 | .92 | .90 | .91 | .89 | .92 | .90 | .84 | .92 | .91 | .93 | .89 | .89 | .91 | .87 | .95 |
| Somatization | .88 | .88 | .86 | .89 | .91 | .88 | .85 | .85 | .86 | .89 | .90 | .88 | .85 | .87 | .84 | .94 |
| Attention Problems | .91 | .88 | .91 | .88 | .88 | .88 | .79 | .77 | .80 | .86 | .90 | .87 | .86 | .86 | .86 | .82 |
| Atypicality | .91 | .89 | .92 | .91 | .90 | .91 | .89 | .85 | .90 | .89 | .92 | .85 | .85 | .87 | .85 | .95 |
| Withdrawal | .87 | .86 | .89 | .91 | .87 | .92 | .89 | .86 | .90 | .88 | .88 | .90 | .88 | .85 | .89 | .88 |
| **Adaptive scale** | | | | | | | | | | | | | | | | |
| Adaptability | .85 | .82 | .86 | .87 | .84 | .87 | .84 | .83 | .84 | .89 | .88 | .90 | .87 | .84 | .88 | .86 |
| Social Skills | .90 | .87 | .90 | .92 | .90 | .92 | .90 | .90 | .90 | .91 | .91 | .92 | .91 | .91 | .92 | .90 |
| Leadership | — | — | — | .84 | .80 | .85 | .78 | .79 | .79 | .88 | .90 | .86 | .84 | .87 | .83 | .86 |
| Activities of Daily Living | .85 | .78 | .87 | .77 | .78 | .76 | .76 | .70 | .77 | .80 | .80 | .80 | .77 | .74 | .79 | .71 |
| Functional Communication | .85 | .83 | .86 | .87 | .86 | .87 | .83 | .82 | .83 | .88 | .88 | .88 | .85 | .83 | .86 | .78 |
| **Content scale** | | | | | | | | | | | | | | | | |
| Anger Control | .87 | .91 | .84 | .90 | .91 | .90 | .90 | .89 | .90 | .91 | .90 | .91 | .89 | .85 | .91 | .93 |
| Bullying | .85 | .70 | .89 | .90 | .90 | .90 | .90 | .91 | .90 | .94 | .95 | .92 | .90 | .93 | .89 | .97 |
| Developmental Social Disorders | .90 | .90 | .91 | .91 | .88 | .92 | .90 | .87 | .91 | .89 | .89 | .90 | .87 | .89 | .87 | .87 |
| Emotional Self-Control | .93 | .94 | .92 | .91 | .91 | .90 | .89 | .86 | .90 | .91 | .91 | .90 | .88 | .86 | .89 | .91 |
| Executive Functioning | .93 | .94 | .93 | .92 | .91 | .92 | .88 | .86 | .88 | .91 | .92 | .91 | .91 | .91 | .91 | .86 |
| Negative Emotionality | .89 | .91 | .88 | .88 | .87 | .88 | .87 | .86 | .87 | .89 | .90 | .88 | .86 | .85 | .87 | .94 |
| Resiliency | .84 | .83 | .85 | .87 | .87 | .87 | .82 | .83 | .82 | .91 | .91 | .91 | .89 | .88 | .90 | .90 |
| **Clinical index** | | | | | | | | | | | | | | | | |
| Clinical Probability Index | .89 | .88 | .89 | — | — | — | — | — | — | — | — | — | — | — | — | — |
| ADHD Probability Index | — | — | — | .89 | .90 | .88 | .85 | .84 | .86 | .84 | .85 | .83 | .81 | .80 | .82 | .78 |
| EBD Probability Index | — | — | — | .93 | .92 | .93 | .93 | .93 | .93 | .93 | .93 | .93 | .93 | .92 | .93 | .92 |
| Autism Probability Index | — | — | — | .88 | .84 | .89 | .86 | .83 | .87 | .88 | .90 | .90 | .88 | .89 | .87 | .83 |
| Functional Impairment Index | .92 | .91 | .93 | .94 | .93 | .94 | .93 | .90 | .94 | .92 | .94 | .93 | .92 | .91 | .92 | .93 |

For the general norm samples, composite scale score reliability coefficients range from good to excellent, with the majority of values above .90. Reliability coefficients of the individual clinical and adaptive scales scores range from adequate to excellent, with the majority of the values above .80. Across all of the norm groups, scores from the Conduct Problems, Atypicality, and Social Skills scales had the highest reliability coefficients. The pattern of score reliability coefficients is fairly consistent across all clinical and adaptive scales, although the Activities of Daily Living scale score reliability coefficients are somewhat lower (but adequate), particularly for the youngest age ranges.

Reliability coefficients for the scores of the content scales are also generally good to excellent; scores on the Developmental Social Disorders, Emotional Self-Control, and Executive Functioning scales have the highest reliability coefficients. Reliability coefficients for the scores on the various clinical indexes are also good to excellent with most in the middle .80s and higher.

Reliability coefficients for the clinical norm samples are generally similar to or higher than the reliability coefficients from the general norm sample. Most coefficients are above .80, with scores from the composite scales in the .90s.

In summary, internal-consistency reliability coefficients for the BASC–3 PRS composite and subscale scores are good to excellent and are generally consistent between females and males, clinical and nonclinical groups, and different age levels. Overall, reliabilities are somewhat lower than those of the TRS, a finding consistent with previous BASC editions (Reynolds & Kamphaus, 1992, 2004).

## Spanish Forms

Separate studies were conducted to determine internal-consistency reliability coefficients for the Spanish-language PRS forms. Demographic characteristics of the Spanish sample are presented in Table 10.3 (see chapter 8 for a more complete description of the demographic characteristics), and reliability coefficient estimates are presented in Table 10.4. In general, composite score reliability coefficients are above .90, and the reliability coefficients for the clinical, adaptive, content, and clinical index scale scores are generally above .80 with only a few exceptions.

**Table 10.3** PRS: Demographic Characteristics of the Spanish-Form Samples

|  | Preschool | Child | Adolescent |
|---|---|---|---|
| N | 78 | 92 | 71 |
| **Age** | | | |
| Mean | 3.9 | 8.7 | 15.6 |
| SD | 1.2 | 1.8 | 2.1 |
| Range | 2–5 | 6–11 | 12–18 |
| **Mother's education level** | | | |
| 1 | 17.9 | 37.0 | 36.6 |
| 2 | 29.5 | 21.7 | 25.4 |
| 3 | 23.1 | 16.3 | 16.9 |
| 4 | 29.5 | 25.0 | 21.1 |
| **Region** | | | |
| Midwest | 1.3 | 5.4 | 8.5 |
| Northeast | 2.6 | 1.1 | 2.8 |
| South | 57.7 | 54.3 | 31.0 |
| West | 38.5 | 39.1 | 57.7 |
| **Gender** | | | |
| Female | 53.8 | 50.0 | 47.9 |
| Male | 46.2 | 50.0 | 52.1 |

**Table 10.4** PRS: Coefficient Alpha Reliabilities of Composites, Scales, and Indexes for the Spanish Form, by Gender and Test Form

| | Preschool | Child | Adolescent |
|---|---|---|---|
| | Ages 2–5 | Ages 6–11 | Ages 12–18 |
| **Composite** | | | |
| Externalizing Problems | .87 | .92 | .93 |
| Internalizing Problems | .90 | .92 | .89 |
| Adaptive Skills | .91 | .95 | .94 |
| Behavioral Symptoms Index | .95 | .96 | .95 |
| **Clinical scale** | | | |
| Hyperactivity | .79 | .80 | .83 |
| Aggression | .79 | .77 | .76 |
| Conduct Problems | — | .87 | .86 |
| Anxiety | .79 | .77 | .76 |
| Depression | .81 | .89 | .78 |
| Somatization | .85 | .85 | .80 |
| Attention Problems | .83 | .87 | .84 |
| Atypicality | .89 | .85 | .86 |
| Withdrawal | .84 | .82 | .77 |
| **Adaptive scale** | | | |
| Adaptability | .79 | .89 | .80 |
| Social Skills | .80 | .87 | .83 |
| Leadership | — | .83 | .71 |
| Activities of Daily Living | .74 | .72 | .70 |
| Functional Communication | .86 | .85 | .84 |
| **Content scale** | | | |
| Anger Control | .81 | .83 | .78 |
| Bullying | .71 | .75 | .84 |
| Developmental Social Disorders | .87 | .88 | .87 |
| Emotional Self-Control | .85 | .86 | .81 |
| Executive Functioning | .90 | .90 | .88 |
| Negative Emotionality | .83 | .84 | .74 |
| Resiliency | .81 | .84 | .83 |
| **Clinical index** | | | |
| Clinical Probability Index | .85 | — | — |
| ADHD Probability Index | — | .83 | .74 |
| EBD Probability Index | — | .91 | .85 |
| Autism Probability Index | — | .71 | .85 |
| Functional Impairment Index | .90 | .93 | .91 |

## EVIDENCE OF TEST–RETEST RELIABILITY

Another method of indicating the consistency of test scores is for the same parent to rate the child twice over a period of several weeks. In this brief period of time, the child's behavior is unlikely to change much and it should also be long enough to avoid bias from a parent recalling his or her prior ratings. Therefore, high test–retest reliability indicates that scores are unlikely to change greatly at different times. However, one can expect a parent's responses to differ somewhat from one occasion to another because the child's most recent behaviors will be uppermost in the parent's mind, and because some children may actually have altered their behavior between ratings.

At each age level of the PRS (preschool, child, adolescent), a sample of children was rated twice by the same parent or caregiver, with an interval of 7 to 70 days between ratings across all age levels. These samples include both children with clinical diagnoses and children from the general population. Demographic characteristics of the retest samples are shown in Table 10.5 (see chapter 8 for a more complete description of the demographic characteristics).

**Table 10.5** PRS: Demographic Characteristics of Test–Retest Reliability Study Samples

| Characteristic | Preschool | Child | Adolescent |
|---|---|---|---|
| *N* | 70 | 70 | 126 |
| **Age** | | | |
| Mean | 4.0 | 9.0 | 14.8 |
| *SD* | 1.1 | 1.6 | 1.9 |
| Range | 2–5 | 6–11 | 12–18 |
| **Test interval** | | | |
| Mean | 21.7 | 22.2 | 20.3 |
| Range | 7–69 | 7–68 | 7–70 |
| **Mother's education level** | | | |
| 1 | 1.4 | 8.6 | 1.6 |
| 2 | 8.6 | 10.0 | 6.3 |
| 3 | 22.9 | 27.1 | 19.8 |
| 4 | 67.1 | 54.3 | 72.2 |
| **Race/ethnicity** | | | |
| African American | 11.4 | 5.7 | 5.6 |
| Asian | 0 | 2.9 | 0.8 |
| Hispanic | 7.1 | 25.7 | 17.5 |
| Other | 10.0 | 2.9 | 4.0 |
| White | 71.4 | 62.9 | 72.2 |
| **Region** | | | |
| Midwest | 31.4 | 10.0 | 14.3 |
| Northeast | 18.6 | 20.0 | 15.1 |
| South | 31.4 | 47.1 | 44.4 |
| West | 18.6 | 22.9 | 26.2 |
| **Rater** | | | |
| Mother | 62 | 62 | 115 |
| Father | 8 | 7 | 9 |
| Other | 0 | 1 | 2 |
| **Gender** | | | |
| Female | 48.6 | 51.4 | 53.2 |
| Male | 51.4 | 48.6 | 46.8 |

The PRS test–retest stability coefficients, both unadjusted and adjusted for restriction of range, are reported in Tables 10.6, 10.7, and 10.8 for the preschool, child, and adolescent levels, respectively. The general combined-gender norms were used in the analyses. Adjusted correlations remove the biasing effect that results from sampling differences in the variability of scale scores. The raw test–retest correlations were adjusted using the standard deviation at Time 1 relative to the norm-sample standard deviation of 10. The result is a correlation that better reflects what one would expect if the variability of scale scores from the obtained sample better matched that of the population. The tables also report the standard differences (i.e., effect sizes) between the first and second testing. The standard difference was calculated using the mean score difference between the two testing sessions, divided by the pooled standard deviation (Cohen, 1996).

**Table 10.6** PRS: Test–Retest Reliabilities of Composites, Scales, and Indexes, Preschool

| | Preschool | | | | | | |
| | First rating | | Second rating | | | Corrected | Standard |
| | Mean | SD | Mean | SD | r | r | difference |
|---|---|---|---|---|---|---|---|
| **Composite** | | | | | | | |
| Externalizing Problems | 48.8 | 8.2 | 47.8 | 6.9 | .86 | .91 | −0.13 |
| Internalizing Problems | 49.6 | 9.3 | 49.9 | 8.6 | .89 | .90 | 0.03 |
| Adaptive Skills | 49.7 | 7.8 | 50.5 | 8.7 | .88 | .93 | 0.10 |
| Behavioral Symptoms Index | 49.2 | 7.9 | 48.9 | 7.1 | .88 | .93 | −0.04 |
| **Clinical scale** | | | | | | | |
| Hyperactivity | 48.2 | 8.1 | 47.1 | 7.3 | .86 | .91 | −0.14 |
| Aggression | 49.6 | 8.6 | 48.9 | 7.4 | .77 | .83 | −0.09 |
| Anxiety | 49.5 | 9.3 | 49.1 | 8.2 | .85 | .87 | −0.05 |
| Depression | 49.4 | 8.0 | 49.8 | 7.0 | .84 | .90 | 0.05 |
| Somatization | 50.3 | 8.7 | 51.0 | 9.4 | .75 | .81 | 0.08 |
| Attention Problems | 48.3 | 8.9 | 48.3 | 7.5 | .75 | .80 | 0.00 |
| Atypicality | 49.8 | 8.6 | 49.3 | 8.4 | .83 | .87 | −0.06 |
| Withdrawal | 51.6 | 10.0 | 51.7 | 10.0 | .85 | .85 | 0.01 |
| **Adaptive scale** | | | | | | | |
| Adaptability | 50.5 | 8.7 | 51.8 | 8.7 | .80 | .85 | 0.15 |
| Social Skills | 50.1 | 8.5 | 50.4 | 8.7 | .80 | .86 | 0.03 |
| Activities of Daily Living | 47.5 | 8.8 | 47.6 | 9.8 | .85 | .88 | 0.01 |
| Functional Communication | 51.3 | 8.6 | 52.1 | 9.0 | .90 | .93 | 0.09 |
| **Content scale** | | | | | | | |
| Anger Control | 49.6 | 7.7 | 49.5 | 7.2 | .86 | .92 | −0.01 |
| Bullying | 50.0 | 8.3 | 49.3 | 7.7 | .76 | .83 | −0.09 |
| Developmental Social Disorders | 49.3 | 9.1 | 48.1 | 9.2 | .87 | .89 | −0.13 |
| Emotional Self-Control | 49.1 | 8.2 | 49.4 | 7.0 | .78 | .85 | 0.04 |
| Executive Functioning | 49.1 | 7.7 | 48.5 | 6.6 | .81 | .89 | −0.08 |
| Negative Emotionality | 50.2 | 7.9 | 49.8 | 7.2 | .77 | .86 | −0.05 |
| Resiliency | 50.1 | 8.6 | 50.1 | 8.4 | .82 | .87 | 0.00 |
| **Clinical index** | | | | | | | |
| Clinical Probability Index | 48.4 | 7.7 | 48.0 | 7.6 | .86 | .92 | −0.05 |
| Functional Impairment Index | 50.0 | 8.0 | 49.4 | 8.0 | .87 | .92 | −0.08 |

**Table 10.7** PRS: Test–Retest Reliabilities of Composites, Scales, and Indexes, Child

| | Child | | | | | | |
| | First rating | | Second rating | | | Corrected | Standard |
| | Mean | SD | Mean | SD | r | r | difference |
|---|---|---|---|---|---|---|---|
| **Composite** | | | | | | | |
| Externalizing Problems | 50.2 | 13.1 | 49.4 | 11.6 | .93 | .88 | −0.06 |
| Internalizing Problems | 52.9 | 12.0 | 51.5 | 12.1 | .91 | .87 | −0.12 |
| Adaptive Skills | 50.0 | 10.2 | 50.7 | 11.0 | .92 | .92 | 0.07 |
| Behavioral Symptoms Index | 49.9 | 12.3 | 49.1 | 11.2 | .92 | .88 | −0.07 |
| **Clinical scale** | | | | | | | |
| Hyperactivity | 49.7 | 11.9 | 48.7 | 10.5 | .91 | .87 | −0.09 |
| Aggression | 50.4 | 12.4 | 49.8 | 11.2 | .89 | .83 | −0.05 |
| Conduct Problems | 50.3 | 12.8 | 49.8 | 11.4 | .91 | .85 | −0.04 |
| Anxiety | 53.1 | 10.9 | 50.5 | 10.3 | .87 | .85 | −0.25 |
| Depression | 51.4 | 12.6 | 50.7 | 12.3 | .89 | .83 | −0.06 |
| Somatization | 52.6 | 11.6 | 52.7 | 12.4 | .87 | .83 | 0.01 |
| Attention Problems | 49.5 | 11.3 | 49.1 | 11.0 | .92 | .90 | −0.04 |
| Atypicality | 49.7 | 10.4 | 49.7 | 10.4 | .85 | .84 | 0.00 |
| Withdrawal | 48.5 | 9.9 | 47.6 | 8.9 | .81 | .81 | −0.10 |
| **Adaptive scale** | | | | | | | |
| Adaptability | 49.2 | 11.3 | 50.3 | 12.0 | .87 | .83 | 0.09 |
| Social Skills | 50.2 | 9.1 | 50.4 | 10.0 | .84 | .87 | 0.02 |
| Leadership | 50.4 | 10.8 | 51.0 | 10.6 | .89 | .87 | 0.06 |
| Activities of Daily Living | 50.1 | 9.9 | 51.4 | 9.7 | .86 | .86 | 0.13 |
| Functional Communication | 49.9 | 10.0 | 50.4 | 10.8 | .88 | .88 | 0.05 |
| **Content scale** | | | | | | | |
| Anger Control | 51.9 | 12.4 | 50.7 | 11.1 | .92 | .88 | −0.10 |
| Bullying | 50.1 | 11.2 | 49.6 | 10.3 | .84 | .80 | −0.05 |
| Developmental Social Disorders | 49.2 | 9.4 | 48.2 | 9.5 | .82 | .84 | −0.11 |
| Emotional Self-Control | 52.2 | 11.9 | 50.4 | 11.3 | .90 | .86 | −0.16 |
| Executive Functioning | 50.8 | 11.6 | 49.4 | 11.6 | .94 | .92 | −0.12 |
| Negative Emotionality | 53.0 | 12.8 | 51.6 | 12.0 | .92 | .87 | −0.11 |
| Resiliency | 50.5 | 11.0 | 51.1 | 11.5 | .89 | .87 | 0.05 |
| **Clinical index** | | | | | | | |
| ADHD Probability Index | 50.2 | 11.6 | 48.8 | 10.6 | .93 | .91 | −0.13 |
| EBD Probability Index | 51.0 | 12.8 | 49.7 | 12.0 | .89 | .82 | −0.10 |
| Autism Probability Index | 49.1 | 9.0 | 48.2 | 8.5 | .83 | .86 | −0.10 |
| Functional Impairment Index | 50.7 | 11.1 | 49.5 | 11.2 | .93 | .91 | −0.11 |

**Table 10.8** PRS: Test–Retest Reliabilities of Composites, Scales, and Indexes, Adolescent

| | Adolescent | | | | | | |
| | First rating | | Second rating | | | Corrected | Standard |
| | Mean | SD | Mean | SD | r | r | difference |
|---|---|---|---|---|---|---|---|
| **Composite** | | | | | | | |
| Externalizing Problems | 47.7 | 5.6 | 48.2 | 6.4 | .79 | .93 | 0.08 |
| Internalizing Problems | 48.6 | 7.6 | 48.4 | 7.5 | .88 | .93 | −0.03 |
| Adaptive Skills | 53.8 | 8.1 | 54.2 | 8.2 | .88 | .92 | 0.05 |
| Behavioral Symptoms Index | 47.6 | 6.7 | 47.5 | 7.1 | .87 | .94 | −0.01 |
| **Clinical scale** | | | | | | | |
| Hyperactivity | 48.4 | 6.8 | 48.6 | 7.4 | .78 | .90 | 0.03 |
| Aggression | 48.1 | 6.1 | 48.7 | 7.5 | .72 | .90 | 0.09 |
| Conduct Problems | 46.9 | 5.8 | 47.5 | 6.1 | .78 | .93 | 0.10 |
| Anxiety | 49.3 | 8.6 | 48.9 | 8.1 | .87 | .90 | −0.05 |
| Depression | 48.6 | 7.1 | 48.3 | 6.7 | .81 | .90 | −0.04 |
| Somatization | 48.5 | 8.7 | 48.9 | 8.8 | .86 | .89 | 0.05 |
| Attention Problems | 46.2 | 8.1 | 45.8 | 8.0 | .85 | .90 | −0.05 |
| Atypicality | 47.6 | 7.5 | 47.5 | 7.3 | .87 | .93 | −0.01 |
| Withdrawal | 49.3 | 9.6 | 49.4 | 9.9 | .88 | .89 | 0.01 |
| **Adaptive scale** | | | | | | | |
| Adaptability | 52.9 | 8.9 | 53.3 | 8.8 | .78 | .83 | 0.05 |
| Social Skills | 52.3 | 8.4 | 52.7 | 8.6 | .82 | .87 | 0.05 |
| Leadership | 53.4 | 8.6 | 53.5 | 8.5 | .87 | .90 | 0.01 |
| Activities of Daily Living | 54.2 | 8.2 | 54.4 | 8.7 | .85 | .90 | 0.02 |
| Functional Communication | 53.5 | 8.1 | 54.1 | 8.4 | .84 | .90 | 0.07 |
| **Content scale** | | | | | | | |
| Anger Control | 48.8 | 7.0 | 49.0 | 7.2 | .78 | .89 | 0.03 |
| Bullying | 48.1 | 5.6 | 48.7 | 7.3 | .67 | .90 | 0.09 |
| Developmental Social Disorders | 46.9 | 8.2 | 46.4 | 8.2 | .86 | .91 | −0.06 |
| Emotional Self-Control | 48.7 | 8.4 | 48.4 | 7.6 | .80 | .86 | −0.04 |
| Executive Functioning | 46.2 | 8.0 | 45.4 | 8.0 | .87 | .92 | −0.10 |
| Negative Emotionality | 48.7 | 7.0 | 48.8 | 6.7 | .71 | .86 | 0.01 |
| Resiliency | 53.6 | 8.2 | 53.9 | 8.4 | .85 | .90 | 0.04 |
| **Clinical index** | | | | | | | |
| ADHD Probability Index | 46.6 | 8.0 | 46.2 | 8.0 | .81 | .88 | −0.05 |
| EBD Probability Index | 47.7 | 7.4 | 47.7 | 7.6 | .85 | .92 | 0.00 |
| Autism Probability Index | 47.5 | 8.9 | 47.1 | 9.1 | .86 | .89 | −0.04 |
| Functional Impairment Index | 46.4 | 7.9 | 46.1 | 8.1 | .88 | .93 | −0.04 |

Test–retest stability coefficients for the various scale scores generally possess adequate stability across time for all scale types and levels, with most corrected stability coefficients in the .80s or higher. Mean scores between administrations are very similar, with most effect sizes under .10, indicating very stable ratings across the testing interval.

# EVIDENCE OF INTERRATER RELIABILITY

The third type of reliability evaluated for the PRS is the agreement of scores obtained from different parents or caregivers who provided ratings at about the same point in time. Different raters are not expected to give identical results because the occasions and settings in which they observe the child vary, and the child may behave differently in the presence of different raters.

An interrater reliability study was completed at each age level of the PRS. Each child included in the study was rated by two different parents or caregivers. Table 10.9 presents the demographic characteristics of the PRS interrater reliability studies (see chapter 8 for a more complete description of the demographic characteristics). The period between parent ratings ranged from 0 to 63 days across all three age levels.

**Table 10.9** PRS: Demographic Characteristics of Interrater Reliability Study Samples

| Characteristic | Preschool | Child | Adolescent |
|---|---|---|---|
| N | 125 | 117 | 114 |
| **Age** | | | |
| Mean | 4.0 | 9.3 | 14.4 |
| SD | 1.1 | 1.7 | 1.8 |
| Range | 2–5 | 6–11 | 12–18 |
| **Test interval** | | | |
| Mean | 8.3 | 10.5 | 10.8 |
| Range | 0–42 | 0–61 | 0–63 |
| **Mother's education level** | | | |
| 1 | 0.8 | 1.7 | 0.9 |
| 2 | 9.6 | 7.7 | 6.1 |
| 3 | 14.4 | 28.2 | 15.8 |
| 4 | 75.2 | 62.4 | 77.2 |
| **Race/ethnicity** | | | |
| African American | 4.0 | 10.3 | 5.3 |
| Asian | 5.6 | 7.7 | 3.5 |
| Hispanic | 10.4 | 13.7 | 9.6 |
| Other | 9.6 | 1.7 | 4.4 |
| White | 70.4 | 66.7 | 77.2 |
| **Region** | | | |
| Midwest | 15.2 | 9.4 | 19.3 |
| Northeast | 16.0 | 16.2 | 12.3 |
| South | 50.4 | 46.2 | 43.9 |
| West | 18.4 | 28.2 | 24.6 |
| **Gender** | | | |
| Female | 56.8 | 54.7 | 57.0 |
| Male | 43.2 | 45.3 | 43.0 |

Tables 10.10, 10.11, and 10.12 show the interrater reliabilities, corrected for restriction of range, for scale scores from the preschool, child, and adolescent levels. Both unadjusted and adjusted correlations are presented. In general, interrater correlations are lower than the estimates obtained in the coefficient alpha and test–retest reliability studies. However, they are generally higher than interrater reliability estimates found on other rating scale instruments (Youngstrom et al., 2000). The range of reliabilities among scale scores varies widely across all PRS levels, a result that is consistent with the findings in previous BASC editions (Reynolds & Kamphaus, 1992, 2004).

**Table 10.10** PRS: Interrater Reliabilities of Composites, Scales, and Indexes, Preschool

| | Preschool | | | | | | |
| | First rater | | Second rater | | | Corrected | Standard |
| | Mean | SD | Mean | SD | r | r | difference |
|---|---|---|---|---|---|---|---|
| **Composite** | | | | | | | |
| Externalizing Problems | 48.7 | 8.4 | 48.7 | 8.8 | .64 | .75 | 0.00 |
| Internalizing Problems | 49.5 | 8.1 | 49.6 | 8.4 | .55 | .70 | 0.01 |
| Adaptive Skills | 51.0 | 8.9 | 50.2 | 9.1 | .77 | .82 | −0.09 |
| Behavioral Symptoms Index | 48.8 | 8.2 | 49.2 | 8.7 | .70 | .80 | 0.05 |
| **Clinical scale** | | | | | | | |
| Hyperactivity | 48.5 | 8.6 | 48.3 | 8.5 | .55 | .67 | −0.02 |
| Aggression | 49.3 | 8.9 | 49.3 | 9.1 | .65 | .72 | 0.00 |
| Anxiety | 49.8 | 8.7 | 49.4 | 9.0 | .50 | .62 | −0.05 |
| Depression | 49.7 | 8.2 | 49.9 | 8.5 | .60 | .73 | 0.02 |
| Somatization | 49.5 | 8.1 | 49.8 | 8.4 | .53 | .69 | 0.04 |
| Attention Problems | 47.9 | 9.6 | 49.1 | 9.3 | .62 | .65 | 0.13 |
| Atypicality | 48.3 | 7.3 | 49.2 | 8.8 | .53 | .75 | 0.11 |
| Withdrawal | 50.7 | 10.0 | 50.6 | 10.4 | .75 | .75 | −0.01 |
| **Adaptive scale** | | | | | | | |
| Adaptability | 52.6 | 9.7 | 51.3 | 9.0 | .58 | .60 | −0.14 |
| Social Skills | 51.4 | 8.9 | 50.1 | 9.2 | .66 | .73 | −0.14 |
| Activities of Daily Living | 48.0 | 8.9 | 48.0 | 9.0 | .63 | .71 | 0.00 |
| Functional Communication | 51.6 | 9.3 | 51.3 | 9.1 | .77 | .80 | −0.03 |
| **Content scale** | | | | | | | |
| Anger Control | 50.2 | 9.0 | 50.0 | 8.9 | .66 | .72 | −0.02 |
| Bullying | 49.5 | 8.0 | 49.3 | 8.8 | .53 | .70 | −0.02 |
| Developmental Social Disorders | 47.8 | 8.6 | 49.7 | 9.0 | .71 | .79 | 0.22 |
| Emotional Self-Control | 49.7 | 8.6 | 50.2 | 9.2 | .60 | .70 | 0.06 |
| Executive Functioning | 49.1 | 8.8 | 49.6 | 9.1 | .72 | .78 | 0.06 |
| Negative Emotionality | 50.3 | 8.8 | 50.3 | 8.7 | .59 | .68 | 0.00 |
| Resiliency | 52.2 | 9.1 | 50.6 | 9.2 | .64 | .70 | −0.17 |
| **Clinical index** | | | | | | | |
| Clinical Probability Index | 48.2 | 9.0 | 49.1 | 8.8 | .75 | .80 | 0.10 |
| Functional Impairment Index | 49.5 | 9.2 | 49.8 | 9.2 | .78 | .81 | 0.03 |

**Table 10.11** PRS: Interrater Reliabilities of Composites, Scales, and Indexes, Child

| | Child | | | | | | |
| | First rater | | Second rater | | | Corrected | Standard |
| | Mean | SD | Mean | SD | r | r | difference |
|---|---|---|---|---|---|---|---|
| **Composite** | | | | | | | |
| Externalizing Problems | 48.7 | 8.8 | 48.2 | 8.5 | .68 | .75 | −0.06 |
| Internalizing Problems | 50.8 | 10.1 | 49.2 | 8.7 | .60 | .59 | −0.17 |
| Adaptive Skills | 53.7 | 9.1 | 52.0 | 9.1 | .70 | .75 | −0.19 |
| Behavioral Symptoms Index | 48.1 | 9.0 | 48.0 | 8.5 | .63 | .70 | −0.01 |
| **Clinical scale** | | | | | | | |
| Hyperactivity | 48.4 | 9.2 | 48.6 | 8.7 | .57 | .64 | 0.02 |
| Aggression | 49.7 | 8.4 | 48.9 | 8.9 | .56 | .69 | −0.09 |
| Conduct Problems | 48.6 | 9.1 | 47.6 | 8.3 | .68 | .74 | −0.11 |
| Anxiety | 52.1 | 10.2 | 50.7 | 9.9 | .56 | .54 | −0.14 |
| Depression | 49.3 | 9.5 | 48.2 | 7.6 | .65 | .68 | −0.13 |
| Somatization | 50.7 | 10.6 | 49.1 | 8.8 | .53 | .47 | −0.16 |
| Attention Problems | 47.2 | 10.1 | 47.4 | 9.0 | .66 | .65 | 0.02 |
| Atypicality | 47.9 | 8.5 | 48.9 | 9.1 | .59 | .70 | 0.11 |
| Withdrawal | 49.2 | 10.5 | 48.9 | 8.7 | .67 | .64 | −0.03 |
| **Adaptive scale** | | | | | | | |
| Adaptability | 53.1 | 10.1 | 51.8 | 10.2 | .59 | .58 | −0.13 |
| Social Skills | 53.3 | 8.9 | 51.8 | 8.9 | .68 | .75 | −0.17 |
| Leadership | 53.5 | 9.5 | 52.4 | 9.6 | .71 | .74 | −0.12 |
| Activities of Daily Living | 52.4 | 9.6 | 51.4 | 9.2 | .65 | .68 | −0.11 |
| Functional Communication | 53.6 | 8.7 | 52.0 | 9.1 | .64 | .73 | −0.18 |
| **Content scale** | | | | | | | |
| Anger Control | 49.2 | 8.3 | 49.1 | 8.7 | .56 | .70 | −0.01 |
| Bullying | 49.3 | 8.3 | 48.3 | 7.9 | .53 | .68 | −0.12 |
| Developmental Social Disorders | 47.0 | 8.9 | 48.6 | 9.2 | .57 | .66 | 0.18 |
| Emotional Self-Control | 50.2 | 9.0 | 49.1 | 8.7 | .58 | .66 | −0.12 |
| Executive Functioning | 47.2 | 9.5 | 47.8 | 9.9 | .63 | .67 | 0.06 |
| Negative Emotionality | 50.3 | 9.1 | 49.2 | 8.6 | .69 | .74 | −0.12 |
| Resiliency | 54.3 | 9.1 | 52.7 | 9.2 | .57 | .64 | −0.17 |
| **Clinical index** | | | | | | | |
| ADHD Probability Index | 47.9 | 9.8 | 48.1 | 9.1 | .65 | .66 | 0.02 |
| EBD Probability Index | 47.8 | 8.8 | 47.7 | 8.5 | .66 | .74 | −0.01 |
| Autism Probability Index | 48.5 | 9.6 | 49.0 | 8.5 | .62 | .65 | 0.06 |
| Functional Impairment Index | 47.2 | 8.9 | 48.2 | 8.9 | .65 | .72 | 0.11 |

**Table 10.12** PRS: Interrater Reliabilities of Composites, Scales, and Indexes, Adolescent

| | Adolescent | | | | | | |
| | First rater | | Second rater | | | Corrected r | Standard difference |
| | Mean | SD | Mean | SD | r | | |
|---|---|---|---|---|---|---|---|
| **Composite** | | | | | | | |
| Externalizing Problems | 49.2 | 6.5 | 49.6 | 6.9 | .67 | .86 | 0.06 |
| Internalizing Problems | 49.0 | 7.7 | 49.1 | 6.7 | .61 | .77 | 0.01 |
| Adaptive Skills | 53.4 | 7.9 | 51.2 | 8.1 | .65 | .78 | −0.27 |
| Behavioral Symptoms Index | 48.3 | 6.7 | 49.3 | 7.2 | .70 | .87 | 0.14 |
| **Clinical scale** | | | | | | | |
| Hyperactivity | 49.6 | 7.4 | 50.5 | 8.5 | .72 | .85 | 0.11 |
| Aggression | 49.2 | 6.2 | 49.7 | 6.9 | .52 | .82 | 0.08 |
| Conduct Problems | 48.8 | 7.3 | 48.6 | 6.9 | .58 | .78 | −0.03 |
| Anxiety | 49.4 | 8.3 | 49.9 | 7.4 | .49 | .65 | 0.06 |
| Depression | 49.1 | 7.2 | 48.7 | 6.5 | .60 | .79 | −0.06 |
| Somatization | 49.1 | 9.4 | 48.9 | 8.0 | .66 | .70 | −0.02 |
| Attention Problems | 47.5 | 9.3 | 49.4 | 9.0 | .70 | .74 | 0.21 |
| Atypicality | 47.7 | 6.5 | 49.1 | 7.5 | .65 | .85 | 0.20 |
| Withdrawal | 48.6 | 7.7 | 49.4 | 7.7 | .64 | .79 | 0.10 |
| **Adaptive scale** | | | | | | | |
| Adaptability | 52.7 | 8.5 | 50.3 | 8.6 | .48 | .62 | −0.28 |
| Social Skills | 52.6 | 8.0 | 51.4 | 7.8 | .57 | .72 | −0.15 |
| Leadership | 53.1 | 8.7 | 51.0 | 8.9 | .59 | .69 | −0.24 |
| Activities of Daily Living | 53.1 | 9.1 | 50.9 | 8.9 | .58 | .65 | −0.24 |
| Functional Communication | 53.4 | 8.4 | 50.7 | 8.4 | .54 | .68 | −0.32 |
| **Content scale** | | | | | | | |
| Anger Control | 50.2 | 7.6 | 50.1 | 8.1 | .59 | .76 | −0.01 |
| Bullying | 49.1 | 6.3 | 49.1 | 6.5 | .53 | .81 | 0.00 |
| Developmental Social Disorders | 46.9 | 7.3 | 49.2 | 7.9 | .59 | .78 | 0.30 |
| Emotional Self-Control | 49.5 | 8.5 | 50.3 | 7.7 | .63 | .73 | 0.10 |
| Executive Functioning | 47.2 | 9.0 | 49.3 | 9.3 | .64 | .71 | 0.23 |
| Negative Emotionality | 49.8 | 7.7 | 50.3 | 7.5 | .59 | .76 | 0.07 |
| Resiliency | 53.6 | 7.8 | 51.5 | 8.4 | .51 | .70 | −0.26 |
| **Clinical index** | | | | | | | |
| ADHD Probability Index | 47.9 | 9.0 | 49.4 | 9.4 | .64 | .71 | 0.16 |
| EBD Probability Index | 48.6 | 7.8 | 49.4 | 7.9 | .66 | .79 | 0.10 |
| Autism Probability Index | 47.4 | 7.7 | 49.1 | 8.0 | .63 | .78 | 0.22 |
| Functional Impairment Index | 47.3 | 8.3 | 48.8 | 8.4 | .64 | .75 | 0.18 |

## STANDARD ERRORS OF MEASUREMENT AND CONFIDENCE INTERVALS

The standard error of measurement *(SEM)* of a test score represents the average amount by which observed scores differ from true scores. The true score, which can never be known with certainty, is the score that would be obtained with a perfectly accurate measuring instrument. The *SEM,* therefore, helps the clinician understand how much error is associated with any observed score. The *SEM* in *T*-score units on each BASC–3 composite and scale (based on internal-consistency reliabilities) is presented in Table 10.13 for the general norm samples and in Table 10.14 for the clinical norm samples. Composite and scale scores with higher reliability coefficients have smaller *SEM*s; the pattern of *SEM*s replicates the pattern of reliability coefficients shown in Tables 10.1 and 10.2. *SEM*s for composite scores are generally 3 or less, while *SEM*s for the other scale scores are generally under 4.5.

**Table 10.13** PRS: *T*-Score Standard Errors of Measurement of Composites, Scales, and Indexes, by Gender and Age, General Norm Samples

| | Preschool | | | | | | | Child | | | | | | |
| --- | --- | --- | --- | --- | --- | --- | --- | --- | --- | --- | --- | --- | --- | --- |
| | Ages 2–3 | | | Ages 4–5 | | | Ages 2–5 | Ages 6–7 | | | Ages 8–11 | | | Ages 6–11 |
| | Combined | Female | Male | Combined | Female | Male | Combined total | Combined | Female | Male | Combined | Female | Male | Combined total |
| **Composite** | | | | | | | | | | | | | | |
| Externalizing Problems | 3.32 | 3.16 | 3.46 | 3.00 | 3.32 | 2.83 | 3.16 | 2.24 | 2.45 | 2.00 | 2.65 | 2.65 | 2.65 | 2.45 |
| Internalizing Problems | 2.65 | 2.45 | 2.83 | 2.83 | 3.00 | 2.83 | 2.74 | 2.83 | 2.83 | 2.83 | 2.65 | 2.45 | 2.65 | 2.74 |
| Adaptive Skills | 2.65 | 2.83 | 2.65 | 2.45 | 2.65 | 2.45 | 2.55 | 1.73 | 2.00 | 1.73 | 2.00 | 2.24 | 2.00 | 1.87 |
| Behavioral Symptoms Index | 2.24 | 2.24 | 2.45 | 2.00 | 2.00 | 1.73 | 2.12 | 2.00 | 2.00 | 1.73 | 2.24 | 2.24 | 2.24 | 2.12 |
| **Clinical scale** | | | | | | | | | | | | | | |
| Hyperactivity | 4.24 | 3.87 | 4.47 | 3.32 | 3.74 | 3.16 | 3.81 | 3.46 | 3.61 | 3.32 | 4.00 | 4.00 | 4.00 | 3.74 |
| Aggression | 4.36 | 4.12 | 4.69 | 4.24 | 4.47 | 4.12 | 4.30 | 3.61 | 4.00 | 3.46 | 4.58 | 4.47 | 4.69 | 4.12 |
| Conduct Problems | — | — | — | — | — | — | — | 3.46 | 4.00 | 3.16 | 3.61 | 3.87 | 3.32 | 3.54 |
| Anxiety | 4.12 | 4.12 | 4.00 | 4.36 | 4.69 | 4.24 | 4.24 | 4.12 | 4.24 | 4.00 | 3.61 | 3.61 | 3.61 | 3.87 |
| Depression | 3.87 | 3.61 | 4.12 | 3.74 | 3.87 | 3.61 | 3.81 | 3.74 | 3.74 | 3.74 | 3.61 | 3.74 | 3.61 | 3.68 |
| Somatization | 3.61 | 3.16 | 4.24 | 3.87 | 4.00 | 3.87 | 3.74 | 4.00 | 4.12 | 3.87 | 3.87 | 4.00 | 3.74 | 3.94 |
| Attention Problems | 4.36 | 4.69 | 4.00 | 3.16 | 3.61 | 3.00 | 3.81 | 3.16 | 3.00 | 3.46 | 3.32 | 3.46 | 3.46 | 3.24 |
| Atypicality | 3.87 | 3.61 | 4.24 | 3.32 | 3.61 | 3.00 | 3.61 | 3.46 | 3.46 | 3.32 | 3.74 | 4.12 | 3.61 | 3.60 |
| Withdrawal | 4.24 | 4.24 | 4.36 | 3.74 | 4.12 | 3.46 | 4.00 | 4.12 | 4.36 | 3.87 | 3.87 | 4.47 | 3.61 | 4.00 |
| **Adaptive scale** | | | | | | | | | | | | | | |
| Adaptability | 4.24 | 4.36 | 4.24 | 3.74 | 3.46 | 4.12 | 4.00 | 3.32 | 3.46 | 3.16 | 3.87 | 4.00 | 3.87 | 3.61 |
| Social Skills | 3.46 | 3.61 | 3.46 | 3.46 | 3.46 | 3.46 | 3.46 | 2.83 | 3.00 | 2.83 | 3.00 | 3.16 | 3.00 | 2.92 |
| Leadership | — | — | — | — | — | — | — | 3.87 | 3.87 | 3.74 | 3.87 | 4.36 | 3.87 | 3.87 |
| Activities of Daily Living | 4.90 | 5.39 | 4.58 | 4.69 | 5.39 | 4.24 | 4.80 | 4.47 | 4.24 | 4.69 | 4.47 | 4.58 | 4.47 | 4.47 |
| Functional Communication | 4.00 | 4.00 | 3.87 | 3.74 | 3.87 | 3.61 | 3.87 | 3.61 | 3.87 | 3.32 | 3.61 | 4.12 | 3.61 | 3.61 |
| **Content scale** | | | | | | | | | | | | | | |
| Anger Control | 4.12 | 4.12 | 4.12 | 3.87 | 4.12 | 3.74 | 4.00 | 3.32 | 3.32 | 3.32 | 4.00 | 4.00 | 4.00 | 3.68 |
| Bullying | 4.58 | 4.58 | 4.69 | 4.80 | 5.20 | 4.58 | 4.69 | 3.46 | 4.24 | 3.00 | 3.87 | 3.87 | 3.87 | 3.67 |
| Developmental Social Disorders | 4.47 | 4.58 | 4.36 | 3.32 | 3.74 | 3.16 | 3.94 | 3.32 | 3.61 | 3.00 | 3.46 | 3.74 | 3.46 | 3.39 |
| Emotional Self-Control | 3.46 | 3.61 | 3.46 | 3.32 | 3.46 | 3.16 | 3.39 | 3.46 | 3.32 | 3.61 | 3.61 | 3.87 | 3.61 | 3.54 |
| Executive Functioning | 3.32 | 3.46 | 3.32 | 2.65 | 2.83 | 2.65 | 3.00 | 2.83 | 2.83 | 2.65 | 3.00 | 3.00 | 3.16 | 2.92 |
| Negative Emotionality | 4.12 | 4.00 | 4.24 | 4.12 | 4.12 | 4.12 | 4.12 | 4.00 | 3.87 | 4.12 | 4.12 | 4.58 | 3.87 | 4.06 |
| Resiliency | 4.47 | 4.69 | 4.36 | 4.00 | 4.00 | 4.00 | 4.24 | 3.46 | 3.61 | 3.32 | 3.61 | 3.87 | 3.74 | 3.54 |
| **Clinical index** | | | | | | | | | | | | | | |
| Clinical Probability Index | 4.00 | 4.36 | 3.74 | 3.16 | 3.32 | 3.16 | 3.60 | — | — | — | — | — | — | — |
| ADHD Probability Index | — | — | — | — | — | — | — | 3.32 | 3.46 | 3.32 | 3.74 | 3.87 | 3.87 | 3.54 |
| EBD Probability Index | — | — | — | — | — | — | — | 2.83 | 3.16 | 2.65 | 3.32 | 3.16 | 3.46 | 3.08 |
| Autism Probability Index | — | — | — | — | — | — | — | 4.58 | 4.90 | 4.36 | 4.12 | 4.47 | 4.00 | 4.36 |
| Functional Impairment Index | 3.46 | 3.61 | 3.32 | 2.83 | 3.32 | 2.65 | 3.16 | 2.45 | 2.65 | 2.45 | 2.65 | 2.65 | 2.65 | 2.55 |

**Table 10.13** PRS: *T*-Score Standard Errors of Measurement of Composites, Scales, and Indexes, by Gender and Age, General Norm Samples *(continued)*

| | Ages 12–14 | | | Adolescent | | | |
| | | | | | Ages 15–18 | | Ages 12–18 |
| | Combined | Female | Male | Combined | Female | Male | Combined total |
|---|---|---|---|---|---|---|---|
| **Composite** | | | | | | | |
| Externalizing Problems | 2.00 | 2.00 | 2.00 | 2.00 | 1.73 | 2.65 | 2.00 |
| Internalizing Problems | 2.24 | 2.24 | 2.24 | 2.00 | 1.73 | 2.45 | 2.12 |
| Adaptive Skills | 1.73 | 1.73 | 1.73 | 1.73 | 2.00 | 1.73 | 1.73 |
| Behavioral Symptoms Index | 1.73 | 1.73 | 1.73 | 1.73 | 1.41 | 1.73 | 1.73 |
| **Clinical scale** | | | | | | | |
| Hyperactivity | 3.46 | 3.74 | 3.32 | 3.61 | 3.16 | 4.12 | 3.54 |
| Aggression | 3.32 | 3.00 | 3.46 | 3.16 | 2.65 | 4.12 | 3.24 |
| Conduct Problems | 3.00 | 2.65 | 3.46 | 2.83 | 2.24 | 3.87 | 2.92 |
| Anxiety | 3.32 | 3.32 | 3.32 | 3.32 | 3.32 | 3.61 | 3.32 |
| Depression | 3.16 | 3.16 | 3.16 | 2.65 | 2.24 | 3.46 | 2.92 |
| Somatization | 3.46 | 3.46 | 3.46 | 3.16 | 2.83 | 4.00 | 3.31 |
| Attention Problems | 3.16 | 3.46 | 3.00 | 3.46 | 3.46 | 3.32 | 3.31 |
| Atypicality | 2.83 | 2.65 | 3.16 | 2.83 | 2.65 | 3.46 | 2.83 |
| Withdrawal | 3.74 | 3.74 | 3.61 | 3.46 | 3.61 | 3.46 | 3.60 |
| **Adaptive scale** | | | | | | | |
| Adaptability | 3.16 | 3.46 | 3.00 | 3.32 | 3.46 | 3.16 | 3.24 |
| Social Skills | 2.83 | 2.65 | 3.00 | 3.16 | 3.32 | 3.00 | 3.00 |
| Leadership | 3.32 | 3.46 | 3.32 | 3.46 | 3.46 | 3.46 | 3.39 |
| Activities of Daily Living | 4.24 | 4.58 | 4.24 | 4.24 | 4.58 | 4.12 | 4.24 |
| Functional Communication | 3.32 | 3.46 | 3.32 | 3.61 | 3.74 | 3.46 | 3.47 |
| **Content scale** | | | | | | | |
| Anger Control | 3.32 | 3.32 | 3.32 | 3.46 | 3.16 | 3.74 | 3.39 |
| Bullying | 2.65 | 2.65 | 2.83 | 2.45 | 2.00 | 3.46 | 2.55 |
| Developmental Social Disorders | 3.00 | 3.00 | 3.00 | 3.32 | 3.32 | 3.16 | 3.16 |
| Emotional Self-Control | 3.16 | 3.00 | 3.16 | 3.16 | 3.16 | 3.16 | 3.16 |
| Executive Functioning | 2.65 | 2.83 | 2.65 | 2.83 | 2.83 | 2.83 | 2.74 |
| Negative Emotionality | 3.46 | 3.46 | 3.46 | 3.46 | 3.00 | 4.00 | 3.46 |
| Resiliency | 2.65 | 2.83 | 2.65 | 2.83 | 2.65 | 2.83 | 2.74 |
| **Clinical index** | | | | | | | |
| Clinical Probability Index | — | — | — | — | — | — | — |
| ADHD Probability Index | 3.61 | 3.87 | 3.61 | 3.74 | 3.87 | 3.61 | 3.68 |
| EBD Probability Index | 2.83 | 2.83 | 2.83 | 3.16 | 3.00 | 3.16 | 3.00 |
| Autism Probability Index | 3.16 | 3.16 | 3.32 | 3.32 | 3.32 | 3.16 | 3.24 |
| Functional Impairment Index | 2.45 | 2.45 | 2.45 | 2.45 | 2.65 | 2.45 | 2.45 |

**Table 10.14** PRS: *T*-Score Standard Errors of Measurement of Composites, Scales, and Indexes, by Gender and Form Level, Clinical Norm Samples

| | Preschool | | | Child | | | | | | Adolescent | | | | | |
| | All clinical | | | All clinical | | | ADHD | | | All clinical | | | ADHD | | |
| | Combined | Female | Male | Combined | Female | Male | Combined | Female | Male | Combined | Female | Male | Combined | Female | Male |
|---|---|---|---|---|---|---|---|---|---|---|---|---|---|---|---|
| **Composite** | | | | | | | | | | | | | | | |
| Externalizing Problems | 2.65 | 3.16 | 2.45 | 2.00 | 2.00 | 2.00 | 2.24 | 2.00 | 2.24 | 2.00 | 1.73 | 2.24 | 2.45 | 2.24 | 2.45 |
| Internalizing Problems | 2.24 | 2.24 | 2.24 | 2.24 | 2.24 | 2.24 | 2.45 | 2.65 | 2.24 | 2.00 | 2.00 | 2.24 | 2.45 | 2.45 | 2.45 |
| Adaptive Skills | 2.24 | 2.65 | 2.24 | 2.00 | 2.24 | 2.00 | 2.24 | 2.45 | 2.24 | 2.00 | 1.73 | 2.00 | 2.24 | 2.24 | 2.00 |
| Behavioral Symptoms Index | 1.73 | 1.73 | 1.73 | 1.73 | 1.73 | 1.73 | 2.00 | 2.45 | 2.00 | 1.73 | 1.41 | 2.00 | 2.00 | 2.00 | 2.00 |
| **Clinical scale** | | | | | | | | | | | | | | | |
| Hyperactivity | 3.16 | 3.16 | 3.16 | 3.00 | 2.83 | 3.00 | 3.32 | 3.32 | 3.32 | 3.32 | 3.16 | 3.32 | 3.74 | 4.00 | 3.61 |
| Aggression | 3.61 | 4.58 | 3.32 | 3.46 | 3.46 | 3.46 | 3.46 | 3.32 | 3.46 | 3.00 | 2.65 | 3.32 | 3.74 | 3.46 | 3.87 |
| Conduct Problems | – | – | – | 3.00 | 2.83 | 3.00 | 2.83 | 2.83 | 2.83 | 3.00 | 2.45 | 3.32 | 3.46 | 2.83 | 3.87 |
| Anxiety | 3.61 | 3.46 | 3.61 | 3.46 | 3.32 | 3.46 | 3.46 | 3.87 | 3.46 | 3.16 | 3.00 | 3.32 | 3.32 | 3.74 | 3.16 |
| Depression | 3.00 | 2.83 | 3.16 | 3.00 | 3.32 | 2.83 | 3.16 | 4.00 | 2.83 | 3.00 | 2.65 | 3.32 | 3.32 | 3.00 | 3.61 |
| Somatization | 3.46 | 3.46 | 3.74 | 3.32 | 3.00 | 3.46 | 3.87 | 3.87 | 3.74 | 3.32 | 3.16 | 3.46 | 3.87 | 3.61 | 4.00 |
| Attention Problems | 3.00 | 3.46 | 3.00 | 3.46 | 3.46 | 3.46 | 4.58 | 4.80 | 4.47 | 3.46 | 3.16 | 3.61 | 3.74 | 3.74 | 3.74 |
| Atypicality | 3.00 | 3.32 | 2.83 | 3.00 | 3.16 | 3.00 | 3.32 | 3.87 | 3.16 | 3.32 | 2.83 | 3.87 | 3.87 | 3.61 | 3.87 |
| Withdrawal | 3.61 | 3.74 | 3.32 | 3.00 | 3.61 | 2.83 | 3.32 | 3.74 | 3.16 | 3.16 | 3.46 | 3.16 | 3.46 | 3.87 | 3.32 |
| **Adaptive scale** | | | | | | | | | | | | | | | |
| Adaptability | 3.87 | 4.24 | 3.74 | 3.61 | 4.00 | 3.61 | 4.00 | 4.12 | 4.00 | 3.32 | 3.46 | 3.16 | 3.61 | 4.00 | 3.46 |
| Social Skills | 3.16 | 3.61 | 3.16 | 2.83 | 3.16 | 2.83 | 3.16 | 3.16 | 3.16 | 2.83 | 3.00 | 2.83 | 3.00 | 3.00 | 2.83 |
| Leadership | – | – | – | 4.00 | 4.47 | 3.87 | 4.69 | 4.58 | 4.58 | 3.46 | 3.16 | 3.74 | 4.00 | 3.61 | 4.12 |
| Activities of Daily Living | 3.87 | 4.69 | 3.61 | 4.80 | 4.69 | 4.90 | 4.90 | 5.48 | 4.80 | 4.47 | 4.47 | 4.47 | 4.80 | 5.10 | 4.58 |
| Functional Communication | 3.87 | 4.12 | 3.74 | 3.61 | 3.74 | 3.61 | 4.12 | 4.24 | 4.12 | 3.46 | 3.46 | 3.46 | 3.87 | 4.12 | 3.74 |
| **Content scale** | | | | | | | | | | | | | | | |
| Anger Control | 3.61 | 3.00 | 4.00 | 3.16 | 3.00 | 3.16 | 3.16 | 3.32 | 3.16 | 3.00 | 3.16 | 3.00 | 3.32 | 3.87 | 3.00 |
| Bullying | 3.87 | 5.48 | 3.32 | 3.16 | 3.16 | 3.00 | 3.16 | 3.00 | 3.16 | 2.45 | 2.24 | 2.83 | 3.16 | 2.65 | 3.32 |
| Developmental Social Disorders | 3.16 | 3.16 | 3.00 | 3.00 | 3.46 | 2.83 | 3.16 | 3.61 | 3.00 | 3.32 | 3.32 | 3.16 | 3.61 | 3.32 | 3.61 |
| Emotional Self-Control | 2.65 | 2.45 | 2.83 | 3.00 | 3.00 | 3.16 | 3.32 | 3.74 | 3.16 | 3.00 | 3.00 | 3.16 | 3.46 | 3.74 | 3.32 |
| Executive Functioning | 2.65 | 2.45 | 2.65 | 2.83 | 3.00 | 3.00 | 3.46 | 3.74 | 3.46 | 3.00 | 2.83 | 3.00 | 3.00 | 3.00 | 3.00 |
| Negative Emotionality | 3.32 | 3.00 | 3.46 | 3.46 | 3.61 | 3.46 | 3.61 | 3.74 | 3.61 | 3.32 | 3.16 | 3.46 | 3.74 | 3.87 | 3.61 |
| Resiliency | 4.00 | 4.12 | 3.87 | 3.61 | 3.61 | 3.61 | 4.24 | 4.12 | 4.24 | 3.00 | 3.00 | 3.00 | 3.32 | 3.46 | 3.16 |
| **Clinical index** | | | | | | | | | | | | | | | |
| Clinical Probability Index | 3.32 | 3.46 | 3.32 | – | – | – | – | – | – | – | – | – | – | – | – |
| ADHD Probability Index | – | – | – | 3.32 | 3.16 | 3.46 | 3.87 | 4.00 | 3.74 | 4.00 | 3.87 | 4.12 | 4.36 | 4.47 | 4.24 |
| EBD Probability Index | – | – | – | 2.65 | 2.83 | 2.65 | 2.65 | 2.65 | 2.65 | 2.65 | 2.65 | 2.65 | 2.65 | 2.83 | 2.65 |
| Autism Probability Index | – | – | – | 3.46 | 4.00 | 3.32 | 3.74 | 4.12 | 3.61 | 3.16 | 3.16 | 3.16 | 3.46 | 3.32 | 3.61 |
| Functional Impairment Index | 2.83 | 3.00 | 2.65 | 2.45 | 2.65 | 2.45 | 2.65 | 3.16 | 2.45 | 2.65 | 2.45 | 2.65 | 2.83 | 3.00 | 2.83 |

As discussed in chapter 2, a confidence interval may be formed around the observed $T$ score to indicate, with a particular level of confidence (e.g., 90%), the range of $T$ scores within which the person's true score is likely to fall. This confidence interval is constructed using a multiple of the *SEM*. The resulting value is added to (and subtracted from) the observed $T$ score, forming 90% confidence intervals (see the bottom row of the norm tables presented in Appendix A).

# Evidence of Validity

Three types of evidence about the validity of the PRS as a measure of multiple behavioral constructs are discussed in this section. The first is the empirical support from scale intercorrelations and factor analysis for the grouping of scales into composites. The second is the pattern of correlations of PRS composite and scale scores with scores obtained on other behavior measures. The last consists of the PRS score profiles of groups of children with particular clinical diagnoses or educational classifications. Additional validity evidence related to test content (i.e., item development and selection) is presented in chapter 7.

## EVIDENCE BASED ON INTERNAL STRUCTURE

One way of evaluating how well a scale measures the dimension it is designed to measure is to see whether its correlations with other scale scores reflect the current scientific understanding of behavioral dimensions. Tables 10.15 through 10.17 show the intercorrelations of scales at each age level of the general and clinical norm samples. Within each PRS level, the pattern and magnitude of correlations are very similar between the two samples. As expected, correlations of scores within clinical scales and of scores within adaptive scales are positive, while correlations between scores from clinical and adaptive scales are negative.

# Table 10.15 PRS–P: Intercorrelation of Composites, Scales, and Indexes, General and Clinical Norm Samples

| | Composite | | | | Clinical scale | | | | | | | |
|---|---|---|---|---|---|---|---|---|---|---|---|---|
| | Externalizing Problems | Internalizing Problems | Adaptive Skills | Behavioral Symptoms Index | Hyper-activity | Aggression | Anxiety | Depression | Somatization | Attention Problems | Atypicality | Withdrawal |
| **Composite** | | | | | | | | | | | | |
| Externalizing Problems | — | .66 | -.48 | .88 | .91 | .91 | .46 | .72 | .53 | .71 | .66 | .30 |
| Internalizing Problems | .65 | — | -.34 | .76 | .54 | .66 | .87 | .87 | .85 | .42 | .57 | .53 |
| Adaptive Skills | -.42 | -.22 | — | -.70 | -.49 | -.39 | -.08 | -.48 | -.33 | -.69 | -.69 | -.59 |
| Behavioral Symptoms Index | .90 | .73 | -.60 | — | .83 | .78 | .52 | .85 | .59 | .80 | .87 | .63 |
| **Clinical scale** | | | | | | | | | | | | |
| Hyperactivity | .91 | .56 | -.39 | .83 | — | .65 | .38 | .66 | .35 | .76 | .65 | .22 |
| Aggression | .91 | .62 | -.38 | .80 | .65 | — | .43 | .65 | .62 | .53 | .54 | .32 |
| Anxiety | .40 | .81 | .02 | .44 | .35 | .38 | — | .65 | .59 | .23 | .32 | .40 |
| Depression | .73 | .84 | -.39 | .83 | .65 | .68 | .52 | — | .61 | .52 | .67 | .54 |
| Somatization | .48 | .82 | -.16 | .53 | .38 | .49 | .49 | .55 | — | .32 | .50 | .43 |
| Attention Problems | .64 | .35 | -.64 | .76 | .66 | .51 | .14 | .52 | .21 | — | .69 | .33 |
| Atypicality | .67 | .60 | -.46 | .83 | .64 | .59 | .38 | .61 | .50 | .53 | — | .61 |
| Withdrawal | .25 | .38 | -.49 | .55 | .20 | .26 | .28 | .36 | .31 | .27 | .45 | — |
| **Adaptive scale** | | | | | | | | | | | | |
| Adaptability | -.35 | -.29 | .75 | -.52 | -.29 | -.35 | -.14 | -.40 | -.16 | -.51 | -.36 | -.51 |
| Social Skills | -.33 | -.12 | .89 | -.48 | -.30 | -.30 | .10 | -.29 | -.10 | -.57 | -.34 | -.39 |
| Activities of Daily Living | -.40 | -.22 | .67 | -.47 | -.41 | -.33 | -.03 | -.33 | -.18 | -.42 | -.38 | -.28 |
| Functional Communication | -.27 | -.08 | .87 | -.44 | -.27 | -.23 | .12 | -.23 | -.09 | -.55 | -.38 | -.37 |
| **Content scale** | | | | | | | | | | | | |
| Anger Control | .82 | .69 | -.49 | .83 | .71 | .77 | .40 | .83 | .47 | .60 | .60 | .32 |
| Bullying | .72 | .66 | -.24 | .67 | .48 | .82 | .48 | .64 | .51 | .35 | .53 | .26 |
| Developmental Social Disorders | .50 | .42 | -.81 | .74 | .46 | .46 | .20 | .50 | .33 | .62 | .71 | .63 |
| Emotional Self-Control | .76 | .78 | -.43 | .84 | .72 | .67 | .51 | .92 | .50 | .58 | .62 | .37 |
| Executive Functioning | .81 | .57 | -.71 | .90 | .80 | .68 | .30 | .75 | .37 | .86 | .66 | .39 |
| Negative Emotionality | .77 | .77 | -.37 | .81 | .67 | .74 | .50 | .90 | .52 | .51 | .58 | .34 |
| Resiliency | -.35 | -.31 | .79 | -.57 | -.31 | -.33 | -.13 | -.44 | -.19 | -.56 | -.41 | -.56 |
| **Clinical index** | | | | | | | | | | | | |
| Clinical Probability Index | .70 | .46 | -.83 | .85 | .68 | .58 | .20 | .62 | .33 | .82 | .71 | .49 |
| Functional Impairment Index | .68 | .55 | -.85 | .87 | .64 | .60 | .28 | .69 | .40 | .76 | .70 | .59 |

| | Adaptive scale | | | | Content scale | | | | | | | Clinical index | |
|---|---|---|---|---|---|---|---|---|---|---|---|---|---|
| | Adapt-ability | Social Skills | Activities of Daily Living | Functional Commu-nication | Anger Control | Bullying | Develop-mental Social Disorders | Emotional Self-Control | Executive Functioning | Negative Emotionality | Resiliency | Clinical Probability Index | Functional Impairment Index |
| **Composite** | | | | | | | | | | | | | |
| Externalizing Problems | −.46 | −.39 | −.42 | −.27 | .83 | .71 | .57 | .79 | .87 | .76 | −.47 | .74 | .69 |
| Internalizing Problems | −.55 | −.19 | −.22 | −.15 | .74 | .60 | .56 | .80 | .69 | .82 | −.51 | .56 | .63 |
| Adaptive Skills | .70 | .92 | .74 | .85 | −.55 | −.23 | −.86 | −.55 | −.74 | −.46 | .81 | −.86 | −.88 |
| Behavioral Symptoms Index | −.66 | −.58 | −.53 | −.48 | .87 | .61 | .85 | .89 | .94 | .84 | −.70 | .90 | .91 |
| **Clinical scale** | | | | | | | | | | | | | |
| Hyperactivity | −.44 | −.38 | −.47 | −.26 | .77 | .41 | .55 | .78 | .88 | .70 | −.44 | .76 | .70 |
| Aggression | −.41 | −.33 | −.30 | −.24 | .75 | .86 | .48 | .65 | .69 | .69 | −.41 | .58 | .57 |
| Anxiety | −.36 | .08 | −.05 | .08 | .50 | .43 | .30 | .60 | .46 | .61 | −.28 | .28 | .39 |
| Depression | −.68 | −.32 | −.27 | −.27 | .88 | .61 | .68 | .92 | .81 | .94 | −.64 | .69 | .76 |
| Somatization | −.39 | −.26 | −.25 | −.21 | .53 | .51 | .46 | .56 | .50 | .56 | −.40 | .46 | .48 |
| Attention Problems | −.47 | −.63 | −.60 | −.52 | .63 | .35 | .68 | .63 | .84 | .51 | −.56 | .84 | .78 |
| Atypicality | −.53 | −.59 | −.55 | −.52 | .68 | .39 | .87 | .73 | .78 | .64 | −.65 | .83 | .84 |
| Withdrawal | −.59 | −.51 | −.34 | −.46 | .44 | .26 | .77 | .51 | .47 | .50 | −.63 | .57 | .69 |
| **Adaptive scale** | | | | | | | | | | | | | |
| Adaptability | — | .56 | .25 | .45 | −.66 | −.40 | −.69 | −.67 | −.69 | −.63 | .90 | −.67 | −.70 |
| Social Skills | .63 | — | .63 | .79 | −.43 | −.19 | −.76 | −.39 | −.61 | −.31 | .72 | −.76 | −.77 |
| Activities of Daily Living | .23 | .44 | — | .52 | −.38 | −.08 | −.57 | −.39 | −.56 | −.29 | .39 | −.67 | −.67 |
| Functional Communication | .54 | .76 | .47 | — | −.31 | −.12 | −.74 | −.32 | −.51 | −.25 | .60 | −.68 | −.70 |
| **Content scale** | | | | | | | | | | | | | |
| Anger Control | −.49 | −.39 | −.38 | −.31 | — | .62 | .66 | .91 | .89 | .90 | −.64 | .75 | .78 |
| Bullying | −.29 | −.19 | −.19 | −.11 | .63 | — | .36 | .50 | .50 | .56 | −.38 | .39 | .41 |
| Developmental Social Disorders | −.72 | −.69 | −.41 | −.76 | .53 | .38 | — | .71 | .79 | .63 | −.81 | .88 | .92 |
| Emotional Self-Control | −.43 | −.32 | −.37 | −.27 | .88 | .56 | .52 | — | .89 | .93 | −.65 | .79 | .82 |
| Executive Functioning | −.62 | −.60 | −.49 | −.57 | .85 | .50 | .72 | .81 | — | .82 | −.72 | .91 | .91 |
| Negative Emotionality | −.38 | −.29 | −.33 | −.19 | .88 | .62 | .45 | .90 | .76 | — | −.58 | .69 | .74 |
| Resiliency | .91 | .71 | .30 | .60 | −.49 | −.28 | −.77 | −.46 | −.66 | −.41 | — | −.75 | −.79 |
| **Clinical index** | | | | | | | | | | | | | |
| Clinical Probability Index | −.65 | −.73 | −.53 | −.73 | .70 | .44 | .84 | .69 | .90 | .61 | −.71 | — | .95 |
| Functional Impairment Index | −.66 | −.74 | −.60 | −.71 | .74 | .47 | .85 | .74 | .89 | .67 | −.74 | .92 | — |

| | Composite | | | | Clinical scale | | | | | | | | |
| --- | --- | --- | --- | --- | --- | --- | --- | --- | --- | --- | --- | --- | --- |
| | Externalizing Problems | Internalizing Problems | Adaptive Skills | Behavioral Symptoms Index | Hyper-activity | Aggression | Conduct Problems | Anxiety | Depression | Somatization | Attention Problems | Atypicality | Withdrawal |
| **Composite** | | | | | | | | | | | | | |
| Externalizing Problems | — | .42 | -.49 | .82 | .86 | .91 | .93 | .22 | .60 | .26 | .57 | .52 | .18 |
| Internalizing Problems | .51 | — | -.32 | .66 | .41 | .40 | .32 | .87 | .85 | .81 | .39 | .46 | .40 |
| Adaptive Skills | -.52 | -.40 | — | -.73 | -.45 | -.45 | -.41 | -.15 | -.47 | -.18 | -.64 | -.63 | -.59 |
| Behavioral Symptoms Index | .84 | .67 | -.74 | — | .78 | .75 | .69 | .46 | .81 | .41 | .73 | .79 | .58 |
| **Clinical scale** | | | | | | | | | | | | | |
| Hyperactivity | .86 | .47 | -.46 | .79 | — | .65 | .69 | .26 | .54 | .24 | .66 | .47 | .12 |
| Aggression | .89 | .46 | -.47 | .75 | .61 | — | .82 | .19 | .59 | .23 | .41 | .47 | .22 |
| Conduct Problems | .92 | .42 | -.45 | .71 | .69 | .76 | — | .13 | .48 | .22 | .48 | .45 | .13 |
| Anxiety | .29 | .85 | -.22 | .46 | .32 | .24 | .21 | — | .66 | .55 | .26 | .31 | .35 |
| Depression | .62 | .84 | -.53 | .81 | .56 | .57 | .52 | .61 | — | .51 | .48 | .54 | .42 |
| Somatization | .36 | .79 | -.25 | .41 | .30 | .35 | .32 | .50 | .48 | — | .25 | .33 | .25 |
| Attention Problems | .61 | .38 | -.74 | .77 | .65 | .46 | .53 | .24 | .52 | .20 | — | .45 | .23 |
| Atypicality | .60 | .51 | -.59 | .83 | .57 | .51 | .54 | .35 | .59 | .33 | .58 | — | .59 |
| Withdrawal | .25 | .39 | -.59 | .60 | .21 | .27 | .19 | .32 | .45 | .20 | .32 | .51 | — |
| **Adaptive scale** | | | | | | | | | | | | | |
| Adaptability | -.48 | -.44 | .85 | -.66 | -.43 | -.44 | -.40 | -.31 | -.56 | -.24 | -.63 | -.49 | -.47 |
| Social Skills | -.41 | -.23 | .88 | -.58 | -.31 | -.42 | -.36 | -.06 | -.37 | -.15 | -.55 | -.44 | -.56 |
| Leadership | -.36 | -.33 | .89 | -.61 | -.33 | -.32 | -.31 | -.20 | -.43 | -.19 | -.64 | -.50 | -.56 |
| Activities of Daily Living | -.60 | -.41 | .84 | -.72 | -.57 | -.49 | -.53 | -.23 | -.51 | -.29 | -.73 | -.56 | -.40 |
| Functional Communication | -.42 | -.34 | .90 | -.67 | -.38 | -.37 | -.36 | -.19 | -.44 | -.21 | -.68 | -.59 | -.58 |
| **Content scale** | | | | | | | | | | | | | |
| Anger Control | .78 | .62 | -.61 | .82 | .67 | .77 | .65 | .40 | .78 | .35 | .58 | .56 | .37 |
| Bullying | .85 | .41 | -.41 | .68 | .55 | .91 | .80 | .21 | .48 | .34 | .40 | .52 | .25 |
| Developmental Social Disorders | .50 | .45 | -.86 | .79 | .47 | .46 | .43 | .30 | .55 | .27 | .65 | .77 | .69 |
| Emotional Self-Control | .66 | .79 | -.55 | .80 | .64 | .59 | .54 | .65 | .86 | .46 | .56 | .60 | .40 |
| Executive Functioning | .69 | .50 | -.88 | .84 | .69 | .56 | .59 | .32 | .63 | .29 | .88 | .64 | .44 |
| Negative Emotionality | .69 | .76 | -.52 | .77 | .60 | .66 | .59 | .54 | .88 | .46 | .51 | .52 | .36 |
| Resiliency | -.38 | -.33 | .90 | -.62 | -.35 | -.34 | -.33 | -.20 | -.45 | -.17 | -.67 | -.50 | -.52 |
| **Clinical index** | | | | | | | | | | | | | |
| ADHD Probability Index | .78 | .45 | -.70 | .83 | .84 | .57 | .67 | .29 | .57 | .26 | .89 | .62 | .30 |
| EBD Probability Index | .86 | .64 | -.77 | .90 | .68 | .82 | .80 | .40 | .77 | .43 | .67 | .67 | .49 |
| Autism Probability Index | .38 | .44 | -.68 | .73 | .35 | .37 | .30 | .34 | .52 | .24 | .46 | .74 | .88 |
| Functional Impairment Index | .66 | .61 | -.91 | .90 | .63 | .57 | .57 | .43 | .72 | .38 | .79 | .74 | .64 |

**Table 10.16** PRS–C: Intercorrelation of Composites, Scales, and Indexes, General and Clinical Norm Samples *(continued)*

| | Adaptive scale | | | | | Content scale | | | | | | | Clinical index | | | |
|---|---|---|---|---|---|---|---|---|---|---|---|---|---|---|---|---|
| | Adapt-ability | Social Skills | Leader-ship | Activities of Daily Living | Functional Commu-nication | Anger Control | Bullying | Develop-mental Social Disorders | Emotional Self-Control | Executive Func-tioning | Negative Emotion-ality | Resiliency | ADHD Probability Index | EBD Probability Index | Autism Probability Index | Functional Impairment Index |
| **Composite** | | | | | | | | | | | | | | | | |
| Externalizing Problems | -.49 | -.38 | -.26 | -.58 | -.32 | .83 | .86 | .46 | .71 | .70 | .69 | -.36 | .77 | .90 | .31 | .64 |
| Internalizing Problems | -.43 | -.12 | -.23 | -.35 | -.21 | .58 | .34 | .41 | .75 | .46 | .74 | -.27 | .40 | .57 | .42 | .59 |
| Adaptive Skills | .82 | .85 | .88 | .79 | .88 | -.56 | -.37 | -.83 | -.55 | -.83 | -.46 | .89 | -.61 | -.67 | -.69 | -.89 |
| Behavioral Symptoms Index | -.68 | -.54 | -.55 | -.69 | -.59 | .83 | .65 | .78 | .85 | .84 | .78 | -.61 | .79 | .89 | .70 | .91 |
| **Clinical scale** | | | | | | | | | | | | | | | | |
| Hyperactivity | -.45 | -.28 | -.27 | -.59 | -.30 | .70 | .57 | .41 | .67 | .74 | .60 | -.34 | .87 | .69 | .27 | .62 |
| Aggression | -.49 | -.41 | -.24 | -.47 | -.28 | .85 | .91 | .44 | .67 | .59 | .70 | -.34 | .57 | .90 | .32 | .58 |
| Conduct Problems | -.39 | -.33 | -.20 | -.52 | -.27 | .69 | .86 | .38 | .57 | .58 | .56 | -.28 | .64 | .84 | .24 | .54 |
| Anxiety | -.31 | .02 | -.12 | -.16 | -.08 | .36 | .15 | .28 | .60 | .29 | .55 | -.15 | .23 | .35 | .33 | .41 |
| Depression | -.55 | -.30 | -.34 | -.46 | -.31 | .77 | .48 | .52 | .85 | .61 | .90 | -.41 | .55 | .75 | .47 | .69 |
| Somatization | -.24 | -.03 | -.11 | -.26 | -.14 | .34 | .22 | .25 | .46 | .27 | .44 | -.12 | .23 | .36 | .28 | .39 |
| Attention Problems | -.54 | -.40 | -.55 | -.70 | -.53 | .53 | .34 | .47 | .56 | .87 | .50 | -.58 | .88 | .57 | .35 | .71 |
| Atypicality | -.50 | -.47 | -.48 | -.53 | -.64 | .53 | .43 | .86 | .60 | .58 | .46 | -.51 | .48 | .63 | .80 | .78 |
| Withdrawal | -.48 | -.53 | -.54 | -.33 | -.58 | .30 | .16 | .75 | .39 | .36 | .31 | -.50 | .17 | .42 | .90 | .67 |
| **Adaptive scale** | | | | | | | | | | | | | | | | |
| Adaptability | — | .67 | .65 | .57 | .60 | -.64 | -.40 | -.72 | -.62 | -.74 | -.56 | .82 | -.53 | -.69 | -.53 | -.76 |
| Social Skills | .67 | — | .69 | .55 | .69 | -.44 | -.36 | -.69 | -.37 | -.59 | -.33 | .70 | -.39 | -.57 | -.57 | -.68 |
| Leadership | .68 | .75 | — | .59 | .78 | -.36 | -.16 | -.68 | -.38 | -.70 | -.30 | .87 | -.45 | -.46 | -.62 | -.72 |
| Activities of Daily Living | .64 | .66 | .69 | — | .63 | -.54 | -.39 | -.60 | -.54 | -.81 | -.49 | .62 | -.74 | -.63 | -.46 | -.78 |
| Functional Communication | .71 | .76 | .80 | .69 | — | -.37 | -.22 | -.82 | -.40 | -.67 | -.28 | .77 | -.46 | -.48 | -.70 | -.82 |
| **Content scale** | | | | | | | | | | | | | | | | |
| Anger Control | -.64 | -.49 | -.46 | -.58 | -.50 | — | .69 | .53 | .87 | .74 | .86 | -.48 | .66 | .88 | .40 | .71 |
| Bullying | -.37 | -.39 | -.27 | -.43 | -.33 | .62 | — | .38 | .55 | .48 | .56 | -.25 | .48 | .85 | .25 | .49 |
| Developmental Social Disorders | -.78 | -.74 | -.73 | -.67 | -.85 | .58 | .43 | — | .58 | .66 | .44 | -.73 | .47 | .65 | .89 | .87 |
| Emotional Self-Control | -.59 | -.38 | -.44 | -.54 | -.47 | .83 | .49 | .58 | — | .73 | .85 | -.47 | .66 | .82 | .49 | .78 |
| Executive Functioning | -.77 | -.69 | -.78 | -.84 | -.79 | .72 | .49 | .76 | .69 | — | .65 | -.78 | .88 | .75 | .49 | .87 |
| Negative Emotionality | -.55 | -.40 | -.39 | -.53 | -.42 | .85 | .53 | .50 | .84 | .64 | — | -.40 | .59 | .80 | .36 | .66 |
| Resiliency | .83 | .75 | .85 | .69 | .83 | -.48 | -.30 | -.79 | -.47 | -.82 | -.42 | — | -.51 | -.56 | -.57 | -.76 |
| **Clinical index** | | | | | | | | | | | | | | | | |
| ADHD Probability Index | -.57 | -.52 | -.57 | -.79 | -.60 | .66 | .50 | .61 | .63 | .88 | .60 | -.58 | — | .68 | .32 | .71 |
| EBD Probability Index | -.72 | -.66 | -.62 | -.70 | -.65 | .85 | .78 | .73 | .79 | .81 | .80 | -.65 | .74 | — | .51 | .80 |
| Autism Probability Index | -.52 | -.60 | -.65 | -.52 | -.69 | .46 | .35 | .82 | .50 | .57 | .43 | -.59 | .45 | .59 | — | .78 |
| Functional Impairment Index | -.78 | -.74 | -.78 | -.82 | -.87 | .74 | .51 | .87 | .76 | .91 | .69 | -.80 | .79 | .86 | .76 | — |

**Table 10.17** PRS–A: Intercorrelation of Composites, Scales, and Indexes, General and Clinical Norm Samples

| | Composite | | | | Clinical scale | | | | | | | | |
|---|---|---|---|---|---|---|---|---|---|---|---|---|---|
| | Externalizing Problems | Internalizing Problems | Adaptive Skills | Behavioral Symptoms Index | Hyper-activity | Aggression | Conduct Problems | Anxiety | Depression | Somatization | Attention Problems | Atypicality | Withdrawal |
| **Composite** | | | | | | | | | | | | | |
| Externalizing Problems | — | .64 | -.40 | .85 | .88 | .93 | .92 | .46 | .70 | .52 | .51 | .63 | .27 |
| Internalizing Problems | .76 | — | -.29 | .76 | .60 | .59 | .56 | .87 | .88 | .84 | .35 | .62 | .46 |
| Adaptive Skills | -.39 | -.33 | — | -.60 | -.42 | -.34 | -.32 | -.21 | -.37 | -.17 | -.64 | -.44 | -.54 |
| Behavioral Symptoms Index | .90 | .83 | -.58 | — | .84 | .78 | .71 | .61 | .84 | .54 | .67 | .82 | .64 |
| **Clinical scale** | | | | | | | | | | | | | |
| Hyperactivity | .92 | .69 | -.42 | .87 | — | .71 | .68 | .47 | .65 | .44 | .57 | .63 | .30 |
| Aggression | .95 | .74 | -.34 | .86 | .81 | — | .83 | .40 | .66 | .47 | .39 | .55 | .26 |
| Conduct Problems | .93 | .69 | -.34 | .79 | .76 | .84 | — | .37 | .58 | .50 | .43 | .53 | .19 |
| Anxiety | .58 | .89 | -.27 | .69 | .56 | .57 | .50 | — | .68 | .59 | .27 | .54 | .44 |
| Depression | .81 | .92 | -.41 | .90 | .74 | .78 | .73 | .77 | — | .61 | .41 | .62 | .50 |
| Somatization | .62 | .86 | -.19 | .63 | .54 | .60 | .60 | .60 | .68 | — | .23 | .46 | .25 |
| Attention Problems | .55 | .44 | -.76 | .71 | .58 | .45 | .51 | .36 | .51 | .32 | — | .39 | .30 |
| Atypicality | .79 | .74 | -.42 | .89 | .75 | .74 | .70 | .62 | .78 | .59 | .50 | — | .56 |
| Withdrawal | .45 | .59 | -.54 | .72 | .42 | .46 | .38 | .56 | .63 | .38 | .44 | .62 | — |
| **Adaptive scale** | | | | | | | | | | | | | |
| Adaptability | -.35 | -.34 | .85 | -.50 | -.38 | -.31 | -.28 | -.29 | -.41 | -.20 | -.57 | -.37 | -.45 |
| Social Skills | -.30 | -.20 | .88 | -.46 | -.31 | -.29 | -.24 | -.14 | -.29 | -.09 | -.56 | -.32 | -.50 |
| Leadership | -.24 | -.23 | .90 | -.45 | -.27 | -.18 | -.20 | -.22 | -.29 | -.10 | -.67 | -.31 | -.50 |
| Activities of Daily Living | -.43 | -.30 | .85 | -.55 | -.46 | -.35 | -.40 | -.21 | -.39 | -.21 | -.80 | -.37 | -.36 |
| Functional Communication | -.40 | -.36 | .91 | -.59 | -.41 | -.34 | -.36 | -.31 | -.43 | -.23 | -.72 | -.49 | -.55 |
| **Content scale** | | | | | | | | | | | | | |
| Anger Control | .87 | .76 | -.44 | .87 | .84 | .86 | .74 | .62 | .84 | .55 | .54 | .72 | .50 |
| Bullying | .91 | .71 | -.30 | .81 | .74 | .95 | .85 | .54 | .74 | .61 | .40 | .73 | .44 |
| Developmental Social Disorders | .58 | .58 | -.84 | .79 | .58 | .54 | .50 | .50 | .64 | .39 | .66 | .73 | .73 |
| Emotional Self-Control | .77 | .85 | -.49 | .85 | .77 | .73 | .65 | .77 | .88 | .61 | .53 | .73 | .56 |
| Executive Functioning | .60 | .48 | -.88 | .74 | .65 | .50 | .53 | .39 | .56 | .33 | .90 | .54 | .49 |
| Negative Emotionality | .85 | .82 | -.42 | .87 | .79 | .83 | .76 | .67 | .90 | .61 | .54 | .70 | .54 |
| Resiliency | -.33 | -.31 | .93 | -.52 | -.37 | -.27 | -.28 | -.27 | -.39 | -.17 | -.67 | -.39 | -.48 |
| **Clinical index** | | | | | | | | | | | | | |
| ADHD Probability Index | .50 | .44 | -.87 | .68 | .57 | .41 | .43 | .39 | .50 | .28 | .90 | .48 | .50 |
| EBD Probability Index | .88 | .72 | -.65 | .90 | .83 | .84 | .79 | .58 | .81 | .53 | .68 | .74 | .57 |
| Autism Probability Index | .47 | .50 | -.86 | .72 | .48 | .45 | .40 | .45 | .57 | .31 | .64 | .64 | .82 |
| Functional Impairment Index | .68 | .70 | -.86 | .86 | .68 | .62 | .61 | .62 | .75 | .49 | .81 | .72 | .72 |

| | Adaptive scale | | | | | Content scale | | | | | | | Clinical index | | | |
|---|---|---|---|---|---|---|---|---|---|---|---|---|---|---|---|---|
| | Adapt-ability | Social Skills | Leader-ship | Activities of Daily Living | Functional Commu-nication | Anger Control | Bullying | Develop-mental Social Disorders | Emotional Self-Control | Executive Func-tioning | Negative Emotion-ality | Resiliency | ADHD Probability Index | EBD Probability Index | Autism Probability Index | Functional Impairment Index |
| **Composite** | | | | | | | | | | | | | | | | |
| Externalizing Problems | -.41 | -.32 | -.19 | -.49 | -.25 | .86 | .89 | .47 | .75 | .62 | .84 | -.32 | .52 | .89 | .35 | .62 |
| Internalizing Problems | -.40 | -.17 | -.16 | -.30 | -.20 | .65 | .57 | .46 | .82 | .42 | .75 | -.30 | .41 | .64 | .39 | .64 |
| Adaptive Skills | .79 | .84 | .90 | .80 | .85 | -.47 | -.28 | -.81 | -.50 | -.84 | -.41 | .92 | -.80 | -.62 | -.82 | -.85 |
| Behavioral Symptoms Index | -.55 | -.47 | -.44 | -.58 | -.48 | .83 | .71 | .75 | .85 | .76 | .84 | -.54 | .71 | .87 | .68 | .86 |
| **Clinical scale** | | | | | | | | | | | | | | | | |
| Hyperactivity | -.40 | -.27 | -.27 | -.51 | -.30 | .78 | .64 | .49 | .74 | .70 | .74 | -.37 | .62 | .77 | .39 | .65 |
| Aggression | -.39 | -.34 | -.13 | -.39 | -.17 | .85 | .94 | .43 | .69 | .49 | .81 | -.26 | .39 | .86 | .31 | .52 |
| Conduct Problems | -.33 | -.26 | -.13 | -.43 | -.20 | .72 | .84 | .37 | .60 | .50 | .73 | -.25 | .40 | .78 | .25 | .52 |
| Anxiety | -.32 | -.06 | -.14 | -.19 | -.19 | .47 | .40 | .42 | .72 | .31 | .56 | -.24 | .36 | .44 | .35 | .56 |
| Depression | -.46 | -.28 | -.22 | -.38 | -.24 | .76 | .61 | .51 | .85 | .51 | .86 | -.37 | .46 | .75 | .46 | .68 |
| Somatization | -.25 | -.11 | -.07 | -.22 | -.08 | .45 | .48 | .27 | .57 | .27 | .54 | -.16 | .25 | .48 | .20 | .42 |
| Attention Problems | -.48 | -.40 | -.55 | -.71 | -.53 | .51 | .32 | .50 | .49 | .85 | .50 | -.56 | .88 | .58 | .46 | .70 |
| Atypicality | -.36 | -.33 | -.32 | -.37 | -.46 | .54 | .54 | .74 | .64 | .50 | .55 | -.39 | .47 | .59 | .65 | .70 |
| Withdrawal | -.44 | -.51 | -.51 | -.30 | -.49 | .35 | .22 | .74 | .49 | .42 | .38 | -.50 | .44 | .43 | .83 | .69 |
| **Adaptive scale** | | | | | | | | | | | | | | | | |
| Adaptability | — | .64 | .60 | .53 | .54 | -.53 | -.35 | -.71 | -.60 | -.68 | -.50 | .84 | -.69 | -.61 | -.63 | -.67 |
| Social Skills | .71 | — | .72 | .56 | .61 | -.40 | -.30 | -.67 | -.39 | -.60 | -.35 | .73 | -.53 | -.59 | -.77 | -.64 |
| Leadership | .67 | .76 | — | .65 | .79 | -.26 | -.07 | -.67 | -.33 | -.74 | -.21 | .87 | -.72 | -.41 | -.76 | -.73 |
| Activities of Daily Living | .63 | .63 | .71 | — | .62 | -.50 | -.32 | -.56 | -.47 | -.83 | -.45 | .66 | -.74 | -.61 | -.53 | -.75 |
| Functional Communication | .70 | .74 | .80 | .73 | — | -.26 | -.14 | -.79 | -.31 | -.69 | -.21 | .77 | -.67 | -.39 | -.76 | -.79 |
| **Content scale** | | | | | | | | | | | | | | | | |
| Anger Control | -.45 | -.34 | -.27 | -.43 | -.41 | — | .72 | .50 | .86 | .64 | .90 | -.41 | .54 | .94 | .42 | .65 |
| Bullying | -.25 | -.27 | -.15 | -.30 | -.32 | .75 | — | .39 | .62 | .41 | .73 | -.21 | .32 | .78 | .26 | .47 |
| Developmental Social Disorders | -.78 | -.71 | -.68 | -.64 | -.85 | .61 | .51 | — | .60 | .67 | .46 | -.76 | .68 | .61 | .92 | .85 |
| Emotional Self-Control | -.54 | -.36 | -.35 | -.43 | -.47 | .88 | .66 | .67 | — | .63 | .86 | -.50 | .58 | .84 | .53 | .75 |
| Executive Functioning | -.73 | -.67 | -.78 | -.84 | -.81 | .61 | .43 | .77 | .62 | — | .59 | -.80 | .91 | .74 | .64 | .86 |
| Negative Emotionality | -.44 | -.32 | -.26 | -.42 | -.40 | .90 | .75 | .59 | .85 | .59 | — | -.36 | .51 | .88 | .39 | .65 |
| Resiliency | .88 | .77 | .87 | .72 | .84 | -.38 | -.23 | -.80 | -.49 | -.83 | -.37 | — | -.78 | -.54 | -.76 | -.79 |
| **Clinical index** | | | | | | | | | | | | | | | | |
| ADHD Probability Index | -.74 | -.67 | -.79 | -.82 | -.80 | .52 | .35 | .77 | .57 | .92 | .52 | -.83 | — | .62 | .63 | .82 |
| EBD Probability Index | -.59 | -.58 | -.48 | -.61 | -.60 | .92 | .77 | .73 | .85 | .76 | .87 | -.57 | .68 | — | .55 | .76 |
| Autism Probability Index | -.72 | -.80 | -.78 | -.62 | -.84 | .52 | .41 | .92 | .59 | .74 | .51 | -.79 | .74 | .67 | — | .83 |
| Functional Impairment Index | -.71 | -.68 | -.74 | -.77 | -.86 | .70 | .57 | .90 | .77 | .88 | .70 | -.79 | .86 | .83 | .87 | — |

The PRS composites assess broader behavioral dimensions than those measured by the individual scales. These broad dimensions are evident in the correlations of scores among the scales. When scales correlate relatively highly, they are measuring a common dimension that is represented by the composite. Factor analysis is the statistical technique used in identifying these broad dimensions. This technique is important not only for providing construct validation of the composite scores but also for validating the scales themselves. The correlations between a scale score and the broad dimensions it measures are shown in factor analysis by the scale's loadings on factors.

The PRS composites were based partly on factor analyses of the scale intercorrelations at the preschool, child, and adolescent levels. In this process, the correlations are derived from the entire item-development sample, which includes a greater proportion of clinical cases than is found in the general population. The item-development sample was used for factor analysis instead of the norm samples because the former more closely resembles the population with whom the PRS is used—that is, children who receive services or who have been referred for evaluation of various behavioral, emotional, or educational difficulties. In general, the item-development samples include cases that have a greater incidence of problems than those found in the general norm samples.

Two types of factor analysis were performed in developing the composites. The primary technique was covariance structure analysis (CSA; also known as confirmatory factor analysis) using the Amos 6.0 program (Arbuckle, 2005). CSA has three important advantages for analyzing an instrument such as the BASC–3 PRS. First, there is a large research base (derived from the previous BASC editions and similar instruments) that points to a starting factor structure that can be tested in the analysis. Second, CSA works well with instruments, such as the PRS, for which some factors are expected to correlate highly. Third, CSA identifies which aspects of a hypothesized factor-structure model are inconsistent with the data. It is important to note that CSA was used not to confirm a hypothesized model but rather to evaluate the model and modify it in appropriate ways according to the results of the analysis.

The second technique was principal-axis analysis, an exploratory factor-analytic method. The results of principal-axis analysis can be more difficult to compare across samples (especially those with highly correlated factors) than those of CSA. However, if several principal-axis analyses point to an alternative structure, then that structure should be strongly considered. Thus, use of the principal-axis method complements CSA because it may reveal a substantially different factor structure not indicated by CSA.

## Covariance Structure Analyses

The starting CSA models were based on the final PRS factor structure models reported in the BASC–2 Manual (Reynolds & Kamphaus, 2004). For each level, scale modification indexes (MIs) were examined to see if possible changes might be evident that would substantially improve the model's overall fit to the data. Scales with high MI value loadings on other composite scales (relative to other modification indexes) were identified, and a new model fit was evaluated after adding a parameter between the scale and the composite. However, these changes to the model did not result in a substantial improvement in model fit. (Consistent with the BASC–2 analyses, fit was evaluated using the chi-square, Comparative Fit Index [CFI] and the Root Mean Squared Error of Approximation [RMSEA] fit indexes.) Therefore, the starting models for each level were retained. Fit indexes for each model are presented in Table 10.18, and standardized loadings and factor correlations for the models are presented in Table 10.19. The primary use of the fit indexes was to evaluate the potential model changes. The overall fit of the models is moderate, a finding that is consistent with analyses conducted on the previous BASC editions.

**Table 10.18** PRS: Fit of Various CSA Models (Item-Development Samples)

| Parent Rating Scales | df | $x^2$ | CFI | RMSEA |
|---|---|---|---|---|
| Preschool | 51 | 1,677.9 | 0.76 | 0.18 |
| Child | 71 | 2,200.1 | 0.85 | 0.15 |
| Adolescent | 72 | 2,049.4 | 0.89 | 0.15 |

**Table 10.19** PRS: CSA Factor Loadings for the Final Models (Item-Development Samples)

| | PRS–P | | | PRS–C | | | PRS–A | | |
|---|---|---|---|---|---|---|---|---|---|
| | Externalizing Problems | Internalizing Problems | Adaptive Skills | Externalizing Problems | Internalizing Problems | Adaptive Skills | Externalizing Problems | Internalizing Problems | Adaptive Skills |
| Hyperactivity | .84 | — | — | .80 | — | — | .87 | — | — |
| Aggression | .76 | — | — | .86 | — | — | .94 | — | — |
| Conduct Problems | — | — | — | .87 | — | — | .93 | — | — |
| Anxiety | — | .56 | — | — | .99 | .43 | — | .80 | — |
| Depression | — | .86 | — | — | .88 | — | — | .94 | — |
| Somatization | — | .62 | — | — | .53 | — | — | .76 | — |
| Attention Problems | .72 | — | — | .31 | — | −.59 | .29 | — | −.68 |
| Atypicality | — | .75 | — | — | .75 | — | — | .85 | — |
| Withdrawal | — | .42 | — | — | .65 | — | — | .70 | — |
| Adaptability | — | — | .67 | — | −.24 | .62 | — | −.09 | .75 |
| Social Skills | — | — | .90 | — | — | .83 | — | — | .80 |
| Leadership | — | — | — | — | — | .88 | — | — | .89 |
| Activities of Daily Living | — | — | .52 | — | — | .80 | — | — | .84 |
| Functional Communication | — | — | .85 | — | — | .90 | — | — | .90 |
| **Factor Correlations** | | | | | | | | | |
| Externalizing Problems | — | .89 | — | — | .74 | — | — | .87 | — |
| Adaptive Skills | −.50 | −.35 | — | −.59 | −.71 | — | −.38 | −.44 | — |

## Principal-Axis Factor Analyses

Principal-axis analyses were carried out at each level of the PRS. Three- and four-factor solutions were obtained using oblique and orthogonal rotations; because the results were similar, only the orthogonal (Varimax) results are reported. Results of these analyses are reported in Table 10.20 for the preschool level, Table 10.21 for the child level, and Table 10.22 for the adolescent level.

**Table 10.20** PRS–P: Principal-Axis Factor Matrix, Varimax Rotation

| | 3-factor | | | 4-factor | | | |
|---|---|---|---|---|---|---|---|
| Scale | I | II | III | I | II | III | IV |
| Hyperactivity | −.15 | .36 | .82 | .34 | −.20 | .81 | −.05 |
| Aggression | −.15 | .52 | .55 | .49 | −.12 | .57 | −.11 |
| Anxiety | .13 | .77 | .08 | .71 | .23 | .16 | −.05 |
| Depression | −.21 | .67 | .49 | .63 | −.12 | .53 | −.19 |
| Somatization | −.09 | .65 | .19 | .68 | −.08 | .18 | −.03 |
| Attention Problems | −.48 | .15 | .61 | .12 | −.39 | .62 | −.32 |
| Atypicality | −.39 | .47 | .47 | .52 | −.42 | .42 | −.13 |
| Withdrawal | −.63 | .36 | −.04 | .40 | −.47 | −.07 | −.39 |
| Adaptability | .67 | −.26 | −.13 | −.18 | .24 | −.19 | .86 |
| Social Skills | .83 | .07 | −.24 | .07 | .63 | −.21 | .53 |
| Activities of Daily Living | .43 | .03 | −.34 | −.04 | .59 | −.24 | .02 |
| Functional Communication | .84 | .15 | −.27 | .10 | .79 | −.17 | .39 |

**Table 10.21** PRS–C: Principal-Axis Factor Matrix, Varimax Rotation

| Scale | 3-factor | | | 4-factor | | | |
|---|---|---|---|---|---|---|---|
| | I | II | III | I | II | III | IV |
| Hyperactivity | −.29 | .73 | .26 | −.22 | .60 | .27 | .50 |
| Aggression | −.25 | .77 | .24 | −.26 | .85 | .24 | .07 |
| Conduct Problems | −.23 | .83 | .17 | −.24 | .80 | .18 | .21 |
| Anxiety | −.12 | .12 | .83 | −.10 | .06 | .84 | .13 |
| Depression | −.35 | .47 | .67 | −.34 | .42 | .67 | .21 |
| Somatization | −.09 | .22 | .59 | −.10 | .21 | .59 | .04 |
| Attention Problems | −.60 | .52 | .19 | −.50 | .33 | .19 | .69 |
| Atypicality | −.47 | .46 | .40 | −.46 | .41 | .41 | .23 |
| Withdrawal | −.58 | .08 | .41 | −.62 | .10 | .42 | −.05 |
| Adaptability | .69 | −.35 | −.24 | .67 | −.30 | −.25 | −.24 |
| Social Skills | .80 | −.29 | −.02 | .84 | −.31 | −.01 | −.05 |
| Leadership | .87 | −.18 | −.14 | .84 | −.12 | −.14 | −.26 |
| Activities of Daily Living | .64 | −.51 | −.19 | .58 | −.39 | −.19 | −.43 |
| Functional Communication | .86 | −.26 | −.16 | .83 | −.20 | −.16 | −.28 |

**Table 10.22** PRS–A: Principal-Axis Factor Matrix, Varimax Rotation

| Scale | 3-factor | | | 4-factor | | | |
|---|---|---|---|---|---|---|---|
| | I | II | III | I | II | III | IV |
| Hyperactivity | .83 | −.30 | .12 | .82 | −.30 | .16 | .12 |
| Aggression | .90 | −.17 | .09 | .93 | −.16 | .08 | −.11 |
| Conduct Problems | .92 | −.17 | .04 | .92 | −.16 | .08 | .02 |
| Anxiety | .58 | −.11 | .61 | .56 | −.11 | .65 | .11 |
| Depression | .76 | −.22 | .50 | .75 | −.22 | .51 | .01 |
| Somatization | .66 | −.02 | .40 | .65 | −.02 | .42 | .05 |
| Attention Problems | .41 | −.73 | .08 | .40 | −.74 | .10 | .31 |
| Atypicality | .74 | −.25 | .38 | .73 | −.24 | .40 | −.02 |
| Withdrawal | .38 | −.46 | .52 | .38 | −.45 | .53 | −.17 |
| Adaptability | −.15 | .77 | −.14 | −.16 | .76 | −.13 | .09 |
| Social Skills | −.09 | .81 | −.03 | −.12 | .85 | .03 | .38 |
| Leadership | .01 | .90 | −.18 | .01 | .89 | −.18 | .00 |
| Activities of Daily Living | −.27 | .82 | .02 | −.26 | .83 | .01 | −.23 |
| Functional Communication | −.19 | .86 | −.20 | −.19 | .85 | −.20 | −.02 |

The principal-axis analyses generally support the factor structures analyzed using CSA and reflect the pattern of results found in the previous BASC editions. The analyses point to an Externalizing Problems factor defined by the Aggression, Hyperactivity, and Conduct Problems scales. The Depression scale has moderate loadings on the Externalizing Problems factor for the preschool and child levels, while on the adolescent level, the Depression scale, along with the Anxiety and Somatization scales, has moderate to high loadings. An Internalizing Problems factor is also indicated, reflecting primarily the Anxiety, Depression, and Somatization scales but with additional loadings for the Withdrawal and Atypicality scales. The factor corresponding to the Adaptive Skills composite has moderate to high loadings for the Adaptability, Social Skills, Leadership, Functional Communication, and Activities of Daily Living scales; the Withdrawal and Attention Problems scales also share moderate loadings with this factor across each of the levels. Overall, the patterns of factor correlations were somewhat higher for the adolescent level than the preschool or child levels, particularly for the internalizing scales.

# CORRELATIONS WITH OTHER MEASURES OF BEHAVIOR

Several studies were carried out in which the PRS and another behavior-rating scale were completed by the same parent or caregiver at about the same time. The correlations between scores on the two instruments indicate the degree to which the instruments measure the same behavioral dimensions. The fact that scales on different instruments have the same or similar names does not ensure that those scales measure the same construct; the scales may define the behavioral dimension differently. Thus, in interpreting the results of correlation studies, it is important to consider the item content of the scales on both instruments.

Demographic information about the samples used for the correlational studies is presented in Table 10.23 (see chapter 8 for a more complete description of the demographic characteristics). In each study, the BASC–3 PRS cases were scored using the general combined-gender norms. Each sample was collected from several sites and composed primarily of children and adolescents from regular school settings.

**Table 10.23** PRS: Demographic Characteristics of BASC–3 and Validity Studies

| Characteristic | PRS–P | | PRS–C | | | | PRS–A | | |
|---|---|---|---|---|---|---|---|---|---|
| | ASEBA | ASRS | ASEBA | ASRS | Conners 3 | D-REF | ASEBA | Conners 3 | D-REF |
| N | 66 | 88 | 61 | 66 | 103 | 49 | 91 | 70 | 65 |
| **Age** | | | | | | | | | |
| Mean | 4.2 | 4.0 | 8.7 | 8.5 | 8.7 | 8.7 | 14.5 | 15.0 | 14.6 |
| SD | 1.1 | 1.2 | 1.7 | 1.3 | 1.7 | 1.8 | 1.7 | 1.9 | 1.8 |
| Range | 2–5 | 2–5 | 6–11 | 6–11 | 6–11 | 6–11 | 12–18 | 12–18 | 12–18 |
| **Test interval** | | | | | | | | | |
| Mean | 17.6 | 18.5 | 16.3 | 16.9 | 6.0 | 10.4 | 17.9 | 12.3 | 12.7 |
| Range | 0–69 | 0–70 | 0–68 | 0–65 | 0–60 | 0–69 | 0–70 | 0–62 | 0–67 |
| **Mother's education level** | | | | | | | | | |
| 1 | 6.1 | 3.4 | 9.8 | 6.1 | 2.9 | 10.2 | 2.2 | 10.0 | 7.7 |
| 2 | 12.1 | 23.9 | 18.0 | 13.6 | 40.8 | 4.1 | 6.6 | 20.0 | 18.5 |
| 3 | 19.7 | 33.0 | 26.2 | 27.3 | 38.8 | 44.9 | 14.3 | 30.0 | 46.2 |
| 4 | 62.1 | 39.8 | 45.9 | 53.0 | 17.5 | 40.8 | 76.9 | 40.0 | 27.7 |
| **Race/ethnicity** | | | | | | | | | |
| African American | 21.2 | 8.0 | 23.0 | 1.5 | 4.9 | 22.4 | 18.7 | 7.1 | 15.4 |
| Asian | 1.5 | 2.3 | 9.8 | 1.5 | 1.0 | 2.0 | — | 4.3 | 4.6 |
| Hispanic | 12.1 | 19.3 | 50.8 | 22.7 | 6.8 | 26.5 | 8.8 | 20.0 | 16.9 |
| Other | 6.1 | 13.6 | — | — | 8.7 | 10.2 | 5.5 | 2.9 | 10.8 |
| White | 59.1 | 56.8 | 16.4 | 74.2 | 78.6 | 38.8 | 67.0 | 65.7 | 52.3 |
| **Region** | | | | | | | | | |
| Midwest | 24.2 | 9.1 | 13.1 | 16.7 | 6.8 | 24.5 | 15.4 | 21.4 | 18.5 |
| Northeast | 18.2 | 21.6 | 27.9 | 24.2 | 6.8 | 6.1 | 8.8 | 31.4 | 1.5 |
| South | 37.9 | 44.3 | 34.4 | 24.2 | 76.7 | 34.7 | 36.3 | 35.7 | 41.5 |
| West | 19.7 | 25.0 | 24.6 | 34.8 | 9.7 | 34.7 | 39.6 | 11.4 | 38.5 |
| **Gender** | | | | | | | | | |
| Female | 43.9 | 63.6 | 49.2 | 37.9 | 58.3 | 53.1 | 65.9 | 51.4 | 63.1 |
| Male | 56.1 | 36.4 | 50.8 | 62.1 | 41.7 | 46.9 | 34.1 | 48.6 | 36.9 |

## Behavior Assessment System for Children, Second Edition

As discussed in chapter 7, the BASC–3 standardization forms contained all of the items found on the BASC–2 forms, as well as newly written BASC–3 items. As such, correlations between the BASC–3 and BASC–2 scales can be derived using a large sample representative of the U.S. population (i.e., the BASC–3 general combined-gender norms); see Table 10.24 for the scales from each PRS level. Correlations between scores from the corresponding BASC–3 and BASC–2 scales for each PRS level are presented in Table 10.24. As expected, correlations between the corresponding scale scores are extremely high. Overall, these results provide a sound basis for generalizing research done on the BASC–2 PRS to the BASC–3 PRS.

**Table 10.24** BASC–3 PRS: Correlations With the BASC–2 Parent Rating Scales, General Combined Norm Samples

| BASC–3 | BASC–2 | | |
| --- | --- | --- | --- |
| | PRS–P | PRS–C | PRS–A |
| **Composite** | | | |
| Externalizing Problems | .98 | .97 | .99 |
| Internalizing Problems | .98 | .98 | .99 |
| Adaptive Skills | .99 | .98 | .98 |
| Behavioral Symptoms Index | .99 | .98 | .98 |
| **Clinical scale** | | | |
| Hyperactivity | .98 | .98 | .97 |
| Aggression | .95 | .91 | .96 |
| Conduct Problems | — | .99 | .99 |
| Anxiety | .97 | .96 | .95 |
| Depression | .98 | .97 | .98 |
| Somatization | .97 | .98 | .98 |
| Attention Problems | .98 | .99 | .97 |
| Atypicality | .96 | .97 | .96 |
| Withdrawal | .98 | .94 | .96 |
| **Adaptive scale** | | | |
| Adaptability | .97 | .92 | .94 |
| Social Skills | .99 | .97 | .97 |
| Leadership | — | .94 | .94 |
| Activities of Daily Living | .97 | .87 | .89 |
| Functional Communication | .98 | .96 | .96 |
| **Content scale** | | | |
| Anger Control | .79 | .79 | .82 |
| Bullying | .79 | .82 | .92 |
| Developmental Social Disorders | .86 | .91 | .89 |
| Emotional Self-Control | .93 | .89 | .92 |
| Executive Functioning | .93 | .85 | .80 |
| Negative Emotionality | .89 | .83 | .84 |
| Resiliency | .80 | .84 | .86 |

## Achenbach System of Empirically Based Assessment Child Behavior Checklist

The PRS and the Achenbach System of Empirically Based Assessment (ASEBA) Child Behavior Checklist for Ages 2–5 (Achenbach & Rescorla, 2000) were completed for 66 children ages 2 through 5 years. The PRS and the ASEBA Child Behavior Checklist for Ages 6–18 (Achenbach & Rescorla, 2001) also were completed for 61 children ages 6 through 11 years and for 91 adolescents ages 12 through 18 years. Demographic characteristics of the sample are presented in Table 10.23 (see chapter 8 for a more complete description of the demographic characteristics). Correlations between the PRS and ASEBA composites and scales, adjusted for restriction of range, are shown in Tables 10.25 through 10.27.

**Table 10.25** PRS–P: Correlations With the ASEBA Child Behavior Checklist for Ages 1.5–5

| BASC-3 | Empirically based scales | | | | | | | | | Composite | |
|---|---|---|---|---|---|---|---|---|---|---|---|
| | Emotionally Reactive | Anxious/ Depressed | Somatic Complaints | Withdrawn | Sleep Problems | Attention Problems | Aggressive Behavior | Stress | Internalizing Problems | Externalizing Problems | Total Problems |
| **Composite** | | | | | | | | | | | |
| Externalizing Problems | .29 | .21 | .12 | .38 | .28 | .50 | .64 | .37 | .29 | .59 | .54 |
| Internalizing Problems | .34 | .50 | .33 | .42 | .47 | .03 | .09 | .29 | .50 | .29 | .46 |
| Adaptive Skills | -.33 | -.21 | -.14 | -.43 | -.18 | -.49 | -.66 | -.50 | -.38 | -.65 | -.56 |
| Behavioral Symptoms Index | .52 | .47 | .30 | .59 | .45 | .47 | .62 | .56 | .54 | .66 | .70 |
| **Clinical scale** | | | | | | | | | | | |
| Hyperactivity | .21 | .10 | .11 | .30 | .12 | .50 | .53 | .30 | .21 | .50 | .43 |
| Aggression | .32 | .32 | .12 | .38 | .40 | .37 | .61 | .37 | .32 | .54 | .52 |
| Anxiety | .20 | .42 | .17 | .25 | .36 | -.02 | -.03 | .14 | .37 | .18 | .34 |
| Depression | .53 | .50 | .30 | .51 | .42 | .11 | .39 | .48 | .50 | .47 | .56 |
| Somatization | .25 | .42 | .42 | .40 | .48 | .03 | .02 | .23 | .48 | .19 | .38 |
| Attention Problems | .17 | .01 | .01 | .27 | .19 | .49 | .47 | .29 | .18 | .48 | .42 |
| Atypicality | .52 | .55 | .48 | .64 | .31 | .33 | .41 | .59 | .57 | .45 | .57 |
| Withdrawal | .50 | .55 | .24 | .41 | .48 | .07 | .19 | .40 | .58 | .41 | .54 |
| **Adaptive scale** | | | | | | | | | | | |
| Adaptability | -.51 | -.37 | -.19 | -.46 | -.34 | -.33 | -.53 | -.50 | -.46 | -.62 | -.61 |
| Social Skills | -.25 | -.10 | .00 | -.28 | .01 | -.40 | -.51 | -.43 | -.21 | -.48 | -.38 |
| Activities of Daily Living | -.10 | -.01 | -.03 | -.29 | -.13 | -.43 | -.49 | -.23 | -.21 | -.47 | -.38 |
| Functional Communication | -.20 | -.17 | -.25 | -.36 | -.09 | -.37 | -.56 | -.43 | -.31 | -.50 | -.43 |
| **Content scale** | | | | | | | | | | | |
| Anger Control | .49 | .38 | .19 | .53 | .38 | .33 | .64 | .55 | .45 | .59 | .60 |
| Bullying | .24 | .48 | .17 | .30 | .36 | .01 | .28 | .31 | .30 | .30 | .38 |
| Developmental Social Disorders | .44 | .48 | .38 | .53 | .29 | .40 | .56 | .61 | .55 | .61 | .63 |
| Emotional Self-Control | .52 | .46 | .31 | .57 | .45 | .22 | .53 | .52 | .53 | .57 | .63 |
| Executive Functioning | .45 | .33 | .22 | .55 | .32 | .55 | .72 | .58 | .47 | .71 | .69 |
| Negative Emotionality | .62 | .48 | .16 | .58 | .45 | .10 | .47 | .59 | .43 | .48 | .54 |
| Resiliency | -.46 | -.44 | -.26 | -.49 | -.30 | -.37 | -.55 | -.55 | -.50 | -.60 | -.60 |
| **Clinical index** | | | | | | | | | | | |
| Clinical Probability Index | .43 | .31 | .21 | .52 | .27 | .51 | .73 | .58 | .45 | .69 | .64 |
| Functional Impairment Index | .44 | .38 | .24 | .52 | .30 | .47 | .65 | .59 | .51 | .68 | .66 |
| **ASEBA mean** | 53.1 | 52.5 | 53.4 | 52.9 | 53.2 | 52.9 | 52.9 | 53.2 | 46.0 | 46.1 | 45.3 |
| **ASEBA SD** | 6.3 | 4.7 | 5.9 | 4.9 | 5.5 | 4.4 | 5.7 | 5.9 | 11.2 | 11.0 | 11.1 |

**Table 10.25** PRS–P: Correlations With the ASEBA Child Behavior Checklist for Ages 1.5–5 *(continued)*

| BASC–3 | DSM-oriented scales | | | | | BASC–3 | |
|---|---|---|---|---|---|---|---|
| | Affective Problems | Anxiety Problems | Pervasive Development Problems | ADHD | Oppositional Defiant Problems | Mean | SD |
| **Composite** | | | | | | | |
| Externalizing Problems | .42 | .21 | .52 | .62 | .55 | 49.9 | 8.8 |
| Internalizing Problems | .48 | .43 | .39 | .05 | .12 | 49.9 | 9.7 |
| Adaptive Skills | -.42 | -.21 | -.46 | -.51 | -.69 | 50.3 | 9.2 |
| Behavioral Symptoms Index | .57 | .49 | .66 | .53 | .62 | 49.4 | 8.0 |
| **Clinical scale** | | | | | | | |
| Hyperactivity | .30 | .12 | .38 | .59 | .44 | 49.4 | 9.4 |
| Aggression | .46 | .29 | .55 | .48 | .54 | 50.5 | 8.6 |
| Anxiety | .31 | .44 | .22 | .01 | -.01 | 50.7 | 10.0 |
| Depression | .54 | .42 | .55 | .21 | .46 | 49.3 | 8.0 |
| Somatization | .46 | .30 | .33 | -.01 | .01 | 49.9 | 9.7 |
| Attention Problems | .20 | .11 | .29 | .52 | .44 | 49.4 | 8.8 |
| Atypicality | .56 | .45 | .59 | .28 | .43 | 49.2 | 7.7 |
| Withdrawal | .41 | .67 | .48 | .05 | .28 | 49.8 | 8.8 |
| **Adaptive scale** | | | | | | | |
| Adaptability | -.46 | -.38 | -.55 | -.42 | -.60 | 50.4 | 9.0 |
| Social Skills | -.21 | -.06 | -.29 | -.39 | -.55 | 49.5 | 8.9 |
| Activities of Daily Living | -.29 | -.11 | -.29 | -.39 | -.47 | 50.0 | 10.1 |
| Functional Communication | -.36 | -.09 | -.33 | -.42 | -.57 | 51.1 | 9.2 |
| **Content scale** | | | | | | | |
| Anger Control | .53 | .33 | .59 | .49 | .66 | 50.1 | 7.9 |
| Bullying | .40 | .28 | .43 | .04 | .35 | 50.7 | 8.2 |
| Developmental Social Disorders | .52 | .38 | .57 | .45 | .57 | 49.3 | 8.5 |
| Emotional Self-Control | .59 | .43 | .57 | .35 | .59 | 49.2 | 8.0 |
| Executive Functioning | .53 | .32 | .60 | .66 | .71 | 49.6 | 8.6 |
| Negative Emotionality | .55 | .45 | .55 | .23 | .54 | 49.4 | 7.9 |
| Resiliency | -.49 | -.38 | -.54 | -.44 | -.59 | 49.8 | 8.9 |
| **Clinical index** | | | | | | | |
| Clinical Probability Index | .49 | .30 | .55 | .59 | .73 | 48.9 | 8.7 |
| Functional Impairment Index | .53 | .37 | .55 | .49 | .69 | 49.8 | 8.8 |
| **ASEBA mean** | 54.0 | 52.6 | 53.7 | 52.6 | 53.7 | — | — |
| **ASEBA SD** | 5.7 | 4.8 | 5.7 | 4.9 | 6.3 | — | — |

**Table 10.26** PRS–C: Correlations With the ASEBA Child Behavior Checklist for Ages 6–18

| | | | | Syndrome scales | | | | | | | |
|---|---|---|---|---|---|---|---|---|---|---|---|
| BASC-3 | Anxious/ Depressed | Withdrawn/ Depressed | Somatic Complaints | Social Problems | Thought Problems | Attention Problems Total | Rule-Breaking Behavior | Aggressive Behavior | Internalizing Problems | Externalizing Problems | Total Problems |
| **Composite** | | | | | | | | | | | |
| Externalizing Problems | .19 | .22 | .24 | .44 | .51 | .57 | .69 | .68 | .24 | .69 | .61 |
| Internalizing Problems | .46 | .39 | .41 | .38 | .32 | .30 | .10 | .22 | .52 | .26 | .48 |
| Adaptive Skills | -.28 | -.38 | -.37 | -.44 | -.35 | -.53 | -.34 | -.50 | -.39 | -.58 | -.59 |
| Behavioral Symptoms Index | .38 | .40 | .30 | .54 | .56 | .69 | .57 | .68 | .39 | .70 | .70 |
| **Clinical scale** | | | | | | | | | | | |
| Hyperactivity | .31 | .17 | .17 | .38 | .56 | .59 | .51 | .56 | .28 | .60 | .57 |
| Aggression | .07 | .20 | .18 | .39 | .41 | .41 | .71 | .66 | .12 | .63 | .47 |
| Conduct Problems | .11 | .22 | .29 | .42 | .40 | .53 | .64 | .63 | .25 | .65 | .61 |
| Anxiety | .46 | .17 | .23 | .19 | .22 | .12 | -.05 | .02 | .40 | .08 | .30 |
| Depression | .49 | .43 | .33 | .45 | .34 | .44 | .16 | .36 | .47 | .39 | .53 |
| Somatization | .20 | .49 | .57 | .43 | .32 | .30 | .26 | .34 | .50 | .31 | .46 |
| Attention Problems | .33 | .26 | .20 | .41 | .32 | .67 | .31 | .48 | .26 | .57 | .59 |
| Atypicality | .18 | .28 | .19 | .30 | .40 | .49 | .43 | .52 | .21 | .45 | .42 |
| Withdrawal | .20 | .40 | .24 | .32 | .27 | .22 | .15 | .16 | .35 | .19 | .35 |
| **Adaptive scale** | | | | | | | | | | | |
| Adaptability | -.28 | -.22 | -.31 | -.38 | -.35 | -.33 | -.29 | -.41 | -.30 | -.51 | -.47 |
| Social Skills | -.13 | -.40 | -.32 | -.31 | -.24 | -.34 | -.27 | -.25 | -.33 | -.40 | -.43 |
| Leadership | -.19 | -.24 | -.18 | -.25 | -.13 | -.36 | -.09 | -.29 | -.26 | -.30 | -.36 |
| Activities of Daily Living | -.22 | -.30 | -.29 | -.38 | -.34 | -.56 | -.41 | -.57 | -.29 | -.63 | -.60 |
| Functional Communication | -.29 | -.41 | -.39 | -.40 | -.35 | -.57 | -.31 | -.46 | -.39 | -.48 | -.55 |
| **Content scale** | | | | | | | | | | | |
| Anger Control | .20 | .32 | .23 | .45 | .47 | .55 | .63 | .61 | .22 | .67 | .55 |
| Bullying | .03 | .19 | .25 | .43 | .38 | .37 | .70 | .62 | .16 | .61 | .49 |
| Developmental Social Disorders | .18 | .39 | .37 | .42 | .42 | .47 | .35 | .53 | .31 | .49 | .51 |
| Emotional Self-Control | .41 | .34 | .39 | .44 | .51 | .47 | .37 | .52 | .42 | .53 | .59 |
| Executive Functioning | .36 | .38 | .31 | .49 | .48 | .71 | .48 | .57 | .39 | .69 | .70 |
| Negative Emotionality | .45 | .31 | .15 | .36 | .45 | .51 | .32 | .41 | .32 | .50 | .54 |
| Resiliency | -.24 | -.32 | -.33 | -.34 | -.31 | -.37 | -.21 | -.41 | -.33 | -.39 | -.41 |
| **Clinical index** | | | | | | | | | | | |
| ADHD Probability Index | .34 | .28 | .20 | .39 | .46 | .74 | .48 | .58 | .29 | .67 | .66 |
| EBD Probability Index | .27 | .39 | .42 | .54 | .51 | .60 | .62 | .69 | .41 | .72 | .70 |
| Autism Probability Index | .26 | .40 | .12 | .35 | .37 | .44 | .27 | .40 | .28 | .28 | .40 |
| Functional Impairment Index | .43 | .46 | .45 | .53 | .50 | .69 | .43 | .62 | .49 | .67 | .74 |
| **ASEBA mean** | 53.3 | 53.0 | 54.4 | 53.2 | 53.6 | 54.7 | 53.0 | 53.0 | 48.3 | 46.8 | 47.3 |
| **ASEBA SD** | 5.6 | 4.7 | 5.8 | 4.1 | 6.2 | 6.3 | 4.7 | 5.0 | 9.8 | 9.8 | 10.5 |

**Table 10.26** PRS–C: Correlations With the ASEBA Child Behavior Checklist for Ages 6–18 (continued)

| BASC–3 | Competence scales | | | DSM-oriented scales | | | | | | BASC–3 | |
|---|---|---|---|---|---|---|---|---|---|---|---|
| | Activities | Social | School | Affective Problems | Anxiety Problems | Somatic Problems | ADHD | Oppositional Defiant Problems | Conduct Problems | Mean | SD |
| **Composite** | | | | | | | | | | | |
| Externalizing Problems | -.18 | -.23 | -.39 | .27 | .26 | .20 | .57 | .69 | .61 | 50.9 | 11.4 |
| Internalizing Problems | .00 | -.10 | -.16 | .49 | .40 | .31 | .17 | .20 | .15 | 50.1 | 10.3 |
| Adaptive Skills | .30 | .32 | .40 | -.45 | -.40 | -.23 | -.45 | -.50 | -.40 | 49.9 | 9.3 |
| Behavioral Symptoms Index | -.24 | -.26 | -.37 | .47 | .40 | .21 | .63 | .65 | .54 | 50.7 | 9.5 |
| **Clinical scale** | | | | | | | | | | | |
| Hyperactivity | -.07 | -.20 | -.35 | .35 | .39 | .16 | .67 | .58 | .41 | 51.3 | 11.3 |
| Aggression | -.20 | -.19 | -.29 | .17 | .14 | .14 | .38 | .64 | .68 | 50.2 | 10.5 |
| Conduct Problems | -.23 | -.26 | -.41 | .20 | .18 | .25 | .49 | .64 | .61 | 50.8 | 11.4 |
| Anxiety | .06 | -.06 | -.06 | .38 | .40 | .13 | .08 | -.02 | -.05 | 50.8 | 12.1 |
| Depression | -.09 | -.15 | -.08 | .52 | .31 | .24 | .28 | .35 | .21 | 49.4 | 8.8 |
| Somatization | -.03 | -.05 | -.31 | .39 | .27 | .52 | .16 | .33 | .33 | 50.2 | 9.2 |
| Attention Problems | -.23 | -.20 | -.32 | .40 | .36 | .14 | .59 | .49 | .29 | 51.1 | 11.1 |
| Atypicality | -.28 | -.25 | -.21 | .18 | .16 | .14 | .48 | .48 | .37 | 49.7 | 8.8 |
| Withdrawal | -.20 | -.15 | -.15 | .32 | .27 | .05 | .12 | .05 | .19 | 51.2 | 8.5 |
| **Adaptive scale** | | | | | | | | | | | |
| Adaptability | .13 | .19 | .28 | -.44 | -.36 | -.16 | -.24 | -.46 | -.34 | 50.1 | 10.0 |
| Social Skills | .24 | .32 | .17 | -.32 | -.29 | -.16 | -.30 | -.26 | -.32 | 50.7 | 9.2 |
| Leadership | .28 | .22 | .33 | -.23 | -.30 | -.10 | -.31 | -.26 | -.15 | 49.5 | 9.4 |
| Activities of Daily Living | .34 | .21 | .35 | -.40 | -.30 | -.21 | -.48 | -.57 | -.44 | 49.9 | 10.3 |
| Functional Communication | .24 | .35 | .47 | -.41 | -.39 | -.27 | -.48 | -.42 | -.34 | 49.4 | 9.7 |
| **Content scale** | | | | | | | | | | | |
| Anger Control | -.16 | -.17 | -.34 | .40 | .28 | .18 | .44 | .67 | .63 | 50.1 | 9.4 |
| Bullying | -.25 | -.25 | -.29 | .12 | .11 | .17 | .33 | .62 | .67 | 50.7 | 9.6 |
| Developmental Social Disorders | -.32 | -.28 | -.33 | .44 | .28 | .23 | .43 | .50 | .42 | 50.7 | 8.9 |
| Emotional Self-Control | -.14 | -.16 | -.33 | .54 | .40 | .32 | .36 | .55 | .41 | 50.8 | 9.3 |
| Executive Functioning | -.29 | -.26 | -.43 | .47 | .46 | .23 | .65 | .59 | .45 | 51.3 | 10.4 |
| Negative Emotionality | .01 | -.09 | -.19 | .52 | .40 | .12 | .41 | .46 | .32 | 49.6 | 9.3 |
| Resiliency | .29 | .22 | .30 | -.40 | -.34 | -.23 | -.33 | -.40 | -.30 | 49.1 | 9.7 |
| **Clinical index** | | | | | | | | | | | |
| ADHD Probability Index | -.25 | -.27 | -.34 | .43 | .38 | .17 | .72 | .58 | .41 | 50.9 | 11.4 |
| EBD Probability Index | -.25 | -.24 | -.45 | .45 | .35 | .31 | .51 | .70 | .64 | 50.4 | 9.3 |
| Autism Probability Index | -.32 | -.26 | -.26 | .31 | .28 | -.04 | .35 | .28 | .31 | 50.2 | 7.7 |
| Functional Impairment Index | -.24 | -.30 | -.48 | .55 | .50 | .32 | .60 | .60 | .45 | 50.0 | 9.2 |
| **ASEBA mean** | 46.0 | 46.7 | 47.4 | 54.0 | 54.0 | 54.3 | 54.3 | 53.4 | 53.0 | — | — |
| **ASEBA SD** | 9.9 | 8.6 | 6.9 | 6.2 | 6.1 | 5.8 | 6.5 | 4.3 | 5.3 | — | — |

**Table 10.27** PRS–A: Correlations With the ASEBA Child Behavior Checklist for Ages 6–18

| BASC-3 | Anxious/ Depressed | Withdrawn/ Depressed | Somatic Complaints | Social Problems | Thought Problems | Attention Problems Total | Rule-Breaking Behavior | Aggressive Behavior | Internalizing Problems | Externalizing Problems | Total Problems |
|---|---|---|---|---|---|---|---|---|---|---|---|
| **Composite** | | | | | | | | | | | |
| Externalizing Problems | .26 | .61 | .40 | .56 | .62 | .61 | .61 | .75 | .50 | .83 | .76 |
| Internalizing Problems | .69 | .53 | .66 | .56 | .56 | .47 | .29 | .48 | .76 | .51 | .71 |
| Adaptive Skills | –.39 | –.68 | –.43 | –.53 | –.49 | –.65 | –.58 | –.65 | –.57 | –.71 | –.72 |
| Behavioral Symptoms Index | .48 | .73 | .56 | .66 | .69 | .76 | .47 | .73 | .67 | .75 | .80 |
| **Clinical scale** | | | | | | | | | | | |
| Hyperactivity | .24 | .40 | .33 | .51 | .57 | .60 | .29 | .58 | .41 | .65 | .62 |
| Aggression | .27 | .57 | .35 | .48 | .53 | .38 | .55 | .72 | .44 | .78 | .66 |
| Conduct Problems | .13 | .57 | .29 | .43 | .47 | .53 | .72 | .64 | .39 | .78 | .69 |
| Anxiety | .63 | .33 | .37 | .41 | .39 | .28 | .03 | .25 | .63 | .27 | .52 |
| Depression | .65 | .74 | .66 | .72 | .65 | .67 | .45 | .71 | .73 | .70 | .77 |
| Somatization | .48 | .26 | .60 | .29 | .35 | .25 | .22 | .25 | .58 | .33 | .51 |
| Attention Problems | .18 | .41 | .28 | .33 | .32 | .65 | .43 | .42 | .35 | .53 | .59 |
| Atypicality | .35 | .66 | .44 | .51 | .66 | .67 | .38 | .66 | .54 | .62 | .65 |
| Withdrawal | .34 | .63 | .34 | .40 | .43 | .39 | .26 | .45 | .50 | .37 | .48 |
| **Adaptive scale** | | | | | | | | | | | |
| Adaptability | –.40 | –.51 | –.42 | –.47 | –.48 | –.46 | –.40 | –.62 | –.49 | –.62 | –.57 |
| Social Skills | –.19 | –.58 | –.25 | –.25 | –.36 | –.32 | –.45 | –.47 | –.40 | –.59 | –.53 |
| Leadership | –.33 | –.53 | –.24 | –.38 | –.27 | –.56 | –.44 | –.40 | –.47 | –.50 | –.58 |
| Activities of Daily Living | –.21 | –.45 | –.28 | –.39 | –.34 | –.57 | –.38 | –.49 | –.35 | –.51 | –.54 |
| Functional Communication | –.35 | –.67 | –.46 | –.58 | –.50 | –.74 | –.62 | –.62 | –.55 | –.66 | –.71 |
| **Content scale** | | | | | | | | | | | |
| Anger Control | .33 | .56 | .37 | .55 | .55 | .52 | .37 | .70 | .46 | .75 | .66 |
| Bullying | .16 | .52 | .21 | .34 | .36 | .34 | .46 | .58 | .37 | .65 | .58 |
| Developmental Social Disorders | .42 | .69 | .49 | .58 | .64 | .66 | .49 | .70 | .59 | .67 | .70 |
| Emotional Self-Control | .54 | .52 | .47 | .57* | .54 | .52 | .23 | .54 | .59 | .58 | .64 |
| Executive Functioning | .29 | .52 | .37 | .51 | .45 | .72 | .50 | .57 | .51 | .65 | .70 |
| Negative Emotionality | .57 | .71 | .58 | .64 | .69 | .53 | .57 | .78 | .67 | .81 | .77 |
| Resiliency | –.49 | –.66 | –.46 | –.54 | –.49 | –.62 | –.54 | –.64 | –.62 | –.68 | –.70 |
| **Clinical index** | | | | | | | | | | | |
| ADHD Probability Index | .36 | .50 | .36 | .45 | .42 | .63 | .46 | .55 | .49 | .63 | .68 |
| EBD Probability Index | .31 | .65 | .39 | .53 | .54 | .55 | .51 | .71 | .51 | .78 | .70 |
| Autism Probability Index | .35 | .70 | .37 | .46 | .48 | .53 | .39 | .57 | .54 | .54 | .60 |
| Functional Impairment Index | .52 | .68 | .57 | .67 | .62 | .79 | .55 | .67 | .67 | .70 | .80 |
| **ASEBA mean** | 53.2 | 54.7 | 54.1 | 52.9 | 53.7 | 52.6 | 52.0 | 52.3 | 49.2 | 45.6 | 46.0 |
| **ASEBA SD** | 6.0 | 6.6 | 6.7 | 5.5 | 6.5 | 4.1 | 3.3 | 4.8 | 10.2 | 8.8 | 10.2 |

**Table 10.27** PRS–A: Correlations With the ASEBA Child Behavior Checklist for Ages 6–18 *(continued)*

| BASC-3 | Competence scales | | | DSM-oriented scales | | | | | | BASC-3 | |
|---|---|---|---|---|---|---|---|---|---|---|---|
| | Activities | Social | School | Affective Problems | Anxiety Problems | Somatic Problems | ADHD | Oppositional Defiant Problems | Conduct Problems | Mean | SD |
| **Composite** | | | | | | | | | | | |
| Externalizing Problems | −.10 | −.46 | −.37 | .58 | .21 | .15 | .52 | .80 | .77 | 48.0 | 6.0 |
| Internalizing Problems | −.08 | −.19 | −.17 | .66 | .58 | .60 | .40 | .40 | .31 | 48.5 | 7.5 |
| Adaptive Skills | .32 | .60 | .46 | −.64 | −.29 | −.27 | −.57 | −.67 | −.63 | 53.9 | 7.7 |
| Behavioral Symptoms Index | −.19 | −.58 | −.42 | .71 | .41 | .30 | .59 | .73 | .66 | 47.6 | 7.2 |
| **Clinical scale** | | | | | | | | | | | |
| Hyperactivity | −.09 | −.35 | −.30 | .46 | .26 | .12 | .48 | .61 | .53 | 48.4 | 7.5 |
| Aggression | −.13 | −.36 | −.18 | .52 | .18 | .13 | .24 | .78 | .73 | 48.5 | 6.1 |
| Conduct Problems | .02 | −.42 | −.39 | .48 | .07 | .15 | .53 | .73 | .77 | 47.4 | 6.1 |
| Anxiety | .06 | −.15 | −.05 | .39 | .53 | .29 | .22 | .18 | .10 | 48.6 | 7.8 |
| Depression | −.25 | −.40 | −.28 | .76 | .50 | .55 | .55 | .64 | .53 | 48.4 | 7.1 |
| Somatization | −.06 | .02 | −.14 | .50 | .39 | .60 | .23 | .19 | .17 | 49.1 | 9.0 |
| Attention Problems | −.22 | −.45 | −.57 | .45 | .14 | .11 | .58 | .48 | .47 | 45.8 | 8.7 |
| Atypicality | −.13 | −.51 | −.42 | .59 | .35 | .12 | .40 | .68 | .63 | 47.8 | 7.4 |
| Withdrawal | −.20 | −.47 | −.13 | .47 | .27 | .17 | .23 | .41 | .37 | 49.9 | 10.0 |
| **Adaptive scale** | | | | | | | | | | | |
| Adaptability | .28 | .39 | .23 | −.57 | −.33 | −.28 | −.36 | −.61 | −.48 | 52.2 | 9.3 |
| Social Skills | .30 | .49 | .17 | −.45 | −.09 | −.16 | −.25 | −.50 | −.46 | 52.5 | 8.2 |
| Leadership | .17 | .53 | .41 | −.43 | −.23 | −.14 | −.45 | −.44 | −.45 | 53.3 | 8.1 |
| Activities of Daily Living | .24 | .34 | .44 | −.56 | −.12 | −.10 | −.57 | −.51 | −.49 | 55.4 | 8.2 |
| Functional Communication | .22 | .62 | .62 | −.57 | −.33 | −.33 | −.64 | −.63 | −.64 | 53.7 | 7.5 |
| **Content scale** | | | | | | | | | | | |
| Anger Control | −.09 | −.29 | −.17 | .58 | .19 | .17 | .34 | .75 | .57 | 48.7 | 7.7 |
| Bullying | −.21 | −.37 | −.28 | .37 | .02 | .02 | .26 | .66 | .65 | 48.8 | 5.6 |
| Developmental Social Disorders | −.23 | −.53 | −.39 | .62 | .39 | .27 | .47 | .69 | .63 | 47.2 | 8.8 |
| Emotional Self-Control | −.16 | −.29 | −.18 | .60 | .43 | .32 | .35 | .50 | .37 | 48.6 | 8.3 |
| Executive Functioning | −.18 | −.53 | −.57 | .56 | .26 | .20 | .66 | .61 | .58 | 46.2 | 8.1 |
| Negative Emotionality | −.18 | −.34 | −.27 | .76 | .42 | .44 | .39 | .78 | .67 | 48.4 | 7.2 |
| Resiliency | .28 | .57 | .41 | −.65 | −.41 | −.30 | −.52 | −.65 | −.59 | 53.2 | 8.0 |
| **Clinical index** | | | | | | | | | | | |
| ADHD Probability Index | −.28 | −.47 | −.50 | .54 | .27 | .19 | .56 | .59 | .53 | 46.1 | 8.5 |
| EBD Probability Index | −.23 | −.44 | −.30 | .62 | .20 | .22 | .43 | .76 | .65 | 47.4 | 7.6 |
| Autism Probability Index | −.22 | −.56 | −.28 | .54 | .28 | .18 | .34 | .57 | .51 | 47.7 | 9.1 |
| Functional Impairment Index | −.22 | −.60 | −.54 | .72 | .44 | .38 | .70 | .65 | .62 | 46.1 | 7.7 |
| **ASEBA mean** | 49.9 | 51.7 | 52.2 | 54.0 | 53.4 | 53.6 | 52.2 | 53.2 | 51.8 | — | — |
| **ASEBA SD** | 8.8 | 8.6 | 4.5 | 6.5 | 5.7 | 6.9 | 3.5 | 4.9 | 3.6 | — | — |

The mean PRS scores indicate that overall the preschool- and child-level samples are about average with respect to their level of behavior problems and variability of scores. The adolescent sample appears to include somewhat smaller proportions of children with behavior problems than is true for the population as a whole. Relatedly, the variability in behavioral ratings of the samples is generally smaller than that of the general population. The adjusted correlations presented in the tables remove the biasing effect that results from sampling differences in the variability of scale scores.

Composite scale and clinical scale correlations between corresponding scores from PRS and ASEBA scales that measure similar constructs are moderate to high. Low to moderate correlations were expected at times, particularly for scales between tests that are not directly comparable (e.g., BASC–3 Anxiety with ASEBA Anxiety/Depression). Scales measuring externalizing behaviors typically demonstrated higher correlations than did scales measuring internalizing behaviors, a finding consistent across the BASC editions.

## Conners 3 Parent Form

The PRS child and adolescent forms were filled out along with the parent form of the Conners 3 (Conners 3rd Edition; Conners, 2008) for 103 children ages 6 through 11 years and for 70 adolescents ages 12 through 18 years. Demographic characteristics of the sample are presented in Table 10.23 (see chapter 8 for a more complete description of the demographic characteristics). Tables 10.28 and 10.29 show correlations between scores from the PRS and Conners rating scales.

# Table 10.28 PRS–C: Correlations With the Conners 3 Parent Form

| BASC-3 | Inattention | Hyperactivity/ Impulsivity | Learning Problems | Executive Functioning | Aggression | Peer Relations | ADHD: Inattentive | ADHD: Impulsive | Conduct Disorder | Oppositional Defiant Disorder | Conners 3 Global Index | Conners 3GI: Emotional Lability | Conners 3GI: Restless-Impulsive | BASC-3 Mean | BASC-3 SD |
|---|---|---|---|---|---|---|---|---|---|---|---|---|---|---|---|
| **Composite** | | | | | | | | | | | | | | | |
| Externalizing Problems | .74 | .71 | .40 | .64 | .74 | .30 | .73 | .71 | .63 | .83 | .78 | .71 | .73 | 47.0 | 7.9 |
| Internalizing Problems | .41 | .14 | .24 | .26 | .28 | .30 | .38 | .12 | .28 | .42 | .43 | .55 | .31 | 47.3 | 8.6 |
| Adaptive Skills | -.51 | -.38 | -.51 | -.55 | -.42 | -.41 | -.51 | -.37 | -.37 | -.49 | -.51 | -.48 | -.46 | 50.5 | 8.7 |
| Behavioral Symptoms Index | .79 | .69 | .53 | .68 | .66 | .49 | .76 | .66 | .55 | .79 | .81 | .76 | .75 | 47.0 | 7.9 |
| **Clinical scale** | | | | | | | | | | | | | | | |
| Hyperactivity | .66 | .73 | .36 | .47 | .49 | .28 | .60 | .73 | .28 | .62 | .74 | .59 | .71 | 48.5 | 9.4 |
| Aggression | .62 | .42 | .36 | .54 | .79 | .22 | .60 | .41 | .73 | .79 | .64 | .72 | .54 | 46.4 | 7.5 |
| Conduct Problems | .58 | .57 | .26 | .58 | .63 | .19 | .65 | .57 | .64 | .73 | .60 | .46 | .59 | 47.2 | 7.9 |
| Anxiety | .27 | .02 | .16 | .10 | .06 | .18 | .21 | .00 | .16 | .16 | .24 | .28 | .17 | 48.2 | 10.2 |
| Depression | .61 | .42 | .41 | .55 | .51 | .53 | .60 | .38 | .34 | .69 | .70 | .76 | .61 | 46.7 | 6.8 |
| Somatization | .23 | .04 | .10 | .14 | .25 | .16 | .23 | .04 | .23 | .30 | .23 | .39 | .11 | 48.5 | 9.0 |
| Attention Problems | .77 | .66 | .58 | .64 | .48 | .37 | .72 | .65 | .42 | .56 | .73 | .55 | .72 | 48.6 | 8.5 |
| Atypicality | .64 | .65 | .37 | .57 | .49 | .36 | .69 | .62 | .42 | .61 | .66 | .53 | .64 | 47.4 | 7.9 |
| Withdrawal | .28 | .07 | .24 | .25 | .17 | .46 | .27 | .01 | .26 | .33 | .24 | .33 | .15 | 48.8 | 8.0 |
| **Adaptive scale** | | | | | | | | | | | | | | | |
| Adaptability | -.41 | -.30 | -.43 | -.34 | -.32 | -.30 | -.38 | -.31 | -.31 | -.39 | -.43 | -.43 | -.37 | 50.2 | 9.2 |
| Social Skills | -.37 | -.26 | -.35 | -.40 | -.41 | -.29 | -.37 | -.24 | -.33 | -.43 | -.39 | -.41 | -.33 | 51.4 | 8.6 |
| Leadership | -.37 | -.24 | -.43 | -.47 | -.31 | -.33 | -.37 | -.23 | -.23 | -.36 | -.35 | -.34 | -.31 | 49.4 | 9.0 |
| Activities of Daily Living | -.61 | -.45 | -.49 | -.73 | -.50 | -.47 | -.64 | -.45 | -.46 | -.59 | -.59 | -.53 | -.55 | 50.6 | 8.1 |
| Functional Communication | -.47 | -.42 | -.50 | -.50 | -.30 | -.36 | -.46 | -.38 | -.28 | -.39 | -.48 | -.39 | -.46 | 50.6 | 9.0 |
| **Content scale** | | | | | | | | | | | | | | | |
| Anger Control | .67 | .55 | .41 | .58 | .77 | .30 | .67 | .52 | .51 | .80 | .77 | .83 | .66 | 47.3 | 7.8 |
| Bullying | .56 | .39 | .29 | .45 | .75 | .07 | .55 | .40 | .71 | .73 | .52 | .52 | .46 | 46.6 | 7.2 |
| Developmental Social Disorders | .54 | .49 | .50 | .51 | .35 | .41 | .53 | .48 | .35 | .45 | .53 | .45 | .50 | 49.1 | 8.2 |
| Emotional Self-Control | .58 | .41 | .29 | .43 | .49 | .21 | .56 | .35 | .33 | .63 | .67 | .75 | .54 | 47.0 | 8.4 |
| Executive Functioning | .69 | .55 | .61 | .67 | .48 | .41 | .67 | .53 | .44 | .60 | .66 | .56 | .63 | 48.7 | 8.8 |
| Negative Emotionality | .62 | .41 | .32 | .50 | .63 | .28 | .61 | .36 | .48 | .79 | .69 | .76 | .59 | 46.8 | 7.3 |
| Resiliency | -.33 | -.25 | -.43 | -.33 | -.24 | -.31 | -.30 | -.24 | -.28 | -.33 | -.36 | -.36 | -.32 | 49.3 | 9.4 |
| **Clinical index** | | | | | | | | | | | | | | | |
| ADHD Probability Index | .77 | .68 | .51 | .66 | .50 | .37 | .73 | .66 | .39 | .63 | .75 | .59 | .74 | 48.4 | 8.9 |
| EBD Probability Index | .66 | .52 | .47 | .60 | .73 | .35 | .66 | .50 | .66 | .82 | .70 | .73 | .62 | 47.5 | 7.4 |
| Autism Probability Index | .50 | .33 | .42 | .50 | .31 | .56 | .51 | .28 | .36 | .49 | .44 | .51 | .35 | 48.5 | 6.7 |
| Functional Impairment Index | .67 | .53 | .57 | .64 | .49 | .50 | .66 | .50 | .45 | .64 | .69 | .66 | .63 | 48.1 | 8.2 |
| **Conners 3 mean** | 52.1 | 52.9 | 51.8 | 51.6 | 50.4 | 49.6 | 51.7 | 53.2 | 49.3 | 50.7 | 50.8 | 49.5 | 51.7 | — | — |
| **Conners 3 SD** | 10.9 | 11.2 | 10.7 | 9.8 | 11.0 | 9.9 | 9.8 | 11.0 | 6.5 | 10.0 | 10.3 | 9.3 | 10.7 | — | — |

**Table 10.29** PRS–A: Correlations With the Conners 3 Parent Form

| BASC-3 | Inattention | Hyper-activity/ Impulsivity | Learning Problems | Executive Functioning | Aggression | Peer Relations | ADHD: Inattentive | ADHD: Impulsive | Conduct Disorder | Oppositional Defiant Disorder | Conners 3 Global Index | Conners 3GI: Emotional Lability | Conners 3GI: Restless-Impulsive | BASC-3 Mean | BASC-3 SD |
|---|---|---|---|---|---|---|---|---|---|---|---|---|---|---|---|
| **Composite** | | | | | | | | | | | | | | | |
| Externalizing Problems | .24 | .30 | .11 | .29 | .43 | .01 | .24 | .30 | .41 | .42 | .40 | .34 | .36 | 49.8 | 10.7 |
| Internalizing Problems | .05 | .06 | .02 | .06 | .24 | -.02 | .03 | .11 | .21 | .27 | .18 | .27 | .09 | 49.3 | 9.5 |
| Adaptive Skills | -.62 | -.35 | -.46 | -.68 | -.61 | -.22 | -.63 | -.25 | -.53 | -.57 | -.47 | -.40 | -.45 | 51.5 | 9.1 |
| Behavioral Symptoms Index | .32 | .33 | .20 | .42 | .48 | .13 | .38 | .32 | .46 | .45 | .41 | .33 | .38 | 49.0 | 8.9 |
| **Clinical scale** | | | | | | | | | | | | | | | |
| Hyperactivity | .31 | .42 | .21 | .32 | .37 | -.02 | .31 | .45 | .38 | .41 | .48 | .40 | .46 | 49.3 | 9.5 |
| Aggression | .16 | .21 | .07 | .26 | .43 | .03 | .19 | .20 | .40 | .40 | .34 | .31 | .29 | 50.8 | 11.7 |
| Conduct Problems | .25 | .26 | .09 | .28 | .40 | .02 | .24 | .24 | .37 | .37 | .34 | .27 | .32 | 49.3 | 10.5 |
| Anxiety | .09 | -.04 | .18 | .03 | .14 | -.12 | .05 | -.04 | .13 | .20 | .14 | .20 | .06 | 48.9 | 9.3 |
| Depression | .04 | .18 | -.03 | .17 | .37 | .12 | .09 | .18 | .36 | .34 | .24 | .30 | .17 | 49.5 | 9.0 |
| Somatization | .02 | .05 | -.08 | -.01 | .15 | -.03 | -.05 | .13 | .10 | .22 | .11 | .23 | .03 | 49.8 | 9.7 |
| Attention Problems | .75 | .43 | .52 | .76 | .47 | .11 | .74 | .36 | .44 | .44 | .54 | .39 | .54 | 48.0 | 9.0 |
| Atypicality | .12 | .20 | .12 | .10 | .29 | .05 | .17 | .23 | .32 | .26 | .17 | .08 | .16 | 48.5 | 8.3 |
| Withdrawal | .02 | .04 | -.01 | .20 | .18 | .37 | .20 | .00 | .17 | .11 | -.05 | -.10 | -.02 | 49.0 | 8.1 |
| **Adaptive scale** | | | | | | | | | | | | | | | |
| Adaptability | -.45 | -.36 | -.29 | -.51 | -.58 | -.19 | -.41 | -.25 | -.48 | -.59 | -.42 | -.37 | -.40 | 51.0 | 9.5 |
| Social Skills | -.48 | -.23 | -.29 | -.50 | -.56 | -.17 | -.45 | -.16 | -.44 | -.51 | -.33 | -.34 | -.29 | 50.6 | 10.1 |
| Leadership | -.49 | -.16 | -.52 | -.57 | -.42 | -.29 | -.55 | -.05 | -.38 | -.37 | -.32 | -.29 | -.31 | 51.2 | 9.1 |
| Activities of Daily Living | -.66 | -.42 | -.42 | -.78 | -.49 | -.09 | -.72 | -.37 | -.50 | -.49 | -.51 | -.35 | -.52 | 51.5 | 8.9 |
| Functional Communication | -.59 | -.37 | -.51 | -.63 | -.55 | -.23 | -.60 | -.26 | -.49 | -.46 | -.46 | -.31 | -.48 | 51.8 | 8.5 |
| **Content scale** | | | | | | | | | | | | | | | |
| Anger Control | .24 | .35 | .09 | .31 | .42 | .02 | .25 | .34 | .44 | .43 | .46 | .44 | .38 | 50.3 | 9.9 |
| Bullying | .13 | .19 | .05 | .26 | .47 | .08 | .18 | .16 | .43 | .41 | .30 | .29 | .26 | 50.8 | 11.7 |
| Developmental Social Disorders | .48 | .44 | .33 | .54 | .55 | .30 | .52 | .33 | .53 | .49 | .42 | .30 | .44 | 48.1 | 7.9 |
| Emotional Self-Control | .19 | .29 | .12 | .22 | .42 | .02 | .16 | .27 | .41 | .46 | .39 | .45 | .30 | 49.4 | 10.1 |
| Executive Functioning | .68 | .47 | .56 | .76 | .56 | .11 | .69 | .38 | .52 | .55 | .60 | .49 | .58 | 47.7 | 8.7 |
| Negative Emotionality | .16 | .29 | .03 | .29 | .43 | .05 | .20 | .27 | .41 | .43 | .37 | .34 | .32 | 50.1 | 10.0 |
| Resiliency | -.49 | -.26 | -.46 | -.54 | -.53 | -.21 | -.46 | -.14 | -.45 | -.51 | -.36 | -.31 | -.36 | 51.8 | 9.0 |
| **Clinical index** | | | | | | | | | | | | | | | |
| ADHD Probability Index | .70 | .47 | .58 | .71 | .55 | .18 | .70 | .38 | .48 | .54 | .57 | .40 | .58 | 48.0 | 9.1 |
| EBD Probability Index | .35 | .36 | .19 | .44 | .53 | .06 | .36 | .32 | .51 | .53 | .48 | .47 | .41 | 49.9 | 10.6 |
| Autism Probability Index | .48 | .30 | .37 | .52 | .51 | .38 | .53 | .20 | .43 | .45 | .31 | .24 | .31 | 48.7 | 8.0 |
| Functional Impairment Index | .58 | .41 | .47 | .65 | .59 | .21 | .60 | .34 | .55 | .57 | .52 | .44 | .50 | 48.2 | 8.4 |
| **Conners 3 mean** | 50.8 | 48.9 | 50.0 | 51.2 | 51.6 | 50.8 | 50.5 | 49.4 | 50.5 | 51.6 | 49.6 | 50.0 | 48.9 | — | — |
| **Conners 3 SD** | 9.9 | 7.9 | 9.1 | 10.3 | 11.7 | 10.5 | 10.1 | 8.4 | 10.1 | 9.0 | 8.8 | 9.5 | 7.9 | — | — |

The mean PRS scores indicate that overall the samples appear to include somewhat smaller proportions of children with behavior problems than is true for the population as a whole. Correlations between PRS and Conners parent form scale scores that measure similar constructs are generally strong across both PRS levels; the child-level correlations are somewhat stronger than the adolescent level across several scales. The BASC–3 content scales and clinical indexes correlate moderately to high across a number of Conners scales.

## Autism Spectrum Rating Scales Parent Forms

As discussed in chapter 5, the BASC–2 has become increasingly used in evaluations involving children suspected of having an autism spectrum disorder. As such, the PRS was compared to the Autism Spectrum Rating Scales (ASRS; Goldstein & Naglieri, 2010) during the BASC–3 standardization project. The PRS–P and PRS–C were completed along with the ASRS parent rating forms for 88 children ages 2 through 5 years and for 66 children ages 6 through 11 years. Demographic characteristics of the sample are presented in Table 10.23 (see chapter 8 for a more complete description of the demographic characteristics). Tables 10.30 and 10.31 show the correlations between the PRS and ASRS scores.

**Table 10.30** PRS-P: Correlations With the Autism Spectrum Rating Scales (2–5) Parent Ratings

| BASC-3 | Social/Commu-nication | Unusual Behaviors | DSM-IV-TR | Peer Social-ization | Adult Social-ization | Social/Emotional Reciprocity | Atypical Language | Stereotypy | Behavioral Rigidity | Sensory Sensitivity | Attention/Self-Regulation | Total | BASC-3 Mean | BASC-3 SD |
|---|---|---|---|---|---|---|---|---|---|---|---|---|---|---|
| **Composite** | | | | | | | | | | | | | | |
| Externalizing Problems | .16 | .32 | .16 | -.01 | .40 | -.06 | .43 | .27 | .22 | .35 | .60 | .28 | 47.4 | 8.2 |
| Internalizing Problems | .05 | .28 | .09 | .07 | .37 | -.15 | .24 | .11 | .32 | .26 | .27 | .19 | 48.0 | 8.0 |
| Adaptive Skills | -.53 | -.34 | -.55 | -.45 | -.38 | -.51 | -.27 | -.28 | -.27 | -.18 | -.34 | -.49 | 51.6 | 8.8 |
| Behavioral Symptoms Index | .40 | .53 | .44 | .28 | .59 | .19 | .51 | .40 | .46 | .46 | .66 | .52 | 47.2 | 7.4 |
| **Clinical scale** | | | | | | | | | | | | | | |
| Hyperactivity | .24 | .42 | .29 | .09 | .41 | .05 | .51 | .38 | .30 | .40 | .60 | .37 | 47.9 | 8.8 |
| Aggression | .03 | .12 | -.04 | -.12 | .30 | -.14 | .20 | .06 | .05 | .24 | .43 | .09 | 47.7 | 7.8 |
| Anxiety | -.07 | .22 | .01 | .01 | .14 | -.19 | .15 | .06 | .31 | .21 | .05 | .08 | 48.8 | 8.5 |
| Depression | .13 | .26 | .18 | .08 | .38 | -.03 | .26 | .15 | .31 | .19 | .34 | .22 | 48.3 | 8.7 |
| Somatization | .05 | .17 | -.01 | .06 | .33 | -.14 | .10 | .08 | .12 | .22 | .23 | .13 | 48.1 | 7.8 |
| Attention Problems | .49 | .46 | .50 | .28 | .42 | .39 | .53 | .46 | .35 | .28 | .68 | .53 | 47.7 | 8.5 |
| Atypicality | .41 | .51 | .42 | .33 | .58 | .21 | .46 | .37 | .46 | .51 | .52 | .52 | 46.9 | 6.5 |
| Withdrawal | .30 | .27 | .35 | .41 | .25 | .27 | .02 | .15 | .29 | .21 | .02 | .31 | 49.3 | 8.8 |
| **Adaptive scale** | | | | | | | | | | | | | | |
| Adaptability | -.32 | -.40 | -.44 | -.22 | -.42 | -.32 | -.19 | -.30 | -.45 | -.27 | -.33 | -.41 | 51.4 | 9.6 |
| Social Skills | -.50 | -.24 | -.48 | -.43 | -.26 | -.50 | -.15 | -.24 | -.20 | -.10 | -.23 | -.42 | 51.5 | 9.7 |
| Activities of Daily Living | -.21 | -.14 | -.21 | -.24 | -.17 | -.14 | -.27 | -.03 | -.06 | -.07 | -.19 | -.19 | 50.8 | 8.8 |
| Functional Communication | -.48 | -.15 | -.44 | -.43 | -.23 | -.48 | -.18 | -.21 | -.03 | -.08 | -.20 | -.37 | 51.7 | 9.1 |
| **Content scale** | | | | | | | | | | | | | | |
| Anger Control | .18 | .25 | .21 | .09 | .40 | .03 | .28 | .16 | .22 | .25 | .37 | .25 | 48.8 | 9.7 |
| Bullying | -.15 | -.01 | -.22 | -.15 | .26 | -.30 | -.01 | -.04 | -.04 | .20 | .20 | -.09 | 47.5 | 6.8 |
| Developmental Social Disorders | .62 | .51 | .66 | .52 | .44 | .58 | .37 | .51 | .42 | .43 | .46 | .63 | 47.4 | 7.3 |
| Emotional Self-Control | .18 | .32 | .24 | .11 | .43 | .03 | .31 | .22 | .31 | .26 | .41 | .29 | 48.3 | 9.2 |
| Executive Functioning | .42 | .44 | .47 | .23 | .51 | .31 | .46 | .41 | .34 | .38 | .61 | .49 | 48.2 | 8.5 |
| Negative Emotionality | .14 | .24 | .16 | .08 | .39 | -.01 | .26 | .13 | .23 | .21 | .38 | .22 | 48.6 | 9.2 |
| Resiliency | -.38 | -.44 | -.48 | -.27 | -.43 | -.35 | -.12 | -.35 | -.47 | -.28 | -.27 | -.46 | 51.1 | 9.1 |
| **Clinical index** | | | | | | | | | | | | | | |
| Clinical Probability Index | .52 | .36 | .51 | .42 | .50 | .43 | .38 | .34 | .30 | .26 | .53 | .50 | 47.5 | 8.1 |
| Functional Impairment Index | .51 | .45 | .54 | .45 | .51 | .40 | .39 | .37 | .38 | .32 | .50 | .53 | 48.2 | 8.2 |
| **ASRS mean** | 47.7 | 52.8 | 49.5 | 49.5 | 51.9 | 46.5 | 50.2 | 51.3 | 53.9 | 53.1 | 48.9 | 50.5 | — | — |
| **ASRS SD** | 9.1 | 8.2 | 8.3 | 10.5 | 8.8 | 10.1 | 8.5 | 9.0 | 9.0 | 9.4 | 9.1 | 8.5 | — | — |

**Table 10.31** PRS–C: Correlations With the Autism Spectrum Rating Scales

| BASC-3 | Social/Communication | Unusual Behaviors | Self-Regulation | DSM–IV–TR | Peer Socialization | Adult Socialization | Social/Emotional Reciprocity | Atypical Language | Stereotypy | Behavioral Rigidity | Sensory Sensitivity | Attention | Total | BASC-3 Mean | BASC-3 SD |
|---|---|---|---|---|---|---|---|---|---|---|---|---|---|---|---|
| **Composite** | | | | | | | | | | | | | | | |
| Externalizing Problems | .20 | .37 | .56 | .33 | .38 | .49 | .24 | .39 | .23 | .36 | .38 | .44 | .42 | 52.0 | 12.1 |
| Internalizing Problems | .30 | .37 | .37 | .34 | .41 | .31 | .27 | .44 | .20 | .38 | .26 | .34 | .40 | 51.0 | 11.2 |
| Adaptive Skills | -.65 | -.64 | -.70 | -.69 | -.63 | -.65 | -.69 | -.60 | -.44 | -.59 | -.58 | -.68 | -.75 | 48.3 | 10.5 |
| Behavioral Symptoms Index | .36 | .48 | .63 | .49 | .51 | .55 | .41 | .54 | .30 | .48 | .38 | .55 | .56 | 52.0 | 12.0 |
| **Clinical scale** | | | | | | | | | | | | | | | |
| Hyperactivity | .14 | .33 | .50 | .30 | .29 | .40 | .20 | .35 | .19 | .35 | .27 | .41 | .36 | 51.2 | 11.5 |
| Aggression | .22 | .38 | .49 | .33 | .38 | .45 | .25 | .41 | .26 | .35 | .38 | .38 | .40 | 52.1 | 12.1 |
| Conduct Problems | .17 | .27 | .49 | .25 | .31 | .45 | .21 | .30 | .17 | .25 | .38 | .38 | .35 | 51.7 | 12.1 |
| Anxiety | .31 | .41 | .39 | .41 | .40 | .32 | .31 | .48 | .24 | .45 | .17 | .37 | .43 | 50.8 | 10.4 |
| Depression | .32 | .42 | .48 | .40 | .47 | .44 | .32 | .46 | .25 | .45 | .32 | .41 | .46 | 51.3 | 11.6 |
| Somatization | .15 | .15 | .10 | .10 | .21 | .06 | .06 | .22 | .03 | .10 | .20 | .12 | .15 | 50.5 | 10.5 |
| Attention Problems | .43 | .51 | .75 | .55 | .48 | .56 | .52 | .57 | .37 | .47 | .42 | .71 | .63 | 50.8 | 11.0 |
| Atypicality | .28 | .36 | .45 | .39 | .43 | .38 | .33 | .43 | .27 | .34 | .18 | .44 | .42 | 51.3 | 10.2 |
| Withdrawal | .42 | .35 | .36 | .43 | .40 | .44 | .43 | .39 | .17 | .35 | .27 | .35 | .44 | 51.9 | 11.5 |
| **Adaptive scale** | | | | | | | | | | | | | | | |
| Adaptability | -.51 | -.59 | -.56 | -.60 | -.55 | -.54 | -.57 | -.54 | -.37 | -.60 | -.49 | -.50 | -.63 | 49.2 | 11.2 |
| Social Skills | -.64 | -.57 | -.63 | -.63 | -.59 | -.63 | -.64 | -.52 | -.38 | -.52 | -.61 | -.60 | -.69 | 48.3 | 10.0 |
| Leadership | -.61 | -.50 | -.61 | -.60 | -.50 | -.53 | -.65 | -.50 | -.37 | -.43 | -.38 | -.61 | -.66 | 47.9 | 10.8 |
| Activities of Daily Living | -.45 | -.54 | -.69 | -.54 | -.55 | -.60 | -.49 | -.51 | -.41 | -.48 | -.58 | -.67 | -.63 | 48.8 | 9.7 |
| Functional Communication | -.61 | -.58 | -.58 | -.63 | -.57 | -.51 | -.66 | -.54 | -.38 | -.53 | -.46 | -.58 | -.67 | 49.0 | 10.8 |
| **Content scale** | | | | | | | | | | | | | | | |
| Anger Control | .22 | .41 | .51 | .34 | .39 | .44 | .24 | .43 | .22 | .44 | .38 | .38 | .43 | 52.0 | 12.1 |
| Bullying | .25 | .36 | .50 | .35 | .41 | .47 | .28 | .41 | .30 | .33 | .37 | .41 | .41 | 51.5 | 11.2 |
| Developmental Social Disorders | .59 | .65 | .61 | .67 | .64 | .59 | .63 | .62 | .43 | .64 | .50 | .58 | .70 | 50.8 | 10.5 |
| Emotional Self-Control | .31 | .50 | .49 | .45 | .49 | .49 | .31 | .55 | .29 | .52 | .37 | .41 | .49 | 51.7 | 10.7 |
| Executive Functioning | .49 | .61 | .76 | .62 | .59 | .61 | .56 | .61 | .41 | .57 | .53 | .71 | .70 | 51.9 | 11.1 |
| Negative Emotionality | .27 | .41 | .50 | .38 | .43 | .46 | .29 | .44 | .23 | .46 | .36 | .40 | .45 | 52.4 | 12.0 |
| Resiliency | -.64 | -.60 | -.58 | -.66 | -.60 | -.55 | -.69 | -.52 | -.42 | -.54 | -.52 | -.58 | -.69 | 49.1 | 11.4 |
| **Clinical index** | | | | | | | | | | | | | | | |
| ADHD Probability Index | .37 | .54 | .75 | .53 | .51 | .59 | .45 | .59 | .36 | .50 | .46 | .70 | .63 | 51.8 | 10.6 |
| EBD Probability Index | .42 | .53 | .65 | .52 | .55 | .61 | .45 | .55 | .36 | .51 | .49 | .55 | .62 | 52.4 | 12.0 |
| Autism Probability Index | .52 | .49 | .53 | .58 | .59 | .57 | .55 | .57 | .33 | .48 | .32 | .52 | .59 | 52.0 | 10.3 |
| Functional Impairment Index | .55 | .61 | .71 | .64 | .63 | .64 | .60 | .62 | .39 | .59 | .51 | .65 | .72 | 51.4 | 10.7 |
| **ASRS mean** | 51.2 | 50.2 | 50.7 | 51.0 | 52.2 | 50.9 | 50.6 | 49.5 | 49.4 | 50.3 | 50.1 | 50.2 | 51.0 | — | — |
| **ASRS SD** | 10.9 | 10.2 | 10.2 | 10.3 | 10.7 | 11.3 | 11.4 | 9.1 | 8.8 | 10.1 | 11.2 | 10.1 | 10.7 | — | — |

The mean scores on most of the PRS composites indicate that these samples are about average with respect to their level of behavior problems. The variability in scores is somewhat lower than the general population at the preschool level but somewhat higher than the general population at the child level. Correlations between similar PRS and ASRS scales (e.g., PRS Developmental Social Disorders and Autism Probability Index scores with the ASRS Total Scores and the *DSM–IV–TR* scores) are moderate to high.

## Delis Rating of Executive Functions Parent Rating Form

The PRS–C and PRS–A forms were completed along with the Delis Rating of Executive Functions (D-REF; Delis, 2012) Parent Rating Form for 49 children ages 6 through 11 years and for 65 children and adolescents ages 12 through 19 years. Demographic characteristics of the sample are provided in Table 10.23 (see chapter 8 for a more complete description of the demographic characteristics). Tables 10.32 and 10.33 present the correlations between the PRS and D-REF core index and clinical index scale scores.

The mean PRS scores indicate that the samples are generally average in their levels of behavior problems. The scale score variability is about average in the PRS–C sample but generally a bit lower than average in the PRS–A sample.

The correlations between the PRS scales that assess various aspects of executive functioning (e.g., Hyperactivity, Attention Problems, Anger Control, Executive Functioning, and Emotional Self-Control) are moderate to high across the various D-REF scales.

**Table 10.32** PRS–C: Correlations With the D-REF Parent Rating Form

| BASC–3 | Behavioral Functioning Index | Emotional Functioning Index | Executive Functioning Index | Total Composite | Attention/Working Memory Index | Activity Level/Impulse Control Index | Compliance/Anger Management Index | Abstract Thinking/Problem Solving Index | BASC–3 Mean | BASC–3 SD |
|---|---|---|---|---|---|---|---|---|---|---|
| **Composite** | | | | | | | | | | |
| Externalizing Problems | .28 | .25 | .26 | .18 | .19 | .20 | .38 | .22 | 49.9 | 10.3 |
| Internalizing Problems | .01 | .22 | .18 | .08 | .13 | .01 | .15 | .26 | 50.5 | 11.0 |
| Adaptive Skills | -.51 | -.62 | -.63 | -.60 | -.59 | -.48 | -.53 | -.62 | 51.2 | 9.3 |
| Behavioral Symptoms Index | .29 | .38 | .41 | .30 | .34 | .26 | .39 | .41 | 50.3 | 11.2 |
| **Clinical scale** | | | | | | | | | | |
| Hyperactivity | .57 | .48 | .50 | .47 | .43 | .51 | .60 | .42 | 50.4 | 9.2 |
| Aggression | .10 | .13 | .10 | .03 | .06 | .04 | .24 | .10 | 49.9 | 10.9 |
| Conduct Problems | .25 | .17 | .23 | .14 | .15 | .13 | .31 | .18 | 49.1 | 9.3 |
| Anxiety | -.01 | .17 | .18 | .08 | .15 | .00 | .05 | .30 | 49.6 | 9.9 |
| Depression | .15 | .41 | .30 | .23 | .26 | .15 | .31 | .31 | 49.9 | 10.9 |
| Somatization | -.02 | .06 | .07 | -.01 | .03 | -.04 | .06 | .12 | 51.2 | 12.5 |
| Attention Problems | .48 | .49 | .66 | .56 | .66 | .49 | .48 | .61 | 49.5 | 10.2 |
| Atypicality | .20 | .20 | .29 | .17 | .21 | .14 | .22 | .34 | 50.4 | 11.7 |
| Withdrawal | .12 | .29 | .28 | .19 | .23 | .14 | .19 | .32 | 49.9 | 11.4 |
| **Adaptive scale** | | | | | | | | | | |
| Adaptability | -.51 | -.64 | -.56 | -.59 | -.49 | -.51 | -.52 | -.52 | 52.4 | 9.3 |
| Social Skills | -.33 | -.53 | -.39 | -.42 | -.39 | -.30 | -.42 | -.41 | 50.0 | 9.5 |
| Leadership | -.35 | -.43 | -.51 | -.45 | -.47 | -.34 | -.34 | -.50 | 51.6 | 9.4 |
| Activities of Daily Living | -.61 | -.52 | -.70 | -.62 | -.67 | -.57 | -.56 | -.63 | 50.6 | 9.7 |
| Functional Communication | -.39 | -.56 | -.57 | -.50 | -.50 | -.34 | -.47 | -.61 | 51.1 | 9.0 |
| **Content scale** | | | | | | | | | | |
| Anger Control | .37 | .60 | .41 | .41 | .33 | .35 | .56 | .39 | 48.3 | 8.8 |
| Bullying | .02 | .04 | .07 | -.04 | .04 | -.05 | .10 | .09 | 50.7 | 12.2 |
| Developmental Social Disorders | .43 | .49 | .56 | .46 | .49 | .37 | .43 | .58 | 50.0 | 9.6 |
| Emotional Self-Control | .33 | .64 | .50 | .47 | .41 | .35 | .50 | .53 | 49.2 | 8.3 |
| Executive Functioning | .57 | .60 | .73 | .64 | .67 | .55 | .57 | .68 | 49.4 | 9.4 |
| Negative Emotionality | .41 | .68 | .46 | .49 | .36 | .33 | .65 | .47 | 50.0 | 7.3 |
| Resiliency | -.46 | -.48 | -.57 | -.52 | -.56 | -.43 | -.37 | -.54 | 51.6 | 8.4 |
| **Clinical index** | | | | | | | | | | |
| ADHD Probability Index | .62 | .57 | .71 | .63 | .66 | .60 | .61 | .61 | 50.4 | 10.0 |
| EBD Probability Index | .21 | .41 | .35 | .25 | .30 | .17 | .35 | .35 | 49.7 | 9.5 |
| Autism Probability Index | .20 | .32 | .36 | .24 | .28 | .18 | .26 | .38 | 49.7 | 11.1 |
| Functional Impairment Index | .45 | .58 | .63 | .53 | .56 | .41 | .51 | .64 | 49.1 | 10.0 |
| **D-REF mean** | 52.0 | 48.1 | 50.3 | 50.2 | 50.7 | 52.5 | 48.3 | 49.8 | — | — |
| **D-REF SD** | 10.1 | 9.6 | 10.7 | 10.1 | 10.6 | 9.4 | 10.0 | 9.6 | — | — |

# Table 10.33 PRS–A: Correlations With the D-REF Parent Rating Form

| BASC–3 | Behavioral Functioning Index | Emotional Functioning Index | Executive Functioning Index | Total Composite | Attention/ Working Memory Index | Activity Level/ Impulse Control Index | Compliance/ Anger Management Index | Abstract Thinking/Problem Solving Index | BASC–3 Mean | BASC–3 SD |
|---|---|---|---|---|---|---|---|---|---|---|
| **Composite** | | | | | | | | | | |
| Externalizing Problems | .70 | .73 | .63 | .73 | .61 | .66 | .79 | .46 | 49.4 | 6.7 |
| Internalizing Problems | .49 | .58 | .53 | .56 | .56 | .44 | .54 | .45 | 49.1 | 7.6 |
| Adaptive Skills | −.53 | −.68 | −.59 | −.64 | −.57 | −.56 | −.66 | −.51 | 50.5 | 7.9 |
| Behavioral Symptoms Index | .75 | .79 | .75 | .80 | .76 | .73 | .80 | .63 | 48.8 | 6.9 |
| **Clinical scale** | | | | | | | | | | |
| Hyperactivity | .76 | .73 | .64 | .74 | .64 | .73 | .76 | .51 | 49.5 | 7.1 |
| Aggression | .58 | .69 | .56 | .64 | .56 | .51 | .74 | .37 | 49.0 | 6.3 |
| Conduct Problems | .56 | .58 | .50 | .58 | .45 | .53 | .66 | .33 | 49.7 | 7.4 |
| Anxiety | .28 | .40 | .30 | .35 | .40 | .21 | .33 | .21 | 48.9 | 7.5 |
| Depression | .53 | .65 | .58 | .62 | .61 | .47 | .64 | .50 | 49.6 | 7.7 |
| Somatization | .37 | .38 | .40 | .40 | .37 | .37 | .34 | .37 | 49.0 | 8.9 |
| Attention Problems | .73 | .62 | .75 | .75 | .76 | .73 | .64 | .62 | 49.7 | 8.9 |
| Atypicality | .76 | .69 | .65 | .73 | .64 | .73 | .68 | .53 | 48.5 | 6.4 |
| Withdrawal | .14 | .38 | .35 | .31 | .33 | .19 | .36 | .31 | 48.2 | 7.9 |
| **Adaptive scale** | | | | | | | | | | |
| Adaptability | −.32 | −.58 | −.36 | −.45 | −.35 | −.33 | −.61 | −.27 | 50.0 | 8.7 |
| Social Skills | −.17 | −.35 | −.22 | −.27 | −.19 | −.19 | −.32 | −.17 | 51.3 | 8.2 |
| Leadership | −.32 | −.50 | −.46 | −.47 | −.46 | −.39 | −.47 | −.38 | 49.5 | 8.2 |
| Activities of Daily Living | −.61 | −.61 | −.63 | −.67 | −.59 | −.62 | −.61 | −.54 | 50.0 | 9.0 |
| Functional Communication | −.58 | −.64 | −.64 | −.66 | −.64 | −.61 | −.61 | −.58 | 50.9 | 8.2 |
| **Content scale** | | | | | | | | | | |
| Anger Control | .70 | .78 | .59 | .73 | .60 | .68 | .80 | .45 | 49.8 | 7.5 |
| Bullying | .41 | .55 | .45 | .49 | .47 | .35 | .60 | .26 | 49.1 | 6.4 |
| Developmental Social Disorders | .54 | .69 | .62 | .65 | .62 | .55 | .67 | .58 | 48.3 | 7.3 |
| Emotional Self-Control | .62 | .71 | .54 | .67 | .58 | .60 | .70 | .41 | 49.9 | 8.4 |
| Executive Functioning | .71 | .71 | .71 | .76 | .69 | .72 | .71 | .60 | 49.9 | 8.6 |
| Negative Emotionality | .55 | .64 | .43 | .59 | .42 | .50 | .67 | .34 | 50.4 | 8.0 |
| Resiliency | −.43 | −.59 | −.49 | −.54 | −.50 | −.48 | −.59 | −.40 | 49.8 | 7.8 |
| **Clinical index** | | | | | | | | | | |
| ADHD Probability Index | .65 | .69 | .69 | .73 | .69 | .65 | .71 | .60 | 50.0 | 8.1 |
| EBD Probability Index | .63 | .74 | .57 | .69 | .57 | .63 | .76 | .44 | 49.0 | 7.9 |
| Autism Probability Index | .36 | .58 | .52 | .53 | .51 | .38 | .54 | .45 | 48.7 | 7.9 |
| Functional Impairment Index | .66 | .73 | .68 | .74 | .68 | .65 | .73 | .60 | 48.8 | 8.3 |
| **D-REF mean** | 50.0 | 49.8 | 50.2 | 50.3 | 50.5 | 49.9 | 49.7 | 49.7 | — | — |
| **D-REF SD** | 9.3 | 9.3 | 10.0 | 9.3 | 10.6 | 8.9 | 9.1 | 9.5 | — | — |

## PROFILES OF CLINICAL GROUPS

When interpreting BASC–3 results, it is helpful to know the profiles of mean scale scores of groups of children and adolescents who have been identified with behavioral or emotional problems. In general, such individuals tend to have various behavioral strengths along with higher than average deficits.

Often, these differences between the strengths and deficits are defining features of the problem area itself; for example, attention-deficit/hyperactivity disorder (ADHD) is defined by hyperactivity and attention problems. An understanding of these profiles is helpful when making complex differential diagnoses. The presentation of group score profiles gives added empirical support for the use of the BASC–3 in identifying behavioral and emotional problems.

As discussed in chapters 7 and 8, the clinical norm samples were created from groups of children and adolescents identified as having one or more behavioral, emotional, physical, or learning problems. There were sufficient cases of each of the following groups to calculate profiles:

- Attention-deficit/hyperactivity disorder (ADHD)

- Autism spectrum disorder

- Emotional/behavioral disturbance (EBD)

- Hearing impairment

- Specific learning disorder

- Speech or language disorder

The mean *T* scores for these groups on the PRS composites and scales appear in Table 10.34 and are displayed graphically in Figures 10.1 through 10.6. General combined-gender norms were used for all cases. The following points summarize the results for each group. For each diagnostic group, results are combined across the child and adolescent levels. Scores from the preschool level are not presented because of the imprecision of diagnoses at such a young age. Selected results of these profiles include:

- ADHD: significant score elevations for the Attention Problems and Hyperactivity scales

- Autism: significant score elevations on the Developmental Social Disorders, Atypicality, and Withdrawal scales, as well as markedly lower scores on several of the adaptive scales

- EBD: significant score elevations for the Aggression, Anxiety, Conduct Problems, and Depression scales, as well other clinical and adaptive scales

**Table 10.34** Mean *T* Scores for Clinical Groups on the PRS Composites, Scales, and Indexes

| | All Clinical | | Attention-Deficit/ Hyperactivity Disorder | | Autism Spectrum Disorder and Pervasive Developmental Disorder | | Emotional/Behavioral Disturbance | | Hearing Impairment | | Learning Disability | | Speech/Language Disorder | |
| | Child/Adolescent | | Child/Adolescent | | Child/Adolescent | | Child/Adolescent | | Child/Adolescent | | Child/Adolescent | | Child/Adolescent | |
| | Mean | SD | Mean | SD | Mean | SD | Mean | SD | Mean | SD | Mean | SD | Mean | SD |
|---|---|---|---|---|---|---|---|---|---|---|---|---|---|---|
| **Composite** | | | | | | | | | | | | | | |
| Externalizing Problems | 58.1 | 13.8 | 60.2 | 12.7 | 55.4 | 13.4 | 66.6 | 16.1 | 55.9 | 13.1 | 50.7 | 9.8 | 50.7 | 11.3 |
| Internalizing Problems | 55.5 | 12.3 | 55.1 | 11.3 | 55.5 | 12.6 | 64.0 | 14.3 | 50.5 | 9.5 | 52.2 | 10.2 | 50.0 | 10.7 |
| Adaptive Skills | 41.0 | 9.7 | 41.4 | 8.4 | 35.2 | 8.5 | 38.5 | 10.1 | 48.9 | 7.3 | 45.1 | 10.2 | 46.1 | 8.9 |
| Behavioral Symptoms Index | 60.5 | 12.8 | 61.3 | 11.6 | 63.3 | 12.5 | 67.7 | 13.8 | 54.6 | 10.2 | 53.0 | 10.7 | 51.9 | 11.2 |
| **Clinical scale** | | | | | | | | | | | | | | |
| Hyperactivity | 59.1 | 13.6 | 61.9 | 12.7 | 57.9 | 14.3 | 65.0 | 14.2 | 54.8 | 11.8 | 51.7 | 11.0 | 50.6 | 10.2 |
| Aggression | 56.9 | 14.7 | 57.7 | 13.9 | 54.0 | 13.3 | 66.9 | 17.5 | 56.6 | 14.1 | 50.1 | 9.8 | 52.3 | 12.8 |
| Conduct Problems | 55.7 | 12.9 | 57.7 | 12.3 | 52.4 | 11.9 | 63.2 | 15.6 | 54.4 | 12.3 | 50.0 | 8.9 | 48.9 | 8.9 |
| Anxiety | 54.6 | 11.7 | 53.9 | 10.7 | 54.4 | 12.5 | 60.9 | 13.2 | 50.1 | 9.3 | 54.0 | 10.7 | 51.7 | 10.8 |
| Depression | 57.2 | 13.5 | 57.5 | 12.9 | 57.2 | 12.8 | 65.9 | 15.1 | 51.6 | 9.5 | 52.5 | 11.3 | 50.8 | 12.2 |
| Somatization | 52.4 | 12.0 | 51.7 | 10.6 | 52.7 | 13.1 | 59.4 | 15.0 | 49.7 | 9.7 | 49.3 | 9.0 | 47.4 | 9.6 |
| Attention Problems | 60.8 | 9.7 | 64.5 | 7.7 | 60.7 | 8.7 | 61.7 | 10.1 | 52.4 | 9.1 | 56.9 | 9.7 | 51.6 | 9.6 |
| Atypicality | 58.0 | 14.0 | 56.4 | 12.2 | 66.4 | 15.7 | 62.3 | 15.6 | 54.0 | 9.6 | 51.5 | 10.1 | 51.0 | 11.8 |
| Withdrawal | 57.0 | 13.2 | 54.7 | 11.4 | 65.6 | 14.9 | 61.2 | 13.4 | 52.0 | 11.8 | 51.5 | 10.2 | 52.2 | 10.5 |
| **Adaptive scale** | | | | | | | | | | | | | | |
| Adaptability | 42.4 | 9.8 | 42.4 | 9.0 | 40.0 | 9.7 | 37.9 | 9.0 | 50.3 | 8.7 | 46.3 | 9.8 | 46.0 | 9.7 |
| Social Skills | 43.7 | 10.6 | 44.9 | 9.7 | 38.4 | 11.2 | 41.4 | 10.6 | 50.4 | 6.9 | 47.1 | 10.2 | 45.9 | 9.1 |
| Leadership | 41.6 | 9.6 | 42.2 | 8.4 | 35.3 | 7.7 | 40.8 | 10.4 | 49.7 | 8.0 | 44.6 | 9.6 | 46.3 | 9.5 |
| Activities of Daily Living | 41.7 | 10.1 | 40.4 | 9.1 | 38.7 | 9.2 | 39.3 | 10.4 | 49.2 | 9.0 | 46.5 | 9.9 | 49.9 | 8.8 |
| Functional Communication | 40.9 | 10.4 | 42.6 | 9.0 | 32.9 | 9.4 | 40.3 | 10.6 | 45.5 | 9.1 | 43.7 | 9.9 | 45.4 | 9.8 |
| **Content scale** | | | | | | | | | | | | | | |
| Anger Control | 58.4 | 13.4 | 59.1 | 12.9 | 57.2 | 12.6 | 68.1 | 13.6 | 54.1 | 11.9 | 52.2 | 10.9 | 53.1 | 12.2 |
| Bullying | 55.1 | 13.7 | 55.6 | 13.0 | 51.6 | 11.7 | 64.7 | 17.0 | 55.6 | 13.4 | 49.3 | 8.9 | 51.9 | 12.4 |
| Developmental Social Disorders | 59.1 | 12.0 | 57.3 | 10.7 | 67.9 | 12.4 | 62.2 | 11.3 | 53.1 | 9.0 | 53.4 | 10.1 | 53.6 | 9.7 |
| Emotional Self-Control | 57.8 | 12.7 | 57.8 | 11.7 | 58.7 | 12.1 | 67.3 | 12.7 | 52.3 | 11.0 | 52.7 | 12.0 | 50.1 | 10.6 |
| Executive Functioning | 61.0 | 10.2 | 62.7 | 8.9 | 63.5 | 8.6 | 64.6 | 11.2 | 53.2 | 8.7 | 55.9 | 10.4 | 52.5 | 10.0 |
| Negative Emotionality | 57.3 | 12.9 | 58.4 | 12.3 | 55.4 | 12.0 | 66.3 | 13.2 | 52.4 | 10.8 | 52.1 | 10.5 | 51.1 | 12.3 |
| Resiliency | 41.7 | 9.2 | 42.2 | 8.0 | 36.4 | 7.4 | 39.5 | 9.9 | 50.1 | 8.6 | 45.2 | 9.7 | 46.0 | 9.5 |
| **Clinical index** | | | | | | | | | | | | | | |
| ADHD Probability Index | 61.0 | 10.8 | 64.4 | 9.4 | 61.5 | 10.0 | 62.7 | 11.4 | 54.2 | 9.3 | 55.8 | 9.9 | 51.2 | 10.1 |
| EBD Probability Index | 58.7 | 13.1 | 59.5 | 12.8 | 58.3 | 11.4 | 68.2 | 14.2 | 53.5 | 10.2 | 52.3 | 10.3 | 51.9 | 10.8 |
| Autism Probability Index | 59.0 | 13.2 | 56.8 | 11.2 | 69.5 | 14.6 | 61.1 | 12.4 | 53.9 | 9.4 | 53.6 | 9.9 | 52.7 | 11.0 |
| Functional Impairment Index | 60.4 | 10.8 | 60.0 | 9.6 | 66.0 | 9.6 | 65.2 | 10.9 | 53.4 | 9.2 | 55.5 | 10.9 | 53.0 | 9.0 |

## Clinical Profile

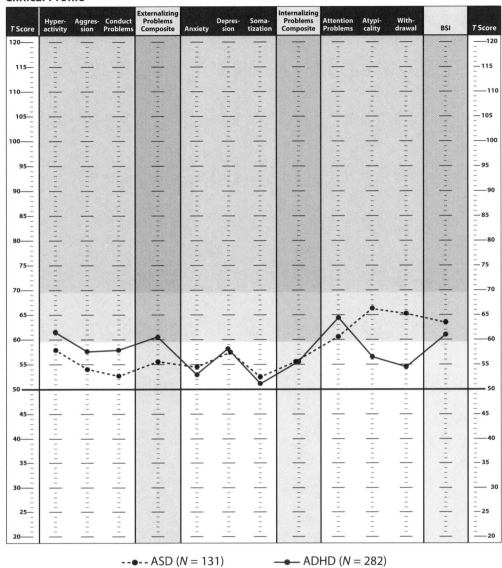

--●-- ASD (N = 131)  ——●—— ADHD (N = 282)

**Figure 10.1** PRS: Clinical group *T* scores for attention-deficit/hyperactivity disorder and autism spectrum disorder in the Clinical Profile

## Adaptive Profile

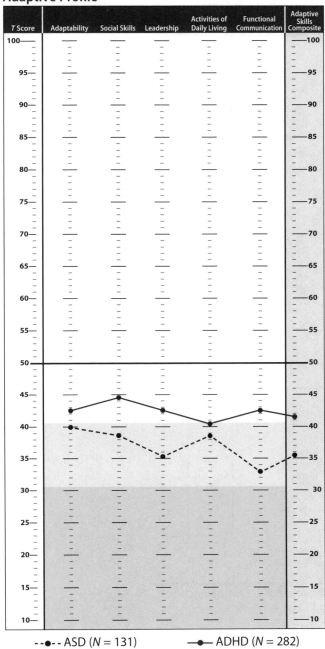

--•-- ASD (N = 131)    —•— ADHD (N = 282)

**Figure 10.2** PRS: Clinical group *T* scores for attention-deficit/hyperactivity disorder and autism spectrum disorder in the Adaptive Profile

## Clinical Profile

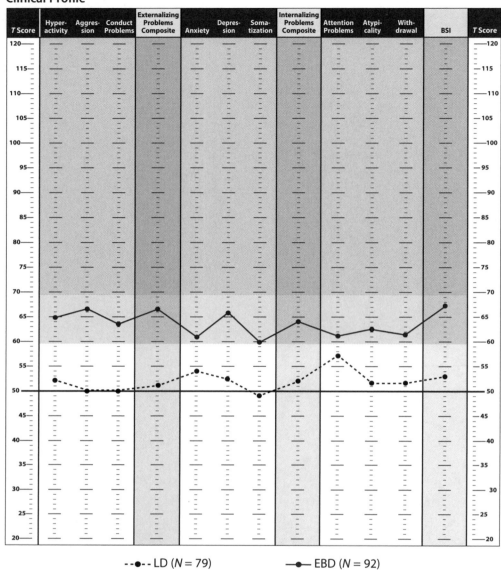

**Figure 10.3** PRS: Clinical group *T* scores for emotional/behavioral disturbance and specific learning disorder in the Clinical Profile

## Adaptive Profile

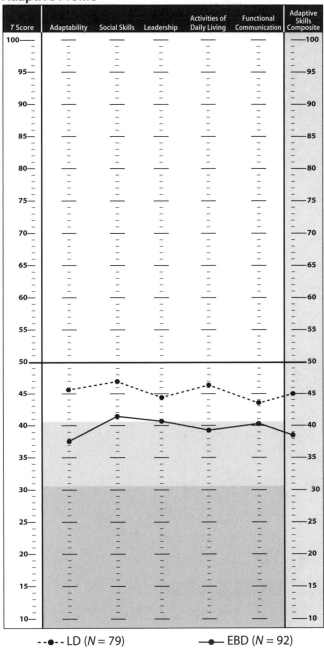

**Figure 10.4** PRS: Clinical group *T* scores for emotional/ behavioral disturbance and specific learning disorder in the Adaptive Profile

## Clinical Profile

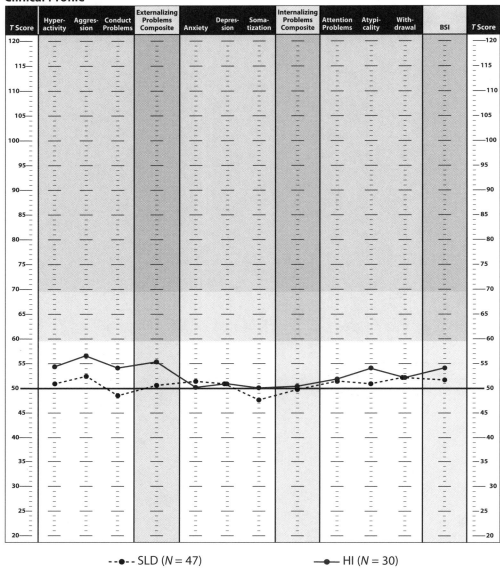

--•-- SLD (N = 47)          —•— HI (N = 30)

**Figure 10.5** PRS: Clinical group *T* scores for hearing impairment and speech or language disorder in the Clinical Profile

## Adaptive Profile

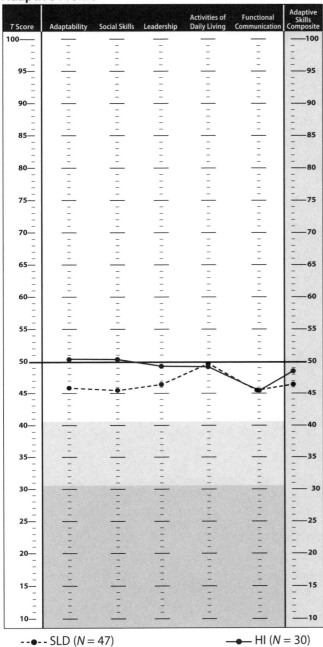

**Figure 10.6** PRS: Clinical group *T* scores for hearing impairment and speech or language disorder in the Adaptive Profile

# Chapter 11

## Self-Report of Personality: Reliability and Validity

This chapter presents technical information about the Self-Report of Personality (SRP), including evidence of reliability (i.e., internal consistency and test–retest), and validity (i.e., factor structure of the scales, correlations with other instruments, score profiles of clinical groups). Technical information about the Teacher Rating Scales (TRS) and the Parent Rating Scales (PRS) is found in chapters 9 and 10, respectively. Technical information about the relationship between the TRS, PRS, and SRP components is presented in chapter 12.

## Evidence of Reliability

The following types of reliability evidence were analyzed for the BASC–3 SRP and are presented in this chapter.

- *Internal consistency:* shows the degree to which all of the items of a scale are measuring the same behavioral or emotional dimension

- *Test–retest reliability:* reflects the consistency of ratings over a brief time interval

### EVIDENCE OF INTERNAL CONSISTENCY

#### English Forms

Tables 11.1 and 11.2 report coefficient alpha of the SRP–Interview (SRP–I) Total Score and the SRP–Child (SRP–C), SRP–Adolescent (SRP–A), and SRP–College (SRP–COL) composite and scale scores, based on all of the cases in each of the general norm groups with complete item data for the scale. Table 11.3 presents the same type of information for the SRP–C and SRP–A clinical norm samples. Because reliability is affected by both the variability of scores in a sample and the quality of the items, each table shows separate reliability coefficients for the scores of the combined, female, and male samples, and for the all clinical, ADHD, and 19- through 21-year-old subsamples.

**Table 11.1** SRP–I: Coefficient Alpha Reliabilities of Composites and Scales, by Gender and Age, General Norm Samples

|  | Ages 6–7 | | |
|---|---|---|---|
|  | Combined | Female | Male |
| Total Score | .73 | .74 | .71 |

For the general norm samples, the SRP–I Total Score reliabilities are adequate. The reliabilities are consistent for both combined-gender and separate-gender groups.

**Table 11.2** SRP: Coefficient Alpha Reliabilities of Composites, Scales, and Indexes, by Gender and Age, General Norm Samples

| | Child | | | | | | Adolescent | | | College | | |
| | Ages 8–11 | | | Ages 12–14 | | | Ages 15–18 | | | Ages 18–25 | | |
| | Combined | Female | Male | Combined | Female | Male | Combined | Female | Male | Combined | Female | Male |
|---|---|---|---|---|---|---|---|---|---|---|---|---|
| **Composite** | | | | | | | | | | | | |
| School Problems | .89 | .86 | .90 | .91 | .92 | .90 | .90 | .91 | .89 | — | — | — |
| Internalizing Problems | .95 | .97 | .94 | .96 | .96 | .95 | .97 | .97 | .96 | .97 | .97 | .96 |
| Inattention/Hyperactivity | .89 | .91 | .87 | .91 | .91 | .91 | .92 | .92 | .92 | .91 | .91 | .90 |
| Emotional Symptoms | .95 | .96 | .93 | .95 | .96 | .95 | .97 | .97 | .96 | .96 | .97 | .96 |
| Personal Adjustment | .93 | .92 | .93 | .93 | .94 | .93 | .94 | .94 | .94 | .94 | .94 | .93 |
| **Clinical scale** | | | | | | | | | | | | |
| Attitude to School | .82 | .75 | .85 | .83 | .82 | .84 | .81 | .84 | .77 | — | — | — |
| Attitude to Teachers | .83 | .82 | .83 | .82 | .83 | .81 | .83 | .83 | .83 | — | — | — |
| Sensation Seeking | — | — | — | .84 | .85 | .83 | .85 | .83 | .86 | .87 | .85 | .88 |
| Atypicality | .86 | .88 | .84 | .84 | .85 | .83 | .83 | .82 | .84 | .81 | .80 | .83 |
| Locus of Control | .73 | .77 | .69 | .78 | .80 | .75 | .80 | .82 | .77 | .82 | .79 | .84 |
| Social Stress | .83 | .85 | .81 | .87 | .87 | .86 | .88 | .89 | .88 | .86 | .86 | .85 |
| Anxiety | .85 | .89 | .79 | .87 | .88 | .84 | .91 | .92 | .88 | .91 | .92 | .89 |
| Depression | .83 | .88 | .72 | .86 | .87 | .84 | .90 | .92 | .88 | .88 | .89 | .86 |
| Sense of Inadequacy | .76 | .81 | .70 | .82 | .84 | .81 | .84 | .87 | .81 | .85 | .86 | .83 |
| Somatization | — | — | — | .71 | .72 | .69 | .82 | .83 | .80 | .79 | .79 | .74 |
| Attention Problems | .81 | .83 | .79 | .86 | .85 | .86 | .88 | .90 | .86 | .87 | .89 | .83 |
| Hyperactivity | .82 | .85 | .78 | .84 | .84 | .84 | .85 | .82 | .87 | .82 | .79 | .84 |
| Alcohol Abuse | — | — | — | — | — | — | — | — | — | .93 | .91 | .95 |
| School Maladjustment | — | — | — | — | — | — | — | — | — | .84 | .83 | .84 |
| **Adaptive scale** | | | | | | | | | | | | |
| Relations With Parents | .87 | .86 | .88 | .90 | .90 | .90 | .90 | .91 | .89 | .91 | .92 | .90 |
| Interpersonal Relations | .81 | .80 | .81 | .81 | .81 | .81 | .84 | .87 | .78 | .83 | .83 | .82 |
| Self-Esteem | .78 | .81 | .76 | .82 | .84 | .80 | .87 | .89 | .83 | .88 | .89 | .85 |
| Self-Reliance | .75 | .73 | .77 | .82 | .81 | .82 | .82 | .76 | .86 | .78 | .81 | .75 |
| **Content scale** | | | | | | | | | | | | |
| Anger Control | — | — | — | .83 | .83 | .83 | .82 | .81 | .84 | .83 | .80 | .86 |
| Ego Strength | — | — | — | .81 | .83 | .80 | .84 | .85 | .83 | .79 | .80 | .77 |
| Mania | — | — | — | .82 | .84 | .79 | .86 | .85 | .87 | .85 | .85 | .86 |
| Test Anxiety | — | — | — | .76 | .77 | .75 | .81 | .83 | .78 | .84 | .82 | .86 |
| **Clinical index** | | | | | | | | | | | | |
| Functional Impairment Index | .85 | .88 | .82 | .87 | .89 | .85 | .89 | .90 | .88 | — | — | — |

For the SRP–C, SRP–A, and SRP–COL general norm samples, overall average composite scale score reliability coefficients are generally excellent, largely ranging from the upper .80s to upper .90s. The composite scale score reliability coefficients are fairly consistent across age levels and for both combined-gender and separate-gender groups.

Overall, average score reliability coefficients of the clinical and adaptive scales are also adequate to good with most being in the .80s. When comparing reliability coefficients between the female and male samples across SRP levels, most are similar; however, for some scale scores (e.g., Anxiety, Depression), reliability coefficients are higher for the female samples than the male samples.

The overall average reliability coefficients of scores for the content scales and clinical scales (i.e., the Functional Impairment Index) are good, with most being in the .80s. The scores of content and clinical scales exhibit consistent reliability coefficients for combined-gender and separate-gender samples.

In the clinical norm samples, most of the internal-consistency reliability coefficients composite scale scores are excellent and similar to those in the general norm samples. Composite scale reliability coefficients for the male and female samples tend to be fairly consistent. Reliability coefficients of the clinical, adaptive, and content scales for the combined-gender samples are generally adequate to good, with most being in the .80s. Reliability coefficients tend to be somewhat higher for the female sample than for the male sample (with a few exceptions).

In summary, internal-consistency reliability coefficients of the composite and scale scores range from adequate to excellent across the various nonclinical and clinical samples.

**Table 11.3** SRP: Coefficient Alpha Reliabilities of Composites, Scales, and Indexes, by Gender and Norm Group, Clinical Norm Samples

| | Child | | | | | | Adolescent | | | | | | Ages 19–21 |
| | All clinical | | | ADHD | | | All clinical | | | ADHD | | | |
| | Combined | Female | Male | Combined | Female | Male | Combined | Female | Male | Combined | Female | Male | Combined |
|---|---|---|---|---|---|---|---|---|---|---|---|---|---|
| **Composite** | | | | | | | | | | | | | |
| School Problems | .90 | .92 | .89 | .90 | .87 | .91 | .91 | .89 | .91 | .91 | .92 | .91 | .85 |
| Internalizing Problems | .95 | .96 | .95 | .95 | .96 | .94 | .96 | .97 | .96 | .96 | .95 | .96 | .96 |
| Inattention/Hyperactivity | .90 | .90 | .90 | .89 | .85 | .90 | .90 | .90 | .90 | .91 | .89 | .91 | .89 |
| Emotional Symptoms | .94 | .96 | .93 | .93 | .96 | .92 | .96 | .96 | .95 | .96 | .97 | .96 | .95 |
| Personal Adjustment | .92 | .94 | .90 | .90 | .93 | .89 | .93 | .93 | .93 | .94 | .94 | .94 | .92 |
| **Clinical scale** | | | | | | | | | | | | | |
| Attitude to School | .86 | .88 | .85 | .85 | .79 | .86 | .84 | .83 | .85 | .86 | .85 | .86 | .57 |
| Attitude to Teachers | .83 | .88 | .81 | .85 | .86 | .85 | .85 | .83 | .85 | .86 | .87 | .86 | .80 |
| Sensation Seeking | — | — | — | — | — | — | .81 | .82 | .81 | .82 | .85 | .80 | .86 |
| Atypicality | .83 | .85 | .83 | .83 | .87 | .81 | .86 | .90 | .83 | .80 | .46 | .83 | .82 |
| Locus of Control | .75 | .79 | .72 | .72 | .80 | .67 | .77 | .77 | .77 | .74 | .74 | .74 | .79 |
| Social Stress | .82 | .84 | .80 | .84 | .85 | .83 | .88 | .90 | .87 | .89 | .91 | .88 | .86 |
| Anxiety | .84 | .87 | .83 | .82 | .87 | .80 | .89 | .91 | .87 | .90 | .94 | .88 | .91 |
| Depression | .83 | .88 | .81 | .83 | .89 | .80 | .88 | .90 | .86 | .88 | .91 | .87 | .91 |
| Sense of Inadequacy | .77 | .80 | .76 | .77 | .75 | .78 | .80 | .83 | .78 | .81 | .86 | .80 | .75 |
| Somatization | — | — | — | — | — | — | .79 | .79 | .76 | .77 | .77 | .77 | .81 |
| Attention Problems | .82 | .81 | .82 | .80 | .68 | .82 | .85 | .88 | .84 | .86 | .89 | .85 | .87 |
| Hyperactivity | .83 | .84 | .82 | .82 | .81 | .82 | .80 | .79 | .81 | .84 | .78 | .85 | .77 |
| **Adaptive scale** | | | | | | | | | | | | | |
| Relations With Parents | .85 | .89 | .83 | .83 | .89 | .81 | .91 | .89 | .91 | .92 | .92 | .92 | .88 |
| Interpersonal Relations | .84 | .85 | .83 | .82 | .80 | .83 | .85 | .87 | .84 | .86 | .89 | .86 | .86 |
| Self-Esteem | .75 | .83 | .69 | .74 | .80 | .71 | .86 | .90 | .81 | .88 | .92 | .85 | .84 |
| Self-Reliance | .74 | .79 | .71 | .61 | .75 | .56 | .78 | .77 | .79 | .79 | .73 | .80 | .76 |
| **Content scale** | | | | | | | | | | | | | |
| Anger Control | — | — | — | — | — | — | .86 | .84 | .86 | .86 | .80 | .88 | .79 |
| Ego Strength | — | — | — | — | — | — | .85 | .87 | .83 | .85 | .89 | .83 | .85 |
| Mania | — | — | — | — | — | — | .80 | .79 | .81 | .85 | .80 | .85 | .79 |
| Test Anxiety | — | — | — | — | — | — | .77 | .80 | .75 | .80 | .87 | .77 | .73 |
| **Clinical index** | | | | | | | | | | | | | |
| Functional Impairment Index | .86 | .87 | .85 | .84 | .78 | .86 | .86 | .87 | .85 | .88 | .86 | .88 | .83 |

## Spanish Forms

Separate studies were conducted to determine internal-consistency reliability coefficients for the Spanish-language SRP–C and SRP–A forms. Demographic characteristics of the Spanish sample are presented in Table 11.4 (see chapter 8 for a more complete description of the demographic characteristics) and reliability coefficients in Table 11.5.

**Table 11.4** SRP: Demographic Characteristics of the SRP Spanish-Form Samples

|  | Child | Adolescent |
|---|---|---|
| *N* | 36 | 77 |
| **Age** | | |
| Mean | 10.0 | 15.3 |
| *SD* | 1.1 | 2.0 |
| Range | 8–11 | 12–18 |
| **Mother's education level** | | |
| 1 | 11.1 | 29.9 |
| 2 | 30.6 | 31.2 |
| 3 | 27.8 | 23.4 |
| 4 | 30.6 | 15.6 |
| **Region** | | |
| Midwest | 8.3 | 6.5 |
| Northeast | 2.8 | 3.9 |
| South | 61.1 | 41.6 |
| West | 27.8 | 48.1 |
| **Gender** | | |
| Female | 66.7 | 50.6 |
| Male | 33.3 | 49.4 |

**Table 11.5** SRP: Coefficient Alpha Reliabilities of Composites, Scales, and Indexes for the Spanish Form, by Gender and Test Form

| | Child | Adolescent |
| --- | --- | --- |
| | Ages 8–11 | Ages 12–18 |
| **Composite** | | |
| School Problems | .90 | .86 |
| Internalizing Problems | .94 | .94 |
| Inattention/Hyperactivity | .94 | .90 |
| Emotional Symptoms | .94 | .95 |
| Personal Adjustment | .92 | .91 |
| **Clinical scale** | | |
| Attitude to School | .83 | .73 |
| Attitude to Teachers | .84 | .79 |
| Sensation Seeking | — | .80 |
| Atypicality | .70 | .74 |
| Locus of Control | .61 | .56 |
| Social Stress | .90 | .86 |
| Anxiety | .82 | .82 |
| Depression | .79 | .87 |
| Sense of Inadequacy | .82 | .76 |
| Somatization | — | .56 |
| Attention Problems | .86 | .82 |
| Hyperactivity | .91 | .84 |
| **Adaptive scale** | | |
| Relations With Parents | .89 | .87 |
| Interpersonal Relations | .75 | .68 |
| Self-Esteem | .73 | .74 |
| Self-Reliance | .69 | .87 |
| **Content scale** | | |
| Anger Control | — | .80 |
| Ego Strength | — | .77 |
| Mania | — | .82 |
| Test Anxiety | — | .70 |
| **Clinical index** | | |
| Functional Impairment Index | .88 | .85 |

In general, reliability coefficients of the composite scale scores are above .90, and the reliability coefficients of scores for the clinical, adaptive, content, and clinical index scales are generally above .70, with only a few exceptions.

## EVIDENCE OF TEST–RETEST RELIABILITY

Another method of indicating the consistency of test scores is for an individual to complete the same test form twice over a period of several weeks. For each SRP age level, children and young adults were selected for inclusion in a test–retest study; each individual selected for this study completed the SRP twice. The samples included both individuals with clinical diagnoses and individuals from the general population. Demographic characteristics and testing intervals of the retest samples are presented in Table 11.6 (see chapter 8 for a more complete description of the demographic characteristics).

**Table 11.6** SRP: Demographic Characteristics of Test–Retest Reliability Study Samples

| Characteristic | Interview | Child | Adolescent | College |
|---|---|---|---|---|
| N | 102 | 81 | 131 | 69 |
| **Age** | | | | |
| Mean | 7.2 | 9.8 | 14.6 | 21.1 |
| SD | 0.5 | 1.1 | 1.8 | 2.2 |
| Range | 6–7 | 8–11 | 12–18 | 18–25 |
| **Test interval** | | | | |
| Mean | 19.3 | 22.8 | 21.9 | 19.0 |
| Range | 7–66 | 7–67 | 7–70 | 7–68 |
| **Mother's education level** | | | | |
| 1 | 10.8 | 11.1 | 3.1 | 5.8 |
| 2 | 6.9 | 19.8 | 11.5 | 21.7 |
| 3 | 29.4 | 25.9 | 19.1 | 30.4 |
| 4 | 52.9 | 43.2 | 66.4 | 42.0 |
| **Race/ethnicity** | | | | |
| African American | 5.9 | 16.0 | 6.9 | 14.5 |
| Asian | 2.0 | 4.9 | — | 1.4 |
| Hispanic | 18.6 | 38.3 | 18.3 | 13.0 |
| Other | 1.0 | — | 4.6 | 10.1 |
| White | 72.5 | 40.7 | 70.2 | 60.9 |
| **Region** | | | | |
| Midwest | 8.8 | 8.6 | 12.2 | 23.2 |
| Northeast | 14.7 | 16.0 | 12.2 | 8.7 |
| South | 34.3 | 44.4 | 40.5 | 52.2 |
| West | 42.2 | 30.9 | 35.1 | 15.9 |
| **Gender** | | | | |
| Female | 49.0 | 46.9 | 61.8 | 58.0 |
| Male | 51.0 | 53.1 | 38.2 | 42.0 |

Overall, the individuals in this study are reasonably representative of the U.S. population, although the numbers of females is higher in the adolescent sample. The general combined-gender norms were used in the analyses.

Table 11.7 presents the uncorrected SRP–I Total Score test–retest stability coefficient. The SRP–I Total Score's test–retest stability is adequate and the mean scores are consistent across the two test administrations.

**Table 11.7** SRP–I: Total Score Test–Retest Reliability

| | Interview | | | | | |
|---|---|---|---|---|---|---|
| | First rating | | Second rating | | | Standard difference |
| | Mean | SD | Mean | SD | r | |
| Total Score | 3.1 | 2.4 | 3.0 | 2.7 | .72 | −0.04 |

Tables 11.8, 11.9, and 11.10 report the uncorrected and corrected SRP test–retest stability coefficients for the SRP–C, SRP–A, and SRP–COL, respectively. Test–retest stability coefficients for scores from the various scales generally possess adequate stability across all scale types and levels, with most corrected stability coefficients in the .70s or higher. Mean scores between administrations are very similar, with most effect sizes under .20, indicating stable performance across the testing interval.

**Table 11.8** SRP: Test–Retest Reliabilities of Composites, Scales, and Indexes, Child

| | Child | | | | | | |
| | First rating | | Second rating | | | Corrected | Standard |
| | Mean | SD | Mean | SD | r | r | difference |
|---|---|---|---|---|---|---|---|
| **Composite** | | | | | | | |
| School Problems | 50.0 | 9.2 | 49.0 | 9.0 | .85 | .87 | −0.11 |
| Internalizing Problems | 48.6 | 9.6 | 46.7 | 9.9 | .81 | .82 | −0.19 |
| Inattention/Hyperactivity | 47.6 | 9.2 | 48.0 | 10.2 | .79 | .82 | 0.04 |
| Emotional Symptoms | 49.1 | 9.5 | 47.3 | 9.8 | .82 | .84 | −0.19 |
| Personal Adjustment | 50.1 | 10.1 | 51.1 | 10.1 | .77 | .77 | 0.10 |
| **Clinical scale** | | | | | | | |
| Attitude to School | 50.7 | 10.2 | 49.3 | 9.4 | .84 | .83 | −0.14 |
| Attitude to Teachers | 49.4 | 9.1 | 49.0 | 8.7 | .77 | .81 | −0.04 |
| Atypicality | 48.7 | 9.4 | 47.1 | 9.3 | .75 | .78 | −0.17 |
| Locus of Control | 48.3 | 10.2 | 46.7 | 9.8 | .75 | .74 | −0.16 |
| Social Stress | 48.9 | 10.5 | 47.3 | 9.5 | .82 | .80 | −0.16 |
| Anxiety | 49.0 | 9.6 | 46.8 | 10.1 | .76 | .78 | −0.22 |
| Depression | 48.8 | 9.4 | 48.2 | 9.4 | .76 | .79 | −0.06 |
| Sense of Inadequacy | 49.3 | 8.6 | 47.8 | 10.3 | .44 | .59 | −0.16 |
| Attention Problems | 48.4 | 9.0 | 48.1 | 9.6 | .75 | .80 | −0.03 |
| Hyperactivity | 47.6 | 9.3 | 48.3 | 10.3 | .74 | .78 | 0.07 |
| **Adaptive scale** | | | | | | | |
| Relations With Parents | 49.3 | 11.5 | 49.7 | 11.3 | .72 | .63 | 0.04 |
| Interpersonal Relations | 51.1 | 10.1 | 51.7 | 8.6 | .69 | .68 | 0.06 |
| Self-Esteem | 49.9 | 10.2 | 51.0 | 9.0 | .65 | .64 | 0.11 |
| Self-Reliance | 50.1 | 9.5 | 51.4 | 10.2 | .59 | .63 | 0.13 |
| **Clinical index** | | | | | | | |
| Functional Impairment Index | 48.4 | 9.0 | 47.9 | 10.3 | .75 | .80 | −0.05 |

**Table 11.9** SRP: Test–Retest Reliabilities of Composites, Scales, and Indexes, Adolescent

| | Adolescent | | | | | | |
| | First rating | | Second rating | | | Corrected | Standard |
| | Mean | SD | Mean | SD | r | r | difference |
|---|---|---|---|---|---|---|---|
| **Composite** | | | | | | | |
| School Problems | 48.2 | 10.0 | 47.6 | 10.0 | .89 | .89 | −0.06 |
| Internalizing Problems | 49.9 | 11.2 | 49.2 | 10.3 | .89 | .86 | −0.07 |
| Inattention/Hyperactivity | 48.7 | 9.7 | 48.8 | 9.5 | .89 | .90 | 0.01 |
| Emotional Symptoms | 49.3 | 11.0 | 49.0 | 11.1 | .91 | .89 | −0.03 |
| Personal Adjustment | 51.9 | 10.3 | 51.6 | 10.6 | .88 | .87 | −0.03 |
| **Clinical scale** | | | | | | | |
| Attitude to School | 48.6 | 9.8 | 48.4 | 10.4 | .82 | .83 | −0.02 |
| Attitude to Teachers | 47.7 | 10.5 | 47.5 | 10.3 | .86 | .85 | −0.02 |
| Sensation Seeking | 49.6 | 10.1 | 48.7 | 9.4 | .85 | .85 | −0.09 |
| Atypicality | 50.1 | 11.1 | 49.6 | 9.9 | .82 | .78 | −0.05 |
| Locus of Control | 49.5 | 10.6 | 48.0 | 9.6 | .80 | .78 | −0.15 |
| Social Stress | 50.0 | 11.5 | 49.9 | 10.7 | .85 | .80 | −0.01 |
| Anxiety | 51.1 | 10.3 | 50.0 | 10.1 | .82 | .81 | −0.11 |
| Depression | 49.5 | 11.2 | 50.0 | 11.0 | .88 | .85 | 0.05 |
| Sense of Inadequacy | 49.2 | 10.4 | 48.1 | 9.7 | .84 | .83 | −0.11 |
| Somatization | 50.1 | 10.8 | 49.9 | 10.6 | .82 | .79 | −0.02 |
| Attention Problems | 48.0 | 9.2 | 48.4 | 9.2 | .84 | .86 | 0.04 |
| Hyperactivity | 49.6 | 10.1 | 49.4 | 9.3 | .86 | .86 | −0.02 |
| **Adaptive scale** | | | | | | | |
| Relations With Parents | 51.8 | 9.8 | 52.2 | 9.7 | .81 | .82 | 0.04 |
| Interpersonal Relations | 50.9 | 11.1 | 50.1 | 11.3 | .88 | .85 | −0.07 |
| Self-Esteem | 50.3 | 10.5 | 50.1 | 11.3 | .87 | .86 | −0.02 |
| Self-Reliance | 53.0 | 8.6 | 52.7 | 8.4 | .73 | .80 | −0.04 |
| **Content scale** | | | | | | | |
| Anger Control | 50.2 | 11.1 | 49.4 | 9.5 | .79 | .74 | −0.08 |
| Ego Strength | 51.5 | 10.5 | 50.7 | 11.3 | .88 | .87 | −0.07 |
| Mania | 51.0 | 11.2 | 49.1 | 10.2 | .82 | .77 | −0.18 |
| Test Anxiety | 50.6 | 11.3 | 49.0 | 10.9 | .78 | .72 | −0.14 |
| **Clinical index** | | | | | | | |
| Functional Impairment Index | 49.2 | 10.7 | 48.8 | 10.8 | .87 | .85 | −0.04 |

**Table 11.10** SRP: Test–Retest Reliabilities of Composites and Scales, College

| | College | | | | | | |
|---|---|---|---|---|---|---|---|
| | First rating | | Second rating | | | Corrected | Standard |
| | Mean | SD | Mean | SD | r | r | difference |
| **Composite** | | | | | | | |
| Internalizing Problems | 47.6 | 8.7 | 47.3 | 10.1 | .90 | .92 | −0.03 |
| Inattention/Hyperactivity | 49.4 | 10.6 | 48.8 | 10.8 | .83 | .81 | −0.06 |
| Emotional Symptoms | 47.6 | 9.3 | 47.4 | 10.9 | .92 | .93 | −0.02 |
| Personal Adjustment | 52.7 | 9.2 | 52.6 | 10.4 | .89 | .91 | −0.01 |
| **Clinical scale** | | | | | | | |
| Atypicality | 48.7 | 10.3 | 48.3 | 9.9 | .80 | .79 | −0.04 |
| Locus of Control | 46.9 | 8.8 | 47.3 | 9.7 | .88 | .91 | 0.04 |
| Social Stress | 48.1 | 9.4 | 47.2 | 10.1 | .87 | .89 | −0.09 |
| Anxiety | 48.3 | 8.8 | 47.3 | 9.8 | .89 | .91 | −0.11 |
| Depression | 47.8 | 8.1 | 48.0 | 10.2 | .76 | .84 | 0.02 |
| Sense of Inadequacy | 48.2 | 9.8 | 48.1 | 10.5 | .81 | .82 | −0.01 |
| Somatization | 48.2 | 7.6 | 47.8 | 8.3 | .78 | .87 | −0.05 |
| Attention Problems | 48.6 | 10.2 | 49.0 | 10.9 | .85 | .84 | 0.04 |
| Hyperactivity | 50.3 | 10.6 | 48.6 | 10.5 | .79 | .76 | −0.16 |
| Sensation Seeking | 49.6 | 10.0 | 48.1 | 9.7 | .84 | .84 | −0.15 |
| Alcohol Abuse | 49.5 | 10.4 | 49.6 | 10.8 | .92 | .91 | 0.01 |
| School Maladjustment | 50.0 | 11.4 | 49.7 | 11.3 | .88 | .84 | −0.03 |
| **Adaptive scale** | | | | | | | |
| Relations With Parents | 52.7 | 8.8 | 53.4 | 7.9 | .77 | .82 | 0.08 |
| Interpersonal Relations | 52.0 | 9.1 | 51.4 | 10.0 | .88 | .90 | −0.06 |
| Self-Esteem | 51.0 | 9.9 | 50.2 | 10.8 | .89 | .89 | −0.08 |
| Self-Reliance | 53.2 | 9.6 | 53.4 | 10.8 | .82 | .83 | 0.02 |
| **Content scale** | | | | | | | |
| Anger Control | 48.5 | 9.8 | 48.5 | 10.0 | .72 | .73 | 0.00 |
| Ego Strength | 51.1 | 10.3 | 51.1 | 11.1 | .79 | .78 | 0.00 |
| Mania | 49.9 | 10.0 | 47.8 | 10.6 | .74 | .74 | −0.20 |
| Test Anxiety | 48.9 | 10.0 | 48.9 | 10.5 | .87 | .87 | 0.00 |

## STANDARD ERRORS OF MEASUREMENT AND CONFIDENCE INTERVALS

The standard error of measurement (SEM) of a test score represents the average amount by which observed scores differ from true scores. The true score, which can never be known with certainty, is the score that would be obtained with a perfectly accurate measuring instrument. The SEM, therefore, helps the clinician understand how much error is associated with any observed score. The SEMs in T-score units of each BASC–3 composite and scale (based on internal-consistency reliabilities) are presented in Table 11.11 for the SRP–I, Table 11.12 for the general norm samples, and in Table 11.13 for the clinical norm samples. Composite and scale scores with higher reliability coefficients have smaller SEMs; thus, the pattern of SEMs replicates the pattern of reliability coefficients shown in Tables 11.1 and 11.2. SEMs for composite scores are generally 3 or less, while SEMs for the other scale scores are generally under 5.

**Table 11.11** SRP–I: T-Score Total Score Standard Error of Measurement

| | Ages 6–7 | | |
|---|---|---|---|
| | Combined | Female | Male |
| Total Score | 1.25 | 1.24 | 1.28 |

# Table 11.12 SRP: T-Score Standard Errors of Measurement of Composites, Scales, and Indexes, by Gender and Age, General Norm Samples

| | Child | | | Adolescent | | | | | | | College | | |
| | Ages 8–11 | | | Ages 12–14 | | | Ages 15–18 | | | Ages 12–18 | Ages 18–25 | | |
| | Combined | Female | Male | Combined | Female | Male | Combined | Female | Male | Combined total | Combined | Female | Male |
|---|---|---|---|---|---|---|---|---|---|---|---|---|---|
| **Composite** | | | | | | | | | | | | | |
| School Problems | 3.32 | 3.74 | 3.16 | 3.00 | 2.83 | 3.16 | 3.16 | 3.00 | 3.32 | 3.08 | — | — | — |
| Internalizing Problems | 2.24 | 1.73 | 2.45 | 2.00 | 2.00 | 2.24 | 1.73 | 1.73 | 2.00 | 1.87 | 1.73 | 1.73 | 2.00 |
| Inattention/Hyperactivity | 3.32 | 3.00 | 3.61 | 3.00 | 3.00 | 3.00 | 2.83 | 2.83 | 2.83 | 2.92 | 3.00 | 3.00 | 3.16 |
| Emotional Symptoms | 2.24 | 2.00 | 2.65 | 2.24 | 2.00 | 2.24 | 1.73 | 1.73 | 2.00 | 2.00 | 2.00 | 1.73 | 2.00 |
| Personal Adjustment | 2.65 | 2.83 | 2.65 | 2.65 | 2.45 | 2.65 | 2.45 | 2.45 | 2.45 | 2.55 | 2.45 | 2.45 | 2.65 |
| **Clinical scale** | | | | | | | | | | | | | |
| Attitude to School | 4.24 | 5.00 | 3.87 | 4.12 | 4.24 | 4.00 | 4.36 | 4.00 | 4.80 | 4.24 | — | — | — |
| Attitude to Teachers | 4.12 | 4.24 | 4.12 | 4.24 | 4.12 | 4.36 | 4.12 | 4.12 | 4.12 | 4.18 | — | — | — |
| Sensation Seeking | — | — | — | 4.00 | 3.87 | 4.12 | 3.87 | 4.12 | 3.74 | 3.94 | 3.61 | 3.87 | 3.46 |
| Atypicality | 3.74 | 3.46 | 4.00 | 4.00 | 3.87 | 4.12 | 4.12 | 4.24 | 4.00 | 4.06 | 4.36 | 4.47 | 4.12 |
| Locus of Control | 5.20 | 4.80 | 5.57 | 4.69 | 4.47 | 5.00 | 4.47 | 4.24 | 4.80 | 4.58 | 4.24 | 4.58 | 4.00 |
| Social Stress | 4.12 | 3.87 | 4.36 | 3.61 | 3.61 | 3.74 | 3.46 | 3.32 | 3.46 | 3.54 | 3.74 | 3.74 | 3.87 |
| Anxiety | 3.87 | 3.32 | 4.58 | 3.61 | 3.46 | 4.00 | 3.00 | 2.83 | 3.46 | 3.32 | 3.00 | 2.83 | 3.32 |
| Depression | 4.12 | 3.46 | 5.29 | 3.74 | 3.61 | 4.00 | 3.16 | 2.83 | 3.46 | 3.46 | 3.46 | 3.32 | 3.74 |
| Sense of Inadequacy | 4.90 | 4.36 | 5.48 | 4.24 | 4.00 | 4.36 | 4.00 | 3.61 | 4.36 | 4.12 | 3.87 | 3.74 | 4.12 |
| Somatization | — | — | — | 5.39 | 5.29 | 5.57 | 4.24 | 4.12 | 4.47 | 4.85 | 4.58 | 4.58 | 5.10 |
| Attention Problems | 4.36 | 4.12 | 4.58 | 3.74 | 3.87 | 3.74 | 3.46 | 3.16 | 3.74 | 3.60 | 3.61 | 3.32 | 4.12 |
| Hyperactivity | 4.24 | 3.87 | 4.69 | 4.00 | 4.00 | 4.00 | 3.87 | 4.24 | 3.61 | 3.94 | 4.24 | 4.58 | 4.00 |
| Alcohol Abuse | — | — | — | — | — | — | — | — | — | — | 2.65 | 3.00 | 2.24 |
| School Maladjustment | — | — | — | — | — | — | — | — | — | — | 4.00 | 4.12 | 4.00 |
| **Adaptive scale** | | | | | | | | | | | | | |
| Relations With Parents | 3.61 | 3.74 | 3.46 | 3.16 | 3.16 | 3.16 | 3.16 | 3.00 | 3.32 | 3.16 | 3.00 | 2.83 | 3.16 |
| Interpersonal Relations | 4.36 | 4.47 | 4.36 | 4.36 | 4.36 | 4.36 | 4.00 | 3.61 | 4.69 | 4.18 | 4.12 | 4.12 | 4.24 |
| Self-Esteem | 4.69 | 4.36 | 4.90 | 4.24 | 4.00 | 4.47 | 3.61 | 3.32 | 4.12 | 3.94 | 3.46 | 3.32 | 3.87 |
| Self-Reliance | 5.00 | 5.20 | 4.80 | 4.24 | 4.36 | 4.24 | 4.24 | 4.90 | 3.74 | 4.24 | 4.69 | 4.36 | 5.00 |
| **Content scale** | | | | | | | | | | | | | |
| Anger Control | — | — | — | 4.12 | 4.12 | 4.12 | 4.24 | 4.36 | 4.00 | 4.18 | 4.12 | 4.47 | 3.74 |
| Ego Strength | — | — | — | 4.36 | 4.12 | 4.47 | 4.00 | 3.87 | 4.12 | 4.18 | 4.58 | 4.47 | 4.80 |
| Mania | — | — | — | 4.24 | 4.00 | 4.58 | 3.74 | 3.87 | 3.61 | 4.00 | 3.87 | 3.87 | 3.74 |
| Test Anxiety | — | — | — | 4.90 | 4.80 | 5.00 | 4.36 | 4.12 | 4.69 | 4.64 | 4.00 | 4.24 | 3.74 |
| **Clinical index** | | | | | | | | | | | | | |
| Functional Impairment Index | 3.87 | 3.46 | 4.24 | 3.61 | 3.32 | 3.87 | 3.32 | 3.16 | 3.46 | 3.47 | — | — | — |

**Table 11.13** SRP: *T*-Score Standard Errors of Measurement of Composites, Scales, and Indexes, by Gender and Form Level, Clinical Norm Samples

| | Child | | | | | | Adolescent | | | | | | Ages 19–21 |
| | All clinical | | | ADHD | | | All clinical | | | ADHD | | | |
| | Combined | Female | Male | Combined | Female | Male | Combined | Female | Male | Combined | Female | Male | Combined |
|---|---|---|---|---|---|---|---|---|---|---|---|---|---|
| **Composite** | | | | | | | | | | | | | |
| School Problems | 3.16 | 2.83 | 3.32 | 3.16 | 3.61 | 3.00 | 3.00 | 3.32 | 3.00 | 3.00 | 2.83 | 3.00 | 3.87 |
| Internalizing Problems | 2.24 | 2.00 | 2.24 | 2.24 | 2.00 | 2.45 | 2.00 | 1.73 | 2.00 | 2.00 | 2.24 | 2.00 | 2.00 |
| Inattention/Hyperactivity | 3.16 | 3.16 | 3.16 | 3.32 | 3.87 | 3.16 | 3.00 | 3.16 | 3.16 | 3.00 | 3.32 | 3.00 | 3.32 |
| Emotional Symptoms | 2.45 | 2.00 | 2.65 | 2.65 | 2.00 | 2.83 | 2.00 | 2.00 | 2.24 | 2.00 | 1.73 | 2.00 | 2.24 |
| Personal Adjustment | 2.83 | 2.45 | 3.16 | 3.16 | 2.65 | 3.32 | 2.65 | 2.65 | 2.65 | 2.45 | 2.45 | 2.45 | 2.83 |
| **Clinical scale** | | | | | | | | | | | | | |
| Attitude to School | 3.74 | 3.46 | 3.87 | 3.87 | 4.58 | 3.74 | 4.00 | 4.12 | 3.87 | 3.74 | 3.87 | 3.74 | 6.56 |
| Attitude to Teachers | 4.12 | 3.46 | 4.36 | 3.87 | 3.74 | 3.87 | 3.87 | 4.12 | 3.87 | 3.74 | 3.61 | 3.74 | 4.47 |
| Sensation Seeking | — | — | — | — | — | — | 4.36 | 4.24 | 4.36 | 4.24 | 3.87 | 4.47 | 3.74 |
| Atypicality | 4.12 | 3.87 | 4.12 | 4.12 | 3.61 | 4.36 | 3.74 | 3.16 | 4.12 | 4.47 | 7.35 | 4.12 | 4.24 |
| Locus of Control | 5.00 | 4.58 | 5.29 | 5.29 | 4.47 | 5.74 | 4.80 | 4.80 | 4.80 | 5.10 | 5.10 | 5.10 | 4.58 |
| Social Stress | 4.24 | 4.00 | 4.47 | 4.00 | 3.87 | 4.12 | 3.46 | 3.16 | 3.61 | 3.32 | 3.00 | 3.46 | 3.74 |
| Anxiety | 4.00 | 3.61 | 4.12 | 4.24 | 3.61 | 4.47 | 3.32 | 3.00 | 3.61 | 3.16 | 2.45 | 3.46 | 3.00 |
| Depression | 4.12 | 3.46 | 4.36 | 4.12 | 3.32 | 4.47 | 3.46 | 3.16 | 3.74 | 3.46 | 3.00 | 3.61 | 3.00 |
| Sense of Inadequacy | 4.80 | 4.47 | 4.90 | 4.80 | 5.00 | 4.69 | 4.47 | 4.12 | 4.69 | 4.36 | 3.74 | 4.47 | 5.00 |
| Somatization | — | — | — | — | — | — | 4.58 | 4.58 | 4.90 | 4.80 | 4.80 | 4.80 | 4.36 |
| Attention Problems | 4.24 | 4.36 | 4.24 | 4.47 | 5.66 | 4.24 | 3.87 | 3.46 | 4.00 | 3.74 | 3.32 | 3.87 | 3.61 |
| Hyperactivity | 4.12 | 4.00 | 4.24 | 4.24 | 4.36 | 4.24 | 4.47 | 4.58 | 4.36 | 4.00 | 4.69 | 3.87 | 4.80 |
| **Adaptive scale** | | | | | | | | | | | | | |
| Relations With Parents | 3.87 | 3.32 | 4.12 | 4.12 | 3.32 | 4.36 | 3.00 | 3.32 | 3.00 | 2.83 | 2.83 | 3.00 | 3.46 |
| Interpersonal Relations | 4.00 | 3.87 | 4.12 | 4.24 | 4.47 | 4.12 | 3.87 | 3.61 | 4.00 | 3.74 | 3.32 | 3.74 | 3.74 |
| Self-Esteem | 5.00 | 4.12 | 5.57 | 5.10 | 4.47 | 5.39 | 3.74 | 3.16 | 4.36 | 3.46 | 2.83 | 3.87 | 4.00 |
| Self-Reliance | 5.10 | 4.58 | 5.39 | 6.24 | 5.00 | 6.63 | 4.69 | 4.80 | 4.58 | 4.58 | 5.20 | 4.47 | 4.90 |
| **Content scale** | | | | | | | | | | | | | |
| Anger Control | — | — | — | — | — | — | 3.74 | 4.00 | 3.74 | 3.74 | 4.47 | 3.46 | 4.58 |
| Ego Strength | — | — | — | — | — | — | 3.87 | 3.61 | 4.12 | 3.87 | 3.32 | 4.12 | 3.87 |
| Mania | — | — | — | — | — | — | 4.47 | 4.58 | 4.36 | 3.87 | 4.47 | 3.87 | 4.58 |
| Test Anxiety | — | — | — | — | — | — | 4.80 | 4.47 | 5.00 | 4.47 | 3.61 | 4.80 | 5.20 |
| **Clinical index** | | | | | | | | | | | | | |
| Functional Impairment Index | 3.74 | 3.61 | 3.87 | 4.00 | 4.69 | 3.74 | 3.74 | 3.61 | 3.87 | 3.46 | 3.74 | 3.46 | 4.12 |

As discussed in chapter 2, a confidence interval may be formed around the observed $T$ score to indicate, with a particular level of confidence (e.g., 90%), the range of $T$ scores within which the person's true score is likely to fall. This confidence interval is constructed using a multiple of the *SEM*. The resulting value is added to (and subtracted from) the observed $T$ score, forming 90% confidence intervals (see the bottom row of the norm tables presented in Appendix A).

# Evidence of Validity

Three types of evidence about the validity of the SRP as a measure of multiple behavioral constructs are discussed in this section. The first is the empirical support from scale intercorrelations and factor analysis for the grouping of scales into composites. The second is the pattern of correlations of SRP composite and scale scores with scores obtained on other behavior measures. The last consists of the SRP score profiles of groups of children with particular clinical diagnoses or educational classifications. Additional validity evidence related to test content (i.e., item development and selection) is presented in chapter 7.

## EVIDENCE BASED ON INTERNAL STRUCTURE

One way of evaluating how well a scale measures the dimensions it is designed to measure is to see whether its correlations with other scale scores reflect the current scientific understanding of behavioral dimensions. Tables 11.14 through 11.16 show the intercorrelations of scale scores at each age level of the general and clinical norm samples. Within each SRP age level, the pattern and magnitude of scale score correlations are very similar between the general and clinical samples. As expected, correlations of scores within clinical scales and adaptive scales are positive, whereas correlations of scores between clinical and adaptive scales are negative.

**Table 11.14** SRP–C: Intercorrelation of Composites, Scales, and Indexes, General and Clinical Norm Samples

| | Composite | | | | | Clinical scale | | | | | | | | | |
|---|---|---|---|---|---|---|---|---|---|---|---|---|---|---|---|
| | School Problems | Internalizing Problems | Inattention/ Hyperactivity | Emotional Symptoms | Personal Adjustment | Attitude to School | Attitude to Teachers | Atypicality | Locus of Control | Social Stress | Anxiety | Depression | Sense of Inadequacy | Attention Problems | Hyperactivity |
| **Composite** | | | | | | | | | | | | | | | |
| School Problems | — | .49 | .49 | .55 | -.58 | .88 | .88 | .19 | .50 | .42 | .32 | .42 | .56 | .50 | .43 |
| Internalizing Problems | .56 | — | .60 | .93 | -.67 | .41 | .45 | .74 | .84 | .84 | .83 | .87 | .82 | .56 | .56 |
| Inattention/Hyperactivity | .61 | .63 | — | .60 | -.49 | .44 | .43 | .36 | .56 | .46 | .47 | .46 | .65 | .94 | .94 |
| Emotional Symptoms | .58 | .94 | .62 | — | -.85 | .43 | .53 | .56 | .74 | .85 | .76 | .86 | .82 | .59 | .54 |
| Personal Adjustment | -.60 | -.69 | -.48 | -.84 | — | -.42 | -.60 | -.33 | -.60 | -.66 | -.45 | -.68 | -.59 | -.52 | -.39 |
| **Clinical scale** | | | | | | | | | | | | | | | |
| Attitude to School | .88 | .48 | .54 | .48 | -.48 | — | .55 | .19 | .42 | .32 | .27 | .35 | .47 | .42 | .41 |
| Attitude to Teachers | .88 | .50 | .54 | .54 | -.59 | .56 | — | .15 | .47 | .43 | .30 | .39 | .52 | .46 | .35 |
| Atypicality | .39 | .81 | .47 | .67 | -.44 | .36 | .32 | — | .50 | .53 | .65 | .52 | .44 | .28 | .38 |
| Locus of Control | .53 | .84 | .55 | .74 | -.64 | .45 | .48 | .62 | — | .63 | .56 | .76 | .69 | .55 | .50 |
| Social Stress | .48 | .87 | .50 | .85 | -.66 | .41 | .44 | .68 | .67 | — | .61 | .74 | .63 | .41 | .45 |
| Anxiety | .42 | .82 | .51 | .78 | -.46 | .37 | .37 | .63 | .59 | .63 | — | .63 | .61 | .41 | .47 |
| Depression | .44 | .88 | .46 | .87 | -.70 | .37 | .39 | .64 | .75 | .78 | .62 | — | .66 | .46 | .40 |
| Sense of Inadequacy | .54 | .80 | .68 | .81 | -.57 | .47 | .49 | .53 | .59 | .63 | .63 | .63 | — | .65 | .56 |
| Attention Problems | .61 | .57 | .93 | .60 | -.52 | .53 | .54 | .37 | .52 | .44 | .42 | .46 | .66 | — | .76 |
| Hyperactivity | .52 | .60 | .93 | .54 | -.36 | .48 | .45 | .50 | .49 | .49 | .52 | .40 | .59 | .72 | — |
| **Adaptive scale** | | | | | | | | | | | | | | | |
| Relations With Parents | -.60 | -.52 | -.39 | -.60 | .83 | -.47 | -.60 | -.30 | -.56 | -.46 | -.32 | -.51 | -.45 | -.43 | -.29 |
| Interpersonal Relations | -.50 | -.68 | -.39 | -.74 | .85 | -.42 | -.47 | -.47 | -.61 | -.71 | -.41 | -.71 | -.50 | -.41 | -.31 |
| Self-Esteem | -.42 | -.64 | -.36 | -.78 | .80 | -.36 | -.38 | -.40 | -.55 | -.60 | -.48 | -.67 | -.49 | -.38 | -.29 |
| Self-Reliance | -.44 | -.43 | -.40 | -.63 | .79 | -.30 | -.48 | -.26 | -.37 | -.40 | -.31 | -.40 | -.42 | -.47 | -.27 |
| **Clinical index** | | | | | | | | | | | | | | | |
| Functional Impairment Index | .63 | .86 | .88 | .84 | -.65 | .55 | .55 | .65 | .72 | .74 | .67 | .70 | .81 | .83 | .81 |

**Table 11.14** SRP–C: Intercorrelation of Composites, Scales, and Indexes, General and Clinical Norm Samples *(continued)*

| | Adaptive scale | | | | Clinical index |
| --- | --- | --- | --- | --- | --- |
| | Relations With Parents | Interpersonal Relations | Self-Esteem | Self-Reliance | Functional Impairment Index |
| **Composite** | | | | | |
| School Problems | –.46 | –.52 | –.39 | –.47 | .58 |
| Internalizing Problems | –.42 | –.71 | –.57 | –.43 | .84 |
| Inattention/Hyperactivity | –.30 | –.44 | –.32 | –.49 | .87 |
| Emotional Symptoms | –.51 | –.79 | –.74 | –.66 | .84 |
| Personal Adjustment | .76 | .82 | .80 | .81 | –.66 |
| **Clinical scale** | | | | | |
| Attitude to School | –.30 | –.41 | –.33 | –.30 | .51 |
| Attitude to Teachers | –.51 | –.51 | –.36 | –.52 | .51 |
| Atypicality | –.17 | –.39 | –.33 | –.16 | .56 |
| Locus of Control | –.49 | –.57 | –.51 | –.35 | .70 |
| Social Stress | –.33 | –.78 | –.56 | –.44 | .70 |
| Anxiety | –.27 | –.47 | –.41 | –.28 | .66 |
| Depression | –.44 | –.71 | –.58 | –.43 | .70 |
| Sense of Inadequacy | –.35 | –.57 | –.45 | –.49 | .83 |
| Attention Problems | –.35 | –.44 | –.32 | –.55 | .82 |
| Hyperactivity | –.21 | –.39 | –.27 | –.37 | .80 |
| **Adaptive scale** | | | | | |
| Relations With Parents | — | .43 | .43 | .56 | –.38 |
| Interpersonal Relations | .61 | — | .63 | .54 | –.66 |
| Self-Esteem | .51 | .64 | — | .48 | –.49 |
| Self-Reliance | .59 | .52 | .46 | — | –.58 |
| **Clinical index** | | | | | |
| Functional Impairment Index | –.49 | –.59 | –.54 | –.50 | — |

| | Composite | | | | | Clinical scale | | | | | | | | | | | |
|---|---|---|---|---|---|---|---|---|---|---|---|---|---|---|---|---|---|
| | School Problems | Internalizing Problems | Inattention/Hyper-activity | Emotional Symptoms | Personal Adjustment | Attitude to School | Attitude to Teachers | Sensation Seeking | Atypicality | Locus of Control | Social Stress | Anxiety | Depression | Sense of Inadequacy | Soma-tization | Attention Problems | Hyper-activity |
| **Composite** | | | | | | | | | | | | | | | | | |
| School Problems | — | .45 | .45 | .42 | -.37 | .82 | .81 | .67 | .38 | .46 | .34 | .26 | .37 | .43 | .26 | .43 | .40 |
| Internalizing Problems | .58 | — | .48 | .92 | -.64 | .42 | .34 | .27 | .80 | .76 | .88 | .82 | .89 | .77 | .71 | .47 | .41 |
| Inattention/Hyperactivity | .56 | .60 | — | .47 | -.32 | .40 | .33 | .32 | .43 | .39 | .40 | .39 | .35 | .49 | .28 | .91 | .91 |
| Emotional Symptoms | .56 | .93 | .54 | — | -.83 | .45 | .39 | .11 | .66 | .65 | .86 | .74 | .89 | .81 | .56 | .49 | .36 |
| Personal Adjustment | -.51 | -.68 | -.38 | -.84 | — | -.43 | -.43 | .03 | -.46 | -.54 | -.65 | -.39 | -.67 | -.56 | -.36 | -.35 | -.24 |
| **Clinical scale** | | | | | | | | | | | | | | | | | |
| Attitude to School | .82 | .58 | .51 | .61 | -.55 | — | .61 | .29 | .33 | .38 | .36 | .25 | .40 | .42 | .21 | .42 | .31 |
| Attitude to Teachers | .81 | .49 | .39 | .53 | -.57 | .60 | — | .26 | .23 | .35 | .27 | .18 | .31 | .37 | .20 | .33 | .28 |
| Sensation Seeking | .68 | .27 | .41 | .16 | -.06 | .30 | .29 | — | .32 | .33 | .16 | .17 | .15 | .20 | .19 | .23 | .35 |
| Atypicality | .51 | .79 | .57 | .65 | -.45 | .46 | .37 | .36 | — | .54 | .68 | .65 | .64 | .49 | .53 | .35 | .43 |
| Locus of Control | .52 | .78 | .52 | .69 | -.56 | .49 | .45 | .26 | .55 | — | .63 | .49 | .64 | .58 | .37 | .38 | .33 |
| Social Stress | .50 | .87 | .52 | .84 | -.65 | .50 | .42 | .25 | .69 | .65 | — | .69 | .82 | .64 | .53 | .40 | .32 |
| Anxiety | .36 | .81 | .46 | .75 | -.43 | .39 | .28 | .16 | .62 | .52 | .63 | — | .66 | .53 | .59 | .37 | .35 |
| Depression | .47 | .87 | .41 | .89 | -.70 | .53 | .43 | .13 | .59 | .64 | .79 | .64 | — | .68 | .56 | .38 | .26 |
| Sense of Inadequacy | .54 | .82 | .57 | .84 | -.61 | .57 | .48 | .19 | .58 | .66 | .64 | .60 | .71 | — | .39 | .53 | .37 |
| Somatization | .37 | .69 | .34 | .58 | -.43 | .36 | .31 | .17 | .45 | .37 | .52 | .55 | .56 | .46 | — | .23 | .28 |
| Attention Problems | .54 | .58 | .92 | .57 | -.45 | .54 | .42 | .30 | .49 | .52 | .48 | .43 | .45 | .60 | .31 | — | .67 |
| Hyperactivity | .48 | .52 | .92 | .42 | -.25 | .40 | .30 | .44 | .55 | .43 | .46 | .42 | .31 | .44 | .31 | .69 | — |
| **Adaptive scale** | | | | | | | | | | | | | | | | | |
| Relations With Parents | -.50 | -.52 | -.31 | -.58 | .78 | -.46 | -.53 | -.16 | -.36 | -.56 | -.47 | -.28 | -.53 | -.43 | -.28 | -.35 | -.22 |
| Interpersonal Relations | -.40 | -.67 | -.33 | -.74 | .82 | -.46 | -.43 | -.04 | -.51 | -.47 | -.72 | -.46 | -.66 | -.54 | -.43 | -.36 | -.26 |
| Self-Esteem | -.38 | -.65 | -.30 | -.80 | .80 | -.44 | -.40 | -.05 | -.39 | -.45 | -.61 | -.52 | -.70 | -.54 | -.45 | -.36 | -.20 |
| Self-Reliance | -.32 | -.30 | -.25 | -.52 | .74 | -.38 | -.43 | .06 | -.18 | -.28 | -.24 | -.10 | -.30 | -.40 | -.17 | -.33 | -.12 |
| **Content scale** | | | | | | | | | | | | | | | | | |
| Anger Control | .62 | .79 | .62 | .71 | -.52 | .56 | .51 | .37 | .68 | .72 | .67 | .65 | .64 | .64 | .47 | .57 | .57 |
| Ego Strength | -.51 | -.67 | -.34 | -.81 | .92 | -.55 | -.56 | -.08 | -.45 | -.54 | -.62 | -.45 | -.72 | -.59 | -.44 | -.39 | -.24 |
| Mania | .56 | .70 | .77 | .57 | -.34 | .45 | .36 | .49 | .73 | .53 | .60 | .62 | .47 | .53 | .43 | .63 | .78 |
| Test Anxiety | .42 | .59 | .46 | .57 | -.34 | .50 | .34 | .14 | .43 | .42 | .45 | .60 | .42 | .65 | .39 | .47 | .38 |
| **Clinical index** | | | | | | | | | | | | | | | | | |
| Functional Impairment Index | .62 | .90 | .77 | .88 | -.67 | .64 | .52 | .27 | .71 | .66 | .76 | .74 | .76 | .81 | .62 | .77 | .65 |

**Table 11.15** SRP–A: Intercorrelation of Composites, Scales, and Indexes, General and Clinical Norm Samples (*continued*)

| | Adaptive scale | | | | Content scale | | | | Clinical index |
|---|---|---|---|---|---|---|---|---|---|
| | Relations With Parents | Interpersonal Relations | Self-Esteem | Self-Reliance | Anger Control | Ego Strength | Mania | Test Anxiety | Functional Impairment Index |
| **Composite** | | | | | | | | | |
| School Problems | -.34 | -.30 | -.35 | -.13 | .54 | -.41 | .45 | .33 | .51 |
| Internalizing Problems | -.45 | -.71 | -.65 | -.15 | .75 | -.66 | .61 | .43 | .87 |
| Inattention/Hyperactivity | -.16 | -.32 | -.31 | -.19 | .49 | -.29 | .73 | .27 | .73 |
| Emotional Symptoms | -.50 | -.78 | -.80 | -.43 | .65 | -.80 | .49 | .45 | .86 |
| Personal Adjustment | .76 | .80 | .80 | .67 | -.49 | .91 | -.28 | -.24 | -.62 |
| **Clinical scale** | | | | | | | | | |
| Attitude to School | -.33 | -.38 | -.36 | -.25 | .49 | -.42 | .35 | .36 | .50 |
| Attitude to Teachers | -.38 | -.31 | -.37 | -.28 | .38 | -.45 | .27 | .26 | .39 |
| Sensation Seeking | -.08 | .00 | -.06 | .23 | .36 | -.05 | .42 | .14 | .27 |
| Atypicality | -.29 | -.58 | -.41 | -.12 | .69 | -.49 | .63 | .28 | .72 |
| Locus of Control | -.57 | -.48 | -.45 | -.16 | .67 | -.53 | .47 | .28 | .60 |
| Social Stress | -.43 | -.77 | -.61 | -.16 | .66 | -.63 | .50 | .34 | .74 |
| Anxiety | -.19 | -.54 | -.50 | .03 | .63 | -.43 | .57 | .47 | .74 |
| Depression | -.47 | -.70 | -.67 | -.19 | .61 | -.68 | .43 | .28 | .76 |
| Sense of Inadequacy | -.35 | -.53 | -.54 | -.30 | .52 | -.55 | .44 | .55 | .75 |
| Somatization | -.23 | -.42 | -.47 | .02 | .46 | -.42 | .38 | .25 | .61 |
| Attention Problems | -.18 | -.32 | -.35 | -.22 | .46 | -.32 | .59 | .30 | .71 |
| Hyperactivity | -.12 | -.27 | -.22 | -.13 | .44 | -.20 | .75 | .19 | .62 |
| **Adaptive scale** | | | | | | | | | |
| Relations With Parents | — | .47 | .50 | .34 | -.41 | .68 | -.20 | -.06 | -.33 |
| Interpersonal Relations | .49 | — | .60 | .38 | -.52 | .73 | -.38 | -.27 | -.66 |
| Self-Esteem | .50 | .62 | — | .32 | -.42 | .84 | -.30 | -.25 | -.60 |
| Self-Reliance | .46 | .47 | .38 | — | -.12 | .50 | .00 | -.15 | -.29 |
| **Content scale** | | | | | | | | | |
| Anger Control | -.46 | -.50 | -.43 | -.24 | — | -.52 | .54 | .32 | .69 |
| Ego Strength | .70 | .77 | .82 | .58 | -.52 | — | -.29 | -.20 | -.60 |
| Mania | -.30 | -.36 | -.33 | -.08 | .65 | -.34 | — | .24 | .70 |
| Test Anxiety | -.20 | -.32 | -.32 | -.21 | .48 | -.31 | .45 | — | .49 |
| **Clinical index** | | | | | | | | | |
| Functional Impairment Index | -.47 | -.62 | -.60 | -.41 | .74 | -.64 | .73 | .66 | — |

**Table 11.16** SRP–COL: Intercorrelation of Composites and Scales, General Norm Samples

| | Composite | | | | Clinical scale | | | | | | | | | | | |
|---|---|---|---|---|---|---|---|---|---|---|---|---|---|---|---|---|
| | Internalizing Problems | Inattention/ Hyperactivity | Emotional Symptoms | Personal Adjustment | Atypicality | Locus of Control | Social Stress | Anxiety | Depression | Sense of Inadequacy | Somatization | Attention Problems | Hyperactivity | Sensation Seeking | Alcohol Abuse | School Maladjustment |
| **Composite** | | | | | | | | | | | | | | | | |
| Internalizing Problems | — | — | — | — | — | — | — | — | — | — | — | — | — | — | — | — |
| Inattention/Hyperactivity | .57 | — | — | — | — | — | — | — | — | — | — | — | — | — | — | — |
| Emotional Symptoms | .93 | .51 | — | — | — | — | — | — | — | — | — | — | — | — | — | — |
| Personal Adjustment | -.70 | -.39 | -.85 | — | — | — | — | — | — | — | — | — | — | — | — | — |
| **Clinical scale** | | | | | | | | | | | | | | | | |
| Atypicality | .76 | .58 | .63 | -.44 | — | — | — | — | — | — | — | — | — | — | — | — |
| Locus of Control | .86 | .47 | .77 | -.59 | .59 | — | — | — | — | — | — | — | — | — | — | — |
| Social Stress | .88 | .50 | .89 | -.72 | .65 | .71 | — | — | — | — | — | — | — | — | — | — |
| Anxiety | .83 | .46 | .79 | -.54 | .56 | .66 | .68 | — | — | — | — | — | — | — | — | — |
| Depression | .89 | .42 | .89 | -.65 | .61 | .76 | .81 | .69 | — | — | — | — | — | — | — | — |
| Sense of Inadequacy | .83 | .52 | .85 | -.66 | .56 | .72 | .72 | .59 | .73 | — | — | — | — | — | — | — |
| Somatization | .65 | .31 | .52 | -.40 | .36 | .47 | .45 | .56 | .49 | .39 | — | — | — | — | — | — |
| Attention Problems | .57 | .92 | .57 | -.46 | .49 | .47 | .52 | .44 | .45 | .61 | .28 | — | — | — | — | — |
| Hyperactivity | .48 | .92 | .38 | -.27 | .59 | .39 | .41 | .40 | .33 | .36 | .29 | .69 | — | — | — | — |
| Sensation Seeking | .12 | .36 | .02 | .05 | .28 | .15 | .09 | .03 | .09 | .06 | -.05 | .29 | .37 | — | — | — |
| Alcohol Abuse | .38 | .33 | .33 | -.21 | .36 | .36 | .29 | .30 | .34 | .32 | .18 | .28 | .33 | .39 | — | — |
| School Maladjustment | .57 | .50 | .62 | -.55 | .39 | .50 | .54 | .46 | .56 | .58 | .24 | .57 | .35 | .20 | .35 | — |
| **Adaptive scale** | | | | | | | | | | | | | | | | |
| Relations With Parents | -.48 | -.31 | -.49 | .72 | -.35 | -.53 | -.42 | -.38 | -.39 | -.38 | -.32 | -.31 | -.26 | -.09 | -.20 | -.38 |
| Interpersonal Relations | -.60 | -.33 | -.72 | .84 | -.38 | -.45 | -.70 | -.43 | -.57 | -.58 | -.30 | -.39 | -.21 | .09 | -.12 | -.46 |
| Self-Esteem | -.68 | -.32 | -.82 | .77 | -.41 | -.52 | -.68 | -.61 | -.66 | -.59 | -.41 | -.38 | -.22 | .08 | -.20 | -.46 |
| Self-Reliance | -.43 | -.28 | -.63 | .79 | -.25 | -.35 | -.43 | -.27 | -.41 | -.52 | -.20 | -.37 | -.15 | .08 | -.13 | -.43 |
| **Content scale** | | | | | | | | | | | | | | | | |
| Anger Control | .68 | .55 | .60 | -.44 | .58 | .68 | .55 | .57 | .58 | .54 | .36 | .49 | .52 | .22 | .39 | .42 |
| Ego Strength | -.72 | -.37 | -.83 | .85 | -.47 | -.59 | -.71 | -.59 | -.68 | -.66 | -.44 | -.43 | -.25 | .02 | -.22 | -.52 |
| Mania | .66 | .76 | .55 | -.36 | .76 | .50 | .56 | .59 | .51 | .48 | .38 | .63 | .77 | .35 | .37 | .38 |
| Test Anxiety | .63 | .41 | .63 | -.48 | .38 | .54 | .49 | .58 | .52 | .69 | .40 | .47 | .28 | .04 | .24 | .52 |

**Table 11.16** SRP–COL: Intercorrelation of Composites and Scales, General Norm Samples *(continued)*

| | Adaptive scale | | | | Content scale | | | |
|---|---|---|---|---|---|---|---|---|
| | Relations With Parents | Interpersonal Relations | Self-Esteem | Self-Reliance | Anger Control | Ego Strength | Mania | Test Anxiety |
| **Composite** | | | | | | | | |
| Internalizing Problems | — | — | — | — | — | — | — | — |
| Inattention/Hyperactivity | — | — | — | — | — | — | — | — |
| Emotional Symptoms | — | — | — | — | — | — | — | — |
| Personal Adjustment | — | — | — | — | — | — | — | — |
| **Clinical scale** | | | | | | | | |
| Atypicality | — | — | — | — | — | — | — | — |
| Locus of Control | — | — | — | — | — | — | — | — |
| Social Stress | — | — | — | — | — | — | — | — |
| Anxiety | — | — | — | — | — | — | — | — |
| Depression | — | — | — | — | — | — | — | — |
| Sense of Inadequacy | — | — | — | — | — | — | — | — |
| Somatization | — | — | — | — | — | — | — | — |
| Attention Problems | — | — | — | — | — | — | — | — |
| Hyperactivity | — | — | — | — | — | — | — | — |
| Sensation Seeking | — | — | — | — | — | — | — | — |
| Alcohol Abuse | — | — | — | — | — | — | — | — |
| School Maladjustment | — | — | — | — | — | — | — | — |
| **Adaptive scale** | | | | | | | | |
| Relations With Parents | — | — | — | — | — | — | — | — |
| Interpersonal Relations | .44 | — | — | — | — | — | — | — |
| Self-Esteem | .39 | .58 | — | — | — | — | — | — |
| Self-Reliance | .42 | .62 | .42 | — | — | — | — | — |
| **Content scale** | | | | | | | | |
| Anger Control | -.39 | -.32 | -.38 | -.28 | — | — | — | — |
| Ego Strength | .55 | .71 | .85 | .56 | -.45 | — | — | — |
| Mania | -.32 | -.27 | -.36 | -.16 | .50 | -.39 | — | — |
| Test Anxiety | -.32 | -.38 | -.46 | -.34 | .40 | -.50 | .37 | — |

The SRP composites assess broader behavioral dimensions than those measured by the individual scales. These broad dimensions are evident in the correlations of scores among the scales. When scales correlate relatively highly, they are measuring a common dimension that is represented by the composite. Factor analysis is the statistical technique used in identifying these broad dimensions. This technique is important not only for providing construct validation of the composite scores but also for validating the scales themselves. The correlations between a scale score and the broad dimensions it measures are shown in factor analysis by the scale's loadings on higher-order factors (which correspond to composites).

The SRP composites were based partly on factor analyses of the scale intercorrelations at the child, adolescent, and college levels and on prevailing behavioral and psychological theory. For the child and adolescent levels, the correlations are derived from the entire item-development sample, which includes a greater proportion of clinical cases than is found in the general population. The item-development sample was used for factor analysis instead of the norm samples because the former more closely represents the population with whom the SRP is used—that is, children who receive services or who have been referred for evaluation of various behavioral, emotional, or educational difficulties. No clinical data were collected at the college level, so the SRP–COL factor analyses are based on the general norm sample.

Two types of factor analysis were performed in developing the composites. The primary technique was covariance structure analysis (CSA; also known as confirmatory factor analysis) using the Amos 6.0 program (Arbuckle, 2005). CSA has three important advantages for analyzing an instrument such as the BASC–3 SRP. First, there is a large research base (derived from the previous BASC editions and similar instruments) that points to a starting factor structure that can be tested in the analysis. Second, CSA works well with instruments, such as the SRP, for which some factors are expected to correlate highly. Third, CSA identifies which aspects of a hypothesized factor-structure model are inconsistent with the data. It is important to note that CSA was used not to confirm a hypothesized model but rather to evaluate the model and modify it in appropriate ways according to the results of the analysis.

The second type of factor analysis, principal-axis analysis, an exploratory factor-analytic method. The results of principal-axis analysis can be more difficult to compare across samples (especially when there are highly correlated factors) than those of CSA. However, if several principal-axis analyses point to an alternative structure, then that structure should be strongly considered. Thus, use of the principal-axis method complements CSA because it may reveal a substantially different factor structure not indicated by CSA.

## Covariance Structure Analyses

The starting CSAs models were based on the final SRP factor structure models reported in the BASC–2 Manual (Reynolds & Kamphaus, 2004). For each level, scale modification indexes (MIs) were examined to see if possible changes might be evident that would substantially improve the model's overall fit to the data. Scales with MI value loadings on other composite scales (relative to other modification indexes) were identified, and a new model fit was evaluated after adding a parameter between the scale and the composite. However, these changes to the model did not result in a substantial improvement in model fit. (Consistent with the BASC–2 analyses, fit was evaluated using the chi-square, Comparative Fit Index [CFI] and the Root Mean Squared Error of Approximation [RMSEA] fit indexes.) Therefore, the starting models for each level were retained. Fit indexes for each model are presented in Table 11.17, and standardized loadings and factor correlations for the models are presented in Table 11.18. The primary use of the fit indexes was to evaluate the potential model changes. The overall fit of the models is moderate, a finding that is consistent with analyses conducted on the previous BASC editions.

**Table 11.17** SRP: Fit of Various CSA Models (Item-Development Samples)

| Self-Report of Personality | df | $x^2$ | CFI | RMSEA |
|---|---|---|---|---|
| Child | 71 | 937.0 | 0.87 | 0.13 |
| Adolescent | 98 | 1,893.1 | 0.85 | 0.13 |
| College | 62 | 523.0 | 0.88 | 0.13 |

**Table 11.18** SRP: CSA Factor Loadings for the Final Models (Item-Development Samples)

| Scale | SRP–C | | | | SRP–A | | | | SRP–COL | | |
|---|---|---|---|---|---|---|---|---|---|---|---|
| | School Problems | Internalizing Problems | Inattention/ Hyperactivity | Personal Adjustment | School Problems | Internalizing Problems | Inattention/ Hyperactivity | Personal Adjustment | Internalizing Problems | Inattention/ Hyperactivity | Personal Adjustment |
| Attitude to School | .72 | — | — | — | .81 | — | — | — | — | — | — |
| Attitude to Teachers | .74 | — | — | — | .74 | — | — | — | — | — | — |
| Sensation Seeking | — | — | — | — | .37 | — | — | — | — | — | — |
| Atypicality | — | .70 | — | — | — | .74 | — | — | .68 | — | — |
| Locus of Control | — | .83 | — | — | — | .74 | — | — | .82 | — | — |
| Social Stress | — | .86 | — | — | — | .88 | — | — | .89 | — | — |
| Anxiety | — | .75 | — | — | — | .74 | — | — | .74 | — | — |
| Depression | — | .89 | — | — | — | .89 | — | — | .90 | — | — |
| Sense of Inadequacy | — | .79 | — | — | — | .81 | — | — | .84 | — | — |
| Somatization | — | — | — | — | — | .64 | — | — | .51 | — | — |
| Attention Problems | — | — | .89 | — | — | — | .89 | — | — | .99 | — |
| Hyperactivity | — | — | .85 | — | — | — | .77 | — | — | .68 | — |
| Relations With Parents | — | — | — | .68 | — | — | — | .65 | — | — | .58 |
| Interpersonal Relations | — | — | — | .84 | — | — | — | .81 | — | — | .81 |
| Self-Esteem | — | — | — | .74 | — | — | — | .78 | — | — | .77 |
| Self-Reliance | — | — | — | .63 | — | — | — | .49 | — | — | .65 |
| **Factor Correlations** | | | | | | | | | | | |
| Internalizing Problems | .71 | — | — | — | .68 | — | — | — | −.88 | — | — |
| Inattention/Hyperactivity | .76 | .74 | — | — | .68 | .64 | — | — | −.52 | .57 | — |
| Personal Adjustment | −.80 | −.88 | −.63 | — | −.75 | −.90 | −.50 | — | — | — | — |

## Principal-Axis Factor Analyses

Principal-axis factor analyses were carried out at each level of the SRP. Across the form levels, three- and four-factor solutions were obtained using oblique and orthogonal rotations; because the results were similar, only the orthogonal (Varimax) results are reported. Results of these analyses are reported for the child level in Table 11.19, for the adolescent level in Table 11.20, and for the college level in Table 11.21.

**Table 11.19** SRP–C: Principal-Axis Factor Matrix, Varimax Rotation

| Scale | 3-factor | | | 4-factor | | | |
|---|---|---|---|---|---|---|---|
| | I | II | III | I | II | III | IV |
| Attitude to School | .26 | .41 | .43 | .31 | .34 | .12 | .48 |
| Attitude to Teachers | .16 | .60 | .36 | .18 | .27 | .20 | .68 |
| Atypicality | .70 | .06 | .31 | .74 | .20 | .13 | .11 |
| Locus of Control | .63 | .39 | .35 | .65 | .24 | .27 | .40 |
| Social Stress | .77 | .36 | .24 | .68 | .22 | .49 | .18 |
| Anxiety | .69 | .12 | .39 | .71 | .30 | .18 | .14 |
| Depression | .76 | .42 | .21 | .66 | .19 | .52 | .24 |
| Sense of Inadequacy | .51 | .34 | .56 | .51 | .52 | .29 | .28 |
| Attention Problems | .23 | .39 | .77 | .23 | .84 | .24 | .30 |
| Hyperactivity | .35 | .16 | .76 | .44 | .68 | .06 | .21 |
| Relations With Parents | −.23 | −.73 | −.16 | −.16 | −.12 | −.42 | −.64 |
| Interpersonal Relations | −.60 | −.57 | −.11 | −.45 | −.14 | −.64 | −.30 |
| Self-Esteem | −.50 | −.52 | −.09 | −.37 | −.12 | −.56 | −.29 |
| Self-Reliance | −.16 | −.64 | −.28 | −.06 | −.35 | −.50 | −.42 |

**Table 11.20** SRP–A: Principal-Axis Factor Matrix, Varimax Rotation

| Scale | 3-factor | | | 4-factor | | | |
|---|---|---|---|---|---|---|---|
| | I | II | III | I | II | III | IV |
| Attitude to School | .29 | .55 | .38 | .31 | .35 | .51 | −.21 |
| Attitude to Teachers | .16 | .66 | .32 | .18 | .28 | .63 | −.24 |
| Sensation Seeking | .06 | .06 | .55 | .04 | .52 | .29 | .27 |
| Atypicality | .61 | .17 | .46 | .61 | .44 | .19 | −.03 |
| Locus of Control | .53 | .40 | .34 | .54 | .29 | .48 | .00 |
| Social Stress | .78 | .30 | .26 | .79 | .25 | .26 | −.12 |
| Anxiety | .79 | .03 | .24 | .79 | .24 | .03 | .01 |
| Depression | .82 | .37 | .13 | .83 | .10 | .35 | −.10 |
| Sense of Inadequacy | .61 | .42 | .33 | .62 | .32 | .34 | −.22 |
| Somatization | .63 | .13 | .18 | .63 | .17 | .12 | −.03 |
| Attention Problems | .29 | .32 | .64 | .30 | .67 | .20 | −.25 |
| Hyperactivity | .24 | .11 | .78 | .25 | .82 | .05 | −.10 |
| Relations With Parents | −.32 | −.63 | −.11 | −.33 | −.05 | −.65 | .19 |
| Interpersonal Relations | −.62 | −.50 | −.05 | −.65 | −.07 | −.28 | .41 |
| Self-Esteem | −.64 | −.45 | −.02 | −.65 | −.02 | −.35 | .24 |
| Self-Reliance | −.12 | −.65 | −.04 | −.12 | −.08 | −.36 | .71 |

**Table 11.21** SRP–COL: Principal-Axis Factor Matrix, Varimax Rotation

| Scale | 3-factor | | | 4-factor | | | |
|---|---|---|---|---|---|---|---|
| | I | II | III | I | II | III | IV |
| Atypicality | .52 | .21 | .52 | .53 | .21 | .37 | .34 |
| Locus of Control | .68 | .32 | .32 | .69 | .34 | .13 | .30 |
| Social Stress | .74 | .43 | .21 | .74 | .42 | .23 | .08 |
| Anxiety | .77 | .17 | .15 | .78 | .14 | .21 | .00 |
| Depression | .79 | .38 | .19 | .79 | .40 | .07 | .19 |
| Sense of Inadequacy | .61 | .51 | .26 | .61 | .51 | .22 | .14 |
| Somatization | .55 | .11 | .09 | .55 | .11 | .08 | .05 |
| Attention Problems | .24 | .44 | .62 | .23 | .41 | .67 | .23 |
| Hyperactivity | .19 | .15 | .69 | .18 | .07 | .82 | .28 |
| Sensation Seeking | −.09 | −.05 | .64 | −.10 | −.02 | .23 | .72 |
| Alcohol Abuse | .22 | .08 | .45 | .23 | .11 | .12 | .51 |
| School Maladjustment | .33 | .50 | .37 | .34 | .51 | .22 | .29 |
| Relations With Parents | −.32 | −.45 | −.21 | −.31 | −.46 | −.09 | −.20 |
| Interpersonal Relations | −.46 | −.68 | .00 | −.46 | −.65 | −.14 | .11 |
| Self-Esteem | −.65 | −.43 | .00 | −.64 | −.43 | −.06 | .04 |
| Self-Reliance | −.17 | −.79 | −.09 | −.17 | −.78 | −.10 | −.03 |

The principal-axis analyses generally support the factor structures derived using CSA and reflect the pattern of results found in the previous BASC editions. An internalizing-problems factor was indicated at all SRP age levels by the Anxiety, Social Stress, Depression, Locus of Control, Somatization, Atypicality, and Sense of Inadequacy scales. The Attitude to School and Attitude to Teachers scales pointed to a school-problems factor. The Attention Problems and Hyperactivity scales also formed a factor, which incorporates the Sensation Seeking scale at the adolescent level. A personal-adjustment factor emerged with moderate to strong loadings for the Relations With Parents, Interpersonal Relations, Self-Esteem, and Self-Reliance scales, although the Self-Esteem scale loads somewhat higher on the internalizing-problems factor on the adolescent level.

# CORRELATIONS WITH OTHER MEASURES OF BEHAVIOR

Several studies were carried out in which the SRP and another self-report scale were completed by the same child at about the same time. The correlations between scores on the two instruments indicate the degree to which the instruments measure the same behavioral dimensions. The fact that scales on different instruments have the same or similar names does not ensure that those scales measure the same construct; the scales may define the behavioral dimension differently. Thus, in interpreting the results of correlation studies, it is important to consider the item content of the scales on both instruments.

Demographic information about the samples used for the correlational studies is presented in Table 11.22 (see chapter 8 for a more complete description of the demographic characteristics). In each study, the BASC–3 SRP cases were scored using the general combined-gender norms; other tests were scored according to the choice of norms recommended in the test manuals for typical use. Each sample was collected from several sites and was composed primarily of children and adolescents from regular school settings or college students seeking a 2- or 4-year degree.

**Table 11.22** SRP: Demographic Characteristics of BASC-3 and Validity Studies

| Characteristic | SRP-I | | SRP-C | | | | | SRP-A | | | | SRP-COL | |
|---|---|---|---|---|---|---|---|---|---|---|---|---|---|
| | CDI 2 | RCMAS-2 | CDI 2 | Conners 3 | RCMAS-2 | ASEBA | BYI-Dep | BYI-Anx | Conners 3 | MMPI-A | D-REF | BYI-II | MMPI-2-RF |
| N | 54 | 72 | 110 | 41 | 39 | 60 | 56 | 57 | 56 | 39 | 33 | 53 | 61 |
| **Age** | | | | | | | | | | | | | |
| Mean | 7.5 | 7.1 | 9.9 | 10.0 | 9.7 | 14.6 | 14.8 | 14.9 | 14.8 | 15.9 | 15.2 | 20.9 | 21.1 |
| SD | 0.3 | 0.6 | 1.1 | 1.0 | 1.3 | 1.8 | 1.7 | 1.8 | 1.9 | 1.3 | 2.0 | 2.0 | 2.1 |
| Range | 6–7 | 6–7 | 8–11 | 8–11 | 8–11 | 12–18 | 12–18 | 12–18 | 12–18 | 14–18 | 12–18 | 18–25 | 18–25 |
| **Test interval** | | | | | | | | | | | | | |
| Mean | 8.9 | 4.7 | 6.7 | 20.2 | 17.9 | 9.7 | 22.4 | 14.3 | 7.7 | 15.7 | 9.7 | 7.8 | 8.5 |
| Range | 0–66 | 0–70 | 0–61 | 0–70 | 0–62 | 0–70 | 0–62 | 0–62 | 0–70 | 0–65 | 0–67 | 0–52 | 0–45 |
| **Mother's education level** | | | | | | | | | | | | | |
| 1 | 5.6 | 4.2 | 9.1 | 7.3 | 2.6 | 6.7 | 1.8 | 3.5 | 8.9 | — | 21.2 | 7.5 | 4.9 |
| 2 | 11.1 | 25.0 | 33.6 | 22.0 | 17.9 | 18.3 | 12.5 | 17.5 | 17.9 | 10.3 | 9.1 | 24.5 | 16.4 |
| 3 | 31.5 | 37.5 | 38.2 | 29.3 | 28.2 | 53.3 | 26.8 | 22.8 | 25.0 | 23.1 | 27.3 | 32.1 | 32.8 |
| 4 | 51.9 | 33.3 | 19.1 | 41.5 | 51.3 | 21.7 | 58.9 | 56.1 | 48.2 | 66.7 | 42.4 | 35.8 | 45.9 |
| **Race/ethnicity** | | | | | | | | | | | | | |
| African American | 5.6 | 11.1 | 6.4 | 29.3 | — | 11.7 | 10.7 | 10.5 | — | 5.1 | 15.2 | 9.4 | 11.5 |
| Asian | 1.9 | 1.4 | 3.6 | 7.3 | — | — | 1.8 | — | 5.4 | 2.6 | — | 7.5 | 6.6 |
| Hispanic | 13.0 | 13.9 | 8.2 | 48.8 | 7.7 | 20.0 | 10.7 | 10.5 | 17.9 | 7.7 | 36.4 | 11.3 | 6.6 |
| Other | 1.9 | 2.8 | 4.5 | 4.9 | 5.1 | 6.7 | — | 10.5 | 12.5 | 2.6 | — | 9.4 | 6.6 |
| White | 77.8 | 70.8 | 77.3 | 9.8 | 87.2 | 61.7 | 76.8 | 68.4 | 64.3 | 82.1 | 48.5 | 62.3 | 68.9 |
| **Region** | | | | | | | | | | | | | |
| Midwest | 11.1 | 22.2 | 8.2 | 9.8 | 10.3 | 13.3 | 16.1 | 26.3 | 23.2 | 17.9 | 21.2 | 41.5 | 27.9 |
| Northeast | 18.5 | 11.1 | 2.7 | 22.0 | 20.5 | 35.0 | 8.9 | 8.8 | 25.0 | 10.3 | 6.1 | 3.8 | 11.5 |
| South | 35.2 | 47.2 | 77.3 | 43.9 | 38.5 | 26.7 | 57.1 | 42.1 | 30.4 | 48.7 | 24.2 | 39.6 | 52.5 |
| West | 35.2 | 19.4 | 11.8 | 24.4 | 30.8 | 25.0 | 17.9 | 22.8 | 21.4 | 23.1 | 48.5 | 15.1 | 8.2 |
| **Gender** | | | | | | | | | | | | | |
| Female | 59.3 | 61.1 | 54.5 | 46.3 | 53.8 | 53.3 | 48.2 | 54.4 | 53.6 | 61.5 | 51.5 | 66.0 | 70.5 |
| Male | 40.7 | 38.9 | 45.5 | 53.7 | 46.2 | 46.7 | 51.8 | 45.6 | 46.4 | 38.5 | 48.5 | 34.0 | 29.5 |

## Behavior Assessment System for Children, Second Edition

As discussed in chapter 7, the BASC–3 standardization forms contained all of the items found on the BASC–2 forms, as well as newly written BASC–3 items. As such, correlations between the BASC–3 and BASC–2 scales can be derived using a large sample representative of the U.S. population (i.e., the BASC–3 general, combined-gender norms); see Table 11.23 for the scales from each SRP level. (Due to the substantial SRP–I changes between editions, the SRP–I was not included in this analysis.) As expected, correlations between the corresponding scale scores are extremely high. Overall, these results provide a sound basis for generalizing research done on the BASC–2 SRP to the BASC–3 SRP.

**Table 11.23** BASC–3 SRP: Correlations With the BASC–2 Self-Report of Personality, General Combined Norm Samples

| | BASC–2 | | |
| BASC–3 | SRP–C | SRP–A | SRP–COL |
|---|---|---|---|
| **Composite** | | | |
| School Problems | .98 | .95 | — |
| Internalizing Problems | .99 | .97 | .99 |
| Inattention/Hyperactivity | .98 | .97 | .98 |
| Emotional Symptoms | .99 | .97 | .99 |
| Personal Adjustment | .98 | .96 | .99 |
| **Clinical scale** | | | |
| Attitude to School | .98 | .98 | — |
| Attitude to Teachers | .95 | .92 | — |
| Sensation Seeking | — | .87 | .97 |
| Atypicality | .98 | .96 | .95 |
| Locus of Control | .96 | .97 | .98 |
| Social Stress | .99 | .99 | .95 |
| Anxiety | .97 | .97 | .98 |
| Depression | .93 | .93 | .94 |
| Sense of Inadequacy | .97 | .95 | .98 |
| Somatization | — | .84 | .82 |
| Attention Problems | .97 | .92 | .94 |
| Hyperactivity | .97 | .99 | .98 |
| Alcohol Abuse | — | — | .99 |
| School Maladjustment | — | — | .98 |
| **Adaptive scale** | | | |
| Relations With Parents | .97 | .98 | .99 |
| Interpersonal Relations | .87 | .93 | .96 |
| Self-Esteem | .96 | .93 | .96 |
| Self-Reliance | .99 | .94 | .95 |
| **Content scale** | | | |
| Anger Control | — | .88 | .89 |
| Ego Strength | — | .86 | .88 |
| Mania | — | .96 | .96 |
| Test Anxiety | — | .95 | .93 |

## Achenbach System of Empirically Based Assessment Youth Self-Report Form

The SRP–A and the Achenbach System of Empirically Based Assessment (ASEBA) Youth Self-Report Form (Achenbach & Rescorla, 2001) were completed by 60 adolescents ages 12 through 18 years. Correlations between the SRP and ASEBA composites and scales are shown in Table 11.24.

**Table 11.24** SRP–A: Correlations With the ASEBA Youth Self-Report

| BASC–3 | Syndrome scales | | | | | | | | | | |
|---|---|---|---|---|---|---|---|---|---|---|---|
| | Anxious/ Depressed | Withdrawn/ Depressed | Somatic Complaints | Social Problems | Thought Problems | Attention Problems Total | Rule-Breaking Behavior | Aggressive Behavior | Internalizing Problems | Externalizing Problems | Total Problems |
| **Composite** | | | | | | | | | | | |
| School Problems | .34 | .37 | .46 | .36 | .32 | .60 | .53 | .62 | .46 | .63 | .61 |
| Internalizing Problems | .62 | .65 | .80 | .63 | .47 | .59 | .50 | .59 | .76 | .60 | .78 |
| Inattention/Hyperactivity | .40 | .16 | .56 | .48 | .33 | .84 | .50 | .55 | .47 | .54 | .65 |
| Emotional Symptoms | .59 | .74 | .74 | .67 | .38 | .53 | .51 | .57 | .76 | .63 | .78 |
| Personal Adjustment | -.36 | -.66 | -.58 | -.59 | -.29 | -.49 | -.54 | -.59 | -.59 | -.62 | -.68 |
| **Clinical scale** | | | | | | | | | | | |
| Attitude to School | .38 | .44 | .41 | .41 | .31 | .54 | .42 | .58 | .46 | .56 | .58 |
| Attitude to Teachers | .28 | .35 | .47 | .35 | .32 | .48 | .51 | .55 | .44 | .58 | .57 |
| Sensation Seeking | .15 | .11 | .25 | .13 | .18 | .48 | .40 | .41 | .22 | .44 | .37 |
| Atypicality | .61 | .48 | .69 | .59 | .56 | .61 | .30 | .54 | .59 | .38 | .61 |
| Locus of Control | .48 | .56 | .66 | .47 | .46 | .65 | .54 | .68 | .60 | .62 | .69 |
| Social Stress | .58 | .65 | .65 | .71 | .48 | .49 | .48 | .44 | .68 | .59 | .74 |
| Anxiety | .50 | .52 | .64 | .35 | .30 | .26 | .24 | .18 | .66 | .34 | .55 |
| Depression | .63 | .72 | .71 | .69 | .43 | .47 | .42 | .58 | .72 | .54 | .71 |
| Sense of Inadequacy | .56 | .66 | .73 | .57 | .34 | .55 | .53 | .62 | .71 | .62 | .74 |
| Somatization | .45 | .40 | .73 | .50 | .29 | .57 | .55 | .54 | .59 | .57 | .66 |
| Attention Problems | .42 | .28 | .65 | .48 | .37 | .80 | .52 | .52 | .55 | .53 | .68 |
| Hyperactivity | .33 | .05 | .42 | .44 | .25 | .76 | .45 | .53 | .35 | .50 | .54 |
| **Adaptive scale** | | | | | | | | | | | |
| Relations With Parents | -.22 | -.50 | -.49 | -.40 | -.27 | -.46 | -.56 | -.65 | -.47 | -.59 | -.58 |
| Interpersonal Relations | -.32 | -.60 | -.46 | -.58 | -.30 | -.25 | -.30 | -.22 | -.52 | -.42 | -.54 |
| Self-Esteem | -.31 | -.55 | -.59 | -.56 | -.12 | -.39 | -.46 | -.42 | -.54 | -.50 | -.57 |
| Self-Reliance | -.39 | -.56 | -.34 | -.44 | -.33 | -.53 | -.44 | -.67 | -.44 | -.58 | -.58 |
| **Content scale** | | | | | | | | | | | |
| Anger Control | .53 | .49 | .63 | .58 | .39 | .69 | .50 | .71 | .61 | .67 | .74 |
| Ego Strength | -.32 | -.62 | -.52 | -.54 | -.22 | -.40 | -.55 | -.55 | -.56 | -.62 | -.63 |
| Mania | .41 | .25 | .67 | .43 | .49 | .67 | .42 | .43 | .54 | .47 | .64 |
| Test Anxiety | .40 | .36 | .50 | .22 | .18 | .21 | .04 | .08 | .47 | .15 | .37 |
| **Clinical index** | | | | | | | | | | | |
| Functional Impairment Index | .58 | .56 | .78 | .60 | .44 | .70 | .56 | .60 | .73 | .66 | .81 |
| **ASEBA mean** | 53.0 | 53.5 | 54.1 | 54.3 | 53.5 | 55.2 | 52.6 | 53.3 | 47.3 | 47.4 | 47.9 |
| **ASEBA SD** | 5.6 | 4.6 | 5.8 | 6.7 | 6.3 | 8.5 | 4.1 | 5.9 | 10.7 | 9.7 | 10.6 |

# Table 11.24 SRP–A: Correlations With the ASEBA Youth Self-Report (continued)

| BASC–3 | DSM-oriented scales | | | | | | BASC–3 | |
|---|---|---|---|---|---|---|---|---|
| | Affective Problems | Anxiety Problems | Somatic Problems | ADHD | Oppositional Defiant Problems | Conduct Problems | Mean | SD |
| **Composite** | | | | | | | | |
| School Problems | .47 | .18 | .50 | .55 | .61 | .57 | 51.7 | 11.5 |
| Internalizing Problems | .73 | .39 | .76 | .55 | .51 | .55 | 49.0 | 10.7 |
| Inattention/Hyperactivity | .42 | .18 | .52 | .80 | .41 | .55 | 48.9 | 10.0 |
| Emotional Symptoms | .74 | .34 | .71 | .49 | .53 | .59 | 48.5 | 10.2 |
| Personal Adjustment | −.58 | −.07 | −.65 | −.47 | −.48 | −.64 | 51.9 | 10.2 |
| **Clinical scale** | | | | | | | | |
| Attitude to School | .54 | .22 | .43 | .53 | .64 | .48 | 51.8 | 11.1 |
| Attitude to Teachers | .41 | .15 | .52 | .47 | .52 | .53 | 50.7 | 12.2 |
| Sensation Seeking | .20 | .04 | .28 | .40 | .35 | .40 | 51.5 | 9.1 |
| Atypicality | .55 | .37 | .69 | .52 | .34 | .41 | 50.0 | 11.3 |
| Locus of Control | .63 | .28 | .69 | .63 | .61 | .56 | 49.1 | 10.9 |
| Social Stress | .61 | .37 | .53 | .46 | .47 | .56 | 47.8 | 9.0 |
| Anxiety | .53 | .52 | .49 | .26 | .25 | .21 | 48.4 | 9.9 |
| Depression | .75 | .36 | .69 | .42 | .52 | .50 | 50.0 | 10.3 |
| Sense of Inadequacy | .73 | .34 | .72 | .52 | .58 | .59 | 49.3 | 9.7 |
| Somatization | .63 | .16 | .71 | .55 | .40 | .56 | 49.4 | 10.1 |
| Attention Problems | .47 | .28 | .55 | .74 | .37 | .56 | 48.1 | 9.3 |
| Hyperactivity | .34 | .10 | .45 | .75 | .40 | .49 | 49.8 | 10.4 |
| **Adaptive scale** | | | | | | | | |
| Relations With Parents | −.47 | .03 | −.61 | −.44 | −.53 | −.59 | 51.0 | 10.6 |
| Interpersonal Relations | −.43 | −.14 | −.39 | −.26 | −.20 | −.42 | 52.5 | 9.0 |
| Self-Esteem | −.50 | .01 | −.65 | −.38 | −.38 | −.52 | 52.0 | 11.1 |
| Self-Reliance | −.55 | −.22 | −.44 | −.46 | −.48 | −.59 | 50.2 | 8.6 |
| **Content scale** | | | | | | | | |
| Anger Control | .61 | .30 | .65 | .65 | .65 | .59 | 49.4 | 11.0 |
| Ego Strength | −.56 | −.06 | −.61 | −.39 | −.50 | −.62 | 51.2 | 10.9 |
| Mania | .38 | .28 | .61 | .63 | .31 | .41 | 50.4 | 10.3 |
| Test Anxiety | .40 | .44 | .36 | .18 | .05 | .08 | 48.8 | 9.8 |
| **Clinical index** | | | | | | | | |
| Functional Impairment Index | .68 | .39 | .71 | .67 | .55 | .62 | 48.8 | 10.2 |
| **ASEBA mean** | 53.6 | 52.0 | 54.2 | 55.0 | 53.6 | 53.5 | — | — |
| **ASEBA SD** | 5.0 | 4.6 | 6.6 | 6.8 | 5.3 | 5.2 | — | — |

The mean SRP scores indicate that overall the samples are about average with respect to their level of behavior problems and variability of scores. Generally, there are moderate or high correlations between the SRP clinical scale scores and conceptually similar ASEBA syndrome scale scores. Particularly high correlations are seen between scores for the Attention and Hyperactivity scales on the SRP and the Attention scale from the ASEBA. As expected, almost all the adaptive skills scale scores on the SRP are negatively correlated with the ASEBA syndrome and *DSM*-oriented scale scores.

## Conners 3 Self-Report Form

The SRP–C and SRP–A forms were filled out with the self-report form of the Conners 3 (Conners 3rd Edition; Conners, 2008) by 41 children ages 8 through 11 years and by 56 adolescents ages 12 through 18 years. Tables 11.25 and 11.26 show correlations between scores from the SRP and Conners scales.

The mean scores from the SRP scales indicate that overall the samples are about average with respect to their level of behavior problems and variability. Correlations between SRP and Conners self-report scale scores that measure similar constructs are generally higher than nonsimilar constructs across both SRP levels; the adolescent-level correlation coefficients are higher than the child level across several scales. The Sensation Seeking and Somatization scales, however, tend to show lower values. As expected, the SRP adaptive scale scores show negative correlations with the Conners scale scores. The SRP Attention and Hyperactivity scale scores demonstrate higher correlations with the Conners Hyperactivity/Impulsivity scale scores, compared to other scores.

**Table 11.25** SRP-C: Correlations With the Conners 3 Child Self-Report Scale

| BASC–3 | Inattention | Hyperactivity/ Impulsivity | Learning Problems | Aggression | Family Relations | ADHD: Inattentive | ADHD: Impulsive | Conduct Disorder | Oppositional Defiant Disorder | BASC–3 Mean | BASC–3 SD |
|---|---|---|---|---|---|---|---|---|---|---|---|
| **Composite** | | | | | | | | | | | |
| School Problems | .22 | .40 | −.15 | .32 | .42 | .25 | .31 | .22 | .40 | 49.9 | 10.2 |
| Internalizing Problems | .44 | .44 | .07 | .45 | .51 | .44 | .37 | .38 | .49 | 49.6 | 12.1 |
| Inattention/Hyperactivity | .42 | .52 | .09 | .42 | .47 | .46 | .48 | .36 | .48 | 48.7 | 10.9 |
| Emotional Symptoms | .44 | .40 | .11 | .42 | .46 | .44 | .34 | .35 | .45 | 50.4 | 11.7 |
| Personal Adjustment | −.34 | −.31 | .00 | −.39 | −.37 | −.36 | −.23 | −.25 | −.40 | 48.9 | 10.5 |
| **Clinical scale** | | | | | | | | | | | |
| Attitude to School | .29 | .52 | −.14 | .37 | .45 | .31 | .48 | .26 | .50 | 49.3 | 10.0 |
| Attitude to Teachers | .11 | .21 | −.11 | .22 | .31 | .15 | .10 | .15 | .23 | 50.6 | 10.2 |
| Atypicality | .39 | .40 | −.03 | .40 | .36 | .36 | .31 | .30 | .45 | 49.1 | 11.7 |
| Locus of Control | .35 | .44 | −.02 | .44 | .50 | .37 | .35 | .37 | .50 | 48.9 | 11.8 |
| Social Stress | .35 | .38 | −.03 | .32 | .42 | .34 | .34 | .23 | .41 | 50.2 | 12.1 |
| Anxiety | .49 | .51 | .15 | .46 | .55 | .46 | .46 | .46 | .50 | 48.9 | 10.3 |
| Depression | .37 | .33 | .09 | .43 | .51 | .37 | .27 | .35 | .42 | 50.1 | 12.9 |
| Sense of Inadequacy | .40 | .32 | .27 | .32 | .37 | .43 | .27 | .33 | .32 | 50.3 | 10.6 |
| Attention Problems | .48 | .45 | .19 | .38 | .40 | .50 | .42 | .30 | .48 | 49.7 | 10.6 |
| Hyperactivity | .34 | .53 | −.02 | .43 | .49 | .38 | .50 | .39 | .45 | 48.2 | 10.7 |
| **Adaptive scale** | | | | | | | | | | | |
| Relations With Parents | −.19 | −.24 | .07 | −.36 | −.50 | −.23 | −.19 | −.23 | −.38 | 49.1 | 10.7 |
| Interpersonal Relations | −.24 | −.22 | .07 | −.30 | −.25 | −.28 | −.13 | −.15 | −.28 | 50.3 | 10.9 |
| Self-Esteem | −.29 | −.31 | −.05 | −.27 | −.30 | −.31 | −.30 | −.21 | −.35 | 48.2 | 12.4 |
| Self-Reliance | −.28 | −.13 | −.06 | −.26 | −.03 | −.29 | −.02 | −.13 | −.17 | 49.0 | 9.5 |
| **Clinical index** | | | | | | | | | | | |
| Functional Impairment Index | .44 | .42 | .13 | .46 | .52 | .45 | .35 | .43 | .48 | 49.4 | 11.6 |
| **Conners 3 mean** | 54.6 | 53.2 | 54.5 | 50.6 | 52.7 | 53.6 | 52.9 | 51.0 | 51.2 | — | — |
| **Conners 3 SD** | 11.9 | 11.1 | 10.5 | 9.6 | 13.3 | 12.2 | 11.5 | 11.2 | 11.6 | — | — |

# Table 11.26 SRP–A: Correlations With the Conners 3 Adolescent Self-Report Scale

| BASC–3 | Inattention | Hyperactivity/ Impulsivity | Learning Problems | Aggression | Family Relations | ADHD: Inattentive | ADHD: Impulsive | Conduct Disorder | Oppositional Defiant Disorder | BASC–3 Mean | BASC–3 SD |
|---|---|---|---|---|---|---|---|---|---|---|---|
| **Composite** | | | | | | | | | | | |
| School Problems | .31 | .49 | .30 | .59 | .49 | .33 | .53 | .60 | .43 | 48.8 | 9.0 |
| Internalizing Problems | .60 | .55 | .64 | .56 | .50 | .57 | .50 | .46 | .43 | 49.5 | 9.2 |
| Inattention/Hyperactivity | .68 | .75 | .51 | .51 | .23 | .72 | .72 | .54 | .26 | 50.0 | 9.1 |
| Emotional Symptoms | .64 | .49 | .66 | .58 | .51 | .60 | .45 | .49 | .43 | 49.3 | 8.9 |
| Personal Adjustment | -.51 | -.34 | -.47 | -.58 | -.60 | -.44 | -.29 | -.50 | -.38 | 51.2 | 8.1 |
| **Clinical scale** | | | | | | | | | | | |
| Attitude to School | .26 | .31 | .32 | .47 | .36 | .27 | .38 | .48 | .29 | 50.0 | 9.7 |
| Attitude to Teachers | .35 | .47 | .22 | .65 | .62 | .34 | .47 | .59 | .57 | 47.5 | 8.1 |
| Sensation Seeking | .13 | .36 | .14 | .27 | .20 | .17 | .37 | .32 | .17 | 49.8 | 9.5 |
| Atypicality | .43 | .67 | .39 | .47 | .42 | .48 | .60 | .48 | .29 | 48.8 | 8.3 |
| Locus of Control | .56 | .50 | .62 | .59 | .73 | .54 | .47 | .45 | .50 | 49.0 | 7.2 |
| Social Stress | .58 | .51 | .55 | .43 | .43 | .55 | .47 | .38 | .28 | 48.9 | 9.1 |
| Anxiety | .54 | .52 | .64 | .41 | .25 | .56 | .47 | .36 | .33 | 50.1 | 9.1 |
| Depression | .50 | .32 | .58 | .46 | .51 | .43 | .30 | .33 | .42 | 49.4 | 8.6 |
| Sense of Inadequacy | .67 | .52 | .63 | .63 | .53 | .61 | .49 | .52 | .50 | 50.5 | 9.8 |
| Somatization | .33 | .27 | .40 | .35 | .20 | .27 | .21 | .25 | .22 | 50.1 | 11.0 |
| Attention Problems | .77 | .70 | .59 | .55 | .24 | .79 | .63 | .57 | .32 | 49.5 | 8.7 |
| Hyperactivity | .55 | .76 | .40 | .47 | .24 | .63 | .77 | .51 | .21 | 50.5 | 8.8 |
| **Adaptive scale** | | | | | | | | | | | |
| Relations With Parents | -.25 | -.21 | -.15 | -.38 | -.73 | -.15 | -.15 | -.29 | -.31 | 50.4 | 8.6 |
| Interpersonal Relations | -.51 | -.39 | -.50 | -.52 | -.32 | -.46 | -.38 | -.44 | -.33 | 51.5 | 8.7 |
| Self-Esteem | -.47 | -.38 | -.55 | -.47 | -.38 | -.43 | -.31 | -.41 | -.25 | 51.4 | 8.0 |
| Self-Reliance | -.38 | .00 | -.29 | -.46 | -.46 | -.34 | .04 | -.41 | -.30 | 50.5 | 7.2 |
| **Content scale** | | | | | | | | | | | |
| Anger Control | .47 | .35 | .56 | .57 | .29 | .42 | .26 | .33 | .61 | 48.8 | 8.1 |
| Ego Strength | -.42 | -.24 | -.39 | -.44 | -.57 | -.36 | -.19 | -.34 | -.27 | 52.5 | 8.7 |
| Mania | .46 | .74 | .37 | .42 | .35 | .57 | .74 | .44 | .21 | 48.7 | 9.0 |
| Test Anxiety | .46 | .51 | .55 | .36 | .20 | .44 | .55 | .40 | .24 | 52.0 | 9.2 |
| **Clinical index** | | | | | | | | | | | |
| Functional Impairment Index | .76 | .66 | .68 | .63 | .43 | .75 | .62 | .57 | .45 | 49.8 | 9.0 |
| Conners 3 mean | 51.5 | 51.6 | 52.9 | 48.6 | 47.7 | 51.2 | 51.1 | 48.7 | 48.0 | — | — |
| Conners 3 *SD* | 10.4 | 9.2 | 12.0 | 8.9 | 8.4 | 10.0 | 9.3 | 10.5 | 8.9 | — | — |

## Delis Rating of Executive Functions

The SRP–A form was completed along with Delis Rating of Executive Functions (D-REF; Delis, 2012) Self Rating Form by 33 adolescents ages 12 through 18 years. Table 11.27 presents the correlations between the SRP and D-REF core index and clinical index scale scores. The mean SRP scores indicate that the samples are generally average in their levels of behavior problems. The scale score variability is generally average as well. As expected, the correlations between the SRP scale scores that assess various aspects of executive functioning (e.g., Hyperactivity, Attention Problems, and Anger Control) are among the highest correlations across the various D-REF scales.

**Table 11.27** SRP–A: Correlations With the D-REF Self Rating Form

| BASC–3 | Core indexes | | | | Clinical indexes | | | BASC–3 | |
|---|---|---|---|---|---|---|---|---|---|
| | Behavioral Functioning Index | Emotional Functioning Index | Executive Functioning Index | Total Composite | Attention/Working Memory Index | Activity Level/Impulse Control Index | Compliance/Anger Management Index | Mean | SD |
| **Composite** | | | | | | | | | |
| School Problems | .68 | .68 | .58 | .66 | .57 | .71 | .70 | 46.8 | 10.9 |
| Internalizing Problems | .68 | .60 | .63 | .65 | .62 | .64 | .64 | 49.2 | 10.7 |
| Inattention/Hyperactivity | .75 | .70 | .67 | .73 | .67 | .73 | .71 | 47.8 | 9.4 |
| Emotional Symptoms | .54 | .52 | .57 | .57 | .55 | .56 | .55 | 50.1 | 12.0 |
| Personal Adjustment | -.52 | -.56 | -.61 | -.59 | -.58 | -.58 | -.58 | 50.7 | 12.0 |
| **Clinical scale** | | | | | | | | | |
| Attitude to School | .63 | .66 | .60 | .64 | .62 | .65 | .65 | 47.2 | 11.2 |
| Attitude to Teachers | .72 | .76 | .68 | .73 | .63 | .74 | .79 | 46.9 | 9.9 |
| Sensation Seeking | .30 | .25 | .15 | .25 | .15 | .32 | .27 | 48.6 | 11.0 |
| Atypicality | .66 | .62 | .66 | .66 | .63 | .67 | .67 | 48.1 | 8.8 |
| Locus of Control | .80 | .67 | .67 | .74 | .68 | .72 | .69 | 48.4 | 9.1 |
| Social Stress | .62 | .58 | .61 | .63 | .57 | .64 | .62 | 49.4 | 11.3 |
| Anxiety | .55 | .53 | .53 | .55 | .48 | .54 | .56 | 50.2 | 10.5 |
| Depression | .38 | .34 | .37 | .37 | .34 | .35 | .37 | 49.8 | 10.4 |
| Sense of Inadequacy | .61 | .53 | .58 | .59 | .59 | .59 | .59 | 49.7 | 10.7 |
| Somatization | .52 | .41 | .49 | .50 | .53 | .43 | .46 | 50.0 | 10.0 |
| Attention Problems | .67 | .66 | .69 | .70 | .64 | .66 | .70 | 47.9 | 9.5 |
| Hyperactivity | .66 | .57 | .50 | .59 | .54 | .63 | .56 | 47.9 | 9.7 |
| **Adaptive scale** | | | | | | | | | |
| Relations With Parents | -.56 | -.61 | -.63 | -.63 | -.55 | -.65 | -.66 | 51.3 | 10.8 |
| Interpersonal Relations | -.53 | -.53 | -.57 | -.56 | -.55 | -.53 | -.57 | 51.6 | 10.6 |
| Self-Esteem | -.24 | -.25 | -.29 | -.27 | -.28 | -.27 | -.25 | 47.1 | 14.2 |
| Self-Reliance | -.49 | -.59 | -.67 | -.63 | -.67 | -.59 | -.58 | 52.0 | 10.0 |
| **Content scale** | | | | | | | | | |
| Anger Control | .78 | .80 | .79 | .81 | .77 | .81 | .80 | 47.5 | 8.9 |
| Ego Strength | -.49 | -.50 | -.52 | -.51 | -.50 | -.52 | -.53 | 50.9 | 10.9 |
| Mania | .66 | .57 | .56 | .63 | .55 | .64 | .60 | 49.1 | 10.1 |
| Test Anxiety | .49 | .36 | .56 | .52 | .56 | .53 | .38 | 48.7 | 10.4 |
| **Clinical index** | | | | | | | | | |
| Functional Impairment Index | .69 | .66 | .70 | .70 | .69 | .69 | .70 | 48.3 | 10.8 |
| **D-REF mean** | 47.8 | 45.8 | 51.5 | 47.8 | 51.6 | 47.5 | 46.5 | — | — |
| **D-REF SD** | 11.3 | 9.6 | 11.9 | 12.4 | 10.9 | 11.0 | 9.9 | — | — |

## Children's Depression Inventory 2

The SRP–I and SRP–C forms were completed along with the Children's Depression Inventory 2™ (CDI™ 2; Kovacs, 2011) by 110 children ages 8 through 11 years. Correlations between the SRP–I and SRP–C with the CDI 2 are presented in Tables 11.28 and 11.29, respectively. The mean SRP composite scores indicate that these samples are about average in their levels of behavior problems. Most SRP composites have correlations in the .60s with the CDI 2 Total Score. The Personal Adjustment composite, as expected, has a negative correlation with the CDI 2 Total Score. The correlation between the SRP Depression scale and the CDI 2 Total Score is in the .60s.

**Table 11.28** SRP–I: Correlations With the Children's Depression Inventory 2

| BASC–3 | Emotional Problems | Negative Mood/ Physical Symptoms | Negative Self-Esteem | Functional Problems | Ineffectiveness | Interpersonal Problems | Total CDI | Mean | SD |
|---|---|---|---|---|---|---|---|---|---|
| | Children's Depression Inventory 2 | | | | | | | BASC–3 | |
| Total Score | .70 | .62 | .58 | .52 | .46 | .50 | .65 | 2.9 | 2.3 |
| CDI 2 mean | 52.1 | 52.6 | 50.2 | 53.4 | 53.3 | 50.6 | 53.0 | — | — |
| CDI 2 SD | 9.1 | 10.9 | 7.4 | 11.0 | 10.1 | 11.2 | 10.3 | — | — |

**Table 11.29** SRP–C: Correlations With the Children's Depression Inventory 2

| BASC–3 | Emotional Problems | Negative Mood/Physical Symptoms | Negative Self-Esteem | Functional Problems | Ineffectiveness | Interpersonal Problems | Total CDI | Mean | SD |
|---|---|---|---|---|---|---|---|---|---|
| | Children's Depression Inventory 2 | | | | | | | BASC–3 | |
| **Composite** | | | | | | | | | |
| School Problems | .37 | .36 | .18 | .49 | .52 | .31 | .47 | 49.4 | 9.1 |
| Internalizing Problems | .54 | .49 | .30 | .58 | .51 | .51 | .62 | 50.6 | 11.6 |
| Inattention/Hyperactivity | .58 | .58 | .23 | .65 | .60 | .52 | .68 | 51.4 | 10.4 |
| Emotional Symptoms | .51 | .45 | .31 | .62 | .55 | .54 | .63 | 49.7 | 11.4 |
| Personal Adjustment | −.51 | −.43 | −.39 | −.65 | −.58 | −.57 | −.63 | 50.8 | 9.8 |
| **Clinical scale** | | | | | | | | | |
| Attitude to School | .37 | .35 | .15 | .46 | .49 | .26 | .46 | 50.9 | 10.2 |
| Attitude to Teachers | .21 | .19 | .13 | .34 | .34 | .23 | .30 | 48.0 | 8.7 |
| Atypicality | .53 | .48 | .35 | .43 | .38 | .40 | .52 | 52.0 | 10.3 |
| Locus of Control | .58 | .53 | .33 | .56 | .49 | .49 | .62 | 50.4 | 10.7 |
| Social Stress | .47 | .40 | .31 | .48 | .39 | .50 | .52 | 49.4 | 10.9 |
| Anxiety | .47 | .44 | .25 | .48 | .44 | .42 | .52 | 50.9 | 11.6 |
| Depression | .53 | .47 | .29 | .61 | .53 | .56 | .63 | 49.6 | 11.5 |
| Sense of Inadequacy | .38 | .35 | .16 | .53 | .50 | .40 | .49 | 50.9 | 12.2 |
| Attention Problems | .51 | .52 | .16 | .68 | .64 | .49 | .65 | 50.4 | 10.7 |
| Hyperactivity | .54 | .53 | .27 | .49 | .45 | .43 | .57 | 52.3 | 10.3 |
| **Adaptive scale** | | | | | | | | | |
| Relations With Parents | −.49 | −.44 | −.36 | −.60 | −.55 | −.50 | −.60 | 50.0 | 10.0 |
| Interpersonal Relations | −.40 | −.32 | −.26 | −.46 | −.39 | −.45 | −.46 | 50.9 | 10.3 |
| Self-Esteem | −.49 | −.39 | −.37 | −.52 | −.44 | −.46 | −.55 | 51.4 | 9.6 |
| Self-Reliance | −.22 | −.18 | −.23 | −.49 | −.45 | −.41 | −.40 | 50.5 | 9.5 |
| **Clinical index** | | | | | | | | | |
| Functional Impairment Index | .55 | .52 | .27 | .66 | .61 | .53 | .67 | 50.7 | 11.1 |
| **CDI 2 mean** | 50.3 | 51.9 | 47.4 | 50.9 | 50.8 | 49.1 | 50.7 | — | — |
| **CDI 2 SD** | 8.6 | 10.3 | 5.7 | 10.6 | 10.4 | 10.1 | 9.4 | — | — |

## Revised Children's Manifest Anxiety Scale: Second Edition

The SRP–I and SRP–C forms and Revised Children's Manifest Anxiety Scale: Second Edition (RCMAS-2™; Reynolds & Richmond, 2008), were completed by 39 children ages 8 through 11 years. SRP–I and SRP–C correlations with RCMAS-2 scale scores are presented in Tables 11.30 and 11.31, respectively. The mean SRP composite scores indicate that these samples are about average in their levels of behavior problems, while the variability in scores is slightly higher than average. Correlations between the Total Scores from the SRP–I and RCMAS-2 and the SRP–C Emotional Symptoms Index and RCMAS-2 Total Score are in the middle .50s. On the SRP–C, the Anxiety scale score exhibited the highest correlations among the other scales.

**Table 11.30** SRP–I: Correlations With the Revised Children's Manifest Anxiety Scale: Second Edition

| BASC–3 | Revised Children's Manifest Anxiety Scale: Second Edition | | | | BASC–3 | |
| | Physiological Anxiety | Worry/ Oversensitivity | Social Concerns/ Concentration | Total Anxiety | Mean | SD |
|---|---|---|---|---|---|---|
| Total Score | .51 | .49 | .55 | .57 | 3.1 | 2.5 |
| RCMAS-2 mean | 46.7 | 43.9 | 43.1 | 44.0 | — | — |
| RCMAS-2 SD | 9.6 | 9.9 | 11.1 | 10.3 | — | — |

**Table 11.31** SRP–C: Correlations With the Revised Children's Manifest Anxiety Scale: Second Edition

| BASC–3 | Revised Children's Manifest Anxiety Scale: Second Edition | | | | BASC–3 | |
| | Physiological Anxiety | Worry/ Oversensitivity | Social Concerns/ Concentration | Total Anxiety | Mean | SD |
|---|---|---|---|---|---|---|
| **Composite** | | | | | | |
| School Problems | .35 | .36 | .48 | .41 | 52.2 | 12.4 |
| Internalizing Problems | .47 | .46 | .48 | .51 | 52.2 | 12.0 |
| Inattention/Hyperactivity | .47 | .33 | .34 | .39 | 47.6 | 10.7 |
| Emotional Symptoms | .55 | .48 | .54 | .55 | 51.9 | 12.2 |
| Personal Adjustment | −.43 | −.34 | −.50 | −.45 | 47.9 | 13.0 |
| **Clinical scale** | | | | | | |
| Attitude to School | .33 | .32 | .42 | .37 | 53.4 | 12.6 |
| Attitude to Teachers | .27 | .29 | .39 | .33 | 50.4 | 12.4 |
| Atypicality | .30 | .39 | .19 | .33 | 53.0 | 11.4 |
| Locus of Control | .37 | .34 | .45 | .42 | 50.7 | 12.3 |
| Social Stress | .40 | .33 | .47 | .40 | 51.4 | 11.5 |
| Anxiety | .50 | .62 | .42 | .59 | 52.3 | 11.4 |
| Depression | .41 | .40 | .52 | .50 | 53.2 | 12.8 |
| Sense of Inadequacy | .48 | .34 | .42 | .40 | 50.9 | 11.2 |
| Attention Problems | .47 | .34 | .40 | .40 | 48.5 | 10.4 |
| Hyperactivity | .48 | .31 | .28 | .37 | 47.5 | 10.0 |
| **Adaptive scale** | | | | | | |
| Relations With Parents | −.27 | −.22 | −.38 | −.32 | 48.2 | 13.5 |
| Interpersonal Relations | −.28 | −.27 | −.38 | −.34 | 46.7 | 14.3 |
| Self-Esteem | −.48 | −.41 | −.43 | −.50 | 47.8 | 12.4 |
| Self-Reliance | −.44 | −.26 | −.42 | −.33 | 50.5 | 11.0 |
| **Clinical index** | | | | | | |
| Functional Impairment Index | .46 | .42 | .41 | .45 | 50.5 | 12.3 |
| **RCMAS-2 mean** | 48.1 | 48.8 | 46.6 | 47.2 | — | — |
| **RCMAS-2 SD** | 11.7 | 12.3 | 11.5 | 12.7 | — | — |

## Beck Youth Inventories–II

The SRP–A form and the Beck Youth Inventories™–II (BYI™–II; Beck, Beck, & Jolly, 2005) were completed by adolescents ages 12 through 18 years, with 56 adolescents completing the BYI–II Depression scale and 57 completing the BYI–II Anxiety scale. Correlations with BYI–II scale scores are presented in Table 11.32. The mean SRP scale scores indicate that these samples are about average in their levels of behavior problems. Correlations between similarly named (e.g., Anxiety and Depression) scale scores on the SRP–A form and BYI–II are moderate. The composite scale scores show positive correlations with the BYI–II scales except for the Personal Adjustment scale which, as expected, has a negative correlation. Among the composite scores, the Internalizing Problems and Emotional Symptoms composites show relatively high correlations with the BYI–II Depression and Anxiety scales.

**Table 11.32** SRP–A: Correlations With the Beck Youth Inventories–II

| | | | BASC–3 | |
| --- | --- | --- | --- | --- |
| BASC–3 | Depression | Anxiety | Mean | SD |
| **Composite** | | | | |
| School Problems | .48 | .58 | 48.9 | 9.7 |
| Internalizing Problems | .63 | .70 | 50.6 | 10.1 |
| Inattention/Hyperactivity | .37 | .60 | 49.1 | 9.7 |
| Emotional Symptoms | .60 | .60 | 49.9 | 10.8 |
| Personal Adjustment | −.61 | −.59 | 51.4 | 9.5 |
| **Clinical scale** | | | | |
| Attitude to School | .53 | .60 | 49.2 | 9.7 |
| Attitude to Teachers | .38 | .39 | 47.9 | 9.4 |
| Sensation Seeking | .22 | .27 | 50.4 | 11.1 |
| Atypicality | .57 | .49 | 51.0 | 10.2 |
| Locus of Control | .53 | .37 | 49.2 | 9.6 |
| Social Stress | .62 | .66 | 50.3 | 9.8 |
| Anxiety | .46 | .58 | 52.6 | 10.6 |
| Depression | .51 | .48 | 50.7 | 11.0 |
| Sense of Inadequacy | .48 | .50 | 48.8 | 10.6 |
| Somatization | .36 | .53 | 50.3 | 10.1 |
| Attention Problems | .42 | .57 | 48.6 | 9.5 |
| Hyperactivity | .28 | .56 | 49.7 | 9.8 |
| **Adaptive scale** | | | | |
| Relations With Parents | −.40 | −.29 | 50.4 | 10.8 |
| Interpersonal Relations | −.45 | −.64 | 51.1 | 9.7 |
| Self-Esteem | −.39 | −.39 | 49.7 | 11.5 |
| Self-Reliance | −.45 | −.35 | 53.4 | 9.1 |
| **Content scale** | | | | |
| Anger Control | .63 | .69 | 49.5 | 9.4 |
| Ego Strength | −.52 | −.56 | 51.3 | 9.9 |
| Mania | .39 | .55 | 50.9 | 9.9 |
| Test Anxiety | .31 | .57 | 49.8 | 10.9 |
| **Clinical index** | | | | |
| Functional Impairment | .58 | .71 | 49.6 | 10.1 |
| **BYI–II mean** | 46.1 | 49.6 | — | — |
| **BYI–II SD** | 7.3 | 9.2 | — | — |

## Beck Depression Inventory–II

The SRP–COL form was completed along with the Beck Depression Inventory®–II (BDI®–II; Beck, Steer, & Brown, 1996) by 53 college students ages 18 through 25 years. Correlations with BDI–II scale scores are presented in Table 11.33. The mean SRP scale scores indicate that these samples are about average in their levels of behavior problems and variability in scores. A number of SRP scale scores correlate at .60 or above with BDI–II Total Score; the correlation with the SRP Depression scale score is .61.

**Table 11.33** SRP–COL: Correlations With the Beck Depression Inventory–II

| | | BASC–3 | |
| --- | --- | --- | --- |
| BASC–3 | Depression | Mean | *SD* |
| **Composite** | | | |
| Internalizing Problems | .73 | 49.9 | 12.2 |
| Inattention/Hyperactivity | .52 | 49.3 | 11.4 |
| Emotional Symptoms | .63 | 49.8 | 12.7 |
| Personal Adjustment | −.56 | 50.6 | 11.8 |
| **Clinical scale** | | | |
| Atypicality | .64 | 49.5 | 10.8 |
| Locus of Control | .71 | 49.6 | 10.9 |
| Social Stress | .54 | 49.3 | 11.7 |
| Anxiety | .65 | 50.2 | 11.6 |
| Depression | .61 | 49.7 | 12.1 |
| Sense of Inadequacy | .61 | 50.5 | 12.0 |
| Somatization | .61 | 50.8 | 11.4 |
| Attention Problems | .57 | 49.6 | 11.1 |
| Hyperactivity | .43 | 49.1 | 11.2 |
| Sensation Seeking | .11 | 48.6 | 10.5 |
| Alcohol Abuse | .37 | 49.6 | 11.7 |
| School Maladjustment | .44 | 51.9 | 12.6 |
| **Adaptive scale** | | | |
| Relations With Parents | −.51 | 51.2 | 10.4 |
| Interpersonal Relations | −.42 | 50.4 | 10.7 |
| Self-Esteem | −.54 | 48.1 | 12.9 |
| Self-Reliance | −.44 | 52.3 | 10.0 |
| **Content scale** | | | |
| Anger Control | .46 | 49.2 | 10.7 |
| Ego Strength | −.60 | 49.0 | 13.1 |
| Mania | .51 | 49.3 | 11.8 |
| Test Anxiety | .43 | 50.3 | 12.7 |
| **BDI–II mean** | 9.1 | — | — |
| **BDI–II *SD*** | 9.0 | — | — |

## Minnesota Multiphasic Personality Inventory-Adolescent

The SRP–A form and Minnesota Multiphasic Personality Inventory®-Adolescent (MMPI®-A; Butcher et al., 1992) forms were completed by 39 adolescents ages 14 through 18 years. Correlations between the SRP–A and MMPI-A are shown in Table 11.34. The mean SRP composite scores indicate that these samples are about average in their levels of problem behaviors. The SRP Internalizing and Emotional Symptoms composites show the highest correlations with MMPI-A scale scores. Correlations between similarly named scale scores (e.g., Anxiety, Depression) are generally in the .50s or higher.

**Table 11.34** SRP–A: Correlations With the MMPI-A

| BASC–3 | Hypochondriasis | Depression | Hysteria | Psychopathic Deviate | Masculinity/Femininity | Paranoia | Psychasthenia | Schizophrenia | Hypomania | Social Introversion | Anxiety | Obsessiveness | Depression |
|---|---|---|---|---|---|---|---|---|---|---|---|---|---|
| **Composite** | | | | | | | | | | | | | |
| School Problems | .29 | .19 | -.10 | .26 | .10 | .26 | .41 | .45 | .47 | .22 | .31 | .39 | .36 |
| Internalizing Problems | .64 | .57 | .17 | .38 | .26 | .53 | .62 | .70 | .25 | .57 | .48 | .54 | .56 |
| Inattention/Hyperactivity | .43 | .41 | .08 | .30 | .22 | .30 | .44 | .49 | .31 | .38 | .32 | .43 | .30 |
| Emotional Symptoms | .62 | .56 | .17 | .36 | .18 | .52 | .70 | .73 | .28 | .67 | .57 | .67 | .61 |
| Personal Adjustment | -.56 | -.52 | -.12 | -.43 | -.06 | -.48 | -.67 | -.70 | -.31 | -.65 | -.54 | -.63 | -.63 |
| **Clinical scale** | | | | | | | | | | | | | |
| Attitude to School | .37 | .31 | .09 | .29 | .02 | .32 | .43 | .41 | .29 | .27 | .34 | .30 | .37 |
| Attitude to Teachers | .27 | .21 | -.10 | .16 | -.01 | .22 | .40 | .43 | .33 | .32 | .25 | .42 | .33 |
| Sensation Seeking | .06 | -.06 | -.22 | .17 | .19 | .06 | .13 | .18 | .44 | -.07 | .15 | .17 | .13 |
| Atypicality | .53 | .57 | .21 | .32 | .30 | .47 | .56 | .60 | .23 | .50 | .45 | .47 | .47 |
| Locus of Control | .39 | .35 | -.04 | .44 | .20 | .43 | .45 | .56 | .25 | .38 | .37 | .46 | .45 |
| Social Stress | .55 | .48 | .16 | .32 | .31 | .47 | .59 | .61 | .24 | .62 | .41 | .53 | .58 |
| Anxiety | .53 | .54 | .17 | .01 | .17 | .33 | .52 | .46 | -.05 | .51 | .56 | .43 | .35 |
| Depression | .61 | .57 | .17 | .48 | .27 | .59 | .67 | .72 | .33 | .64 | .54 | .61 | .67 |
| Sense of Inadequacy | .58 | .47 | .10 | .34 | .10 | .51 | .61 | .71 | .35 | .50 | .49 | .63 | .49 |
| Somatization | .52 | .39 | .23 | .31 | .20 | .39 | .32 | .46 | .20 | .28 | .17 | .16 | .34 |
| Attention Problems | .45 | .42 | .01 | .28 | .21 | .33 | .45 | .55 | .30 | .43 | .37 | .49 | .33 |
| Hyperactivity | .35 | .35 | .13 | .29 | .20 | .25 | .37 | .38 | .28 | .30 | .25 | .33 | .24 |
| **Adaptive scale** | | | | | | | | | | | | | |
| Relations With Parents | -.48 | -.45 | -.02 | -.45 | -.09 | -.44 | -.53 | -.62 | -.27 | -.46 | -.49 | -.42 | -.55 |
| Interpersonal Relations | -.58 | -.56 | -.14 | -.39 | -.11 | -.50 | -.67 | -.71 | -.27 | -.75 | -.50 | -.67 | -.64 |
| Self-Esteem | -.55 | -.48 | -.20 | -.44 | -.10 | -.46 | -.70 | -.63 | -.32 | -.62 | -.54 | -.62 | -.61 |
| Self-Reliance | -.27 | -.30 | -.06 | -.20 | .22 | -.23 | -.38 | -.45 | -.25 | -.40 | -.32 | -.44 | -.33 |
| **Content scale** | | | | | | | | | | | | | |
| Anger Control | .37 | .28 | -.09 | .35 | .28 | .39 | .44 | .56 | .28 | .35 | .27 | .39 | .41 |
| Ego Strength | -.53 | -.52 | -.17 | -.38 | -.07 | -.45 | -.64 | -.65 | -.24 | -.60 | -.53 | -.54 | -.59 |
| Mania | .51 | .45 | .20 | .24 | .28 | .37 | .53 | .49 | .30 | .34 | .48 | .41 | .34 |
| Test Anxiety | .44 | .38 | .15 | .14 | .19 | .26 | .38 | .38 | .10 | .31 | .29 | .35 | .21 |
| **Clinical index** | | | | | | | | | | | | | |
| Functional Impairment Index | .60 | .55 | .16 | .37 | .30 | .45 | .62 | .68 | .31 | .53 | .47 | .56 | .50 |
| **MMPI-A mean** | 45.5 | 49.7 | 48.3 | 47.3 | 49.3 | 45.5 | 44.5 | 44.7 | 45.3 | 46.2 | 46.1 | 45.8 | 45.2 |
| **MMPI-A *SD*** | 11.4 | 9.2 | 8.0 | 8.9 | 11.6 | 8.0 | 9.8 | 11.6 | 9.1 | 11.1 | 10.4 | 8.6 | 10.7 |

**Table 11.34** SRP–A: Correlations With the MMPI-A (continued)

| BASC-3 | Health Concerns | Alienation | Bizarre Mentation | Anger | Cynicism | Conduct Problems | Low Self-Esteem | Low Aspirations | Social Discomfort | Family Problems | School Problems | Negative Treatment Indicators |
|---|---|---|---|---|---|---|---|---|---|---|---|---|
| **Composite** | | | | | | | | | | | | |
| School Problems | .14 | .41 | .46 | .50 | .49 | .63 | .39 | .29 | .24 | .50 | .49 | .45 |
| Internalizing Problems | .55 | .55 | .64 | .23 | .39 | .31 | .67 | .32 | .47 | .55 | .31 | .62 |
| Inattention/Hyperactivity | .35 | .37 | .45 | .11 | .29 | .40 | .39 | .18 | .32 | .45 | .24 | .32 |
| Emotional Symptoms | .54 | .63 | .62 | .33 | .48 | .40 | .74 | .37 | .52 | .64 | .35 | .71 |
| Personal Adjustment | -.45 | -.68 | -.53 | -.44 | -.51 | -.43 | -.67 | -.28 | -.50 | -.73 | -.38 | -.68 |
| **Clinical scale** | | | | | | | | | | | | |
| Attitude to School | .20 | .39 | .45 | .45 | .37 | .48 | .33 | .21 | .33 | .51 | .56 | .35 |
| Attitude to Teachers | .16 | .41 | .42 | .41 | .51 | .53 | .37 | .41 | .29 | .46 | .56 | .48 |
| Sensation Seeking | -.01 | .17 | .20 | .31 | .25 | .44 | .19 | .07 | -.04 | .20 | .06 | .22 |
| Atypicality | .41 | .47 | .58 | .10 | .33 | .36 | .56 | .32 | .46 | .50 | .26 | .56 |
| Locus of Control | .29 | .48 | .51 | .42 | .36 | .26 | .51 | .19 | .23 | .55 | .20 | .52 |
| Social Stress | .45 | .58 | .61 | .22 | .44 | .34 | .66 | .28 | .57 | .47 | .24 | .68 |
| Anxiety | .47 | .29 | .47 | .09 | .27 | .15 | .50 | .22 | .38 | .41 | .17 | .45 |
| Depression | .55 | .64 | .62 | .36 | .46 | .35 | .73 | .34 | .49 | .57 | .34 | .71 |
| Sense of Inadequacy | .51 | .51 | .60 | .26 | .40 | .38 | .66 | .45 | .40 | .61 | .43 | .60 |
| Somatization | .54 | .31 | .37 | -.01 | .17 | .09 | .36 | .19 | .29 | .23 | .27 | .24 |
| Attention Problems | .39 | .37 | .41 | .12 | .30 | .41 | .47 | .28 | .34 | .48 | .32 | .42 |
| Hyperactivity | .29 | .32 | .42 | .09 | .25 | .34 | .29 | .08 | .27 | .38 | .14 | .22 |
| **Adaptive scale** | | | | | | | | | | | | |
| Relations With Parents | -.36 | -.57 | -.45 | -.49 | -.44 | -.36 | -.53 | -.21 | -.33 | -.73 | -.36 | -.56 |
| Interpersonal Relations | -.46 | -.68 | -.57 | -.31 | -.51 | -.40 | -.68 | -.23 | -.65 | -.65 | -.35 | -.76 |
| Self-Esteem | -.42 | -.60 | -.52 | -.41 | -.52 | -.40 | -.68 | -.16 | -.46 | -.64 | -.30 | -.61 |
| Self-Reliance | -.32 | -.52 | -.24 | -.31 | -.29 | -.35 | -.38 | -.47 | -.29 | -.53 | -.32 | -.41 |
| **Content scale** | | | | | | | | | | | | |
| Anger Control | .23 | .45 | .56 | .43 | .40 | .37 | .48 | .24 | .32 | .51 | .28 | .52 |
| Ego Strength | -.42 | -.62 | -.50 | -.39 | -.46 | -.39 | -.58 | -.24 | -.47 | -.68 | -.29 | -.60 |
| Mania | .42 | .36 | .54 | .15 | .37 | .46 | .47 | .23 | .27 | .50 | .28 | .39 |
| Test Anxiety | .42 | .20 | .37 | .00 | .16 | .17 | .40 | .29 | .29 | .24 | .38 | .23 |
| **Clinical index** | | | | | | | | | | | | |
| Functional Impairment Index | .53 | .50 | .58 | .19 | .39 | .41 | .62 | .32 | .45 | .52 | .36 | .53 |
| **MMPI-A mean** | 45.9 | 45.5 | 43.4 | 44.3 | 46.8 | 42.2 | 46.7 | 46.3 | 50.8 | 44.6 | 45.5 | 45.3 |
| **MMPI-A SD** | 11.5 | 11.2 | 7.0 | 9.2 | 10.4 | 8.4 | 10.5 | 8.8 | 13.7 | 8.9 | 8.7 | 10.4 |

Table 11.34 SRP–A: Correlations With the MMPI-A *(continued)*

| BASC–3 | MacAndrew-Revised | Alcohol/Drug Problem Acknowledgment | Alcohol/Drug Problem Proneness | Immaturity | Anxiety | Repression | Aggressiveness | Psychoticism | Disconstraint | Negative Emotionality/Neuroticism | Introversion/Low Positive Emotionality | BASC–3 Mean | BASC–3 SD |
|---|---|---|---|---|---|---|---|---|---|---|---|---|---|
| **Composite** | | | | | | | | | | | | | |
| School Problems | .23 | .37 | .31 | .60 | .39 | -.37 | .56 | .53 | .51 | .24 | .21 | 52.6 | 10.6 |
| Internalizing Problems | .10 | .31 | .16 | .55 | .59 | -.03 | .25 | .63 | .27 | .34 | .49 | 52.8 | 11.5 |
| Inattention/Hyperactivity | -.02 | .28 | .16 | .41 | .43 | -.04 | .22 | .37 | .35 | .14 | .21 | 51.7 | 11.3 |
| Emotional Symptoms | .07 | .26 | .25 | .59 | .71 | -.08 | .32 | .62 | .27 | .47 | .48 | 51.8 | 10.7 |
| Personal Adjustment | -.15 | -.29 | -.28 | -.60 | -.69 | .14 | -.42 | -.59 | -.35 | -.47 | -.45 | 49.6 | 11.2 |
| **Clinical scale** | | | | | | | | | | | | | |
| Attitude to School | .24 | .39 | .36 | .56 | .35 | -.25 | .48 | .49 | .50 | .18 | .33 | 51.7 | 9.7 |
| Attitude to Teachers | .31 | .29 | .27 | .55 | .39 | -.21 | .48 | .57 | .40 | .26 | .26 | 51.1 | 10.9 |
| Sensation Seeking | .00 | .19 | .13 | .29 | .17 | -.39 | .34 | .18 | .29 | .11 | -.08 | 53.5 | 10.9 |
| Atypicality | -.03 | .28 | .16 | .48 | .51 | .07 | .18 | .55 | .24 | .25 | .45 | 52.6 | 10.7 |
| Locus of Control | .21 | .24 | .15 | .43 | .47 | -.23 | .33 | .52 | .20 | .32 | .25 | 51.9 | 11.6 |
| Social Stress | .05 | .25 | .10 | .55 | .58 | -.01 | .27 | .61 | .21 | .35 | .55 | 53.5 | 11.3 |
| Anxiety | -.17 | .07 | .14 | .32 | .42 | .16 | .08 | .42 | .00 | .43 | .39 | 53.9 | 10.3 |
| Depression | .22 | .33 | .25 | .58 | .68 | -.08 | .34 | .66 | .28 | .47 | .52 | 51.3 | 10.5 |
| Sense of Inadequacy | .11 | .32 | .27 | .56 | .63 | -.18 | .26 | .57 | .35 | .30 | .36 | 50.2 | 10.2 |
| Somatization | .16 | .30 | .04 | .34 | .28 | .06 | .10 | .39 | .31 | .04 | .35 | 52.9 | 13.6 |
| Attention Problems | .05 | .33 | .16 | .45 | .47 | -.06 | .20 | .39 | .38 | .15 | .26 | 50.6 | 10.4 |
| Hyperactivity | -.07 | .21 | .13 | .33 | .34 | -.02 | .22 | .31 | .28 | .12 | .16 | 52.5 | 11.7 |
| **Adaptive scale** | | | | | | | | | | | | | |
| Relations With Parents | -.25 | -.32 | -.27 | -.53 | -.51 | .19 | -.46 | -.52 | -.37 | -.40 | -.37 | 49.5 | 11.0 |
| Interpersonal Relations | -.13 | -.29 | -.16 | -.61 | -.71 | .04 | -.34 | -.64 | -.30 | -.44 | -.58 | 48.7 | 11.4 |
| Self-Esteem | -.10 | -.19 | -.28 | -.52 | -.71 | .23 | -.41 | -.54 | -.26 | -.49 | -.37 | 47.7 | 10.7 |
| Self-Reliance | .02 | -.20 | -.29 | -.39 | -.45 | .04 | -.23 | -.26 | -.32 | -.31 | -.20 | 53.1 | 8.3 |
| **Content scale** | | | | | | | | | | | | | |
| Anger Control | .25 | .27 | .15 | .53 | .39 | -.26 | .43 | .59 | .31 | .21 | .30 | 52.6 | 10.3 |
| Ego Strength | -.05 | -.20 | -.23 | -.55 | -.63 | .10 | -.38 | -.53 | -.28 | -.45 | -.44 | 49.2 | 10.7 |
| Mania | -.13 | .31 | .28 | .45 | .44 | -.05 | .28 | .43 | .35 | .33 | .24 | 54.9 | 10.1 |
| Test Anxiety | .13 | .22 | .19 | .33 | .31 | .06 | .04 | .33 | .23 | .09 | .24 | 50.8 | 12.1 |
| **Clinical index** | | | | | | | | | | | | | |
| Functional Impairment Index | .12 | .33 | .22 | .56 | .58 | -.03 | .26 | .57 | .35 | .32 | .40 | 52.3 | 11.3 |
| **MMPI-A mean** | 48.7 | 43.0 | 42.7 | 45.6 | 42.8 | 51.6 | 43.9 | 44.3 | 42.6 | 46.5 | 49.7 | — | — |
| **MMPI-A SD** | 8.6 | 7.0 | 7.5 | 10.1 | 9.4 | 9.9 | 9.7 | 9.1 | 7.5 | 8.9 | 10.6 | — | — |

## Minnesota Multiphasic Personality Inventory-2-Restructured Form

The SRP–COL and the Minnesota Multiphasic Personality Inventory-2-Restructured Form® (MMPI-2-RF®; Tellegen & Ben-Porath, 2008, 2011) were completed by 61 college students ages 18 through 25 years. Correlations between the SRP–COL and MMPI-2-RF scales are shown in Table 11.35.

A comprehensive review of these results would require a more extensive discussion of MMPI-2-RF scale attributes than the scope of this manual allows. However, a few generalities can be made: the SRP Emotional Symptoms Index score indicates correlations in the .50s or higher with several of the MMPI-2-RF scales that indicate broad emotional problems, such as Emotional/Internalizing Dysfunction, Dysfunctional Negative Emotions, and Negative Emotionality/Neuroticism Revised and similarly named scale scores, such as Anxiety; Somatization with Somatic Complaints and Gastrointestinal Complaints; and Alcohol Abuse with Substance Abuse, indicate correlations in the .40s or higher.

Table 11.35 SRP-COL: Correlations With the MMPI-2-RF

| BASC-3 | Emotional/ Internalizing Dysfunction | Thought Dysfunction | Behavioral/ Externalizing Dysfunction | Demoral-ization | Somatic Complaints | Low Positive Emotions | Cynicism | Antisocial Behavior | Ideas of Persecution | Dysfunctional Negative Emotions | Aberrant Experiences | Hypomanic Activation |
|---|---|---|---|---|---|---|---|---|---|---|---|---|
| **Composite** | | | | | | | | | | | | |
| Internalizing Problems | .65 | .37 | .45 | .63 | .52 | .47 | .29 | .44 | .35 | .63 | .49 | .27 |
| Inattention/Hyperactivity | .34 | .34 | .47 | .39 | .36 | .09 | .30 | .38 | .25 | .41 | .49 | .41 |
| Emotional Symptoms | .73 | .30 | .40 | .68 | .47 | .54 | .33 | .42 | .33 | .63 | .40 | .19 |
| Personal Adjustment | -.72 | -.30 | -.38 | -.64 | -.32 | -.53 | -.42 | -.42 | -.36 | -.55 | -.33 | -.18 |
| **Clinical scale** | | | | | | | | | | | | |
| Atypicality | .43 | .51 | .56 | .41 | .43 | .31 | .34 | .50 | .37 | .47 | .69 | .48 |
| Locus of Control | .64 | .43 | .48 | .62 | .44 | .49 | .34 | .49 | .44 | .63 | .47 | .29 |
| Social Stress | .68 | .28 | .34 | .64 | .37 | .50 | .38 | .35 | .31 | .53 | .40 | .19 |
| Anxiety | .63 | .26 | .31 | .61 | .46 | .43 | .16 | .34 | .23 | .64 | .38 | .16 |
| Depression | .63 | .26 | .39 | .62 | .50 | .45 | .21 | .39 | .28 | .55 | .35 | .20 |
| Sense of Inadequacy | .58 | .28 | .38 | .54 | .45 | .45 | .30 | .35 | .32 | .55 | .38 | .21 |
| Somatization | .30 | .23 | .23 | .30 | .45 | .20 | .07 | .19 | .16 | .42 | .29 | .15 |
| Attention Problems | .42 | .31 | .48 | .45 | .32 | .22 | .36 | .44 | .27 | .39 | .45 | .32 |
| Hyperactivity | .24 | .35 | .43 | .30 | .36 | -.02 | .22 | .29 | .22 | .39 | .49 | .45 |
| Sensation Seeking | -.09 | .31 | .55 | -.03 | .23 | -.26 | .29 | .38 | .34 | .11 | .38 | .59 |
| Alcohol Abuse | .14 | .24 | .54 | .17 | .24 | .02 | .07 | .54 | .24 | .30 | .29 | .36 |
| School Maladjustment | .65 | .35 | .53 | .61 | .38 | .49 | .47 | .54 | .40 | .62 | .43 | .31 |
| **Adaptive scale** | | | | | | | | | | | | |
| Relations With Parents | -.59 | -.41 | -.45 | -.55 | -.27 | -.38 | -.45 | -.46 | -.46 | -.47 | -.41 | -.41 |
| Interpersonal Relations | -.61 | -.08 | -.22 | -.52 | -.22 | -.50 | -.29 | -.23 | -.17 | -.44 | -.13 | .00 |
| Self-Esteem | -.69 | -.21 | -.25 | -.67 | -.33 | -.53 | -.23 | -.33 | -.23 | -.54 | -.31 | -.10 |
| Self-Reliance | -.47 | -.26 | -.34 | -.40 | -.26 | -.40 | -.39 | -.38 | -.32 | -.38 | -.24 | -.10 |
| **Content scale** | | | | | | | | | | | | |
| Anger Control | .40 | .55 | .63 | .41 | .42 | .22 | .38 | .61 | .42 | .52 | .63 | .55 |
| Ego Strength | -.71 | -.26 | -.26 | -.68 | -.32 | -.54 | -.38 | -.28 | -.29 | -.51 | -.34 | -.12 |
| Mania | .49 | .45 | .61 | .50 | .44 | .25 | .37 | .51 | .40 | .54 | .58 | .56 |
| Test Anxiety | .44 | .19 | .27 | .41 | .37 | .22 | .27 | .25 | .25 | .49 | .25 | .14 |
| **MMPI-2-RF mean** | 51.9 | 51.5 | 48.4 | 53.3 | 53.9 | 49.7 | 50.7 | 48.7 | 54.2 | 53.2 | 51.5 | 50.2 |
| **MMPI-2-RF SD** | 12.4 | 13.9 | 9.6 | 11.7 | 11.3 | 11.7 | 8.8 | 10.8 | 13.0 | 11.0 | 13.5 | 8.7 |

**Table 11.35** SRP-COL: Correlations With the MMPI-2-RF *(continued)*

| BASC-3 | Malaise | Head Pain Complaints | Neurological Complaints | Gastro-intestinal Complaints | Suicidal/Death Ideation | Helplessness/Hopelessness | Self-Doubt | Inefficacy | Cognitive Complaints | Stress/Worry | Anxiety | Anger Proneness |
|---|---|---|---|---|---|---|---|---|---|---|---|---|
| **Composite** | | | | | | | | | | | | |
| Internalizing Problems | .46 | .29 | .50 | .44 | .43 | .35 | .47 | .52 | .60 | .55 | .55 | .34 |
| Inattention/Hyperactivity | .10 | .20 | .45 | .27 | .24 | .26 | .26 | .35 | .73 | .29 | .26 | .39 |
| Emotional Symptoms | .49 | .25 | .39 | .43 | .42 | .42 | .53 | .55 | .58 | .58 | .55 | .31 |
| Personal Adjustment | -.45 | -.16 | -.20 | -.31 | -.26 | -.40 | -.49 | -.44 | -.51 | -.50 | -.44 | -.33 |
| **Clinical scale** | | | | | | | | | | | | |
| Atypicality | .27 | .14 | .53 | .20 | .31 | .20 | .36 | .33 | .63 | .32 | .41 | .34 |
| Locus of Control | .48 | .24 | .45 | .35 | .43 | .43 | .48 | .47 | .56 | .52 | .50 | .43 |
| Social Stress | .52 | .22 | .31 | .36 | .34 | .34 | .55 | .45 | .53 | .49 | .42 | .26 |
| Anxiety | .52 | .26 | .37 | .38 | .35 | .26 | .41 | .55 | .53 | .70 | .65 | .28 |
| Depression | .41 | .33 | .42 | .49 | .51 | .37 | .49 | .50 | .51 | .54 | .54 | .31 |
| Sense of Inadequacy | .29 | .22 | .47 | .40 | .40 | .39 | .38 | .56 | .54 | .44 | .46 | .29 |
| Somatization | .30 | .35 | .44 | .47 | .27 | .12 | .18 | .26 | .27 | .35 | .31 | .14 |
| Attention Problems | .16 | .18 | .38 | .31 | .23 | .32 | .30 | .40 | .77 | .29 | .26 | .40 |
| Hyperactivity | .05 | .20 | .46 | .22 | .24 | .20 | .22 | .27 | .60 | .27 | .26 | .35 |
| Sensation Seeking | -.09 | .02 | .42 | .01 | .22 | -.10 | -.02 | -.06 | .27 | -.05 | .13 | .16 |
| Alcohol Abuse | .08 | .05 | .33 | .22 | .37 | .17 | .07 | .14 | .39 | .19 | .26 | .20 |
| School Maladjustment | .38 | .14 | .36 | .30 | .40 | .45 | .48 | .58 | .66 | .55 | .52 | .37 |
| **Adaptive scale** | | | | | | | | | | | | |
| Relations With Parents | -.32 | -.10 | -.19 | -.18 | -.20 | -.23 | -.36 | -.31 | -.46 | -.43 | -.42 | -.33 |
| Interpersonal Relations | -.42 | -.16 | -.04 | -.34 | -.15 | -.32 | -.45 | -.40 | -.42 | -.45 | -.29 | -.30 |
| Self-Esteem | -.54 | -.16 | -.24 | -.31 | -.34 | -.46 | -.57 | -.40 | -.40 | -.52 | -.47 | -.13 |
| Self-Reliance | -.20 | -.13 | -.18 | -.23 | -.20 | -.34 | -.26 | -.37 | -.44 | -.30 | -.27 | -.31 |
| **Content scale** | | | | | | | | | | | | |
| Anger Control | .29 | .20 | .50 | .24 | .39 | .23 | .20 | .31 | .64 | .25 | .43 | .51 |
| Ego Strength | -.51 | -.12 | -.24 | -.28 | -.35 | -.38 | -.60 | -.36 | -.44 | -.54 | -.41 | -.16 |
| Mania | .34 | .17 | .52 | .27 | .39 | .22 | .43 | .36 | .69 | .46 | .46 | .41 |
| Test Anxiety | .24 | .25 | .32 | .30 | .25 | .30 | .24 | .41 | .46 | .51 | .35 | .28 |
| **MMPI-2-RF mean** | 50.0 | 51.0 | 54.7 | 51.7 | 51.8 | 49.7 | 52.5 | 54.5 | 57.2 | 54.8 | 54.3 | 53.1 |
| **MMPI-2-RF *SD*** | 9.7 | 10.9 | 12.7 | 10.9 | 12.1 | 11.5 | 12.4 | 10.1 | 13.0 | 12.1 | 12.7 | 9.7 |

**Table 11.35** SRP–COL: Correlations With the MMPI-2-RF (continued)

| BASC–3 | Behavior-Restricting Fears | Multiple Specific Fears | Juvenile Conduct Problems | Substance Abuse | Aggression | Activation | Family Problems | Interpersonal Passivity | Social Avoidance | Shyness | Disaffilia-tiveness | Aesthetic-Literary Interests |
|---|---|---|---|---|---|---|---|---|---|---|---|---|
| **Composite** | | | | | | | | | | | | |
| Internalizing Problems | .18 | .14 | .33 | .29 | .49 | .14 | .50 | .09 | .30 | .43 | .36 | -.02 |
| Inattention/Hyperactivity | .21 | .14 | .23 | .37 | .47 | .30 | .33 | -.04 | .03 | .33 | .14 | -.08 |
| Emotional Symptoms | .20 | .14 | .29 | .26 | .45 | .06 | .52 | .22 | .37 | .54 | .42 | .03 |
| Personal Adjustment | -.25 | -.18 | -.26 | -.22 | -.46 | .03 | -.56 | -.25 | -.48 | -.63 | -.51 | -.10 |
| **Clinical scale** | | | | | | | | | | | | |
| Atypicality | .10 | .13 | .34 | .39 | .51 | .33 | .40 | -.07 | .09 | .33 | .20 | -.06 |
| Locus of Control | .21 | .14 | .42 | .30 | .56 | .09 | .57 | .15 | .33 | .41 | .45 | -.03 |
| Social Stress | .09 | .07 | .23 | .22 | .35 | .08 | .47 | .15 | .38 | .49 | .39 | .05 |
| Anxiety | .22 | .09 | .18 | .29 | .39 | .10 | .42 | .05 | .18 | .49 | .12 | -.02 |
| Depression | .18 | .09 | .36 | .27 | .38 | .14 | .46 | .14 | .27 | .37 | .37 | -.06 |
| Sense of Inadequacy | .22 | .21 | .28 | .18 | .49 | .08 | .45 | .17 | .36 | .40 | .49 | .03 |
| Somatization | .10 | .10 | .19 | .11 | .28 | .02 | .24 | -.09 | .15 | .12 | .09 | .01 |
| Attention Problems | .22 | .22 | .25 | .39 | .49 | .19 | .39 | .06 | .16 | .44 | .30 | -.03 |
| Hyperactivity | .18 | .05 | .21 | .31 | .42 | .38 | .26 | -.10 | -.08 | .22 | .00 | -.13 |
| Sensation Seeking | -.06 | -.06 | .31 | .36 | .33 | .31 | .15 | -.24 | -.24 | -.10 | .09 | -.10 |
| Alcohol Abuse | .03 | -.09 | .41 | .64 | .43 | .13 | .27 | -.08 | -.15 | .16 | .05 | -.18 |
| School Maladjustment | .21 | .08 | .42 | .40 | .54 | .00 | .50 | .12 | .33 | .65 | .44 | -.04 |
| **Adaptive scale** | | | | | | | | | | | | |
| Relations With Parents | -.23 | -.14 | -.34 | -.20 | -.53 | -.14 | -.57 | -.08 | -.39 | -.53 | -.52 | -.12 |
| Interpersonal Relations | -.27 | -.17 | -.13 | -.11 | -.30 | .13 | -.40 | -.15 | -.51 | -.59 | -.43 | -.07 |
| Self-Esteem | -.07 | .03 | -.20 | -.09 | -.29 | .01 | -.46 | -.30 | -.40 | -.52 | -.36 | -.08 |
| Self-Reliance | -.28 | -.31 | -.21 | -.33 | -.39 | .12 | -.45 | -.34 | -.30 | -.48 | -.40 | -.08 |
| **Content scale** | | | | | | | | | | | | |
| Anger Control | .16 | .09 | .47 | .47 | .74 | .26 | .39 | -.10 | .07 | .36 | .18 | -.02 |
| Ego Strength | -.09 | -.07 | -.13 | -.14 | -.34 | -.02 | -.48 | -.33 | -.39 | -.52 | -.39 | -.13 |
| Mania | .11 | .10 | .40 | .42 | .56 | .35 | .41 | .00 | .09 | .37 | .19 | -.06 |
| Test Anxiety | .37 | .31 | .19 | .14 | .41 | .07 | .40 | .03 | .23 | .35 | .28 | .05 |
| **MMPI-2-RF mean** | 52.2 | 48.6 | 47.7 | 49.8 | 48.0 | 54.1 | 50.6 | 47.3 | 49.3 | 50.0 | 53.7 | 46.2 |
| **MMPI-2-RF SD** | 12.7 | 8.6 | 10.4 | 10.3 | 9.1 | 11.2 | 11.3 | 8.1 | 11.1 | 11.0 | 13.3 | 9.7 |

**Table 11.35** SRP–COL: Correlations With the MMPI-2-RF (continued)

| BASC-3 | Mechanical-Physical Interests | Aggressive-ness–Revised | Psychoticism–Revised | Disconstraint–Revised | Negative Emotionality/ Neuroticism–Revised | Introversion/ Low Positive Emotionality–Revised | BASC-3 Mean | BASC-3 SD |
|---|---|---|---|---|---|---|---|---|
| **Composite** | | | | | | | | |
| Internalizing Problems | .15 | .14 | .38 | .38 | .64 | .32 | 48.9 | 11.1 |
| Inattention/Hyperactivity | .31 | .32 | .37 | .42 | .35 | .01 | 49.4 | 10.7 |
| Emotional Symptoms | .11 | .05 | .31 | .30 | .63 | .43 | 49.1 | 11.2 |
| Personal Adjustment | -.13 | -.08 | -.29 | -.25 | -.55 | -.53 | 51.6 | 10.7 |
| **Clinical scale** | | | | | | | | |
| Atypicality | .33 | .27 | .54 | .55 | .44 | .05 | 48.2 | 10.8 |
| Locus of Control | .24 | .17 | .45 | .38 | .63 | .36 | 48.0 | 9.9 |
| Social Stress | .16 | .04 | .31 | .28 | .53 | .40 | 49.6 | 11.2 |
| Anxiety | -.06 | .08 | .23 | .23 | .74 | .25 | 49.4 | 9.8 |
| Depression | .11 | .06 | .28 | .31 | .58 | .29 | 50.0 | 11.8 |
| Sense of Inadequacy | .12 | .13 | .32 | .28 | .51 | .38 | 49.0 | 11.2 |
| Somatization | .04 | .16 | .23 | .19 | .41 | .18 | 49.5 | 10.7 |
| Attention Problems | .28 | .30 | .35 | .38 | .31 | .19 | 48.4 | 10.1 |
| Hyperactivity | .31 | .31 | .36 | .42 | .35 | -.15 | 50.3 | 11.0 |
| Sensation Seeking | .42 | .44 | .34 | .57 | .06 | -.34 | 47.6 | 9.9 |
| Alcohol Abuse | .28 | .26 | .25 | .53 | .28 | -.14 | 49.3 | 12.2 |
| School Maladjustment | .19 | .22 | .36 | .42 | .61 | .39 | 48.3 | 9.0 |
| **Adaptive scale** | | | | | | | | |
| Relations With Parents | -.15 | -.31 | -.41 | -.30 | -.53 | -.36 | 51.4 | 10.6 |
| Interpersonal Relations | -.08 | -.04 | -.11 | -.13 | -.44 | -.55 | 51.4 | 9.9 |
| Self-Esteem | -.06 | .11 | -.17 | -.20 | -.53 | -.42 | 50.2 | 10.4 |
| Self-Reliance | -.15 | -.04 | -.25 | -.22 | -.34 | -.46 | 52.1 | 10.3 |
| **Content scale** | | | | | | | | |
| Anger Control | .30 | .47 | .55 | .56 | .48 | .05 | 48.4 | 10.2 |
| Ego Strength | -.08 | .07 | -.25 | -.18 | -.53 | -.42 | 50.9 | 10.5 |
| Mania | .29 | .33 | .49 | .56 | .57 | .07 | 49.5 | 10.0 |
| Test Anxiety | -.01 | .21 | .25 | .17 | .53 | .25 | 50.5 | 11.5 |
| **MMPI-2-RF mean** | 46.0 | 51.0 | 51.5 | 47.8 | 53.6 | 47.6 | — | — |
| **MMPI-2-RF SD** | 7.6 | 9.5 | 14.0 | 9.5 | 10.3 | 10.4 | — | — |

# PROFILES OF CLINICAL GROUPS

When interpreting BASC–3 results, it is helpful to know the profiles of mean scale scores of groups of children and adolescents who have been identified with behavioral or emotional problems. In general, such individuals will tend to have various behavioral strengths along with higher than average deficits.

Often, these differences between the strengths and deficits are defining features of the problem area itself; for example, attention-deficit/hyperactivity disorder (ADHD) is defined by hyperactivity and attention problems. An understanding of these profiles is helpful when making complex differential diagnoses. The presentation of group score profiles gives added empirical support for the use of the BASC–3 in identifying behavioral and emotional problems.

As discussed in chapters 7 and 8, the clinical norm samples were created from groups of children and adolescents who were identified as having one or more behavioral, emotional, physical, or learning problems. There were sufficient cases of each of the following groups to calculate profiles:

- Attention-deficit/hyperactivity disorder (ADHD)

- Autism spectrum disorder

- Emotional/behavioral disturbance (EBD)

- Hearing impairment

- Specific learning disorder

- Speech or language disorder

The mean $T$ scores for these groups on the SRP composites and scales appear in Table 11.36 and are displayed graphically in Figures 11.1 through 11.6. General combined-gender norms were used for all cases. For each diagnostic group, results are combined across the child and adolescent levels. Overall, none of the average scale scores reached a level of At-Risk (i.e., 60 or higher); however, several patterns of scale score elevations were evident for several clinical groups. Selected results of these profiles include:

- ADHD: elevated scale scores for the Attention Problems and Hyperactivity scales

- Autism: elevated scale scores for several composite and clinical scales, along with markedly lower than average scores on several of the adaptive scales

- EBD: elevated scale scores for several of the Internalizing Problems scales, including the Depression, Somatization, Anxiety, and Sense of Inadequacy scales.

# Table 11.36 Mean *T* Scores for Clinical Groups on the SRP Composites, Scales, and Indexes

| | All Clinical | | Attention-Deficit/ Hyperactivity Disorder | | Autism Spectrum Disorder and Pervasive Developmental Disorder | | Emotional/Behavioral Disturbance | | Hearing Impairment | | Learning Disability | | Speech/Language Disorder | |
|---|---|---|---|---|---|---|---|---|---|---|---|---|---|---|
| | Child/Adolescent | | Child/Adolescent | | Child/Adolescent | | Child/Adolescent | | Child/Adolescent | | Child/Adolescent | | Child/Adolescent | |
| | Mean | SD | Mean | SD | Mean | SD | Mean | SD | Mean | SD | Mean | SD | Mean | SD |
| **Composite** | | | | | | | | | | | | | | |
| School Problems | 52.8 | 11.1 | 53.9 | 11.5 | 52.0 | 11.3 | 53.6 | 11.5 | 50.6 | 10.7 | 51.6 | 9.9 | 51.0 | 9.9 |
| Internalizing Problems | 54.6 | 11.2 | 54.0 | 10.6 | 55.8 | 10.7 | 57.6 | 13.0 | 54.7 | 10.1 | 53.6 | 12.4 | 50.1 | 8.4 |
| Inattention/Hyperactivity | 55.8 | 10.9 | 58.0 | 10.9 | 56.2 | 10.0 | 54.7 | 10.8 | 52.3 | 8.8 | 53.3 | 11.3 | 50.6 | 10.1 |
| Emotional Symptoms | 54.7 | 10.9 | 54.1 | 10.7 | 56.8 | 10.4 | 56.3 | 11.9 | 54.7 | 9.6 | 54.5 | 11.4 | 50.7 | 9.4 |
| Personal Adjustment | 45.8 | 10.7 | 46.2 | 10.4 | 43.0 | 11.9 | 45.8 | 10.9 | 46.9 | 9.8 | 45.7 | 10.9 | 49.5 | 8.1 |
| **Clinical scale** | | | | | | | | | | | | | | |
| Attitude to School | 53.6 | 11.9 | 54.4 | 12.0 | 54.2 | 12.1 | 53.8 | 13.2 | 51.7 | 11.0 | 52.4 | 10.5 | 52.1 | 11.6 |
| Attitude to Teachers | 51.8 | 10.8 | 52.8 | 11.6 | 50.5 | 10.1 | 52.4 | 10.7 | 50.5 | 10.2 | 50.9 | 10.3 | 50.7 | 9.4 |
| Sensation Seeking | 50.8 | 9.8 | 51.6 | 9.9 | 48.0 | 9.6 | 51.6 | 10.2 | 49.4 | 10.3 | 51.4 | 8.7 | 46.8 | 10.7 |
| Atypicality | 53.7 | 11.6 | 52.8 | 10.1 | 54.6 | 11.1 | 56.0 | 14.3 | 55.7 | 13.5 | 53.9 | 13.4 | 49.5 | 8.1 |
| Locus of Control | 53.7 | 11.1 | 54.2 | 10.6 | 54.7 | 11.8 | 55.7 | 12.6 | 52.6 | 10.6 | 51.6 | 10.6 | 49.1 | 8.4 |
| Social Stress | 53.0 | 11.1 | 52.4 | 11.2 | 55.0 | 10.9 | 54.5 | 11.3 | 54.3 | 9.7 | 52.2 | 12.3 | 49.9 | 7.6 |
| Anxiety | 53.0 | 11.0 | 52.6 | 10.8 | 54.0 | 10.0 | 56.0 | 12.0 | 51.7 | 8.3 | 51.3 | 11.6 | 49.7 | 9.9 |
| Depression | 54.5 | 12.0 | 53.6 | 11.5 | 57.1 | 12.2 | 57.7 | 13.4 | 54.5 | 10.3 | 53.1 | 12.4 | 49.3 | 8.2 |
| Sense of Inadequacy | 54.9 | 11.1 | 54.5 | 11.3 | 55.2 | 11.1 | 55.7 | 12.3 | 55.3 | 9.8 | 55.9 | 10.4 | 52.4 | 9.9 |
| Somatization | 52.6 | 11.9 | 50.2 | 10.2 | 51.5 | 11.1 | 58.7 | 15.1 | 54.2 | 7.4 | 53.1 | 12.1 | 53.6 | 12.6 |
| Attention Problems | 56.4 | 10.7 | 58.7 | 10.7 | 56.7 | 9.9 | 54.5 | 11.4 | 52.5 | 9.7 | 54.7 | 10.2 | 51.9 | 10.2 |
| Hyperactivity | 54.2 | 10.8 | 56.1 | 10.9 | 54.6 | 10.4 | 54.1 | 9.8 | 51.8 | 8.1 | 51.4 | 12.2 | 49.4 | 10.0 |
| **Adaptive scale** | | | | | | | | | | | | | | |
| Relations with Parents | 47.8 | 10.6 | 47.7 | 10.5 | 45.8 | 11.6 | 48.0 | 11.4 | 50.4 | 9.4 | 48.6 | 9.8 | 49.8 | 8.7 |
| Interpersonal Relations | 45.7 | 12.4 | 46.3 | 12.2 | 42.5 | 12.7 | 44.4 | 13.2 | 46.1 | 11.9 | 45.8 | 12.8 | 51.0 | 6.9 |
| Self-Esteem | 48.0 | 10.8 | 48.8 | 10.4 | 46.2 | 10.9 | 46.9 | 12.1 | 48.5 | 8.4 | 48.0 | 11.2 | 50.0 | 9.5 |
| Self-Reliance | 45.3 | 10.1 | 45.2 | 9.2 | 43.2 | 10.9 | 47.1 | 10.5 | 45.6 | 10.1 | 43.9 | 10.4 | 47.9 | 10.6 |
| **Content scale** | | | | | | | | | | | | | | |
| Anger Control | 54.2 | 12.1 | 52.7 | 11.3 | 55.2 | 13.0 | 56.8 | 13.6 | 55.5 | 13.1 | 55.0 | 11.8 | 50.6 | 8.4 |
| Ego Strength | 46.2 | 11.2 | 48.1 | 10.3 | 42.9 | 11.5 | 45.5 | 12.1 | 46.5 | 11.7 | 44.0 | 11.9 | 47.7 | 7.9 |
| Mania | 54.3 | 10.3 | 55.0 | 10.8 | 55.6 | 10.3 | 54.2 | 9.0 | 52.5 | 10.3 | 52.3 | 10.4 | 50.8 | 10.2 |
| Test Anxiety | 52.2 | 10.0 | 51.3 | 10.2 | 50.8 | 10.3 | 51.9 | 9.5 | 53.0 | 9.7 | 56.0 | 9.4 | 55.0 | 8.3 |
| **Clinical index** | | | | | | | | | | | | | | |
| Functional Impairment Index | 56.0 | 10.9 | 56.8 | 10.9 | 56.8 | 9.7 | 57.5 | 11.6 | 55.1 | 10.8 | 53.7 | 11.1 | 50.9 | 9.8 |

## Clinical Profile

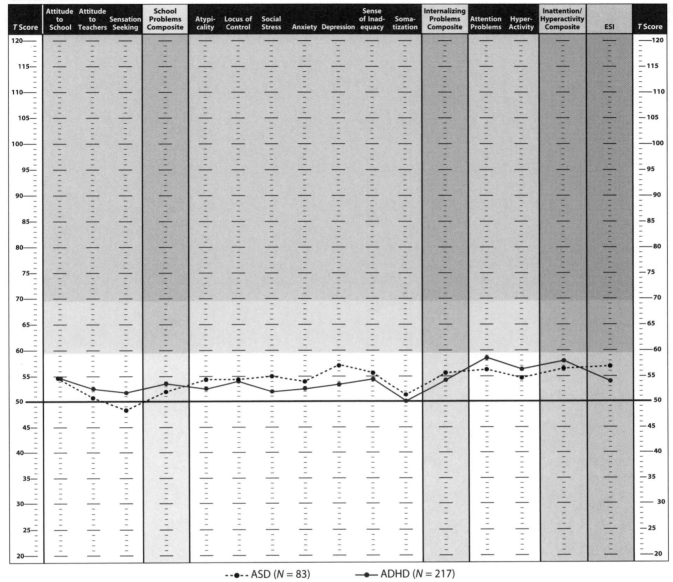

**Figure 11.1** SRP: Clinical group *T* scores for attention-deficit/hyperactivity disorder and autism spectrum disorder in the Clinical Profile

## Adaptive Profile

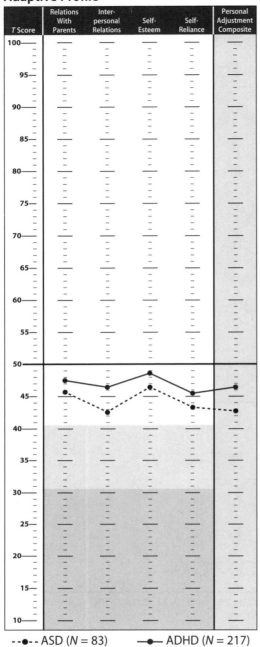

**Figure 11.2** SRP: Clinical group *T* scores for attention-deficit/hyperactivity disorder and autism spectrum disorder in the Adaptive Profile

## Clinical Profile

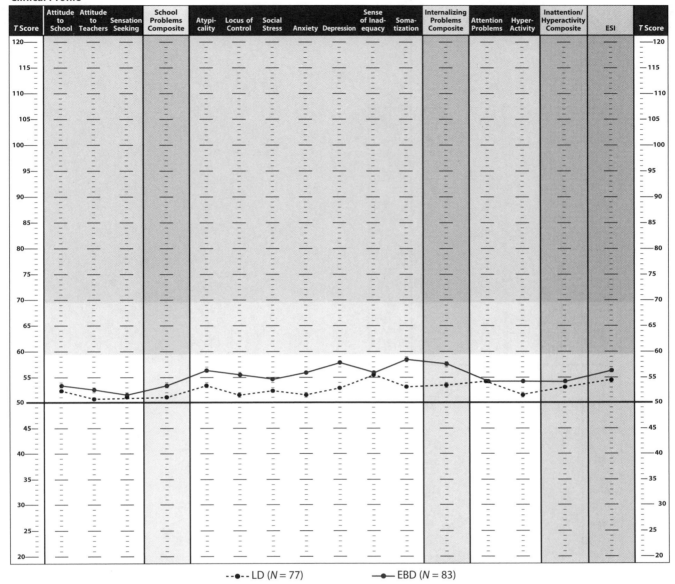

**Figure 11.3** SRP: Clinical group *T* scores for emotional/behavioral disturbance and specific learning disorder in the Clinical Profile

## Adaptive Profile

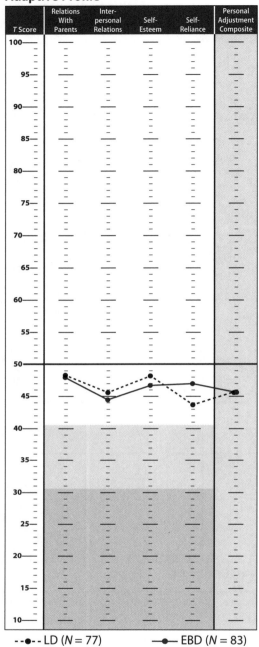

--●-- LD (*N* = 77)      —●— EBD (*N* = 83)

**Figure 11.4** SRP: Clinical group *T* scores for emotional/
behavioral disturbance and specific learning
disorder in the Adaptive Profile

**Clinical Profile**

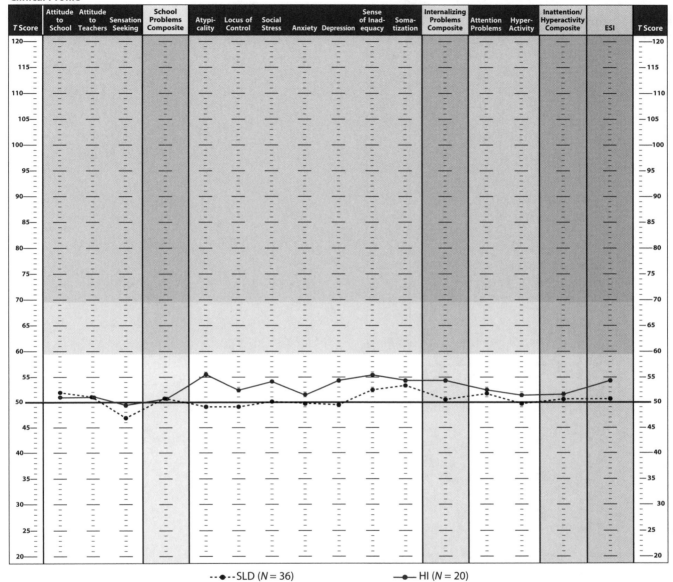

**Figure 11.5** SRP: Clinical group *T* scores for hearing impairment and speech or language disorder in the Clinical Profile

## Adaptive Profile

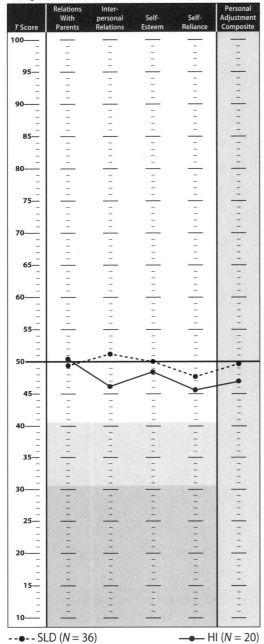

**Figure 11.6** SRP: Clinical group *T* scores for hearing impairment and speech or language disorder in the Adaptive Profile

# Chapter 12

# Relationships Among BASC–3 Components

The Teacher Rating Scales (TRS), Parent Rating Scales (PRS), and Self-Report of Personality (SRP) are measures of a variety of behaviors that may be viewed as manifestations of individual traits. Expression of these behaviors (their type and intensity) may depend on the setting and be perceived differently by teachers, parents, and individuals. The items on each BASC–3 form are suited both to the specific setting in which the behavior is observed and to the respondent's perspective. For example, the TRS includes a clinical measure of learning problems and an adaptive measure of study skills that do not appear on the PRS, yet much of the content is similar across components. For instance, both the TRS and PRS include a clinical measure of aggression. Aggression may manifest at different levels in various environments; however, a child who is highly aggressive in one environment can be expected to be so in other environments. This chapter presents the similarities and differences among the BASC–3 TRS, PRS, and SRP, with correlations between scales and composites for each form. All correlations presented are based on samples that include both clinical and nonclinical cases.

## Evidence of Multitrait-Multimethod Validity

One type of validity evidence often reported with measures of many traits is the multitrait-multimethod correlation matrix. This matrix shows correlations between different measures of the same trait (multimethod) as well as correlations between different traits (multitrait). The pattern of correlations shown by this method is more important for analysis than the magnitude of the correlation. The validity of this matrix is evident when the correlations between measures of the same trait are moderate to high and correlations between measures of different traits are low. The same pattern should be expected when behavior observations are made in different settings and by different raters (as with the teacher and parent ratings).

### RELATIONSHIP BETWEEN TEACHERS' AND PARENTS' RATINGS

The TRS and PRS are useful for assessing multiple traits because they require different types of respondents (teachers and parents) who rate behaviors observed in different settings (school and home). Because some behaviors can be observed across settings, the TRS and PRS contain many similar items and scales. For example, the child levels of the TRS and PRS both have 12 items, 7 that occur on both forms. The similarities in scale content should lead to moderate correlations between forms. On the other hand, some scales measure very different behaviors, and the correlations between these scales should be low. Tables 12.1 through 12.3 show the correlations of *T* scores on each scale for individuals who were rated by both a teacher and a parent. The sample sizes for the preschool, child, and adolescent levels were 259, 392, and 343, respectively. Three patterns among the correlation clusters are particularly important for evaluating validity:

1.  Correlations between scales that measure the same construct should be higher than correlations between scales that measure different constructs.

2.  Correlations between clinical and adaptive scales should be negative.

3.  Correlations between the composites and the scales composing the composites should be higher than correlations between composites and scales that are not part of those composites.

**Table 12.1** Correlations Between TRS–P and PRS–P Forms (Combined General and Clinical Samples)

| TRS scales | PRS scales | | | | | | | | | | | |
|---|---|---|---|---|---|---|---|---|---|---|---|---|
| | Composite | | | | Clinical scale | | | | | | | |
| | Externalizing Problems | Internalizing Problems | Adaptive Skills | Behavioral Symptoms Index | Hyperactivity | Aggression | Anxiety | Depression | Somatization | Attention Problems | Atypicality | Withdrawal |
| **Composite** | | | | | | | | | | | | |
| Externalizing Problems | .43 | .13 | −.37 | .39 | .43 | .35 | −.01 | .30 | .04 | .48 | .30 | −.02 |
| Internalizing Problems | .22 | .18 | −.20 | .22 | .17 | .24 | .04 | .22 | .19 | .21 | .16 | .02 |
| Adaptive Skills | −.24 | −.08 | .41 | −.32 | −.23 | −.22 | .01 | −.16 | −.05 | −.34 | −.26 | −.23 |
| Behavioral Symptoms Index | .39 | .15 | −.45 | .44 | .39 | .32 | .00 | .30 | .08 | .50 | .39 | .16 |
| **Clinical scale** | | | | | | | | | | | | |
| Hyperactivity | .40 | .10 | −.32 | .38 | .42 | .30 | −.04 | .27 | .02 | .47 | .32 | −.01 |
| Aggression | .40 | .16 | −.34 | .36 | .38 | .36 | .02 | .29 | .07 | .43 | .24 | −.02 |
| Anxiety | .19 | .19 | −.17 | .20 | .15 | .20 | .09 | .21 | .16 | .17 | .14 | .07 |
| Depression | .26 | .13 | −.29 | .25 | .22 | .25 | .00 | .24 | .07 | .29 | .17 | .01 |
| Somatization | .10 | .13 | −.02 | .08 | .06 | .14 | .02 | .10 | .21 | .07 | .09 | −.09 |
| Attention Problems | .23 | .06 | −.34 | .31 | .25 | .18 | −.03 | .19 | .01 | .43 | .28 | .10 |
| Atypicality | .26 | .11 | −.33 | .36 | .31 | .19 | .00 | .19 | .06 | .37 | .39 | .24 |
| Withdrawal | .21 | .13 | −.36 | .33 | .20 | .18 | .05 | .18 | .11 | .28 | .32 | .36 |
| **Adaptive scale** | | | | | | | | | | | | |
| Adaptability | −.28 | −.15 | .27 | −.29 | −.25 | −.28 | −.08 | −.19 | −.10 | −.30 | −.19 | −.17 |
| Social Skills | −.16 | −.03 | .38 | −.24 | −.15 | −.15 | .03 | −.12 | .00 | −.24 | −.24 | −.23 |
| Functional Communication | −.20 | −.02 | .46 | −.28 | −.22 | −.16 | .08 | −.13 | −.02 | −.33 | −.26 | −.23 |
| **Content scale** | | | | | | | | | | | | |
| Anger Control | .37 | .19 | −.36 | .37 | .35 | .34 | .06 | .34 | .07 | .40 | .25 | .04 |
| Bullying | .40 | .09 | −.41 | .38 | .39 | .34 | −.03 | .23 | .02 | .47 | .30 | .05 |
| Developmental Social Disorders | .29 | .11 | −.40 | .37 | .30 | .22 | −.01 | .19 | .09 | .38 | .34 | .26 |
| Emotional Self-Control | .32 | .18 | −.35 | .33 | .30 | .29 | .04 | .30 | .08 | .36 | .24 | .05 |
| Executive Functioning | .38 | .17 | −.45 | .42 | .39 | .30 | .03 | .32 | .07 | .50 | .36 | .11 |
| Negative Emotionality | .31 | .14 | −.32 | .29 | .27 | .31 | −.01 | .27 | .08 | .29 | .22 | .02 |
| Resiliency | −.28 | −.16 | .31 | −.30 | −.25 | −.27 | −.06 | −.24 | −.09 | −.32 | −.20 | −.14 |
| **Clinical index** | | | | | | | | | | | | |
| Clinical Probability Index | .33 | .14 | −.50 | .44 | .37 | .24 | .01 | .27 | .08 | .50 | .45 | .26 |
| Functional Impairment Index | .30 | .10 | −.50 | .39 | .33 | .21 | −.03 | .22 | .04 | .46 | .36 | .23 |

| TRS scales | PRS scales | | | | | | | | | | | | |
| --- | --- | --- | --- | --- | --- | --- | --- | --- | --- | --- | --- | --- | --- |
| | Adaptive scale | | | | Content scale | | | | | | | Clinical index | |
| | Adaptability | Social Skills | Activities of Daily Living | Functional Communication | Anger Control | Bullying | Developmental Social Disorders | Emotional Self-Control | Executive Functioning | Negative Emotionality | Resiliency | Clinical Probability Index | Functional Impairment Index |
| **Composite** | | | | | | | | | | | | | |
| Externalizing Problems | -.30 | -.31 | -.28 | -.28 | .37 | .19 | .31 | .35 | .46 | .30 | -.30 | .44 | .37 |
| Internalizing Problems | -.18 | -.18 | -.16 | -.09 | .25 | .12 | .11 | .21 | .22 | .26 | -.13 | .19 | .21 |
| Adaptive Skills | .30 | .41 | .23 | .41 | -.22 | -.11 | -.40 | -.21 | -.36 | -.16 | .34 | -.40 | -.41 |
| Behavioral Symptoms Index | -.37 | -.41 | -.31 | -.37 | .37 | .16 | .44 | .36 | .48 | .30 | -.38 | .50 | .46 |
| **Clinical scale** | | | | | | | | | | | | | |
| Hyperactivity | -.27 | -.30 | -.25 | -.28 | .33 | .16 | .30 | .32 | .43 | .27 | -.27 | .43 | .33 |
| Aggression | -.30 | -.29 | -.28 | -.24 | .35 | .21 | .28 | .34 | .43 | .30 | -.29 | .39 | .33 |
| Anxiety | -.18 | -.14 | -.14 | -.05 | .23 | .09 | .07 | .21 | .20 | .24 | -.13 | .15 | .20 |
| Depression | -.22 | -.26 | -.24 | -.19 | .27 | .15 | .21 | .24 | .30 | .27 | -.19 | .28 | .28 |
| Somatization | -.06 | -.02 | .00 | .02 | .13 | .07 | -.02 | .07 | .08 | .13 | -.02 | .04 | .04 |
| Attention Problems | -.32 | -.31 | -.22 | -.32 | .23 | .09 | .37 | .24 | .37 | .14 | -.34 | .39 | .33 |
| Atypicality | -.25 | -.32 | -.23 | -.26 | .23 | .04 | .35 | .24 | .35 | .20 | -.29 | .37 | .37 |
| Withdrawal | -.30 | -.37 | -.20 | -.33 | .23 | .09 | .42 | .23 | .31 | .20 | -.32 | .36 | .41 |
| **Adaptive scale** | | | | | | | | | | | | | |
| Adaptability | .31 | .22 | .15 | .18 | -.24 | -.17 | -.26 | -.22 | -.32 | -.21 | .26 | -.28 | -.30 |
| Social Skills | .21 | .41 | .22 | .39 | -.17 | -.07 | -.37 | -.16 | -.26 | -.11 | .29 | -.35 | -.36 |
| Functional Communication | .27 | .46 | .25 | .52 | -.18 | -.06 | -.44 | -.18 | -.35 | -.11 | .35 | -.42 | -.41 |
| **Content scale** | | | | | | | | | | | | | |
| Anger Control | -.34 | -.31 | -.23 | -.25 | .38 | .20 | .33 | .37 | .43 | .33 | -.33 | .42 | .38 |
| Bullying | -.33 | -.37 | -.29 | -.34 | .31 | .16 | .37 | .29 | .45 | .24 | -.32 | .45 | .39 |
| Developmental Social Disorders | -.32 | -.41 | -.23 | -.36 | .25 | .09 | .43 | .25 | .38 | .20 | -.35 | .42 | .43 |
| Emotional Self-Control | -.32 | -.30 | -.25 | -.24 | .34 | .15 | .28 | .32 | .38 | .31 | -.29 | .36 | .34 |
| Executive Functioning | -.39 | -.41 | -.30 | -.39 | .38 | .16 | .43 | .38 | .49 | .30 | -.41 | .49 | .45 |
| Negative Emotionality | -.23 | -.26 | -.29 | -.21 | .31 | .16 | .22 | .27 | .33 | .30 | -.19 | .30 | .29 |
| Resiliency | .31 | .27 | .21 | .22 | -.27 | -.18 | -.27 | -.26 | -.34 | -.23 | .28 | -.30 | -.33 |
| **Clinical index** | | | | | | | | | | | | | |
| Clinical Probability Index | -.38 | -.48 | -.31 | -.49 | .31 | .09 | .53 | .33 | .48 | .24 | -.44 | .54 | .51 |
| Functional Impairment Index | -.37 | -.49 | -.28 | -.51 | .29 | .07 | .50 | .30 | .46 | .19 | -.43 | .51 | .49 |

**Table 12.2** Correlations Between TRS–C and PRS–C Forms (Combined General and Clinical Samples)

| TRS scales | PRS scales | | | | | | | | | | | | |
|---|---|---|---|---|---|---|---|---|---|---|---|---|---|
| | Composite | | | | Clinical scale | | | | | | | | |
| | Externalizing Problems | Internalizing Problems | Adaptive Skills | Behavioral Symptoms Index | Hyperactivity | Aggression | Conduct Problems | Anxiety | Depression | Somatization | Attention Problems | Atypicality | Withdrawal |
| **Composite** | | | | | | | | | | | | | |
| Externalizing Problems | .43 | .13 | −.29 | .37 | .41 | .38 | .35 | .04 | .24 | .03 | .36 | .21 | .11 |
| Internalizing Problems | .18 | .28 | −.21 | .28 | .19 | .18 | .10 | .24 | .26 | .17 | .23 | .21 | .22 |
| School Problems | .24 | .18 | −.40 | .35 | .30 | .17 | .19 | .13 | .22 | .10 | .48 | .31 | .23 |
| Adaptive Skills | −.27 | −.14 | .49 | −.42 | −.27 | −.27 | −.19 | −.07 | −.23 | −.04 | −.44 | −.37 | −.37 |
| Behavioral Symptoms Index | .35 | .20 | −.43 | .46 | .37 | .33 | .25 | .12 | .29 | .07 | .44 | .37 | .33 |
| **Clinical scale** | | | | | | | | | | | | | |
| Hyperactivity | .40 | .15 | −.29 | .37 | .44 | .32 | .31 | .07 | .24 | .05 | .40 | .23 | .12 |
| Aggression | .37 | .09 | −.23 | .30 | .32 | .37 | .28 | .01 | .19 | −.01 | .26 | .16 | .09 |
| Conduct Problems | .40 | .11 | −.27 | .32 | .36 | .36 | .35 | .02 | .20 | .04 | .32 | .16 | .09 |
| Anxiety | .08 | .27 | −.17 | .22 | .12 | .08 | .01 | .29 | .21 | .18 | .19 | .19 | .21 |
| Depression | .25 | .21 | −.26 | .33 | .24 | .25 | .16 | .14 | .28 | .09 | .24 | .25 | .25 |
| Somatization | .11 | .18 | −.08 | .13 | .11 | .10 | .07 | .16 | .15 | .16 | .11 | .07 | .06 |
| Attention Problems | .32 | .19 | −.41 | .41 | .39 | .24 | .25 | .13 | .24 | .12 | .53 | .33 | .24 |
| Learning Problems | .12 | .13 | −.31 | .25 | .17 | .08 | .10 | .12 | .16 | .06 | .36 | .22 | .19 |
| Atypicality | .20 | .14 | −.40 | .37 | .22 | .19 | .13 | .09 | .21 | .06 | .34 | .37 | .36 |
| Withdrawal | .12 | .13 | −.31 | .31 | .13 | .15 | .04 | .11 | .19 | .01 | .22 | .30 | .41 |
| **Adaptive scale** | | | | | | | | | | | | | |
| Adaptability | −.32 | −.17 | .39 | −.42 | −.30 | −.32 | −.23 | −.08 | −.28 | −.03 | −.35 | −.34 | −.32 |
| Social Skills | −.21 | −.08 | .38 | −.32 | −.20 | −.24 | −.13 | −.02 | −.16 | .01 | −.26 | −.28 | −.32 |
| Leadership | −.21 | −.17 | .46 | −.37 | −.21 | −.21 | −.14 | −.11 | −.22 | −.08 | −.43 | −.34 | −.34 |
| Study Skills | −.28 | −.14 | .46 | −.38 | −.30 | −.23 | −.21 | −.06 | −.21 | −.08 | −.48 | −.33 | −.29 |
| Functional Communication | −.15 | −.07 | .41 | −.32 | −.16 | −.15 | −.10 | −.03 | −.14 | .00 | −.36 | −.33 | −.35 |
| **Content scale** | | | | | | | | | | | | | |
| Anger Control | .34 | .14 | −.29 | .37 | .32 | .35 | .24 | .05 | .26 | .02 | .32 | .26 | .19 |
| Bullying | .34 | .07 | −.16 | .24 | .27 | .35 | .29 | .00 | .16 | −.01 | .20 | .09 | .04 |
| Developmental Social Disorders | .17 | .13 | −.41 | .37 | .18 | .18 | .08 | .08 | .20 | .03 | .32 | .38 | .43 |
| Emotional Self-Control | .30 | .20 | −.33 | .40 | .32 | .30 | .20 | .12 | .29 | .06 | .34 | .32 | .26 |
| Executive Functioning | .37 | .19 | −.47 | .46 | .38 | .32 | .27 | .10 | .28 | .07 | .52 | .37 | .29 |
| Negative Emotionality | .31 | .17 | −.26 | .35 | .29 | .31 | .21 | .09 | .26 | .04 | .28 | .22 | .21 |
| Resiliency | −.28 | −.19 | .49 | −.45 | −.29 | −.27 | −.18 | −.12 | −.27 | −.07 | −.45 | −.39 | −.38 |
| **Clinical index** | | | | | | | | | | | | | |
| ADHD Probability Index | .36 | .19 | −.46 | .46 | .40 | .30 | .27 | .12 | .27 | .08 | .51 | .37 | .28 |
| EBD Probability Index | .39 | .17 | −.34 | .39 | .37 | .36 | .30 | .08 | .27 | .04 | .37 | .25 | .21 |
| Autism Probability Index | .23 | .16 | −.47 | .41 | .24 | .23 | .13 | .10 | .24 | .04 | .39 | .39 | .40 |
| Functional Impairment Index | .27 | .19 | −.45 | .42 | .29 | .24 | .18 | .13 | .26 | .08 | .45 | .38 | .35 |

**Table 12.2** Correlations Between TRS–C and PRS–C Forms (Combined General and Clinical Samples) (continued)

| | PRS scales | | | | | | | | | | | | | | | |
| --- | --- | --- | --- | --- | --- | --- | --- | --- | --- | --- | --- | --- | --- | --- | --- | --- |
| | Adaptive scale | | | | | Content scale | | | | | | | Clinical index | | | |
| TRS scales | Adaptability | Social Skills | Leadership | Activities of Daily Living | Functional Communication | Anger Control | Bullying | Developmental Social Disorders | Emotional Self-Control | Executive Functioning | Negative Emotionality | Resiliency | ADHD Probability Index | EBD Probability Index | Autism Probability Index | Functional Impairment Index |
| **Composite** | | | | | | | | | | | | | | | | |
| Externalizing Problems | -.29 | -.24 | -.21 | -.28 | -.26 | .35 | .35 | .27 | .24 | .37 | .25 | -.26 | .40 | .36 | .15 | .32 |
| Internalizing Problems | -.24 | -.14 | -.16 | -.17 | -.21 | .21 | .12 | .26 | .28 | .24 | .22 | -.22 | .22 | .22 | .22 | .28 |
| School Problems | -.32 | -.25 | -.40 | -.33 | -.44 | .22 | .13 | .37 | .22 | .45 | .16 | -.38 | .41 | .28 | .31 | .42 |
| Adaptive Skills | .37 | .41 | .46 | .36 | .51 | -.27 | -.20 | -.48 | -.22 | -.46 | -.18 | .44 | -.37 | -.34 | -.43 | -.46 |
| Behavioral Symptoms Index | -.39 | -.34 | -.35 | -.35 | -.43 | .35 | .25 | .46 | .31 | .46 | .26 | -.40 | .43 | .38 | .38 | .46 |
| **Clinical scale** | | | | | | | | | | | | | | | | |
| Hyperactivity | -.28 | -.20 | -.21 | -.30 | -.27 | .32 | .26 | .28 | .26 | .39 | .26 | -.27 | .44 | .32 | .17 | .33 |
| Aggression | -.26 | -.21 | -.15 | -.20 | -.19 | .32 | .32 | .23 | .21 | .28 | .22 | -.21 | .30 | .31 | .12 | .25 |
| Conduct Problems | -.27 | -.22 | -.20 | -.26 | -.25 | .30 | .35 | .23 | .19 | .33 | .21 | -.24 | .36 | .33 | .12 | .28 |
| Anxiety | -.20 | -.09 | -.15 | -.11 | -.19 | .14 | .03 | .21 | .24 | .21 | .17 | -.19 | .17 | .15 | .20 | .24 |
| Depression | -.27 | -.21 | -.19 | -.21 | -.25 | .25 | .20 | .31 | .26 | .28 | .23 | -.26 | .25 | .28 | .28 | .30 |
| Somatization | -.11 | -.05 | -.04 | -.11 | -.07 | .12 | .07 | .10 | .16 | .11 | .12 | -.09 | .11 | .12 | .07 | .13 |
| Attention Problems | -.34 | -.28 | -.39 | -.37 | -.42 | .29 | .19 | .39 | .26 | .49 | .21 | -.39 | .49 | .32 | .31 | .44 |
| Learning Problems | -.24 | -.18 | -.33 | -.23 | -.39 | .11 | .06 | .28 | .15 | .33 | .09 | -.31 | .28 | .19 | .24 | .33 |
| Atypicality | -.33 | -.32 | -.36 | -.30 | -.44 | .24 | .13 | .47 | .23 | .38 | .16 | -.36 | .31 | .28 | .42 | .42 |
| Withdrawal | -.28 | -.30 | -.28 | -.19 | -.35 | .19 | .08 | .40 | .20 | .26 | .15 | -.30 | .18 | .21 | .41 | .33 |
| **Adaptive scale** | | | | | | | | | | | | | | | | |
| Adaptability | .36 | .35 | .31 | .30 | .38 | -.34 | -.24 | -.43 | -.27 | -.39 | -.24 | .36 | -.33 | -.36 | -.37 | -.40 |
| Social Skills | .27 | .39 | .34 | .27 | .37 | -.21 | -.17 | -.39 | -.14 | -.31 | -.14 | .31 | -.25 | -.27 | -.36 | -.34 |
| Leadership | .34 | .37 | .47 | .35 | .50 | -.21 | -.16 | -.44 | -.20 | -.43 | -.15 | .43 | -.35 | -.29 | -.39 | -.44 |
| Study Skills | .35 | .34 | .44 | .39 | .48 | -.24 | -.20 | -.41 | -.19 | -.47 | -.16 | .43 | -.42 | -.32 | -.35 | -.44 |
| Functional Communication | .29 | .35 | .42 | .27 | .49 | -.17 | -.12 | -.43 | -.13 | -.37 | -.08 | .38 | -.28 | -.24 | -.41 | -.39 |
| **Content scale** | | | | | | | | | | | | | | | | |
| Anger Control | -.31 | -.25 | -.22 | -.23 | -.27 | .36 | .27 | .32 | .28 | .34 | .27 | -.28 | .33 | .34 | .23 | .32 |
| Bullying | -.21 | -.16 | -.08 | -.16 | -.13 | .27 | .35 | .15 | .15 | .22 | .18 | -.15 | .24 | .27 | .05 | .18 |
| Developmental Social Disorders | -.34 | -.37 | -.37 | -.27 | -.46 | .21 | .11 | .49 | .20 | .36 | .14 | -.39 | .27 | .27 | .47 | .41 |
| Emotional Self-Control | -.32 | -.28 | -.26 | -.27 | -.32 | .33 | .22 | .38 | .31 | .37 | .26 | -.31 | .34 | .32 | .30 | .38 |
| Executive Functioning | -.39 | -.36 | -.42 | -.40 | -.48 | .34 | .25 | .45 | .29 | .52 | .24 | -.44 | .48 | .38 | .37 | .48 |
| Negative Emotionality | -.29 | -.21 | -.20 | -.20 | -.25 | .30 | .25 | .30 | .26 | .32 | .25 | -.27 | .30 | .31 | .23 | .30 |
| Resiliency | .40 | .42 | .44 | .37 | .50 | -.30 | -.21 | -.50 | -.26 | -.47 | -.21 | .45 | -.39 | -.36 | -.44 | -.48 |
| **Clinical index** | | | | | | | | | | | | | | | | |
| ADHD Probability Index | -.38 | -.33 | -.42 | -.39 | -.47 | .32 | .24 | .45 | .28 | .50 | .24 | -.43 | .48 | .37 | .23 | .47 |
| EBD Probability Index | -.34 | -.27 | -.26 | -.29 | -.33 | .34 | .32 | .34 | .26 | .38 | .26 | -.32 | .39 | .36 | .24 | .36 |
| Autism Probability Index | -.37 | -.40 | -.43 | -.34 | -.50 | .26 | .16 | .50 | .24 | .43 | .18 | -.43 | .34 | .32 | .46 | .46 |
| Functional Impairment Index | -.38 | -.35 | -.42 | -.35 | -.50 | .27 | .17 | .47 | .26 | .46 | .19 | -.43 | .39 | .33 | .41 | .47 |

**Table 12.3** Correlations Between TRS-A and PRS-A Forms (Combined General and Clinical Samples)

| | PRS scales | | | | | | | | | | | | |
|---|---|---|---|---|---|---|---|---|---|---|---|---|---|
| | Composite | | | | Clinical scale | | | | | | | | |
| TRS scales | Externalizing Problems | Internalizing Problems | Adaptive Skills | Behavioral Symptoms Index | Hyperactivity | Aggression | Conduct Problems | Anxiety | Depression | Somatization | Attention Problems | Atypicality | Withdrawal |
| **Composite** | | | | | | | | | | | | | |
| Externalizing Problems | .46 | .25 | -.35 | .42 | .46 | .34 | .42 | .18 | .27 | .19 | .42 | .35 | .18 |
| Internalizing Problems | .31 | .44 | -.38 | .45 | .33 | .19 | .29 | .40 | .41 | .30 | .35 | .40 | .40 |
| School Problems | .37 | .34 | -.58 | .52 | .43 | .22 | .33 | .32 | .36 | .18 | .59 | .45 | .35 |
| Adaptive Skills | -.31 | -.33 | .58 | -.49 | -.34 | -.20 | -.28 | -.30 | -.35 | -.19 | -.52 | -.44 | -.44 |
| Behavioral Symptoms Index | .38 | .32 | -.48 | .51 | .43 | .25 | .32 | .30 | .35 | .18 | .48 | .47 | .41 |
| **Clinical scale** | | | | | | | | | | | | | |
| Hyperactivity | .38 | .20 | -.27 | .34 | .43 | .24 | .33 | .16 | .21 | .12 | .38 | .30 | .08 |
| Aggression | .39 | .22 | -.30 | .38 | .38 | .33 | .33 | .14 | .26 | .17 | .35 | .31 | .20 |
| Conduct Problems | .46 | .23 | -.36 | .41 | .43 | .36 | .46 | .15 | .25 | .20 | .41 | .31 | .19 |
| Anxiety | .21 | .39 | -.31 | .37 | .26 | .11 | .19 | .44 | .33 | .23 | .30 | .31 | .36 |
| Depression | .30 | .33 | -.36 | .41 | .31 | .20 | .26 | .30 | .36 | .20 | .33 | .35 | .34 |
| Somatization | .24 | .34 | -.24 | .32 | .24 | .15 | .25 | .24 | .32 | .30 | .22 | .32 | .26 |
| Attention Problems | .41 | .34 | -.56 | .54 | .49 | .24 | .37 | .31 | .36 | .18 | .63 | .46 | .33 |
| Learning Problems | .29 | .30 | -.51 | .42 | .33 | .18 | .25 | .29 | .31 | .17 | .47 | .38 | .30 |
| Atypicality | .21 | .20 | -.34 | .34 | .27 | .12 | .17 | .23 | .19 | .10 | .26 | .37 | .36 |
| Withdrawal | .10 | .20 | -.35 | .31 | .14 | .06 | .06 | .21 | .22 | .07 | .25 | .31 | .47 |
| **Adaptive scale** | | | | | | | | | | | | | |
| Adaptability | -.31 | -.34 | .46 | -.46 | -.33 | -.22 | -.27 | -.31 | -.36 | -.20 | -.44 | -.39 | -.41 |
| Social Skills | -.19 | -.21 | .43 | -.34 | -.20 | -.14 | -.15 | -.20 | -.25 | -.08 | -.34 | -.29 | -.38 |
| Leadership | -.27 | -.31 | .57 | -.45 | -.30 | -.17 | -.24 | -.30 | -.32 | -.17 | -.50 | -.40 | -.42 |
| Study Skills | -.37 | -.29 | .59 | -.48 | -.40 | -.23 | -.34 | -.24 | -.32 | -.18 | -.59 | -.44 | -.32 |
| Functional Communication | -.22 | -.29 | .50 | -.40 | -.27 | -.11 | -.19 | -.27 | -.28 | -.18 | -.42 | -.38 | -.39 |
| **Content scale** | | | | | | | | | | | | | |
| Anger Control | .44 | .32 | -.35 | .47 | .43 | .37 | .37 | .20 | .37 | .25 | .40 | .39 | .25 |
| Bullying | .33 | .20 | -.28 | .34 | .31 | .29 | .29 | .14 | .22 | .16 | .31 | .27 | .20 |
| Developmental Social Disorders | .18 | .22 | -.44 | .38 | .24 | .09 | .15 | .24 | .23 | .09 | .36 | .38 | .46 |
| Emotional Self-Control | .42 | .40 | -.38 | .50 | .44 | .31 | .37 | .32 | .43 | .27 | .41 | .44 | .32 |
| Executive Functioning | .43 | .38 | -.61 | .57 | .47 | .29 | .38 | .32 | .42 | .23 | .62 | .52 | .38 |
| Negative Emotionality | .38 | .34 | -.36 | .42 | .38 | .30 | .34 | .25 | .35 | .25 | .36 | .34 | .27 |
| Resiliency | -.29 | -.35 | .55 | -.48 | -.31 | -.20 | -.26 | -.32 | -.37 | -.19 | -.49 | -.43 | -.43 |
| **Clinical index** | | | | | | | | | | | | | |
| ADHD Probability Index | .39 | .30 | -.53 | .50 | .45 | .23 | .34 | .26 | .32 | .18 | .60 | .39 | .29 |
| EBD Probability Index | .45 | .35 | -.46 | .51 | .45 | .35 | .40 | .28 | .38 | .24 | .46 | .41 | .35 |
| Autism Probability Index | .19 | .25 | -.46 | .39 | .24 | .09 | .15 | .29 | .24 | .10 | .36 | .39 | .46 |
| Functional Impairment Index | .37 | .39 | -.60 | .55 | .42 | .22 | .32 | .37 | .40 | .22 | .55 | .50 | .47 |

| TRS scales | PRS scales | | | | | | | | | | | | | | | |
|---|---|---|---|---|---|---|---|---|---|---|---|---|---|---|---|---|
| | Adaptive scale | | | | | Content scale | | | | | | | Clinical index | | | |
| | Adaptability | Social Skills | Leadership | Activities of Daily Living | Functional Communication | Anger Control | Bullying | Developmental Social Disorders | Emotional Self-Control | Executive Functioning | Negative Emotionality | Resiliency | ADHD Probability Index | EBD Probability Index | Autism Probability Index | Functional Impairment Index |
| **Composite** | | | | | | | | | | | | | | | | |
| Externalizing Problems | -.32 | -.20 | -.32 | -.39 | -.30 | .38 | .29 | .31 | .32 | .45 | .31 | -.37 | .41 | .39 | .26 | .39 |
| Internalizing Problems | -.32 | -.22 | -.37 | -.34 | -.35 | .25 | .19 | .42 | .37 | .37 | .28 | -.38 | .37 | .31 | .40 | .47 |
| School Problems | -.40 | -.34 | -.58 | -.56 | -.59 | .28 | .20 | .50 | .35 | .62 | .27 | -.58 | .60 | .37 | .47 | .61 |
| Adaptive Skills | .43 | .41 | .60 | .51 | .56 | -.27 | -.19 | -.52 | -.37 | -.57 | -.27 | .58 | -.56 | -.37 | -.53 | -.58 |
| Behavioral Symptoms Index | -.38 | -.32 | -.47 | -.46 | -.44 | .30 | .23 | .48 | .36 | .51 | .28 | -.47 | .49 | .38 | .46 | .53 |
| **Clinical scale** | | | | | | | | | | | | | | | | |
| Hyperactivity | -.24 | -.10 | -.27 | -.35 | -.24 | .27 | .20 | .23 | .25 | .39 | .25 | -.28 | .37 | .28 | .18 | .31 |
| Aggression | -.29 | -.19 | -.25 | -.32 | -.24 | .37 | .25 | .29 | .30 | .38 | .26 | -.32 | .34 | .37 | .24 | .34 |
| Conduct Problems | -.34 | -.23 | -.32 | -.37 | -.31 | .39 | .33 | .31 | .32 | .44 | .32 | -.38 | .39 | .41 | .26 | .39 |
| Anxiety | -.27 | -.17 | -.31 | -.27 | -.32 | .17 | .12 | .37 | .32 | .30 | .21 | -.30 | .33 | .23 | .33 | .40 |
| Depression | -.32 | -.24 | -.34 | -.33 | -.32 | .27 | .19 | .37 | .33 | .35 | .28 | -.35 | .34 | .32 | .36 | .41 |
| Somatization | -.21 | -.13 | -.24 | -.24 | -.23 | .17 | .17 | .29 | .25 | .25 | .19 | -.26 | .23 | .23 | .27 | .32 |
| Attention Problems | -.42 | -.32 | -.55 | -.57 | -.53 | .31 | .22 | .48 | .36 | .63 | .31 | -.55 | .62 | .39 | .45 | .59 |
| Learning Problems | -.33 | -.30 | -.52 | -.47 | -.56 | .22 | .16 | .44 | .28 | .52 | .21 | -.51 | .49 | .30 | .42 | .54 |
| Atypicality | -.24 | -.24 | -.34 | -.27 | -.34 | .13 | .13 | .38 | .23 | .30 | .11 | -.32 | .31 | .20 | .38 | .37 |
| Withdrawal | -.24 | -.32 | -.37 | -.26 | -.33 | .10 | .06 | .38 | .20 | .26 | .12 | -.31 | .28 | .17 | .44 | .35 |
| **Adaptive scale** | | | | | | | | | | | | | | | | |
| Adaptability | .40 | .32 | .45 | .40 | .41 | -.28 | -.20 | -.47 | -.38 | -.48 | -.30 | .48 | -.47 | -.35 | -.45 | -.48 |
| Social Skills | .34 | .38 | .44 | .34 | .38 | -.21 | -.12 | -.39 | -.28 | -.40 | -.20 | .43 | -.39 | -.28 | -.43 | -.40 |
| Leadership | .40 | .41 | .61 | .49 | .56 | -.24 | -.15 | -.50 | -.34 | -.55 | -.25 | .57 | -.54 | -.33 | -.52 | -.56 |
| Study Skills | .43 | .39 | .58 | .57 | .57 | -.29 | -.21 | -.48 | -.33 | -.61 | -.28 | .58 | -.59 | -.39 | -.46 | -.58 |
| Functional Communication | .32 | .31 | .55 | .42 | .54 | -.15 | -.12 | -.46 | -.27 | -.47 | -.16 | .50 | -.46 | -.24 | -.46 | -.51 |
| **Content scale** | | | | | | | | | | | | | | | | |
| Anger Control | -.34 | -.22 | -.33 | -.35 | -.29 | .43 | .30 | .34 | .39 | .44 | .35 | -.36 | .39 | .43 | .31 | .41 |
| Bullying | -.26 | -.21 | -.23 | -.28 | -.24 | .32 | .25 | .27 | .26 | .34 | .22 | -.29 | .30 | .32 | .23 | .31 |
| Developmental Social Disorders | -.29 | -.33 | -.46 | -.36 | -.44 | .15 | .09 | .46 | .26 | .39 | .14 | -.42 | .39 | .23 | .48 | .45 |
| Emotional Self-Control | -.34 | -.22 | -.36 | -.38 | -.33 | .39 | .27 | .39 | .44 | .45 | .36 | -.39 | .42 | .42 | .35 | .46 |
| Executive Functioning | -.45 | -.39 | -.61 | -.58 | -.59 | .37 | .25 | .53 | .42 | .65 | .35 | -.61 | .63 | .45 | .52 | .63 |
| Negative Emotionality | -.34 | -.25 | -.33 | -.34 | -.30 | .36 | .25 | .34 | .36 | .40 | .34 | -.36 | .37 | .38 | .32 | .40 |
| Resiliency | .41 | .38 | .57 | .46 | .53 | -.26 | -.18 | -.51 | -.37 | -.54 | -.27 | .56 | -.53 | -.35 | -.52 | -.56 |
| **Clinical index** | | | | | | | | | | | | | | | | |
| ADHD Probability Index | -.39 | -.30 | -.52 | -.56 | -.50 | .30 | .20 | .44 | .34 | .60 | .30 | -.52 | .59 | .37 | .42 | .55 |
| EBD Probability Index | -.41 | -.31 | -.43 | -.44 | -.41 | .41 | .30 | .44 | .41 | .51 | .35 | -.47 | .48 | .45 | .41 | .50 |
| Autism Probability Index | -.32 | -.36 | -.49 | -.36 | -.45 | .15 | .09 | .47 | .28 | .40 | .15 | -.43 | .41 | .24 | .51 | .47 |
| Functional Impairment Index | -.44 | -.39 | -.61 | -.53 | -.59 | .30 | .21 | .56 | .40 | .60 | .30 | -.59 | .58 | .40 | .56 | .64 |

In each section of the tables, correlation coefficients between scales that measure the same construct are higher on average than correlation coefficients between scales that measure different constructs. Additional evidence of the validity of the clinical scales is that in most cases, the correlation between the scores of clinical scales of the same construct is higher than all correlations between those scales and clinical scales for different constructs. The correlation coefficients between teachers' and parents' ratings on most of the clinical scales become higher as the age level increases. This increase may suggest that, as the child advances in age, behaviors associated with clinical scales become more salient, pervasive, and easily observable as well as more consistent across settings. The relationship between teachers' and parents' ratings of adaptive behaviors remain generally consistent across levels, with some modest increases. Composite scales, which are aggregates of the clinical and adaptive scales, display a pattern of correlation coefficients across forms consistent with that observed on the clinical and adaptive scales.

The relationship between clinical and adaptive scales derived from teachers' and parents' ratings show the expected pattern. At all three form levels, the scores from teachers' ratings of clinical behaviors have low to moderate negative relationships with the scores from parents' ratings of adaptive behaviors. Likewise, the scores from parents' ratings of clinical behaviors have low to moderate negative relationships with the scores from teachers' ratings of adaptive behaviors. Scores from the content scales and clinical indexes generally show negative correlations with the adaptive scales, while the Resiliency scale has a positive correlation with the adaptive scales.

In summary, the following conclusions may be drawn about the relationship between TRS and PRS ratings:

- Overall, the correlation coefficients between the TRS and PRS scale scores are generally low to moderate, indicating perceived behavioral differences between teachers and parents across settings.

- The pattern of correlation coefficients between teachers' and parents' ratings generally provides evidence of convergent and discriminant validity of the BASC–3 scales. Scales measuring the same construct correlate more highly across forms than scales measuring different constructs.

- Among the clinical scales, the correlation coefficients between the TRS and PRS scale scores become higher as age level of the form increases.

- Internalizing scale scores generally demonstrate lower correlation coefficients between TRS and PRS ratings.

## RELATIONSHIP BETWEEN BEHAVIOR RATINGS AND SELF-REPORTS

Previous research has shown relatively low correlations between a child's self-report and others' ratings of the child's behavior, with correlation coefficients typically under .30 (Achenbach, McConaughy, & Howell, 1987; Youngstrom et al., 2000). In the BASC–3 standardization study, students who completed an SRP were also rated by a teacher using the TRS. In addition, students who completed the SRP were also rated by a parent using the PRS. Correlation coefficients between teacher ratings and self-reports are shown in Table 12.4 for children ($n = 237$) and in Table 12.5 for adolescents ($n = 450$); correlation coefficients between parent ratings and self-reports are shown in Table 12.6 for children ($n = 333$) and in Table 12.7 for adolescents ($n = 453$).

**Table 12.4** Correlations Between TRS–C and SRP–C Forms (Combined General and Clinical Samples)

| | SRP scales | | | | | | | | | | | | | | |
| | Composite | | | | | Clinical scale | | | | | | | | | |
| TRS scales | School Problems | Internalizing Problems | Inattention/ Hyperactivity | Emotional Symptoms | Personal Adjustment | Attitude to School | Attitude to Teachers | Atypicality | Locus of Control | Social Stress | Anxiety | Depression | Sense of Inadequacy | Attention Problems | Hyperactivity |
|---|---|---|---|---|---|---|---|---|---|---|---|---|---|---|---|
| **Composite** | | | | | | | | | | | | | | | |
| Externalizing Problems | .32 | .19 | .27 | .21 | −.25 | .24 | .33 | .16 | .19 | .15 | .07 | .18 | .21 | .29 | .22 |
| Internalizing Problems | .21 | .21 | .14 | .21 | −.15 | .20 | .17 | .11 | .14 | .14 | .16 | .21 | .27 | .16 | .10 |
| School Problems | .25 | .31 | .31 | .31 | −.27 | .17 | .29 | .26 | .26 | .21 | .18 | .29 | .38 | .37 | .21 |
| Adaptive Skills | −.33 | −.27 | −.27 | −.29 | .34 | −.26 | −.35 | −.19 | −.25 | −.20 | −.07 | −.28 | −.32 | −.35 | −.17 |
| Behavioral Symptoms Index | .32 | .26 | .28 | .28 | −.30 | .25 | .32 | .19 | .22 | .22 | .11 | .27 | .28 | .31 | .20 |
| **Clinical scale** | | | | | | | | | | | | | | | |
| Hyperactivity | .32 | .22 | .30 | .21 | −.22 | .26 | .32 | .20 | .19 | .18 | .10 | .20 | .20 | .31 | .25 |
| Aggression | .27 | .15 | .22 | .17 | −.24 | .20 | .29 | .11 | .15 | .12 | .04 | .14 | .17 | .24 | .18 |
| Conduct Problems | .28 | .17 | .24 | .18 | −.23 | .19 | .32 | .13 | .18 | .12 | .05 | .17 | .20 | .25 | .20 |
| Anxiety | .16 | .20 | .11 | .20 | −.10 | .17 | .11 | .11 | .11 | .11 | .20 | .19 | .26 | .14 | .06 |
| Depression | .28 | .24 | .18 | .25 | −.23 | .24 | .27 | .13 | .20 | .20 | .12 | .26 | .26 | .20 | .14 |
| Somatization | .05 | .06 | .04 | .04 | −.02 | .05 | .04 | .03 | .03 | .02 | .03 | .04 | .11 | .05 | .03 |
| Attention Problems | .29 | .31 | .34 | .30 | −.29 | .21 | .32 | .28 | .26 | .21 | .16 | .28 | .33 | .40 | .23 |
| Learning Problems | .18 | .28 | .25 | .28 | −.21 | .11 | .21 | .20 | .23 | .18 | .18 | .25 | .38 | .29 | .16 |
| Atypicality | .19 | .19 | .17 | .23 | −.24 | .16 | .19 | .13 | .13 | .17 | .10 | .23 | .21 | .19 | .13 |
| Withdrawal | .15 | .13 | .08 | .16 | −.19 | .13 | .12 | .08 | .09 | .15 | .04 | .17 | .14 | .11 | .04 |
| **Adaptive scale** | | | | | | | | | | | | | | | |
| Adaptability | −.38 | −.23 | −.27 | −.26 | .32 | −.30 | −.38 | −.17 | −.23 | −.19 | −.06 | −.24 | −.26 | −.30 | −.19 |
| Social Skills | −.29 | −.15 | −.16 | −.19 | .27 | −.22 | −.29 | −.07 | −.15 | −.15 | .02 | −.19 | −.20 | −.20 | −.09 |
| Leadership | −.31 | −.29 | −.29 | −.31 | .33 | −.24 | −.32 | −.22 | −.25 | −.20 | −.10 | −.29 | −.37 | −.38 | −.17 |
| Study Skills | −.31 | −.32 | −.34 | −.33 | .34 | −.22 | −.35 | −.24 | −.29 | −.22 | −.14 | −.32 | −.37 | −.40 | −.21 |
| Functional Communication | −.22 | −.21 | −.18 | −.23 | .27 | −.15 | −.24 | −.15 | −.17 | −.16 | −.04 | −.23 | −.25 | −.25 | −.09 |
| **Content scale** | | | | | | | | | | | | | | | |
| Anger Control | .29 | .17 | .23 | .19 | −.24 | .24 | .29 | .13 | .16 | .14 | .06 | .17 | .18 | .24 | .18 |
| Bullying | .18 | .13 | .16 | .14 | −.18 | .12 | .21 | .09 | .14 | .09 | .02 | .12 | .16 | .18 | .13 |
| Developmental Social Disorders | .21 | .18 | .16 | .21 | −.25 | .16 | .21 | .12 | .15 | .16 | .05 | .21 | .20 | .21 | .09 |
| Emotional Self-Control | .33 | .23 | .26 | .25 | −.26 | .27 | .31 | .16 | .19 | .19 | .10 | .23 | .24 | .28 | .20 |
| Executive Functioning | .34 | .28 | .35 | .30 | −.32 | .27 | .36 | .23 | .26 | .21 | .12 | .28 | .33 | .40 | .24 |
| Negative Emotionality | .35 | .22 | .26 | .24 | −.25 | .27 | .34 | .12 | .23 | .17 | .09 | .22 | .25 | .27 | .21 |
| Resiliency | −.34 | −.29 | −.30 | −.31 | .34 | −.27 | −.34 | −.22 | −.25 | −.20 | −.10 | −.29 | −.34 | −.36 | −.19 |
| **Clinical index** | | | | | | | | | | | | | | | |
| ADHD Probability Index | .34 | .31 | .34 | .31 | −.31 | .25 | .36 | .25 | .26 | .22 | .14 | .30 | .34 | .39 | .24 |
| EBD Probability Index | .32 | .23 | .28 | .24 | −.28 | .25 | .33 | .17 | .22 | .17 | .09 | .23 | .27 | .31 | .21 |
| Autism Probability Index | .26 | .23 | .21 | .26 | −.30 | .21 | .26 | .15 | .19 | .19 | .07 | .26 | .26 | .27 | .12 |
| Functional Impairment Index | .30 | .29 | .28 | .30 | −.30 | .23 | .30 | .20 | .23 | .21 | .13 | .29 | .35 | .33 | .17 |

**Table 12.4** Correlations Between TRS–C and SRP–C Forms (Combined General and Clinical Samples) *(continued)*

| TRS scales | SRP scales | | | | | |
|---|---|---|---|---|---|---|
| | | Adaptive scale | | | Clinical index | |
| | Relations With Parents | Interpersonal Relations | Self-Esteem | Self-Reliance | Functional Impairment Index | |
| **Composite** | | | | | | |
| Externalizing Problems | –.23 | –.26 | –.11 | –.22 | .26 | |
| Internalizing Problems | –.11 | –.18 | –.07 | –.12 | .18 | |
| School Problems | –.18 | –.30 | –.09 | –.30 | .35 | |
| Adaptive Skills | .28 | .33 | .14 | .35 | –.32 | |
| Behavioral Symptoms Index | –.25 | –.33 | –.13 | –.28 | .30 | |
| **Clinical scale** | | | | | | |
| Hyperactivity | –.17 | –.26 | –.09 | –.21 | .29 | |
| Aggression | –.23 | –.22 | –.11 | –.20 | .21 | |
| Conduct Problems | –.23 | –.23 | –.08 | –.21 | .23 | |
| Anxiety | –.02 | –.14 | –.07 | –.07 | .15 | |
| Depression | –.21 | –.25 | –.12 | –.19 | .23 | |
| Somatization | –.03 | –.03 | .01 | –.01 | .04 | |
| Attention Problems | –.22 | –.32 | –.11 | –.29 | .36 | |
| Learning Problems | –.12 | –.24 | –.06 | –.27 | .29 | |
| Atypicality | –.18 | –.27 | –.11 | –.23 | .23 | |
| Withdrawal | –.15 | –.22 | –.05 | –.19 | .11 | |
| **Adaptive scale** | | | | | | |
| Adaptability | .27 | .31 | .16 | .29 | –.29 | |
| Social Skills | .27 | .26 | .10 | .25 | –.20 | |
| Leadership | .27 | .31 | .12 | .36 | –.34 | |
| Study Skills | .25 | .36 | .14 | .35 | –.37 | |
| Functional Communication | .21 | .27 | .09 | .31 | –.23 | |
| **Content scale** | | | | | | |
| Anger Control | –.22 | –.23 | –.13 | –.22 | .23 | |
| Bullying | –.18 | –.18 | –.07 | –.15 | .17 | |
| Developmental Social Disorders | –.21 | –.27 | –.09 | –.25 | .20 | |
| Emotional Self-Control | –.22 | –.26 | –.14 | –.23 | .26 | |
| Executive Functioning | –.26 | –.32 | –.14 | –.32 | .36 | |
| Negative Emotionality | –.25 | –.24 | –.12 | –.22 | .25 | |
| Resiliency | .28 | .33 | .16 | .34 | –.34 | |
| **Clinical index** | | | | | | |
| ADHD Probability Index | –.24 | –.32 | –.12 | –.31 | .37 | |
| EBD Probability Index | –.25 | –.28 | –.11 | –.26 | .30 | |
| Autism Probability Index | –.25 | –.30 | –.11 | –.31 | .26 | |
| Functional Impairment Index | –.23 | –.31 | –.12 | –.30 | .32 | |

**Table 12.5** Correlations Between TRS–A and SRP–A Forms (Combined General and Clinical Samples)

| | SRP scales | | | | | | | | | | | | | | | | |
| | Composite | | | | | Clinical scale | | | | | | | | | | | |
| TRS scales | School Problems | Internalizing Problems | Inattention/ Hyperactivity | Emotional Symptoms | Personal Adjustment | Attitude to School | Attitude to Teachers | Sensation Seeking | Atypicality | Locus of Control | Social Stress | Anxiety | Depression | Sense of Inadequacy | Somatization | Attention Problems | Hyperactivity |
|---|---|---|---|---|---|---|---|---|---|---|---|---|---|---|---|---|---|
| **Composite** | | | | | | | | | | | | | | | | | |
| Externalizing Problems | .32 | .08 | .25 | .09 | -.22 | .23 | .36 | .16 | .09 | .17 | .08 | -.07 | .07 | .07 | .08 | .23 | .23 |
| Internalizing Problems | .08 | .14 | .16 | .16 | -.19 | .05 | .14 | -.01 | .14 | .12 | .13 | .07 | .11 | .14 | .13 | .17 | .14 |
| School Problems | .27 | .15 | .27 | .20 | -.28 | .22 | .32 | .10 | .13 | .17 | .11 | -.05 | .14 | .25 | .10 | .31 | .18 |
| Adaptive Skills | -.25 | -.16 | -.23 | -.22 | .31 | -.21 | -.31 | -.06 | -.13 | -.18 | -.14 | .01 | -.16 | -.22 | -.12 | -.27 | -.14 |
| Behavioral Symptoms Index | .23 | .15 | .27 | .18 | -.27 | .17 | .28 | .07 | .16 | .17 | .15 | .00 | .15 | .15 | .11 | .28 | .22 |
| **Clinical scale** | | | | | | | | | | | | | | | | | |
| Hyperactivity | .26 | .06 | .25 | .07 | -.20 | .17 | .30 | .15 | .08 | .12 | .06 | -.07 | .05 | .06 | .07 | .22 | .23 |
| Aggression | .29 | .08 | .22 | .08 | -.18 | .23 | .32 | .15 | .08 | .16 | .08 | -.07 | .05 | .06 | .07 | .20 | .21 |
| Conduct Problems | .34 | .11 | .24 | .12 | -.21 | .25 | .37 | .16 | .11 | .18 | .08 | -.04 | .09 | .10 | .10 | .23 | .21 |
| Anxiety | .00 | .12 | .13 | .12 | -.10 | -.02 | .03 | -.01 | .13 | .06 | .08 | .09 | .08 | .14 | .07 | .14 | .09 |
| Depression | .11 | .14 | .19 | .15 | -.21 | .08 | .17 | .01 | .15 | .14 | .12 | .05 | .11 | .12 | .09 | .20 | .14 |
| Somatization | .08 | .12 | .09 | .13 | -.15 | .07 | .13 | -.01 | .09 | .10 | .11 | .04 | .09 | .09 | .15 | .08 | .08 |
| Attention Problems | .33 | .15 | .31 | .20 | -.29 | .26 | .36 | .13 | .13 | .18 | .12 | -.06 | .14 | .23 | .10 | .34 | .23 |
| Learning Problems | .19 | .15 | .20 | .19 | -.24 | .17 | .24 | .04 | .13 | .15 | .09 | -.03 | .14 | .25 | .11 | .26 | .12 |
| Atypicality | .07 | .12 | .16 | .12 | -.15 | .03 | .10 | .02 | .15 | .09 | .12 | .05 | .10 | .10 | .09 | .17 | .13 |
| Withdrawal | .05 | .17 | .15 | .19 | -.23 | .07 | .11 | -.06 | .14 | .13 | .17 | .09 | .18 | .16 | .09 | .18 | .09 |
| **Adaptive scale** | | | | | | | | | | | | | | | | | |
| Adaptability | -.23 | -.16 | -.21 | -.19 | .29 | -.19 | -.27 | -.06 | -.13 | -.19 | -.16 | -.01 | -.14 | -.16 | -.13 | -.22 | -.17 |
| Social Skills | -.26 | -.13 | -.16 | -.19 | .29 | -.21 | -.30 | -.07 | -.12 | -.16 | -.13 | -.01 | -.13 | -.14 | -.08 | -.21 | -.09 |
| Leadership | -.23 | -.16 | -.21 | -.22 | .29 | -.20 | -.28 | -.03 | -.12 | -.16 | -.12 | -.01 | -.17 | -.23 | -.11 | -.26 | -.12 |
| Study Skills | -.34 | -.14 | -.28 | -.20 | .30 | -.26 | -.39 | -.12 | -.10 | -.19 | -.11 | .08 | -.14 | -.24 | -.11 | -.32 | -.19 |
| Functional Communication | -.10 | -.14 | -.15 | -.17 | .23 | -.07 | -.17 | .01 | -.11 | -.12 | -.09 | -.02 | -.13 | -.19 | -.12 | -.20 | -.07 |
| **Content scale** | | | | | | | | | | | | | | | | | |
| Anger Control | .24 | .10 | .23 | .11 | -.21 | .17 | .28 | .09 | .11 | .16 | .10 | -.03 | .08 | .08 | .08 | .21 | .21 |
| Bullying | .26 | .09 | .17 | .08 | -.16 | .21 | .25 | .15 | .10 | .17 | .08 | -.03 | .06 | .07 | .07 | .16 | .16 |
| Developmental Social Disorders | .11 | .15 | .18 | .18 | -.24 | .09 | .17 | -.01 | .15 | .15 | .14 | .04 | .15 | .16 | .09 | .21 | .13 |
| Emotional Self-Control | .16 | .11 | .22 | .12 | -.20 | .11 | .22 | .05 | .14 | .14 | .10 | .01 | .07 | .09 | .08 | .20 | .21 |
| Executive Functioning | .30 | .16 | .29 | .20 | -.30 | .23 | .36 | .11 | .14 | .18 | .12 | -.04 | .15 | .21 | .13 | .32 | .21 |
| Negative Emotionality | .24 | .13 | .22 | .14 | -.23 | .20 | .29 | .07 | .11 | .18 | .12 | .01 | .10 | .11 | .08 | .22 | .20 |
| Resiliency | -.23 | -.17 | -.22 | -.21 | .29 | -.19 | -.27 | -.05 | -.13 | -.17 | -.13 | -.01 | -.17 | -.21 | -.14 | -.26 | -.15 |
| **Clinical index** | | | | | | | | | | | | | | | | | |
| ADHD Probability Index | .34 | .13 | .32 | .17 | -.28 | .24 | .38 | .15 | .12 | .17 | .12 | -.08 | .13 | .19 | .10 | .33 | .25 |
| EBD Probability Index | .29 | .15 | .25 | .16 | -.25 | .23 | .32 | .12 | .14 | .19 | .13 | -.01 | .11 | .14 | .11 | .25 | .21 |
| Autism Probability Index | .10 | .15 | .17 | .18 | -.23 | .10 | .16 | -.01 | .14 | .12 | .14 | .05 | .16 | .17 | .07 | .20 | .11 |
| Functional Impairment Index | .21 | .17 | .23 | .21 | -.28 | .15 | .27 | .04 | .15 | .17 | .13 | .01 | .15 | .21 | .12 | .27 | .16 |

**Table 12.5** Correlations Between TRS–A and SRP–A Forms (Combined General and Clinical Samples) (continued)

| | SRP scales | | | | | | | | Clinical index |
|---|---|---|---|---|---|---|---|---|---|
| | Adaptive scale | | | | Content scale | | | | |
| TRS scales | Relations With Parents | Interpersonal Relations | Self-Esteem | Self-Reliance | Anger Control | Ego Strength | Mania | Test Anxiety | Functional Impairment Index |
| **Composite** | | | | | | | | | |
| Externalizing Problems | –.17 | –.21 | –.03 | –.26 | .20 | –.18 | .13 | –.02 | .18 |
| Internalizing Problems | –.10 | –.18 | –.08 | –.23 | .11 | –.15 | .10 | .10 | .18 |
| School Problems | –.19 | –.21 | –.10 | –.37 | .17 | –.23 | .10 | .13 | .23 |
| Adaptive Skills | .24 | .25 | .12 | .39 | –.16 | .26 | –.11 | –.08 | –.23 |
| Behavioral Symptoms Index | –.20 | –.27 | –.07 | –.32 | .17 | –.22 | .15 | .02 | .23 |
| **Clinical scale** | | | | | | | | | |
| Hyperactivity | –.16 | –.19 | –.03 | –.24 | .14 | –.16 | .13 | –.03 | .17 |
| Aggression | –.15 | –.19 | –.01 | –.23 | .19 | –.15 | .11 | –.02 | .15 |
| Conduct Problems | –.17 | –.18 | –.05 | –.26 | .22 | –.19 | .12 | .01 | .19 |
| Anxiety | –.03 | –.12 | –.05 | –.13 | .06 | –.08 | .08 | .11 | .14 |
| Depression | –.14 | –.21 | –.08 | –.24 | .14 | –.17 | .12 | .05 | .19 |
| Somatization | –.08 | –.12 | –.08 | –.19 | .08 | –.14 | .05 | .11 | .14 |
| Attention Problems | –.23 | –.23 | –.10 | –.36 | .19 | –.24 | .14 | .10 | .24 |
| Learning Problems | –.16 | –.17 | –.08 | –.36 | .15 | –.20 | .06 | .16 | .20 |
| Atypicality | –.09 | –.19 | –.03 | –.17 | .09 | –.11 | .11 | .00 | .15 |
| Withdrawal | –.16 | –.25 | –.10 | –.22 | .09 | –.17 | .10 | –.01 | .18 |
| **Adaptive scale** | | | | | | | | | |
| Adaptability | .24 | .26 | .12 | .30 | –.16 | .24 | –.13 | –.05 | –.20 |
| Social Skills | .22 | .23 | .11 | .34 | –.15 | .24 | –.10 | –.01 | –.18 |
| Leadership | .21 | .23 | .12 | .37 | –.14 | .24 | –.09 | –.09 | –.22 |
| Study Skills | .26 | .21 | .11 | .39 | –.17 | .25 | –.12 | –.11 | –.23 |
| Functional Communication | .15 | .19 | .07 | .32 | –.09 | .18 | –.07 | –.07 | –.18 |
| **Content scale** | | | | | | | | | |
| Anger Control | –.15 | –.22 | –.05 | –.24 | .20 | –.18 | .13 | .00 | .17 |
| Bullying | –.13 | –.16 | .00 | –.20 | .19 | –.14 | .09 | –.01 | .15 |
| Developmental Social Disorders | –.17 | –.24 | –.07 | –.27 | .10 | –.19 | .11 | .02 | .19 |
| Emotional Self-Control | –.13 | –.23 | –.05 | –.24 | .17 | –.17 | .14 | .02 | .17 |
| Executive Functioning | –.22 | –.24 | –.10 | –.39 | .18 | –.25 | .14 | .09 | .25 |
| Negative Emotionality | –.20 | –.22 | –.06 | –.26 | .19 | –.19 | .13 | .03 | .19 |
| Resiliency | .23 | .25 | .13 | .34 | –.16 | .26 | –.11 | –.07 | –.22 |
| **Clinical index** | | | | | | | | | |
| ADHD Probability Index | –.22 | –.22 | –.08 | –.37 | .16 | –.22 | .15 | .09 | .24 |
| EBD Probability Index | –.19 | –.24 | –.06 | –.29 | .22 | –.21 | .14 | .03 | .22 |
| Autism Probability Index | –.16 | –.23 | –.08 | –.26 | .10 | –.17 | .10 | .01 | .18 |
| Functional Impairment Index | –.20 | –.25 | –.09 | –.37 | .15 | –.23 | .12 | .07 | .23 |

**Table 12.6** Correlations Between PRS–C and SRP–C Forms (Combined General and Clinical Samples)

| | SRP scales | | | | | | | | | | | | | | |
|---|---|---|---|---|---|---|---|---|---|---|---|---|---|---|---|
| | Composite | | | | | Clinical scale | | | | | | | | | |
| PRS scales | School Problems | Internalizing Problems | Inattention/ Hyperactivity | Emotional Symptoms | Personal Adjustment | Attitude to School | Attitude to Teachers | Atypicality | Locus of Control | Social Stress | Anxiety | Depression | Sense of Inadequacy | Attention Problems | Hyperactivity |
| **Composite** | | | | | | | | | | | | | | | |
| Externalizing Problems | .15 | .32 | .32 | .30 | −.24 | .11 | .16 | .26 | .24 | .24 | .25 | .30 | .30 | .30 | .30 |
| Internalizing Problems | .14 | .38 | .19 | .35 | −.22 | .14 | .10 | .30 | .26 | .31 | .35 | .35 | .32 | .18 | .19 |
| Adaptive Skills | −.23 | −.39 | −.39 | −.45 | .44 | −.19 | −.23 | −.27 | −.32 | −.32 | −.24 | −.39 | −.41 | −.43 | −.29 |
| Behavioral Symptoms Index | .19 | .40 | .36 | .40 | −.31 | .16 | .16 | .31 | .28 | .31 | .30 | .38 | .37 | .35 | .32 |
| **Clinical scale** | | | | | | | | | | | | | | | |
| Hyperactivity | .19 | .32 | .40 | .30 | −.20 | .16 | .18 | .24 | .23 | .24 | .26 | .30 | .31 | .35 | .38 |
| Aggression | .10 | .26 | .20 | .26 | −.22 | .06 | .11 | .21 | .19 | .20 | .20 | .25 | .23 | .19 | .18 |
| Conduct Problems | .12 | .28 | .27 | .25 | −.22 | .06 | .15 | .23 | .22 | .18 | .19 | .25 | .27 | .25 | .24 |
| Anxiety | .13 | .31 | .15 | .29 | −.17 | .15 | .08 | .21 | .19 | .25 | .34 | .27 | .27 | .12 | .16 |
| Depression | .15 | .39 | .24 | .37 | −.26 | .15 | .12 | .31 | .27 | .32 | .31 | .36 | .34 | .22 | .22 |
| Somatization | .07 | .27 | .09 | .21 | −.12 | .06 | .06 | .25 | .20 | .21 | .24 | .22 | .20 | .09 | .09 |
| Attention Problems | .20 | .38 | .48 | .38 | −.29 | .19 | .16 | .28 | .30 | .25 | .29 | .34 | .40 | .50 | .39 |
| Atypicality | .11 | .30 | .29 | .31 | −.25 | .09 | .11 | .26 | .20 | .22 | .22 | .30 | .28 | .28 | .25 |
| Withdrawal | .15 | .24 | .16 | .27 | −.28 | .14 | .11 | .14 | .17 | .23 | .16 | .26 | .22 | .18 | .12 |
| **Adaptive scale** | | | | | | | | | | | | | | | |
| Adaptability | −.27 | −.40 | −.36 | −.44 | .41 | −.23 | −.24 | −.26 | −.33 | −.34 | −.26 | −.37 | −.41 | −.40 | −.28 |
| Social Skills | −.16 | −.26 | −.24 | −.32 | .37 | −.12 | −.17 | −.14 | −.22 | −.24 | −.14 | −.26 | −.26 | −.28 | −.17 |
| Leadership | −.21 | −.35 | −.33 | −.40 | .39 | −.17 | −.19 | −.25 | −.27 | −.29 | −.22 | −.35 | −.34 | −.38 | −.23 |
| Activities of Daily Living | −.21 | −.39 | −.43 | −.40 | .36 | −.17 | −.19 | −.31 | −.31 | −.29 | −.29 | −.36 | −.39 | −.44 | −.36 |
| Functional Communication | −.18 | −.29 | −.31 | −.35 | .36 | −.14 | −.18 | −.18 | −.23 | −.22 | −.15 | −.31 | −.34 | −.36 | −.22 |
| **Content scale** | | | | | | | | | | | | | | | |
| Anger Control | .16 | .35 | .26 | .34 | −.26 | .14 | .15 | .27 | .26 | .28 | .26 | .33 | .31 | .25 | .24 |
| Bullying | .07 | .24 | .18 | .23 | −.20 | .02 | .11 | .20 | .18 | .18 | .18 | .21 | .23 | .17 | .16 |
| Developmental Social Disorders | .16 | .32 | .28 | .36 | −.34 | .13 | .15 | .21 | .22 | .25 | .22 | .33 | .31 | .31 | .22 |
| Emotional Self-Control | .17 | .40 | .26 | .37 | −.25 | .15 | .13 | .30 | .27 | .31 | .33 | .37 | .33 | .25 | .23 |
| Executive Functioning | .23 | .41 | .45 | .43 | −.35 | .19 | .21 | .31 | .32 | .32 | .29 | .38 | .42 | .46 | .36 |
| Negative Emotionality | .18 | .35 | .25 | .34 | −.24 | .17 | .13 | .28 | .26 | .30 | .29 | .32 | .32 | .23 | .22 |
| Resiliency | −.23 | −.35 | −.36 | −.41 | .40 | −.18 | −.22 | −.24 | −.28 | −.29 | −.22 | −.35 | −.37 | −.42 | −.26 |
| **Clinical index** | | | | | | | | | | | | | | | |
| ADHD Probability Index | .22 | .39 | .47 | .39 | −.29 | .19 | .20 | .27 | .30 | .28 | .28 | .33 | .40 | .47 | .41 |
| EBD Probability Index | .17 | .39 | .30 | .39 | −.33 | .11 | .18 | .30 | .29 | .30 | .28 | .37 | .36 | .30 | .26 |
| Autism Probability Index | .14 | .27 | .20 | .30 | −.28 | .12 | .11 | .20 | .18 | .24 | .19 | .28 | .24 | .20 | .17 |
| Functional Impairment Index | .23 | .42 | .38 | .45 | −.40 | .18 | .20 | .31 | .31 | .33 | .30 | .41 | .41 | .40 | .31 |

**Table 12.6** Correlations Between PRS–C and SRP–C Forms (Combined General and Clinical Samples) *(continued)*

| | SRP scales | | | | |
| | Adaptive scale | | | | Clinical index |
| PRS scales | Relations With Parents | Interpersonal Relations | Self-Esteem | Self-Reliance | Functional Impairment Index |
|---|---|---|---|---|---|
| **Composite** | | | | | |
| Externalizing Problems | –.19 | –.24 | –.13 | –.20 | .35 |
| Internalizing Problems | –.10 | –.27 | –.19 | –.13 | .31 |
| Adaptive Skills | .30 | .38 | .28 | .46 | –.45 |
| Behavioral Symptoms Index | –.19 | –.32 | –.21 | –.27 | .43 |
| **Clinical scale** | | | | | |
| Hyperactivity | –.12 | –.22 | –.12 | –.17 | .39 |
| Aggression | –.19 | –.20 | –.12 | –.18 | .25 |
| Conduct Problems | –.18 | –.22 | –.10 | –.18 | .29 |
| Anxiety | –.06 | –.21 | –.16 | –.11 | .25 |
| Depression | –.14 | –.29 | –.21 | –.19 | .35 |
| Somatization | –.06 | –.18 | –.13 | –.03 | .18 |
| Attention Problems | –.15 | –.28 | –.17 | –.33 | .48 |
| Atypicality | –.16 | –.25 | –.19 | –.22 | .32 |
| Withdrawal | –.16 | –.30 | –.19 | –.24 | .24 |
| **Adaptive scale** | | | | | |
| Adaptability | .29 | .38 | .27 | .39 | –.44 |
| Social Skills | .28 | .29 | .23 | .40 | –.29 |
| Leadership | .24 | .33 | .25 | .44 | –.39 |
| Activities of Daily Living | .25 | .33 | .24 | .33 | –.45 |
| Functional Communication | .24 | .30 | .22 | .41 | –.34 |
| **Content scale** | | | | | |
| Anger Control | –.20 | –.24 | –.17 | –.22 | .33 |
| Bullying | –.17 | –.19 | –.11 | –.16 | .23 |
| Developmental Social Disorders | –.22 | –.32 | –.22 | –.32 | .34 |
| Emotional Self-Control | –.15 | –.27 | –.19 | –.18 | .35 |
| Executive Functioning | –.21 | –.33 | –.22 | –.36 | .47 |
| Negative Emotionality | –.16 | –.24 | –.17 | –.21 | .32 |
| Resiliency | .28 | .32 | .25 | .44 | –.41 |
| **Clinical index** | | | | | |
| ADHD Probability Index | –.16 | –.29 | –.17 | –.29 | .48 |
| EBD Probability Index | –.24 | –.31 | –.20 | –.29 | .38 |
| Autism Probability Index | –.17 | –.30 | –.20 | –.25 | .27 |
| Functional Impairment Index | –.24 | –.38 | –.26 | –.37 | .45 |

**Table 12.7** Correlations Between PRS–A and SRP–A Forms (Combined General and Clinical Samples)

| | SRP scales | | | | | | | | | | | | | | | | |
|---|---|---|---|---|---|---|---|---|---|---|---|---|---|---|---|---|---|
| | Composite | | | | | Clinical scale | | | | | | | | | | | |
| PRS scales | School Problems | Internalizing Problems | Inattention/ Hyperactivity | Emotional Symptoms | Personal Adjustment | Attitude to School | Attitude to Teachers | Sensation Seeking | Atypicality | Locus of Control | Social Stress | Anxiety | Depression | Sense of Inadequacy | Somatization | Attention Problems | Hyperactivity |
| **Composite** | | | | | | | | | | | | | | | | | |
| Externalizing Problems | .39 | .32 | .38 | .31 | -.37 | .34 | .36 | .20 | .21 | .37 | .26 | .15 | .24 | .29 | .24 | .37 | .33 |
| Internalizing Problems | .17 | .39 | .26 | .40 | -.38 | .25 | .15 | .01 | .23 | .30 | .33 | .34 | .34 | .32 | .40 | .26 | .23 |
| Adaptive Skills | -.31 | -.32 | -.30 | -.36 | .43 | -.32 | -.32 | -.07 | -.22 | -.34 | -.24 | -.16 | -.28 | -.37 | -.19 | -.35 | -.21 |
| Behavioral Symptoms Index | .31 | .38 | .38 | .39 | -.43 | .32 | .30 | .10 | .28 | .37 | .34 | .21 | .32 | .35 | .26 | .38 | .31 |
| **Clinical scale** | | | | | | | | | | | | | | | | | |
| Hyperactivity | .32 | .28 | .37 | .27 | -.30 | .29 | .29 | .14 | .23 | .29 | .24 | .14 | .19 | .24 | .21 | .34 | .35 |
| Aggression | .31 | .24 | .25 | .24 | -.31 | .27 | .29 | .12 | .13 | .32 | .22 | .12 | .19 | .22 | .18 | .25 | .21 |
| Conduct Problems | .42 | .32 | .34 | .31 | -.38 | .34 | .39 | .25 | .17 | .40 | .23 | .14 | .26 | .33 | .24 | .35 | .26 |
| Anxiety | .07 | .27 | .18 | .29 | -.25 | .16 | .05 | -.05 | .18 | .15 | .22 | .30 | .23 | .23 | .23 | .17 | .15 |
| Depression | .22 | .40 | .29 | .41 | -.41 | .27 | .20 | .03 | .25 | .37 | .37 | .27 | .38 | .33 | .32 | .29 | .23 |
| Somatization | .14 | .29 | .16 | .28 | -.26 | .16 | .12 | .04 | .13 | .21 | .20 | .26 | .21 | .22 | .45 | .14 | .16 |
| Attention Problems | .33 | .27 | .41 | .29 | -.32 | .32 | .31 | .14 | .22 | .28 | .20 | .11 | .22 | .34 | .15 | .45 | .29 |
| Atypicality | .23 | .33 | .28 | .31 | -.33 | .22 | .23 | .08 | .30 | .29 | .27 | .17 | .28 | .27 | .27 | .27 | .25 |
| Withdrawal | .09 | .26 | .14 | .29 | -.32 | .15 | .11 | -.06 | .19 | .21 | .28 | .16 | .25 | .23 | .13 | .17 | .10 |
| **Adaptive scale** | | | | | | | | | | | | | | | | | |
| Adaptability | -.29 | -.33 | -.25 | -.35 | .39 | -.28 | -.32 | -.06 | -.20 | -.31 | -.27 | -.19 | -.28 | -.32 | -.25 | -.25 | -.21 |
| Social Skills | -.23 | -.20 | -.16 | -.25 | .35 | -.26 | -.26 | -.02 | -.14 | -.24 | -.17 | -.07 | -.20 | -.24 | -.09 | -.20 | -.08 |
| Leadership | -.23 | -.26 | -.25 | -.33 | .41 | -.27 | -.27 | .02 | -.17 | -.27 | -.19 | -.13 | -.25 | -.35 | -.14 | -.31 | -.14 |
| Activities of Daily Living | -.36 | -.29 | -.37 | -.30 | .36 | -.33 | -.30 | -.19 | -.25 | -.34 | -.22 | -.10 | -.23 | -.34 | -.18 | -.40 | -.28 |
| Functional Communication | -.23 | -.30 | -.28 | -.34 | .34 | -.26 | -.23 | -.03 | -.20 | -.28 | -.20 | -.17 | -.25 | -.36 | -.18 | -.32 | -.18 |
| **Content scale** | | | | | | | | | | | | | | | | | |
| Anger Control | .28 | .27 | .30 | .26 | -.30 | .27 | .27 | .10 | .18 | .28 | .24 | .15 | .22 | .22 | .20 | .28 | .27 |
| Bullying | .31 | .25 | .22 | .24 | -.31 | .29 | .29 | .14 | .13 | .31 | .19 | .13 | .20 | .23 | .20 | .24 | .16 |
| Developmental Social Disorders | .23 | .34 | .26 | .34 | -.38 | .26 | .25 | .03 | .26 | .32 | .28 | .19 | .28 | .33 | .22 | .28 | .20 |
| Emotional Self-Control | .21 | .32 | .27 | .33 | -.35 | .25 | .22 | .02 | .22 | .29 | .29 | .24 | .28 | .26 | .27 | .26 | .24 |
| Executive Functioning | .33 | .30 | .36 | .33 | -.38 | .32 | .32 | .11 | .22 | .33 | .22 | .13 | .24 | .35 | .18 | .39 | .28 |
| Negative Emotionality | .27 | .33 | .28 | .33 | -.36 | .28 | .24 | .09 | .19 | .33 | .30 | .21 | .29 | .27 | .26 | .27 | .24 |
| Resiliency | -.27 | -.32 | -.26 | -.36 | .43 | -.28 | -.32 | -.02 | -.21 | -.32 | -.23 | -.16 | -.28 | -.37 | -.22 | -.29 | -.18 |
| **Clinical index** | | | | | | | | | | | | | | | | | |
| ADHD Probability Index | .28 | .28 | .34 | .30 | -.35 | .29 | .28 | .08 | .22 | .29 | .21 | .13 | .23 | .33 | .16 | .37 | .25 |
| EBD Probability Index | .31 | .29 | .31 | .30 | -.37 | .30 | .30 | .11 | .20 | .34 | .24 | .15 | .24 | .27 | .21 | .31 | .25 |
| Autism Probability Index | .20 | .31 | .23 | .33 | -.38 | .25 | .24 | -.03 | .24 | .28 | .27 | .17 | .27 | .31 | .18 | .26 | .17 |
| Functional Impairment Index | .28 | .35 | .33 | .38 | -.42 | .30 | .27 | .06 | .25 | .33 | .28 | .20 | .30 | .38 | .22 | .36 | .25 |

**Table 12.7** Correlations Between PRS–A and SRP–A Forms (Combined General and Clinical Samples) *(continued)*

| PRS scales | Adaptive scale | | | | Anger Control | Content scale | | | Clinical index |
|---|---|---|---|---|---|---|---|---|---|
| | Relations With Parents | Interpersonal Relations | Self-Esteem | Self-Reliance | | Ego Strength | Mania | Test Anxiety | Functional Impairment Index |
| **Composite** | | | | | | | | | |
| Externalizing Problems | –.38 | –.28 | –.21 | –.28 | .40 | –.33 | .29 | .18 | .37 |
| Internalizing Problems | –.24 | –.35 | –.36 | –.24 | .36 | –.36 | .23 | .27 | .42 |
| Adaptive Skills | .34 | .33 | .23 | .42 | –.31 | .35 | –.20 | –.24 | –.38 |
| Behavioral Symptoms Index | –.34 | –.39 | –.27 | –.33 | .39 | –.37 | .29 | .21 | .43 |
| **Clinical scale** | | | | | | | | | |
| Hyperactivity | –.24 | –.27 | –.17 | –.26 | .34 | –.26 | .30 | .15 | .34 |
| Aggression | –.34 | –.23 | –.18 | –.20 | .36 | –.27 | .21 | .13 | .27 |
| Conduct Problems | –.43 | –.24 | –.22 | –.28 | .38 | –.35 | .24 | .20 | .35 |
| Anxiety | –.10 | –.28 | –.24 | –.17 | .23 | –.24 | .13 | .26 | .31 |
| Depression | –.30 | –.38 | –.35 | –.24 | .40 | –.39 | .24 | .18 | .41 |
| Somatization | –.18 | –.19 | –.28 | –.16 | .24 | –.25 | .17 | .20 | .30 |
| Attention Problems | –.27 | –.23 | –.17 | –.33 | .29 | –.27 | .27 | .22 | .38 |
| Atypicality | –.25 | –.33 | –.21 | –.27 | .28 | –.27 | .22 | .14 | .33 |
| Withdrawal | –.19 | –.38 | –.21 | –.21 | .18 | –.27 | .13 | .12 | .26 |
| **Adaptive scale** | | | | | | | | | |
| Adaptability | .32 | .33 | .25 | .32 | –.32 | .36 | –.21 | –.25 | –.36 |
| Social Skills | .32 | .27 | .17 | .32 | –.23 | .29 | –.11 | –.13 | –.23 |
| Leadership | .29 | .33 | .22 | .43 | –.23 | .33 | –.13 | –.22 | –.34 |
| Activities of Daily Living | .31 | .27 | .21 | .35 | –.33 | .31 | –.27 | –.21 | –.36 |
| Functional Communication | .25 | .26 | .18 | .39 | –.24 | .26 | –.15 | –.26 | –.35 |
| **Content scale** | | | | | | | | | |
| Anger Control | –.28 | –.26 | –.19 | –.21 | .37 | –.27 | .26 | .14 | .31 |
| Bullying | –.34 | –.23 | –.19 | –.19 | .31 | –.27 | .18 | .12 | .26 |
| Developmental Social Disorders | –.28 | –.34 | –.23 | –.34 | .28 | –.32 | .19 | .22 | .35 |
| Emotional Self-Control | –.27 | –.32 | –.27 | –.24 | .37 | –.32 | .24 | .17 | .36 |
| Executive Functioning | –.31 | –.29 | –.21 | –.37 | .34 | –.33 | .24 | .22 | .38 |
| Negative Emotionality | –.33 | –.30 | –.27 | –.21 | .38 | –.35 | .26 | .17 | .36 |
| Resiliency | .33 | .34 | .24 | .42 | –.30 | .36 | –.17 | –.24 | –.36 |
| **Clinical index** | | | | | | | | | |
| ADHD Probability Index | –.27 | –.27 | –.20 | –.34 | .29 | –.30 | .23 | .23 | .36 |
| EBD Probability Index | –.35 | –.29 | –.23 | –.27 | .39 | –.33 | .24 | .17 | .34 |
| Autism Probability Index | –.26 | –.37 | –.21 | –.33 | .24 | –.31 | .17 | .18 | .32 |
| Functional Impairment Index | –.31 | –.36 | –.27 | –.38 | .33 | –.36 | .23 | .26 | .41 |

*SRP scales*

There is some overlap between the SRP scales and those found on the TRS and PRS. At the child level, five clinical scales overlap (Anxiety, Attention Problems, Atypicality, Depression, and Hyperactivity), and on the adolescent level, six scales overlap (with the addition of Somatization). In general, correlation coefficients are higher (generally in the .30s to .40s) for the PRS comparisons compared to the TRS comparisons (generally in the .10s to .20s). The pattern of correlation coefficients demonstrate that self-report ratings provide distinct information that is not obtained in teacher and parent ratings. Such differences in information often prove useful when conducting behavioral and emotional functioning assessments.

# References

Abelkop, A. S. (2001). Somatic complaints in young school children: The relationship with internalizing distress, behavior problems, academic achievement, and school adjustment. *Dissertation Abstracts International: Section B. Sciences and Engineering, 62*(9-B), 4207.

Achenbach, T. M., McConaughy, S. H., & Howell, C. T. (1987). Child/adolescent behavioral and emotional problems: Implications of cross-informant correlations for situational specificity. *Psychological Bulletin, 101*(2), 213–232.

Achenbach, T. M., & Rescorla, L. A. (2000). *Manual for the ASEBA preschool forms and profiles.* Burlington, VT: University of Vermont, Research Center for Children, Youth, & Families.

Achenbach, T. M., & Rescorla, L. A. (2001). *Manual for the ASEBA school-age forms and profiles.* Burlington, VT: University of Vermont, Research Center for Children, Youth, & Families.

Altmann, R., & Reynolds, C. R. (2005, March). *It's as easy as ABC (i.e., ASEBA, BASC–2, CRS-R): A comparison.* Paper presented at the annual meeting of the National Association of School Psychologists, Atlanta, GA.

American Educational Research Association, American Psychological Association, & National Council on Measurement in Education. (2014). *Standards for educational and psychological testing.* Washington, DC: American Educational Research Association.

American Psychiatric Association. (2000). *Diagnostic and statistical manual of mental disorders* (4th ed., text revision). Washington, DC: Author.

American Psychiatric Association. (2013). *Diagnostic and statistical manual of mental disorders* (5th ed.). Washington, DC: Author.

Americans With Disabilities Act of 1990, 42 U.S.C.A. §§ 12101–12213 (1990).

Anastasi, A., & Urbina, S. (1997). *Psychological testing* (7th ed.). Upper Saddle River, NJ: Prentice Hall.

Arbuckle, J. L. (2005). *AMOS 6.0 user's guide.* Spring House, PA: Amos Development Corporation.

Asher, S. R., & Wheeler, V. A. (1985). Children's loneliness: A comparison of rejected and neglected peer status. *Journal of Consulting and Clinical Psychology, 53*(4), 500–505.

Bassarath, L. (2003). Medication strategies in childhood aggression: A review. *Canadian Journal of Psychiatry, 48*(6), 367–373.

Beck, J. S., Beck, A. T., & Jolly, J. B. (2005). *Beck Youth Inventories–second edition.* Bloomington, MN: NCS Pearson, Inc.

Beck, A. T., Steer, R. A., & Brown, G. K. (1996). *Beck Depression Inventory–II.* Bloomington, MN: NCS Pearson, Inc.

Bhatia, S. K., & Bhatia, S. C. (2007). Childhood and adolescent depression. *American Family Physician, 75*(1), 73–80.

Booth-LaForce, C., & Oxford, M. L. (2008). Trajectories of social withdrawal from grades 1 to 6: Prediction from early parenting, attachment, and temperament. *Developmental Psychology, 44*(5), 1298–1313.

Broidy, L. M., Nagin, D. S., Tremblay, R. E., Bates, J. E., Brame, B., Dodge, K. A., . . . Vitaro, F. (2003). Developmental trajectories of childhood disruptive behaviors and adolescent delinquency: A six-site, cross-national study. *Developmental Psychology, 39*(2), 222–245.

Butcher, J. N., Williams, C. L., Graham, J. R., Archer, R. P., Tellegen, A., Ben-Porath, Y. S., & Kaemmer, B. (1992). *MMPI-A (Minnesota Multiphasic Personality Inventory–Adolescent) manual for administration, scoring, and interpretation.* Minneapolis, MN: University of Minnesota Press.

Cantwell, D. P. (1996). Classification of child and adolescent psychopathology. *Journal of Child Psychology and Psychiatry, 37*(1), 3–12. doi: 10.1111/j.1469-7610.1996.tb01377.x

Charnigo, R., Noar, S. M., Garnett, C., Crosby, R., Palmgreen, P., & Zimmerman, R. S. (2013). Sensation seeking and impulsivity: Combined associations with risky sexual behavior in a large sample of young adults. *Journal of Sex Research, 50*(5), 480–488.

Cohen, B. (1996). *Explaining psychological statistics.* Pacific Grove, CA: Brooks/Cole Publishing Company.

Comrey, A. L. (1988). Factor-analytic methods of scale development in personality and clinical psychology. *Journal of Consulting and Clinical Psychology, 56*(5), 754–761.

Conners, C. K. (2008). *Conners 3rd edition.* Toronto, ON: Multi-Health Systems Inc.

Cummings, C. M., Caporino, N. E., & Kendall, P. C. (2014). Comorbidity of anxiety and depression in children and adolescents: 20 years after. *Psychological Bulletin, 140*(3), 816–845.

Daubert v. Merrell Dow Pharmaceuticals. (92-102) 509 U.S. 579. (1993).

Delis, D. C. (2012). *Delis Rating of Executive Function.* Bloomington, MN: NCS Pearson, Inc.

DeRosier, M. E., & Mercer, S. H. (2009). Perceived behavioral atypicality as a predictor of social rejection and peer victimization: Implications for emotional adjustment and academic achievement. *Psychology in the Schools, 46*(4), 375–387.

DiStefano, C., Kamphaus, R. W., Horne, A. M., & Winsor, A. P. (2003). Behavioral adjustment in the U.S. elementary school: Cross-validation of a person-oriented typology of risk. *Journal of Psychoeducational Assessment, 21*(4), 338–357.

Doll, E. A. (1953). *Measurement of social competence: A manual for the Vineland social maturity scale.* Circle Pines, MN: American Guidance Service.

Doran, N., Sanders, P. E., Bekman, N. M., Worley, M. J., Monreal, T. K., McGee, E., . . . Brown, S. A. (2011). Mediating influences of negative affect and risk perception on the relationship between sensation seeking and adolescent cigarette smoking. *Nicotine & Tobacco Research, 13*(6), 457–465.

Draba, R. E. (1977). *The identification and interpretation of item bias* (Research Memorandum No. 25). Chicago, IL: Statistical Laboratory, Department of Education, University of Chicago. Retrieved from http://www.rasch.org/rmt/rmt261d.htm

Farrington, D. P., & Ttofi, M. M. (2011). Bullying as a predictor of offending, violence and later life outcomes [Special issue]. *Criminal Behaviour and Mental Health, 21*(2), 90–98.

Fletcher-Janzen, E., & Reynolds, C. R. (2003). *Childhood disorders diagnostic desk reference.* New York, NY: Wiley.

Frick, P. J., Burns, C., & Kamphaus, R. W. (2009). *Clinical assessment of child and adolescent personality and behavior* (3rd ed.). New York, NY: Springer.

Galéra, C., Melchior, M., Chastang, J.-F., Bouvard, M.-P., & Fombonne, E. (2009). Childhood and adolescent hyperactivity-inattention symptoms and academic achievement 8 years later: The GAZEL Youth study. *Psychological Medicine, 39*(11), 1895–1906.

Garber, J., Walker, L. S., & Zeman, J. (1991). Somatization symptoms in a community sample of children and adolescents: Further validation of the children's somatization inventory. *Psychological Assessment, 3*(4), 588–595.

Garcia-Barrera, M. A., Kamphaus, R. W., & Bandalos, D. (2011). Theoretical and statistical derivation of a screener for the behavioral assessment of executive functions in children. *Psychological Assessment, 23*(1), 64–79.

Garcia-Barrera, M. A., Karr, J. E., Duran, V., Direnfeld, E., & Pineda, D. A. (2015). Cross-cultural validation of a behavioral screener for executive functions: Guidelines for clinical use among Colombian children with and without ADHD. *Psychological Assessment.* Advance online publication. http://dx.doi.org/10.1037/pas0000117

Garcia-Barrera, M. A., Karr, J. E., & Kamphaus, R. W. (2013). Longitudinal applications of a behavioral screener of executive functioning: Assessing factorial invariance and exploring latent growth. *Psychological Assessment, 25*(4), 1300–1313.

Gledhill, J., & Garralda, M. E. (2006). Functional symptoms and somatoform disorders in children and adolescents: The role of standardised measures in assessment. *Child and Adolescent Mental Health, 11*(4), 208–214.

Goldstein, S., & Naglieri, J. A. (2010). *Autism Spectrum Rating Scales.* Toronto, ON: Multi-Health Systems Inc.

Goldstein, S., & Reynolds, C. R. (Eds.). (1999). *Handbook of neurodevelopmental and genetic disorders in children.* New York, NY: Guilford Press.

Gulliksen, H. (1950). *Theory of mental tests.* New York, NY: Wiley.

Hartley, M. M. M. (1999). The relationship among disruptive behaviors, attention, and academic achievement in a clinical referral sample. *Dissertation Abstracts International: Section A. Humanities and Social Sciences, 60*(2-A), 0333.

Harty, S. C., Galanopoulos, S., Newcorn, J. H., & Halperin, J. M. (2013). Delinquency, aggression, and attention-related problem behaviors differentially predict adolescent substance use in individuals diagnosed with ADHD. *The American Journal on Addictions, 22*(6), 543–550. doi: 10.1111/j.1521-0391.2013.12015.x

Hass, M. R., Brown, R. S., Brady, J., & Johnson, D. B. (2012). Validating the BASC-TRS for use with children and adolescents with an educational diagnosis of autism. *Remedial and Special Education, 33*(3), 173–183. doi: 10.1177/0741932510383160

Henker, B., & Whalen, C. K. (1989). Hyperactivity and attention deficits. *American Psychologist, 44*(2), 216–223.

Hill, I. D. (1976). Statistical algorithms: Algorithm AS 100: Normal-Johnson and Johnson-Normal transformations. *Applied Statistics, 25*(2), 190–192. Retrieved from http://ftp.math.utah.edu/pub/tex/bib/toc/as1980.html#25(2):June:1976

Hill, I. D., Hill, R., & Holder, R. L. (1976). Statistical algorithms: Algorithm AS 99: Fitting Johnson curves by moments. *Applied Statistics, 25*(2), 180–189. Retrieved from http://ftp.math.utah.edu/pub/tex/bib/toc/as1980.html#25(2):June:1976

Holland, P. W., & Thayer, D. T. (1988). Differential item performance and the Mantel-Haenszel procedure. In H. Wainer & H. I. Braun (Eds.), *Test validity* (pp. 129–145). Hillsdale, NJ: Erlbaum.

Hope, T. L., Adams, C., Reynolds, L., Powers, D., Perez, R. A., & Kelley, M. L. (1999). Parent vs. self-report: Contributions toward diagnosis of adolescent psychopathology. *Journal of Psychopathology and Behavioral Assessment, 21*(4), 349–363.

Hoyle, R. H. (1991). Evaluating measurement models in clinical research: Covariance structure analysis of latent variable models of self-conception [Special section]. *Journal of Consulting and Clinical Psychology, 59*(1), 67–76.

Hughes, A. A., Lourea-Waddell, B., & Kendall, P. C. (2008). Somatic complaints in children with anxiety disorders and their unique prediction of poorer academic performance. *Child Psychiatry and Human Development, 39*(2), 211–220. doi: 10.1007/s10578-007-0082-5

Individuals With Disabilities Education Act, 20 U.S.C.A. § 1400 et seq. (2004).

Johnson, N. L. (1949). Systems of frequency curves generated by methods of translation. *Biometrika, 36*(1–2), 149–176. doi: 10.1093/biomet/36.1-2.149

Kamphaus, R. W. (1987). Conceptual and psychometric issues in the assessment of adaptive behavior. *Journal of Special Education 21*(1), 27–35. doi: 10.1177/002246698702100107

Kamphaus, R. W. (2003). Adaptive behavior scales. In C. R. Reynolds & R. W. Kamphaus (Eds.), *Handbook of psychological and educational assessment of children: Personality, behavior, and context* (2nd ed.). New York, NY: Guilford Press.

Kamphaus, R. W., DiStefano, C., & Lease, A. M. (2003). A self-report typology of behavioral adjustment for young children. *Psychological Assessment, 15*(1), 17–28.

Kim, M. J., Catalano, R. F., Haggerty, K. P., & Abbott, R. D. (2011). Bullying at elementary school and problem behaviour in young adulthood: A study of bullying, violence, and substance use from age 11 to age 21 [Special issue]. *Criminal Behaviour and Mental Health, 21*(2), 136–144.

Kovacs, M. (2011). *Children's Depression Inventory 2.* Toronto, ON: Multi-Health Systems Inc.

Kreutzer, M. A., Leonard, C., & Flavell, J. H. (1975). An interview study of children's knowledge about memory. *Monographs of the Society for Research in Child Development, 40*(1, Serial No. 159).

Kugler, B. B., Bloom, M., Kaercher, L. B., Truax, T. V., & Storch, E. A. (2012). Somatic symptoms in traumatized children and adolescents. *Child Psychiatry & Human Development, 43*(5), 661–673. doi: 10.1007/s10578-012-0289-y

Lewis, A. J., Bertino, M. D., Bailey, C. M., Skewes, J., Lubman, D. I., & Toumbourou, J. W. (2014). Depression and suicidal behavior in adolescents: A multi-informant and multi-methods approach to diagnostic classification. *Frontiers in Psychology, 5,* 776. doi: 10.3389/fpsyg.2014.00766

Liguori, G., & Lonbaken, B. (2015). Alcohol consumption and academic retention in first-year college students. *College Student Journal, 49*(1), 69–77.

Loevinger, J. (1957). Objective tests as instruments of psychological theory [Monograph Supplement 9]. *Psychological Reports, 3*(3), 635–694. doi: 10.2466/pr0.1957.3.3.635

Lopata, C., Smith, R. A., Volker, M. A., Thomeer, M. L., Lee, G. K., & McDonald, C. A. (2013). Comparison of adaptive behavior measures for children with HFASDs. *Autism Research and Treatment, 2013,* 1–10.

Maag, J. W., & Katsiyannis, A. (2012). Bullying and students with disabilities: Legal and practice considerations. *Behavioral Disorders, 37*(2), 78–86.

MacPherson, L., Magidson, J. F., Reynolds, E. K., Kahler, C. W., & Lejuez, C. W. (2010). Changes in sensation seeking and risk-taking propensity predict increases in alcohol use among early adolescents. *Alcoholism: Clinical & Experimental Research, 34*(8), 1400–1408. doi: 10.1111/j.1530-0277.2010.01223.x

Martin, S., Wolters, P., Baldwin, A., Gillespie, A., Dombi, E., Walker, K., & Widemann, B. (2012). Social–emotional functioning of children and adolescents with neurofibromatosis type 1 and plexiform neurofibromas: Relationships with cognitive, disease, and environmental variables. *Journal of Pediatric Psychology, 37*(7), 713–724. doi: 10.1093/jpepsy/jsr124

Mellenbergh, G. J. (1982). Contingency table models for assessing item bias. *Journal of Educational and Behavioral Statistics, 7*(2), 105–107. doi: 10.3102/10769986007002105

Miranda, A., Berenguer, C., Colomer, C., & Roselló, R. (2014). Influence of the symptoms of attention deficit hyperactivity disorder (ADHD) and comorbid disorders on functioning in adulthood. *Psicothema, 26*(4), 471–476. doi: 10.7334/psicothema2014.121

Molina, B. S. G., & Pelham, W. E., Jr. (2003). Childhood predictors of adolescent substance use in a longitudinal study of children with ADHD. *Journal of Abnormal Psychology, 112*(3), 497–507.

Morgan, R. B. (1989). Reliability and validity of a factor analytically derived measure of leadership behavior and characteristics. *Educational and Psychological Measurements, 49*(4), 911–919. doi: 10.1177/001316448904900414

Neul, S. K. T., Applegate, H., & Drabman, R. (2003). Assessment of attention-deficit/hyperactivity disorder. In C. R. Reynolds & R. W. Kamphaus (Eds.), *Handbook of psychological and educational assessment of children: Personality, behavior, and context* (2nd ed.). New York, NY: Guilford Press.

Obeid, N., Buchholz, A., Boerner, K., Henderson, K. A., & Norris, M. (2013). Self-esteem and social anxiety in an adolescent female eating disorder population: Age and diagnostic effects. *Eating Disorders: The Journal of Treatment & Prevention, 21*(2), 140–153.

Oehler-Stinnett, J., & Boykin, C. (2001). Convergent, discriminant, and predictive validity of the Teacher Rating of Academic Achievement Motivation (TRAMM) with the ACTeRS-TF and the BASC–TRS. *Journal of Psychoeducational Assessment, 19*(1), 4–18. doi: 10.1177/073428290101900101

Ostrander, R., Weinfurt, K. P., Yarnold, P. R., & August, G. J. (1998). Diagnosing attention deficit disorders with the Behavioral Assessment System for Children and the Child Behavior Checklist: Test and construct validity and analyses using optimal discriminant classification trees. *Journal of Consulting and Clinical Psychology, 66*(4), 660–672.

Patterson, G. R., DeBaryshe, B. D., & Ramsey, E. (1989). A developmental perspective on antisocial behavior. *American Psychologist, 44*(2), 329–335.

Podeszwa, D. A., Richard, H. M., Nguyen, D. C., De La Rocha, A., & Shapiro, E. L. (2015). Preoperative psychological findings in adolescents undergoing hip preservation surgery. *Journal of Pediatric Orthopaedics, 35*(3), 253–257. doi: 10.1097/BPO.0000000000000243

Ramsay, M. C., Reynolds, C. R., & Kamphaus, R. W. (2002). *Essentials of behavioral assessment.* New York, NY: Wiley.

Rehabilitation Act, 29 U.S.C.A. §. 701 et seq. (1973).

Reynolds, C. R. (1997). *Detection of malingering in head injury litigation.* New York, NY: Kluwer Academic Press.

Reynolds, C. R. (2001a, June). *Understanding and defending against the Daubert challenge to expert testimony.* Workshop presented at the annual convention of the American Psychological Society, Toronto, ON, Canada.

Reynolds, C. R. (2001b, October). *Forensic neuropsychological evaluation.* Workshop presented at the annual convention of the American Board of Forensic Examiners, Nashville, TN.

Reynolds, C. R. (2014, August*). A case for combined gender norms in clinical assessment: Separate equates but is still not equal.* Invited address to the annual meeting of the American Psychological Association, Washington, DC.

Reynolds, C. R., & French, C. L. (2003). The neuropsychological basis of intelligence revised: Some false starts and a clinical model. In A. M. Horton, Jr. & L. C. Hartlage (Eds.), *Handbook of forensic neuropsychology* (pp. 35–92). New York, NY: Springer Publishing.

Reynolds, C. R., & Kamphaus, R. W. (1992). *Behavior Assessment System for Children.* Circle Pines, MN: American Guidance Service.

Reynolds, C. R., & Kamphaus, R. W. (2002). *A clinician's guide to the Behavioral Assessment System for Children* (BASC). New York, NY: Guilford Press.

Reynolds, C. R., & Kamphaus, R. W. (2004). *Behavior Assessment System for Children, second edition.* Bloomington, MN: NCS Pearson, Inc.

Reynolds, C. R., & Richmond, B. O. (2008). *Revised Children's Manifest Anxiety Scale: second edition.* Torrance, CA: Western Psychological Services.

Robers, S., Kemp, J., Rathbun, A., & Morgan, R. E. (2014). *Indicators of school crime and safety: 2013* (NCES 2014-042/NCJ 243299). Retrieved from http://www.bjs.gov/content/pub/pdf/iscs13.pdf

Roid, G. H. (1989). *Programs to fit skewed distributions and generate percentile norms for skewed or kurtotic distributions: Continuous norming with the first four moments* (Technical Report No. 89-02). Salem, OR: Assessment Research.

Rowe, C. L. (1999). Externalizing and internalizing problems and adolescent substance abuse. *Dissertation Abstracts International: Section B. Sciences and Engineering, 59*(10-B), 5586.

Sandoval, J., & Echandia, A. (1994). Behavior assessment system for children. *Journal of School Psychology, 32*(4), 419–425. doi: 10.1016/0022-4405(94)90037-X

Sargent, J. D., Tanski, S., Stoolmiller, M., & Hanewinkel, R. (2010). Using sensation seeking to target adolescents for substance use interventions. *Addiction, 105*(3), 506–514. doi: 10.1111/j.1360-0443.2009.02782.x

Sassaroli, S., & Ruggiero, G. M. (2005). The role of stress in the association between low self-esteem, perfectionism, and worry, and eating disorders. *International Journal of Eating Disorders, 37*(2), 135–141. doi: 10.1002/eat.20079

Sattler, J. M. (2008). *Assessment of children: Cognitive foundations* (5th ed.). La Mesa, CA: Author.

Sattler, J. M. (2014). *Foundations of behavioral, social, and clinical assessment of children* (6th ed.). La Mesa, CA: Author.

Scahill, L., Schwab-Stone, M., Merikangas, K. R., Leckman, J. F., Zhang, H., & Kasl, S. (1999). Psychosocial and clinical correlates of ADHD in a community sample of school-age children. *Journal of the American Academy of Child and Adolescent Psychiatry, 38*(8), 976–984.

Schaefer, E. S. (1971). Development of hierarchical configurational models for parent behavior and child behavior. In J. P. Hill (Ed.), *Minnesota symposia on child psychology, Volume 5* (pp. 130–161). Minneapolis, MN: University of Minnesota Press.

Schopler, E. S., & Van Bourgondien, M. E. (2010). *Childhood Autism Rating Scale, second edition.* Torrance, CA: Western Psychological Services.

Schwanz, K. A., Palm, L. J., & Brallier, S. A. (2007). Attention problems and hyperactivity as predictors of college grade point average. *Journal of Attention Disorders, 11*(3), 368–373.

Semrud-Clikeman, M., Bennett, L., & Guli, L. (2003). Assessment of childhood depression. In C. R. Reynolds & R. W. Kamphaus (Eds.), *Handbook of psychological and educational assessment of children: Personality, behavior, and context* (2nd ed., pp. 259–290). New York, NY: Guilford Press.

Smith, B. H., Pelham, W. E., Jr., Gnagy, E., Molina, B., & Evans, S. (2000). The reliability, validity, and unique contributions of self-report by adolescents receiving treatment for attention-deficit/hyperactivity disorder. *Journal of Consulting and Clinical Psychology, 68*(3), 489–499.

Sparrow, S. S., Balla, D. A., & Cicchetti, D. V. (1984). *Vineland adaptive behavior scales: Interview edition, survey form.* Circle Pines, MN: American Guidance Service.

Strauss, C. S. (1990). Anxiety disorders of childhood and adolescence. *School Psychology Review, 19*(2), 142–167.

Stroud, K. C., & Reynolds, C. R. (2006). *School motivation and learning strategies inventory.* Los Angeles, CA: Western Psychological Services.

Sullivan, J. R., & Riccio, C. A. (2006). An empirical analysis of the BASC frontal lobe/executive control scale with a clinical sample. *Archives of Clinical Neuropsychology, 21*(5), 495–501.

Tarter, R. E., Butters, M., & Beers, S. R. (2001). *Medical neuropsychology: The impact of disease on behavior* (2nd ed.). New York, NY: Kluwer Academic/Plenum Publishers.

Tellegen, A., & Ben-Porath, Y. S. (2008, 2011). *MMPI-2-RF (Minnesota Multiphasic Personality Inventory-2-Restructured Form) technical manual--corrected reprinting.* Minneapolis, MN: University of Minnesota Press.

Thaler, N. S., Mayfield, J., Reynolds, C. R., Hadland, C., & Allen, D. A. (2012). Teacher-reported behavioral disturbances in children with traumatic brain injury: An examination of the BASC–2. *Applied Neuropsychology Child, 1*(1), 30–37.

Thorpe, J. S. (2004). *Emotion and inhibitory control in child social development: A behavioral systems approach* (Unpublished doctoral dissertation). University of Georgia, Athens, GA.

Tiffen, K., & Spence, S. H. (1986). Responsiveness of isolated versus rejected children to social skills training. *Journal of Child Psychology and Psychiatry, 27*(3), 343–355. doi: 10.1111/j.1469-7610.1986.tb01837.x

U.S. Census Bureau. (2013). *American community survey, 2013 1-year period estimates.* Washington DC: Author.

U.S. Department of Health and Human Services, Centers for Disease Control and Prevention. (2014). Retrieved from http://www.cdc.gov/alcohol/fact-sheets/alcohol-use.htm

Vaughn, M. L., Riccio, C. A., Hynd, G. W., & Hall, J. (1997). Diagnosing ADHD (predominantly inattentive and combine type subtypes): Discriminant validity of the behavior assessment system for children and the Achenbach parent and teacher rating scales. *Journal of Clinical Child Psychology, 26*(4), 349–357. doi: 10.1207/s15374424jccp2604_3

Volker, M. A., Lopata, C., Smerbeck, A. M., Knoll, V. A., Thomeer, M. L., Toomey, J. A., & Rodgers, J. D. (2010). BASC–2 PRS profiles for students with high-functioning autism spectrum disorders. *Journal of Autism Developmental Disorders, 40*(2), 188–199.

Weinstein, C. E., & Macdonald, J. D. (1986). Why does a school psychologist need to know about learning strategies? *Journal of School Psychology, 24*(3), 257–265. doi:10.1016/0022-4405(86)90058-0

Yen, C.-J., Konold, T. R., & McDermott, P. A. (2004). Does learning behavior augment cognitive ability as an indicator of academic achievement? *Journal of School Psychology, 42*(2), 157–169. doi:10.1016/j.jsp.2003.12.001

Youngstrom, E., Loeber, R., & Stouthamer-Loeber, M. (2000). Patterns and correlates of agreement between parent, teacher, and male adolescent ratings of externalizing and internalizing problems. *Journal of Consulting and Clinical Psychology, 68*(6), 1038–1050.

Zuckerman, M. (1994). *Behavioral expressions and biosocial bases of sensation seeking.* New York, NY: Cambridge University Press.

Zwick, R., Thayer, D. T., & Mazzeo, J. (1997). Descriptive and inferential procedures for assessing differential item functioning in polytomous items. *Applied Measurement in Education, 10*(4), 321–344. doi: 10.1207/s15324818ame1004_2

# Appendix A

## Norm Tables

## Table A.1a TRS–P *T* Scores and Percentiles

| Raw score | Hyperactivity T | Hyperactivity %ile | Aggression T | Aggression %ile | Anxiety T | Anxiety %ile | Depression T | Depression %ile | Somatization T | Somatization %ile | Attention Problems T | Attention Problems %ile | Atypicality T | Atypicality %ile | Withdrawal T | Withdrawal %ile | Adaptability T | Adaptability %ile | Social Skills T | Social Skills %ile | Functional Communication T | Functional Communication %ile | Raw score |
|---|---|---|---|---|---|---|---|---|---|---|---|---|---|---|---|---|---|---|---|---|---|---|---|
| 30 | — | — | 102 | 99 | — | — | — | — | 120 | 99 | — | — | — | — | — | — | — | — | — | — | — | — | 30 |
| 29 | — | — | 100 | 99 | — | — | — | — | 120 | 99 | — | — | — | — | — | — | — | — | — | — | — | — | 29 |
| 28 | — | — | 97 | 99 | — | — | — | — | 120 | 99 | — | — | — | — | — | — | — | — | — | — | — | — | 28 |
| 27 | 88 | 99 | 95 | 99 | 120 | 99 | 112 | 99 | 120 | 99 | — | — | — | — | — | — | — | — | — | — | 76 | 99 | 27 |
| 26 | 86 | 99 | 93 | 99 | 117 | 99 | 109 | 99 | 120 | 99 | — | — | — | — | — | — | — | — | — | — | 75 | 99 | 26 |
| 25 | 84 | 99 | 91 | 99 | 114 | 99 | 106 | 99 | 120 | 99 | — | — | — | — | — | — | — | — | — | — | 73 | 99 | 25 |
| 24 | 82 | 99 | 89 | 99 | 111 | 99 | 103 | 99 | 120 | 99 | — | — | 114 | 99 | — | — | — | — | — | — | 71 | 99 | 24 |
| 23 | 80 | 99 | 87 | 99 | 108 | 99 | 100 | 99 | 116 | 99 | — | — | 111 | 99 | — | — | — | — | — | — | 70 | 97 | 23 |
| 22 | 78 | 98 | 85 | 99 | 105 | 99 | 98 | 99 | 113 | 99 | — | — | 108 | 99 | — | — | — | — | — | — | 68 | 95 | 22 |
| 21 | 76 | 98 | 83 | 99 | 102 | 99 | 95 | 99 | 109 | 99 | 80 | 99 | 105 | 99 | 113 | 99 | 72 | 99 | — | — | 66 | 93 | 21 |
| 20 | 74 | 97 | 81 | 99 | 98 | 99 | 92 | 99 | 106 | 99 | 78 | 99 | 102 | 99 | 109 | 99 | 70 | 98 | — | — | 65 | 90 | 20 |
| 19 | 72 | 97 | 78 | 98 | 95 | 99 | 89 | 99 | 102 | 99 | 75 | 99 | 99 | 99 | 106 | 99 | 68 | 96 | — | — | 63 | 87 | 19 |
| 18 | 70 | 96 | 76 | 98 | 92 | 99 | 86 | 99 | 99 | 99 | 73 | 99 | 96 | 99 | 102 | 99 | 66 | 93 | 73 | 99 | 61 | 84 | 18 |
| 17 | 69 | 94 | 74 | 97 | 89 | 99 | 83 | 99 | 95 | 99 | 71 | 98 | 93 | 99 | 98 | 99 | 63 | 90 | 71 | 97 | 59 | 80 | 17 |
| 16 | 67 | 93 | 72 | 96 | 86 | 99 | 81 | 99 | 92 | 99 | 68 | 96 | 90 | 99 | 95 | 99 | 61 | 85 | 69 | 96 | 58 | 75 | 16 |
| 15 | 65 | 91 | 70 | 95 | 83 | 99 | 78 | 99 | 88 | 99 | 66 | 94 | 87 | 99 | 91 | 99 | 59 | 80 | 67 | 93 | 56 | 71 | 15 |
| 14 | 63 | 89 | 68 | 93 | 80 | 99 | 75 | 99 | 85 | 99 | 64 | 91 | 84 | 98 | 88 | 99 | 57 | 74 | 64 | 90 | 54 | 66 | 14 |
| 13 | 61 | 86 | 66 | 92 | 77 | 99 | 72 | 98 | 81 | 99 | 61 | 87 | 81 | 98 | 84 | 99 | 55 | 68 | 62 | 86 | 53 | 61 | 13 |
| 12 | 59 | 83 | 64 | 90 | 74 | 98 | 69 | 96 | 78 | 99 | 59 | 81 | 78 | 97 | 80 | 99 | 53 | 60 | 60 | 82 | 51 | 56 | 12 |
| 11 | 57 | 79 | 62 | 87 | 71 | 96 | 66 | 94 | 74 | 99 | 56 | 74 | 75 | 97 | 77 | 99 | 51 | 53 | 58 | 77 | 49 | 51 | 11 |
| 10 | 55 | 75 | 59 | 84 | 68 | 94 | 64 | 90 | 71 | 97 | 54 | 66 | 72 | 96 | 73 | 97 | 48 | 45 | 55 | 71 | 48 | 45 | 10 |
| 9 | 53 | 69 | 57 | 80 | 65 | 91 | 61 | 86 | 68 | 95 | 52 | 57 | 69 | 94 | 69 | 95 | 46 | 38 | 53 | 64 | 46 | 39 | 9 |
| 8 | 51 | 63 | 55 | 76 | 62 | 87 | 58 | 79 | 64 | 90 | 49 | 47 | 66 | 93 | 66 | 92 | 44 | 30 | 51 | 57 | 44 | 33 | 8 |
| 7 | 49 | 56 | 53 | 70 | 59 | 81 | 55 | 72 | 61 | 84 | 47 | 38 | 63 | 91 | 62 | 87 | 42 | 23 | 49 | 49 | 42 | 27 | 7 |
| 6 | 47 | 48 | 51 | 64 | 56 | 74 | 52 | 62 | 57 | 76 | 44 | 29 | 60 | 88 | 58 | 80 | 40 | 17 | 47 | 41 | 41 | 21 | 6 |
| 5 | 46 | 40 | 49 | 56 | 53 | 65 | 49 | 51 | 54 | 66 | 42 | 21 | 57 | 84 | 55 | 72 | 38 | 12 | 44 | 33 | 39 | 15 | 5 |
| 4 | 44 | 31 | 47 | 47 | 50 | 55 | 47 | 40 | 50 | 54 | 40 | 15 | 54 | 78 | 51 | 61 | 36 | 7 | 42 | 25 | 37 | 10 | 4 |
| 3 | 42 | 21 | 45 | 37 | 46 | 42 | 44 | 29 | 47 | 41 | 37 | 10 | 51 | 70 | 48 | 47 | 33 | 4 | 40 | 17 | 36 | 5 | 3 |
| 2 | 40 | 13 | 43 | 25 | 43 | 29 | 41 | 19 | 43 | 29 | 35 | 6 | 48 | 58 | 44 | 32 | 31 | 2 | 38 | 10 | 34 | 2 | 2 |
| 1 | 38 | 6 | 40 | 13 | 40 | 17 | 38 | 11 | 40 | 17 | 33 | 4 | 45 | 40 | 40 | 17 | 29 | 1 | 35 | 5 | 32 | 1 | 1 |
| 0 | 36 | 1 | 38 | 3 | 37 | 7 | 35 | 5 | 36 | 7 | 30 | 2 | 42 | 14 | 37 | 5 | 27 | 1 | 33 | 1 | 30 | 1 | 0 |
| **Raw mean** | 7.31 | | 5.51 | | 4.15 | | 5.20 | | 3.95 | | 8.33 | | 2.59 | | 3.68 | | 10.74 | | 7.57 | | 11.45 | | **Raw mean** |
| **Raw SD** | 5.22 | | 4.74 | | 3.27 | | 3.53 | | 2.88 | | 4.19 | | 3.37 | | 2.75 | | 4.65 | | 4.49 | | 5.87 | | **Raw SD** |
| **T: 90% Conf. int.** | 5 | | 5 | | 8 | | 7 | | 8 | | 6 | | 6 | | 8 | | 6 | | 5 | | 6 | | **T: 90% Conf. int.** |

## Table A.1b TRS–P *T* Scores and Percentiles

| Raw score | Hyperactivity T | Hyperactivity %ile | Aggression T | Aggression %ile | Anxiety T | Anxiety %ile | Depression T | Depression %ile | Somatization T | Somatization %ile | Attention Problems T | Attention Problems %ile | Atypicality T | Atypicality %ile | Withdrawal T | Withdrawal %ile | Adaptability T | Adaptability %ile | Social Skills T | Social Skills %ile | Functional Communication T | Functional Communication %ile | Raw score |
|---|---|---|---|---|---|---|---|---|---|---|---|---|---|---|---|---|---|---|---|---|---|---|---|
| 30 | — | — | 107 | 99 | — | — | — | — | 120 | 99 | — | — | — | — | — | — | — | — | — | — | — | — | 30 |
| 29 | — | — | 105 | 99 | — | — | — | — | 120 | 99 | — | — | — | — | — | — | — | — | — | — | — | — | 29 |
| 28 | — | — | 102 | 99 | — | — | — | — | 120 | 99 | — | — | — | — | — | — | — | — | — | — | — | — | 28 |
| 27 | 90 | 99 | 100 | 99 | 120 | 99 | 108 | 99 | 120 | 99 | — | — | — | — | — | — | — | — | — | — | 77 | 99 | 27 |
| 26 | 88 | 99 | 98 | 99 | 119 | 99 | 105 | 99 | 120 | 99 | — | — | — | — | — | — | — | — | — | — | 75 | 99 | 26 |
| 25 | 86 | 99 | 96 | 99 | 116 | 99 | 102 | 99 | 120 | 99 | — | — | — | — | — | — | — | — | — | — | 74 | 99 | 25 |
| 24 | 84 | 99 | 93 | 99 | 113 | 99 | 100 | 99 | 116 | 99 | — | — | 108 | 99 | — | — | — | — | — | — | 72 | 99 | 24 |
| 23 | 82 | 99 | 91 | 99 | 110 | 99 | 97 | 99 | 113 | 99 | — | — | 105 | 99 | — | — | — | — | — | — | 70 | 98 | 23 |
| 22 | 80 | 99 | 89 | 99 | 107 | 99 | 95 | 99 | 110 | 99 | — | — | 102 | 99 | — | — | — | — | — | — | 68 | 96 | 22 |
| 21 | 78 | 98 | 87 | 99 | 104 | 99 | 92 | 99 | 106 | 99 | 82 | 99 | 100 | 99 | 115 | 99 | 70 | 98 | — | — | 66 | 94 | 21 |
| 20 | 76 | 98 | 84 | 99 | 100 | 99 | 89 | 99 | 103 | 99 | 79 | 99 | 97 | 99 | 111 | 99 | 68 | 97 | — | — | 65 | 91 | 20 |
| 19 | 74 | 97 | 82 | 99 | 97 | 99 | 87 | 99 | 100 | 99 | 77 | 99 | 94 | 99 | 107 | 99 | 66 | 95 | — | — | 63 | 87 | 19 |
| 18 | 72 | 96 | 80 | 98 | 94 | 99 | 84 | 99 | 97 | 99 | 75 | 99 | 91 | 99 | 104 | 99 | 64 | 91 | 72 | 99 | 61 | 84 | 18 |
| 17 | 70 | 95 | 78 | 98 | 91 | 99 | 81 | 99 | 93 | 99 | 72 | 98 | 89 | 99 | 100 | 99 | 62 | 88 | 70 | 97 | 59 | 79 | 17 |
| 16 | 68 | 94 | 75 | 97 | 88 | 99 | 79 | 99 | 90 | 99 | 70 | 97 | 86 | 99 | 96 | 99 | 60 | 83 | 67 | 95 | 57 | 75 | 16 |
| 15 | 66 | 92 | 73 | 97 | 85 | 99 | 76 | 99 | 87 | 99 | 67 | 95 | 83 | 98 | 93 | 99 | 58 | 78 | 65 | 92 | 56 | 70 | 15 |
| 14 | 64 | 91 | 71 | 96 | 82 | 99 | 74 | 98 | 83 | 99 | 65 | 93 | 81 | 98 | 89 | 99 | 56 | 72 | 63 | 88 | 54 | 64 | 14 |
| 13 | 62 | 88 | 69 | 94 | 79 | 99 | 71 | 97 | 80 | 99 | 62 | 89 | 78 | 97 | 85 | 99 | 54 | 65 | 61 | 84 | 52 | 59 | 13 |
| 12 | 61 | 86 | 66 | 93 | 75 | 98 | 68 | 95 | 77 | 99 | 60 | 85 | 75 | 97 | 81 | 99 | 52 | 59 | 58 | 79 | 50 | 53 | 12 |
| 11 | 59 | 82 | 64 | 91 | 72 | 97 | 66 | 93 | 73 | 98 | 57 | 78 | 72 | 96 | 78 | 99 | 50 | 52 | 56 | 73 | 48 | 47 | 11 |
| 10 | 57 | 79 | 62 | 88 | 69 | 95 | 63 | 89 | 70 | 96 | 55 | 71 | 70 | 95 | 74 | 98 | 48 | 44 | 54 | 66 | 47 | 41 | 10 |
| 9 | 55 | 74 | 60 | 85 | 66 | 92 | 61 | 85 | 67 | 93 | 52 | 61 | 67 | 93 | 70 | 96 | 46 | 37 | 52 | 58 | 45 | 35 | 9 |
| 8 | 53 | 69 | 57 | 81 | 63 | 88 | 58 | 80 | 63 | 89 | 50 | 51 | 64 | 92 | 67 | 93 | 44 | 30 | 49 | 51 | 43 | 29 | 8 |
| 7 | 51 | 62 | 55 | 76 | 60 | 83 | 55 | 73 | 60 | 83 | 48 | 41 | 62 | 89 | 63 | 88 | 42 | 24 | 47 | 43 | 41 | 23 | 7 |
| 6 | 49 | 55 | 53 | 70 | 57 | 76 | 53 | 65 | 57 | 76 | 45 | 31 | 59 | 86 | 59 | 82 | 40 | 18 | 45 | 34 | 39 | 17 | 6 |
| 5 | 47 | 47 | 51 | 63 | 54 | 68 | 50 | 56 | 54 | 67 | 43 | 22 | 56 | 83 | 55 | 73 | 38 | 13 | 43 | 27 | 38 | 12 | 5 |
| 4 | 45 | 37 | 48 | 54 | 50 | 57 | 48 | 45 | 50 | 56 | 40 | 15 | 53 | 77 | 52 | 62 | 36 | 9 | 40 | 19 | 36 | 7 | 4 |
| 3 | 43 | 27 | 46 | 43 | 47 | 45 | 45 | 34 | 47 | 44 | 38 | 10 | 51 | 70 | 48 | 48 | 34 | 5 | 38 | 13 | 34 | 3 | 3 |
| 2 | 41 | 17 | 44 | 31 | 44 | 32 | 42 | 24 | 44 | 31 | 35 | 6 | 48 | 58 | 44 | 33 | 32 | 3 | 36 | 7 | 32 | 1 | 2 |
| 1 | 39 | 8 | 42 | 19 | 41 | 19 | 40 | 14 | 40 | 19 | 33 | 4 | 45 | 41 | 41 | 17 | 30 | 1 | 34 | 4 | 31 | 1 | 1 |
| 0 | 37 | 2 | 39 | 8 | 38 | 9 | 37 | 7 | 37 | 7 | 30 | 2 | 43 | 13 | 37 | 5 | 28 | 1 | 32 | 1 | 29 | 1 | 0 |
| Raw mean | 6.61 | | 4.74 | | 3.85 | | 4.95 | | 3.91 | | 8.00 | | 2.73 | | 3.55 | | 10.89 | | 8.23 | | 11.87 | | Raw mean |
| Raw SD | 5.13 | | 4.45 | | 3.20 | | 3.83 | | 3.03 | | 4.07 | | 3.68 | | 2.69 | | 4.94 | | 4.45 | | 5.58 | | Raw SD |
| T: 90% Conf. int. | 5 | | 6 | | 8 | | 7 | | 7 | | 6 | | 5 | | 8 | | 6 | | 5 | | 6 | | T: 90% Conf. int. |

## Table A.1c TRS-P T Scores and Percentiles

| Raw score | Hyperactivity T | Hyperactivity %ile | Aggression T | Aggression %ile | Anxiety T | Anxiety %ile | Depression T | Depression %ile | Somatization T | Somatization %ile | Attention Problems T | Attention Problems %ile | Atypicality T | Atypicality %ile | Withdrawal T | Withdrawal %ile | Adaptability T | Adaptability %ile | Social Skills T | Social Skills %ile | Functional Communication T | Functional Communication %ile | Raw score |
|---|---|---|---|---|---|---|---|---|---|---|---|---|---|---|---|---|---|---|---|---|---|---|---|
| 30 | — | — | 98 | 99 | — | — | — | — | 120 | 99 | — | — | — | — | — | — | — | — | — | — | — | — | 30 |
| 29 | — | — | 96 | 99 | — | — | — | — | 120 | 99 | — | — | — | — | — | — | — | — | — | — | — | — | 29 |
| 28 | — | — | 94 | 99 | — | — | — | — | 120 | 99 | — | — | — | — | — | — | — | — | — | — | — | — | 28 |
| 27 | 86 | 99 | 92 | 99 | 118 | 99 | 117 | 99 | 120 | 99 | — | — | — | — | — | — | — | — | — | — | 76 | 99 | 27 |
| 26 | 84 | 99 | 90 | 99 | 115 | 99 | 114 | 99 | 120 | 99 | — | — | — | — | — | — | — | — | — | — | 74 | 99 | 26 |
| 25 | 82 | 99 | 88 | 99 | 112 | 99 | 111 | 99 | 120 | 99 | — | — | — | — | — | — | — | — | — | — | 73 | 99 | 25 |
| 24 | 80 | 99 | 86 | 99 | 109 | 99 | 108 | 99 | 120 | 99 | — | — | 120 | 99 | — | — | — | — | — | — | 71 | 98 | 24 |
| 23 | 79 | 99 | 84 | 99 | 106 | 99 | 105 | 99 | 120 | 99 | — | — | 117 | 99 | — | — | — | — | — | — | 69 | 97 | 23 |
| 22 | 77 | 98 | 82 | 99 | 103 | 99 | 102 | 99 | 116 | 99 | — | — | 114 | 99 | — | — | — | — | — | — | 68 | 95 | 22 |
| 21 | 75 | 98 | 80 | 99 | 100 | 99 | 98 | 99 | 112 | 99 | 79 | 99 | 111 | 99 | 111 | 99 | 74 | 99 | — | — | 66 | 92 | 21 |
| 20 | 73 | 97 | 78 | 98 | 97 | 99 | 95 | 99 | 109 | 99 | 76 | 99 | 108 | 99 | 107 | 99 | 72 | 99 | — | — | 65 | 90 | 20 |
| 19 | 71 | 96 | 76 | 98 | 94 | 99 | 92 | 99 | 105 | 99 | 74 | 99 | 104 | 99 | 104 | 99 | 69 | 97 | — | — | 63 | 87 | 19 |
| 18 | 69 | 95 | 74 | 97 | 91 | 99 | 89 | 99 | 101 | 99 | 72 | 99 | 101 | 99 | 100 | 99 | 67 | 95 | 75 | 99 | 61 | 84 | 18 |
| 17 | 67 | 93 | 72 | 96 | 88 | 99 | 86 | 99 | 98 | 99 | 69 | 97 | 98 | 99 | 97 | 99 | 65 | 92 | 73 | 98 | 60 | 80 | 17 |
| 16 | 65 | 92 | 70 | 94 | 85 | 99 | 83 | 99 | 94 | 99 | 67 | 96 | 94 | 99 | 93 | 99 | 62 | 88 | 70 | 96 | 58 | 77 | 16 |
| 15 | 63 | 90 | 68 | 93 | 82 | 99 | 80 | 99 | 90 | 99 | 65 | 93 | 91 | 99 | 90 | 99 | 60 | 83 | 68 | 94 | 56 | 73 | 15 |
| 14 | 61 | 87 | 66 | 91 | 79 | 99 | 77 | 99 | 87 | 99 | 62 | 89 | 88 | 99 | 86 | 99 | 58 | 77 | 66 | 92 | 55 | 68 | 14 |
| 13 | 60 | 84 | 64 | 89 | 76 | 98 | 74 | 99 | 83 | 99 | 60 | 84 | 85 | 99 | 83 | 99 | 56 | 70 | 64 | 89 | 53 | 64 | 13 |
| 12 | 58 | 80 | 62 | 87 | 73 | 97 | 70 | 98 | 79 | 99 | 58 | 78 | 81 | 98 | 79 | 99 | 53 | 63 | 61 | 85 | 52 | 59 | 12 |
| 11 | 56 | 76 | 60 | 84 | 70 | 96 | 67 | 95 | 76 | 99 | 55 | 71 | 78 | 98 | 75 | 98 | 51 | 55 | 59 | 81 | 50 | 54 | 11 |
| 10 | 54 | 70 | 58 | 80 | 67 | 93 | 64 | 91 | 72 | 99 | 53 | 62 | 75 | 97 | 72 | 97 | 49 | 47 | 57 | 76 | 48 | 49 | 10 |
| 9 | 52 | 64 | 56 | 76 | 64 | 90 | 61 | 86 | 68 | 97 | 51 | 53 | 72 | 96 | 68 | 94 | 46 | 39 | 55 | 70 | 47 | 44 | 9 |
| 8 | 50 | 57 | 54 | 72 | 61 | 85 | 58 | 78 | 65 | 92 | 48 | 44 | 68 | 94 | 65 | 91 | 44 | 30 | 52 | 64 | 45 | 38 | 8 |
| 7 | 48 | 50 | 51 | 66 | 58 | 79 | 55 | 69 | 61 | 85 | 46 | 35 | 65 | 92 | 61 | 86 | 42 | 23 | 50 | 57 | 43 | 32 | 7 |
| 6 | 46 | 41 | 49 | 59 | 55 | 71 | 52 | 58 | 57 | 75 | 44 | 27 | 62 | 89 | 58 | 79 | 39 | 16 | 48 | 49 | 42 | 26 | 6 |
| 5 | 44 | 33 | 47 | 51 | 52 | 62 | 49 | 46 | 54 | 64 | 42 | 20 | 58 | 85 | 54 | 70 | 37 | 10 | 46 | 40 | 40 | 20 | 5 |
| 4 | 42 | 24 | 45 | 42 | 49 | 51 | 46 | 35 | 50 | 52 | 39 | 14 | 55 | 79 | 51 | 59 | 35 | 6 | 43 | 31 | 39 | 14 | 4 |
| 3 | 40 | 16 | 43 | 31 | 46 | 38 | 42 | 24 | 46 | 39 | 37 | 10 | 52 | 70 | 47 | 45 | 33 | 3 | 41 | 22 | 37 | 8 | 3 |
| 2 | 39 | 9 | 41 | 19 | 43 | 25 | 39 | 15 | 43 | 26 | 35 | 6 | 49 | 58 | 44 | 31 | 30 | 1 | 39 | 13 | 35 | 3 | 2 |
| 1 | 37 | 4 | 39 | 6 | 40 | 14 | 36 | 8 | 39 | 15 | 32 | 4 | 45 | 40 | 40 | 16 | 28 | 1 | 37 | 6 | 34 | 1 | 1 |
| 0 | 35 | 1 | 37 | 1 | 37 | 5 | 33 | 3 | 35 | 7 | 30 | 2 | 42 | 17 | 36 | 4 | 26 | 1 | 35 | 1 | 32 | 1 | 0 |
| **Raw mean** | 8.00 | | 6.28 | | 4.44 | | 5.44 | | 3.99 | | 8.65 | | 2.44 | | 3.81 | | 10.59 | | 6.91 | | 11.03 | | **Raw mean** |
| **Raw SD** | 5.25 | | 4.91 | | 3.33 | | 3.21 | | 2.73 | | 4.30 | | 3.05 | | 2.82 | | 4.35 | | 4.46 | | 6.15 | | **Raw SD** |
| **T: 90% Conf. int.** | 6 | | 5 | | 8 | | 8 | | 8 | | 6 | | 7 | | 8 | | 6 | | 5 | | 5 | | **T: 90% Conf. int.** |

## Table A.1d  TRS–P Composite T Scores

| T score | Externalizing Problems | | | Internalizing Problems | | | Adaptive Skills | | | Behavioral Symptoms Index | | | T score |
|---|---|---|---|---|---|---|---|---|---|---|---|---|---|
| | Combined | Female | Male | Combined | Female | Male | Combined | Female | Male | Combined | Female | Male | |
| 120 | — | — | — | 319–352 | 324–348 | 310–355 | — | — | — | — | — | — | 120 |
| 119 | — | — | — | 317–318 | 321–323 | 308–309 | — | — | — | — | — | 610–611 | 119 |
| 118 | — | — | — | 314–316 | 319–320 | 305–307 | — | — | — | — | — | 605–609 | 118 |
| 117 | — | — | — | 312–313 | 316–318 | 303–304 | — | — | — | 606–609 | — | 601–604 | 117 |
| 116 | — | — | — | 309–311 | 314–315 | 301–302 | — | — | — | 602–605 | 608–610 | 596–600 | 116 |
| 115 | — | — | — | 307–308 | 311–313 | 299–300 | — | — | — | 597–601 | 603–607 | 592–595 | 115 |
| 114 | — | — | — | 304–306 | 309–310 | 296–298 | — | — | — | 593–596 | 598–602 | 587–591 | 114 |
| 113 | — | — | — | 302–303 | 306–308 | 294–295 | — | — | — | 588–592 | 594–597 | 583–586 | 113 |
| 112 | — | — | — | 300–301 | 304–305 | 292–293 | — | — | — | 583–587 | 589–593 | 578–582 | 112 |
| 111 | — | — | — | 297–299 | 301–303 | 289–291 | — | — | — | 579–582 | 584–588 | 574–577 | 111 |
| 110 | — | — | — | 295–296 | 299–300 | 287–288 | — | — | — | 574–578 | 579–583 | 569–573 | 110 |
| 109 | — | — | — | 292–294 | 296–298 | 285–286 | — | — | — | 570–573 | 575–578 | 565–568 | 109 |
| 108 | — | — | — | 290–291 | 294–295 | 283–284 | — | — | — | 565–569 | 570–574 | 560–564 | 108 |
| 107 | — | — | — | 287–289 | 291–293 | 280–282 | — | — | — | 560–564 | 565–569 | 556–559 | 107 |
| 106 | — | — | — | 285–286 | 289–290 | 278–279 | — | — | — | 556–559 | 561–564 | 551–555 | 106 |
| 105 | — | — | — | 283–284 | 286–288 | 276–277 | — | — | — | 551–555 | 556–560 | 547–550 | 105 |
| 104 | — | — | — | 280–282 | 284–285 | 273–275 | — | — | — | 547–550 | 551–555 | 542–546 | 104 |
| 103 | — | — | — | 278–279 | 281–283 | 271–272 | — | — | — | 542–546 | 547–550 | 538–541 | 103 |
| 102 | — | 197 | — | 275–277 | 279–280 | 269–270 | — | — | — | 537–541 | 542–546 | 533–537 | 102 |
| 101 | — | — | — | 273–274 | 276–278 | 266–268 | — | — | — | 533–536 | 537–541 | 529–532 | 101 |
| 100 | — | 195–196 | — | 270–272 | 274–275 | 264–265 | — | — | — | 528–532 | 533–536 | 524–528 | 100 |
| 99 | — | 193–194 | — | 268–269 | 271–273 | 262–263 | — | — | — | 524–527 | 528–532 | 519–523 | 99 |
| 98 | 190 | 191–192 | — | 266–267 | 269–270 | 260–261 | — | — | — | 519–523 | 523–527 | 515–518 | 98 |
| 97 | 188–189 | 190 | — | 263–265 | 266–268 | 257–259 | — | — | — | 514–518 | 519–522 | 510–514 | 97 |
| 96 | 186–187 | 188–189 | — | 261–262 | 264–265 | 255–256 | — | — | — | 510–513 | 514–518 | 506–509 | 96 |
| 95 | 185 | 186–187 | 183–184 | 258–260 | 261–263 | 253–254 | — | — | — | 505–509 | 509–513 | 501–505 | 95 |
| 94 | 183–184 | 184–185 | 181–182 | 256–257 | 259–260 | 250–252 | — | — | — | 501–504 | 505–508 | 497–500 | 94 |
| 93 | 181–182 | 182–183 | 179–180 | 253–255 | 256–258 | 248–249 | — | — | — | 496–500 | 500–504 | 492–496 | 93 |
| 92 | 179–180 | 180–181 | 177–178 | 251–252 | 254–255 | 246–247 | — | — | — | 491–495 | 495–499 | 488–491 | 92 |
| 91 | 177–178 | 178–179 | 175–176 | 249–250 | 251–253 | 244–245 | — | — | — | 487–490 | 490–494 | 483–487 | 91 |
| 90 | 175–176 | 176–177 | 173–174 | 246–248 | 249–250 | 241–243 | — | — | — | 482–486 | 486–489 | 479–482 | 90 |
| 89 | 173–174 | 174–175 | 171–172 | 244–245 | 246–248 | 239–240 | — | — | — | 477–481 | 481–485 | 474–478 | 89 |
| 88 | 171–172 | 172–173 | 170 | 241–243 | 244–245 | 237–238 | — | — | — | 473–476 | 476–480 | 470–473 | 88 |
| 87 | 169–170 | 170–171 | 168–169 | 239–240 | 241–243 | 234–236 | — | — | — | 468–472 | 472–475 | 465–469 | 87 |
| 86 | 168 | 169 | 166–167 | 237–238 | 239–240 | 232–233 | — | — | — | 464–467 | 467–471 | 461–464 | 86 |
| 85 | 166–167 | 167–168 | 164–165 | 234–236 | 236–238 | 230–231 | — | — | — | 459–463 | 462–466 | 456–460 | 85 |
| 84 | 164–165 | 165–166 | 162–163 | 232–233 | 234–235 | 228–229 | — | — | — | 454–458 | 458–461 | 452–455 | 84 |
| 83 | 162–163 | 163–164 | 160–161 | 229–231 | 232–233 | 225–227 | — | — | — | 450–453 | 453–457 | 447–451 | 83 |
| 82 | 160–161 | 161–162 | 158–159 | 227–228 | 229–231 | 223–224 | — | — | — | 445–449 | 448–452 | 443–446 | 82 |
| 81 | 158–159 | 159–160 | 156–157 | 224–226 | 227–228 | 221–222 | — | — | — | 441–444 | 444–447 | 438–442 | 81 |
| 80 | 156–157 | 157–158 | 154–155 | 222–223 | 224–226 | 218–220 | — | — | 224–225 | 436–440 | 439–443 | 434–437 | 80 |
| 79 | 154–155 | 155–156 | 152–153 | 220–221 | 222–223 | 216–217 | — | — | 221–223 | 431–435 | 434–438 | 429–433 | 79 |
| 78 | 152–153 | 153–154 | 151 | 217–219 | 219–221 | 214–215 | 219–221 | — | 219–220 | 427–430 | 430–433 | 425–428 | 78 |
| 77 | 151 | 151–152 | 149–150 | 215–216 | 217–218 | 212–213 | 217–218 | — | 216–218 | 422–426 | 425–429 | 420–424 | 77 |
| 76 | 149–150 | 149–150 | 147–148 | 212–214 | 214–216 | 209–211 | 214–216 | 217–219 | 214–215 | 418–421 | 420–424 | 416–419 | 76 |
| 75 | 147–148 | 147–148 | 145–146 | 210–211 | 212–213 | 207–208 | 212–213 | 214–216 | 211–213 | 413–417 | 416–419 | 411–415 | 75 |
| 74 | 145–146 | 146 | 143–144 | 207–209 | 209–211 | 205–206 | 210–211 | 212–213 | 208–210 | 408–412 | 411–415 | 407–410 | 74 |
| 73 | 143–144 | 144–145 | 141–142 | 205–206 | 207–208 | 202–204 | 207–209 | 209–211 | 206–207 | 404–407 | 406–410 | 402–406 | 73 |
| 72 | 141–142 | 142–143 | 139–140 | 203–204 | 204–206 | 200–201 | 205–206 | 206–208 | 203–205 | 399–403 | 402–405 | 397–401 | 72 |
| 71 | 139–140 | 140–141 | 137–138 | 200–202 | 202–203 | 198–199 | 203–204 | 204–205 | 201–202 | 395–398 | 397–401 | 393–396 | 71 |
| 70 | 137–138 | 138–139 | 135–136 | 198–199 | 199–201 | 195–197 | 200–202 | 201–203 | 198–200 | 390–394 | 392–396 | 388–392 | 70 |
| 69 | 135–136 | 136–137 | 134 | 195–197 | 197–198 | 193–194 | 198–199 | 199–200 | 196–197 | 385–389 | 387–391 | 384–387 | 69 |
| 68 | 134 | 134–135 | 132–133 | 193–194 | 194–196 | 191–192 | 196–197 | 196–198 | 193–195 | 381–384 | 383–386 | 379–383 | 68 |
| 67 | 132–133 | 132–133 | 130–131 | 190–192 | 192–193 | 189–190 | 193–195 | 193–195 | 190–192 | 376–380 | 378–382 | 375–378 | 67 |
| 66 | 130–131 | 130–131 | — | 188–189 | 189–191 | 186–188 | 191–192 | 191–192 | — | 372–375 | 373–377 | 370–374 | 66 |

**Table A.1d** TRS–P Composite T Scores (continued)

| T score | Externalizing Problems Combined | Externalizing Problems Female | Externalizing Problems Male | Internalizing Problems Combined | Internalizing Problems Female | Internalizing Problems Male | Adaptive Skills Combined | Adaptive Skills Female | Adaptive Skills Male | Behavioral Symptoms Index Combined | Behavioral Symptoms Index Female | Behavioral Symptoms Index Male | T score |
|---|---|---|---|---|---|---|---|---|---|---|---|---|---|
| 65 | 128–129 | 128–129 | 128–129 | 186–187 | 187–188 | 184–185 | 188–190 | 188–190 | 188–189 | 367–371 | 369–372 | 366–369 | 65 |
| 64 | 126–127 | 126–127 | 126–127 | 183–185 | 184–186 | 182–183 | 186–187 | 186–187 | 185–187 | 362–366 | 364–368 | 361–365 | 64 |
| 63 | 124–125 | 125 | 124–125 | 181–182 | 182–183 | 179–181 | 183–185 | 183–185 | 183–184 | 358–361 | 359–363 | 357–360 | 63 |
| 62 | 122–123 | 123–124 | 122–123 | 178–180 | 179–181 | 177–178 | 180–182 | 180–182 | 180–182 | 353–357 | 355–358 | 352–356 | 62 |
| 61 | 120–121 | 121–122 | 120–121 | 176–177 | 177–178 | 175–176 | 178–179 | 178–179 | 178–179 | 349–352 | 350–354 | 348–351 | 61 |
| 60 | 118–119 | 119–120 | 118–119 | 173–175 | 174–176 | 173–174 | 175–177 | 175–177 | 175–177 | 344–348 | 345–349 | 343–347 | 60 |
| 59 | 117 | 117–118 | 116–117 | 171–172 | 172–173 | 170–172 | 173–174 | 172–174 | 172–174 | 339–343 | 341–344 | 339–342 | 59 |
| 58 | 115–116 | 115–116 | 115 | 169–170 | 169–171 | 168–169 | 170–172 | 170–171 | 170–171 | 335–338 | 336–340 | 334–338 | 58 |
| 57 | 113–114 | 113–114 | 113–114 | 166–168 | 167–168 | 166–167 | 167–169 | 167–169 | 167–169 | 330–334 | 331–335 | 330–333 | 57 |
| 56 | 111–112 | 111–112 | 111–112 | 164–165 | 164–166 | 163–165 | 165–166 | 165–166 | 165–166 | 325–329 | 327–330 | 325–329 | 56 |
| 55 | 109–110 | 109–110 | 109–110 | 161–163 | 162–163 | 161–162 | 162–164 | 162–164 | 162–164 | 321–324 | 322–326 | 321–324 | 55 |
| 54 | 107–108 | 107–108 | 107–108 | 159–160 | 159–161 | 159–160 | 160–161 | 159–161 | 159–161 | 316–320 | 317–321 | 316–320 | 54 |
| 53 | 105–106 | 105–106 | 105–106 | 156–158 | 157–158 | 157–158 | 157–159 | 157–158 | 157–158 | 312–315 | 313–316 | 312–315 | 53 |
| 52 | 103–104 | 103–104 | 103–104 | 154–155 | 154–156 | 154–156 | 154–156 | 154–156 | 154–156 | 307–311 | 308–312 | 307–311 | 52 |
| 51 | 101–102 | 102 | 101–102 | 152–153 | 152–153 | 152–153 | 152–153 | 151–153 | 152–153 | 302–306 | 303–307 | 303–306 | 51 |
| 50 | 100 | 100–101 | 99–100 | 149–151 | 149–151 | 150–151 | 149–151 | 149–150 | 149–151 | 298–301 | 298–302 | 298–302 | 50 |
| 49 | 98–99 | 98–99 | 98 | 147–148 | 147–148 | 147–149 | 147–148 | 146–148 | 147–148 | 293–297 | 294–297 | 294–297 | 49 |
| 48 | 96–97 | 96–97 | 96–97 | 144–146 | 144–146 | 145–146 | 144–146 | 144–145 | 144–146 | 289–292 | 289–293 | 289–293 | 48 |
| 47 | 94–95 | 94–95 | 94–95 | 142–143 | 142–143 | 143–144 | 141–143 | 141–143 | 141–143 | 284–288 | 284–288 | 285–288 | 47 |
| 46 | 92–93 | 92–93 | 92–93 | 140–141 | 139–141 | 141–142 | 139–140 | 138–140 | 139–140 | 279–283 | 280–283 | 280–284 | 46 |
| 45 | 90–91 | 90–91 | 90–91 | 137–139 | 137–138 | 138–140 | 136–138 | 136–137 | 136–138 | 275–278 | 275–279 | 276–279 | 45 |
| 44 | 88–89 | 88–89 | 88–89 | 135–136 | 134–136 | 136–137 | 134–135 | 133–135 | 134–135 | 270–274 | 270–274 | 271–275 | 44 |
| 43 | 86–87 | 86–87 | 86–87 | 132–134 | 132–133 | 134–135 | 131–133 | 131–132 | 131–133 | 266–269 | 266–269 | 266–270 | 43 |
| 42 | 84–85 | 84–85 | 84–85 | 130–131 | 129–131 | 131–133 | 128–130 | 128–130 | 129–130 | 261–265 | 261–265 | 262–265 | 42 |
| 41 | 83 | 82–83 | 82–83 | 127–129 | 127–128 | 129–130 | 126–127 | 125–127 | 126–128 | 256–260 | 256–260 | 257–261 | 41 |
| 40 | 81–82 | 81 | 80–81 | 125–126 | 124–126 | 127–128 | 123–125 | 123–124 | 123–125 | 252–255 | 252–255 | 253–256 | 40 |
| 39 | 79–80 | 79–80 | 79 | 123–124 | 122–123 | 124–126 | 121–122 | 120–122 | 121–122 | 247–251 | 247–251 | 248–252 | 39 |
| 38 | 77–78 | 77–78 | 77–78 | 120–122 | 119–121 | 122–123 | 118–120 | 117–119 | 118–120 | 243–246 | 242–246 | 244–247 | 38 |
| 37 | 75–76 | 76 | 75–76 | 118–119 | 117–118 | 120–121 | 115–117 | 115–116 | 116–117 | 238–242 | 238–241 | 239–243 | 37 |
| 36 | 74 | — | 73–74 | 115–117 | 114–116 | 118–119 | 113–114 | 112–114 | 113–115 | 233–237 | 233–237 | 235–238 | 36 |
| 35 | — | — | 72 | 113–114 | 112–113 | 115–117 | 110–112 | 110–111 | 110–112 | 229–232 | 228–232 | 230–234 | 35 |
| 34 | — | — | — | 110–112 | — | 113–114 | 108–109 | 107–109 | 108–109 | 224–228 | 224–227 | 226–229 | 34 |
| 33 | — | — | — | 108–109 | — | 111–112 | 105–107 | 104–106 | 105–107 | 220–223 | 223 | 221–225 | 33 |
| 32 | — | — | — | — | — | 108–110 | 102–104 | 102–103 | 103–104 | 218–219 | — | 217–220 | 32 |
| 31 | — | — | — | — | — | 106–107 | 100–101 | 99–101 | 100–102 | — | — | 213–216 | 31 |
| 30 | — | — | — | — | — | 105 | 97–99 | 97–98 | 98–99 | — | — | — | 30 |
| 29 | — | — | — | — | — | — | 95–96 | 94–96 | 95–97 | — | — | — | 29 |
| 28 | — | — | — | — | — | — | 92–94 | 91–93 | 93–94 | — | — | — | 28 |
| 27 | — | — | — | — | — | — | 90–91 | 89–90 | — | — | — | — | 27 |
| 26 | — | — | — | — | — | — | — | — | — | — | — | — | 26 |
| 25 | — | — | — | — | — | — | — | — | — | — | — | — | 25 |
| 24 | — | — | — | — | — | — | — | — | — | — | — | — | 24 |
| 23 | — | — | — | — | — | — | — | — | — | — | — | — | 23 |
| 22 | — | — | — | — | — | — | — | — | — | — | — | — | 22 |
| 21 | — | — | — | — | — | — | — | — | — | — | — | — | 21 |
| 20 | — | — | — | — | — | — | — | — | — | — | — | — | 20 |
| 19 | — | — | — | — | — | — | — | — | — | — | — | — | 19 |
| 18 | — | — | — | — | — | — | — | — | — | — | — | — | 18 |
| 17 | — | — | — | — | — | — | — | — | — | — | — | — | 17 |
| 16 | — | — | — | — | — | — | — | — | — | — | — | — | 16 |
| 15 | — | — | — | — | — | — | — | — | — | — | — | — | 15 |
| 14 | — | — | — | — | — | — | — | — | — | — | — | — | 14 |
| 13 | — | — | — | — | — | — | — | — | — | — | — | — | 13 |
| 12 | — | — | — | — | — | — | — | — | — | — | — | — | 12 |
| 11 | — | — | — | — | — | — | — | — | — | — | — | — | 11 |
| 10 | — | — | — | — | — | — | — | — | — | — | — | — | 10 |
| T: 90% Conf. int. | 4 | 4 | 4 | 5 | 5 | 6 | 4 | 4 | 4 | 3 | 3 | 4 | T: 90% Conf. int. |

## Table A.1e TRS–P Composite Percentiles

| %ile | Externalizing Problems Combined | Externalizing Problems Female | Externalizing Problems Male | Internalizing Problems Combined | Internalizing Problems Female | Internalizing Problems Male | Adaptive Skills Combined | Adaptive Skills Female | Adaptive Skills Male | Behavioral Symptoms Index Combined | Behavioral Symptoms Index Female | Behavioral Symptoms Index Male | %ile |
|---|---|---|---|---|---|---|---|---|---|---|---|---|---|
| 99 | 155–190 | 157–197 | 154–184 | 202–352 | 207–348 | 196–355 | 207–221 | 205–219 | 208–225 | 422–609 | 430–610 | 415–611 | 99 |
| 98 | 148–154 | 149–156 | 148–153 | 199–201 | 203–206 | 193–195 | 203–206 | 202–204 | 204–207 | 407–421 | 414–429 | 402–414 | 98 |
| 97 | 143–147 | 144–148 | 144–147 | 196–198 | 200–202 | 191–192 | 200–202 | 199–201 | 201–203 | 397–406 | 403–413 | 393–401 | 97 |
| 96 | 139–142 | 140–143 | 140–143 | 193–195 | 197–199 | 189–190 | 197–199 | 197–198 | 198–200 | 390–396 | 395–402 | 386–392 | 96 |
| 95 | 136–138 | 136–139 | 137–139 | 191–192 | 195–196 | 188 | 195–196 | 194–196 | 195–197 | 383–389 | 388–394 | 380–385 | 95 |
| 94 | 134–135 | 134–135 | 134–136 | 189–190 | 193–194 | 186–187 | 193–194 | 192–193 | 193–194 | 378–382 | 382–387 | 375–379 | 94 |
| 93 | 131–133 | 131–133 | 132–133 | 188 | 191–192 | 185 | 191–192 | 191 | 191–192 | 373–377 | 377–381 | 370–374 | 93 |
| 92 | 129–130 | 129–130 | 130–131 | 186–187 | 189–190 | 184 | 190 | 189–190 | 190 | 369–372 | 372–376 | 366–369 | 92 |
| 91 | 127–128 | 127–128 | 128–129 | 185 | 187–188 | 182–183 | 188–189 | 188 | 188–189 | 365–368 | 368–371 | 363–365 | 91 |
| 90 | 126 | 126 | 127 | 183–184 | 185–186 | 181 | 186–187 | 186–187 | 186–187 | 361–364 | 364–367 | 360–362 | 90 |
| 89 | 124–125 | 124–125 | 125–126 | 182 | 184 | 180 | 185 | 185 | 185 | 358–360 | 360–363 | 357–359 | 89 |
| 88 | 123 | 123 | 123–124 | 181 | 182–183 | 179 | 184 | 183–184 | 183–184 | 355–357 | 357–359 | 354–356 | 88 |
| 87 | 121–122 | 121–122 | 122 | 179–180 | 181 | 178 | 182–183 | 182 | 182 | 352–354 | 354–356 | 351–353 | 87 |
| 86 | 120 | 120 | 121 | 178 | 180 | 177 | 181 | 181 | 181 | 349–351 | 351–353 | 349–350 | 86 |
| 85 | 119 | 119 | 120 | 177 | 179 | 176 | 180 | 180 | 179–180 | 347–348 | 348–350 | 346–348 | 85 |
| 84 | 118 | 118 | 118–119 | 176 | 177–178 | 175 | 178–179 | 178–179 | 178 | 344–346 | 346–347 | 344–345 | 84 |
| 83 | 117 | 117 | 117 | 175 | 176 | 174 | 177 | 177 | 177 | 342–343 | 343–345 | 342–343 | 83 |
| 82 | 116 | 116 | 116 | 174 | 175 | 173 | 176 | 176 | 176 | 340–341 | 341–342 | 340–341 | 82 |
| 81 | 115 | 115 | 115 | 173 | 174 | — | 175 | 175 | 175 | 338–339 | 339–340 | 338–339 | 81 |
| 80 | 114 | 114 | 114 | 172 | 173 | 172 | 174 | 174 | 173–174 | 336–337 | 336–338 | 336–337 | 80 |
| 79 | 113 | 113 | 113 | 171 | 172 | 171 | 173 | 173 | 172 | 334–335 | 334–335 | 334–335 | 79 |
| 78 | 112 | 112 | — | 170 | 171 | 170 | 172 | 172 | 171 | 332–333 | 332–333 | 332–333 | 78 |
| 77 | 111 | 111 | 112 | 169 | 170 | 169 | 171 | 171 | 170 | 330–331 | 330–331 | 331 | 77 |
| 76 | 110 | 110 | 111 | 168 | 169 | 168 | 170 | 170 | 169 | 328–329 | 328–329 | 329–330 | 76 |
| 75 | — | 109 | 110 | 167 | 168 | — | 169 | 169 | 168 | 326–327 | 327 | 327–328 | 75 |
| 74 | 109 | 109 | 109 | — | 167 | 167 | 168 | 168 | 167 | 325 | 325–326 | 326 | 74 |
| 73 | 108 | 108 | — | 166 | 166 | 166 | 167 | 167 | 166 | 323–324 | 323–324 | 324–325 | 73 |
| 72 | — | — | 108 | 165 | 165 | 165 | 166 | 166 | 165 | 321–322 | 321–322 | 323 | 72 |
| 71 | 107 | 107 | 107 | 164 | 164 | — | 165 | 165 | 164 | 320 | 320 | 321–322 | 71 |
| 70 | 106 | 106 | 106 | 163 | 163 | 164 | 164 | 164 | — | 318–319 | 318–319 | 320 | 70 |
| 69 | — | — | — | 162 | 162 | 163 | 163 | — | 163 | 317 | 317 | 318–319 | 69 |
| 68 | 105 | 105 | 105 | — | 161 | — | 162 | 163 | 162 | 315–316 | 315–316 | 317 | 68 |
| 67 | 104 | — | — | 161 | 160 | 162 | — | 162 | 161 | 314 | 314 | 315–316 | 67 |
| 66 | — | 104 | 104 | 160 | — | 161 | 161 | 161 | 160 | 313 | 312–313 | 314 | 66 |
| 65 | 103 | 103 | 103 | 159 | 159 | 160 | 160 | 160 | 159 | 311–312 | 311 | 313 | 65 |
| 64 | — | — | — | — | 158 | 159 | 159 | 159 | 158 | 310 | 309–310 | 312 | 64 |
| 63 | 102 | 102 | 102 | 158 | 157 | 159 | 158 | 158 | — | 309 | 308 | 310–311 | 63 |
| 62 | — | — | — | 157 | 156 | 158 | 157 | — | 157 | 307–308 | 307 | 309 | 62 |
| 61 | 101 | 101 | 101 | 156 | 155 | — | — | 157 | 156 | 306 | 305–306 | 308 | 61 |
| 60 | — | — | 100 | — | — | 157 | 156 | 156 | 155 | 305 | 304 | 306–307 | 60 |
| 59 | 100 | 100 | — | 155 | 154 | 156 | 155 | 155 | 154 | 304 | 303 | 305 | 59 |
| 58 | — | — | 99 | 154 | 153 | — | 154 | 154 | 153 | 302–303 | 302 | 304 | 58 |
| 57 | 99 | 99 | — | 153 | 152 | 155 | 153 | 153 | 152 | 301 | 300–301 | 303 | 57 |
| 56 | — | — | 98 | — | — | 154 | — | 152 | 151 | 300 | 299 | 302 | 56 |
| 55 | 98 | 98 | — | 152 | 151 | — | 152 | 151 | 150 | 299 | 298 | 301 | 55 |
| 54 | — | — | 97 | 151 | 150 | 153 | 151 | — | — | 297–298 | 297 | 299–300 | 54 |
| 53 | 97 | 97 | — | — | 149 | 152 | 150 | — | 149 | 296 | 296 | 298 | 53 |
| 52 | — | — | — | 150 | — | — | — | 150 | 149 | 295 | 294–295 | 297 | 52 |
| 51 | 96 | — | 96 | 149 | 148 | 151 | 149 | 149 | 148 | 294 | 293 | 296 | 51 |

**Table A.1e** TRS–P Composite Percentiles *(continued)*

| %ile | Externalizing Problems | | | Internalizing Problems | | | Adaptive Skills | | | Behavioral Symptoms Index | | | %ile |
|---|---|---|---|---|---|---|---|---|---|---|---|---|---|
| | Combined | Female | Male | Combined | Female | Male | Combined | Female | Male | Combined | Female | Male | |
| 50 | – | 96 | – | – | 147 | 150 | 148 | 148 | 147 | 293 | 292 | 295 | 50 |
| 49 | 95 | – | 95 | 148 | – | – | 147 | 147 | – | 292 | 291 | 294 | 49 |
| 48 | – | 95 | – | 147 | 146 | 149 | – | – | 146 | 291 | 290 | 293 | 48 |
| 47 | 94 | – | 94 | 146 | 145 | 148 | 146 | 146 | 145 | 290 | 289 | 291–292 | 47 |
| 46 | 94 | – | – | – | 144 | – | 145 | 145 | 144 | 288–289 | 288 | 290 | 46 |
| 45 | – | 94 | 93 | 145 | – | 147 | 144 | 144 | – | 287 | 287 | 289 | 45 |
| 44 | 93 | – | – | 144 | 143 | 146 | – | – | 143 | 286 | 286 | 288 | 44 |
| 43 | – | 93 | – | – | 142 | – | 143 | 143 | 142 | 285 | 284–285 | 287 | 43 |
| 42 | 92 | – | 92 | 143 | – | 145 | 142 | 142 | 141 | 284 | 283 | 286 | 42 |
| 41 | 92 | – | – | 142 | 141 | 144 | 141 | 141 | 141 | 283 | 282 | 285 | 41 |
| 40 | – | 92 | 91 | – | 140 | – | 140 | 140 | 140 | 282 | 281 | 284 | 40 |
| 39 | 91 | – | – | 141 | – | 143 | 139 | 139 | 139 | 281 | 280 | 283 | 39 |
| 38 | – | 91 | – | 140 | 139 | 142 | 138 | 138 | – | 280 | 279 | 282 | 38 |
| 37 | 90 | – | 90 | – | 138 | – | 137 | 137 | 138 | 279 | 278 | 281 | 37 |
| 36 | 90 | – | – | 139 | – | 141 | – | 136 | 137 | 278 | 277 | 279–280 | 36 |
| 35 | – | 90 | 89 | 138 | 137 | 140 | 136 | 135 | 136 | 277 | 276 | 278 | 35 |
| 34 | 89 | – | – | – | 136 | – | 135 | 134 | – | 275–276 | 275 | 277 | 34 |
| 33 | – | 89 | – | 137 | – | 139 | 134 | 133 | 135 | 274 | 274 | 276 | 33 |
| 32 | – | – | 88 | 136 | 135 | 138 | – | 132 | 134 | 273 | 273 | 275 | 32 |
| 31 | 88 | – | – | 135 | 134 | 137 | 133 | 131 | – | 272 | 272 | 274 | 31 |
| 30 | – | 88 | – | – | – | – | 132 | 130 | 133 | 271 | 271 | 273 | 30 |
| 29 | 87 | – | 87 | 134 | 133 | 136 | 131 | 129 | 132 | 270 | 270 | 272 | 29 |
| 28 | 87 | – | – | 133 | 132 | 135 | – | 128 | 131 | 269 | 269 | 270–271 | 28 |
| 27 | – | 87 | – | – | – | 134 | 130 | – | – | 268 | 268 | 269 | 27 |
| 26 | – | – | 86 | 132 | 131 | – | 129 | 127 | 130 | 267 | 267 | 268 | 26 |
| 25 | 86 | 86 | – | 131 | 130 | 133 | 128 | 126 | 129 | 266 | 266 | 267 | 25 |
| 24 | – | – | 85 | 130 | – | 132 | – | 125 | 128 | 264–265 | 265 | 266 | 24 |
| 23 | 85 | 85 | – | – | 129 | 131 | 127 | 124 | – | 263 | 264 | 264–265 | 23 |
| 22 | – | – | 84 | 129 | 128 | – | 126 | 123 | 127 | 262 | 263 | 263 | 22 |
| 21 | 84 | – | – | 128 | – | 130 | 125 | – | 126 | 261 | 262 | 262 | 21 |
| 20 | 84 | – | – | 127 | 127 | 129 | – | 122 | 125 | 260 | 260–261 | 261 | 20 |
| 19 | – | 84 | – | – | 126 | 128 | 124 | 121 | – | 259 | 259 | 259–260 | 19 |
| 18 | 83 | – | 83 | 126 | 125 | 127 | 123 | 120 | 124 | 257–258 | 258 | 258 | 18 |
| 17 | – | – | – | 125 | – | 126 | 122 | 119 | 123 | 256 | 257 | 257 | 17 |
| 16 | 83 | – | – | 124 | 124 | 125 | – | 118 | 122 | 255 | 256 | 255–256 | 16 |
| 15 | 82 | 82 | 82 | 123 | 123 | – | 121 | 117 | – | 253–254 | 255 | 254 | 15 |
| 14 | – | – | – | 122 | 122 | 124 | 120 | 116 | 121 | 252 | 254 | 252–253 | 14 |
| 13 | 81 | 81 | – | 121 | – | 123 | 119 | 115 | 120 | 251 | 252–253 | 251 | 13 |
| 12 | 81 | – | 81 | – | 121 | 122 | 118 | 114 | 119 | 249–250 | 251 | 249–250 | 12 |
| 11 | – | – | – | 120 | 120 | 121 | 117 | 112–113 | 118 | 248 | 250 | 247–248 | 11 |
| 10 | 80 | 80 | 80 | 119 | 119 | 120 | 117 | 116 | 117 | 246–247 | 248–249 | 245–246 | 10 |
| 9 | – | – | – | 117–118 | 118 | 118–119 | 116 | 115 | 116 | 244–245 | 247 | 243–244 | 9 |
| 8 | 79 | 79 | 79 | 116 | 117 | 117 | 115 | 114 | 115 | 243 | 245–246 | 241–242 | 8 |
| 7 | – | – | – | 115 | 116 | 116 | 114 | 112–113 | 114 | 241–242 | 244 | 239–240 | 7 |
| 6 | 78 | 78 | 78 | 114 | 115 | 115 | 112–113 | 111 | 113 | 239–240 | 242–243 | 237–238 | 6 |
| 5 | – | – | – | 112–113 | 114 | 113–114 | 111 | 110 | 112 | 236–238 | 240–241 | 234–236 | 5 |
| 4 | 77 | 77 | 77 | 111 | 113 | 111–112 | 110 | 108–109 | 111 | 234–235 | 238–239 | 231–233 | 4 |
| 3 | 76 | 76 | 77 | 109–110 | 112 | 109–110 | 108–109 | 106–107 | 109–110 | 230–233 | 235–237 | 227–230 | 3 |
| 2 | 75 | – | 76 | 108 | – | 106–108 | 106–107 | 104–105 | 107–108 | 226–229 | 232–234 | 221–226 | 2 |
| 1 | 74 | – | 72–75 | – | – | 105 | 90–105 | 89–103 | 93–106 | 218–225 | 223–231 | 213–220 | 1 |

## Table A.2a  TRS–P T Scores and Percentiles

| Raw score | Hyperactivity T | Hyperactivity %ile | Aggression T | Aggression %ile | Anxiety T | Anxiety %ile | Depression T | Depression %ile | Somatization T | Somatization %ile | Attention Problems T | Attention Problems %ile | Atypicality T | Atypicality %ile | Withdrawal T | Withdrawal %ile | Adaptability T | Adaptability %ile | Social Skills T | Social Skills %ile | Functional Communication T | Functional Communication %ile | Raw score |
|---|---|---|---|---|---|---|---|---|---|---|---|---|---|---|---|---|---|---|---|---|---|---|---|
| 30 | — | — | 103 | 99 | — | — | — | — | 120 | 99 | — | — | — | — | — | — | — | — | — | — | — | — | 30 |
| 29 | — | — | 101 | 99 | — | — | — | — | 120 | 99 | — | — | — | — | — | — | — | — | — | — | — | — | 29 |
| 28 | — | — | 99 | 99 | — | — | — | — | 119 | 99 | — | — | — | — | — | — | — | — | — | — | — | — | 28 |
| 27 | 87 | 99 | 97 | 99 | 112 | 99 | 106 | 99 | 116 | 99 | — | — | — | — | — | — | — | — | — | — | 67 | 99 | 27 |
| 26 | 85 | 99 | 95 | 99 | 109 | 99 | 103 | 99 | 113 | 99 | — | — | — | — | — | — | — | — | — | — | 66 | 98 | 26 |
| 25 | 83 | 99 | 93 | 99 | 106 | 99 | 101 | 99 | 110 | 99 | — | — | — | — | — | — | — | — | — | — | 64 | 95 | 25 |
| 24 | 82 | 99 | 91 | 99 | 103 | 99 | 98 | 99 | 107 | 99 | — | — | 108 | 99 | — | — | — | — | — | — | 63 | 90 | 24 |
| 23 | 80 | 99 | 89 | 99 | 101 | 99 | 96 | 99 | 104 | 99 | — | — | 105 | 99 | — | — | — | — | — | — | 61 | 85 | 23 |
| 22 | 78 | 98 | 87 | 99 | 98 | 99 | 93 | 99 | 102 | 99 | — | — | 102 | 99 | — | — | — | — | — | — | 60 | 80 | 22 |
| 21 | 76 | 98 | 85 | 99 | 95 | 99 | 91 | 99 | 99 | 99 | 76 | 99 | 100 | 99 | 103 | 99 | 66 | 96 | — | — | 58 | 74 | 21 |
| 20 | 74 | 97 | 83 | 99 | 93 | 99 | 88 | 99 | 96 | 99 | 74 | 99 | 97 | 99 | 100 | 99 | 64 | 91 | — | — | 56 | 69 | 20 |
| 19 | 73 | 96 | 81 | 98 | 90 | 99 | 86 | 99 | 93 | 99 | 72 | 98 | 94 | 99 | 97 | 99 | 62 | 86 | — | — | 55 | 63 | 19 |
| 18 | 71 | 95 | 79 | 98 | 87 | 99 | 83 | 99 | 90 | 99 | 70 | 97 | 92 | 99 | 94 | 99 | 60 | 81 | 68 | 97 | 53 | 58 | 18 |
| 17 | 69 | 94 | 76 | 97 | 85 | 99 | 81 | 99 | 87 | 99 | 68 | 95 | 89 | 99 | 91 | 99 | 58 | 75 | 66 | 94 | 52 | 52 | 17 |
| 16 | 67 | 93 | 74 | 96 | 82 | 99 | 79 | 98 | 85 | 99 | 66 | 93 | 86 | 99 | 88 | 99 | 56 | 68 | 64 | 90 | 50 | 47 | 16 |
| 15 | 66 | 91 | 72 | 96 | 79 | 99 | 76 | 98 | 82 | 99 | 64 | 90 | 84 | 98 | 85 | 99 | 54 | 62 | 62 | 85 | 49 | 42 | 15 |
| 14 | 64 | 89 | 70 | 95 | 77 | 98 | 74 | 97 | 79 | 99 | 62 | 86 | 81 | 98 | 82 | 99 | 52 | 56 | 60 | 80 | 47 | 37 | 14 |
| 13 | 62 | 87 | 68 | 93 | 74 | 97 | 71 | 96 | 76 | 98 | 61 | 82 | 78 | 97 | 79 | 98 | 50 | 49 | 58 | 74 | 45 | 32 | 13 |
| 12 | 60 | 85 | 66 | 92 | 71 | 96 | 69 | 94 | 73 | 97 | 59 | 78 | 76 | 97 | 76 | 97 | 48 | 43 | 55 | 68 | 44 | 28 | 12 |
| 11 | 58 | 82 | 64 | 90 | 68 | 94 | 66 | 92 | 71 | 96 | 57 | 74 | 73 | 96 | 73 | 96 | 46 | 37 | 53 | 61 | 42 | 24 | 11 |
| 10 | 57 | 78 | 62 | 88 | 66 | 92 | 64 | 90 | 68 | 94 | 55 | 69 | 70 | 95 | 70 | 95 | 44 | 31 | 51 | 55 | 41 | 20 | 10 |
| 9 | 55 | 74 | 60 | 86 | 63 | 89 | 61 | 87 | 65 | 92 | 53 | 63 | 68 | 94 | 67 | 93 | 43 | 26 | 49 | 48 | 39 | 17 | 9 |
| 8 | 53 | 69 | 58 | 83 | 60 | 85 | 59 | 82 | 62 | 88 | 51 | 58 | 65 | 92 | 64 | 91 | 41 | 20 | 47 | 41 | 38 | 13 | 8 |
| 7 | 51 | 64 | 56 | 79 | 58 | 80 | 56 | 77 | 59 | 84 | 49 | 52 | 62 | 90 | 61 | 88 | 39 | 16 | 45 | 34 | 36 | 11 | 7 |
| 6 | 49 | 58 | 54 | 75 | 55 | 74 | 54 | 70 | 56 | 77 | 47 | 45 | 60 | 87 | 58 | 84 | 37 | 11 | 43 | 27 | 34 | 8 | 6 |
| 5 | 48 | 51 | 52 | 70 | 52 | 66 | 51 | 62 | 54 | 69 | 45 | 39 | 57 | 83 | 55 | 79 | 35 | 8 | 41 | 21 | 33 | 6 | 5 |
| 4 | 46 | 43 | 50 | 64 | 50 | 57 | 49 | 52 | 51 | 60 | 44 | 32 | 54 | 79 | 53 | 71 | 33 | 5 | 39 | 15 | 31 | 4 | 4 |
| 3 | 44 | 34 | 48 | 55 | 47 | 46 | 47 | 40 | 48 | 48 | 42 | 25 | 52 | 72 | 50 | 61 | 31 | 2 | 36 | 10 | 30 | 3 | 3 |
| 2 | 42 | 24 | 46 | 45 | 44 | 34 | 44 | 29 | 45 | 35 | 40 | 18 | 49 | 63 | 47 | 48 | 29 | 1 | 34 | 5 | 28 | 1 | 2 |
| 1 | 40 | 14 | 44 | 32 | 41 | 21 | 42 | 17 | 42 | 22 | 38 | 11 | 46 | 49 | 44 | 29 | 27 | 1 | 32 | 2 | 27 | 1 | 1 |
| 0 | 39 | 5 | 42 | 15 | 39 | 9 | 39 | 8 | 39 | 12 | 36 | 5 | 44 | 27 | 41 | 8 | 25 | 1 | 30 | 1 | 25 | 1 | 0 |
| Raw mean | 6.36 | | 4.06 | | 4.16 | | 4.41 | | 3.73 | | 7.41 | | 2.38 | | 3.16 | | 12.87 | | 9.40 | | 15.92 | | Raw mean |
| Raw SD | 5.57 | | 4.89 | | 3.71 | | 4.06 | | 3.54 | | 5.30 | | 3.76 | | 3.35 | | 5.18 | | 4.73 | | 6.38 | | Raw SD |
| T:90% Conf. int. | 5 | | 5 | | 7 | | 6 | | 6 | | 4 | | 5 | | 7 | | 5 | | 5 | | 6 | | T:90% Conf. int. |

**Table A.2b** TRS-P T Scores and Percentiles

| Raw score | Hyperactivity T | Hyperactivity %ile | Aggression T | Aggression %ile | Anxiety T | Anxiety %ile | Depression T | Depression %ile | Somatization T | Somatization %ile | Attention Problems T | Attention Problems %ile | Atypicality T | Atypicality %ile | Withdrawal T | Withdrawal %ile | Adaptability T | Adaptability %ile | Social Skills T | Social Skills %ile | Functional Communication T | Functional Communication %ile | Raw score |
|---|---|---|---|---|---|---|---|---|---|---|---|---|---|---|---|---|---|---|---|---|---|---|---|
| 30 | — | — | 110 | 99 | — | — | — | — | 120 | 99 | — | — | — | — | — | — | — | — | — | — | — | — | 30 |
| 29 | — | — | 107 | 99 | — | — | — | — | 119 | 99 | — | — | — | — | — | — | — | — | — | — | — | — | 29 |
| 28 | — | — | 105 | 99 | — | — | — | — | 116 | 99 | — | — | — | — | — | — | — | — | — | — | — | — | 28 |
| 27 | 98 | 99 | 103 | 99 | 110 | 99 | 103 | 99 | 113 | 99 | — | — | — | — | — | — | — | — | — | — | 66 | 99 | 27 |
| 26 | 96 | 99 | 101 | 99 | 107 | 99 | 101 | 99 | 110 | 99 | — | — | — | — | — | — | — | — | — | — | 64 | 97 | 26 |
| 25 | 93 | 99 | 98 | 99 | 105 | 99 | 98 | 99 | 108 | 99 | — | — | — | — | — | — | — | — | — | — | 63 | 92 | 25 |
| 24 | 91 | 99 | 96 | 99 | 102 | 99 | 96 | 99 | 105 | 99 | — | — | 109 | 99 | — | — | — | — | — | — | 61 | 86 | 24 |
| 23 | 89 | 99 | 94 | 99 | 99 | 99 | 94 | 99 | 102 | 99 | — | — | 106 | 99 | — | — | — | — | — | — | 60 | 80 | 23 |
| 22 | 87 | 99 | 92 | 99 | 97 | 99 | 91 | 99 | 99 | 99 | — | — | 104 | 99 | — | — | — | — | — | — | 58 | 74 | 22 |
| 21 | 85 | 99 | 90 | 99 | 94 | 99 | 89 | 99 | 97 | 99 | 80 | 99 | 101 | 99 | 106 | 99 | 64 | 93 | — | — | 56 | 67 | 21 |
| 20 | 83 | 99 | 87 | 99 | 91 | 99 | 87 | 99 | 94 | 99 | 78 | 99 | 98 | 99 | 103 | 99 | 62 | 88 | — | — | 55 | 61 | 20 |
| 19 | 81 | 98 | 85 | 99 | 89 | 99 | 84 | 99 | 91 | 99 | 76 | 99 | 95 | 99 | 100 | 99 | 60 | 82 | — | — | 53 | 55 | 19 |
| 18 | 78 | 98 | 83 | 98 | 86 | 99 | 82 | 99 | 88 | 99 | 74 | 98 | 93 | 99 | 97 | 99 | 58 | 75 | 68 | 97 | 51 | 49 | 18 |
| 17 | 76 | 97 | 81 | 98 | 83 | 99 | 80 | 98 | 86 | 99 | 72 | 97 | 90 | 99 | 94 | 99 | 56 | 68 | 65 | 94 | 50 | 44 | 17 |
| 16 | 74 | 97 | 78 | 98 | 81 | 99 | 77 | 98 | 83 | 99 | 70 | 95 | 87 | 99 | 91 | 99 | 54 | 62 | 63 | 89 | 48 | 39 | 16 |
| 15 | 72 | 96 | 76 | 97 | 78 | 99 | 75 | 97 | 80 | 99 | 68 | 93 | 85 | 98 | 87 | 99 | 52 | 55 | 61 | 83 | 46 | 34 | 15 |
| 14 | 70 | 95 | 74 | 96 | 75 | 98 | 73 | 97 | 78 | 99 | 66 | 91 | 82 | 98 | 84 | 99 | 50 | 48 | 58 | 76 | 45 | 30 | 14 |
| 13 | 68 | 94 | 72 | 96 | 73 | 97 | 70 | 96 | 75 | 98 | 64 | 88 | 79 | 97 | 81 | 99 | 49 | 42 | 56 | 70 | 43 | 26 | 13 |
| 12 | 66 | 92 | 69 | 95 | 70 | 95 | 68 | 94 | 72 | 97 | 62 | 85 | 76 | 97 | 78 | 98 | 47 | 36 | 54 | 62 | 42 | 22 | 12 |
| 11 | 63 | 90 | 67 | 93 | 67 | 93 | 66 | 93 | 69 | 95 | 60 | 82 | 74 | 96 | 75 | 97 | 45 | 31 | 51 | 55 | 40 | 18 | 11 |
| 10 | 61 | 88 | 65 | 92 | 65 | 91 | 63 | 91 | 67 | 93 | 58 | 78 | 71 | 95 | 72 | 96 | 43 | 25 | 49 | 47 | 38 | 15 | 10 |
| 9 | 59 | 85 | 63 | 90 | 62 | 87 | 61 | 88 | 64 | 90 | 56 | 73 | 68 | 94 | 68 | 94 | 41 | 20 | 47 | 40 | 37 | 12 | 9 |
| 8 | 57 | 81 | 61 | 88 | 59 | 83 | 59 | 84 | 61 | 86 | 54 | 68 | 66 | 93 | 65 | 92 | 39 | 16 | 44 | 32 | 35 | 10 | 8 |
| 7 | 55 | 77 | 58 | 85 | 57 | 77 | 56 | 80 | 58 | 81 | 52 | 63 | 63 | 91 | 62 | 88 | 37 | 12 | 42 | 25 | 33 | 7 | 7 |
| 6 | 53 | 71 | 56 | 81 | 54 | 71 | 54 | 74 | 56 | 75 | 50 | 57 | 60 | 88 | 59 | 84 | 35 | 9 | 40 | 19 | 32 | 5 | 6 |
| 5 | 51 | 64 | 54 | 76 | 51 | 63 | 52 | 66 | 53 | 67 | 48 | 50 | 58 | 85 | 56 | 78 | 33 | 6 | 38 | 13 | 30 | 4 | 5 |
| 4 | 48 | 56 | 52 | 70 | 49 | 53 | 49 | 57 | 50 | 57 | 46 | 43 | 55 | 81 | 53 | 70 | 31 | 3 | 35 | 8 | 29 | 2 | 4 |
| 3 | 46 | 45 | 49 | 62 | 46 | 42 | 47 | 46 | 47 | 46 | 44 | 35 | 52 | 75 | 50 | 60 | 29 | 2 | 33 | 4 | 27 | 1 | 3 |
| 2 | 44 | 33 | 47 | 52 | 43 | 30 | 44 | 34 | 45 | 34 | 42 | 26 | 49 | 66 | 46 | 46 | 27 | 1 | 31 | 1 | 25 | 1 | 2 |
| 1 | 42 | 20 | 45 | 38 | 41 | 18 | 42 | 21 | 42 | 22 | 40 | 17 | 47 | 52 | 43 | 29 | 25 | 1 | 28 | 1 | 24 | 1 | 1 |
| 0 | 40 | 7 | 43 | 20 | 38 | 8 | 40 | 9 | 39 | 11 | 38 | 8 | 44 | 28 | 40 | 11 | 23 | 1 | 26 | 1 | 22 | 1 | 0 |
| **Raw mean** | 4.73 | | 3.29 | | 4.47 | | 4.35 | | 3.95 | | 6.01 | | 2.23 | | 3.12 | | 13.77 | | 10.38 | | 17.15 | | **Raw mean** |
| **Raw SD** | 4.67 | | 4.48 | | 3.76 | | 4.27 | | 3.65 | | 5.06 | | 3.69 | | 3.18 | | 5.14 | | 4.32 | | 6.13 | | **Raw SD** |
| **T: 90% Conf. int.** | 5 | | 5 | | 7 | | 6 | | 6 | | 4 | | 5 | | 7 | | 5 | | 6 | | 6 | | **T: 90% Conf. int.** |

**Table A.2c** TRS–P *T* Scores and Percentiles

| Raw score | Hyperactivity T | Hyperactivity %ile | Aggression T | Aggression %ile | Anxiety T | Anxiety %ile | Depression T | Depression %ile | Somatization T | Somatization %ile | Attention Problems T | Attention Problems %ile | Atypicality T | Atypicality %ile | Withdrawal T | Withdrawal %ile | Adaptability T | Adaptability %ile | Social Skills T | Social Skills %ile | Functional Communication T | Functional Communication %ile | Raw score |
|---|---|---|---|---|---|---|---|---|---|---|---|---|---|---|---|---|---|---|---|---|---|---|---|
| 30 | — | — | 99 | 99 | — | — | — | — | 120 | 99 | — | — | — | — | — | — | — | — | — | — | — | — | 30 |
| 29 | — | — | 97 | 99 | — | — | — | — | 120 | 99 | — | — | — | — | — | — | — | — | — | — | — | — | 29 |
| 28 | — | — | 95 | 99 | — | — | — | — | 120 | 99 | — | — | — | — | — | — | — | — | — | — | — | — | 28 |
| 27 | 82 | 99 | 93 | 99 | 114 | 99 | 109 | 99 | 118 | 99 | — | — | — | — | — | — | — | — | — | — | 69 | 99 | 27 |
| 26 | 80 | 99 | 91 | 99 | 111 | 99 | 106 | 99 | 116 | 99 | — | — | — | — | — | — | — | — | — | — | 68 | 99 | 26 |
| 25 | 79 | 99 | 89 | 99 | 108 | 99 | 103 | 99 | 113 | 99 | — | — | — | — | — | — | — | — | — | — | 66 | 97 | 25 |
| 24 | 77 | 99 | 87 | 99 | 105 | 99 | 101 | 99 | 110 | 99 | — | — | 106 | 99 | — | — | — | — | — | — | 65 | 94 | 24 |
| 23 | 75 | 98 | 85 | 99 | 103 | 99 | 98 | 99 | 107 | 99 | — | — | 103 | 99 | — | — | — | — | — | — | 63 | 90 | 23 |
| 22 | 74 | 98 | 83 | 99 | 100 | 99 | 96 | 99 | 104 | 99 | — | — | 101 | 99 | — | — | — | — | — | — | 61 | 86 | 22 |
| 21 | 72 | 97 | 81 | 99 | 97 | 99 | 93 | 99 | 101 | 99 | 74 | 99 | 98 | 99 | 101 | 99 | 68 | 98 | — | — | 60 | 81 | 21 |
| 20 | 70 | 96 | 79 | 98 | 94 | 99 | 90 | 99 | 98 | 99 | 72 | 99 | 95 | 99 | 98 | 99 | 66 | 95 | — | — | 58 | 76 | 20 |
| 19 | 69 | 94 | 77 | 98 | 92 | 99 | 88 | 99 | 95 | 99 | 70 | 98 | 93 | 99 | 95 | 99 | 64 | 91 | — | — | 57 | 71 | 19 |
| 18 | 67 | 93 | 75 | 97 | 89 | 99 | 85 | 99 | 92 | 99 | 68 | 96 | 90 | 99 | 92 | 99 | 62 | 86 | 69 | 97 | 55 | 66 | 18 |
| 17 | 65 | 91 | 74 | 96 | 86 | 99 | 83 | 99 | 89 | 99 | 66 | 93 | 88 | 99 | 89 | 99 | 60 | 81 | 67 | 95 | 54 | 60 | 17 |
| 16 | 64 | 89 | 72 | 95 | 83 | 99 | 80 | 99 | 86 | 99 | 64 | 90 | 85 | 99 | 86 | 99 | 58 | 75 | 65 | 92 | 52 | 55 | 16 |
| 15 | 62 | 86 | 70 | 94 | 81 | 99 | 77 | 99 | 83 | 99 | 62 | 86 | 82 | 98 | 83 | 98 | 56 | 69 | 63 | 88 | 50 | 50 | 15 |
| 14 | 60 | 83 | 68 | 92 | 78 | 98 | 75 | 98 | 81 | 99 | 60 | 82 | 80 | 98 | 81 | 98 | 54 | 63 | 61 | 84 | 49 | 44 | 14 |
| 13 | 58 | 80 | 66 | 91 | 75 | 98 | 72 | 97 | 78 | 98 | 58 | 77 | 77 | 97 | 78 | 97 | 52 | 56 | 59 | 79 | 47 | 39 | 13 |
| 12 | 57 | 76 | 64 | 89 | 72 | 96 | 70 | 95 | 75 | 98 | 56 | 71 | 75 | 97 | 75 | 97 | 50 | 50 | 57 | 74 | 46 | 35 | 12 |
| 11 | 55 | 72 | 62 | 87 | 70 | 95 | 67 | 93 | 72 | 97 | 54 | 65 | 72 | 96 | 72 | 96 | 48 | 44 | 55 | 69 | 44 | 30 | 11 |
| 10 | 53 | 68 | 60 | 84 | 67 | 93 | 64 | 91 | 69 | 95 | 52 | 59 | 69 | 94 | 69 | 94 | 46 | 37 | 53 | 63 | 43 | 26 | 10 |
| 9 | 52 | 63 | 58 | 81 | 64 | 90 | 62 | 87 | 66 | 93 | 50 | 53 | 67 | 93 | 66 | 93 | 44 | 31 | 51 | 57 | 41 | 21 | 9 |
| 8 | 50 | 57 | 56 | 78 | 61 | 87 | 59 | 83 | 63 | 90 | 48 | 46 | 64 | 91 | 64 | 90 | 42 | 25 | 49 | 50 | 40 | 18 | 8 |
| 7 | 48 | 51 | 54 | 74 | 59 | 82 | 57 | 77 | 60 | 86 | 46 | 39 | 62 | 89 | 61 | 88 | 40 | 20 | 47 | 43 | 38 | 14 | 7 |
| 6 | 47 | 44 | 52 | 69 | 56 | 77 | 54 | 70 | 57 | 80 | 45 | 33 | 59 | 86 | 58 | 84 | 38 | 15 | 45 | 36 | 36 | 11 | 6 |
| 5 | 45 | 37 | 50 | 64 | 53 | 69 | 51 | 62 | 54 | 72 | 43 | 26 | 56 | 82 | 55 | 79 | 36 | 10 | 43 | 30 | 35 | 8 | 5 |
| 4 | 43 | 30 | 48 | 57 | 50 | 60 | 49 | 52 | 51 | 63 | 41 | 20 | 54 | 76 | 52 | 72 | 34 | 6 | 41 | 23 | 33 | 6 | 4 |
| 3 | 42 | 22 | 46 | 49 | 48 | 50 | 46 | 41 | 49 | 50 | 39 | 15 | 51 | 69 | 49 | 63 | 32 | 3 | 39 | 16 | 32 | 4 | 3 |
| 2 | 40 | 15 | 45 | 38 | 45 | 37 | 44 | 29 | 46 | 37 | 37 | 10 | 49 | 60 | 47 | 49 | 30 | 1 | 37 | 10 | 30 | 2 | 2 |
| 1 | 38 | 8 | 43 | 25 | 42 | 23 | 41 | 18 | 43 | 23 | 35 | 6 | 46 | 46 | 44 | 29 | 28 | 1 | 35 | 4 | 29 | 1 | 1 |
| 0 | 37 | 3 | 41 | 9 | 39 | 11 | 38 | 9 | 40 | 12 | 33 | 3 | 43 | 27 | 41 | 4 | 26 | 1 | 33 | 1 | 27 | 1 | 0 |
| **Raw mean** | 7.99 | | 4.83 | | 3.85 | | 4.47 | | 3.51 | | 8.81 | | 2.54 | | 3.21 | | 11.96 | | 8.41 | | 14.69 | | **Raw mean** |
| **Raw SD** | 5.92 | | 5.17 | | 3.64 | | 3.85 | | 3.43 | | 5.17 | | 3.84 | | 3.52 | | 5.08 | | 4.92 | | 6.42 | | **Raw SD** |
| **T: 90% Conf. int.** | 5 | | 5 | | 7 | | 6 | | 6 | | 5 | | 5 | | 7 | | 6 | | 5 | | 6 | | **T: 90% Conf. int.** |

## Table A.2d TRS–P Composite T Scores

| T score | Externalizing Problems | | | Internalizing Problems | | | Adaptive Skills | | | Behavioral Symptoms Index | | | T score |
|---|---|---|---|---|---|---|---|---|---|---|---|---|---|
| | Combined | Female | Male | Combined | Female | Male | Combined | Female | Male | Combined | Female | Male | |
| 120 | — | — | — | 324–338 | 328–333 | 320–343 | — | — | — | — | — | — | 120 |
| 119 | — | — | — | 321–323 | 325–327 | 318–319 | — | — | — | — | — | — | 119 |
| 118 | — | — | — | 319–320 | 323–324 | 316–317 | — | — | — | — | — | — | 118 |
| 117 | — | — | — | 316–318 | 320–322 | 313–315 | — | — | — | — | — | — | 117 |
| 116 | — | — | — | 314–315 | 317–319 | 311–312 | — | — | — | — | — | — | 116 |
| 115 | — | — | — | 311–313 | 315–316 | 308–310 | — | — | — | — | — | — | 115 |
| 114 | — | — | — | 309–310 | 312–314 | 306–307 | — | — | — | — | — | — | 114 |
| 113 | — | — | — | 306–308 | 310–311 | 303–305 | — | — | — | — | 606 | — | 113 |
| 112 | — | — | — | 304–305 | 307–309 | 301–302 | — | — | — | — | — | — | 112 |
| 111 | — | — | — | 301–303 | 305–306 | 298–300 | — | — | — | 583 | 601–605 | — | 111 |
| 110 | — | — | — | 299–300 | 302–304 | 296–297 | — | — | — | 578–582 | 596–600 | 568–571 | 110 |
| 109 | — | — | — | 296–298 | 300–301 | 294–295 | — | — | — | 573–577 | 591–595 | 564–567 | 109 |
| 108 | — | — | — | 294–295 | 297–299 | 291–293 | — | — | — | 569–572 | 586–590 | 559–563 | 108 |
| 107 | — | 208 | — | 291–293 | 294–296 | 289–290 | — | — | — | 564–568 | 581–585 | 555–558 | 107 |
| 106 | — | 206–207 | — | 289–290 | 292–293 | 286–288 | — | — | — | 559–563 | 576–580 | 550–554 | 106 |
| 105 | — | 204–205 | — | 286–288 | 289–291 | 284–285 | — | — | — | 555–558 | 571–575 | 546–549 | 105 |
| 104 | — | 202–203 | — | 284–285 | 287–288 | 281–283 | — | — | — | 550–554 | 566–570 | 541–545 | 104 |
| 103 | — | 200–201 | — | 281–283 | 284–286 | 279–280 | — | — | — | 545–549 | 561–565 | 537–540 | 103 |
| 102 | — | 199 | — | 279–280 | 282–283 | 276–278 | — | — | — | 541–544 | 556–560 | 532–536 | 102 |
| 101 | — | 197–198 | — | 276–278 | 279–281 | 274–275 | — | — | — | 536–540 | 551–555 | 528–531 | 101 |
| 100 | — | 195–196 | — | 274–275 | 277–278 | 272–273 | — | — | — | 531–535 | 546–550 | 523–527 | 100 |
| 99 | — | 193–194 | — | 271–273 | 274–276 | 269–271 | — | — | — | 527–530 | 541–545 | 519–522 | 99 |
| 98 | 189–190 | 191–192 | — | 269–270 | 272–273 | 267–268 | — | — | — | 522–526 | 537–540 | 514–518 | 98 |
| 97 | 188 | 189–190 | — | 266–268 | 269–271 | 264–266 | — | — | — | 518–521 | 532–536 | 510–513 | 97 |
| 96 | 186–187 | 187–188 | — | 264–265 | 266–268 | 262–263 | — | — | — | 513–517 | 527–531 | 505–509 | 96 |
| 95 | 184–185 | 185–186 | — | 261–263 | 264–265 | 259–261 | — | — | — | 508–512 | 522–526 | 501–504 | 95 |
| 94 | 182–183 | 183–184 | 181 | 259–260 | 261–263 | 257–258 | — | — | — | 504–507 | 517–521 | 496–500 | 94 |
| 93 | 180–181 | 181–182 | 179–180 | 256–258 | 259–260 | 254–256 | — | — | — | 499–503 | 512–516 | 492–495 | 93 |
| 92 | 178–179 | 180 | 177–178 | 254–255 | 256–258 | 252–253 | — | — | — | 494–498 | 507–511 | 487–491 | 92 |
| 91 | 176–177 | 178–179 | 175–176 | 251–253 | 254–255 | 250–251 | — | — | — | 490–493 | 502–506 | 483–486 | 91 |
| 90 | 175 | 176–177 | 174 | 249–250 | 251–253 | 247–249 | — | — | — | 485–489 | 497–501 | 478–482 | 90 |
| 89 | 173–174 | 174–175 | 172–173 | 246–248 | 249–250 | 245–246 | — | — | — | 480–484 | 492–496 | 474–477 | 89 |
| 88 | 171–172 | 172–173 | 170–171 | 244–245 | 246–248 | 242–244 | — | — | — | 476–479 | 487–491 | 469–473 | 88 |
| 87 | 169–170 | 170–171 | 168–169 | 241–243 | 243–245 | 240–241 | — | — | — | 471–475 | 482–486 | 465–468 | 87 |
| 86 | 167–168 | 168–169 | 166–167 | 239–240 | 241–242 | 237–239 | — | — | — | 466–470 | 477–481 | 460–464 | 86 |
| 85 | 165–166 | 166–167 | 164–165 | 236–238 | 238–240 | 235–236 | — | — | — | 462–465 | 472–476 | 456–459 | 85 |
| 84 | 163–164 | 164–165 | 163 | 234–235 | 236–237 | 232–234 | — | — | — | 457–461 | 467–471 | 451–455 | 84 |
| 83 | 161–162 | 162–163 | 161–162 | 231–233 | 233–235 | 230–231 | — | — | — | 452–456 | 462–466 | 447–450 | 83 |
| 82 | 160 | 160–161 | 159–160 | 229–230 | 231–232 | 227–229 | — | — | — | 448–451 | 457–461 | 442–446 | 82 |
| 81 | 158–159 | 159 | 157–158 | 226–228 | 228–230 | 225–226 | — | — | — | 443–447 | 452–456 | 438–441 | 81 |
| 80 | 156–157 | 157–158 | 155–156 | 224–225 | 226–227 | 223–224 | — | — | — | 438–442 | 447–451 | 433–437 | 80 |
| 79 | 154–155 | 155–156 | 153–154 | 221–223 | 223–225 | 220–222 | — | — | — | 434–437 | 442–446 | 429–432 | 79 |
| 78 | 152–153 | 153–154 | 151–152 | 219–220 | 220–222 | 218–219 | — | — | — | 429–433 | 437–441 | 424–428 | 78 |
| 77 | 150–151 | 151–152 | 150 | 216–218 | 218–219 | 215–217 | — | — | — | 424–428 | 432–436 | 420–423 | 77 |
| 76 | 148–149 | 149–150 | 148–149 | 214–215 | 215–217 | 213–214 | — | — | — | 420–423 | 427–431 | 415–419 | 76 |
| 75 | 146–147 | 147–148 | 146–147 | 211–213 | 213–214 | 210–212 | — | — | — | 415–419 | 422–426 | 411–414 | 75 |
| 74 | 145 | 145–146 | 144–145 | 209–210 | 210–212 | 208–209 | — | — | — | 410–414 | 417–421 | 406–410 | 74 |
| 73 | 143–144 | 143–144 | 142–143 | 207–208 | 208–209 | 205–207 | — | — | — | 406–409 | 412–416 | 402–405 | 73 |
| 72 | 141–142 | 141–142 | 140–141 | 204–206 | 205–207 | 203–204 | — | — | 206 | 401–405 | 407–411 | 397–401 | 72 |
| 71 | 139–140 | 140 | 138–139 | 202–203 | 203–204 | 201–202 | — | — | 204–205 | 396–400 | 402–406 | 393–396 | 71 |
| 70 | 137–138 | 138–139 | 137 | 199–201 | 200–202 | 198–200 | — | — | 201–203 | 392–395 | 397–401 | 388–392 | 70 |
| 69 | 135–136 | 136–137 | 135–136 | 197–198 | 198–199 | 196–197 | 199–201 | — | 198–200 | 387–391 | 393–396 | 384–387 | 69 |
| 68 | 133–134 | 134–135 | 133–134 | 194–196 | 195–197 | 193–195 | 197–198 | 196–198 | 196–197 | 383–386 | 388–392 | 379–383 | 68 |
| 67 | 132 | 132–133 | 131–132 | 192–194 | 192–194 | 191–192 | 194–196 | 194–195 | 193–195 | 378–382 | 383–387 | 375–378 | 67 |
| 66 | 130–131 | 130–131 | 129–130 | 189–191 | 190–191 | 188–190 | 191–193 | 191–193 | 191–192 | 373–377 | 378–382 | 370–374 | 66 |

## Table A.2d  TRS–P Composite T Scores (continued)

| T score | Externalizing Problems Combined | Externalizing Problems Female | Externalizing Problems Male | Internalizing Problems Combined | Internalizing Problems Female | Internalizing Problems Male | Adaptive Skills Combined | Adaptive Skills Female | Adaptive Skills Male | Behavioral Symptoms Index Combined | Behavioral Symptoms Index Female | Behavioral Symptoms Index Male | T score |
|---|---|---|---|---|---|---|---|---|---|---|---|---|---|
| 65 | 128–129 | 128–129 | 127–128 | 187–188 | 187–189 | 186–187 | 189–190 | 189–190 | 188–190 | 369–372 | 373–377 | 366–369 | 65 |
| 64 | 126–127 | 126–127 | 126 | 184–186 | 185–186 | 183–185 | 186–188 | 186–188 | 185–187 | 364–368 | 368–372 | 361–365 | 64 |
| 63 | 124–125 | 124–125 | 124–125 | 182–183 | 182–184 | 181–182 | 183–185 | 183–185 | 183–184 | 359–363 | 363–367 | 357–360 | 63 |
| 62 | 122–123 | 122–123 | 122–123 | 179–181 | 180–181 | 179–180 | 181–182 | 181–182 | 180–182 | 355–358 | 358–362 | 352–356 | 62 |
| 61 | 120–121 | 121 | 120–121 | 177–178 | 177–179 | 176–178 | 178–180 | 178–180 | 178–179 | 350–354 | 353–357 | 348–351 | 61 |
| 60 | 118–119 | 119–120 | 118–119 | 174–176 | 175–176 | 174–175 | 176–177 | 175–177 | 175–177 | 345–349 | 348–352 | 343–347 | 60 |
| 59 | 117 | 117–118 | 116–117 | 172–173 | 172–174 | 171–173 | 173–175 | 173–174 | 172–174 | 341–344 | 343–347 | 339–342 | 59 |
| 58 | 115–116 | 115–116 | 114–115 | 169–171 | 169–171 | 169–170 | 170–172 | 170–172 | 170–171 | 336–340 | 338–342 | 334–338 | 58 |
| 57 | 113–114 | 113–114 | 113 | 167–168 | 167–168 | 166–168 | 168–169 | 168–169 | 167–169 | 331–335 | 333–337 | 330–333 | 57 |
| 56 | 111–112 | 111–112 | 111–112 | 164–166 | 164–166 | 164–165 | 165–167 | 165–167 | 165–166 | 327–330 | 328–332 | 325–329 | 56 |
| 55 | 109–110 | 109–110 | 109–110 | 162–163 | 162–163 | 161–163 | 162–164 | 162–164 | 162–164 | 322–326 | 323–327 | 321–324 | 55 |
| 54 | 107–108 | 107–108 | 107–108 | 159–161 | 159–161 | 159–160 | 160–161 | 160–161 | 159–161 | 317–321 | 318–322 | 316–320 | 54 |
| 53 | 105–106 | 105–106 | 105–106 | 157–158 | 157–158 | 157–158 | 157–159 | 157–159 | 157–158 | 313–316 | 313–317 | 312–315 | 53 |
| 52 | 104 | 103–104 | 103–104 | 154–156 | 154–156 | 154–156 | 154–156 | 154–156 | 154–156 | 308–312 | 308–312 | 307–311 | 52 |
| 51 | 102–103 | 102 | 102 | 152–153 | 152–153 | 152–153 | 152–153 | 152–153 | 152–153 | 303–307 | 303–307 | 303–306 | 51 |
| 50 | 100–101 | 100–101 | 100–101 | 149–151 | 149–151 | 149–151 | 149–151 | 149–151 | 149–151 | 299–302 | 298–302 | 298–302 | 50 |
| 49 | 98–99 | 98–99 | 98–99 | 147–148 | 147–148 | 147–148 | 147–148 | 147–148 | 146–148 | 294–298 | 293–297 | 294–297 | 49 |
| 48 | 96–97 | 96–97 | 96–97 | 144–146 | 144–146 | 144–146 | 144–146 | 144–146 | 144–145 | 289–293 | 288–292 | 289–293 | 48 |
| 47 | 94–95 | 94–95 | 94–95 | 142–143 | 141–143 | 142–143 | 141–143 | 141–143 | 141–143 | 285–288 | 283–287 | 285–288 | 47 |
| 46 | 92–93 | 92–93 | 92–93 | 139–141 | 139–140 | 139–141 | 139–140 | 139–140 | 139–140 | 280–284 | 278–282 | 280–284 | 46 |
| 45 | 90–91 | 90–91 | 90–91 | 137–138 | 136–138 | 137–138 | 136–138 | 136–138 | 136–138 | 275–279 | 273–277 | 276–279 | 45 |
| 44 | 89 | 88–89 | 89 | 134–136 | 134–135 | 135–136 | 133–135 | 133–135 | 133–135 | 271–274 | 268–272 | 271–275 | 44 |
| 43 | 87–88 | 86–87 | 87–88 | 132–133 | 131–133 | 132–134 | 131–132 | 131–132 | 131–132 | 266–270 | 263–267 | 267–270 | 43 |
| 42 | 85–86 | 84–85 | 85–86 | 129–131 | 129–130 | 130–131 | 128–130 | 128–130 | 128–130 | 262–265 | 258–262 | 262–266 | 42 |
| 41 | 83–84 | 83 | 83–84 | 127–128 | 126–128 | 127–129 | 125–127 | 126–127 | 126–127 | 257–261 | 253–257 | 258–261 | 41 |
| 40 | 81–82 | — | 81–82 | 124–126 | 124–125 | 125–126 | 123–124 | 123–125 | 123–125 | 252–256 | 248–252 | 253–257 | 40 |
| 39 | — | — | 79–80 | 122–123 | 122–123 | 122–124 | 120–122 | 120–122 | 118–119 | 248–251 | 245–247 | 249–252 | 39 |
| 38 | — | — | 78 | 119–121 | 118–120 | 120–121 | 118–119 | 118–119 | 115–117 | 243–247 | — | 244–248 | 38 |
| 37 | — | — | — | 117–118 | 117 | 117–119 | 115–117 | 115–117 | 112–114 | 241–242 | — | 240–243 | 37 |
| 36 | — | — | — | — | — | — | 112–114 | 112–114 | 110–111 | — | — | 235–239 | 36 |
| 35 | — | — | — | — | — | — | 110–111 | 110–111 | 107–109 | — | — | 233–234 | 35 |
| 34 | — | — | — | — | — | — | 107–109 | 107–109 | 105–106 | — | — | — | 34 |
| 33 | — | — | — | — | — | — | 104–106 | 105–106 | 102–104 | — | — | — | 33 |
| 32 | — | — | — | — | — | — | 102–103 | 102–104 | 99–101 | — | — | — | 32 |
| 31 | — | — | — | — | — | — | 99–101 | 99–101 | 97–98 | — | — | — | 31 |
| 30 | — | — | — | — | — | — | 96–98 | 97–98 | 94–96 | — | — | — | 30 |
| 29 | — | — | — | — | — | — | 94–95 | 94–96 | 92–93 | — | — | — | 29 |
| 28 | — | — | — | — | — | — | 91–93 | 91–93 | 89–91 | — | — | — | 28 |
| 27 | — | — | — | — | — | — | 89–90 | 89–90 | 86–88 | — | — | — | 27 |
| 26 | — | — | — | — | — | — | 86–88 | 86–88 | — | — | — | — | 26 |
| 25 | — | — | — | — | — | — | 83–85 | 83–85 | — | — | — | — | 25 |
| 24 | — | — | — | — | — | — | 81–82 | 81–82 | — | — | — | — | 24 |
| 23 | — | — | — | — | — | — | 80 | 78–80 | — | — | — | — | 23 |
| 22 | — | — | — | — | — | — | — | 76–77 | — | — | — | — | 22 |
| 21 | — | — | — | — | — | — | — | 73–75 | — | — | — | — | 21 |
| 20 | — | — | — | — | — | — | — | 71–72 | — | — | — | — | 20 |
| 19 | — | — | — | — | — | — | — | — | — | — | — | — | 19 |
| 18 | — | — | — | — | — | — | — | — | — | — | — | — | 18 |
| 17 | — | — | — | — | — | — | — | — | — | — | — | — | 17 |
| 16 | — | — | — | — | — | — | — | — | — | — | — | — | 16 |
| 15 | — | — | — | — | — | — | — | — | — | — | — | — | 15 |
| 14 | — | — | — | — | — | — | — | — | — | — | — | — | 14 |
| 13 | — | — | — | — | — | — | — | — | — | — | — | — | 13 |
| 12 | — | — | — | — | — | — | — | — | — | — | — | — | 12 |
| 11 | — | — | — | — | — | — | — | — | — | — | — | — | 11 |
| 10 | — | — | — | — | — | — | — | — | — | — | — | — | 10 |
| T: 90% Conf. int. | 4 | 4 | 4 | 5 | 4 | 5 | 4 | 4 | 4 | 3 | 3 | 3 | T: 90% Conf. int. |

**Table A.2e** TRS–P Composite Percentiles

| %ile | Externalizing Problems | | | Internalizing Problems | | | Adaptive Skills | | | Behavioral Symptoms Index | | | %ile |
|---|---|---|---|---|---|---|---|---|---|---|---|---|---|
| | Combined | Female | Male | Combined | Female | Male | Combined | Female | Male | Combined | Female | Male | |
| 99 | 158–190 | 163–208 | 153–181 | 220–338 | 224–333 | 213–343 | 196–201 | 193–198 | 200–206 | 437–583 | 458–606 | 419–571 | 99 |
| 98 | 150–157 | 153–162 | 148–152 | 211–219 | 214–223 | 207–212 | 194–195 | 191–192 | 197–199 | 417–436 | 432–457 | 407–418 | 98 |
| 97 | 145–149 | 146–152 | 144–147 | 204–210 | 207–213 | 203–206 | 193 | 190 | 195–196 | 404–416 | 415–431 | 398–406 | 97 |
| 96 | 141–144 | 141–145 | 140–143 | 200–203 | 202–206 | 199–202 | 191–192 | 189 | 193–194 | 394–403 | 403–414 | 391–397 | 96 |
| 95 | 138–140 | 137–140 | 137–139 | 196–199 | 198–201 | 196–198 | 190 | 188 | 192 | 386–393 | 393–402 | 385–390 | 95 |
| 94 | 135–137 | 134–136 | 135–136 | 193–195 | 194–197 | 193–195 | 189 | 187 | 190–191 | 380–385 | 385–392 | 380–384 | 94 |
| 93 | 132–134 | 131–133 | 133–134 | 190–192 | 191–193 | 191–192 | 188 | 186 | 189 | 374–379 | 378–384 | 375–379 | 93 |
| 92 | 130–131 | 128–130 | 131–132 | 187–189 | 188–190 | 188–190 | 187 | 185 | 188 | 369–373 | 372–377 | 371–374 | 92 |
| 91 | 128–129 | 126–127 | 129–130 | 185–186 | 186–187 | 186–187 | 186 | 184 | 186–187 | 364–368 | 367–371 | 367–370 | 91 |
| 90 | 126–127 | 124–125 | 127–128 | 183–184 | 184–185 | 184–185 | 185 | 183 | 185 | 360–363 | 362–366 | 363–366 | 90 |
| 89 | 124–125 | 122–123 | 125–126 | 181–182 | 182–183 | 183 | 184 | 182 | 184 | 356–359 | 357–361 | 360–362 | 89 |
| 88 | 123 | 121 | 124 | 179–180 | 180–181 | 181–182 | 183 | 181 | 183 | 353–355 | 354–356 | 357–359 | 88 |
| 87 | 121–122 | 119–120 | 122–123 | 178 | 178–179 | 179–180 | 182 | 181 | 182 | 350–352 | 350–353 | 354–356 | 87 |
| 86 | 120 | 118 | 121 | 176–177 | 177 | 178 | 181 | 180 | 181 | 347–349 | 347–349 | 351–353 | 86 |
| 85 | 119 | 117 | 120 | 175 | 175–176 | 176–177 | 180 | 179 | 180 | 344–346 | 343–346 | 348–350 | 85 |
| 84 | 117–118 | 115–116 | 119 | 173–174 | 174 | 175 | 179 | – | 179 | 342–343 | 341–342 | 346–347 | 84 |
| 83 | 116 | 114 | 118 | 172 | 172–173 | 174 | 178 | 178 | 178 | 339–341 | 338–340 | 343–345 | 83 |
| 82 | 115 | 113 | 117 | 171 | 171 | 172–173 | 177 | 177 | 177 | 337–338 | 335–337 | 341–342 | 82 |
| 81 | 114 | 112 | 115–116 | 170 | 170 | 171 | – | 176 | 176 | 334–336 | 333–334 | 339–340 | 81 |
| 80 | 113 | 111 | 114 | 169 | 169 | 170 | 176 | – | 175 | 332–333 | 330–332 | 336–338 | 80 |
| 79 | 112 | 110 | – | 168 | 167–168 | 169 | 175 | 175 | 174 | 330–331 | 328–329 | 334–335 | 79 |
| 78 | 111 | 109 | 113 | 166–167 | 166 | 168 | 174 | 174 | 173 | 328–329 | 326–327 | 332–333 | 78 |
| 77 | – | – | 112 | 165 | 165 | 167 | 173 | 173 | 172 | 326–327 | 324–325 | 330–331 | 77 |
| 76 | 110 | 108 | 111 | – | 164 | 166 | 172 | – | 171 | 325 | 322–323 | 328–329 | 76 |
| 75 | 109 | 107 | 110 | 164 | 163 | 165 | – | 172 | 170 | 323–324 | 320–321 | 326–327 | 75 |
| 74 | 108 | 106 | 109 | 163 | 162 | 164 | 171 | 171 | 169 | 321–322 | 318–319 | 325 | 74 |
| 73 | 107 | – | – | 162 | – | 163 | 170 | 170 | – | 320 | 317 | 323–324 | 73 |
| 72 | – | 105 | 108 | 161 | 161 | 162 | 169 | – | 168 | 318–319 | 315–316 | 321–322 | 72 |
| 71 | 106 | 104 | 107 | 160 | 160 | 161 | 168 | 169 | 167 | 316–317 | 313–314 | 320 | 71 |
| 70 | 105 | – | 106 | 159 | 159 | 160 | 167 | 168 | 166 | 315 | 312 | 318–319 | 70 |
| 69 | 104 | 103 | – | 158 | 158 | 159 | 166 | 167 | 165 | 313–314 | 310–311 | 316–317 | 69 |
| 68 | – | – | 105 | – | 157 | – | 165 | – | 164 | 312 | 309 | 315 | 68 |
| 67 | 103 | 102 | 104 | 157 | – | 158 | 164 | 166 | 163 | 311 | 308 | 313–314 | 67 |
| 66 | – | – | – | 156 | 156 | 157 | – | 165 | – | 309–310 | 306–307 | 312 | 66 |
| 65 | 102 | 101 | 103 | 155 | 155 | 156 | 163 | – | 162 | 308 | 305 | 310–311 | 65 |
| 64 | – | – | – | – | 154 | 155 | – | 164 | 161 | 307 | 304 | 309 | 64 |
| 63 | 101 | 100 | 102 | 154 | – | – | 162 | 163 | 160 | 305–306 | 302–303 | 307–308 | 63 |
| 62 | – | – | 101 | – | 153 | 154 | 161 | 162 | 159 | 304 | 301 | 306 | 62 |
| 61 | 100 | 99 | 100 | 153 | 152 | 153 | 160 | – | 158 | 303 | 300 | 305 | 61 |
| 60 | – | – | – | 152 | – | 152 | 159 | 161 | – | 302 | 299 | 303–304 | 60 |
| 59 | 99 | 98 | 99 | 151 | 151 | – | – | 160 | 157 | 301 | 297–298 | 302 | 59 |
| 58 | – | – | – | – | 150 | 151 | 158 | 159 | 156 | 299–300 | 296 | 301 | 58 |
| 57 | 98 | 97 | 98 | 150 | – | 150 | 157 | 158 | 155 | 298 | 295 | 299–300 | 57 |
| 56 | – | – | – | 149 | 149 | – | 156 | – | 154 | 297 | 294 | 298 | 56 |
| 55 | 97 | 96 | 97 | – | 148 | 149 | 155 | 157 | – | 296 | 293 | 297 | 55 |
| 54 | – | – | – | 148 | – | 148 | – | 156 | 153 | 295 | 292 | 296 | 54 |
| 53 | – | – | 96 | – | 147 | – | 154 | 155 | 152 | 294 | 291 | 295 | 53 |
| 52 | 96 | 95 | – | 147 | – | 147 | 153 | – | 151 | 293 | 290 | 293–294 | 52 |
| 51 | – | – | – | 146 | 146 | 146 | 152 | 154 | 150 | 292 | 289 | 292 | 51 |

## Table A.2e  TRS–P Composite Percentiles (continued)

| %ile | Externalizing Problems — Combined | Externalizing Problems — Female | Externalizing Problems — Male | Internalizing Problems — Combined | Internalizing Problems — Female | Internalizing Problems — Male | Adaptive Skills — Combined | Adaptive Skills — Female | Adaptive Skills — Male | Behavioral Symptoms Index — Combined | Behavioral Symptoms Index — Female | Behavioral Symptoms Index — Male | %ile |
|---|---|---|---|---|---|---|---|---|---|---|---|---|---|
| 50 | 95 | 95 | 95 | — | 145 | — | 151 | 153 | — | 291 | 288 | 291 | 50 |
| 49 | — | 94 | — | 145 | — | 145 | — | 152 | 149 | 290 | 287 | 290 | 49 |
| 48 | — | — | — | — | 144 | 144 | 150 | 151 | 148 | 289 | 286 | 289 | 48 |
| 47 | 94 | — | 94 | 144 | — | — | 149 | — | 147 | 288 | 285 | 288 | 47 |
| 46 | — | 93 | — | 143 | 143 | 143 | 148 | 150 | 146 | 287 | 284 | 287 | 46 |
| 45 | 93 | — | 93 | — | — | — | 147 | 149 | — | 286 | 283 | 285–286 | 45 |
| 44 | — | — | — | 142 | 142 | 142 | 146 | 148 | 145 | 285 | 282 | 284 | 44 |
| 43 | 92 | 92 | — | — | 141 | 141 | — | 147 | 144 | 284 | 281 | 283 | 43 |
| 42 | — | — | 92 | 141 | — | — | 145 | 146 | 143 | 283 | — | 282 | 42 |
| 41 | — | — | — | — | 140 | 140 | 144 | — | 142 | 282 | 280 | 281 | 41 |
| 40 | — | 91 | 91 | 140 | — | — | 143 | 145 | 141 | 281 | 279 | 280 | 40 |
| 39 | 91 | — | — | — | 139 | 139 | 142 | 144 | 140 | 280 | 278 | 279 | 39 |
| 38 | — | — | — | 139 | 138 | 138 | 141 | 143 | 139 | 279 | 277 | 278 | 38 |
| 37 | — | — | 90 | 138 | — | 137 | — | 142 | 138 | 278 | 276 | 277 | 37 |
| 36 | 90 | 90 | — | — | — | — | 140 | 141 | — | 277 | 275 | 276 | 36 |
| 35 | — | — | — | 137 | 137 | — | 139 | 140 | 137 | 276 | — | 275 | 35 |
| 34 | — | — | 89 | — | — | 136 | 138 | 139 | 136 | 275 | 274 | 274 | 34 |
| 33 | 89 | 89 | — | 136 | 136 | 135 | 137 | 138 | 135 | — | 273 | 273 | 33 |
| 32 | — | — | — | — | — | — | 136 | 137 | 134 | 274 | 272 | 272 | 32 |
| 31 | — | — | 88 | 135 | 135 | 134 | 135 | — | 133 | 273 | 271 | 271 | 31 |
| 30 | 88 | — | — | — | — | — | 134 | 136 | — | 272 | 270 | 270 | 30 |
| 29 | — | 88 | — | 134 | 134 | 133 | 133 | 135 | 132 | 271 | — | 269 | 29 |
| 28 | 87 | — | 87 | — | — | — | 132 | 134 | 131 | 270 | 269 | 268 | 28 |
| 27 | — | — | — | 133 | 133 | 132 | 131 | 133 | 130 | 269 | 268 | 267 | 27 |
| 26 | — | — | — | 132 | 132 | — | 130 | 132 | 129 | 268 | 267 | 266 | 26 |
| 25 | — | 87 | 86 | — | 131 | 131 | 129 | 131 | 128 | 267 | 266 | 265 | 25 |
| 24 | 86 | — | — | 131 | — | 130 | 129 | 129–130 | 127 | 266 | — | 264 | 24 |
| 23 | — | — | — | — | 130 | — | 128 | 128 | 126 | 265 | 265 | 263 | 23 |
| 22 | — | — | 85 | 130 | — | 129 | 127 | 127 | — | 264 | 264 | 262 | 22 |
| 21 | 85 | 86 | — | — | — | — | 126 | 126 | 125 | 263 | 263 | 261 | 21 |
| 20 | — | — | — | 129 | 129 | 128 | 124–125 | 125 | 124 | 262 | 262 | 260 | 20 |
| 19 | — | — | 84 | 128 | 128 | 127 | 123 | 124 | 123 | 261 | — | 259 | 19 |
| 18 | — | — | — | — | — | — | 122 | 123 | 122 | 260 | 261 | 258 | 18 |
| 17 | 84 | 85 | — | 127 | 127 | 126 | 121 | 121–122 | 121 | 259 | 260 | 257 | 17 |
| 16 | — | — | 83 | 126 | — | — | 120 | 120 | 120 | 258 | 259 | 256 | 16 |
| 15 | — | — | — | 125 | 126 | 125 | 119 | 119 | 119 | 257 | 258 | 255 | 15 |
| 14 | 83 | 84 | 82 | 124 | 125 | 124 | 118 | 118 | 118 | 256 | 257 | 254 | 14 |
| 13 | — | — | — | — | — | — | 117 | 116–117 | 117 | 255 | 256 | 253 | 13 |
| 12 | — | — | — | 123 | 124 | 123 | 115–116 | 115 | 116 | 254 | 255 | 251–252 | 12 |
| 11 | 82 | — | — | 122 | 123 | 122 | 114 | 113–114 | 114–115 | 253 | 254 | 250 | 11 |
| 10 | — | — | 81 | 121 | 122 | 121 | 113 | 112 | 113 | 251–252 | 253 | 249 | 10 |
| 9 | — | 83 | — | — | 121 | 120 | 111–112 | 110–111 | 112 | 250 | 252 | 248 | 9 |
| 8 | 81 | — | 80 | 120 | 120 | 119 | 110 | 108–109 | 111 | 249 | 251 | 247 | 8 |
| 7 | — | — | — | 119 | 119 | 118 | 108–109 | 107 | 109–110 | 247–248 | 250 | 245–246 | 7 |
| 6 | — | — | — | — | — | 117 | 107 | 105–106 | 108 | 246 | 249 | 244 | 6 |
| 5 | — | — | — | 117–118 | 118 | — | 105–106 | 102–104 | 106–107 | 244–245 | 248 | 242–243 | 5 |
| 4 | — | — | 79 | — | 117 | — | 103–104 | 100–101 | 104–105 | 242–243 | 246–247 | 241 | 4 |
| 3 | — | — | — | — | — | — | 101–102 | 97–99 | 102–103 | 241 | 245 | 239–240 | 3 |
| 2 | — | — | 78 | — | — | — | 98–100 | 94–96 | 86–101 | — | — | 236–238 | 2 |
| 1 | — | — | — | — | — | — | 80–97 | 71–93 | — | — | — | 233–235 | 1 |

**Table A.3a** TRS-C *T* Scores and Percentiles

| Raw score | Hyperactivity T | Hyperactivity %ile | Aggression T | Aggression %ile | Conduct Problems T | Conduct Problems %ile | Anxiety T | Anxiety %ile | Depression T | Depression %ile | Somatization T | Somatization %ile | Attention Problems T | Attention Problems %ile | Learning Problems T | Learning Problems %ile | Atypicality T | Atypicality %ile | Withdrawal T | Withdrawal %ile | Adaptability T | Adaptability %ile | Social Skills T | Social Skills %ile | Leadership T | Leadership %ile | Study Skills T | Study Skills %ile | Functional Communication T | Functional Communication %ile | Raw score |
|---|---|---|---|---|---|---|---|---|---|---|---|---|---|---|---|---|---|---|---|---|---|---|---|---|---|---|---|---|---|---|---|
| 33 | 87 | 99 | — | — | — | — | — | — | 120 | 99 | — | — | — | — | — | — | — | — | — | — | — | — | — | — | — | — | — | — | — | — | 33 |
| 32 | 86 | 99 | — | — | — | — | — | — | 120 | 99 | — | — | — | — | — | — | — | — | — | — | — | — | — | — | — | — | — | — | — | — | 32 |
| 31 | 84 | 99 | — | — | — | — | — | — | 120 | 99 | — | — | — | — | — | — | — | — | — | — | — | — | — | — | — | — | — | — | — | — | 31 |
| 30 | 83 | 99 | 120 | 99 | — | — | — | — | 120 | 99 | — | — | — | — | — | — | — | — | — | — | — | — | 68 | 98 | — | — | — | — | 66 | 98 | 30 |
| 29 | 82 | 99 | 117 | 99 | — | — | — | — | 120 | 99 | — | — | — | — | — | — | — | — | — | — | — | — | 67 | 96 | — | — | — | — | 64 | 95 | 29 |
| 28 | 80 | 99 | 115 | 99 | — | — | — | — | 120 | 99 | — | — | — | — | — | — | 120 | 99 | — | — | — | — | 65 | 94 | — | — | — | — | 63 | 90 | 28 |
| 27 | 79 | 99 | 112 | 99 | 113 | 99 | 119 | 99 | 119 | 99 | — | — | — | — | — | — | 120 | 99 | — | — | 65 | 96 | 64 | 91 | — | — | — | — | 61 | 85 | 27 |
| 26 | 77 | 98 | 110 | 99 | 110 | 99 | 116 | 99 | 116 | 99 | — | — | — | — | — | — | 120 | 99 | — | — | 63 | 92 | 62 | 88 | — | — | — | — | 59 | 79 | 26 |
| 25 | 76 | 98 | 107 | 99 | 108 | 99 | 114 | 99 | 113 | 99 | 120 | 99 | — | — | — | — | 117 | 99 | — | — | 61 | 86 | 61 | 85 | — | — | — | — | 57 | 73 | 25 |
| 24 | 74 | 97 | 104 | 99 | 105 | 99 | 111 | 99 | 110 | 99 | 120 | 99 | 75 | 99 | 84 | 99 | 114 | 99 | 114 | 99 | 59 | 80 | 60 | 81 | — | — | 66 | 99 | 56 | 67 | 24 |
| 23 | 73 | 96 | 102 | 99 | 102 | 99 | 108 | 99 | 108 | 99 | 120 | 99 | 74 | 99 | 82 | 99 | 111 | 99 | 111 | 99 | 57 | 73 | 58 | 77 | — | — | 64 | 95 | 54 | 61 | 23 |
| 22 | 71 | 96 | 99 | 99 | 100 | 99 | 105 | 99 | 105 | 99 | 120 | 99 | 72 | 99 | 81 | 99 | 108 | 99 | 108 | 99 | 56 | 66 | 57 | 72 | — | — | 63 | 89 | 52 | 54 | 22 |
| 21 | 70 | 95 | 97 | 99 | 97 | 99 | 102 | 99 | 102 | 99 | 119 | 99 | 71 | 97 | 79 | 98 | 105 | 99 | 105 | 99 | 54 | 59 | 55 | 68 | 70 | 99 | 61 | 84 | 51 | 48 | 21 |
| 20 | 69 | 93 | 94 | 99 | 94 | 99 | 99 | 99 | 99 | 99 | 115 | 99 | 69 | 95 | 77 | 98 | 102 | 99 | 102 | 99 | 52 | 52 | 54 | 63 | 68 | 97 | 59 | 78 | 49 | 43 | 20 |
| 19 | 67 | 92 | 92 | 99 | 92 | 99 | 96 | 99 | 96 | 99 | 112 | 99 | 67 | 93 | 75 | 97 | 99 | 99 | 99 | 99 | 50 | 46 | 52 | 58 | 66 | 95 | 57 | 72 | 47 | 37 | 19 |
| 18 | 66 | 91 | 89 | 99 | 89 | 99 | 93 | 99 | 93 | 99 | 108 | 99 | 66 | 91 | 73 | 96 | 96 | 99 | 96 | 99 | 48 | 40 | 51 | 53 | 64 | 92 | 56 | 66 | 45 | 32 | 18 |
| 17 | 64 | 89 | 87 | 99 | 86 | 99 | 90 | 99 | 90 | 99 | 104 | 99 | 64 | 88 | 71 | 95 | 93 | 99 | 93 | 99 | 46 | 34 | 50 | 48 | 62 | 88 | 54 | 60 | 44 | 27 | 17 |
| 16 | 63 | 87 | 84 | 99 | 84 | 99 | 88 | 99 | 88 | 99 | 100 | 99 | 63 | 86 | 70 | 93 | 90 | 99 | 90 | 99 | 45 | 29 | 48 | 43 | 60 | 83 | 52 | 54 | 42 | 23 | 16 |
| 15 | 61 | 85 | 82 | 98 | 81 | 99 | 85 | 99 | 85 | 99 | 97 | 99 | 61 | 82 | 68 | 92 | 86 | 99 | 86 | 99 | 43 | 24 | 47 | 38 | 58 | 78 | 51 | 49 | 40 | 19 | 15 |
| 14 | 60 | 83 | 79 | 97 | 78 | 98 | 82 | 99 | 82 | 98 | 93 | 99 | 59 | 79 | 66 | 90 | 83 | 99 | 83 | 99 | 41 | 20 | 45 | 34 | 57 | 72 | 49 | 43 | 39 | 15 | 14 |
| 13 | 59 | 81 | 76 | 96 | 76 | 97 | 79 | 98 | 79 | 98 | 89 | 99 | 58 | 76 | 64 | 89 | 80 | 98 | 80 | 98 | 39 | 16 | 44 | 29 | 55 | 65 | 47 | 38 | 37 | 12 | 13 |
| 12 | 57 | 78 | 74 | 95 | 73 | 96 | 76 | 97 | 76 | 97 | 85 | 98 | 56 | 72 | 62 | 87 | 77 | 98 | 77 | 98 | 37 | 13 | 42 | 25 | 53 | 59 | 45 | 33 | 35 | 9 | 12 |
| 11 | 56 | 75 | 71 | 94 | 70 | 95 | 73 | 96 | 73 | 96 | 82 | 98 | 54 | 68 | 60 | 84 | 74 | 97 | 74 | 97 | 36 | 10 | 41 | 21 | 51 | 52 | 44 | 29 | 33 | 7 | 11 |
| 10 | 54 | 72 | 69 | 93 | 68 | 93 | 70 | 95 | 70 | 95 | 78 | 97 | 53 | 64 | 58 | 82 | 71 | 96 | 71 | 96 | 34 | 7 | 40 | 17 | 49 | 46 | 42 | 24 | 32 | 5 | 10 |
| 9 | 53 | 68 | 66 | 91 | 65 | 90 | 67 | 93 | 68 | 93 | 74 | 95 | 51 | 59 | 57 | 78 | 68 | 95 | 68 | 94 | 32 | 5 | 38 | 14 | 47 | 39 | 40 | 20 | 30 | 3 | 9 |
| 8 | 51 | 64 | 64 | 89 | 62 | 87 | 64 | 91 | 65 | 89 | 70 | 94 | 50 | 54 | 55 | 75 | 65 | 93 | 65 | 92 | 30 | 4 | 37 | 11 | 45 | 32 | 39 | 16 | 28 | 2 | 8 |
| 7 | 50 | 60 | 61 | 87 | 60 | 84 | 61 | 88 | 62 | 89 | 66 | 89 | 48 | 49 | 53 | 66 | 62 | 91 | 62 | 89 | 28 | 2 | 35 | 8 | 43 | 26 | 37 | 13 | 27 | 1 | 7 |
| 6 | 48 | 55 | 59 | 85 | 57 | 79 | 59 | 83 | 59 | 85 | 63 | 89 | 46 | 44 | 51 | 66 | 59 | 88 | 59 | 84 | 27 | 1 | 34 | 6 | 41 | 20 | 35 | 9 | 25 | 1 | 6 |
| 5 | 47 | 50 | 56 | 81 | 54 | 73 | 56 | 78 | 56 | 80 | 59 | 86 | 45 | 38 | 49 | 61 | 56 | 85 | 55 | 78 | 25 | 1 | 33 | 4 | 39 | 15 | 33 | 6 | 23 | 1 | 5 |
| 4 | 46 | 43 | 53 | 77 | 52 | 66 | 53 | 70 | 53 | 74 | 55 | 81 | 43 | 32 | 47 | 54 | 53 | 80 | 52 | 69 | 23 | 1 | 31 | 3 | 37 | 10 | 32 | 4 | 21 | 1 | 4 |
| 3 | 44 | 36 | 51 | 72 | 49 | 58 | 50 | 60 | 50 | 65 | 51 | 74 | 42 | 25 | 46 | 45 | 50 | 74 | 49 | 58 | 21 | 1 | 30 | 2 | 35 | 6 | 30 | 2 | 20 | 1 | 3 |
| 2 | 43 | 29 | 48 | 64 | 46 | 47 | 47 | 48 | 48 | 54 | 48 | 61 | 40 | 18 | 44 | 35 | 46 | 64 | 46 | 43 | 19 | 1 | 28 | 1 | 33 | 4 | 28 | 1 | 18 | 1 | 2 |
| 1 | 41 | 20 | 46 | 51 | 44 | 33 | 44 | 32 | 45 | 37 | 44 | 29 | 38 | 11 | 42 | 21 | 43 | 51 | 43 | 26 | 17 | 1 | 27 | 1 | 31 | 2 | 27 | 1 | 16 | 1 | 1 |
| 0 | 40 | 11 | 43 | 22 | 41 | 16 | 41 | 15 | 42 | 16 | — | — | 37 | 4 | 40 | 2 | 40 | 28 | 40 | 10 | 16 | 1 | 25 | 1 | 29 | 1 | 25 | 0 | 15 | 1 | 0 |
| **Raw mean** | 7.08 | | 2.65 | | 3.36 | | 3.06 | | 2.85 | | 1.62 | | 8.25 | | 5.40 | | 2.16 | | 3.25 | | 18.93 | | 17.26 | | 10.72 | | 14.66 | | 20.67 | | **Raw mean** |
| **Raw SD** | 6.95 | | 3.92 | | 3.75 | | 3.45 | | 3.50 | | 2.66 | | 6.19 | | 5.42 | | 3.25 | | 3.22 | | 5.51 | | 7.01 | | 5.04 | | 5.85 | | 5.84 | | **Raw SD** |
| **T:90% Conf. int.** | 4 | | 5 | | 5 | | 6 | | 7 | | 6 | | 4 | | 5 | | 6 | | 7 | | 5 | | 4 | | 5 | | 5 | | 6 | | **T:90% Conf. int.** |

## Table A.3b TRS-C T Scores and Percentiles

| Raw score | Hyperactivity T | %ile | Aggression T | %ile | Conduct Problems T | %ile | Anxiety T | %ile | Depression T | %ile | Somatization T | %ile | Attention Problems T | %ile | Learning Problems T | %ile | Atypicality T | %ile | Withdrawal T | %ile | Adaptability T | %ile | Social Skills T | %ile | Leadership T | %ile | Study Skills T | %ile | Functional Communication T | %ile | Raw score |
|---|---|---|---|---|---|---|---|---|---|---|---|---|---|---|---|---|---|---|---|---|---|---|---|---|---|---|---|---|---|---|---|---|
| 33 | 94 | 99 | — | — | — | — | — | — | 120 | 99 | — | — | — | — | — | — | — | — | — | — | — | — | — | — | — | — | — | — | — | — | 33 |
| 32 | 92 | 99 | — | — | — | — | — | — | 120 | 99 | — | — | — | — | — | — | — | — | — | — | — | — | — | — | — | — | — | — | — | — | 32 |
| 31 | 90 | 99 | — | — | — | — | — | — | 120 | 99 | — | — | — | — | — | — | — | — | — | — | — | — | — | — | — | — | — | — | — | — | 31 |
| 30 | 89 | 99 | 120 | 99 | — | — | — | — | 120 | 99 | — | — | — | — | — | — | — | — | — | — | — | — | 67 | 97 | — | — | — | — | 66 | 98 | 30 |
| 29 | 87 | 99 | 120 | 99 | — | — | — | — | 120 | 99 | — | — | — | — | — | — | — | — | — | — | — | — | 65 | 95 | — | — | — | — | 64 | 95 | 29 |
| 28 | 86 | 99 | 120 | 99 | — | — | — | — | 120 | 99 | — | — | — | — | — | — | — | — | — | — | — | — | 64 | 92 | — | — | — | — | 62 | 91 | 28 |
| 27 | 84 | 99 | 119 | 99 | 113 | 99 | 115 | 99 | 120 | 99 | — | — | — | — | — | — | 120 | 99 | — | — | 64 | 97 | 63 | 89 | — | — | — | — | 61 | 85 | 27 |
| 26 | 82 | 99 | 116 | 99 | 110 | 99 | 113 | 99 | 120 | 99 | — | — | — | — | — | — | 120 | 99 | — | — | 62 | 92 | 61 | 85 | — | — | — | — | 59 | 79 | 26 |
| 25 | 81 | 98 | 113 | 99 | 108 | 99 | 110 | 99 | 117 | 99 | 120 | 99 | — | — | — | — | 120 | 99 | 115 | 99 | 60 | 86 | 60 | 81 | — | — | — | — | 57 | 72 | 25 |
| 24 | 79 | 98 | 110 | 99 | 105 | 99 | 107 | 99 | 114 | 99 | 120 | 99 | 81 | 99 | 88 | 99 | 120 | 99 | 111 | 99 | 59 | 78 | 58 | 77 | — | — | 64 | 98 | 55 | 65 | 24 |
| 23 | 78 | 97 | 108 | 99 | 103 | 99 | 105 | 99 | 111 | 99 | 120 | 99 | 79 | 99 | 86 | 99 | 120 | 99 | 108 | 99 | 57 | 70 | 57 | 73 | — | — | 62 | 92 | 54 | 58 | 23 |
| 22 | 76 | 97 | 105 | 99 | 100 | 99 | 102 | 99 | 108 | 99 | 120 | 99 | 77 | 99 | 84 | 99 | 118 | 99 | 105 | 99 | 55 | 62 | 56 | 68 | — | — | 61 | 85 | 52 | 52 | 22 |
| 21 | 75 | 96 | 102 | 99 | 97 | 99 | 99 | 99 | 105 | 99 | 120 | 99 | 75 | 98 | 82 | 99 | 114 | 99 | 102 | 99 | 53 | 55 | 54 | 63 | 69 | 99 | 59 | 77 | 50 | 45 | 21 |
| 20 | 73 | 96 | 99 | 99 | 95 | 99 | 96 | 99 | 102 | 99 | 120 | 99 | 73 | 97 | 80 | 98 | 111 | 99 | 99 | 99 | 51 | 48 | 53 | 58 | 67 | 97 | 57 | 70 | 48 | 39 | 20 |
| 19 | 71 | 95 | 97 | 99 | 92 | 99 | 94 | 99 | 99 | 99 | 119 | 99 | 72 | 96 | 78 | 98 | 108 | 99 | 96 | 99 | 49 | 41 | 51 | 53 | 65 | 94 | 56 | 63 | 47 | 34 | 19 |
| 18 | 70 | 94 | 94 | 99 | 89 | 99 | 91 | 99 | 96 | 99 | 115 | 99 | 70 | 95 | 76 | 97 | 104 | 99 | 93 | 99 | 48 | 35 | 50 | 48 | 63 | 90 | 54 | 57 | 45 | 29 | 18 |
| 17 | 68 | 93 | 91 | 98 | 87 | 99 | 88 | 99 | 93 | 99 | 111 | 99 | 68 | 94 | 74 | 96 | 101 | 99 | 90 | 99 | 46 | 30 | 49 | 43 | 61 | 85 | 52 | 51 | 43 | 24 | 17 |
| 16 | 67 | 92 | 88 | 98 | 84 | 99 | 85 | 99 | 90 | 99 | 107 | 99 | 66 | 92 | 72 | 95 | 98 | 99 | 87 | 99 | 44 | 25 | 47 | 39 | 59 | 80 | 50 | 45 | 41 | 20 | 16 |
| 15 | 65 | 91 | 86 | 98 | 82 | 99 | 83 | 99 | 87 | 99 | 103 | 99 | 65 | 90 | 70 | 93 | 94 | 99 | 83 | 99 | 42 | 20 | 46 | 34 | 57 | 74 | 49 | 40 | 39 | 16 | 15 |
| 14 | 64 | 90 | 83 | 98 | 79 | 98 | 80 | 98 | 84 | 99 | 99 | 99 | 63 | 88 | 68 | 93 | 91 | 99 | 80 | 98 | 40 | 17 | 45 | 30 | 55 | 67 | 47 | 35 | 38 | 13 | 14 |
| 13 | 62 | 88 | 80 | 97 | 76 | 97 | 77 | 97 | 81 | 98 | 95 | 99 | 61 | 85 | 66 | 91 | 88 | 99 | 77 | 98 | 38 | 14 | 43 | 26 | 54 | 61 | 45 | 31 | 36 | 10 | 13 |
| 12 | 60 | 86 | 77 | 96 | 74 | 96 | 74 | 97 | 78 | 97 | 91 | 99 | 59 | 82 | 64 | 90 | 84 | 99 | 74 | 97 | 37 | 11 | 42 | 22 | 52 | 54 | 43 | 27 | 34 | 8 | 12 |
| 11 | 59 | 84 | 75 | 96 | 71 | 95 | 72 | 95 | 75 | 97 | 87 | 99 | 58 | 79 | 62 | 88 | 81 | 98 | 71 | 95 | 35 | 9 | 40 | 19 | 50 | 48 | 42 | 23 | 32 | 6 | 11 |
| 10 | 57 | 82 | 72 | 95 | 68 | 93 | 69 | 94 | 72 | 96 | 83 | 98 | 56 | 75 | 60 | 86 | 78 | 97 | 68 | 94 | 33 | 7 | 39 | 16 | 48 | 41 | 40 | 19 | 31 | 4 | 10 |
| 9 | 56 | 79 | 69 | 94 | 66 | 91 | 66 | 92 | 69 | 94 | 79 | 97 | 54 | 70 | 58 | 83 | 74 | 96 | 65 | 91 | 31 | 5 | 38 | 13 | 46 | 35 | 38 | 16 | 29 | 3 | 9 |
| 8 | 54 | 76 | 66 | 92 | 63 | 89 | 63 | 90 | 66 | 93 | 75 | 96 | 52 | 65 | 56 | 80 | 71 | 95 | 62 | 88 | 29 | 4 | 36 | 10 | 44 | 29 | 37 | 12 | 27 | 2 | 8 |
| 7 | 52 | 72 | 63 | 91 | 61 | 86 | 61 | 87 | 63 | 90 | 71 | 94 | 50 | 60 | 54 | 76 | 68 | 94 | 59 | 83 | 27 | 3 | 35 | 8 | 42 | 23 | 35 | 10 | 25 | 1 | 7 |
| 6 | 51 | 67 | 61 | 89 | 58 | 82 | 58 | 83 | 60 | 87 | 67 | 92 | 49 | 54 | 52 | 72 | 64 | 92 | 55 | 77 | 26 | 2 | 33 | 6 | 40 | 18 | 33 | 7 | 24 | 1 | 6 |
| 5 | 49 | 62 | 58 | 87 | 55 | 78 | 55 | 78 | 57 | 83 | 63 | 90 | 47 | 47 | 50 | 66 | 61 | 89 | 52 | 69 | 24 | 1 | 32 | 4 | 38 | 14 | 31 | 5 | 22 | 1 | 5 |
| 4 | 48 | 56 | 55 | 84 | 53 | 72 | 52 | 71 | 54 | 77 | 60 | 86 | 45 | 39 | 48 | 60 | 58 | 85 | 49 | 58 | 22 | 1 | 31 | 3 | 36 | 10 | 30 | 3 | 20 | 1 | 4 |
| 3 | 46 | 48 | 52 | 79 | 50 | 65 | 50 | 62 | 51 | 69 | 56 | 81 | 43 | 31 | 46 | 51 | 54 | 80 | 46 | 44 | 20 | 1 | 29 | 2 | 34 | 6 | 28 | 2 | 18 | 1 | 3 |
| 2 | 45 | 39 | 50 | 72 | 47 | 55 | 47 | 50 | 48 | 56 | 52 | 74 | 42 | 23 | 44 | 39 | 51 | 71 | 43 | 27 | 18 | 1 | 28 | 1 | 32 | 4 | 26 | 1 | 17 | 1 | 2 |
| 1 | 43 | 27 | 47 | 60 | 45 | 41 | 44 | 34 | 45 | 38 | 48 | 61 | 40 | 14 | 42 | 22 | 47 | 57 | 40 | 9 | 16 | 1 | 27 | 1 | 30 | 2 | 25 | 1 | 15 | 1 | 1 |
| 0 | 41 | 13 | 44 | 21 | 42 | 21 | 42 | 15 | 42 | 13 | 44 | 27 | 38 | 7 | 40 | 10 | 44 | 30 | — | — | 14 | 1 | 25 | 1 | 28 | 1 | 23 | 1 | 13 | 1 | 0 |
| **Raw mean** | 5.44 | | 2.12 | | 2.96 | | 3.10 | | 2.65 | | 1.60 | | 6.72 | | 4.79 | | 1.75 | | 3.23 | | 19.35 | | 17.94 | | 11.18 | | 15.79 | | 20.99 | | **Raw mean** |
| **Raw SD** | 6.33 | | 3.62 | | 3.81 | | 3.65 | | 3.33 | | 2.52 | | 5.66 | | 4.99 | | 2.99 | | 3.22 | | 5.45 | | 7.23 | | 5.15 | | 5.80 | | 5.69 | | **Raw SD** |
| **T:90% Conf. int.** | 4 | | 5 | | 5 | | 6 | | 7 | | 6 | | 4 | | 5 | | 6 | | 7 | | 5 | | 4 | | 5 | | 5 | | 6 | | **T:90% Conf. int.** |

## Table A.3c TRS-C T Scores and Percentiles

| Raw score | Hyperactivity T | Hyperactivity %ile | Aggression T | Aggression %ile | Conduct Problems T | Conduct Problems %ile | Anxiety T | Anxiety %ile | Depression T | Depression %ile | Somatization T | Somatization %ile | Attention Problems T | Attention Problems %ile | Learning Problems T | Learning Problems %ile | Atypicality T | Atypicality %ile | Withdrawal T | Withdrawal %ile | Adaptability T | Adaptability %ile | Social Skills T | Social Skills %ile | Leadership T | Leadership %ile | Study Skills T | Study Skills %ile | Functional Communication T | Functional Communication %ile | Raw score |
|---|---|---|---|---|---|---|---|---|---|---|---|---|---|---|---|---|---|---|---|---|---|---|---|---|---|---|---|---|---|---|---|
| 33 | 84 | 99 | — | — | — | — | — | — | 120 | 99 | — | — | — | — | — | — | — | — | — | — | — | — | — | — | — | — | — | — | — | — | 33 |
| 32 | 83 | 99 | — | — | — | — | — | — | 120 | 99 | — | — | — | — | — | — | — | — | — | — | — | — | — | — | — | — | — | — | — | — | 32 |
| 31 | 81 | 99 | — | — | — | — | — | — | 120 | 99 | — | — | — | — | — | — | — | — | — | — | — | — | — | — | — | — | — | — | — | — | 31 |
| 30 | 80 | 99 | 115 | 99 | — | — | — | — | 120 | 99 | — | — | — | — | — | — | — | — | — | — | — | — | 70 | 98 | — | — | — | — | 66 | 97 | 30 |
| 29 | 78 | 99 | 112 | 99 | — | — | — | — | 120 | 99 | — | — | — | — | — | — | — | — | — | — | — | — | 68 | 97 | — | — | — | — | 64 | 94 | 29 |
| 28 | 77 | 99 | 110 | 99 | — | — | — | — | 118 | 99 | — | — | — | — | — | — | — | — | — | — | — | — | 67 | 95 | — | — | — | — | 63 | 89 | 28 |
| 27 | 76 | 99 | 108 | 99 | 113 | 99 | 120 | 99 | 115 | 99 | — | — | — | — | — | — | 120 | 99 | — | — | 65 | 95 | 65 | 93 | — | — | — | — | 61 | 84 | 27 |
| 26 | 74 | 99 | 105 | 99 | 111 | 99 | 120 | 99 | 113 | 99 | — | — | — | — | — | — | 118 | 99 | — | — | 63 | 91 | 64 | 91 | — | — | — | — | 59 | 79 | 26 |
| 25 | 73 | 98 | 103 | 99 | 108 | 99 | 117 | 99 | 110 | 99 | — | — | — | — | — | — | 115 | 99 | — | — | 62 | 86 | 62 | 88 | — | — | — | — | 58 | 74 | 25 |
| 24 | 71 | 97 | 100 | 99 | 105 | 99 | 114 | 99 | 107 | 99 | 120 | 99 | 72 | 99 | 81 | 99 | 112 | 99 | 114 | 99 | 60 | 80 | 61 | 84 | — | — | 68 | 99 | 56 | 68 | 24 |
| 23 | 70 | 96 | 98 | 99 | 103 | 99 | 111 | 99 | 105 | 99 | 120 | 99 | 71 | 99 | 79 | 99 | 109 | 99 | 111 | 99 | 58 | 74 | 59 | 81 | — | — | 67 | 97 | 54 | 62 | 23 |
| 22 | 69 | 94 | 95 | 99 | 100 | 99 | 108 | 99 | 102 | 99 | 120 | 99 | 69 | 99 | 78 | 99 | 106 | 99 | 108 | 99 | 56 | 68 | 58 | 77 | — | — | 65 | 94 | 53 | 57 | 22 |
| 21 | 67 | 93 | 93 | 99 | 97 | 99 | 105 | 99 | 99 | 99 | 119 | 99 | 68 | 97 | 76 | 99 | 103 | 99 | 105 | 99 | 54 | 63 | 57 | 72 | 72 | 99 | 63 | 89 | 51 | 51 | 21 |
| 20 | 66 | 91 | 91 | 99 | 94 | 99 | 102 | 99 | 96 | 99 | 115 | 99 | 66 | 94 | 74 | 98 | 101 | 99 | 102 | 99 | 53 | 57 | 55 | 67 | 70 | 98 | 61 | 85 | 49 | 46 | 20 |
| 19 | 64 | 89 | 88 | 99 | 92 | 99 | 99 | 99 | 94 | 99 | 112 | 99 | 65 | 91 | 73 | 97 | 98 | 99 | 99 | 99 | 51 | 51 | 54 | 63 | 68 | 96 | 60 | 79 | 48 | 41 | 19 |
| 18 | 63 | 87 | 86 | 99 | 89 | 99 | 96 | 99 | 91 | 99 | 108 | 99 | 63 | 87 | 71 | 96 | 95 | 99 | 96 | 99 | 49 | 45 | 52 | 58 | 66 | 93 | 58 | 74 | 46 | 35 | 18 |
| 17 | 62 | 84 | 83 | 99 | 86 | 98 | 93 | 99 | 88 | 99 | 105 | 99 | 61 | 83 | 69 | 95 | 92 | 99 | 93 | 99 | 47 | 39 | 51 | 53 | 64 | 90 | 56 | 68 | 44 | 31 | 17 |
| 16 | 60 | 82 | 81 | 99 | 83 | 96 | 90 | 99 | 85 | 99 | 101 | 99 | 60 | 79 | 67 | 92 | 89 | 99 | 89 | 99 | 45 | 34 | 49 | 47 | 62 | 86 | 54 | 63 | 43 | 26 | 16 |
| 15 | 59 | 79 | 79 | 98 | 81 | 95 | 87 | 99 | 83 | 99 | 98 | 99 | 58 | 75 | 66 | 90 | 86 | 99 | 86 | 99 | 44 | 29 | 48 | 42 | 60 | 81 | 53 | 57 | 41 | 22 | 15 |
| 14 | 57 | 76 | 76 | 97 | 78 | 99 | 84 | 99 | 80 | 98 | 94 | 99 | 57 | 71 | 64 | 88 | 83 | 99 | 83 | 99 | 42 | 24 | 46 | 37 | 58 | 76 | 51 | 51 | 39 | 18 | 14 |
| 13 | 56 | 73 | 74 | 95 | 75 | 98 | 81 | 99 | 77 | 97 | 90 | 99 | 55 | 66 | 62 | 86 | 80 | 98 | 80 | 98 | 40 | 19 | 45 | 32 | 56 | 70 | 49 | 45 | 38 | 14 | 13 |
| 12 | 55 | 69 | 71 | 94 | 73 | 96 | 78 | 98 | 74 | 96 | 87 | 99 | 53 | 62 | 60 | 84 | 77 | 97 | 77 | 98 | 38 | 15 | 43 | 27 | 54 | 64 | 47 | 40 | 36 | 11 | 12 |
| 11 | 53 | 66 | 69 | 92 | 70 | 95 | 74 | 97 | 72 | 95 | 83 | 99 | 52 | 57 | 59 | 81 | 74 | 96 | 74 | 97 | 36 | 11 | 42 | 23 | 51 | 57 | 46 | 35 | 34 | 8 | 11 |
| 10 | 52 | 62 | 66 | 90 | 67 | 92 | 71 | 96 | 69 | 94 | 80 | 97 | 50 | 53 | 57 | 78 | 72 | 95 | 71 | 96 | 35 | 8 | 40 | 19 | 49 | 50 | 44 | 29 | 33 | 5 | 10 |
| 9 | 50 | 58 | 64 | 88 | 64 | 90 | 68 | 94 | 66 | 89 | 76 | 96 | 49 | 48 | 55 | 75 | 69 | 93 | 68 | 94 | 33 | 5 | 39 | 15 | 47 | 43 | 42 | 24 | 31 | 3 | 9 |
| 8 | 49 | 53 | 62 | 86 | 62 | 86 | 65 | 92 | 64 | 86 | 73 | 95 | 47 | 44 | 53 | 71 | 66 | 91 | 65 | 92 | 31 | 3 | 37 | 11 | 45 | 35 | 40 | 20 | 29 | 2 | 8 |
| 7 | 48 | 49 | 59 | 83 | 59 | 81 | 62 | 88 | 61 | 82 | 69 | 93 | 46 | 39 | 52 | 67 | 63 | 88 | 62 | 89 | 29 | 1 | 36 | 8 | 43 | 29 | 39 | 15 | 28 | 1 | 7 |
| 6 | 46 | 44 | 57 | 80 | 56 | 76 | 59 | 83 | 58 | 77 | 66 | 91 | 44 | 34 | 50 | 62 | 60 | 84 | 58 | 84 | 28 | 1 | 34 | 6 | 41 | 22 | 37 | 12 | 26 | 1 | 6 |
| 5 | 45 | 38 | 54 | 76 | 53 | 69 | 56 | 77 | 55 | 71 | 62 | 89 | 42 | 29 | 48 | 56 | 57 | 80 | 55 | 78 | 26 | 1 | 33 | 4 | 39 | 16 | 35 | 8 | 24 | 1 | 5 |
| 4 | 43 | 33 | 52 | 71 | 51 | 61 | 53 | 69 | 53 | 63 | 58 | 86 | 41 | 24 | 47 | 49 | 54 | 75 | 52 | 69 | 24 | 1 | 31 | 2 | 37 | 11 | 33 | 5 | 23 | 1 | 4 |
| 3 | 42 | 27 | 50 | 65 | 48 | 52 | 50 | 59 | 50 | 52 | 55 | 81 | 39 | 18 | 45 | 42 | 51 | 68 | 49 | 57 | 22 | 1 | 30 | 1 | 35 | 6 | 32 | 3 | 21 | 1 | 3 |
| 2 | 41 | 20 | 47 | 57 | 45 | 40 | 47 | 47 | 47 | 44 | 51 | 74 | 38 | 13 | 43 | 32 | 48 | 58 | 46 | 42 | 20 | 1 | 28 | 1 | 33 | 3 | 30 | 1 | 19 | 1 | 2 |
| 1 | 39 | 14 | 45 | 44 | 42 | 27 | 44 | 32 | 44 | 37 | 48 | 61 | 36 | 7 | 41 | 20 | 45 | 45 | 43 | 24 | 19 | 1 | 27 | 1 | 31 | 1 | 28 | 1 | 18 | 1 | 1 |
| 0 | 38 | 8 | 42 | 19 | 40 | 12 | 41 | 16 | 42 | 18 | 44 | 33 | 35 | 2 | 40 | 5 | 43 | 24 | 40 | 8 | 17 | 1 | 25 | 1 | 29 | 1 | 26 | 1 | 16 | 1 | 0 |
| Raw mean | 8.73 | | 3.19 | | 3.76 | | 3.02 | | 3.05 | | 1.64 | | 9.79 | | 6.01 | | 2.57 | | 3.27 | | 18.51 | | 16.59 | | 10.27 | | 13.53 | | 20.35 | | Raw mean |
| Raw SD | 7.16 | | 4.14 | | 3.66 | | 3.26 | | 3.66 | | 2.81 | | 6.33 | | 5.77 | | 3.45 | | 3.23 | | 5.56 | | 6.75 | | 4.92 | | 5.70 | | 6.00 | | Raw SD |
| T:90% Conf. int. | 4 | | 5 | | 5 | | 7 | | 6 | | 5 | | 4 | | 4 | | 7 | | 7 | | 5 | | 5 | | 6 | | 5 | | 6 | | T:90% Conf. int. |

## Table A.3d TRS–C Composite *T* Scores

| T score | Externalizing Problems Combined | Female | Male | Internalizing Problems Combined | Female | Male | School Problems Combined | Female | Male | Adaptive Skills Combined | Female | Male | Behavioral Symptoms Index Combined | Female | Male | T score |
|---|---|---|---|---|---|---|---|---|---|---|---|---|---|---|---|---|
| 120 | — | — | — | 318–359 | 319–355 | 316–360 | — | — | — | — | — | — | 618–636 | 636–650 | 600–625 | 120 |
| 119 | — | — | — | 315–317 | 316–318 | 313–315 | — | — | — | — | — | — | 614–617 | 632–635 | 596–599 | 119 |
| 118 | — | — | — | 313–314 | 314–315 | 311–312 | — | — | — | — | — | — | 609–613 | 627–631 | 592–595 | 118 |
| 117 | — | — | — | 311–312 | 312–313 | 309–310 | — | — | — | — | — | — | 604–608 | 622–626 | 587–591 | 117 |
| 116 | — | — | — | 308–310 | 309–311 | 306–308 | — | — | — | — | — | — | 600–603 | 617–621 | 583–586 | 116 |
| 115 | — | — | — | 306–307 | 307–308 | 304–305 | — | — | — | — | — | — | 595–599 | 612–616 | 579–582 | 115 |
| 114 | — | 327 | — | 303–305 | 304–306 | 301–303 | — | — | — | — | — | — | 591–594 | 607–611 | 574–578 | 114 |
| 113 | — | 324–326 | — | 301–302 | 302–303 | 299–300 | — | — | — | — | — | — | 586–590 | 603–606 | 570–573 | 113 |
| 112 | 320 | 321–323 | — | 299–300 | 299–301 | 297–298 | — | — | — | — | — | — | 582–585 | 598–602 | 566–569 | 112 |
| 111 | 317–319 | 318–320 | — | 296–298 | 297–298 | 294–296 | — | — | — | — | — | — | 577–581 | 593–597 | 562–565 | 111 |
| 110 | 314–316 | 316–317 | — | 294–295 | 295–296 | 292–293 | — | — | — | — | — | — | 572–576 | 588–592 | 557–561 | 110 |
| 109 | 311–313 | 313–315 | 312 | 291–293 | 292–294 | 290–291 | — | — | — | — | — | — | 568–571 | 583–587 | 553–556 | 109 |
| 108 | 309–310 | 310–312 | 309–311 | 289–290 | 290–291 | 287–289 | — | — | — | — | — | — | 563–567 | 578–582 | 549–552 | 108 |
| 107 | 306–308 | 307–309 | 306–308 | 287–288 | 287–289 | 285–286 | — | — | — | — | — | — | 559–562 | 574–577 | 544–548 | 107 |
| 106 | 303–305 | 304–306 | 303–305 | 284–286 | 285–286 | 282–284 | — | — | — | — | — | — | 554–558 | 569–573 | 540–543 | 106 |
| 105 | 300–302 | 302–303 | 301–302 | 282–283 | 283–284 | 280–281 | — | — | — | — | — | — | 550–553 | 564–568 | 536–539 | 105 |
| 104 | 298–299 | 299–301 | 298–300 | 279–281 | 280–282 | 278–279 | — | — | — | — | — | — | 545–549 | 559–563 | 531–535 | 104 |
| 103 | 295–297 | 296–298 | 295–297 | 277–278 | 278–279 | 275–277 | — | — | — | — | — | — | 540–544 | 554–558 | 527–530 | 103 |
| 102 | 292–294 | 293–295 | 292–294 | 274–276 | 275–277 | 273–274 | — | — | — | — | — | — | 536–539 | 549–553 | 523–526 | 102 |
| 101 | 289–291 | 291–292 | 290–291 | 272–273 | 273–274 | 271–272 | — | — | — | — | — | — | 531–535 | 544–548 | 518–522 | 101 |
| 100 | 287–288 | 288–290 | 287–289 | 270–271 | 270–272 | 268–270 | — | — | — | — | — | — | 527–530 | 540–543 | 514–517 | 100 |
| 99 | 284–286 | 285–287 | 284–286 | 267–269 | 268–269 | 266–267 | — | — | — | — | — | — | 522–526 | 535–539 | 510–513 | 99 |
| 98 | 281–283 | 282–284 | 281–283 | 265–266 | 266–267 | 263–265 | — | — | — | — | — | — | 518–521 | 530–534 | 505–509 | 98 |
| 97 | 278–280 | 279–281 | 279–280 | 262–264 | 263–265 | 261–262 | — | — | — | — | — | — | 513–517 | 525–529 | 501–504 | 97 |
| 96 | 276–277 | 277–278 | 276–278 | 260–261 | 261–262 | 259–260 | — | — | — | — | — | — | 508–512 | 520–524 | 497–500 | 96 |
| 95 | 273–275 | 274–276 | 273–275 | 258–259 | 258–260 | 256–258 | — | — | — | — | — | — | 504–507 | 515–519 | 493–496 | 95 |
| 94 | 270–272 | 271–273 | 270–272 | 255–257 | 256–257 | 254–255 | — | — | — | — | — | — | 499–503 | 511–514 | 488–492 | 94 |
| 93 | 267–269 | 268–270 | 267–269 | 253–254 | 254–255 | 252–253 | — | — | — | — | — | — | 495–498 | 506–510 | 484–487 | 93 |
| 92 | 265–266 | 266–267 | 265–267 | 250–252 | 251–253 | 249–251 | — | — | — | — | — | — | 490–494 | 501–505 | 480–483 | 92 |
| 91 | 262–264 | 263–265 | 262–264 | 248–249 | 249–250 | 247–248 | — | — | — | — | — | — | 486–489 | 496–500 | 475–479 | 91 |
| 90 | 259–261 | 260–262 | 259–261 | 246–247 | 246–248 | 244–246 | — | — | — | — | — | — | 481–485 | 491–495 | 471–474 | 90 |
| 89 | 256–258 | 257–259 | 257–258 | 243–245 | 244–245 | 242–243 | — | — | — | — | — | — | 476–480 | 486–490 | 467–470 | 89 |
| 88 | 254–255 | 254–256 | 254–256 | 241–242 | 241–243 | 240–241 | — | 169 | — | — | — | — | 472–475 | 482–485 | 462–466 | 88 |
| 87 | 251–253 | 252–253 | 251–253 | 238–240 | 239–240 | 237–239 | — | 167–168 | — | — | — | — | 467–471 | 477–481 | 458–461 | 87 |
| 86 | 248–250 | 249–251 | 248–250 | 236–237 | 237–238 | 235–236 | — | 165–166 | — | — | — | — | 463–466 | 472–476 | 454–457 | 86 |
| 85 | 245–247 | 246–248 | 246–247 | 234–235 | 234–236 | 233–234 | — | 164 | — | — | — | — | 458–462 | 467–471 | 449–453 | 85 |
| 84 | 243–244 | 243–245 | 243–245 | 231–233 | 232–233 | 230–232 | — | 162–163 | — | — | — | — | 454–457 | 462–466 | 445–448 | 84 |
| 83 | 240–242 | 241–242 | 240–242 | 229–230 | 229–231 | 228–229 | — | 160–161 | — | — | — | — | 449–453 | 457–461 | 441–444 | 83 |
| 82 | 237–239 | 238–240 | 237–239 | 226–228 | 227–228 | 225–227 | 158–159 | 158–159 | — | — | — | — | 444–448 | 453–456 | 436–440 | 82 |
| 81 | 234–236 | 235–237 | 235–236 | 224–225 | 225–226 | 223–224 | 156–157 | 156–157 | 153 | — | — | — | 440–443 | 448–452 | 432–435 | 81 |
| 80 | 232–233 | 232–234 | 232–234 | 222–223 | 222–224 | 221–222 | 154–155 | 154–155 | 152 | — | — | — | 435–439 | 443–447 | 428–431 | 80 |
| 79 | 229–231 | 229–231 | 229–231 | 219–221 | 220–221 | 218–220 | 152–153 | 152–153 | 150–151 | — | — | — | 431–434 | 438–442 | 424–427 | 79 |
| 78 | 226–228 | 227–228 | 226–228 | 217–219 | 217–219 | 216–217 | 151 | 151 | 148–149 | — | — | — | 426–430 | 433–437 | 419–423 | 78 |
| 77 | 223–225 | 224–226 | 224–225 | 214–216 | 215–216 | 214–215 | 149–150 | 149–150 | 146–147 | — | — | — | 422–425 | 428–432 | 415–418 | 77 |
| 76 | 221–222 | 221–223 | 221–223 | 212–213 | 212–214 | 211–213 | 147–148 | 147–148 | 145 | — | — | — | 417–421 | 423–427 | 411–414 | 76 |
| 75 | 218–220 | 218–220 | 218–220 | 210–211 | 210–211 | 209–210 | 145–146 | 145–146 | 143–144 | — | — | — | 412–416 | 419–422 | 406–410 | 75 |
| 74 | 215–217 | 216–217 | 215–217 | 207–209 | 208–209 | 206–208 | 143–144 | 143–144 | 141–142 | — | — | — | 408–411 | 414–418 | 402–405 | 74 |
| 73 | 212–214 | 213–215 | 213–214 | 205–206 | 205–207 | 204–205 | 141–142 | 141–142 | 139–140 | — | — | — | 403–407 | 409–413 | 398–401 | 73 |
| 72 | 210–211 | 210–212 | 210–212 | 202–204 | 203–204 | 202–203 | 140 | 140 | 137–138 | — | — | — | 399–402 | 404–408 | 393–397 | 72 |
| 71 | 207–209 | 207–209 | 207–209 | 200–201 | 200–202 | 199–201 | 138–139 | 138–139 | 136 | — | — | 337–341 | 394–398 | 399–403 | 389–392 | 71 |
| 70 | 204–206 | 204–206 | 204–206 | 198–199 | 198–199 | 197–198 | 136–137 | 136–137 | 134–135 | 335 | — | 333–336 | 390–393 | 394–398 | 385–388 | 70 |
| 69 | 201–203 | 202–203 | 202–203 | 195–197 | 196–197 | 195–196 | 134–135 | 134–135 | 132–133 | 331–334 | — | 329–332 | 385–389 | 390–393 | 380–384 | 69 |
| 68 | 199–200 | 199–201 | 199–201 | 193–194 | 193–195 | 192–194 | 132–133 | 132–133 | 130–131 | 326–330 | 328–330 | 325–328 | 380–384 | 385–389 | 376–379 | 68 |
| 67 | 196–198 | 196–198 | 196–198 | 190–192 | 191–192 | 190–191 | 131 | 130–131 | 128–129 | 322–325 | 324–327 | 320–324 | 376–379 | 380–384 | 372–375 | 67 |
| 66 | 193–195 | 193–195 | 193–195 | 188–189 | 188–190 | 187–189 | 129–130 | 129 | — | 318–321 | 319–323 | 316–319 | 371–375 | 375–379 | 367–371 | 66 |

**Table A.3d** TRS-C Composite *T* Scores *(continued)*

| T score | Externalizing Problems Combined | Externalizing Problems Female | Externalizing Problems Male | Internalizing Problems Combined | Internalizing Problems Female | Internalizing Problems Male | School Problems Combined | School Problems Female | School Problems Male | Adaptive Skills Combined | Adaptive Skills Female | Adaptive Skills Male | Behavioral Symptoms Index Combined | Behavioral Symptoms Index Female | Behavioral Symptoms Index Male | T score |
|---|---|---|---|---|---|---|---|---|---|---|---|---|---|---|---|---|
| 65 | 190–192 | 191–192 | 190–192 | 185–187 | 186–187 | 185–186 | 127–128 | 127–128 | 127 | 313–317 | 315–318 | 312–315 | 367–370 | 370–374 | 363–366 | 65 |
| 64 | 188–189 | 188–190 | 188–189 | 183–184 | 183–185 | 183–184 | 125–126 | 125–126 | 125–126 | 309–312 | 311–314 | 308–311 | 362–366 | 365–369 | 359–362 | 64 |
| 63 | 185–187 | 185–187 | 185–187 | 181–182 | 181–182 | 180–182 | 123–124 | 123–124 | 123–124 | 305–308 | 306–310 | 303–307 | 358–361 | 361–364 | 355–358 | 63 |
| 62 | 182–184 | 182–184 | 182–184 | 178–180 | 179–180 | 178–179 | 121–122 | 121–122 | 121–122 | 300–304 | 302–305 | 299–302 | 353–357 | 356–360 | 350–354 | 62 |
| 61 | 179–181 | 179–181 | 179–181 | 176–177 | 176–178 | 176–177 | 120 | 119–120 | 119–120 | 296–299 | 297–301 | 295–298 | 348–352 | 351–355 | 346–349 | 61 |
| 60 | 177–178 | 177–178 | 177–178 | 173–175 | 174–175 | 173–175 | 118–119 | 118 | 118 | 292–295 | 293–296 | 291–294 | 344–347 | 346–350 | 342–345 | 60 |
| 59 | 174–176 | 174–176 | 174–176 | 171–172 | 171–173 | 171–172 | 116–117 | 116–117 | 116–117 | 287–291 | 288–292 | 286–290 | 339–343 | 341–345 | 337–341 | 59 |
| 58 | 171–173 | 171–173 | 171–173 | 169–170 | 169–170 | 168–170 | 114–115 | 114–115 | 114–115 | 283–286 | 284–287 | 282–285 | 335–338 | 336–340 | 333–336 | 58 |
| 57 | 168–170 | 168–170 | 168–170 | 166–168 | 167–168 | 166–167 | 112–113 | 112–113 | 112–113 | 279–282 | 279–283 | 278–281 | 330–334 | 332–335 | 329–332 | 57 |
| 56 | 166–167 | 166–167 | 166–167 | 164–165 | 164–166 | 164–165 | 111 | 110–111 | 110–111 | 274–278 | 275–278 | 274–277 | 326–329 | 327–331 | 324–328 | 56 |
| 55 | 163–165 | 163–165 | 163–165 | 161–163 | 162–163 | 161–163 | 109–110 | 108–109 | 109 | 270–273 | 271–274 | 269–273 | 321–325 | 322–326 | 320–323 | 55 |
| 54 | 160–162 | 160–162 | 160–162 | 159–160 | 159–161 | 159–160 | 107–108 | 106–107 | 107–108 | 266–269 | 266–270 | 265–268 | 316–320 | 317–321 | 316–319 | 54 |
| 53 | 157–159 | 157–159 | 157–159 | 157–158 | 157–158 | 156–158 | 105–106 | 105 | 105–106 | 261–265 | 262–265 | 261–264 | 312–315 | 312–316 | 311–315 | 53 |
| 52 | 155–156 | 154–156 | 155–156 | 154–156 | 154–156 | 154–155 | 103–104 | 103–104 | 103–104 | 257–260 | 257–261 | 257–260 | 307–311 | 307–311 | 307–310 | 52 |
| 51 | 152–154 | 152–153 | 152–154 | 152–153 | 152–153 | 152–153 | 101–102 | 101–102 | 101–102 | 253–256 | 253–256 | 252–256 | 303–306 | 302–306 | 303–306 | 51 |
| 50 | 149–151 | 149–151 | 149–151 | 149–151 | 150–151 | 149–151 | 100 | 99–100 | 100 | 248–252 | 248–252 | 248–251 | 298–302 | 298–301 | 298–302 | 50 |
| 49 | 146–148 | 146–148 | 146–148 | 147–148 | 147–149 | 147–148 | 98–99 | 97–98 | 98–99 | 244–247 | 244–247 | 244–247 | 294–297 | 293–297 | 294–297 | 49 |
| 48 | 144–145 | 143–145 | 144–145 | 145–146 | 145–146 | 145–146 | 96–97 | 95–96 | 96–97 | 240–243 | 240–243 | 240–243 | 289–293 | 288–292 | 290–293 | 48 |
| 47 | 141–143 | 141–142 | 141–143 | 142–144 | 142–144 | 142–144 | 94–95 | 94 | 94–95 | 235–239 | 235–239 | 235–239 | 284–288 | 283–287 | 286–289 | 47 |
| 46 | 138–140 | 138–140 | 138–140 | 140–141 | 140–141 | 140–141 | 92–93 | 92–93 | 92–93 | 231–234 | 231–234 | 231–234 | 280–283 | 278–282 | 281–285 | 46 |
| 45 | 135–137 | 135–137 | 135–137 | 137–139 | 138–139 | 137–139 | 91 | 90–91 | 91 | 227–230 | 226–230 | 227–230 | 275–279 | 273–277 | 277–280 | 45 |
| 44 | 133–134 | 132–134 | 133–134 | 135–136 | 135–137 | 135–136 | 89–90 | 88–89 | 89–90 | 223–226 | 222–225 | 223–226 | 271–274 | 269–272 | 273–276 | 44 |
| 43 | 130–132 | 129–131 | 130–132 | 133–134 | 133–134 | 133–134 | 87–88 | 86–87 | 87–88 | 218–222 | 217–221 | 218–222 | 266–270 | 264–268 | 268–272 | 43 |
| 42 | 127–129 | 127–128 | 127–129 | 130–132 | 130–132 | 130–132 | 85–86 | 84–85 | 85–86 | 214–217 | 213–216 | 214–217 | 262–265 | 259–263 | 264–267 | 42 |
| 41 | 124–126 | — | 124–126 | 128–129 | 128–129 | 128–129 | 83–84 | 83 | 83–84 | 210–213 | 208–212 | 210–213 | 257–261 | 254–258 | 260–263 | 41 |
| 40 | — | — | 122–123 | 127 | — | 127 | 81–82 | 81–82 | 82 | 205–209 | 204–207 | 206–209 | 252–256 | 249–253 | 255–259 | 40 |
| 39 | — | — | 120–121 | — | — | — | 80 | 79–80 | 80–81 | 201–204 | 200–203 | 201–205 | 248–251 | — | 251–254 | 39 |
| 38 | — | — | — | — | — | — | 78–79 | 78 | 78–79 | 197–200 | 195–199 | 197–200 | 245–247 | — | 247–250 | 38 |
| 37 | — | — | — | — | — | — | 77 | — | 76–77 | 192–196 | 191–194 | 193–196 | — | — | 242–246 | 37 |
| 36 | — | — | — | — | — | — | — | — | 75 | 188–191 | 186–190 | 189–192 | — | — | 240–241 | 36 |
| 35 | — | — | — | — | — | — | — | — | — | 184–187 | 182–185 | 184–188 | — | — | — | 35 |
| 34 | — | — | — | — | — | — | — | — | — | 179–183 | 177–181 | 180–183 | — | — | — | 34 |
| 33 | — | — | — | — | — | — | — | — | — | 175–178 | 173–176 | 176–179 | — | — | — | 33 |
| 32 | — | — | — | — | — | — | — | — | — | 171–174 | 169–172 | 172–175 | — | — | — | 32 |
| 31 | — | — | — | — | — | — | — | — | — | 166–170 | 164–168 | 167–171 | — | — | — | 31 |
| 30 | — | — | — | — | — | — | — | — | — | 162–165 | 160–163 | 163–166 | — | — | — | 30 |
| 29 | — | — | — | — | — | — | — | — | — | 158–161 | 155–159 | 159–162 | — | — | — | 29 |
| 28 | — | — | — | — | — | — | — | — | — | 153–157 | 151–154 | 155–158 | — | — | — | 28 |
| 27 | — | — | — | — | — | — | — | — | — | 149–152 | 146–150 | 150–154 | — | — | — | 27 |
| 26 | — | — | — | — | — | — | — | — | — | 145–148 | 142–145 | 146–149 | — | — | — | 26 |
| 25 | — | — | — | — | — | — | — | — | — | 140–144 | 137–141 | 142–145 | — | — | — | 25 |
| 24 | — | — | — | — | — | — | — | — | — | 136–139 | 133–136 | 138–141 | — | — | — | 24 |
| 23 | — | — | — | — | — | — | — | — | — | 132–135 | 129–132 | 133–137 | — | — | — | 23 |
| 22 | — | — | — | — | — | — | — | — | — | 127–131 | 124–128 | 129–132 | — | — | — | 22 |
| 21 | — | — | — | — | — | — | — | — | — | 123–126 | 120–123 | 125–128 | — | — | — | 21 |
| 20 | — | — | — | — | — | — | — | — | — | 119–122 | 115–119 | 121–124 | — | — | — | 20 |
| 19 | — | — | — | — | — | — | — | — | — | 114–118 | 111–114 | 116–120 | — | — | — | 19 |
| 18 | — | — | — | — | — | — | — | — | — | 110–113 | 106–110 | 113–115 | — | — | — | 18 |
| 17 | — | — | — | — | — | — | — | — | — | — | 103–105 | — | — | — | — | 17 |
| 16 | — | — | — | — | — | — | — | — | — | — | — | — | — | — | — | 16 |
| 15 | — | — | — | — | — | — | — | — | — | — | — | — | — | — | — | 15 |
| 14 | — | — | — | — | — | — | — | — | — | — | — | — | — | — | — | 14 |
| 13 | — | — | — | — | — | — | — | — | — | — | — | — | — | — | — | 13 |
| 12 | — | — | — | — | — | — | — | — | — | — | — | — | — | — | — | 12 |
| 11 | — | — | — | — | — | — | — | — | — | — | — | — | — | — | — | 11 |
| 10 | — | — | — | — | — | — | — | — | — | — | — | — | — | — | — | 10 |
| *T*: 90% Conf. int. | 3 | 3 | 3 | 4 | 4 | 4 | 3 | 3 | 3 | 3 | 2 | 3 | 3 | 3 | 3 | *T*: 90% Conf. int. |

## Table A.3e  TRS–C Composite Percentiles

| %ile | Externalizing Problems Combined | Externalizing Problems Female | Externalizing Problems Male | Internalizing Problems Combined | Internalizing Problems Female | Internalizing Problems Male | School Problems Combined | School Problems Female | School Problems Male | Adaptive Skills Combined | Adaptive Skills Female | Adaptive Skills Male | Behavioral Symptoms Index Combined | Behavioral Symptoms Index Female | Behavioral Symptoms Index Male | %ile |
|---|---|---|---|---|---|---|---|---|---|---|---|---|---|---|---|---|
| 99 | 232–320 | 244–327 | 223–312 | 226–359 | 231–355 | 221–360 | 147–159 | 152–169 | 143–153 | 328–335 | 321–330 | 335–341 | 429–636 | 458–650 | 396–625 | 99 |
| 98 | 223–231 | 231–243 | 217–222 | 215–225 | 218–230 | 213–220 | 143–146 | 146–151 | 140–142 | 324–327 | 318–320 | 329–334 | 416–428 | 437–457 | 392–395 | 98 |
| 97 | 216–222 | 221–230 | 212–216 | 208–214 | 209–217 | 207–212 | 140–142 | 143–145 | 138–139 | 321–323 | 316–317 | 325–328 | 406–415 | 421–436 | 388–391 | 97 |
| 96 | 211–215 | 214–220 | 208–211 | 202–207 | 203–208 | 202–206 | 138–139 | 139–142 | 136–137 | 318–320 | 314–315 | 321–324 | 398–405 | 409–420 | 384–387 | 96 |
| 95 | 206–210 | 208–213 | 204–207 | 197–201 | 197–202 | 198–201 | 136–137 | 137–138 | 134–135 | 316–317 | 312–313 | 318–320 | 391–397 | 399–408 | 381–383 | 95 |
| 94 | 202–205 | 202–207 | 201–203 | 193–196 | 193–196 | 194–197 | 134–135 | 134–136 | 132–133 | 313–315 | 310–311 | 315–317 | 385–390 | 391–398 | 377–380 | 94 |
| 93 | 198–201 | 198–201 | 198–200 | 190–192 | 189–192 | 191–193 | 132–133 | 132–133 | 130–131 | 311–312 | 308–309 | 313–314 | 380–384 | 383–390 | 374–376 | 93 |
| 92 | 195–197 | 194–197 | 195–197 | 187–189 | 186–188 | 188–190 | 130–131 | 130–131 | 129 | 309–310 | 307 | 310–312 | 375–379 | 376–382 | 371–373 | 92 |
| 91 | 192–194 | 190–193 | 193–194 | 184–186 | 183–185 | 186–187 | 129 | 128–129 | 128 | 307–308 | 305–306 | 308–309 | 370–374 | 370–375 | 368–370 | 91 |
| 90 | 189–191 | 187–189 | 190–192 | 182–183 | 181–182 | 183–185 | 127–128 | 126–127 | 126–127 | 306 | 304 | 306–307 | 366–369 | 365–369 | 366–367 | 90 |
| 89 | 187–188 | 184–186 | 188–189 | 180–181 | 179–180 | 181–182 | 126 | 125 | 125 | 304–305 | 303 | 304–305 | 362–365 | 360–364 | 363–365 | 89 |
| 88 | 184–186 | 181–183 | 186–187 | 178–179 | 176–178 | 179–180 | 124–125 | 123–124 | 124 | 302–303 | 301–302 | 302–303 | 358–361 | 356–359 | 360–362 | 88 |
| 87 | 182–183 | 179–180 | 184–185 | 176–177 | 175 | 177–178 | 123 | 122 | 123 | 301 | 300 | 300–301 | 355–357 | 351–355 | 358–359 | 87 |
| 86 | 180–181 | 177–178 | 182–183 | 174–175 | 173–174 | 176 | 122 | 121 | 122 | 299–300 | 299 | 298–299 | 352–354 | 348–350 | 355–357 | 86 |
| 85 | 178–179 | 175–176 | 181 | 172–173 | 171–172 | 174–175 | 121 | 119–120 | 121 | 298 | 297–298 | 297 | 349–351 | 344–347 | 353–354 | 85 |
| 84 | 176–177 | 173–174 | 179–180 | 171 | 170 | 172–173 | 120 | 118 | 120 | 296–297 | 296 | 295–296 | 346–348 | 340–343 | 351–352 | 84 |
| 83 | 174–175 | 171–172 | 177–178 | 169–170 | 168–169 | 171 | 119 | 117 | 119 | 295 | 295 | 293–294 | 343–345 | 337–339 | 348–350 | 83 |
| 82 | 173 | 169–170 | 176 | 168 | 167 | 170 | 118 | 116 | 118 | 293–294 | 294 | 292 | 340–342 | 334–336 | 346–347 | 82 |
| 81 | 171–172 | 167–168 | 174–175 | 167 | 166 | 168–169 | 117 | 115 | 117 | 292 | 292–293 | 290–291 | 338–339 | 331–333 | 344–345 | 81 |
| 80 | 169–170 | 166 | 173 | 166 | 164–165 | 167 | 116 | 114 | 116 | 290–291 | 291 | 289 | 335–337 | 329–330 | 342–343 | 80 |
| 79 | 168 | 164–165 | 171–172 | 164–165 | 163 | 166 | 115 | 113 | — | 289 | 290 | 287–288 | 333–334 | 326–328 | 340–341 | 79 |
| 78 | 167 | 163 | 170 | 163 | 162 | 165 | 114 | 112 | 115 | 288 | 289 | 286 | 331–332 | 324–325 | 337–339 | 78 |
| 77 | 165–166 | 162 | 169 | 162 | 161 | 164 | 113 | 111 | 114 | 286–287 | 288 | 284–285 | 328–330 | 322–323 | 335–336 | 77 |
| 76 | 164 | 160–161 | 167–168 | 161 | 160 | 162–163 | 112 | 110 | 113 | 285 | 286–287 | 283 | 326–327 | 319–321 | 333–334 | 76 |
| 75 | 163 | 159 | 166 | 160 | 159 | 161 | 111 | 109 | 112 | 284 | 285 | 281–282 | 324–325 | 317–318 | 331–332 | 75 |
| 74 | 162 | 158 | 165 | 159 | 158 | 160 | — | — | — | 283 | 284 | 280 | 322–323 | 315–316 | 329–330 | 74 |
| 73 | 160–161 | 157 | 164 | 158 | 157 | 159 | 110 | 108 | 111 | 281–282 | 283 | 279 | 320–321 | 313–314 | 327–328 | 73 |
| 72 | 159 | 156 | 163 | 157 | 156 | — | 109 | 107 | 110 | 280 | 282 | 277–278 | 318–319 | 311–312 | 326 | 72 |
| 71 | 158 | 155 | 161–162 | — | — | 158 | 108 | 106 | — | 279 | 281 | 276 | 317 | 310 | 324–325 | 71 |
| 70 | 157 | 154 | 160 | 156 | 155 | 157 | 107 | 105 | 109 | 278 | 280 | 275 | 315–316 | 308–309 | 322–323 | 70 |
| 69 | 156 | 153 | 159 | 155 | 154 | 156 | 106 | 104 | 108 | 276–277 | 278–279 | 273–274 | 313–314 | 306–307 | 320–321 | 69 |
| 68 | 155 | 152 | 158 | 154 | 153 | 155 | 105 | — | — | 275 | 277 | 272 | 311–312 | 305 | 318–319 | 68 |
| 67 | 154 | 151 | 157 | 153 | 152 | 154 | 104 | 103 | 107 | 274 | 276 | 271 | 310 | 303–304 | 317 | 67 |
| 66 | 153 | 150 | 156 | 152 | 151 | — | 103 | 102 | 106 | 273 | 275 | 270 | 308–309 | 302 | 315–316 | 66 |
| 65 | 152 | 149 | 155 | 151 | — | 153 | 104 | — | — | 271–272 | 274 | 268–269 | 307 | 300–301 | 313–314 | 65 |
| 64 | — | — | 154 | — | 150 | 152 | 103 | 101 | 105 | 270 | 273 | 267 | 305–306 | 299 | 311–312 | 64 |
| 63 | 151 | 148 | — | 150 | — | 151 | — | — | 104 | 269 | 272 | 266 | 304 | 298 | 310 | 63 |
| 62 | 150 | 147 | 153 | 149 | 149 | 150 | 102 | 101 | — | 268 | 270–271 | 265 | 302–303 | 296–297 | 308–309 | 62 |
| 61 | 149 | — | 152 | 148 | — | — | — | 100 | 103 | 266–267 | 269 | 263–264 | 301 | 295 | 307 | 61 |
| 60 | 148 | 146 | 151 | — | 148 | 150 | 101 | — | — | 265 | 268 | 262 | 300 | 294 | 305–306 | 60 |
| 59 | — | 145 | 150 | 147 | — | 149 | — | 99 | 102 | 264 | 267 | 261 | 298–299 | 293 | 304 | 59 |
| 58 | 147 | — | 149 | 146 | 147 | 148 | 100 | 98 | — | 263 | 266 | 260 | 297 | 291–292 | 302–303 | 58 |
| 57 | 146 | 144 | — | — | — | 147 | — | — | 101 | 262 | 264–265 | 258–259 | 296 | 290 | 301 | 57 |
| 56 | 145 | 143 | 148 | 145 | 146 | — | 99 | — | 100 | 260–261 | 263 | 257 | 294–295 | 289 | 299–300 | 56 |
| 55 | — | — | — | — | — | 146 | — | 96 | — | 259 | 262 | 256 | 293 | 288 | 298 | 55 |
| 54 | 144 | 142 | 147 | 144 | 145 | 145 | 98 | — | 99 | 258 | 261 | 255 | 292 | 287 | 296–297 | 54 |
| 53 | 143 | 141 | 146 | — | — | — | 97 | — | — | 257 | 260 | 254 | 291 | 286 | 295 | 53 |
| 52 | — | — | 145 | 144 | 144 | 144 | — | 95 | 98 | 256 | 258–259 | 252–253 | 290 | 285 | 293–294 | 52 |
| 51 | 142 | — | 144 | — | — | — | — | — | — | 254–255 | 257 | 251 | 289 | 284 | 292 | 51 |

**Table A.3e** TRS–C Composite Percentiles (continued)

| | Externalizing Problems | | | Internalizing Problems | | | School Problems | | | Adaptive Skills | | | Behavioral Symptoms Index | | | |
|---|---|---|---|---|---|---|---|---|---|---|---|---|---|---|---|---|
| **%ile** | Combined | Female | Male | Combined | Female | Male | Combined | Female | Male | Combined | Female | Male | Combined | Female | Male | **%ile** |
| 50 | – | 140 | 143 | 143 | 143 | 143 | 96 | – | 97 | 253 | 256 | 250 | 287–288 | 283 | 291 | 50 |
| 49 | 141 | – | – | 142 | 142 | 142 | – | 94 | – | 252 | 255 | 249 | 286 | 282 | 290 | 49 |
| 48 | 140 | 139 | 142 | – | – | 141 | 95 | – | 96 | 251 | 253–254 | 248 | 285 | – | 288–289 | 48 |
| 47 | – | – | 141 | 141 | 141 | – | – | 93 | – | 249–250 | 252 | 246–247 | 284 | 281 | 287 | 47 |
| 46 | 139 | 138 | – | 140 | 140 | 140 | 94 | – | 95 | 248 | 251 | 245 | 283 | 280 | 286 | 46 |
| 45 | – | – | 140 | – | – | 139 | – | 92 | – | 247 | 250 | 244 | 282 | 279 | 284–285 | 45 |
| 44 | 138 | – | 139 | 139 | 139 | – | 93 | – | 94 | 246 | 248–249 | 243 | 281 | 278 | 283 | 44 |
| 43 | – | 137 | – | 138 | – | 138 | – | – | – | 244–245 | 247 | 242 | 280 | 277 | 282 | 43 |
| 42 | 137 | – | 138 | – | 138 | – | 92 | 91 | 93 | 243 | 246 | 240–241 | 279 | – | 281 | 42 |
| 41 | – | 136 | 137 | 137 | – | 137 | – | – | – | 242 | 244–245 | 239 | 278 | 276 | 280 | 41 |
| 40 | 136 | – | – | 136 | 137 | 136 | 91 | 90 | 92 | 240–241 | 243 | 238 | 277 | 275 | 279 | 40 |
| 39 | 135 | 135 | 136 | – | – | – | – | – | – | 239 | 241–242 | 237 | 276 | 274 | 277–278 | 39 |
| 38 | – | – | – | 135 | 136 | 135 | 90 | 89 | 91 | 238 | 240 | 235–236 | 275 | – | 276 | 38 |
| 37 | 134 | 134 | 135 | – | – | – | – | – | – | 236–237 | 239 | 234 | 274 | 273 | 275 | 37 |
| 36 | – | – | 134 | 134 | 135 | 134 | – | – | – | 235 | 237–238 | 233 | – | 272 | 274 | 36 |
| 35 | 133 | 133 | – | – | – | – | 89 | 88 | 90 | 234 | 236 | 232 | 273 | – | 273 | 35 |
| 34 | – | – | 133 | 133 | 134 | 133 | – | – | – | 232–233 | 234–235 | 230–231 | 272 | 271 | 272 | 34 |
| 33 | 132 | – | – | – | 133 | – | 88 | – | 89 | 231 | 233 | 229 | 271 | 270 | 271 | 33 |
| 32 | – | 132 | 132 | 132 | – | 132 | – | 87 | – | 229–230 | 231–232 | 228 | 270 | – | 270 | 32 |
| 31 | – | – | – | – | 132 | – | – | – | 88 | 228 | 230 | 226–227 | 269 | 269 | 269 | 31 |
| 30 | 131 | 131 | 131 | 131 | – | 131 | 87 | – | – | 226–227 | 228–229 | 225 | 268 | 268 | 268 | 30 |
| 29 | – | – | 130 | – | 131 | 130 | – | 86 | – | 225 | 226–227 | 224 | – | – | 267 | 29 |
| 28 | – | 130 | – | 130 | – | – | – | – | 87 | 223–224 | 225 | 222–223 | 267 | 267 | 266 | 28 |
| 27 | 130 | – | 129 | – | 130 | 129 | 86 | – | – | 222 | 223–224 | 221 | 266 | – | 265 | 27 |
| 26 | – | – | – | 129 | – | – | – | 85 | 86 | 220–221 | 221–222 | 220 | 265 | 266 | 264 | 26 |
| 25 | 129 | 129 | 128 | – | 129 | 128 | 85 | – | 85 | 219 | 220 | 218–219 | 264 | 265 | 263 | 25 |
| 24 | – | – | 127 | 128 | – | 127 | – | 84 | – | 217–218 | 218–219 | 217 | – | 264 | 262 | 24 |
| 23 | 128 | – | – | – | 128 | – | – | – | – | 216 | 216–217 | 215–216 | 263 | – | – | 23 |
| 22 | – | 128 | 126 | 127 | – | – | 84 | – | 84 | 214–215 | 214–215 | 214 | 262 | – | 261 | 22 |
| 21 | 127 | – | – | – | – | – | – | – | – | 212–213 | 212–213 | 212–213 | 261 | 263 | 260 | 21 |
| 20 | – | 127 | 125 | – | – | – | – | 83 | – | 210–211 | 210–211 | 211 | 260 | – | 259 | 20 |
| 19 | 126 | – | – | – | – | – | 83 | – | 83 | 209 | 208–209 | 209–210 | – | 262 | 258 | 19 |
| 18 | – | – | 124 | – | – | – | – | – | – | 207–208 | 206–207 | 207–208 | 259 | – | 257 | 18 |
| 17 | 125 | – | – | – | – | – | – | 82 | 82 | 205–206 | 204–205 | 206 | 258 | 261 | 256 | 17 |
| 16 | – | – | 123 | – | – | – | 82 | – | – | 203–204 | 202–203 | 204–205 | 257 | – | – | 16 |
| 15 | 124 | – | – | – | – | – | – | – | 81 | 201–202 | 199–201 | 202–203 | – | 260 | 255 | 15 |
| 14 | – | – | 122 | – | – | – | – | 81 | – | 199–200 | 197–198 | 200–201 | 256 | – | 254 | 14 |
| 13 | – | – | – | – | – | – | 81 | – | 80 | 196–198 | 194–196 | 199 | 255 | 259 | 253 | 13 |
| 12 | – | – | 121 | – | – | – | – | – | – | 194–195 | 191–193 | 197–198 | 254 | – | 252 | 12 |
| 11 | – | – | – | – | – | – | – | 80 | – | 192–193 | 189–190 | 194–196 | 253 | 258 | – | 11 |
| 10 | – | – | 120 | – | – | – | 80 | – | 79 | 189–191 | 186–188 | 192–193 | 252 | – | 251 | 10 |
| 9 | – | – | – | – | – | – | – | – | – | 187–188 | 182–185 | 190–191 | 251 | 257 | 250 | 9 |
| 8 | – | – | – | – | – | – | – | 79 | 78 | 184–186 | 179–181 | 187–189 | 250 | – | 249 | 8 |
| 7 | – | – | – | – | – | – | – | – | – | 181–183 | 175–178 | 185–186 | – | 256 | 248 | 7 |
| 6 | – | – | – | – | – | – | 79 | – | 77 | 177–180 | 171–174 | 182–184 | 249 | – | – | 6 |
| 5 | – | – | – | – | – | – | 78 | 78 | 76 | 173–176 | 167–170 | 179–181 | 248 | 255 | 247 | 5 |
| 4 | – | – | – | – | – | – | – | – | – | 169–172 | 162–166 | 175–178 | 247 | 254 | 246 | 4 |
| 3 | – | – | – | – | – | – | 77 | – | 75 | 164–168 | 155–161 | 171–174 | 246 | – | 245 | 3 |
| 2 | – | – | – | – | – | – | – | – | – | 157–163 | 147–154 | 165–170 | 245 | 253 | 244 | 2 |
| 1 | – | – | – | – | – | – | – | – | – | 110–156 | 103–146 | 113–164 | – | 249–252 | 240–243 | 1 |

## Table A.4a TRS–C *T* Scores and Percentiles

| Raw score | Hyperactivity T | Hyperactivity %ile | Aggression T | Aggression %ile | Conduct Problems T | Conduct Problems %ile | Anxiety T | Anxiety %ile | Depression T | Depression %ile | Somatization T | Somatization %ile | Attention Problems T | Attention Problems %ile | Learning Problems T | Learning Problems %ile | Atypicality T | Atypicality %ile | Withdrawal T | Withdrawal %ile | Adaptability T | Adaptability %ile | Social Skills T | Social Skills %ile | Leadership T | Leadership %ile | Study Skills T | Study Skills %ile | Functional Communication T | Functional Communication %ile | Raw score |
|---|---|---|---|---|---|---|---|---|---|---|---|---|---|---|---|---|---|---|---|---|---|---|---|---|---|---|---|---|---|---|---|
| 33 | 94 | 99 | — | — | — | — | — | — | 120 | 99 | — | — | — | — | — | — | — | — | — | — | — | — | — | — | — | — | — | — | — | — | 33 |
| 32 | 92 | 99 | — | — | — | — | — | — | 120 | 99 | — | — | — | — | — | — | — | — | — | — | — | — | — | — | — | — | — | — | — | — | 32 |
| 31 | 91 | 99 | — | — | — | — | — | — | 120 | 99 | — | — | — | — | — | — | — | — | — | — | — | — | — | — | — | — | — | — | — | — | 31 |
| 30 | 89 | 99 | 119 | 99 | — | — | — | — | 120 | 99 | — | — | — | — | — | — | — | — | — | — | — | — | 67 | 96 | — | — | — | — | 65 | 96 | 30 |
| 29 | 87 | 99 | 116 | 99 | — | — | — | — | 119 | 99 | — | — | — | — | — | — | — | — | — | — | — | — | 65 | 94 | — | — | — | — | 63 | 93 | 29 |
| 28 | 86 | 99 | 114 | 99 | — | — | — | — | 116 | 99 | — | — | — | — | — | — | — | — | — | — | — | — | 64 | 91 | — | — | — | — | 61 | 88 | 28 |
| 27 | 84 | 99 | 111 | 99 | 118 | 99 | 108 | 99 | 114 | 99 | — | — | — | — | — | — | 120 | 99 | — | — | 64 | 95 | 62 | 88 | — | — | — | — | 59 | 82 | 27 |
| 26 | 83 | 99 | 109 | 99 | 116 | 99 | 105 | 99 | 111 | 99 | — | — | — | — | — | — | 120 | 99 | — | — | 62 | 90 | 61 | 85 | — | — | — | — | 58 | 76 | 26 |
| 25 | 81 | 99 | 106 | 99 | 113 | 99 | 103 | 99 | 108 | 99 | 120 | 99 | — | — | — | — | 117 | 99 | — | — | 60 | 84 | 59 | 81 | — | — | — | — | 56 | 68 | 25 |
| 24 | 79 | 98 | 104 | 99 | 110 | 99 | 100 | 99 | 106 | 99 | 120 | 99 | 80 | 99 | 89 | 99 | 114 | 99 | 99 | 99 | 58 | 77 | 58 | 77 | — | — | 65 | 97 | 54 | 61 | 24 |
| 23 | 78 | 98 | 101 | 99 | 107 | 99 | 98 | 99 | 103 | 99 | 120 | 99 | 78 | 99 | 86 | 99 | 111 | 99 | 97 | 99 | 57 | 70 | 57 | 72 | — | — | 63 | 92 | 52 | 54 | 23 |
| 22 | 76 | 97 | 99 | 99 | 104 | 99 | 95 | 99 | 100 | 99 | 119 | 99 | 76 | 99 | 84 | 99 | 108 | 99 | 95 | 99 | 55 | 63 | 55 | 67 | — | — | 61 | 86 | 51 | 47 | 22 |
| 21 | 75 | 97 | 96 | 99 | 102 | 99 | 92 | 99 | 98 | 99 | 116 | 99 | 74 | 99 | 82 | 99 | 105 | 99 | 92 | 99 | 53 | 56 | 54 | 62 | 70 | 98 | 59 | 79 | 49 | 41 | 21 |
| 20 | 73 | 96 | 94 | 99 | 99 | 99 | 90 | 99 | 95 | 99 | 112 | 99 | 73 | 98 | 80 | 99 | 102 | 99 | 90 | 99 | 51 | 50 | 52 | 57 | 68 | 96 | 58 | 72 | 47 | 34 | 20 |
| 19 | 71 | 95 | 91 | 99 | 96 | 99 | 87 | 99 | 92 | 99 | 109 | 99 | 71 | 97 | 78 | 99 | 99 | 99 | 87 | 99 | 49 | 43 | 51 | 52 | 65 | 93 | 56 | 66 | 45 | 29 | 19 |
| 18 | 70 | 94 | 89 | 99 | 93 | 99 | 85 | 99 | 90 | 99 | 106 | 99 | 69 | 95 | 76 | 98 | 96 | 99 | 85 | 99 | 47 | 37 | 49 | 47 | 63 | 90 | 54 | 59 | 44 | 24 | 18 |
| 17 | 68 | 93 | 86 | 99 | 90 | 99 | 82 | 99 | 87 | 99 | 102 | 99 | 67 | 93 | 74 | 97 | 93 | 99 | 82 | 99 | 46 | 32 | 48 | 42 | 61 | 86 | 52 | 53 | 42 | 20 | 17 |
| 16 | 67 | 92 | 84 | 99 | 88 | 99 | 80 | 98 | 84 | 99 | 99 | 99 | 65 | 91 | 72 | 96 | 90 | 99 | 80 | 99 | 44 | 27 | 47 | 37 | 59 | 80 | 50 | 47 | 40 | 16 | 16 |
| 15 | 65 | 90 | 81 | 98 | 85 | 99 | 77 | 98 | 82 | 98 | 95 | 99 | 63 | 89 | 70 | 95 | 88 | 99 | 77 | 98 | 42 | 22 | 45 | 33 | 57 | 75 | 48 | 41 | 38 | 13 | 15 |
| 14 | 63 | 89 | 79 | 97 | 82 | 98 | 75 | 97 | 79 | 98 | 92 | 99 | 62 | 86 | 68 | 93 | 85 | 98 | 75 | 97 | 40 | 18 | 44 | 28 | 55 | 68 | 47 | 35 | 37 | 10 | 14 |
| 13 | 62 | 87 | 76 | 96 | 79 | 98 | 72 | 96 | 77 | 97 | 88 | 99 | 60 | 82 | 66 | 91 | 82 | 98 | 73 | 96 | 38 | 14 | 42 | 24 | 53 | 61 | 45 | 30 | 35 | 8 | 13 |
| 12 | 60 | 84 | 73 | 95 | 76 | 97 | 70 | 94 | 74 | 96 | 85 | 99 | 58 | 78 | 64 | 89 | 79 | 98 | 70 | 95 | 36 | 11 | 41 | 20 | 51 | 54 | 43 | 25 | 33 | 6 | 12 |
| 11 | 58 | 82 | 71 | 94 | 74 | 96 | 67 | 93 | 71 | 95 | 81 | 98 | 56 | 74 | 62 | 86 | 76 | 97 | 68 | 93 | 35 | 9 | 40 | 17 | 49 | 46 | 41 | 21 | 31 | 5 | 11 |
| 10 | 57 | 79 | 68 | 92 | 71 | 94 | 65 | 90 | 69 | 94 | 78 | 98 | 54 | 69 | 60 | 83 | 73 | 96 | 65 | 92 | 33 | 6 | 38 | 13 | 47 | 39 | 39 | 17 | 29 | 4 | 10 |
| 9 | 55 | 76 | 66 | 90 | 68 | 93 | 62 | 88 | 66 | 92 | 74 | 97 | 53 | 63 | 57 | 79 | 70 | 95 | 63 | 89 | 31 | 4 | 37 | 11 | 44 | 31 | 37 | 13 | 28 | 3 | 9 |
| 8 | 54 | 72 | 63 | 88 | 65 | 91 | 59 | 84 | 63 | 90 | 71 | 95 | 51 | 57 | 55 | 75 | 67 | 94 | 60 | 87 | 29 | 3 | 35 | 8 | 42 | 25 | 35 | 10 | 26 | 2 | 8 |
| 7 | 52 | 68 | 61 | 86 | 62 | 88 | 57 | 80 | 61 | 87 | 67 | 94 | 49 | 51 | 53 | 70 | 64 | 92 | 58 | 83 | 27 | 2 | 34 | 6 | 40 | 19 | 34 | 7 | 24 | 1 | 7 |
| 6 | 50 | 63 | 58 | 84 | 59 | 85 | 54 | 74 | 58 | 84 | 64 | 91 | 47 | 44 | 51 | 64 | 61 | 90 | 56 | 79 | 25 | 1 | 32 | 4 | 38 | 13 | 32 | 5 | 22 | 1 | 6 |
| 5 | 49 | 58 | 56 | 80 | 57 | 81 | 52 | 67 | 55 | 79 | 60 | 88 | 45 | 38 | 49 | 57 | 58 | 87 | 53 | 74 | 24 | 1 | 31 | 3 | 36 | 9 | 30 | 3 | 21 | 1 | 5 |
| 4 | 47 | 51 | 53 | 76 | 54 | 75 | 49 | 58 | 53 | 74 | 57 | 82 | 43 | 30 | 47 | 49 | 55 | 83 | 51 | 67 | 22 | 1 | 30 | 2 | 34 | 5 | 28 | 1 | 19 | 1 | 4 |
| 3 | 46 | 43 | 51 | 71 | 51 | 68 | 47 | 48 | 50 | 66 | 53 | 75 | 42 | 23 | 45 | 30 | 53 | 78 | 48 | 57 | 20 | 1 | 28 | 1 | 32 | 3 | 26 | 1 | 17 | 1 | 3 |
| 2 | 44 | 34 | 48 | 64 | 48 | 58 | 44 | 35 | 47 | 55 | 50 | 64 | 40 | 16 | 43 | 18 | 50 | 69 | 46 | 45 | 18 | 1 | 27 | 1 | 30 | 1 | 24 | 1 | 15 | 1 | 2 |
| 1 | 42 | 24 | 46 | 52 | 45 | 44 | 42 | 19 | 45 | 39 | 46 | 47 | 38 | 10 | 41 | 7 | 47 | 54 | 43 | 29 | 16 | 1 | 25 | 1 | 28 | 1 | 22 | 1 | 14 | 1 | 1 |
| 0 | 41 | 13 | 43 | 27 | 43 | 23 | 39 | 5 | 42 | 16 | 43 | 24 | 36 | 5 | 39 | — | 44 | 21 | 41 | 9 | 15 | 1 | 24 | 1 | 26 | 1 | 21 | 1 | 12 | 1 | 0 |
| **Raw mean** | 5.75 | | 2.65 | | 2.62 | | 4.30 | | 2.96 | | 2.01 | | 7.61 | | 5.38 | | 2.13 | | 3.73 | | 19.38 | | 18.36 | | 11.63 | | 15.88 | | 21.69 | | **Raw mean** |
| **Raw SD** | 6.21 | | 3.98 | | 3.56 | | 3.93 | | 3.78 | | 2.88 | | 5.49 | | 4.83 | | 3.43 | | 4.10 | | 5.46 | | 7.02 | | 4.77 | | 5.41 | | 5.70 | | **Raw SD** |
| **T:90% Conf. int.** | 4 | | 5 | | 5 | | 6 | | 6 | | 6 | | 4 | | 5 | | 6 | | 5 | | 5 | | 4 | | 6 | | 5 | | 6 | | **T:90% Conf. int.** |

Table A.4b TRS–C T Scores and Percentiles

| Raw score | Hyperactivity | | Aggression | | Conduct Problems | | Anxiety | | Depression | | Somatization | | Attention Problems | | Learning Problems | | Atypicality | | Withdrawal | | Adaptability | | Social Skills | | Leadership | | Study Skills | | Functional Communication | | Raw score |
|---|---|---|---|---|---|---|---|---|---|---|---|---|---|---|---|---|---|---|---|---|---|---|---|---|---|---|---|---|---|---|---|---|---|
| | T | %ile | T | %ile | T | %ile | T | %ile | T | %ile | T | %ile | T | %ile | T | %ile | T | %ile | T | %ile | T | %ile | T | %ile | T | %ile | T | %ile | T | %ile | |
| 33 | 112 | 99 | — | — | — | — | — | — | 120 | 99 | — | — | — | — | — | — | — | — | — | — | — | — | — | — | — | — | — | — | — | — | 33 |
| 32 | 110 | 99 | — | — | — | — | — | — | 120 | 99 | — | — | — | — | — | — | — | — | — | — | — | — | — | — | — | — | — | — | — | — | 32 |
| 31 | 108 | 99 | — | — | — | — | — | — | 120 | 99 | — | — | — | — | — | — | — | — | — | — | — | — | — | — | — | — | — | — | — | — | 31 |
| 30 | 105 | 99 | 120 | 99 | — | — | — | — | 120 | 99 | — | — | — | — | — | — | — | — | — | — | — | — | 65 | 94 | — | — | — | — | 64 | 95 | 30 |
| 29 | 103 | 99 | 120 | 99 | — | — | — | — | 120 | 99 | — | — | — | — | — | — | — | — | — | — | — | — | 63 | 91 | — | — | — | — | 62 | 90 | 29 |
| 28 | 101 | 99 | 120 | 99 | — | — | — | — | 120 | 99 | — | — | — | — | — | — | — | — | — | — | — | — | 62 | 86 | — | — | — | — | 60 | 83 | 28 |
| 27 | 99 | 99 | 120 | 99 | 120 | 99 | 108 | 99 | 120 | 99 | 117 | 99 | — | — | — | — | — | — | — | — | 63 | 95 | 60 | 82 | — | — | — | — | 58 | 76 | 27 |
| 26 | 97 | 99 | 120 | 99 | 120 | 99 | 105 | 99 | 120 | 99 | 114 | 99 | — | — | — | — | 120 | 99 | — | — | 61 | 86 | 58 | 77 | — | — | — | — | 56 | 68 | 26 |
| 25 | 95 | 99 | 120 | 99 | 120 | 99 | 103 | 99 | 120 | 99 | 111 | 99 | — | — | — | — | 120 | 99 | — | — | 59 | 77 | 57 | 71 | — | — | — | — | 54 | 61 | 25 |
| 24 | 93 | 99 | 118 | 99 | 120 | 99 | 100 | 99 | 118 | 99 | 108 | 99 | 85 | 99 | 92 | 99 | 120 | 99 | 113 | 99 | 56 | 67 | 55 | 66 | — | — | 63 | 95 | 52 | 53 | 24 |
| 23 | 91 | 99 | 115 | 99 | 120 | 99 | 98 | 99 | 114 | 99 | 105 | 99 | 83 | 99 | 90 | 99 | 120 | 99 | 110 | 99 | 54 | 59 | 54 | 61 | — | — | 61 | 87 | 50 | 46 | 23 |
| 22 | 88 | 99 | 112 | 99 | 120 | 99 | 95 | 99 | 111 | 99 | 102 | 99 | 81 | 99 | 87 | 99 | 120 | 99 | 107 | 99 | 52 | 51 | 52 | 55 | — | — | 59 | 79 | 48 | 39 | 22 |
| 21 | 86 | 99 | 109 | 99 | 118 | 99 | 92 | 99 | 108 | 99 | 99 | 99 | 79 | 99 | 85 | 99 | 120 | 99 | 104 | 99 | 50 | 44 | 51 | 50 | 68 | 96 | 57 | 71 | 46 | 32 | 21 |
| 20 | 84 | 99 | 106 | 99 | 115 | 99 | 90 | 99 | 105 | 99 | 96 | 99 | 77 | 99 | 83 | 99 | 120 | 99 | 101 | 99 | 48 | 37 | 49 | 45 | 65 | 93 | 55 | 63 | 44 | 27 | 20 |
| 19 | 82 | 98 | 103 | 99 | 111 | 99 | 87 | 99 | 102 | 99 | 92 | 99 | 75 | 98 | 81 | 99 | 120 | 99 | 98 | 99 | 46 | 31 | 48 | 40 | 63 | 90 | 53 | 55 | 42 | 21 | 19 |
| 18 | 80 | 98 | 100 | 99 | 107 | 99 | 85 | 99 | 99 | 99 | 89 | 99 | 73 | 97 | 79 | 99 | 120 | 99 | 95 | 99 | 44 | 26 | 46 | 35 | 61 | 85 | 51 | 48 | 40 | 17 | 18 |
| 17 | 78 | 98 | 97 | 99 | 104 | 99 | 82 | 99 | 96 | 99 | 86 | 99 | 71 | 96 | 77 | 98 | 120 | 99 | 92 | 99 | 42 | 21 | 45 | 30 | 59 | 79 | 49 | 42 | 38 | 13 | 17 |
| 16 | 76 | 97 | 94 | 99 | 100 | 99 | 80 | 98 | 93 | 99 | 83 | 98 | 69 | 95 | 74 | 97 | 116 | 99 | 89 | 99 | 40 | 17 | 43 | 26 | 57 | 73 | 47 | 36 | 36 | 10 | 16 |
| 15 | 74 | 96 | 91 | 99 | 97 | 99 | 77 | 98 | 89 | 99 | 80 | 98 | 67 | 93 | 72 | 96 | 111 | 99 | 86 | 99 | 37 | 14 | 41 | 22 | 55 | 67 | 45 | 31 | 34 | 7 | 15 |
| 14 | 71 | 95 | 87 | 99 | 93 | 99 | 74 | 97 | 86 | 99 | 77 | 97 | 65 | 91 | 70 | 95 | 106 | 99 | 83 | 99 | 35 | 10 | 40 | 18 | 53 | 59 | 43 | 26 | 32 | 5 | 14 |
| 13 | 69 | 94 | 84 | 98 | 90 | 99 | 72 | 96 | 83 | 99 | 74 | 96 | 63 | 88 | 68 | 93 | 102 | 99 | 80 | 98 | 33 | 8 | 38 | 15 | 50 | 52 | 41 | 21 | 30 | 4 | 13 |
| 12 | 67 | 93 | 81 | 97 | 86 | 99 | 69 | 94 | 80 | 98 | 71 | 95 | 61 | 85 | 66 | 91 | 97 | 99 | 77 | 98 | 31 | 5 | 37 | 12 | 48 | 45 | 39 | 17 | 28 | 2 | 12 |
| 11 | 65 | 91 | 78 | 96 | 83 | 99 | 67 | 92 | 77 | 97 | 68 | 94 | 59 | 81 | 63 | 88 | 92 | 99 | 74 | 97 | 29 | 4 | 35 | 9 | 46 | 37 | 37 | 13 | 26 | 2 | 11 |
| 10 | 63 | 89 | 75 | 95 | 79 | 97 | 64 | 90 | 74 | 96 | 65 | 92 | 57 | 77 | 61 | 85 | 87 | 99 | 71 | 96 | 27 | 2 | 34 | 7 | 44 | 30 | 35 | 10 | 24 | 1 | 10 |
| 9 | 61 | 87 | 72 | 94 | 76 | 96 | 61 | 87 | 71 | 95 | 62 | 89 | 55 | 72 | 59 | 82 | 82 | 98 | 68 | 94 | 25 | 1 | 32 | 5 | 42 | 23 | 33 | 7 | 22 | 1 | 9 |
| 8 | 59 | 84 | 69 | 93 | 72 | 95 | 59 | 83 | 67 | 93 | 59 | 86 | 53 | 67 | 57 | 78 | 77 | 97 | 65 | 92 | 23 | 1 | 31 | 3 | 40 | 17 | 31 | 5 | 20 | 1 | 8 |
| 7 | 57 | 81 | 66 | 91 | 68 | 92 | 56 | 78 | 64 | 91 | 56 | 81 | 51 | 61 | 55 | 74 | 72 | 95 | 62 | 89 | 21 | 1 | 29 | 2 | 38 | 12 | 29 | 3 | 18 | 1 | 7 |
| 6 | 55 | 76 | 63 | 90 | 65 | 90 | 54 | 72 | 61 | 88 | 52 | 74 | 50 | 54 | 53 | 68 | 68 | 93 | 59 | 85 | 18 | 1 | 28 | 1 | 35 | 8 | 27 | 2 | 16 | 1 | 6 |
| 5 | 52 | 71 | 60 | 87 | 61 | 87 | 51 | 64 | 58 | 83 | 49 | 64 | 48 | 47 | 50 | 62 | 63 | 90 | 56 | 79 | 16 | 1 | 26 | 1 | 33 | 4 | 25 | 1 | 14 | 1 | 5 |
| 4 | 50 | 65 | 57 | 85 | 58 | 83 | 49 | 54 | 55 | 77 | 46 | 48 | 46 | 39 | 48 | 55 | 58 | 85 | 53 | 71 | 14 | 1 | 24 | 1 | 31 | 2 | 23 | 1 | 12 | 1 | 4 |
| 3 | 48 | 57 | 54 | 81 | 54 | 77 | 46 | 43 | 52 | 70 | 43 | 23 | 44 | 31 | 46 | 46 | 53 | 77 | 50 | 61 | 12 | 1 | 23 | 1 | 29 | 1 | 21 | 1 | 10 | 1 | 3 |
| 2 | 46 | 47 | 51 | 75 | 51 | 69 | 43 | 29 | 49 | 58 | — | — | 42 | 23 | 44 | 35 | 48 | 62 | 47 | 47 | 10 | 1 | 21 | 1 | 27 | 1 | 19 | 1 | 10 | 1 | 2 |
| 1 | 44 | 34 | 48 | 65 | 47 | 57 | 41 | 15 | 46 | 43 | — | — | 40 | 15 | 42 | 23 | 43 | 24 | 44 | 29 | 10 | 1 | 20 | 1 | 25 | 1 | 17 | 1 | 10 | 1 | 1 |
| 0 | 42 | 17 | 45 | 33 | 44 | 32 | 38 | 3 | 42 | 20 | — | — | 38 | 8 | 39 | 8 | — | — | 41 | 11 | 10 | 1 | 18 | 1 | 23 | 1 | 15 | 1 | 10 | 1 | 0 |
| Raw mean | 3.86 | | 1.78 | | 1.80 | | 4.58 | | 2.43 | | 2.21 | | 6.25 | | 4.83 | | 1.37 | | 3.05 | | 20.95 | | 20.51 | | 12.78 | | 17.41 | | 23.02 | | Raw mean |
| Raw SD | 4.72 | | 3.26 | | 2.82 | | 3.87 | | 3.19 | | 3.25 | | 5.12 | | 4.58 | | 2.06 | | 3.30 | | 4.74 | | 6.46 | | 4.66 | | 5.00 | | 5.00 | | Raw SD |
| T:90% Conf. int. | 5 | | 6 | | 6 | | 6 | | 7 | | 6 | | 4 | | 6 | | 9 | | 6 | | 6 | | 4 | | 5 | | 5 | | 6 | | T:90% Conf. int. |

## Table A.4c TRS–C T Scores and Percentiles

### Clinical Scales

| Raw score | Hyperactivity | | Aggression | | Conduct Problems | | Anxiety | | Depression | | Somatization | | Attention Problems | | Learning Problems | | Atypicality | | Withdrawal | |
|---|---|---|---|---|---|---|---|---|---|---|---|---|---|---|---|---|---|---|---|---|
| | T | %ile | T | %ile | T | %ile | T | %ile | T | %ile | T | %ile | T | %ile | T | %ile | T | %ile | T | %ile |
| 33 | 87 | 99 | — | — | — | — | — | — | 120 | 99 | — | — | — | — | — | — | — | — | — | — |
| 32 | 85 | 99 | — | — | — | — | — | — | 117 | 99 | — | — | — | — | — | — | — | — | — | — |
| 31 | 84 | 99 | — | — | — | — | — | — | 115 | 99 | — | — | — | — | — | — | — | — | — | — |
| 30 | 82 | 99 | 110 | 99 | — | — | — | — | 113 | 99 | — | — | — | — | — | — | — | — | — | — |
| 29 | 81 | 99 | 108 | 99 | — | — | — | — | 110 | 99 | — | — | — | — | — | — | — | — | — | — |
| 28 | 79 | 99 | 105 | 99 | — | — | — | — | 108 | 99 | — | — | — | — | — | — | — | — | — | — |
| 27 | 78 | 99 | 103 | 99 | 109 | 99 | 108 | 99 | 106 | 99 | — | — | — | — | — | — | 106 | 99 | — | — |
| 26 | 77 | 98 | 101 | 99 | 106 | 99 | 105 | 99 | 103 | 99 | — | — | — | — | — | — | 104 | 99 | — | — |
| 25 | 75 | 98 | 99 | 99 | 104 | 99 | 103 | 99 | 101 | 99 | — | — | — | — | — | — | 102 | 99 | — | — |
| 24 | 74 | 97 | 96 | 99 | 101 | 99 | 100 | 99 | 98 | 99 | — | — | 77 | 99 | 86 | 99 | 99 | 99 | 92 | 99 |
| 23 | 72 | 96 | 94 | 99 | 99 | 99 | 98 | 99 | 96 | 99 | — | — | 75 | 99 | 84 | 99 | 97 | 99 | 90 | 99 |
| 22 | 71 | 95 | 92 | 99 | 96 | 99 | 95 | 99 | 94 | 99 | 120 | 99 | 74 | 99 | 82 | 99 | 95 | 99 | 88 | 99 |
| 21 | 69 | 94 | 89 | 99 | 94 | 99 | 93 | 99 | 91 | 99 | 120 | 99 | 72 | 99 | 80 | 99 | 92 | 99 | 85 | 99 |
| 20 | 68 | 93 | 87 | 99 | 91 | 99 | 90 | 99 | 89 | 99 | 120 | 99 | 70 | 97 | 78 | 99 | 90 | 99 | 83 | 99 |
| 19 | 66 | 92 | 85 | 99 | 89 | 99 | 88 | 99 | 87 | 99 | 120 | 99 | 68 | 95 | 76 | 98 | 88 | 99 | 81 | 98 |
| 18 | 65 | 90 | 83 | 99 | 86 | 99 | 85 | 99 | 84 | 99 | 116 | 99 | 66 | 93 | 74 | 97 | 85 | 99 | 79 | 98 |
| 17 | 64 | 89 | 80 | 99 | 84 | 99 | 83 | 99 | 82 | 98 | 112 | 99 | 65 | 91 | 72 | 96 | 83 | 99 | 77 | 97 |
| 16 | 62 | 87 | 78 | 98 | 81 | 99 | 80 | 98 | 80 | 98 | 108 | 99 | 63 | 88 | 70 | 95 | 81 | 98 | 75 | 96 |
| 15 | 61 | 84 | 76 | 97 | 79 | 99 | 78 | 98 | 77 | 97 | 104 | 99 | 61 | 84 | 68 | 93 | 78 | 98 | 73 | 96 |
| 14 | 59 | 82 | 74 | 96 | 76 | 98 | 75 | 97 | 75 | 96 | 100 | 99 | 59 | 80 | 66 | 91 | 76 | 97 | 70 | 94 |
| 13 | 58 | 79 | 71 | 94 | 74 | 97 | 73 | 96 | 72 | 95 | 96 | 99 | 57 | 76 | 64 | 89 | 74 | 96 | 68 | 93 |
| 12 | 56 | 76 | 69 | 93 | 71 | 95 | 70 | 95 | 70 | 94 | 92 | 99 | 55 | 71 | 62 | 87 | 71 | 95 | 66 | 91 |
| 11 | 55 | 73 | 67 | 91 | 69 | 93 | 68 | 93 | 68 | 93 | 88 | 99 | 54 | 66 | 60 | 83 | 69 | 94 | 64 | 90 |
| 10 | 53 | 69 | 65 | 89 | 66 | 91 | 65 | 91 | 65 | 91 | 83 | 99 | 52 | 60 | 58 | 80 | 67 | 92 | 62 | 87 |
| 9 | 52 | 65 | 62 | 86 | 64 | 89 | 63 | 88 | 63 | 89 | 79 | 99 | 50 | 54 | 56 | 76 | 64 | 91 | 60 | 85 |
| 8 | 51 | 61 | 60 | 84 | 61 | 86 | 60 | 85 | 61 | 87 | 75 | 97 | 48 | 47 | 54 | 71 | 62 | 89 | 58 | 82 |
| 7 | 49 | 56 | 58 | 81 | 59 | 83 | 57 | 81 | 58 | 84 | 71 | 93 | 46 | 41 | 52 | 66 | 60 | 87 | 56 | 78 |
| 6 | 48 | 51 | 56 | 77 | 56 | 79 | 55 | 76 | 56 | 80 | 67 | 90 | 45 | 34 | 50 | 59 | 57 | 84 | 53 | 73 |
| 5 | 46 | 45 | 53 | 73 | 54 | 74 | 52 | 70 | 54 | 75 | 63 | 86 | 43 | 27 | 48 | 52 | 55 | 81 | 51 | 68 |
| 4 | 45 | 38 | 51 | 68 | 51 | 67 | 50 | 62 | 51 | 70 | 59 | 81 | 41 | 21 | 46 | 44 | 53 | 76 | 49 | 61 |
| 3 | 43 | 31 | 49 | 62 | 49 | 59 | 47 | 52 | 49 | 62 | 55 | 76 | 39 | 15 | 44 | 35 | 50 | 70 | 47 | 52 |
| 2 | 42 | 23 | 47 | 53 | 46 | 49 | 45 | 39 | 46 | 51 | 51 | 69 | 37 | 10 | 42 | 25 | 48 | 61 | 45 | 41 |
| 1 | 40 | 16 | 44 | 41 | 44 | 35 | 42 | 24 | 44 | 35 | 47 | 57 | 36 | 5 | 40 | 15 | 46 | 47 | 43 | 26 |
| 0 | 39 | 8 | 42 | 21 | 41 | 16 | 40 | 7 | 42 | 9 | 43 | 24 | 34 | 2 | 38 | 5 | 43 | 20 | 41 | 6 |
| Raw mean | 7.64 | | 3.51 | | 3.44 | | 4.02 | | 3.50 | | 1.80 | | 8.97 | | 5.94 | | 2.89 | | 4.41 | |
| Raw SD | 6.92 | | 4.43 | | 4.02 | | 3.98 | | 4.23 | | 2.45 | | 5.52 | | 5.03 | | 4.27 | | 4.68 | |
| T:90% Conf. int. | 4 | | 5 | | 5 | | 6 | | 6 | | 7 | | 4 | | 5 | | 5 | | 5 | |

### Adaptive Scales

| Raw score | Adaptability | | Social Skills | | Leadership | | Study Skills | | Functional Communication | |
|---|---|---|---|---|---|---|---|---|---|---|
| | T | %ile | T | %ile | T | %ile | T | %ile | T | %ile |
| 33 | — | — | — | — | — | — | — | — | — | — |
| 32 | — | — | — | — | — | — | — | — | — | — |
| 31 | — | — | — | — | — | — | — | — | — | — |
| 30 | — | — | 70 | 98 | — | — | — | — | 66 | 98 |
| 29 | — | — | 68 | 97 | — | — | — | — | 64 | 95 |
| 28 | — | — | 67 | 95 | — | — | — | — | 63 | 92 |
| 27 | 66 | 96 | 66 | 94 | — | — | — | — | 61 | 87 |
| 26 | 64 | 93 | 64 | 92 | — | — | — | — | 59 | 82 |
| 25 | 63 | 89 | 63 | 89 | — | — | — | — | 58 | 76 |
| 24 | 61 | 85 | 61 | 86 | — | — | — | — | 56 | 69 |
| 23 | 59 | 80 | 60 | 82 | — | — | 68 | 99 | 54 | 62 |
| 22 | 57 | 74 | 58 | 79 | — | — | 66 | 97 | 53 | 56 |
| 21 | 56 | 68 | 57 | 74 | 73 | 99 | 64 | 93 | 51 | 49 |
| 20 | 54 | 62 | 55 | 70 | 71 | 98 | 62 | 88 | 49 | 43 |
| 19 | 52 | 56 | 54 | 65 | 69 | 97 | 61 | 83 | 48 | 37 |
| 18 | 50 | 49 | 53 | 60 | 66 | 94 | 59 | 77 | 46 | 32 |
| 17 | 49 | 43 | 51 | 55 | 64 | 91 | 57 | 70 | 44 | 27 |
| 16 | 47 | 37 | 50 | 49 | 62 | 87 | 55 | 64 | 43 | 22 |
| 15 | 45 | 32 | 48 | 44 | 60 | 82 | 53 | 58 | 41 | 19 |
| 14 | 43 | 26 | 47 | 39 | 58 | 76 | 51 | 52 | 40 | 15 |
| 13 | 42 | 21 | 45 | 34 | 55 | 70 | 48 | 46 | 38 | 12 |
| 12 | 40 | 17 | 44 | 29 | 53 | 63 | 46 | 40 | 36 | 10 |
| 11 | 38 | 13 | 42 | 24 | 51 | 55 | 44 | 34 | 35 | 8 |
| 10 | 36 | 10 | 41 | 20 | 49 | 47 | 42 | 29 | 33 | 6 |
| 9 | 35 | 7 | 40 | 16 | 47 | 39 | 40 | 24 | 31 | 5 |
| 8 | 33 | 5 | 38 | 13 | 45 | 32 | 38 | 19 | 30 | 4 |
| 7 | 31 | 3 | 37 | 10 | 42 | 25 | 36 | 15 | 28 | 3 |
| 6 | 29 | 2 | 35 | 7 | 40 | 18 | 34 | 11 | 26 | 2 |
| 5 | 28 | 1 | 34 | 5 | 38 | 13 | 33 | 8 | 25 | 2 |
| 4 | 26 | 1 | 32 | 4 | 36 | 8 | 31 | 5 | 23 | 1 |
| 3 | 24 | 1 | 31 | 2 | 34 | 5 | 29 | 3 | 21 | 1 |
| 2 | 22 | 1 | 29 | 1 | 32 | 2 | 27 | 1 | 20 | 1 |
| 1 | 20 | 1 | 28 | 1 | 29 | 1 | 25 | 1 | 18 | 1 |
| 0 | 19 | 1 | 27 | 1 | 27 | 1 | 23 | 1 | 16 | 1 |
| Raw mean | 17.80 | | 16.22 | | 10.47 | | 14.34 | | 20.35 | |
| Raw SD | 5.69 | | 6.93 | | 4.61 | | 5.37 | | 6.06 | |
| T:90% Conf. int. | 5 | | 4 | | 6 | | 5 | | 5 | |

**Table A.4d** TRS–C Composite T Scores

| T score | Externalizing Problems | | | Internalizing Problems | | | School Problems | | | Adaptive Skills | | | Behavioral Symptoms Index | | | T score |
| --- | --- | --- | --- | --- | --- | --- | --- | --- | --- | --- | --- | --- | --- | --- | --- | --- |
| | Combined | Female | Male | Combined | Female | Male | Combined | Female | Male | Combined | Female | Male | Combined | Female | Male | |
| 120 | — | 335–352 | — | 312–348 | 312–345 | 316–348 | — | — | — | — | — | — | 631–632 | 607–670 | — | 120 |
| 119 | — | 332–334 | — | 310–311 | 310–311 | 314–315 | — | — | — | — | — | — | 626–630 | 602–606 | — | 119 |
| 118 | — | 330–331 | — | 308–309 | 308–309 | 311–313 | — | — | — | — | — | — | 622–625 | 598–601 | — | 118 |
| 117 | — | 327–329 | — | 305–307 | 305–307 | 309–310 | — | — | — | — | — | — | 617–621 | 593–597 | — | 117 |
| 116 | 331 | 324–326 | — | 303–304 | 303–304 | 307–308 | — | — | — | — | — | — | 612–616 | 589–592 | — | 116 |
| 115 | 328–330 | 322–323 | — | 301–302 | 301–302 | 304–306 | — | — | — | — | — | — | 607–611 | 585–588 | — | 115 |
| 114 | 326–327 | 319–321 | — | 298–300 | 298–300 | 302–303 | — | — | — | — | — | — | 603–606 | 580–584 | — | 114 |
| 113 | 323–325 | 316–318 | — | 296–297 | 296–297 | 300–301 | — | — | — | — | — | — | 598–602 | 576–579 | — | 113 |
| 112 | 320–322 | 314–315 | — | 294–295 | 294–295 | 297–299 | — | — | — | — | — | — | 593–597 | 571–575 | — | 112 |
| 111 | 317–319 | 311–313 | — | 291–293 | 291–293 | 295–296 | — | — | — | — | — | — | 588–592 | 567–570 | — | 111 |
| 110 | 315–316 | 308–310 | — | 289–290 | 289–290 | 292–294 | — | — | — | — | — | — | 584–587 | 563–566 | 589–592 | 110 |
| 109 | 312–314 | 306–307 | — | 287–288 | 287–288 | 290–291 | — | — | — | — | — | — | 579–583 | 558–562 | 584–588 | 109 |
| 108 | 309–311 | 303–305 | — | 284–286 | 284–286 | 288–289 | — | — | — | — | — | — | 574–578 | 554–557 | 580–583 | 108 |
| 107 | 306–308 | 301–302 | — | 282–283 | 282–283 | 285–287 | — | — | — | — | — | — | 569–573 | 549–553 | 575–579 | 107 |
| 106 | 304–305 | 298–300 | 306 | 280–281 | 280–281 | 283–284 | — | — | — | — | — | — | 565–568 | 545–548 | 570–574 | 106 |
| 105 | 301–303 | 295–297 | 303–305 | 277–279 | 277–279 | 280–282 | — | — | — | — | — | — | 560–564 | 541–544 | 565–569 | 105 |
| 104 | 298–300 | 293–294 | 300–302 | 275–276 | 275–276 | 278–279 | — | — | — | — | — | — | 555–559 | 536–540 | 560–564 | 104 |
| 103 | 295–297 | 290–292 | 297–299 | 273–274 | 273–274 | 276–277 | — | — | — | — | — | — | 550–554 | 532–535 | 555–559 | 103 |
| 102 | 292–294 | 287–289 | 295–296 | 270–272 | 270–272 | 273–275 | — | — | — | — | — | — | 546–549 | 527–531 | 550–554 | 102 |
| 101 | 290–291 | 285–286 | 292–294 | 268–269 | 268–269 | 271–272 | — | — | — | — | — | — | 541–545 | 523–526 | 546–549 | 101 |
| 100 | 287–289 | 282–284 | 289–291 | 266–267 | 266–267 | 269–270 | — | — | — | — | — | — | 536–540 | 519–522 | 541–545 | 100 |
| 99 | 284–286 | 279–281 | 286–288 | 263–265 | 263–265 | 266–268 | — | — | — | — | — | — | 531–535 | 514–518 | 536–540 | 99 |
| 98 | 281–283 | 277–278 | 283–285 | 261–262 | 261–262 | 264–265 | — | — | — | — | — | — | 526–530 | 510–513 | 531–535 | 98 |
| 97 | 279–280 | 274–276 | 281–282 | 259–260 | 259–260 | 261–263 | — | — | — | — | — | — | 522–525 | 505–509 | 526–530 | 97 |
| 96 | 276–278 | 271–273 | 278–280 | 256–258 | 256–258 | 259–260 | — | — | — | — | — | — | 517–521 | 501–504 | 521–525 | 96 |
| 95 | 273–275 | 269–270 | 275–277 | 254–255 | 254–255 | 257–258 | — | — | — | — | — | — | 512–516 | 497–500 | 516–520 | 95 |
| 94 | 270–272 | 266–268 | 272–274 | 252–253 | 252–253 | 254–256 | — | — | — | — | — | — | 507–511 | 492–496 | 512–515 | 94 |
| 93 | 268–269 | 264–265 | 269–271 | 249–251 | 249–251 | 252–253 | — | — | — | — | — | — | 503–506 | 488–491 | 507–511 | 93 |
| 92 | 265–267 | 261–263 | 267–268 | 247–248 | 247–248 | 249–251 | — | 176–177 | — | — | — | — | 498–502 | 483–487 | 502–506 | 92 |
| 91 | 262–264 | 258–260 | 264–266 | 245–246 | 245–246 | 247–248 | — | 175 | — | — | — | — | 493–497 | 479–482 | 497–501 | 91 |
| 90 | 259–261 | 256–257 | 261–263 | 242–244 | 242–244 | 245–246 | — | 173–174 | — | — | — | — | 488–492 | 475–478 | 492–496 | 90 |
| 89 | 257–258 | 253–255 | 258–260 | 240–241 | 240–241 | 242–244 | — | 171–172 | — | — | — | — | 484–487 | 470–474 | 487–491 | 89 |
| 88 | 254–256 | 250–252 | 255–257 | 238–239 | 238–239 | 240–241 | 169 | 169–170 | — | — | — | — | 479–483 | 466–469 | 482–486 | 88 |
| 87 | 251–253 | 248–249 | 253–254 | 235–237 | 235–237 | 238–239 | 167–168 | 167–168 | — | — | — | — | 474–478 | 461–465 | 478–481 | 87 |
| 86 | 248–250 | 245–247 | 250–252 | 233–234 | 233–234 | 235–237 | 165–166 | 165–166 | — | — | — | — | 469–473 | 457–460 | 473–477 | 86 |
| 85 | 246–247 | 242–244 | 247–249 | 231–232 | 231–232 | 233–234 | 164 | 164 | 163 | — | — | — | 465–468 | 453–456 | 468–472 | 85 |
| 84 | 243–245 | 240–241 | 244–246 | 228–230 | 228–230 | 230–232 | 162–163 | 162–163 | 161–162 | — | — | — | 460–464 | 448–452 | 463–467 | 84 |
| 83 | 240–242 | 237–239 | 241–243 | 226–227 | 226–227 | 228–229 | 160–161 | 160–161 | 159–160 | — | — | — | 455–459 | 444–447 | 458–462 | 83 |
| 82 | 237–239 | 234–236 | 239–240 | 224–225 | 224–225 | 226–227 | 158–159 | 158–159 | 158 | — | — | — | 450–454 | 439–443 | 453–457 | 82 |
| 81 | 235–236 | 232–233 | 236–238 | 221–223 | 221–223 | 223–225 | 156–157 | 156–157 | 156–157 | — | — | — | 446–449 | 435–438 | 449–452 | 81 |
| 80 | 232–234 | 229–231 | 233–235 | 219–220 | 219–220 | 221–222 | 154–155 | 154–155 | 154–155 | — | — | — | 441–445 | 431–434 | 444–448 | 80 |
| 79 | 229–231 | 226–228 | 230–232 | 217–218 | 217–218 | 218–220 | 153 | 153 | 152–153 | — | — | — | 436–440 | 426–430 | 439–443 | 79 |
| 78 | 226–228 | 224–225 | 227–229 | 214–216 | 214–216 | 216–217 | 151–152 | 151–152 | 150–151 | — | — | — | 431–435 | 422–425 | 434–438 | 78 |
| 77 | 224–225 | 221–223 | 225–226 | 212–213 | 212–213 | 214–215 | 149–150 | 149–150 | 149 | — | — | — | 427–430 | 417–421 | 429–433 | 77 |
| 76 | 221–223 | 219–220 | 222–224 | 210–211 | 210–211 | 211–213 | 147–148 | 147–148 | 147–148 | — | — | — | 422–426 | 413–416 | 424–428 | 76 |
| 75 | 218–220 | 216–218 | 219–221 | 207–209 | 207–209 | 209–210 | 145–146 | 145–146 | 145–146 | — | — | — | 417–421 | 409–412 | 419–423 | 75 |
| 74 | 215–217 | 213–215 | 216–218 | 205–206 | 205–206 | 207–208 | 143–144 | 143–144 | 143–144 | — | — | — | 412–416 | 404–408 | 415–418 | 74 |
| 73 | 212–214 | 211–212 | 213–215 | 203–204 | 203–204 | 204–206 | 142 | 142 | 141–142 | — | — | — | 407–411 | 400–403 | 410–414 | 73 |
| 72 | 210–211 | 208–210 | 210–212 | 200–202 | 200–202 | 202–203 | 140–141 | 140–141 | 139–140 | — | — | 343 | 403–406 | 395–399 | 405–409 | 72 |
| 71 | 207–209 | 205–207 | 208–209 | 198–199 | 198–199 | 199–201 | 138–139 | 138–139 | 138 | — | — | 339–342 | 398–402 | 391–394 | 400–404 | 71 |
| 70 | 204–206 | 203–204 | 205–207 | 196–197 | 196–197 | 197–198 | 136–137 | 136–137 | 136–137 | — | — | 334–338 | 393–397 | 387–390 | 395–399 | 70 |
| 69 | 201–203 | 200–202 | 202–204 | 193–195 | 193–195 | 195–196 | 134–135 | 134–135 | 134–135 | 331 | — | 330–333 | 388–392 | 382–386 | 390–394 | 69 |
| 68 | 199–200 | 197–199 | 199–201 | 191–192 | 191–192 | 192–194 | 132–133 | 133 | 132–133 | 327–330 | — | 326–329 | 384–387 | 378–381 | 385–389 | 68 |
| 67 | 196–198 | 195–196 | 196–198 | 189–190 | 189–190 | 190–191 | 131 | 131–132 | 130–131 | 322–326 | 321–323 | 322–325 | 379–383 | 373–377 | 381–384 | 67 |
| 66 | 193–195 | 192–194 | 194–195 | 186–188 | 186–188 | 188–189 | 129–130 | 129–130 | 129 | 318–321 | 317–320 | 317–321 | 374–378 | 369–372 | 376–380 | 66 |

**Table A.4d** TRS–C Composite *T* Scores *(continued)*

| T score | Externalizing Problems Combined | Externalizing Female | Externalizing Male | Internalizing Problems Combined | Internalizing Female | Internalizing Male | School Problems Combined | School Problems Female | School Problems Male | Adaptive Skills Combined | Adaptive Skills Female | Adaptive Skills Male | Behavioral Symptoms Index Combined | BSI Female | BSI Male | T score |
|---|---|---|---|---|---|---|---|---|---|---|---|---|---|---|---|---|
| 65 | 190–192 | 189–191 | 191–193 | 184–185 | 184–185 | 185–187 | 127–128 | 127–128 | 127–128 | 314–317 | 313–316 | 313–316 | 369–373 | 365–368 | 371–375 | 65 |
| 64 | 188–189 | 187–188 | 188–190 | 182–183 | 182–183 | 183–184 | 125–126 | 125–126 | 125–126 | 309–313 | 309–312 | 309–312 | 365–368 | 360–364 | 366–370 | 64 |
| 63 | 185–187 | 184–186 | 185–187 | 179–181 | 179–181 | 180–182 | 123–124 | 123–124 | 123–124 | 305–308 | 304–308 | 304–308 | 360–364 | 356–359 | 361–365 | 63 |
| 62 | 182–184 | 181–183 | 182–184 | 177–178 | 177–178 | 178–179 | 121–122 | 122 | 121–122 | 301–304 | 300–303 | 300–303 | 355–359 | 351–355 | 356–360 | 62 |
| 61 | 179–181 | 179–180 | 180–181 | 175–176 | 175–176 | 176–177 | 120 | 120–121 | 119–120 | 296–300 | 296–299 | 296–299 | 350–354 | 347–350 | 352–355 | 61 |
| 60 | 177–178 | 176–178 | 177–179 | 172–174 | 172–174 | 173–175 | 118–119 | 118–119 | 118 | 292–295 | 291–295 | 291–295 | 346–349 | 343–346 | 347–351 | 60 |
| 59 | 174–176 | 174–175 | 174–176 | 170–171 | 170–171 | 171–172 | 116–117 | 116–117 | 116–117 | 287–291 | 287–290 | 287–290 | 341–345 | 338–342 | 342–346 | 59 |
| 58 | 171–173 | 171–173 | 171–173 | 168–169 | 168–169 | 168–170 | 114–115 | 114–115 | 114–115 | 283–286 | 283–286 | 283–286 | 336–340 | 334–337 | 337–341 | 58 |
| 57 | 168–170 | 168–170 | 168–170 | 165–167 | 165–167 | 166–167 | 112–113 | 112–113 | 112–113 | 279–282 | 278–282 | 278–282 | 331–335 | 329–333 | 332–336 | 57 |
| 56 | 166–167 | 166–167 | 166–167 | 163–164 | 163–164 | 164–165 | 110–111 | 111 | 110–111 | 274–278 | 274–277 | 274–277 | 327–330 | 325–328 | 327–331 | 56 |
| 55 | 163–165 | 163–165 | 163–165 | 161–162 | 161–162 | 161–163 | 109 | 109–110 | 109 | 270–273 | 270–273 | 270–273 | 322–326 | 321–324 | 322–326 | 55 |
| 54 | 160–162 | 160–162 | 160–162 | 158–160 | 159–160 | 159–160 | 107–108 | 107–108 | 107–108 | 266–269 | 265–269 | 266–269 | 317–321 | 316–320 | 318–321 | 54 |
| 53 | 157–159 | 158–159 | 157–159 | 156–157 | 156–158 | 157–158 | 105–106 | 105–106 | 105–106 | 261–265 | 261–264 | 261–265 | 312–316 | 312–315 | 313–317 | 53 |
| 52 | 155–156 | 155–157 | 154–156 | 154–155 | 154–155 | 154–156 | 103–104 | 103–104 | 103–104 | 257–260 | 257–260 | 257–260 | 308–311 | 307–311 | 308–312 | 52 |
| 51 | 152–154 | 152–154 | 152–153 | 151–153 | 152–153 | 152–153 | 101–102 | 101–102 | 101–102 | 253–256 | 253–256 | 253–256 | 303–307 | 303–306 | 303–307 | 51 |
| 50 | 149–151 | 150–151 | 149–151 | 149–150 | 149–151 | 149–151 | 100 | 100 | 99–100 | 248–252 | 248–252 | 248–252 | 298–302 | 299–302 | 298–302 | 50 |
| 49 | 146–148 | 147–149 | 146–148 | 147–148 | 147–148 | 147–148 | 98–99 | 98–99 | 98 | 244–247 | 244–247 | 244–247 | 293–297 | 294–298 | 293–297 | 49 |
| 48 | 144–145 | 144–146 | 143–145 | 144–146 | 145–146 | 145–146 | 96–97 | 96–97 | 96–97 | 240–243 | 240–243 | 240–243 | 289–292 | 290–293 | 288–292 | 48 |
| 47 | 141–143 | 142–143 | 140–142 | 142–143 | 142–144 | 142–144 | 94–95 | 94–95 | 94–95 | 235–239 | 235–239 | 235–239 | 284–288 | 285–289 | 284–287 | 47 |
| 46 | 138–140 | 139–141 | 138–139 | 140–141 | 140–141 | 140–141 | 92–93 | 92–93 | 92–93 | 231–234 | 231–234 | 231–234 | 279–283 | 281–284 | 279–283 | 46 |
| 45 | 135–137 | 137–138 | 135–137 | 137–139 | 138–139 | 137–139 | 90–91 | 90–91 | 90–91 | 227–230 | 227–230 | 227–230 | 274–278 | 277–280 | 274–278 | 45 |
| 44 | 132–134 | 134–136 | 132–134 | 135–136 | 135–137 | 135–136 | 89 | 89 | 89 | 222–226 | 222–226 | 222–226 | 269–273 | 272–276 | 269–273 | 44 |
| 43 | 130–131 | 131–133 | 129–131 | 133–134 | 133–134 | 133–134 | 87–88 | 87–88 | 87–88 | 218–221 | 218–221 | 218–221 | 265–268 | 268–271 | 264–268 | 43 |
| 42 | 127–129 | — | 126–128 | 131–132 | 131–132 | 130–132 | 85–86 | 85–86 | 85–86 | 214–217 | 214–217 | 214–217 | 260–264 | 263–267 | 259–263 | 42 |
| 41 | — | — | 124–125 | 128–130 | 128–130 | 128–129 | 83–84 | 83–84 | 83–84 | 209–213 | 210–213 | 210–213 | 255–259 | 259–262 | 254–258 | 41 |
| 40 | — | — | 122–123 | 126–127 | 126–127 | 126–127 | 81–82 | 81–82 | 81–82 | 205–208 | 205–209 | 205–209 | 250–254 | 255–258 | 250–253 | 40 |
| 39 | — | — | — | 124–125 | 124–125 | 125 | 79–80 | 80 | 79–80 | 201–204 | 201–204 | 201–204 | 247–249 | 251–254 | 245–249 | 39 |
| 38 | — | — | — | — | 123 | — | 78 | 78–79 | 78 | 196–199 | 197–200 | 197–200 | — | — | 241–244 | 38 |
| 37 | — | — | — | — | — | — | 76–77 | 77 | 76–77 | 192–195 | 192–196 | 192–196 | — | — | — | 37 |
| 36 | — | — | — | — | — | — | 75 | — | 74–75 | 187–191 | 188–191 | 188–191 | — | — | — | 36 |
| 35 | — | — | — | — | — | — | — | — | 72–73 | 183–186 | 184–187 | 184–187 | — | — | — | 35 |
| 34 | — | — | — | — | — | — | — | — | — | 179–182 | 179–183 | 179–183 | — | — | — | 34 |
| 33 | — | — | — | — | — | — | — | — | — | 174–178 | 175–178 | 175–178 | — | — | — | 33 |
| 32 | — | — | — | — | — | — | — | — | — | 170–173 | 171–174 | 171–174 | — | — | — | 32 |
| 31 | — | — | — | — | — | — | — | — | — | 166–169 | 166–170 | 167–170 | — | — | — | 31 |
| 30 | — | — | — | — | — | — | — | — | — | 161–165 | 162–166 | 162–166 | — | — | — | 30 |
| 29 | — | — | — | — | — | — | — | — | — | 157–160 | 158–161 | 158–161 | — | — | — | 29 |
| 28 | — | — | — | — | — | — | — | — | — | 153–156 | 154–157 | 154–157 | — | — | — | 28 |
| 27 | — | — | — | — | — | — | — | — | — | 148–152 | 149–153 | 149–153 | — | — | — | 27 |
| 26 | — | — | — | — | — | — | — | — | — | 144–147 | 145–148 | 145–148 | — | — | — | 26 |
| 25 | — | — | — | — | — | — | — | — | — | 140–143 | 141–144 | 141–144 | — | — | — | 25 |
| 24 | — | — | — | — | — | — | — | — | — | 135–139 | 136–140 | 136–140 | — | — | — | 24 |
| 23 | — | — | — | — | — | — | — | — | — | 131–134 | 132–135 | 132–135 | — | — | — | 23 |
| 22 | — | — | — | — | — | — | — | — | — | 127–130 | 128–131 | 128–131 | — | — | — | 22 |
| 21 | — | — | — | — | — | — | — | — | — | 122–126 | 123–127 | 123–127 | — | — | — | 21 |
| 20 | — | — | — | — | — | — | — | — | — | 118–121 | 119–122 | 119–122 | — | — | — | 20 |
| 19 | — | — | — | — | — | — | — | — | — | 113–117 | 115–118 | 115–118 | — | — | — | 19 |
| 18 | — | — | — | — | — | — | — | — | — | 109–112 | 111–114 | 112–114 | — | — | — | 18 |
| 17 | — | — | — | — | — | — | — | — | — | 105–108 | 106–110 | — | — | — | — | 17 |
| 16 | — | — | — | — | — | — | — | — | — | 100–104 | 102–105 | — | — | — | — | 16 |
| 15 | — | — | — | — | — | — | — | — | — | 98–99 | 98–101 | — | — | — | — | 15 |
| 14 | — | — | — | — | — | — | — | — | — | — | 93–97 | — | — | — | — | 14 |
| 13 | — | — | — | — | — | — | — | — | — | — | 89–92 | — | — | — | — | 13 |
| 12 | — | — | — | — | — | — | — | — | — | — | 85–88 | — | — | — | — | 12 |
| 11 | — | — | — | — | — | — | — | — | — | — | 80–84 | — | — | — | — | 11 |
| 10 | — | — | — | — | — | — | — | — | — | — | 76–79 | — | — | — | — | 10 |
| **T: 90% Conf. int.** | 3 | 4 | 3 | 5 | 5 | 4 | 4 | 4 | 4 | 3 | 3 | 3 | 3 | 3 | 2 | **T: 90% Conf. int.** |

## Table A.4e TRS-C Composite Percentiles

| %ile | Externalizing Problems | | | Internalizing Problems | | | School Problems | | | Adaptive Skills | | | Behavioral Symptoms Index | | | %ile |
|---|---|---|---|---|---|---|---|---|---|---|---|---|---|---|---|---|
| | Combined | Female | Male | Combined | Female | Male | Combined | Female | Male | Combined | Female | Male | Combined | Female | Male | |
| 99 | 235–331 | 234–352 | 230–306 | 220–348 | 216–345 | 224–348 | 148–169 | 149–177 | 146–163 | – | – | 331–343 | 447–632 | 432–670 | 439–592 | 99 |
| 98 | 226–234 | 227–233 | 222–229 | 212–219 | 209–215 | 215–223 | 143–147 | 144–148 | 142–145 | 327–331 | – | 325–330 | 429–446 | 415–431 | 426–438 | 98 |
| 97 | 219–225 | 221–226 | 216–221 | 206–211 | 205–208 | 209–214 | 140–142 | 141–143 | 139–141 | 322–326 | 323 | 321–324 | 415–428 | 403–414 | 415–425 | 97 |
| 96 | 213–218 | 215–220 | 211–215 | 202–205 | 200–204 | 204–208 | 137–139 | 138–140 | 136–138 | 319–321 | 320–322 | 318–320 | 405–414 | 394–402 | 407–414 | 96 |
| 95 | 208–212 | 210–214 | 207–210 | 197–201 | 197–199 | 199–203 | 135–136 | 136–137 | 134–135 | 316–318 | 317–319 | 315–317 | 396–404 | 387–393 | 399–406 | 95 |
| 94 | 204–207 | 206–209 | 203–206 | 194–196 | 194–196 | 196–198 | 133–134 | 133–135 | 132–133 | 313–315 | 315–316 | 312–314 | 388–395 | 380–386 | 393–398 | 94 |
| 93 | 200–203 | 201–205 | 200–202 | 191–193 | 191–193 | 192–195 | 131–132 | 131–132 | 130–131 | 311–312 | 312–314 | 310–311 | 381–387 | 374–379 | 387–392 | 93 |
| 92 | 196–199 | 197–200 | 196–199 | 188–190 | 188–190 | 189–191 | 129–130 | 130 | 129 | 308–310 | 310–311 | 308–309 | 375–380 | 369–373 | 381–386 | 92 |
| 91 | 193–195 | 194–196 | 194–195 | 186–187 | 186–187 | 186–188 | 128 | 128–129 | 127–128 | 306–307 | 308–309 | 306–307 | 370–374 | 365–368 | 376–380 | 91 |
| 90 | 190–192 | 191–193 | 191–193 | 183–185 | 184–185 | 184–185 | 126–127 | 127 | 126 | 304–305 | 306–307 | 304–305 | 365–369 | 361–364 | 371–375 | 90 |
| 89 | 187–189 | 187–190 | 188–190 | 181–182 | 182–183 | 182–183 | 125 | 125–126 | 124–125 | 302–303 | 304–305 | 302–303 | 361–364 | 357–360 | 367–370 | 89 |
| 88 | 185–186 | 184–186 | 186–187 | 179–180 | 180–181 | 179–181 | 124 | 124 | 123 | 300–301 | 302–303 | 300–301 | 356–360 | 353–356 | 363–366 | 88 |
| 87 | 182–184 | 182–183 | 184–185 | 177–178 | 178–179 | 177–178 | 122–123 | 122–123 | 122 | 299 | 301 | 298–299 | 353–355 | 350–352 | 359–362 | 87 |
| 86 | 180–181 | 179–181 | 182–183 | 175–176 | 177 | 176 | 121 | 121 | 121 | 297–298 | 299–300 | 297 | 349–352 | 347–349 | 355–358 | 86 |
| 85 | 178–179 | 177–178 | 180–181 | 174 | 175–176 | 174–175 | 120 | 120 | 120 | 295–296 | 297–298 | 295–296 | 345–348 | 344–346 | 352–354 | 85 |
| 84 | 176–177 | 175–176 | 178–179 | 172–173 | 173–174 | 172–173 | 119 | 119 | 119 | 294 | 296 | 294 | 342–344 | 341–343 | 348–351 | 84 |
| 83 | 174–175 | 172–174 | 176–177 | 171 | 172 | 171 | 118 | 118 | 118 | 292–293 | 294–295 | 292–293 | 339–341 | 339–340 | 345–347 | 83 |
| 82 | 172–173 | 170–171 | 174–175 | 169–170 | 171 | 169–170 | 117 | 117 | 117 | 291 | 293 | 291 | 336–338 | 336–338 | 342–344 | 82 |
| 81 | 170–171 | 169 | 173 | 168 | 169–170 | 168 | 116 | 116 | 116 | 289–290 | 291–292 | 289–290 | 334–335 | 334–335 | 339–341 | 81 |
| 80 | 169 | 167–168 | 171–172 | 167 | 168 | 166–167 | 115 | 115 | 115 | 288 | 290 | 288 | 331–333 | 332–333 | 337–338 | 80 |
| 79 | 167–168 | 165–166 | 170 | 166 | 167 | 165 | – | 114 | 114 | 287 | 288–289 | 287 | 329–330 | 329–331 | 334–336 | 79 |
| 78 | 166 | 164 | 168–169 | 164–165 | 166 | 164 | 114 | 113 | – | 285–286 | 287 | 285–286 | 326–328 | 327–328 | 332–333 | 78 |
| 77 | 164–165 | 162–163 | 167 | 163 | 164–165 | 163 | 113 | – | 113 | 284 | 286 | 284 | 324–325 | 325–326 | 329–331 | 77 |
| 76 | 163 | 161 | 166 | 162 | 163 | 162 | 112 | 112 | 112 | 283 | 284–285 | 283 | 322–323 | 323–324 | 327–328 | 76 |
| 75 | 162 | 159–160 | 164–165 | 161 | 162 | 160–161 | 111 | 111 | 111 | 281–282 | 283 | 281–282 | 320–321 | 322 | 324–326 | 75 |
| 74 | 161 | 158 | 163 | 160 | 161 | 159 | – | 110 | – | 280 | 282 | 280 | 318–319 | 320–321 | 322–323 | 74 |
| 73 | 159–160 | 157 | 162 | 159 | 160 | 158 | 110 | 109 | 110 | 279 | 280–281 | 279 | 316–317 | 318–319 | 320–321 | 73 |
| 72 | 158 | 155–156 | 161 | 158 | 159 | 157 | 109 | – | 109 | 278 | 279 | 278 | 314–315 | 317 | 318–319 | 72 |
| 71 | 157 | 154 | 160 | 157 | 158 | – | – | 108 | – | 276–277 | 278 | 276–277 | 312–313 | 315–316 | 316–317 | 71 |
| 70 | 156 | 153 | 158–159 | 156 | 157 | 156 | 108 | 107 | 108 | 275 | 276–277 | 275 | 311 | 313–314 | 314–315 | 70 |
| 69 | 155 | 152 | 157 | – | – | 155 | 107 | – | 107 | 274 | 275 | 274 | 309–310 | 312 | 312–313 | 69 |
| 68 | 154 | 151 | 156 | 155 | 156 | 154 | 106 | 106 | – | 273 | 274 | 273 | 307–308 | 310–311 | 311 | 68 |
| 67 | 153 | 150 | 155 | 154 | 155 | 153 | – | 105 | 106 | 272 | 273 | 272 | 306 | 309 | 309–310 | 67 |
| 66 | 152 | – | 154 | 153 | 154 | 152 | 105 | – | – | 270–271 | 271–272 | 271 | 304–305 | 308 | 307–308 | 66 |
| 65 | 151 | 149 | 153 | 152 | 153 | – | 104 | 104 | 105 | 269 | 270 | 269–270 | 303 | 306–307 | 305–306 | 65 |
| 64 | 150 | 148 | 152 | – | – | 151 | – | 103 | 104 | 268 | 269 | 268 | 301–302 | 305 | 304 | 64 |
| 63 | – | 147 | – | 151 | 152 | 150 | 103 | – | – | 267 | 268 | 267 | 300 | 304 | 302–303 | 63 |
| 62 | 149 | 146 | 151 | 150 | 151 | 149 | – | 102 | 103 | 266 | 266–267 | 266 | 299 | 302–303 | 301 | 62 |
| 61 | 148 | – | 150 | – | 150 | – | 102 | – | – | 265 | 265 | 265 | 297–298 | 301 | 299–300 | 61 |
| 60 | 147 | 145 | 149 | 149 | 149 | 148 | – | 101 | 102 | 264 | 264 | 264 | 296 | 300 | 298 | 60 |
| 59 | 146 | 144 | 148 | 148 | – | – | 101 | – | – | 262–263 | 263 | 263 | 295 | 299 | 296–297 | 59 |
| 58 | – | – | 147 | – | 148 | 147 | – | 100 | 101 | 261 | 261–262 | 261–262 | 294 | 298 | 295 | 58 |
| 57 | 145 | 143 | – | 147 | – | 146 | 100 | – | – | 260 | 260 | 260 | 292–293 | 296–297 | 294 | 57 |
| 56 | 144 | – | 146 | 146 | 147 | – | – | 99 | 100 | 259 | 259 | 259 | 291 | 295 | 292–293 | 56 |
| 55 | – | 142 | 145 | – | 146 | 145 | 99 | – | – | 258 | 258 | 258 | 290 | 294 | 291 | 55 |
| 54 | 143 | 141 | 144 | 145 | – | – | – | 98 | 99 | 257 | 257 | 257 | 289 | 293 | 290 | 54 |
| 53 | – | – | – | – | 145 | 144 | 98 | – | – | 256 | 255–256 | 256 | 288 | 292 | 289 | 53 |
| 52 | 142 | 140 | 143 | 144 | – | – | – | 97 | 98 | 254–255 | 254 | 255 | 287 | 291 | 287–288 | 52 |
| 51 | 141 | – | 142 | – | 144 | 143 | 97 | – | – | 253 | 253 | 253–254 | 286 | 290 | 286 | 51 |

## Table A.4e TRS-C Composite Percentiles (continued)

| %ile | Externalizing Problems Combined | Externalizing Problems Female | Externalizing Problems Male | Internalizing Problems Combined | Internalizing Problems Female | Internalizing Problems Male | School Problems Combined | School Problems Female | School Problems Male | Adaptive Skills Combined | Adaptive Skills Female | Adaptive Skills Male | Behavioral Symptoms Index Combined | Behavioral Symptoms Index Female | Behavioral Symptoms Index Male | %ile |
|---|---|---|---|---|---|---|---|---|---|---|---|---|---|---|---|---|
| 50 | – | – | – | 143 | 143 | – | – | 96 | 97 | 252 | 252 | 252 | 285 | 289 | 285 | 50 |
| 49 | 140 | 139 | 141 | – | – | 142 | 96 | – | – | 251 | 250–251 | 251 | 284 | 288 | 284 | 49 |
| 48 | – | 138 | 140 | 142 | 142 | – | – | 95 | 96 | 250 | 249 | 250 | 283 | 287 | 283 | 48 |
| 47 | 139 | – | – | – | – | 141 | 95 | – | – | 249 | 248 | 249 | 282 | 286 | 282 | 47 |
| 46 | – | – | 139 | 141 | 141 | – | – | 94 | 95 | 248 | 247 | 248 | 281 | 285 | 281 | 46 |
| 45 | 138 | – | 138 | – | – | 140 | 94 | 93 | – | 246–247 | 245–246 | 247 | 280 | 284 | 280 | 45 |
| 44 | 137 | 137 | – | 140 | 140 | – | – | – | 94 | 245 | 244 | 245–246 | 279 | 283 | 279 | 44 |
| 43 | – | – | 137 | – | – | 139 | 93 | 92 | – | 244 | 243 | 244 | 278 | – | 278 | 43 |
| 42 | – | – | – | 139 | 139 | – | – | – | 93 | 243 | 242 | 243 | 277 | 282 | 277 | 42 |
| 41 | 136 | 136 | 136 | – | – | – | – | – | – | 242 | 240–241 | 242 | – | 281 | 276 | 41 |
| 40 | – | – | – | 138 | 138 | 138 | 92 | – | – | 240–241 | 239 | 241 | 276 | 280 | 275 | 40 |
| 39 | 135 | – | 135 | – | – | – | – | 91 | 92 | 239 | 238 | 239–240 | 275 | 279 | 274 | 39 |
| 38 | 134 | 135 | 134 | 137 | 137 | 137 | 91 | – | – | 238 | 237 | 238 | 274 | 278 | 273 | 38 |
| 37 | – | – | – | – | – | – | – | 90 | 91 | 237 | 235–236 | 237 | 273 | 277 | 272 | 37 |
| 36 | – | – | 133 | – | – | – | – | – | – | 235–236 | 234 | 236 | – | – | 271 | 36 |
| 35 | – | – | – | 136 | 136 | 136 | 90 | – | 90 | 234 | 233 | 234–235 | 272 | 276 | 270 | 35 |
| 34 | 133 | 134 | 132 | – | – | – | – | 89 | – | 233 | 231–232 | 233 | 271 | 275 | – | 34 |
| 33 | – | – | – | – | 135 | 135 | 89 | – | 89 | 232 | 230 | 232 | 270 | 274 | 269 | 33 |
| 32 | 132 | – | 131 | 135 | – | – | – | 88 | – | 230–231 | 229 | 230–231 | – | 273 | 268 | 32 |
| 31 | – | – | – | – | – | – | 88 | – | – | 229 | 227–228 | 229 | 269 | 272 | 267 | 31 |
| 30 | – | 133 | 130 | 134 | 134 | 134 | – | – | 88 | 228 | 226 | 228 | 268 | – | 266 | 30 |
| 29 | 131 | – | – | – | – | – | 87 | 87 | 87 | 226–227 | 224–225 | 226–227 | 267 | 271 | – | 29 |
| 28 | – | – | 129 | 133 | 133 | – | – | – | 87 | 225 | 223 | 225 | – | 270 | 265 | 28 |
| 27 | – | – | – | – | – | 133 | – | – | – | 223–224 | 221–222 | 223–224 | 266 | 269 | 264 | 27 |
| 26 | 130 | – | – | – | 132 | – | 86 | 86 | 86 | 222 | 220 | 222 | 265 | – | 263 | 26 |
| 25 | – | 132 | 128 | 132 | – | – | 85 | 85 | – | 220–221 | 218–219 | 220–221 | – | 268 | – | 25 |
| 24 | – | – | – | – | – | 132 | – | – | 85 | 219 | 217 | 219 | 264 | 267 | 262 | 24 |
| 23 | 129 | – | 127 | – | 131 | – | – | – | – | 217–218 | 215–216 | 217–218 | 263 | 266 | 261 | 23 |
| 22 | – | – | – | – | – | – | – | – | – | 215–216 | 214 | 216 | – | 265 | 260 | 22 |
| 21 | – | – | 126 | 131 | 130 | – | 84 | 84 | 84 | 214 | 212–213 | 214–215 | 262 | – | – | 21 |
| 20 | 128 | – | – | – | – | 131 | – | – | – | 212–213 | 210–211 | 212–213 | 261 | 264 | 259 | 20 |
| 19 | – | 131 | – | – | – | – | 83 | 83 | 83 | 210–211 | 209 | 210–211 | – | 263 | 258 | 19 |
| 18 | – | – | 125 | 130 | 129 | – | – | – | – | 208–209 | 207–208 | 208–209 | 260 | 262 | – | 18 |
| 17 | 127 | – | – | – | – | 130 | 82 | – | 82 | 207 | 205–206 | 207 | 259 | – | 257 | 17 |
| 16 | – | – | 124 | – | – | – | – | 82 | – | 205–206 | 203–204 | 205–206 | – | 261 | 256 | 16 |
| 15 | – | – | – | 129 | 128 | – | 81 | – | 81 | 203–204 | 201–202 | 203–204 | 258 | 260 | – | 15 |
| 14 | – | – | – | – | – | – | – | 81 | – | 200–201 | 199–200 | 200–202 | 257 | 259 | 255 | 14 |
| 13 | – | – | 123 | – | – | 129 | – | – | 80 | 198–199 | 197–198 | 198–199 | – | 258 | 254 | 13 |
| 12 | – | – | – | 128 | 127 | – | – | – | – | 196–197 | 195–196 | 196–197 | 256 | – | – | 12 |
| 11 | – | – | 122 | – | – | – | 80 | 80 | 79 | 193–195 | 193–194 | 193–195 | 255 | 257 | 253 | 11 |
| 10 | – | – | – | – | 126 | 128 | 79 | – | – | 190–192 | 190–192 | 190–192 | – | 256 | 252 | 10 |
| 9 | – | – | – | 127 | – | – | – | – | – | 187–189 | 188–189 | 188–189 | 254 | 255 | – | 9 |
| 8 | – | – | – | – | – | – | 78 | 79 | 78 | 184–186 | 185–187 | 184–187 | 253 | 254 | 251 | 8 |
| 7 | – | – | – | 126 | 125 | – | – | – | 77 | 181–183 | 182–184 | 181–183 | – | 253 | 250 | 7 |
| 6 | – | – | – | – | – | 127 | 77 | 78 | 76 | 177–180 | 179–181 | 177–180 | 252 | 252 | 249 | 6 |
| 5 | – | – | – | – | 124 | – | – | 77 | – | 172–176 | 175–178 | 173–176 | 251 | 251 | 248 | 5 |
| 4 | – | – | – | 125 | – | – | 76 | – | 75 | 167–171 | 171–174 | 167–172 | 250 | – | – | 4 |
| 3 | – | – | – | – | – | 126 | 75 | – | 74 | 160–166 | 166–170 | 161–166 | 248–249 | – | 247 | 3 |
| 2 | – | – | – | 124 | 123 | – | – | – | 73 | 151–159 | 160–165 | 152–160 | 247 | – | 246 | 2 |
| 1 | – | – | – | – | – | 125 | – | – | 72 | 98–150 | 76–159 | 112–151 | – | – | 241–245 | 1 |

## Table A.5a TRS-A T Scores and Percentiles

| Raw score | Hyperactivity | | Aggression | | Conduct Problems | | Anxiety | | Depression | | Somatization | | Attention Problems | | Learning Problems | | Atypicality | | Withdrawal | | Adaptability | | Social Skills | | Leadership | | Study Skills | | Functional Communication | | Raw score |
|---|---|---|---|---|---|---|---|---|---|---|---|---|---|---|---|---|---|---|---|---|---|---|---|---|---|---|---|---|---|---|---|
| | T | %ile | T | %ile | T | %ile | T | %ile | T | %ile | T | %ile | T | %ile | T | %ile | T | %ile | T | %ile | T | %ile | T | %ile | T | %ile | T | %ile | T | %ile | |
| 36 | — | — | — | — | — | — | — | — | 120 | 99 | — | — | — | — | — | — | — | — | — | — | — | — | — | — | — | — | — | — | — | — | 36 |
| 35 | — | — | — | — | — | — | — | — | 120 | 99 | — | — | — | — | — | — | — | — | — | — | — | — | — | — | — | — | — | — | — | — | 35 |
| 34 | — | — | — | — | — | — | — | — | 120 | 99 | — | — | — | — | — | — | — | — | — | — | — | — | — | — | — | — | — | — | — | — | 34 |
| 33 | 100 | 99 | 120 | 99 | — | — | — | — | 120 | 99 | — | — | — | — | — | — | — | — | — | — | — | — | — | — | — | — | 65 | 97 | — | — | 33 |
| 32 | 99 | 99 | 117 | 99 | — | — | — | — | 120 | 99 | — | — | — | — | — | — | — | — | — | — | — | — | — | — | — | — | 64 | 93 | — | — | 32 |
| 31 | 97 | 99 | 115 | 99 | — | — | — | — | 120 | 99 | — | — | — | — | — | — | — | — | — | — | — | — | — | — | — | — | 63 | 88 | — | — | 31 |
| 30 | 95 | 99 | 113 | 99 | 120 | 99 | — | — | 120 | 99 | — | — | 83 | 99 | — | — | 120 | 99 | — | — | — | — | 68 | 98 | — | — | 61 | 84 | — | — | 30 |
| 29 | 93 | 99 | 110 | 99 | 119 | 99 | — | — | 120 | 99 | — | — | 81 | 99 | — | — | 120 | 99 | — | — | — | — | 67 | 96 | — | — | 60 | 80 | — | — | 29 |
| 28 | 91 | 99 | 108 | 99 | 116 | 99 | — | — | 120 | 99 | — | — | 80 | 99 | — | — | 120 | 99 | — | — | — | — | 65 | 94 | — | — | 59 | 76 | — | — | 28 |
| 27 | 90 | 99 | 106 | 99 | 113 | 99 | 113 | 99 | 120 | 99 | — | — | 78 | 99 | — | — | 120 | 99 | — | — | — | — | 64 | 91 | — | — | 58 | 71 | 65 | 96 | 27 |
| 26 | 88 | 99 | 103 | 99 | 111 | 99 | 111 | 99 | 118 | 99 | — | — | 77 | 99 | — | — | 120 | 99 | — | — | — | — | 62 | 88 | — | — | 56 | 67 | 63 | 92 | 26 |
| 25 | 86 | 99 | 101 | 99 | 108 | 99 | 108 | 99 | 115 | 99 | — | — | 75 | 99 | — | — | 118 | 99 | — | — | — | — | 61 | 84 | — | — | 55 | 63 | 61 | 86 | 25 |
| 24 | 84 | 99 | 99 | 99 | 106 | 99 | 105 | 99 | 112 | 99 | — | — | 73 | 99 | 95 | 99 | 115 | 99 | 104 | 99 | 65 | 96 | 60 | 80 | — | — | 54 | 59 | 59 | 80 | 24 |
| 23 | 82 | 99 | 96 | 99 | 103 | 99 | 102 | 99 | 109 | 99 | — | — | 72 | 98 | 93 | 99 | 112 | 99 | 101 | 99 | 63 | 91 | 58 | 76 | — | — | 53 | 56 | 57 | 73 | 23 |
| 22 | 81 | 98 | 94 | 99 | 100 | 99 | 100 | 99 | 106 | 99 | — | — | 70 | 97 | 90 | 99 | 109 | 99 | 99 | 99 | 61 | 84 | 57 | 72 | — | — | 52 | 52 | 55 | 66 | 22 |
| 21 | 79 | 98 | 92 | 99 | 98 | 99 | 97 | 99 | 103 | 99 | 120 | 99 | 69 | 95 | 88 | 99 | 106 | 99 | 96 | 99 | 59 | 77 | 56 | 68 | 70 | 99 | 50 | 48 | 53 | 59 | 21 |
| 20 | 77 | 97 | 89 | 99 | 95 | 99 | 94 | 99 | 100 | 99 | 120 | 99 | 67 | 94 | 85 | 99 | 103 | 99 | 93 | 99 | 57 | 70 | 54 | 63 | 68 | 97 | 49 | 45 | 51 | 52 | 20 |
| 19 | 75 | 97 | 87 | 99 | 93 | 99 | 91 | 99 | 97 | 99 | 117 | 99 | 66 | 92 | 83 | 99 | 100 | 99 | 91 | 99 | 55 | 63 | 53 | 59 | 66 | 95 | 48 | 41 | 49 | 45 | 19 |
| 18 | 73 | 96 | 85 | 98 | 90 | 99 | 89 | 99 | 94 | 99 | 113 | 99 | 64 | 89 | 81 | 99 | 97 | 99 | 88 | 99 | 53 | 56 | 51 | 54 | 64 | 92 | 47 | 38 | 47 | 38 | 18 |
| 17 | 72 | 96 | 82 | 98 | 87 | 99 | 86 | 99 | 91 | 99 | 110 | 99 | 63 | 87 | 78 | 99 | 94 | 99 | 85 | 99 | 50 | 49 | 50 | 49 | 62 | 87 | 45 | 34 | 46 | 32 | 17 |
| 16 | 70 | 95 | 80 | 98 | 85 | 99 | 83 | 99 | 89 | 99 | 106 | 99 | 61 | 84 | 76 | 98 | 91 | 99 | 83 | 99 | 48 | 42 | 49 | 45 | 60 | 82 | 44 | 31 | 44 | 27 | 16 |
| 15 | 68 | 94 | 78 | 97 | 82 | 98 | 80 | 99 | 86 | 99 | 102 | 99 | 60 | 81 | 74 | 97 | 88 | 99 | 80 | 98 | 46 | 36 | 47 | 40 | 58 | 76 | 43 | 28 | 42 | 22 | 15 |
| 14 | 66 | 93 | 75 | 97 | 79 | 98 | 78 | 99 | 83 | 99 | 98 | 99 | 58 | 77 | 71 | 96 | 85 | 99 | 77 | 98 | 44 | 30 | 46 | 36 | 56 | 70 | 42 | 25 | 40 | 17 | 14 |
| 13 | 65 | 91 | 73 | 96 | 77 | 97 | 75 | 98 | 80 | 98 | 94 | 99 | 57 | 74 | 69 | 94 | 82 | 98 | 75 | 97 | 42 | 24 | 44 | 32 | 54 | 64 | 41 | 22 | 38 | 13 | 13 |
| 12 | 63 | 90 | 71 | 95 | 74 | 96 | 72 | 97 | 77 | 98 | 90 | 99 | 55 | 70 | 67 | 92 | 79 | 98 | 72 | 96 | 40 | 19 | 43 | 27 | 52 | 57 | 39 | 19 | 36 | 10 | 12 |
| 11 | 61 | 88 | 68 | 94 | 72 | 95 | 69 | 95 | 74 | 97 | 87 | 99 | 53 | 65 | 64 | 90 | 77 | 97 | 69 | 94 | 38 | 14 | 42 | 23 | 50 | 50 | 38 | 16 | 34 | 7 | 11 |
| 10 | 59 | 85 | 66 | 92 | 69 | 93 | 67 | 93 | 71 | 95 | 83 | 98 | 52 | 61 | 62 | 87 | 74 | 96 | 67 | 93 | 36 | 10 | 40 | 20 | 48 | 43 | 37 | 13 | 32 | 4 | 10 |
| 9 | 57 | 82 | 64 | 90 | 66 | 92 | 64 | 90 | 68 | 93 | 79 | 97 | 50 | 56 | 60 | 83 | 71 | 95 | 64 | 90 | 34 | 6 | 39 | 16 | 46 | 36 | 36 | 10 | 30 | 3 | 9 |
| 8 | 56 | 79 | 62 | 88 | 64 | 90 | 61 | 86 | 65 | 91 | 75 | 96 | 49 | 51 | 57 | 79 | 68 | 94 | 61 | 87 | 31 | 3 | 38 | 13 | 44 | 29 | 35 | 8 | 28 | 1 | 8 |
| 7 | 54 | 75 | 59 | 86 | 61 | 87 | 58 | 81 | 62 | 88 | 71 | 95 | 47 | 46 | 55 | 74 | 65 | 92 | 59 | 84 | 29 | 1 | 36 | 10 | 42 | 23 | 33 | 6 | 26 | 1 | 7 |
| 6 | 52 | 70 | 57 | 82 | 59 | 84 | 56 | 75 | 59 | 84 | 67 | 93 | 46 | 41 | 53 | 68 | 62 | 90 | 56 | 79 | 27 | 1 | 35 | 7 | 40 | 18 | 32 | 3 | 24 | 1 | 6 |
| 5 | 50 | 63 | 55 | 78 | 56 | 80 | 53 | 68 | 56 | 79 | 64 | 91 | 44 | 35 | 50 | 60 | 59 | 86 | 53 | 73 | 25 | 1 | 33 | 5 | 38 | 13 | 31 | 2 | 22 | 1 | 5 |
| 4 | 48 | 56 | 52 | 73 | 53 | 75 | 50 | 59 | 53 | 72 | 60 | 88 | 43 | 29 | 48 | 52 | 56 | 81 | 51 | 64 | 23 | 1 | 32 | 3 | 36 | 9 | 30 | 1 | 20 | 1 | 4 |
| 3 | 47 | 47 | 50 | 66 | 51 | 68 | 47 | 48 | 50 | 63 | 56 | 84 | 41 | 23 | 46 | 43 | 53 | 74 | 48 | 54 | 21 | 1 | 31 | 2 | 34 | 5 | 28 | 1 | 18 | 1 | 3 |
| 2 | 45 | 37 | 48 | 56 | 48 | 59 | 45 | 36 | 47 | 51 | 52 | 76 | 40 | 16 | 43 | 32 | 50 | 64 | 45 | 40 | 19 | 1 | 29 | 1 | 32 | 3 | 27 | 1 | 16 | 1 | 2 |
| 1 | 43 | 25 | 45 | 43 | 46 | 46 | 42 | 23 | 44 | 36 | 48 | 63 | 38 | 10 | 41 | 20 | 47 | 49 | 42 | 23 | 17 | 1 | 28 | 1 | 30 | 1 | 26 | 1 | 14 | 1 | 1 |
| 0 | 41 | 13 | 43 | 24 | 43 | 25 | 39 | 11 | 41 | 18 | 44 | 32 | 37 | 5 | 39 | 8 | 44 | 27 | 40 | 5 | 14 | 1 | 27 | 1 | 28 | 1 | 25 | 1 | 12 | 1 | 0 |
| Raw mean | 4.90 | | 3.04 | | 2.72 | | 3.92 | | 2.91 | | 1.45 | | 8.77 | | 4.81 | | 2.09 | | 3.81 | | 16.77 | | 17.00 | | 11.00 | | 20.71 | | 19.27 | | Raw mean |
| Raw SD | 5.58 | | 4.31 | | 3.83 | | 3.64 | | 3.40 | | 2.61 | | 6.50 | | 4.28 | | 3.36 | | 3.73 | | 4.72 | | 7.27 | | 4.95 | | 8.21 | | 5.05 | | Raw SD |
| T: 90% Conf. int. | 4 | | 5 | | 5 | | 6 | | 7 | | 5 | | 4 | | 6 | | 6 | | 6 | | 5 | | 4 | | 5 | | 4 | | 6 | | T: 90% Conf. int. |

## Table A.5b TRS-A T Scores and Percentiles

| Raw score | Hyperactivity T | Hyperactivity %ile | Aggression T | Aggression %ile | Conduct Problems T | Conduct Problems %ile | Anxiety T | Anxiety %ile | Depression T | Depression %ile | Somatization T | Somatization %ile | Attention Problems T | Attention Problems %ile | Learning Problems T | Learning Problems %ile | Atypicality T | Atypicality %ile | Withdrawal T | Withdrawal %ile | Adaptability T | Adaptability %ile | Social Skills T | Social Skills %ile | Leadership T | Leadership %ile | Study Skills T | Study Skills %ile | Functional Communication T | Functional Communication %ile | Raw score |
|---|---|---|---|---|---|---|---|---|---|---|---|---|---|---|---|---|---|---|---|---|---|---|---|---|---|---|---|---|---|---|---|
| 36 | — | — | — | — | — | — | — | — | 120 | 99 | — | — | — | — | — | — | — | — | — | — | — | — | — | — | — | — | — | — | — | — | 36 |
| 35 | — | — | — | — | — | — | — | — | 120 | 99 | — | — | — | — | — | — | — | — | — | — | — | — | — | — | — | — | — | — | — | — | 35 |
| 34 | — | — | — | — | — | — | — | — | 120 | 99 | — | — | — | — | — | — | — | — | — | — | — | — | — | — | — | — | — | — | — | — | 34 |
| 33 | 117 | 99 | 120 | 99 | — | — | — | — | 120 | 99 | — | — | — | — | — | — | — | — | — | — | — | — | — | — | — | — | 64 | 95 | — | — | 33 |
| 32 | 115 | 99 | 120 | 99 | — | — | — | — | 120 | 99 | — | — | — | — | — | — | — | — | — | — | — | — | — | — | — | — | 63 | 91 | — | — | 32 |
| 31 | 113 | 99 | 120 | 99 | — | — | — | — | 120 | 99 | — | — | — | — | — | — | — | — | — | — | — | — | — | — | — | — | 61 | 86 | — | — | 31 |
| 30 | 110 | 99 | 120 | 99 | 120 | 99 | — | — | 120 | 99 | — | — | 92 | 99 | — | — | 120 | 99 | — | — | — | — | 66 | 97 | — | — | 60 | 82 | — | — | 30 |
| 29 | 108 | 99 | 120 | 99 | 120 | 99 | — | — | 120 | 99 | — | — | 90 | 99 | — | — | 120 | 99 | — | — | — | — | 65 | 94 | — | — | 59 | 77 | — | — | 29 |
| 28 | 106 | 99 | 120 | 99 | 120 | 99 | — | — | 120 | 99 | — | — | 88 | 99 | — | — | 120 | 99 | — | — | — | — | 63 | 91 | — | — | 57 | 72 | — | — | 28 |
| 27 | 104 | 99 | 120 | 99 | 120 | 99 | 111 | 99 | 119 | 99 | — | — | 86 | 99 | — | — | 120 | 99 | — | — | — | — | 62 | 87 | — | — | 56 | 66 | 64 | 94 | 27 |
| 26 | 101 | 99 | 120 | 99 | 120 | 99 | 108 | 99 | 116 | 99 | — | — | 85 | 99 | — | — | 120 | 99 | — | — | — | — | 61 | 83 | — | — | 55 | 62 | 62 | 89 | 26 |
| 25 | 99 | 99 | 118 | 99 | 120 | 99 | 106 | 99 | 113 | 99 | — | — | 83 | 99 | — | — | 120 | 99 | — | — | — | — | 59 | 78 | — | — | 53 | 57 | 60 | 83 | 25 |
| 24 | 97 | 99 | 115 | 99 | 118 | 99 | 103 | 99 | 110 | 99 | — | — | 81 | 99 | 100 | 99 | 120 | 99 | 104 | 99 | 65 | 96 | 58 | 74 | — | — | 52 | 52 | 58 | 76 | 24 |
| 23 | 94 | 99 | 112 | 99 | 115 | 99 | 100 | 99 | 108 | 99 | — | — | 79 | 99 | 98 | 99 | 120 | 99 | 102 | 99 | 63 | 91 | 56 | 69 | — | — | 50 | 47 | 56 | 69 | 23 |
| 22 | 92 | 99 | 109 | 99 | 112 | 99 | 98 | 99 | 105 | 99 | 119 | 99 | 77 | 99 | 95 | 99 | 120 | 99 | 99 | 99 | 61 | 84 | 55 | 64 | — | — | 49 | 43 | 54 | 61 | 22 |
| 21 | 90 | 99 | 106 | 99 | 109 | 99 | 95 | 99 | 102 | 99 | 115 | 99 | 75 | 99 | 93 | 99 | 117 | 99 | 97 | 99 | 58 | 77 | 53 | 59 | 69 | 99 | 48 | 39 | 52 | 54 | 21 |
| 20 | 87 | 99 | 103 | 99 | 106 | 99 | 92 | 99 | 99 | 99 | 112 | 99 | 74 | 99 | 90 | 99 | 113 | 99 | 94 | 99 | 56 | 68 | 52 | 55 | 67 | 97 | 46 | 35 | 50 | 46 | 20 |
| 19 | 85 | 99 | 100 | 99 | 103 | 99 | 90 | 99 | 96 | 99 | 108 | 99 | 72 | 98 | 87 | 99 | 110 | 99 | 91 | 99 | 53 | 60 | 50 | 50 | 65 | 94 | 45 | 31 | 48 | 40 | 19 |
| 18 | 83 | 99 | 97 | 99 | 100 | 99 | 87 | 99 | 93 | 99 | 105 | 99 | 70 | 96 | 85 | 99 | 106 | 99 | 89 | 99 | 51 | 51 | 49 | 45 | 63 | 90 | 44 | 27 | 46 | 33 | 18 |
| 17 | 81 | 98 | 94 | 99 | 97 | 99 | 84 | 99 | 90 | 99 | 101 | 99 | 68 | 94 | 82 | 99 | 103 | 99 | 86 | 99 | 49 | 43 | 48 | 40 | 61 | 85 | 42 | 24 | 44 | 27 | 17 |
| 16 | 78 | 98 | 91 | 99 | 93 | 99 | 82 | 99 | 88 | 99 | 98 | 99 | 66 | 92 | 80 | 99 | 99 | 99 | 83 | 99 | 46 | 36 | 46 | 36 | 59 | 78 | 41 | 20 | 42 | 22 | 16 |
| 15 | 76 | 97 | 88 | 99 | 90 | 99 | 79 | 99 | 85 | 99 | 94 | 99 | 64 | 90 | 77 | 99 | 96 | 99 | 81 | 98 | 44 | 28 | 45 | 31 | 56 | 72 | 39 | 17 | 40 | 18 | 15 |
| 14 | 74 | 96 | 85 | 99 | 87 | 99 | 76 | 99 | 82 | 99 | 90 | 99 | 63 | 87 | 75 | 98 | 92 | 99 | 78 | 98 | 42 | 22 | 43 | 27 | 54 | 64 | 38 | 14 | 38 | 14 | 14 |
| 13 | 71 | 95 | 82 | 99 | 84 | 99 | 73 | 99 | 79 | 98 | 87 | 99 | 61 | 83 | 72 | 96 | 89 | 99 | 75 | 97 | 39 | 17 | 42 | 23 | 52 | 56 | 37 | 12 | 36 | 11 | 13 |
| 12 | 69 | 94 | 79 | 99 | 81 | 99 | 71 | 98 | 76 | 97 | 83 | 99 | 59 | 79 | 70 | 95 | 86 | 99 | 73 | 97 | 37 | 12 | 40 | 20 | 50 | 49 | 35 | 10 | 34 | 8 | 12 |
| 11 | 67 | 92 | 76 | 99 | 78 | 99 | 68 | 97 | 73 | 96 | 80 | 99 | 57 | 75 | 67 | 92 | 82 | 98 | 70 | 96 | 35 | 8 | 39 | 16 | 48 | 41 | 34 | 7 | 32 | 6 | 11 |
| 10 | 65 | 90 | 73 | 95 | 75 | 96 | 65 | 90 | 70 | 95 | 76 | 98 | 55 | 71 | 65 | 90 | 79 | 97 | 67 | 95 | 32 | 5 | 38 | 13 | 46 | 34 | 32 | 6 | 30 | 4 | 10 |
| 9 | 62 | 88 | 70 | 93 | 72 | 94 | 63 | 87 | 68 | 93 | 73 | 96 | 53 | 66 | 62 | 86 | 75 | 96 | 65 | 93 | 30 | 3 | 36 | 10 | 44 | 27 | 31 | 4 | 28 | 3 | 9 |
| 8 | 60 | 85 | 67 | 91 | 69 | 93 | 60 | 82 | 65 | 91 | 69 | 94 | 52 | 60 | 60 | 82 | 72 | 94 | 62 | 91 | 28 | 1 | 35 | 8 | 42 | 21 | 30 | 3 | 26 | 2 | 8 |
| 7 | 58 | 81 | 64 | 89 | 66 | 91 | 57 | 77 | 62 | 88 | 66 | 93 | 50 | 54 | 57 | 78 | 68 | 93 | 59 | 89 | 25 | 1 | 33 | 5 | 40 | 16 | 28 | 2 | 24 | 1 | 7 |
| 6 | 55 | 77 | 61 | 86 | 63 | 88 | 55 | 70 | 59 | 84 | 62 | 91 | 48 | 48 | 54 | 72 | 65 | 91 | 57 | 86 | 23 | 1 | 32 | 3 | 37 | 12 | 27 | 1 | 22 | 1 | 6 |
| 5 | 53 | 72 | 58 | 82 | 59 | 85 | 52 | 63 | 56 | 79 | 59 | 88 | 46 | 42 | 52 | 65 | 61 | 88 | 54 | 82 | 21 | 1 | 30 | 2 | 35 | 8 | 26 | 1 | 20 | 1 | 5 |
| 4 | 51 | 66 | 55 | 77 | 56 | 81 | 49 | 55 | 53 | 72 | 55 | 84 | 44 | 35 | 49 | 57 | 58 | 85 | 51 | 77 | 18 | 1 | 29 | 1 | 33 | 5 | 24 | 1 | 18 | 1 | 4 |
| 3 | 48 | 58 | 52 | 71 | 53 | 76 | 46 | 45 | 50 | 64 | 52 | 78 | 42 | 28 | 47 | 47 | 55 | 81 | 49 | 70 | 16 | 1 | 28 | 1 | 31 | 3 | 23 | 1 | 16 | 1 | 3 |
| 2 | 46 | 48 | 49 | 63 | 50 | 69 | 44 | 34 | 48 | 52 | 48 | 66 | 41 | 20 | 44 | 36 | 51 | 74 | 46 | 60 | 14 | 1 | 26 | 1 | 29 | 2 | 21 | 1 | 14 | 1 | 2 |
| 1 | 44 | 35 | 46 | 50 | 47 | 57 | 41 | 22 | 45 | 38 | 45 | 31 | 39 | 13 | 42 | 23 | 48 | 62 | 43 | 46 | 11 | 1 | 25 | 1 | 27 | 1 | 20 | 1 | 13 | 1 | 1 |
| 0 | 42 | 18 | 43 | 28 | 44 | 34 | 38 | 9 | 42 | 20 | — | — | 37 | 7 | 39 | 10 | 44 | 31 | 41 | 26 | 10 | 1 | 23 | 1 | 25 | 1 | 19 | 1 | 11 | 1 | 0 |
| **Raw mean** | 3.66 | | 2.32 | | 1.96 | | 4.31 | | 2.84 | | 1.51 | | 7.11 | | 4.23 | | 1.69 | | 3.51 | | 17.51 | | 18.67 | | 11.95 | | 22.69 | | 19.93 | | **Raw mean** |
| **Raw SD** | 4.36 | | 3.33 | | 3.23 | | 3.71 | | 3.50 | | 2.84 | | 5.47 | | 3.94 | | 2.90 | | 3.76 | | 4.26 | | 6.97 | | 4.72 | | 7.24 | | 5.05 | | **Raw SD** |
| **T: 90% Conf. int.** | 5 | | 6 | | 5 | | 6 | | 7 | | 5 | | 5 | | 7 | | 7 | | 6 | | 6 | | 4 | | 5 | | 5 | | 6 | | **T: 90% Conf. int.** |

**Table A.5c** TRS–A *T* Scores and Percentiles

| Raw score | Hyperactivity T | Hyper. %ile | Aggression T | Aggr. %ile | Conduct Problems T | Conduct %ile | Anxiety T | Anxiety %ile | Depression T | Depr. %ile | Somatization T | Somat. %ile | Attention Problems T | Attn. %ile | Learning Problems T | Learn. %ile | Atypicality T | Atyp. %ile | Withdrawal T | With. %ile | Adaptability T | Adapt. %ile | Social Skills T | Social %ile | Leadership T | Lead. %ile | Study Skills T | Study %ile | Functional Communication T | Func. %ile | Raw score |
|---|---|---|---|---|---|---|---|---|---|---|---|---|---|---|---|---|---|---|---|---|---|---|---|---|---|---|---|---|---|---|---|
| 36 | — | — | — | — | — | — | — | — | 120 | 99 | — | — | — | — | — | — | — | — | — | — | — | — | — | — | — | — | — | — | — | — | 36 |
| 35 | — | — | — | — | — | — | — | — | **120** | **99** | — | — | — | — | — | — | — | — | — | — | — | — | — | — | — | — | — | — | — | — | 35 |
| 34 | — | — | — | — | — | — | — | — | **120** | **99** | — | — | — | — | — | — | — | — | — | — | — | — | — | — | — | — | — | — | — | — | 34 |
| 33 | 92 | 99 | 108 | 99 | — | — | — | — | 120 | 99 | — | — | — | — | — | — | — | — | — | — | — | — | — | — | — | — | 66 | 98 | — | — | 33 |
| 32 | 91 | 99 | 106 | 99 | — | — | — | — | 120 | 99 | — | — | — | — | — | — | — | — | — | — | — | — | — | — | — | — | 65 | 94 | — | — | 32 |
| 31 | 89 | 99 | 104 | 99 | — | — | — | — | 120 | 99 | — | — | — | — | — | — | — | — | — | — | — | — | — | — | — | — | 64 | 91 | — | — | 31 |
| 30 | 88 | 99 | 102 | 99 | 113 | 99 | — | — | 120 | 99 | — | — | 78 | 99 | — | — | 120 | 99 | — | — | — | — | 70 | 99 | — | — | 63 | 87 | — | — | 30 |
| 29 | 86 | 99 | 100 | 99 | 110 | 99 | — | — | 120 | 99 | — | — | 76 | 99 | — | — | 120 | 99 | — | — | — | — | 69 | 99 | — | — | 62 | 84 | — | — | 29 |
| 28 | 84 | 99 | 98 | 99 | 108 | 99 | — | — | 120 | 99 | — | — | 75 | 99 | — | — | 118 | 99 | — | — | — | — | 68 | 98 | — | — | 61 | 80 | — | — | 28 |
| 27 | 83 | 99 | 96 | 99 | 106 | 99 | 116 | 99 | 120 | 99 | — | — | 74 | 99 | — | — | 116 | 99 | — | — | — | — | 66 | 96 | — | — | 60 | 77 | 67 | 98 | 27 |
| 26 | 81 | 98 | 94 | 99 | 103 | 99 | 113 | 99 | 119 | 99 | — | — | 72 | 99 | — | — | 113 | 99 | — | — | — | — | 65 | 95 | — | — | 58 | 74 | 65 | 95 | 26 |
| 25 | 80 | 98 | 92 | 99 | 101 | 99 | 110 | 99 | 116 | 99 | — | — | 71 | 99 | — | — | 110 | 99 | — | — | — | — | 63 | 92 | — | — | 57 | 70 | 63 | 90 | 25 |
| 24 | 78 | 98 | 90 | 99 | 99 | 99 | 108 | 99 | 113 | 99 | — | — | 69 | 98 | 91 | 99 | 108 | 99 | 104 | 99 | 66 | 96 | 62 | 90 | — | — | 56 | 67 | 61 | 84 | 24 |
| 23 | 77 | 97 | 88 | 99 | 96 | 99 | 105 | 99 | 110 | 99 | — | — | 68 | 96 | 89 | 99 | 105 | 99 | 101 | 99 | 64 | 91 | 61 | 87 | — | — | 55 | 64 | 59 | 77 | 23 |
| 22 | 75 | 97 | 86 | 99 | 94 | 99 | 102 | 99 | 107 | 99 | — | — | 66 | 94 | 87 | 99 | 102 | 99 | 99 | 99 | 62 | 85 | 59 | 83 | — | — | 54 | 61 | 57 | 71 | 22 |
| 21 | 73 | 96 | 84 | 99 | 92 | 99 | 99 | 99 | 104 | 99 | — | — | 65 | 91 | 84 | 99 | 100 | 99 | 96 | 99 | 60 | 79 | 58 | 80 | — | — | 53 | 58 | 55 | 64 | 21 |
| 20 | 72 | 96 | 82 | 99 | 89 | 99 | 96 | 99 | 101 | 99 | 120 | 99 | 64 | 88 | 82 | 99 | 97 | 99 | 93 | 99 | 58 | 73 | 56 | 76 | 72 | 99 | 51 | 55 | 53 | 57 | 20 |
| 19 | 70 | 95 | 80 | 98 | 87 | 99 | 94 | 99 | 98 | 99 | 120 | 99 | 62 | 85 | 80 | 99 | 94 | 99 | 90 | 99 | 56 | 67 | 55 | 72 | 70 | 98 | 50 | 51 | 51 | 50 | 19 |
| 18 | 69 | 94 | 78 | 97 | 84 | 99 | 91 | 99 | 95 | 99 | 120 | 99 | 61 | 82 | 78 | 98 | 91 | 99 | 88 | 99 | 54 | 61 | 54 | 67 | 68 | 96 | 49 | 48 | 49 | 44 | 18 |
| 17 | 67 | 93 | 76 | 97 | 82 | 99 | 88 | 99 | 92 | 99 | 116 | 99 | 59 | 78 | 76 | 98 | 89 | 99 | 85 | 99 | 52 | 55 | 52 | 63 | 66 | 93 | 48 | 45 | 47 | 37 | 17 |
| 16 | 66 | 92 | 74 | 96 | 80 | 98 | 85 | 99 | 89 | 99 | 112 | 99 | 58 | 75 | 73 | 97 | 86 | 99 | 82 | 99 | 50 | 49 | 51 | 58 | 64 | 90 | 47 | 42 | 45 | 31 | 16 |
| 15 | 64 | 90 | 72 | 95 | 77 | 97 | 82 | 99 | 86 | 99 | 107 | 99 | 57 | 71 | 71 | 96 | 83 | 98 | 80 | 99 | 48 | 43 | 50 | 54 | 62 | 86 | 46 | 39 | 43 | 26 | 15 |
| 14 | 62 | 89 | 70 | 94 | 75 | 96 | 79 | 99 | 83 | 99 | 103 | 99 | 55 | 68 | 69 | 94 | 81 | 98 | 77 | 98 | 46 | 38 | 48 | 49 | 60 | 81 | 45 | 35 | 41 | 20 | 14 |
| 13 | 61 | 87 | 68 | 93 | 73 | 95 | 77 | 98 | 80 | 98 | 99 | 99 | 54 | 64 | 67 | 92 | 78 | 98 | 74 | 97 | 44 | 32 | 47 | 44 | 58 | 76 | 43 | 32 | 39 | 16 | 13 |
| 12 | 59 | 85 | 66 | 92 | 70 | 94 | 74 | 97 | 77 | 98 | 95 | 99 | 52 | 60 | 65 | 90 | 75 | 97 | 71 | 96 | 42 | 26 | 45 | 40 | 56 | 70 | 42 | 29 | 37 | 11 | 12 |
| 11 | 58 | 82 | 64 | 90 | 68 | 92 | 71 | 96 | 74 | 97 | 91 | 99 | 51 | 56 | 62 | 87 | 73 | 96 | 69 | 94 | 40 | 21 | 44 | 35 | 54 | 64 | 41 | 25 | 35 | 8 | 11 |
| 10 | 56 | 79 | 62 | 88 | 65 | 91 | 68 | 94 | 71 | 95 | 86 | 99 | 49 | 51 | 60 | 83 | 70 | 95 | 66 | 92 | 38 | 15 | 43 | 30 | 52 | 58 | 40 | 22 | 33 | 5 | 10 |
| 9 | 55 | 76 | 60 | 86 | 63 | 88 | 65 | 92 | 68 | 93 | 82 | 98 | 48 | 47 | 58 | 79 | 67 | 94 | 63 | 89 | 36 | 10 | 41 | 26 | 50 | 51 | 39 | 18 | 31 | 3 | 9 |
| 8 | 53 | 72 | 58 | 84 | 61 | 86 | 63 | 89 | 65 | 91 | 78 | 96 | 47 | 42 | 56 | 74 | 65 | 92 | 61 | 85 | 34 | 5 | 40 | 22 | 48 | 45 | 38 | 14 | 29 | 1 | 8 |
| 7 | 51 | 67 | 56 | 81 | 58 | 83 | 60 | 85 | 62 | 88 | 74 | 95 | 45 | 38 | 54 | 69 | 62 | 90 | 58 | 81 | 32 | 1 | 38 | 18 | 46 | 38 | 36 | 10 | 27 | 1 | 7 |
| 6 | 50 | 62 | 54 | 77 | 56 | 79 | 57 | 79 | 59 | 84 | 69 | 93 | 44 | 33 | 51 | 63 | 59 | 87 | 55 | 75 | 30 | 1 | 37 | 14 | 44 | 31 | 35 | 6 | 25 | 1 | 6 |
| 5 | 48 | 55 | 52 | 73 | 54 | 74 | 54 | 73 | 56 | 78 | 65 | 91 | 42 | 28 | 49 | 55 | 57 | 83 | 52 | 68 | 28 | 1 | 36 | 11 | 42 | 24 | 34 | 2 | 23 | 1 | 5 |
| 4 | 47 | 48 | 50 | 68 | 51 | 68 | 51 | 64 | 53 | 71 | 61 | 87 | 41 | 23 | 47 | 47 | 54 | 78 | 50 | 59 | 26 | 1 | 34 | 8 | 40 | 18 | 33 | 1 | 21 | 1 | 4 |
| 3 | 45 | 39 | 49 | 61 | 49 | 60 | 49 | 53 | 50 | 61 | 57 | 83 | 39 | 18 | 45 | 37 | 51 | 70 | 47 | 49 | 24 | 1 | 33 | 6 | 38 | 12 | 31 | 1 | 19 | 1 | 3 |
| 2 | 43 | 29 | 47 | 52 | 46 | 50 | 46 | 40 | 47 | 49 | 53 | 77 | 38 | 13 | 43 | 27 | 49 | 59 | 44 | 36 | 22 | 1 | 31 | 4 | 36 | 8 | 30 | 1 | 17 | 1 | 2 |
| 1 | 42 | 18 | 45 | 39 | 44 | 36 | 43 | 26 | 44 | 33 | 48 | 65 | 37 | 8 | 40 | 16 | 46 | 44 | 42 | 21 | 20 | 1 | 30 | 2 | 34 | 4 | 28 | 1 | 15 | 1 | 1 |
| 0 | 40 | 8 | 43 | 20 | 42 | 16 | 40 | 12 | 41 | 14 | 44 | 32 | 35 | 4 | 38 | 6 | 43 | 24 | 39 | 6 | 18 | 1 | 29 | 1 | 30 | 1 | — | — | 13 | 1 | 0 |
| **Raw mean** | 6.14 | | 3.75 | | 3.48 | | 3.53 | | 2.98 | | 1.39 | | 10.43 | | 5.39 | | 2.48 | | 4.12 | | 16.04 | | 15.33 | | 10.05 | | 18.73 | | 18.61 | | **Raw mean** |
| **Raw SD** | 6.35 | | 5.02 | | 4.22 | | 3.55 | | 3.32 | | 2.37 | | 7.03 | | 4.54 | | 3.74 | | 3.68 | | 5.04 | | 7.20 | | 5.01 | | 8.67 | | 4.97 | | **Raw SD** |
| **T: 90% Conf. int.** | 4 | | 4 | | 5 | | 6 | | 7 | | 6 | | 4 | | 6 | | 6 | | 6 | | 5 | | 4 | | 5 | | 4 | | 6 | | **T: 90% Conf. int.** |

**Table A.5d** TRS–A Composite *T* Scores

| T score | Externalizing Problems Combined | Externalizing Problems Female | Externalizing Problems Male | Internalizing Problems Combined | Internalizing Problems Female | Internalizing Problems Male | School Problems Combined | School Problems Female | School Problems Male | Adaptive Skills Combined | Adaptive Skills Female | Adaptive Skills Male | Behavioral Symptoms Index Combined | Behavioral Symptoms Index Female | Behavioral Symptoms Index Male | T score |
|---|---|---|---|---|---|---|---|---|---|---|---|---|---|---|---|---|
| 120 | — | 343–357 | — | 327–353 | 330–350 | 321–356 | — | — | — | — | — | — | 628–647 | 625–673 | — | 120 |
| 119 | — | 340–342 | — | 325–326 | 327–329 | 319–320 | — | — | — | — | — | — | 623–627 | 620–624 | 620–622 | 119 |
| 118 | 340 | 338–339 | — | 322–324 | 325–326 | 316–318 | — | — | — | — | — | — | 618–622 | 616–619 | 616–619 | 118 |
| 117 | 337–339 | 335–337 | — | 319–321 | 322–324 | 314–315 | — | — | — | — | — | — | 613–617 | 611–615 | 611–615 | 117 |
| 116 | 334–336 | 332–334 | — | 317–318 | 320–321 | 311–313 | — | — | — | — | — | — | 609–612 | 606–610 | 606–610 | 116 |
| 115 | 331–333 | 329–331 | — | 314–316 | 317–319 | 309–310 | — | — | — | — | — | — | 604–608 | 602–605 | 602–605 | 115 |
| 114 | 328–330 | 326–328 | — | 312–313 | 314–316 | 306–308 | — | — | — | — | — | — | 599–603 | 597–601 | 597–601 | 114 |
| 113 | 326–327 | 324–325 | — | 309–311 | 312–313 | 304–305 | — | — | — | — | — | — | 595–598 | 592–596 | 592–596 | 113 |
| 112 | 323–325 | 321–323 | — | 307–308 | 309–311 | 301–303 | — | — | — | — | — | — | 590–594 | 588–591 | 588–591 | 112 |
| 111 | 320–322 | 318–320 | — | 304–306 | 307–308 | 299–300 | — | — | — | — | — | — | 585–589 | 583–587 | 583–587 | 111 |
| 110 | 317–319 | 315–317 | — | 302–303 | 304–306 | 296–298 | — | — | — | — | — | — | 580–584 | 578–582 | 578–582 | 110 |
| 109 | 314–316 | 313–314 | 313 | 299–301 | 301–303 | 294–295 | — | — | — | — | — | — | 576–579 | 574–577 | 574–577 | 109 |
| 108 | 312–313 | 310–312 | 310–312 | 296–298 | 299–300 | 292–293 | — | — | — | — | — | — | 571–575 | 569–573 | 569–573 | 108 |
| 107 | 309–311 | 307–309 | 307–309 | 294–295 | 296–298 | 289–291 | — | — | — | — | — | — | 566–570 | 564–568 | 564–568 | 107 |
| 106 | 306–308 | 304–306 | 305–306 | 291–293 | 294–295 | 287–288 | — | — | — | — | — | — | 562–565 | 560–563 | 560–563 | 106 |
| 105 | 303–305 | 302–303 | 302–304 | 289–290 | 291–293 | 284–286 | — | — | — | — | — | — | 557–561 | 555–559 | 555–559 | 105 |
| 104 | 300–302 | 299–301 | 299–301 | 286–288 | 289–290 | 282–283 | — | — | — | — | — | — | 552–556 | 550–554 | 550–554 | 104 |
| 103 | 298–299 | 296–298 | 296–298 | 284–285 | 286–288 | 279–281 | — | — | — | — | — | — | 548–551 | 546–549 | 546–549 | 103 |
| 102 | 295–297 | 293–295 | 294–295 | 281–283 | 283–285 | 277–278 | — | — | — | — | — | — | 543–547 | 541–545 | 541–545 | 102 |
| 101 | 292–294 | 290–292 | 291–293 | 279–280 | 281–282 | 274–276 | — | — | — | — | — | — | 538–542 | 536–540 | 536–540 | 101 |
| 100 | 289–291 | 288–289 | 288–290 | 276–278 | 278–280 | 272–273 | — | 192 | — | — | — | — | 533–537 | 532–535 | 532–535 | 100 |
| 99 | 286–288 | 285–287 | 285–287 | 274–275 | 276–277 | 269–271 | — | 190–191 | — | — | — | — | 529–532 | 527–531 | 527–531 | 99 |
| 98 | 284–285 | 282–284 | 282–284 | 271–273 | 273–275 | 267–268 | — | 188–189 | — | — | — | — | 524–528 | 522–526 | 522–526 | 98 |
| 97 | 281–283 | 279–281 | 280–281 | 268–270 | 271–272 | 265–266 | — | 186–187 | — | — | — | — | 519–523 | 518–521 | 518–521 | 97 |
| 96 | 278–280 | 277–278 | 277–279 | 266–267 | 268–270 | 262–264 | — | 184–185 | — | — | — | — | 515–518 | 513–517 | 513–517 | 96 |
| 95 | 275–277 | 274–276 | 274–276 | 263–265 | 265–267 | 260–261 | — | 182–183 | — | — | — | — | 510–514 | 508–512 | 508–512 | 95 |
| 94 | 272–274 | 271–273 | 271–273 | 261–262 | 263–264 | 257–259 | 163 | 180–181 | 164 | — | — | — | 505–509 | 504–507 | 504–507 | 94 |
| 93 | 270–271 | 268–270 | 269–270 | 258–260 | 260–262 | 255–256 | — | 179 | — | — | — | — | 501–504 | 499–503 | 499–503 | 93 |
| 92 | 267–269 | 266–267 | 266–268 | 256–257 | 258–259 | 252–254 | 177–178 | 177–178 | — | — | — | — | 496–500 | 494–498 | 494–498 | 92 |
| 91 | 264–266 | 263–265 | 263–265 | 253–255 | 255–257 | 250–251 | 175–176 | 175–176 | — | — | — | — | 491–495 | 490–493 | 490–493 | 91 |
| 90 | 261–263 | 260–262 | 260–262 | 251–252 | 252–254 | 247–249 | 174 | 173–174 | — | — | — | — | 486–490 | 485–489 | 485–489 | 90 |
| 89 | 258–260 | 257–259 | 257–259 | 248–250 | 250–251 | 245–246 | 172–173 | 171–172 | — | — | — | — | 482–485 | 480–484 | 480–484 | 89 |
| 88 | 256–257 | 254–256 | 255–256 | 245–247 | 247–249 | 242–244 | 170–171 | 169–170 | — | — | — | — | 477–481 | 476–479 | 476–479 | 88 |
| 87 | 253–255 | 252–253 | 252–254 | 243–244 | 245–246 | 240–241 | 168–169 | 168 | — | — | — | — | 472–476 | 471–475 | 471–475 | 87 |
| 86 | 250–252 | 249–251 | 249–251 | 240–242 | 242–244 | 238–239 | 166–167 | 166–167 | 169 | — | — | — | 468–471 | 466–470 | 466–470 | 86 |
| 85 | 247–249 | 246–248 | 246–248 | 238–239 | 240–241 | 235–237 | 164–165 | 164–165 | 167–168 | — | — | — | 463–467 | 462–465 | 462–465 | 85 |
| 84 | 244–246 | 243–245 | 244–245 | 235–237 | 237–239 | 233–234 | 163 | 162–163 | 165–166 | — | — | — | 458–462 | 457–461 | 457–461 | 84 |
| 83 | 242–243 | 241–242 | 241–243 | 233–234 | 234–236 | 230–232 | 161–162 | 160–161 | 162–163 | — | — | — | 453–457 | 452–456 | 452–456 | 83 |
| 82 | 239–241 | 238–240 | 238–240 | 230–232 | 232–233 | 228–229 | 159–160 | 158–159 | 160–161 | — | — | — | 449–452 | 448–451 | 448–451 | 82 |
| 81 | 236–238 | 235–237 | 235–237 | 228–229 | 229–231 | 225–227 | 157–158 | 157 | 158–159 | — | — | — | 444–448 | 443–447 | 443–447 | 81 |
| 80 | 233–235 | 232–234 | 232–234 | 225–227 | 227–228 | 223–224 | 155–156 | 155–156 | 156–157 | — | — | — | 439–443 | 438–442 | 438–442 | 80 |
| 79 | 230–232 | 229–231 | 230–231 | 222–224 | 224–226 | 220–222 | 153–154 | 153–154 | 154–155 | — | — | — | 435–438 | 434–437 | 434–437 | 79 |
| 78 | 228–229 | 227–229 | 227–229 | 220–221 | 222–223 | 218–219 | 151–152 | 151–152 | 152–153 | — | — | — | 430–434 | 429–433 | 429–433 | 78 |
| 77 | 225–227 | 224–226 | 224–226 | 217–219 | 219–221 | 215–217 | 150 | 149–150 | 150–151 | — | — | — | 425–429 | 424–428 | 424–428 | 77 |
| 76 | 222–224 | 221–223 | 221–223 | 215–216 | 216–218 | 213–214 | 148–149 | 147–148 | 148–149 | — | — | — | 421–424 | 420–423 | 420–423 | 76 |
| 75 | 219–221 | 218–220 | 219–220 | 212–214 | 214–215 | 211–212 | 146–147 | 146 | 147 | — | — | — | 416–420 | 415–419 | 415–419 | 75 |
| 74 | 216–218 | 216–217 | 216–218 | 210–211 | 211–213 | 208–210 | 144–145 | 144–145 | 145–146 | — | — | — | 411–415 | 410–414 | 410–414 | 74 |
| 73 | 214–215 | 213–215 | 213–215 | 207–209 | 209–210 | 206–207 | 142–143 | 142–143 | 143–144 | — | — | — | 406–410 | 406–409 | 406–409 | 73 |
| 72 | 211–213 | 210–212 | 210–212 | 205–206 | 206–208 | 203–205 | 140–141 | 140–141 | 141–142 | — | — | — | 402–405 | 401–405 | 401–405 | 72 |
| 71 | 208–210 | 207–209 | 207–209 | 202–204 | 203–205 | 201–202 | 138–139 | 138–139 | 139–140 | — | — | — | 397–401 | 396–400 | 396–400 | 71 |
| 70 | 205–207 | 205–206 | 205–206 | 200–201 | 201–202 | 198–200 | 137 | 136–137 | 137–138 | 332–333 | — | 338–341 | 392–396 | 392–395 | 392–395 | 70 |
| 69 | 202–204 | 202–204 | 202–204 | 197–199 | 198–200 | 196–197 | 135–136 | 134–135 | 135–136 | 327–331 | — | 333–337 | 388–391 | 387–391 | 387–391 | 69 |
| 68 | 200–201 | 199–201 | 199–201 | 194–196 | 196–197 | 193–195 | 133–134 | 133 | 133–134 | — | 326–328 | 329–332 | 383–387 | 382–386 | 382–386 | 68 |
| 67 | 197–199 | 196–198 | 196–198 | 192–193 | 193–195 | 191–192 | 131–132 | 131–132 | 132 | 323–326 | 322–325 | 324–328 | 378–382 | 378–381 | 378–381 | 67 |
| 66 | 194–196 | 193–195 | 194–195 | 189–191 | 191–192 | 188–190 | 129–130 | 129–130 | 130–131 | 318–322 | 318–321 | 320–323 | 373–377 | 373–377 | 373–377 | 66 |

## Table A.5d  TRS–A Composite T Scores (continued)

| T score | Externalizing Problems | | | Internalizing Problems | | | School Problems | | | Adaptive Skills | | | Behavioral Symptoms Index | | | T score |
|---|---|---|---|---|---|---|---|---|---|---|---|---|---|---|---|---|
| | Combined | Female | Male | Combined | Female | Male | Combined | Female | Male | Combined | Female | Male | Combined | Female | Male | |
| 65 | 191–193 | 191–192 | 191–193 | 187–188 | 188–190 | 186–187 | 127–128 | 127–128 | 128–129 | 314–317 | 313–317 | 315–319 | 369–372 | 368–372 | 368–372 | 65 |
| 64 | 188–190 | 188–190 | 188–190 | 184–186 | 185–187 | 184–185 | 125–126 | 125–126 | 126–127 | 310–313 | 309–312 | 311–314 | 364–368 | 364–367 | 363–367 | 64 |
| 63 | 186–187 | 185–187 | 185–187 | 182–183 | 183–184 | 181–183 | 124 | 123–124 | 124–125 | 305–309 | 305–308 | 306–310 | 359–363 | 359–363 | 359–362 | 63 |
| 62 | 183–185 | 182–184 | 182–184 | 179–181 | 180–182 | 179–180 | 122–123 | 122 | 122–123 | 301–304 | 300–304 | 302–305 | 355–358 | 354–358 | 354–358 | 62 |
| 61 | 180–182 | 180–181 | 180–181 | 177–178 | 178–179 | 176–178 | 120–121 | 120–121 | 120–121 | 296–300 | 296–299 | 298–301 | 350–354 | 350–353 | 349–353 | 61 |
| 60 | 177–179 | 177–179 | 177–179 | 174–176 | 175–177 | 174–175 | 118–119 | 118–119 | 118–119 | 292–295 | 292–295 | 293–297 | 345–349 | 345–349 | 345–348 | 60 |
| 59 | 174–176 | 174–176 | 174–176 | 171–173 | 173–174 | 171–173 | 116–117 | 116–117 | 117 | 288–291 | 287–291 | 289–292 | 341–344 | 340–344 | 340–344 | 59 |
| 58 | 172–173 | 171–173 | 171–173 | 169–170 | 170–172 | 169–170 | 114–115 | 114–115 | 115–116 | 283–287 | 283–286 | 284–288 | 336–340 | 336–339 | 335–339 | 58 |
| 57 | 169–171 | 169–170 | 169–170 | 166–168 | 167–169 | 166–168 | 113 | 112–113 | 113–114 | 279–282 | 279–282 | 280–283 | 331–335 | 331–334 | 331–334 | 57 |
| 56 | 166–168 | 166–168 | 166–168 | 164–165 | 165–166 | 164–165 | 111–112 | 111 | 111–112 | 275–278 | 274–278 | 275–279 | 326–330 | 326–330 | 326–330 | 56 |
| 55 | 163–165 | 163–165 | 163–165 | 161–163 | 162–164 | 161–163 | 109–110 | 109–110 | 109–110 | 270–274 | 270–273 | 271–274 | 322–325 | 322–325 | 321–325 | 55 |
| 54 | 160–162 | 160–162 | 160–162 | 159–160 | 160–161 | 159–160 | 107–108 | 107–108 | 107–108 | 266–269 | 265–269 | 266–270 | 317–321 | 317–321 | 317–320 | 54 |
| 53 | 158–159 | 157–159 | 158–159 | 156–158 | 157–159 | 157–158 | 105–106 | 105–106 | 105–106 | 261–265 | 261–264 | 262–265 | 312–316 | 312–316 | 312–316 | 53 |
| 52 | 155–157 | 155–156 | 155–157 | 154–155 | 154–156 | 154–156 | 103–104 | 103–104 | 103–104 | 257–260 | 257–260 | 258–261 | 308–311 | 308–311 | 307–311 | 52 |
| 51 | 152–154 | 152–154 | 152–154 | 151–153 | 152–153 | 152–153 | 101–102 | 101–102 | 101–102 | 253–256 | 252–256 | 253–257 | 303–307 | 303–307 | 303–306 | 51 |
| 50 | 149–151 | 149–151 | 149–151 | 149–150 | 149–151 | 149–151 | 100 | 99–100 | 100 | 248–252 | 248–251 | 249–252 | 298–302 | 298–302 | 298–302 | 50 |
| 49 | 146–148 | 146–148 | 146–148 | 146–148 | 147–148 | 147–148 | 98–99 | 98 | 98–99 | 244–247 | 244–247 | 244–248 | 293–297 | 294–297 | 293–297 | 49 |
| 48 | 144–145 | 144–145 | 144–146 | 143–145 | 144–146 | 144–146 | 96–97 | 96–97 | 96–97 | 239–243 | 239–243 | 240–243 | 289–292 | 289–293 | 289–292 | 48 |
| 47 | 141–143 | 141–143 | 141–143 | 141–142 | 142–143 | 142–143 | 94–95 | 94–95 | 94–95 | 235–238 | 235–238 | 235–239 | 284–288 | 284–288 | 284–288 | 47 |
| 46 | 138–140 | 138–140 | 138–140 | 138–140 | 139–141 | 139–141 | 92–93 | 92–93 | 92–93 | 231–234 | 231–234 | 231–234 | 279–283 | 280–283 | 279–283 | 46 |
| 45 | 135–137 | 135–137 | 135–137 | 136–137 | 136–138 | 137–138 | 90–91 | 90–91 | 90–91 | 226–230 | 226–230 | 226–230 | 275–278 | 275–279 | 275–278 | 45 |
| 44 | 132–134 | 133–134 | 133–134 | 133–135 | 133–135 | 134–136 | 88–89 | 88–89 | 88–89 | 222–225 | 222–225 | 222–225 | 270–274 | 270–274 | 270–274 | 44 |
| 43 | 130–131 | 130–132 | 130–132 | 131–133 | 131–133 | 132–133 | 87 | 87 | 86–87 | 218–221 | 218–221 | 218–221 | 265–269 | 266–269 | 265–269 | 43 |
| 42 | 127–129 | 129 | 127–129 | 128–130 | 129–130 | 130–131 | 85–86 | 85–86 | 85 | 213–217 | 213–217 | 213–217 | 261–264 | 261–265 | 261–264 | 42 |
| 41 | 124–125 | — | 125–126 | 126–127 | 126–128 | 127–129 | 83–84 | 83–84 | 83–84 | 209–212 | 209–212 | 209–212 | 256–260 | 256–260 | 256–260 | 41 |
| 40 | 124–125 | — | — | 124–125 | 125 | 125–126 | 81–82 | 81–82 | 81–82 | 204–208 | 205–208 | 204–208 | 251–255 | 252–255 | 251–255 | 40 |
| 39 | — | — | — | — | — | — | 79–80 | 79–80 | 79–80 | 200–203 | 200–204 | 200–203 | 246–250 | 249–251 | 247–250 | 39 |
| 38 | — | — | — | — | — | — | 77–78 | 77–78 | 77–78 | 196–199 | 196–199 | 195–199 | — | — | 242–246 | 38 |
| 37 | — | — | — | — | — | — | 76 | 76 | 75–76 | 191–195 | 191–195 | 191–194 | — | — | 241 | 37 |
| 36 | — | — | — | — | — | — | — | — | 73–74 | 187–190 | 187–190 | 186–190 | — | — | — | 36 |
| 35 | — | — | — | — | — | — | — | — | — | 182–186 | 183–186 | 182–185 | — | — | — | 35 |
| 34 | — | — | — | — | — | — | — | — | — | 178–181 | 178–182 | 178–181 | — | — | — | 34 |
| 33 | — | — | — | — | — | — | — | — | — | 174–177 | 174–177 | 173–177 | — | — | — | 33 |
| 32 | — | — | — | — | — | — | — | — | — | 169–173 | 170–173 | 169–172 | — | — | — | 32 |
| 31 | — | — | — | — | — | — | — | — | — | 165–168 | 165–169 | 164–168 | — | — | — | 31 |
| 30 | — | — | — | — | — | — | — | — | — | 161–164 | 161–164 | 160–163 | — | — | — | 30 |
| 29 | — | — | — | — | — | — | — | — | — | 156–160 | 157–160 | 155–159 | — | — | — | 29 |
| 28 | — | — | — | — | — | — | — | — | — | 152–155 | 152–156 | 151–154 | — | — | — | 28 |
| 27 | — | — | — | — | — | — | — | — | — | 147–151 | 148–151 | 146–150 | — | — | — | 27 |
| 26 | — | — | — | — | — | — | — | — | — | 143–146 | 144–147 | 142–145 | — | — | — | 26 |
| 25 | — | — | — | — | — | — | — | — | — | 139–142 | 139–143 | 138–141 | — | — | — | 25 |
| 24 | — | — | — | — | — | — | — | — | — | 134–138 | 135–138 | 133–137 | — | — | — | 24 |
| 23 | — | — | — | — | — | — | — | — | — | 130–133 | 131–134 | 129–132 | — | — | — | 23 |
| 22 | — | — | — | — | — | — | — | — | — | 125–129 | 126–130 | 124–128 | — | — | — | 22 |
| 21 | — | — | — | — | — | — | — | — | — | 121–124 | 122–125 | 120–123 | — | — | — | 21 |
| 20 | — | — | — | — | — | — | — | — | — | 117–120 | 117–121 | 118–119 | — | — | — | 20 |
| 19 | — | — | — | — | — | — | — | — | — | 112–116 | 113–116 | — | — | — | — | 19 |
| 18 | — | — | — | — | — | — | — | — | — | 108–111 | 109–112 | — | — | — | — | 18 |
| 17 | — | — | — | — | — | — | — | — | — | 106–107 | 104–108 | — | — | — | — | 17 |
| 16 | — | — | — | — | — | — | — | — | — | — | 100–103 | — | — | — | — | 16 |
| 15 | — | — | — | — | — | — | — | — | — | — | 96–99 | — | — | — | — | 15 |
| 14 | — | — | — | — | — | — | — | — | — | — | 91–95 | — | — | — | — | 14 |
| 13 | — | — | — | — | — | — | — | — | — | — | 88–90 | — | — | — | — | 13 |
| 12 | — | — | — | — | — | — | — | — | — | — | — | — | — | — | — | 12 |
| 11 | — | — | — | — | — | — | — | — | — | — | — | — | — | — | — | 11 |
| 10 | — | — | — | — | — | — | — | — | — | — | — | — | — | — | — | 10 |
| **T: 90% Conf. int.** | 3 | 4 | 3 | 4 | 4 | 5 | 4 | 4 | 4 | 2 | 3 | 2 | 3 | 3 | 3 | **T: 90% Conf. int.** |

## Table A.5e TRS–A Composite Percentiles

| %ile | Externalizing Problems | | | Internalizing Problems | | | School Problems | | | Adaptive Skills | | | Behavioral Symptoms Index | | | %ile |
|---|---|---|---|---|---|---|---|---|---|---|---|---|---|---|---|---|
| | Combined | Female | Male | Combined | Female | Male | Combined | Female | Male | Combined | Female | Male | Combined | Female | Male | |
| 99 | 241–340 | 236–357 | 239–313 | 227–353 | 232–350 | 217–356 | 145–178 | 146–192 | 143–169 | 330–333 | – | 334–341 | 438–647 | 436–673 | 433–622 | 99 |
| 98 | 229–240 | 228–235 | 227–238 | 217–226 | 221–231 | 212–216 | 142–144 | 142–145 | 140–142 | 326–329 | 325–328 | 330–333 | 420–437 | 421–435 | 416–432 | 98 |
| 97 | 220–228 | 221–227 | 219–226 | 210–216 | 213–220 | 207–211 | 139–141 | 139–141 | 138–139 | 323–325 | 321–324 | 327–329 | 408–419 | 410–420 | 404–415 | 97 |
| 96 | 213–219 | 215–220 | 213–218 | 205–209 | 207–212 | 204–206 | 137–138 | 137–138 | 136–137 | 320–322 | 319–320 | 324–326 | 398–407 | 401–409 | 395–403 | 96 |
| 95 | 207–212 | 210–214 | 207–212 | 200–204 | 202–206 | 200–203 | 135–136 | 134–136 | 134–135 | 318–319 | 316–318 | 322–323 | 391–397 | 393–400 | 388–394 | 95 |
| 94 | 202–206 | 206–209 | 202–206 | 196–199 | 198–201 | 197–199 | 133–134 | 133 | 133 | 316–317 | 314–315 | 319–321 | 384–390 | 386–392 | 382–387 | 94 |
| 93 | 198–201 | 202–205 | 198–201 | 193–195 | 194–197 | 194–196 | 131–132 | 131–132 | 131–132 | 313–315 | 312–313 | 317–318 | 378–383 | 381–385 | 376–381 | 93 |
| 92 | 194–197 | 198–201 | 195–197 | 190–192 | 191–193 | 192–193 | 130 | 129–130 | 130 | 311–312 | 310–311 | 315–316 | 373–377 | 375–380 | 371–375 | 92 |
| 91 | 191–193 | 194–197 | 191–194 | 187–189 | 188–190 | 190–191 | 129 | 128 | 129 | 310 | 308–309 | 313–314 | 368–372 | 370–374 | 367–370 | 91 |
| 90 | 188–190 | 191–193 | 188–190 | 185–186 | 186–187 | 187–189 | 127–128 | 127 | 127–128 | 308–309 | 306–307 | 311–312 | 364–367 | 366–369 | 363–366 | 90 |
| 89 | 185–187 | 188–190 | 186–187 | 182–184 | 183–185 | 185–186 | 126 | 125–126 | 126 | 306–307 | 304–305 | 309–310 | 360–363 | 362–365 | 359–362 | 89 |
| 88 | 182–184 | 185–187 | 183–185 | 180–181 | 181–182 | 183–184 | 125 | 124 | 125 | 304–305 | 302–303 | 307–308 | 357–359 | 358–361 | 355–358 | 88 |
| 87 | 180–181 | 183–184 | 181–182 | 178–179 | 179–180 | 181–182 | 124 | 123 | 124 | 302–303 | 301 | 305–306 | 353–356 | 354–357 | 352–354 | 87 |
| 86 | 178–179 | 180–182 | 179–180 | 176–177 | 177–178 | 179–180 | 122–123 | 122 | 123 | 301 | 299–300 | 303–304 | 350–352 | 351–353 | 349–351 | 86 |
| 85 | 176–177 | 178–179 | 177–178 | 174–175 | 175–176 | 178 | 121 | 121 | 122 | 299–300 | 298 | 301–302 | 347–349 | 348–350 | 346–348 | 85 |
| 84 | 174–175 | 176–177 | 175–176 | 173 | 173–174 | 176–177 | 120 | 120 | 121 | 298 | 296–297 | 300 | 344–346 | 344–347 | 344–345 | 84 |
| 83 | 172–173 | 174–175 | 173–174 | 171–172 | 172 | 174–175 | 119 | 119 | 120 | 296–297 | 295 | 298–299 | 341–343 | 342–343 | 341–343 | 83 |
| 82 | 171 | 172–173 | 171–172 | 170 | 170–171 | 173 | 118 | 118 | 119 | 295 | 293–294 | 296–297 | 339–340 | 339–341 | 339–340 | 82 |
| 81 | 169–170 | 170–171 | 169–170 | 168–169 | 169 | 171–172 | 117 | 117 | – | 293–294 | 292 | 295 | 337–338 | 336–338 | 336–338 | 81 |
| 80 | 167–168 | 169 | 168 | 167 | 167–168 | 170 | – | 116 | 118 | 292 | 290–291 | 293–294 | 334–336 | 334–335 | 334–335 | 80 |
| 79 | 166 | 167–168 | 167 | 166 | 166 | 169 | 116 | 115 | 117 | 290–291 | 289 | 292 | 332–333 | 331–333 | 332–333 | 79 |
| 78 | 165 | 165–166 | 165–166 | 165 | 165 | 167–168 | 115 | 114 | 116 | 289 | 288 | 290–291 | 330–331 | 329–330 | 330–331 | 78 |
| 77 | 163–164 | 164 | 164 | 163–164 | 164 | 166 | 114 | – | 115 | 287–288 | 286–287 | 289 | 328–329 | 327–328 | 328–329 | 77 |
| 76 | 162 | 162–163 | 163 | 162 | 162–163 | 165 | 113 | 113 | 114 | 286 | 285 | 287–288 | 326–327 | 325–326 | 326–327 | 76 |
| 75 | 161 | 161 | 161–162 | 161 | 161 | 164 | 112 | 112 | – | 285 | 283–284 | 285–286 | 324–325 | 323–324 | 324–325 | 75 |
| 74 | 160 | 160 | 160 | 160 | 160 | 162–163 | – | 111 | 113 | 283–284 | 282 | 284 | 322–323 | 321–322 | 323 | 74 |
| 73 | 159 | 158–159 | 159 | 159 | 159 | 161 | 111 | – | 112 | 282 | 281 | 282–283 | 320–321 | 319–320 | 321–322 | 73 |
| 72 | 158 | 157 | 158 | 158 | 158 | 160 | 110 | 110 | 111 | 280–281 | 280 | 281 | 319 | 317–318 | 319–320 | 72 |
| 71 | 157 | 156 | 157 | 157 | 157 | 159 | – | 109 | – | 279 | 278–279 | 280 | 317–318 | 315–316 | 318 | 71 |
| 70 | 156 | 155 | 156 | 156 | 156 | 158 | 109 | 108 | 110 | 278 | 277 | 278–279 | 315–316 | 313–314 | 316–317 | 70 |
| 69 | 155 | 154 | 155 | 155 | 155 | 157 | 108 | 108 | 109 | 276–277 | 276 | 277 | 314 | 312 | 315 | 69 |
| 68 | 154 | 153 | 154 | 154 | – | 156 | 107 | 107 | – | 275 | 274–275 | 275–276 | 312–313 | 310–311 | 313–314 | 68 |
| 67 | 153 | 152 | 153 | 153 | 154 | 155 | – | – | 108 | 274 | 273 | 274 | 311 | 308–309 | 312 | 67 |
| 66 | 152 | 151 | 152 | 152 | 153 | 154 | 106 | 106 | 107 | 272–273 | 272 | 272–273 | 309–310 | 307 | 310–311 | 66 |
| 65 | 151 | 150 | 151 | 151 | 152 | 153 | 105 | 105 | – | 271 | 271 | 271 | 308 | 305–306 | 309 | 65 |
| 64 | 150 | 149 | – | 150 | 151 | – | – | – | 106 | 270 | 269–270 | 270 | 306–307 | 304 | 307–308 | 64 |
| 63 | – | 148 | 150 | – | – | 152 | 104 | 104 | 105 | 269 | 268 | 268–269 | 305 | 302–303 | 306 | 63 |
| 62 | 149 | – | 149 | 150 | 150 | 151 | – | – | 104 | 267–268 | 267 | 267 | 304 | 301 | 305 | 62 |
| 61 | 148 | 147 | 148 | 149 | 149 | 150 | 103 | 103 | – | 266 | 266 | 265–266 | 302–303 | 300 | 303–304 | 61 |
| 60 | 147 | 146 | – | 148 | – | 149 | 102 | 102 | 104 | 265 | 264–265 | 264 | 301 | 298–299 | 302 | 60 |
| 59 | – | 145 | 147 | – | 148 | – | – | – | 103 | 263–264 | 263 | 263 | 300 | 297 | 301 | 59 |
| 58 | 146 | – | 146 | 148 | 147 | 148 | 101 | 101 | 102 | 262 | 262 | 261–262 | 298–299 | 296 | 300 | 58 |
| 57 | 145 | – | – | 147 | – | 147 | – | – | – | 261 | 261 | 260 | 297 | 294–295 | 298–299 | 57 |
| 56 | – | – | 145 | 146 | 146 | – | 100 | 100 | 101 | 260 | 260 | 258–259 | 296 | 293 | 297 | 56 |
| 55 | 144 | – | 144 | 145 | 145 | 146 | – | 99 | 100 | 258 | 258–259 | 257 | 295 | 292 | 296 | 55 |
| 54 | – | 142 | – | – | – | 145 | 99 | – | 99 | 257 | 257 | 256 | 294 | 291 | 295 | 54 |
| 53 | 143 | 141 | 143 | 144 | 144 | 144 | 98 | 98 | – | 256 | 256 | 254–255 | 293 | 290 | 294 | 53 |
| 52 | 142 | – | 142 | 143 | – | – | – | – | – | 254–255 | 255 | 253 | 291–292 | 289 | 293 | 52 |
| 51 | – | 140 | – | – | 143 | 143 | 97 | – | 98 | 253 | 253–254 | 252 | 290 | 287–288 | 292 | 51 |

**Table A.5e** TRS–A Composite Percentiles (continued)

| %ile | Externalizing Problems Combined | Externalizing Problems Female | Externalizing Problems Male | Internalizing Problems Combined | Internalizing Problems Female | Internalizing Problems Male | School Problems Combined | School Problems Female | School Problems Male | Adaptive Skills Combined | Adaptive Skills Female | Adaptive Skills Male | Behavioral Symptoms Index Combined | Behavioral Symptoms Index Female | Behavioral Symptoms Index Male | %ile |
|---|---|---|---|---|---|---|---|---|---|---|---|---|---|---|---|---|
| 50 | 141 | – | 141 | 142 | – | 142 | – | 97 | – | 252 | 252 | 250–251 | 289 | 286 | 290–291 | 50 |
| 49 | – | 139 | – | – | 142 | – | – | – | 97 | 250–251 | 251 | 249 | 288 | 285 | 289 | 49 |
| 48 | 140 | – | 140 | 141 | 141 | 141 | 96 | 96 | – | 249 | 250 | 247–248 | 287 | 284 | 288 | 48 |
| 47 | – | 138 | – | – | – | – | – | – | 96 | 248 | 248–249 | 246 | 286 | 283 | 287 | 47 |
| 46 | 139 | – | 139 | 140 | 140 | 140 | 95 | 95 | – | 246–247 | 247 | 245 | 285 | 282 | 286 | 46 |
| 45 | – | 137 | – | – | – | – | 94 | – | 95 | 245 | 246 | 243–244 | 284 | 281 | 285 | 45 |
| 44 | 138 | – | 138 | 139 | 139 | 139 | – | 94 | 94 | 244 | 244–245 | 242 | 283 | 280 | 284 | 44 |
| 43 | – | 136 | – | – | – | – | – | – | – | 242–243 | 243 | 241 | 282 | 279 | 283 | 43 |
| 42 | 137 | – | 137 | 138 | 138 | 138 | 93 | 93 | 93 | 241 | 242 | 239–240 | 281 | 278 | 282 | 42 |
| 41 | – | 135 | – | – | – | – | – | – | – | 240 | 241 | 238 | 280 | – | 281 | 41 |
| 40 | 136 | – | 136 | 137 | 137 | 137 | 92 | 92 | 92 | 238–239 | 239–240 | 236–237 | 279 | 277 | 280 | 40 |
| 39 | – | – | 135 | – | – | – | – | – | – | 237 | 238 | 235 | 278 | 276 | 279 | 39 |
| 38 | 135 | 134 | – | 136 | 136 | 136 | 91 | 91 | 91 | 236 | 237 | 234 | 277 | 275 | 278 | 38 |
| 37 | – | – | – | – | – | – | – | – | – | 234–235 | 235–236 | 232–233 | 276 | 274 | 277 | 37 |
| 36 | – | – | – | 135 | – | 135 | 90 | – | 90 | 233 | 234 | 231 | 275 | 273 | 276 | 36 |
| 35 | – | 133 | 134 | 134 | 135 | 134 | – | 90 | – | 231–232 | 232–233 | 230 | 274 | 272 | 275 | 35 |
| 34 | 134 | – | – | – | – | – | 89 | – | 89 | 230 | 231 | 228–229 | 273 | 271 | 274 | 34 |
| 33 | – | 132 | 133 | 133 | 134 | 133 | – | 89 | – | 229 | 230 | 227 | – | – | 273 | 33 |
| 32 | 133 | – | – | – | – | – | 88 | – | 88 | 227–228 | 228–229 | 225–226 | 272 | 270 | 272 | 32 |
| 31 | – | – | – | – | – | – | – | 88 | – | 226 | 227 | 224 | 271 | 269 | 271 | 31 |
| 30 | 132 | – | 132 | 132 | 133 | 132 | 87 | – | 87 | 224–225 | 225–226 | 222–223 | 270 | 268 | 270 | 30 |
| 29 | – | 131 | – | – | – | – | – | 87 | – | 223 | 224 | 221 | 269 | 267 | 269 | 29 |
| 28 | 131 | – | 131 | 131 | – | 131 | 86 | – | 86 | 221–222 | 222–223 | 219–220 | 268 | – | 268 | 28 |
| 27 | – | – | – | – | 132 | – | – | – | – | 220 | 221 | 218 | 267 | 266 | 267 | 27 |
| 26 | – | 130 | – | – | – | – | – | 86 | 85 | 218–219 | 219–220 | 216–217 | 266 | 265 | 266 | 26 |
| 25 | – | – | 130 | 130 | 131 | 130 | 85 | – | – | 217 | 218 | 215 | 265 | 264 | 265 | 25 |
| 24 | 130 | – | – | – | – | – | 84 | 85 | 84 | 215–216 | 216–217 | 213–214 | 264 | 263 | 264 | 24 |
| 23 | – | – | – | – | – | – | – | – | – | 213–214 | 214–215 | 212 | – | – | – | 23 |
| 22 | – | 129 | 129 | 129 | 130 | 129 | – | 84 | 83 | 212 | 213 | 210–211 | 263 | 262 | 263 | 22 |
| 21 | 129 | – | – | – | – | – | – | – | – | 210–211 | 211–212 | 209 | 262 | 261 | 262 | 21 |
| 20 | – | – | – | – | – | – | 83 | 83 | – | 208–209 | 209–210 | 207–208 | 261 | – | 261 | 20 |
| 19 | 128 | – | 128 | 128 | 129 | 128 | – | – | 82 | 207 | 207–208 | 206 | 260 | 260 | 259–260 | 19 |
| 18 | – | – | – | – | – | – | 82 | 82 | 81 | 205–206 | 206 | 204–205 | 259 | 259 | 258 | 18 |
| 17 | – | – | 127 | – | – | – | – | – | – | 203–204 | 204–205 | 202–203 | 258 | 258 | 257 | 17 |
| 16 | – | – | – | – | 128 | 127 | 81 | – | 80 | 201–202 | 202–203 | 201 | 257 | – | 256 | 16 |
| 15 | 127 | – | – | 127 | – | – | – | 81 | – | 199–200 | 200–201 | 199–200 | 256 | 257 | 255 | 15 |
| 14 | – | – | – | – | 127 | – | – | – | 79 | 197–198 | 198–199 | 197–198 | 255 | 256 | 254 | 14 |
| 13 | – | – | 126 | 126 | – | 126 | 80 | 80 | – | 195–196 | 196–197 | 195–196 | 254 | 255 | 253 | 13 |
| 12 | – | – | – | 125 | – | – | – | – | 78 | 193–194 | 193–195 | 194 | 253 | 254 | 252 | 12 |
| 11 | – | – | – | – | 126 | – | 79 | 79 | – | 191–192 | 191–192 | 192–193 | 252 | – | 251 | 11 |
| 10 | – | – | 125 | – | – | – | – | – | 77 | 189–190 | 189–190 | 190–191 | 251 | 253 | 249–250 | 10 |
| 9 | – | – | – | – | – | 125 | 78 | 78 | – | 186–188 | 186–188 | 188–189 | 250 | 252 | 248 | 9 |
| 8 | – | – | – | – | – | – | – | 77 | 76 | 184–185 | 183–185 | 185–187 | 249 | – | 247 | 8 |
| 7 | – | – | – | – | 125 | – | 77 | – | 75 | 181–183 | 180–182 | 183–184 | 248 | 251 | 245–246 | 7 |
| 6 | – | – | – | 124 | – | – | 76 | 76 | 74 | 178–180 | 177–179 | 181–182 | 246–247 | 250 | 244 | 6 |
| 5 | – | – | – | – | – | – | – | – | 73 | 175–177 | 173–176 | 178–180 | – | 249 | 242–243 | 5 |
| 4 | – | – | – | – | – | – | – | – | – | 171–174 | 169–172 | 175–177 | – | – | 241 | 4 |
| 3 | – | – | – | – | – | – | – | – | – | 167–170 | 164–168 | 172–174 | – | – | – | 3 |
| 2 | – | – | – | – | – | – | – | – | – | 162–166 | 158–163 | 168–171 | – | – | – | 2 |
| 1 | – | – | – | – | – | – | – | – | – | 106–161 | 88–157 | 118–167 | – | – | – | 1 |

## Table A.6a  TRS-A T Scores and Percentiles

| Raw score | Hyperactivity | | Aggression | | Conduct Problems | | Anxiety | | Depression | | Somatization | | Attention Problems | | Learning Problems | | Atypicality | | Withdrawal | | Adaptability | | Social Skills | | Leadership | | Study Skills | | Functional Communication | | Raw score |
|---|---|---|---|---|---|---|---|---|---|---|---|---|---|---|---|---|---|---|---|---|---|---|---|---|---|---|---|---|---|---|---|---|
| | T | %ile | T | %ile | T | %ile | T | %ile | T | %ile | T | %ile | T | %ile | T | %ile | T | %ile | T | %ile | T | %ile | T | %ile | T | %ile | T | %ile | T | %ile | |
| 36 | — | — | — | — | — | — | — | — | 120 | 99 | — | — | — | — | — | — | — | — | — | — | — | — | — | — | — | — | — | — | — | — | 36 |
| 35 | — | — | — | — | — | — | — | — | 120 | 99 | — | — | — | — | — | — | — | — | — | — | — | — | — | — | — | — | — | — | — | — | 35 |
| 34 | — | — | — | — | — | — | — | — | 120 | 99 | — | — | — | — | — | — | — | — | — | — | — | — | — | — | — | — | — | — | — | — | 34 |
| 33 | 105 | 99 | 120 | 99 | — | — | — | — | 120 | 99 | — | — | — | — | — | — | — | — | — | — | — | — | — | — | — | — | 63 | 93 | — | — | 33 |
| 32 | 103 | 99 | 120 | 99 | — | — | — | — | 120 | 99 | — | — | — | — | — | — | — | — | — | — | — | — | — | — | — | — | 62 | 88 | — | — | 32 |
| 31 | 101 | 99 | 120 | 99 | — | — | — | — | 119 | 99 | — | — | — | — | — | — | — | — | — | — | — | — | — | — | — | — | 60 | 82 | — | — | 31 |
| 30 | 99 | 99 | 118 | 99 | — | — | — | — | 117 | 99 | — | — | 83 | 99 | — | — | 120 | 99 | — | — | — | — | — | — | — | — | 59 | 77 | — | — | 30 |
| 29 | 97 | 99 | 116 | 99 | 115 | 99 | — | — | 115 | 99 | — | — | 81 | 99 | — | — | 120 | 99 | — | — | — | — | 64 | 95 | — | — | 58 | 72 | — | — | 29 |
| 28 | 95 | 99 | 113 | 99 | 112 | 99 | — | — | 112 | 99 | — | — | 80 | 99 | — | — | 120 | 99 | — | — | — | — | 63 | 91 | — | — | 57 | 68 | — | — | 28 |
| 27 | 93 | 99 | 111 | 99 | 108 | 99 | 106 | 99 | 110 | 99 | — | — | 78 | 99 | — | — | 120 | 99 | — | — | — | — | 62 | 87 | — | — | 56 | 63 | 62 | 94 | 27 |
| 26 | 91 | 99 | 108 | 99 | 105 | 99 | 104 | 99 | 107 | 99 | — | — | 77 | 99 | — | — | 120 | 99 | — | — | — | — | 60 | 82 | — | — | 54 | 59 | 60 | 87 | 26 |
| 25 | 90 | 99 | 106 | 99 | 103 | 99 | 102 | 99 | 105 | 99 | — | — | 75 | 98 | — | — | 117 | 99 | — | — | — | — | 59 | 78 | — | — | 53 | 55 | 58 | 79 | 25 |
| 24 | 88 | 99 | 103 | 99 | 100 | 99 | 99 | 99 | 102 | 99 | — | — | 74 | 98 | 96 | 99 | 114 | 99 | 98 | 99 | 63 | 93 | 58 | 73 | — | — | 52 | 51 | 57 | 70 | 24 |
| 23 | 86 | 99 | 101 | 99 | 98 | 99 | 97 | 99 | 100 | 99 | — | — | 72 | 97 | 94 | 99 | 111 | 99 | 96 | 99 | 61 | 86 | 57 | 68 | — | — | 51 | 47 | 55 | 62 | 23 |
| 22 | 84 | 99 | 98 | 99 | 96 | 99 | 94 | 99 | 97 | 99 | — | — | 71 | 96 | 91 | 99 | 108 | 99 | 93 | 99 | 59 | 78 | 55 | 64 | — | — | 50 | 44 | 53 | 54 | 22 |
| 21 | 82 | 99 | 96 | 99 | 93 | 99 | 92 | 99 | 95 | 99 | — | — | 69 | 95 | 89 | 99 | 105 | 99 | 91 | 99 | 57 | 71 | 54 | 59 | 66 | 97 | 48 | 40 | 51 | 46 | 21 |
| 20 | 80 | 98 | 93 | 99 | 91 | 99 | 89 | 99 | 92 | 99 | 120 | 99 | 68 | 93 | 87 | 99 | 102 | 99 | 89 | 99 | 55 | 63 | 53 | 55 | 64 | 93 | 47 | 37 | 49 | 40 | 20 |
| 19 | 78 | 98 | 91 | 99 | 89 | 99 | 87 | 99 | 90 | 99 | 120 | 99 | 66 | 92 | 85 | 99 | 99 | 99 | 86 | 99 | 53 | 56 | 51 | 51 | 63 | 89 | 46 | 34 | 48 | 34 | 19 |
| 18 | 76 | 97 | 88 | 99 | 86 | 99 | 84 | 99 | 87 | 99 | 120 | 99 | 65 | 90 | 82 | 99 | 96 | 99 | 84 | 99 | 51 | 49 | 50 | 47 | 61 | 83 | 45 | 31 | 46 | 29 | 18 |
| 17 | 74 | 96 | 86 | 99 | 84 | 99 | 82 | 98 | 85 | 99 | 120 | 99 | 63 | 88 | 80 | 98 | 94 | 99 | 82 | 99 | 49 | 42 | 48 | 43 | 59 | 77 | 44 | 28 | 44 | 24 | 17 |
| 16 | 72 | 95 | 83 | 98 | 81 | 99 | 80 | 98 | 82 | 98 | 117 | 99 | 62 | 86 | 78 | 98 | 91 | 99 | 79 | 98 | 48 | 36 | 46 | 39 | 57 | 71 | 42 | 25 | 42 | 20 | 16 |
| 15 | 70 | 94 | 81 | 98 | 79 | 98 | 77 | 97 | 80 | 98 | 113 | 99 | 60 | 84 | 75 | 97 | 88 | 98 | 77 | 97 | 46 | 31 | 45 | 35 | 55 | 65 | 41 | 22 | 40 | 17 | 15 |
| 14 | 68 | 93 | 78 | 97 | 77 | 97 | 75 | 97 | 77 | 97 | 108 | 99 | 59 | 81 | 73 | 96 | 85 | 98 | 74 | 96 | 44 | 26 | 44 | 32 | 53 | 58 | 40 | 20 | 38 | 14 | 14 |
| 13 | 67 | 92 | 76 | 96 | 74 | 97 | 72 | 96 | 75 | 96 | 103 | 99 | 58 | 78 | 71 | 95 | 82 | 97 | 72 | 95 | 42 | 22 | 42 | 28 | 51 | 52 | 39 | 17 | 37 | 11 | 13 |
| 12 | 65 | 90 | 73 | 95 | 72 | 96 | 70 | 95 | 73 | 96 | 99 | 99 | 56 | 75 | 69 | 94 | 79 | 96 | 70 | 94 | 40 | 18 | 41 | 25 | 49 | 46 | 38 | 15 | 35 | 9 | 12 |
| 11 | 63 | 88 | 71 | 94 | 69 | 95 | 67 | 93 | 70 | 95 | 94 | 99 | 55 | 71 | 66 | 92 | 76 | 95 | 67 | 93 | 38 | 14 | 40 | 22 | 47 | 40 | 36 | 12 | 33 | 7 | 11 |
| 10 | 61 | 86 | 68 | 92 | 67 | 93 | 65 | 92 | 68 | 93 | 90 | 99 | 53 | 67 | 64 | 90 | 73 | 94 | 65 | 91 | 36 | 11 | 39 | 19 | 46 | 34 | 35 | 10 | 31 | 6 | 10 |
| 9 | 59 | 83 | 66 | 91 | 65 | 92 | 63 | 89 | 65 | 92 | 85 | 98 | 52 | 63 | 62 | 87 | 70 | 93 | 63 | 89 | 34 | 9 | 37 | 16 | 44 | 29 | 34 | 8 | 29 | 4 | 9 |
| 8 | 57 | 80 | 63 | 89 | 62 | 90 | 60 | 86 | 63 | 90 | 81 | 97 | 50 | 58 | 59 | 84 | 67 | 91 | 60 | 87 | 32 | 6 | 36 | 13 | 42 | 24 | 33 | 7 | 28 | 3 | 8 |
| 7 | 55 | 76 | 61 | 86 | 60 | 85 | 58 | 83 | 60 | 88 | 76 | 96 | 49 | 53 | 57 | 81 | 64 | 89 | 58 | 84 | 31 | 4 | 35 | 11 | 40 | 19 | 32 | 5 | 26 | 3 | 7 |
| 6 | 53 | 72 | 58 | 83 | 57 | 83 | 55 | 78 | 58 | 85 | 72 | 95 | 47 | 47 | 55 | 76 | 62 | 86 | 55 | 80 | 29 | 3 | 33 | 9 | 38 | 15 | 30 | 3 | 24 | 2 | 6 |
| 5 | 51 | 67 | 56 | 80 | 55 | 79 | 53 | 72 | 55 | 82 | 67 | 93 | 46 | 41 | 52 | 70 | 59 | 82 | 53 | 75 | 27 | 2 | 32 | 7 | 36 | 11 | 29 | 2 | 22 | 1 | 5 |
| 4 | 49 | 61 | 53 | 75 | 53 | 74 | 50 | 64 | 53 | 77 | 63 | 91 | 44 | 34 | 50 | 63 | 56 | 77 | 51 | 68 | 25 | 1 | 31 | 5 | 34 | 7 | 28 | 1 | 20 | 1 | 4 |
| 3 | 47 | 54 | 51 | 70 | 50 | 68 | 48 | 54 | 50 | 70 | 58 | 87 | 43 | 28 | 48 | 54 | 53 | 70 | 48 | 59 | 23 | 1 | 29 | 3 | 32 | 5 | 27 | 1 | 18 | 1 | 3 |
| 2 | 45 | 45 | 48 | 62 | 48 | 60 | 45 | 41 | 48 | 60 | 53 | 81 | 41 | 21 | 46 | 43 | 50 | 57 | 46 | 46 | 21 | 1 | 28 | 2 | 31 | 3 | 26 | 1 | 17 | 1 | 2 |
| 1 | 44 | 33 | 46 | 49 | 46 | 48 | 43 | 25 | 45 | 43 | 49 | 68 | 40 | 14 | 43 | 29 | 47 | 44 | 44 | 28 | 19 | 1 | 27 | 1 | 29 | 1 | 24 | 1 | 15 | 1 | 1 |
| 0 | 42 | 18 | 43 | 27 | 43 | 27 | 41 | 8 | 43 | 13 | 44 | 26 | 38 | 7 | 41 | 13 | 44 | 32 | 41 | 4 | 17 | 1 | 26 | 1 | 27 | 1 | 23 | 1 | 13 | 1 | 0 |
| Raw mean | 4.35 | | 2.69 | | 2.86 | | 3.86 | | 2.87 | | 1.24 | | 7.94 | | 3.93 | | 2.02 | | 3.71 | | 17.30 | | 18.93 | | 12.34 | | 22.40 | | 20.36 | | Raw mean |
| Raw SD | 5.22 | | 4.01 | | 4.19 | | 4.10 | | 4.05 | | 2.20 | | 6.73 | | 4.36 | | 3.44 | | 4.21 | | 5.29 | | 7.77 | | 5.32 | | 8.33 | | 5.51 | | Raw SD |
| T:90% Conf. int. | 5 | | 5 | | 5 | | 5 | | 6 | | 6 | | 4 | | 5 | | 5 | | 5 | | 5 | | 4 | | 5 | | 3 | | 5 | | T:90% Conf. int. |

**Table A.6b** TRS–A *T* Scores and Percentiles

| Raw score | Hyperactivity T | Hyperactivity %ile | Aggression T | Aggression %ile | Conduct Problems T | Conduct Problems %ile | Anxiety T | Anxiety %ile | Depression T | Depression %ile | Somatization T | Somatization %ile | Attention Problems T | Attention Problems %ile | Learning Problems T | Learning Problems %ile | Atypicality T | Atypicality %ile | Withdrawal T | Withdrawal %ile | Adaptability T | Adaptability %ile | Social Skills T | Social Skills %ile | Leadership T | Leadership %ile | Study Skills T | Study Skills %ile | Functional Communication T | Functional Communication %ile | Raw score |
|---|---|---|---|---|---|---|---|---|---|---|---|---|---|---|---|---|---|---|---|---|---|---|---|---|---|---|---|---|---|---|---|
| 36 | — | — | — | — | — | — | — | — | 120 | 99 | — | — | — | — | — | — | — | — | — | — | — | — | — | — | — | — | — | — | — | — | 36 |
| 35 | — | — | — | — | — | — | — | — | 120 | 99 | — | — | — | — | — | — | — | — | — | — | — | — | — | — | — | — | — | — | — | — | 35 |
| 34 | — | — | — | — | — | — | — | — | 120 | 99 | — | — | — | — | — | — | — | — | — | — | — | — | — | — | — | — | — | — | — | — | 34 |
| 33 | 110 | 99 | 120 | 99 | — | — | — | — | 120 | 99 | — | — | — | — | — | — | — | — | — | — | — | — | — | — | — | — | 61 | 90 | — | — | 33 |
| 32 | 108 | 99 | 120 | 99 | — | — | — | — | 120 | 99 | — | — | — | — | — | — | — | — | — | — | — | — | — | — | — | — | 60 | 82 | — | — | 32 |
| 31 | 106 | 99 | 120 | 99 | — | — | — | — | 118 | 99 | — | — | — | — | — | — | — | — | — | — | — | — | — | — | — | — | 59 | 75 | — | — | 31 |
| 30 | 104 | 99 | 120 | 99 | 120 | 99 | — | — | 116 | 99 | — | — | 89 | 99 | — | — | 120 | 99 | — | — | — | — | 63 | 94 | — | — | 57 | 69 | — | — | 30 |
| 29 | 102 | 99 | 120 | 99 | 117 | 99 | — | — | 113 | 99 | — | — | 87 | 99 | — | — | 120 | 99 | — | — | — | — | 62 | 88 | — | — | 56 | 63 | — | — | 29 |
| 28 | 100 | 99 | 118 | 99 | 115 | 99 | — | — | 111 | 99 | — | — | 85 | 99 | — | — | 120 | 99 | — | — | — | — | 61 | 83 | — | — | 55 | 58 | — | — | 28 |
| 27 | 98 | 99 | 115 | 99 | 112 | 99 | 102 | 99 | 108 | 99 | — | — | 84 | 99 | — | — | 120 | 99 | — | — | — | — | 59 | 77 | — | — | 53 | 53 | 62 | 94 | 27 |
| 26 | 96 | 99 | 113 | 99 | 110 | 99 | 100 | 99 | 106 | 99 | — | — | 82 | 99 | — | — | 120 | 99 | — | — | — | — | 58 | 72 | — | — | 52 | 49 | 60 | 85 | 26 |
| 25 | 94 | 99 | 110 | 99 | 107 | 99 | 97 | 99 | 104 | 99 | — | — | 81 | 99 | — | — | 120 | 99 | — | — | — | — | 56 | 67 | — | — | 51 | 44 | 58 | 75 | 25 |
| 24 | 92 | 99 | 107 | 99 | 105 | 99 | 95 | 99 | 101 | 99 | — | — | 79 | 99 | 100 | 99 | 120 | 99 | 108 | 99 | 62 | 92 | 55 | 62 | — | — | 50 | 41 | 56 | 66 | 24 |
| 23 | 90 | 99 | 105 | 99 | 102 | 99 | 93 | 99 | 99 | 99 | — | — | 77 | 99 | 97 | 99 | 118 | 99 | 105 | 99 | 60 | 84 | 54 | 57 | — | — | 48 | 37 | 54 | 57 | 23 |
| 22 | 88 | 99 | 102 | 99 | 100 | 99 | 90 | 99 | 96 | 99 | — | — | 76 | 98 | 95 | 99 | 115 | 99 | 102 | 99 | 58 | 75 | 52 | 53 | — | — | 47 | 34 | 52 | 49 | 22 |
| 21 | 86 | 99 | 99 | 99 | 97 | 99 | 88 | 99 | 94 | 99 | — | — | 74 | 97 | 92 | 99 | 112 | 99 | 99 | 99 | 56 | 67 | 51 | 49 | 65 | 97 | 46 | 31 | 50 | 41 | 21 |
| 20 | 84 | 98 | 97 | 99 | 95 | 99 | 86 | 99 | 92 | 99 | 120 | 99 | 72 | 96 | 90 | 99 | 109 | 99 | 97 | 99 | 54 | 59 | 50 | 44 | 63 | 92 | 44 | 28 | 48 | 35 | 20 |
| 19 | 82 | 98 | 94 | 99 | 92 | 99 | 84 | 99 | 89 | 99 | 120 | 99 | 71 | 95 | 88 | 99 | 105 | 99 | 94 | 99 | 53 | 52 | 48 | 40 | 61 | 87 | 43 | 25 | 46 | 29 | 19 |
| 18 | 80 | 97 | 92 | 99 | 89 | 99 | 81 | 98 | 87 | 99 | 120 | 99 | 69 | 94 | 85 | 99 | 102 | 99 | 91 | 99 | 51 | 46 | 47 | 37 | 60 | 80 | 42 | 22 | 44 | 25 | 18 |
| 17 | 78 | 97 | 89 | 98 | 87 | 99 | 79 | 98 | 84 | 98 | 119 | 99 | 68 | 93 | 83 | 98 | 99 | 99 | 88 | 99 | 49 | 40 | 45 | 33 | 58 | 74 | 41 | 20 | 42 | 20 | 17 |
| 16 | 76 | 96 | 86 | 98 | 84 | 98 | 77 | 97 | 82 | 98 | 114 | 99 | 66 | 91 | 80 | 97 | 96 | 99 | 85 | 99 | 47 | 35 | 44 | 29 | 56 | 67 | 39 | 18 | 40 | 17 | 16 |
| 15 | 74 | 96 | 84 | 98 | 82 | 97 | 75 | 97 | 79 | 97 | 110 | 99 | 64 | 90 | 78 | 96 | 93 | 98 | 83 | 98 | 45 | 30 | 43 | 26 | 54 | 59 | 38 | 15 | 39 | 14 | 15 |
| 14 | 72 | 95 | 81 | 97 | 79 | 97 | 72 | 96 | 77 | 97 | 106 | 99 | 63 | 88 | 76 | 95 | 89 | 98 | 80 | 97 | 44 | 26 | 41 | 23 | 52 | 53 | 37 | 13 | 37 | 11 | 14 |
| 13 | 70 | 94 | 78 | 97 | 77 | 96 | 70 | 95 | 75 | 96 | 101 | 99 | 61 | 86 | 73 | 93 | 86 | 97 | 77 | 97 | 42 | 22 | 40 | 20 | 50 | 46 | 35 | 12 | 35 | 9 | 13 |
| 12 | 68 | 93 | 76 | 96 | 74 | 95 | 68 | 94 | 72 | 95 | 97 | 99 | 59 | 83 | 71 | 92 | 83 | 97 | 74 | 95 | 40 | 18 | 38 | 17 | 48 | 40 | 34 | 10 | 33 | 7 | 12 |
| 11 | 66 | 91 | 73 | 95 | 72 | 94 | 65 | 92 | 70 | 94 | 93 | 99 | 58 | 81 | 68 | 90 | 80 | 96 | 71 | 94 | 38 | 12 | 37 | 14 | 46 | 34 | 33 | 8 | 31 | 6 | 11 |
| 10 | 64 | 90 | 71 | 94 | 69 | 93 | 63 | 90 | 67 | 93 | 88 | 97 | 56 | 78 | 66 | 87 | 77 | 95 | 68 | 92 | 36 | 9 | 36 | 11 | 44 | 28 | 32 | 7 | 29 | 4 | 10 |
| 9 | 61 | 88 | 68 | 93 | 67 | 92 | 61 | 88 | 65 | 92 | 84 | 96 | 55 | 74 | 64 | 85 | 74 | 94 | 66 | 89 | 34 | 7 | 34 | 9 | 42 | 23 | 30 | 5 | 27 | 3 | 9 |
| 8 | 59 | 86 | 65 | 92 | 64 | 90 | 59 | 85 | 63 | 90 | 79 | 95 | 53 | 70 | 61 | 81 | 70 | 92 | 63 | 86 | 33 | 5 | 33 | 6 | 40 | 19 | 29 | 4 | 25 | 2 | 8 |
| 7 | 57 | 84 | 63 | 90 | 62 | 89 | 56 | 81 | 60 | 88 | 75 | 93 | 51 | 65 | 59 | 77 | 67 | 90 | 60 | 85 | 31 | 4 | 32 | 4 | 38 | 15 | 28 | 3 | 23 | 2 | 7 |
| 6 | 55 | 81 | 60 | 88 | 59 | 87 | 54 | 77 | 58 | 86 | 71 | 90 | 50 | 60 | 56 | 71 | 64 | 87 | 57 | 82 | 29 | 2 | 30 | 2 | 36 | 11 | 27 | 2 | 21 | 1 | 6 |
| 5 | 53 | 77 | 57 | 85 | 57 | 84 | 52 | 71 | 55 | 82 | 66 | 86 | 48 | 54 | 54 | 63 | 61 | 83 | 54 | 76 | 27 | 1 | 29 | 1 | 34 | 8 | 25 | 1 | 19 | 1 | 5 |
| 4 | 51 | 72 | 55 | 81 | 54 | 81 | 50 | 63 | 53 | 77 | 62 | 80 | 47 | 47 | 52 | 53 | 58 | 76 | 52 | 68 | 25 | 1 | 27 | 1 | 33 | 6 | 24 | 1 | 17 | 1 | 4 |
| 3 | 49 | 66 | 52 | 76 | 52 | 77 | 47 | 53 | 51 | 71 | 57 | 76 | 45 | 39 | 49 | 42 | 55 | 64 | 49 | 58 | 23 | 1 | 26 | 1 | 31 | 4 | 23 | 1 | 15 | 1 | 3 |
| 2 | 47 | 58 | 50 | 69 | 49 | 71 | 45 | 40 | 48 | 61 | 53 | 64 | 43 | 31 | 47 | 31 | 51 | 56 | 46 | 44 | 22 | 1 | 25 | 1 | 29 | 2 | 21 | 1 | 14 | 1 | 2 |
| 1 | 45 | 45 | 47 | 57 | 47 | 60 | 43 | 22 | 46 | 46 | 49 | 44 | 42 | 21 | 45 | 21 | 48 | 48 | 43 | 27 | 20 | 1 | 23 | 1 | 27 | 1 | 20 | 1 | 12 | 1 | 1 |
| 0 | 43 | 23 | 44 | 32 | 44 | 36 | 40 | 3 | 43 | 15 | 44 | 25 | 40 | 11 | 42 | 16 | 45 | 35 | 40 | 8 | 18 | 1 | 22 | 1 | 25 | 1 | 19 | 1 | 10 | 1 | 0 |
| **Raw mean** | 3.33 | | 2.17 | | 2.24 | | 4.20 | | 2.79 | | 1.31 | | 6.13 | | 3.29 | | 1.57 | | 3.43 | | 17.54 | | 20.37 | | 13.05 | | 24.35 | | 20.99 | | **Raw mean** |
| **Raw SD** | 4.94 | | 3.81 | | 3.99 | | 4.40 | | 4.14 | | 2.28 | | 6.18 | | 4.18 | | 3.15 | | 3.56 | | 5.47 | | 7.24 | | 5.19 | | 7.82 | | 5.21 | | **Raw SD** |
| **T: 90% Conf. int.** | 5 | | 5 | | 4 | | 5 | | 5 | | 6 | | 4 | | 5 | | 5 | | 6 | | 4 | | 4 | | 5 | | 4 | | 5 | | **T: 90% Conf. int.** |

## Table A.6c  TRS-A T Scores and Percentiles

| Raw score | Hyperactivity T | %ile | Aggression T | %ile | Conduct Problems T | %ile | Anxiety T | %ile | Depression T | %ile | Somatization T | %ile | Attention Problems T | %ile | Learning Problems T | %ile | Atypicality T | %ile | Withdrawal T | %ile | Adaptability T | %ile | Social Skills T | %ile | Leadership T | %ile | Study Skills T | %ile | Functional Communication T | %ile | Raw score |
|---|---|---|---|---|---|---|---|---|---|---|---|---|---|---|---|---|---|---|---|---|---|---|---|---|---|---|---|---|---|---|---|
| 36 | — | — | — | — | — | — | — | — | 120 | 99 | — | — | — | — | — | — | — | — | — | — | — | — | — | — | — | — | — | — | — | — | 36 |
| 35 | — | — | — | — | — | — | — | — | 120 | 99 | — | — | — | — | — | — | — | — | — | — | — | — | — | — | — | — | — | — | — | — | 35 |
| 34 | — | — | — | — | — | — | — | — | 120 | 99 | — | — | — | — | — | — | — | — | — | — | — | — | — | — | — | — | 65 | 96 | — | — | 34 |
| 33 | 102 | 99 | 120 | 99 | — | — | — | — | 120 | 99 | — | — | — | — | — | — | — | — | — | — | — | — | — | — | — | — | 64 | 93 | — | — | 33 |
| 32 | 100 | 99 | 120 | 99 | — | — | — | — | 120 | 99 | — | — | — | — | — | — | — | — | — | — | — | — | — | — | — | — | 63 | 89 | — | — | 32 |
| 31 | 98 | 99 | 117 | 99 | — | — | — | — | 120 | 99 | — | — | — | — | — | — | — | — | — | — | — | — | — | — | — | — | 61 | 85 | — | — | 31 |
| 30 | 96 | 99 | 115 | 99 | 112 | 99 | — | — | 118 | 99 | — | — | 80 | 99 | — | — | 120 | 99 | — | — | — | — | 66 | 97 | — | — | 60 | 81 | — | — | 30 |
| 29 | 95 | 99 | 112 | 99 | 109 | 99 | — | — | 116 | 99 | — | — | 78 | 99 | — | — | 120 | 99 | — | — | — | — | 64 | 94 | — | — | 59 | 77 | — | — | 29 |
| 28 | 93 | 99 | 110 | 99 | 107 | 99 | — | — | 113 | 99 | — | — | 77 | 99 | — | — | 120 | 99 | — | — | — | — | 63 | 90 | — | — | 58 | 73 | — | — | 28 |
| 27 | 91 | 99 | 107 | 99 | 105 | 99 | 112 | 99 | 111 | 99 | — | — | 75 | 99 | — | — | 117 | 99 | — | — | — | — | 62 | 87 | — | — | 57 | 69 | 63 | 95 | 27 |
| 26 | 89 | 99 | 105 | 99 | 102 | 99 | 110 | 99 | 108 | 99 | — | — | 74 | 98 | — | — | 114 | 99 | — | — | — | — | 61 | 83 | — | — | 55 | 65 | 61 | 89 | 26 |
| 25 | 87 | 99 | 103 | 99 | 100 | 99 | 107 | 99 | 106 | 99 | — | — | 72 | 98 | 94 | 99 | 112 | 99 | — | — | 64 | 94 | 59 | 78 | — | — | 54 | 61 | 59 | 82 | 25 |
| 24 | 85 | 99 | 100 | 99 | 98 | 99 | 104 | 99 | 103 | 99 | — | — | 71 | 97 | 91 | 99 | 109 | 99 | 92 | 99 | 62 | 89 | 58 | 74 | — | — | 53 | 57 | 57 | 74 | 24 |
| 23 | 83 | 99 | 98 | 99 | 95 | 99 | 102 | 99 | 101 | 99 | — | — | 70 | 96 | 89 | 99 | 106 | 99 | 90 | 99 | 60 | 82 | 57 | 70 | — | — | 52 | 53 | 56 | 66 | 23 |
| 22 | 81 | 99 | 95 | 99 | 93 | 99 | 99 | 99 | 98 | 99 | — | — | 68 | 94 | 87 | 99 | 103 | 99 | 88 | 99 | 58 | 75 | 56 | 66 | — | — | 51 | 50 | 54 | 58 | 22 |
| 21 | 79 | 99 | 93 | 99 | 91 | 99 | 96 | 99 | 96 | 99 | 120 | 99 | 67 | 93 | 85 | 99 | 101 | 99 | 86 | 99 | 56 | 67 | 54 | 62 | 67 | 97 | 49 | 46 | 52 | 51 | 21 |
| 20 | 78 | 99 | 91 | 99 | 88 | 99 | 94 | 99 | 93 | 99 | 120 | 99 | 65 | 91 | 82 | 99 | 98 | 99 | 84 | 98 | 54 | 59 | 53 | 57 | 66 | 94 | 48 | 42 | 50 | 44 | 20 |
| 19 | 76 | 98 | 88 | 99 | 86 | 99 | 91 | 99 | 91 | 99 | 120 | 99 | 64 | 89 | 80 | 99 | 95 | 99 | 81 | 98 | 52 | 52 | 52 | 53 | 64 | 90 | 47 | 39 | 49 | 38 | 19 |
| 18 | 74 | 97 | 86 | 99 | 84 | 99 | 88 | 99 | 88 | 99 | 120 | 99 | 62 | 87 | 78 | 98 | 92 | 99 | 79 | 97 | 50 | 45 | 51 | 49 | 62 | 86 | 46 | 35 | 47 | 33 | 18 |
| 17 | 72 | 96 | 83 | 99 | 81 | 99 | 86 | 99 | 85 | 98 | 120 | 99 | 61 | 84 | 76 | 97 | 90 | 99 | 77 | 97 | 48 | 38 | 49 | 46 | 60 | 81 | 45 | 32 | 45 | 28 | 17 |
| 16 | 70 | 95 | 81 | 99 | 79 | 98 | 83 | 99 | 83 | 98 | 115 | 99 | 59 | 81 | 73 | 97 | 87 | 99 | 75 | 96 | 46 | 32 | 48 | 42 | 58 | 75 | 44 | 29 | 43 | 23 | 16 |
| 15 | 68 | 93 | 78 | 98 | 77 | 97 | 81 | 98 | 80 | 98 | 110 | 99 | 58 | 78 | 71 | 96 | 84 | 99 | 73 | 95 | 44 | 27 | 47 | 38 | 56 | 69 | 42 | 26 | 42 | 19 | 15 |
| 14 | 66 | 91 | 76 | 97 | 74 | 96 | 78 | 98 | 78 | 97 | 106 | 99 | 56 | 74 | 69 | 94 | 81 | 98 | 71 | 94 | 42 | 22 | 46 | 34 | 54 | 64 | 41 | 22 | 40 | 16 | 14 |
| 13 | 64 | 89 | 74 | 96 | 72 | 95 | 75 | 97 | 75 | 97 | 101 | 99 | 55 | 71 | 67 | 93 | 79 | 97 | 69 | 93 | 40 | 17 | 44 | 31 | 53 | 58 | 40 | 20 | 38 | 13 | 13 |
| 12 | 62 | 87 | 71 | 94 | 70 | 94 | 73 | 96 | 73 | 96 | 96 | 99 | 53 | 66 | 64 | 91 | 76 | 96 | 67 | 92 | 38 | 14 | 43 | 28 | 51 | 52 | 39 | 17 | 37 | 11 | 12 |
| 11 | 61 | 84 | 69 | 92 | 67 | 92 | 70 | 95 | 70 | 95 | 91 | 99 | 52 | 62 | 62 | 88 | 73 | 95 | 65 | 91 | 36 | 10 | 42 | 24 | 49 | 46 | 38 | 14 | 35 | 9 | 11 |
| 10 | 59 | 81 | 66 | 90 | 65 | 90 | 67 | 93 | 68 | 94 | 87 | 99 | 50 | 57 | 60 | 85 | 71 | 93 | 63 | 89 | 34 | 8 | 41 | 21 | 47 | 40 | 36 | 12 | 33 | 7 | 10 |
| 9 | 57 | 77 | 64 | 88 | 63 | 88 | 65 | 91 | 65 | 92 | 82 | 98 | 49 | 51 | 58 | 81 | 68 | 92 | 61 | 87 | 32 | 6 | 39 | 18 | 45 | 34 | 35 | 9 | 31 | 6 | 9 |
| 8 | 55 | 73 | 62 | 86 | 60 | 85 | 62 | 88 | 63 | 90 | 77 | 97 | 47 | 46 | 55 | 76 | 65 | 90 | 58 | 84 | 30 | 4 | 38 | 15 | 43 | 28 | 34 | 7 | 30 | 4 | 8 |
| 7 | 53 | 68 | 59 | 83 | 58 | 82 | 59 | 84 | 60 | 88 | 73 | 95 | 46 | 40 | 53 | 71 | 62 | 87 | 56 | 82 | 28 | 3 | 37 | 13 | 41 | 23 | 33 | 5 | 28 | 3 | 7 |
| 6 | 51 | 63 | 57 | 79 | 56 | 78 | 57 | 80 | 58 | 85 | 68 | 94 | 44 | 34 | 51 | 64 | 60 | 85 | 54 | 78 | 26 | 2 | 36 | 10 | 40 | 18 | 32 | 3 | 26 | 3 | 6 |
| 5 | 49 | 57 | 54 | 75 | 54 | 73 | 54 | 74 | 55 | 81 | 63 | 91 | 43 | 28 | 49 | 56 | 57 | 82 | 52 | 73 | 24 | 1 | 34 | 8 | 38 | 13 | 30 | 2 | 24 | 2 | 5 |
| 4 | 47 | 50 | 52 | 70 | 51 | 67 | 51 | 67 | 53 | 75 | 59 | 88 | 42 | 22 | 46 | 46 | 54 | 77 | 50 | 67 | 22 | 1 | 33 | 6 | 36 | 9 | 29 | 1 | 23 | 1 | 4 |
| 3 | 46 | 42 | 49 | 64 | 49 | 59 | 49 | 57 | 50 | 67 | 54 | 81 | 40 | 17 | 44 | 34 | 51 | 72 | 48 | 59 | 21 | 1 | 32 | 4 | 34 | 6 | 28 | 1 | 21 | 1 | 3 |
| 2 | 44 | 33 | 47 | 55 | 47 | 49 | 46 | 45 | 48 | 56 | 49 | 69 | 39 | 12 | 42 | 22 | 49 | 65 | 46 | 48 | 19 | 1 | 31 | 3 | 32 | 3 | 27 | 1 | 19 | 1 | 2 |
| 1 | 42 | 24 | 45 | 43 | 44 | 37 | 43 | 29 | 45 | 39 | 45 | 28 | 37 | 7 | 40 | 10 | 46 | 53 | 44 | 30 | 17 | 1 | 29 | 1 | 30 | 1 | 26 | 1 | 17 | 1 | 1 |
| 0 | 40 | 13 | 42 | 22 | 42 | 20 | 41 | 11 | 43 | 11 | — | — | 36 | 4 | — | — | 43 | 26 | 42 | 1 | — | — | 28 | 1 | — | — | — | — | 16 | 1 | 0 |
| **Raw mean** | 5.37 | | 3.21 | | 3.48 | | 3.53 | | 2.95 | | 1.17 | | 9.76 | | 4.57 | | 2.48 | | 3.98 | | 17.07 | | 17.49 | | 11.63 | | 20.44 | | 19.73 | | **Raw mean** |
| **Raw SD** | 5.31 | | 4.14 | | 4.31 | | 3.76 | | 3.96 | | 2.13 | | 6.78 | | 4.46 | | 3.66 | | 4.77 | | 5.11 | | 8.03 | | 5.37 | | 8.38 | | 5.73 | | **Raw SD** |
| **T:90% Conf. int.** | 5 | | 5 | | 5 | | 6 | | 6 | | 6 | | 4 | | 5 | | 5 | | 5 | | 5 | | 4 | | 5 | | 4 | | 5 | | **T:90% Conf. int.** |

**Table A.6d** TRS–A Composite T Scores

| T score | Externalizing Problems | | | Internalizing Problems | | | School Problems | | | Adaptive Skills | | | Behavioral Symptoms Index | | | T score |
|---|---|---|---|---|---|---|---|---|---|---|---|---|---|---|---|---|
| | Combined | Female | Male | Combined | Female | Male | Combined | Female | Male | Combined | Female | Male | Combined | Female | Male | |
| 120 | — | 346–350 | — | 335–346 | — | 325–352 | — | — | — | — | — | — | 638–646 | 650–667 | 629–634 | 120 |
| 119 | — | 343–345 | — | 332–334 | 340–342 | 323–324 | — | — | — | — | — | — | 634–637 | 645–649 | 625–628 | 119 |
| 118 | 338–340 | 340–342 | — | 330–331 | 338–339 | 320–322 | — | — | — | — | — | — | 629–633 | 640–644 | 620–624 | 118 |
| 117 | 336–337 | 337–339 | 334 | 327–329 | 335–337 | 318–319 | — | — | — | — | — | — | 624–628 | 635–639 | 615–619 | 117 |
| 116 | 333–335 | 334–336 | 331–333 | 324–326 | 332–334 | 315–317 | — | — | — | — | — | — | 619–623 | 630–634 | 610–614 | 116 |
| 115 | 330–332 | 332–333 | 329–330 | 322–323 | 329–331 | 313–314 | — | — | — | — | — | — | 614–618 | 625–629 | 606–609 | 115 |
| 114 | 327–329 | 329–331 | 326–328 | 319–321 | 327–328 | 310–312 | — | — | — | — | — | — | 609–613 | 620–624 | 601–605 | 114 |
| 113 | 324–326 | 326–328 | 323–325 | 317–318 | 324–326 | 308–309 | — | — | — | — | — | — | 604–608 | 615–619 | 596–600 | 113 |
| 112 | 322–323 | 323–325 | 320–322 | 314–316 | 321–323 | 305–307 | — | — | — | — | — | — | 599–603 | 610–614 | 592–595 | 112 |
| 111 | 319–321 | 320–322 | 318–319 | 311–313 | 318–320 | 303–304 | — | — | — | — | — | — | 595–598 | 605–609 | 587–591 | 111 |
| 110 | 316–318 | 318–319 | 315–317 | 309–310 | 315–317 | 300–302 | — | — | — | — | — | — | 590–594 | 600–604 | 582–586 | 110 |
| 109 | 313–315 | 315–317 | 312–314 | 306–308 | 313–314 | 298–299 | — | — | — | — | — | — | 585–589 | 595–599 | 577–581 | 109 |
| 108 | 311–312 | 312–314 | 309–311 | 303–305 | 310–312 | 295–297 | — | — | — | — | — | — | 580–584 | 590–594 | 573–576 | 108 |
| 107 | 308–310 | 309–311 | 307–308 | 301–302 | 307–309 | 293–294 | — | — | — | — | — | — | 575–579 | 585–589 | 568–572 | 107 |
| 106 | 305–307 | 306–308 | 304–306 | 298–300 | 304–306 | 290–292 | — | — | — | — | — | — | 570–574 | 580–584 | 563–567 | 106 |
| 105 | 302–304 | 303–305 | 301–303 | 295–297 | 302–303 | 288–289 | — | — | — | — | — | — | 565–569 | 575–579 | 558–562 | 105 |
| 104 | 299–301 | 301–302 | 298–300 | 293–294 | 299–301 | 285–287 | — | — | — | — | — | — | 561–564 | 570–574 | 554–557 | 104 |
| 103 | 297–298 | 298–300 | 295–297 | 290–292 | 296–298 | 283–284 | — | — | — | — | — | — | 556–560 | 565–569 | 549–553 | 103 |
| 102 | 294–296 | 295–297 | 293–294 | 287–289 | 293–295 | 280–282 | — | — | — | — | — | — | 551–555 | 559–564 | 544–548 | 102 |
| 101 | 291–293 | 292–294 | 290–292 | 285–286 | 290–292 | 278–279 | — | — | — | — | — | — | 546–550 | 554–558 | 540–543 | 101 |
| 100 | 288–290 | 289–291 | 287–289 | 282–284 | 288–289 | 275–277 | — | — | — | — | — | — | 541–545 | 549–553 | 535–539 | 100 |
| 99 | 285–287 | 287–288 | 284–286 | 279–281 | 285–287 | 273–274 | — | — | — | — | — | — | 536–540 | 544–548 | 530–534 | 99 |
| 98 | 283–284 | 284–286 | 282–283 | 277–278 | 282–284 | 270–272 | — | — | — | — | — | — | 531–535 | 539–543 | 525–529 | 98 |
| 97 | 280–282 | 281–283 | 279–281 | 274–276 | 279–281 | 268–269 | — | — | — | — | — | — | 527–530 | 534–538 | 521–524 | 97 |
| 96 | 277–279 | 278–280 | 276–278 | 271–273 | 277–278 | 265–267 | — | 188–189 | — | — | — | — | 522–526 | 529–533 | 516–520 | 96 |
| 95 | 274–276 | 275–277 | 273–275 | 269–270 | 274–276 | 263–264 | — | 186–187 | — | — | — | — | 517–521 | 524–528 | 511–515 | 95 |
| 94 | 272–273 | 272–274 | 271–272 | 266–268 | 271–273 | 260–262 | — | 184–185 | — | — | — | — | 512–516 | 519–523 | 506–510 | 94 |
| 93 | 269–271 | 270–271 | 268–270 | 263–265 | 268–270 | 258–259 | — | 182–183 | — | — | — | — | 507–511 | 514–518 | 502–505 | 93 |
| 92 | 266–268 | 267–269 | 265–267 | 261–262 | 266–267 | 255–257 | 179 | 180–181 | — | — | — | — | 502–506 | 509–513 | 497–501 | 92 |
| 91 | 263–265 | 264–266 | 262–264 | 258–260 | 263–265 | 253–254 | 177–178 | 178–179 | — | — | — | — | 497–501 | 504–508 | 492–496 | 91 |
| 90 | 260–262 | 261–263 | 260–261 | 255–257 | 260–262 | 250–252 | 176 | 176–177 | 173–174 | — | — | — | 492–496 | 499–503 | 487–491 | 90 |
| 89 | 258–259 | 258–260 | 257–259 | 253–254 | 257–259 | 248–249 | 174–175 | 174–175 | 171–172 | — | — | — | 488–491 | 494–498 | 483–486 | 89 |
| 88 | 255–257 | 256–257 | 254–256 | 250–252 | 254–256 | 245–247 | 172–173 | 172–173 | 169–170 | — | — | — | 483–487 | 489–493 | 478–482 | 88 |
| 87 | 252–254 | 253–255 | 251–253 | 247–249 | 252–253 | 243–244 | 170–171 | 171 | 167–168 | — | — | — | 478–482 | 484–488 | 473–477 | 87 |
| 86 | 249–251 | 250–252 | 249–250 | 245–246 | 249–251 | 240–242 | 168–169 | 169–170 | 165–166 | — | — | — | 473–477 | 479–483 | 469–472 | 86 |
| 85 | 246–248 | 247–249 | 246–248 | 242–244 | 246–248 | 238–239 | 166–167 | 167–168 | 163–164 | — | — | — | 468–472 | 474–478 | 464–468 | 85 |
| 84 | 244–245 | 244–246 | 243–245 | 239–241 | 243–245 | 235–237 | 164–165 | 165–166 | 161–162 | — | — | — | 463–467 | 469–473 | 459–463 | 84 |
| 83 | 241–243 | 241–243 | 240–242 | 237–238 | 241–242 | 233–234 | 162–163 | 163–164 | 160 | — | — | — | 458–462 | 464–468 | 454–458 | 83 |
| 82 | 238–240 | 239–240 | 237–239 | 234–236 | 238–240 | 230–232 | 160–161 | 161–162 | 158–159 | — | — | — | 454–457 | 459–463 | 450–453 | 82 |
| 81 | 235–237 | 236–238 | 235–236 | 231–233 | 235–237 | 228–229 | 158–159 | 159–160 | 156–157 | — | — | — | 449–453 | 454–458 | 445–449 | 81 |
| 80 | 233–234 | 233–235 | 232–234 | 229–230 | 232–234 | 225–227 | 157 | 157–158 | 154–155 | — | — | — | 444–448 | 449–453 | 440–444 | 80 |
| 79 | 230–232 | 230–232 | 229–231 | 226–228 | 227–229 | 223–224 | 155–156 | 155–156 | 152–153 | — | — | — | 439–443 | 444–448 | 435–439 | 79 |
| 78 | 227–229 | 227–229 | 226–228 | 223–225 | 224–226 | 220–222 | 153–154 | 153–154 | 150–151 | — | — | — | 434–438 | 439–443 | 431–434 | 78 |
| 77 | 224–226 | 225–226 | 224–225 | 221–222 | 221–223 | 218–219 | 151–152 | 151–152 | 148–149 | — | — | — | 429–433 | 434–438 | 426–430 | 77 |
| 76 | 221–223 | 222–224 | 221–223 | 218–220 | 218–220 | 215–217 | 149–150 | 149–150 | 146–147 | — | — | — | 424–428 | 429–433 | 421–425 | 76 |
| 75 | 219–220 | 219–221 | 218–220 | 215–217 | 216–217 | 213–214 | 147–148 | 148 | 145 | — | — | — | 420–423 | 423–428 | 417–420 | 75 |
| 74 | 216–218 | 216–218 | 215–217 | 213–214 | 213–215 | 210–212 | 145–146 | 146–147 | 143–144 | — | — | — | 415–419 | 418–422 | 412–416 | 74 |
| 73 | 213–215 | 213–215 | 213–214 | 210–212 | 210–212 | 208–209 | 143–144 | 144–145 | 141–142 | — | — | — | 410–414 | 413–417 | 407–411 | 73 |
| 72 | 210–212 | 210–212 | 210–212 | 207–209 | 207–209 | 205–207 | 141–142 | 142–143 | 139–140 | — | — | — | 405–409 | 408–412 | 402–406 | 72 |
| 71 | 208–209 | 208–209 | 207–209 | 205–206 | 205–206 | 202–204 | 139–140 | 140–141 | 137–138 | — | — | — | 400–404 | 403–407 | 398–401 | 71 |
| 70 | 205–207 | 205–207 | 204–206 | 202–204 | 202–204 | 200–201 | 138 | 138–139 | 135–136 | — | — | — | 395–399 | 398–402 | 393–397 | 70 |
| 69 | 202–204 | 202–204 | 202–203 | 199–201 | 199–201 | 197–199 | 136–137 | 136–137 | 133–134 | — | — | — | 390–394 | 393–397 | 388–392 | 69 |
| 68 | 199–201 | 199–201 | 199–201 | 197–198 | 196–198 | 195–196 | 134–135 | 134–135 | 131–132 | — | — | — | 385–389 | 388–392 | 383–387 | 68 |
| 67 | 196–198 | 196–198 | 196–198 | 194–196 | 193–195 | 192–194 | 132–133 | 132–133 | 130 | — | — | — | 381–384 | 383–387 | 379–382 | 67 |
| 66 | 194–195 | 194–195 | 193–195 | 191–193 | — | 190–191 | 130–131 | 130–131 | — | — | — | 321–325 | 376–380 | 378–382 | 374–378 | 66 |

## Table A.6d TRS–A Composite T Scores (continued)

| T score | Externalizing Problems Combined | Female | Male | Internalizing Problems Combined | Female | Male | School Problems Combined | Female | Male | Adaptive Skills Combined | Female | Male | Behavioral Symptoms Index Combined | Female | Male | T score |
|---|---|---|---|---|---|---|---|---|---|---|---|---|---|---|---|---|
| 65 | 191–193 | 191–193 | 191–192 | 189–190 | 191–192 | 187–189 | 128–129 | 128–129 | 128–129 | 317–318 | — | 317–320 | 371–375 | 373–377 | 369–373 | 65 |
| 64 | 188–190 | 188–190 | 188–190 | 186–188 | 188–190 | 185–186 | 126–127 | 126–127 | 126–127 | 312–316 | 313 | 312–316 | 366–370 | 368–372 | 365–368 | 64 |
| 63 | 185–187 | 185–187 | 185–187 | 184–185 | 185–187 | 182–184 | 124–125 | 125 | 124–125 | 308–311 | 308–312 | 307–311 | 361–365 | 363–367 | 360–364 | 63 |
| 62 | 182–184 | 182–184 | 182–184 | 181–183 | 182–184 | 180–181 | 122–123 | 123–124 | 122–123 | 303–307 | 304–307 | 303–306 | 356–360 | 358–362 | 355–359 | 62 |
| 61 | 180–181 | 179–181 | 180–181 | 178–180 | 180–181 | 177–179 | 120–121 | 121–122 | 120–121 | 298–302 | 299–303 | 298–302 | 351–355 | 353–357 | 350–354 | 61 |
| 60 | 177–179 | 177–178 | 177–179 | 176–177 | 177–179 | 175–176 | 119 | 119–120 | 118–119 | 294–297 | 294–298 | 294–297 | 347–350 | 348–352 | 346–349 | 60 |
| 59 | 174–176 | 174–176 | 174–176 | 173–175 | 174–176 | 172–174 | 117–118 | 117–118 | 116–117 | 289–293 | 290–293 | 289–293 | 342–346 | 343–347 | 341–345 | 59 |
| 58 | 171–173 | 171–173 | 171–173 | 170–172 | 171–173 | 170–171 | 115–116 | 115–116 | 115 | 285–288 | 285–289 | 285–288 | 337–341 | 338–342 | 336–340 | 58 |
| 57 | 169–170 | 168–170 | 168–170 | 168–169 | 169–170 | 167–169 | 113–114 | 113–114 | 113–114 | 280–284 | 281–284 | 280–284 | 332–336 | 333–337 | 331–335 | 57 |
| 56 | 166–168 | 165–167 | 166–167 | 165–167 | 166–168 | 165–166 | 111–112 | 111–112 | 111–112 | 276–279 | 276–280 | 276–279 | 327–331 | 328–332 | 327–330 | 56 |
| 55 | 163–165 | 163–164 | 163–165 | 162–164 | 163–165 | 162–164 | 109–110 | 109–110 | 109–110 | 271–275 | 271–275 | 271–275 | 322–326 | 323–327 | 322–326 | 55 |
| 54 | 160–162 | 160–162 | 160–162 | 160–161 | 160–162 | 160–161 | 107–108 | 107–108 | 107–108 | 267–270 | 267–270 | 267–270 | 317–321 | 318–322 | 317–321 | 54 |
| 53 | 157–159 | 157–159 | 157–159 | 157–159 | 157–159 | 157–159 | 105–106 | 105–106 | 105–106 | 262–266 | 262–266 | 262–266 | 313–316 | 313–317 | 312–316 | 53 |
| 52 | 155–156 | 154–156 | 155–156 | 154–156 | 155–156 | 155–156 | 103–104 | 103–104 | 103–104 | 257–261 | 258–261 | 257–261 | 308–312 | 308–312 | 308–311 | 52 |
| 51 | 152–154 | 151–153 | 152–154 | 152–153 | 152–154 | 152–154 | 101–102 | 101–102 | 101–102 | 253–256 | 253–257 | 253–256 | 303–307 | 303–307 | 303–307 | 51 |
| 50 | 149–151 | 149–150 | 149–151 | 149–151 | 149–151 | 150–151 | 100 | 100 | 100 | 248–252 | 248–252 | 248–252 | 298–302 | 298–302 | 298–302 | 50 |
| 49 | 146–148 | 146–148 | 146–148 | 146–148 | 146–148 | 147–149 | 98–99 | 98–99 | 98–99 | 244–247 | 244–247 | 244–247 | 293–297 | 293–297 | 294–297 | 49 |
| 48 | 143–145 | 143–145 | 144–145 | 144–145 | 144–145 | 145–146 | 96–97 | 96–97 | 96–97 | 239–243 | 239–243 | 239–243 | 288–292 | 287–292 | 289–293 | 48 |
| 47 | 141–142 | 140–142 | 141–143 | 141–143 | 141–143 | 142–144 | 94–95 | 94–95 | 94–95 | 235–238 | 235–238 | 235–238 | 283–287 | 282–286 | 284–288 | 47 |
| 46 | 138–140 | 137–139 | 138–140 | 138–140 | 138–140 | 140–141 | 92–93 | 92–93 | 92–93 | 230–234 | 230–234 | 230–234 | 278–282 | 277–281 | 279–283 | 46 |
| 45 | 135–137 | 134–136 | 135–137 | 136–137 | 135–137 | 137–139 | 90–91 | 90–91 | 90–91 | 226–229 | 225–229 | 226–229 | 274–277 | 272–276 | 275–278 | 45 |
| 44 | 132–134 | 132–133 | 133–134 | 133–135 | 132–134 | 135–136 | 88–89 | 88–89 | 88–89 | 221–225 | 221–224 | 221–225 | 269–273 | 267–271 | 270–274 | 44 |
| 43 | 130–131 | 131 | 130–132 | 130–132 | 130–131 | 132–134 | 86–87 | 86–87 | 86–87 | 216–220 | 216–220 | 217–220 | 264–268 | 262–266 | 265–269 | 43 |
| 42 | 128–129 | — | 127–129 | 128–129 | 127–129 | 130–131 | 84–85 | 84–85 | 85 | 212–215 | 212–215 | 212–216 | 259–263 | 257–261 | 260–264 | 42 |
| 41 | — | — | 124–126 | — | — | 129 | 82–83 | 82–83 | 83–84 | 207–211 | 207–211 | 207–211 | 254–258 | 255–256 | 256–259 | 41 |
| 40 | — | — | — | — | — | — | 81 | — | 81–82 | 203–206 | 202–206 | 203–206 | 251–253 | — | 251–255 | 40 |
| 39 | — | — | — | — | — | — | 79–80 | — | 79–80 | 198–202 | 198–201 | 198–202 | — | — | 246–250 | 39 |
| 38 | — | — | — | — | — | — | — | — | 77–78 | 194–197 | 193–197 | 194–197 | — | — | — | 38 |
| 37 | — | — | — | — | — | — | — | — | 76 | 189–193 | 189–192 | 189–193 | — | — | — | 37 |
| 36 | — | — | — | — | — | — | — | — | — | 184–188 | 184–188 | 185–188 | — | — | — | 36 |
| 35 | — | — | — | — | — | — | — | — | — | 180–183 | 179–183 | 180–184 | — | — | — | 35 |
| 34 | — | — | — | — | — | — | — | — | — | 175–179 | 175–178 | 176–179 | — | — | — | 34 |
| 33 | — | — | — | — | — | — | — | — | — | 171–174 | 170–174 | 171–175 | — | — | — | 33 |
| 32 | — | — | — | — | — | — | — | — | — | 166–170 | 166–169 | 167–170 | — | — | — | 32 |
| 31 | — | — | — | — | — | — | — | — | — | 162–165 | 161–165 | 162–166 | — | — | — | 31 |
| 30 | — | — | — | — | — | — | — | — | — | 157–161 | 156–160 | 158–161 | — | — | — | 30 |
| 29 | — | — | — | — | — | — | — | — | — | 153–156 | 152–155 | 153–157 | — | — | — | 29 |
| 28 | — | — | — | — | — | — | — | — | — | 148–152 | 147–151 | 148–152 | — | — | — | 28 |
| 27 | — | — | — | — | — | — | — | — | — | 143–147 | 143–146 | 144–147 | — | — | — | 27 |
| 26 | — | — | — | — | — | — | — | — | — | 139–142 | 138–142 | 139–143 | — | — | — | 26 |
| 25 | — | — | — | — | — | — | — | — | — | 134–138 | 133–137 | 135–138 | — | — | — | 25 |
| 24 | — | — | — | — | — | — | — | — | — | 130–133 | 129–132 | 130–134 | — | — | — | 24 |
| 23 | — | — | — | — | — | — | — | — | — | 125–129 | 124–128 | 126–129 | — | — | — | 23 |
| 22 | — | — | — | — | — | — | — | — | — | 121–124 | 120–123 | 121–125 | — | — | — | 22 |
| 21 | — | — | — | — | — | — | — | — | — | 116–120 | 115–119 | 117–120 | — | — | — | 21 |
| 20 | — | — | — | — | — | — | — | — | — | 112–115 | 110–114 | 115–116 | — | — | — | 20 |
| 19 | — | — | — | — | — | — | — | — | — | 107–111 | 106–109 | — | — | — | — | 19 |
| 18 | — | — | — | — | — | — | — | — | — | 106 | 101–105 | — | — | — | — | 18 |
| 17 | — | — | — | — | — | — | — | — | — | — | 97–100 | — | — | — | — | 17 |
| 16 | — | — | — | — | — | — | — | — | — | — | 94–96 | — | — | — | — | 16 |
| 15 | — | — | — | — | — | — | — | — | — | — | — | — | — | — | — | 15 |
| 14 | — | — | — | — | — | — | — | — | — | — | — | — | — | — | — | 14 |
| 13 | — | — | — | — | — | — | — | — | — | — | — | — | — | — | — | 13 |
| 12 | — | — | — | — | — | — | — | — | — | — | — | — | — | — | — | 12 |
| 11 | — | — | — | — | — | — | — | — | — | — | — | — | — | — | — | 11 |
| 10 | — | — | — | — | — | — | — | — | — | — | — | — | — | — | — | 10 |
| T: 90% Conf. int. | 3 | 3 | 3 | 4 | 3 | 4 | 3 | 3 | 4 | 2 | 2 | 2 | 2 | 2 | 3 | T: 90% Conf. int. |

**Table A.6e** TRS–A Composite Percentiles

| %ile | Externalizing Problems Combined | Externalizing Problems Female | Externalizing Problems Male | Internalizing Problems Combined | Internalizing Problems Female | Internalizing Problems Male | School Problems Combined | School Problems Female | School Problems Male | Adaptive Skills Combined | Adaptive Skills Female | Adaptive Skills Male | Behavioral Symptoms Index Combined | Behavioral Symptoms Index Female | Behavioral Symptoms Index Male | %ile |
|---|---|---|---|---|---|---|---|---|---|---|---|---|---|---|---|---|
| 99 | 236–340 | 249–350 | 226–334 | 244–346 | 253–342 | 235–352 | 155–179 | 161–189 | 151–174 | – | – | – | 452–646 | 471–667 | 439–634 | 99 |
| 98 | 228–235 | 237–248 | 220–225 | 228–243 | 235–252 | 222–234 | 149–154 | 153–160 | 145–150 | 318 | – | 325 | 433–451 | 447–470 | 422–438 | 98 |
| 97 | 222–227 | 228–236 | 215–219 | 217–227 | 223–234 | 214–221 | 144–148 | 147–152 | 141–144 | 316–317 | 312–313 | 322–324 | 419–432 | 429–446 | 410–421 | 97 |
| 96 | 217–221 | 220–227 | 211–214 | 209–216 | 214–222 | 207–213 | 140–143 | 143–146 | 138–140 | 314–315 | 311 | 319–321 | 408–418 | 415–428 | 400–409 | 96 |
| 95 | 212–216 | 213–219 | 208–210 | 203–208 | 206–213 | 202–206 | 137–139 | 139–142 | 135–137 | 313 | 309–310 | 317–318 | 398–407 | 404–414 | 392–399 | 95 |
| 94 | 207–211 | 207–212 | 204–207 | 197–202 | 200–205 | 197–201 | 135–136 | 136–138 | 133–134 | 311–312 | 308 | 315–316 | 390–397 | 394–403 | 385–391 | 94 |
| 93 | 203–206 | 201–206 | 201–203 | 193–196 | 195–199 | 193–196 | 132–135 | 133–135 | 131–132 | 309–310 | 307 | 313–314 | 384–389 | 385–393 | 379–384 | 93 |
| 92 | 199–202 | 196–200 | 198–200 | 189–192 | 190–194 | 190–192 | 130–131 | 131–132 | 129–130 | 308 | 306 | 311–312 | 377–383 | 378–384 | 374–378 | 92 |
| 91 | 196–198 | 192–195 | 195–197 | 185–188 | 186–189 | 186–189 | 128–129 | 129–130 | 127–128 | 307 | 305 | 309–310 | 372–376 | 371–377 | 369–373 | 91 |
| 90 | 192–195 | 188–191 | 193–194 | 182–184 | 183–185 | 184–185 | 127 | 127–128 | 126 | 305–306 | 304 | 307–308 | 367–371 | 365–370 | 365–368 | 90 |
| 89 | 189–191 | 184–187 | 190–192 | 179–181 | 179–182 | 181–183 | 125–126 | 125–126 | 124–125 | 304 | 302–303 | 306 | 362–366 | 360–364 | 361–364 | 89 |
| 88 | 186–188 | 181–183 | 188–189 | 177–178 | 177–178 | 179–180 | 124 | 123–124 | 123 | 303 | 301 | 304–305 | 358–361 | 355–359 | 357–360 | 88 |
| 87 | 184–185 | 178–180 | 186–187 | 174–176 | 174–176 | 177–178 | 122–123 | 122 | 122 | 301–302 | 300 | 302–303 | 354–357 | 350–354 | 354–356 | 87 |
| 86 | 181–183 | 175–177 | 183–185 | 172–173 | 172–173 | 175–176 | 121 | 120–121 | 120–121 | 300 | 299 | 301 | 350–353 | 346–349 | 351–353 | 86 |
| 85 | 179–180 | 172–174 | 181–182 | 170–171 | 170–171 | 173–174 | 120 | 119 | 119 | 299 | 298 | 299–300 | 347–349 | 342–345 | 347–350 | 85 |
| 84 | 176–178 | 170–171 | 179–180 | 169 | 168–169 | 171–172 | 119 | 117–118 | 118 | 298 | 297 | 298 | 343–346 | 338–341 | 345–346 | 84 |
| 83 | 174–175 | 168–169 | 177–178 | 167–168 | 166–167 | 169–170 | 118 | 116 | 117 | 296–297 | 296 | 297 | 340–342 | 335–337 | 342–344 | 83 |
| 82 | 172–173 | 166–167 | 176 | 165–166 | 164–165 | 168 | 116–117 | 115 | 116 | 295 | 295 | 295–296 | 337–339 | 332–334 | 339–341 | 82 |
| 81 | 170–171 | 164–165 | 174–175 | 164 | 162–163 | 166–167 | 115 | 114 | 115 | 294 | 294 | 294 | 335–336 | 329–331 | 337–338 | 81 |
| 80 | 168–169 | 162–163 | 172–173 | 162–163 | 161 | 165 | – | 113 | – | 293 | 293 | 292–293 | 332–334 | 326–328 | 334–336 | 80 |
| 79 | 167 | 160–161 | 171 | 161 | 160 | 164 | 114 | 112 | 114 | 292 | 292 | 291 | 329–331 | 323–325 | 332–333 | 79 |
| 78 | 165–166 | 159 | 169–170 | 160 | 158–159 | 163 | 113 | 111 | 113 | 290–291 | 291 | 290 | 327–328 | 321–322 | 330–331 | 78 |
| 77 | 163–164 | 157–158 | 167–168 | 159 | 157 | 161–162 | 112 | 110 | 112 | 289 | 290 | 288–289 | 325–326 | 318–320 | 328–329 | 77 |
| 76 | 162 | 156 | 166 | 158 | 156 | 160 | 111 | 109 | 111 | 288 | 289 | 287 | 323–324 | 316–317 | 326–327 | 76 |
| 75 | 160–161 | 155 | 165 | 157 | 155 | 159 | 110 | 108 | – | 287 | 288 | 286 | 320–322 | 314–315 | 324–325 | 75 |
| 74 | 159 | 153–154 | 163–164 | 156 | 154 | 158 | 109 | 107 | 110 | 286 | 287 | 284–285 | 318–319 | 312–313 | 322–323 | 74 |
| 73 | 158 | 152 | 162 | 155 | 153 | 157 | – | – | 109 | 285 | 286 | 283 | 317 | 310–311 | 320–321 | 73 |
| 72 | 156–157 | 151 | 161 | 154 | 152 | 156 | 108 | 106 | – | 283–284 | 285 | 282 | 315–316 | 308–309 | 318–319 | 72 |
| 71 | 155 | 150 | 159–160 | 153 | 151 | 155 | 107 | 105 | 108 | 282 | 284 | 281 | 313–314 | 306–307 | 317 | 71 |
| 70 | 154 | 149 | 158 | 152 | 150 | – | – | – | 107 | 281 | 283 | 279–280 | 311–312 | 304–305 | 315–316 | 70 |
| 69 | 153 | 148 | 157 | 151 | – | 154 | 106 | 104 | – | 280 | 282 | 278 | 309–310 | 303 | 313–314 | 69 |
| 68 | 152 | 147 | 156 | 150 | 149 | 153 | 105 | 103 | 106 | 279 | 280–281 | 277 | 308 | 301–302 | 312 | 68 |
| 67 | 151 | – | 155 | – | 148 | 152 | – | – | 105 | 277–278 | 279 | 275–276 | 306–307 | 300 | 310–311 | 67 |
| 66 | 150 | 146 | 154 | 149 | 147 | 151 | 104 | 102 | – | 276 | 278 | 274 | 305 | 298–299 | 309 | 66 |
| 65 | 149 | 145 | 153 | 148 | – | 150 | 103 | 101 | 104 | 275 | 277 | 273 | 303–304 | 297 | 307–308 | 65 |
| 64 | 148 | 144 | 152 | 147 | 146 | – | 102 | – | – | 274 | 276 | 272 | 302 | 295–296 | 306 | 64 |
| 63 | 147 | – | 151 | 146 | – | 149 | – | 100 | 103 | 273 | 275 | 270–271 | 300–301 | 294 | 304–305 | 63 |
| 62 | 146 | 143 | 150 | 145 | 145 | – | 101 | – | – | 272 | 274 | 269 | 299 | 293 | 303 | 62 |
| 61 | – | 142 | 149 | – | 144 | 148 | – | 99 | 102 | 270–271 | 273 | 268 | 298 | 292 | 302 | 61 |
| 60 | 145 | – | 148 | 144 | – | – | 100 | – | – | 269 | 271–272 | 267 | 296–297 | 290–291 | 300–301 | 60 |
| 59 | 144 | 141 | 147 | – | 143 | 147 | – | 98 | 101 | 268 | 270 | 265–266 | 295 | 289 | 299 | 59 |
| 58 | 143 | – | 146 | 143 | – | 146 | 99 | – | – | 267 | 269 | 264 | 294 | 288 | 298 | 58 |
| 57 | – | 140 | – | – | 142 | – | – | 97 | 100 | 265–266 | 268 | 263 | 293 | 287 | 297 | 57 |
| 56 | 142 | – | 145 | 142 | – | 145 | 98 | – | – | 264 | 267 | 261–262 | 291–292 | 286 | 295–296 | 56 |
| 55 | 141 | 139 | 144 | – | 141 | 144 | – | 96 | 99 | 263 | 265–266 | 260 | 290 | 285 | 294 | 55 |
| 54 | – | – | 143 | 141 | – | 144 | 97 | – | – | 262 | 264 | 259 | 289 | 284 | 293 | 54 |
| 53 | 140 | – | 142 | – | 140 | 143 | – | 95 | 98 | 260–261 | 263 | 258 | 288 | 283 | 292 | 53 |
| 52 | – | 138 | – | – | – | – | 96 | – | – | 259 | 262 | 256–257 | 287 | 282 | 291 | 52 |
| 51 | 139 | – | 141 | – | – | 143 | – | – | 97 | 258 | 260–261 | 255 | 286 | 281 | 290 | 51 |

## Table A.6e TRS-A Composite Percentiles (continued)

| %ile | Externalizing Problems | | | Internalizing Problems | | | School Problems | | | Adaptive Skills | | | Behavioral Symptoms Index | | | %ile |
|---|---|---|---|---|---|---|---|---|---|---|---|---|---|---|---|---|
| | Combined | Female | Male | Combined | Female | Male | Combined | Female | Male | Combined | Female | Male | Combined | Female | Male | |
| 50 | – | 137 | 140 | – | – | 142 | – | 94 | – | 256–257 | 259 | 254 | 285 | – | 289 | 50 |
| 49 | 138 | – | – | 140 | 139 | – | 95 | – | 96 | 255 | 258 | 252–253 | 284 | 280 | 288 | 49 |
| 48 | – | – | 139 | – | – | 141 | – | – | – | 254 | 257 | 251 | 283 | 279 | 286–287 | 48 |
| 47 | 137 | – | – | 139 | – | – | – | 93 | 95 | 252–253 | 255–256 | 250 | 282 | 278 | 285 | 47 |
| 46 | – | 136 | 138 | – | 138 | – | 94 | – | – | 251 | 254 | 248–249 | 281 | 277 | 284 | 46 |
| 45 | 136 | – | 137 | 138 | – | 140 | 93 | 92 | 94 | 250 | 252–253 | 247 | 280 | – | 283 | 45 |
| 44 | – | – | – | – | – | – | – | – | – | 248–249 | 251 | 246 | 279 | 276 | 282 | 44 |
| 43 | 135 | 135 | 136 | 137 | 137 | 139 | 92 | – | 93 | 247 | 250 | 244–245 | 278 | 275 | 281 | 43 |
| 42 | – | – | – | – | – | – | – | 91 | – | 245–246 | 248–249 | 243 | – | – | 280 | 42 |
| 41 | – | – | 135 | – | – | – | – | – | – | 244 | 247 | 241–242 | 277 | 274 | 279 | 41 |
| 40 | 134 | – | – | – | 136 | 138 | 91 | 90 | 92 | 243 | 245–246 | 240 | 276 | 273 | 278 | 40 |
| 39 | – | 134 | 134 | 136 | – | – | – | – | – | 241–242 | 244 | 239 | 275 | – | – | 39 |
| 38 | 133 | – | – | – | – | – | 90 | – | 91 | 240 | 242–243 | 237–238 | 274 | 272 | 277 | 38 |
| 37 | – | – | 133 | – | – | 137 | – | – | – | 238–239 | 241 | 236 | 273 | – | 276 | 37 |
| 36 | – | – | – | – | – | – | – | 89 | – | 237 | 239–240 | 234–235 | – | 271 | 275 | 36 |
| 35 | 132 | – | 132 | 135 | 135 | – | 89 | – | 90 | 235–236 | 237–238 | 233 | 272 | 270 | 274 | 35 |
| 34 | – | 133 | – | – | – | 136 | – | 88 | – | 233–234 | 236 | 231–232 | 271 | – | 273 | 34 |
| 33 | 131 | – | 131 | – | – | – | 88 | – | 89 | 232 | 234–235 | 230 | 270 | 269 | 272 | 33 |
| 32 | – | – | – | – | – | – | – | – | – | 230–231 | 232–233 | 228–229 | – | – | 271 | 32 |
| 31 | – | – | 130 | 134 | 134 | 135 | – | – | 88 | 229 | 231 | 227 | 269 | 268 | 270 | 31 |
| 30 | – | – | – | – | – | – | 87 | 87 | – | 227–228 | 229–230 | 225–226 | 268 | – | 269 | 30 |
| 29 | – | 132 | – | – | – | – | – | – | 87 | 225–226 | 227–228 | 224 | 267 | 267 | 268 | 29 |
| 28 | – | – | 129 | 133 | – | 134 | – | – | – | 223–224 | 225–226 | 222–223 | – | – | 267 | 28 |
| 27 | 130 | – | – | – | 133 | – | – | – | – | 222 | 223–224 | 220–221 | 266 | 266 | – | 27 |
| 26 | – | – | – | – | – | – | 86 | 86 | 86 | 220–221 | 221–222 | 219 | 265 | – | 266 | 26 |
| 25 | – | – | 128 | – | – | 133 | – | – | – | 218–219 | 219–220 | 217–218 | – | 265 | 265 | 25 |
| 24 | – | – | – | – | – | – | – | – | 85 | 216–217 | 217–218 | 215–216 | 264 | – | 264 | 24 |
| 23 | 129 | – | 127 | – | – | – | 85 | – | – | 214–215 | 215–216 | 213–214 | 263 | 264 | 263 | 23 |
| 22 | – | – | – | 132 | – | – | – | 85 | – | 212–213 | 213–214 | 212 | – | – | 262 | 22 |
| 21 | – | – | – | – | 132 | 132 | 84 | – | 84 | 210–211 | 211–212 | 210–211 | 262 | – | 261 | 21 |
| 20 | – | 131 | 126 | – | – | – | – | – | – | 208–209 | 208–210 | 208–209 | 261 | 263 | 260 | 20 |
| 19 | – | – | – | – | – | – | – | – | – | 206–207 | 206–207 | 206–207 | – | – | – | 19 |
| 18 | 128 | – | – | 131 | – | – | 83 | 84 | 83 | 204–205 | 204–205 | 204–205 | 260 | 262 | 259 | 18 |
| 17 | – | – | 125 | – | – | 131 | – | – | – | 201–203 | 201–203 | 202–203 | 259 | – | 258 | 17 |
| 16 | – | – | – | – | – | – | – | – | 82 | 199–200 | 199–200 | 200–201 | – | – | 257 | 16 |
| 15 | – | – | – | – | – | – | 82 | – | 81 | 197–198 | 196–198 | 197–199 | 258 | 261 | 256 | 15 |
| 14 | – | – | – | – | – | – | – | – | – | 194–196 | 193–195 | 195–196 | 257 | – | 255 | 14 |
| 13 | – | – | 124 | 130 | 131 | 130 | 81 | 83 | 80 | 192–193 | 190–192 | 193–194 | – | 260 | 254 | 13 |
| 12 | – | – | – | – | – | – | – | – | – | 189–191 | 187–189 | 190–192 | 256 | – | 253 | 12 |
| 11 | – | – | – | – | – | – | – | – | – | 186–188 | 184–186 | 186–189 | 255 | – | 252 | 11 |
| 10 | – | – | – | 129 | – | 129 | 80 | – | 79 | 183–185 | 180–183 | 185–187 | 254 | 259 | 251 | 10 |
| 9 | – | – | – | – | – | – | – | 82 | 78 | 180–182 | 177–179 | 182–184 | – | – | 250 | 9 |
| 8 | – | – | – | – | – | – | – | – | – | 176–179 | 173–176 | 178–181 | 253 | – | 249 | 8 |
| 7 | – | – | – | – | – | – | 79 | – | 77 | 173–175 | 169–172 | 176–178 | 252 | 258 | 248 | 7 |
| 6 | – | – | – | – | – | – | – | – | 76 | 169–172 | 164–168 | 172–175 | – | – | 247 | 6 |
| 5 | – | – | – | – | 130 | – | – | – | – | 164–168 | 159–163 | 168–171 | 251 | 257 | 246 | 5 |
| 4 | – | – | – | 128 | – | – | – | – | – | 159–163 | 153–158 | 163–167 | – | – | – | 4 |
| 3 | – | – | – | – | – | – | – | – | – | 153–158 | 147–152 | 158–162 | – | – | – | 3 |
| 2 | – | – | – | – | 129 | – | – | – | – | 146–152 | 138–146 | 151–157 | – | 256 | – | 2 |
| 1 | – | – | – | – | 127–128 | – | – | – | – | 106–145 | 94–137 | 115–150 | – | 255 | – | 1 |

## Table A.7a  PRS-P T Scores and Percentiles

| Raw score | Hyperactivity T | Hyperactivity %ile | Aggression T | Aggression %ile | Anxiety T | Anxiety %ile | Depression T | Depression %ile | Somatization T | Somatization %ile | Attention Problems T | Attention Problems %ile | Atypicality T | Atypicality %ile | Withdrawal T | Withdrawal %ile | Adaptability T | Adaptability %ile | Social Skills T | Social Skills %ile | Activities of Daily Living T | Activities of Daily Living %ile | Functional Communication T | Functional Communication %ile | Raw score |
|---|---|---|---|---|---|---|---|---|---|---|---|---|---|---|---|---|---|---|---|---|---|---|---|---|---|
| 39 | — | — | — | — | — | — | — | — | 120 | 99 | — | — | — | — | — | — | — | — | — | — | — | — | — | — | 39 |
| 38 | — | — | — | — | — | — | — | — | 120 | 99 | — | — | — | — | — | — | — | — | — | — | — | — | — | — | 38 |
| 37 | — | — | — | — | — | — | — | — | 120 | 99 | — | — | — | — | — | — | — | — | — | — | — | — | — | — | 37 |
| 36 | — | — | — | — | — | — | — | — | 120 | 99 | — | — | — | — | 102 | 99 | — | — | — | — | — | — | — | — | 36 |
| 35 | — | — | — | — | — | — | — | — | 119 | 99 | — | — | — | — | 100 | 99 | — | — | — | — | — | — | — | — | 35 |
| 34 | — | — | — | — | — | — | — | — | 116 | 99 | — | — | — | — | 98 | 99 | — | — | — | — | — | — | — | — | 34 |
| 33 | 92 | 99 | — | — | 117 | 99 | 109 | 99 | 114 | 99 | — | — | — | — | 96 | 99 | — | — | — | — | — | — | 73 | 99 | 33 |
| 32 | 90 | 99 | — | — | 114 | 99 | 107 | 99 | 112 | 99 | — | — | — | — | 94 | 99 | — | — | — | — | — | — | 72 | 99 | 32 |
| 31 | 88 | 99 | — | — | 112 | 99 | 104 | 99 | 109 | 99 | — | — | — | — | 92 | 99 | — | — | — | — | — | — | 70 | 99 | 31 |
| 30 | 86 | 99 | — | — | 110 | 99 | 102 | 99 | 107 | 99 | — | — | 120 | 99 | 90 | 99 | — | — | — | — | — | — | 69 | 99 | 30 |
| 29 | 84 | 99 | — | — | 107 | 99 | 100 | 99 | 105 | 99 | — | — | 118 | 99 | 88 | 99 | — | — | — | — | — | — | 67 | 97 | 29 |
| 28 | 82 | 99 | — | — | 105 | 99 | 97 | 99 | 102 | 99 | — | — | 115 | 99 | 86 | 99 | — | — | — | — | — | — | 66 | 95 | 28 |
| 27 | 80 | 99 | — | — | 103 | 99 | 95 | 99 | 100 | 99 | — | — | 113 | 99 | 84 | 99 | 73 | 99 | 71 | 99 | — | — | 64 | 93 | 27 |
| 26 | 78 | 99 | — | — | 100 | 99 | 93 | 99 | 98 | 99 | — | — | 110 | 99 | 82 | 99 | 70 | 98 | 69 | 98 | — | — | 63 | 89 | 26 |
| 25 | 77 | 99 | — | — | 98 | 99 | 90 | 99 | 95 | 99 | — | — | 107 | 99 | 80 | 99 | 68 | 97 | 67 | 96 | — | — | 61 | 86 | 25 |
| 24 | 75 | 98 | 119 | 99 | 95 | 99 | 88 | 99 | 93 | 99 | — | — | 105 | 99 | 78 | 99 | 66 | 95 | 66 | 94 | — | — | 60 | 81 | 24 |
| 23 | 73 | 98 | 115 | 99 | 93 | 99 | 86 | 99 | 91 | 99 | — | — | 102 | 99 | 76 | 99 | 64 | 92 | 64 | 92 | — | — | 58 | 77 | 23 |
| 22 | 71 | 97 | 112 | 99 | 91 | 99 | 83 | 99 | 88 | 99 | — | — | 99 | 99 | 74 | 98 | 62 | 88 | 62 | 89 | — | — | 57 | 72 | 22 |
| 21 | 69 | 95 | 109 | 99 | 88 | 99 | 81 | 99 | 86 | 99 | 87 | 99 | 97 | 99 | 72 | 97 | 60 | 82 | 61 | 85 | 78 | 99 | 55 | 67 | 21 |
| 20 | 67 | 94 | 105 | 99 | 86 | 99 | 79 | 99 | 84 | 99 | 85 | 99 | 94 | 99 | 70 | 96 | 58 | 77 | 59 | 80 | 75 | 99 | 54 | 61 | 20 |
| 19 | 65 | 92 | 102 | 99 | 84 | 99 | 76 | 98 | 81 | 98 | 82 | 99 | 91 | 99 | 68 | 95 | 56 | 70 | 57 | 75 | 73 | 99 | 52 | 56 | 19 |
| 18 | 63 | 86 | 99 | 99 | 81 | 99 | 74 | 98 | 79 | 98 | 79 | 99 | 89 | 99 | 66 | 93 | 53 | 62 | 55 | 69 | 71 | 98 | 51 | 50 | 18 |
| 17 | 61 | 83 | 95 | 99 | 79 | 99 | 72 | 97 | 77 | 98 | 76 | 99 | 86 | 99 | 64 | 91 | 51 | 55 | 54 | 63 | 68 | 96 | 49 | 45 | 17 |
| 16 | 59 | 79 | 92 | 99 | 77 | 98 | 69 | 96 | 74 | 97 | 73 | 98 | 83 | 99 | 62 | 88 | 49 | 47 | 52 | 56 | 66 | 93 | 48 | 40 | 16 |
| 15 | 58 | 78 | 89 | 99 | 74 | 97 | 67 | 94 | 72 | 96 | 71 | 96 | 81 | 98 | 60 | 84 | 47 | 39 | 50 | 50 | 63 | 90 | 46 | 35 | 15 |
| 14 | 56 | 73 | 85 | 99 | 72 | 97 | 65 | 93 | 70 | 95 | 68 | 93 | 78 | 98 | 58 | 79 | 45 | 32 | 48 | 43 | 61 | 85 | 45 | 30 | 14 |
| 13 | 54 | 68 | 82 | 99 | 70 | 96 | 62 | 90 | 67 | 94 | 65 | 88 | 75 | 97 | 56 | 74 | 43 | 25 | 47 | 37 | 59 | 80 | 43 | 26 | 13 |
| 12 | 52 | 61 | 79 | 98 | 67 | 94 | 60 | 87 | 65 | 93 | 62 | 81 | 73 | 96 | 54 | 68 | 41 | 19 | 45 | 31 | 56 | 73 | 41 | 21 | 12 |
| 11 | 50 | 54 | 75 | 97 | 65 | 93 | 58 | 82 | 63 | 91 | 59 | 73 | 70 | 95 | 52 | 61 | 39 | 14 | 43 | 25 | 54 | 65 | 40 | 18 | 11 |
| 10 | 48 | 46 | 72 | 96 | 63 | 90 | 55 | 76 | 60 | 89 | 56 | 64 | 67 | 94 | 50 | 53 | 36 | 9 | 41 | 20 | 51 | 56 | 38 | 14 | 10 |
| 9 | 46 | 38 | 69 | 95 | 60 | 88 | 53 | 69 | 58 | 85 | 54 | 53 | 65 | 92 | 48 | 45 | 34 | 6 | 40 | 16 | 49 | 47 | 37 | 11 | 9 |
| 8 | 44 | 31 | 65 | 93 | 58 | 84 | 51 | 59 | 56 | 81 | 51 | 42 | 62 | 90 | 46 | 37 | 32 | 4 | 38 | 12 | 46 | 38 | 35 | 8 | 8 |
| 7 | 42 | 23 | 62 | 89 | 56 | 79 | 48 | 48 | 54 | 76 | 48 | 32 | 59 | 86 | 44 | 29 | 30 | 2 | 36 | 9 | 44 | 29 | 34 | 6 | 7 |
| 6 | 40 | 16 | 58 | 85 | 53 | 73 | 46 | 36 | 51 | 68 | 45 | 23 | 57 | 82 | 42 | 22 | 28 | 1 | 34 | 6 | 42 | 21 | 32 | 4 | 6 |
| 5 | 38 | 11 | 55 | 78 | 51 | 65 | 44 | 24 | 49 | 58 | 42 | 15 | 54 | 76 | 40 | 15 | 26 | 1 | 33 | 4 | 39 | 14 | 31 | 3 | 5 |
| 4 | 37 | 6 | 52 | 68 | 49 | 55 | 41 | 15 | 47 | 45 | 39 | 9 | 51 | 68 | 38 | 10 | 24 | 1 | 31 | 3 | 37 | 9 | 29 | 2 | 4 |
| 3 | 35 | 3 | 48 | 54 | 46 | 43 | 39 | 9 | 44 | 30 | 37 | 5 | 49 | 57 | 36 | 6 | 22 | 1 | 29 | 2 | 34 | 5 | 28 | 1 | 3 |
| 2 | 33 | 1 | 45 | 37 | 44 | 30 | 37 | 5 | 42 | 13 | 34 | 2 | 46 | 43 | 34 | 3 | 19 | 1 | 28 | 1 | 32 | 2 | 26 | 1 | 2 |
| 1 | 31 | 1 | 42 | 18 | 42 | 18 | 34 | 2 | 40 | 1 | 31 | 1 | 43 | 26 | 32 | 1 | 17 | 1 | 26 | 1 | 30 | 1 | 25 | 1 | 1 |
| 0 | 29 | 1 | 38 | 4 | 39 | 8 | 32 | 1 | 37 | 1 | 28 | 1 | 41 | 10 | 30 | 1 | 15 | 1 | 24 | 1 | 27 | 1 | 23 | 1 | 0 |
| Raw mean | 11.07 | | 3.46 | | 4.53 | | 7.76 | | 5.49 | | 7.75 | | 3.48 | | 10.06 | | 16.38 | | 14.95 | | 9.48 | | 17.62 | | Raw mean |
| Raw SD | 5.24 | | 2.99 | | 4.28 | | 4.27 | | 4.30 | | 3.54 | | 3.75 | | 5.00 | | 4.71 | | 5.76 | | 4.14 | | 6.59 | | Raw SD |
| T: 90% Conf. int. | 7 | | 7 | | 7 | | 6 | | 6 | | 7 | | 6 | | 7 | | 7 | | 6 | | 8 | | 7 | | T: 90% Conf. int. |

**Table A.7b** PRS-P *T* Scores and Percentiles

| Raw score | Hyperactivity T | Hyperactivity %ile | Aggression T | Aggression %ile | Anxiety T | Anxiety %ile | Depression T | Depression %ile | Somatization T | Somatization %ile | Attention Problems T | Attention Problems %ile | Atypicality T | Atypicality %ile | Withdrawal T | Withdrawal %ile | Adaptability T | Adaptability %ile | Social Skills T | Social Skills %ile | Activities of Daily Living T | Activities of Daily Living %ile | Functional Communication T | Functional Communication %ile | Raw score |
|---|---|---|---|---|---|---|---|---|---|---|---|---|---|---|---|---|---|---|---|---|---|---|---|---|---|
| 39 | — | — | — | — | — | — | — | — | 118 | 99 | — | — | — | — | — | — | — | — | — | — | — | — | — | — | 39 |
| 38 | — | — | — | — | — | — | — | — | 116 | 99 | — | — | — | — | — | — | — | — | — | — | — | — | — | — | 38 |
| 37 | — | — | — | — | — | — | — | — | 114 | 99 | — | — | — | — | — | — | — | — | — | — | — | — | — | — | 37 |
| 36 | — | — | — | — | — | — | — | — | 112 | 99 | — | — | — | — | 100 | 99 | — | — | — | — | — | — | — | — | 36 |
| 35 | — | — | — | — | — | — | — | — | 110 | 99 | — | — | — | — | 98 | 99 | — | — | — | — | — | — | — | — | 35 |
| 34 | — | — | — | — | — | — | — | — | 108 | 99 | — | — | — | — | 96 | 99 | — | — | — | — | — | — | — | — | 34 |
| 33 | 93 | 99 | — | — | 118 | 99 | 107 | 99 | 106 | 99 | — | — | — | — | 94 | 99 | — | — | — | — | — | — | 73 | 99 | 33 |
| 32 | 91 | 99 | — | — | 116 | 99 | 105 | 99 | 104 | 99 | — | — | — | — | 92 | 99 | — | — | — | — | — | — | 71 | 99 | 32 |
| 31 | 89 | 99 | — | — | 113 | 99 | 103 | 99 | 102 | 99 | — | — | — | — | 90 | 99 | — | — | — | — | — | — | 70 | 99 | 31 |
| 30 | 87 | 99 | — | — | 111 | 99 | 100 | 99 | 100 | 99 | — | — | 118 | 99 | 88 | 99 | — | — | — | — | — | — | 68 | 98 | 30 |
| 29 | 86 | 99 | — | — | 108 | 99 | 98 | 99 | 98 | 99 | — | — | 116 | 99 | 86 | 99 | — | — | — | — | — | — | 67 | 96 | 29 |
| 28 | 84 | 99 | — | — | 106 | 99 | 96 | 99 | 96 | 99 | — | — | 113 | 99 | 84 | 99 | — | — | — | — | — | — | 65 | 94 | 28 |
| 27 | 82 | 99 | — | — | 104 | 99 | 94 | 99 | 94 | 99 | — | — | 111 | 99 | 82 | 99 | 73 | 99 | — | — | — | — | 64 | 91 | 27 |
| 26 | 80 | 99 | — | — | 101 | 99 | 91 | 99 | 92 | 99 | — | — | 108 | 99 | 80 | 99 | 71 | 98 | 70 | 98 | — | — | 62 | 88 | 26 |
| 25 | 78 | 99 | — | — | 99 | 99 | 89 | 99 | 90 | 99 | — | — | 105 | 99 | 78 | 99 | 68 | 96 | 68 | 97 | — | — | 60 | 84 | 25 |
| 24 | 76 | 98 | 118 | 99 | 97 | 99 | 87 | 99 | 88 | 99 | — | — | 103 | 99 | 76 | 99 | 66 | 94 | 67 | 95 | — | — | 59 | 79 | 24 |
| 23 | 74 | 98 | 114 | 99 | 94 | 99 | 85 | 99 | 86 | 99 | — | — | 100 | 99 | 75 | 99 | 64 | 91 | 65 | 92 | — | — | 57 | 74 | 23 |
| 22 | 72 | 97 | 111 | 99 | 92 | 99 | 82 | 99 | 84 | 98 | — | — | 98 | 99 | 73 | 98 | 62 | 87 | 63 | 89 | — | — | 56 | 69 | 22 |
| 21 | 70 | 96 | 108 | 99 | 89 | 99 | 80 | 98 | 81 | 98 | 91 | 99 | 95 | 99 | 71 | 97 | 60 | 82 | 61 | 86 | 78 | 99 | 54 | 64 | 21 |
| 20 | 68 | 95 | 105 | 99 | 87 | 99 | 78 | 98 | 79 | 98 | 88 | 99 | 93 | 99 | 69 | 96 | 57 | 77 | 59 | 81 | 76 | 99 | 53 | 58 | 20 |
| 19 | 66 | 93 | 101 | 99 | 85 | 99 | 76 | 98 | 77 | 98 | 85 | 99 | 90 | 99 | 67 | 94 | 55 | 70 | 57 | 76 | 73 | 99 | 51 | 52 | 19 |
| 18 | 64 | 91 | 98 | 99 | 82 | 99 | 73 | 97 | 75 | 97 | 82 | 99 | 88 | 99 | 65 | 92 | 53 | 62 | 56 | 71 | 70 | 98 | 49 | 46 | 18 |
| 17 | 63 | 89 | 95 | 99 | 80 | 98 | 71 | 96 | 73 | 97 | 79 | 99 | 85 | 99 | 63 | 89 | 51 | 54 | 54 | 64 | 68 | 96 | 48 | 41 | 17 |
| 16 | 61 | 86 | 91 | 99 | 78 | 98 | 69 | 95 | 71 | 96 | 76 | 99 | 83 | 98 | 61 | 86 | 49 | 46 | 52 | 58 | 65 | 93 | 46 | 35 | 16 |
| 15 | 59 | 83 | 88 | 99 | 75 | 97 | 67 | 94 | 69 | 95 | 73 | 98 | 80 | 98 | 59 | 82 | 47 | 37 | 50 | 51 | 63 | 89 | 45 | 30 | 15 |
| 14 | 57 | 78 | 85 | 99 | 73 | 97 | 64 | 92 | 67 | 94 | 70 | 97 | 77 | 97 | 57 | 77 | 44 | 30 | 48 | 44 | 60 | 84 | 43 | 25 | 14 |
| 13 | 55 | 73 | 82 | 98 | 70 | 96 | 62 | 90 | 65 | 93 | 67 | 95 | 75 | 97 | 55 | 71 | 42 | 23 | 46 | 37 | 57 | 77 | 41 | 21 | 13 |
| 12 | 53 | 67 | 78 | 98 | 68 | 94 | 60 | 87 | 63 | 92 | 64 | 91 | 72 | 96 | 53 | 64 | 40 | 16 | 44 | 31 | 55 | 69 | 40 | 17 | 12 |
| 11 | 51 | 60 | 75 | 97 | 66 | 93 | 58 | 84 | 61 | 90 | 61 | 86 | 70 | 95 | 51 | 57 | 38 | 11 | 43 | 25 | 52 | 60 | 38 | 13 | 11 |
| 10 | 49 | 53 | 72 | 96 | 63 | 90 | 55 | 79 | 59 | 87 | 58 | 79 | 67 | 94 | 49 | 50 | 36 | 7 | 41 | 19 | 50 | 50 | 37 | 10 | 10 |
| 9 | 47 | 44 | 69 | 95 | 61 | 88 | 53 | 73 | 57 | 85 | 55 | 70 | 65 | 92 | 47 | 42 | 33 | 4 | 39 | 14 | 47 | 40 | 35 | 8 | 9 |
| 8 | 45 | 36 | 65 | 93 | 58 | 84 | 51 | 65 | 55 | 81 | 52 | 59 | 62 | 90 | 45 | 34 | 31 | 2 | 37 | 10 | 44 | 30 | 34 | 6 | 8 |
| 7 | 43 | 27 | 62 | 90 | 56 | 79 | 49 | 55 | 53 | 76 | 49 | 47 | 60 | 88 | 43 | 26 | 29 | 1 | 35 | 7 | 42 | 21 | 32 | 4 | 7 |
| 6 | 42 | 20 | 59 | 86 | 54 | 73 | 46 | 43 | 51 | 69 | 46 | 35 | 57 | 84 | 41 | 20 | 27 | 1 | 33 | 4 | 39 | 14 | 30 | 3 | 6 |
| 5 | 40 | 13 | 55 | 80 | 51 | 65 | 44 | 29 | 49 | 60 | 43 | 24 | 55 | 80 | 39 | 14 | 25 | 1 | 30 | 3 | 37 | 9 | 29 | 2 | 5 |
| 4 | 38 | 7 | 52 | 72 | 49 | 55 | 42 | 16 | 46 | 47 | 40 | 15 | 52 | 73 | 37 | 9 | 22 | 1 | 28 | 1 | 34 | 5 | 27 | 1 | 4 |
| 3 | 36 | 4 | 49 | 59 | 47 | 43 | 40 | 7 | 44 | 31 | 37 | 9 | 49 | 64 | 36 | 6 | 20 | 1 | 26 | 1 | 31 | 3 | 26 | 1 | 3 |
| 2 | 34 | 2 | 46 | 41 | 44 | 30 | 37 | 2 | 42 | 11 | 34 | 5 | 47 | 50 | 34 | 3 | 18 | 1 | 24 | 1 | 29 | 1 | 24 | 1 | 2 |
| 1 | 32 | 1 | 42 | 17 | 42 | 17 | 35 | 1 | 40 | 1 | 31 | 2 | 44 | 31 | 32 | 2 | 16 | 1 | 22 | 1 | 26 | 1 | 23 | 1 | 1 |
| 0 | 30 | 1 | 39 | 1 | 39 | 6 | 33 | 1 | 38 | 1 | 28 | 1 | 42 | 7 | 30 | 1 | 14 | 1 | 20 | 1 | 24 | 1 | 21 | 1 | 0 |
| Raw mean | 10.43 | | 3.32 | | 4.45 | | 7.64 | | 5.71 | | 7.38 | | 3.20 | | 10.43 | | 16.60 | | 15.99 | | 10.13 | | 18.40 | | Raw mean |
| Raw *SD* | 5.23 | | 3.06 | | 4.20 | | 4.43 | | 4.86 | | 3.35 | | 3.93 | | 5.13 | | 4.58 | | 5.42 | | 3.84 | | 6.33 | | Raw *SD* |
| *T*:90% Conf. int. | 6 | | 7 | | 7 | | 6 | | 5 | | 8 | | 6 | | 7 | | 7 | | 6 | | 9 | | 7 | | *T*:90% Conf. int. |

**Table A.7c** PRS–P *T* Scores and Percentiles

| Raw score | Hyperactivity T | Hyperactivity %ile | Aggression T | Aggression %ile | Anxiety T | Anxiety %ile | Depression T | Depression %ile | Somatization T | Somatization %ile | Attention Problems T | Attention Problems %ile | Atypicality T | Atypicality %ile | Withdrawal T | Withdrawal %ile | Adaptability T | Adaptability %ile | Social Skills T | Social Skills %ile | Activities of Daily Living T | Activities of Daily Living %ile | Functional Communication T | Functional Communication %ile | Raw score |
|---|---|---|---|---|---|---|---|---|---|---|---|---|---|---|---|---|---|---|---|---|---|---|---|---|---|
| 39 | — | — | — | — | — | — | — | — | 120 | 99 | — | — | — | — | — | — | — | — | — | — | — | — | — | — | 39 |
| 38 | — | — | — | — | — | — | — | — | 120 | 99 | — | — | — | — | — | — | — | — | — | — | — | — | — | — | 38 |
| 37 | — | — | — | — | — | — | — | — | 120 | 99 | — | — | — | — | — | — | — | — | — | — | — | — | — | — | 37 |
| 36 | — | — | — | — | — | — | — | — | 120 | 99 | — | — | — | — | 104 | 99 | — | — | — | — | — | — | — | — | 36 |
| 35 | — | — | — | — | — | — | — | — | 120 | 99 | — | — | — | — | 102 | 99 | — | — | — | — | — | — | — | — | 35 |
| 34 | — | — | — | — | — | — | — | — | 120 | 99 | — | — | — | — | 100 | 99 | — | — | — | — | — | — | — | — | 34 |
| 33 | 91 | 99 | — | — | 115 | 99 | 111 | 99 | 120 | 99 | — | — | — | — | 98 | 99 | — | — | — | — | — | — | 74 | 99 | 33 |
| 32 | 89 | 99 | — | — | 113 | 99 | 109 | 99 | 120 | 99 | — | — | — | — | 96 | 99 | — | — | — | — | — | — | 72 | 99 | 32 |
| 31 | 87 | 99 | — | — | 110 | 99 | 106 | 99 | 120 | 99 | — | — | — | — | 94 | 99 | — | — | — | — | — | — | 71 | 99 | 31 |
| 30 | 85 | 99 | — | — | 108 | 99 | 104 | 99 | 118 | 99 | — | — | 120 | 99 | 92 | 99 | — | — | — | — | — | — | 69 | 99 | 30 |
| 29 | 83 | 99 | — | — | 106 | 99 | 101 | 99 | 115 | 99 | — | — | 120 | 99 | 90 | 99 | — | — | — | — | — | — | 68 | 99 | 29 |
| 28 | 81 | 99 | — | — | 104 | 99 | 99 | 99 | 112 | 99 | — | — | 118 | 99 | 88 | 99 | — | — | — | — | — | — | 66 | 97 | 28 |
| 27 | 79 | 99 | — | — | 101 | 99 | 96 | 99 | 109 | 99 | — | — | 115 | 99 | 86 | 99 | 72 | 98 | 72 | 98 | — | — | 65 | 94 | 27 |
| 26 | 77 | 99 | — | — | 99 | 99 | 94 | 99 | 107 | 99 | — | — | 112 | 99 | 84 | 99 | 70 | 95 | 70 | 97 | — | — | 64 | 91 | 26 |
| 25 | 76 | 99 | — | — | 97 | 99 | 92 | 99 | 104 | 99 | — | — | 110 | 99 | 82 | 99 | 68 | 92 | 69 | 94 | — | — | 62 | 87 | 25 |
| 24 | 74 | 99 | 120 | 99 | 94 | 99 | 89 | 99 | 101 | 99 | — | — | 107 | 99 | 80 | 99 | 66 | 88 | 67 | 91 | — | — | 61 | 83 | 24 |
| 23 | 72 | 98 | 116 | 99 | 92 | 99 | 87 | 99 | 98 | 99 | — | — | 104 | 99 | 77 | 99 | 64 | 83 | 65 | 88 | — | — | 59 | 79 | 23 |
| 22 | 70 | 97 | 113 | 99 | 90 | 99 | 84 | 99 | 96 | 99 | — | — | 101 | 99 | 75 | 99 | 62 | 77 | 64 | 84 | — | — | 58 | 74 | 22 |
| 21 | 68 | 95 | 109 | 99 | 87 | 99 | 82 | 99 | 93 | 99 | 85 | 99 | 98 | 99 | 73 | 99 | 60 | 70 | 62 | 79 | 78 | 99 | 56 | 69 | 21 |
| 20 | 66 | 93 | 106 | 99 | 85 | 99 | 79 | 99 | 90 | 99 | 82 | 99 | 96 | 99 | 71 | 98 | 58 | 63 | 60 | 73 | 76 | 99 | 55 | 64 | 20 |
| 19 | 64 | 90 | 103 | 99 | 83 | 99 | 77 | 99 | 88 | 99 | 80 | 99 | 93 | 99 | 69 | 97 | 56 | 56 | 59 | 68 | 74 | 98 | 53 | 59 | 19 |
| 18 | 62 | 87 | 99 | 99 | 81 | 99 | 75 | 99 | 85 | 99 | 77 | 99 | 90 | 99 | 67 | 96 | 54 | 48 | 57 | 62 | 71 | 96 | 52 | 54 | 18 |
| 17 | 60 | 83 | 96 | 99 | 78 | 99 | 72 | 98 | 82 | 99 | 74 | 99 | 87 | 99 | 65 | 94 | 52 | 41 | 55 | 56 | 69 | 94 | 50 | 49 | 17 |
| 16 | 58 | 78 | 92 | 99 | 76 | 99 | 70 | 97 | 79 | 99 | 71 | 99 | 84 | 99 | 63 | 92 | 50 | 34 | 54 | 49 | 67 | 91 | 49 | 44 | 16 |
| 15 | 56 | 73 | 89 | 99 | 74 | 97 | 67 | 95 | 77 | 98 | 69 | 97 | 82 | 99 | 61 | 89 | 48 | 27 | 52 | 43 | 64 | 87 | 47 | 39 | 15 |
| 14 | 54 | 67 | 85 | 99 | 71 | 96 | 65 | 92 | 74 | 97 | 66 | 95 | 79 | 98 | 59 | 86 | 46 | 21 | 50 | 37 | 62 | 82 | 46 | 35 | 14 |
| 13 | 52 | 61 | 82 | 99 | 69 | 95 | 62 | 89 | 71 | 96 | 63 | 90 | 76 | 98 | 57 | 82 | 43 | 16 | 48 | 32 | 60 | 76 | 44 | 30 | 13 |
| 12 | 51 | 55 | 79 | 99 | 67 | 94 | 60 | 84 | 68 | 95 | 61 | 84 | 73 | 97 | 55 | 77 | 41 | 12 | 47 | 27 | 57 | 70 | 43 | 26 | 12 |
| 11 | 49 | 48 | 75 | 98 | 65 | 92 | 58 | 78 | 66 | 93 | 58 | 77 | 70 | 96 | 53 | 71 | 39 | 8 | 45 | 22 | 55 | 62 | 41 | 22 | 11 |
| 10 | 47 | 41 | 72 | 96 | 62 | 90 | 55 | 70 | 63 | 91 | 55 | 68 | 68 | 94 | 51 | 64 | 37 | 5 | 43 | 17 | 53 | 54 | 40 | 18 | 10 |
| 9 | 45 | 34 | 68 | 94 | 60 | 87 | 53 | 62 | 60 | 87 | 52 | 58 | 65 | 92 | 49 | 57 | 35 | 3 | 42 | 14 | 50 | 46 | 38 | 15 | 9 |
| 8 | 43 | 27 | 65 | 91 | 58 | 83 | 50 | 53 | 57 | 82 | 50 | 48 | 62 | 88 | 47 | 49 | 33 | 2 | 40 | 10 | 48 | 37 | 37 | 12 | 8 |
| 7 | 41 | 20 | 62 | 87 | 55 | 78 | 48 | 44 | 55 | 76 | 47 | 38 | 59 | 84 | 44 | 41 | 31 | 1 | 38 | 8 | 46 | 28 | 35 | 9 | 7 |
| 6 | 39 | 14 | 58 | 81 | 53 | 71 | 45 | 34 | 52 | 67 | 44 | 29 | 56 | 79 | 42 | 32 | 29 | 1 | 37 | 5 | 43 | 21 | 34 | 7 | 6 |
| 5 | 37 | 9 | 55 | 73 | 51 | 63 | 43 | 25 | 49 | 55 | 42 | 21 | 53 | 71 | 40 | 24 | 27 | 1 | 35 | 4 | 41 | 14 | 33 | 5 | 5 |
| 4 | 35 | 5 | 51 | 63 | 49 | 53 | 41 | 18 | 47 | 41 | 39 | 14 | 51 | 62 | 38 | 17 | 25 | 1 | 33 | 2 | 39 | 8 | 31 | 3 | 4 |
| 3 | 33 | 2 | 48 | 50 | 46 | 41 | 38 | 12 | 44 | 27 | 36 | 9 | 48 | 50 | 36 | 11 | 23 | 1 | 32 | 1 | 37 | 4 | 30 | 2 | 3 |
| 2 | 31 | 1 | 45 | 34 | 44 | 29 | 36 | 7 | 41 | 14 | 33 | 5 | 45 | 37 | 34 | 6 | 21 | 1 | 30 | 1 | 34 | 1 | 28 | 1 | 2 |
| 1 | 29 | 1 | 41 | 18 | 42 | 17 | 33 | 4 | 38 | 6 | 31 | 3 | 42 | 22 | 32 | 3 | 19 | 1 | 28 | 1 | 32 | 1 | 27 | 1 | 1 |
| 0 | 27 | 1 | 38 | 5 | 39 | 8 | 31 | 2 | 36 | 2 | 28 | 1 | 39 | 9 | 30 | 1 | 17 | 1 | 27 | 1 | 30 | 1 | 25 | 1 | 0 |
| Raw mean | 11.72 | | 3.61 | | 4.62 | | 7.89 | | 5.27 | | 8.11 | | 3.76 | | 9.69 | | 16.15 | | 13.91 | | 8.82 | | 16.84 | | Raw mean |
| Raw SD | 5.20 | | 2.93 | | 4.37 | | 4.12 | | 3.66 | | 3.69 | | 3.56 | | 4.85 | | 4.84 | | 5.92 | | 4.33 | | 6.77 | | Raw SD |
| T: 90% Conf. int. | 7 | | 8 | | 7 | | 7 | | 7 | | 7 | | 7 | | 7 | | 7 | | 6 | | 8 | | 6 | | T: 90% Conf. int. |

## Table A.7d  PRS-P Composite T Scores

| T score | Externalizing Problems | | | Internalizing Problems | | | Adaptive Skills | | | Behavioral Symptoms Index | | | T score |
|---|---|---|---|---|---|---|---|---|---|---|---|---|---|
| | Combined | Female | Male | Combined | Female | Male | Combined | Female | Male | Combined | Female | Male | |
| 120 | — | — | — | 326–346 | 333–343 | 323–346 | — | — | — | 618–629 | 622–627 | 616–631 | 120 |
| 119 | — | — | — | 324–325 | 330–332 | 321–322 | — | — | — | 613–617 | 617–621 | 611–615 | 119 |
| 118 | — | — | — | 321–323 | 328–329 | 318–320 | — | — | — | 609–612 | 612–616 | 607–610 | 118 |
| 117 | — | — | — | 319–320 | 325–327 | 316–317 | — | — | — | 604–608 | 608–611 | 602–606 | 117 |
| 116 | — | — | — | 316–318 | 322–324 | 313–315 | — | — | — | 599–603 | 603–607 | 597–601 | 116 |
| 115 | — | — | — | 314–315 | 320–321 | 311–312 | — | — | — | 595–598 | 599–602 | 593–596 | 115 |
| 114 | — | — | — | 311–313 | 317–319 | 308–310 | — | — | — | 590–594 | 594–598 | 588–592 | 114 |
| 113 | — | — | — | 309–310 | 314–316 | 306–307 | — | — | — | 586–589 | 589–593 | 584–587 | 113 |
| 112 | — | — | — | 306–308 | 312–313 | 303–305 | — | — | — | 581–585 | 585–588 | 579–583 | 112 |
| 111 | — | 211 | 211 | 304–305 | 309–311 | 301–302 | — | — | — | 577–580 | 580–584 | 575–578 | 111 |
| 110 | 210–211 | 209–210 | 210 | 301–303 | 307–308 | 298–300 | — | — | — | 572–576 | 575–579 | 570–574 | 110 |
| 109 | 208–209 | 207–208 | 208–209 | 298–300 | 304–306 | 296–297 | — | — | — | 567–571 | 571–574 | 566–569 | 109 |
| 108 | 206–207 | 205–206 | 206–207 | 296–297 | 301–303 | 293–295 | — | — | — | 563–566 | 566–570 | 561–565 | 108 |
| 107 | 204–205 | 204 | 204–205 | 293–295 | 299–300 | 291–292 | — | — | — | 558–562 | 562–565 | 557–560 | 107 |
| 106 | 202–203 | 202–203 | 202–203 | 291–292 | 296–298 | 288–290 | — | — | — | 554–557 | 557–561 | 552–556 | 106 |
| 105 | 201 | 200–201 | 200–201 | 288–290 | 293–295 | 286–287 | — | — | — | 549–553 | 552–556 | 548–551 | 105 |
| 104 | 199–200 | 198–199 | 199 | 286–287 | 291–292 | 283–285 | — | — | — | 545–548 | 548–551 | 543–547 | 104 |
| 103 | 197–198 | 196–197 | 197–198 | 283–285 | 288–290 | 281–282 | — | — | — | 540–544 | 543–547 | 539–542 | 103 |
| 102 | 195–196 | 194–195 | 195–196 | 281–282 | 286–287 | 278–280 | — | — | — | 536–539 | 538–542 | 534–538 | 102 |
| 101 | 193–194 | 193 | 193–194 | 278–280 | 283–285 | 276–277 | — | — | — | 531–535 | 534–537 | 529–533 | 101 |
| 100 | 191–192 | 191–192 | 191–192 | 276–277 | 280–282 | 274–275 | — | — | — | 526–530 | 529–533 | 525–528 | 100 |
| 99 | 190 | 189–190 | 189–190 | 273–275 | 278–279 | 271–273 | — | — | — | 522–525 | 525–528 | 520–524 | 99 |
| 98 | 188–189 | 187–188 | 188 | 271–272 | 275–277 | 269–270 | — | — | — | 517–521 | 520–524 | 516–519 | 98 |
| 97 | 186–187 | 185–186 | 186–187 | 268–270 | 272–274 | 266–268 | — | — | — | 513–516 | 515–519 | 511–515 | 97 |
| 96 | 184–185 | 183–184 | 184–185 | 266–267 | 270–271 | 264–265 | — | — | — | 508–512 | 511–514 | 507–510 | 96 |
| 95 | 182–183 | 182 | 182–183 | 263–265 | 267–269 | 261–263 | — | — | — | 504–507 | 506–510 | 502–506 | 95 |
| 94 | 180–181 | 180–181 | 180–181 | 261–262 | 265–266 | 259–260 | — | — | — | 499–503 | 501–505 | 498–501 | 94 |
| 93 | 178–179 | 178–179 | 178–179 | 258–260 | 262–264 | 256–258 | — | — | — | 495–498 | 497–500 | 493–497 | 93 |
| 92 | 177 | 176–177 | 177 | 255–257 | 259–261 | 254–255 | — | — | — | 490–494 | 492–496 | 489–492 | 92 |
| 91 | 175–176 | 174–175 | 175–176 | 253–254 | 257–258 | 251–253 | — | — | — | 485–489 | 488–491 | 484–488 | 91 |
| 90 | 173–174 | 173 | 173–174 | 250–252 | 254–256 | 249–250 | — | — | — | 481–484 | 483–487 | 480–483 | 90 |
| 89 | 171–172 | 171–172 | 171–172 | 248–249 | 252–253 | 246–248 | — | — | — | 476–480 | 478–482 | 475–479 | 89 |
| 88 | 169–170 | 169–170 | 169–170 | 245–247 | 249–251 | 244–245 | — | — | — | 472–475 | 474–477 | 471–474 | 88 |
| 87 | 167–168 | 167–168 | 167–168 | 243–244 | 246–248 | 241–243 | — | — | — | 467–471 | 469–473 | 466–470 | 87 |
| 86 | 166 | 165–166 | 166 | 240–242 | 244–245 | 239–240 | — | — | — | 463–466 | 464–466 | 461–465 | 86 |
| 85 | 164–165 | 163–164 | 164–165 | 238–239 | 241–243 | 236–238 | — | — | — | 458–462 | 460–463 | 457–460 | 85 |
| 84 | 162–163 | 162 | 162–163 | 235–237 | 238–240 | 234–235 | — | — | — | 453–457 | 455–459 | 452–456 | 84 |
| 83 | 160–161 | 160–161 | 160–161 | 233–234 | 236–237 | 231–233 | — | — | — | 449–452 | 451–454 | 448–451 | 83 |
| 82 | 158–159 | 158–159 | 158–159 | 230–232 | 233–235 | 229–230 | — | 294 | — | 444–448 | 446–450 | 443–447 | 82 |
| 81 | 156–157 | 156–157 | 156–157 | 228–229 | 231–232 | 226–228 | — | — | — | 440–443 | 441–445 | 439–442 | 81 |
| 80 | 155 | 154–155 | 155 | 225–227 | 228–230 | 224–225 | 293–295 | 291–293 | 294–296 | 435–439 | 437–440 | 434–438 | 80 |
| 79 | 153–154 | 152–153 | 153–154 | 223–224 | 225–227 | 221–223 | 290–292 | 288–290 | 291–293 | 431–434 | 432–436 | 430–433 | 79 |
| 78 | 151–152 | 151 | 151–152 | 220–222 | 223–224 | 219–220 | 287–289 | 285–287 | 288–290 | 426–430 | 428–431 | 425–429 | 78 |
| 77 | 149–150 | 149–150 | 149–150 | 218–219 | 220–222 | 216–218 | 284–286 | 282–284 | 284–287 | 422–425 | 423–427 | 421–424 | 77 |
| 76 | 147–148 | 147–148 | 147–148 | 215–217 | 217–219 | 214–215 | 280–283 | 279–281 | 281–283 | 417–421 | 418–422 | 416–420 | 76 |
| 75 | 145–146 | 145–146 | 145–146 | 213–214 | 215–216 | 211–213 | 277–279 | 276–278 | 278–280 | 412–416 | 414–417 | 412–415 | 75 |
| 74 | 144 | 143–144 | 144 | 210–212 | 212–214 | 209–210 | 274–276 | 273–275 | 275–277 | 408–411 | 409–413 | 407–411 | 74 |
| 73 | 142–143 | 141–142 | 142–143 | 207–209 | 210–211 | 206–208 | 271–273 | 269–272 | 272–274 | 403–407 | 404–408 | 403–406 | 73 |
| 72 | 140–141 | 140 | 140–141 | 205–206 | 207–209 | 204–205 | 268–270 | 266–268 | 269–271 | 399–402 | 400–403 | 398–402 | 72 |
| 71 | 138–139 | 138–139 | 138–139 | 202–204 | 204–206 | 201–203 | 265–267 | 263–265 | 265–268 | 394–398 | 395–399 | 393–397 | 71 |
| 70 | 136–137 | 136–137 | 136–137 | 200–201 | 202–203 | 199–200 | 262–264 | 260–262 | 262–264 | 390–393 | 391–394 | 389–392 | 70 |
| 69 | 134–135 | 134–135 | 134–135 | 197–199 | 199–201 | 196–198 | 259–261 | 257–259 | 259–261 | 385–389 | 386–390 | 384–388 | 69 |
| 68 | 133 | 132–133 | 133 | 195–196 | 196–198 | 194–195 | 255–258 | 254–256 | 255–258 | 380–384 | 381–385 | 380–383 | 68 |
| 67 | 131–132 | 131 | 131–132 | 192–194 | 194–195 | 191–193 | 252–254 | 251–253 | 253–255 | 376–379 | 377–380 | 375–379 | 67 |
| 66 | 129–130 | 129–130 | 129–130 | 190–191 | 191–193 | 189–190 | 249–251 | 248–250 | 250–252 | 371–375 | 372–376 | 371–374 | 66 |

**Table A.7d** PRS–P Composite T Scores *(continued)*

| T score | Externalizing Problems Combined | Externalizing Problems Female | Externalizing Problems Male | Internalizing Problems Combined | Internalizing Problems Female | Internalizing Problems Male | Adaptive Skills Combined | Adaptive Skills Female | Adaptive Skills Male | Behavioral Symptoms Index Combined | Behavioral Symptoms Index Female | Behavioral Symptoms Index Male | T score |
|---|---|---|---|---|---|---|---|---|---|---|---|---|---|
| 65 | 127–128 | 127–128 | 127–128 | 187–189 | 189–190 | 187–188 | 246–248 | 245–247 | 246–249 | 367–370 | 367–371 | 366–370 | 65 |
| 64 | 125–126 | 125–126 | 125–126 | 185–186 | 186–188 | 184–186 | 243–245 | 242–244 | 243–245 | 362–366 | 363–366 | 362–365 | 64 |
| 63 | 123–124 | 123–124 | 123–124 | 182–184 | 183–185 | 182–183 | 240–242 | 239–241 | 240–242 | 358–361 | 358–362 | 357–361 | 63 |
| 62 | 120–121 | 121–122 | 122 | 180–181 | 181–182 | 179–181 | 237–239 | 236–238 | 237–239 | 353–357 | 354–357 | 353–356 | 62 |
| 61 | — | 120 | 120–121 | 177–179 | 178–180 | 177–178 | 233–236 | 233–235 | 234–236 | 349–352 | 349–353 | 348–352 | 61 |
| 60 | 118–119 | 118–119 | 118–119 | 175–176 | 175–177 | 174–176 | 230–232 | 230–232 | 231–233 | 344–348 | 344–348 | 344–347 | 60 |
| 59 | 116–117 | 116–117 | 116–117 | 172–174 | 173–174 | 172–173 | 227–229 | 227–229 | 227–230 | 339–343 | 340–343 | 339–343 | 59 |
| 58 | 114–115 | 114–115 | 114–115 | 170–171 | 170–172 | 169–171 | 224–226 | 223–226 | 224–226 | 335–338 | 335–339 | 334–338 | 58 |
| 57 | 112–113 | 112–113 | 113 | 167–169 | 168–169 | 167–168 | 221–223 | 220–222 | 221–223 | 330–334 | 330–334 | 330–333 | 57 |
| 56 | 111 | 110–111 | 111–112 | 164–166 | 165–167 | 164–166 | 218–220 | 217–219 | 218–220 | 326–329 | 326–329 | 325–329 | 56 |
| 55 | 109–110 | 109 | 109–110 | 162–163 | 162–164 | 162–163 | 215–217 | 214–216 | 215–217 | 321–325 | 321–325 | 321–324 | 55 |
| 54 | 107–108 | 107–108 | 107–108 | 159–161 | 160–161 | 159–161 | 212–214 | 211–213 | 212–214 | 317–320 | 317–320 | 316–320 | 54 |
| 53 | 105–106 | 105–106 | 105–106 | 157–158 | 157–159 | 157–158 | 208–211 | 208–210 | 208–211 | 312–316 | 312–316 | 312–315 | 53 |
| 52 | 103–104 | 103–104 | 103–104 | 154–156 | 154–156 | 154–156 | 205–207 | 205–207 | 205–207 | 307–311 | 307–311 | 307–311 | 52 |
| 51 | 101–102 | 101–102 | 102 | 152–153 | 152–153 | 152–153 | 202–204 | 202–204 | 202–204 | 303–306 | 303–306 | 303–306 | 51 |
| 50 | 99–100 | 99–100 | 100–101 | 149–151 | 149–151 | 149–151 | 199–201 | 199–201 | 199–201 | 298–302 | 298–302 | 298–302 | 50 |
| 49 | 98 | 98 | 98–99 | 147–148 | 147–148 | 147–148 | 196–198 | 196–198 | 196–198 | 294–297 | 293–297 | 294–297 | 49 |
| 48 | 96–97 | 96–97 | 96–97 | 144–146 | 144–146 | 144–146 | 193–195 | 193–195 | 193–195 | 289–293 | 289–292 | 289–293 | 48 |
| 47 | 94–95 | 94–95 | 94–95 | 142–143 | 141–143 | 142–143 | 190–192 | 190–192 | 189–192 | 285–288 | 284–288 | 285–288 | 47 |
| 46 | 92–93 | 92–93 | 92–93 | 139–141 | 139–140 | 139–141 | 187–189 | 187–189 | 186–188 | 280–284 | 280–283 | 280–284 | 46 |
| 45 | 90–91 | 90–91 | 91 | 137–138 | 136–138 | 137–138 | 183–186 | 184–186 | 183–185 | 276–279 | 275–279 | 276–279 | 45 |
| 44 | 88–89 | 89 | 89–90 | 134–136 | 133–135 | 134–136 | 180–182 | 180–183 | 180–182 | 271–275 | 270–274 | 271–275 | 44 |
| 43 | 87 | 87–88 | 87–88 | 132–133 | 131–132 | 132–133 | 177–179 | 177–179 | 177–179 | 266–270 | 266–269 | 266–270 | 43 |
| 42 | 85–86 | 85–86 | 85–86 | 129–131 | 128–130 | 129–131 | 174–176 | 174–176 | 174–176 | 262–265 | 261–265 | 262–265 | 42 |
| 41 | 83–84 | 83–84 | 83–84 | 127–128 | 126–127 | 127–128 | 171–173 | 171–173 | 170–173 | 257–261 | 257–260 | 257–261 | 41 |
| 40 | 81–82 | 81–82 | 81–82 | 124–126 | 123–125 | 124–126 | 168–170 | 168–170 | 167–169 | 253–256 | 252–256 | 253–256 | 40 |
| 39 | 79–80 | 79–80 | 80 | 121–123 | 120–122 | 122–123 | 165–167 | 165–167 | 164–166 | 248–252 | 247–251 | 248–252 | 39 |
| 38 | 77–78 | 78 | 78–79 | 119–120 | 118–119 | 119–121 | 161–164 | 162–164 | 161–163 | 244–247 | 243–246 | 244–247 | 38 |
| 37 | 76 | 76–77 | 76–77 | 116–118 | 115–117 | 117–118 | 158–160 | 159–161 | 158–160 | 239–243 | 238–242 | 239–243 | 37 |
| 36 | 74–75 | 74–75 | 74–75 | 114–115 | 110–111 | 114–116 | 155–157 | 156–158 | 155–157 | 234–238 | 233–237 | 235–238 | 36 |
| 35 | 72–73 | 72–73 | 72–73 | 111–113 | — | 112–113 | 152–154 | 153–155 | 151–154 | 230–233 | 229–232 | 230–234 | 35 |
| 34 | 70–71 | 70–71 | 70–71 | 109–110 | — | 109–111 | 149–151 | 150–152 | 148–150 | 225–229 | 224–228 | 226–229 | 34 |
| 33 | 68–69 | 69 | 69 | 108 | — | 107–108 | 146–148 | 147–149 | 145–147 | 221–224 | 220–223 | 221–225 | 33 |
| 32 | 67 | — | 67–68 | — | — | 106 | 143–145 | 144–146 | 142–144 | 216–220 | 215–219 | 217–220 | 32 |
| 31 | — | — | 65–66 | — | — | — | 140–142 | 141–143 | 139–141 | 212–215 | 210–214 | 212–216 | 31 |
| 30 | — | — | — | — | — | — | 136–139 | 137–140 | 136–138 | 207–211 | 206–209 | 208–211 | 30 |
| 29 | — | — | — | — | — | — | 133–135 | 134–136 | 132–135 | 203–206 | 202–205 | 203–207 | 29 |
| 28 | — | — | — | — | — | — | 130–132 | 131–133 | 129–131 | 198–202 | — | 198–202 | 28 |
| 27 | — | — | — | — | — | — | 127–129 | 128–130 | 126–128 | — | — | 194–197 | 27 |
| 26 | — | — | — | — | — | — | 124–126 | 125–127 | 123–125 | — | — | 193 | 26 |
| 25 | — | — | — | — | — | — | 121–123 | 122–124 | 120–122 | — | — | — | 25 |
| 24 | — | — | — | — | — | — | 118–120 | 119–121 | 116–119 | — | — | — | 24 |
| 23 | — | — | — | — | — | — | 114–117 | 116–118 | 113–115 | — | — | — | 23 |
| 22 | — | — | — | — | — | — | 111–113 | 113–115 | 110–112 | — | — | — | 22 |
| 21 | — | — | — | — | — | — | 108–110 | 110–112 | 107–109 | — | — | — | 21 |
| 20 | — | — | — | — | — | — | 105–107 | 107–109 | 104–106 | — | — | — | 20 |
| 19 | — | — | — | — | — | — | 102–104 | 104–106 | 101–103 | — | — | — | 19 |
| 18 | — | — | — | — | — | — | 99–101 | 101–103 | 99–100 | — | — | — | 18 |
| 17 | — | — | — | — | — | — | 96–98 | 98–100 | — | — | — | — | 17 |
| 16 | — | — | — | — | — | — | 93–95 | 94–97 | — | — | — | — | 16 |
| 15 | — | — | — | — | — | — | 89–92 | 91–93 | — | — | — | — | 15 |
| 14 | — | — | — | — | — | — | — | 88–90 | — | — | — | — | 14 |
| 13 | — | — | — | — | — | — | — | 85–87 | — | — | — | — | 13 |
| 12 | — | — | — | — | — | — | — | 82–84 | — | — | — | — | 12 |
| 11 | — | — | — | — | — | — | — | 79–81 | — | — | — | — | 11 |
| 10 | — | — | — | — | — | — | — | — | — | — | — | — | 10 |
| T: 90% Conf. int. | 5 | 5 | 6 | 4 | 4 | 5 | 4 | 5 | 4 | 4 | 4 | 4 | T: 90% Conf. int. |

**Table A.7e** PRS–P Composite Percentiles

| %ile | Externalizing Problems Combined | Externalizing Problems Female | Externalizing Problems Male | Internalizing Problems Combined | Internalizing Problems Female | Internalizing Problems Male | Adaptive Skills Combined | Adaptive Skills Female | Adaptive Skills Male | Behavioral Symptoms Index Combined | Behavioral Symptoms Index Female | Behavioral Symptoms Index Male | %ile |
|---|---|---|---|---|---|---|---|---|---|---|---|---|---|
| 99 | 153–211 | 157–211 | 148–211 | 231–346 | 239–343 | 223–346 | 269–295 | 271–294 | 266–296 | 429–629 | 441–627 | 410–631 | 99 |
| 98 | 145–152 | 147–156 | 143–147 | 216–230 | 221–238 | 211–222 | 262–268 | 264–270 | 261–265 | 409–428 | 417–440 | 399–409 | 98 |
| 97 | 140–144 | 141–146 | 139–142 | 207–215 | 210–220 | 204–210 | 258–261 | 259–263 | 257–260 | 396–408 | 402–416 | 390–398 | 97 |
| 96 | 136–139 | 137–140 | 136–138 | 200–206 | 202–209 | 198–203 | 254–257 | 255–258 | 254–256 | 387–395 | 391–401 | 384–389 | 96 |
| 95 | 133–135 | 133–136 | 134–135 | 195–199 | 196–201 | 194–197 | 251–253 | 252–254 | 252–253 | 379–386 | 382–390 | 379–383 | 95 |
| 94 | 130–132 | 130–132 | 132–133 | 191–194 | 191–195 | 190–193 | 249–250 | 249–251 | 249–251 | 373–378 | 375–381 | 374–378 | 94 |
| 93 | 128–129 | 128–129 | 130–131 | 187–190 | 187–190 | 187–189 | 246–248 | 247–248 | 247–248 | 368–372 | 369–374 | 370–373 | 93 |
| 92 | 126–127 | 126–127 | 128–129 | 184–186 | 184–186 | 184–186 | 244–245 | 244–246 | 245–246 | 363–367 | 364–368 | 366–369 | 92 |
| 91 | 125 | 124–125 | 127 | 182–183 | 181–183 | 182–183 | 242–243 | 242–243 | 243–244 | 359–362 | 359–363 | 363–365 | 91 |
| 90 | 123–124 | 122–123 | 125–126 | 179–181 | 178–180 | 180–181 | 241 | 240–241 | 242 | 355–358 | 355–358 | 360–362 | 90 |
| 89 | 122 | 121 | 124 | 177–178 | 176–177 | 178–179 | 239–240 | 239 | 240–241 | 352–354 | 352–354 | 357–359 | 89 |
| 88 | 120–121 | 119–120 | 123 | 175–176 | 174–175 | 176–177 | 237–238 | 237–238 | 238–239 | 349–351 | 348–351 | 354–356 | 88 |
| 87 | 119 | 118 | 122 | 173–174 | 172–173 | 175 | 236 | 235–236 | 237 | 346–348 | 345–347 | 352–353 | 87 |
| 86 | 118 | 117 | 121 | 172 | 170–171 | 173–174 | 234–235 | 234 | 236 | 343–345 | 342–344 | 349–351 | 86 |
| 85 | 117 | 116 | 120 | 170–171 | 168–169 | 172 | 233 | 232–233 | 234–235 | 341–342 | 340–341 | 347–348 | 85 |
| 84 | 116 | 115 | 119 | 169 | 167 | 171 | 232 | 231 | 233 | 339–340 | 337–339 | 345–346 | 84 |
| 83 | 115 | 114 | 118 | 167–168 | 165–166 | 169–170 | 230–231 | 230 | 232 | 337–338 | 335–336 | 343–344 | 83 |
| 82 | 114 | 113 | 117 | 166 | 164 | 168 | 229 | 228–229 | 230–231 | 334–336 | 332–334 | 341–342 | 82 |
| 81 | – | 112 | 116 | 165 | 163 | 167 | 228 | 227 | 229 | 333 | 330–331 | 339–340 | 81 |
| 80 | 113 | 111 | 115 | 164 | 161–162 | 166 | 227 | 226 | 228 | 331–332 | 328–329 | 337–338 | 80 |
| 79 | 112 | – | 114 | 163 | 160 | 165 | 226 | 225 | 227 | 329–330 | 326–327 | 336 | 79 |
| 78 | 111 | 110 | – | 162 | 159 | 164 | 225 | 224 | 226 | 327–328 | 325 | 334–335 | 78 |
| 77 | – | 109 | 113 | 161 | 158 | 163 | 224 | 222–223 | 225 | 326 | 323–324 | 332–333 | 77 |
| 76 | 110 | 108 | 112 | 160 | 157 | 162 | 222–223 | 221 | 224 | 324–325 | 321–322 | 330–331 | 76 |
| 75 | 109 | – | 111 | 159 | 156 | – | 221 | 220 | 223 | 322–323 | 319–320 | 329 | 75 |
| 74 | – | 107 | – | 158 | – | 161 | 220 | 219 | 222 | 321 | 318 | 327–328 | 74 |
| 73 | 108 | 106 | 110 | 157 | 155 | 160 | 219 | 218 | 221 | 319–320 | 316–317 | 326 | 73 |
| 72 | 107 | – | 109 | – | 154 | 159 | – | 217 | 220 | 318 | 315 | 324–325 | 72 |
| 71 | – | 105 | – | 156 | 153 | – | 218 | 216 | 219 | 317 | 314 | 323 | 71 |
| 70 | 106 | – | 108 | 155 | 152 | 158 | 217 | 215 | 218 | 315–316 | 312–313 | 321–322 | 70 |
| 69 | – | 104 | – | 154 | – | 157 | 216 | 214 | 217 | 314 | 311 | 320 | 69 |
| 68 | 105 | – | 107 | – | 151 | 156 | 215 | – | 216 | 313 | 310 | 319 | 68 |
| 67 | – | 103 | 106 | 153 | 150 | – | 214 | 213 | 215 | 312 | 308–309 | 317–318 | 67 |
| 66 | 104 | – | – | 152 | – | 155 | 213 | 212 | 214 | 310–311 | 307 | 316 | 66 |
| 65 | – | 102 | 105 | – | 149 | – | 212 | 211 | 213 | 309 | 306 | 315 | 65 |
| 64 | 103 | – | – | 151 | – | 154 | 211 | 210 | 212 | 308 | 305 | 313–314 | 64 |
| 63 | – | 101 | 104 | – | 148 | 153 | 210 | 209 | 211 | 307 | 304 | 312 | 63 |
| 62 | 102 | – | – | 150 | – | – | – | 208 | 210 | 306 | 303 | 311 | 62 |
| 61 | – | 100 | 103 | 149 | 147 | 152 | 209 | 207 | – | 305 | 301–302 | 310 | 61 |
| 60 | 101 | – | – | – | – | – | 208 | – | 209 | 304 | 300 | 308–309 | 60 |
| 59 | – | – | 102 | 148 | 146 | 151 | 207 | 206 | 208 | 303 | 299 | 307 | 59 |
| 58 | 100 | 99 | – | – | – | 150 | 206 | 205 | 207 | 302 | 298 | 306 | 58 |
| 57 | – | – | 101 | 147 | 145 | – | 205 | 204 | 206 | 301 | 297 | 305 | 57 |
| 56 | – | 98 | – | – | – | 149 | – | 203 | 205 | 300 | 296 | 304 | 56 |
| 55 | 99 | – | 100 | 146 | 144 | – | 204 | 202 | 204 | 299 | 295 | 302–303 | 55 |
| 54 | – | – | – | – | – | 148 | 203 | – | 203 | 298 | 294 | 301 | 54 |
| 53 | 98 | 97 | 99 | 145 | 143 | – | 202 | 201 | – | 297 | 293 | 300 | 53 |
| 52 | – | – | – | – | – | 147 | 201 | 200 | 202 | 296 | – | 299 | 52 |
| 51 | 97 | 96 | 98 | 144 | 142 | – | – | 199 | 201 | 295 | 292 | 298 | 51 |

**Table A.7e** PRS–P Composite Percentiles (*continued*)

| %ile | Externalizing Problems Combined | Externalizing Problems Female | Externalizing Problems Male | Internalizing Problems Combined | Internalizing Problems Female | Internalizing Problems Male | Adaptive Skills Combined | Adaptive Skills Female | Adaptive Skills Male | Behavioral Symptoms Index Combined | Behavioral Symptoms Index Female | Behavioral Symptoms Index Male | %ile |
|---|---|---|---|---|---|---|---|---|---|---|---|---|---|
| 50 | – | – | – | – | – | 146 | 200 | 198 | 200 | 294 | 291 | 297 | 50 |
| 49 | – | – | 97 | – | – | – | 199 | – | 199 | 293 | 290 | 295–296 | 49 |
| 48 | 96 | 95 | – | 143 | 141 | 145 | 198 | 197 | 198 | 292 | 289 | 294 | 48 |
| 47 | – | – | 96 | 142 | – | – | 197 | 196 | 197 | 291 | 288 | 293 | 47 |
| 46 | – | – | – | – | – | 144 | 196 | 195 | – | 290 | 287 | 292 | 46 |
| 45 | 95 | 94 | 95 | – | 140 | – | – | 194 | 196 | 289 | 286 | 291 | 45 |
| 44 | – | – | – | 141 | – | 143 | 195 | – | 195 | 288 | 285 | 290 | 44 |
| 43 | 94 | 93 | 94 | – | – | – | 194 | 193 | 194 | 287 | – | 289 | 43 |
| 42 | – | – | – | 140 | 139 | 142 | 193 | 192 | 193 | 286 | 284 | 287–288 | 42 |
| 41 | – | – | – | – | – | – | 192 | 191 | 192 | – | 283 | 286 | 41 |
| 40 | 93 | – | 93 | – | – | – | 191 | 190 | 191 | 285 | 282 | 285 | 40 |
| 39 | – | 92 | 92 | 139 | 138 | 141 | 190 | 189 | 190 | 284 | 281 | 284 | 39 |
| 38 | – | – | – | – | – | – | 189 | 188 | – | 283 | 280 | 283 | 38 |
| 37 | 92 | – | – | 138 | 137 | 140 | 188 | 187 | 189 | 282 | – | 282 | 37 |
| 36 | – | 91 | 91 | – | – | – | – | – | 188 | 281 | 279 | 281 | 36 |
| 35 | 91 | – | – | 137 | – | 139 | 187 | 186 | 187 | 280 | 278 | 279–280 | 35 |
| 34 | – | – | – | – | – | – | 186 | 185 | 186 | 279 | 277 | 278 | 34 |
| 33 | – | 90 | 90 | 136 | 136 | 138 | – | – | 185 | 278 | 276 | 277 | 33 |
| 32 | 90 | – | – | – | – | – | 185 | 184 | 184 | 277 | 275 | 276 | 32 |
| 31 | – | – | – | – | – | 137 | 184 | 183 | 183 | 276 | – | 275 | 31 |
| 30 | – | 89 | – | 135 | 135 | – | 183 | 182 | 182 | 275 | 274 | 274 | 30 |
| 29 | 89 | – | 88 | – | – | 136 | 182 | 181 | 181 | 274 | 273 | 272–273 | 29 |
| 28 | – | 88 | – | – | – | – | 181 | – | 180 | 273 | 272 | 271 | 28 |
| 27 | 88 | – | 87 | 134 | – | 135 | 180 | 180 | 179 | 272 | 271 | 270 | 27 |
| 26 | – | – | – | – | 134 | – | 179 | 179 | 178 | 271 | 270 | 269 | 26 |
| 25 | 87 | – | 86 | – | – | 134 | 178 | 178 | 177 | 270 | 269 | 267–268 | 25 |
| 24 | – | 87 | – | 133 | – | – | 177 | 177 | 176 | 269 | – | 266 | 24 |
| 23 | 86 | – | 85 | – | 133 | 133 | 176 | 176 | 175 | 268 | 268 | 265 | 23 |
| 22 | – | – | – | 132 | – | – | 175 | 175 | 174 | 267 | 267 | 263–264 | 22 |
| 21 | – | – | 84 | – | – | 132 | 174 | 174 | 173 | 266 | 266 | 262 | 21 |
| 20 | 85 | 86 | – | 131 | 132 | 131 | 173 | 173 | 172 | 265 | 265 | 261 | 20 |
| 19 | – | – | 83 | – | – | – | 172 | 172 | 171 | 264 | 264 | 259–260 | 19 |
| 18 | 84 | 85 | – | – | – | 130 | 171 | 171 | 169–170 | 263 | 263 | 258 | 18 |
| 17 | – | – | – | 130 | – | – | 169–170 | 170 | 168 | 261–262 | 262 | 256–257 | 17 |
| 16 | – | – | 82 | – | – | 129 | 168 | 169 | 167 | 260 | 261 | 255 | 16 |
| 15 | 83 | 84 | – | – | 131 | 128 | 167 | 168 | 166 | 259 | 260 | 253–254 | 15 |
| 14 | – | – | 81 | 129 | – | – | 165–166 | 167 | 164–165 | 257–258 | 259 | 251–252 | 14 |
| 13 | 82 | – | 80 | – | – | 127 | 164 | 165–166 | 163 | 256 | 258 | 250 | 13 |
| 12 | – | 83 | – | 128 | 130 | 126 | 163 | 164 | 161–162 | 254–255 | 257 | 248–249 | 12 |
| 11 | 81 | – | 79 | – | – | 125 | 161–162 | 163 | 160 | 252–253 | 255–256 | 246–247 | 11 |
| 10 | 80 | 82 | – | 127 | – | 124 | 159–160 | 161–162 | 158–159 | 251 | 254 | 244–245 | 10 |
| 9 | – | – | 78 | – | 129 | 123 | 157–158 | 160 | 156–157 | 249–250 | 252–253 | 242–243 | 9 |
| 8 | 79 | – | 77 | 126 | – | 122 | 156 | 158–159 | 154–155 | 247–248 | 251 | 240–241 | 8 |
| 7 | 78 | 81 | – | – | – | 121 | 153–155 | 156–157 | 152–153 | 244–246 | 249–250 | 237–239 | 7 |
| 6 | – | 80 | 76 | 125 | – | 120 | 151–152 | 154–155 | 150–151 | 241–243 | 247–248 | 234–236 | 6 |
| 5 | 77 | – | 75 | – | 128 | 118–119 | 148–150 | 152–153 | 147–149 | 238–240 | 245–246 | 231–233 | 5 |
| 4 | 75–76 | 79 | 74 | 124 | – | 116–117 | 145–147 | 149–151 | 144–146 | 234–237 | 242–244 | 227–230 | 4 |
| 3 | 74 | 78 | 73 | 123 | – | 114–115 | 141–144 | 146–148 | 141–143 | 229–233 | 239–241 | 223–226 | 3 |
| 2 | 72–73 | 77 | 71–72 | 122 | 127 | 110–113 | 135–140 | 141–145 | 136–140 | 222–228 | 234–238 | 217–222 | 2 |
| 1 | 67–71 | 69–76 | 65–70 | 108–121 | 110–126 | 106–109 | 89–134 | 79–140 | 99–135 | 198–221 | 202–233 | 193–216 | 1 |

## Table A.8a PRS-P T Scores and Percentiles

| Raw score | Hyperactivity T | %ile | Aggression T | %ile | Anxiety T | %ile | Depression T | %ile | Somatization T | %ile | Attention Problems T | %ile | Atypicality T | %ile | Withdrawal T | %ile | Adaptability T | %ile | Social Skills T | %ile | Activities of Daily Living T | %ile | Functional Communication T | %ile | Raw score |
|---|---|---|---|---|---|---|---|---|---|---|---|---|---|---|---|---|---|---|---|---|---|---|---|---|---|
| 39 | — | — | — | — | — | — | — | — | 120 | 99 | — | — | — | — | — | — | — | — | — | — | — | — | — | — | 39 |
| 38 | — | — | — | — | — | — | — | — | 120 | 99 | — | — | — | — | — | — | — | — | — | — | — | — | — | — | 38 |
| 37 | — | — | — | — | — | — | — | — | 120 | 99 | — | — | — | — | — | 99 | — | — | — | — | — | — | — | — | 37 |
| 36 | — | — | — | — | — | — | — | — | 119 | 99 | — | — | — | — | 100 | 99 | — | — | — | — | — | — | — | — | 36 |
| 35 | — | — | — | — | — | — | — | — | 117 | 99 | — | — | — | — | 98 | 99 | — | — | — | — | — | — | — | — | 35 |
| 34 | — | — | — | — | — | — | — | — | 114 | 99 | — | — | — | — | 96 | 99 | — | — | — | — | — | — | — | — | 34 |
| 33 | 85 | 99 | — | — | 104 | 99 | 103 | 99 | 112 | 99 | — | — | — | — | 95 | 99 | — | — | — | — | — | — | 67 | 99 | 33 |
| 32 | 83 | 99 | — | — | 102 | 99 | 101 | 99 | 110 | 99 | — | — | — | — | 93 | 99 | — | — | — | — | — | — | 65 | 99 | 32 |
| 31 | 82 | 99 | — | — | 100 | 99 | 99 | 99 | 107 | 99 | — | — | — | — | 91 | 99 | — | — | — | — | — | — | 64 | 96 | 31 |
| 30 | 80 | 99 | — | — | 97 | 99 | 97 | 99 | 105 | 99 | — | — | 110 | 99 | 89 | 99 | — | — | — | — | — | — | 62 | 91 | 30 |
| 29 | 78 | 99 | — | — | 95 | 99 | 94 | 99 | 103 | 99 | — | — | 108 | 99 | 87 | 99 | — | — | — | — | — | — | 60 | 85 | 29 |
| 28 | 77 | 98 | — | — | 93 | 99 | 92 | 99 | 100 | 99 | — | — | 105 | 99 | 85 | 99 | — | — | — | — | — | — | 59 | 79 | 28 |
| 27 | 75 | 98 | — | — | 91 | 99 | 90 | 99 | 98 | 99 | — | — | 103 | 99 | 84 | 99 | 69 | 98 | 67 | 98 | — | — | 57 | 73 | 27 |
| 26 | 74 | 97 | — | — | 89 | 99 | 88 | 99 | 96 | 99 | — | — | 101 | 99 | 82 | 99 | 67 | 97 | 65 | 96 | — | — | 56 | 66 | 26 |
| 25 | 72 | 97 | — | — | 87 | 99 | 86 | 99 | 93 | 99 | — | — | 98 | 99 | 80 | 99 | 65 | 94 | 63 | 93 | — | — | 54 | 60 | 25 |
| 24 | 70 | 96 | 114 | 99 | 85 | 99 | 84 | 99 | 91 | 99 | — | — | 96 | 99 | 78 | 99 | 63 | 90 | 62 | 88 | — | — | 53 | 54 | 24 |
| 23 | 69 | 95 | 111 | 99 | 83 | 99 | 82 | 99 | 89 | 99 | — | — | 94 | 99 | 76 | 98 | 61 | 86 | 60 | 83 | — | — | 51 | 48 | 23 |
| 22 | 67 | 94 | 108 | 99 | 80 | 99 | 79 | 99 | 86 | 99 | — | — | 92 | 99 | 74 | 98 | 59 | 80 | 58 | 77 | — | — | 50 | 43 | 22 |
| 21 | 66 | 92 | 105 | 99 | 78 | 99 | 77 | 98 | 84 | 99 | 81 | 99 | 89 | 99 | 72 | 97 | 57 | 74 | 56 | 70 | 69 | 99 | 48 | 38 | 21 |
| 20 | 64 | 90 | 102 | 99 | 76 | 99 | 75 | 98 | 82 | 99 | 79 | 99 | 87 | 99 | 71 | 96 | 56 | 68 | 55 | 63 | 66 | 99 | 46 | 33 | 20 |
| 19 | 63 | 88 | 99 | 99 | 74 | 98 | 73 | 97 | 79 | 99 | 77 | 99 | 85 | 99 | 69 | 95 | 54 | 62 | 53 | 57 | 64 | 95 | 45 | 29 | 19 |
| 18 | 61 | 86 | 95 | 99 | 72 | 97 | 71 | 96 | 77 | 99 | 74 | 98 | 83 | 98 | 67 | 94 | 52 | 55 | 51 | 50 | 61 | 90 | 43 | 25 | 18 |
| 17 | 59 | 83 | 92 | 99 | 70 | 96 | 69 | 95 | 75 | 98 | 72 | 97 | 80 | 98 | 65 | 92 | 50 | 48 | 49 | 44 | 59 | 82 | 42 | 21 | 17 |
| 16 | 58 | 80 | 89 | 99 | 68 | 94 | 66 | 93 | 72 | 98 | 70 | 96 | 78 | 98 | 63 | 90 | 48 | 41 | 48 | 38 | 57 | 72 | 40 | 18 | 16 |
| 15 | 56 | 77 | 86 | 99 | 66 | 93 | 64 | 91 | 70 | 96 | 67 | 94 | 76 | 97 | 61 | 88 | 46 | 35 | 46 | 32 | 54 | 61 | 39 | 15 | 15 |
| 14 | 55 | 72 | 83 | 99 | 64 | 90 | 62 | 89 | 68 | 94 | 65 | 92 | 73 | 96 | 59 | 85 | 44 | 29 | 44 | 27 | 52 | 50 | 37 | 13 | 14 |
| 13 | 53 | 68 | 80 | 99 | 61 | 87 | 60 | 85 | 65 | 92 | 63 | 89 | 71 | 96 | 58 | 81 | 42 | 23 | 42 | 22 | 49 | 41 | 36 | 10 | 13 |
| 12 | 51 | 63 | 76 | 98 | 59 | 83 | 58 | 81 | 63 | 90 | 61 | 85 | 69 | 94 | 56 | 76 | 40 | 18 | 41 | 18 | 47 | 32 | 34 | 8 | 12 |
| 11 | 50 | 57 | 73 | 97 | 57 | 78 | 56 | 76 | 60 | 86 | 58 | 80 | 67 | 93 | 54 | 71 | 38 | 13 | 39 | 15 | 44 | 25 | 33 | 7 | 11 |
| 10 | 48 | 50 | 70 | 96 | 55 | 72 | 54 | 70 | 58 | 82 | 56 | 74 | 64 | 91 | 52 | 65 | 36 | 9 | 37 | 11 | 42 | 19 | 31 | 5 | 10 |
| 9 | 47 | 44 | 67 | 94 | 53 | 66 | 51 | 62 | 56 | 76 | 54 | 67 | 62 | 89 | 50 | 58 | 34 | 6 | 35 | 9 | 39 | 14 | 29 | 4 | 9 |
| 8 | 45 | 37 | 64 | 91 | 51 | 58 | 49 | 53 | 53 | 69 | 51 | 60 | 60 | 87 | 48 | 50 | 32 | 4 | 33 | 7 | 37 | 10 | 28 | 3 | 8 |
| 7 | 43 | 29 | 61 | 88 | 49 | 49 | 47 | 44 | 51 | 61 | 49 | 51 | 58 | 83 | 47 | 42 | 30 | 2 | 32 | 5 | 34 | 8 | 26 | 2 | 7 |
| 6 | 42 | 22 | 57 | 82 | 47 | 40 | 45 | 34 | 49 | 52 | 47 | 43 | 55 | 79 | 45 | 33 | 28 | 1 | 30 | 3 | 32 | 5 | 25 | 1 | 6 |
| 5 | 40 | 15 | 54 | 75 | 44 | 32 | 43 | 24 | 46 | 41 | 45 | 33 | 53 | 73 | 43 | 25 | 26 | 1 | 28 | 2 | 29 | 4 | 23 | 1 | 5 |
| 4 | 39 | 9 | 51 | 64 | 42 | 23 | 41 | 15 | 44 | 30 | 42 | 25 | 51 | 66 | 41 | 18 | 24 | 1 | 26 | 2 | 27 | 3 | 22 | 1 | 4 |
| 3 | 37 | 5 | 48 | 51 | 40 | 15 | 39 | 9 | 42 | 20 | 40 | 17 | 48 | 57 | 39 | 11 | 22 | 1 | 25 | 1 | 25 | 2 | 20 | 1 | 3 |
| 2 | 36 | 2 | 45 | 34 | 38 | 9 | 36 | 4 | 39 | 12 | 38 | 10 | 46 | 45 | 37 | 6 | 20 | 1 | 23 | 1 | 22 | 1 | 19 | 1 | 2 |
| 1 | 34 | 1 | 42 | 18 | 36 | 5 | 34 | 1 | 37 | 6 | 36 | 5 | 44 | 30 | 35 | 3 | 19 | 1 | 21 | 1 | 20 | 1 | 17 | 1 | 1 |
| 0 | 32 | 1 | 38 | 5 | 34 | 2 | 32 | 1 | 35 | 2 | 33 | 2 | 42 | 13 | 34 | 1 | 17 | 1 | 19 | 1 | 17 | 1 | 15 | 1 | 0 |
| **Raw mean** | 11.12 | | 3.64 | | 7.64 | | 8.34 | | 6.51 | | 7.36 | | 3.69 | | 8.87 | | 17.17 | | 17.38 | | 13.35 | | 22.27 | | **Raw mean** |
| **Raw SD** | 6.30 | | 3.16 | | 4.71 | | 4.65 | | 4.28 | | 4.39 | | 4.40 | | 5.41 | | 5.14 | | 5.67 | | 4.07 | | 6.45 | | **Raw SD** |
| **T: 90% Conf. int.** | 5 | | 7 | | 7 | | 6 | | 6 | | 5 | | 5 | | 6 | | 6 | | 6 | | 8 | | 6 | | **T: 90% Conf. int.** |

## Table A.8b  PRS–P T Scores and Percentiles

| Raw score | Hyperactivity T | Hyperactivity %ile | Aggression T | Aggression %ile | Anxiety T | Anxiety %ile | Depression T | Depression %ile | Somatization T | Somatization %ile | Attention Problems T | Attention Problems %ile | Atypicality T | Atypicality %ile | Withdrawal T | Withdrawal %ile | Adaptability T | Adaptability %ile | Social Skills T | Social Skills %ile | Activities of Daily Living T | Activities of Daily Living %ile | Functional Communication T | Functional Communication %ile | Raw score |
|---|---|---|---|---|---|---|---|---|---|---|---|---|---|---|---|---|---|---|---|---|---|---|---|---|---|
| 39 | — | — | — | — | — | — | — | — | 120 | 99 | — | — | — | — | — | — | — | — | — | — | — | — | — | — | 39 |
| 38 | — | — | — | — | — | — | — | — | 120 | 99 | — | — | — | — | — | — | — | — | — | — | — | — | — | — | 38 |
| 37 | — | — | — | — | — | — | — | — | 120 | 99 | — | — | — | — | — | — | — | — | — | — | — | — | — | — | 37 |
| 36 | — | — | — | — | — | — | — | — | 120 | 99 | — | — | — | — | 108 | 99 | — | — | — | — | — | — | — | — | 36 |
| 35 | — | — | — | — | — | — | — | — | 120 | 99 | — | — | — | — | 106 | 99 | — | — | — | — | — | — | — | — | 35 |
| 34 | — | — | — | — | — | — | — | — | 119 | 99 | — | — | — | — | 104 | 99 | — | — | — | — | — | — | — | — | 34 |
| 33 | 92 | 99 | — | — | 110 | 99 | 110 | 99 | 117 | 99 | — | — | — | — | 101 | 99 | — | — | — | — | — | — | 67 | 99 | 33 |
| 32 | 90 | 99 | — | — | 108 | 99 | 107 | 99 | 114 | 99 | — | — | — | — | 99 | 99 | — | — | — | — | — | — | 65 | 98 | 32 |
| 31 | 88 | 99 | — | — | 106 | 99 | 105 | 99 | 112 | 99 | — | — | — | — | 97 | 99 | — | — | — | — | — | — | 63 | 94 | 31 |
| 30 | 86 | 99 | — | — | 103 | 99 | 102 | 99 | 109 | 99 | — | — | 120 | 99 | 95 | 99 | — | — | — | — | — | — | 62 | 89 | 30 |
| 29 | 84 | 99 | — | — | 101 | 99 | 100 | 99 | 107 | 99 | — | — | 120 | 99 | 93 | 99 | — | — | — | — | — | — | 60 | 83 | 29 |
| 28 | 83 | 99 | — | — | 99 | 99 | 98 | 99 | 104 | 99 | — | — | 118 | 99 | 91 | 99 | — | — | — | — | — | — | 58 | 77 | 28 |
| 27 | 81 | 99 | — | — | 96 | 99 | 95 | 99 | 102 | 99 | — | — | 115 | 99 | 89 | 99 | 68 | 99 | 66 | 99 | — | — | 56 | 70 | 27 |
| 26 | 79 | 99 | — | — | 94 | 99 | 93 | 99 | 99 | 99 | — | — | 113 | 99 | 87 | 99 | 66 | 96 | 64 | 96 | — | — | 55 | 63 | 26 |
| 25 | 77 | 99 | — | — | 92 | 99 | 91 | 99 | 97 | 99 | — | — | 110 | 99 | 85 | 99 | 64 | 92 | 63 | 90 | — | — | 53 | 56 | 25 |
| 24 | 75 | 98 | 120 | 99 | 89 | 99 | 88 | 99 | 94 | 99 | — | — | 107 | 99 | 82 | 98 | 62 | 87 | 61 | 84 | — | — | 51 | 50 | 24 |
| 23 | 74 | 97 | 120 | 99 | 87 | 99 | 86 | 99 | 92 | 99 | — | — | 104 | 99 | 80 | 97 | 61 | 82 | 59 | 77 | — | — | 50 | 44 | 23 |
| 22 | 72 | 97 | 119 | 99 | 84 | 99 | 83 | 99 | 89 | 99 | — | 99 | 102 | 99 | 78 | 96 | 59 | 77 | 57 | 71 | — | — | 48 | 38 | 22 |
| 21 | 70 | 96 | 115 | 99 | 82 | 99 | 81 | 99 | 87 | 99 | 85 | 99 | 99 | 99 | 76 | 95 | 57 | 71 | 55 | 64 | 70 | 99 | 46 | 33 | 21 |
| 20 | 68 | 94 | 112 | 99 | 80 | 99 | 79 | 99 | 84 | 99 | 83 | 99 | 96 | 99 | 74 | 93 | 55 | 64 | 53 | 58 | 68 | 98 | 45 | 28 | 20 |
| 19 | 66 | 93 | 108 | 99 | 77 | 99 | 76 | 98 | 82 | 99 | 80 | 99 | 94 | 99 | 72 | 91 | 53 | 58 | 52 | 51 | 65 | 95 | 43 | 24 | 19 |
| 18 | 65 | 91 | 104 | 99 | 75 | 99 | 74 | 98 | 79 | 99 | 78 | 99 | 91 | 99 | 70 | 88 | 51 | 52 | 50 | 45 | 62 | 90 | 41 | 20 | 18 |
| 17 | 63 | 88 | 101 | 99 | 73 | 98 | 72 | 97 | 77 | 98 | 75 | 99 | 88 | 99 | 68 | 84 | 49 | 46 | 48 | 40 | 59 | 82 | 40 | 16 | 17 |
| 16 | 61 | 85 | 97 | 99 | 70 | 97 | 69 | 95 | 74 | 98 | 73 | 98 | 85 | 99 | 66 | 79 | 47 | 40 | 46 | 34 | 56 | 72 | 38 | 13 | 16 |
| 15 | 59 | 82 | 93 | 99 | 68 | 95 | 67 | 94 | 72 | 97 | 70 | 97 | 83 | 99 | 63 | 73 | 45 | 34 | 44 | 29 | 53 | 59 | 36 | 11 | 15 |
| 14 | 57 | 78 | 90 | 99 | 66 | 92 | 65 | 92 | 69 | 96 | 68 | 95 | 80 | 98 | 61 | 66 | 43 | 29 | 42 | 24 | 50 | 46 | 35 | 9 | 14 |
| 13 | 55 | 74 | 86 | 99 | 63 | 89 | 62 | 89 | 67 | 94 | 65 | 92 | 77 | 97 | 59 | 58 | 42 | 23 | 41 | 20 | 47 | 34 | 33 | 7 | 13 |
| 12 | 54 | 69 | 82 | 99 | 61 | 85 | 60 | 85 | 64 | 92 | 63 | 89 | 74 | 97 | 57 | 49 | 40 | 18 | 39 | 16 | 44 | 24 | 31 | 5 | 12 |
| 11 | 52 | 63 | 79 | 98 | 58 | 80 | 57 | 80 | 62 | 89 | 61 | 85 | 72 | 96 | 55 | 40 | 38 | 14 | 37 | 13 | 41 | 17 | 30 | 4 | 11 |
| 10 | 50 | 57 | 75 | 97 | 56 | 74 | 55 | 74 | 59 | 85 | 58 | 79 | 69 | 94 | 53 | 31 | 36 | 9 | 35 | 9 | 38 | 11 | 28 | 3 | 10 |
| 9 | 48 | 50 | 71 | 96 | 54 | 67 | 53 | 67 | 57 | 79 | 56 | 72 | 66 | 92 | 51 | 22 | 34 | 6 | 33 | 7 | 35 | 8 | 26 | 2 | 9 |
| 8 | 46 | 42 | 68 | 93 | 51 | 59 | 50 | 58 | 54 | 72 | 53 | 65 | 64 | 90 | 49 | 15 | 32 | 3 | 31 | 4 | 32 | 5 | 24 | 1 | 8 |
| 7 | 45 | 34 | 64 | 90 | 49 | 50 | 48 | 48 | 52 | 64 | 51 | 56 | 61 | 87 | 47 | 9 | 30 | 1 | 30 | 2 | 30 | 3 | 23 | 1 | 7 |
| 6 | 43 | 27 | 60 | 85 | 47 | 41 | 46 | 37 | 49 | 53 | 48 | 47 | 58 | 83 | 44 | 5 | 28 | 1 | 28 | 1 | 27 | 2 | 21 | 1 | 6 |
| 5 | 41 | 19 | 57 | 79 | 44 | 31 | 43 | 26 | 47 | 42 | 46 | 38 | 55 | 78 | 42 | 3 | 26 | 1 | 26 | 1 | 24 | 1 | 19 | 1 | 5 |
| 4 | 39 | 12 | 53 | 70 | 42 | 22 | 41 | 17 | 44 | 30 | 43 | 28 | 53 | 72 | 40 | 1 | 24 | 1 | 24 | 1 | 21 | 1 | 18 | 1 | 4 |
| 3 | 37 | 6 | 49 | 58 | 40 | 15 | 38 | 9 | 42 | 19 | 41 | 20 | 50 | 63 | 38 | 1 | 23 | 1 | 22 | 1 | 18 | 1 | 16 | 1 | 3 |
| 2 | 36 | 2 | 46 | 43 | 37 | 8 | 36 | 4 | 39 | 11 | 39 | 12 | 47 | 51 | 36 | 1 | 21 | 1 | 20 | 1 | 15 | 1 | 14 | 1 | 2 |
| 1 | 34 | 1 | 42 | 23 | 35 | 4 | 34 | 1 | 37 | 5 | 36 | 7 | 45 | 36 | 34 | 1 | 19 | 1 | 19 | 1 | 12 | 1 | 13 | 1 | 1 |
| 0 | 32 | 1 | 38 | 4 | 32 | 2 | 31 | 1 | 34 | 2 | 34 | 3 | 42 | 17 | 32 | 1 | 17 | 1 | 17 | 1 | 10 | 1 | 11 | 1 | 0 |

| Scale | Raw mean | Raw SD | T:90% Conf. int. |
|---|---|---|---|
| Hyperactivity | 9.98 | 5.53 | 6 |
| Aggression | 3.14 | 2.73 | 7 |
| Anxiety | 7.42 | 4.23 | 8 |
| Depression | 7.87 | 4.22 | 6 |
| Somatization | 6.31 | 4.01 | 7 |
| Attention Problems | 6.69 | 4.08 | 6 |
| Atypicality | 2.99 | 3.68 | 6 |
| Withdrawal | 8.61 | 4.74 | 7 |
| Adaptability | 17.46 | 5.26 | 6 |
| Social Skills | 18.14 | 5.45 | 6 |
| Activities of Daily Living | 14.00 | 3.42 | 9 |
| Functional Communication | 23.15 | 5.93 | 6 |

## Table A.8c PRS-P T Scores and Percentiles

| Raw score | Hyperactivity T | Hyperactivity %ile | Aggression T | Aggression %ile | Anxiety T | Anxiety %ile | Depression T | Depression %ile | Somatization T | Somatization %ile | Attention Problems T | Attention Problems %ile | Atypicality T | Atypicality %ile | Withdrawal T | Withdrawal %ile | Adaptability T | Adaptability %ile | Social Skills T | Social Skills %ile | Activities of Daily Living T | Activities of Daily Living %ile | Functional Communication T | Functional Communication %ile | Raw score |
|---|---|---|---|---|---|---|---|---|---|---|---|---|---|---|---|---|---|---|---|---|---|---|---|---|---|
| 39 | — | — | — | — | — | — | — | — | 120 | 99 | — | — | — | — | — | — | — | — | — | — | — | — | — | — | 39 |
| 38 | — | — | — | — | — | — | — | — | 119 | 99 | — | — | — | — | — | — | — | — | — | — | — | — | — | — | 38 |
| 37 | — | — | — | — | — | — | — | — | 117 | 99 | — | — | — | — | — | — | — | — | — | — | — | — | — | — | 37 |
| 36 | — | — | — | — | — | — | — | — | 114 | 99 | — | — | — | — | — | — | — | — | — | — | — | — | — | — | 36 |
| 35 | — | — | — | — | — | — | — | — | 112 | 99 | — | — | — | — | — | — | — | — | — | — | — | — | — | — | 35 |
| 34 | — | — | — | — | — | — | — | — | 110 | 99 | — | — | — | — | — | — | — | — | — | — | — | — | — | — | 34 |
| 33 | 80 | 99 | — | — | 99 | 99 | 98 | 99 | 108 | 99 | — | — | — | — | 90 | 99 | — | — | — | — | — | — | 67 | 99 | 33 |
| 32 | 79 | 99 | — | — | 97 | 99 | 96 | 99 | 106 | 99 | — | — | — | — | 88 | 99 | — | — | — | — | — | — | 66 | 99 | 32 |
| 31 | 77 | 99 | — | — | 95 | 99 | 94 | 99 | 103 | 99 | — | — | — | — | 86 | 99 | — | — | — | — | — | — | 64 | 97 | 31 |
| 30 | 76 | 98 | — | — | 93 | 99 | 92 | 99 | 101 | 99 | — | — | 102 | 99 | 85 | 99 | — | — | — | — | — | — | 63 | 93 | 30 |
| 29 | 75 | 98 | — | — | 91 | 99 | 90 | 99 | 99 | 99 | — | — | 100 | 99 | 83 | 99 | — | — | — | — | — | — | 61 | 87 | 29 |
| 28 | 73 | 97 | — | — | 89 | 99 | 88 | 99 | 97 | 99 | — | — | 98 | 99 | 81 | 99 | — | — | — | — | — | — | 60 | 82 | 28 |
| 27 | 72 | 96 | — | — | 87 | 99 | 86 | 99 | 95 | 99 | — | — | 96 | 99 | 80 | 99 | 70 | 99 | 68 | 99 | — | — | 58 | 76 | 27 |
| 26 | 70 | 96 | — | — | 85 | 99 | 84 | 99 | 92 | 99 | — | — | 94 | 99 | 78 | 99 | 68 | 97 | 66 | 97 | — | — | 57 | 69 | 26 |
| 25 | 69 | 95 | — | — | 83 | 99 | 82 | 99 | 90 | 99 | — | — | 92 | 99 | 76 | 98 | 66 | 95 | 64 | 95 | — | — | 55 | 64 | 25 |
| 24 | 67 | 93 | 107 | 99 | 81 | 99 | 80 | 99 | 88 | 99 | — | — | 90 | 99 | 75 | 98 | 64 | 92 | 63 | 91 | — | — | 54 | 58 | 24 |
| 23 | 66 | 92 | 104 | 99 | 79 | 99 | 78 | 99 | 86 | 99 | — | — | 88 | 99 | 73 | 97 | 62 | 88 | 61 | 87 | — | — | 52 | 52 | 23 |
| 22 | 64 | 90 | 101 | 99 | 77 | 99 | 76 | 99 | 84 | 99 | — | — | 86 | 99 | 71 | 96 | 60 | 84 | 59 | 81 | — | — | 51 | 47 | 22 |
| 21 | 63 | 89 | 98 | 99 | 76 | 99 | 74 | 98 | 81 | 99 | 78 | 99 | 84 | 99 | 70 | 96 | 58 | 78 | 58 | 75 | 68 | 99 | 49 | 42 | 21 |
| 20 | 61 | 87 | 96 | 99 | 74 | 98 | 72 | 97 | 79 | 99 | 76 | 99 | 82 | 98 | 68 | 94 | 56 | 72 | 56 | 69 | 66 | 99 | 48 | 38 | 20 |
| 19 | 60 | 84 | 93 | 99 | 72 | 97 | 70 | 96 | 77 | 98 | 74 | 98 | 80 | 98 | 66 | 93 | 54 | 65 | 54 | 62 | 64 | 97 | 47 | 33 | 19 |
| 18 | 58 | 81 | 90 | 99 | 70 | 96 | 68 | 95 | 75 | 98 | 72 | 97 | 78 | 98 | 65 | 92 | 52 | 58 | 52 | 55 | 62 | 91 | 45 | 29 | 18 |
| 17 | 57 | 78 | 87 | 99 | 68 | 94 | 66 | 93 | 73 | 97 | 70 | 96 | 76 | 97 | 63 | 90 | 50 | 50 | 51 | 49 | 59 | 83 | 44 | 26 | 17 |
| 16 | 55 | 75 | 84 | 99 | 66 | 93 | 64 | 92 | 70 | 96 | 67 | 94 | 74 | 96 | 61 | 87 | 48 | 43 | 49 | 42 | 57 | 73 | 42 | 22 | 16 |
| 15 | 54 | 71 | 81 | 99 | 64 | 90 | 62 | 89 | 68 | 95 | 65 | 92 | 72 | 96 | 60 | 85 | 46 | 36 | 47 | 36 | 55 | 64 | 41 | 19 | 15 |
| 14 | 53 | 66 | 78 | 98 | 62 | 88 | 60 | 86 | 66 | 93 | 63 | 89 | 69 | 95 | 58 | 82 | 44 | 29 | 45 | 31 | 53 | 55 | 39 | 16 | 14 |
| 13 | 51 | 62 | 75 | 98 | 60 | 85 | 58 | 82 | 64 | 91 | 61 | 85 | 67 | 94 | 56 | 78 | 42 | 23 | 44 | 26 | 51 | 46 | 38 | 14 | 13 |
| 12 | 50 | 56 | 73 | 97 | 58 | 81 | 56 | 78 | 62 | 88 | 59 | 80 | 65 | 92 | 55 | 74 | 40 | 17 | 42 | 21 | 48 | 38 | 36 | 11 | 12 |
| 11 | 48 | 51 | 70 | 96 | 56 | 76 | 54 | 72 | 59 | 84 | 56 | 75 | 63 | 91 | 53 | 69 | 38 | 13 | 40 | 17 | 46 | 31 | 35 | 9 | 11 |
| 10 | 47 | 44 | 67 | 94 | 54 | 71 | 52 | 66 | 57 | 80 | 54 | 69 | 61 | 89 | 51 | 63 | 36 | 9 | 39 | 14 | 44 | 25 | 33 | 7 | 10 |
| 9 | 45 | 38 | 64 | 92 | 52 | 64 | 50 | 58 | 55 | 74 | 52 | 62 | 59 | 86 | 50 | 57 | 34 | 6 | 37 | 11 | 42 | 20 | 32 | 6 | 9 |
| 8 | 44 | 31 | 61 | 88 | 50 | 57 | 48 | 50 | 53 | 67 | 50 | 54 | 57 | 83 | 48 | 50 | 32 | 4 | 35 | 9 | 40 | 16 | 30 | 4 | 8 |
| 7 | 42 | 24 | 58 | 84 | 48 | 50 | 46 | 41 | 51 | 59 | 48 | 46 | 55 | 79 | 46 | 43 | 30 | 3 | 33 | 7 | 38 | 12 | 29 | 3 | 7 |
| 6 | 41 | 18 | 55 | 78 | 46 | 41 | 44 | 31 | 48 | 50 | 46 | 38 | 53 | 75 | 45 | 35 | 28 | 2 | 32 | 5 | 35 | 9 | 28 | 2 | 6 |
| 5 | 39 | 12 | 53 | 69 | 44 | 33 | 42 | 23 | 46 | 40 | 43 | 29 | 51 | 69 | 43 | 27 | 26 | 1 | 30 | 4 | 33 | 7 | 26 | 2 | 5 |
| 4 | 38 | 7 | 50 | 58 | 42 | 25 | 40 | 15 | 44 | 30 | 41 | 21 | 49 | 61 | 41 | 20 | 24 | 1 | 28 | 3 | 31 | 5 | 25 | 1 | 4 |
| 3 | 36 | 3 | 47 | 45 | 41 | 17 | 38 | 9 | 42 | 21 | 39 | 13 | 47 | 52 | 40 | 13 | 22 | 1 | 27 | 2 | 29 | 4 | 23 | 1 | 3 |
| 2 | 35 | 1 | 44 | 29 | 39 | 10 | 36 | 5 | 40 | 13 | 37 | 7 | 45 | 40 | 38 | 8 | 20 | 1 | 25 | 1 | 27 | 3 | 22 | 1 | 2 |
| 1 | 34 | 1 | 41 | 14 | 37 | 5 | 34 | 2 | 37 | 7 | 35 | 3 | 43 | 25 | 37 | 4 | 18 | 1 | 23 | 1 | 24 | 2 | 20 | 1 | 1 |
| 0 | 32 | 1 | 38 | 4 | 35 | 2 | 32 | 1 | 35 | 3 | 33 | 1 | 41 | 9 | 35 | 1 | 16 | 1 | 21 | 1 | 22 | 1 | 19 | 1 | 0 |
| Raw mean | 12.25 | | 4.13 | | 7.87 | | 8.80 | | 6.71 | | 8.03 | | 4.39 | | 9.12 | | 16.88 | | 16.62 | | 12.69 | | 21.39 | | Raw mean |
| Raw SD | 6.82 | | 3.48 | | 5.14 | | 5.02 | | 4.55 | | 4.60 | | 4.93 | | 6.02 | | 5.01 | | 5.81 | | 4.56 | | 6.84 | | Raw SD |
| T: 90% Conf. int. | 5 | | 7 | | 7 | | 6 | | 6 | | 5 | | 5 | | 6 | | 7 | | 6 | | 7 | | 6 | | T: 90% Conf. int. |

**Table A.8d** PRS–P Composite T Scores

| T score | Externalizing Problems Combined | Externalizing Problems Female | Externalizing Problems Male | Internalizing Problems Combined | Internalizing Problems Female | Internalizing Problems Male | Adaptive Skills Combined | Adaptive Skills Female | Adaptive Skills Male | Behavioral Symptoms Index Combined | Behavioral Symptoms Index Female | Behavioral Symptoms Index Male | T score |
|---|---|---|---|---|---|---|---|---|---|---|---|---|---|
| 120 | — | — | — | 317–327 | 318–340 | 317 | — | — | — | — | 620–635 | — | 120 |
| 119 | — | — | — | 315–316 | 315–317 | 314–316 | — | — | — | — | 616–619 | — | 119 |
| 118 | — | — | — | 312–314 | 313–314 | 312–313 | — | — | — | — | 611–615 | — | 118 |
| 117 | — | — | — | 310–311 | 310–312 | 309–311 | — | — | — | — | 606–610 | — | 117 |
| 116 | — | — | — | 308–309 | 308–309 | 307–308 | — | — | — | — | 602–605 | — | 116 |
| 115 | — | — | — | 305–307 | 306–307 | 305–306 | — | — | — | — | 597–601 | — | 115 |
| 114 | — | — | — | 303–304 | 303–305 | 302–304 | — | — | — | — | 593–596 | — | 114 |
| 113 | — | 212 | — | 300–302 | 301–302 | 300–301 | — | — | — | 590–593 | 588–592 | — | 113 |
| 112 | — | 211 | — | 298–299 | 298–300 | 297–299 | — | — | — | 585–589 | 583–587 | — | 112 |
| 111 | — | 209–210 | — | 296–297 | 296–297 | 295–296 | — | — | — | 581–584 | 579–582 | — | 111 |
| 110 | — | 207–208 | — | 293–295 | 294–295 | 293–294 | — | — | — | 576–580 | 574–578 | — | 110 |
| 109 | — | 205–206 | — | 291–292 | 291–293 | 290–292 | — | — | — | 571–575 | 570–573 | — | 109 |
| 108 | — | 203–204 | — | 288–290 | 289–290 | 288–289 | — | — | — | 567–570 | 565–569 | — | 108 |
| 107 | — | 202 | — | 286–287 | 286–288 | 285–287 | — | — | — | 562–566 | 560–564 | — | 107 |
| 106 | — | 200–201 | — | 284–285 | 284–285 | 283–284 | — | — | — | 558–561 | 556–559 | 557–560 | 106 |
| 105 | 199 | 198–199 | — | 281–283 | 282–283 | 281–282 | — | — | — | 553–557 | 551–555 | 553–556 | 105 |
| 104 | 197–198 | 196–197 | — | 279–280 | 279–281 | 278–280 | — | — | — | 548–552 | 547–550 | 548–552 | 104 |
| 103 | 195–196 | 194–195 | — | 276–278 | 277–278 | 276–277 | — | — | — | 544–547 | 542–546 | 543–547 | 103 |
| 102 | 193–194 | 193 | — | 274–275 | 274–276 | 273–275 | — | — | — | 539–543 | 537–541 | 539–542 | 102 |
| 101 | 191–192 | 191–192 | — | 272–273 | 272–273 | 271–272 | — | — | — | 534–538 | 533–536 | 534–538 | 101 |
| 100 | 190 | 189–190 | — | 269–271 | 270–271 | 269–270 | — | — | — | 530–533 | 528–532 | 530–533 | 100 |
| 99 | 188–189 | 187–188 | — | 267–268 | 267–269 | 266–268 | — | — | — | 525–529 | 524–527 | 525–529 | 99 |
| 98 | 186–187 | 186 | 186–187 | 264–266 | 265–266 | 264–265 | — | — | — | 520–524 | 519–523 | 520–524 | 98 |
| 97 | 184–185 | 184–185 | 185 | 262–263 | 262–264 | 261–263 | — | — | — | 516–519 | 514–518 | 516–519 | 97 |
| 96 | 182–183 | 182–183 | 183–184 | 260–261 | 260–261 | 259–260 | — | — | — | 511–515 | 510–513 | 511–515 | 96 |
| 95 | 181 | 180–181 | 181–182 | 257–259 | 258–259 | 257–258 | — | — | — | 507–510 | 505–509 | 506–510 | 95 |
| 94 | 179–180 | 178–179 | 179–180 | 255–256 | 255–257 | 254–256 | — | — | — | 502–506 | 501–504 | 502–505 | 94 |
| 93 | 177–178 | 177 | 177–178 | 252–254 | 253–254 | 252–253 | — | — | — | 497–501 | 496–500 | 497–501 | 93 |
| 92 | 175–176 | 175–176 | 176 | 250–251 | 250–252 | 249–251 | — | — | — | 493–496 | 491–495 | 492–496 | 92 |
| 91 | 173–174 | 173–174 | 174–175 | 248–249 | 248–249 | 247–248 | — | — | — | 488–492 | 487–490 | 488–491 | 91 |
| 90 | 172 | 171–172 | 172–173 | 245–247 | 246–247 | 245–246 | — | — | — | 483–487 | 482–486 | 483–487 | 90 |
| 89 | 170–171 | 169–170 | 170–171 | 243–244 | 243–245 | 242–244 | — | — | — | 479–482 | 478–481 | 479–482 | 89 |
| 88 | 168–169 | 168 | 168–169 | 240–242 | 241–242 | 240–241 | — | — | — | 474–478 | 473–477 | 474–478 | 88 |
| 87 | 166–167 | 166–167 | 167 | 238–239 | 238–240 | 237–239 | — | — | — | 470–473 | 468–472 | 469–473 | 87 |
| 86 | 164–165 | 164–165 | 165–166 | 236–237 | 236–237 | 235–236 | — | — | — | 465–469 | 464–467 | 465–468 | 86 |
| 85 | 163 | 162–163 | 163–164 | 233–235 | 234–235 | 233–234 | — | — | — | 460–464 | 459–463 | 460–464 | 85 |
| 84 | 161–162 | 160–161 | 161–162 | 231–232 | 231–233 | 230–232 | — | — | — | 456–459 | 455–458 | 455–459 | 84 |
| 83 | 159–160 | 159 | 159–160 | 228–230 | 229–230 | 228–229 | — | — | — | 451–455 | 450–454 | 451–454 | 83 |
| 82 | 157–158 | 157–158 | 158 | 226–227 | 226–228 | 225–227 | — | — | — | 446–450 | 445–449 | 446–450 | 82 |
| 81 | 155–156 | 155–156 | 156–157 | 224–225 | 224–225 | 223–224 | — | — | — | 442–445 | 441–444 | 441–445 | 81 |
| 80 | 154 | 153–154 | 154–155 | 221–223 | 221–223 | 221–222 | — | — | — | 437–441 | 436–440 | 437–440 | 80 |
| 79 | 152–153 | 151–152 | 152–153 | 219–220 | 219–220 | 218–220 | — | — | — | 433–436 | 432–435 | 432–436 | 79 |
| 78 | 150–151 | 150 | 150–151 | 216–218 | 217–218 | 216–217 | — | — | — | 428–432 | 427–431 | 428–431 | 78 |
| 77 | 148–149 | 148–149 | 149 | 214–215 | 214–216 | 214–215 | — | — | — | 423–427 | 422–426 | 423–427 | 77 |
| 76 | 146–147 | 146–147 | 147–148 | 212–213 | 212–213 | 211–213 | — | — | — | 419–422 | 418–421 | 418–422 | 76 |
| 75 | 145 | 144–145 | 145–146 | 209–211 | 209–211 | 209–210 | — | — | — | 414–418 | 413–417 | 414–417 | 75 |
| 74 | 143–144 | 142–143 | 143–144 | 207–208 | 207–208 | 206–208 | — | — | — | 409–413 | 409–412 | 409–413 | 74 |
| 73 | 141–142 | 141 | 141–142 | 204–206 | 205–206 | 204–205 | — | 271 | — | 405–408 | 404–408 | 404–408 | 73 |
| 72 | 139–140 | 139–140 | 139–140 | 202–203 | 203–204 | 202–203 | 270–272 | 268–270 | 271–273 | 400–404 | 399–403 | 400–403 | 72 |
| 71 | 137–138 | 137–138 | 138 | 200–201 | 200–201 | 199–201 | 267–269 | 265–267 | 268–270 | 396–399 | 395–398 | 395–399 | 71 |
| 70 | 136 | 135–136 | 136–137 | 197–199 | 197–199 | 197–198 | 264–266 | 262–264 | 264–267 | 391–395 | 390–394 | 390–394 | 70 |
| 69 | 134–135 | 134 | 134–135 | 195–196 | 195–196 | 194–196 | 261–263 | 259–261 | 261–263 | 386–390 | 386–389 | 386–389 | 69 |
| 68 | 132–133 | 132–133 | 132–133 | 192–194 | 193–194 | 192–193 | 257–260 | 256–258 | 258–260 | 382–385 | 381–385 | 381–385 | 68 |
| 67 | 130–131 | 130–131 | 130–131 | 190–191 | 190–192 | 190–191 | 254–256 | 253–255 | 254–257 | 377–381 | 376–380 | 377–380 | 67 |
| 66 | 128–129 | 128–129 | 129 | 188–189 | 188–189 | 187–189 | 251–253 | 249–252 | 251–253 | 372–376 | 372–375 | 372–376 | 66 |

**Table A.8d** PRS–P Composite T Scores (continued)

| T score | Externalizing Problems Combined | Female | Male | Internalizing Problems Combined | Female | Male | Adaptive Skills Combined | Female | Male | Behavioral Symptoms Index Combined | Female | Male | T score |
|---|---|---|---|---|---|---|---|---|---|---|---|---|---|
| 65 | 127 | 126–127 | 127–128 | 185–187 | 185–187 | 185–186 | 248–250 | 246–248 | 248–250 | 368–371 | 367–371 | 367–371 | 65 |
| 64 | 125–126 | 125 | 125–126 | 183–184 | 183–184 | 182–184 | 244–247 | 243–245 | 245–247 | 363–367 | 363–366 | 363–366 | 64 |
| 63 | 123–124 | 123–124 | 123–124 | 180–182 | 181–182 | 180–181 | 241–243 | 240–242 | 241–244 | 359–362 | 358–362 | 358–362 | 63 |
| 62 | 121–122 | 121–122 | 121–122 | 178–179 | 178–180 | 178–179 | 238–240 | 237–239 | 238–240 | 354–358 | 353–357 | 353–357 | 62 |
| 61 | 119–120 | 119–120 | 120 | 176–177 | 176–177 | 175–177 | 235–237 | 234–236 | 235–237 | 349–353 | 349–352 | 349–352 | 61 |
| 60 | 118 | 117–118 | 118–119 | 173–175 | 173–175 | 173–174 | 231–234 | 231–233 | 231–234 | 345–348 | 344–348 | 344–348 | 60 |
| 59 | 116–117 | 116 | 116–117 | 171–172 | 171–172 | 170–172 | 228–230 | 227–230 | 228–230 | 340–344 | 340–343 | 339–343 | 59 |
| 58 | 114–115 | 114–115 | 114–115 | 168–170 | 169–170 | 168–169 | 225–227 | 224–226 | 225–227 | 335–339 | 335–339 | 335–338 | 58 |
| 57 | 112–113 | 112–113 | 112–113 | 166–167 | 166–168 | 166–167 | 222–224 | 221–223 | 222–224 | 331–334 | 330–334 | 330–334 | 57 |
| 56 | 110–111 | 110–111 | 111 | 164–165 | 164–165 | 163–165 | 218–221 | 218–220 | 218–221 | 326–330 | 326–329 | 326–329 | 56 |
| 55 | 109 | 108–109 | 109–110 | 161–163 | 161–163 | 161–162 | 215–217 | 215–217 | 215–217 | 321–325 | 321–325 | 321–325 | 55 |
| 54 | 107–108 | 107 | 107–108 | 159–160 | 159–160 | 158–160 | 212–214 | 212–214 | 212–214 | 317–320 | 317–320 | 316–320 | 54 |
| 53 | 105–106 | 105–106 | 105–106 | 156–158 | 157–158 | 156–157 | 209–211 | 208–211 | 208–211 | 312–316 | 312–316 | 312–315 | 53 |
| 52 | 103–104 | 103–104 | 103–104 | 154–155 | 154–156 | 154–155 | 205–208 | 205–207 | 205–207 | 308–311 | 307–311 | 307–311 | 52 |
| 51 | 101–102 | 101–102 | 102 | 152–153 | 152–153 | 151–153 | 202–204 | 202–204 | 202–204 | 303–307 | 303–306 | 302–306 | 51 |
| 50 | 100 | 99–100 | 100–101 | 149–151 | 149–151 | 149–150 | 199–201 | 199–201 | 199–201 | 298–302 | 298–302 | 298–301 | 50 |
| 49 | 98–99 | 98 | 98–99 | 147–148 | 147–148 | 146–148 | 196–198 | 196–198 | 195–198 | 294–297 | 294–297 | 293–297 | 49 |
| 48 | 96–97 | 96–97 | 96–97 | 144–146 | 145–146 | 144–145 | 193–195 | 193–195 | 192–194 | 289–293 | 289–293 | 288–292 | 48 |
| 47 | 94–95 | 94–95 | 94–95 | 142–143 | 142–144 | 142–143 | 190–192 | 190–192 | 189–191 | 284–288 | 284–287 | 284–287 | 47 |
| 46 | 92–93 | 92–93 | 93 | 140–141 | 140–141 | 139–141 | 186–189 | 186–189 | 185–188 | 280–283 | 280–283 | 279–283 | 46 |
| 45 | 91 | 90–91 | 91–92 | 137–139 | 137–139 | 137–138 | 183–185 | 183–185 | 182–184 | 275–279 | 275–279 | 275–278 | 45 |
| 44 | 89–90 | 89 | 89–90 | 135–136 | 135–136 | 134–136 | 180–182 | 180–182 | 179–181 | 271–274 | 271–274 | 270–274 | 44 |
| 43 | 87–88 | 87–88 | 87–88 | 132–134 | 132–134 | 132–133 | 176–179 | 177–179 | 176–178 | 266–270 | 266–270 | 265–269 | 43 |
| 42 | 85–86 | 85–86 | 85–86 | 130–131 | 130–131 | 130–131 | 173–175 | 174–176 | 172–175 | 261–265 | 261–265 | 261–264 | 42 |
| 41 | 83–84 | 83–84 | 84 | 128–129 | 128–129 | 127–129 | 170–172 | 171–173 | 169–171 | 257–260 | 257–260 | 256–260 | 41 |
| 40 | 82 | 82 | 82–83 | 125–127 | 125–127 | 125–126 | 167–169 | 167–170 | 166–168 | 252–256 | 252–256 | 251–255 | 40 |
| 39 | 80–81 | 80–81 | 80–81 | 123–124 | 123–124 | 122–124 | 163–166 | 164–166 | 162–165 | 247–251 | 248–251 | 247–250 | 39 |
| 38 | 78–79 | 78–79 | 78–79 | 120–122 | 120–122 | 120–121 | 160–162 | 161–163 | 159–161 | 243–246 | 243–247 | 242–246 | 38 |
| 37 | 76–77 | 76–77 | 76–77 | 118–119 | 118–119 | 118–119 | 157–159 | 158–160 | 156–158 | 238–242 | 238–242 | 237–241 | 37 |
| 36 | 74–75 | 74–75 | 74–75 | 116–117 | 116–117 | 115–117 | 154–156 | 155–157 | 152–155 | 234–237 | 234–237 | 233–236 | 36 |
| 35 | 73 | 73 | 73 | 113–115 | 113–115 | 113–114 | 150–153 | 152–154 | 149–151 | 229–233 | 229–233 | 228–232 | 35 |
| 34 | 71–72 | 71–72 | 71–72 | 111–112 | 111–112 | 110–112 | 147–149 | 149–151 | 146–148 | 224–228 | 225–228 | 224–227 | 34 |
| 33 | 70 | 70 | 70 | 108–110 | 108–110 | 108–109 | 144–146 | 145–148 | 143–145 | 220–223 | 220–224 | 219–223 | 33 |
| 32 | — | — | — | 106–107 | 106–107 | 106–107 | 141–143 | 142–144 | 139–142 | 215–219 | 215–219 | 214–218 | 32 |
| 31 | — | — | — | 104–105 | 104–105 | 103–105 | 137–140 | 139–141 | 136–138 | 211–214 | 211–214 | 211–213 | 31 |
| 30 | — | — | — | 101–103 | 101–103 | 102 | 134–136 | 136–138 | 133–135 | — | 209–210 | — | 30 |
| 29 | — | — | — | — | 99–100 | — | 131–133 | 133–135 | 129–132 | — | — | — | 29 |
| 28 | — | — | — | — | 97–98 | — | 128–130 | 130–132 | 126–128 | — | — | — | 28 |
| 27 | — | — | — | — | — | — | 124–127 | 127–129 | 123–125 | — | — | — | 27 |
| 26 | — | — | — | — | — | — | 121–123 | 123–126 | 120–122 | — | — | — | 26 |
| 25 | — | — | — | — | — | — | 118–120 | 120–122 | 116–119 | — | — | — | 25 |
| 24 | — | — | — | — | — | — | 115–117 | 117–119 | 113–115 | — | — | — | 24 |
| 23 | — | — | — | — | — | — | 111–114 | 114–116 | 110–112 | — | — | — | 23 |
| 22 | — | — | — | — | — | — | 108–110 | 111–113 | 106–109 | — | — | — | 22 |
| 21 | — | — | — | — | — | — | 105–107 | 108–110 | 103–105 | — | — | — | 21 |
| 20 | — | — | — | — | — | — | 102–104 | 104–107 | 100–102 | — | — | — | 20 |
| 19 | — | — | — | — | — | — | 99–101 | 101–103 | 97–99 | — | — | — | 19 |
| 18 | — | — | — | — | — | — | 95–98 | 98–100 | 93–96 | — | — | — | 18 |
| 17 | — | — | — | — | — | — | 92–94 | 95–97 | 90–92 | — | — | — | 17 |
| 16 | — | — | — | — | — | — | 89–91 | 92–94 | 87–89 | — | — | — | 16 |
| 15 | — | — | — | — | — | — | 86–88 | 89–91 | 83–86 | — | — | — | 15 |
| 14 | — | — | — | — | — | — | 82–85 | 86–88 | 80–82 | — | — | — | 14 |
| 13 | — | — | — | — | — | — | 79–81 | 82–85 | 78–79 | — | — | — | 13 |
| 12 | — | — | — | — | — | — | 76–78 | 79–81 | — | — | — | — | 12 |
| 11 | — | — | — | — | — | — | 73–75 | 76–78 | — | — | — | — | 11 |
| 10 | — | — | — | — | — | — | 68–72 | 55–75 | — | — | — | — | 10 |
| T: 90% Conf. int. | 5 | 5 | 5 | 5 | 5 | 5 | 4 | 4 | 4 | 3 | 3 | 3 | T: 90% Conf. int. |

**Table A.8e** PRS-P Composite Percentiles

| %ile | Externalizing Problems | | | Internalizing Problems | | | Adaptive Skills | | | Behavioral Symptoms Index | | | %ile |
|---|---|---|---|---|---|---|---|---|---|---|---|---|---|
| | Combined | Female | Male | Combined | Female | Male | Combined | Female | Male | Combined | Female | Male | |
| 99 | 153–199 | 151–212 | 153–187 | 215–327 | 216–340 | 214–317 | 254–272 | 252–271 | 257–273 | 440–593 | 438–635 | 440–560 | 99 |
| 98 | 146–152 | 145–150 | 146–152 | 206–214 | 207–215 | 205–213 | 251–253 | 249–251 | 253–256 | 418–439 | 417–437 | 418–439 | 98 |
| 97 | 141–145 | 140–144 | 141–145 | 200–205 | 201–206 | 199–204 | 249–250 | 247–248 | 251–252 | 403–417 | 403–416 | 404–417 | 97 |
| 96 | 137–140 | 137–139 | 137–140 | 196–199 | 197–200 | 195–198 | 247–248 | 246 | 248–250 | 393–402 | 393–402 | 394–403 | 96 |
| 95 | 134–136 | 134–136 | 134–136 | 192–195 | 193–196 | 192–194 | 245–246 | 244–245 | 247 | 385–392 | 385–392 | 385–393 | 95 |
| 94 | 131–133 | 131–133 | 131–133 | 189–191 | 190–192 | 189–191 | 244 | 243 | 245–246 | 378–384 | 378–384 | 378–384 | 94 |
| 93 | 129–130 | 129–130 | 129–130 | 187–188 | 187–189 | 186–188 | 242–243 | 242 | 243–244 | 372–377 | 372–377 | 373–377 | 93 |
| 92 | 127–128 | 127–128 | 127–128 | 184–186 | 185–186 | 184–185 | 241 | 241 | 242 | 367–371 | 367–372 | 367–372 | 92 |
| 91 | 125–126 | 126 | 125–126 | 182–183 | 183–184 | 182–183 | 240 | 239–240 | 241 | 362–366 | 363–366 | 363–366 | 91 |
| 90 | 124 | 124–125 | 124 | 180–181 | 181–182 | 180–181 | 239 | 238 | 239–240 | 358–361 | 358–362 | 359–362 | 90 |
| 89 | 122–123 | 123 | 122–123 | 179 | 179–180 | 178–179 | 237–238 | 237 | 238 | 354–357 | 355–357 | 355–358 | 89 |
| 88 | 121 | 121–122 | 121 | 177–178 | 178 | 177 | 236 | 236 | 237 | 351–353 | 351–354 | 351–354 | 88 |
| 87 | 120 | 120 | 120 | 176 | 176–177 | 175–176 | 235 | 235 | 236 | 348–350 | 348–350 | 348–350 | 87 |
| 86 | 119 | 119 | 119 | 174–175 | 175 | 174 | 234 | 234 | 235 | 345–347 | 345–347 | 345–347 | 86 |
| 85 | 117–118 | 118 | 118 | 173 | 174 | 173 | 233 | 233 | 234 | 342–344 | 342–344 | 343–344 | 85 |
| 84 | 116 | 117 | 117 | 172 | 173 | 172 | 232 | – | 233 | 339–341 | 340–341 | 340–342 | 84 |
| 83 | 115 | 116 | 116 | 171 | 171–172 | 171 | 231 | 232 | 232 | 337–338 | 337–339 | 338–339 | 83 |
| 82 | – | 115 | 115 | 170 | 170 | 169–170 | – | 231 | 231 | 335–336 | 335–336 | 335–337 | 82 |
| 81 | 114 | 114 | 114 | 169 | 169 | 168 | 230 | 230 | 230 | 332–334 | 333–334 | 333–334 | 81 |
| 80 | 113 | 113 | 113 | 168 | 168 | 167 | 229 | 229 | 229 | 330–331 | 331–332 | 331–332 | 80 |
| 79 | 112 | – | 112 | 167 | 167 | 166 | 228 | 228 | 228 | 328–329 | 329–330 | 329–330 | 79 |
| 78 | 111 | 112 | – | 166 | 166 | – | 227 | 227 | 227 | 326–327 | 327–328 | 327–328 | 78 |
| 77 | – | 111 | 111 | 165 | 165 | 165 | 226 | 226 | 226 | 324–325 | 325–326 | 325–326 | 77 |
| 76 | 110 | 110 | 110 | 164 | 164 | 164 | 225 | – | 225 | 323 | 323–324 | 323–324 | 76 |
| 75 | 109 | – | 109 | 163 | – | 163 | 224 | 225 | 224 | 321–322 | 321–322 | 322 | 75 |
| 74 | – | 109 | – | 162 | 163 | 162 | – | 224 | 223 | 319–320 | 320 | 320–321 | 74 |
| 73 | 108 | 108 | 108 | – | 162 | 161 | 223 | 223 | – | 318 | 318–319 | 318–319 | 73 |
| 72 | 107 | – | – | 161 | 161 | 160 | 222 | 222 | 222 | 316–317 | 317 | 317 | 72 |
| 71 | – | 107 | 107 | 160 | 160 | 160 | 221 | 221 | 221 | 315 | 315–316 | 315–316 | 71 |
| 70 | 106 | 106 | 106 | 159 | – | 159 | 220 | – | 220 | 313–314 | 314 | 314 | 70 |
| 69 | 105 | – | – | – | 159 | 158 | 219 | 220 | 219 | 312 | 312–313 | 312–313 | 69 |
| 68 | 105 | 105 | 105 | 158 | 158 | – | 218 | 219 | 218 | 311 | 311 | 311 | 68 |
| 67 | 104 | – | – | 157 | 157 | 157 | 217 | 218 | – | 309–310 | 309–310 | 310 | 67 |
| 66 | – | 104 | 104 | – | – | 156 | – | 217 | 217 | 308 | 308 | 308–309 | 66 |
| 65 | 103 | – | – | 156 | 156 | – | 216 | – | 216 | 307 | 307 | 307 | 65 |
| 64 | – | 103 | 103 | 155 | 155 | 155 | 215 | 216 | 215 | 305–306 | 306 | 306 | 64 |
| 63 | 102 | – | – | 154 | – | 154 | 214 | 215 | 214 | 304 | 304–305 | 305 | 63 |
| 62 | – | 102 | 102 | – | 154 | – | – | 214 | – | 303 | 303 | 303–304 | 62 |
| 61 | 101 | – | – | 153 | 153 | 153 | 213 | 213 | 213 | 302 | 302 | 302 | 61 |
| 60 | – | 101 | 101 | – | – | – | 212 | 212 | 212 | 301 | 301 | 301 | 60 |
| 59 | 100 | – | – | 152 | 152 | 152 | – | – | 211 | 300 | 300 | 300 | 59 |
| 58 | 100 | 100 | 100 | – | – | – | 211 | 211 | 210 | 298–299 | 299 | 299 | 58 |
| 57 | – | – | – | 151 | 151 | 151 | 210 | 210 | – | 297 | 297–298 | 298 | 57 |
| 56 | 99 | – | 99 | 150 | 150 | 150 | 209 | 209 | 209 | 296 | 296 | 297 | 56 |
| 55 | – | – | – | – | – | – | 208 | 208 | 208 | 295 | 295 | 296 | 55 |
| 54 | 98 | 98 | – | 149 | 149 | 149 | 207 | 207 | 207 | 294 | 294 | 295 | 54 |
| 53 | – | – | 98 | – | – | – | 207 | – | 206 | 293 | 293 | 294 | 53 |
| 52 | – | – | – | 148 | 148 | 148 | 206 | 206 | 205 | 292 | 292 | 293 | 52 |
| 51 | 97 | 97 | 97 | – | – | – | 205 | 205 | – | 291 | 291 | 292 | 51 |

## Table A.8e  PRS–P Composite Percentiles (continued)

| %ile | Externalizing Problems | | | Internalizing Problems | | | Adaptive Skills | | | Behavioral Symptoms Index | | | %ile |
| --- | --- | --- | --- | --- | --- | --- | --- | --- | --- | --- | --- | --- | --- |
| | Combined | Female | Male | Combined | Female | Male | Combined | Female | Male | Combined | Female | Male | |
| 50 | – | – | – | 147 | 147 | 147 | 204 | 204 | 204 | 290 | 290 | 291 | 50 |
| 49 | 96 | 96 | – | – | 146 | 146 | – | 203 | 203 | 289 | 289 | 290 | 49 |
| 48 | – | – | 96 | 146 | – | – | 203 | 202 | 202 | 288 | 288 | 289 | 48 |
| 47 | – | 95 | – | 145 | 145 | 145 | 202 | 201 | 201 | 287 | 287 | 288 | 47 |
| 46 | 95 | – | 95 | – | – | – | 201 | 200 | 200 | 286 | 286 | 287 | 46 |
| 45 | – | – | – | 144 | 144 | 144 | 200 | – | 199 | 285 | 285 | 286 | 45 |
| 44 | 94 | 94 | – | 143 | – | 143 | 199 | 199 | – | 284 | 284 | 285 | 44 |
| 43 | – | – | 94 | – | 143 | – | 198 | 198 | 198 | 283 | – | 284 | 43 |
| 42 | – | 93 | – | 142 | 142 | 142 | 197 | 197 | 197 | 282 | 283 | 283 | 42 |
| 41 | 93 | – | 93 | – | – | – | – | 196 | 196 | – | 282 | 282 | 41 |
| 40 | – | – | – | 141 | 141 | 141 | 196 | 195 | 195 | 281 | 281 | 281 | 40 |
| 39 | – | 92 | – | – | 140 | – | 195 | 194 | 194 | 280 | 280 | 280 | 39 |
| 38 | 92 | – | 92 | 140 | – | – | 194 | 193 | 193 | 279 | 279 | 279 | 38 |
| 37 | – | – | – | – | – | 140 | 193 | 192 | 192 | 278 | 278 | 278 | 37 |
| 36 | 91 | 91 | – | – | 139 | 139 | 192 | 191 | 191 | 277 | 277 | – | 36 |
| 35 | – | – | 91 | 139 | 138 | – | 191 | 190 | 190 | – | 276 | 277 | 35 |
| 34 | – | 90 | – | – | – | 138 | 190 | 189 | 189 | 276 | 275 | 276 | 34 |
| 33 | 90 | – | 90 | 138 | 137 | – | 189 | 188 | 188 | 275 | – | 275 | 33 |
| 32 | – | – | – | 137 | – | 137 | 188 | 187 | 187 | 274 | 274 | 274 | 32 |
| 31 | – | 89 | – | – | 136 | – | 187 | 186 | 186 | 273 | 273 | 273 | 31 |
| 30 | 89 | – | 89 | 136 | – | 136 | 186 | 185 | 185 | 272 | 272 | 272 | 30 |
| 29 | – | – | – | – | 135 | – | 184–185 | 183–184 | 184 | 271 | 271 | 271 | 29 |
| 28 | 88 | 88 | 88 | 135 | – | 135 | 183 | 182 | 183 | – | 270 | 270 | 28 |
| 27 | – | – | – | – | 134 | – | 182 | 181 | 181–182 | 270 | 269 | – | 27 |
| 26 | – | 87 | – | 134 | – | 134 | 181 | 180 | 180 | 269 | 268 | 269 | 26 |
| 25 | 87 | – | – | 133 | 133 | 133 | 180 | 179 | 179 | 268 | – | 268 | 25 |
| 24 | – | 86 | 87 | 132 | 132 | 132 | 178–179 | 177–178 | 178 | 267 | 267 | 267 | 24 |
| 23 | 86 | – | – | – | 131 | 131 | 177 | 176 | 177 | 266 | 266 | 266 | 23 |
| 22 | – | – | 86 | 131 | – | – | 176 | 175 | 175–176 | 265 | 265 | 265 | 22 |
| 21 | – | 85 | – | – | 130 | 130 | 174–175 | 173–174 | 174 | 264 | 264 | 264 | 21 |
| 20 | – | – | – | 130 | – | 129 | 173 | 172 | 172–173 | 263 | 263 | 263 | 20 |
| 19 | 85 | – | 85 | – | 129 | – | 172 | 171 | 171 | 262 | 262 | 262 | 19 |
| 18 | – | 84 | – | 129 | 128 | 128 | 170–171 | 169–170 | 169–170 | 261 | 261 | 261 | 18 |
| 17 | 84 | – | 84 | 128 | – | – | 168–169 | 167–168 | 168 | 260 | 260 | 260 | 17 |
| 16 | – | 83 | – | – | 127 | 127 | 167 | 166 | 166–167 | 259 | 259 | 259 | 16 |
| 15 | – | – | – | 127 | 126 | – | 165–166 | 164–165 | 164–165 | 258–259 | 258 | 258 | 15 |
| 14 | 83 | – | 83 | 126 | 125 | 126 | 163–164 | 162–163 | 163 | 257 | 257 | 257 | 14 |
| 13 | – | 82 | – | 125 | 124 | 125 | 161–162 | 161 | 161–162 | 256 | 256 | 256 | 13 |
| 12 | 82 | – | 82 | 124 | – | 124 | 159–160 | 159–160 | 159–160 | 255 | 255 | 255 | 12 |
| 11 | – | 81 | – | – | – | 123 | 157–158 | 157–158 | 156–158 | 254 | 254 | 254 | 11 |
| 10 | 81 | – | 81 | 123 | 123 | 122 | 155–156 | 155–156 | 154–155 | 253 | 253 | 252–253 | 10 |
| 9 | – | 80 | – | 122 | 122 | 121 | 152–154 | 152–154 | 151–153 | 252 | 251–252 | 251 | 9 |
| 8 | 80 | – | 80 | 120–121 | 121 | 120 | 149–151 | 150–151 | 149–150 | 250–251 | 250 | 250 | 8 |
| 7 | – | 79 | – | 119 | 119–120 | 119 | 146–148 | 147–149 | 145–148 | 249 | 249 | 248–249 | 7 |
| 6 | 79 | 78 | 79 | 118 | 118 | 117–118 | 142–145 | 144–146 | 142–144 | 247–248 | 247–248 | 247 | 6 |
| 5 | 78 | 77 | 78 | 116–117 | 117 | 115–116 | 138–141 | 141–143 | 138–141 | 246 | 245–246 | 245–246 | 5 |
| 4 | 77 | 77 | 77 | 115 | 115–116 | 113–114 | 133–137 | 137–140 | 133–137 | 244–245 | 243–244 | 243–244 | 4 |
| 3 | – | 76 | 76 | 112–114 | 113–114 | 111–112 | 127–132 | 132–136 | 127–132 | 242–243 | 241–242 | 241–242 | 3 |
| 2 | 75–76 | 75 | 75 | 109–111 | 110–112 | 107–110 | 119–126 | 126–131 | 118–126 | 239–241 | 238–240 | 237–240 | 2 |
| 1 | 70–74 | 70–74 | 70–74 | 101–108 | 97–109 | 102–106 | 68–118 | 55–125 | 78–117 | 211–238 | 209–237 | 211–236 | 1 |

## Table A.9a PRS-C T Scores and Percentiles

| Raw score | Hyperactivity T | Hyperactivity %ile | Aggression T | Aggression %ile | Conduct Problems T | Conduct Problems %ile | Anxiety T | Anxiety %ile | Depression T | Depression %ile | Somatization T | Somatization %ile | Attention Problems T | Attention Problems %ile | Atypicality T | Atypicality %ile | Withdrawal T | Withdrawal %ile | Adaptability T | Adaptability %ile | Social Skills T | Social Skills %ile | Leadership T | Leadership %ile | Activities of Daily Living T | Activities of Daily Living %ile | Functional Communication T | Functional Communication %ile | Raw score |
|---|---|---|---|---|---|---|---|---|---|---|---|---|---|---|---|---|---|---|---|---|---|---|---|---|---|---|---|---|---|
| 42 | — | — | — | — | — | — | 111 | 99 | — | — | — | — | — | — | 120 | 99 | — | — | — | — | — | — | — | — | — | — | — | — | 42 |
| 41 | — | — | — | — | — | — | 109 | 99 | — | — | — | — | — | — | 120 | 99 | — | — | — | — | — | — | — | — | — | — | — | — | 41 |
| 40 | — | — | — | — | — | — | 107 | 99 | — | — | — | — | — | — | 120 | 99 | — | — | — | — | — | — | — | — | — | — | — | — | 40 |
| 39 | — | — | — | — | — | — | 105 | 99 | 118 | 99 | — | — | — | — | 120 | 99 | — | — | — | — | — | — | — | — | — | — | — | — | 39 |
| 38 | — | — | — | — | — | — | 103 | 99 | 116 | 99 | — | — | — | — | 120 | 99 | — | — | — | — | — | — | — | — | — | — | — | — | 38 |
| 37 | — | — | — | — | — | — | 101 | 99 | 114 | 99 | — | — | — | — | 118 | 99 | — | — | — | — | — | — | — | — | — | — | — | — | 37 |
| 36 | — | — | — | — | — | — | 99 | 99 | 112 | 99 | 120 | 99 | — | — | 116 | 99 | — | — | — | — | — | — | — | — | — | — | 68 | 98 | 36 |
| 35 | — | — | — | — | — | — | 97 | 99 | 110 | 99 | 120 | 99 | — | — | 114 | 99 | — | — | — | — | — | — | — | — | — | — | 66 | 97 | 35 |
| 34 | — | — | — | — | — | — | 95 | 99 | 108 | 99 | 120 | 99 | — | — | 112 | 99 | — | — | — | — | — | — | — | — | — | — | 65 | 95 | 34 |
| 33 | 90 | 99 | — | — | — | — | 93 | 99 | 106 | 99 | 120 | 99 | — | — | 110 | 99 | — | — | — | — | — | — | — | — | — | — | 63 | 92 | 33 |
| 32 | 88 | 99 | — | — | — | — | 91 | 99 | 104 | 99 | 119 | 99 | — | — | 108 | 99 | — | — | — | — | — | — | — | — | — | — | 62 | 88 | 32 |
| 31 | 86 | 99 | — | — | — | — | 90 | 99 | 102 | 99 | 117 | 99 | — | — | 106 | 99 | — | — | — | — | — | — | — | — | — | — | 60 | 84 | 31 |
| 30 | 84 | 99 | — | — | 112 | 99 | 88 | 99 | 100 | 99 | 114 | 99 | — | — | 104 | 99 | — | — | — | — | 66 | 97 | — | — | — | — | 59 | 79 | 30 |
| 29 | 83 | 99 | — | — | 109 | 99 | 86 | 99 | 98 | 99 | 111 | 99 | — | — | 102 | 99 | — | — | — | — | 64 | 94 | — | — | — | — | 57 | 74 | 29 |
| 28 | 81 | 99 | — | — | 106 | 99 | 84 | 99 | 95 | 99 | 109 | 99 | — | — | 99 | 99 | — | — | — | — | 63 | 90 | — | — | — | — | 56 | 69 | 28 |
| 27 | 79 | 99 | 115 | 99 | 104 | 99 | 82 | 99 | 93 | 99 | 106 | 99 | — | — | 97 | 99 | 106 | 99 | — | — | 61 | 86 | — | — | 72 | 99 | 54 | 63 | 27 |
| 26 | 78 | 98 | 112 | 99 | 101 | 99 | 80 | 99 | 91 | 99 | 104 | 99 | — | — | 95 | 99 | 104 | 99 | — | — | 60 | 81 | — | — | 70 | 99 | 53 | 57 | 26 |
| 25 | 76 | 98 | 109 | 99 | 99 | 99 | 78 | 99 | 89 | 99 | 101 | 99 | — | — | 93 | 99 | 101 | 99 | — | — | 58 | 76 | — | — | 68 | 98 | 51 | 51 | 25 |
| 24 | 74 | 97 | 106 | 99 | 96 | 99 | 76 | 99 | 87 | 99 | 99 | 99 | — | — | 91 | 99 | 98 | 99 | 69 | 97 | 56 | 70 | — | — | 66 | 95 | 49 | 45 | 24 |
| 23 | 72 | 97 | 103 | 99 | 94 | 99 | 74 | 98 | 85 | 99 | 96 | 99 | — | — | 89 | 99 | 96 | 99 | 67 | 95 | 55 | 64 | — | — | 64 | 92 | 48 | 40 | 23 |
| 22 | 71 | 96 | 101 | 99 | 91 | 99 | 72 | 98 | 83 | 99 | 94 | 99 | — | — | 87 | 99 | 93 | 99 | 65 | 92 | 53 | 58 | — | — | 61 | 87 | 46 | 35 | 22 |
| 21 | 69 | 94 | 98 | 99 | 89 | 99 | 70 | 97 | 81 | 99 | 91 | 99 | 81 | 99 | 85 | 99 | 91 | 99 | 63 | 88 | 52 | 52 | 71 | 99 | 59 | 80 | 45 | 30 | 21 |
| 20 | 67 | 93 | 95 | 99 | 86 | 99 | 68 | 96 | 79 | 98 | 89 | 99 | 79 | 99 | 83 | 99 | 88 | 99 | 61 | 84 | 50 | 47 | 69 | 98 | 57 | 74 | 43 | 25 | 20 |
| 19 | 66 | 92 | 92 | 99 | 84 | 99 | 67 | 94 | 77 | 98 | 86 | 99 | 76 | 99 | 81 | 99 | 86 | 99 | 59 | 78 | 48 | 41 | 67 | 95 | 55 | 66 | 42 | 21 | 19 |
| 18 | 64 | 90 | 90 | 99 | 81 | 99 | 65 | 93 | 75 | 97 | 83 | 99 | 74 | 99 | 79 | 99 | 83 | 99 | 57 | 73 | 47 | 36 | 64 | 92 | 53 | 58 | 40 | 17 | 18 |
| 17 | 62 | 87 | 87 | 99 | 78 | 99 | 63 | 90 | 73 | 96 | 81 | 99 | 72 | 98 | 76 | 99 | 81 | 99 | 55 | 66 | 45 | 31 | 62 | 88 | 51 | 50 | 39 | 14 | 17 |
| 16 | 61 | 85 | 84 | 99 | 76 | 98 | 61 | 87 | 70 | 95 | 78 | 99 | 70 | 97 | 74 | 98 | 78 | 99 | 53 | 60 | 44 | 26 | 60 | 83 | 48 | 42 | 37 | 11 | 16 |
| 15 | 59 | 82 | 81 | 99 | 73 | 97 | 59 | 84 | 68 | 94 | 76 | 98 | 68 | 95 | 72 | 96 | 76 | 98 | 51 | 53 | 42 | 22 | 58 | 76 | 46 | 35 | 36 | 9 | 15 |
| 14 | 57 | 79 | 78 | 98 | 71 | 96 | 57 | 79 | 66 | 93 | 73 | 97 | 65 | 92 | 70 | 95 | 73 | 97 | 49 | 46 | 40 | 18 | 55 | 69 | 44 | 28 | 34 | 7 | 14 |
| 13 | 55 | 75 | 76 | 97 | 68 | 94 | 55 | 73 | 64 | 91 | 71 | 96 | 63 | 88 | 68 | 94 | 71 | 96 | 47 | 39 | 39 | 15 | 53 | 62 | 42 | 22 | 33 | 5 | 13 |
| 12 | 54 | 70 | 73 | 96 | 66 | 92 | 53 | 67 | 62 | 88 | 68 | 94 | 61 | 84 | 66 | 92 | 68 | 94 | 45 | 33 | 37 | 12 | 51 | 53 | 40 | 16 | 31 | 4 | 12 |
| 11 | 52 | 65 | 70 | 95 | 63 | 89 | 51 | 59 | 60 | 86 | 66 | 92 | 59 | 79 | 64 | 91 | 66 | 93 | 43 | 26 | 35 | 9 | 49 | 45 | 37 | 12 | 29 | 3 | 11 |
| 10 | 50 | 60 | 67 | 93 | 61 | 86 | 49 | 51 | 58 | 82 | 63 | 89 | 56 | 73 | 62 | 88 | 63 | 90 | 41 | 20 | 34 | 7 | 47 | 37 | 35 | 8 | 28 | 2 | 10 |
| 9 | 49 | 53 | 65 | 90 | 58 | 81 | 47 | 42 | 56 | 78 | 61 | 86 | 54 | 67 | 60 | 86 | 61 | 87 | 39 | 15 | 32 | 5 | 44 | 30 | 33 | 5 | 26 | 1 | 9 |
| 8 | 47 | 46 | 62 | 87 | 56 | 75 | 46 | 34 | 54 | 73 | 58 | 82 | 52 | 60 | 58 | 83 | 58 | 82 | 37 | 10 | 31 | 4 | 42 | 23 | 31 | 3 | 25 | 1 | 8 |
| 7 | 45 | 39 | 59 | 84 | 53 | 68 | 44 | 26 | 52 | 66 | 55 | 76 | 50 | 52 | 56 | 79 | 56 | 77 | 35 | 6 | 29 | 3 | 40 | 17 | 29 | 2 | 23 | 1 | 7 |
| 6 | 43 | 30 | 56 | 79 | 50 | 59 | 42 | 19 | 50 | 59 | 53 | 70 | 47 | 44 | 54 | 74 | 53 | 70 | 33 | 3 | 27 | 2 | 38 | 12 | 27 | 1 | 22 | 1 | 6 |
| 5 | 42 | 22 | 54 | 73 | 48 | 49 | 40 | 13 | 48 | 50 | 50 | 61 | 45 | 36 | 51 | 68 | 51 | 62 | 31 | 1 | 26 | 1 | 36 | 8 | 24 | 1 | 20 | 1 | 5 |
| 4 | 40 | 14 | 51 | 64 | 45 | 37 | 38 | 9 | 45 | 40 | 48 | 51 | 43 | 28 | 49 | 60 | 48 | 52 | 29 | 1 | 24 | 1 | 33 | 5 | 22 | 1 | 19 | 1 | 4 |
| 3 | 38 | 7 | 48 | 54 | 43 | 26 | 36 | 6 | 43 | 29 | 45 | 39 | 41 | 20 | 47 | 51 | 46 | 40 | 27 | 1 | 23 | 1 | 31 | 3 | 20 | 1 | 17 | 1 | 3 |
| 2 | 37 | 2 | 45 | 41 | 40 | 15 | 34 | 4 | 41 | 17 | 43 | 26 | 39 | 13 | 45 | 40 | 43 | 28 | 25 | 1 | 21 | 1 | 29 | 1 | 18 | 1 | 16 | 1 | 2 |
| 1 | 35 | 1 | 42 | 24 | 38 | 6 | 32 | 2 | 39 | 7 | 40 | 13 | 36 | 7 | 43 | 27 | 41 | 16 | 23 | 1 | 19 | 1 | 27 | 1 | 16 | 1 | 14 | 1 | 1 |
| 0 | 33 | 1 | 40 | 6 | 35 | 1 | 30 | 1 | 37 | 1 | 38 | 4 | 34 | 3 | 41 | 12 | 38 | 6 | 21 | 1 | 18 | 1 | 24 | 1 | 13 | 1 | 13 | 1 | 0 |
| Raw mean | 9.82 | | 3.71 | | 5.83 | | 10.34 | | 6.19 | | 4.84 | | 7.13 | | 4.31 | | 4.70 | | 14.67 | | 20.04 | | 11.52 | | 16.77 | | 24.33 | | Raw mean |
| Raw SD | 5.86 | | 3.61 | | 3.93 | | 5.23 | | 4.80 | | 3.93 | | 4.49 | | 4.79 | | 3.98 | | 5.03 | | 6.23 | | 4.51 | | 4.59 | | 6.50 | | Raw SD |
| T: 90% Conf. int. | 6 | | 6 | | 6 | | 7 | | 6 | | 7 | | 5 | | 6 | | 7 | | 5 | | 5 | | 6 | | 7 | | 6 | | T: 90% Conf. int. |

# Table A.9b PRS–C T Scores and Percentiles

| Raw score | Hyperactivity T | Hyperactivity %ile | Aggression T | Aggression %ile | Conduct Problems T | Conduct Problems %ile | Anxiety T | Anxiety %ile | Depression T | Depression %ile | Somatization T | Somatization %ile | Attention Problems T | Attention Problems %ile | Atypicality T | Atypicality %ile | Withdrawal T | Withdrawal %ile | Adaptability T | Adaptability %ile | Social Skills T | Social Skills %ile | Leadership T | Leadership %ile | Activities of Daily Living T | Activities of Daily Living %ile | Functional Communication T | Functional Communication %ile | Raw score |
|---|---|---|---|---|---|---|---|---|---|---|---|---|---|---|---|---|---|---|---|---|---|---|---|---|---|---|---|---|---|
| 42 | — | — | — | — | — | — | 112 | 99 | — | — | — | — | — | — | 120 | 99 | — | — | — | — | — | — | — | — | — | — | — | — | 42 |
| 41 | — | — | — | — | — | — | 110 | 99 | — | — | — | — | — | — | 120 | 99 | — | — | — | — | — | — | — | — | — | — | — | — | 41 |
| 40 | — | — | — | — | — | — | 108 | 99 | 120 | 99 | — | — | — | — | 120 | 99 | — | — | — | — | — | — | — | — | — | — | — | — | 40 |
| 39 | — | — | — | — | — | — | 106 | 99 | 120 | 99 | — | — | — | — | 120 | 99 | — | — | — | — | — | — | — | — | — | — | — | — | 39 |
| 38 | — | — | — | — | — | — | 104 | 99 | 118 | 99 | — | — | — | — | 120 | 99 | — | — | — | — | — | — | — | — | — | — | — | — | 38 |
| 37 | — | — | — | — | — | — | 102 | 99 | 116 | 99 | — | — | — | — | 120 | 99 | — | — | — | — | — | — | — | — | — | — | — | — | 37 |
| 36 | — | — | — | — | — | — | 100 | 99 | 114 | 99 | 120 | 99 | — | — | 120 | 99 | — | — | — | — | — | — | — | — | — | — | 68 | 99 | 36 |
| 35 | — | — | — | — | — | — | 98 | 99 | 112 | 99 | 120 | 99 | — | — | 119 | 99 | — | — | — | — | — | — | — | — | — | — | 67 | 97 | 35 |
| 34 | — | — | — | — | — | — | 96 | 99 | 109 | 99 | 120 | 99 | — | — | 117 | 99 | — | — | — | — | — | — | — | — | — | — | 65 | 95 | 34 |
| 33 | 93 | 99 | — | — | — | — | 94 | 99 | 107 | 99 | 120 | 99 | — | — | 115 | 99 | — | — | — | — | — | — | — | — | — | — | 63 | 92 | 33 |
| 32 | 91 | 99 | — | — | — | — | 93 | 99 | 105 | 99 | 120 | 99 | — | — | 112 | 99 | — | — | — | — | — | — | — | — | — | — | 62 | 88 | 32 |
| 31 | 89 | 99 | — | — | — | — | 91 | 99 | 103 | 99 | 117 | 99 | — | — | 110 | 99 | — | — | — | — | — | — | — | — | — | — | 60 | 84 | 31 |
| 30 | 88 | 99 | — | — | 120 | 99 | 89 | 99 | 101 | 99 | 115 | 99 | — | — | 108 | 99 | — | — | — | — | 65 | 96 | — | — | — | — | 58 | 79 | 30 |
| 29 | 86 | 99 | — | — | 117 | 99 | 87 | 99 | 99 | 99 | 112 | 99 | — | — | 106 | 99 | — | — | — | — | 64 | 93 | — | — | — | — | 57 | 73 | 29 |
| 28 | 84 | 99 | 120 | 99 | 114 | 99 | 85 | 99 | 97 | 99 | 110 | 99 | — | — | 104 | 99 | — | — | — | — | 62 | 89 | — | — | — | — | 55 | 67 | 28 |
| 27 | 82 | 99 | 120 | 99 | 112 | 99 | 83 | 99 | 95 | 99 | 107 | 99 | — | — | 101 | 99 | 113 | 99 | — | — | 60 | 85 | — | — | 71 | 99 | 53 | 60 | 27 |
| 26 | 80 | 99 | 120 | 99 | 109 | 99 | 81 | 99 | 93 | 99 | 104 | 99 | — | — | 99 | 99 | 110 | 99 | — | — | 59 | 79 | — | — | 69 | 99 | 52 | 54 | 26 |
| 25 | 79 | 99 | 118 | 99 | 106 | 99 | 79 | 99 | 90 | 99 | 102 | 99 | — | — | 97 | 99 | 107 | 99 | — | — | 57 | 73 | — | — | 67 | 97 | 50 | 47 | 25 |
| 24 | 77 | 98 | 115 | 99 | 103 | 99 | 77 | 99 | 88 | 99 | 99 | 99 | — | — | 95 | 99 | 104 | 99 | 68 | 97 | 55 | 67 | — | — | 65 | 94 | 48 | 41 | 24 |
| 23 | 75 | 98 | 112 | 99 | 100 | 99 | 75 | 99 | 86 | 99 | 97 | 99 | — | — | 92 | 99 | 102 | 99 | 66 | 94 | 54 | 60 | — | — | 63 | 90 | 47 | 35 | 23 |
| 22 | 73 | 97 | 109 | 99 | 97 | 99 | 73 | 98 | 84 | 99 | 94 | 99 | — | — | 90 | 99 | 99 | 99 | 64 | 91 | 52 | 54 | — | — | 60 | 84 | 45 | 30 | 22 |
| 21 | 71 | 96 | 106 | 99 | 94 | 99 | 71 | 97 | 82 | 99 | 91 | 99 | 81 | 99 | 88 | 99 | 96 | 99 | 62 | 87 | 50 | 47 | 71 | 97 | 58 | 78 | 44 | 25 | 21 |
| 20 | 70 | 95 | 103 | 99 | 92 | 99 | 69 | 96 | 80 | 99 | 89 | 99 | 78 | 99 | 86 | 99 | 93 | 99 | 60 | 81 | 49 | 41 | 69 | 95 | 56 | 70 | 42 | 21 | 20 |
| 19 | 68 | 94 | 99 | 99 | 89 | 99 | 67 | 95 | 78 | 99 | 86 | 99 | 76 | 99 | 83 | 99 | 91 | 99 | 58 | 76 | 47 | 35 | 66 | 92 | 54 | 63 | 40 | 17 | 19 |
| 18 | 66 | 92 | 96 | 99 | 86 | 99 | 65 | 93 | 76 | 99 | 83 | 99 | 74 | 99 | 81 | 99 | 88 | 99 | 56 | 70 | 45 | 30 | 64 | 87 | 52 | 54 | 39 | 14 | 18 |
| 17 | 64 | 90 | 93 | 99 | 83 | 99 | 63 | 91 | 74 | 99 | 81 | 99 | 72 | 98 | 79 | 98 | 85 | 99 | 54 | 63 | 44 | 25 | 62 | 82 | 50 | 46 | 37 | 11 | 17 |
| 16 | 62 | 88 | 90 | 99 | 80 | 99 | 61 | 87 | 71 | 98 | 79 | 99 | 70 | 96 | 77 | 97 | 82 | 99 | 52 | 56 | 42 | 21 | 60 | 76 | 48 | 39 | 35 | 9 | 16 |
| 15 | 60 | 85 | 87 | 99 | 77 | 99 | 59 | 83 | 69 | 95 | 76 | 98 | 68 | 94 | 75 | 96 | 80 | 99 | 50 | 49 | 40 | 17 | 57 | 69 | 45 | 32 | 34 | 7 | 15 |
| 14 | 59 | 82 | 84 | 99 | 74 | 98 | 57 | 79 | 67 | 94 | 73 | 97 | 65 | 92 | 72 | 95 | 77 | 98 | 48 | 42 | 39 | 14 | 55 | 61 | 43 | 25 | 32 | 5 | 14 |
| 13 | 57 | 78 | 81 | 98 | 71 | 97 | 55 | 73 | 65 | 92 | 71 | 96 | 63 | 88 | 70 | 94 | 74 | 97 | 46 | 35 | 37 | 11 | 53 | 52 | 41 | 20 | 30 | 4 | 13 |
| 12 | 55 | 74 | 77 | 98 | 69 | 95 | 53 | 66 | 63 | 90 | 68 | 94 | 61 | 85 | 68 | 92 | 71 | 96 | 44 | 29 | 35 | 9 | 51 | 44 | 39 | 15 | 29 | 3 | 12 |
| 11 | 53 | 69 | 74 | 97 | 66 | 93 | 51 | 58 | 61 | 87 | 66 | 92 | 59 | 80 | 66 | 90 | 69 | 94 | 42 | 22 | 34 | 7 | 48 | 36 | 37 | 11 | 27 | 2 | 11 |
| 10 | 51 | 63 | 71 | 95 | 63 | 89 | 49 | 50 | 59 | 84 | 63 | 89 | 57 | 75 | 63 | 88 | 66 | 91 | 39 | 17 | 32 | 5 | 46 | 28 | 35 | 7 | 26 | 1 | 10 |
| 9 | 50 | 57 | 68 | 93 | 60 | 85 | 47 | 42 | 57 | 80 | 60 | 85 | 55 | 69 | 61 | 86 | 63 | 87 | 37 | 12 | 30 | 4 | 44 | 21 | 32 | 5 | 24 | 1 | 9 |
| 8 | 48 | 50 | 65 | 91 | 57 | 78 | 45 | 34 | 55 | 75 | 58 | 81 | 53 | 63 | 59 | 83 | 60 | 83 | 35 | 8 | 29 | 3 | 42 | 15 | 30 | 3 | 22 | 1 | 8 |
| 7 | 46 | 42 | 62 | 87 | 54 | 71 | 44 | 26 | 52 | 69 | 55 | 75 | 50 | 56 | 57 | 79 | 58 | 78 | 33 | 5 | 27 | 2 | 39 | 10 | 28 | 2 | 21 | 1 | 7 |
| 6 | 44 | 34 | 59 | 83 | 51 | 61 | 42 | 19 | 50 | 62 | 53 | 68 | 48 | 48 | 55 | 75 | 55 | 73 | 31 | 2 | 25 | 1 | 37 | 7 | 26 | 1 | 19 | 1 | 6 |
| 5 | 42 | 25 | 55 | 77 | 49 | 50 | 40 | 14 | 48 | 53 | 50 | 59 | 46 | 41 | 52 | 70 | 52 | 65 | 29 | 1 | 24 | 1 | 35 | 5 | 24 | 1 | 17 | 1 | 5 |
| 4 | 41 | 17 | 52 | 69 | 46 | 38 | 38 | 9 | 46 | 43 | 48 | 49 | 44 | 32 | 50 | 64 | 49 | 57 | 27 | 1 | 22 | 1 | 33 | 4 | 22 | 1 | 16 | 1 | 4 |
| 3 | 39 | 9 | 49 | 59 | 43 | 25 | 36 | 6 | 44 | 32 | 45 | 38 | 42 | 24 | 48 | 56 | 47 | 47 | 25 | 1 | 20 | 1 | 30 | 2 | 19 | 1 | 14 | 1 | 3 |
| 2 | 37 | 4 | 46 | 45 | 40 | 15 | 34 | 4 | 42 | 21 | 42 | 25 | 40 | 16 | 46 | 46 | 44 | 34 | 23 | 1 | 19 | 1 | 28 | 1 | 17 | 1 | 12 | 1 | 2 |
| 1 | 35 | 1 | 43 | 26 | 37 | 7 | 32 | 2 | 40 | 10 | 40 | 13 | 37 | 9 | 43 | 32 | 41 | 20 | 21 | 1 | 17 | 1 | 26 | 1 | 15 | 1 | 11 | 1 | 1 |
| 0 | 33 | 1 | 40 | 6 | 34 | 2 | 30 | 1 | 38 | 2 | 37 | 4 | 35 | 4 | 41 | 12 | 38 | 5 | 19 | 1 | 15 | 1 | 24 | 1 | 13 | 1 | 10 | 1 | 0 |
| Raw mean | 9.19 | | 3.25 | | 5.50 | | 10.31 | | 5.83 | | 4.94 | | 6.83 | | 3.96 | | 4.26 | | 15.17 | | 20.81 | | 11.72 | | 17.15 | | 24.92 | | Raw mean |
| Raw SD | 5.54 | | 3.19 | | 3.49 | | 5.10 | | 4.74 | | 3.87 | | 4.64 | | 4.49 | | 3.63 | | 4.91 | | 5.98 | | 4.44 | | 4.62 | | 6.10 | | Raw SD |
| T:90% Conf. int. | 6 | | 7 | | 7 | | 7 | | 6 | | 7 | | 5 | | 6 | | 7 | | 6 | | 5 | | 6 | | 7 | | 6 | | T:90% Conf. int. |

## Table A.9c PRS-C T Scores and Percentiles

| Raw score | Hyperactivity T | Hyperactivity %ile | Aggression T | Aggression %ile | Conduct Problems T | Conduct Problems %ile | Anxiety T | Anxiety %ile | Depression T | Depression %ile | Somatization T | Somatization %ile | Attention Problems T | Attention Problems %ile | Atypicality T | Atypicality %ile | Withdrawal T | Withdrawal %ile | Adaptability T | Adaptability %ile | Social Skills T | Social Skills %ile | Leadership T | Leadership %ile | Activities of Daily Living T | Activities of Daily Living %ile | Functional Communication T | Functional Communication %ile | Raw score |
|---|---|---|---|---|---|---|---|---|---|---|---|---|---|---|---|---|---|---|---|---|---|---|---|---|---|---|---|---|---|
| 42 | — | — | — | — | — | — | 109 | 99 | — | — | — | — | — | — | 120 | 99 | — | — | — | — | — | — | — | — | — | — | — | — | 42 |
| 41 | — | — | — | — | — | — | 107 | 99 | — | — | — | — | — | — | 120 | 99 | — | — | — | — | — | — | — | — | — | — | — | — | 41 |
| 40 | — | — | — | — | — | — | 105 | 99 | — | — | — | — | — | — | 120 | 99 | — | — | — | — | — | — | — | — | — | — | — | — | 40 |
| 39 | — | — | — | — | — | — | 103 | 99 | 117 | 99 | — | — | — | — | 118 | 99 | — | — | — | — | — | — | — | — | — | — | — | — | 39 |
| 38 | — | — | — | — | — | — | 101 | 99 | 115 | 99 | — | — | — | — | 116 | 99 | — | — | — | — | — | — | — | — | — | — | — | — | 38 |
| 37 | — | — | — | — | — | — | 100 | 99 | 113 | 99 | 120 | 99 | — | — | 114 | 99 | — | — | — | — | — | — | — | — | — | — | — | — | 37 |
| 36 | — | — | — | — | — | — | 98 | 99 | 111 | 99 | 120 | 99 | — | — | 112 | 99 | — | — | — | — | — | — | — | — | — | — | 68 | 98 | 36 |
| 35 | — | — | — | — | — | — | 96 | 99 | 109 | 99 | 120 | 99 | — | — | 110 | 99 | — | — | — | — | — | — | — | — | — | — | 66 | 96 | 35 |
| 34 | — | — | — | — | — | — | 94 | 99 | 107 | 99 | 120 | 99 | — | — | 108 | 99 | — | — | — | — | — | — | — | — | — | — | 65 | 94 | 34 |
| 33 | 87 | 99 | — | — | — | — | 92 | 99 | 105 | 99 | 120 | 99 | — | — | 106 | 99 | — | — | — | — | — | — | — | — | — | — | 64 | 91 | 33 |
| 32 | 85 | 99 | — | — | — | — | 90 | 99 | 102 | 99 | 118 | 99 | — | — | 104 | 99 | — | — | — | — | — | — | — | — | — | — | 62 | 88 | 32 |
| 31 | 84 | 99 | — | — | — | — | 88 | 99 | 100 | 99 | 116 | 99 | — | — | 102 | 99 | — | — | — | — | — | — | — | — | — | — | 61 | 84 | 31 |
| 30 | 82 | 99 | — | — | 105 | 99 | 87 | 99 | 98 | 99 | 113 | 99 | — | — | 100 | 99 | — | — | — | — | 67 | 97 | — | — | — | — | 59 | 80 | 30 |
| 29 | 80 | 99 | — | — | 103 | 99 | 85 | 99 | 96 | 99 | 111 | 99 | — | — | 98 | 99 | — | — | — | — | 65 | 95 | — | — | — | — | 58 | 75 | 29 |
| 28 | 79 | 99 | 108 | 99 | 101 | 99 | 83 | 99 | 94 | 99 | 108 | 99 | — | — | 96 | 99 | — | — | — | — | 64 | 92 | — | — | — | — | 56 | 70 | 28 |
| 27 | 77 | 98 | 105 | 99 | 98 | 99 | 81 | 99 | 92 | 99 | 106 | 99 | — | — | 94 | 99 | 101 | 99 | — | — | 62 | 88 | — | — | 73 | 99 | 55 | 65 | 27 |
| 26 | 75 | 98 | 103 | 99 | 96 | 99 | 79 | 99 | 90 | 99 | 103 | 99 | — | — | 92 | 99 | 99 | 99 | — | — | 61 | 83 | — | — | 71 | 99 | 53 | 60 | 26 |
| 25 | 74 | 97 | 100 | 99 | 94 | 99 | 77 | 99 | 88 | 99 | 101 | 99 | — | — | 90 | 99 | 97 | 97 | — | — | 59 | 79 | — | — | 69 | 98 | 52 | 54 | 25 |
| 24 | 72 | 96 | 98 | 99 | 91 | 99 | 75 | 98 | 86 | 99 | 98 | 99 | — | — | 88 | 99 | 94 | 94 | 69 | 97 | 57 | 74 | — | — | 67 | 96 | 50 | 49 | 24 |
| 23 | 70 | 95 | 95 | 99 | 89 | 99 | 74 | 98 | 84 | 99 | 96 | 99 | — | — | 86 | 99 | 92 | 92 | 67 | 95 | 56 | 68 | — | — | 65 | 93 | 49 | 44 | 23 |
| 22 | 69 | 94 | 93 | 99 | 87 | 99 | 72 | 97 | 82 | 99 | 93 | 99 | — | — | 84 | 99 | 90 | 90 | 65 | 93 | 54 | 63 | — | — | 62 | 89 | 47 | 39 | 22 |
| 21 | 67 | 93 | 90 | 99 | 84 | 99 | 70 | 96 | 80 | 99 | 91 | 99 | 81 | 99 | 82 | 98 | 87 | 87 | 63 | 89 | 53 | 57 | 71 | 99 | 60 | 83 | 46 | 34 | 21 |
| 20 | 66 | 91 | 88 | 99 | 82 | 99 | 68 | 95 | 78 | 98 | 88 | 99 | 79 | 99 | 80 | 98 | 85 | 85 | 61 | 85 | 51 | 52 | 69 | 98 | 58 | 77 | 45 | 30 | 20 |
| 19 | 64 | 89 | 85 | 99 | 80 | 99 | 66 | 94 | 76 | 97 | 86 | 99 | 77 | 99 | 78 | 98 | 83 | 83 | 59 | 81 | 50 | 47 | 67 | 96 | 56 | 69 | 43 | 25 | 19 |
| 18 | 62 | 87 | 82 | 99 | 77 | 98 | 64 | 92 | 74 | 97 | 83 | 99 | 74 | 99 | 76 | 97 | 80 | 80 | 58 | 75 | 48 | 41 | 65 | 93 | 54 | 61 | 42 | 21 | 18 |
| 17 | 61 | 85 | 80 | 99 | 75 | 98 | 62 | 90 | 72 | 96 | 81 | 99 | 72 | 98 | 74 | 97 | 78 | 78 | 56 | 70 | 46 | 36 | 62 | 88 | 51 | 53 | 40 | 18 | 17 |
| 16 | 59 | 82 | 77 | 98 | 73 | 97 | 61 | 87 | 70 | 95 | 78 | 98 | 70 | 97 | 72 | 96 | 75 | 75 | 54 | 63 | 45 | 32 | 60 | 83 | 49 | 45 | 39 | 15 | 16 |
| 15 | 57 | 79 | 75 | 97 | 71 | 96 | 59 | 84 | 67 | 93 | 76 | 97 | 68 | 95 | 70 | 95 | 73 | 73 | 52 | 57 | 43 | 27 | 58 | 77 | 47 | 37 | 37 | 12 | 15 |
| 14 | 56 | 75 | 72 | 96 | 68 | 94 | 57 | 79 | 65 | 92 | 73 | 97 | 65 | 92 | 68 | 94 | 71 | 71 | 50 | 50 | 42 | 23 | 56 | 70 | 45 | 30 | 36 | 9 | 14 |
| 13 | 54 | 71 | 70 | 94 | 66 | 92 | 55 | 74 | 63 | 90 | 71 | 95 | 63 | 89 | 66 | 93 | 68 | 68 | 48 | 43 | 40 | 19 | 54 | 62 | 43 | 23 | 34 | 7 | 13 |
| 12 | 53 | 67 | 67 | 93 | 64 | 90 | 53 | 67 | 61 | 87 | 68 | 94 | 61 | 84 | 64 | 91 | 66 | 66 | 46 | 36 | 39 | 15 | 52 | 54 | 40 | 18 | 33 | 5 | 12 |
| 11 | 51 | 62 | 65 | 90 | 61 | 87 | 51 | 60 | 59 | 84 | 66 | 92 | 58 | 78 | 63 | 89 | 64 | 64 | 44 | 30 | 37 | 12 | 49 | 46 | 38 | 13 | 31 | 4 | 11 |
| 10 | 49 | 56 | 62 | 88 | 59 | 83 | 49 | 52 | 57 | 81 | 63 | 90 | 56 | 72 | 61 | 87 | 61 | 61 | 42 | 23 | 36 | 9 | 47 | 39 | 36 | 9 | 30 | 3 | 10 |
| 9 | 48 | 50 | 60 | 84 | 57 | 78 | 47 | 43 | 55 | 76 | 61 | 87 | 54 | 64 | 59 | 85 | 59 | 59 | 40 | 17 | 34 | 7 | 45 | 31 | 34 | 6 | 28 | 2 | 9 |
| 8 | 46 | 43 | 57 | 80 | 54 | 72 | 46 | 34 | 53 | 71 | 58 | 83 | 51 | 56 | 57 | 81 | 57 | 57 | 38 | 12 | 32 | 5 | 43 | 25 | 32 | 4 | 27 | 1 | 8 |
| 7 | 44 | 35 | 55 | 75 | 52 | 65 | 44 | 26 | 51 | 64 | 56 | 78 | 49 | 48 | 55 | 77 | 54 | 54 | 36 | 8 | 31 | 3 | 41 | 19 | 29 | 2 | 26 | 1 | 7 |
| 6 | 43 | 27 | 52 | 68 | 50 | 57 | 42 | 19 | 49 | 57 | 53 | 71 | 47 | 39 | 53 | 72 | 52 | 52 | 34 | 4 | 29 | 2 | 38 | 14 | 27 | 1 | 24 | 1 | 6 |
| 5 | 41 | 19 | 50 | 60 | 47 | 48 | 40 | 13 | 47 | 48 | 51 | 63 | 44 | 31 | 51 | 66 | 50 | 50 | 32 | 2 | 28 | 1 | 36 | 9 | 25 | 1 | 23 | 1 | 5 |
| 4 | 39 | 11 | 47 | 50 | 45 | 37 | 38 | 9 | 45 | 37 | 48 | 53 | 42 | 23 | 49 | 58 | 47 | 47 | 30 | 1 | 26 | 1 | 34 | 6 | 23 | 1 | 21 | 1 | 4 |
| 3 | 38 | 4 | 44 | 37 | 43 | 26 | 36 | 6 | 43 | 26 | 46 | 41 | 40 | 16 | 47 | 49 | 45 | 45 | 28 | 1 | 25 | 1 | 32 | 4 | 21 | 1 | 20 | 1 | 3 |
| 2 | 36 | 1 | 42 | 22 | 40 | 15 | 34 | 4 | 41 | 14 | 43 | 28 | 37 | 11 | 45 | 37 | 43 | 43 | 26 | 1 | 23 | 1 | 30 | 2 | 18 | 1 | 18 | 1 | 2 |
| 1 | 35 | 1 | 39 | 6 | 38 | 6 | 33 | 2 | 39 | 4 | 41 | 14 | 35 | 6 | 43 | 24 | 40 | 40 | 24 | 1 | 21 | 1 | 27 | 1 | 16 | 1 | 17 | 1 | 1 |
| 0 | 33 | 1 | — | — | 36 | 1 | 31 | 1 | 37 | 1 | 38 | 3 | 33 | 3 | 41 | 9 | 38 | 38 | 22 | 1 | 20 | 1 | 25 | 1 | 14 | 1 | 15 | 1 | 0 |
| **Raw mean** | 10.45 | | 4.18 | | 6.15 | | 10.36 | | 6.54 | | 4.75 | | 7.44 | | 4.65 | | 5.15 | | 14.17 | | 19.27 | | 11.31 | | 16.39 | | 23.75 | | **Raw mean** |
| **Raw SD** | 6.13 | | 3.95 | | 4.31 | | 5.37 | | 4.85 | | 4.00 | | 4.32 | | 5.07 | | 4.26 | | 5.10 | | 6.40 | | 4.58 | | 4.54 | | 6.85 | | **Raw SD** |
| **T: 90% Conf. int.** | 5 | | 6 | | 5 | | 7 | | 6 | | 6 | | 6 | | 5 | | 6 | | 5 | | 5 | | 6 | | 8 | | 5 | | **T: 90% Conf. int.** |

## Table A.9d  PRS–C Composite T Scores

| T score | Externalizing Problems | | | Internalizing Problems | | | Adaptive Skills | | | Behavioral Symptoms Index | | | T score |
|---|---|---|---|---|---|---|---|---|---|---|---|---|---|
| | Combined | Female | Male | Combined | Female | Male | Combined | Female | Male | Combined | Female | Male | |
| 120 | — | — | — | 322–349 | 324–352 | 318–346 | — | — | — | 627–630 | 625–647 | — | 120 |
| 119 | — | — | — | 320–321 | 322–323 | 315–317 | — | — | — | 622–626 | 620–624 | — | 119 |
| 118 | — | 333 | — | 317–319 | 319–321 | 313–314 | — | — | — | 617–621 | 616–619 | 612–614 | 118 |
| 117 | — | 330–332 | — | 315–316 | 317–318 | 311–312 | — | — | — | 613–616 | 611–615 | 607–611 | 117 |
| 116 | — | 328–329 | — | 312–314 | 314–316 | 308–310 | — | — | — | 608–612 | 606–610 | 603–606 | 116 |
| 115 | — | 325–327 | — | 310–311 | 312–313 | 306–307 | — | — | — | 603–607 | 602–605 | 598–602 | 115 |
| 114 | — | 322–324 | — | 307–309 | 309–311 | 303–305 | — | — | — | 599–602 | 597–601 | 593–597 | 114 |
| 113 | — | 320–321 | — | 305–306 | 307–308 | 301–302 | — | — | — | 594–598 | 592–596 | 588–592 | 113 |
| 112 | — | 317–319 | — | 302–304 | 304–306 | 299–300 | — | — | — | 589–593 | 588–591 | 584–587 | 112 |
| 111 | 316–317 | 314–316 | — | 300–301 | 302–303 | 296–298 | — | — | — | 585–588 | 583–587 | 579–583 | 111 |
| 110 | 313–315 | 311–313 | — | 298–299 | 299–301 | 294–295 | — | — | — | 580–584 | 578–582 | 574–578 | 110 |
| 109 | 310–312 | 309–310 | — | 295–297 | 297–298 | 291–293 | — | — | — | 575–579 | 574–577 | 570–573 | 109 |
| 108 | 307–309 | 306–308 | — | 293–294 | 294–296 | 289–290 | — | — | — | 570–574 | 569–573 | 565–569 | 108 |
| 107 | 305–306 | 303–305 | — | 290–292 | 292–293 | 287–288 | — | — | — | 566–569 | 564–568 | 560–564 | 107 |
| 106 | 302–304 | 301–302 | — | 288–289 | 289–291 | 284–286 | — | — | — | 561–565 | 560–563 | 556–559 | 106 |
| 105 | 299–301 | 298–300 | 300 | 285–287 | 287–288 | 282–283 | — | — | — | 556–560 | 555–559 | 551–555 | 105 |
| 104 | 297–298 | 295–297 | 297–299 | 283–284 | 284–286 | 279–281 | — | — | — | 552–555 | 550–554 | 546–550 | 104 |
| 103 | 294–296 | 292–294 | 294–296 | 280–282 | 282–283 | 277–278 | — | — | — | 547–551 | 546–549 | 542–545 | 103 |
| 102 | 291–293 | 290–291 | 291–293 | 278–279 | 279–281 | 275–276 | — | — | — | 542–546 | 541–545 | 537–541 | 102 |
| 101 | 288–290 | 287–289 | 289–290 | 275–277 | 277–278 | 272–274 | — | — | — | 538–541 | 536–540 | 532–536 | 101 |
| 100 | 286–287 | 284–286 | 286–288 | 273–274 | 274–276 | 270–271 | — | — | — | 533–537 | 532–535 | 528–531 | 100 |
| 99 | 283–285 | 282–283 | 283–285 | 270–272 | 272–273 | 267–269 | — | — | — | 528–532 | 527–531 | 523–527 | 99 |
| 98 | 280–282 | 279–281 | 280–282 | 268–269 | 269–271 | 265–266 | — | — | — | 524–527 | 522–526 | 518–522 | 98 |
| 97 | 277–279 | 276–278 | 278–279 | 265–267 | 267–268 | 263–264 | — | — | — | 519–523 | 518–521 | 514–517 | 97 |
| 96 | 275–276 | 274–275 | 275–277 | 263–264 | 264–266 | 260–262 | — | — | — | 514–518 | 513–517 | 509–513 | 96 |
| 95 | 272–274 | 271–273 | 272–274 | 260–262 | 262–263 | 258–259 | — | — | — | 509–513 | 508–512 | 504–508 | 95 |
| 94 | 269–271 | 268–270 | 269–271 | 258–259 | 259–261 | 255–257 | — | — | — | 505–508 | 504–507 | 500–503 | 94 |
| 93 | 266–268 | 265–267 | 267–268 | 256–257 | 257–258 | 253–254 | — | — | — | 500–504 | 499–503 | 495–499 | 93 |
| 92 | 264–265 | 263–264 | 264–266 | 253–255 | 254–256 | 251–252 | — | — | — | 495–499 | 494–498 | 490–494 | 92 |
| 91 | 261–263 | 260–262 | 261–263 | 251–252 | 252–253 | 248–250 | — | — | — | 491–494 | 490–493 | 486–489 | 91 |
| 90 | 258–260 | 257–259 | 259–260 | 248–250 | 249–251 | 246–247 | — | — | — | 486–490 | 485–489 | 481–485 | 90 |
| 89 | 256–257 | 255–256 | 256–258 | 246–247 | 247–248 | 243–245 | — | — | — | 481–485 | 480–484 | 476–480 | 89 |
| 88 | 253–255 | 252–254 | 253–255 | 243–245 | 244–246 | 241–242 | — | — | — | 477–480 | 476–479 | 472–475 | 88 |
| 87 | 250–252 | 249–251 | 250–252 | 241–242 | 242–243 | 239–240 | — | — | — | 472–476 | 471–475 | 467–471 | 87 |
| 86 | 247–249 | 246–248 | 248–249 | 238–240 | 239–241 | 236–238 | — | — | — | 467–471 | 466–470 | 462–466 | 86 |
| 85 | 245–246 | 244–245 | 245–247 | 236–237 | 237–238 | 234–235 | — | — | — | 462–466 | 462–465 | 458–461 | 85 |
| 84 | 242–244 | 241–243 | 242–244 | 233–235 | 234–236 | 231–233 | — | — | — | 458–461 | 457–461 | 453–457 | 84 |
| 83 | 239–241 | 238–240 | 239–241 | 231–232 | 232–233 | 229–230 | — | — | — | 453–457 | 452–456 | 448–452 | 83 |
| 82 | 236–238 | 236–237 | 237–238 | 228–230 | 229–231 | 227–228 | — | — | — | 448–452 | 448–451 | 444–447 | 82 |
| 81 | 234–235 | 233–235 | 234–236 | 226–227 | 227–228 | 224–226 | — | — | — | 444–447 | 443–447 | 439–443 | 81 |
| 80 | 231–233 | 230–232 | 231–233 | 223–225 | 224–226 | 222–223 | — | — | — | 439–443 | 438–442 | 434–438 | 80 |
| 79 | 228–230 | 228–229 | 228–230 | 221–222 | 222–223 | 219–221 | — | — | — | 434–438 | 434–437 | 430–433 | 79 |
| 78 | 226–227 | 225–227 | 226–227 | 218–220 | 219–221 | 217–218 | — | — | — | 430–433 | 429–433 | 425–429 | 78 |
| 77 | 223–225 | 222–224 | 223–225 | 216–217 | 217–218 | 215–216 | — | — | — | 425–429 | 424–428 | 420–424 | 77 |
| 76 | 220–222 | 219–221 | 220–222 | 214–215 | 214–216 | 212–214 | — | — | — | 420–424 | 420–423 | 416–419 | 76 |
| 75 | 217–219 | 217–218 | 217–219 | 211–213 | 212–213 | 210–211 | — | — | — | 415–419 | 415–419 | 411–415 | 75 |
| 74 | 215–216 | 214–216 | 215–216 | 209–210 | 209–211 | 207–209 | — | — | — | 411–414 | 410–414 | 406–410 | 74 |
| 73 | 212–214 | 211–213 | 212–214 | 206–208 | 207–208 | 205–206 | — | — | — | 406–410 | 406–409 | 402–405 | 73 |
| 72 | 209–211 | 209–210 | 209–211 | 204–205 | 204–206 | 203–204 | 346 | — | 347–348 | 401–405 | 401–405 | 397–401 | 72 |
| 71 | 206–208 | 206–208 | 207–208 | 201–203 | 202–203 | 200–202 | 341–345 | 339–343 | 343–346 | 397–400 | 396–400 | 392–396 | 71 |
| 70 | 204–205 | 203–205 | 204–206 | 199–200 | 199–201 | 198–199 | 337–340 | 335–338 | 338–342 | 392–396 | 392–395 | 388–391 | 70 |
| 69 | 201–203 | 200–202 | 201–203 | 196–198 | 197–198 | 195–197 | 333–336 | 331–334 | 334–337 | 387–391 | 387–391 | 383–387 | 69 |
| 68 | 198–200 | 198–199 | 198–200 | 194–195 | 194–196 | 193–194 | 328–332 | 326–330 | 329–333 | 383–386 | 382–386 | 378–382 | 68 |
| 67 | 195–197 | 195–197 | 196–197 | 191–193 | 192–193 | 191–192 | 324–327 | 322–325 | 325–328 | 378–382 | 378–381 | 374–377 | 67 |
| 66 | 193–194 | 192–194 | 193–195 | 189–190 | 189–191 | 188–190 | 319–323 | 318–321 | 320–324 | 373–377 | 373–377 | — | 66 |

**Table A.9d** PRS–C Composite *T* Scores *(continued)*

| T score | Externalizing Problems Combined | Externalizing Problems Female | Externalizing Problems Male | Internalizing Problems Combined | Internalizing Problems Female | Internalizing Problems Male | Adaptive Skills Combined | Adaptive Skills Female | Adaptive Skills Male | Behavioral Symptoms Index Combined | Behavioral Symptoms Index Female | Behavioral Symptoms Index Male | T score |
|---|---|---|---|---|---|---|---|---|---|---|---|---|---|
| 65 | 190–192 | 190–191 | 190–192 | 186–188 | 187–188 | 186–187 | 315–318 | 313–317 | 316–319 | 369–372 | 368–372 | 369–373 | 65 |
| 64 | 187–189 | 187–189 | 187–189 | 184–185 | 184–186 | 183–185 | 311–314 | 309–312 | 311–315 | 364–368 | 364–367 | 364–368 | 64 |
| 63 | 185–186 | 184–186 | 185–186 | 181–183 | 182–183 | 181–182 | 306–310 | 305–308 | 307–310 | 359–363 | 359–363 | 360–363 | 63 |
| 62 | 182–184 | 182–183 | 182–184 | 179–180 | 179–181 | 179–180 | 302–305 | 300–304 | 302–306 | 354–358 | 354–358 | 355–359 | 62 |
| 61 | 179–181 | 179–181 | 179–181 | 176–178 | 177–178 | 176–178 | 297–301 | 296–299 | 298–301 | 350–353 | 350–353 | 350–354 | 61 |
| 60 | 176–178 | 176–178 | 176–178 | 174–175 | 174–176 | 174–175 | 293–296 | 292–295 | 293–297 | 345–349 | 345–349 | 346–349 | 60 |
| 59 | 174–175 | 173–175 | 174–175 | 172–173 | 172–173 | 171–173 | 288–292 | 288–291 | 289–292 | 340–344 | 340–344 | 341–345 | 59 |
| 58 | 171–173 | 171–172 | 171–173 | 169–171 | 169–171 | 169–170 | 284–287 | 283–287 | 284–288 | 336–339 | 336–339 | 336–340 | 58 |
| 57 | 168–170 | 168–170 | 168–170 | 167–168 | 167–168 | 167–168 | 280–283 | 279–282 | 280–283 | 331–335 | 331–335 | 331–335 | 57 |
| 56 | 165–167 | 165–167 | 166–167 | 164–166 | 164–166 | 164–166 | 275–279 | 275–278 | 276–279 | 326–330 | 326–330 | 327–330 | 56 |
| 55 | 163–164 | 163–164 | 163–165 | 162–163 | 162–163 | 162–163 | 271–275 | 270–274 | 271–275 | 322–325 | 321–325 | 322–326 | 55 |
| 54 | 160–162 | 160–162 | 160–162 | 159–161 | 159–161 | 159–161 | 266–270 | 266–269 | 267–270 | 317–321 | 317–320 | 317–321 | 54 |
| 53 | 157–159 | 157–159 | 157–159 | 157–158 | 157–158 | 157–158 | 262–265 | 262–265 | 262–266 | 312–316 | 312–316 | 313–316 | 53 |
| 52 | 154–156 | 154–156 | 155–156 | 154–156 | 154–156 | 155–156 | 257–261 | 257–261 | 258–261 | 307–311 | 307–311 | 308–312 | 52 |
| 51 | 152–153 | 152–153 | 152–154 | 152–153 | 152–153 | 152–154 | 253–256 | 253–256 | 253–257 | 303–306 | 303–306 | 303–307 | 51 |
| 50 | 149–151 | 149–151 | 149–151 | 149–151 | 149–151 | 150–151 | 249–252 | 249–252 | 249–252 | 298–302 | 298–302 | 299–302 | 50 |
| 49 | 146–148 | 146–148 | 146–148 | 147–148 | 147–148 | 147–149 | 244–248 | 244–248 | 244–248 | 293–297 | 293–297 | 294–298 | 49 |
| 48 | 144–145 | 144–145 | 144–145 | 144–146 | 144–146 | 145–146 | 240–243 | 240–243 | 240–243 | 289–292 | 289–292 | 289–293 | 48 |
| 47 | 141–143 | 141–143 | 141–143 | 142–143 | 142–143 | 143–144 | 235–239 | 236–239 | 235–239 | 284–288 | 284–288 | 285–288 | 47 |
| 46 | 138–140 | 138–140 | 138–140 | 139–141 | 139–141 | 140–142 | 231–234 | 231–235 | 231–234 | 279–283 | 279–283 | 280–284 | 46 |
| 45 | 135–137 | 136–137 | 135–137 | 137–138 | 137–138 | 138–139 | 226–230 | 227–230 | 226–230 | 275–278 | 275–278 | 275–279 | 45 |
| 44 | 133–134 | 133–135 | 133–134 | 134–136 | 134–136 | 135–137 | 222–225 | 223–226 | 222–225 | 270–274 | 270–274 | 271–274 | 44 |
| 43 | 130–132 | 130–132 | 130–132 | 132–133 | 132–133 | 133–134 | 218–221 | 218–222 | 217–221 | 265–269 | 265–269 | 266–270 | 43 |
| 42 | 127–129 | 127–129 | 127–129 | 130–131 | 129–131 | 131–132 | 213–217 | 214–217 | 213–216 | 260–264 | 261–264 | 261–265 | 42 |
| 41 | 124–126 | 125–126 | 124–126 | 127–129 | 127–128 | 128–130 | 209–212 | 210–213 | 208–212 | 256–259 | 256–260 | 257–260 | 41 |
| 40 | 122–123 | 122–124 | 122–123 | 125–126 | 124–126 | 126–127 | 204–208 | 205–209 | 204–207 | 251–255 | 251–255 | 252–256 | 40 |
| 39 | 119–121 | 119–121 | 119–121 | 122–124 | 122–123 | 123–125 | 200–203 | 201–204 | 199–203 | 246–250 | 247–250 | 247–251 | 39 |
| 38 | 116–118 | 117–118 | 116–118 | 120–121 | 119–121 | 121–122 | 196–199 | 197–200 | 195–198 | 242–245 | 242–246 | 243–246 | 38 |
| 37 | 113–115 | 114–116 | 114–115 | 117–119 | 117–118 | 119–120 | 191–195 | 192–196 | 190–194 | 237–241 | 237–241 | 238–242 | 37 |
| 36 | 111–112 | 111–113 | 111–113 | 115–116 | 114–116 | 116–118 | 187–190 | 188–191 | 186–189 | 232–236 | 233–236 | 233–237 | 36 |
| 35 | 108–110 | 108–110 | 108–110 | 112–114 | 112–113 | 114–115 | 182–186 | 184–187 | 181–185 | 228–231 | 228–232 | 229–232 | 35 |
| 34 | — | 107 | — | 110–111 | 109–111 | 111–113 | 178–181 | 179–183 | 177–180 | 223–227 | 225–227 | 224–228 | 34 |
| 33 | — | — | — | 107–109 | 107–108 | 109–110 | 173–177 | 175–178 | 172–176 | — | — | 221–223 | 33 |
| 32 | — | — | — | 105–106 | 105–106 | 107–108 | 169–172 | 171–174 | 168–171 | — | — | — | 32 |
| 31 | — | — | — | — | — | 106 | 165–168 | 166–170 | 163–167 | — | — | — | 31 |
| 30 | — | — | — | — | — | — | 160–164 | 162–165 | 159–162 | — | — | — | 30 |
| 29 | — | — | — | — | — | — | 156–159 | 158–161 | 154–158 | — | — | — | 29 |
| 28 | — | — | — | — | — | — | 151–155 | 153–157 | 150–153 | — | — | — | 28 |
| 27 | — | — | — | — | — | — | 147–150 | 149–152 | 145–149 | — | — | — | 27 |
| 26 | — | — | — | — | — | — | 142–146 | 145–148 | 141–144 | — | — | — | 26 |
| 25 | — | — | — | — | — | — | 138–141 | 140–144 | 136–140 | — | — | — | 25 |
| 24 | — | — | — | — | — | — | 134–137 | 136–139 | 132–135 | — | — | — | 24 |
| 23 | — | — | — | — | — | — | 129–133 | 132–135 | 127–131 | — | — | — | 23 |
| 22 | — | — | — | — | — | — | 125–128 | 127–131 | 123–126 | — | — | — | 22 |
| 21 | — | — | — | — | — | — | 120–124 | 123–126 | 119–122 | — | — | — | 21 |
| 20 | — | — | — | — | — | — | 116–119 | 119–122 | 114–118 | — | — | — | 20 |
| 19 | — | — | — | — | — | — | 111–115 | 114–118 | 110–113 | — | — | — | 19 |
| 18 | — | — | — | — | — | — | 107–110 | 110–113 | 105–109 | — | — | — | 18 |
| 17 | — | — | — | — | — | — | 103–106 | 106–109 | 101–104 | — | — | — | 17 |
| 16 | — | — | — | — | — | — | 98–102 | 101–105 | 96–100 | — | — | — | 16 |
| 15 | — | — | — | — | — | — | 94–97 | 97–100 | — | — | — | — | 15 |
| 14 | — | — | — | — | — | — | 89–93 | 93–96 | — | — | — | — | 14 |
| 13 | — | — | — | — | — | — | — | 88–92 | — | — | — | — | 13 |
| 12 | — | — | — | — | — | — | — | 84–87 | — | — | — | — | 12 |
| 11 | — | — | — | — | — | — | — | 81–83 | — | — | — | — | 11 |
| 10 | — | — | — | — | — | — | — | — | — | — | — | — | 10 |
| *T:* 90% Conf. int. | 4 | 4 | 3 | 5 | 5 | 5 | 3 | 3 | 3 | 3 | 3 | 3 | *T:* 90% Conf. int. |

## Table A.9e  PRS-C Composite Percentiles

| %ile | Externalizing Problems Combined | Female | Male | Internalizing Problems Combined | Female | Male | Adaptive Skills Combined | Female | Male | Behavioral Symptoms Index Combined | Female | Male | %ile |
|---|---|---|---|---|---|---|---|---|---|---|---|---|---|
| 99 | 230–317 | 229–333 | 231–300 | 220–349 | 219–352 | 220–346 | 335–346 | 336–343 | 334–348 | 434–630 | 431–647 | 435–614 | 99 |
| 98 | 220–229 | 218–228 | 221–230 | 211–219 | 211–218 | 212–219 | 329–334 | 329–335 | 329–333 | 417–433 | 415–430 | 418–434 | 98 |
| 97 | 213–219 | 211–217 | 214–220 | 205–210 | 205–210 | 205–211 | 325–328 | 324–328 | 326–328 | 405–416 | 404–414 | 406–417 | 97 |
| 96 | 207–212 | 206–210 | 208–213 | 200–204 | 200–204 | 201–204 | 321–324 | 320–323 | 322–325 | 396–404 | 396–403 | 396–405 | 96 |
| 95 | 203–206 | 202–205 | 204–207 | 196–199 | 196–199 | 197–200 | 318–320 | 317–319 | 319–321 | 389–395 | 388–395 | 389–395 | 95 |
| 94 | 199–202 | 198–201 | 200–203 | 193–195 | 193–195 | 193–196 | 316–317 | 314–316 | 317–318 | 382–388 | 382–387 | 382–388 | 94 |
| 93 | 195–198 | 194–197 | 196–199 | 190–192 | 190–192 | 190–192 | 313–315 | 311–313 | 314–316 | 377–381 | 377–381 | 377–381 | 93 |
| 92 | 192–194 | 192–193 | 193–195 | 188–189 | 188–189 | 188–189 | 311–312 | 309–310 | 312–313 | 372–376 | 372–376 | 372–376 | 92 |
| 91 | 190–191 | 189–191 | 190–192 | 185–187 | 186–187 | 185–187 | 309–310 | 306–308 | 310–311 | 368–371 | 368–371 | 367–371 | 91 |
| 90 | 187–189 | 187–188 | 188–189 | 183–184 | 184–185 | 183–184 | 306–308 | 304–305 | 308–309 | 363–367 | 364–367 | 363–366 | 90 |
| 89 | 185–186 | 184–186 | 185–187 | 181–182 | 182–183 | 181–182 | 304–305 | 302–303 | 306–307 | 360–362 | 360–363 | 360–362 | 89 |
| 88 | 183–184 | 182–183 | 183–184 | 180 | 180–181 | 180 | 303 | 300–301 | 304–305 | 356–359 | 357–359 | 356–359 | 88 |
| 87 | 181–182 | 180–181 | 181–182 | 178–179 | 178–179 | 178–179 | 301–302 | 299 | 303 | 353–355 | 353–356 | 353–355 | 87 |
| 86 | 179–180 | 179 | 179–180 | 176–177 | 177 | 176–177 | 299–300 | 297–298 | 301–302 | 350–352 | 350–352 | 350–352 | 86 |
| 85 | 177–178 | 177–178 | 177–178 | 175 | 175–176 | 175 | 297–298 | 295–296 | 299–300 | 347–349 | 348–349 | 347–349 | 85 |
| 84 | 175–176 | 175–176 | 176 | 173–174 | 174 | 173–174 | 296 | 294 | 298 | 344–346 | 345–347 | 344–346 | 84 |
| 83 | 174 | 174 | 174–175 | 172 | 172–173 | 172 | 294–295 | 292–293 | 296–297 | 342–343 | 342–344 | 342–343 | 83 |
| 82 | 172–173 | 173 | 173 | 171 | 171 | 171 | 293 | 290–291 | 294–295 | 339–341 | 340–341 | 339–341 | 82 |
| 81 | 171 | 171–172 | 171–172 | 170 | 170 | 170 | 291–292 | 289 | 293 | 337–338 | 338–339 | 337–338 | 81 |
| 80 | 169–170 | 170 | 170 | 168–169 | 169 | 168–169 | 290 | 288 | 291–292 | 335–336 | 335–337 | 335–336 | 80 |
| 79 | 168 | 169 | 168–169 | 167 | 168 | 167 | 288–289 | 286–287 | 290 | 333–334 | 333–334 | 333–334 | 79 |
| 78 | 167 | 167–168 | 167 | 166 | 167 | 166 | 287 | 285 | 289 | 331–332 | 331–332 | 331–332 | 78 |
| 77 | 166 | 166 | 166 | 165 | 166 | 165 | 286 | 283–284 | 287–288 | 329–330 | 329–330 | 329–330 | 77 |
| 76 | 164–165 | 165 | 165 | 164 | 165 | 164 | 284–285 | 282 | 286 | 327–328 | 327–328 | 327–328 | 76 |
| 75 | 163 | 164 | 163–164 | 163 | 164 | 163 | 283 | 281 | 284–285 | 325–326 | 325–326 | 325–326 | 75 |
| 74 | 162 | 163 | 162 | 162 | 163 | 162 | 282 | 279–280 | 283 | 323–324 | 324 | 323–324 | 74 |
| 73 | 161 | 162 | 161 | 161 | 162 | 161 | 280–281 | 278 | 282 | 321–322 | 322–323 | 321–322 | 73 |
| 72 | 160 | 161 | 160 | — | 161 | 160 | 279 | 277 | 280–281 | 320 | 320–321 | 320 | 72 |
| 71 | 159 | 160 | 159 | 160 | 160 | — | 278 | 276 | 279 | 318–319 | 318–319 | 318–319 | 71 |
| 70 | 158 | 159 | 158 | 159 | 159 | 159 | 276–277 | 275 | 278 | 317 | 317 | 317 | 70 |
| 69 | 157 | 158 | 157 | 158 | 158 | 158 | 275 | 273–274 | 276–277 | 315–316 | 315–316 | 315–316 | 69 |
| 68 | 156 | — | 156 | 157 | — | 157 | 274 | 272 | 275 | 313–314 | 314 | 314 | 68 |
| 67 | 155 | 157 | 155 | 156 | 157 | 156 | 273 | 271 | 274 | 312 | 312–313 | 312–313 | 67 |
| 66 | — | 156 | 154 | — | 156 | — | 271–272 | 270 | 272–273 | 311 | 311 | 311 | 66 |
| 65 | 154 | 155 | 155 | 155 | 155 | 155 | 270 | 269 | 271 | 309–310 | 309–310 | 309–310 | 65 |
| 64 | 153 | 154 | 154 | 154 | — | 154 | 269 | 268 | 270 | 308 | 308 | 308 | 64 |
| 63 | 152 | 153 | 152 | 153 | 154 | — | 268 | 266–267 | 269 | 306–307 | 306–307 | 307 | 63 |
| 62 | 151 | — | 151 | — | 153 | 153 | 267 | 265 | 267–268 | 305 | 305 | 305–306 | 62 |
| 61 | — | 152 | 150 | 152 | 152 | 152 | 265–266 | 264 | 266 | 304 | 304 | 304 | 61 |
| 60 | 150 | 151 | — | 151 | — | — | 264 | 263 | 265 | 302–303 | 302–303 | 303 | 60 |
| 59 | 149 | 150 | 149 | — | 151 | 151 | 263 | 262 | 264 | 301 | 301 | 301–302 | 59 |
| 58 | 148 | — | 148 | 150 | 150 | 150 | 262 | 261 | 262–263 | 300 | 300 | 300 | 58 |
| 57 | — | 149 | 147 | 149 | — | — | 261 | 260 | 261 | 299 | 299 | 299 | 57 |
| 56 | 147 | 148 | 146 | — | 149 | 149 | 259–260 | 259 | 260 | 298 | 297–298 | 298 | 56 |
| 55 | 146 | — | 146 | 148 | 148 | 148 | 258 | 257–258 | 259 | 296–297 | 296 | 297 | 55 |
| 54 | — | 147 | 145 | — | — | — | 257 | 256 | 257–258 | 295 | 295 | 296 | 54 |
| 53 | 145 | 146 | 144 | 147 | 147 | 147 | 256 | 255 | 256 | 294 | 294 | 294–295 | 53 |
| 52 | 144 | — | 144 | 146 | — | — | 255 | 254 | 255 | 293 | 293 | 293 | 52 |
| 51 | — | 145 | 143 | — | 146 | 146 | 253–254 | 253 | 254 | 292 | 292 | 292 | 51 |

**Table A.9e** PRS-C Composite Percentiles (continued)

| %ile | Externalizing Problems Combined | Female | Male | Internalizing Problems Combined | Female | Male | Adaptive Skills Combined | Female | Male | Behavioral Symptoms Index Combined | Female | Male | %ile |
|---|---|---|---|---|---|---|---|---|---|---|---|---|---|
| 50 | 143 | — | — | 145 | 145 | — | 252 | 252 | 252–253 | 291 | 291 | 291 | 50 |
| 49 | — | 144 | 142 | — | — | 145 | 251 | 251 | 251 | 290 | 289–290 | 290 | 49 |
| 48 | 142 | 143 | 141 | 144 | 144 | — | 250 | 250 | 250 | 288–289 | 288 | 289 | 48 |
| 47 | 141 | — | — | 143 | — | 144 | 249 | 249 | 248–249 | 287 | 287 | 288 | 47 |
| 46 | — | 142 | 140 | — | 143 | 143 | 247–248 | 247–248 | 247 | 286 | 286 | 287 | 46 |
| 45 | 140 | 141 | — | 142 | 142 | 142 | 246 | 246 | 246 | 285 | 285 | 286 | 45 |
| 44 | — | — | 139 | — | — | — | 245 | 245 | 245 | 284 | 284 | 285 | 44 |
| 43 | 139 | 140 | — | 141 | 141 | 141 | 244 | 244 | 243–244 | 283 | 283 | 284 | 43 |
| 42 | 138 | — | 138 | — | — | — | 243 | 243 | 242 | 282 | 282 | 283 | 42 |
| 41 | — | 139 | 137 | 140 | 140 | 140 | 241–242 | 242 | 241 | 281 | 281 | 282 | 41 |
| 40 | 137 | — | 136 | — | — | — | 240 | 240–241 | 239–240 | 280 | 280 | 281 | 40 |
| 39 | 136 | 138 | — | 139 | 139 | 139 | 239 | 239 | 238 | 279 | 279 | 280 | 39 |
| 38 | — | 137 | 135 | 138 | 138 | — | 237–238 | 238 | 237 | 278 | 278 | 279 | 38 |
| 37 | 135 | — | — | 137 | 137 | 138 | 236 | 237 | 235–236 | 277 | 277 | 278 | 37 |
| 36 | — | 136 | 134 | — | — | — | 235 | 236 | 234 | 276 | 276 | 277 | 36 |
| 35 | 134 | — | — | 136 | 136 | 137 | 234 | 234–235 | 233 | 275 | 275 | 276 | 35 |
| 34 | — | 135 | 133 | — | — | — | 232–233 | 233 | 231–232 | 274 | 274 | 275 | 34 |
| 33 | 133 | — | — | 135 | 135 | 136 | 231 | 232 | 230 | 273 | 273 | 274 | 33 |
| 32 | — | 134 | 132 | — | — | — | 229–230 | 231 | 228–229 | 272 | 272 | 273 | 32 |
| 31 | 132 | — | — | 134 | 134 | 135 | 228 | 229–230 | 227 | 271 | 271 | 272 | 31 |
| 30 | — | 133 | 131 | — | — | — | 227 | 228 | 225–226 | 270 | 270 | 271 | 30 |
| 29 | 131 | — | — | 133 | 133 | 134 | 225–226 | 227 | 224 | 269 | 269 | 270 | 29 |
| 28 | — | 132 | 130 | — | — | — | 224 | 225–226 | 222–223 | 268 | 268 | 269 | 28 |
| 27 | 130 | 131 | — | 132 | 132 | 133 | 222–223 | 224 | 221 | 267 | 267 | 268 | 27 |
| 26 | — | — | 129 | — | — | — | 221 | 222–223 | 219–220 | 266 | 266 | 267 | 26 |
| 25 | 129 | 130 | — | 131 | 131 | 132 | 219–220 | 221 | 218 | 265 | 265 | 266 | 25 |
| 24 | — | 129 | 128 | — | — | — | 218 | 219–220 | 216–217 | 264 | 264 | — | 24 |
| 23 | 128 | — | — | 130 | 130 | 131 | 216–217 | 218 | 214–215 | 263 | 263 | 265 | 23 |
| 22 | — | 128 | 127 | — | — | — | 214–215 | 216–217 | 213 | 262 | 262 | 264 | 22 |
| 21 | 127 | — | — | 129 | 129 | 130 | 213 | 215 | 211–212 | 261 | 261 | 263 | 21 |
| 20 | — | — | — | 128 | 128 | 129 | 211–212 | 213–214 | 209–210 | 260 | 260 | 262 | 20 |
| 19 | 126 | 127 | 126 | 127 | 127 | 128 | 209–210 | 211–212 | 207–208 | 259 | 259 | 261 | 19 |
| 18 | — | 126 | — | 126 | 126 | 127 | 207–208 | 209–210 | 205–206 | 258 | 258 | 260 | 18 |
| 17 | 125 | — | 125 | — | — | — | 205–206 | 208 | 204 | 257 | 257 | 259 | 17 |
| 16 | — | 125 | — | 125 | 125 | 126 | 203–204 | 206–207 | 202–203 | 256 | 256 | 258 | 16 |
| 15 | 124 | — | 124 | 124 | 124 | 125 | 201–202 | 204–205 | 200–201 | 255 | 255 | 256–257 | 15 |
| 14 | — | 124 | — | 123 | 123 | 124 | 199–200 | 202–203 | 197–199 | 254 | 254 | 255 | 14 |
| 13 | 123 | 123 | 123 | 122 | 122 | 123 | 197–198 | 199–201 | 195–196 | 253 | 253 | 254 | 13 |
| 12 | 122 | — | 122 | 121 | 121 | 122 | 194–196 | 197–198 | 193–194 | 252 | 251–252 | 253 | 12 |
| 11 | — | 122 | — | 120 | 120 | 121 | 192–193 | 195–196 | 190–192 | 251 | 250 | 252 | 11 |
| 10 | 121 | 121 | 121 | 119 | 119 | 120 | 189–191 | 192–194 | 188–189 | 249–250 | 249 | 251 | 10 |
| 9 | — | — | — | 118 | 118 | 119 | 186–188 | 189–191 | 185–187 | 248 | 248 | 249–250 | 9 |
| 8 | 120 | 120 | 120 | 117 | — | — | 183–185 | 186–188 | 182–184 | 247 | 246–247 | 248 | 8 |
| 7 | — | 119 | — | — | — | — | 180–182 | 182–185 | 179–181 | 245–246 | 245 | 247 | 7 |
| 6 | 119 | 118 | 119 | — | — | — | 176–179 | 178–181 | 176–178 | 244 | 243–244 | 245–246 | 6 |
| 5 | — | 117 | — | — | — | — | 172–175 | 174–177 | 172–175 | 242–243 | 242 | 243–244 | 5 |
| 4 | 118 | 116 | 118 | — | 116–117 | — | 167–171 | 168–173 | 167–171 | 240–241 | 240–241 | 242 | 4 |
| 3 | 117 | 115 | 117 | — | 115 | — | 160–166 | 162–167 | 162–166 | 238–239 | 238–239 | 239–241 | 3 |
| 2 | 116 | 114 | — | 115–116 | 113–114 | — | 152–159 | 152–161 | 155–161 | 235–237 | 235–237 | 237–238 | 2 |
| 1 | 108–115 | 107–113 | 108–116 | 105–114 | 105–112 | 106–118 | 89–151 | 81–151 | 96–154 | 223–234 | 225–234 | 221–236 | 1 |

## Table A.10a PRS-C T Scores and Percentiles

| Raw score | Hyperactivity | | Aggression | | Conduct Problems | | Anxiety | | Depression | | Somatization | | Attention Problems | | Atypicality | | Withdrawal | | Adaptability | | Social Skills | | Leadership | | Activities of Daily Living | | Functional Communication | | Raw score |
|---|---|---|---|---|---|---|---|---|---|---|---|---|---|---|---|---|---|---|---|---|---|---|---|---|---|---|---|---|---|
| | T | %ile | T | %ile | T | %ile | T | %ile | T | %ile | T | %ile | T | %ile | T | %ile | T | %ile | T | %ile | T | %ile | T | %ile | T | %ile | T | %ile | |
| 42 | — | — | — | — | — | — | 99 | 99 | — | — | — | — | — | — | 120 | 99 | — | — | — | — | — | — | — | — | — | — | — | — | 42 |
| 41 | — | — | — | — | — | — | 98 | 99 | — | — | — | — | — | — | 120 | 99 | — | — | — | — | — | — | — | — | — | — | — | — | 41 |
| 40 | — | — | — | — | — | — | 96 | 99 | — | — | — | — | — | — | 120 | 99 | — | — | — | — | — | — | — | — | — | — | — | — | 40 |
| 39 | — | — | — | — | — | — | 94 | 99 | 119 | 99 | — | — | — | — | 120 | 99 | — | — | — | — | — | — | — | — | — | — | — | — | 39 |
| 38 | — | — | — | — | — | — | 93 | 99 | 117 | 99 | — | — | — | — | 120 | 99 | — | — | — | — | — | — | — | — | — | — | — | — | 38 |
| 37 | — | — | — | — | — | — | 91 | 99 | 115 | 99 | — | — | — | — | 120 | 99 | — | — | — | — | — | — | — | — | — | — | — | — | 37 |
| 36 | — | — | — | — | — | — | 89 | 99 | 113 | 99 | 120 | 99 | — | — | 120 | 99 | — | — | — | — | — | — | — | — | — | — | 66 | 98 | 36 |
| 35 | — | — | — | — | — | — | 88 | 99 | 111 | 99 | 120 | 99 | — | — | 120 | 99 | — | — | — | — | — | — | — | — | — | — | 64 | 96 | 35 |
| 34 | — | — | — | — | — | — | 86 | 99 | 109 | 99 | 119 | 99 | — | — | 120 | 99 | — | — | — | — | — | — | — | — | — | — | 63 | 93 | 34 |
| 33 | 103 | 99 | — | — | — | — | 85 | 99 | 107 | 99 | 117 | 99 | — | — | 119 | 99 | — | — | — | — | — | — | — | — | — | — | 61 | 88 | 33 |
| 32 | 100 | 99 | — | — | — | — | 83 | 99 | 105 | 99 | 114 | 99 | — | — | 116 | 99 | — | — | — | — | — | — | — | — | — | — | 60 | 83 | 32 |
| 31 | 98 | 99 | — | — | — | — | 81 | 99 | 103 | 99 | 112 | 99 | — | — | 114 | 99 | — | — | — | — | — | — | — | — | — | — | 58 | 77 | 31 |
| 30 | 96 | 99 | — | — | 120 | 99 | 80 | 99 | 101 | 99 | 109 | 99 | — | — | 112 | 99 | — | — | — | — | 64 | 96 | — | — | — | — | 56 | 71 | 30 |
| 29 | 94 | 99 | — | — | 117 | 99 | 78 | 99 | 98 | 99 | 107 | 99 | — | — | 109 | 99 | — | — | — | — | 63 | 92 | — | — | — | — | 55 | 64 | 29 |
| 28 | 92 | 99 | — | — | 114 | 99 | 76 | 99 | 96 | 99 | 104 | 99 | — | — | 107 | 99 | — | — | — | — | 61 | 87 | — | — | — | — | 53 | 58 | 28 |
| 27 | 90 | 99 | — | — | 112 | 99 | 75 | 99 | 94 | 99 | 102 | 99 | — | — | 105 | 99 | 103 | 99 | — | — | 59 | 82 | — | — | 70 | 99 | 52 | 51 | 27 |
| 26 | 88 | 99 | — | — | 109 | 99 | 73 | 99 | 92 | 99 | 100 | 99 | — | — | 102 | 99 | 100 | 99 | — | — | 58 | 75 | — | — | 68 | 98 | 50 | 45 | 26 |
| 25 | 86 | 99 | 120 | 99 | 106 | 99 | 72 | 97 | 90 | 99 | 97 | 99 | — | — | 100 | 99 | 98 | 99 | — | — | 56 | 69 | — | — | 66 | 96 | 48 | 39 | 25 |
| 24 | 84 | 99 | 120 | 99 | 103 | 99 | 70 | 96 | 88 | 99 | 95 | 99 | — | — | 98 | 99 | 96 | 99 | 68 | 98 | 54 | 62 | — | — | 64 | 93 | 47 | 34 | 24 |
| 23 | 82 | 99 | 120 | 99 | 101 | 99 | 68 | 95 | 86 | 99 | 92 | 99 | — | — | 95 | 99 | 93 | 99 | 66 | 95 | 53 | 56 | — | — | 61 | 88 | 45 | 29 | 23 |
| 22 | 80 | 99 | 119 | 99 | 98 | 99 | 67 | 94 | 84 | 99 | 90 | 99 | — | — | 93 | 99 | 91 | 99 | 64 | 92 | 51 | 49 | — | — | 59 | 81 | 44 | 24 | 22 |
| 21 | 78 | 98 | 116 | 99 | 95 | 99 | 65 | 92 | 82 | 99 | 88 | 99 | 84 | 99 | 91 | 99 | 89 | 99 | 62 | 88 | 50 | 43 | 70 | 99 | 57 | 73 | 42 | 20 | 21 |
| 20 | 76 | 98 | 112 | 99 | 92 | 99 | 64 | 91 | 80 | 98 | 85 | 99 | 81 | 99 | 88 | 99 | 86 | 99 | 60 | 82 | 48 | 38 | 68 | 99 | 55 | 65 | 40 | 17 | 20 |
| 19 | 74 | 97 | 109 | 99 | 90 | 99 | 62 | 89 | 78 | 98 | 83 | 99 | 79 | 99 | 86 | 99 | 84 | 99 | 58 | 76 | 46 | 32 | 66 | 96 | 52 | 56 | 39 | 14 | 19 |
| 18 | 72 | 97 | 105 | 99 | 87 | 99 | 60 | 86 | 75 | 97 | 80 | 99 | 77 | 99 | 84 | 99 | 81 | 99 | 55 | 69 | 45 | 28 | 63 | 91 | 50 | 47 | 37 | 11 | 18 |
| 17 | 70 | 96 | 101 | 99 | 84 | 99 | 59 | 83 | 73 | 97 | 78 | 99 | 74 | 99 | 81 | 99 | 79 | 98 | 53 | 61 | 43 | 23 | 61 | 86 | 48 | 39 | 36 | 9 | 17 |
| 16 | 68 | 94 | 98 | 99 | 81 | 98 | 57 | 80 | 71 | 96 | 76 | 99 | 72 | 98 | 79 | 99 | 77 | 97 | 51 | 54 | 41 | 19 | 59 | 78 | 46 | 31 | 34 | 7 | 16 |
| 15 | 66 | 92 | 94 | 99 | 78 | 98 | 55 | 76 | 69 | 95 | 73 | 99 | 70 | 96 | 77 | 99 | 74 | 97 | 49 | 46 | 40 | 16 | 56 | 70 | 43 | 25 | 33 | 6 | 15 |
| 14 | 63 | 90 | 90 | 99 | 76 | 97 | 54 | 71 | 67 | 93 | 71 | 99 | 67 | 94 | 74 | 99 | 72 | 96 | 47 | 38 | 38 | 13 | 54 | 62 | 41 | 19 | 31 | 5 | 14 |
| 13 | 61 | 87 | 87 | 99 | 73 | 97 | 52 | 66 | 65 | 92 | 68 | 99 | 65 | 91 | 72 | 99 | 70 | 95 | 45 | 31 | 36 | 11 | 52 | 53 | 39 | 14 | 29 | 4 | 13 |
| 12 | 59 | 84 | 83 | 99 | 70 | 95 | 51 | 60 | 63 | 90 | 66 | 99 | 63 | 88 | 70 | 99 | 67 | 93 | 42 | 24 | 35 | 8 | 49 | 45 | 37 | 10 | 28 | 3 | 12 |
| 11 | 57 | 80 | 80 | 99 | 67 | 94 | 49 | 53 | 61 | 87 | 64 | 99 | 61 | 84 | 67 | 99 | 65 | 91 | 40 | 18 | 33 | 7 | 47 | 37 | 34 | 7 | 26 | 2 | 11 |
| 10 | 55 | 75 | 76 | 98 | 65 | 92 | 47 | 46 | 59 | 84 | 61 | 99 | 58 | 79 | 65 | 99 | 63 | 89 | 38 | 13 | 31 | 5 | 45 | 30 | 32 | 5 | 25 | 2 | 10 |
| 9 | 53 | 69 | 72 | 96 | 62 | 89 | 46 | 39 | 57 | 80 | 59 | 99 | 56 | 73 | 62 | 99 | 60 | 86 | 36 | 9 | 30 | 4 | 43 | 23 | 30 | 3 | 23 | 1 | 9 |
| 8 | 51 | 61 | 69 | 95 | 59 | 85 | 44 | 31 | 55 | 75 | 56 | 99 | 54 | 66 | 60 | 99 | 58 | 82 | 34 | 6 | 28 | 3 | 40 | 18 | 28 | 2 | 21 | 1 | 8 |
| 7 | 49 | 53 | 65 | 92 | 56 | 79 | 42 | 24 | 53 | 70 | 54 | 99 | 51 | 58 | 58 | 99 | 55 | 78 | 32 | 3 | 27 | 2 | 38 | 13 | 25 | 1 | 20 | 1 | 7 |
| 6 | 47 | 44 | 61 | 88 | 54 | 72 | 41 | 17 | 50 | 63 | 52 | 99 | 49 | 50 | 55 | 99 | 53 | 72 | 29 | 2 | 25 | 1 | 36 | 9 | 23 | 1 | 18 | 1 | 6 |
| 5 | 45 | 35 | 58 | 83 | 51 | 63 | 39 | 11 | 48 | 54 | 49 | 99 | 47 | 41 | 53 | 99 | 51 | 64 | 27 | 1 | 23 | 1 | 33 | 6 | 21 | 1 | 17 | 1 | 5 |
| 4 | 43 | 26 | 54 | 75 | 48 | 51 | 38 | 7 | 46 | 44 | 47 | 99 | 44 | 32 | 51 | 99 | 48 | 55 | 25 | 1 | 22 | 1 | 31 | 4 | 19 | 1 | 15 | 1 | 4 |
| 3 | 41 | 17 | 51 | 63 | 45 | 36 | 36 | 3 | 44 | 33 | 44 | 99 | 42 | 24 | 48 | 98 | 46 | 44 | 23 | 1 | 20 | 1 | 29 | 2 | 16 | 1 | 13 | 1 | 3 |
| 2 | 39 | 10 | 47 | 48 | 42 | 21 | 34 | 1 | 42 | 21 | 42 | 99 | 40 | 16 | 46 | 98 | 44 | 30 | 21 | 1 | 18 | 1 | 26 | 1 | 14 | 1 | 12 | 1 | 2 |
| 1 | 37 | 5 | 43 | 28 | 40 | 8 | 33 | 1 | 40 | 10 | 40 | 99 | 37 | 9 | 44 | 97 | 41 | 15 | 19 | 1 | 17 | 1 | 24 | 1 | 12 | 1 | 11 | 1 | 1 |
| 0 | 35 | 2 | 40 | 9 | 37 | 1 | 31 | 1 | 38 | 2 | 37 | 99 | 35 | 4 | 41 | 97 | 39 | 3 | 16 | 1 | 15 | 1 | 22 | 1 | 10 | 1 | 10 | 1 | 0 |
| Raw mean | 7.43 | | 2.83 | | 4.72 | | 11.64 | | 5.79 | | 5.33 | | 6.48 | | 3.67 | | 4.69 | | 15.48 | | 21.29 | | 12.24 | | 17.95 | | 25.98 | | Raw mean |
| Raw SD | 4.87 | | 2.76 | | 3.61 | | 6.18 | | 4.79 | | 4.16 | | 4.30 | | 4.27 | | 4.23 | | 4.61 | | 6.09 | | 4.34 | | 4.43 | | 6.29 | | Raw SD |
| T: 90% Conf. int. | 7 | | 8 | | 6 | | 6 | | 6 | | 6 | | 5 | | 6 | | 6 | | 6 | | 5 | | 6 | | 7 | | 6 | | T: 90% Conf. int. |

# Table A.10b PRS–C T Scores and Percentiles

| Raw score | Hyperactivity T | Hyperactivity %ile | Aggression T | Aggression %ile | Conduct Problems T | Conduct Problems %ile | Anxiety T | Anxiety %ile | Depression T | Depression %ile | Somatization T | Somatization %ile | Attention Problems T | Attention Problems %ile | Atypicality T | Atypicality %ile | Withdrawal T | Withdrawal %ile | Adaptability T | Adaptability %ile | Social Skills T | Social Skills %ile | Leadership T | Leadership %ile | Activities of Daily Living T | Activities of Daily Living %ile | Functional Communication T | Functional Communication %ile | Raw score |
|---|---|---|---|---|---|---|---|---|---|---|---|---|---|---|---|---|---|---|---|---|---|---|---|---|---|---|---|---|---|
| 42 | — | — | — | — | — | — | 100 | 99 | — | — | — | — | — | — | 120 | 99 | — | — | — | — | — | — | — | — | — | — | — | — | 42 |
| 41 | — | — | — | — | — | — | 99 | 99 | — | — | — | — | — | — | 120 | 99 | — | — | — | — | — | — | — | — | — | — | — | — | 41 |
| 40 | — | — | — | — | — | — | 97 | 99 | 120 | 99 | — | — | — | — | 120 | 99 | — | — | — | — | — | — | — | — | — | — | — | — | 40 |
| 39 | — | — | — | — | — | — | 95 | 99 | 120 | 99 | — | — | — | — | 120 | 99 | — | — | — | — | — | — | — | — | — | — | — | — | 39 |
| 38 | — | — | — | — | — | — | 94 | 99 | 120 | 99 | — | — | — | — | 120 | 99 | — | — | — | — | — | — | — | — | — | — | — | — | 38 |
| 37 | — | — | — | — | — | — | 92 | 99 | 120 | 99 | — | — | — | — | 120 | 99 | — | — | — | — | — | — | — | — | — | — | — | — | 37 |
| 36 | — | — | — | — | — | — | 91 | 99 | 120 | 99 | — | — | — | — | 120 | 99 | — | — | — | — | — | — | — | — | — | — | 65 | 97 | 36 |
| 35 | — | — | — | — | — | — | 89 | 99 | 118 | 99 | 120 | 99 | — | — | 120 | 99 | — | — | — | — | — | — | — | — | — | — | 63 | 94 | 35 |
| 34 | — | — | — | — | — | — | 87 | 99 | 116 | 99 | 120 | 99 | — | — | 120 | 99 | — | — | — | — | — | — | — | — | — | — | 61 | 90 | 34 |
| 33 | 108 | 99 | — | — | — | — | 86 | 99 | 114 | 99 | 119 | 99 | — | — | 120 | 99 | — | — | — | — | — | — | — | — | — | — | 60 | 84 | 33 |
| 32 | 106 | 99 | — | — | — | — | 84 | 99 | 111 | 99 | 116 | 99 | — | — | 120 | 99 | — | — | — | — | — | — | — | — | — | — | 58 | 78 | 32 |
| 31 | 104 | 99 | — | — | — | — | 82 | 99 | 109 | 99 | 114 | 99 | — | — | 120 | 99 | — | — | — | — | — | — | — | — | — | — | 56 | 70 | 31 |
| 30 | 102 | 99 | — | — | 120 | 99 | 81 | 99 | 107 | 99 | 111 | 99 | — | — | 120 | 99 | — | — | — | — | 63 | 95 | — | — | — | — | 54 | 62 | 30 |
| 29 | 99 | 99 | — | — | 120 | 99 | 79 | 97 | 104 | 99 | 109 | 99 | — | — | 120 | 99 | — | — | — | — | 61 | 89 | — | — | — | — | 52 | 54 | 29 |
| 28 | 97 | 99 | — | — | 120 | 99 | 77 | 97 | 102 | 99 | 106 | 99 | — | — | 118 | 99 | 114 | 99 | — | — | 59 | 83 | — | — | — | — | 51 | 47 | 28 |
| 27 | 95 | 98 | — | — | 120 | 99 | 76 | 96 | 100 | 99 | 104 | 99 | — | — | 116 | 99 | 111 | 99 | — | — | 58 | 75 | — | — | 69 | 99 | 49 | 40 | 27 |
| 26 | 93 | 96 | — | — | 117 | 99 | 74 | 95 | 98 | 99 | 101 | 99 | — | — | 113 | 99 | 109 | 99 | — | — | 56 | 67 | — | — | 67 | 98 | 47 | 33 | 26 |
| 25 | 91 | 95 | — | — | 114 | 99 | 72 | 94 | 95 | 99 | 98 | 99 | — | — | 110 | 99 | 106 | 99 | 69 | 96 | 54 | 59 | — | — | 64 | 95 | 45 | 28 | 25 |
| 24 | 88 | 93 | — | — | 111 | 99 | 71 | 93 | 93 | 99 | 96 | 99 | — | — | 107 | 99 | 103 | 99 | 67 | 93 | 52 | 51 | — | — | 62 | 90 | 43 | 23 | 24 |
| 23 | 86 | 91 | — | — | 108 | 99 | 69 | 91 | 91 | 99 | 93 | 99 | — | — | 105 | 99 | 101 | 99 | 65 | 88 | 50 | 44 | — | — | 60 | 83 | 42 | 18 | 23 |
| 22 | 84 | 88 | 120 | 99 | 105 | 99 | 67 | 89 | 88 | 99 | 91 | 99 | — | — | 102 | 99 | 98 | 99 | 62 | 82 | 48 | 38 | 72 | 99 | 57 | 74 | 40 | 15 | 22 |
| 21 | 82 | 85 | 120 | 99 | 102 | 99 | 66 | 87 | 86 | 99 | 88 | 99 | 89 | 99 | 99 | 99 | 95 | 99 | 60 | 75 | 47 | 32 | 70 | 98 | 55 | 65 | 38 | 12 | 21 |
| 20 | 79 | 81 | 118 | 99 | 99 | 99 | 64 | 84 | 84 | 99 | 86 | 99 | 86 | 99 | 96 | 99 | 93 | 99 | 58 | 68 | 45 | 27 | 67 | 95 | 52 | 55 | 36 | 9 | 20 |
| 19 | 77 | 99 | 114 | 99 | 96 | 99 | 62 | 81 | 81 | 99 | 83 | 99 | 84 | 99 | 94 | 99 | 90 | 99 | 56 | 60 | 43 | 22 | 65 | 89 | 50 | 46 | 34 | 7 | 19 |
| 18 | 75 | 98 | 111 | 99 | 92 | 99 | 61 | 77 | 79 | 98 | 81 | 99 | 81 | 99 | 91 | 99 | 87 | 99 | 53 | 53 | 41 | 18 | 62 | 82 | 48 | 37 | 33 | 6 | 18 |
| 17 | 73 | 96 | 107 | 99 | 89 | 99 | 59 | 73 | 77 | 98 | 78 | 99 | 79 | 99 | 88 | 99 | 84 | 99 | 51 | 45 | 39 | 15 | 59 | 73 | 45 | 29 | 31 | 5 | 17 |
| 16 | 71 | 95 | 103 | 99 | 86 | 99 | 58 | 67 | 75 | 97 | 76 | 99 | 76 | 99 | 85 | 99 | 82 | 99 | 49 | 37 | 37 | 12 | 57 | 63 | 43 | 23 | 29 | 4 | 16 |
| 15 | 68 | 93 | 99 | 99 | 83 | 99 | 56 | 62 | 72 | 96 | 73 | 98 | 74 | 98 | 83 | 99 | 79 | 98 | 47 | 30 | 36 | 9 | 54 | 53 | 40 | 17 | 27 | 3 | 15 |
| 14 | 66 | 91 | 95 | 99 | 80 | 99 | 54 | 55 | 70 | 95 | 71 | 97 | 71 | 97 | 80 | 98 | 76 | 97 | 44 | 24 | 34 | 8 | 52 | 43 | 38 | 12 | 25 | 2 | 14 |
| 13 | 64 | 88 | 91 | 99 | 77 | 98 | 53 | 48 | 68 | 94 | 68 | 95 | 69 | 95 | 77 | 97 | 74 | 97 | 42 | 18 | 32 | 6 | 49 | 35 | 36 | 9 | 24 | 2 | 13 |
| 12 | 62 | 85 | 87 | 99 | 74 | 97 | 51 | 40 | 65 | 92 | 66 | 93 | 66 | 93 | 74 | 96 | 71 | 95 | 40 | 12 | 30 | 5 | 47 | 27 | 33 | 6 | 22 | 1 | 12 |
| 11 | 60 | 81 | 83 | 98 | 71 | 96 | 49 | 32 | 63 | 90 | 63 | 90 | 64 | 90 | 72 | 95 | 68 | 94 | 38 | 8 | 28 | 3 | 44 | 20 | 31 | 4 | 20 | 1 | 11 |
| 10 | 57 | 75 | 79 | 97 | 67 | 94 | 48 | 25 | 61 | 87 | 61 | 86 | 61 | 86 | 69 | 94 | 66 | 92 | 35 | 5 | 26 | 3 | 41 | 15 | 28 | 3 | 18 | 1 | 10 |
| 9 | 55 | 69 | 76 | 96 | 64 | 92 | 46 | 17 | 59 | 83 | 58 | 81 | 59 | 81 | 66 | 92 | 63 | 89 | 33 | 3 | 25 | 2 | 39 | 10 | 26 | 2 | 16 | 1 | 9 |
| 8 | 53 | 61 | 72 | 94 | 61 | 88 | 44 | 11 | 56 | 78 | 56 | 75 | 56 | 75 | 63 | 89 | 60 | 86 | 31 | 1 | 23 | 1 | 36 | 7 | 24 | 1 | 14 | 1 | 8 |
| 7 | 51 | 52 | 68 | 91 | 58 | 83 | 43 | 6 | 54 | 73 | 53 | 67 | 54 | 69 | 61 | 86 | 58 | 81 | 29 | 1 | 21 | 1 | 34 | 4 | 21 | 1 | 13 | 1 | 7 |
| 6 | 49 | 42 | 64 | 86 | 55 | 75 | 41 | 3 | 52 | 66 | 51 | 58 | 51 | 61 | 58 | 83 | 55 | 76 | 26 | 1 | 19 | 1 | 31 | 3 | 19 | 1 | 11 | 1 | 6 |
| 5 | 46 | 32 | 60 | 80 | 52 | 64 | 39 | 1 | 49 | 57 | 48 | 48 | 49 | 52 | 55 | 78 | 52 | 69 | 24 | 1 | 17 | 1 | 29 | 2 | 16 | 1 | 10 | 1 | 5 |
| 4 | 44 | 21 | 56 | 70 | 49 | 51 | 38 | 1 | 47 | 47 | 46 | 38 | 46 | 43 | 53 | 72 | 50 | 60 | 22 | 1 | 16 | 1 | 26 | 1 | 14 | 1 | 10 | 1 | 4 |
| 3 | 42 | 13 | 52 | 55 | 46 | 36 | 36 | 1 | 45 | 36 | 43 | 28 | 44 | 33 | 50 | 63 | 47 | 49 | 20 | 1 | 14 | 1 | 23 | 1 | 11 | 1 | 10 | 1 | 3 |
| 2 | 40 | 6 | 48 | 34 | 42 | 21 | 34 | 1 | 43 | 24 | 41 | 18 | 41 | 22 | 47 | 52 | 44 | 35 | 17 | 1 | 12 | 1 | 21 | 1 | 10 | 1 | 10 | 1 | 2 |
| 1 | 38 | 2 | 44 | 10 | 39 | 10 | 33 | 1 | 40 | 12 | 38 | 11 | 39 | 13 | 44 | 36 | 41 | 18 | 15 | 1 | 10 | 1 | 18 | 1 | 10 | 1 | 10 | 1 | 1 |
| 0 | 35 | 1 | 41 | 4 | 36 | 4 | 31 | 1 | 38 | 4 | 36 | 5 | 36 | 5 | 42 | 14 | 39 | 4 | 13 | 1 | 10 | 1 | 16 | 1 | 10 | 1 | 10 | 1 | 0 |
| **Raw mean** | 6.61 | | 2.43 | | 4.44 | | 11.43 | | 5.27 | | 5.65 | | 5.41 | | 3.08 | | 4.14 | | 16.51 | | 22.89 | | 13.33 | | 18.99 | | 27.68 | | Raw mean |
| **Raw SD** | 4.54 | | 2.57 | | 3.20 | | 6.06 | | 4.36 | | 3.99 | | 4.00 | | 3.65 | | 3.73 | | 4.45 | | 5.48 | | 3.89 | | 4.15 | | 5.54 | | Raw SD |
| **T: 90% Conf. int.** | 7 | | 7 | | 6 | | 6 | | 6 | | 7 | | 6 | | 7 | | 7 | | 7 | | 5 | | 7 | | 8 | | 7 | | T: 90% Conf. int. |

## Table A.10c  PRS-C T Scores and Percentiles

| Raw score | Hyperactivity T | Hyperactivity %ile | Aggression T | Aggression %ile | Conduct Problems T | Conduct Problems %ile | Anxiety T | Anxiety %ile | Depression T | Depression %ile | Somatization T | Somatization %ile | Attention Problems T | Attention Problems %ile | Atypicality T | Atypicality %ile | Withdrawal T | Withdrawal %ile | Adaptability T | Adaptability %ile | Social Skills T | Social Skills %ile | Leadership T | Leadership %ile | Activities of Daily Living T | Activities of Daily Living %ile | Functional Communication T | Functional Communication %ile |
|---|---|---|---|---|---|---|---|---|---|---|---|---|---|---|---|---|---|---|---|---|---|---|---|---|---|---|---|---|
| 42 | — | — | — | — | — | — | 98 | 99 | — | — | — | — | — | — | 120 | 99 | — | — | — | — | — | — | — | — | — | — | — | — |
| 41 | — | — | — | — | — | — | 96 | 99 | — | — | — | — | — | — | 120 | 99 | — | — | — | — | — | — | — | — | — | — | — | — |
| 40 | — | — | — | — | — | — | 95 | 99 | — | — | — | — | — | — | 120 | 99 | — | — | — | — | — | — | — | — | — | — | — | — |
| 39 | — | — | — | — | — | — | 93 | 99 | 113 | 99 | — | — | — | — | 120 | 99 | — | — | — | — | — | — | — | — | — | — | — | — |
| 38 | — | — | — | — | — | — | 91 | 99 | 112 | 99 | — | — | — | — | 120 | 99 | — | — | — | — | — | — | — | — | — | — | — | — |
| 37 | — | — | — | — | — | — | 90 | 99 | 110 | 99 | — | — | — | — | 119 | 99 | — | — | — | — | — | — | — | — | — | — | — | — |
| 36 | — | — | — | — | — | — | 88 | 99 | 108 | 99 | 120 | 99 | — | — | 117 | 99 | — | — | — | — | — | — | — | — | — | — | 68 | 96 |
| 35 | — | — | — | — | — | — | 87 | 99 | 106 | 99 | 120 | 99 | — | — | 115 | 99 | — | — | — | — | — | — | — | — | — | — | 66 | 95 |
| 34 | — | — | — | — | — | — | 85 | 99 | 104 | 99 | 117 | 99 | — | — | 113 | 99 | — | — | — | — | — | — | — | — | — | — | 65 | 93 |
| 33 | 99 | 99 | — | — | — | — | 84 | 99 | 102 | 99 | 115 | 99 | — | — | 110 | 99 | — | — | — | — | — | — | — | — | — | — | 63 | 91 |
| 32 | 97 | 99 | — | — | — | — | 82 | 99 | 100 | 99 | 113 | 99 | — | — | 108 | 99 | — | — | — | — | — | — | — | — | — | — | 62 | 88 |
| 31 | 95 | 99 | — | — | — | — | 80 | 99 | 98 | 99 | 110 | 99 | — | — | 106 | 99 | — | — | — | — | — | — | — | — | — | — | 60 | 85 |
| 30 | 93 | 99 | — | — | 113 | 99 | 79 | 99 | 96 | 99 | 108 | 99 | — | — | 104 | 99 | — | — | — | — | 66 | 95 | — | — | — | — | 59 | 81 |
| 29 | 91 | 99 | — | — | 110 | 99 | 77 | 99 | 94 | 99 | 106 | 99 | — | — | 102 | 99 | — | — | — | — | 65 | 93 | — | — | — | — | 57 | 76 |
| 28 | 89 | 99 | — | — | 108 | 99 | 76 | 99 | 92 | 99 | 103 | 99 | — | — | 100 | 99 | 99 | 99 | — | — | 63 | 91 | — | — | — | — | 56 | 71 |
| 27 | 87 | 99 | — | — | 105 | 99 | 74 | 99 | 90 | 99 | 101 | 99 | — | — | 98 | 99 | 97 | 99 | — | — | 62 | 88 | — | — | 73 | 99 | 54 | 66 |
| 26 | 85 | 99 | — | — | 103 | 99 | 72 | 99 | 88 | 99 | 99 | 99 | — | — | 96 | 99 | 95 | 99 | — | — | 60 | 84 | — | — | 70 | 98 | 53 | 60 |
| 25 | 83 | 99 | 120 | 99 | 100 | 99 | 71 | 98 | 86 | 99 | 97 | 99 | — | — | 94 | 99 | 93 | 99 | 73 | 99 | 58 | 80 | — | — | 68 | 96 | 51 | 54 |
| 24 | 81 | 99 | 120 | 99 | 98 | 99 | 69 | 97 | 84 | 99 | 94 | 99 | — | — | 92 | 99 | 91 | 99 | 71 | 98 | 57 | 75 | — | — | 66 | 94 | 50 | 48 |
| 23 | 79 | 99 | 118 | 99 | 95 | 99 | 68 | 96 | 82 | 99 | 92 | 99 | — | — | 90 | 99 | 88 | 99 | 69 | 97 | 55 | 70 | — | — | 64 | 91 | 48 | 42 |
| 22 | 77 | 99 | 115 | 99 | 93 | 99 | 66 | 95 | 80 | 99 | 90 | 99 | — | — | 87 | 99 | 86 | 99 | 67 | 95 | 54 | 64 | — | — | 61 | 87 | 46 | 36 |
| 21 | 75 | 99 | 111 | 99 | 90 | 99 | 64 | 93 | 79 | 99 | 87 | 99 | 81 | 99 | 85 | 99 | 84 | 99 | 64 | 93 | 52 | 58 | 72 | 99 | 59 | 82 | 45 | 31 |
| 20 | 73 | 99 | 108 | 99 | 88 | 99 | 63 | 90 | 77 | 99 | 85 | 99 | 79 | 99 | 83 | 99 | 82 | 99 | 62 | 89 | 50 | 52 | 70 | 98 | 57 | 75 | 43 | 26 |
| 19 | 71 | 98 | 105 | 99 | 85 | 99 | 61 | 87 | 75 | 99 | 83 | 99 | 76 | 99 | 81 | 99 | 80 | 99 | 60 | 84 | 49 | 46 | 67 | 96 | 55 | 68 | 42 | 21 |
| 18 | 69 | 97 | 101 | 99 | 83 | 99 | 60 | 84 | 73 | 99 | 80 | 99 | 74 | 99 | 79 | 99 | 78 | 99 | 58 | 78 | 47 | 39 | 65 | 94 | 52 | 60 | 40 | 17 |
| 17 | 67 | 96 | 98 | 99 | 80 | 99 | 58 | 79 | 71 | 98 | 78 | 99 | 72 | 99 | 77 | 99 | 75 | 99 | 56 | 71 | 46 | 33 | 63 | 90 | 50 | 51 | 39 | 13 |
| 16 | 65 | 94 | 94 | 99 | 78 | 99 | 57 | 75 | 69 | 97 | 76 | 99 | 69 | 97 | 75 | 99 | 73 | 99 | 53 | 63 | 44 | 28 | 61 | 86 | 48 | 42 | 37 | 10 |
| 15 | 63 | 91 | 91 | 99 | 75 | 99 | 55 | 69 | 67 | 95 | 73 | 99 | 67 | 96 | 73 | 99 | 71 | 98 | 51 | 55 | 42 | 23 | 59 | 80 | 46 | 33 | 36 | 8 |
| 14 | 61 | 87 | 87 | 99 | 73 | 99 | 53 | 63 | 65 | 93 | 71 | 98 | 65 | 93 | 71 | 98 | 69 | 97 | 49 | 46 | 41 | 18 | 56 | 74 | 43 | 26 | 34 | 6 |
| 13 | 59 | 83 | 84 | 99 | 70 | 98 | 52 | 57 | 63 | 90 | 69 | 97 | 63 | 89 | 68 | 97 | 67 | 95 | 47 | 37 | 39 | 14 | 54 | 66 | 41 | 19 | 33 | 4 |
| 12 | 57 | 77 | 80 | 99 | 68 | 96 | 50 | 51 | 61 | 86 | 66 | 95 | 60 | 85 | 66 | 95 | 65 | 93 | 45 | 29 | 38 | 11 | 52 | 56 | 39 | 14 | 31 | 3 |
| 11 | 55 | 71 | 77 | 99 | 65 | 93 | 49 | 45 | 59 | 82 | 64 | 92 | 58 | 78 | 64 | 92 | 62 | 89 | 42 | 22 | 36 | 8 | 50 | 49 | 37 | 9 | 30 | 2 |
| 10 | 53 | 64 | 73 | 99 | 63 | 90 | 47 | 39 | 57 | 76 | 62 | 88 | 56 | 71 | 62 | 89 | 60 | 85 | 40 | 16 | 35 | 6 | 47 | 40 | 35 | 6 | 28 | 1 |
| 9 | 51 | 56 | 70 | 98 | 60 | 84 | 46 | 33 | 55 | 70 | 59 | 82 | 53 | 63 | 60 | 84 | 58 | 79 | 38 | 11 | 33 | 4 | 45 | 32 | 32 | 4 | 27 | 1 |
| 8 | 50 | 48 | 66 | 95 | 58 | 78 | 44 | 27 | 53 | 63 | 57 | 76 | 51 | 54 | 58 | 79 | 56 | 73 | 36 | 8 | 31 | 3 | 43 | 24 | 30 | 2 | 25 | 1 |
| 7 | 48 | 40 | 63 | 90 | 55 | 69 | 42 | 22 | 51 | 55 | 55 | 68 | 49 | 45 | 56 | 72 | 54 | 65 | 34 | 5 | 30 | 2 | 41 | 18 | 28 | 1 | 24 | 1 |
| 6 | 46 | 33 | 60 | 83 | 53 | 60 | 41 | 18 | 49 | 48 | 52 | 59 | 46 | 36 | 54 | 64 | 52 | 56 | 31 | 3 | 28 | 1 | 39 | 13 | 26 | 1 | 22 | 1 |
| 5 | 44 | 26 | 56 | 73 | 50 | 50 | 39 | 14 | 47 | 40 | 50 | 50 | 44 | 28 | 52 | 56 | 49 | 48 | 29 | 2 | 27 | 1 | 36 | 9 | 23 | 1 | 21 | 1 |
| 4 | 42 | 20 | 53 | 60 | 47 | 40 | 38 | 11 | 46 | 33 | 48 | 41 | 42 | 21 | 49 | 48 | 47 | 39 | 27 | 1 | 25 | 1 | 34 | 6 | 21 | 1 | 19 | 1 |
| 3 | 40 | 15 | 49 | 47 | 45 | 31 | 36 | 8 | 44 | 26 | 45 | 32 | 39 | 15 | 47 | 39 | 45 | 31 | 25 | 1 | 23 | 1 | 32 | 4 | 19 | 1 | 18 | 1 |
| 2 | 38 | 11 | 46 | 33 | 42 | 22 | 34 | 6 | 42 | 20 | 43 | 24 | 37 | 10 | 45 | 32 | 43 | 24 | 23 | 1 | 22 | 1 | 30 | 2 | 17 | 1 | 16 | 1 |
| 1 | 36 | 8 | 42 | 22 | 40 | 16 | 33 | 4 | 40 | 15 | 41 | 18 | 35 | 7 | 43 | 25 | 41 | 18 | 20 | 1 | 20 | 1 | 27 | 1 | 14 | 1 | 14 | 1 |
| 0 | 34 | 5 | 39 | 13 | 37 | 10 | 31 | 3 | 38 | 11 | 38 | 12 | 33 | 4 | 41 | 18 | 39 | 13 | 18 | 1 | 19 | 1 | 25 | 1 | 12 | 1 | 13 | 1 |
| **Raw mean** | 8.25 | | 3.24 | | 5.00 | | 11.85 | | 6.31 | | 5.00 | | 7.56 | | 4.27 | | 5.24 | | 14.45 | | 19.70 | | 11.15 | | 16.91 | | 24.29 | |
| **Raw SD** | 5.06 | | 2.89 | | 3.97 | | 6.31 | | 5.15 | | 4.30 | | 4.34 | | 4.75 | | 4.62 | | 4.54 | | 6.26 | | 4.50 | | 4.47 | | 6.55 | |
| **T: 90% Conf. int.** | 7 | | 8 | | 5 | | 6 | | 6 | | 6 | | 6 | | 6 | | 6 | | 6 | | 5 | | 6 | | 7 | | 6 | |

**Table A.10d** PRS–C Composite T Scores

| T score | Externalizing Problems | | | Internalizing Problems | | | Adaptive Skills | | | Behavioral Symptoms Index | | | T score |
|---|---|---|---|---|---|---|---|---|---|---|---|---|---|
| | Combined | Female | Male | Combined | Female | Male | Combined | Female | Male | Combined | Female | Male | |
| 120 | 331–343 | 333–348 | 330–332 | 325–338 | 329–340 | 322–331 | — | — | — | 608–649 | 615–668 | 594–630 | 120 |
| 119 | 329–330 | 330–332 | 327–329 | 323–324 | 327–328 | 319–321 | — | — | — | 603–607 | 611–614 | 590–593 | 119 |
| 118 | 326–328 | 328–329 | 325–326 | 320–322 | 324–326 | 317–318 | — | — | — | 599–602 | 606–610 | 586–589 | 118 |
| 117 | 323–325 | 325–327 | 322–324 | 318–319 | 322–323 | 314–316 | — | — | — | 595–598 | 602–605 | 582–585 | 117 |
| 116 | 321–322 | 322–324 | 320–321 | 315–317 | 319–321 | 312–313 | — | — | — | 590–594 | 597–601 | 577–581 | 116 |
| 115 | 318–320 | 320–321 | 317–319 | 313–314 | 316–318 | 309–311 | — | — | — | 586–589 | 593–596 | 573–576 | 115 |
| 114 | 316–317 | 317–319 | 314–316 | 310–312 | 314–315 | 307–308 | — | — | — | 581–585 | 588–592 | 569–572 | 114 |
| 113 | 313–315 | 315–316 | 312–313 | 308–309 | 311–313 | 304–306 | — | — | — | 577–580 | 584–587 | 565–568 | 113 |
| 112 | 310–312 | 312–314 | 309–311 | 305–307 | 309–310 | 302–303 | — | — | — | 572–576 | 579–583 | 561–564 | 112 |
| 111 | 308–309 | 309–311 | 307–308 | 303–304 | 306–308 | 300–301 | — | — | — | 568–571 | 575–578 | 556–560 | 111 |
| 110 | 305–307 | 307–308 | 304–306 | 300–302 | 304–305 | 297–299 | — | — | — | 564–567 | 570–574 | 552–555 | 110 |
| 109 | 303–304 | 304–306 | 302–303 | 298–299 | 301–303 | 295–296 | — | — | — | 559–563 | 566–569 | 548–551 | 109 |
| 108 | 300–302 | 301–303 | 299–301 | 295–297 | 298–300 | 292–294 | — | — | — | 555–558 | 561–565 | 544–547 | 108 |
| 107 | 297–299 | 299–300 | 296–298 | 292–294 | 296–297 | 290–291 | — | — | — | 550–554 | 556–560 | 539–543 | 107 |
| 106 | 295–296 | 296–298 | 294–295 | 290–291 | 293–295 | 287–289 | — | — | — | 546–549 | 552–555 | 535–538 | 106 |
| 105 | 292–294 | 294–295 | 291–293 | 287–289 | 291–292 | 285–286 | — | — | — | 542–545 | 547–551 | 531–534 | 105 |
| 104 | 290–291 | 291–293 | 289–290 | 285–286 | 288–290 | 282–284 | — | — | — | 537–541 | 543–546 | 527–530 | 104 |
| 103 | 287–289 | 288–290 | 286–288 | 282–284 | 286–287 | 280–281 | — | — | — | 533–536 | 538–542 | 522–526 | 103 |
| 102 | 284–286 | 286–287 | 283–285 | 280–281 | 283–285 | 277–279 | — | — | — | 528–532 | 534–537 | 518–521 | 102 |
| 101 | 282–283 | 283–285 | 281–282 | 277–279 | 280–282 | 275–276 | — | — | — | 524–527 | 529–533 | 514–517 | 101 |
| 100 | 279–281 | 280–282 | 278–280 | 275–276 | 278–279 | 272–274 | — | — | — | 519–523 | 525–528 | 510–513 | 100 |
| 99 | 277–278 | 278–279 | 276–277 | 272–274 | 275–277 | 270–271 | — | — | — | 515–518 | 520–524 | 506–509 | 99 |
| 98 | 274–276 | 275–277 | 273–275 | 270–271 | 273–274 | 268–269 | — | — | — | 511–514 | 516–519 | 501–505 | 98 |
| 97 | 271–273 | 273–274 | 271–272 | 267–269 | 270–272 | 265–267 | — | — | — | 506–510 | 511–515 | 497–500 | 97 |
| 96 | 269–270 | 270–272 | 268–270 | 265–266 | 268–269 | 263–264 | — | — | — | 502–505 | 507–510 | 493–496 | 96 |
| 95 | 266–268 | 267–269 | 265–267 | 262–264 | 265–267 | 260–262 | — | — | — | 497–501 | 502–506 | 489–492 | 95 |
| 94 | 264–265 | 265–266 | 263–264 | 260–261 | 262–264 | 258–259 | — | — | — | 493–496 | 498–501 | 484–488 | 94 |
| 93 | 261–263 | 262–264 | 260–262 | 257–259 | 260–261 | 255–257 | — | — | — | 488–492 | 493–497 | 480–483 | 93 |
| 92 | 258–260 | 259–261 | 258–259 | 255–256 | 257–259 | 253–254 | — | — | — | 484–487 | 488–492 | 476–479 | 92 |
| 91 | 256–257 | 257–258 | 255–257 | 252–254 | 255–256 | 250–252 | — | — | — | 480–483 | 484–487 | 472–475 | 91 |
| 90 | 253–255 | 254–256 | 252–254 | 250–251 | 252–254 | 248–249 | — | — | — | 475–479 | 479–483 | 468–471 | 90 |
| 89 | 251–252 | 252–253 | 250–251 | 247–249 | 250–251 | 245–247 | — | — | — | 471–474 | 475–478 | 463–467 | 89 |
| 88 | 248–250 | 249–251 | 247–249 | 245–246 | 247–249 | 243–244 | — | — | — | 466–470 | 470–474 | 459–462 | 88 |
| 87 | 245–247 | 246–248 | 245–246 | 242–244 | 244–246 | 240–242 | — | — | — | 462–465 | 466–469 | 455–458 | 87 |
| 86 | 243–244 | 244–245 | 242–244 | 240–241 | 242–243 | 238–239 | — | — | — | 457–461 | 461–465 | 451–454 | 86 |
| 85 | 240–242 | 241–243 | 240–241 | 237–239 | 239–241 | 235–237 | — | — | — | 453–456 | 457–460 | 446–450 | 85 |
| 84 | 238–239 | 238–240 | 237–239 | 235–236 | 237–238 | 233–234 | — | — | — | 449–452 | 452–456 | 442–445 | 84 |
| 83 | 235–237 | 236–237 | 234–236 | 232–234 | 234–236 | 231–232 | — | — | — | 444–448 | 448–451 | 438–441 | 83 |
| 82 | 232–234 | 233–235 | 232–233 | 230–231 | 231–233 | 228–230 | — | — | — | 440–443 | 443–447 | 434–437 | 82 |
| 81 | 230–231 | 231–232 | 229–231 | 227–229 | 229–230 | 226–227 | — | — | — | 435–439 | 439–442 | 429–433 | 81 |
| 80 | 227–229 | 228–230 | 227–228 | 225–226 | 226–228 | 223–225 | — | — | — | 431–434 | 434–438 | 425–428 | 80 |
| 79 | 225–226 | 225–227 | 224–226 | 222–224 | 224–225 | 221–222 | — | — | — | 426–430 | 430–433 | 421–424 | 79 |
| 78 | 222–224 | 223–224 | 222–223 | 220–221 | 221–223 | 218–220 | — | — | — | 422–425 | 425–429 | 417–420 | 78 |
| 77 | 219–221 | 220–222 | 219–221 | 217–219 | 219–220 | 216–217 | — | — | — | 418–421 | 420–424 | 413–416 | 77 |
| 76 | 217–218 | 217–219 | 216–218 | 215–216 | 216–218 | 213–215 | — | — | — | 413–417 | 416–419 | 408–412 | 76 |
| 75 | 214–216 | 215–216 | 214–215 | 212–214 | 213–215 | 211–212 | — | — | — | 409–412 | 411–415 | 404–407 | 75 |
| 74 | 212–213 | 212–214 | 211–213 | 210–211 | 211–212 | 208–210 | — | — | — | 404–408 | 407–410 | 400–403 | 74 |
| 73 | 209–211 | 210–211 | 209–210 | 207–209 | 208–210 | 206–207 | — | — | 347–350 | 400–403 | 402–406 | 396–399 | 73 |
| 72 | 206–208 | 207–209 | 206–208 | 204–206 | 206–207 | 203–205 | — | — | 343–346 | 395–399 | 398–401 | 391–395 | 72 |
| 71 | 204–205 | 204–206 | 203–205 | 202–203 | 203–205 | 201–202 | — | — | 339–342 | 391–394 | 393–397 | 387–390 | 71 |
| 70 | 201–203 | 202–203 | 201–202 | 199–201 | 201–202 | 199–200 | 335–338 | 334 | 335–338 | 387–390 | 389–392 | 383–386 | 70 |
| 69 | 199–200 | 199–201 | 198–200 | 197–198 | 198–200 | 196–198 | 331–334 | 330–333 | 330–334 | 382–386 | 384–388 | 379–382 | 69 |
| 68 | 196–198 | 196–198 | 196–197 | 194–196 | 195–197 | 194–195 | 326–330 | 325–329 | 326–329 | 378–381 | 380–383 | 374–378 | 68 |
| 67 | 193–195 | 194–195 | 193–195 | 192–193 | 193–194 | 191–193 | 322–325 | 321–324 | 322–325 | 373–377 | 375–379 | 370–373 | 67 |
| 66 | 191–192 | 191–193 | 191–192 | 189–191 | 190–192 | 189–190 | 318–321 | 317–320 | 317–321 | 369–372 | 371–374 | 366–369 | 66 |

## Table A.10d  PRS-C Composite T Scores (continued)

| T score | Externalizing Problems — Combined | — Female | — Male | Internalizing Problems — Combined | — Female | — Male | Adaptive Skills — Combined | — Female | — Male | Behavioral Symptoms Index — Combined | — Female | — Male | T score |
|---|---|---|---|---|---|---|---|---|---|---|---|---|---|
| 65 | 188–190 | 189–190 | 188–190 | 187–188 | 188–189 | 186–188 | 313–317 | 313–316 | 313–316 | 365–368 | 366–370 | 362–365 | 65 |
| 64 | 186–187 | 186–188 | 185–187 | 184–186 | 185–187 | 184–185 | 309–312 | 308–312 | 309–312 | 360–364 | 362–365 | 358–361 | 64 |
| 63 | 183–185 | 183–185 | 183–184 | 182–183 | 183–184 | 181–183 | 305–308 | 304–307 | 304–308 | 356–359 | 357–361 | 353–357 | 63 |
| 62 | 180–182 | 181–182 | 180–182 | 179–181 | 180–182 | 179–180 | 300–304 | 300–303 | 300–303 | 351–355 | 352–356 | 349–352 | 62 |
| 61 | 178–179 | 178–180 | 178–179 | 177–178 | 177–179 | 176–178 | 296–299 | 295–299 | 296–299 | 347–350 | 348–351 | 345–348 | 61 |
| 60 | 175–177 | 175–177 | 175–177 | 174–176 | 175–176 | 174–175 | 292–295 | 291–294 | 291–295 | 342–346 | 343–347 | 341–344 | 60 |
| 59 | 173–174 | 173–174 | 172–174 | 172–173 | 172–174 | 171–173 | 287–291 | 287–290 | 287–290 | 338–341 | 339–342 | 336–340 | 59 |
| 58 | 170–172 | 170–172 | 170–171 | 169–171 | 170–171 | 169–170 | 283–286 | 283–286 | 283–286 | 334–337 | 334–338 | 332–335 | 58 |
| 57 | 167–169 | 168–169 | 167–169 | 167–168 | 167–169 | 167–168 | 279–282 | 278–282 | 279–282 | 329–333 | 330–333 | 328–331 | 57 |
| 56 | 165–166 | 165–167 | 165–166 | 164–166 | 165–166 | 164–166 | 274–278 | 274–277 | 274–278 | 325–328 | 325–329 | 324–327 | 56 |
| 55 | 162–164 | 162–164 | 162–164 | 162–163 | 162–164 | 162–163 | 270–273 | 270–273 | 270–273 | 320–324 | 321–324 | 320–323 | 55 |
| 54 | 160–161 | 160–161 | 160–161 | 159–161 | 159–161 | 159–161 | 266–269 | 266–269 | 266–269 | 316–319 | 316–320 | 315–319 | 54 |
| 53 | 157–159 | 157–159 | 157–159 | 157–158 | 157–158 | 157–158 | 261–265 | 261–265 | 261–265 | 311–315 | 312–315 | 311–314 | 53 |
| 52 | 154–156 | 154–156 | 154–156 | 154–156 | 154–156 | 154–156 | 257–260 | 257–260 | 257–260 | 307–310 | 307–311 | 307–310 | 52 |
| 51 | 152–153 | 152–153 | 152–153 | 152–153 | 152–153 | 152–153 | 253–256 | 253–256 | 253–256 | 303–306 | 303–306 | 303–306 | 51 |
| 50 | 149–151 | 149–151 | 149–151 | 149–151 | 149–151 | 149–151 | 248–252 | 248–252 | 248–252 | 298–302 | 298–302 | 298–302 | 50 |
| 49 | 147–148 | 147–148 | 147–148 | 147–148 | 147–148 | 147–148 | 244–247 | 244–247 | 244–247 | 294–297 | 294–297 | 294–297 | 49 |
| 48 | 144–146 | 144–146 | 144–146 | 144–146 | 144–146 | 144–146 | 240–243 | 240–243 | 240–243 | 289–293 | 289–293 | 290–293 | 48 |
| 47 | 141–143 | 141–143 | 142–143 | 142–143 | 141–143 | 142–143 | 235–239 | 236–239 | 235–239 | 285–288 | 284–288 | 286–289 | 47 |
| 46 | 139–140 | 139–140 | 139–141 | 139–141 | 139–140 | 139–141 | 231–235 | 231–235 | 231–234 | 280–284 | 280–283 | 281–285 | 46 |
| 45 | 136–138 | 136–138 | 136–138 | 137–138 | 136–138 | 137–138 | 227–230 | 227–230 | 227–230 | 276–279 | 275–279 | 277–280 | 45 |
| 44 | 134–135 | 133–135 | 134–135 | 134–136 | 134–135 | 134–136 | 222–226 | 223–226 | 222–226 | 272–275 | 271–274 | 273–276 | 44 |
| 43 | 131–133 | 131–132 | 131–133 | 132–133 | 131–133 | 132–133 | 218–221 | 218–222 | 218–221 | 267–271 | 266–270 | 269–272 | 43 |
| 42 | 128–130 | 128–130 | 129–130 | 129–131 | 129–130 | 130–131 | 214–217 | 214–217 | 214–217 | 263–266 | 262–265 | 265–268 | 42 |
| 41 | 126–127 | 126–127 | 126–128 | 127–128 | 126–128 | 127–129 | 209–213 | 210–213 | 210–213 | 258–262 | 257–261 | 260–264 | 41 |
| 40 | 123–125 | 123–125 | 123–125 | 124–126 | 123–125 | 125–126 | 205–208 | 206–209 | 205–209 | 254–257 | 253–256 | 256–259 | 40 |
| 39 | 121–122 | 120–122 | 121–122 | 122–123 | 121–122 | 122–124 | 201–204 | 201–205 | 201–204 | 249–253 | 248–252 | 252–255 | 39 |
| 38 | 118–119 | 118–119 | 118–120 | 119–121 | 118–120 | 120–121 | 196–200 | 197–200 | 197–200 | 245–248 | 244–247 | 248–251 | 38 |
| 37 | 115–117 | 115–117 | 116–117 | 117–118 | 116–117 | 117–119 | 192–195 | 193–196 | 192–196 | 241–244 | 239–243 | 243–247 | 37 |
| 36 | 112–114 | 112–114 | 113–115 | 114–116 | 113–115 | 115–116 | 188–191 | 189–192 | 188–191 | 236–240 | 235–238 | 239–242 | 36 |
| 35 | 112 | — | 111–112 | 111–113 | 111–112 | 112–114 | 183–187 | 184–188 | 184–187 | 232–235 | 231–234 | 235–238 | 35 |
| 34 | — | — | 110 | 109–110 | 108–110 | 110–111 | 179–182 | 180–183 | 179–183 | 228–231 | — | 231–234 | 34 |
| 33 | — | — | — | 106–108 | 105–107 | 107–109 | 175–178 | 176–179 | 175–178 | — | — | 227–230 | 33 |
| 32 | — | — | — | — | — | — | 170–174 | 171–175 | 171–174 | — | — | 224–226 | 32 |
| 31 | — | — | — | — | — | — | 166–169 | 167–170 | 166–170 | — | — | — | 31 |
| 30 | — | — | — | — | — | — | 162–165 | 163–166 | 162–165 | — | — | — | 30 |
| 29 | — | — | — | — | — | — | 157–161 | 159–162 | 158–161 | — | — | — | 29 |
| 28 | — | — | — | — | — | — | 153–156 | 154–158 | 154–157 | — | — | — | 28 |
| 27 | — | — | — | — | — | — | 149–152 | 150–153 | 149–153 | — | — | — | 27 |
| 26 | — | — | — | — | — | — | 144–148 | 146–149 | 145–148 | — | — | — | 26 |
| 25 | — | — | — | — | — | — | 140–143 | 142–145 | 141–144 | — | — | — | 25 |
| 24 | — | — | — | — | — | — | 136–139 | 137–141 | 136–140 | — | — | — | 24 |
| 23 | — | — | — | — | — | — | 131–135 | 133–136 | 132–135 | — | — | — | 23 |
| 22 | — | — | — | — | — | — | 127–130 | 129–132 | 128–131 | — | — | — | 22 |
| 21 | — | — | — | — | — | — | 123–126 | 124–128 | 123–127 | — | — | — | 21 |
| 20 | — | — | — | — | — | — | 118–122 | 120–123 | 119–122 | — | — | — | 20 |
| 19 | — | — | — | — | — | — | 114–117 | 116–119 | 115–118 | — | — | — | 19 |
| 18 | — | — | — | — | — | — | 110–113 | 112–115 | 110–114 | — | — | — | 18 |
| 17 | — | — | — | — | — | — | 105–109 | 107–111 | 106–109 | — | — | — | 17 |
| 16 | — | — | — | — | — | — | 101–104 | 103–106 | 102–105 | — | — | — | 16 |
| 15 | — | — | — | — | — | — | 97–100 | 99–102 | 98–101 | — | — | — | 15 |
| 14 | — | — | — | — | — | — | 92–96 | 94–98 | 93–97 | — | — | — | 14 |
| 13 | — | — | — | — | — | — | 88–91 | 90–93 | 89–92 | — | — | — | 13 |
| 12 | — | — | — | — | — | — | 84–87 | 86–89 | 87–88 | — | — | — | 12 |
| 11 | — | — | — | — | — | — | 79–83 | 82–85 | — | — | — | — | 11 |
| 10 | — | — | — | — | — | — | 73–78 | 59–81 | — | — | — | — | 10 |
| T: 90% Conf. int. | 4 | 4 | 4 | 4 | 4 | 4 | 3 | 4 | 3 | 4 | 4 | 4 | T: 90% Conf. int. |

**Table A.10e** PRS-C Composite Percentiles

| %ile | Externalizing Problems | | | Internalizing Problems | | | Adaptive Skills | | | Behavioral Symptoms Index | | | %ile |
|---|---|---|---|---|---|---|---|---|---|---|---|---|---|
| | Combined | Female | Male | Combined | Female | Male | Combined | Female | Male | Combined | Female | Male | |
| 99 | 227–343 | 226–348 | 227–332 | 223–338 | 223–340 | 223–331 | 327–338 | 321–334 | 335–350 | 423–649 | 429–668 | 417–630 | 99 |
| 98 | 215–226 | 215–225 | 215–226 | 212–222 | 212–222 | 212–222 | 322–326 | 317–320 | 329–334 | 407–422 | 412–428 | 401–416 | 98 |
| 97 | 207–214 | 208–214 | 207–214 | 205–211 | 206–211 | 205–211 | 319–321 | 314–316 | 324–328 | 396–406 | 401–411 | 391–400 | 97 |
| 96 | 202–206 | 202–207 | 202–206 | 200–204 | 201–205 | 200–204 | 316–318 | 312–313 | 320–323 | 388–395 | 392–400 | 383–390 | 96 |
| 95 | 197–201 | 198–201 | 197–201 | 196–199 | 197–200 | 195–199 | 313–315 | 309–311 | 316–319 | 381–387 | 385–391 | 376–382 | 95 |
| 94 | 194–196 | 194–197 | 194–196 | 193–195 | 193–196 | 192–194 | 311–312 | 307–308 | 313–315 | 375–380 | 379–384 | 371–375 | 94 |
| 93 | 190–193 | 191–193 | 190–193 | 190–192 | 190–192 | 189–191 | 309–310 | 306 | 311–312 | 370–374 | 374–378 | 366–370 | 93 |
| 92 | 188–189 | 188–190 | 187–189 | 187–189 | 188–189 | 186–188 | 307–308 | 304–305 | 308–310 | 366–369 | 369–373 | 362–365 | 92 |
| 91 | 185–187 | 185–187 | 185–186 | 185–186 | 185–187 | 184–185 | 305–306 | 302–303 | 306–307 | 362–365 | 365–368 | 358–361 | 91 |
| 90 | 183–184 | 184–185 | 183–184 | 183–184 | 183–184 | 182–183 | 303–304 | 301 | 304–305 | 358–361 | 361–364 | 355–357 | 90 |
| 89 | 181–182 | 182–183 | 181–182 | 181–182 | 181–182 | 180–181 | 302 | 299–300 | 302–303 | 355–357 | 357–360 | 352–354 | 89 |
| 88 | 179–180 | 180–181 | 179–180 | 179–180 | 180 | 178–179 | 300–301 | 298 | 300–301 | 352–354 | 354–356 | 349–351 | 88 |
| 87 | 177–178 | 178–179 | 177–178 | 177–178 | 178–179 | 176–177 | 298–299 | 297 | 298–299 | 349–351 | 351–353 | 346–348 | 87 |
| 86 | 175–176 | 176–177 | 175–176 | 176 | 176–177 | 175 | 297 | 295–296 | 297 | 346–348 | 348–350 | 344–345 | 86 |
| 85 | 174 | 175 | 174 | 174–175 | 175 | 173–174 | 295–296 | 294 | 295–296 | 344–345 | 345–347 | 341–343 | 85 |
| 84 | 173 | 173–174 | 172–173 | 173 | 173–174 | 172 | 294 | 293 | 293–294 | 341–343 | 343–344 | 339–340 | 84 |
| 83 | 171–172 | 172 | 171 | 172 | 172 | 171 | 293 | 291–292 | 292 | 339–340 | 340–342 | 337–338 | 83 |
| 82 | 170 | 171 | 170 | 170–171 | 171 | 169–170 | 291–292 | 290 | 290–291 | 337–338 | 338–339 | 335–336 | 82 |
| 81 | 169 | 169–170 | 169 | 169 | 170 | 168 | 290 | 289 | 289 | 335–336 | 336–337 | 333–334 | 81 |
| 80 | 167–168 | 168 | 167–168 | 168 | 169 | 167 | 289 | 288 | 287–288 | 333–334 | 333–335 | 331–332 | 80 |
| 79 | 166 | 167 | 166 | 167 | 168 | 166 | 287–288 | 287 | 286 | 331–332 | 331–332 | 329–330 | 79 |
| 78 | 165 | 166 | 165 | 166 | 166–167 | 165 | 286 | 286 | 285 | 329–330 | 329–330 | 328 | 78 |
| 77 | 164 | 165 | 164 | 165 | 165 | 164 | 285 | 285 | 283–284 | 327–328 | 327–328 | 326–327 | 77 |
| 76 | 163 | 164 | 163 | 164 | — | 163 | 284 | 283–284 | 282 | 325–326 | 326 | 324–325 | 76 |
| 75 | 162 | 163 | 162 | 163 | 164 | 162 | 283 | 282 | 281 | 324 | 324–325 | 323 | 75 |
| 74 | 161 | 162 | 161 | 162 | 163 | 161 | 281–282 | 281 | 279–280 | 322–323 | 322–323 | 321–322 | 74 |
| 73 | — | 161 | — | 161 | 162 | — | 280 | 280 | 278 | 320–321 | 320–321 | 320 | 73 |
| 72 | 160 | 160 | 160 | 160 | 161 | 160 | 279 | 279 | 277 | 319 | 319 | 318–319 | 72 |
| 71 | 159 | 159 | 159 | — | 160 | 159 | 278 | 278 | 276 | 317–318 | 317–318 | 317 | 71 |
| 70 | 158 | 158 | 158 | 159 | 159 | 158 | 277 | 277 | 274–275 | 316 | 316 | 316 | 70 |
| 69 | 157 | — | 157 | 158 | 158 | 157 | 276 | 276 | 273 | 315 | 314–315 | 314–315 | 69 |
| 68 | 156 | 157 | — | 157 | — | — | 274–275 | 275 | 272 | 313–314 | 313 | 313 | 68 |
| 67 | — | 156 | 156 | 156 | 157 | 156 | 273 | 274 | 271 | 312 | 311–312 | 312 | 67 |
| 66 | 155 | 155 | 155 | — | 156 | 155 | 272 | 273 | 270 | 311 | 310 | 311 | 66 |
| 65 | 154 | — | 154 | 155 | 155 | — | 271 | 272 | 269 | 309–310 | 308–309 | 309–310 | 65 |
| 64 | 153 | 154 | — | 154 | — | 154 | 270 | 271 | 267–268 | 308 | 307 | 308 | 64 |
| 63 | — | 153 | 153 | — | 154 | 153 | 269 | 270 | 266 | 307 | 306 | 307 | 63 |
| 62 | 152 | 152 | 152 | 153 | 153 | — | 268 | 269 | 265 | 305–306 | 304–305 | 306 | 62 |
| 61 | 151 | — | — | 152 | — | 152 | 266–267 | 268 | 264 | 304 | 303 | 305 | 61 |
| 60 | — | 151 | 151 | — | 152 | 151 | 265 | 267 | 263 | 303 | 302 | 304 | 60 |
| 59 | 150 | 150 | 150 | 151 | 151 | — | 264 | 265–266 | 262 | 302 | 301 | 303 | 59 |
| 58 | — | — | — | 150 | — | 150 | 263 | 264 | 261 | 301 | 299–300 | 301–302 | 58 |
| 57 | 149 | 149 | 149 | — | 150 | 149 | 262 | 263 | 260 | 300 | 298 | 300 | 57 |
| 56 | 148 | 148 | 148 | 149 | 149 | — | 261 | 262 | 259 | 299 | 297 | 299 | 56 |
| 55 | — | — | — | — | — | 148 | 260 | 261 | 257–258 | 297–298 | 296 | 298 | 55 |
| 54 | 147 | 147 | 147 | 148 | 148 | — | 259 | 260 | 256 | 296 | 295 | 297 | 54 |
| 53 | — | — | — | 147 | — | 147 | 257–258 | 259 | 255 | 295 | 294 | 296 | 53 |
| 52 | 146 | 146 | 146 | 146 | 147 | — | 256 | 258 | 254 | 294 | 293 | 295 | 52 |
| 51 | 145 | 145 | — | 146 | 146 | 146 | 255 | 257 | 253 | 293 | 292 | 294 | 51 |

## Table A.10e  PRS-C Composite Percentiles (continued)

| %ile | Externalizing Problems Combined | Externalizing Problems Female | Externalizing Problems Male | Internalizing Problems Combined | Internalizing Problems Female | Internalizing Problems Male | Adaptive Skills Combined | Adaptive Skills Female | Adaptive Skills Male | Behavioral Symptoms Index Combined | Behavioral Symptoms Index Female | Behavioral Symptoms Index Male | %ile |
|---|---|---|---|---|---|---|---|---|---|---|---|---|---|
| 50 | – | – | 145 | – | – | – | 254 | 256 | 252 | 292 | 291 | 293 | 50 |
| 49 | 144 | 144 | 144 | 145 | 145 | 145 | 253 | 255 | 251 | 291 | 289–290 | 292 | 49 |
| 48 | – | – | – | 144 | – | 144 | 252 | 254 | 250 | 290 | 288 | 291 | 48 |
| 47 | 143 | 143 | 143 | 144 | 144 | 143 | 251 | 252–253 | 248–249 | 289 | 287 | 290 | 47 |
| 46 | – | – | – | 143 | 143 | 143 | 249–250 | 251 | 247 | 288 | 286 | 289 | 46 |
| 45 | 142 | 142 | 142 | 143 | 142 | 142 | 248 | 250 | 246 | 287 | 285 | 288 | 45 |
| 44 | – | 141 | – | 142 | 142 | 142 | 247 | 249 | 245 | 286 | 284 | 287 | 44 |
| 43 | 141 | – | 141 | 141 | 141 | 141 | 246 | 248 | 244 | 285 | 283 | – | 43 |
| 42 | 140 | 140 | – | 141 | 141 | 141 | 245 | 247 | 243 | 284 | 282 | 286 | 42 |
| 41 | – | – | 140 | 140 | 140 | 140 | 243–244 | 245–246 | 242 | 283 | 281 | 285 | 41 |
| 40 | 139 | 139 | – | 140 | 140 | 140 | 242 | 244 | 240–241 | 282 | 280 | 284 | 40 |
| 39 | – | – | 139 | 139 | 139 | 139 | 241 | 243 | 239 | 281 | 279 | 283 | 39 |
| 38 | 138 | 138 | – | 139 | 139 | 139 | 240 | 242 | 238 | 280 | 278 | 282 | 38 |
| 37 | – | 137 | 138 | 138 | 138 | 138 | 238–239 | 240–241 | 237 | 279 | 277 | 281 | 37 |
| 36 | 137 | – | – | 138 | 138 | 138 | 237 | 239 | 236 | 278 | 276 | 280 | 36 |
| 35 | – | – | 137 | 137 | 137 | 137 | 236 | 238 | 234–235 | 277 | – | 279 | 35 |
| 34 | 136 | 136 | – | 137 | – | 137 | 234–235 | 236–237 | 233 | 276 | 275 | 278 | 34 |
| 33 | – | – | 136 | 136 | 136 | 136 | 233 | 235 | 232 | 275 | 274 | 277 | 33 |
| 32 | 135 | 135 | – | 136 | 136 | 136 | 232 | 234 | 231 | 274 | 273 | 276 | 32 |
| 31 | 134 | 134 | 135 | 135 | 135 | 135 | 230–231 | 232–233 | 229–230 | 273 | 272 | 275 | 31 |
| 30 | 134 | – | – | 135 | – | 135 | 229 | 231 | 228 | 272 | 271 | 274 | 30 |
| 29 | 133 | 133 | 134 | 134 | 134 | 134 | 227–228 | 229–230 | 227 | 271 | 270 | 273 | 29 |
| 28 | – | – | – | 134 | 133 | 134 | 226 | 228 | 225–226 | 270 | 269 | 272 | 28 |
| 27 | 132 | 132 | 133 | 133 | – | 133 | 224–225 | 226–227 | 224 | 269 | 268 | 271 | 27 |
| 26 | – | – | – | 133 | 132 | – | 223 | 225 | 222–223 | 268 | 267 | 270 | 26 |
| 25 | 131 | 131 | 132 | 132 | 131 | 132 | 221–222 | 223–224 | 221 | 267 | 266 | 269 | 25 |
| 24 | 131 | – | – | 132 | – | – | 219–220 | 222 | 219–220 | 266 | 265 | 268 | 24 |
| 23 | – | 130 | 131 | 131 | 131 | 131 | 218 | 220–221 | 218 | 265 | 264 | 267 | 23 |
| 22 | 130 | – | – | 131 | – | – | 216–217 | 218–219 | 216–217 | 264 | 263 | 266 | 22 |
| 21 | – | 129 | 130 | 130 | 130 | 131 | 214–215 | 216–217 | 215 | 263 | 262 | 265 | 21 |
| 20 | 129 | 128 | – | 130 | 129 | 130 | 212–213 | 214–215 | 213–214 | 262 | 261 | 264 | 20 |
| 19 | 128 | – | 129 | 129 | 128 | 129 | 210–211 | 212–213 | 211–212 | 261 | 260 | 263 | 19 |
| 18 | – | 127 | 128 | 128 | 127 | 129 | 209 | 210–211 | 209–210 | 260 | 259 | 262 | 18 |
| 17 | 127 | – | – | 127 | – | – | 207–208 | 208–209 | 208 | 259 | 258 | 261 | 17 |
| 16 | – | 126 | 127 | 127 | 126 | 128 | 204–206 | 206–207 | 206–207 | 258 | 257 | 260 | 16 |
| 15 | 126 | 125 | – | 126 | 125 | – | 202–203 | 204–205 | 204–205 | 257 | 256 | 259 | 15 |
| 14 | 125 | – | 126 | 125 | 124 | 126 | 200–201 | 201–203 | 202–203 | 256 | 255 | 257–258 | 14 |
| 13 | – | 124 | 125 | 125 | 124 | – | 197–199 | 199–200 | 199–201 | 254–255 | 254 | 256 | 13 |
| 12 | 124 | 123 | – | 124 | 123 | 125 | 195–196 | 196–198 | 197–198 | 253 | 253 | 255 | 12 |
| 11 | 123 | – | 124 | 124 | 122 | 125 | 192–194 | 193–195 | 195–196 | 252 | 252 | 254 | 11 |
| 10 | – | 122 | 123 | 123 | 121 | 124 | 189–191 | 190–192 | 192–194 | 250–251 | 250–251 | 252–253 | 10 |
| 9 | 122 | 121 | – | 122 | 120 | – | 186–188 | 186–189 | 189–191 | 249 | 249 | 251 | 9 |
| 8 | 121 | 120 | 122 | 121 | 119 | 123 | 183–185 | 183–185 | 186–188 | 247–248 | 248 | 249–250 | 8 |
| 7 | – | 119 | 121 | 120 | 118 | 122 | 179–182 | 179–182 | 182–185 | 246 | 246–247 | 247–248 | 7 |
| 6 | 120 | 118 | 120 | 119 | 118 | 121 | 174–178 | 174–178 | 179–181 | 244–245 | 245 | 245–246 | 6 |
| 5 | 118 | 117 | 119 | 118 | 116–117 | 120 | 170–173 | 169–173 | 174–178 | 242–243 | 243–244 | 243–244 | 5 |
| 4 | 117 | 116 | 118 | 117 | 115 | 119 | 164–169 | 162–168 | 169–173 | 240–241 | 241–242 | 241–242 | 4 |
| 3 | 116 | 114–115 | 117 | 115–116 | 113–114 | 118 | 157–163 | 154–161 | 162–168 | 237–239 | 239–240 | 238–240 | 3 |
| 2 | 114–115 | 112–113 | 115–116 | 113–114 | 111–112 | 116–117 | 147–156 | 143–153 | 153–161 | 233–236 | 236–238 | 234–237 | 2 |
| 1 | 112–113 | – | 110–114 | 106–112 | 105–110 | 107–115 | 73–146 | 59–142 | 87–152 | 228–232 | 231–235 | 224–233 | 1 |

**Table A.11a** PRS–A T Scores and Percentiles

| Raw score | Hyperactivity T | Hyperactivity %ile | Aggression T | Aggression %ile | Conduct Problems T | Conduct Problems %ile | Anxiety T | Anxiety %ile | Depression T | Depression %ile | Somatization T | Somatization %ile | Attention Problems T | Attention Problems %ile | Atypicality T | Atypicality %ile | Withdrawal T | Withdrawal %ile | Adaptability T | Adaptability %ile | Social Skills T | Social Skills %ile | Leadership T | Leadership %ile | Activities of Daily Living T | Activities of Daily Living %ile | Functional Communication T | Functional Communication %ile | Raw score |
|---|---|---|---|---|---|---|---|---|---|---|---|---|---|---|---|---|---|---|---|---|---|---|---|---|---|---|---|---|---|
| 42 | — | — | — | — | 120 | 99 | — | — | — | — | — | — | — | — | — | — | — | — | — | — | — | — | — | — | — | — | — | — | 42 |
| 41 | — | — | — | — | 120 | 99 | — | — | — | — | — | — | — | — | — | — | — | — | — | — | — | — | — | — | — | — | — | — | 41 |
| 40 | — | — | — | — | 119 | 99 | — | — | — | — | — | — | — | — | — | — | — | — | — | — | — | — | — | — | — | — | — | — | 40 |
| 39 | — | — | — | — | 117 | 99 | 96 | 99 | 110 | 99 | — | — | — | — | — | — | — | — | — | — | — | — | — | — | — | — | — | — | 39 |
| 38 | — | — | — | — | 115 | 99 | 95 | 99 | 108 | 99 | — | — | — | — | — | — | — | — | — | — | — | — | — | — | — | — | — | — | 38 |
| 37 | — | — | — | — | 113 | 99 | 93 | 99 | 106 | 99 | — | — | — | — | — | — | — | — | — | — | — | — | — | — | — | — | — | — | 37 |
| 36 | — | — | — | — | 111 | 99 | 92 | 99 | 105 | 99 | — | — | — | — | — | — | — | — | — | — | — | — | — | — | — | — | 66 | 98 | 36 |
| 35 | — | — | — | — | 109 | 99 | 90 | 99 | 103 | 99 | — | — | — | — | — | — | — | — | — | — | — | — | — | — | — | — | 64 | 95 | 35 |
| 34 | — | — | — | — | 107 | 99 | 88 | 99 | 101 | 99 | — | — | — | — | — | — | — | — | — | — | — | — | — | — | — | — | 63 | 91 | 34 |
| 33 | — | — | — | — | 105 | 99 | 87 | 99 | 99 | 99 | — | — | — | — | 108 | 99 | — | — | — | — | — | — | — | — | — | — | 61 | 87 | 33 |
| 32 | — | — | — | — | 103 | 99 | 85 | 99 | 97 | 99 | — | — | — | — | 106 | 99 | — | — | — | — | — | — | — | — | — | — | 60 | 82 | 32 |
| 31 | — | — | — | — | 101 | 99 | 84 | 99 | 96 | 99 | — | — | — | — | 104 | 99 | — | — | — | — | — | — | — | — | — | — | 58 | 77 | 31 |
| 30 | — | — | 113 | 99 | 99 | 99 | 82 | 99 | 94 | 99 | 109 | 99 | — | — | 102 | 99 | — | — | — | — | 64 | 95 | — | — | — | — | 57 | 71 | 30 |
| 29 | — | — | 111 | 99 | 97 | 99 | 80 | 99 | 92 | 99 | 107 | 99 | — | — | 100 | 99 | — | — | — | — | 62 | 91 | — | — | — | — | 55 | 65 | 29 |
| 28 | — | — | 109 | 99 | 95 | 99 | 79 | 99 | 90 | 99 | 105 | 99 | — | — | 98 | 99 | — | — | — | — | 61 | 86 | — | — | — | — | 54 | 59 | 28 |
| 27 | — | — | 106 | 99 | 93 | 99 | 77 | 98 | 88 | 98 | 102 | 99 | 84 | 99 | 96 | 99 | — | — | — | — | 59 | 81 | — | — | — | — | 52 | 54 | 27 |
| 26 | — | — | 104 | 99 | 91 | 99 | 75 | 98 | 86 | 98 | 100 | 99 | 82 | 99 | 94 | 99 | — | — | — | — | 58 | 75 | — | — | — | — | 51 | 48 | 26 |
| 25 | 98 | 99 | 102 | 99 | 90 | 99 | 74 | 97 | 85 | 97 | 98 | 99 | 80 | 99 | 92 | 99 | 95 | 99 | — | — | 56 | 69 | — | — | — | — | 49 | 43 | 25 |
| 24 | 96 | 99 | 99 | 99 | 88 | 99 | 72 | 97 | 83 | 97 | 95 | 99 | 78 | 99 | 90 | 99 | 93 | 99 | 66 | 97 | 55 | 63 | 68 | 98 | 69 | 99 | 48 | 38 | 24 |
| 23 | 93 | 99 | 97 | 98 | 86 | 99 | 71 | 96 | 81 | 96 | 93 | 99 | 76 | 99 | 88 | 99 | 91 | 99 | 64 | 93 | 53 | 57 | 66 | 96 | 67 | 97 | 46 | 33 | 23 |
| 22 | 91 | 99 | 94 | 98 | 84 | 99 | 69 | 95 | 79 | 95 | 91 | 99 | 75 | 98 | 86 | 99 | 88 | 99 | 62 | 88 | 52 | 52 | 64 | 93 | 65 | 95 | 45 | 29 | 22 |
| 21 | 88 | 99 | 92 | 98 | 82 | 99 | 67 | 94 | 77 | 94 | 88 | 99 | 73 | 98 | 84 | 98 | 86 | 99 | 60 | 83 | 50 | 46 | 62 | 89 | 62 | 90 | 43 | 25 | 21 |
| 20 | 86 | 99 | 90 | 99 | 80 | 98 | 66 | 92 | 75 | 93 | 86 | 99 | 71 | 97 | 82 | 98 | 84 | 99 | 58 | 76 | 49 | 41 | 61 | 85 | 60 | 85 | 42 | 21 | 20 |
| 19 | 83 | 99 | 87 | 99 | 78 | 98 | 64 | 91 | 74 | 92 | 84 | 99 | 69 | 96 | 80 | 98 | 81 | 99 | 56 | 69 | 47 | 36 | 59 | 79 | 58 | 78 | 40 | 18 | 19 |
| 18 | 81 | 98 | 85 | 98 | 76 | 97 | 63 | 89 | 72 | 91 | 81 | 99 | 67 | 94 | 78 | 97 | 79 | 98 | 54 | 62 | 46 | 32 | 57 | 73 | 56 | 70 | 39 | 15 | 18 |
| 17 | 78 | 98 | 83 | 98 | 74 | 97 | 61 | 86 | 70 | 89 | 79 | 98 | 66 | 92 | 76 | 97 | 77 | 98 | 52 | 55 | 44 | 28 | 55 | 67 | 54 | 62 | 37 | 12 | 17 |
| 16 | 76 | 97 | 80 | 98 | 72 | 96 | 59 | 84 | 68 | 86 | 76 | 98 | 64 | 90 | 75 | 96 | 74 | 97 | 50 | 47 | 43 | 24 | 53 | 60 | 52 | 53 | 36 | 10 | 16 |
| 15 | 73 | 97 | 78 | 97 | 70 | 95 | 58 | 80 | 66 | 83 | 74 | 97 | 62 | 87 | 73 | 95 | 72 | 96 | 48 | 41 | 41 | 20 | 52 | 54 | 49 | 44 | 34 | 8 | 15 |
| 14 | 71 | 96 | 76 | 97 | 68 | 94 | 56 | 77 | 65 | 79 | 72 | 96 | 60 | 84 | 71 | 95 | 69 | 95 | 46 | 35 | 40 | 17 | 50 | 47 | 47 | 37 | 33 | 6 | 14 |
| 13 | 68 | 94 | 73 | 96 | 66 | 93 | 54 | 72 | 63 | 75 | 69 | 95 | 58 | 80 | 69 | 94 | 67 | 94 | 45 | 29 | 38 | 14 | 48 | 41 | 45 | 29 | 31 | 5 | 13 |
| 12 | 66 | 93 | 71 | 95 | 64 | 92 | 53 | 67 | 61 | 69 | 67 | 93 | 57 | 76 | 67 | 92 | 65 | 92 | 43 | 24 | 37 | 12 | 46 | 35 | 43 | 23 | 30 | 4 | 12 |
| 11 | 63 | 90 | 68 | 94 | 62 | 90 | 51 | 62 | 59 | 63 | 65 | 91 | 55 | 71 | 65 | 90 | 62 | 89 | 41 | 19 | 35 | 10 | 44 | 29 | 41 | 18 | 28 | 3 | 11 |
| 10 | 61 | 87 | 66 | 93 | 60 | 88 | 50 | 56 | 57 | 55 | 62 | 89 | 53 | 65 | 63 | 88 | 60 | 86 | 39 | 15 | 34 | 8 | 43 | 24 | 39 | 13 | 27 | 2 | 10 |
| 9 | 58 | 83 | 64 | 92 | 58 | 86 | 48 | 49 | 55 | 45 | 60 | 86 | 51 | 60 | 61 | 86 | 58 | 82 | 37 | 11 | 32 | 6 | 41 | 19 | 36 | 10 | 26 | 1 | 9 |
| 8 | 56 | 79 | 61 | 90 | 56 | 82 | 46 | 42 | 54 | 34 | 58 | 82 | 50 | 53 | 59 | 84 | 55 | 77 | 35 | 9 | 31 | 4 | 39 | 15 | 34 | 7 | 24 | 1 | 8 |
| 7 | 53 | 72 | 59 | 87 | 54 | 78 | 45 | 34 | 52 | 22 | 55 | 77 | 48 | 47 | 57 | 80 | 53 | 70 | 33 | 6 | 29 | 3 | 37 | 11 | 32 | 5 | 23 | 1 | 7 |
| 6 | 51 | 64 | 57 | 84 | 52 | 73 | 43 | 27 | 50 | 10 | 53 | 71 | 46 | 40 | 55 | 76 | 50 | 62 | 31 | 4 | 28 | 2 | 35 | 8 | 30 | 4 | 21 | 1 | 6 |
| 5 | 48 | 54 | 54 | 80 | 50 | 66 | 42 | 20 | 48 | 1 | 51 | 63 | 44 | 32 | 53 | 71 | 48 | 53 | 29 | 3 | 26 | 2 | 33 | 6 | 28 | 2 | 20 | 1 | 5 |
| 4 | 46 | 41 | 52 | 75 | 48 | 58 | 40 | 13 | 46 | 1 | 48 | 53 | 42 | 25 | 51 | 64 | 46 | 46 | 27 | 2 | 25 | 1 | 32 | 4 | 26 | 2 | 18 | 1 | 4 |
| 3 | 43 | 26 | 50 | 67 | 46 | 46 | 38 | 8 | 44 | 1 | 46 | 42 | 41 | 19 | 49 | 53 | 44 | 29 | 25 | 1 | 23 | 1 | 30 | 2 | 24 | 1 | 17 | 1 | 3 |
| 2 | 41 | 12 | 47 | 55 | 44 | 32 | 37 | 4 | 43 | 1 | 44 | 29 | 39 | 13 | 47 | 36 | 41 | 16 | 23 | 1 | 22 | 1 | 28 | 1 | 21 | 1 | 15 | 1 | 2 |
| 1 | 38 | 2 | 45 | 35 | 42 | 15 | 35 | 1 | 41 | 1 | 41 | 15 | 37 | 7 | 45 | 7 | 39 | 5 | 21 | 1 | 20 | 1 | 26 | 1 | 19 | 1 | 14 | 1 | 1 |
| 0 | — | — | 42 | 2 | 41 | 1 | 33 | 1 | 39 | 1 | 39 | 4 | 35 | 4 | 43 | 1 | — | — | 19 | 1 | 19 | 1 | 24 | 1 | 17 | 1 | 12 | 1 | 0 |
| **Raw mean** | 4.73 | | 3.19 | | 4.84 | | 10.26 | | 6.05 | | 4.76 | | 8.26 | | 3.70 | | 4.79 | | 15.84 | | 20.74 | | 14.12 | | 15.27 | | 25.48 | | **Raw mean** |
| **Raw SD** | 3.98 | | 4.23 | | 5.10 | | 6.19 | | 5.48 | | 4.25 | | 5.59 | | 5.02 | | 4.23 | | 5.19 | | 6.62 | | 5.51 | | 4.64 | | 6.73 | | **Raw SD** |
| **T: 90% Conf. int.** | 6 | | 5 | | 5 | | 5 | | 5 | | 6 | | 5 | | 5 | | 6 | | 5 | | 5 | | 5 | | 7 | | 5 | | **T: 90% Conf. int.** |

## Table A.11b  PRS–A T Scores and Percentiles

| Raw score | Hyperactivity T | Hyperactivity %ile | Aggression T | Aggression %ile | Conduct Problems T | Conduct Problems %ile | Anxiety T | Anxiety %ile | Depression T | Depression %ile | Somatization T | Somatization %ile | Attention Problems T | Attention Problems %ile | Atypicality T | Atypicality %ile | Withdrawal T | Withdrawal %ile | Adaptability T | Adaptability %ile | Social Skills T | Social Skills %ile | Leadership T | Leadership %ile | Activities of Daily Living T | Activities of Daily Living %ile | Functional Communication T | Functional Communication %ile | Raw score |
|---|---|---|---|---|---|---|---|---|---|---|---|---|---|---|---|---|---|---|---|---|---|---|---|---|---|---|---|---|---|
| 42 | — | — | — | — | 120 | 99 | — | — | — | — | — | — | — | — | — | — | — | — | — | — | — | — | — | — | — | — | — | — | 42 |
| 41 | — | — | — | — | 120 | 99 | — | — | — | — | — | — | — | — | — | — | — | — | — | — | — | — | — | — | — | — | — | — | 41 |
| 40 | — | — | — | — | 118 | 99 | — | — | — | — | — | — | — | — | — | — | — | — | — | — | — | — | — | — | — | — | — | — | 40 |
| 39 | — | — | — | — | 116 | 99 | 96 | 99 | 111 | 99 | — | — | — | — | — | — | — | — | — | — | — | — | — | — | — | — | — | — | 39 |
| 38 | — | — | — | — | 114 | 99 | 95 | 99 | 109 | 99 | — | — | — | — | — | — | — | — | — | — | — | — | — | — | — | — | — | — | 38 |
| 37 | — | — | — | — | 112 | 99 | 93 | 99 | 107 | 99 | — | — | — | — | — | — | — | — | — | — | — | — | — | — | — | — | — | — | 37 |
| 36 | — | — | — | — | 110 | 99 | 91 | 99 | 105 | 99 | — | — | — | — | — | — | — | — | — | — | — | — | — | — | — | — | 64 | 97 | 36 |
| 35 | — | — | — | — | 108 | 99 | 90 | 99 | 104 | 99 | — | — | — | — | — | — | — | — | — | — | — | — | — | — | — | — | 63 | 92 | 35 |
| 34 | — | — | — | — | 106 | 99 | 88 | 99 | 102 | 99 | — | — | — | — | — | — | — | — | — | — | — | — | — | — | — | — | 61 | 87 | 34 |
| 33 | — | — | — | — | 105 | 99 | 86 | 99 | 100 | 99 | — | — | — | — | 108 | 99 | — | — | — | — | — | — | — | — | — | — | 60 | 81 | 33 |
| 32 | — | — | — | — | 103 | 99 | 85 | 99 | 98 | 99 | — | — | — | — | 106 | 99 | — | — | — | — | — | — | — | — | — | — | 58 | 75 | 32 |
| 31 | — | — | — | — | 101 | 99 | 83 | 99 | 96 | 99 | — | — | — | — | 104 | 99 | — | — | — | — | — | — | — | — | — | — | 57 | 69 | 31 |
| 30 | — | — | 115 | 99 | 99 | 99 | 82 | 99 | 94 | 99 | 110 | 99 | — | — | 102 | 99 | — | — | — | — | 62 | 94 | — | — | — | — | 55 | 63 | 30 |
| 29 | — | — | 113 | 99 | 97 | 99 | 80 | 99 | 92 | 99 | 108 | 99 | — | — | 100 | 99 | — | — | — | — | 61 | 87 | — | — | — | — | 54 | 57 | 29 |
| 28 | — | — | 110 | 99 | 95 | 98 | 78 | 98 | 91 | 99 | 106 | 99 | — | — | 98 | 99 | — | — | — | — | 59 | 79 | — | — | — | — | 52 | 52 | 28 |
| 27 | — | — | 108 | 99 | 93 | 98 | 77 | 98 | 89 | 99 | 103 | 99 | 88 | 99 | 96 | 99 | — | — | — | — | 57 | 72 | — | — | — | — | 51 | 47 | 27 |
| 26 | — | — | 106 | 99 | 91 | 98 | 75 | 97 | 87 | 99 | 101 | 99 | 86 | 99 | 94 | 99 | — | — | — | — | 56 | 65 | — | — | — | — | 49 | 42 | 26 |
| 25 | — | — | 103 | 99 | 89 | 97 | 74 | 97 | 85 | 99 | 98 | 99 | 84 | 99 | 92 | 99 | — | — | — | — | 54 | 58 | — | — | — | — | 48 | 37 | 25 |
| 24 | 106 | 99 | 101 | 99 | 87 | 97 | 72 | 96 | 83 | 99 | 96 | 99 | 82 | 99 | 91 | 99 | 96 | 99 | 65 | 96 | 53 | 52 | 66 | 97 | 67 | 99 | 46 | 33 | 24 |
| 23 | 103 | 99 | 98 | 99 | 86 | 97 | 70 | 96 | 81 | 98 | 94 | 99 | 80 | 99 | 89 | 99 | 94 | 99 | 63 | 92 | 51 | 46 | 64 | 94 | 65 | 96 | 45 | 29 | 23 |
| 22 | 100 | 99 | 96 | 99 | 84 | 97 | 69 | 95 | 79 | 98 | 91 | 99 | 79 | 99 | 87 | 98 | 91 | 99 | 61 | 87 | 49 | 40 | 62 | 89 | 63 | 91 | 43 | 25 | 22 |
| 21 | 97 | 99 | 93 | 99 | 82 | 96 | 67 | 93 | 78 | 97 | 89 | 99 | 77 | 99 | 85 | 98 | 89 | 99 | 59 | 80 | 48 | 36 | 60 | 84 | 60 | 84 | 42 | 22 | 21 |
| 20 | 95 | 99 | 91 | 99 | 80 | 96 | 65 | 92 | 76 | 97 | 86 | 99 | 75 | 99 | 83 | 98 | 87 | 99 | 57 | 73 | 46 | 31 | 59 | 78 | 58 | 76 | 40 | 18 | 20 |
| 19 | 92 | 99 | 89 | 99 | 78 | 95 | 64 | 89 | 74 | 97 | 84 | 99 | 73 | 99 | 81 | 98 | 84 | 99 | 55 | 65 | 45 | 27 | 57 | 72 | 56 | 68 | 38 | 16 | 19 |
| 18 | 89 | 99 | 86 | 98 | 76 | 94 | 62 | 89 | 72 | 96 | 82 | 99 | 71 | 98 | 79 | 97 | 82 | 99 | 53 | 58 | 43 | 23 | 55 | 65 | 54 | 59 | 37 | 13 | 18 |
| 17 | 86 | 99 | 84 | 98 | 74 | 94 | 61 | 87 | 70 | 95 | 79 | 98 | 69 | 96 | 77 | 97 | 80 | 98 | 51 | 50 | 41 | 20 | 53 | 58 | 51 | 51 | 35 | 10 | 17 |
| 16 | 83 | 99 | 81 | 98 | 72 | 93 | 59 | 84 | 68 | 95 | 77 | 98 | 67 | 95 | 75 | 96 | 77 | 98 | 49 | 43 | 40 | 17 | 51 | 51 | 49 | 43 | 34 | 8 | 16 |
| 15 | 80 | 99 | 79 | 97 | 70 | 92 | 57 | 81 | 67 | 94 | 74 | 97 | 65 | 93 | 73 | 96 | 75 | 97 | 47 | 36 | 38 | 14 | 49 | 44 | 47 | 35 | 32 | 6 | 15 |
| 14 | 78 | 98 | 77 | 97 | 68 | 91 | 56 | 77 | 65 | 92 | 72 | 96 | 63 | 91 | 71 | 95 | 72 | 96 | 45 | 30 | 37 | 12 | 47 | 38 | 44 | 29 | 31 | 5 | 14 |
| 13 | 75 | 97 | 74 | 96 | 67 | 89 | 54 | 73 | 63 | 91 | 70 | 95 | 62 | 88 | 69 | 94 | 70 | 95 | 43 | 24 | 35 | 10 | 46 | 32 | 42 | 23 | 29 | 3 | 13 |
| 12 | 72 | 96 | 72 | 96 | 65 | 87 | 53 | 68 | 61 | 89 | 67 | 94 | 60 | 85 | 67 | 93 | 68 | 94 | 41 | 19 | 33 | 8 | 44 | 27 | 40 | 17 | 28 | 2 | 12 |
| 11 | 69 | 95 | 69 | 95 | 63 | 85 | 51 | 62 | 59 | 87 | 65 | 92 | 58 | 82 | 65 | 92 | 65 | 92 | 39 | 15 | 32 | 5 | 42 | 22 | 38 | 13 | 26 | 1 | 11 |
| 10 | 66 | 93 | 67 | 93 | 61 | 81 | 49 | 56 | 57 | 84 | 63 | 90 | 56 | 78 | 63 | 91 | 63 | 89 | 37 | 11 | 30 | 4 | 40 | 17 | 35 | 8 | 25 | 1 | 10 |
| 9 | 63 | 91 | 65 | 91 | 59 | 77 | 48 | 49 | 55 | 80 | 60 | 87 | 54 | 74 | 61 | 90 | 60 | 86 | 35 | 8 | 29 | 3 | 38 | 14 | 33 | 6 | 23 | 1 | 9 |
| 8 | 61 | 88 | 62 | 89 | 57 | 70 | 46 | 41 | 54 | 76 | 58 | 83 | 52 | 69 | 59 | 88 | 58 | 83 | 33 | 6 | 27 | 2 | 36 | 10 | 31 | 4 | 22 | 1 | 8 |
| 7 | 58 | 83 | 60 | 87 | 55 | 59 | 44 | 33 | 52 | 70 | 55 | 78 | 50 | 63 | 57 | 86 | 56 | 78 | 30 | 4 | 25 | 1 | 34 | 8 | 28 | 2 | 20 | 1 | 7 |
| 6 | 55 | 77 | 57 | 85 | 53 | 42 | 43 | 25 | 50 | 63 | 53 | 71 | 48 | 57 | 55 | 83 | 53 | 72 | 28 | 2 | 24 | 1 | 32 | 5 | 26 | 1 | 19 | 1 | 6 |
| 5 | 52 | 68 | 55 | 83 | 51 | 8 | 41 | 17 | 48 | 55 | 51 | 63 | 46 | 50 | 53 | 79 | 51 | 65 | 26 | 1 | 22 | 1 | 31 | 4 | 24 | 1 | 17 | 1 | 5 |
| 4 | 49 | 57 | 53 | 79 | 49 | 3 | 40 | 10 | 46 | 44 | 48 | 53 | 44 | 43 | 51 | 74 | 49 | 56 | 24 | 1 | 21 | 1 | 29 | 2 | 22 | 1 | 16 | 1 | 4 |
| 3 | 46 | 44 | 50 | 71 | 48 | — | 38 | 5 | 44 | 32 | 46 | 41 | 43 | 35 | 49 | 68 | 46 | 45 | 22 | 1 | 19 | 1 | 27 | 1 | 19 | 1 | 14 | 1 | 3 |
| 2 | 43 | 29 | 48 | 59 | 46 | — | 36 | 1 | 42 | 18 | 43 | 27 | 41 | 27 | 47 | 58 | 44 | 32 | 20 | 1 | 17 | 1 | 25 | 1 | 17 | 1 | 13 | 1 | 2 |
| 1 | 41 | 14 | 45 | 37 | 44 | — | 35 | 1 | 41 | 5 | 41 | 13 | 39 | 12 | 45 | 43 | 41 | 17 | 18 | 1 | 16 | 1 | 23 | 1 | 15 | 1 | 11 | 1 | 1 |
| 0 | 38 | — | 43 | 20 | 42 | — | 33 | 1 | 39 | 1 | 39 | 3 | 37 | 5 | 43 | 13 | 39 | 5 | 16 | 1 | 14 | 1 | 21 | 1 | 12 | 1 | 10 | 1 | 0 |
| **Raw mean** | 4.25 | | 2.95 | | 4.27 | | 10.41 | | 6.09 | | 4.74 | | 6.91 | | 3.34 | | 4.60 | | 16.48 | | 22.37 | | 15.39 | | 16.43 | | 26.64 | | **Raw mean** |
| **Raw SD** | 3.53 | | 4.15 | | 5.27 | | 6.19 | | 5.40 | | 4.19 | | 5.28 | | 5.10 | | 4.20 | | 4.86 | | 6.26 | | 5.36 | | 4.37 | | 6.64 | | **Raw SD** |
| **T: 90% Conf. int.** | 6 | | 5 | | 4 | | 5 | | 5 | | 6 | | 6 | | 4 | | 6 | | 6 | | 4 | | 6 | | 8 | | 6 | | **T: 90% Conf. int.** |

**Table A.11c PRS-A T Scores and Percentiles**

| Raw score | Hyperactivity T | Hyperactivity %ile | Aggression T | Aggression %ile | Conduct Problems T | Conduct Problems %ile | Anxiety T | Anxiety %ile | Depression T | Depression %ile | Somatization T | Somatization %ile | Attention Problems T | Attention Problems %ile | Atypicality T | Atypicality %ile | Withdrawal T | Withdrawal %ile | Adaptability T | Adaptability %ile | Social Skills T | Social Skills %ile | Leadership T | Leadership %ile | Activities of Daily Living T | Activities of Daily Living %ile | Functional Communication T | Functional Communication %ile | Raw score |
|---|---|---|---|---|---|---|---|---|---|---|---|---|---|---|---|---|---|---|---|---|---|---|---|---|---|---|---|---|---|
| 42 | — | — | — | — | 120 | 99 | — | — | — | — | — | — | — | — | — | — | — | — | — | — | — | — | — | — | — | — | — | — | 42 |
| 41 | — | — | — | — | 120 | 99 | — | — | — | — | — | — | — | — | — | — | — | — | — | — | — | — | — | — | — | — | — | — | 41 |
| 40 | — | — | — | — | 120 | 99 | — | — | — | — | — | — | — | — | — | — | — | — | — | — | — | — | — | — | — | — | — | — | 40 |
| 39 | — | — | — | — | 119 | 99 | 97 | 99 | 109 | 99 | — | — | — | — | — | — | — | — | — | — | — | — | — | — | — | — | — | — | 39 |
| 38 | — | — | — | — | 117 | 99 | 95 | 99 | 107 | 99 | — | — | — | — | — | — | — | — | — | — | — | — | — | — | — | — | — | — | 38 |
| 37 | — | — | — | — | 115 | 99 | 93 | 99 | 106 | 99 | — | — | — | — | — | — | — | — | — | — | — | — | — | — | — | — | — | — | 37 |
| 36 | — | — | — | — | 113 | 99 | 92 | 99 | 104 | 99 | — | — | — | — | — | — | — | — | — | — | — | — | — | — | — | — | 68 | 99 | 36 |
| 35 | — | — | — | — | 111 | 99 | 90 | 99 | 102 | 99 | — | — | — | — | — | — | — | — | — | — | — | — | — | — | — | — | 66 | 97 | 35 |
| 34 | — | — | — | — | 109 | 99 | 89 | 99 | 100 | 99 | — | — | — | — | — | — | — | — | — | — | — | — | — | — | — | — | 65 | 95 | 34 |
| 33 | — | — | — | — | 107 | 99 | 87 | 99 | 98 | 99 | — | — | — | — | 109 | 99 | — | — | — | — | — | — | — | — | — | — | 63 | 92 | 33 |
| 32 | — | — | — | — | 105 | 99 | 85 | 99 | 97 | 99 | — | — | — | — | 107 | 99 | — | — | — | — | — | — | — | — | — | — | 62 | 88 | 32 |
| 31 | — | — | — | — | 102 | 99 | 84 | 99 | 95 | 99 | — | — | — | — | 105 | 99 | — | — | — | — | — | — | — | — | — | — | 60 | 84 | 31 |
| 30 | — | — | 112 | 99 | 100 | 99 | 82 | 99 | 93 | 99 | 108 | 99 | — | — | 103 | 99 | — | — | — | — | 67 | 97 | — | — | — | — | 59 | 78 | 30 |
| 29 | — | — | 109 | 99 | 98 | 99 | 80 | 99 | 91 | 99 | 106 | 99 | — | — | 101 | 99 | — | — | — | — | 65 | 95 | — | — | — | — | 57 | 73 | 29 |
| 28 | — | — | 107 | 99 | 96 | 99 | 79 | 99 | 89 | 99 | 104 | 99 | — | — | 99 | 99 | — | — | — | — | 64 | 92 | — | — | — | — | 56 | 67 | 28 |
| 27 | — | — | 105 | 99 | 94 | 99 | 77 | 99 | 88 | 99 | 101 | 99 | 81 | 99 | 97 | 99 | — | — | — | — | 62 | 89 | — | — | — | — | 54 | 61 | 27 |
| 26 | — | — | 103 | 99 | 92 | 99 | 76 | 99 | 86 | 99 | 99 | 99 | 79 | 99 | 95 | 99 | — | — | — | — | 60 | 84 | — | — | — | — | 53 | 55 | 26 |
| 25 | — | — | 100 | 99 | 90 | 99 | 74 | 98 | 84 | 99 | 97 | 99 | 78 | 98 | 92 | 98 | — | — | — | — | 59 | 80 | — | — | — | — | 51 | 50 | 25 |
| 24 | 93 | 99 | 98 | 99 | 88 | 99 | 72 | 97 | 82 | 99 | 94 | 99 | 76 | 98 | 90 | 98 | 95 | 99 | 66 | 97 | 57 | 75 | 71 | 99 | 71 | 99 | 50 | 44 | 24 |
| 23 | 91 | 99 | 96 | 99 | 86 | 99 | 71 | 96 | 81 | 99 | 92 | 99 | 74 | 97 | 88 | 97 | 92 | 99 | 64 | 94 | 56 | 69 | 69 | 98 | 69 | 99 | 48 | 39 | 23 |
| 22 | 89 | 99 | 93 | 99 | 84 | 99 | 69 | 95 | 79 | 99 | 90 | 99 | 72 | 95 | 86 | 96 | 90 | 99 | 62 | 90 | 54 | 63 | 67 | 97 | 67 | 98 | 47 | 34 | 22 |
| 21 | 86 | 99 | 91 | 99 | 82 | 99 | 68 | 94 | 77 | 98 | 88 | 99 | 70 | 94 | 84 | 95 | 88 | 99 | 61 | 85 | 53 | 58 | 65 | 94 | 65 | 95 | 45 | 29 | 21 |
| 20 | 84 | 99 | 89 | 99 | 80 | 98 | 66 | 92 | 75 | 97 | 85 | 99 | 69 | 92 | 82 | 94 | 85 | 99 | 59 | 79 | 51 | 52 | 63 | 91 | 63 | 91 | 44 | 25 | 20 |
| 19 | 82 | 99 | 86 | 99 | 78 | 98 | 64 | 90 | 73 | 96 | 83 | 99 | 67 | 89 | 80 | 92 | 83 | 99 | 57 | 72 | 50 | 46 | 61 | 87 | 61 | 86 | 42 | 21 | 19 |
| 18 | 80 | 98 | 84 | 99 | 76 | 97 | 63 | 88 | 72 | 95 | 81 | 99 | 65 | 86 | 78 | 90 | 81 | 99 | 55 | 65 | 48 | 41 | 60 | 82 | 58 | 79 | 40 | 18 | 18 |
| 17 | 77 | 98 | 82 | 98 | 74 | 97 | 61 | 86 | 70 | 94 | 78 | 99 | 63 | 83 | 76 | 89 | 78 | 99 | 53 | 59 | 47 | 36 | 58 | 76 | 56 | 72 | 39 | 15 | 17 |
| 16 | 75 | 97 | 79 | 98 | 72 | 96 | 59 | 83 | 68 | 93 | 76 | 98 | 61 | 79 | 74 | 87 | 76 | 98 | 51 | 52 | 45 | 31 | 56 | 70 | 54 | 63 | 37 | 12 | 16 |
| 15 | 73 | 96 | 77 | 97 | 70 | 95 | 58 | 80 | 66 | 92 | 74 | 97 | 60 | 74 | 72 | 85 | 73 | 97 | 50 | 45 | 44 | 27 | 54 | 63 | 52 | 54 | 36 | 10 | 15 |
| 14 | 70 | 95 | 75 | 97 | 68 | 93 | 56 | 76 | 64 | 91 | 71 | 96 | 58 | 69 | 70 | 82 | 71 | 96 | 48 | 39 | 42 | 22 | 52 | 56 | 50 | 45 | 34 | 8 | 14 |
| 13 | 68 | 94 | 72 | 96 | 66 | 92 | 55 | 71 | 63 | 89 | 69 | 94 | 56 | 63 | 68 | 80 | 69 | 95 | 46 | 33 | 41 | 19 | 50 | 50 | 48 | 37 | 33 | 6 | 13 |
| 12 | 66 | 92 | 70 | 95 | 64 | 90 | 53 | 67 | 61 | 87 | 67 | 93 | 54 | 57 | 66 | 78 | 66 | 93 | 44 | 28 | 39 | 15 | 48 | 43 | 45 | 30 | 31 | 5 | 12 |
| 11 | 63 | 90 | 68 | 93 | 61 | 88 | 51 | 61 | 59 | 84 | 64 | 91 | 52 | 50 | 64 | 74 | 64 | 91 | 42 | 23 | 38 | 13 | 47 | 37 | 43 | 23 | 30 | 4 | 11 |
| 10 | 61 | 87 | 65 | 92 | 59 | 85 | 50 | 55 | 57 | 81 | 62 | 88 | 51 | 43 | 62 | 72 | 62 | 88 | 40 | 18 | 36 | 10 | 45 | 30 | 41 | 18 | 28 | 3 | 10 |
| 9 | 59 | 84 | 63 | 90 | 57 | 81 | 48 | 49 | 55 | 78 | 60 | 85 | 49 | 36 | 60 | 68 | 59 | 85 | 39 | 15 | 35 | 8 | 43 | 25 | 39 | 13 | 27 | 2 | 9 |
| 8 | 56 | 80 | 61 | 88 | 55 | 77 | 47 | 42 | 54 | 74 | 57 | 81 | 47 | 29 | 58 | 64 | 57 | 80 | 37 | 11 | 33 | 6 | 41 | 20 | 37 | 10 | 25 | 1 | 8 |
| 7 | 54 | 75 | 58 | 85 | 53 | 72 | 45 | 36 | 52 | 69 | 55 | 76 | 45 | 22 | 56 | 60 | 55 | 75 | 35 | 8 | 32 | 5 | 39 | 15 | 35 | 7 | 24 | 1 | 7 |
| 6 | 52 | 68 | 56 | 82 | 51 | 66 | 43 | 29 | 50 | 63 | 53 | 70 | 44 | 16 | 54 | 54 | 52 | 68 | 33 | 6 | 30 | 3 | 37 | 11 | 32 | 5 | 22 | 1 | 6 |
| 5 | 49 | 60 | 54 | 78 | 49 | 59 | 42 | 22 | 48 | 56 | 51 | 63 | 42 | 11 | 52 | 49 | 50 | 59 | 31 | 4 | 29 | 2 | 35 | 8 | 30 | 4 | 21 | 1 | 5 |
| 4 | 47 | 50 | 51 | 73 | 47 | 50 | 40 | 16 | 46 | 48 | 48 | 54 | 40 | 7 | 50 | 44 | 48 | 49 | 29 | 3 | 27 | 2 | 34 | 6 | 28 | 3 | 19 | 1 | 4 |
| 3 | 45 | 38 | 49 | 65 | 45 | 42 | 39 | 10 | 45 | 38 | 46 | 43 | 38 | 4 | 48 | 38 | 45 | 38 | 28 | 2 | 26 | 1 | 32 | 4 | 26 | 2 | 18 | 1 | 3 |
| 2 | 43 | 24 | 47 | 54 | 43 | 27 | 37 | 6 | 43 | 25 | 44 | 31 | 36 | 2 | 46 | 31 | 43 | 25 | 26 | 1 | 24 | 1 | 30 | 2 | 24 | 1 | 16 | 1 | 2 |
| 1 | 40 | 9 | 44 | 35 | 41 | 13 | 35 | 2 | 41 | 12 | 41 | 17 | 35 | 1 | 44 | 24 | 41 | 14 | 24 | 1 | 23 | 1 | 28 | 1 | 22 | 1 | 15 | 1 | 1 |
| 0 | 38 | 1 | 42 | 1 | 39 | 3 | 34 | 1 | 39 | 1 | 39 | 5 | 33 | 1 | 42 | 16 | 38 | 5 | 22 | 1 | 21 | 1 | 26 | 1 | 20 | 1 | 13 | 1 | 0 |
| **Raw mean** | 5.22 | | 3.42 | | 5.40 | | 10.12 | | 6.01 | | 4.78 | | 9.62 | | 4.06 | | 4.99 | | 15.19 | | 19.10 | | 12.86 | | 14.11 | | 24.32 | | **Raw mean** |
| **Raw SD** | 4.33 | | 4.30 | | 4.88 | | 6.20 | | 5.57 | | 4.32 | | 5.59 | | 4.93 | | 4.26 | | 5.45 | | 6.59 | | 5.38 | | 4.63 | | 6.65 | | **Raw SD** |
| **T: 90% Conf. int.** | 5 | | 6 | | 6 | | 5 | | 5 | | 6 | | 5 | | 5 | | 6 | | 5 | | 5 | | 5 | | 7 | | 5 | | **T: 90% Conf. int.** |

**Table A.11d** PRS–A Composite *T* Scores

| T score | Externalizing Problems Combined | Externalizing Problems Female | Externalizing Problems Male | Internalizing Problems Combined | Internalizing Problems Female | Internalizing Problems Male | Adaptive Skills Combined | Adaptive Skills Female | Adaptive Skills Male | Behavioral Symptoms Index Combined | Behavioral Symptoms Index Female | Behavioral Symptoms Index Male | T score |
|---|---|---|---|---|---|---|---|---|---|---|---|---|---|
| 120 | — | — | — | — | — | — | — | — | — | — | — | — | 120 |
| 119 | — | — | — | — | — | — | — | — | — | — | — | — | 119 |
| 118 | — | 339–341 | — | — | — | — | — | — | — | — | — | — | 118 |
| 117 | — | 337–338 | — | — | — | — | — | — | — | — | — | — | 117 |
| 116 | — | 334–336 | — | — | — | — | — | — | — | — | — | — | 116 |
| 115 | 331 | 331–333 | — | — | — | — | — | — | — | — | 622–624 | — | 115 |
| 114 | 328–330 | 328–330 | — | — | 317 | — | — | — | — | — | 617–621 | — | 114 |
| 113 | 326–327 | 325–327 | — | 314–315 | 315–316 | 313–314 | — | — | — | — | 612–616 | — | 113 |
| 112 | 323–325 | 323–324 | 323–325 | 311–313 | 312–314 | 311–312 | — | — | — | 605–608 | 607–611 | — | 112 |
| 111 | 320–322 | 320–322 | 320–322 | 308–310 | 309–311 | 308–310 | — | — | — | 600–604 | 602–606 | 599 | 111 |
| 110 | 317–319 | 317–319 | 317–319 | 306–307 | 307–308 | 305–307 | — | — | — | 595–599 | 597–601 | 594–598 | 110 |
| 109 | 314–316 | 314–316 | 315–316 | 303–305 | 304–306 | 303–304 | — | — | — | 590–594 | 592–596 | 589–593 | 109 |
| 108 | 312–313 | 311–313 | 312–314 | 301–302 | 301–303 | 300–302 | — | — | — | 585–589 | 587–591 | 584–588 | 108 |
| 107 | 309–311 | 309–311 | 309–311 | 298–300 | 299–300 | 298–299 | — | — | — | 580–584 | 582–586 | 579–583 | 107 |
| 106 | 306–308 | 306–308 | 306–308 | 295–297 | 296–298 | 295–297 | — | — | — | 575–579 | 577–581 | 574–578 | 106 |
| 105 | 303–305 | 303–305 | 303–305 | 293–294 | 294–295 | 292–294 | — | — | — | 570–574 | 572–576 | 569–573 | 105 |
| 104 | 300–302 | 300–302 | 301–302 | 290–292 | 291–293 | 290–291 | — | — | — | 566–569 | 567–571 | 564–568 | 104 |
| 103 | 298–299 | 297–299 | 298–300 | 288–289 | 288–290 | 287–289 | — | — | — | 561–565 | 562–566 | 560–563 | 103 |
| 102 | 295–297 | 295–296 | 295–297 | 285–287 | 286–287 | 285–286 | — | — | — | 556–560 | 557–561 | 555–559 | 102 |
| 101 | 292–294 | 292–294 | 292–294 | 282–284 | 283–285 | 282–284 | — | — | — | 551–555 | 552–556 | 550–554 | 101 |
| 100 | 289–291 | 289–291 | 289–291 | 280–281 | 280–282 | 279–281 | — | — | — | 546–550 | 547–551 | 545–549 | 100 |
| 99 | 286–288 | 286–288 | 286–288 | 277–279 | 278–279 | 277–278 | — | — | — | 541–545 | 542–546 | 540–544 | 99 |
| 98 | 284–285 | 283–285 | 284–285 | 275–276 | 275–277 | 274–276 | — | — | — | 536–540 | 537–541 | 535–539 | 98 |
| 97 | 281–283 | 281–283 | 281–283 | 272–274 | 273–274 | 272–273 | — | — | — | 531–535 | 532–536 | 530–534 | 97 |
| 96 | 278–280 | 278–280 | 278–280 | 269–271 | 270–272 | 269–271 | — | — | — | 526–530 | 527–531 | 525–529 | 96 |
| 95 | 275–277 | 275–277 | 275–277 | 267–268 | 267–269 | 266–268 | — | — | — | 521–525 | 522–526 | 520–524 | 95 |
| 94 | 272–274 | 272–274 | 272–274 | 264–266 | 265–266 | 264–265 | — | — | — | 516–520 | 517–521 | 515–519 | 94 |
| 93 | 270–271 | 269–271 | 270–271 | 261–263 | 262–264 | 261–263 | — | — | — | 511–515 | 512–516 | 510–514 | 93 |
| 92 | 267–269 | 267–268 | 267–269 | 259–260 | 259–261 | 259–260 | — | — | — | 506–510 | 507–511 | 505–509 | 92 |
| 91 | 264–266 | 264–266 | 264–266 | 256–258 | 257–258 | 256–258 | — | — | — | 501–505 | 502–506 | 500–504 | 91 |
| 90 | 261–263 | 261–263 | 261–263 | 254–255 | 254–256 | 253–255 | — | — | — | 496–500 | 497–501 | 495–499 | 90 |
| 89 | 258–260 | 258–260 | 258–260 | 251–253 | 252–253 | 251–252 | — | — | — | 491–495 | 492–496 | 490–494 | 89 |
| 88 | 256–257 | 255–257 | 256–257 | 248–250 | 249–251 | 248–250 | — | — | — | 486–490 | 487–491 | 486–489 | 88 |
| 87 | 253–255 | 253–254 | 253–255 | 246–247 | 246–248 | 246–247 | — | — | — | 481–485 | 482–486 | 481–485 | 87 |
| 86 | 250–252 | 250–252 | 250–252 | 243–245 | 244–245 | 243–245 | — | — | — | 476–480 | 477–481 | 476–480 | 86 |
| 85 | 247–249 | 247–249 | 247–249 | 241–242 | 241–243 | 240–242 | — | — | — | 472–475 | 472–476 | 471–475 | 85 |
| 84 | 244–246 | 244–246 | 244–246 | 238–240 | 238–240 | 238–239 | — | — | — | 467–471 | 467–471 | 466–470 | 84 |
| 83 | 242–243 | 241–243 | 242–243 | 235–237 | 236–237 | 235–237 | — | — | — | 462–466 | 462–466 | 461–465 | 83 |
| 82 | 239–241 | 239–240 | 239–241 | 233–234 | 233–235 | 233–234 | — | — | — | 457–461 | 457–461 | 456–460 | 82 |
| 81 | 236–238 | 236–238 | 236–238 | 230–232 | 231–232 | 230–232 | — | — | — | 452–456 | 452–456 | 451–455 | 81 |
| 80 | 233–235 | 233–235 | 233–235 | 228–229 | 228–230 | 227–229 | — | — | — | 447–451 | 447–451 | 446–450 | 80 |
| 79 | 230–232 | 230–232 | 230–232 | 225–227 | 225–227 | 225–226 | — | — | — | 442–446 | 442–446 | 441–445 | 79 |
| 78 | 227–229 | 227–229 | 228–229 | 222–224 | 223–224 | 222–224 | — | — | — | 437–441 | 437–441 | 436–440 | 78 |
| 77 | 225–226 | 225–226 | 225–227 | 220–221 | 220–222 | 220–221 | — | — | — | 432–436 | 432–436 | 431–435 | 77 |
| 76 | 222–224 | 222–224 | 222–224 | 217–219 | 217–219 | 217–219 | — | — | — | 427–431 | 427–431 | 426–430 | 76 |
| 75 | 219–221 | 219–221 | 219–221 | 215–216 | 215–216 | 214–216 | — | — | — | 422–426 | 422–426 | 421–425 | 75 |
| 74 | 216–218 | 216–218 | 216–218 | 212–214 | 212–214 | 212–213 | — | — | — | 417–421 | 417–421 | 416–420 | 74 |
| 73 | 213–215 | 213–215 | 213–215 | 209–211 | 210–211 | 209–211 | — | — | — | 412–416 | 412–416 | 412–415 | 73 |
| 72 | 211–212 | 211–212 | 211–212 | 207–208 | 207–209 | 206–208 | — | — | 340–343 | 407–411 | 407–411 | 407–411 | 72 |
| 71 | 208–210 | 208–210 | 208–210 | 204–206 | 204–206 | 204–205 | — | — | 336–339 | 402–406 | 402–406 | 402–406 | 71 |
| 70 | 205–207 | 205–207 | 205–207 | 201–203 | 202–203 | 201–203 | 332–333 | — | 332–335 | 397–401 | 397–401 | 397–401 | 70 |
| 69 | 202–204 | 202–204 | 202–204 | 199–200 | 199–201 | 199–200 | 328–331 | — | 327–331 | 392–396 | 392–396 | 392–396 | 69 |
| 68 | 199–201 | 199–201 | 199–201 | 196–198 | 196–198 | 196–198 | 323–327 | 323–324 | 323–326 | 387–391 | 387–391 | 387–391 | 68 |
| 67 | 197–198 | 197–198 | 197–198 | 194–195 | 194–195 | 193–195 | 319–322 | 319–322 | 319–322 | 382–386 | 382–386 | 382–386 | 67 |
| 66 | 194–196 | 194–196 | 194–196 | 191–193 | 191–193 | 191–192 | — | — | — | 378–381 | 377–381 | 377–381 | 66 |

**Table A.11d** PRS–A Composite T Scores *(continued)*

| T score | Externalizing Problems | | | Internalizing Problems | | | Adaptive Skills | | | Behavioral Symptoms Index | | | T score |
| --- | --- | --- | --- | --- | --- | --- | --- | --- | --- | --- | --- | --- | --- |
| | Combined | Female | Male | Combined | Female | Male | Combined | Female | Male | Combined | Female | Male | |
| 65 | 191–193 | 191–193 | 191–193 | 188–190 | 189–190 | 188–190 | 314–318 | 314–318 | 314–318 | 373–377 | 372–376 | 372–376 | 65 |
| 64 | 188–190 | 188–190 | 188–190 | 186–187 | 186–188 | 186–187 | 310–313 | 310–313 | 310–313 | 368–372 | 367–371 | 367–371 | 64 |
| 63 | 185–187 | 185–187 | 185–187 | 183–185 | 183–185 | 183–185 | 306–309 | 306–309 | 305–309 | 363–367 | 362–366 | 362–366 | 63 |
| 62 | 183–184 | 183–184 | 183–184 | 181–182 | 181–182 | 180–182 | 301–305 | 301–305 | 301–305 | 358–362 | 357–361 | 357–361 | 62 |
| 61 | 180–182 | 180–182 | 180–182 | 178–180 | 178–180 | 178–179 | 297–300 | 297–300 | 297–300 | 353–357 | 353–356 | 352–356 | 61 |
| 60 | 177–179 | 177–179 | 177–179 | 175–177 | 175–177 | 175–177 | 292–296 | 292–296 | 292–296 | 348–352 | 348–352 | 347–351 | 60 |
| 59 | 174–176 | 174–176 | 174–176 | 173–174 | 173–174 | 173–174 | 288–291 | 288–291 | 288–291 | 343–347 | 343–347 | 342–346 | 59 |
| 58 | 171–173 | 171–173 | 171–173 | 170–172 | 170–172 | 170–172 | 283–287 | 284–287 | 283–287 | 338–342 | 338–342 | 338–341 | 58 |
| 57 | 169–170 | 169–170 | 169–170 | 168–169 | 168–169 | 167–169 | 279–282 | 279–283 | 279–282 | 333–337 | 333–337 | 333–337 | 57 |
| 56 | 166–168 | 166–168 | 166–168 | 165–167 | 165–167 | 165–166 | 275–278 | 275–278 | 275–278 | 328–332 | 328–332 | 328–332 | 56 |
| 55 | 163–165 | 163–165 | 163–165 | 162–164 | 162–164 | 162–164 | 270–274 | 270–274 | 270–274 | 323–327 | 323–327 | 323–327 | 55 |
| 54 | 160–162 | 160–162 | 160–162 | 160–161 | 160–161 | 160–161 | 266–269 | 266–269 | 266–269 | 318–322 | 318–322 | 318–322 | 54 |
| 53 | 157–159 | 157–159 | 157–159 | 157–159 | 157–159 | 157–159 | 261–265 | 261–265 | 262–265 | 313–317 | 313–317 | 313–317 | 53 |
| 52 | 155–156 | 155–156 | 155–156 | 155–156 | 154–156 | 154–156 | 257–260 | 257–260 | 257–261 | 308–312 | 308–312 | 308–312 | 52 |
| 51 | 152–154 | 152–154 | 152–154 | 152–154 | 152–153 | 152–153 | 253–256 | 253–256 | 253–256 | 303–307 | 303–307 | 303–307 | 51 |
| 50 | 149–151 | 149–151 | 149–151 | 149–151 | 149–151 | 149–151 | 248–252 | 248–252 | 248–252 | 298–302 | 298–302 | 298–302 | 50 |
| 49 | 146–148 | 146–148 | 146–148 | 147–148 | 147–148 | 147–148 | 244–247 | 244–247 | 244–247 | 293–297 | 293–297 | 293–297 | 49 |
| 48 | 143–145 | 143–145 | 143–145 | 144–146 | 144–146 | 144–146 | 239–243 | 239–243 | 240–243 | 288–292 | 288–292 | 288–292 | 48 |
| 47 | 140–142 | 141–142 | 140–142 | 141–143 | 141–143 | 141–143 | 235–238 | 235–238 | 235–239 | 284–287 | 283–287 | 283–287 | 47 |
| 46 | 138–139 | 138–140 | 138–139 | 139–140 | 139–140 | 139–140 | 230–234 | 231–234 | 231–234 | 279–283 | 278–282 | 278–282 | 46 |
| 45 | 135–137 | 135–137 | 135–137 | 136–138 | 136–138 | 136–138 | 226–229 | 226–230 | 227–230 | 274–278 | 273–277 | 273–277 | 45 |
| 44 | 132–134 | 132–134 | 132–134 | 134–135 | 133–135 | 134–135 | 222–225 | 222–225 | 222–226 | 269–273 | 268–272 | 268–272 | 44 |
| 43 | 129–131 | 129–131 | 129–131 | 131–133 | 131–132 | 131–133 | 217–221 | 217–221 | 218–221 | 264–268 | 263–267 | 264–267 | 43 |
| 42 | 126–128 | 127–128 | 126–128 | 128–130 | 128–130 | 128–130 | 213–216 | 213–216 | 213–217 | 259–263 | 258–262 | 259–263 | 42 |
| 41 | 121–125 | 124–126 | 124–125 | 126–127 | 126–127 | 126–127 | 209–212 | 209–212 | 209–212 | 254–258 | 253–257 | 254–258 | 41 |
| 40 | — | 123 | 121–123 | 123–125 | 123–125 | 123–125 | 204–207 | 204–208 | 205–208 | 249–253 | 248–252 | 249–253 | 40 |
| 39 | — | — | 119–120 | 121–122 | 120–122 | 121–122 | 199–203 | 200–203 | 200–204 | 244–248 | 243–247 | 244–248 | 39 |
| 38 | — | — | — | 118–120 | 118–119 | 118–120 | 195–198 | 195–199 | 196–199 | 239–243 | 239–242 | 239–243 | 38 |
| 37 | — | — | — | 115–117 | 115–117 | 115–117 | 191–194 | 191–194 | 191–195 | 236–238 | — | 234–238 | 37 |
| 36 | — | — | — | 113–114 | 112–114 | 113–114 | 186–190 | 186–190 | 187–190 | — | — | 232–233 | 36 |
| 35 | — | — | — | 111–112 | 111 | 112 | 182–185 | 182–185 | 183–186 | — | — | — | 35 |
| 34 | — | — | — | — | — | — | 177–181 | 178–181 | 178–182 | — | — | — | 34 |
| 33 | — | — | — | — | — | — | 173–176 | 173–177 | 174–177 | — | — | — | 33 |
| 32 | — | — | — | — | — | — | 168–172 | 169–172 | 170–173 | — | — | — | 32 |
| 31 | — | — | — | — | — | — | 164–167 | 164–168 | 165–169 | — | — | — | 31 |
| 30 | — | — | — | — | — | — | 160–163 | 160–163 | 161–164 | — | — | — | 30 |
| 29 | — | — | — | — | — | — | 155–159 | 156–159 | 156–160 | — | — | — | 29 |
| 28 | — | — | — | — | — | — | 151–154 | 152–155 | 152–155 | — | — | — | 28 |
| 27 | — | — | — | — | — | — | 146–150 | 147–150 | 148–151 | — | — | — | 27 |
| 26 | — | — | — | — | — | — | 142–145 | 142–146 | 143–147 | — | — | — | 26 |
| 25 | — | — | — | — | — | — | 138–141 | 138–141 | 139–142 | — | — | — | 25 |
| 24 | — | — | — | — | — | — | 133–137 | 134–137 | 135–138 | — | — | — | 24 |
| 23 | — | — | — | — | — | — | 129–132 | 129–133 | 130–134 | — | — | — | 23 |
| 22 | — | — | — | — | — | — | 124–128 | 125–128 | 126–129 | — | — | — | 22 |
| 21 | — | — | — | — | — | — | 120–123 | 120–124 | 121–125 | — | — | — | 21 |
| 20 | — | — | — | — | — | — | 115–119 | 116–119 | 117–120 | — | — | — | 20 |
| 19 | — | — | — | — | — | — | 111–114 | 111–115 | 113–116 | — | — | — | 19 |
| 18 | — | — | — | — | — | — | 107–110 | 107–110 | 108–112 | — | — | — | 18 |
| 17 | — | — | — | — | — | — | 102–106 | 103–106 | 104–107 | — | — | — | 17 |
| 16 | — | — | — | — | — | — | 98–101 | 98–102 | 102–103 | — | — | — | 16 |
| 15 | — | — | — | — | — | — | 93–97 | 94–97 | — | — | — | — | 15 |
| 14 | — | — | — | — | — | — | 91–92 | 89–93 | — | — | — | — | 14 |
| 13 | — | — | — | — | — | — | — | 85–88 | — | — | — | — | 13 |
| 12 | — | — | — | — | — | — | — | 81–84 | — | — | — | — | 12 |
| 11 | — | — | — | — | — | — | — | 76–80 | — | — | — | — | 11 |
| 10 | — | — | — | — | — | — | — | 73–75 | — | — | — | — | 10 |
| **T: 90% Conf. int.** | 3 | 3 | 3 | 4 | 4 | 4 | 3 | 3 | 3 | 3 | 3 | 3 | **T: 90% Conf. int.** |

## Table A.11e  PRS–A Composite Percentiles

| %ile | Externalizing Problems | | | Internalizing Problems | | | Adaptive Skills | | | Behavioral Symptoms Index | | | %ile |
|---|---|---|---|---|---|---|---|---|---|---|---|---|---|
| | Combined | Female | Male | Combined | Female | Male | Combined | Female | Male | Combined | Female | Male | |
| 99 | 248–331 | 251–341 | 244–325 | 230–315 | 234–317 | 228–314 | 326–333 | 320–324 | 326–343 | 462–608 | 464–624 | 460–599 | 99 |
| 98 | 230–247 | 230–250 | 231–243 | 217–229 | 220–233 | 217–227 | 322–325 | 317–319 | 321–325 | 436–461 | 435–463 | 436–459 | 98 |
| 97 | 218–229 | 217–229 | 222–230 | 209–216 | 211–219 | 210–216 | 318–321 | 314–316 | 318–320 | 419–435 | 417–434 | 420–435 | 97 |
| 96 | 210–217 | 208–216 | 215–221 | 203–208 | 204–210 | 204–209 | 315–317 | 312–313 | 315–317 | 406–418 | 404–416 | 407–419 | 96 |
| 95 | 203–209 | 201–207 | 209–214 | 198–202 | 199–203 | 200–203 | 313–314 | 311 | 312–314 | 395–405 | 393–403 | 397–406 | 95 |
| 94 | 198–202 | 195–200 | 203–208 | 194–197 | 194–198 | 196–199 | 311–312 | 309–310 | 310–311 | 387–394 | 384–392 | 389–396 | 94 |
| 93 | 193–197 | 190–194 | 199–202 | 191–193 | 191–193 | 193–195 | 309–310 | 307–308 | 308–309 | 379–386 | 377–383 | 381–388 | 93 |
| 92 | 190–192 | 186–189 | 195–198 | 188–190 | 188–190 | 190–192 | 307–308 | 306 | 306–307 | 373–378 | 370–376 | 375–380 | 92 |
| 91 | 186–189 | 182–185 | 191–194 | 185–187 | 185–187 | 187–189 | 305–306 | 304–305 | 304–305 | 367–372 | 365–369 | 369–374 | 91 |
| 90 | 183–185 | 179–181 | 188–190 | 183–184 | 182–184 | 185–186 | 303–304 | 303 | 302–303 | 362–366 | 360–364 | 364–368 | 90 |
| 89 | 180–182 | 177–178 | 185–187 | 181–182 | 180–181 | 182–184 | 302 | 302 | 301 | 357–361 | 355–359 | 360–363 | 89 |
| 88 | 178–179 | 174–176 | 182–184 | 179–180 | 178–179 | 180–181 | 300–301 | 300–301 | 299–300 | 353–356 | 351–354 | 355–359 | 88 |
| 87 | 175–177 | 172–173 | 180–181 | 177–178 | 176–177 | 179 | 298–299 | 299 | 298 | 349–352 | 347–350 | 351–354 | 87 |
| 86 | 173–174 | 170–171 | 177–179 | 175–176 | 175 | 177–178 | 297 | 298 | 296–297 | 346–348 | 343–346 | 348–350 | 86 |
| 85 | 171–172 | 168–169 | 175–176 | 174 | 173–174 | 175–176 | 296 | 297 | 295 | 342–345 | 340–342 | 344–347 | 85 |
| 84 | 170 | 166–167 | 173–174 | 172–173 | 171–172 | 174 | 294–295 | 295–296 | 293–294 | 339–341 | 337–339 | 341–343 | 84 |
| 83 | 168–169 | 165 | 171–172 | 171 | 170 | 172–173 | 293 | 294 | 292 | 336–338 | 334–336 | 338–340 | 83 |
| 82 | 166–167 | 163–164 | 169–170 | 169–170 | 169 | 171 | 291–292 | 293 | 291 | 334–335 | 332–333 | 335–337 | 82 |
| 81 | 165 | 162 | 168 | 168 | 167–168 | 169–170 | 290 | 292 | 290 | 331–333 | 329–331 | 333–334 | 81 |
| 80 | 164 | 161 | 166–167 | 167 | 166 | 168 | 289 | 291 | 288–289 | 328–330 | 327–328 | 330–332 | 80 |
| 79 | 162–163 | 159–160 | 164–165 | 166 | 165 | 167 | 288 | 289–290 | 287 | 326–327 | 324–326 | 328–329 | 79 |
| 78 | 161 | 158 | 163 | 165 | 164 | 166 | 286–287 | 288 | 286 | 324–325 | 322–323 | 325–327 | 78 |
| 77 | 160 | 157 | 162 | 164 | 163 | 165 | 285 | 287 | 285 | 322–323 | 320–321 | 323–324 | 77 |
| 76 | 159 | 156 | 160–161 | 163 | 162 | 164 | 284 | 286 | 284 | 320–321 | 318–319 | 321–322 | 76 |
| 75 | 158 | 155 | 159 | 162 | 161 | 163 | 283 | 285 | 282–283 | 318–319 | 316–317 | 319–320 | 75 |
| 74 | 157 | 154 | 158 | 161 | 160 | 162 | 282 | 284 | 281 | 316–317 | 315 | 317–318 | 74 |
| 73 | 156 | – | 157 | 160 | 159 | 161 | 280–281 | 283 | 280 | 314–315 | 313–314 | 315–316 | 73 |
| 72 | 155 | 153 | 156 | 159 | 158 | 160 | 279 | 281–282 | 279 | 312–313 | 311–312 | 313–314 | 72 |
| 71 | 154 | 152 | 155 | 158 | 157 | 159 | 278 | 280 | 278 | 311 | 310 | 312 | 71 |
| 70 | 153 | 151 | 154 | 157 | – | 158 | 277 | 279 | 277 | 309–310 | 308–309 | 310–311 | 70 |
| 69 | 152 | – | 153 | 156 | 156 | 157 | 276 | 278 | 276 | 308 | 307 | 309 | 69 |
| 68 | – | 150 | 152 | – | 155 | 156 | 275 | 277 | 275 | 306–307 | 305–306 | 307–308 | 68 |
| 67 | 151 | 149 | 151 | 155 | 154 | – | 274 | 276 | 273–274 | 305 | 304 | 305–306 | 67 |
| 66 | 150 | – | 150 | 154 | – | 155 | 272–273 | 275 | 272 | 303–304 | 302–303 | 304 | 66 |
| 65 | 149 | 148 | 149 | – | 153 | 154 | 271 | 274 | 271 | 302 | 301 | 303 | 65 |
| 64 | – | 147 | – | 153 | 152 | 153 | 270 | 272–273 | 270 | 301 | 300 | 301–302 | 64 |
| 63 | 148 | – | 148 | 152 | – | 152 | 269 | 271 | 269 | 299–300 | 299 | 300 | 63 |
| 62 | 147 | 146 | 147 | 151 | 151 | – | 268 | 270 | 268 | 298 | 297–298 | 299 | 62 |
| 61 | – | – | 146 | – | 150 | 151 | 267 | 269 | 267 | 297 | 296 | 297–298 | 61 |
| 60 | 146 | 145 | – | 150 | – | 150 | 266 | 268 | 266 | 296 | 295 | 296 | 60 |
| 59 | – | – | 145 | – | 149 | – | 265 | 267 | 265 | 295 | 294 | 295 | 59 |
| 58 | 145 | 144 | 144 | 149 | 148 | 149 | 263–264 | 265–266 | 264 | 294 | 293 | 294 | 58 |
| 57 | – | – | – | 148 | – | 148 | 262 | 264 | 263 | 292–293 | 292 | 293 | 57 |
| 56 | 144 | 143 | 143 | – | 147 | – | 261 | 263 | 262 | 291 | 291 | 291–292 | 56 |
| 55 | – | – | – | 147 | – | 147 | 260 | 262 | 260–261 | 290 | 290 | 290 | 55 |
| 54 | 143 | – | 142 | – | 146 | 146 | 259 | 261 | 259 | 289 | 289 | 289 | 54 |
| 53 | – | 142 | 141 | 146 | – | – | 258 | 259–260 | 258 | 288 | 288 | 288 | 53 |
| 52 | 142 | – | – | 145 | 145 | 145 | 257 | 258 | 257 | 287 | 287 | 287 | 52 |
| 51 | – | 141 | 140 | – | – | – | 256 | 257 | 256 | 286 | 286 | 286 | 51 |

**Table A.11e** PRS–A Composite Percentiles (continued)

| %ile | Externalizing Problems | | | Internalizing Problems | | | Adaptive Skills | | | Behavioral Symptoms Index | | | %ile |
|---|---|---|---|---|---|---|---|---|---|---|---|---|---|
| | Combined | Female | Male | Combined | Female | Male | Combined | Female | Male | Combined | Female | Male | |
| 50 | 141 | – | – | 144 | 144 | 144 | 254–255 | 256 | 255 | 285 | 285 | 285 | 50 |
| 49 | – | – | 139 | – | – | – | 253 | 255 | 254 | – | 284 | 284 | 49 |
| 48 | 140 | 140 | – | 143 | 143 | 143 | 252 | 253–254 | 253 | 284 | 283 | 283 | 48 |
| 47 | – | – | – | – | – | 142 | 251 | 252 | 251–252 | 283 | 282 | – | 47 |
| 46 | 139 | – | 138 | 142 | 142 | – | 250 | 251 | 250 | 282 | 281 | 282 | 46 |
| 45 | – | 139 | – | 141 | – | 141 | 248–249 | 249–250 | 249 | 281 | – | 281 | 45 |
| 44 | – | – | 137 | – | 141 | – | 247 | 248 | 248 | 280 | 280 | 280 | 44 |
| 43 | 138 | 138 | – | 140 | – | 140 | 246 | 247 | 247 | 279 | 279 | 279 | 43 |
| 42 | – | – | 136 | – | 140 | – | 245 | 245–246 | 246 | – | 278 | 278 | 42 |
| 41 | 137 | – | – | – | – | 139 | 244 | 244 | 244–245 | 278 | 277 | 277 | 41 |
| 40 | – | – | – | 139 | 139 | – | 242–243 | 243 | 243 | 277 | – | – | 40 |
| 39 | – | 137 | 135 | 138 | – | 138 | 241 | 241–242 | 242 | 276 | 276 | 276 | 39 |
| 38 | 136 | – | – | – | 138 | – | 240 | 240 | 241 | 275 | 275 | 275 | 38 |
| 37 | – | – | 134 | – | – | 137 | 238–239 | 238–239 | 239–240 | 274 | 274 | 274 | 37 |
| 36 | – | – | – | 137 | 137 | – | 237 | 237 | 238 | – | – | 273 | 36 |
| 35 | 135 | 136 | – | – | – | 136 | 236 | 236 | 237 | 273 | 273 | – | 35 |
| 34 | – | – | 133 | 136 | 136 | – | 234–235 | 234–235 | 236 | 272 | 272 | 272 | 34 |
| 33 | – | – | – | – | – | 135 | 233 | 233 | 234–235 | – | 271 | 271 | 33 |
| 32 | 134 | – | – | 135 | 135 | – | 232 | 231–232 | 233 | 271 | – | 270 | 32 |
| 31 | – | 135 | 132 | – | – | 134 | 230–231 | 229–230 | 231–232 | 270 | 270 | – | 31 |
| 30 | – | – | – | 134 | 134 | 133 | 229 | 228 | 230 | 269 | – | 269 | 30 |
| 29 | 133 | – | – | – | – | – | 227–228 | 226–227 | 229 | 268 | 269 | 268 | 29 |
| 28 | – | – | – | 133 | – | 132 | 226 | 225 | 227–228 | – | 268 | – | 28 |
| 27 | 132 | 134 | 131 | – | – | – | 224–225 | 223–224 | 225–226 | 267 | 267 | 267 | 27 |
| 26 | – | – | – | 132 | 133 | – | 222–223 | 221–222 | 224 | 266 | – | 266 | 26 |
| 25 | – | – | – | – | – | 131 | 221 | 219–220 | 222–223 | 265 | 266 | 265 | 25 |
| 24 | – | – | 130 | 131 | 132 | – | 219–220 | 218 | 221 | 264 | 265 | 264 | 24 |
| 23 | – | 133 | – | – | – | 130 | 217–218 | 216–217 | 219–220 | 263 | – | 263 | 23 |
| 22 | 131 | – | – | 130 | 131 | – | 216 | 214–215 | 217–218 | – | 264 | – | 22 |
| 21 | – | – | – | – | – | 129 | 214–215 | 212–213 | 215–216 | 262 | 263 | 262 | 21 |
| 20 | 130 | – | 129 | – | – | – | 212–213 | 210–211 | 214 | 261 | – | 261 | 20 |
| 19 | – | – | – | 129 | 130 | 128 | 210–211 | 208–209 | 212–213 | 260 | 262 | – | 19 |
| 18 | – | – | – | – | – | – | 208–209 | 206–207 | 210–211 | – | 261 | 260 | 18 |
| 17 | – | 132 | – | 128 | 129 | 127 | 206–207 | 203–205 | 207–209 | 259 | 260 | 259 | 17 |
| 16 | – | – | 128 | – | – | – | 204–205 | 201–202 | 205–206 | 258 | 259 | – | 16 |
| 15 | 129 | – | – | 127 | 128 | 126 | 201–203 | 199–200 | 203–204 | – | – | 258 | 15 |
| 14 | – | – | – | – | – | – | 199–200 | 196–198 | 201–202 | 257 | 258 | 257 | 14 |
| 13 | – | – | 127 | 126 | 127 | 125 | 196–198 | 194–195 | 198–200 | 256 | 257 | – | 13 |
| 12 | 128 | 131 | – | 125 | – | 124 | 194–195 | 191–193 | 195–197 | – | 256 | 256 | 12 |
| 11 | – | – | – | – | 126 | – | 191–193 | 188–190 | 192–194 | 255 | – | – | 11 |
| 10 | – | – | – | 124 | – | 123 | 188–190 | 185–187 | 189–191 | 254 | 255 | 255 | 10 |
| 9 | – | – | – | – | 125 | – | 184–187 | 182–184 | 186–188 | – | 254 | 254 | 9 |
| 8 | 127 | – | 126 | 123 | 124 | 122 | 181–183 | 178–181 | 182–185 | 253 | 253 | – | 8 |
| 7 | – | 130 | – | 122 | – | 121 | 177–180 | 175–177 | 178–181 | – | 252 | 253 | 7 |
| 6 | 126 | – | – | – | 123 | – | 172–176 | 171–174 | 173–177 | – | 251 | 252 | 6 |
| 5 | – | – | – | 121 | 122 | 120 | 167–171 | 166–170 | 168–172 | 252 | 250 | 251 | 5 |
| 4 | 125 | – | 125 | 120 | – | 119 | 161–166 | 161–165 | 161–167 | 251 | 249 | 250 | 4 |
| 3 | – | 129 | – | 118–119 | 121 | 118 | 153–160 | 154–160 | 153–160 | 250 | 248 | 249 | 3 |
| 2 | – | – | – | 117 | 119–120 | 116–117 | 142–152 | 146–153 | 141–152 | 248–249 | – | 248 | 2 |
| 1 | 121–124 | 123–128 | 119–124 | 111–116 | 111–118 | 112–115 | 91–141 | 73–145 | 102–140 | 236–247 | 239–247 | 232–247 | 1 |

## Table A.12a PRS–A *T* Scores and Percentiles

| Raw score | Hyperactivity | | Aggression | | Conduct Problems | | Anxiety | | Depression | | Somatization | | Attention Problems | | Atypicality | | Withdrawal | | Adaptability | | Social Skills | | Leadership | | Activities of Daily Living | | Functional Communication | | Raw score |
|---|---|---|---|---|---|---|---|---|---|---|---|---|---|---|---|---|---|---|---|---|---|---|---|---|---|---|---|---|---|
| | *T* | %ile | *T* | %ile | *T* | %ile | *T* | %ile | *T* | %ile | *T* | %ile | *T* | %ile | *T* | %ile | *T* | %ile | *T* | %ile | *T* | %ile | *T* | %ile | *T* | %ile | *T* | %ile | |
| 42 | — | — | — | — | 113 | 99 | — | — | — | — | — | — | — | — | — | — | — | — | — | — | — | — | — | — | — | — | — | — | 42 |
| 41 | — | — | — | — | 112 | 99 | — | — | — | — | — | — | — | — | — | — | — | — | — | — | — | — | — | — | — | — | — | — | 41 |
| 40 | — | — | — | — | 110 | 99 | — | — | — | — | — | — | — | — | — | — | — | — | — | — | — | — | — | — | — | — | — | — | 40 |
| 39 | — | — | — | — | 108 | 99 | 96 | 99 | 104 | 99 | — | — | — | — | — | — | — | — | — | — | — | — | — | — | — | — | — | — | 39 |
| 38 | — | — | — | — | 106 | 99 | 94 | 99 | 102 | 99 | — | — | — | — | — | — | — | — | — | — | — | — | — | — | — | — | — | — | 38 |
| 37 | — | — | — | — | 105 | 99 | 93 | 99 | 100 | 99 | — | — | — | — | — | — | — | — | — | — | — | — | — | — | — | — | — | — | 37 |
| 36 | — | — | — | — | 103 | 99 | 91 | 99 | 99 | 99 | — | — | — | — | — | — | — | — | — | — | — | — | — | — | — | — | 66 | 99 | 36 |
| 35 | — | — | — | — | 101 | 99 | 89 | 99 | 97 | 99 | — | — | — | — | — | — | — | — | — | — | — | — | — | — | — | — | 65 | 98 | 35 |
| 34 | — | — | — | — | 99 | 99 | 88 | 99 | 95 | 99 | — | — | — | — | — | — | — | — | — | — | — | — | — | — | — | — | 63 | 94 | 34 |
| 33 | — | — | — | — | 98 | 99 | 86 | 99 | 94 | 99 | — | — | — | — | 103 | 99 | — | — | — | — | — | — | — | — | — | — | 62 | 90 | 33 |
| 32 | — | — | — | — | 96 | 99 | 85 | 99 | 92 | 99 | — | — | — | — | 101 | 99 | — | — | — | — | — | — | — | — | — | — | 60 | 84 | 32 |
| 31 | — | — | — | — | 94 | 99 | 83 | 99 | 90 | 99 | — | — | — | — | 99 | 99 | — | — | — | — | — | — | — | — | — | — | 59 | 78 | 31 |
| 30 | — | — | 111 | 99 | 93 | 99 | 81 | 99 | 89 | 99 | 105 | 99 | — | — | 97 | 99 | — | — | — | — | 66 | 99 | — | — | — | — | 57 | 72 | 30 |
| 29 | — | — | 109 | 99 | 91 | 99 | 80 | 99 | 87 | 99 | 103 | 99 | — | — | 95 | 99 | — | — | — | — | 64 | 95 | — | — | — | — | 56 | 65 | 29 |
| 28 | — | — | 107 | 99 | 89 | 99 | 78 | 98 | 86 | 99 | 101 | 99 | — | — | 94 | 99 | — | — | — | — | 62 | 91 | — | — | — | — | 54 | 59 | 28 |
| 27 | — | — | 104 | 99 | 87 | 99 | 77 | 98 | 84 | 98 | 98 | 99 | 85 | 99 | 92 | 99 | — | — | — | — | 61 | 85 | — | — | — | — | 52 | 53 | 27 |
| 26 | — | — | 102 | 99 | 86 | 99 | 75 | 98 | 82 | 98 | 96 | 99 | 83 | 99 | 90 | 99 | — | — | — | — | 59 | 79 | — | — | — | — | 51 | 47 | 26 |
| 25 | — | — | 100 | 99 | 84 | 98 | 73 | 97 | 81 | 98 | 94 | 99 | 81 | 99 | 88 | 99 | — | — | — | — | 57 | 72 | — | — | — | — | 49 | 42 | 25 |
| 24 | 99 | 99 | 98 | 99 | 82 | 98 | 72 | 96 | 79 | 98 | 92 | 99 | 79 | 99 | 86 | 99 | 91 | 99 | 66 | 97 | 56 | 66 | 68 | 99 | 68 | 98 | 48 | 37 | 24 |
| 23 | 97 | 99 | 95 | 99 | 81 | 98 | 70 | 96 | 77 | 97 | 89 | 99 | 77 | 99 | 84 | 98 | 88 | 99 | 64 | 93 | 54 | 59 | 66 | 97 | 66 | 96 | 46 | 32 | 23 |
| 22 | 94 | 99 | 93 | 99 | 79 | 98 | 69 | 95 | 76 | 97 | 87 | 99 | 75 | 99 | 83 | 98 | 86 | 99 | 62 | 88 | 52 | 53 | 65 | 94 | 64 | 92 | 45 | 28 | 22 |
| 21 | 92 | 99 | 91 | 99 | 77 | 97 | 67 | 93 | 74 | 96 | 85 | 99 | 74 | 98 | 81 | 98 | 84 | 99 | 60 | 82 | 51 | 47 | 63 | 90 | 61 | 87 | 43 | 24 | 21 |
| 20 | 89 | 99 | 88 | 99 | 75 | 97 | 65 | 92 | 72 | 96 | 83 | 99 | 72 | 98 | 79 | 97 | 82 | 99 | 58 | 76 | 49 | 42 | 61 | 85 | 59 | 81 | 41 | 20 | 20 |
| 19 | 87 | 99 | 86 | 98 | 74 | 96 | 64 | 90 | 71 | 95 | 81 | 98 | 70 | 97 | 77 | 97 | 80 | 99 | 56 | 69 | 47 | 37 | 59 | 79 | 57 | 73 | 40 | 17 | 19 |
| 18 | 84 | 99 | 84 | 98 | 72 | 96 | 62 | 88 | 69 | 95 | 78 | 98 | 68 | 95 | 75 | 97 | 77 | 98 | 54 | 62 | 46 | 32 | 57 | 73 | 55 | 65 | 38 | 14 | 18 |
| 17 | 82 | 99 | 81 | 98 | 70 | 95 | 61 | 86 | 68 | 94 | 76 | 98 | 66 | 93 | 73 | 96 | 75 | 98 | 52 | 55 | 44 | 27 | 55 | 67 | 53 | 57 | 37 | 12 | 17 |
| 16 | 79 | 98 | 79 | 97 | 68 | 94 | 59 | 83 | 66 | 93 | 74 | 97 | 64 | 91 | 72 | 95 | 73 | 97 | 50 | 48 | 42 | 23 | 53 | 60 | 50 | 49 | 35 | 9 | 16 |
| 15 | 77 | 98 | 77 | 97 | 67 | 94 | 57 | 80 | 64 | 92 | 72 | 96 | 62 | 88 | 70 | 95 | 71 | 96 | 48 | 41 | 41 | 19 | 52 | 53 | 48 | 41 | 34 | 7 | 15 |
| 14 | 74 | 97 | 75 | 96 | 65 | 93 | 56 | 76 | 63 | 90 | 70 | 95 | 61 | 84 | 68 | 94 | 69 | 94 | 46 | 35 | 39 | 16 | 50 | 47 | 46 | 34 | 32 | 6 | 14 |
| 13 | 72 | 96 | 72 | 96 | 63 | 91 | 54 | 72 | 61 | 89 | 67 | 94 | 59 | 80 | 66 | 93 | 67 | 92 | 44 | 29 | 37 | 13 | 48 | 40 | 44 | 27 | 30 | 4 | 13 |
| 12 | 69 | 95 | 70 | 95 | 62 | 90 | 53 | 66 | 59 | 87 | 65 | 92 | 57 | 75 | 64 | 91 | 64 | 90 | 42 | 24 | 36 | 11 | 46 | 34 | 42 | 21 | 29 | 3 | 12 |
| 11 | 67 | 93 | 68 | 94 | 60 | 88 | 51 | 61 | 58 | 84 | 63 | 90 | 55 | 70 | 62 | 90 | 62 | 87 | 40 | 19 | 34 | 8 | 44 | 28 | 40 | 16 | 27 | 2 | 11 |
| 10 | 64 | 91 | 65 | 93 | 58 | 86 | 49 | 54 | 56 | 82 | 61 | 87 | 53 | 64 | 61 | 88 | 60 | 84 | 38 | 14 | 32 | 6 | 42 | 23 | 37 | 12 | 26 | 2 | 10 |
| 9 | 62 | 88 | 63 | 91 | 56 | 83 | 48 | 47 | 54 | 78 | 59 | 84 | 51 | 58 | 59 | 86 | 58 | 80 | 36 | 11 | 31 | 5 | 40 | 19 | 35 | 8 | 24 | 1 | 9 |
| 8 | 59 | 85 | 61 | 89 | 55 | 80 | 46 | 40 | 53 | 74 | 56 | 80 | 49 | 51 | 57 | 84 | 56 | 75 | 34 | 8 | 29 | 3 | 39 | 14 | 33 | 6 | 23 | 1 | 8 |
| 7 | 57 | 81 | 58 | 87 | 53 | 76 | 45 | 32 | 51 | 69 | 54 | 74 | 47 | 44 | 55 | 80 | 53 | 70 | 32 | 5 | 28 | 2 | 37 | 11 | 31 | 4 | 21 | 1 | 7 |
| 6 | 54 | 75 | 56 | 83 | 51 | 71 | 43 | 25 | 49 | 63 | 52 | 67 | 46 | 37 | 53 | 77 | 51 | 63 | 30 | 3 | 26 | 1 | 35 | 8 | 29 | 2 | 20 | 1 | 6 |
| 5 | 52 | 68 | 54 | 79 | 49 | 64 | 41 | 17 | 48 | 56 | 50 | 59 | 44 | 30 | 51 | 72 | 49 | 55 | 28 | 2 | 24 | 1 | 33 | 6 | 27 | 1 | 18 | 1 | 5 |
| 4 | 49 | 58 | 51 | 73 | 48 | 56 | 40 | 11 | 46 | 47 | 47 | 49 | 42 | 23 | 50 | 65 | 47 | 47 | 26 | 1 | 23 | 1 | 31 | 4 | 24 | 1 | 16 | 1 | 4 |
| 3 | 47 | 47 | 49 | 65 | 46 | 45 | 38 | 6 | 45 | 35 | 45 | 37 | 40 | 17 | 48 | 57 | 45 | 37 | 24 | 1 | 21 | 1 | 29 | 2 | 22 | 1 | 15 | 1 | 3 |
| 2 | 44 | 32 | 47 | 53 | 44 | 31 | 37 | 3 | 43 | 21 | 43 | 25 | 38 | 11 | 46 | 46 | 43 | 26 | 22 | 1 | 19 | 1 | 27 | 1 | 20 | 1 | 13 | 1 | 2 |
| 1 | 42 | 17 | 45 | 33 | 43 | 14 | 35 | 1 | 41 | 6 | 41 | 13 | 36 | 7 | 44 | 30 | 40 | 16 | 20 | 1 | 18 | 1 | 26 | 1 | 18 | 1 | 12 | 1 | 1 |
| 0 | 39 | 3 | 42 | 2 | 41 | 1 | 33 | 1 | 40 | 2 | 39 | 4 | 34 | 3 | 42 | 9 | 38 | 6 | 18 | 1 | 16 | 1 | 24 | 1 | 16 | 1 | 10 | 1 | 0 |
| **Raw mean** | 4.37 | | 3.35 | | 5.34 | | 10.43 | | 6.31 | | 5.15 | | 8.36 | | 4.24 | | 5.40 | | 15.89 | | 20.59 | | 14.14 | | 15.78 | | 25.48 | | **Raw mean** |
| **Raw *SD*** | 3.98 | | 4.34 | | 5.79 | | 6.25 | | 6.10 | | 4.52 | | 5.35 | | 5.45 | | 4.59 | | 5.02 | | 6.04 | | 5.38 | | 4.60 | | 6.39 | | **Raw *SD*** |
| ***T*: 90% Conf. int.** | 6 | | 5 | | 5 | | 5 | | 4 | | 5 | | 6 | | 5 | | 6 | | 5 | | 5 | | 6 | | 7 | | 6 | | ***T*: 90% Conf. int.** |

## Table A.12b PRS-A T Scores and Percentiles

| Raw score | Hyperactivity T | Hyperactivity %ile | Aggression T | Aggression %ile | Conduct Problems T | Conduct Problems %ile | Anxiety T | Anxiety %ile | Depression T | Depression %ile | Somatization T | Somatization %ile | Attention Problems T | Attention Problems %ile | Atypicality T | Atypicality %ile | Withdrawal T | Withdrawal %ile | Adaptability T | Adaptability %ile | Social Skills T | Social Skills %ile | Leadership T | Leadership %ile | Activities of Daily Living T | Activities of Daily Living %ile | Functional Communication T | Functional Communication %ile | Raw score |
|---|---|---|---|---|---|---|---|---|---|---|---|---|---|---|---|---|---|---|---|---|---|---|---|---|---|---|---|---|---|
| 42 | — | — | — | — | 103 | 99 | — | — | — | — | — | — | — | — | — | — | — | — | — | — | — | — | — | — | — | — | — | — | 42 |
| 41 | — | — | — | — | 102 | 99 | — | — | — | — | — | — | — | — | — | — | — | — | — | — | — | — | — | — | — | — | — | — | 41 |
| 40 | — | — | — | — | 100 | 99 | — | — | 94 | 99 | — | — | — | — | — | — | — | — | — | — | — | — | — | — | — | — | — | — | 40 |
| 39 | — | — | — | — | 99 | 99 | 92 | 99 | 93 | 99 | — | — | — | — | — | — | — | — | — | — | — | — | — | — | — | — | — | — | 39 |
| 38 | — | — | — | — | 97 | 99 | 90 | 99 | 91 | 99 | — | — | — | — | — | — | — | — | — | — | — | — | — | — | — | — | — | — | 38 |
| 37 | — | — | — | — | 96 | 99 | 89 | 99 | 90 | 99 | — | — | — | — | — | — | — | — | — | — | — | — | — | — | — | — | — | — | 37 |
| 36 | — | — | — | — | 94 | 99 | 87 | 99 | 88 | 99 | — | — | — | — | — | — | — | — | — | — | — | — | — | — | — | — | 66 | 99 | 36 |
| 35 | — | — | — | — | 93 | 99 | 85 | 99 | 87 | 99 | — | — | — | — | — | — | — | — | — | — | — | — | — | — | — | — | 64 | 97 | 35 |
| 34 | — | — | — | — | 92 | 99 | 84 | 99 | 86 | 99 | — | — | — | — | — | — | — | — | — | — | — | — | — | — | — | — | 63 | 93 | 34 |
| 33 | — | — | — | — | 90 | 99 | 82 | 99 | 84 | 98 | — | — | — | — | 95 | 99 | — | — | — | — | — | — | — | — | — | — | 61 | 87 | 33 |
| 32 | — | — | — | — | 89 | 99 | 81 | 99 | 83 | 98 | — | — | — | — | 94 | 99 | — | — | — | — | — | — | — | — | — | — | 60 | 81 | 32 |
| 31 | — | — | — | — | 87 | 98 | 79 | 98 | 81 | 98 | — | — | — | — | 92 | 99 | — | — | — | — | — | — | — | — | — | — | 58 | 75 | 31 |
| 30 | — | — | 100 | 99 | 86 | 98 | 78 | 98 | 80 | 98 | 96 | 99 | 87 | 99 | 90 | 99 | — | — | — | — | 65 | 99 | — | — | — | — | 56 | 68 | 30 |
| 29 | — | — | 98 | 99 | 84 | 98 | 76 | 98 | 79 | 97 | 94 | 99 | 85 | 99 | 89 | 99 | — | — | — | — | 63 | 93 | — | — | — | — | 55 | 62 | 29 |
| 28 | — | — | 97 | 99 | 83 | 98 | 75 | 97 | 77 | 97 | 92 | 99 | 83 | 99 | 87 | 99 | — | — | — | — | 62 | 87 | — | — | — | — | 53 | 56 | 28 |
| 27 | — | — | 95 | 99 | 81 | 98 | 73 | 97 | 76 | 97 | 90 | 99 | 81 | 99 | 86 | 98 | — | — | — | — | 60 | 80 | — | — | — | — | 52 | 50 | 27 |
| 26 | — | — | 93 | 99 | 80 | 97 | 72 | 96 | 74 | 96 | 88 | 99 | 79 | 99 | 84 | 98 | — | — | — | — | 58 | 73 | — | — | — | — | 50 | 45 | 26 |
| 25 | — | — | 91 | 99 | 79 | 97 | 70 | 95 | 73 | 96 | 86 | 99 | 77 | 99 | 82 | 98 | — | — | — | — | 56 | 67 | — | — | — | — | 49 | 40 | 25 |
| 24 | 95 | 99 | 89 | 99 | 77 | 97 | 69 | 94 | 72 | 95 | 84 | 99 | 75 | 99 | 81 | 98 | 89 | 99 | 67 | 99 | 54 | 60 | 68 | 99 | 67 | 99 | 47 | 35 | 24 |
| 23 | 93 | 99 | 87 | 99 | 76 | 96 | 67 | 93 | 70 | 95 | 83 | 98 | 74 | 98 | 79 | 97 | 87 | 99 | 65 | 95 | 53 | 54 | 66 | 97 | 65 | 96 | 45 | 31 | 23 |
| 22 | 91 | 99 | 85 | 98 | 74 | 96 | 65 | 92 | 69 | 94 | 81 | 98 | 72 | 97 | 78 | 97 | 85 | 99 | 63 | 91 | 51 | 48 | 64 | 93 | 63 | 91 | 44 | 27 | 22 |
| 21 | 88 | 99 | 83 | 98 | 73 | 96 | 64 | 91 | 67 | 93 | 79 | 98 | 70 | 96 | 76 | 97 | 83 | 99 | 61 | 83 | 49 | 43 | 62 | 88 | 61 | 84 | 42 | 23 | 21 |
| 20 | 86 | 99 | 81 | 97 | 71 | 95 | 62 | 89 | 66 | 92 | 77 | 98 | 68 | 95 | 74 | 96 | 81 | 99 | 59 | 77 | 47 | 38 | 60 | 82 | 58 | 77 | 41 | 19 | 20 |
| 19 | 84 | 99 | 79 | 97 | 70 | 95 | 61 | 87 | 65 | 91 | 75 | 97 | 66 | 93 | 73 | 96 | 79 | 99 | 57 | 70 | 46 | 33 | 58 | 76 | 56 | 68 | 39 | 16 | 19 |
| 18 | 81 | 98 | 77 | 97 | 68 | 94 | 59 | 85 | 63 | 90 | 73 | 96 | 64 | 90 | 71 | 95 | 77 | 98 | 55 | 64 | 44 | 28 | 56 | 69 | 54 | 60 | 38 | 13 | 18 |
| 17 | 79 | 98 | 75 | 96 | 67 | 93 | 58 | 82 | 62 | 89 | 71 | 96 | 62 | 87 | 69 | 94 | 74 | 97 | 53 | 57 | 42 | 24 | 55 | 63 | 51 | 51 | 36 | 11 | 17 |
| 16 | 77 | 97 | 74 | 96 | 65 | 93 | 56 | 79 | 60 | 88 | 69 | 95 | 60 | 83 | 68 | 93 | 72 | 97 | 51 | 51 | 40 | 20 | 53 | 56 | 49 | 43 | 34 | 9 | 16 |
| 15 | 75 | 97 | 72 | 95 | 64 | 92 | 55 | 75 | 59 | 86 | 67 | 93 | 58 | 79 | 66 | 93 | 70 | 95 | 49 | 45 | 39 | 16 | 51 | 50 | 47 | 36 | 33 | 7 | 15 |
| 14 | 72 | 96 | 70 | 94 | 62 | 91 | 53 | 71 | 57 | 84 | 65 | 92 | 56 | 74 | 65 | 92 | 68 | 94 | 47 | 38 | 37 | 13 | 49 | 44 | 44 | 29 | 31 | 5 | 14 |
| 13 | 70 | 95 | 68 | 94 | 61 | 90 | 52 | 66 | 56 | 82 | 63 | 90 | 54 | 69 | 63 | 91 | 66 | 92 | 45 | 33 | 35 | 10 | 47 | 38 | 42 | 23 | 30 | 4 | 13 |
| 12 | 68 | 93 | 66 | 93 | 60 | 89 | 50 | 60 | 55 | 79 | 61 | 88 | 53 | 63 | 62 | 89 | 64 | 90 | 43 | 27 | 33 | 7 | 45 | 31 | 40 | 18 | 28 | 3 | 12 |
| 11 | 65 | 92 | 64 | 92 | 58 | 87 | 49 | 54 | 53 | 76 | 59 | 86 | 51 | 56 | 60 | 88 | 62 | 87 | 40 | 21 | 31 | 5 | 43 | 27 | 38 | 13 | 26 | 2 | 11 |
| 10 | 63 | 90 | 62 | 90 | 57 | 85 | 47 | 47 | 52 | 73 | 58 | 83 | 49 | 49 | 58 | 86 | 60 | 83 | 38 | 16 | 30 | 3 | 41 | 22 | 35 | 9 | 25 | 1 | 10 |
| 9 | 61 | 87 | 60 | 89 | 55 | 83 | 45 | 39 | 50 | 68 | 56 | 79 | 47 | 42 | 57 | 84 | 57 | 79 | 36 | 11 | 28 | 1 | 39 | 17 | 33 | 6 | 23 | 1 | 9 |
| 8 | 58 | 84 | 58 | 87 | 54 | 81 | 44 | 31 | 49 | 63 | 54 | 74 | 45 | 35 | 55 | 81 | 55 | 75 | 34 | 7 | 26 | 1 | 38 | 13 | 31 | 4 | 22 | 1 | 8 |
| 7 | 56 | 80 | 56 | 85 | 52 | 78 | 42 | 23 | 48 | 57 | 52 | 69 | 43 | 27 | 54 | 78 | 53 | 69 | 32 | 3 | 24 | 1 | 36 | 10 | 28 | 2 | 20 | 1 | 7 |
| 6 | 54 | 75 | 54 | 82 | 51 | 74 | 41 | 15 | 46 | 49 | 50 | 62 | 41 | 20 | 52 | 74 | 51 | 62 | 30 | 1 | 23 | 1 | 34 | 7 | 26 | 1 | 19 | 1 | 6 |
| 5 | 51 | 68 | 52 | 78 | 50 | 69 | 39 | 9 | 45 | 38 | 48 | 54 | 39 | 14 | 50 | 70 | 49 | 55 | 28 | 1 | 21 | 1 | 32 | 4 | 24 | 1 | 17 | 1 | 5 |
| 4 | 49 | 60 | 50 | 74 | 48 | 63 | 38 | 3 | 43 | 25 | 46 | 44 | 37 | 9 | 49 | 64 | 47 | 46 | 24 | 1 | 19 | 1 | 30 | 3 | 21 | 1 | 15 | 1 | 4 |
| 3 | 47 | 49 | 49 | 67 | 47 | 54 | 36 | 1 | 42 | 8 | 44 | 32 | 35 | 5 | 47 | 56 | 45 | 36 | 22 | 1 | 17 | 1 | 28 | 1 | 19 | 1 | 14 | 1 | 3 |
| 2 | 45 | 36 | 47 | 55 | 45 | 40 | 35 | 1 | 41 | 3 | 42 | 20 | — | — | 45 | 45 | 43 | 26 | 20 | 1 | 16 | 1 | 26 | 1 | 17 | 1 | 12 | 1 | 2 |
| 1 | 42 | 20 | 45 | 34 | 44 | 15 | 33 | 1 | 39 | 1 | 40 | 8 | — | — | 44 | 28 | 40 | 16 | 18 | 1 | 14 | 1 | 24 | 1 | 15 | 1 | 11 | 1 | 1 |
| 0 | 40 | 5 | 43 | 18 | 42 | 6 | 32 | 1 | — | — | 38 | 1 | — | — | 42 | 3 | 38 | 7 | — | — | 12 | 1 | 23 | 1 | 12 | 1 | 10 | 1 | 0 |
| **Raw mean** | 4.36 | | 3.75 | | 5.31 | | 11.96 | | 7.67 | | 6.09 | | 7.65 | | 4.82 | | 5.49 | | 15.67 | | 21.49 | | 14.59 | | 16.42 | | 25.93 | | **Raw mean** |
| **Raw SD** | 4.34 | | 5.21 | | 6.90 | | 6.50 | | 7.12 | | 5.20 | | 5.25 | | 6.22 | | 4.70 | | 4.90 | | 5.66 | | 5.32 | | 4.35 | | 6.35 | | **Raw SD** |
| **T: 90% Conf. int.** | 5 | | 4 | | 4 | | 5 | | 4 | | 5 | | 6 | | 4 | | 6 | | 6 | | 5 | | 6 | | 8 | | 6 | | **T: 90% Conf. int.** |

## Table A.12c  PRS–A T Scores and Percentiles

| Raw score | Hyperactivity T | Hyperactivity %ile | Aggression T | Aggression %ile | Conduct Problems T | Conduct Problems %ile | Anxiety T | Anxiety %ile | Depression T | Depression %ile | Somatization T | Somatization %ile | Attention Problems T | Attention Problems %ile | Atypicality T | Atypicality %ile | Withdrawal T | Withdrawal %ile | Adaptability T | Adaptability %ile | Social Skills T | Social Skills %ile | Leadership T | Leadership %ile | Activities of Daily Living T | Activities of Daily Living %ile | Functional Communication T | Functional Communication %ile | Raw score |
|---|---|---|---|---|---|---|---|---|---|---|---|---|---|---|---|---|---|---|---|---|---|---|---|---|---|---|---|---|---|
| 42 | — | — | — | — | — | — | — | — | — | — | — | — | — | — | — | — | — | — | — | — | — | — | — | — | — | — | — | — | 42 |
| 41 | — | — | — | — | — | — | — | — | — | — | — | — | — | — | — | — | — | — | — | — | — | — | — | — | — | — | — | — | 41 |
| 40 | — | — | — | — | 120 | 99 | — | — | — | — | — | — | — | — | — | — | — | — | — | — | — | — | — | — | — | — | — | — | 40 |
| 39 | — | — | — | — | 120 | 99 | 104 | 99 | 120 | 99 | — | — | — | — | — | — | — | — | — | — | — | — | — | — | — | — | — | — | 39 |
| 38 | — | — | — | — | 120 | 99 | 102 | 99 | 120 | 99 | — | — | — | — | — | — | — | — | — | — | — | — | — | — | — | — | — | — | 38 |
| 37 | — | — | — | — | 120 | 99 | 100 | 99 | 120 | 99 | — | — | — | — | — | — | — | — | — | — | — | — | — | — | — | — | — | — | 37 |
| 36 | — | — | — | — | 120 | 99 | 98 | 99 | 119 | 99 | — | — | — | — | — | — | — | — | — | — | — | — | — | — | — | — | 67 | 99 | 36 |
| 35 | — | — | — | — | 119 | 99 | 96 | 99 | 117 | 99 | — | — | — | — | — | — | — | — | — | — | — | — | — | — | — | — | 66 | 98 | 35 |
| 34 | — | — | — | — | 117 | 99 | 95 | 99 | 115 | 99 | — | — | — | — | 115 | 99 | — | — | — | — | — | — | — | — | — | — | 64 | 95 | 34 |
| 33 | — | — | — | — | 115 | 99 | 93 | 99 | 112 | 99 | — | — | — | — | 113 | 99 | — | — | — | — | — | — | — | — | — | — | 62 | 92 | 33 |
| 32 | — | — | — | — | 112 | 99 | 91 | 99 | 110 | 99 | — | — | — | — | 111 | 99 | — | — | — | — | — | — | — | — | — | — | 61 | 87 | 32 |
| 31 | — | — | — | — | 110 | 99 | 89 | 99 | 108 | 99 | — | — | — | — | 108 | 99 | — | — | — | — | — | — | — | — | — | — | 59 | 81 | 31 |
| 30 | — | — | 120 | 99 | 108 | 99 | 88 | 99 | 106 | 99 | 120 | 99 | — | — | 106 | 99 | — | — | — | — | 66 | 99 | — | — | — | — | 58 | 75 | 30 |
| 29 | — | — | 120 | 99 | 106 | 99 | 86 | 99 | 104 | 99 | 120 | 99 | — | — | 104 | 99 | — | — | — | — | 65 | 98 | — | — | — | — | 56 | 69 | 29 |
| 28 | — | — | 120 | 99 | 103 | 99 | 84 | 99 | 101 | 99 | 118 | 99 | — | — | 102 | 99 | — | — | — | — | 63 | 94 | — | — | — | — | 55 | 62 | 28 |
| 27 | — | — | 120 | 99 | 101 | 99 | 82 | 99 | 99 | 99 | 115 | 99 | 83 | 99 | 100 | 99 | — | — | — | — | 62 | 89 | — | — | — | — | 53 | 56 | 27 |
| 26 | — | — | 120 | 99 | 99 | 99 | 80 | 99 | 97 | 99 | 112 | 99 | 81 | 99 | 98 | 99 | — | — | — | — | 60 | 83 | — | — | — | — | 51 | 50 | 26 |
| 25 | — | — | 118 | 99 | 97 | 99 | 79 | 99 | 95 | 99 | 110 | 99 | 80 | 99 | 97 | 99 | — | — | — | — | 58 | 76 | — | — | — | — | 50 | 44 | 25 |
| 24 | 105 | 99 | 115 | 99 | 94 | 99 | 77 | 99 | 92 | 99 | 107 | 99 | 78 | 99 | 95 | 99 | 92 | 99 | 65 | 96 | 57 | 70 | 69 | 99 | 69 | 98 | 48 | 39 | 24 |
| 23 | 102 | 99 | 112 | 99 | 92 | 99 | 75 | 98 | 90 | 99 | 104 | 99 | 76 | 99 | 93 | 99 | 89 | 99 | 63 | 92 | 55 | 63 | 67 | 97 | 66 | 96 | 47 | 34 | 23 |
| 22 | 99 | 99 | 109 | 99 | 90 | 99 | 73 | 98 | 88 | 99 | 101 | 99 | 74 | 99 | 91 | 99 | 87 | 99 | 61 | 87 | 54 | 57 | 65 | 95 | 64 | 93 | 45 | 30 | 22 |
| 21 | 96 | 99 | 106 | 99 | 88 | 99 | 72 | 97 | 86 | 99 | 98 | 99 | 72 | 98 | 88 | 99 | 85 | 99 | 59 | 81 | 52 | 51 | 64 | 91 | 62 | 89 | 44 | 25 | 21 |
| 20 | 93 | 99 | 103 | 99 | 85 | 99 | 70 | 96 | 84 | 99 | 95 | 99 | 70 | 97 | 86 | 99 | 83 | 99 | 58 | 74 | 50 | 46 | 62 | 87 | 60 | 84 | 42 | 22 | 20 |
| 19 | 91 | 99 | 100 | 99 | 83 | 99 | 68 | 95 | 81 | 99 | 92 | 99 | 68 | 96 | 84 | 99 | 81 | 99 | 56 | 67 | 49 | 41 | 60 | 82 | 58 | 78 | 41 | 18 | 19 |
| 18 | 88 | 99 | 97 | 99 | 81 | 98 | 66 | 93 | 79 | 99 | 89 | 99 | 67 | 94 | 82 | 99 | 78 | 99 | 54 | 60 | 47 | 36 | 58 | 77 | 56 | 71 | 39 | 15 | 18 |
| 17 | 85 | 99 | 94 | 99 | 79 | 98 | 64 | 91 | 77 | 99 | 87 | 99 | 65 | 91 | 80 | 99 | 76 | 98 | 52 | 52 | 46 | 31 | 56 | 70 | 54 | 63 | 37 | 13 | 17 |
| 16 | 82 | 99 | 90 | 99 | 76 | 97 | 63 | 89 | 75 | 99 | 84 | 99 | 63 | 89 | 77 | 99 | 74 | 97 | 50 | 45 | 44 | 27 | 54 | 64 | 52 | 55 | 36 | 10 | 16 |
| 15 | 80 | 98 | 87 | 99 | 74 | 96 | 61 | 87 | 72 | 96 | 81 | 99 | 61 | 85 | 75 | 97 | 72 | 96 | 48 | 39 | 43 | 23 | 52 | 57 | 50 | 47 | 34 | 8 | 15 |
| 14 | 77 | 98 | 84 | 99 | 72 | 95 | 59 | 84 | 70 | 95 | 78 | 99 | 59 | 81 | 73 | 96 | 69 | 94 | 46 | 32 | 41 | 20 | 51 | 50 | 48 | 39 | 33 | 6 | 14 |
| 13 | 74 | 97 | 81 | 99 | 70 | 94 | 57 | 80 | 68 | 94 | 75 | 98 | 57 | 77 | 71 | 95 | 67 | 93 | 44 | 27 | 39 | 16 | 49 | 43 | 46 | 32 | 31 | 5 | 13 |
| 12 | 71 | 96 | 78 | 98 | 67 | 92 | 56 | 75 | 66 | 92 | 72 | 97 | 55 | 71 | 69 | 94 | 65 | 90 | 42 | 22 | 38 | 14 | 47 | 37 | 43 | 25 | 30 | 4 | 12 |
| 11 | 68 | 94 | 75 | 97 | 65 | 89 | 54 | 70 | 63 | 90 | 69 | 95 | 54 | 66 | 66 | 92 | 63 | 88 | 40 | 17 | 36 | 11 | 45 | 30 | 41 | 20 | 28 | 3 | 11 |
| 10 | 66 | 92 | 72 | 95 | 63 | 86 | 52 | 64 | 61 | 87 | 67 | 92 | 52 | 59 | 64 | 91 | 60 | 84 | 38 | 13 | 35 | 9 | 43 | 25 | 39 | 15 | 27 | 2 | 10 |
| 9 | 63 | 89 | 69 | 93 | 60 | 82 | 50 | 57 | 59 | 84 | 64 | 89 | 50 | 53 | 62 | 89 | 58 | 80 | 36 | 10 | 33 | 7 | 41 | 20 | 37 | 11 | 25 | 1 | 9 |
| 8 | 60 | 86 | 66 | 91 | 58 | 77 | 48 | 49 | 57 | 80 | 61 | 85 | 48 | 46 | 60 | 86 | 56 | 76 | 34 | 8 | 31 | 5 | 39 | 16 | 35 | 8 | 23 | 1 | 8 |
| 7 | 57 | 81 | 63 | 88 | 56 | 71 | 47 | 41 | 55 | 75 | 58 | 79 | 46 | 38 | 57 | 83 | 54 | 70 | 32 | 5 | 30 | 4 | 38 | 12 | 33 | 5 | 20 | 1 | 7 |
| 6 | 54 | 75 | 59 | 84 | 54 | 64 | 45 | 33 | 52 | 69 | 55 | 73 | 44 | 31 | 55 | 79 | 52 | 64 | 30 | 4 | 28 | 3 | 36 | 9 | 31 | 4 | 19 | 1 | 6 |
| 5 | 52 | 67 | 56 | 79 | 51 | 55 | 43 | 25 | 50 | 62 | 52 | 65 | 42 | 25 | 53 | 74 | 49 | 57 | 28 | 2 | 27 | 2 | 34 | 6 | 29 | 2 | 17 | 1 | 5 |
| 4 | 49 | 57 | 53 | 72 | 49 | 45 | 41 | 18 | 48 | 53 | 49 | 55 | 41 | 19 | 51 | 68 | 47 | 48 | 26 | 2 | 25 | 1 | 32 | 4 | 27 | 1 | 16 | 1 | 4 |
| 3 | 46 | 44 | 50 | 64 | 47 | 34 | 40 | 12 | 46 | 42 | 47 | 44 | 39 | 13 | 49 | 60 | 45 | 38 | 25 | 1 | 23 | 1 | 30 | 3 | 25 | 1 | 14 | 1 | 3 |
| 2 | 43 | 28 | 47 | 52 | 45 | 23 | 38 | 7 | 43 | 29 | 44 | 32 | 37 | 8 | 46 | 49 | 43 | 27 | 23 | 1 | 22 | 1 | 28 | 2 | 22 | 1 | 12 | 1 | 2 |
| 1 | 41 | 13 | 44 | 35 | 42 | 13 | 36 | 4 | 41 | 16 | 41 | 19 | 35 | 5 | 44 | 34 | 40 | 16 | 21 | 1 | 20 | 1 | 27 | 1 | 20 | 1 | 11 | 1 | 1 |
| 0 | 38 | 2 | 41 | 8 | 38 | 5 | 34 | 2 | 39 | 4 | 38 | 7 | 33 | 2 | 42 | 15 | 38 | 5 | 19 | 1 | 19 | 1 | 25 | 1 | 18 | 1 | 11 | 1 | 0 |
| Raw mean | 4.39 | | 2.96 | | 5.36 | | 8.90 | | 4.94 | | 4.22 | | 9.07 | | 3.65 | | 5.31 | | 16.11 | | 19.69 | | 13.69 | | 15.14 | | 25.04 | | Raw mean |
| Raw SD | 3.59 | | 3.22 | | 4.43 | | 5.62 | | 4.49 | | 3.49 | | 5.38 | | 4.51 | | 4.48 | | 5.15 | | 6.29 | | 5.41 | | 4.77 | | 6.41 | | Raw SD |
| T:90% Conf. int. | 7 | | 7 | | 6 | | 6 | | 6 | | 7 | | 5 | | 6 | | 6 | | 5 | | 5 | | 6 | | 7 | | 6 | | T:90% Conf. int. |

**Table A.12d** PRS–A Composite T Scores

| T score | Externalizing Problems Combined | Female | Male | Internalizing Problems Combined | Female | Male | Adaptive Skills Combined | Female | Male | Behavioral Symptoms Index Combined | Female | Male | T score |
|---|---|---|---|---|---|---|---|---|---|---|---|---|---|
| 120 | — | — | 333–345 | — | — | 331–344 | — | — | — | — | — | — | 120 |
| 119 | — | — | 331–332 | — | — | 329–330 | — | — | — | — | — | 631–635 | 119 |
| 118 | — | — | 328–330 | — | — | 326–328 | — | — | — | — | — | 626–630 | 118 |
| 117 | — | — | 326–327 | — | — | 323–325 | — | — | — | — | — | 621–625 | 117 |
| 116 | — | — | 323–325 | — | — | 321–322 | — | — | — | — | — | 617–620 | 116 |
| 115 | — | — | 320–322 | — | — | 318–320 | — | — | — | — | — | 612–616 | 115 |
| 114 | — | — | 318–319 | — | — | 316–317 | — | — | — | — | — | 607–611 | 114 |
| 113 | — | — | 315–317 | — | — | 313–315 | — | — | — | — | — | 602–606 | 113 |
| 112 | 322–323 | — | 312–314 | — | — | 310–312 | — | — | — | — | — | 597–601 | 112 |
| 111 | 319–321 | — | 310–311 | — | — | 308–309 | — | — | — | — | — | 593–596 | 111 |
| 110 | 316–318 | — | 307–309 | — | — | 305–307 | — | — | — | 589–593 | — | 588–592 | 110 |
| 109 | 313–315 | — | 304–306 | — | — | 303–304 | — | — | — | 584–588 | — | 583–587 | 109 |
| 108 | 311–312 | — | 302–303 | — | — | 300–302 | — | — | — | 579–583 | — | 578–582 | 108 |
| 107 | 308–310 | — | 299–301 | 304–305 | — | 297–299 | — | — | — | 574–578 | — | 573–577 | 107 |
| 106 | 305–307 | — | 297–298 | 301–303 | — | 295–296 | — | — | — | — | — | 568–572 | 106 |
| 105 | 302–304 | — | 294–296 | 298–300 | — | 292–294 | — | — | — | 569–573 | — | 564–567 | 105 |
| 104 | 300–301 | — | 291–293 | 296–297 | — | 290–291 | — | — | — | 565–568 | — | 559–563 | 104 |
| 103 | 297–299 | — | 289–290 | 293–295 | — | 287–289 | — | — | — | 560–564 | — | 554–558 | 103 |
| 102 | 294–296 | 298 | 286–288 | 290–292 | — | 284–286 | — | — | — | 555–559 | 560 | 549–553 | 102 |
| 101 | 291–293 | 295–297 | 283–285 | 287–289 | — | 282–283 | — | — | — | 550–554 | 555–559 | 544–548 | 101 |
| 100 | 288–290 | 292–294 | 281–282 | 285–286 | — | 279–281 | — | — | — | 545–549 | 550–554 | 539–543 | 100 |
| 99 | 286–287 | 289–291 | 278–280 | 282–284 | — | 277–278 | — | — | — | 540–544 | 545–549 | 535–538 | 99 |
| 98 | 283–285 | 286–288 | 275–277 | 279–281 | 282 | 274–276 | — | — | — | 535–539 | 540–544 | 530–534 | 98 |
| 97 | 280–282 | 284–285 | 273–274 | 277–278 | 279–281 | 271–273 | — | — | — | 530–534 | 535–539 | 525–529 | 97 |
| 96 | 277–279 | 281–283 | 270–272 | 274–276 | 276–278 | 269–270 | — | — | — | 525–529 | 530–534 | 520–524 | 96 |
| 95 | 275–276 | 278–280 | 268–269 | 271–273 | 273–275 | 266–268 | — | — | — | 520–524 | 525–529 | 515–519 | 95 |
| 94 | 272–274 | 275–277 | 265–267 | 268–270 | 271–272 | 264–265 | — | — | — | 515–519 | 520–524 | 510–514 | 94 |
| 93 | 269–271 | 272–274 | 262–264 | 266–267 | 268–270 | 261–263 | — | — | — | 510–514 | 515–519 | 506–509 | 93 |
| 92 | 266–268 | 269–271 | 260–261 | 263–265 | 265–267 | 258–260 | — | — | — | 505–509 | 510–514 | 501–505 | 92 |
| 91 | 263–265 | 266–268 | 257–259 | 260–262 | 262–264 | 256–257 | — | — | — | 500–504 | 505–509 | 496–500 | 91 |
| 90 | 261–262 | 264–265 | 254–256 | 258–259 | 260–261 | 253–255 | — | — | — | 495–499 | 500–504 | 491–495 | 90 |
| 89 | 258–260 | 261–263 | 252–253 | 255–257 | 257–259 | 251–252 | — | — | — | 491–494 | 495–499 | 486–490 | 89 |
| 88 | 255–257 | 258–260 | 249–251 | 252–254 | 254–256 | 248–250 | — | — | — | 486–490 | 490–494 | 481–485 | 88 |
| 87 | 252–254 | 255–257 | 246–248 | 249–251 | 251–253 | 245–247 | — | — | — | 481–485 | 485–489 | 477–480 | 87 |
| 86 | 249–251 | 252–254 | 244–246 | 247–248 | 249–250 | 243–244 | — | — | — | 476–480 | 480–484 | 472–476 | 86 |
| 85 | 247–248 | 249–251 | 241–243 | 244–246 | 246–248 | 240–242 | — | — | — | 471–475 | 475–479 | 467–471 | 85 |
| 84 | 244–246 | 246–248 | 239–240 | 241–243 | 243–245 | 238–239 | — | — | — | 466–470 | 470–474 | 462–466 | 84 |
| 83 | 241–243 | 244–245 | 236–238 | 239–240 | 240–242 | 235–237 | — | — | — | 461–465 | 464–469 | 457–461 | 83 |
| 82 | 238–240 | 241–243 | 233–235 | 236–238 | 238–239 | 232–234 | — | — | — | 456–460 | 459–463 | 453–456 | 82 |
| 81 | 236–237 | 238–240 | 231–232 | 233–235 | 235–237 | 230–231 | — | — | — | 451–455 | 454–458 | 448–452 | 81 |
| 80 | 233–235 | 235–237 | 228–230 | 231–232 | 232–234 | 227–229 | — | — | — | 446–450 | 449–453 | 443–447 | 80 |
| 79 | 230–232 | 232–234 | 225–227 | 228–230 | 229–231 | 225–226 | — | — | — | 441–445 | 444–448 | 438–442 | 79 |
| 78 | 227–229 | 229–231 | 223–224 | 225–227 | 226–228 | 222–224 | — | — | — | 436–440 | 439–443 | 433–437 | 78 |
| 77 | 224–226 | 226–228 | 220–222 | 222–224 | 224–225 | 219–221 | — | — | — | 431–435 | 434–438 | 428–432 | 77 |
| 76 | 222–223 | 224–225 | 218–219 | 220–221 | 221–223 | 217–218 | — | — | — | 426–430 | 429–433 | 424–427 | 76 |
| 75 | 219–221 | 221–223 | 215–217 | 217–219 | 218–220 | 214–216 | — | — | — | 421–425 | 424–428 | 419–423 | 75 |
| 74 | 216–218 | 218–220 | 212–214 | 214–216 | 215–217 | 212–213 | — | — | — | 417–420 | 419–423 | 414–418 | 74 |
| 73 | 213–215 | 215–217 | 210–211 | 212–213 | 213–214 | 209–211 | — | — | — | 412–416 | 414–418 | 409–413 | 73 |
| 72 | 211–213 | 212–214 | 207–209 | 209–211 | 210–212 | 206–208 | — | — | — | 407–411 | 409–413 | 404–408 | 72 |
| 71 | 208–210 | 209–211 | 204–206 | 206–208 | 207–209 | 204–205 | — | — | — | 402–406 | 404–408 | 399–403 | 71 |
| 70 | 205–207 | 206–208 | 202–203 | 203–205 | 204–206 | 201–203 | — | — | 336 | 397–401 | 399–403 | 395–398 | 70 |
| 69 | 202–204 | 203–205 | 199–201 | 201–202 | 202–203 | 199–200 | 331–334 | 331–333 | 331–335 | 392–396 | 394–398 | 390–394 | 69 |
| 68 | 199–201 | 201–202 | 197–198 | 198–200 | 199–201 | 196–198 | 326–330 | 327–330 | 327–330 | 387–391 | 389–393 | 385–389 | 68 |
| 67 | 197–198 | 198–200 | 194–196 | 195–197 | 196–198 | 194–195 | 322–325 | 323–326 | 323–326 | 382–386 | 384–388 | 380–384 | 67 |
| 66 | 194–196 | 195–197 | 191–193 | 193–194 | 193–195 | 191–193 | 318–321 | 318–322 | 318–322 | 377–381 | 379–383 | 375–379 | 66 |

**Table A.12d** PRS–A Composite *T* Scores (*continued*)

| T score | Externalizing Problems Combined | Externalizing Problems Female | Externalizing Problems Male | Internalizing Problems Combined | Internalizing Problems Female | Internalizing Problems Male | Adaptive Skills Combined | Adaptive Skills Female | Adaptive Skills Male | Behavioral Symptoms Index Combined | Behavioral Symptoms Index Female | Behavioral Symptoms Index Male | T score |
|---|---|---|---|---|---|---|---|---|---|---|---|---|---|
| 65 | 191–193 | 192–194 | 189–190 | 190–192 | 191–192 | 188–190 | 313–317 | 314–317 | 314–317 | 372–376 | 374–378 | 370–374 | 65 |
| 64 | 188–190 | 189–191 | 186–188 | 187–189 | 188–190 | 186–187 | 309–312 | 309–313 | 309–313 | 367–371 | 369–373 | 366–369 | 64 |
| 63 | 185–187 | 186–188 | 183–185 | 184–186 | 185–187 | 183–185 | 305–308 | 305–308 | 305–308 | 362–366 | 363–368 | 361–365 | 63 |
| 62 | 183–184 | 183–185 | 181–182 | 182–183 | 182–184 | 181–182 | 300–304 | 301–304 | 301–304 | 357–361 | 358–362 | 356–360 | 62 |
| 61 | 180–182 | 181–182 | 178–180 | 179–181 | 180–181 | 178–180 | 296–299 | 296–300 | 296–300 | 352–356 | 353–357 | 351–355 | 61 |
| 60 | 177–179 | 178–180 | 175–177 | 176–178 | 177–179 | 175–177 | 292–295 | 292–295 | 292–295 | 347–351 | 348–352 | 346–350 | 60 |
| 59 | 174–176 | 175–177 | 173–174 | 174–175 | 174–176 | 173–174 | 287–291 | 288–291 | 288–291 | 343–346 | 343–347 | 342–345 | 59 |
| 58 | 172–173 | 172–174 | 170–172 | 171–173 | 171–173 | 170–172 | 283–286 | 283–287 | 283–287 | 338–342 | 338–342 | 337–341 | 58 |
| 57 | 169–171 | 169–171 | 168–169 | 168–170 | 168–170 | 168–169 | 279–282 | 279–282 | 279–282 | 333–337 | 333–337 | 332–336 | 57 |
| 56 | 166–168 | 166–168 | 165–167 | 166–167 | 166–167 | 165–167 | 274–278 | 275–278 | 274–278 | 328–332 | 328–332 | 327–331 | 56 |
| 55 | 163–165 | 163–165 | 162–164 | 163–165 | 163–165 | 162–164 | 270–273 | 270–274 | 270–273 | 323–327 | 323–327 | 322–326 | 55 |
| 54 | 160–162 | 161–162 | 160–161 | 160–162 | 160–162 | 160–161 | 266–269 | 266–269 | 266–269 | 318–322 | 318–322 | 317–321 | 54 |
| 53 | 158–159 | 158–160 | 157–159 | 157–159 | 157–159 | 157–159 | 261–265 | 262–265 | 261–265 | 313–317 | 313–317 | 313–316 | 53 |
| 52 | 155–157 | 155–157 | 154–156 | 155–156 | 155–156 | 155–156 | 257–260 | 257–261 | 257–260 | 308–312 | 308–312 | 308–312 | 52 |
| 51 | 152–154 | 152–154 | 152–153 | 152–154 | 152–154 | 152–154 | 252–256 | 253–256 | 253–256 | 303–307 | 303–307 | 303–307 | 51 |
| 50 | 149–151 | 149–151 | 149–151 | 149–151 | 149–151 | 149–151 | 248–251 | 249–252 | 248–252 | 298–302 | 298–302 | 298–302 | 50 |
| 49 | 147–148 | 146–148 | 146–148 | 147–148 | 146–148 | 147–148 | 244–247 | 244–248 | 244–247 | 293–297 | 293–297 | 293–297 | 49 |
| 48 | 144–146 | 143–145 | 144–145 | 144–146 | 144–145 | 144–146 | 239–243 | 240–243 | 239–243 | 288–292 | 288–292 | 288–292 | 48 |
| 47 | 141–143 | 141–142 | 141–143 | 141–143 | 141–143 | 142–143 | 235–238 | 236–239 | 235–238 | 283–287 | 283–287 | 284–287 | 47 |
| 46 | 138–140 | 138–140 | 139–140 | 138–140 | 138–140 | 139–141 | 231–234 | 231–235 | 231–234 | 278–282 | 278–282 | 279–283 | 46 |
| 45 | 135–137 | 135–137 | 136–138 | 136–137 | 135–137 | 136–138 | 226–230 | 227–230 | 226–230 | 273–277 | 273–277 | 274–278 | 45 |
| 44 | 133–134 | 132–134 | 133–135 | 133–135 | 133–134 | 134–135 | 222–225 | 223–226 | 222–225 | 269–272 | 268–272 | 269–273 | 44 |
| 43 | 130–132 | 129–131 | 131–132 | 130–132 | 130–132 | 131–133 | 218–221 | 218–222 | 218–221 | 264–268 | 263–267 | 264–268 | 43 |
| 42 | 127–129 | 126–128 | 128–130 | 128–130 | 127–129 | 129–130 | 213–217 | 214–217 | 213–217 | 259–263 | 257–262 | 259–263 | 42 |
| 41 | 124–126 | 125 | 125–127 | 125–127 | 124–126 | 126–128 | 209–212 | 209–213 | 209–212 | 254–258 | 252–256 | 255–258 | 41 |
| 40 | 122–123 | — | 123–124 | 122–124 | 121–123 | 123–125 | 205–208 | 205–208 | 204–208 | 249–253 | 247–251 | 250–254 | 40 |
| 39 | — | — | 120–122 | 119–121 | 119–120 | 121–122 | 200–204 | 201–204 | 200–203 | 244–248 | 242–246 | 245–249 | 39 |
| 38 | — | — | 118–119 | 117–118 | 116–118 | 118–120 | 196–199 | 196–199 | 196–199 | 239–243 | 237–241 | 240–244 | 38 |
| 37 | — | — | 117 | 114–116 | 113–115 | 116–117 | 192–195 | 192–195 | 191–195 | 235–238 | — | 235–239 | 37 |
| 36 | — | — | — | 112–113 | 110–112 | 113–115 | 187–191 | 188–191 | 187–190 | — | — | 231–234 | 36 |
| 35 | — | — | — | — | 109 | 111–112 | 183–186 | 183–187 | 182–186 | — | — | — | 35 |
| 34 | — | — | — | — | — | — | 179–182 | 179–182 | 178–181 | — | — | — | 34 |
| 33 | — | — | — | — | — | — | 174–178 | 175–178 | 174–177 | — | — | — | 33 |
| 32 | — | — | — | — | — | — | 170–173 | 170–174 | 169–173 | — | — | — | 32 |
| 31 | — | — | — | — | — | — | 165–169 | 166–169 | 165–168 | — | — | — | 31 |
| 30 | — | — | — | — | — | — | 161–164 | 162–165 | 161–164 | — | — | — | 30 |
| 29 | — | — | — | — | — | — | 157–160 | 157–161 | 156–160 | — | — | — | 29 |
| 28 | — | — | — | — | — | — | 152–156 | 153–156 | 152–155 | — | — | — | 28 |
| 27 | — | — | — | — | — | — | 148–151 | 149–152 | 147–151 | — | — | — | 27 |
| 26 | — | — | — | — | — | — | 144–147 | 144–148 | 143–146 | — | — | — | 26 |
| 25 | — | — | — | — | — | — | 139–143 | 140–143 | 139–142 | — | — | — | 25 |
| 24 | — | — | — | — | — | — | 135–138 | 136–139 | 134–138 | — | — | — | 24 |
| 23 | — | — | — | — | — | — | 131–134 | 131–135 | 130–133 | — | — | — | 23 |
| 22 | — | — | — | — | — | — | 126–130 | 127–130 | 126–129 | — | — | — | 22 |
| 21 | — | — | — | — | — | — | 122–125 | 123–126 | 121–125 | — | — | — | 21 |
| 20 | — | — | — | — | — | — | 118–121 | 118–122 | 117–120 | — | — | — | 20 |
| 19 | — | — | — | — | — | — | 113–117 | 114–117 | 112–116 | — | — | — | 19 |
| 18 | — | — | — | — | — | — | 109–112 | 109–113 | 108–111 | — | — | — | 18 |
| 17 | — | — | — | — | — | — | 105–108 | 105–108 | 104–107 | — | — | — | 17 |
| 16 | — | — | — | — | — | — | 100–104 | 101–104 | 99–103 | — | — | — | 16 |
| 15 | — | — | — | — | — | — | 96–99 | 96–100 | 95–98 | — | — | — | 15 |
| 14 | — | — | — | — | — | — | 92–95 | 92–95 | 92–94 | — | — | — | 14 |
| 13 | — | — | — | — | — | — | 87–91 | 88–91 | — | — | — | — | 13 |
| 12 | — | — | — | — | — | — | 84–86 | 83–87 | — | — | — | — | 12 |
| 11 | — | — | — | — | — | — | — | 79–82 | — | — | — | — | 11 |
| 10 | — | — | — | — | — | — | — | 75–78 | — | — | — | — | 10 |
| T: 90% Conf. int. | 3 | 3 | 4 | 3 | 3 | 4 | 3 | 3 | 3 | 3 | 2 | 3 | T: 90% Conf. int. |

## Table A.12e   PRS-A Composite Percentiles

| %ile | Externalizing Problems Combined | Female | Male | Internalizing Problems Combined | Female | Male | Adaptive Skills Combined | Female | Male | Behavioral Symptoms Index Combined | Female | Male | %ile |
|---|---|---|---|---|---|---|---|---|---|---|---|---|---|
| 99 | 247–323 | 256–298 | 229–345 | 237–305 | 241–282 | 224–344 | 321–334 | 317–333 | 322–336 | 460–593 | 468–560 | 447–635 | 99 |
| 98 | 230–246 | 237–255 | 220–228 | 222–236 | 226–240 | 214–223 | 318–320 | 315–316 | 318–321 | 434–459 | 443–467 | 426–446 | 98 |
| 97 | 218–229 | 224–236 | 213–219 | 213–221 | 216–225 | 207–213 | 316–317 | 313–314 | 316–317 | 417–433 | 425–442 | 412–425 | 97 |
| 96 | 210–217 | 214–223 | 208–212 | 206–212 | 209–215 | 202–206 | 313–315 | 312 | 313–315 | 404–416 | 412–424 | 401–411 | 96 |
| 95 | 203–209 | 207–213 | 203–207 | 200–205 | 203–208 | 197–201 | 311–312 | 310–311 | 311–312 | 394–403 | 401–411 | 392–400 | 95 |
| 94 | 198–202 | 200–206 | 199–202 | 196–199 | 198–202 | 194–196 | 309–310 | 309 | 309–310 | 386–393 | 391–400 | 385–391 | 94 |
| 93 | 193–197 | 195–199 | 196–198 | 192–195 | 194–197 | 191–193 | 308 | 308 | 307–308 | 378–385 | 384–390 | 378–384 | 93 |
| 92 | 189–192 | 190–194 | 192–195 | 189–191 | 190–193 | 188–190 | 306–307 | 307 | 306 | 372–377 | 377–383 | 373–377 | 92 |
| 91 | 186–188 | 186–189 | 190–191 | 186–188 | 187–189 | 186–187 | 305 | 305–306 | 304–305 | 366–371 | 371–376 | 368–372 | 91 |
| 90 | 183–185 | 183–185 | 187–189 | 183–185 | 184–186 | 184–185 | 303–304 | 304 | 303 | 361–365 | 365–370 | 363–367 | 90 |
| 89 | 180–182 | 180–182 | 184–186 | 181–182 | 182–183 | 182–183 | 302 | 303 | 301–302 | 357–360 | 360–364 | 359–362 | 89 |
| 88 | 178–179 | 177–179 | 182–183 | 179–180 | 179–181 | 180–181 | 300–301 | 302 | 300 | 353–356 | 355–359 | 355–358 | 88 |
| 87 | 175–177 | 174–176 | 180–181 | 177–178 | 177–178 | 178–179 | 299 | 301 | 298–299 | 349–352 | 351–354 | 351–354 | 87 |
| 86 | 173–174 | 172–173 | 178–179 | 175–176 | 175–176 | 177 | 298 | 300 | 297 | 345–348 | 347–350 | 348–350 | 86 |
| 85 | 172 | 170–171 | 176–177 | 173–174 | 173–174 | 175–176 | 296–297 | 299 | 296 | 342–344 | 344–346 | 345–347 | 85 |
| 84 | 170–171 | 168–169 | 175 | 171–172 | 171–172 | 174 | 295 | 297–298 | 294–295 | 339–341 | 340–343 | 342–344 | 84 |
| 83 | 168–169 | 166–167 | 173–174 | 170 | 170 | 172–173 | 294 | 296 | 293 | 336–338 | 337–339 | 339–341 | 83 |
| 82 | 167 | 164–165 | 171–172 | 169 | 168–169 | 171 | 292–293 | 295 | 292 | 333–335 | 334–336 | 337–338 | 82 |
| 81 | 165–166 | 163 | 170 | 167–168 | 167 | 170 | 291 | 294 | 291 | 331–332 | 331–333 | 334–336 | 81 |
| 80 | 164 | 161–162 | 168–169 | 166 | 165–166 | 169 | 290 | 293 | 289–290 | 328–330 | 329–330 | 332–333 | 80 |
| 79 | 163 | 160 | 167 | 165 | 164 | 168 | 289 | 292 | 288 | 326–327 | 326–328 | 330–331 | 79 |
| 78 | 161–162 | 159 | 166 | 164 | 163 | 167 | 288 | 291 | 287 | 324–325 | 324–325 | 327–329 | 78 |
| 77 | 160 | 157–158 | 165 | 163 | 162 | 166 | 286–287 | 289–290 | 286 | 321–323 | 321–323 | 325–326 | 77 |
| 76 | 159 | 156 | 163–164 | 161–162 | 161 | 165 | 285 | 288 | 285 | 319–320 | 319–320 | 323–324 | 76 |
| 75 | 158 | 155 | 162 | 160 | 160 | 164 | 284 | 287 | 284 | 318 | 317–318 | 322 | 75 |
| 74 | 157 | 154 | 161 | — | 159 | 163 | 283 | 286 | 282–283 | 316–317 | 315–316 | 320–321 | 74 |
| 73 | 156 | 153 | 160 | 159 | 158 | 162 | 282 | 285 | 281 | 314–315 | 313–314 | 318–319 | 73 |
| 72 | 155 | 152 | 159 | 158 | 157 | 161 | 281 | 284 | 280 | 312–313 | 311–312 | 316–317 | 72 |
| 71 | 154 | 151 | 158 | 157 | 156 | 160 | 279–280 | 282–283 | 279 | 311 | 310 | 314–315 | 71 |
| 70 | — | — | 157 | 156 | 155 | 159 | 278 | 281 | 278 | 309–310 | 308–309 | 313 | 70 |
| 69 | 153 | 150 | 156 | 155 | 154 | 158 | 277 | 280 | 277 | 307–308 | 306–307 | 311–312 | 69 |
| 68 | 152 | 149 | 155 | 154 | 153 | — | 276 | 279 | 276 | 306 | 305 | 310 | 68 |
| 67 | 151 | 148 | 154 | — | 152 | 157 | 275 | 278 | 275 | 304–305 | 303–304 | 308–309 | 67 |
| 66 | 150 | — | 153 | 153 | — | 156 | 274 | 277 | 273–274 | 303 | 302 | 307 | 66 |
| 65 | — | 147 | — | 152 | 151 | 155 | 273 | 275–276 | 272 | 302 | 300–301 | 305–306 | 65 |
| 64 | 149 | 146 | 152 | 151 | 150 | — | 271–272 | 274 | 271 | 300–301 | 299 | 304 | 64 |
| 63 | 148 | — | 151 | — | 149 | 154 | 270 | 273 | 270 | 299 | 298 | 303 | 63 |
| 62 | — | 145 | 150 | 150 | — | 153 | 269 | 272 | 269 | 298 | 296–297 | 301–302 | 62 |
| 61 | 147 | — | 149 | 149 | 148 | — | 268 | 270–271 | 268 | 297 | 295 | 300 | 61 |
| 60 | — | 144 | — | — | 147 | 152 | 267 | 269 | 267 | 296 | 294 | 299 | 60 |
| 59 | 146 | 143 | 148 | 148 | — | 151 | 266 | 268 | 266 | 294–295 | 293 | 298 | 59 |
| 58 | — | — | 147 | — | 146 | — | 265 | 267 | 264–265 | 293 | 292 | 296–297 | 58 |
| 57 | 145 | — | 146 | 147 | — | 150 | 263–264 | 265–266 | 263 | 292 | 291 | 295 | 57 |
| 56 | — | 142 | 145 | 146 | 145 | 149 | 262 | 264 | 262 | 291 | 290 | 294 | 56 |
| 55 | 144 | — | 145 | — | 144 | — | 261 | 263 | 261 | 290 | 288–289 | 293 | 55 |
| 54 | 143 | 141 | 144 | 145 | — | 148 | 260 | 261–262 | 260 | 289 | 287 | 292 | 54 |
| 53 | — | — | 144 | — | 143 | 147 | 259 | 260 | 259 | 288 | 286 | 291 | 53 |
| 52 | — | 140 | 143 | 144 | — | — | 257–258 | 259 | 257–258 | 287 | 285 | 290 | 52 |
| 51 | 142 | — | — | — | 142 | 146 | 256 | 257–258 | 256 | 286 | — | 289 | 51 |

**Table A.12e** PRS–A Composite Percentiles (continued)

| %ile | Externalizing Problems Combined | Externalizing Problems Female | Externalizing Problems Male | Internalizing Problems Combined | Internalizing Problems Female | Internalizing Problems Male | Adaptive Skills Combined | Adaptive Skills Female | Adaptive Skills Male | Behavioral Symptoms Index Combined | Behavioral Symptoms Index Female | Behavioral Symptoms Index Male | %ile |
|---|---|---|---|---|---|---|---|---|---|---|---|---|---|
| 50 | – | – | – | 143 | – | – | 255 | 256 | 255 | 285 | 284 | 288 | 50 |
| 49 | 141 | 139 | 142 | – | 141 | 145 | 254 | 255 | 254 | 284 | 283 | 287 | 49 |
| 48 | 140 | – | 141 | 142 | – | 144 | 253 | 253–254 | 253 | 283 | 282 | 286 | 48 |
| 47 | – | – | – | – | – | – | 251–252 | 252 | 252 | 282 | 281 | 285 | 47 |
| 46 | – | 138 | 140 | 141 | 140 | 143 | 250 | 250–251 | 250–251 | – | 280 | 284 | 46 |
| 45 | – | – | – | – | 139 | – | 249 | 249 | 249 | 281 | 279 | 283 | 45 |
| 44 | 139 | – | 139 | 140 | – | 142 | 247–248 | 247–248 | 248 | 280 | 278 | 282 | 44 |
| 43 | – | 137 | 138 | – | – | – | 246 | 246 | 247 | 279 | – | 281 | 43 |
| 42 | 138 | – | – | 139 | 138 | 141 | 245 | 245 | 245–246 | 278 | 277 | 280 | 42 |
| 41 | – | – | 137 | – | – | – | 244 | 243–244 | 244 | 277 | 276 | 279 | 41 |
| 40 | – | 136 | – | 138 | 137 | 140 | 242–243 | 242 | 243 | – | 275 | 278 | 40 |
| 39 | 137 | – | 136 | – | – | 139 | 241 | 240–241 | 241–242 | 276 | – | 277 | 39 |
| 38 | – | – | – | 137 | 136 | 138 | 240 | 238–239 | 240 | 275 | 274 | 276 | 38 |
| 37 | – | – | – | – | – | – | 238–239 | 237 | 239 | 274 | 273 | 275 | 37 |
| 36 | 136 | 135 | 135 | 136 | 135 | – | 237 | 235–236 | 237–238 | – | 272 | 274 | 36 |
| 35 | – | – | – | – | – | 137 | 235–236 | 234 | 236 | 273 | – | 273 | 35 |
| 34 | – | – | 134 | 135 | 134 | – | 234 | 232–233 | 235 | 272 | 271 | – | 34 |
| 33 | 135 | 134 | – | – | – | 136 | 232–233 | 231 | 233–234 | 271 | 270 | 272 | 33 |
| 32 | – | – | 133 | – | – | – | 231 | 229–230 | 232 | – | – | 271 | 32 |
| 31 | – | – | – | 134 | 133 | 135 | 229–230 | 227–228 | 230–231 | 270 | 269 | 270 | 31 |
| 30 | 134 | – | 132 | – | – | 134 | 228 | 226 | 229 | 269 | 268 | 269 | 30 |
| 29 | – | – | – | 133 | 132 | – | 226–227 | 224–225 | 227–228 | – | – | 268 | 29 |
| 28 | – | 133 | – | – | – | 133 | 225 | 222–223 | 225–226 | 268 | 267 | 267 | 28 |
| 27 | 133 | – | 131 | – | – | – | 223–224 | 220–221 | 224 | 267 | 266 | – | 27 |
| 26 | – | – | – | 132 | 131 | 132 | 221–222 | 219 | 222–223 | 266 | – | 266 | 26 |
| 25 | – | – | 130 | – | – | – | 220 | 217–218 | 220–221 | 265 | 265 | 265 | 25 |
| 24 | 132 | – | – | 131 | – | 131 | 218–219 | 215–216 | 219 | – | 264 | 264 | 24 |
| 23 | – | 132 | – | – | 130 | 130 | 216–217 | 213–214 | 217–218 | 264 | 263 | 263 | 23 |
| 22 | – | – | 129 | – | – | – | 214–215 | 211–212 | 215–216 | 263 | – | 262 | 22 |
| 21 | – | – | – | 130 | – | 129 | 213 | 209–210 | 213–214 | – | 262 | – | 21 |
| 20 | 131 | – | 128 | – | 129 | – | 211–212 | 207–208 | 211–212 | 262 | – | 261 | 20 |
| 19 | – | – | – | 129 | – | 128 | 209–210 | 205–206 | 209–210 | – | 261 | 260 | 19 |
| 18 | – | – | – | – | 128 | 127 | 207–208 | 203–204 | 207–208 | 261 | – | 259 | 18 |
| 17 | – | – | 127 | – | – | – | 204–206 | 201–202 | 205–206 | 260 | 260 | 258 | 17 |
| 16 | 130 | 131 | – | 128 | – | 126 | 202–203 | 199–200 | 203–204 | – | – | 257 | 16 |
| 15 | – | – | 126 | – | 127 | – | 200–201 | 197–198 | 200–202 | 259 | 259 | 256 | 15 |
| 14 | – | – | – | 127 | – | 125 | 198–199 | 195–196 | 198–199 | 258 | – | 255 | 14 |
| 13 | – | – | 125 | – | – | 124 | 195–197 | 192–194 | 195–197 | – | 258 | 254 | 13 |
| 12 | 129 | – | – | 126 | 126 | 123 | 193–194 | 190–191 | 193–194 | 257 | – | 253 | 12 |
| 11 | – | – | – | – | – | 122 | 190–192 | 188–189 | 190–192 | 256 | 257 | – | 11 |
| 10 | 128 | 130 | 124 | 125 | 125 | – | 187–189 | 185–187 | 187–189 | 255 | 256 | 252 | 10 |
| 9 | – | – | – | – | – | 121 | 184–186 | 183–184 | 184–186 | – | 255 | 250–251 | 9 |
| 8 | – | – | – | 124 | – | 120 | 180–183 | 180–182 | 180–183 | 254 | – | 249 | 8 |
| 7 | 127 | – | 123 | – | 124 | 119 | 177–179 | 177–179 | 176–179 | 253 | 254 | 248 | 7 |
| 6 | – | – | – | 123 | – | 118 | 173–176 | 174–176 | 172–175 | 252 | – | 247 | 6 |
| 5 | – | – | – | 122 | 123 | 117 | 168–172 | 171–173 | 167–171 | 251 | 253 | 246 | 5 |
| 4 | – | 129 | 122 | – | – | 115–116 | 163–167 | 167–170 | 161–166 | 250 | 252 | 244–245 | 4 |
| 3 | 126 | – | 121 | 121 | – | 114 | 157–162 | 163–166 | 154–160 | 249 | 251 | 243 | 3 |
| 2 | – | – | – | 120 | 122 | 111–113 | 149–156 | 158–162 | 144–153 | 248 | 237–250 | 240–242 | 2 |
| 1 | 122–125 | 125–128 | 117–120 | 112–119 | 109–121 | – | 84–148 | 75–157 | 92–143 | 235–247 | – | 231–239 | 1 |

## Table A.13a  SRP–C *T* Scores and Percentiles

| Raw score | Attitude to School T | %ile | Attitude to Teachers T | %ile | Atypicality T | %ile | Locus of Control T | %ile | Social Stress T | %ile | Anxiety T | %ile | Depression T | %ile | Sense of Inadequacy T | %ile | Attention Problems T | %ile | Hyperactivity T | %ile | Relations With Parents T | %ile | Interpersonal Relations T | %ile | Self-Esteem T | %ile | Self-Reliance T | %ile | Raw score |
|---|---|---|---|---|---|---|---|---|---|---|---|---|---|---|---|---|---|---|---|---|---|---|---|---|---|---|---|---|---|
| 32 | — | — | — | — | — | — | — | — | — | — | 89 | 99 | — | — | — | — | — | — | — | — | — | — | — | — | — | — | — | — | 32 |
| 31 | — | — | — | — | — | — | — | — | — | — | 87 | 99 | — | — | — | — | — | — | — | — | — | — | — | — | — | — | — | — | 31 |
| 30 | — | — | — | — | — | — | — | — | — | — | 85 | 99 | — | — | — | — | — | — | — | — | 61 | 92 | — | — | — | — | — | — | 30 |
| 29 | — | — | — | — | 88 | 99 | — | — | — | — | 83 | 99 | — | — | — | — | — | — | — | — | 59 | 82 | — | — | — | — | — | — | 29 |
| 28 | — | — | — | — | 86 | 99 | — | — | — | — | 82 | 99 | — | — | — | — | — | — | — | — | 57 | 72 | — | — | — | — | — | — | 28 |
| 27 | — | — | — | — | — | — | — | — | — | — | 80 | 99 | — | — | — | — | — | — | — | — | 55 | 63 | — | — | — | — | — | — | 27 |
| 26 | — | — | — | — | 84 | 99 | — | — | 94 | 99 | 78 | 99 | 101 | 99 | — | — | — | — | — | — | 54 | 54 | — | — | — | — | — | — | 26 |
| 25 | — | — | — | — | 82 | 99 | — | — | 92 | 99 | 77 | 99 | 98 | 99 | — | — | — | — | — | — | 52 | 47 | — | — | — | — | — | — | 25 |
| 24 | — | — | — | — | 81 | 99 | — | — | 90 | 99 | 75 | 98 | 96 | 99 | — | — | 85 | 99 | — | — | 50 | 40 | — | — | — | — | — | — | 24 |
| 23 | — | — | — | — | 79 | 99 | — | — | 87 | 99 | 73 | 98 | 94 | 99 | 99 | 99 | 83 | 99 | 84 | 99 | 48 | 34 | — | — | — | — | — | — | 23 |
| 22 | — | — | — | — | 77 | 98 | — | — | 85 | 99 | 71 | 97 | 91 | 99 | 96 | 99 | 81 | 99 | 82 | 99 | 46 | 29 | — | — | — | — | — | — | 22 |
| 21 | 84 | 99 | — | — | 75 | 98 | — | — | 83 | 99 | 70 | 96 | 89 | 99 | 93 | 99 | 79 | 99 | 80 | 99 | 44 | 24 | 60 | 92 | — | — | — | — | 21 |
| 20 | 82 | 99 | 93 | 99 | 74 | 97 | 91 | 99 | 81 | 99 | 68 | 95 | 87 | 99 | 90 | 99 | 77 | 99 | 78 | 99 | 42 | 20 | 57 | 73 | — | — | 67 | 98 | 20 |
| 19 | 80 | 99 | 90 | 99 | 72 | 96 | 88 | 99 | 79 | 99 | 66 | 93 | 84 | 99 | 88 | 99 | 75 | 99 | 76 | 98 | 41 | 17 | 54 | 56 | — | — | 64 | 94 | 19 |
| 18 | 78 | 99 | 87 | 99 | 70 | 95 | 86 | 99 | 76 | 98 | 64 | 91 | 82 | 99 | 85 | 99 | 72 | 98 | 74 | 98 | 39 | 14 | 51 | 42 | 58 | 85 | 61 | 87 | 18 |
| 17 | 76 | 98 | 85 | 99 | 68 | 94 | 83 | 99 | 74 | 98 | 63 | 89 | 80 | 98 | 82 | 99 | 70 | 97 | 71 | 97 | 37 | 12 | 49 | 32 | 55 | 61 | 59 | 78 | 17 |
| 16 | 73 | 97 | 82 | 99 | 67 | 92 | 80 | 99 | 72 | 97 | 61 | 86 | 77 | 98 | 79 | 98 | 68 | 95 | 69 | 96 | 35 | 10 | 46 | 24 | 52 | 44 | 56 | 68 | 16 |
| 15 | 71 | 96 | 79 | 99 | 65 | 91 | 78 | 98 | 70 | 96 | 59 | 83 | 75 | 97 | 76 | 98 | 66 | 93 | 67 | 94 | 33 | 8 | 43 | 19 | 49 | 33 | 53 | 58 | 15 |
| 14 | 69 | 95 | 77 | 98 | 63 | 89 | 75 | 98 | 68 | 94 | 57 | 79 | 73 | 96 | 73 | 96 | 64 | 90 | 65 | 92 | 31 | 6 | 40 | 14 | 46 | 25 | 51 | 48 | 14 |
| 13 | 67 | 93 | 74 | 97 | 61 | 87 | 72 | 96 | 66 | 92 | 56 | 74 | 70 | 95 | 70 | 95 | 62 | 86 | 63 | 89 | 29 | 5 | 38 | 11 | 43 | 19 | 48 | 39 | 13 |
| 12 | 64 | 90 | 72 | 95 | 60 | 84 | 70 | 95 | 63 | 90 | 54 | 69 | 68 | 94 | 67 | 92 | 60 | 82 | 60 | 85 | 28 | 4 | 35 | 8 | 40 | 14 | 45 | 31 | 12 |
| 11 | 62 | 87 | 69 | 93 | 58 | 81 | 67 | 93 | 61 | 87 | 52 | 63 | 66 | 92 | 65 | 89 | 58 | 77 | 58 | 80 | 26 | 3 | 32 | 6 | 37 | 11 | 43 | 24 | 11 |
| 10 | 60 | 83 | 66 | 91 | 56 | 77 | 65 | 90 | 59 | 83 | 51 | 57 | 63 | 90 | 62 | 84 | 56 | 72 | 56 | 75 | 24 | 2 | 29 | 5 | 34 | 8 | 40 | 18 | 10 |
| 9 | 58 | 79 | 64 | 88 | 54 | 73 | 62 | 87 | 57 | 78 | 49 | 50 | 61 | 87 | 59 | 77 | 54 | 65 | 54 | 69 | 22 | 1 | 27 | 4 | 31 | 6 | 37 | 12 | 9 |
| 8 | 55 | 73 | 61 | 85 | 53 | 68 | 59 | 83 | 55 | 72 | 47 | 42 | 59 | 84 | 56 | 67 | 51 | 59 | 52 | 61 | 20 | 1 | 24 | 3 | 28 | 5 | 35 | 8 | 8 |
| 7 | 53 | 67 | 58 | 80 | 51 | 63 | 57 | 78 | 52 | 65 | 45 | 35 | 56 | 80 | 53 | 56 | 49 | 51 | 50 | 53 | 18 | 1 | 21 | 2 | 25 | 3 | 32 | 5 | 7 |
| 6 | 51 | 60 | 56 | 75 | 49 | 57 | 54 | 71 | 50 | 57 | 44 | 28 | 54 | 75 | 50 | 43 | 47 | 43 | 47 | 44 | 16 | 1 | 18 | 2 | 21 | 2 | 29 | 3 | 6 |
| 5 | 49 | 53 | 53 | 69 | 48 | 50 | 51 | 63 | 48 | 48 | 42 | 21 | 52 | 68 | 47 | 30 | 45 | 35 | 45 | 35 | 15 | 1 | 16 | 1 | 18 | 2 | 27 | 1 | 5 |
| 4 | 47 | 44 | 50 | 62 | 46 | 42 | 49 | 54 | 46 | 39 | 40 | 15 | 49 | 60 | 44 | 18 | 43 | 28 | 43 | 26 | 13 | 1 | 13 | 1 | 15 | 1 | 24 | 1 | 4 |
| 3 | 44 | 35 | 48 | 53 | 44 | 33 | 46 | 43 | 44 | 29 | 38 | 10 | 47 | 49 | 42 | 10 | 41 | 20 | 41 | 18 | 11 | 1 | 10 | 1 | 12 | 1 | 21 | 1 | 3 |
| 2 | 42 | 25 | 45 | 42 | 42 | 24 | 44 | 30 | 41 | 19 | 37 | 7 | 45 | 36 | 39 | 5 | 39 | 13 | 39 | 11 | 10 | 1 | 10 | 1 | 10 | 1 | 19 | 1 | 2 |
| 1 | 40 | 15 | 43 | 28 | 41 | 15 | 41 | 17 | 39 | 11 | 35 | 4 | 42 | 21 | 36 | 2 | 37 | 7 | 36 | 6 | 10 | 1 | 10 | 1 | 10 | 1 | 16 | 1 | 1 |
| 0 | 38 | 7 | 40 | 10 | 39 | 6 | 38 | 5 | 37 | 5 | 33 | 2 | 40 | 5 | 33 | 1 | 35 | 3 | 34 | 3 | 10 | 1 | 10 | 1 | 10 | 1 | 13 | 1 | 0 |
| **Raw mean** | 5.55 | | 3.82 | | 6.43 | | 4.47 | | 5.93 | | 9.71 | | 4.31 | | 5.93 | | 7.34 | | 7.21 | | 24.10 | | 17.52 | | 15.31 | | 13.79 | | **Raw mean** |
| **Raw *SD*** | 4.49 | | 3.79 | | 5.72 | | 3.81 | | 4.56 | | 5.76 | | 4.27 | | 3.48 | | 4.74 | | 4.58 | | 5.39 | | 3.64 | | 3.26 | | 3.76 | | **Raw *SD*** |
| **T: 90% Conf. int.** | 7 | | 7 | | 6 | | 9 | | 7 | | 6 | | 7 | | 8 | | 7 | | 7 | | 6 | | 7 | | 8 | | 8 | | **T: 90% Conf. int.** |

## Table A.13b SRP–C *T* Scores and Percentiles

| Raw score | Attitude to School T | %ile | Attitude to Teachers T | %ile | Atypicality T | %ile | Locus of Control T | %ile | Social Stress T | %ile | Anxiety T | %ile | Depression T | %ile | Sense of Inadequacy T | %ile | Attention Problems T | %ile | Hyperactivity T | %ile | Relations With Parents T | %ile | Interpersonal Relations T | %ile | Self-Esteem T | %ile | Self-Reliance T | %ile | Raw score |
|---|---|---|---|---|---|---|---|---|---|---|---|---|---|---|---|---|---|---|---|---|---|---|---|---|---|---|---|---|---|
| 32 | — | — | — | — | — | — | — | — | — | — | 84 | 99 | — | — | — | — | — | — | — | — | — | — | — | — | — | — | — | — | 32 |
| 31 | — | — | — | — | — | — | — | — | — | — | 82 | 99 | — | — | — | — | — | — | — | — | — | — | — | — | — | — | — | — | 31 |
| 30 | — | — | — | — | — | — | — | — | — | — | 81 | 99 | — | — | — | — | — | — | — | — | 60 | 91 | — | — | — | — | — | — | 30 |
| 29 | — | — | — | — | — | — | — | — | — | — | 79 | 99 | — | — | — | — | — | — | — | — | 58 | 77 | — | — | — | — | — | — | 29 |
| 28 | — | — | — | — | 88 | 99 | — | — | — | — | 78 | 99 | — | — | — | — | — | — | — | — | 56 | 65 | — | — | — | — | — | — | 28 |
| 27 | — | — | — | — | 87 | 99 | — | — | — | — | 76 | 98 | — | — | — | — | — | — | — | — | 54 | 55 | — | — | — | — | — | — | 27 |
| 26 | — | — | — | — | 85 | 99 | — | — | 92 | 99 | 75 | 98 | 94 | 99 | — | — | — | — | — | — | 52 | 47 | — | — | — | — | — | — | 26 |
| 25 | — | — | — | — | 83 | 99 | — | — | 90 | 99 | 73 | 97 | 92 | 99 | — | — | — | — | — | — | 50 | 40 | — | — | — | — | — | — | 25 |
| 24 | — | — | — | — | 81 | 99 | — | — | 88 | 99 | 72 | 97 | 90 | 99 | — | — | 87 | 99 | — | — | 48 | 34 | — | — | — | — | — | — | 24 |
| 23 | — | — | — | — | 80 | 99 | — | — | 86 | 99 | 70 | 96 | 88 | 99 | 97 | 99 | 85 | 99 | 84 | 99 | 46 | 29 | — | — | — | — | — | — | 23 |
| 22 | — | — | — | — | 78 | 98 | — | — | 84 | 99 | 68 | 95 | 86 | 99 | 94 | 99 | 83 | 99 | 82 | 99 | 44 | 24 | — | — | — | — | — | — | 22 |
| 21 | 92 | 99 | — | — | 76 | 98 | — | — | 82 | 99 | 67 | 94 | 84 | 99 | 91 | 99 | 81 | 99 | 80 | 99 | 42 | 20 | 59 | 95 | — | — | — | — | 21 |
| 20 | 90 | 99 | 96 | 99 | 74 | 97 | 89 | 99 | 80 | 99 | 65 | 92 | 82 | 98 | 89 | 99 | 79 | 99 | 78 | 99 | 40 | 17 | 56 | 72 | — | — | 66 | 99 | 20 |
| 19 | 87 | 99 | 93 | 99 | 73 | 96 | 87 | 99 | 78 | 98 | 64 | 90 | 80 | 98 | 86 | 99 | 77 | 99 | 75 | 98 | 38 | 14 | 54 | 52 | — | — | 63 | 94 | 19 |
| 18 | 85 | 99 | 90 | 99 | 71 | 95 | 84 | 99 | 76 | 98 | 62 | 88 | 78 | 97 | 83 | 99 | 74 | 98 | 73 | 98 | 36 | 12 | 51 | 38 | 58 | 86 | 60 | 86 | 18 |
| 17 | 82 | 99 | 88 | 99 | 69 | 94 | 82 | 99 | 74 | 97 | 61 | 86 | 76 | 97 | 81 | 98 | 72 | 97 | 71 | 97 | 34 | 9 | 48 | 28 | 55 | 59 | 58 | 75 | 17 |
| 16 | 79 | 99 | 85 | 99 | 68 | 93 | 79 | 99 | 71 | 96 | 59 | 83 | 74 | 96 | 78 | 98 | 70 | 96 | 69 | 95 | 32 | 7 | 45 | 21 | 52 | 42 | 55 | 64 | 16 |
| 15 | 77 | 98 | 82 | 99 | 66 | 92 | 77 | 98 | 69 | 95 | 58 | 80 | 72 | 95 | 75 | 97 | 68 | 94 | 67 | 93 | 30 | 6 | 42 | 16 | 49 | 31 | 52 | 52 | 15 |
| 14 | 74 | 98 | 79 | 99 | 64 | 90 | 74 | 97 | 67 | 94 | 56 | 76 | 70 | 94 | 72 | 96 | 66 | 92 | 65 | 91 | 28 | 4 | 39 | 12 | 46 | 23 | 49 | 42 | 14 |
| 13 | 72 | 96 | 77 | 98 | 62 | 88 | 72 | 96 | 65 | 92 | 55 | 72 | 68 | 93 | 70 | 94 | 64 | 90 | 63 | 88 | 26 | 3 | 36 | 9 | 43 | 17 | 47 | 33 | 13 |
| 12 | 69 | 95 | 74 | 96 | 61 | 86 | 69 | 94 | 63 | 89 | 53 | 67 | 66 | 92 | 67 | 92 | 62 | 86 | 61 | 85 | 24 | 2 | 34 | 7 | 40 | 13 | 44 | 25 | 12 |
| 11 | 66 | 92 | 71 | 94 | 59 | 83 | 67 | 92 | 61 | 87 | 52 | 62 | 64 | 90 | 64 | 89 | 59 | 82 | 59 | 81 | 22 | 1 | 31 | 5 | 37 | 10 | 41 | 18 | 11 |
| 10 | 64 | 89 | 68 | 92 | 57 | 80 | 64 | 90 | 59 | 83 | 50 | 57 | 62 | 88 | 62 | 84 | 57 | 78 | 56 | 76 | 20 | 1 | 28 | 4 | 34 | 8 | 38 | 13 | 10 |
| 9 | 61 | 86 | 66 | 90 | 55 | 76 | 62 | 87 | 57 | 79 | 49 | 51 | 60 | 86 | 59 | 79 | 55 | 72 | 54 | 70 | 18 | 1 | 25 | 3 | 31 | 6 | 35 | 9 | 9 |
| 8 | 59 | 81 | 63 | 87 | 54 | 72 | 59 | 83 | 55 | 74 | 47 | 45 | 58 | 83 | 56 | 71 | 53 | 66 | 52 | 63 | 16 | 1 | 22 | 2 | 28 | 4 | 33 | 6 | 8 |
| 7 | 56 | 75 | 60 | 84 | 52 | 67 | 57 | 79 | 53 | 68 | 46 | 38 | 56 | 79 | 54 | 62 | 51 | 59 | 50 | 56 | 14 | 1 | 19 | 2 | 25 | 3 | 30 | 4 | 7 |
| 6 | 53 | 68 | 57 | 80 | 50 | 62 | 54 | 73 | 51 | 61 | 44 | 31 | 54 | 75 | 51 | 51 | 49 | 51 | 48 | 48 | 12 | 1 | 16 | 2 | 22 | 3 | 27 | 3 | 6 |
| 5 | 51 | 60 | 55 | 75 | 49 | 56 | 52 | 67 | 48 | 53 | 42 | 25 | 51 | 70 | 48 | 38 | 47 | 42 | 46 | 39 | 10 | 1 | 14 | 1 | 19 | 2 | 24 | 2 | 5 |
| 4 | 48 | 50 | 52 | 69 | 47 | 48 | 49 | 58 | 46 | 43 | 41 | 19 | 49 | 63 | 46 | 25 | 44 | 33 | 44 | 31 | 10 | 1 | 11 | 1 | 16 | 1 | 22 | 1 | 4 |
| 3 | 45 | 39 | 49 | 61 | 45 | 40 | 47 | 48 | 44 | 33 | 39 | 13 | 47 | 55 | 43 | 13 | 42 | 24 | 42 | 22 | 10 | 1 | 10 | 1 | 13 | 1 | 19 | 1 | 3 |
| 2 | 43 | 27 | 46 | 51 | 43 | 31 | 44 | 36 | 42 | 23 | 38 | 8 | 45 | 44 | 40 | 5 | 40 | 16 | 40 | 14 | 10 | 1 | 10 | 1 | 10 | 1 | 16 | 1 | 2 |
| 1 | 40 | 16 | 44 | 36 | 42 | 21 | 42 | 22 | 40 | 13 | 36 | 5 | 43 | 29 | 38 | 2 | 38 | 9 | 37 | 7 | 10 | 1 | 10 | 1 | 10 | 1 | 13 | 1 | 1 |
| 0 | 38 | 6 | 41 | 12 | 40 | 11 | 39 | 7 | 38 | 5 | 35 | 2 | 41 | 9 | 35 | 2 | 36 | 3 | 35 | 3 | 10 | 1 | 10 | 1 | 10 | 1 | 11 | 1 | 0 |
| **Raw mean** | 4.73 | | 3.30 | | 5.83 | | 4.26 | | 5.73 | | 9.92 | | 4.27 | | 5.59 | | 6.60 | | 6.96 | | 24.91 | | 17.77 | | 15.37 | | 14.25 | | **Raw mean** |
| **Raw SD** | 3.84 | | 3.65 | | 5.80 | | 4.01 | | 4.79 | | 6.53 | | 4.89 | | 3.74 | | 4.66 | | 4.74 | | 4.96 | | 3.51 | | 3.30 | | 3.61 | | **Raw SD** |
| **T: 90% Conf. int.** | 8 | | 7 | | 6 | | 8 | | 6 | | 5 | | 6 | | 7 | | 7 | | 6 | | 6 | | 7 | | 7 | | 9 | | **T: 90% Conf. int.** |

**Table A.13c** SRP–C *T* Scores and Percentiles

| Raw score | Attitude to School T | %ile | Attitude to Teachers T | %ile | Atypicality T | %ile | Locus of Control T | %ile | Social Stress T | %ile | Anxiety T | %ile | Depression T | %ile | Sense of Inadequacy T | %ile | Attention Problems T | %ile | Hyperactivity T | %ile | Relations With Parents T | %ile | Interpersonal Relations T | %ile | Self-Esteem T | %ile | Self-Reliance T | %ile | Raw score |
|---|---|---|---|---|---|---|---|---|---|---|---|---|---|---|---|---|---|---|---|---|---|---|---|---|---|---|---|---|---|
| 32 | — | — | — | — | — | — | — | — | — | — | 96 | 99 | — | — | — | — | — | — | — | — | — | — | — | — | — | — | — | — | 32 |
| 31 | — | — | — | — | — | — | — | — | — | — | 94 | 99 | — | — | — | — | — | — | — | — | — | — | — | — | — | — | — | — | 31 |
| 30 | — | — | — | — | — | — | — | — | — | — | 92 | 99 | — | — | — | — | — | — | — | — | 62 | 94 | — | — | — | — | — | — | 30 |
| 29 | — | — | — | — | — | — | — | — | — | — | 90 | 99 | — | — | — | — | — | — | — | — | 60 | 86 | — | — | — | — | — | — | 29 |
| 28 | — | — | — | — | 88 | 99 | — | — | — | — | 88 | 99 | — | — | — | — | — | — | — | — | 58 | 77 | — | — | — | — | — | — | 28 |
| 27 | — | — | — | — | 86 | 99 | — | — | — | — | 86 | 99 | — | — | — | — | — | — | — | — | 57 | 69 | — | — | — | — | — | — | 27 |
| 26 | — | — | — | — | 84 | 99 | — | — | 96 | 99 | 84 | 99 | 111 | 99 | — | — | — | — | — | — | 55 | 60 | — | — | — | — | — | — | 26 |
| 25 | — | — | — | — | 82 | 99 | — | — | 94 | 99 | 82 | 99 | 108 | 99 | — | — | — | — | — | — | 53 | 53 | — | — | — | — | — | — | 25 |
| 24 | — | — | — | — | 80 | 99 | — | — | 91 | 99 | 80 | 99 | 105 | 99 | — | — | 84 | 99 | — | — | 51 | 46 | — | — | — | — | — | — | 24 |
| 23 | — | — | — | — | 79 | 99 | — | — | 89 | 99 | 78 | 99 | 102 | 99 | 103 | 99 | 82 | 99 | 85 | 99 | 49 | 39 | — | — | — | — | — | — | 23 |
| 22 | — | — | — | — | 77 | 98 | — | — | 87 | 99 | 76 | 99 | 100 | 99 | 100 | 99 | 79 | 99 | 83 | 99 | 48 | 34 | — | — | — | — | — | — | 22 |
| 21 | 80 | 99 | — | — | 75 | 97 | — | — | 84 | 99 | 74 | 99 | 97 | 99 | 96 | 99 | 77 | 99 | 81 | 99 | 46 | 29 | 60 | 90 | — | — | — | — | 21 |
| 20 | 78 | 99 | 90 | 99 | 73 | 97 | 93 | 99 | 82 | 99 | 72 | 98 | 94 | 99 | 93 | 99 | 75 | 99 | 78 | 99 | 44 | 24 | 57 | 74 | — | — | 67 | 98 | 20 |
| 19 | 76 | 99 | 88 | 99 | 71 | 96 | 90 | 99 | 80 | 99 | 69 | 97 | 91 | 99 | 90 | 99 | 73 | 99 | 76 | 99 | 42 | 21 | 55 | 59 | — | — | 65 | 94 | 19 |
| 18 | 74 | 98 | 85 | 99 | 70 | 95 | 87 | 99 | 77 | 99 | 67 | 95 | 88 | 99 | 87 | 99 | 71 | 98 | 74 | 98 | 41 | 17 | 52 | 46 | 58 | 84 | 62 | 87 | 18 |
| 17 | 72 | 97 | 83 | 99 | 68 | 93 | 84 | 99 | 75 | 98 | 65 | 93 | 86 | 99 | 84 | 99 | 69 | 97 | 72 | 97 | 39 | 14 | 49 | 36 | 55 | 60 | 60 | 80 | 17 |
| 16 | 69 | 96 | 80 | 99 | 66 | 92 | 81 | 99 | 73 | 98 | 63 | 90 | 83 | 99 | 81 | 99 | 67 | 94 | 69 | 96 | 37 | 12 | 47 | 28 | 52 | 45 | 57 | 71 | 16 |
| 15 | 67 | 94 | 78 | 99 | 64 | 90 | 79 | 99 | 70 | 96 | 61 | 87 | 80 | 99 | 78 | 99 | 65 | 91 | 67 | 94 | 35 | 10 | 44 | 22 | 49 | 34 | 54 | 63 | 15 |
| 14 | 65 | 91 | 75 | 98 | 62 | 88 | 76 | 98 | 68 | 95 | 59 | 82 | 77 | 98 | 74 | 99 | 63 | 88 | 65 | 92 | 34 | 8 | 41 | 17 | 46 | 26 | 52 | 54 | 14 |
| 13 | 63 | 89 | 72 | 97 | 61 | 85 | 73 | 97 | 66 | 93 | 57 | 77 | 74 | 97 | 71 | 98 | 60 | 83 | 63 | 89 | 32 | 6 | 39 | 13 | 43 | 20 | 49 | 45 | 13 |
| 12 | 61 | 85 | 70 | 95 | 59 | 82 | 70 | 96 | 64 | 90 | 55 | 71 | 71 | 96 | 68 | 96 | 58 | 78 | 60 | 85 | 30 | 5 | 36 | 10 | 40 | 16 | 47 | 37 | 12 |
| 11 | 59 | 81 | 67 | 93 | 57 | 79 | 68 | 93 | 61 | 86 | 53 | 64 | 69 | 94 | 65 | 93 | 56 | 72 | 58 | 80 | 28 | 4 | 33 | 8 | 37 | 12 | 44 | 29 | 11 |
| 10 | 57 | 77 | 65 | 90 | 55 | 75 | 65 | 91 | 59 | 82 | 51 | 56 | 66 | 92 | 62 | 88 | 54 | 66 | 56 | 74 | 27 | 3 | 31 | 6 | 34 | 9 | 41 | 22 | 10 |
| 9 | 55 | 72 | 62 | 86 | 54 | 70 | 62 | 87 | 57 | 76 | 49 | 48 | 63 | 89 | 59 | 81 | 52 | 59 | 53 | 67 | 25 | 2 | 28 | 4 | 31 | 7 | 39 | 16 | 9 |
| 8 | 53 | 66 | 59 | 82 | 52 | 65 | 59 | 82 | 54 | 70 | 47 | 40 | 60 | 85 | 55 | 71 | 50 | 51 | 51 | 59 | 23 | 2 | 25 | 3 | 28 | 5 | 36 | 10 | 8 |
| 7 | 51 | 60 | 57 | 77 | 50 | 59 | 56 | 76 | 52 | 62 | 45 | 32 | 57 | 81 | 52 | 60 | 48 | 44 | 49 | 50 | 21 | 1 | 23 | 2 | 25 | 3 | 34 | 6 | 7 |
| 6 | 49 | 53 | 54 | 71 | 48 | 52 | 54 | 69 | 50 | 54 | 43 | 25 | 55 | 74 | 49 | 47 | 46 | 36 | 47 | 40 | 20 | 1 | 20 | 2 | 21 | 2 | 31 | 3 | 6 |
| 5 | 47 | 46 | 52 | 64 | 46 | 45 | 51 | 61 | 47 | 44 | 41 | 18 | 52 | 66 | 46 | 35 | 44 | 29 | 44 | 31 | 18 | 1 | 17 | 1 | 18 | 1 | 28 | 1 | 5 |
| 4 | 45 | 38 | 49 | 55 | 45 | 36 | 48 | 51 | 45 | 35 | 39 | 13 | 49 | 56 | 43 | 24 | 41 | 22 | 42 | 22 | 16 | 1 | 15 | 1 | 15 | 1 | 26 | 1 | 4 |
| 3 | 43 | 30 | 47 | 46 | 43 | 27 | 45 | 39 | 43 | 25 | 37 | 8 | 46 | 44 | 40 | 15 | 39 | 16 | 40 | 15 | 14 | 1 | 12 | 1 | 12 | 1 | 23 | 1 | 3 |
| 2 | 41 | 22 | 44 | 34 | 41 | 18 | 43 | 26 | 40 | 17 | 35 | 5 | 43 | 29 | 37 | 9 | 37 | 11 | 38 | 9 | 13 | 1 | 10 | 1 | 10 | 1 | 21 | 1 | 2 |
| 1 | 39 | 14 | 41 | 22 | 39 | 9 | 40 | 14 | 38 | 10 | 33 | 3 | 41 | 14 | 33 | 5 | 35 | 6 | 35 | 5 | 11 | 1 | 10 | 1 | 10 | 1 | 18 | 1 | 1 |
| 0 | 37 | 7 | 39 | 9 | 37 | 3 | 37 | 4 | 36 | 5 | 31 | 2 | 38 | 2 | 30 | 2 | 33 | 3 | 33 | 2 | 10 | 1 | 10 | 1 | 10 | 1 | 15 | 1 | 0 |
| **Raw mean** | 6.37 | | 4.33 | | 7.03 | | 4.67 | | 6.13 | | 9.50 | | 4.35 | | 6.27 | | 8.07 | | 7.46 | | 23.29 | | 17.27 | | 15.26 | | 13.33 | | **Raw mean** |
| **Raw SD** | 4.94 | | 3.88 | | 5.59 | | 3.60 | | 4.33 | | 4.88 | | 3.56 | | 3.17 | | 4.73 | | 4.42 | | 5.70 | | 3.75 | | 3.24 | | 3.85 | | **Raw SD** |
| **T: 90% Conf. int.** | 6 | | 7 | | 7 | | 9 | | 7 | | 8 | | 9 | | 9 | | 8 | | 8 | | 6 | | 7 | | 8 | | 8 | | **T: 90% Conf. int.** |

## Table A.13d SRP-C Composite T Scores

| T score | School Problems | | | Internalizing Problems | | | Inattention/Hyperactivity | | | Emotional Symptoms | | | Personal Adjustment | | | T score |
|---|---|---|---|---|---|---|---|---|---|---|---|---|---|---|---|---|
| | Combined | Female | Male | Combined | Female | Male | Combined | Female | Male | Combined | Female | Male | Combined | Female | Male | |
| 120 | — | — | — | — | — | — | — | — | — | — | — | — | — | — | — | 120 |
| 119 | — | — | — | — | — | — | — | — | — | — | — | — | — | — | — | 119 |
| 118 | — | — | — | — | — | — | — | — | — | — | — | — | — | — | — | 118 |
| 117 | — | — | — | — | — | — | — | — | — | — | — | — | — | — | — | 117 |
| 116 | — | — | — | — | — | — | — | — | — | — | — | — | — | — | — | 116 |
| 115 | — | — | — | — | — | — | — | — | — | — | — | — | — | — | — | 115 |
| 114 | — | — | — | — | — | — | — | — | — | — | — | — | — | — | — | 114 |
| 113 | — | — | — | — | — | — | — | — | — | — | — | 577–581 | — | — | — | 113 |
| 112 | — | — | — | — | — | — | — | — | — | — | — | 573–576 | — | — | — | 112 |
| 111 | — | — | — | — | — | — | — | — | — | — | — | — | — | — | — | 111 |
| 110 | — | — | — | — | — | 586–587 | — | — | — | — | — | 568–572 | — | — | — | 110 |
| 109 | — | — | — | — | — | 581–585 | — | — | — | — | — | 564–567 | — | — | — | 109 |
| 108 | — | — | — | — | — | 576–580 | — | — | — | — | — | 559–563 | — | — | — | 108 |
| 107 | — | — | — | — | — | 571–575 | — | — | — | — | — | 555–558 | — | — | — | 107 |
| 106 | — | — | — | — | — | 567–570 | — | — | — | — | — | 550–554 | — | — | — | 106 |
| 105 | — | — | — | — | — | 562–566 | — | — | — | 557–560 | — | 546–549 | — | — | — | 105 |
| 104 | — | — | — | — | — | 557–561 | — | — | — | 553–556 | — | 541–545 | — | — | — | 104 |
| 103 | — | 188 | — | — | — | 552–556 | — | — | — | 548–552 | — | 537–540 | — | — | — | 103 |
| 102 | — | — | — | 559–562 | — | 547–551 | — | — | — | 543–547 | — | 532–536 | — | — | — | 102 |
| 101 | — | — | — | 554–558 | — | 543–546 | — | — | — | 539–542 | 546 | 528–531 | — | — | — | 101 |
| 100 | — | — | — | 549–553 | — | 538–542 | — | — | — | 534–538 | 541–545 | 523–527 | — | — | — | 100 |
| 99 | — | 184–185 | 169–170 | 544–548 | — | 533–537 | — | — | — | 529–533 | 536–540 | 519–522 | — | — | — | 99 |
| 98 | — | 183 | 167–168 | 539–543 | — | 528–532 | — | — | — | 524–528 | 531–535 | 514–518 | — | — | — | 98 |
| 97 | — | 181–182 | 165–166 | 534–538 | 542–544 | 523–527 | — | — | — | 520–523 | 527–530 | 510–513 | — | — | — | 97 |
| 96 | — | 179–180 | 164 | 529–533 | 537–541 | 519–522 | — | — | — | 515–519 | 522–526 | 505–509 | — | — | — | 96 |
| 95 | — | 177–178 | 162–163 | 524–528 | 532–536 | 514–518 | — | — | — | 510–514 | 517–521 | 501–504 | — | — | — | 95 |
| 94 | 177 | 176 | 160–161 | 519–523 | 526–531 | 509–513 | — | — | — | 506–509 | 512–516 | 496–500 | — | — | — | 94 |
| 93 | 175–176 | 174–175 | 158–159 | 514–518 | 521–525 | 504–508 | — | — | — | 501–505 | 507–511 | 492–495 | — | — | — | 93 |
| 92 | 174 | 172–173 | 156–157 | 509–513 | 516–520 | 499–503 | — | — | — | 496–500 | 502–506 | 487–491 | — | — | — | 92 |
| 91 | 172–173 | 171 | 155 | 504–508 | 511–515 | 495–498 | — | — | — | 491–495 | 497–501 | 483–486 | — | — | — | 91 |
| 90 | 170–171 | 169–170 | 153–154 | 499–503 | 506–510 | 490–494 | — | — | — | 487–490 | 492–496 | 478–482 | — | — | — | 90 |
| 89 | 168–169 | 167–168 | 151–152 | 494–498 | 500–505 | 485–489 | — | — | — | 482–486 | 488–491 | 474–477 | — | — | — | 89 |
| 88 | 167 | 165–166 | 149–150 | 489–493 | 495–499 | 480–484 | — | 171 | 169 | 477–481 | 483–487 | 469–473 | — | — | — | 88 |
| 87 | 165–166 | 164 | 148 | 484–488 | 490–494 | 476–479 | 168–169 | 169–170 | 168 | 473–476 | 478–482 | 465–468 | — | — | — | 87 |
| 86 | 163–164 | 162–163 | 146–147 | 479–483 | 485–489 | 471–475 | 166–167 | 167–168 | 166–167 | 468–472 | 473–477 | 460–464 | — | — | — | 86 |
| 85 | 161–162 | 160–161 | 144–145 | 474–478 | 480–484 | 466–470 | 164–165 | 165–166 | 164–165 | 463–467 | 468–472 | 456–459 | — | — | — | 85 |
| 84 | 159–160 | 158–159 | 142–143 | 469–473 | 474–479 | 461–465 | 162–163 | 163–164 | 162–163 | 458–462 | 463–467 | 451–455 | — | — | — | 84 |
| 83 | 158 | 157 | 140–141 | 464–468 | 469–473 | 456–460 | 161 | 162 | 160–161 | 454–457 | 458–462 | 447–450 | — | — | — | 83 |
| 82 | 156–157 | 155–156 | 139 | 459–463 | 464–468 | 452–455 | 159–160 | 160–161 | 158–159 | 449–453 | 453–457 | 442–446 | — | — | — | 82 |
| 81 | 154–155 | 153–154 | 137–138 | 454–458 | 459–463 | 447–451 | 157–158 | 158–159 | 157 | 444–448 | 449–452 | 438–441 | — | — | — | 81 |
| 80 | 152–153 | 152 | 135–136 | 449–453 | 454–458 | 442–446 | 155–156 | 156–157 | 155–156 | 440–443 | 444–448 | 433–437 | — | — | — | 80 |
| 79 | 151 | 150–151 | 133–134 | 444–448 | 448–453 | 437–441 | 153–154 | 154–155 | 153–154 | 435–439 | 439–443 | 429–432 | — | — | — | 79 |
| 78 | 149–150 | 148–149 | 131–132 | 439–443 | 443–447 | 432–436 | 151–152 | 152–153 | 151–152 | 430–434 | 434–438 | 424–428 | — | — | — | 78 |
| 77 | 147–148 | 146–147 | 130 | 434–438 | 438–442 | 428–431 | 150 | 150–151 | 149–150 | 425–429 | 429–433 | 420–423 | — | — | — | 77 |
| 76 | 145–146 | 145 | 128–129 | 429–433 | 433–437 | 423–427 | 148–149 | 148–149 | 147–148 | 421–424 | 424–428 | 415–419 | — | — | — | 76 |
| 75 | 144 | 143–144 | — | 424–428 | 427–432 | 418–422 | 146–147 | 147 | 146 | 416–420 | 419–423 | 411–414 | — | — | — | 75 |
| 74 | 142–143 | 141–142 | — | 418–423 | 422–426 | 413–417 | 144–145 | 145–146 | 144–145 | 411–415 | 414–418 | 406–410 | — | — | — | 74 |
| 73 | 140–141 | 139–140 | — | 413–417 | 417–421 | 408–412 | 142–143 | 143–144 | 142–143 | 407–410 | 410–413 | 402–405 | — | — | — | 73 |
| 72 | 138–139 | 138 | — | 408–412 | 412–416 | 404–407 | 140–141 | 141–142 | 140–141 | 402–406 | 405–409 | 397–401 | — | — | — | 72 |
| 71 | 137 | 136–137 | — | 403–407 | 407–411 | 399–403 | 138–139 | 139–140 | 138–139 | 397–401 | 400–404 | 393–396 | — | — | — | 71 |
| 70 | 135–136 | 134–135 | — | 398–402 | 401–406 | 394–398 | 137 | 137–138 | 136–137 | 392–396 | 395–399 | 388–392 | — | — | — | 70 |
| 69 | 133–134 | 132–133 | — | 393–397 | 396–400 | 389–393 | 135–136 | 135 | 135 | 388–391 | 390–394 | 384–387 | — | — | — | 69 |
| 68 | 131–132 | 131 | — | 388–392 | 391–395 | 384–388 | 133–134 | 133–134 | 133–134 | 383–387 | 385–389 | 379–383 | — | — | — | 68 |
| 67 | 130 | 129–130 | — | 383–387 | 386–390 | 380–383 | 131–132 | 131–132 | 131–132 | 378–382 | 380–384 | 375–378 | — | — | — | 67 |
| 66 | 128–129 | 127–128 | — | 378–382 | 381–385 | 375–379 | 129–130 | 130 | 129–130 | 374–377 | 376–379 | 370–374 | — | — | — | 66 |

**Table A.13d** SRP–C Composite T Scores (continued)

| T score | Personal Adjustment Combined | PA Female | PA Male | Emotional Symptoms Combined | ES Female | ES Male | Inattention/Hyperactivity Combined | IH Female | IH Male | Internalizing Problems Combined | IP Female | IP Male | School Problems Combined | SP Female | SP Male | T score |
|---|---|---|---|---|---|---|---|---|---|---|---|---|---|---|---|---|
| 65 | – | – | – | 369–373 | 371–375 | 366–369 | 127–128 | 128–129 | 127–128 | 373–377 | 375–380 | 370–374 | 126–127 | 126 | 126–127 | 65 |
| 64 | 245–246 | – | 244–247 | 364–368 | 366–370 | 361–365 | 126 | 126–127 | 125–126 | 368–372 | 370–374 | 365–369 | 124–125 | 124–125 | 124–125 | 64 |
| 63 | 241–244 | 240–243 | 241–243 | 359–363 | 361–365 | 357–360 | 124–125 | 124–125 | 124 | 363–367 | 365–369 | 360–364 | 123 | 122–123 | 123 | 63 |
| 62 | 238–240 | 237–239 | 238–240 | 355–358 | 356–360 | 352–356 | 122–123 | 122–123 | 122–123 | 358–362 | 360–364 | 356–359 | 121–122 | 120–121 | 121–122 | 62 |
| 61 | 235–237 | 234–236 | 235–237 | 350–354 | 351–355 | 348–351 | 120–121 | 120–121 | 120–121 | 353–357 | 355–359 | 351–355 | 119–120 | 119 | 119–120 | 61 |
| 60 | 232–234 | 231–233 | 231–234 | 345–349 | 346–350 | 343–347 | 118–119 | 118–119 | 118–119 | 348–352 | 349–354 | 346–350 | 117–118 | 117–118 | 117–120 | 60 |
| 59 | 228–231 | 228–230 | 228–230 | 341–344 | 341–345 | 339–342 | 116–117 | 116–117 | 116–117 | 343–347 | 344–348 | 341–345 | 116 | 115–116 | 115–116 | 59 |
| 58 | 225–227 | 225–227 | 225–227 | 336–340 | 337–340 | 334–338 | 114–115 | 115 | 114–115 | 338–342 | 339–343 | 336–340 | 114–115 | 113–114 | 114 | 58 |
| 57 | 222–224 | 221–224 | 222–224 | 331–335 | 332–336 | 330–333 | 113 | 113–114 | 112–113 | 333–337 | 334–338 | 332–335 | 112–113 | 112 | 112–113 | 57 |
| 56 | 219–221 | 218–220 | 218–221 | 326–330 | 327–331 | 325–329 | 111–112 | 111–112 | 111 | 328–332 | 329–333 | 327–331 | 110–111 | 110–111 | 110–111 | 56 |
| 55 | 215–218 | 215–217 | 215–217 | 322–325 | 322–326 | 321–324 | 109–110 | 109–110 | 109–110 | 323–327 | 323–328 | 322–326 | 109 | 108–109 | 108–109 | 55 |
| 54 | 212–214 | 212–214 | 212–214 | 317–321 | 317–321 | 316–320 | 107–108 | 107–108 | 107–108 | 318–322 | 318–322 | 317–321 | 107–108 | 107 | 107 | 54 |
| 53 | 209–211 | 209–211 | 209–211 | 312–316 | 312–316 | 312–315 | 105–106 | 105–106 | 105–106 | 313–317 | 313–317 | 312–316 | 105–106 | 105–106 | 105–106 | 53 |
| 52 | 206–208 | 205–208 | 205–208 | 308–311 | 307–311 | 307–311 | 103–104 | 103–104 | 103–104 | 308–312 | 308–312 | 308–311 | 103–104 | 103–104 | 103–104 | 52 |
| 51 | 202–205 | 202–204 | 202–204 | 303–307 | 302–306 | 303–306 | 102 | 101–102 | 101–102 | 303–307 | 303–307 | 303–307 | 101–102 | 101–102 | 101–102 | 51 |
| 50 | 199–201 | 199–201 | 199–201 | 298–302 | 298–301 | 298–302 | 100–101 | 100 | 100 | 298–302 | 297–302 | 298–302 | 100 | 100 | 99–100 | 50 |
| 49 | 196–198 | 196–198 | 195–198 | 293–297 | 293–297 | 294–297 | 98–99 | 98–99 | 98–99 | 293–297 | 292–296 | 293–297 | 98–99 | 98–99 | 98 | 49 |
| 48 | 193–195 | 193–195 | 192–194 | 289–292 | 288–292 | 289–293 | 96–97 | 96–97 | 96–97 | 288–292 | 287–291 | 288–292 | 96–97 | 96–97 | 96–97 | 48 |
| 47 | 189–192 | 189–192 | 189–191 | 284–288 | 283–287 | 285–288 | 94–95 | 94–95 | 94–95 | 283–287 | 282–286 | 284–287 | 94–95 | 94–95 | 94–95 | 47 |
| 46 | 186–188 | 186–188 | 186–188 | 279–283 | 278–282 | 280–284 | 92–93 | 92–93 | 92–93 | 278–282 | 277–281 | 279–283 | 93 | 93 | 92–93 | 46 |
| 45 | 183–185 | 183–185 | 182–185 | 275–278 | 273–277 | 276–279 | 90–91 | 90–91 | 90–91 | 273–277 | 271–276 | 274–278 | 91–92 | 91–92 | 90–91 | 45 |
| 44 | 180–182 | 180–182 | 179–181 | 270–274 | 268–272 | 271–275 | 89 | 88–89 | 89 | 268–272 | 266–270 | 269–273 | 89–90 | 89–90 | 89 | 44 |
| 43 | 176–179 | 177–179 | 176–178 | 265–269 | 263–267 | 267–270 | 87–88 | 86–87 | 87–88 | 263–267 | 261–265 | 264–268 | 87–88 | 87–88 | 87–88 | 43 |
| 42 | 173–175 | 173–176 | 173–175 | 261–264 | 259–262 | 262–266 | 85–86 | 85 | 85–86 | 258–262 | 256–260 | 260–263 | 86 | 86 | 85–86 | 42 |
| 41 | 170–172 | 170–172 | 169–172 | 256–260 | 254–258 | 258–261 | 83–84 | 83–84 | 83–84 | 253–257 | 251–255 | 255–259 | 84–85 | 84–85 | 83–84 | 41 |
| 40 | 167–169 | 167–169 | 166–168 | 251–255 | 249–253 | 253–257 | 81–82 | 81–82 | 81–82 | 248–252 | 245–250 | 250–254 | 82–83 | 82–83 | 82 | 40 |
| 39 | 163–166 | 164–166 | 163–165 | 246–250 | 244–248 | 249–252 | 79–80 | 79–80 | 79–80 | 243–247 | 240–244 | 245–249 | 80–81 | 81 | 80–81 | 39 |
| 38 | 160–162 | 161–163 | 159–162 | 242–245 | 239–243 | 244–248 | 77–78 | 77–78 | 78 | 238–242 | 235–239 | 241–244 | 79 | 79–80 | 78–79 | 38 |
| 37 | 157–159 | 157–159 | 156–158 | 237–241 | 234–238 | 240–243 | 76 | 75–76 | 76–77 | 233–237 | 230–234 | 236–240 | 78 | – | 76–77 | 37 |
| 36 | 154–156 | 154–156 | 153–155 | 232–236 | 229–233 | 235–239 | 74–75 | 73–74 | 74–75 | 228–232 | 228–229 | 231–235 | – | – | – | 36 |
| 35 | 150–153 | 151–153 | 150–152 | 228–231 | 225–228 | 231–234 | 72–73 | 71–72 | 72–73 | 223–227 | – | 226–230 | – | – | – | 35 |
| 34 | 147–149 | 148–150 | 146–149 | 223–227 | – | 226–230 | 70–71 | – | 70–71 | 220–222 | – | 221–225 | – | – | – | 34 |
| 33 | 144–146 | 145–147 | 143–145 | 218–222 | – | 222–225 | 69 | – | 68–69 | – | – | 217–220 | – | – | – | 33 |
| 32 | 141–143 | 142–144 | 140–142 | – | – | 217–221 | – | – | 66–67 | – | – | 212–216 | – | – | – | 32 |
| 31 | 137–140 | 138–141 | 137–139 | – | – | 213–216 | – | – | – | – | – | 209–211 | – | – | – | 31 |
| 30 | 134–136 | 135–137 | 133–136 | – | – | 210–212 | – | – | – | – | – | – | – | – | – | 30 |
| 29 | 131–133 | 132–134 | 130–132 | – | – | – | – | – | – | – | – | – | – | – | – | 29 |
| 28 | 127–130 | 129–131 | 127–129 | – | – | – | – | – | – | – | – | – | – | – | – | 28 |
| 27 | 124–126 | 126–128 | 124–126 | – | – | – | – | – | – | – | – | – | – | – | – | 27 |
| 26 | 121–123 | 122–125 | 120–123 | – | – | – | – | – | – | – | – | – | – | – | – | 26 |
| 25 | 118–120 | 119–121 | 117–119 | – | – | – | – | – | – | – | – | – | – | – | – | 25 |
| 24 | 114–117 | 116–118 | 114–116 | – | – | – | – | – | – | – | – | – | – | – | – | 24 |
| 23 | 111–113 | 113–115 | 110–113 | – | – | – | – | – | – | – | – | – | – | – | – | 23 |
| 22 | 108–110 | 110–112 | 107–109 | – | – | – | – | – | – | – | – | – | – | – | – | 22 |
| 21 | 105–107 | 106–109 | 104–106 | – | – | – | – | – | – | – | – | – | – | – | – | 21 |
| 20 | 101–104 | 103–105 | 101–103 | – | – | – | – | – | – | – | – | – | – | – | – | 20 |
| 19 | 98–100 | 100–102 | 97–100 | – | – | – | – | – | – | – | – | – | – | – | – | 19 |
| 18 | 95–97 | 97–99 | 94–96 | – | – | – | – | – | – | – | – | – | – | – | – | 18 |
| 17 | 92–94 | 94–96 | 91–93 | – | – | – | – | – | – | – | – | – | – | – | – | 17 |
| 16 | 88–91 | 90–93 | 88–90 | – | – | – | – | – | – | – | – | – | – | – | – | 16 |
| 15 | 85–87 | 87–89 | 84–87 | – | – | – | – | – | – | – | – | – | – | – | – | 15 |
| 14 | 82–84 | 84–86 | 81–83 | – | – | – | – | – | – | – | – | – | – | – | – | 14 |
| 13 | 79–81 | 81–83 | 78–80 | – | – | – | – | – | – | – | – | – | – | – | – | 13 |
| 12 | 75–78 | 78–80 | 74–77 | – | – | – | – | – | – | – | – | – | – | – | – | 12 |
| 11 | 72–74 | 75–77 | 71–73 | – | – | – | – | – | – | – | – | – | – | – | – | 11 |
| 10 | 43–71 | 41–74 | 45–70 | – | – | – | – | – | – | – | – | – | – | – | – | 10 |
| T: 90% Conf. int. | 4 | 5 | 4 | 4 | 3 | 4 | 5 | 5 | 6 | 4 | 3 | 4 | 5 | 6 | 5 | T: 90% Conf. int. |

## Table A.13e  SRP-C Composite Percentiles

| %ile | School Problems | | | Internalizing Problems | | | Inattention/Hyperactivity | | | Emotional Symptoms | | | Personal Adjustment | | | %ile |
|---|---|---|---|---|---|---|---|---|---|---|---|---|---|---|---|---|
| | Combined | Female | Male | Combined | Female | Male | Combined | Female | Male | Combined | Female | Male | Combined | Female | Male | |
| 99 | 146–177 | 144–188 | 146–170 | 446–562 | 457–544 | 429–587 | 146–169 | 149–171 | 145–169 | 430–560 | 442–546 | 414–581 | 245–246 | 241–243 | 246–247 | 99 |
| 98 | 142–145 | 141–143 | 141–145 | 425–445 | 434–456 | 413–428 | 142–145 | 144–148 | 140–144 | 412–429 | 422–441 | 401–413 | 243–244 | 239–240 | 244–245 | 98 |
| 97 | 139–141 | 138–140 | 138–140 | 411–424 | 418–433 | 401–412 | 138–141 | 140–143 | 137–139 | 400–411 | 408–421 | 392–400 | 242 | 238 | 243 | 97 |
| 96 | 136–138 | 136–137 | 135–137 | 401–410 | 407–417 | 393–400 | 136–137 | 137–139 | 134–136 | 391–399 | 398–407 | 385–391 | 241 | 237 | 242 | 96 |
| 95 | 134–135 | 134–135 | 133–134 | 392–400 | 397–406 | 386–392 | 133–135 | 135–136 | 132–133 | 384–390 | 390–397 | 380–384 | 240 | 236 | 241 | 95 |
| 94 | 132–133 | 133 | 131–132 | 385–391 | 389–396 | 380–385 | 131–132 | 133–134 | 130–131 | 378–383 | 383–389 | 375–379 | 239 | 235 | 240 | 94 |
| 93 | 130–131 | 131–132 | 129–130 | 379–384 | 383–388 | 375–379 | 130 | 131–132 | 128–129 | 373–377 | 377–382 | 371–374 | 238 | – | 239 | 93 |
| 92 | 129 | 129–130 | 128 | 374–378 | 377–382 | 370–374 | 128–129 | 129–130 | 127 | 368–372 | 371–376 | 367–370 | 237 | 234 | – | 92 |
| 91 | 127–128 | 128 | 126–127 | 369–373 | 371–376 | 366–369 | 127 | 127–128 | 126 | 364–367 | 367–370 | 363–366 | 236 | 233 | 238 | 91 |
| 90 | 126 | 127 | 125 | 365–368 | 367–370 | 362–365 | 125–126 | 126 | 124–125 | 360–363 | 362–366 | 360–362 | 235 | 232 | 237 | 90 |
| 89 | 124–125 | 125–126 | 124 | 361–364 | 362–366 | 359–361 | 124 | 125 | 123 | 357–359 | 358–361 | 357–359 | – | – | 236 | 89 |
| 88 | 123 | 124 | 122–123 | 358–360 | 358–361 | 355–358 | 123 | 123–124 | 122 | 353–356 | 355–357 | 354–356 | 234 | 231 | 235 | 88 |
| 87 | 122 | 123 | 121 | 354–357 | 355–357 | 353–354 | 122 | 122 | 121 | 350–352 | 351–354 | 352–353 | 233 | 230 | 234 | 87 |
| 86 | 121 | 122 | 120 | 351–353 | 351–354 | 350–352 | 121 | 121 | 120 | 348–349 | 348–350 | 349–351 | 232 | – | 234 | 86 |
| 85 | 120 | 121 | 119 | 348–350 | 348–350 | 347–349 | 120 | 120 | 119 | 345–347 | 345–347 | 347–348 | – | 229 | 233 | 85 |
| 84 | 119 | 119–120 | 118 | 346–347 | 345–347 | 345–346 | 119 | 119 | 118 | 343–344 | 343–344 | 344–346 | 231 | – | – | 84 |
| 83 | 118 | 118 | 117 | 343–345 | 342–344 | 342–344 | 118 | 118 | 117 | 340–342 | 340–342 | 342–343 | 230 | 228 | 232 | 83 |
| 82 | 117 | 117 | 116 | 340–342 | 339–341 | 340–341 | 117 | 117 | 117 | 338–339 | 338–339 | 340–341 | – | 227 | 231 | 82 |
| 81 | 116 | 116 | – | 338–339 | 337–338 | 338–339 | 116 | 116 | 116 | 336–337 | 335–337 | 338–339 | 229 | – | – | 81 |
| 80 | 115 | 115 | 115 | 336–337 | 334–336 | 336–337 | – | 115 | 115 | 334–335 | 333–334 | 336–337 | 228 | 226 | 230 | 80 |
| 79 | 114 | 114 | 114 | 334–335 | 332–333 | 334–335 | 115 | – | – | 332–333 | 331–332 | 335 | 227 | – | 229 | 79 |
| 78 | 113 | – | 113 | 332–333 | 330–331 | 332–333 | 114 | 114 | 114 | 330–331 | 329–330 | 333–334 | 226 | 225 | 228 | 78 |
| 77 | 112 | 113 | 112 | 330–331 | 327–329 | 330–331 | 113 | 113 | 113 | 328–329 | 327–328 | 331–332 | – | 224 | 227 | 77 |
| 76 | – | 112 | – | 328–329 | 325–326 | 328–329 | 112 | 112 | – | 327 | 325–326 | 329–330 | 225 | – | 226 | 76 |
| 75 | 111 | 111 | 111 | 326–327 | 323–324 | 326–327 | 112 | – | 112 | 325–326 | 323–324 | 328 | 225 | 223 | 226 | 75 |
| 74 | 110 | 110 | 110 | 324–325 | 321–322 | 325 | 111 | 111 | 111 | 323–324 | 321–322 | 326–327 | 224 | 222 | 225 | 74 |
| 73 | 109 | 109 | – | 322–323 | 320 | 323–324 | 110 | 110 | 110 | 322 | 319–320 | 325 | – | – | 224 | 73 |
| 72 | – | – | 109 | 321 | 318–319 | 321–322 | 110 | 109 | 110 | 320–321 | 318 | 323–324 | 223 | 221 | 223 | 72 |
| 71 | 108 | 108 | 108 | 319–320 | 316–317 | 320 | 109 | – | – | 319 | 316–317 | 322 | 222 | 221 | 222 | 71 |
| 70 | 107 | 107 | – | 317–318 | 314–315 | 318–319 | 108 | 108 | 109 | 317–318 | 315 | 320–321 | – | 220 | – | 70 |
| 69 | – | 106 | 107 | 316 | 313 | 317 | 108 | – | 108 | 316 | 313–314 | 319 | 221 | 220 | 222 | 69 |
| 68 | 106 | 106 | 106 | 314–315 | 311–312 | 315–316 | 107 | 107 | 107 | 314–315 | 312 | 318 | 220 | 219 | 221 | 68 |
| 67 | 105 | 105 | – | 313 | 309–310 | 314 | 107 | 106 | 107 | 313 | 310–311 | 316–317 | – | 218 | – | 67 |
| 66 | – | 104 | 105 | 311–312 | 308 | 313 | 106 | – | – | 311–312 | 309 | 315 | 219 | 218 | 220 | 66 |
| 65 | 104 | – | – | 310 | 306–307 | 311–312 | 106 | 105 | 106 | 310 | 307–308 | 314 | 218 | – | 219 | 65 |
| 64 | – | 103 | 104 | 309 | 305 | 310 | 105 | – | – | 309 | 306 | 312–313 | – | 217 | 218 | 64 |
| 63 | 103 | – | – | 307–308 | 304 | 309 | – | 104 | 105 | 308 | 305 | 311 | 217 | – | – | 63 |
| 62 | – | 102 | 103 | 306 | 302–303 | 307–308 | 104 | 103 | – | 306–307 | 303–304 | 310 | 216 | 216 | 217 | 62 |
| 61 | 102 | 101 | 102 | 305 | 301 | 306 | – | – | 104 | 305 | 302 | 308–309 | – | 215 | 216 | 61 |
| 60 | 101 | 100 | 101 | 303–304 | 299–300 | 305 | 103 | 102 | 103 | 304 | 301 | 307 | 215 | – | 215 | 60 |
| 59 | – | 100 | – | 302 | 298 | 303–304 | – | – | – | 303 | 299–300 | 306 | 214 | 214 | 214 | 59 |
| 58 | 100 | 99 | 100 | 301 | 297 | 302 | 102 | 101 | – | 302 | 298 | 305 | 213 | 213 | 213 | 58 |
| 57 | – | – | – | 300 | 296 | 301 | – | – | 102 | 300–301 | 297 | 304 | – | – | – | 57 |
| 56 | 99 | 99 | – | 298–299 | 294–295 | 300 | 101 | 100 | – | 299 | 296 | 302–303 | 212 | 212 | 212 | 56 |
| 55 | – | 98 | 99 | 297 | 293 | 299 | – | – | 101 | 298 | 295 | 301 | 211 | – | 211 | 55 |
| 54 | 98 | 97 | – | 296 | 292 | 297–298 | 100 | 99 | 100 | 297 | 294 | 300 | – | 211 | 210 | 54 |
| 53 | – | – | 98 | 295 | 291 | 296 | – | – | – | 296 | 292–293 | 299 | 210 | 210 | 209 | 53 |
| 52 | 97 | 96 | – | 294 | 290 | 295 | 99 | 98 | 100 | 295 | 291 | 298 | 209 | – | – | 52 |
| 51 | – | – | – | 292–293 | 289 | 294 | – | – | 99 | 294 | 290 | 297 | 208 | 209 | 208 | 51 |

**Table A.13e** SRP–C Composite Percentiles (continued)

| %ile | School Problems Combined | School Problems Female | School Problems Male | Internalizing Problems Combined | Internalizing Problems Female | Internalizing Problems Male | Inattention/Hyperactivity Combined | Inattention/Hyperactivity Female | Inattention/Hyperactivity Male | Emotional Symptoms Combined | Emotional Symptoms Female | Emotional Symptoms Male | Personal Adjustment Combined | Personal Adjustment Female | Personal Adjustment Male | %ile |
|---|---|---|---|---|---|---|---|---|---|---|---|---|---|---|---|---|
| 50 | 96 | – | 97 | 291 | 287–288 | 293 | 98 | 97 | – | 293 | 289 | 296 | 207 | 208 | 207 | 50 |
| 49 | – | 95 | – | 290 | 286 | 292 | – | – | – | 292 | 288 | 294–295 | – | – | 206 | 49 |
| 48 | 95 | 94 | 96 | 289 | 285 | 291 | 97 | 96 | 98 | 290–291 | 287 | 293 | 206 | 207 | 205 | 48 |
| 47 | – | – | – | 288 | 284 | 289–290 | – | – | 97 | 289 | 286 | 292 | 205 | 206 | 204 | 47 |
| 46 | – | – | 95 | 287 | 283 | 288 | 96 | 95 | – | 288 | 285 | 291 | 204 | 205 | 203 | 46 |
| 45 | 94 | 93 | – | 286 | 282 | 287 | – | – | – | 287 | 284 | 290 | 203 | – | 202 | 45 |
| 44 | – | – | 94 | 285 | 281 | 286 | – | – | 96 | 286 | 283 | 289 | – | 204 | 201 | 44 |
| 43 | 93 | 92 | – | 284 | 280 | 285 | 95 | 94 | – | 285 | 282 | 288 | 202 | 203 | 200 | 43 |
| 42 | – | – | 93 | 283 | 279 | 284 | – | – | 95 | 284 | 281 | 287 | 201 | 202 | 199 | 42 |
| 41 | – | – | – | 282 | 278 | 283 | 94 | 93 | – | 283 | 280 | 286 | 200 | – | 198 | 41 |
| 40 | 92 | 91 | – | 281 | 277 | 282 | – | – | 94 | 282 | 279 | 284–285 | 199 | 201 | 197 | 40 |
| 39 | 91 | 90 | 92 | 280 | 276 | 281 | 93 | 92 | – | 281 | 278 | 283 | 198 | 200 | 196 | 39 |
| 38 | – | – | – | 278–279 | 275 | 280 | – | – | 93 | 280 | 277 | 282 | 197 | 199 | 195 | 38 |
| 37 | – | – | 91 | 277 | 274 | 278–279 | 92 | 91 | – | 279 | 276 | 281 | 196 | 198 | 194 | 37 |
| 36 | – | – | – | 276 | 273 | 277 | – | – | – | 278 | 275 | 280 | 195 | 197 | 193 | 36 |
| 35 | 90 | 89 | 90 | 275 | 272 | 276 | 91 | 90 | 92 | 277 | 274 | 279 | 194 | 196 | 192 | 35 |
| 34 | – | – | – | 274 | 271 | 275 | – | – | – | 276 | 273 | 278 | 193 | 195 | 191 | 34 |
| 33 | 89 | 88 | 89 | 273 | 270 | 274 | 90 | 89 | 91 | 275 | 272 | 277 | 192 | 194 | 190 | 33 |
| 32 | – | – | – | 272 | 269 | 273 | – | – | – | 274 | 271 | 276 | 191 | 193 | 188–189 | 32 |
| 31 | – | – | – | 271 | 268 | 272 | 89 | – | 90 | 273 | 270 | 274–275 | 190 | 192 | 187 | 31 |
| 30 | 88 | – | 88 | 270 | 267 | 271 | – | 88 | – | 272 | 269 | 273 | 189 | 191 | 186 | 30 |
| 29 | – | 87 | – | 269 | 266 | 270 | – | – | 89 | 271 | 268 | 272 | 188 | 190 | 185 | 29 |
| 28 | 87 | – | – | 268 | 265 | 269 | 88 | 87 | – | 270 | 267 | 271 | 186–187 | 189 | 183–184 | 28 |
| 27 | – | – | 87 | 267 | 264 | 267–268 | – | – | 88 | 269 | 266 | 270 | 185 | 188 | 182 | 27 |
| 26 | – | 86 | – | 266 | 263 | 266 | 87 | 86 | – | 268 | 265 | 269 | 184 | 187 | 181 | 26 |
| 25 | 86 | – | 86 | 265 | 262 | 265 | 86 | – | 87 | 266–267 | 264 | 267–268 | 183 | 185–186 | 179–180 | 25 |
| 24 | – | – | – | 264 | 261 | 264 | – | – | 86 | 265 | 263 | 266 | 181–182 | 184 | 178 | 24 |
| 23 | 85 | 85 | 85 | 263 | 260 | 263 | 85 | 85 | – | 264 | 262 | 265 | 180 | 183 | 176–177 | 23 |
| 22 | – | – | – | 262 | 259 | 262 | – | – | 85 | 263 | 261 | 264 | 178–179 | 181–182 | 175 | 22 |
| 21 | – | – | – | 260–261 | 258 | 260–261 | 84 | 84 | – | 262 | 260 | 263 | 177 | 180 | 173–174 | 21 |
| 20 | 84 | 84 | 84 | 259 | 257 | 259 | 83 | 83 | 84 | 261 | 259 | 261–262 | 175–176 | 178–179 | 172 | 20 |
| 19 | – | – | – | 258 | 256 | 258 | – | – | – | 260 | 258 | 260 | 174 | 177 | 170–171 | 19 |
| 18 | 83 | – | 83 | 257 | 255 | 257 | 82 | 82 | 83 | 258–259 | 257 | 259 | 172–173 | 175–176 | 168–169 | 18 |
| 17 | – | 83 | – | 256 | 254 | 255–256 | – | – | – | 257 | 256 | 257–258 | 170–171 | 173–174 | 166–167 | 17 |
| 16 | – | – | 82 | 255 | 253 | 254 | – | 79 | 82 | 256 | 255 | 256 | 168–169 | 171–172 | 164–165 | 16 |
| 15 | 82 | – | – | 253–254 | 252 | 252–253 | 81 | 78 | 81 | 254–255 | 254 | 254–255 | 166–167 | 169–170 | 162–163 | 15 |
| 14 | – | 82 | 81 | 252 | 251 | 251 | – | – | 80 | 253 | 253 | 253 | 164–165 | 167–168 | 160–161 | 14 |
| 13 | 81 | – | – | 251 | 250 | 249–250 | 80 | 77 | 79 | 252 | 252 | 251–252 | 162–163 | 165–166 | 158–159 | 13 |
| 12 | – | – | 80 | 249–250 | 249 | 248 | 79 | 76 | 78 | 250–251 | 250–251 | 249–250 | 159–161 | 162–164 | 156–157 | 12 |
| 11 | – | 81 | – | 248 | 248 | 246–247 | – | – | 77 | 249 | 249 | 248 | 157–158 | 160–161 | 154–155 | 11 |
| 10 | 80 | – | 79 | 246–247 | 247 | 245 | 78 | 75 | 76 | 247–248 | 248 | 246–247 | 154–156 | 157–159 | 151–153 | 10 |
| 9 | – | – | – | 245 | 245–246 | 243–244 | 77 | – | 75 | 245–246 | 247 | 244–245 | 151–153 | 153–156 | 148–150 | 9 |
| 8 | – | 80 | 78 | 243–244 | 244 | 241–242 | 76 | 74 | 74 | 243–244 | 245–246 | 242–243 | 147–150 | 150–152 | 145–147 | 8 |
| 7 | 79 | – | – | 241–242 | 243 | 239–240 | – | 73 | 73 | 241–242 | 244 | 240–241 | 143–146 | 145–149 | 142–144 | 7 |
| 6 | – | – | 77 | 239–240 | 241–242 | 236–238 | 75 | – | – | 239–240 | 242–243 | 237–239 | 139–142 | 140–144 | 138–141 | 6 |
| 5 | 78 | 79 | 76 | 237–238 | 240 | 234–235 | 74 | – | 70–71 | 237–238 | 240–241 | 234–236 | 134–138 | 135–139 | 134–137 | 5 |
| 4 | – | – | – | 235–236 | 238–239 | 231–233 | 72–73 | 71–72 | 68–69 | 234–236 | 238–239 | 231–233 | 128–133 | 127–134 | 130–133 | 4 |
| 3 | – | 79 | – | 231–234 | 236–237 | 227–230 | 71 | – | – | 230–233 | 236–237 | 227–230 | 120–127 | 118–126 | 124–129 | 3 |
| 2 | – | – | – | 227–230 | 233–235 | 222–226 | 69–70 | – | 66–67 | 225–229 | 233–235 | 222–226 | 109–119 | 104–117 | 117–123 | 2 |
| 1 | – | – | – | 220–226 | 228–232 | 209–221 | – | – | – | 218–224 | 225–232 | 210–221 | 43–108 | 41–103 | 45–116 | 1 |

Table A.14a  SRP-A T Scores and Percentiles

| Raw score | Self-Reliance T | Self-Reliance %ile | Self-Esteem T | Self-Esteem %ile | Interpersonal Relations T | Interpersonal Relations %ile | Relations With Parents T | Relations With Parents %ile | Hyperactivity T | Hyperactivity %ile | Attention Problems T | Attention Problems %ile | Somatization T | Somatization %ile | Sense of Inadequacy T | Sense of Inadequacy %ile | Depression T | Depression %ile | Anxiety T | Anxiety %ile | Social Stress T | Social Stress %ile | Locus of Control T | Locus of Control %ile | Atypicality T | Atypicality %ile | Sensation Seeking T | Sensation Seeking %ile | Attitude to Teachers T | Attitude to Teachers %ile | Attitude to School T | Attitude to School %ile | Raw score |
|---|---|---|---|---|---|---|---|---|---|---|---|---|---|---|---|---|---|---|---|---|---|---|---|---|---|---|---|---|---|---|---|---|---|
| 36 | — | — | — | — | — | — | — | — | — | — | — | — | — | — | — | — | — | — | 91 | 99 | — | — | — | — | — | — | — | — | — | — | — | — | 36 |
| 35 | — | — | — | — | — | — | — | — | — | — | — | — | — | — | — | — | — | — | 90 | 99 | — | — | — | — | — | — | — | — | — | — | — | — | 35 |
| 34 | — | — | — | — | — | — | — | — | — | — | — | — | — | — | — | — | — | — | 88 | 99 | — | — | — | — | — | — | — | — | — | — | — | — | 34 |
| 33 | — | — | — | — | — | — | — | — | — | — | — | — | — | — | — | — | — | — | 87 | 99 | — | — | — | — | — | — | — | — | — | — | — | — | 33 |
| 32 | — | — | — | — | — | — | 62 | 96 | — | — | — | — | — | — | — | — | — | — | 85 | 99 | — | — | — | — | — | — | — | — | — | — | — | — | 32 |
| 31 | — | — | — | — | — | — | 61 | 89 | — | — | — | — | — | — | 95 | 99 | 108 | 99 | 83 | 99 | 99 | 99 | — | — | — | — | — | — | — | — | — | — | 31 |
| 30 | — | — | — | — | — | — | 59 | 81 | — | — | — | — | — | — | 93 | 99 | 105 | 99 | 82 | 99 | 97 | 99 | — | — | — | — | — | — | — | — | — | — | 30 |
| 29 | — | — | — | — | — | — | 57 | 72 | — | — | — | — | — | — | 91 | 99 | 103 | 99 | 80 | 99 | 95 | 99 | — | — | 103 | 99 | — | — | — | — | — | — | 29 |
| 28 | — | — | — | — | — | — | 56 | 65 | — | — | — | — | — | — | 89 | 99 | 101 | 99 | 78 | 99 | 93 | 99 | — | — | 100 | 99 | — | — | — | — | — | — | 28 |
| 27 | — | — | — | — | — | — | 54 | 58 | — | — | — | — | — | — | 87 | 99 | 99 | 99 | 77 | 99 | 91 | 99 | — | — | 98 | 99 | — | — | — | — | — | — | 27 |
| 26 | 69 | 99 | — | — | — | — | 53 | 51 | — | — | — | — | — | — | 85 | 99 | 97 | 99 | 75 | 99 | 89 | 99 | — | — | 96 | 99 | 80 | 99 | — | — | 94 | 99 | 26 |
| 25 | 66 | 98 | — | — | — | — | 51 | 45 | — | — | — | — | — | — | 83 | 99 | 95 | 99 | 74 | 99 | 87 | 99 | — | — | 94 | 99 | 78 | 99 | 94 | 99 | 91 | 99 | 25 |
| 24 | 64 | 94 | — | — | 61 | 94 | 49 | 40 | 89 | 99 | — | — | — | — | 81 | 99 | 92 | 99 | 72 | 99 | 85 | 99 | — | — | 92 | 99 | 76 | 99 | 91 | 99 | 89 | 99 | 24 |
| 23 | 62 | 90 | — | — | 58 | 78 | 48 | 35 | 87 | 99 | — | — | — | — | 79 | 99 | 90 | 99 | 70 | 98 | 83 | 99 | — | — | 90 | 99 | 75 | 98 | 89 | 99 | 87 | 99 | 23 |
| 22 | 60 | 83 | — | — | 55 | 63 | 46 | 31 | 85 | 99 | — | — | — | — | 77 | 98 | 88 | 99 | 69 | 98 | 81 | 99 | — | — | 87 | 99 | 73 | 98 | 87 | 99 | 85 | 99 | 22 |
| 21 | 58 | 76 | — | — | 53 | 50 | 45 | 27 | 82 | 99 | 81 | 99 | — | — | 76 | 98 | 86 | 99 | 67 | 97 | 79 | 99 | — | — | 85 | 99 | 71 | 97 | 85 | 99 | 82 | 99 | 21 |
| 20 | 56 | 68 | — | — | 50 | 39 | 43 | 23 | 80 | 99 | 79 | 99 | — | — | 74 | 97 | 84 | 99 | 66 | 96 | 77 | 99 | 91 | 99 | 83 | 99 | 69 | 96 | 82 | 99 | 80 | 99 | 20 |
| 19 | 53 | 59 | — | — | 47 | 31 | 41 | 20 | 78 | 99 | 77 | 99 | — | — | 72 | 96 | 82 | 98 | 64 | 95 | 75 | 98 | 88 | 99 | 81 | 99 | 67 | 94 | 80 | 99 | 78 | 99 | 19 |
| 18 | 51 | 51 | 60 | 91 | 45 | 24 | 40 | 17 | 76 | 98 | 74 | 98 | — | — | 70 | 95 | 79 | 98 | 62 | 93 | 73 | 97 | 86 | 99 | 79 | 98 | 65 | 92 | 78 | 99 | 76 | 98 | 18 |
| 17 | 49 | 43 | 57 | 71 | 42 | 19 | 38 | 14 | 73 | 98 | 72 | 97 | 106 | 99 | 68 | 94 | 77 | 97 | 61 | 92 | 71 | 96 | 83 | 99 | 77 | 98 | 63 | 89 | 76 | 98 | 74 | 97 | 17 |
| 16 | 47 | 35 | 54 | 55 | 39 | 15 | 37 | 12 | 71 | 97 | 70 | 95 | 102 | 99 | 66 | 92 | 75 | 97 | 59 | 90 | 69 | 95 | 80 | 99 | 74 | 97 | 61 | 86 | 73 | 96 | 71 | 96 | 16 |
| 15 | 45 | 29 | 51 | 42 | 37 | 11 | 35 | 10 | 69 | 95 | 68 | 93 | 98 | 99 | 64 | 90 | 73 | 96 | 57 | 88 | 67 | 93 | 78 | 99 | 72 | 96 | 59 | 82 | 71 | 95 | 69 | 95 | 15 |
| 14 | 42 | 23 | 48 | 32 | 34 | 9 | 33 | 8 | 66 | 93 | 66 | 91 | 95 | 99 | 62 | 88 | 71 | 95 | 56 | 85 | 65 | 91 | 75 | 98 | 70 | 95 | 57 | 78 | 69 | 92 | 67 | 93 | 14 |
| 13 | 40 | 18 | 45 | 24 | 31 | 6 | 32 | 6 | 64 | 90 | 63 | 88 | 91 | 99 | 60 | 85 | 69 | 93 | 54 | 82 | 63 | 88 | 72 | 98 | 68 | 93 | 55 | 72 | 66 | 90 | 65 | 90 | 13 |
| 12 | 38 | 13 | 43 | 19 | 29 | 5 | 30 | 5 | 62 | 87 | 61 | 84 | 87 | 99 | 58 | 82 | 67 | 91 | 53 | 79 | 61 | 85 | 70 | 96 | 66 | 91 | 54 | 66 | 64 | 86 | 62 | 87 | 12 |
| 11 | 36 | 10 | 40 | 14 | 26 | 3 | 29 | 4 | 60 | 83 | 59 | 80 | 83 | 99 | 56 | 78 | 64 | 90 | 51 | 75 | 59 | 81 | 67 | 93 | 64 | 89 | 52 | 60 | 62 | 82 | 60 | 84 | 11 |
| 10 | 34 | 7 | 37 | 11 | 23 | 2 | 27 | 3 | 57 | 78 | 57 | 76 | 80 | 98 | 55 | 73 | 62 | 88 | 49 | 61 | 57 | 77 | 65 | 91 | 61 | 87 | 50 | 52 | 60 | 78 | 58 | 79 | 10 |
| 9 | 31 | 5 | 34 | 8 | 21 | 2 | 25 | 2 | 55 | 72 | 54 | 70 | 76 | 97 | 53 | 68 | 60 | 85 | 48 | 55 | 55 | 72 | 62 | 87 | 59 | 83 | 48 | 45 | 57 | 72 | 56 | 74 | 9 |
| 8 | 29 | 3 | 31 | 6 | 18 | 1 | 24 | 1 | 53 | 65 | 52 | 64 | 72 | 95 | 51 | 62 | 58 | 82 | 46 | 48 | 53 | 67 | 59 | 83 | 57 | 80 | 46 | 37 | 55 | 66 | 53 | 68 | 8 |
| 7 | 27 | 2 | 28 | 5 | 16 | 1 | 22 | 1 | 51 | 57 | 50 | 58 | 68 | 93 | 49 | 55 | 56 | 78 | 45 | 42 | 51 | 61 | 57 | 78 | 55 | 75 | 44 | 30 | 53 | 58 | 51 | 62 | 7 |
| 6 | 25 | 1 | 25 | 3 | 13 | 1 | 21 | 1 | 48 | 49 | 48 | 50 | 64 | 90 | 47 | 47 | 54 | 74 | 43 | 35 | 49 | 54 | 54 | 72 | 53 | 70 | 42 | 23 | 51 | 50 | 49 | 54 | 6 |
| 5 | 23 | 1 | 23 | 2 | 10 | 1 | 19 | 1 | 46 | 40 | 46 | 42 | 61 | 86 | 45 | 38 | 51 | 68 | 41 | 27 | 47 | 47 | 51 | 64 | 51 | 63 | 40 | 16 | 48 | 41 | 47 | 45 | 5 |
| 4 | 21 | 1 | 20 | 2 | 10 | 1 | 17 | 1 | 44 | 30 | 43 | 32 | 57 | 81 | 43 | 28 | 49 | 61 | 40 | 20 | 45 | 39 | 49 | 55 | 48 | 55 | 38 | 11 | 46 | 32 | 44 | 35 | 4 |
| 3 | 18 | 1 | 17 | 1 | 10 | 1 | 16 | 1 | 41 | 21 | 41 | 22 | 53 | 74 | 41 | 18 | 47 | 51 | 38 | 14 | 43 | 31 | 46 | 44 | 46 | 46 | 36 | 7 | 44 | 22 | 42 | 24 | 3 |
| 2 | 16 | 1 | 14 | 1 | 10 | 1 | 14 | 1 | 39 | 13 | 39 | 13 | 49 | 63 | 39 | 9 | 45 | 40 | 37 | 8 | 41 | 22 | 44 | 31 | 44 | 35 | 34 | 4 | 41 | 13 | 40 | 13 | 2 |
| 1 | 14 | 1 | 11 | 1 | 10 | 1 | 13 | 1 | 37 | 6 | 37 | 4 | 46 | 46 | 37 | 2 | 43 | 25 | 35 | 4 | 39 | 14 | 41 | 18 | 42 | 21 | 33 | 2 | 39 | 6 | 37 | 4 | 1 |
| 0 | 12 | 1 | 10 | 1 | 10 | 1 | 11 | 1 | 35 | 2 | 35 | 1 | 42 | 15 | 35 | 1 | 41 | 7 | 33 | 1 | 37 | 6 | 38 | 6 | 40 | 7 | 31 | 1 | 37 | 1 | 35 | 1 | 0 |
| **Raw mean** | 17.46 | | 14.64 | | 19.97 | | 24.33 | | 6.78 | | 6.96 | | 2.18 | | 7.65 | | 4.36 | | 10.37 | | 6.35 | | 4.45 | | 4.73 | | 10.15 | | 5.75 | | 6.54 | | Raw mean |
| **Raw SD** | 4.57 | | 3.52 | | 3.76 | | 6.23 | | 4.38 | | 4.54 | | 2.65 | | 5.22 | | 4.63 | | 6.20 | | 5.07 | | 3.81 | | 4.61 | | 5.24 | | 4.40 | | 4.43 | | Raw SD |
| **T: 90% Conf. int.** | 7 | | 7 | | 7 | | 5 | | 7 | | 6 | | 9 | | 7 | | 6 | | 6 | | 6 | | 8 | | 7 | | 7 | | 7 | | 7 | | T: 90% Conf. int. |

**Table A.14b** SRP-A *T* Scores and Percentiles

| Raw score | Attitude to School T | %ile | Attitude to Teachers T | %ile | Sensation Seeking T | %ile | Atypicality T | %ile | Locus of Control T | %ile | Social Stress T | %ile | Anxiety T | %ile | Depression T | %ile | Sense of Inadequacy T | %ile | Somatization T | %ile | Attention Problems T | %ile | Hyperactivity T | %ile | Relations With Parents T | %ile | Interpersonal Relations T | %ile | Self-Esteem T | %ile | Self-Reliance T | %ile |
|---|---|---|---|---|---|---|---|---|---|---|---|---|---|---|---|---|---|---|---|---|---|---|---|---|---|---|---|---|---|---|---|---|
| 36 | — | — | — | — | — | — | — | — | — | — | — | — | 87 | 99 | — | — | — | — | — | — | — | — | — | — | — | — | — | — | — | — | — | — |
| 35 | — | — | — | — | — | — | — | — | — | — | — | — | 86 | 99 | — | — | — | — | — | — | — | — | — | — | — | — | — | — | — | — | — | — |
| 34 | — | — | — | — | — | — | — | — | — | — | — | — | 84 | 99 | — | — | — | — | — | — | — | — | — | — | — | — | — | — | — | — | — | — |
| 33 | — | — | — | — | — | — | — | — | — | — | — | — | 83 | 99 | — | — | — | — | — | — | — | — | — | — | — | — | — | — | — | — | — | — |
| 32 | — | — | — | — | — | — | — | — | — | — | — | — | 81 | 99 | — | — | — | — | — | — | — | — | — | — | 62 | 99 | — | — | — | — | — | — |
| 31 | — | — | — | — | — | — | — | — | — | — | 97 | 99 | 80 | 99 | 107 | 99 | 93 | 99 | — | — | — | — | — | — | 60 | 96 | — | — | — | — | — | — |
| 30 | — | — | — | — | — | — | — | — | — | — | 95 | 99 | 78 | 99 | 105 | 99 | 92 | 99 | — | — | — | — | — | — | 59 | 87 | — | — | — | — | — | — |
| 29 | — | — | — | — | — | — | 103 | 99 | — | — | 93 | 99 | 77 | 98 | 103 | 99 | 90 | 99 | — | — | — | — | — | — | 57 | 78 | — | — | — | — | — | — |
| 28 | — | — | — | — | — | — | 101 | 99 | — | — | 91 | 99 | 75 | 97 | 101 | 99 | 88 | 99 | — | — | — | — | — | — | 55 | 69 | — | — | — | — | — | — |
| 27 | — | — | — | — | — | — | 98 | 99 | — | — | 89 | 99 | 74 | 96 | 98 | 99 | 86 | 99 | — | — | — | — | — | — | 54 | 62 | — | — | — | — | — | — |
| 26 | — | — | — | — | 82 | 99 | 96 | 99 | — | — | 87 | 99 | 72 | 94 | 96 | 99 | 84 | 99 | — | — | — | — | — | — | 52 | 54 | — | — | — | — | 67 | 99 |
| 25 | 95 | 99 | 95 | 99 | 80 | 99 | 94 | 99 | — | — | 85 | 99 | 71 | 93 | 94 | 99 | 82 | 99 | — | — | — | — | — | — | 50 | 48 | — | — | — | — | 65 | 96 |
| 24 | 93 | 99 | 93 | 99 | 78 | 99 | 92 | 99 | — | — | 83 | 99 | 69 | 92 | 92 | 99 | 80 | 99 | — | — | — | — | 91 | 99 | 49 | 42 | 60 | 99 | — | — | 63 | 91 |
| 23 | 90 | 99 | 90 | 99 | 76 | 98 | 90 | 99 | — | — | 81 | 99 | 68 | 90 | 90 | 99 | 78 | 98 | — | — | — | — | 89 | 99 | 47 | 37 | 57 | 93 | — | — | 60 | 85 |
| 22 | 88 | 99 | 88 | 99 | 74 | 98 | 88 | 99 | — | — | 79 | 99 | 66 | 88 | 88 | 99 | 77 | 98 | — | — | — | — | 86 | 99 | 45 | 33 | 55 | 74 | — | — | 58 | 77 |
| 21 | 86 | 99 | 86 | 99 | 72 | 97 | 85 | 99 | — | — | 78 | 99 | 65 | 86 | 86 | 99 | 75 | 97 | — | — | 82 | 99 | 84 | 99 | 44 | 29 | 52 | 58 | — | — | 56 | 68 |
| 20 | 83 | 99 | 84 | 99 | 70 | 96 | 83 | 99 | 90 | 99 | 76 | 98 | 63 | 84 | 83 | 99 | 73 | 96 | — | — | 80 | 99 | 82 | 99 | 42 | 25 | 49 | 45 | — | — | 54 | 59 |
| 19 | 81 | 98 | 81 | 99 | 68 | 95 | 81 | 98 | 87 | 99 | 74 | 97 | 62 | 81 | 81 | 98 | 71 | 94 | — | — | 78 | 99 | 79 | 99 | 41 | 22 | 47 | 35 | — | — | 51 | 51 |
| 18 | 79 | 98 | 79 | 98 | 66 | 93 | 79 | 98 | 85 | 99 | 72 | 96 | 60 | 78 | 79 | 97 | 69 | 93 | — | — | 75 | 99 | 77 | 99 | 39 | 18 | 44 | 28 | 60 | 99 | 49 | 43 |
| 17 | 76 | 97 | 77 | 98 | 64 | 91 | 77 | 97 | 82 | 99 | 70 | 94 | 59 | 75 | 77 | 96 | 67 | 91 | 103 | 99 | 73 | 97 | 75 | 98 | 37 | 16 | 41 | 22 | 57 | 89 | 47 | 35 |
| 16 | 74 | 96 | 74 | 97 | 62 | 88 | 75 | 96 | 80 | 98 | 68 | 92 | 57 | 71 | 75 | 95 | 65 | 89 | 99 | 99 | 71 | 96 | 72 | 97 | 36 | 13 | 38 | 17 | 54 | 73 | 45 | 29 |
| 15 | 71 | 94 | 72 | 95 | 61 | 85 | 72 | 94 | 77 | 97 | 66 | 89 | 56 | 67 | 73 | 94 | 64 | 87 | 96 | 99 | 69 | 94 | 70 | 96 | 34 | 11 | 36 | 13 | 52 | 58 | 42 | 23 |
| 14 | 69 | 93 | 70 | 94 | 59 | 81 | 70 | 93 | 75 | 96 | 64 | 86 | 54 | 62 | 70 | 93 | 62 | 84 | 92 | 99 | 66 | 92 | 68 | 94 | 32 | 9 | 33 | 10 | 49 | 46 | 40 | 18 |
| 13 | 67 | 90 | 68 | 91 | 57 | 77 | 68 | 91 | 72 | 95 | 62 | 83 | 52 | 57 | 68 | 91 | 60 | 81 | 89 | 99 | 64 | 89 | 65 | 92 | 31 | 7 | 30 | 8 | 46 | 35 | 38 | 13 |
| 12 | 64 | 87 | 65 | 88 | 55 | 72 | 66 | 89 | 69 | 93 | 60 | 79 | 51 | 51 | 66 | 89 | 58 | 77 | 85 | 99 | 62 | 86 | 63 | 89 | 29 | 6 | 28 | 6 | 44 | 27 | 36 | 10 |
| 11 | 62 | 84 | 63 | 85 | 53 | 66 | 64 | 86 | 67 | 90 | 58 | 74 | 49 | 45 | 64 | 87 | 56 | 73 | 81 | 98 | 60 | 82 | 60 | 85 | 27 | 4 | 25 | 4 | 41 | 21 | 33 | 7 |
| 10 | 59 | 79 | 61 | 80 | 51 | 59 | 62 | 83 | 64 | 87 | 56 | 69 | 48 | 38 | 62 | 84 | 54 | 67 | 78 | 97 | 57 | 77 | 58 | 80 | 26 | 3 | 22 | 3 | 38 | 16 | 31 | 5 |
| 9 | 57 | 74 | 58 | 75 | 49 | 52 | 59 | 79 | 62 | 83 | 54 | 64 | 46 | 31 | 60 | 81 | 52 | 61 | 74 | 96 | 55 | 72 | 56 | 74 | 24 | 2 | 20 | 2 | 35 | 12 | 29 | 3 |
| 8 | 55 | 67 | 56 | 69 | 47 | 44 | 57 | 75 | 59 | 78 | 53 | 58 | 45 | 23 | 58 | 77 | 51 | 54 | 70 | 94 | 53 | 66 | 53 | 67 | 22 | 2 | 17 | 2 | 33 | 9 | 27 | 2 |
| 7 | 52 | 59 | 54 | 62 | 45 | 36 | 55 | 70 | 57 | 72 | 51 | 52 | 43 | 15 | 55 | 73 | 49 | 47 | 67 | 92 | 51 | 59 | 51 | 58 | 21 | 1 | 14 | 1 | 30 | 7 | 24 | 1 |
| 6 | 50 | 50 | 52 | 54 | 43 | 27 | 53 | 64 | 54 | 65 | 49 | 45 | 42 | 8 | 53 | 67 | 47 | 38 | 63 | 89 | 48 | 52 | 49 | 49 | 19 | 1 | 12 | 1 | 27 | 5 | 22 | 1 |
| 5 | 47 | 39 | 49 | 45 | 41 | 19 | 51 | 57 | 52 | 56 | 47 | 37 | 40 | 2 | 51 | 60 | 45 | 29 | 59 | 85 | 46 | 43 | 46 | 40 | 18 | 1 | 10 | 1 | 24 | 4 | 20 | 1 |
| 4 | 45 | 26 | 47 | 35 | 39 | 12 | 49 | 48 | 49 | 45 | 45 | 29 | 39 | 1 | 49 | 51 | 43 | 19 | 56 | 79 | 44 | 34 | 44 | 30 | 16 | 1 | 10 | 1 | 22 | 3 | 18 | 1 |
| 3 | 43 | 14 | 45 | 26 | 37 | 6 | 46 | 37 | 46 | 32 | 43 | 21 | 37 | 1 | 47 | 40 | 41 | 10 | 52 | 71 | 42 | 24 | 41 | 21 | 14 | 1 | 10 | 1 | 19 | 2 | 15 | 1 |
| 2 | 40 | 4 | 42 | 16 | 35 | 2 | 44 | 23 | 44 | 19 | 41 | 14 | 36 | 1 | 45 | 24 | 39 | 3 | 49 | 59 | 39 | 14 | 39 | 13 | 13 | 1 | 10 | 1 | 16 | 1 | 13 | 1 |
| 1 | 38 | 1 | 40 | 8 | 33 | 1 | 42 | 7 | 41 | 7 | 39 | 6 | 34 | 1 | 43 | 4 | 38 | 1 | 45 | 41 | 37 | 5 | 37 | 7 | 11 | 1 | 10 | 1 | 13 | 1 | 11 | 1 |
| 0 | 35 | — | 38 | — | 31 | 1 | 40 | — | 39 | 1 | 37 | — | 33 | 1 | 40 | — | 36 | — | 41 | 13 | 35 | 1 | 34 | 3 | 10 | 1 | 10 | 1 | 11 | 1 | 10 | 1 |
| **Raw mean** | 6.05 | | 5.34 | | 9.61 | | 4.65 | | 4.39 | | 6.67 | | 11.37 | | 4.47 | | 7.67 | | 2.39 | | 6.69 | | 6.61 | | 24.74 | | 20.27 | | 14.37 | | 18.37 | |
| **Raw SD** | 4.17 | | 4.37 | | 5.13 | | 4.61 | | 3.92 | | 5.21 | | 6.58 | | 4.65 | | 5.38 | | 2.75 | | 4.44 | | 4.22 | | 6.08 | | 3.71 | | 3.66 | | 4.45 | |
| **T: 90% Conf. int.** | 7 | | 7 | | 6 | | 6 | | 7 | | 6 | | 6 | | 6 | | 7 | | 9 | | 6 | | 7 | | 5 | | 7 | | 7 | | 7 | |

## Table A.14c  SRP-A T Scores and Percentiles

| Raw score | Att. to School T | %ile | Att. to Teachers T | %ile | Sensation Seeking T | %ile | Atypicality T | %ile | Locus of Control T | %ile | Social Stress T | %ile | Anxiety T | %ile | Depression T | %ile | Sense of Inadequacy T | %ile | Somatization T | %ile | Attention Problems T | %ile | Hyperactivity T | %ile | Relations With Parents T | %ile | Interpersonal Relations T | %ile | Self-Esteem T | %ile | Self-Reliance T | %ile | Raw score |
|---|---|---|---|---|---|---|---|---|---|---|---|---|---|---|---|---|---|---|---|---|---|---|---|---|---|---|---|---|---|---|---|---|---|
| 36 | — | — | — | — | — | — | — | — | — | — | — | — | 97 | 99 | — | — | — | — | — | — | — | — | — | — | — | — | — | — | — | — | — | — | 36 |
| 35 | — | — | — | — | — | — | — | — | — | — | — | — | 95 | 99 | — | — | — | — | — | — | — | — | — | — | — | — | — | — | — | — | — | — | 35 |
| 34 | — | — | — | — | — | — | — | — | — | — | — | — | 94 | 99 | — | — | — | — | — | — | — | — | — | — | — | — | — | — | — | — | — | — | 34 |
| 33 | — | — | — | — | — | — | — | — | — | — | — | — | 92 | 99 | — | — | — | — | — | — | — | — | — | — | — | — | — | — | — | — | — | — | 33 |
| 32 | — | — | — | — | — | — | — | — | — | — | — | — | 90 | 99 | — | — | — | — | — | — | — | — | — | — | 63 | 96 | — | — | — | — | — | — | 32 |
| 31 | — | — | — | — | — | — | — | — | — | — | 101 | 99 | 88 | 99 | 108 | 99 | 96 | 99 | — | — | — | — | — | — | 61 | 90 | — | — | — | — | — | — | 31 |
| 30 | — | — | — | — | — | — | — | — | — | — | 99 | 99 | 87 | 99 | 106 | 99 | 94 | 99 | — | — | — | — | — | — | 60 | 83 | — | — | — | — | — | — | 30 |
| 29 | — | — | — | — | — | — | 102 | 99 | — | — | 97 | 99 | 85 | 99 | 104 | 99 | 92 | 99 | — | — | — | — | — | — | 58 | 76 | — | — | — | — | — | — | 29 |
| 28 | — | — | — | — | — | — | 100 | 99 | — | — | 95 | 99 | 83 | 99 | 101 | 99 | 90 | 99 | — | — | — | — | — | — | 56 | 68 | — | — | — | — | — | — | 28 |
| 27 | — | — | — | — | — | — | 98 | 99 | — | — | 93 | 99 | 81 | 99 | 99 | 99 | 88 | 99 | — | — | — | — | — | — | 55 | 61 | — | — | — | — | — | — | 27 |
| 26 | — | — | — | — | 79 | 99 | 96 | 99 | — | — | 91 | 99 | 79 | 98 | 97 | 99 | 86 | 99 | — | — | — | — | — | — | 53 | 54 | — | — | — | — | 71 | 99 | 26 |
| 25 | — | — | 93 | 99 | 77 | 99 | 94 | 99 | — | — | 88 | 99 | 78 | 97 | 95 | 99 | 84 | 99 | — | — | — | — | — | — | 52 | 48 | — | — | — | — | 69 | 99 | 25 |
| 24 | — | — | 91 | 99 | 75 | 98 | 91 | 99 | — | — | 86 | 99 | 76 | 96 | 93 | 99 | 82 | 99 | — | — | — | — | 88 | 99 | 50 | 43 | 61 | 95 | — | — | 67 | 97 | 24 |
| 23 | — | — | 88 | 99 | 73 | 98 | 89 | 99 | — | — | 84 | 99 | 74 | 95 | 91 | 99 | 80 | 99 | — | — | — | — | 85 | 99 | 49 | 37 | 59 | 82 | — | — | 64 | 94 | 23 |
| 22 | 82 | 99 | 86 | 99 | 71 | 97 | 87 | 99 | — | — | 82 | 99 | 72 | 94 | 88 | 99 | 78 | 99 | — | — | — | — | 83 | 99 | 47 | 33 | 56 | 67 | — | — | 62 | 89 | 22 |
| 21 | 80 | 99 | 84 | 99 | 69 | 95 | 85 | 99 | — | — | 80 | 99 | 71 | 92 | 86 | 99 | 76 | 99 | — | — | 80 | 99 | 81 | 99 | 45 | 28 | 54 | 54 | — | — | 60 | 83 | 21 |
| 20 | 78 | 99 | 81 | 99 | 68 | 94 | 83 | 99 | 92 | 99 | 78 | 99 | 69 | 90 | 84 | 99 | 74 | 99 | — | — | 78 | 99 | 79 | 99 | 44 | 25 | 51 | 43 | — | — | 58 | 76 | 20 |
| 19 | 76 | 99 | 79 | 99 | 66 | 91 | 81 | 99 | 89 | 99 | 76 | 98 | 67 | 87 | 82 | 99 | 72 | 99 | — | — | 75 | 99 | 77 | 99 | 42 | 21 | 48 | 34 | — | — | 55 | 67 | 19 |
| 18 | 74 | 98 | 77 | 99 | 64 | 88 | 78 | 99 | 86 | 99 | 74 | 98 | 65 | 84 | 80 | 98 | 70 | 97 | — | — | 73 | 98 | 74 | 98 | 41 | 18 | 46 | 27 | 59 | 92 | 53 | 59 | 18 |
| 17 | 71 | 97 | 75 | 98 | 62 | 84 | 76 | 99 | 84 | 99 | 72 | 97 | 64 | 80 | 78 | 98 | 69 | 96 | 109 | 99 | 71 | 97 | 72 | 97 | 39 | 15 | 43 | 21 | 56 | 69 | 51 | 50 | 17 |
| 16 | 69 | 95 | 72 | 96 | 60 | 80 | 74 | 97 | 81 | 99 | 70 | 95 | 62 | 76 | 75 | 97 | 67 | 95 | 105 | 99 | 69 | 95 | 70 | 96 | 38 | 13 | 40 | 16 | 53 | 50 | 49 | 42 | 16 |
| 15 | 67 | 93 | 70 | 94 | 58 | 74 | 72 | 96 | 78 | 99 | 68 | 94 | 60 | 71 | 73 | 97 | 65 | 93 | 101 | 99 | 67 | 92 | 68 | 94 | 36 | 11 | 38 | 12 | 50 | 37 | 47 | 34 | 15 |
| 14 | 65 | 90 | 68 | 91 | 56 | 68 | 70 | 95 | 76 | 99 | 66 | 92 | 58 | 65 | 71 | 96 | 63 | 91 | 97 | 99 | 65 | 90 | 66 | 92 | 34 | 9 | 35 | 7 | 47 | 28 | 44 | 28 | 14 |
| 13 | 63 | 87 | 66 | 88 | 54 | 61 | 68 | 93 | 73 | 98 | 64 | 90 | 56 | 59 | 69 | 95 | 61 | 89 | 93 | 99 | 62 | 86 | 63 | 89 | 33 | 8 | 32 | 5 | 44 | 21 | 42 | 22 | 13 |
| 12 | 61 | 84 | 63 | 85 | 52 | 54 | 66 | 91 | 70 | 97 | 62 | 87 | 55 | 53 | 67 | 94 | 59 | 86 | 89 | 99 | 60 | 83 | 61 | 85 | 31 | 7 | 30 | 4 | 41 | 16 | 40 | 16 | 12 |
| 11 | 59 | 80 | 61 | 80 | 51 | 46 | 63 | 89 | 67 | 95 | 60 | 83 | 53 | 46 | 65 | 93 | 57 | 84 | 85 | 99 | 58 | 78 | 59 | 81 | 30 | 6 | 27 | 3 | 38 | 12 | 38 | 12 | 11 |
| 10 | 56 | 75 | 59 | 75 | 49 | 39 | 61 | 87 | 65 | 91 | 58 | 80 | 51 | 38 | 62 | 89 | 55 | 79 | 82 | 98 | 56 | 73 | 57 | 76 | 28 | 5 | 25 | 2 | 35 | 9 | 35 | 9 | 10 |
| 9 | 54 | 69 | 56 | 69 | 47 | 31 | 59 | 83 | 62 | 87 | 56 | 75 | 49 | 31 | 60 | 86 | 53 | 74 | 78 | 97 | 54 | 68 | 55 | 71 | 27 | 4 | 22 | 1 | 32 | 7 | 33 | 6 | 9 |
| 8 | 52 | 63 | 54 | 62 | 45 | 25 | 57 | 80 | 59 | 83 | 54 | 70 | 48 | 24 | 58 | 83 | 51 | 68 | 74 | 96 | 52 | 62 | 52 | 64 | 25 | 3 | 19 | 1 | 29 | 5 | 31 | 4 | 8 |
| 7 | 50 | 56 | 52 | 55 | 43 | 19 | 55 | 75 | 57 | 77 | 52 | 64 | 46 | 18 | 56 | 79 | 49 | 62 | 70 | 94 | 50 | 55 | 50 | 57 | 23 | 2 | 17 | 1 | 26 | 4 | 29 | 3 | 7 |
| 6 | 48 | 48 | 50 | 50 | 41 | 14 | 53 | 69 | 54 | 71 | 50 | 57 | 44 | 12 | 54 | 75 | 47 | 55 | 66 | 91 | 47 | 47 | 48 | 49 | 22 | 1 | 14 | 1 | 23 | 3 | 27 | 2 | 6 |
| 5 | 46 | 40 | 47 | 46 | 39 | 10 | 50 | 62 | 51 | 62 | 48 | 49 | 42 | 7 | 52 | 69 | 45 | 46 | 62 | 88 | 45 | 39 | 46 | 40 | 20 | 1 | 11 | 1 | 21 | 2 | 24 | 1 | 5 |
| 4 | 43 | 31 | 45 | 37 | 37 | 7 | 48 | 54 | 49 | 53 | 46 | 41 | 40 | 4 | 49 | 61 | 43 | 37 | 58 | 83 | 43 | 30 | 44 | 30 | 19 | 1 | 10 | 1 | 18 | 2 | 22 | 1 | 4 |
| 3 | 41 | 22 | 43 | 28 | 35 | 4 | 46 | 44 | 46 | 42 | 44 | 32 | 39 | 2 | 47 | 52 | 41 | 27 | 54 | 76 | 41 | 21 | 41 | 21 | 17 | 1 | 10 | 1 | 15 | 1 | 20 | 1 | 3 |
| 2 | 39 | 13 | 41 | 19 | 34 | 3 | 44 | 33 | 43 | 29 | 42 | 23 | 37 | 1 | 45 | 40 | 39 | 17 | 50 | 67 | 39 | 11 | 39 | 12 | 16 | 1 | 10 | 1 | 12 | 1 | 18 | 1 | 2 |
| 1 | 37 | 5 | 38 | 10 | 32 | 2 | 42 | 20 | 41 | 17 | 40 | 14 | 35 | 1 | 43 | 26 | 37 | 8 | 46 | 50 | 37 | 4 | 37 | 5 | 14 | 1 | 10 | 1 | 10 | 1 | 16 | 1 | 1 |
| 0 | 35 | 1 | 36 | 3 | 30 | 2 | 40 | 7 | 38 | 6 | 38 | 6 | 33 | 1 | 41 | 9 | 35 | 2 | 42 | 18 | 34 | 1 | 35 | 1 | 12 | 1 | 10 | 1 | 10 | 1 | 13 | 1 | 0 |
| **Raw mean** | 7.03 | | 6.17 | | 10.70 | | 4.81 | | 4.51 | | 6.03 | | 9.37 | | 4.25 | | 7.62 | | 1.96 | | 7.23 | | 6.95 | | 23.91 | | 19.67 | | 14.91 | | 16.55 | | **Raw mean** |
| **Raw SD** | 4.64 | | 4.40 | | 5.30 | | 4.63 | | 3.71 | | 4.93 | | 5.64 | | 4.62 | | 5.07 | | 2.55 | | 4.63 | | 4.54 | | 6.36 | | 3.80 | | 3.36 | | 4.51 | | **Raw SD** |
| **T: 90% Conf. int.** | 7 | | 7 | | 7 | | 7 | | 8 | | 6 | | 7 | | 7 | | 7 | | 9 | | 6 | | 7 | | 5 | | 7 | | 7 | | 7 | | **T: 90% Conf. int.** |

**Table A.14d** SRP–A Composite T Scores

| T score | School Problems Combined | School Problems Female | School Problems Male | Internalizing Problems Combined | Internalizing Problems Female | Internalizing Problems Male | Inattention/Hyperactivity Combined | Inattention/Hyperactivity Female | Inattention/Hyperactivity Male | Emotional Symptoms Combined | Emotional Symptoms Female | Emotional Symptoms Male | Personal Adjustment Combined | Personal Adjustment Female | Personal Adjustment Male | T score |
|---|---|---|---|---|---|---|---|---|---|---|---|---|---|---|---|---|
| 120 | — | — | — | — | — | — | — | — | — | — | — | — | — | — | — | 120 |
| 119 | — | — | — | — | — | — | — | — | — | — | — | — | — | — | — | 119 |
| 118 | — | — | — | — | — | — | — | — | — | — | — | — | — | — | — | 118 |
| 117 | — | — | — | — | — | — | — | — | — | — | — | — | — | — | — | 117 |
| 116 | — | — | — | — | — | 703–705 | — | — | — | — | — | — | — | — | — | 116 |
| 115 | — | — | — | — | — | 698–702 | — | — | — | — | — | — | — | — | — | 115 |
| 114 | — | — | — | — | — | 692–697 | — | — | — | — | — | — | — | — | — | 114 |
| 113 | — | — | — | — | — | 687–691 | — | — | — | — | — | 577–579 | — | — | — | 113 |
| 112 | — | — | — | 691–693 | — | 682–686 | — | — | — | — | — | 573–576 | — | — | — | 112 |
| 111 | — | — | — | 686–690 | — | 676–681 | — | — | — | — | — | 568–572 | — | — | — | 111 |
| 110 | — | — | — | 680–685 | — | 671–675 | — | — | — | 568–571 | — | 564–567 | — | — | — | 110 |
| 109 | — | — | — | 674–679 | — | 665–670 | — | — | — | 563–567 | — | 560–563 | — | — | — | 109 |
| 108 | — | — | — | 669–673 | 678–680 | 660–664 | — | — | — | 559–562 | — | 555–559 | — | — | — | 108 |
| 107 | — | — | — | 663–668 | 672–677 | 655–659 | — | — | — | 554–558 | — | 551–554 | — | — | — | 107 |
| 106 | — | — | — | 658–662 | 667–671 | 649–654 | — | — | — | 550–553 | 562–563 | 546–550 | — | — | — | 106 |
| 105 | — | — | — | 652–657 | 661–666 | 644–648 | — | — | — | 545–549 | 557–561 | 542–545 | — | — | — | 105 |
| 104 | — | — | — | 647–651 | 655–660 | 639–643 | — | — | — | 540–544 | 553–556 | 538–541 | — | — | — | 104 |
| 103 | — | — | — | 641–646 | 649–654 | 633–638 | — | — | — | 536–539 | 548–552 | 533–537 | — | — | — | 103 |
| 102 | — | — | — | 636–640 | 644–648 | 628–632 | — | — | — | 531–535 | 543–547 | 529–532 | — | — | — | 102 |
| 101 | — | — | — | 630–635 | 638–643 | 622–627 | — | — | — | 527–530 | 539–542 | 524–528 | — | — | — | 101 |
| 100 | — | — | — | 625–629 | 632–637 | 617–621 | — | — | — | 522–526 | 534–538 | 520–523 | — | — | — | 100 |
| 99 | — | — | — | 619–624 | 627–631 | 612–616 | — | — | — | 518–521 | 529–533 | 515–519 | — | — | — | 99 |
| 98 | — | 264–265 | — | 614–618 | 621–626 | 606–611 | — | — | — | 513–517 | 524–528 | 511–514 | — | — | — | 98 |
| 97 | — | 262–263 | — | 608–613 | 615–620 | 601–605 | — | — | — | 508–512 | 520–523 | 507–510 | — | — | — | 97 |
| 96 | 259 | — | — | 602–607 | 610–614 | 596–600 | — | — | — | 504–507 | 515–519 | 502–506 | — | — | — | 96 |
| 95 | 256–258 | 259–261 | 253–254 | 597–601 | 604–609 | 590–595 | — | — | — | 499–503 | 510–514 | 498–501 | — | — | — | 95 |
| 94 | 254–255 | 257–258 | 251–252 | 591–596 | 598–603 | 585–589 | — | — | — | 495–498 | 506–509 | 493–497 | — | — | — | 94 |
| 93 | 252–253 | 254–256 | 249–250 | 586–590 | 592–597 | 579–584 | — | — | — | 490–494 | 501–505 | 489–492 | — | — | — | 93 |
| 92 | 249–251 | 252–253 | 246–248 | 580–585 | 587–591 | 574–578 | — | — | — | 486–489 | 496–500 | 484–488 | — | — | — | 92 |
| 91 | 247–248 | 250–251 | 244–245 | 575–579 | 581–586 | 569–573 | — | — | — | 481–485 | 491–495 | 480–483 | — | — | — | 91 |
| 90 | 245–246 | 247–249 | 242–243 | 569–574 | 575–580 | 563–568 | — | 172–173 | — | 476–480 | 487–490 | 476–479 | — | — | — | 90 |
| 89 | 242–244 | 245–246 | 239–241 | 564–568 | 570–574 | 558–562 | 170 | 170–171 | — | 472–475 | 482–486 | 471–475 | — | — | — | 89 |
| 88 | 240–241 | 242–244 | 237–238 | 558–563 | 564–569 | 552–557 | 168–169 | 168–169 | 168 | 467–471 | 477–481 | 467–470 | — | — | — | 88 |
| 87 | 237–239 | 240–241 | 235–236 | 553–557 | 558–563 | 547–551 | 166–167 | 166–167 | 166–167 | 463–466 | 473–476 | 462–466 | — | — | — | 87 |
| 86 | 235–236 | 237–239 | 232–234 | 547–552 | 553–557 | 542–546 | 164–165 | 165 | 164–165 | 458–462 | 468–472 | 458–461 | — | — | — | 86 |
| 85 | 233–234 | 235–236 | 230–231 | 542–546 | 547–552 | 536–541 | 162–163 | 163–164 | 162–163 | 454–457 | 463–467 | 454–457 | — | — | — | 85 |
| 84 | 230–232 | 232–234 | 228–229 | 536–541 | 541–546 | 531–535 | 161 | 161–162 | 160–161 | 449–453 | 458–462 | 449–453 | — | — | — | 84 |
| 83 | 228–229 | 230–231 | 225–227 | 530–535 | 536–540 | 526–530 | 159–160 | 159–160 | 159 | 444–448 | 454–457 | 445–448 | — | — | — | 83 |
| 82 | 225–227 | 228–229 | 223–224 | 525–529 | 530–535 | 520–525 | 157–158 | 157–158 | 157–158 | 440–443 | 449–453 | 440–444 | — | — | — | 82 |
| 81 | 223–224 | 225–227 | 221–222 | 519–524 | 524–529 | 515–519 | 155–156 | 155–156 | 155–156 | 435–439 | 444–448 | 436–439 | — | — | — | 81 |
| 80 | 221–222 | 223–224 | 219–220 | 514–518 | 518–523 | 509–514 | 153–154 | 153–154 | 153–154 | 431–434 | 440–443 | 431–435 | — | — | — | 80 |
| 79 | 218–220 | 220–222 | 216–218 | 508–513 | 513–517 | 504–508 | 151–152 | 152 | 151–152 | 426–430 | 435–439 | 427–430 | — | — | — | 79 |
| 78 | 216–217 | 218–219 | 212–215 | 503–507 | 507–512 | 499–503 | 149–150 | 150–151 | 149–150 | 421–425 | 430–434 | 423–426 | — | — | — | 78 |
| 77 | 214–215 | 215–217 | 209–211 | 497–502 | 501–506 | 493–498 | 148 | 148–149 | 148 | 417–420 | 425–429 | 418–422 | — | — | — | 77 |
| 76 | 211–213 | 213–214 | 207–208 | 492–496 | 496–500 | 488–492 | 146–147 | 146–147 | 146–147 | 412–416 | 421–424 | 414–417 | — | — | — | 76 |
| 75 | 209–210 | 210–212 | 205–206 | 486–491 | 490–495 | 482–487 | 144–145 | 144–145 | 144–145 | 408–411 | 416–420 | 409–413 | — | — | — | 75 |
| 74 | 206–208 | 208–209 | 202–204 | 481–485 | 484–489 | 477–481 | 142–143 | 142–143 | 142–143 | 403–407 | 411–415 | 405–408 | — | — | — | 74 |
| 73 | 204–205 | 206–207 | 200–201 | 475–480 | 479–483 | 472–476 | 140–141 | 140–141 | 140–141 | 399–402 | 407–410 | 400–404 | — | — | — | 73 |
| 72 | 202–203 | 203–205 | 198–199 | 470–474 | 473–478 | 466–471 | 138–139 | 138–139 | 138–139 | 394–398 | 402–406 | 396–399 | — | — | — | 72 |
| 71 | 199–201 | 201–202 | 195–197 | 464–469 | 467–472 | 461–465 | 137 | 137 | 137 | 389–393 | 397–401 | 392–395 | — | — | — | 71 |
| 70 | 197–198 | 198–200 | 193–194 | 458–463 | 461–466 | 456–460 | 135–136 | 135–136 | 135–136 | 385–388 | 392–396 | 387–391 | — | — | — | 70 |
| 69 | 195–196 | 196–197 | 191–192 | 453–457 | 456–460 | 450–455 | 133–134 | 133–134 | 133–134 | 380–384 | 388–391 | 383–386 | — | — | — | 69 |
| 68 | 192–194 | 193–195 | 189–190 | 447–452 | 450–455 | 445–449 | 131–132 | 131–132 | 131–132 | 376–379 | 383–387 | 378–382 | — | — | 254 | 68 |
| 67 | 190–191 | 191–192 | 186–188 | 442–446 | 444–449 | 439–444 | 129–130 | 129–130 | 129–130 | 371–375 | 378–382 | 374–377 | 252 | — | 251–253 | 67 |
| 66 | 187–189 | 188–190 | — | 436–441 | 439–443 | 434–438 | — | — | — | — | 374–377 | 369–373 | 249–251 | — | 248–250 | 66 |

**Table A.14d** SRP-A Composite *T* Scores (*continued*)

| T score | School Problems | | | Internalizing Problems | | | Inattention/Hyperactivity | | | Emotional Symptoms | | | Personal Adjustment | | | T score |
|---|---|---|---|---|---|---|---|---|---|---|---|---|---|---|---|---|
| | Combined | Female | Male | Combined | Female | Male | Combined | Female | Male | Combined | Female | Male | Combined | Female | Male | |
| 65 | 185–186 | 186–187 | 184–185 | 431–435 | 433–438 | 429–433 | 127–128 | 127–128 | 127–128 | 367–370 | 369–373 | 365–368 | 246–248 | 246–249 | 245–247 | 65 |
| 64 | 183–184 | 184–185 | 182–183 | 425–430 | 427–432 | 423–428 | 125–126 | 125–126 | 125–126 | 362–366 | 364–368 | 361–364 | 243–245 | 243–245 | 242–244 | 64 |
| 63 | 180–182 | 181–183 | 179–181 | 420–424 | 422–426 | 418–422 | 124 | 124 | 124 | 357–361 | 359–363 | 356–360 | 240–242 | 240–242 | 239–241 | 63 |
| 62 | 178–179 | 179–180 | 177–178 | 414–419 | 416–421 | 413–417 | 122–123 | 122–123 | 122–123 | 353–356 | 355–358 | 352–355 | 236–239 | 237–239 | 236–238 | 62 |
| 61 | 176–177 | 176–178 | 175–176 | 409–413 | 410–415 | 407–412 | 120–121 | 120–121 | 120–121 | 348–352 | 350–354 | 347–351 | 233–235 | 234–236 | 232–235 | 61 |
| 60 | 173–175 | 174–175 | 172–174 | 403–408 | 405–409 | 402–406 | 118–119 | 118–119 | 118–119 | 344–347 | 345–349 | 343–346 | 230–232 | 231–233 | 229–231 | 60 |
| 59 | 171–172 | 171–173 | 170–171 | 398–402 | 399–404 | 396–401 | 116–117 | 116–117 | 116–117 | 339–343 | 341–344 | 339–342 | 227–229 | 227–230 | 226–228 | 59 |
| 58 | 168–170 | 169–170 | 168–169 | 392–397 | 393–398 | 391–395 | 114–115 | 114–115 | 114–115 | 335–338 | 336–340 | 334–338 | 224–226 | 224–226 | 223–225 | 58 |
| 57 | 166–167 | 166–168 | 166–167 | 386–391 | 387–392 | 386–390 | 112–113 | 112–113 | 113 | 330–334 | 331–335 | 330–333 | 221–223 | 221–223 | 220–222 | 57 |
| 56 | 164–165 | 164–165 | 163–165 | 381–385 | 382–386 | 380–385 | 111 | 111 | 111–112 | 325–329 | 326–330 | 325–329 | 218–220 | 218–220 | 217–219 | 56 |
| 55 | 161–163 | 162–163 | 161–162 | 375–380 | 376–381 | 375–379 | 109–110 | 109–110 | 109–110 | 321–324 | 322–325 | 321–324 | 215–217 | 215–217 | 214–216 | 55 |
| 54 | 159–160 | 159–161 | 159–160 | 370–374 | 370–375 | 369–374 | 107–108 | 107–108 | 107–108 | 316–320 | 317–321 | 316–320 | 211–214 | 211–214 | 211–213 | 54 |
| 53 | 157–158 | 157–158 | 156–158 | 364–369 | 365–369 | 364–368 | 105–106 | 105–106 | 105–106 | 312–315 | 312–316 | 312–315 | 208–210 | 208–210 | 208–210 | 53 |
| 52 | 154–156 | 154–156 | 154–155 | 359–363 | 359–364 | 359–363 | 103–104 | 103–104 | 103–104 | 307–311 | 308–311 | 308–311 | 205–207 | 205–207 | 205–207 | 52 |
| 51 | 152–153 | 152–153 | 152–153 | 353–358 | 353–358 | 353–358 | 101–102 | 101–102 | 102 | 303–306 | 303–307 | 303–307 | 202–204 | 202–204 | 202–204 | 51 |
| 50 | 149–151 | 149–151 | 149–151 | 348–352 | 348–352 | 348–352 | 100 | 99–100 | 100–101 | 298–302 | 298–302 | 299–302 | 199–201 | 199–201 | 199–201 | 50 |
| 49 | 147–148 | 147–148 | 147–148 | 342–347 | 342–347 | 343–347 | 98–99 | 98 | 98–99 | 293–297 | 293–297 | 294–298 | 196–198 | 196–198 | 196–198 | 49 |
| 48 | 145–146 | 145–146 | 145–146 | 337–341 | 336–341 | 337–342 | 96–97 | 96–97 | 96–97 | 289–292 | 289–292 | 290–293 | 193–195 | 192–195 | 193–195 | 48 |
| 47 | 142–144 | 142–144 | 142–144 | 331–336 | 330–335 | 332–336 | 94–95 | 94–95 | 94–95 | 284–288 | 284–288 | 285–289 | 190–192 | 189–191 | 190–192 | 47 |
| 46 | 140–141 | 140–141 | 140–141 | 326–330 | 325–329 | 326–331 | 92–93 | 92–93 | 92–93 | 280–283 | 279–283 | 281–284 | 186–189 | 186–188 | 187–189 | 46 |
| 45 | 138–139 | 137–139 | 138–139 | 320–325 | 319–324 | 321–325 | 90–91 | 90–91 | 91 | 275–279 | 275–278 | 277–280 | 183–185 | 183–185 | 183–186 | 45 |
| 44 | 135–137 | 135–136 | 136–137 | 314–319 | 313–318 | 316–320 | 88–89 | 88–89 | 89–90 | 271–274 | 270–274 | 272–276 | 180–182 | 180–182 | 180–182 | 44 |
| 43 | 133–134 | 132–134 | 133–135 | 309–313 | 308–312 | 310–315 | 87 | 86–87 | 87–88 | 266–270 | 265–269 | 268–271 | 177–179 | 176–179 | 177–179 | 43 |
| 42 | 130–132 | 130–131 | 131–132 | 303–308 | 302–307 | 305–309 | 85–86 | 85 | 85–86 | 261–265 | 260–264 | 263–267 | 174–176 | 173–175 | 174–176 | 42 |
| 41 | 128–129 | 127–129 | 129–130 | 298–302 | 296–301 | 299–304 | 83–84 | 83–84 | 83–84 | 257–260 | 256–259 | 259–262 | 171–173 | 170–172 | 171–173 | 41 |
| 40 | 126–127 | 125–126 | 127–128 | 292–297 | 291–295 | 294–298 | 81–82 | 81–82 | 81–82 | 252–256 | 251–255 | 255–258 | 168–170 | 167–169 | 168–170 | 40 |
| 39 | 123–125 | 123–124 | 124–125 | 287–291 | 285–290 | 289–293 | 79–80 | 79–80 | 79–80 | 248–251 | 246–250 | 250–254 | 165–167 | 164–166 | 165–167 | 39 |
| 38 | 121–122 | 120–122 | 122–123 | 281–286 | 279–284 | 283–288 | 77–78 | 77–78 | 78 | 243–247 | 242–245 | 246–249 | 161–164 | 161–163 | 162–164 | 38 |
| 37 | 118–120 | 118–119 | 119–121 | 276–280 | 273–278 | 278–282 | 76 | 75–76 | 76–77 | 238–242 | 237–241 | 241–245 | 158–160 | 157–160 | 159–161 | 37 |
| 36 | 116–117 | 115–117 | 117–118 | 270–275 | 268–272 | 273–277 | 74–75 | 74–75 | 74–75 | 234–237 | 232–236 | 237–240 | 155–157 | 154–156 | 156–158 | 36 |
| 35 | 114–115 | 113–114 | 115–116 | 266–269 | 266–267 | 267–272 | 72–73 | 72 | 72–73 | 229–233 | 227–231 | 232–236 | 152–154 | 151–153 | 153–155 | 35 |
| 34 | 111–113 | 110–112 | 112–114 | — | — | — | 70–71 | 70–71 | 70–71 | 225–228 | 223–226 | 228–231 | 149–151 | 148–150 | 150–152 | 34 |
| 33 | 109–110 | 108–109 | 110–111 | — | — | — | — | 69 | 69 | 220–224 | 219–222 | 224–227 | 146–148 | 145–147 | 147–149 | 33 |
| 32 | 107–108 | 105–107 | 108–109 | — | — | — | — | — | — | 217–219 | — | 219–223 | 143–145 | 141–144 | 144–146 | 32 |
| 31 | 104–106 | 104 | 106–107 | — | — | — | — | — | — | — | — | 217–218 | 140–142 | 138–140 | 141–143 | 31 |
| 30 | 103 | — | 103–105 | — | — | — | — | — | — | — | — | — | 136–139 | 135–137 | 138–140 | 30 |
| 29 | — | — | 101–102 | — | — | — | — | — | — | — | — | — | 133–135 | 132–134 | 134–137 | 29 |
| 28 | — | — | — | — | — | — | — | — | — | — | — | — | 130–132 | 129–131 | 131–133 | 28 |
| 27 | — | — | — | — | — | — | — | — | — | — | — | — | 127–129 | 126–128 | 128–130 | 27 |
| 26 | — | — | — | — | — | — | — | — | — | — | — | — | 124–126 | 122–125 | 125–127 | 26 |
| 25 | — | — | — | — | — | — | — | — | — | — | — | — | 121–123 | 119–121 | 122–124 | 25 |
| 24 | — | — | — | — | — | — | — | — | — | — | — | — | 118–120 | 116–118 | 119–121 | 24 |
| 23 | — | — | — | — | — | — | — | — | — | — | — | — | 115–117 | 113–115 | 116–118 | 23 |
| 22 | — | — | — | — | — | — | — | — | — | — | — | — | 111–114 | 110–112 | 113–115 | 22 |
| 21 | — | — | — | — | — | — | — | — | — | — | — | — | 108–110 | 106–109 | 110–112 | 21 |
| 20 | — | — | — | — | — | — | — | — | — | — | — | — | 105–107 | 103–105 | 107–109 | 20 |
| 19 | — | — | — | — | — | — | — | — | — | — | — | — | 102–104 | 100–102 | 104–106 | 19 |
| 18 | — | — | — | — | — | — | — | — | — | — | — | — | 99–101 | 97–99 | 101–103 | 18 |
| 17 | — | — | — | — | — | — | — | — | — | — | — | — | 96–98 | 94–96 | 98–100 | 17 |
| 16 | — | — | — | — | — | — | — | — | — | — | — | — | 93–95 | 91–93 | 95–97 | 16 |
| 15 | — | — | — | — | — | — | — | — | — | — | — | — | 90–92 | 87–90 | 92–94 | 15 |
| 14 | — | — | — | — | — | — | — | — | — | — | — | — | 86–89 | 84–86 | 89–91 | 14 |
| 13 | — | — | — | — | — | — | — | — | — | — | — | — | 83–85 | 81–83 | 85–88 | 13 |
| 12 | — | — | — | — | — | — | — | — | — | — | — | — | 80–82 | 78–80 | 82–84 | 12 |
| 11 | — | — | — | — | — | — | — | — | — | — | — | — | 77–79 | 75–77 | 79–81 | 11 |
| 10 | — | — | — | — | — | — | — | — | — | — | — | — | 43–76 | 41–74 | 45–78 | 10 |
| T: 90% Conf. int. | 5 | 5 | 5 | 3 | 3 | 4 | 5 | 5 | 5 | 4 | 3 | 4 | 4 | 4 | 4 | T: 90% Conf. int. |

## Table A.14e  SRP–A Composite Percentiles

| %ile | School Problems Combined | School Problems Female | School Problems Male | Internalizing Problems Combined | Internalizing Problems Female | Internalizing Problems Male | Inattention/Hyperactivity Combined | Inattention/Hyperactivity Female | Inattention/Hyperactivity Male | Emotional Symptoms Combined | Emotional Symptoms Female | Emotional Symptoms Male | Personal Adjustment Combined | Personal Adjustment Female | Personal Adjustment Male | %ile |
|---|---|---|---|---|---|---|---|---|---|---|---|---|---|---|---|---|
| 99 | 210–259 | 216–265 | 204–254 | 505–693 | 506–680 | 502–705 | 148–170 | 149–173 | 147–168 | 427–571 | 430–563 | 423–579 | 246–252 | 243–249 | 247–254 | 99 |
| 98 | 204–209 | 207–215 | 199–203 | 488–504 | 489–505 | 483–501 | 143–147 | 144–148 | 143–146 | 412–426 | 415–429 | 408–422 | 244–245 | 241–242 | 244–246 | 98 |
| 97 | 199–203 | 202–206 | 196–198 | 475–487 | 477–488 | 470–482 | 140–142 | 140–143 | 140–142 | 401–411 | 404–414 | 398–407 | 243 | 240 | 243 | 97 |
| 96 | 196–198 | 198–201 | 193–195 | 465–474 | 468–476 | 460–469 | 137–139 | 137–139 | 137–139 | 393–400 | 396–403 | 390–397 | 241–242 | 239 | 241–242 | 96 |
| 95 | 193–195 | 194–197 | 191–192 | 456–464 | 459–467 | 451–459 | 135–136 | 134–136 | 135–136 | 386–392 | 389–395 | 383–389 | 240 | 238 | 240 | 95 |
| 94 | 190–192 | 191–193 | 189–190 | 449–455 | 452–458 | 444–450 | 133–134 | 132–133 | 133–134 | 380–385 | 383–388 | 378–382 | 239 | – | 239 | 94 |
| 93 | 188–189 | 189–190 | 187–188 | 443–448 | 446–451 | 438–443 | 131–132 | 130–131 | 131–132 | 375–378 | 378–382 | 373–377 | 238 | 237 | 238 | 93 |
| 92 | 186–187 | 186–188 | 185–186 | 437–442 | 440–445 | 432–437 | 129–130 | 129 | 130 | 370–374 | 373–377 | 368–372 | 237 | 236 | 237 | 92 |
| 91 | 184–185 | 184–185 | 183–184 | 431–436 | 435–439 | 427–431 | 128 | 127–128 | 128–129 | 366–369 | 369–372 | 364–367 | 236 | 235 | 236 | 91 |
| 90 | 182–183 | 182–183 | 182 | 427–430 | 430–434 | 422–426 | 126–127 | 126 | 127 | 362–365 | 365–368 | 361–363 | 235 | – | 235 | 90 |
| 89 | 181 | 181 | 181 | 422–426 | 426–429 | 418–421 | 125 | 124–125 | 125–126 | 359–361 | 361–364 | 357–360 | – | 234 | 234 | 89 |
| 88 | 179–180 | 179–180 | 179–180 | 418–421 | 421–425 | 414–417 | 123–124 | 123 | 124 | 355–358 | 358–360 | 354–356 | 234 | 233 | 233 | 88 |
| 87 | 178 | 178 | 178 | 414–417 | 417–420 | 411–413 | 122 | 122 | 123 | 352–354 | 354–357 | 351–353 | 233 | – | 232 | 87 |
| 86 | 177 | 176–177 | 177 | 410–413 | 414–416 | 407–410 | 121 | 121 | 122 | 349–351 | 351–353 | 348–350 | 232 | 232 | 231 | 86 |
| 85 | 175–176 | 175 | 176 | 407–409 | 410–413 | 404–406 | 120 | 120 | 121 | 347–348 | 349–350 | 346–347 | – | 231 | 230 | 85 |
| 84 | 174 | 173–174 | 175 | 404–406 | 407–409 | 401–403 | 119 | 119 | 120 | 344–346 | 346–348 | 343–345 | 231 | – | – | 84 |
| 83 | 173 | 172 | 173–174 | 401–403 | 403–406 | 398–400 | 118 | 118 | 119 | 342–343 | 343–345 | 341–342 | 230 | 230 | 229 | 83 |
| 82 | 172 | 171 | 172 | 398–400 | 400–402 | 395–397 | 117 | 117 | 118 | 339–341 | 341–342 | 339–340 | 229 | 229 | 228 | 82 |
| 81 | 171 | 170 | 171 | 395–397 | 397–399 | 393–394 | 116 | 116 | 117 | 337–338 | 339–340 | 337–338 | – | – | 227 | 81 |
| 80 | 170 | 169 | 170 | 392–394 | 395–396 | 390–392 | 115 | 115 | 116 | 335–336 | 336–338 | 334–336 | 228 | 228 | – | 80 |
| 79 | 169 | 168 | – | 389–391 | 392–394 | 388–389 | – | 114 | 115 | 333–334 | 334–335 | 333 | 227 | 227 | 226 | 79 |
| 78 | 168 | 167 | 169 | 387–388 | 389–391 | 385–387 | 114 | – | 114 | 331–332 | 332–333 | 331–332 | 226 | – | 225 | 78 |
| 77 | 167 | 166 | 168 | 384–386 | 387–388 | 383–384 | 113 | 113 | – | 329–330 | 330–331 | 329–330 | – | 226 | 224 | 77 |
| 76 | 166 | 165 | 167 | 382–383 | 384–386 | 381–382 | 112 | 112 | 113 | 327–328 | 328–329 | 327–328 | 225 | – | – | 76 |
| 75 | 165 | 164 | 166 | 380–381 | 382–383 | 379–380 | 111 | 111 | 112 | 325–326 | 326–327 | 325–326 | 224 | 225 | 223 | 75 |
| 74 | 164 | 163 | 165 | 378–379 | 379–381 | 377–378 | – | – | 111 | 323–324 | 324–325 | 324 | – | 224 | 222 | 74 |
| 73 | 163 | 162 | 164 | 375–377 | 377–378 | 375–376 | 110 | 110 | – | 322 | 323 | 322–323 | 223 | – | – | 73 |
| 72 | – | – | 163 | 373–374 | 375–376 | 373–374 | 109 | 109 | 110 | 320–321 | 321–322 | 320–321 | 222 | 223 | 221 | 72 |
| 71 | 162 | 161 | – | 371–372 | 373–374 | 371–372 | – | – | 109 | 318–319 | 319–320 | 319 | – | 222 | 220 | 71 |
| 70 | 161 | 160 | 162 | 369–370 | 371–372 | 369–370 | 108 | 108 | 108 | 317 | 318 | 317–318 | 221 | – | – | 70 |
| 69 | 160 | 159 | 161 | 367–368 | 369–370 | 367–368 | 107 | 107 | – | 315–316 | 316–317 | 316 | 220 | 221 | 219 | 69 |
| 68 | – | 158 | 160 | 366 | 367–368 | 365–366 | – | – | 107 | 314 | 314–315 | 314–315 | – | 220 | 218 | 68 |
| 67 | 159 | – | – | 364–365 | 365–366 | 364 | 106 | 106 | – | 312–313 | 313 | 313 | 219 | – | 217 | 67 |
| 66 | 158 | 157 | 159 | 362–363 | 363–364 | 362–363 | 105 | – | 106 | 311 | 311–312 | 312 | 218 | 219 | – | 66 |
| 65 | 157 | 156 | 158 | 360–361 | 361–362 | 360–361 | – | 105 | 105 | 309–310 | 310 | 310–311 | 217 | 218 | 216 | 65 |
| 64 | – | – | 157 | 358–359 | 359–360 | 359 | 104 | 104 | – | 308 | 308–309 | 309 | – | 217 | 215 | 64 |
| 63 | 156 | 155 | – | 357 | 357–358 | 357–358 | – | – | 104 | 307 | 307 | 308 | 216 | – | – | 63 |
| 62 | 155 | 154 | 156 | 355–356 | 356 | 356 | 103 | 103 | – | 305–306 | 306 | 307 | 215 | 216 | 214 | 62 |
| 61 | – | – | 155 | 354 | 354–355 | 354–355 | – | – | 103 | 304 | 304–305 | 305–306 | – | 215 | 213 | 61 |
| 60 | 154 | 153 | – | 352–353 | 352–353 | 353 | 102 | 102 | 102 | 303 | 303 | 304 | 214 | – | – | 60 |
| 59 | 153 | 152 | 154 | 350–351 | 351 | 351–352 | – | – | – | 302 | 302 | 303 | 213 | 214 | 212 | 59 |
| 58 | – | – | 153 | 349 | 349–350 | 350 | – | – | – | 300–301 | 300–301 | 302 | 212 | 213 | 211 | 58 |
| 57 | 152 | 151 | – | 347–348 | 348 | 349 | 101 | 101 | 101 | 299 | 299 | 301 | – | 212 | 210 | 57 |
| 56 | 151 | 150 | 152 | 346 | 346–347 | 347–348 | 100 | 100 | 100 | 298 | 298 | 299–300 | 211 | – | – | 56 |
| 55 | – | – | 151 | 344–345 | 344–345 | 344–345 | 99 | 99 | 99 | 297 | 297 | 298 | 210 | 211 | 209 | 55 |
| 54 | 150 | 149 | – | 343 | 343 | 343 | – | – | – | 296 | 295–296 | 297 | 209 | 210 | 208 | 54 |
| 53 | 149 | – | 150 | 342 | 341–342 | 342 | 98 | 98 | 98 | 294–295 | 294 | 296 | – | 209 | 207 | 53 |
| 52 | – | 148 | 149 | 340–341 | 340 | 341 | – | – | – | 293 | 293 | 295 | 208 | – | 206 | 52 |
| 51 | 148 | 147 | – | 339 | 339 | – | 97 | – | – | 292 | 292 | 294 | 207 | 208 | 206 | 51 |

## Table A.14e SRP–A Composite Percentiles (continued)

| %ile | School Problems | | | Internalizing Problems | | | Inattention/Hyperactivity | | | Emotional Symptoms | | | Personal Adjustment | | | %ile |
|---|---|---|---|---|---|---|---|---|---|---|---|---|---|---|---|---|
| | Combined | Female | Male | Combined | Female | Male | Combined | Female | Male | Combined | Female | Male | Combined | Female | Male | |
| 50 | – | – | 148 | 338 | 337–338 | 339–340 | – | 97 | 97 | 291 | 291 | 293 | 206 | 207 | 205 | 50 |
| 49 | 147 | 146 | 147 | 336–337 | 336 | 338 | 96 | – | – | 290 | 290 | 292 | 205 | 206 | 204 | 49 |
| 48 | 146 | – | 146 | 335 | 334–335 | 337 | – | 96 | 96 | 289 | 288–289 | 291 | – | 205 | – | 48 |
| 47 | – | 145 | – | 334 | 333 | 336 | – | – | – | 288 | 287 | 290 | 204 | 204 | 203 | 47 |
| 46 | 145 | 144 | 145 | 332–333 | 332 | 334–335 | 95 | 95 | 95 | 287 | 286 | 289 | 203 | 203 | 202 | 46 |
| 45 | – | – | 145 | 331 | 330–331 | 333 | – | – | – | 286 | 285 | 288 | 202 | – | 201 | 45 |
| 44 | 144 | 143 | 144 | 330 | 329 | 332 | 94 | 94 | 94 | 285 | 284 | 287 | 201 | 202 | 200 | 44 |
| 43 | 143 | – | 143 | 329 | 328 | 331 | – | – | – | 283–284 | 283 | 286 | 200 | 201 | – | 43 |
| 42 | – | 142 | – | 327–328 | 326–327 | 330 | 93 | – | 93 | 282 | 282 | 285 | 199 | 200 | 199 | 42 |
| 41 | 142 | – | 142 | 326 | 325 | 328–329 | – | 93 | – | 281 | 281 | 284 | – | 199 | 198 | 41 |
| 40 | – | 141 | 142 | 325 | 324 | 327 | 92 | – | – | 280 | 280 | 283 | 198 | 198 | 197 | 40 |
| 39 | 141 | 140 | 141 | 324 | 323 | 326 | – | 92 | 92 | 279 | 279 | 282 | 197 | 197 | 196 | 39 |
| 38 | 140 | – | 140 | 323 | 321–322 | 325 | 91 | – | – | 278 | 278 | 281 | 196 | 196 | 195 | 38 |
| 37 | – | 139 | – | 321–322 | 320 | 324 | – | 91 | 91 | 277 | 277 | 280 | 195 | 195 | 194 | 37 |
| 36 | 139 | – | 139 | 320 | 319 | 323 | – | – | – | 276 | 276 | 279 | 194 | 194 | – | 36 |
| 35 | – | 138 | 138 | 319 | 318 | 321–322 | 90 | – | 90 | 275 | 275 | 278 | 193 | 193 | 193 | 35 |
| 34 | 138 | – | – | 318 | 316–317 | 320 | – | 90 | – | 274 | 274 | 277 | 192 | 192 | 192 | 34 |
| 33 | 137 | 137 | – | 317 | 315 | 319 | 89 | – | 89 | 273 | 273 | 276 | 191 | 191 | 191 | 33 |
| 32 | – | 136 | 137 | 316 | 314 | 318 | – | 89 | – | 272 | 272 | 275 | 190 | 189–190 | 190 | 32 |
| 31 | 136 | – | 136 | 314–315 | 313 | 317 | 88 | – | – | 271 | 270–271 | 274 | 189 | 188 | 189 | 31 |
| 30 | – | 135 | – | 313 | 312 | 316 | – | 88 | 88 | 270 | 269 | 273 | 187–188 | 187 | 188 | 30 |
| 29 | 135 | – | 135 | 312 | 310–311 | 315 | – | – | – | 269 | 268 | 272 | 186 | 186 | 187 | 29 |
| 28 | 134 | 134 | 134 | 311 | 309 | 314 | 87 | 87 | 87 | 268 | 267 | 271 | 185 | 185 | 185–186 | 28 |
| 27 | – | – | – | 310 | 308 | 312–313 | – | – | – | 267 | 266 | 270 | 184 | 183–184 | 184 | 27 |
| 26 | 133 | 133 | 133 | 309 | 307 | 311 | 86 | – | 86 | 266 | 265 | 269 | 183 | 182 | 183 | 26 |
| 25 | – | 132 | 132 | 308 | 306 | 310 | – | 86 | – | 265 | 264 | 268 | 181–182 | 181 | 182 | 25 |
| 24 | 132 | – | – | 307 | 305 | 309 | 85 | – | – | 264 | 263 | 267 | 180 | 179–180 | 181 | 24 |
| 23 | 131 | 131 | 131 | 305–306 | 303–304 | 308 | – | 85 | 85 | 263 | 262 | 266 | 179 | 178 | 179–180 | 23 |
| 22 | – | – | – | 304 | 302 | 307 | – | – | – | 262 | 261 | 265 | 177–178 | 176–177 | 178 | 22 |
| 21 | 130 | 130 | 130 | 303 | 301 | 305–306 | 84 | 84 | 84 | 261 | 260 | 264 | 176 | 175 | 177 | 21 |
| 20 | 129 | 129 | 129 | 302 | 300 | 304 | – | – | – | 260 | 259 | 263 | 174–175 | 173–174 | 175–176 | 20 |
| 19 | – | – | 128 | 301 | 299 | 303 | 83 | 83 | 83 | 259 | 258 | 262 | 173 | 171–172 | 174 | 19 |
| 18 | 128 | 128 | – | 300 | 298 | 302 | – | – | – | 258 | 257 | 261 | 171–172 | 170 | 172–173 | 18 |
| 17 | 127 | 127 | 127 | 299 | 296–297 | 301 | 82 | 82 | – | 257 | 256 | 260 | 170 | 168–169 | 171 | 17 |
| 16 | 126 | – | 126 | 297–298 | 295 | 299–300 | – | – | 82 | 256 | 255 | 259 | 168–169 | 166–167 | 169–170 | 16 |
| 15 | – | 126 | – | 296 | 294 | 298 | 81 | 81 | – | 255 | 254 | 257–258 | 166–167 | 164–165 | 167–168 | 15 |
| 14 | 125 | 125 | 125 | 295 | 293 | 297 | – | – | 81 | 254 | 253 | 256 | 164–165 | 162–163 | 165–166 | 14 |
| 13 | 124 | 124 | 124 | 294 | 291–292 | 295–296 | 80 | 80 | – | 253 | 252 | 255 | 162–163 | 160–161 | 163–164 | 13 |
| 12 | 123 | – | 123 | 292–293 | 290 | 294 | – | – | 80 | 252 | 250–251 | 254 | 160–161 | 157–159 | 161–162 | 12 |
| 11 | 122 | 123 | 122 | 291 | 289 | 293 | 79 | 79 | – | 250–251 | 249 | 253 | 157–159 | 155–156 | 159–160 | 11 |
| 10 | 121 | 122 | 121 | 290 | 288 | 291–292 | – | – | 79 | 249 | 248 | 251–252 | 155–156 | 152–154 | 157–158 | 10 |
| 9 | – | 121 | 120 | 289 | 286–287 | 290 | 78 | 78 | – | 248 | 247 | 250 | 152–154 | 149–151 | 154–156 | 9 |
| 8 | 119–120 | 120 | 119 | 287–288 | 285 | 288–289 | 77 | 77 | 78 | 246–247 | 245–246 | 249 | 149–151 | 146–148 | 151–153 | 8 |
| 7 | 118 | 119 | 118 | 286 | 283–284 | 286–287 | 76 | – | 77 | 245 | 244 | 247–248 | 146–148 | 143–145 | 148–150 | 7 |
| 6 | 117 | 118 | 117 | 284–285 | 282 | 285 | – | 76 | – | 243–244 | 242–243 | 245–246 | 142–145 | 139–142 | 144–147 | 6 |
| 5 | 116 | 116–117 | 116 | 282–283 | 280–281 | 283–284 | 75 | 75 | 76 | 241–242 | 240–241 | 244 | 138–141 | 135–138 | 140–143 | 5 |
| 4 | 114–115 | 115 | 114–115 | 280–281 | 278–279 | 280–282 | 74 | 74 | 75 | 240 | 239 | 241–243 | 132–137 | 130–134 | 134–139 | 4 |
| 3 | 112–113 | 113–114 | 113 | 278–279 | 276–277 | 278–279 | 73 | 73 | – | 237–239 | 236–238 | 239–240 | 126–131 | 124–129 | 128–133 | 3 |
| 2 | 110–111 | 111–112 | 111–112 | 275–277 | 274–275 | 274–277 | – | 71–72 | 74 | 234–236 | 234–235 | 236–238 | 117–125 | 116–123 | 118–127 | 2 |
| 1 | 103–109 | 104–110 | 101–110 | 266–274 | 266–273 | 267–273 | 70–72 | 69–70 | 69–73 | 217–233 | 219–233 | 217–235 | 43–116 | 41–115 | 45–117 | 1 |

## Table A.15a SRP–A T Scores and Percentiles

| Raw score | Attitude to School | | Attitude to Teachers | | Sensation Seeking | | Atypicality | | Locus of Control | | Social Stress | | Anxiety | | Depression | | Sense of Inadequacy | | Somatization | | Attention Problems | | Hyperactivity | | Relations With Parents | | Interpersonal Relations | | Self-Esteem | | Self-Reliance | |
| --- | --- | --- | --- | --- | --- | --- | --- | --- | --- | --- | --- | --- | --- | --- | --- | --- | --- | --- | --- | --- | --- | --- | --- | --- | --- | --- | --- | --- | --- | --- | --- | --- |
| | T | %ile | T | %ile | T | %ile | T | %ile | T | %ile | T | %ile | T | %ile | T | %ile | T | %ile | T | %ile | T | %ile | T | %ile | T | %ile | T | %ile | T | %ile | T | %ile |
| 36 | — | — | — | — | — | — | — | — | — | — | — | — | 82 | 99 | — | — | — | — | — | — | — | — | — | — | — | — | — | — | — | — | — | — |
| 35 | — | — | — | — | — | — | — | — | — | — | — | — | 80 | 99 | — | — | — | — | — | — | — | — | — | — | — | — | — | — | — | — | — | — |
| 34 | — | — | — | — | — | — | — | — | — | — | — | — | 79 | 99 | — | — | — | — | — | — | — | — | — | — | — | — | — | — | — | — | — | — |
| 33 | — | — | — | — | — | — | — | — | — | — | — | — | 78 | 99 | — | — | — | — | — | — | — | — | — | — | — | — | — | — | — | — | — | — |
| 32 | — | — | — | — | — | — | — | — | — | — | — | — | 77 | 99 | — | — | — | — | — | — | — | — | — | — | 64 | 97 | — | — | — | — | — | — |
| 31 | — | — | — | — | — | — | — | — | — | — | 92 | 99 | 75 | 98 | 92 | 99 | 91 | 99 | — | — | — | — | — | — | 63 | 93 | — | — | — | — | — | — |
| 30 | — | — | — | — | — | — | — | — | — | — | 90 | 99 | 74 | 98 | 91 | 99 | 89 | 99 | — | — | — | — | — | — | 61 | 88 | — | — | — | — | — | — |
| 29 | — | — | — | — | — | — | 107 | 99 | — | — | 89 | 99 | 73 | 97 | 89 | 99 | 87 | 99 | — | — | — | — | — | — | 60 | 82 | — | — | — | — | — | — |
| 28 | — | — | — | — | — | — | 105 | 99 | — | — | 87 | 99 | 71 | 96 | 87 | 99 | 85 | 99 | — | — | — | — | — | — | 58 | 76 | — | — | — | — | — | — |
| 27 | — | — | — | — | — | — | 103 | 99 | — | — | 85 | 99 | 70 | 95 | 86 | 99 | 83 | 99 | — | — | — | — | — | — | 57 | 69 | — | — | — | — | — | — |
| 26 | — | — | — | — | 82 | 99 | 100 | 99 | — | — | 83 | 99 | 69 | 94 | 84 | 99 | 82 | 99 | — | — | — | — | — | — | 55 | 63 | — | — | — | — | 68 | 98 |
| 25 | — | — | 91 | 99 | 80 | 99 | 98 | 99 | — | — | 82 | 99 | 67 | 93 | 82 | 99 | 80 | 99 | — | — | — | — | — | — | 54 | 57 | — | — | — | — | 66 | 96 |
| 24 | — | — | 88 | 99 | 78 | 99 | 96 | 99 | — | — | 80 | 99 | 66 | 91 | 81 | 99 | 78 | 98 | — | — | — | — | 88 | 99 | 52 | 51 | 61 | 94 | — | — | 63 | 93 |
| 23 | — | — | 86 | 99 | 76 | 99 | 94 | 99 | — | — | 78 | 99 | 65 | 90 | 79 | 98 | 76 | 98 | — | — | — | — | 86 | 99 | 51 | 46 | 58 | 81 | — | — | 61 | 88 |
| 22 | 84 | 99 | 84 | 99 | 74 | 99 | 91 | 99 | — | — | 76 | 98 | 63 | 88 | 77 | 98 | 75 | 97 | — | — | — | — | 84 | 99 | 49 | 40 | 56 | 67 | — | — | 59 | 81 |
| 21 | 82 | 99 | 82 | 99 | 72 | 98 | 89 | 99 | — | — | 75 | 98 | 62 | 86 | 76 | 97 | 73 | 97 | — | — | 76 | 99 | 82 | 99 | 48 | 36 | 53 | 54 | — | — | 57 | 73 |
| 20 | 80 | 99 | 80 | 99 | 70 | 96 | 87 | 99 | 88 | 99 | 73 | 97 | 61 | 84 | 74 | 97 | 71 | 96 | — | — | 74 | 99 | 79 | 99 | 46 | 31 | 51 | 43 | — | — | 55 | 65 |
| 19 | 77 | 99 | 78 | 99 | 68 | 96 | 84 | 99 | 86 | 99 | 71 | 97 | 59 | 81 | 72 | 96 | 69 | 95 | — | — | 72 | 98 | 77 | 99 | 45 | 27 | 48 | 34 | — | — | 52 | 56 |
| 18 | 75 | 98 | 76 | 98 | 66 | 94 | 82 | 98 | 83 | 99 | 69 | 95 | 58 | 79 | 71 | 95 | 67 | 93 | — | — | 70 | 97 | 75 | 98 | 43 | 23 | 46 | 26 | 60 | 90 | 50 | 47 |
| 17 | 73 | 97 | 73 | 97 | 64 | 91 | 80 | 98 | 81 | 99 | 67 | 94 | 57 | 76 | 69 | 94 | 66 | 92 | 93 | 99 | 68 | 95 | 73 | 97 | 42 | 20 | 43 | 20 | 58 | 76 | 48 | 39 |
| 16 | 70 | 96 | 71 | 96 | 62 | 88 | 77 | 97 | 78 | 99 | 66 | 92 | 55 | 73 | 67 | 93 | 64 | 90 | 90 | 99 | 66 | 92 | 71 | 96 | 40 | 17 | 41 | 16 | 56 | 62 | 46 | 32 |
| 15 | 68 | 94 | 69 | 95 | 60 | 85 | 75 | 97 | 76 | 98 | 64 | 90 | 54 | 69 | 66 | 91 | 62 | 88 | 87 | 99 | 64 | 90 | 68 | 94 | 39 | 14 | 38 | 12 | 53 | 51 | 44 | 25 |
| 14 | 66 | 92 | 67 | 93 | 58 | 80 | 73 | 96 | 73 | 97 | 62 | 87 | 53 | 65 | 64 | 90 | 60 | 85 | 84 | 99 | 62 | 86 | 66 | 92 | 37 | 12 | 36 | 9 | 51 | 42 | 41 | 19 |
| 13 | 64 | 89 | 65 | 91 | 57 | 75 | 71 | 95 | 71 | 96 | 60 | 85 | 51 | 61 | 62 | 88 | 58 | 82 | 81 | 99 | 60 | 83 | 64 | 90 | 36 | 10 | 33 | 7 | 48 | 35 | 39 | 15 |
| 12 | 61 | 86 | 63 | 88 | 55 | 69 | 68 | 94 | 68 | 94 | 59 | 81 | 50 | 57 | 61 | 87 | 57 | 78 | 78 | 98 | 58 | 78 | 62 | 87 | 34 | 8 | 31 | 5 | 46 | 28 | 37 | 11 |
| 11 | 59 | 81 | 61 | 85 | 53 | 62 | 66 | 92 | 66 | 92 | 57 | 78 | 49 | 52 | 59 | 84 | 55 | 74 | 75 | 96 | 56 | 74 | 60 | 83 | 33 | 7 | 28 | 4 | 44 | 23 | 35 | 8 |
| 10 | 57 | 76 | 58 | 81 | 51 | 54 | 64 | 90 | 64 | 89 | 55 | 73 | 47 | 47 | 57 | 82 | 53 | 69 | 72 | 94 | 54 | 69 | 58 | 79 | 31 | 5 | 26 | 3 | 41 | 19 | 33 | 5 |
| 9 | 54 | 70 | 56 | 76 | 49 | 47 | 61 | 88 | 61 | 86 | 53 | 68 | 46 | 42 | 56 | 79 | 51 | 63 | 69 | 92 | 53 | 63 | 55 | 74 | 30 | 4 | 23 | 2 | 39 | 15 | 30 | 4 |
| 8 | 52 | 63 | 54 | 70 | 47 | 39 | 59 | 85 | 59 | 82 | 52 | 63 | 45 | 36 | 54 | 76 | 50 | 57 | 66 | 90 | 51 | 57 | 53 | 68 | 28 | 3 | 21 | 2 | 37 | 12 | 28 | 2 |
| 7 | 50 | 55 | 52 | 63 | 45 | 32 | 57 | 81 | 56 | 77 | 50 | 56 | 43 | 30 | 52 | 72 | 48 | 50 | 63 | 87 | 49 | 51 | 51 | 61 | 27 | 2 | 18 | 1 | 34 | 9 | 26 | 2 |
| 6 | 48 | 47 | 50 | 55 | 43 | 25 | 54 | 76 | 54 | 71 | 48 | 50 | 42 | 24 | 51 | 67 | 46 | 42 | 60 | 84 | 47 | 44 | 49 | 53 | 25 | 2 | 16 | 1 | 32 | 7 | 24 | 1 |
| 5 | 45 | 38 | 48 | 47 | 41 | 18 | 52 | 70 | 51 | 63 | 46 | 42 | 41 | 18 | 49 | 62 | 44 | 33 | 57 | 80 | 45 | 36 | 47 | 45 | 24 | 1 | 13 | 1 | 30 | 5 | 21 | 1 |
| 4 | 43 | 28 | 45 | 38 | 39 | 13 | 50 | 63 | 49 | 55 | 44 | 34 | 39 | 12 | 47 | 55 | 42 | 25 | 54 | 76 | 43 | 28 | 45 | 35 | 22 | 1 | 10 | 1 | 27 | 4 | 19 | 1 |
| 3 | 41 | 18 | 43 | 29 | 37 | 8 | 48 | 53 | 46 | 44 | 43 | 26 | 38 | 7 | 46 | 47 | 41 | 16 | 51 | 71 | 41 | 20 | 42 | 26 | 21 | 1 | 10 | 1 | 25 | 3 | 17 | 1 |
| 2 | 38 | 10 | 41 | 20 | 35 | 5 | 45 | 41 | 44 | 32 | 41 | 19 | 37 | 2 | 44 | 36 | 39 | 9 | 48 | 63 | 39 | 13 | 40 | 16 | 19 | 1 | 10 | 1 | 23 | 2 | 15 | 1 |
| 1 | 36 | 4 | 39 | 12 | 33 | 3 | 43 | 26 | 41 | 19 | 39 | 11 | 35 | 1 | 42 | 22 | 37 | 3 | 45 | 50 | 37 | 6 | 38 | 8 | 18 | 1 | 10 | 1 | 20 | 1 | 13 | 1 |
| 0 | 34 | 1 | 37 | 5 | 31 | 1 | 41 | 9 | 39 | 7 | 37 | 5 | 34 | 1 | 41 | — | 35 | 1 | 42 | 15 | 35 | 1 | 36 | 2 | 16 | 1 | 10 | 1 | 18 | 1 | 10 | 1 |
| **Raw mean** | 7.07 | | 6.10 | | 9.71 | | 4.06 | | 4.53 | | 7.12 | | 12.07 | | 5.52 | | 8.23 | | 2.55 | | 7.73 | | 6.50 | | 22.62 | | 19.65 | | 13.65 | | 17.91 | |
| **Raw SD** | 4.38 | | 4.65 | | 5.05 | | 4.35 | | 4.05 | | 5.65 | | 7.52 | | 6.00 | | 5.62 | | 3.37 | | 5.07 | | 4.61 | | 6.70 | | 3.96 | | 4.27 | | 4.52 | |
| **T:90% Conf. int.** | 7 | | 7 | | 6 | | 7 | | 7 | | 6 | | 5 | | 5 | | 7 | | 7 | | 6 | | 6 | | 5 | | 7 | | 6 | | 7 | |

## Table A.15b  SRP–A T Scores and Percentiles

| Raw score | Attitude to School | | Attitude to Teachers | | Sensation Seeking | | Atypicality | | Locus of Control | | Social Stress | | Anxiety | | Depression | | Sense of Inadequacy | | Somatization | | Attention Problems | | Hyperactivity | | Relations With Parents | | Interpersonal Relations | | Self-Esteem | | Self-Reliance | | Raw score |
|---|---|---|---|---|---|---|---|---|---|---|---|---|---|---|---|---|---|---|---|---|---|---|---|---|---|---|---|---|---|---|---|---|---|
| | T | %ile | T | %ile | T | %ile | T | %ile | T | %ile | T | %ile | T | %ile | T | %ile | T | %ile | T | %ile | T | %ile | T | %ile | T | %ile | T | %ile | T | %ile | T | %ile | |
| 36 | — | — | — | — | — | — | — | — | — | — | — | — | 78 | 99 | — | — | — | — | — | — | — | — | — | — | — | — | — | — | — | — | — | — | 36 |
| 35 | — | — | — | — | — | — | — | — | — | — | — | — | 77 | 99 | — | — | — | — | — | — | — | — | — | — | — | — | — | — | — | — | — | — | 35 |
| 34 | — | — | — | — | — | — | — | — | — | — | — | — | 75 | 99 | — | — | — | — | — | — | — | — | — | — | — | — | — | — | — | — | — | — | 34 |
| 33 | — | — | — | — | — | — | — | — | — | — | — | — | 74 | 98 | — | — | — | — | — | — | — | — | — | — | — | — | — | — | — | — | — | — | 33 |
| 32 | — | — | — | — | — | — | — | — | — | — | — | — | 73 | 97 | — | — | — | — | — | — | — | — | — | — | 63 | 95 | — | — | — | — | — | — | 32 |
| 31 | — | — | — | — | — | — | — | — | — | — | 90 | 99 | 72 | 97 | 88 | 99 | 88 | 99 | — | — | — | — | — | — | 62 | 91 | — | — | — | — | — | — | 31 |
| 30 | — | — | — | — | — | — | — | — | — | — | 88 | 99 | 70 | 96 | 86 | 99 | 86 | 99 | — | — | — | — | — | — | 60 | 86 | — | — | — | — | — | — | 30 |
| 29 | — | — | — | — | — | — | 109 | 99 | — | — | 87 | 99 | 69 | 94 | 84 | 99 | 85 | 99 | — | — | — | — | — | — | 59 | 80 | — | — | — | — | — | — | 29 |
| 28 | — | — | — | — | — | — | 107 | 99 | — | — | 85 | 99 | 68 | 93 | 83 | 99 | 83 | 99 | — | — | — | — | — | — | 57 | 74 | — | — | — | — | — | — | 28 |
| 27 | — | — | — | — | — | — | 104 | 99 | — | — | 83 | 99 | 67 | 92 | 81 | 98 | 81 | 99 | — | — | — | — | — | — | 56 | 68 | — | — | — | — | — | — | 27 |
| 26 | — | — | — | — | 87 | 99 | 102 | 99 | — | — | 81 | 99 | 65 | 90 | 80 | 98 | 80 | 98 | — | — | — | — | — | — | 55 | 62 | — | — | — | — | — | 99 | 26 |
| 25 | — | — | 93 | 99 | 85 | 99 | 100 | 99 | — | — | 80 | 99 | 64 | 89 | 78 | 98 | 78 | 98 | — | — | — | — | — | — | 53 | 56 | — | — | — | — | 68 | 99 | 25 |
| 24 | — | — | 91 | 99 | 83 | 99 | 97 | 99 | — | — | 78 | 98 | 63 | 87 | 77 | 97 | 76 | 97 | — | — | — | — | 89 | 99 | 52 | 50 | 61 | 94 | — | — | 66 | 96 | 24 |
| 23 | — | — | 88 | 99 | 81 | 99 | 95 | 99 | — | — | 76 | 98 | 62 | 85 | 75 | 96 | 75 | 97 | — | — | — | — | 87 | 99 | 50 | 45 | 58 | 81 | — | — | 63 | 92 | 23 |
| 22 | 82 | 99 | 86 | 99 | 79 | 99 | 93 | 99 | — | — | 75 | 97 | 60 | 83 | 74 | 96 | 73 | 97 | — | — | — | — | 85 | 99 | 49 | 40 | 56 | 66 | — | — | 61 | 86 | 22 |
| 21 | 80 | 99 | 84 | 99 | 77 | 99 | 90 | 99 | — | — | 73 | 96 | 59 | 80 | 72 | 95 | 71 | 96 | — | — | 76 | 99 | 83 | 99 | 48 | 36 | 54 | 54 | — | — | 58 | 78 | 21 |
| 20 | 77 | 99 | 82 | 99 | 74 | 99 | 88 | 99 | 86 | 99 | 71 | 95 | 58 | 78 | 71 | 94 | 70 | 94 | — | — | 74 | 98 | 80 | 99 | 46 | 31 | 51 | 43 | — | — | 56 | 69 | 20 |
| 19 | 75 | 99 | 80 | 99 | 72 | 98 | 86 | 99 | 84 | 99 | 70 | 94 | 57 | 75 | 69 | 94 | 68 | 93 | — | — | 72 | 97 | 78 | 99 | 45 | 27 | 49 | 34 | — | — | 53 | 59 | 19 |
| 18 | 73 | 98 | 77 | 99 | 70 | 97 | 83 | 99 | 81 | 99 | 68 | 92 | 55 | 72 | 68 | 93 | 66 | 92 | — | — | 70 | 95 | 76 | 98 | 43 | 24 | 47 | 27 | 61 | 90 | 51 | 50 | 18 |
| 17 | 71 | 97 | 75 | 98 | 68 | 96 | 81 | 98 | 79 | 99 | 66 | 90 | 54 | 69 | 66 | 91 | 65 | 91 | 88 | 99 | 68 | 94 | 74 | 97 | 42 | 21 | 44 | 22 | 58 | 78 | 48 | 41 | 17 |
| 16 | 69 | 95 | 73 | 97 | 66 | 93 | 78 | 97 | 77 | 98 | 64 | 88 | 53 | 66 | 65 | 90 | 63 | 89 | 85 | 99 | 66 | 91 | 71 | 96 | 40 | 18 | 42 | 17 | 56 | 66 | 46 | 33 | 16 |
| 15 | 67 | 93 | 71 | 96 | 64 | 90 | 76 | 96 | 74 | 97 | 63 | 86 | 52 | 62 | 63 | 89 | 61 | 87 | 82 | 99 | 64 | 89 | 69 | 95 | 39 | 15 | 40 | 14 | 54 | 56 | 43 | 25 | 15 |
| 14 | 64 | 90 | 69 | 94 | 61 | 87 | 74 | 95 | 72 | 96 | 61 | 83 | 50 | 58 | 62 | 87 | 60 | 84 | 80 | 99 | 62 | 86 | 67 | 93 | 38 | 13 | 37 | 11 | 52 | 47 | 41 | 19 | 14 |
| 13 | 62 | 87 | 66 | 92 | 59 | 82 | 71 | 94 | 70 | 94 | 59 | 80 | 49 | 54 | 60 | 86 | 58 | 82 | 77 | 98 | 60 | 82 | 64 | 90 | 36 | 11 | 35 | 9 | 50 | 39 | 38 | 14 | 13 |
| 12 | 60 | 83 | 64 | 89 | 57 | 76 | 69 | 92 | 67 | 93 | 58 | 76 | 48 | 50 | 59 | 84 | 56 | 78 | 74 | 96 | 58 | 79 | 62 | 88 | 35 | 9 | 33 | 7 | 48 | 33 | 36 | 9 | 12 |
| 11 | 58 | 78 | 62 | 86 | 55 | 70 | 67 | 90 | 65 | 90 | 56 | 72 | 47 | 45 | 57 | 81 | 55 | 75 | 71 | 94 | 56 | 75 | 60 | 84 | 33 | 7 | 30 | 5 | 45 | 27 | 33 | 6 | 11 |
| 10 | 56 | 73 | 60 | 83 | 53 | 63 | 64 | 87 | 63 | 88 | 54 | 67 | 45 | 40 | 56 | 79 | 53 | 71 | 69 | 92 | 55 | 70 | 58 | 80 | 32 | 6 | 28 | 4 | 43 | 22 | 31 | 4 | 10 |
| 9 | 54 | 67 | 58 | 78 | 51 | 55 | 62 | 84 | 60 | 84 | 52 | 61 | 44 | 35 | 54 | 76 | 51 | 66 | 66 | 89 | 53 | 65 | 55 | 74 | 30 | 5 | 26 | 3 | 41 | 18 | 28 | 2 | 9 |
| 8 | 52 | 61 | 55 | 73 | 49 | 47 | 59 | 80 | 58 | 80 | 51 | 55 | 43 | 29 | 53 | 72 | 50 | 60 | 63 | 86 | 51 | 59 | 53 | 68 | 29 | 4 | 24 | 2 | 39 | 15 | 26 | 1 | 8 |
| 7 | 49 | 53 | 53 | 67 | 46 | 39 | 57 | 75 | 56 | 76 | 49 | 48 | 42 | 24 | 51 | 68 | 48 | 53 | 61 | 83 | 49 | 53 | 51 | 61 | 28 | 3 | 21 | 1 | 37 | 12 | 23 | 1 | 7 |
| 6 | 47 | 45 | 51 | 61 | 44 | 31 | 55 | 70 | 53 | 70 | 47 | 41 | 40 | 18 | 50 | 64 | 46 | 46 | 58 | 80 | 47 | 46 | 49 | 53 | 26 | 2 | 19 | 1 | 34 | 7 | 21 | 1 | 6 |
| 5 | 45 | 37 | 49 | 53 | 42 | 23 | 52 | 63 | 51 | 63 | 46 | 32 | 39 | 11 | 48 | 58 | 45 | 37 | 55 | 76 | 45 | 39 | 46 | 43 | 25 | 2 | 17 | 1 | 32 | 5 | 18 | 1 | 5 |
| 4 | 43 | 28 | 46 | 44 | 40 | 17 | 50 | 54 | 49 | 55 | 44 | 24 | 38 | 6 | 46 | 51 | 43 | 28 | 53 | 72 | 43 | 31 | 44 | 33 | 23 | 1 | 14 | 1 | 30 | 5 | 16 | 1 | 4 |
| 3 | 41 | 20 | 44 | 35 | 38 | 11 | 48 | 42 | 46 | 46 | 42 | 16 | 37 | 1 | 45 | 42 | 41 | 18 | 50 | 66 | 41 | 22 | 42 | 22 | 22 | 1 | 12 | 1 | 28 | 4 | 13 | 1 | 3 |
| 2 | 39 | 12 | 42 | 24 | 36 | 7 | 45 | 28 | 44 | 35 | 41 | 9 | 35 | 1 | 43 | 31 | 40 | 8 | 47 | 58 | 39 | 13 | 40 | 12 | 21 | 1 | 10 | 1 | 26 | 3 | 11 | 1 | 2 |
| 1 | 36 | 5 | 40 | 14 | 34 | 4 | 43 | 9 | 42 | 22 | 39 | 3 | 34 | 1 | 42 | 15 | 38 | 1 | 44 | 45 | 37 | 5 | 37 | 5 | 19 | 1 | 10 | 1 | 24 | 2 | 10 | 1 | 1 |
| 0 | 34 | 1 | 38 | 5 | 31 | 2 | 40 | 2 | 39 | 8 | 37 | — | 33 | 1 | 40 | 6 | 36 | 1 | 42 | 10 | 35 | 1 | 35 | 1 | 18 | 1 | 10 | 1 | 21 | 1 | 10 | 1 | 0 |
| **Raw mean** | 7.28 | | 5.61 | | 8.65 | | 4.01 | | 4.59 | | 7.54 | | 13.77 | | 6.35 | | 8.21 | | 3.06 | | 7.63 | | 6.63 | | 22.73 | | 19.45 | | 13.15 | | 18.68 | | **Raw mean** |
| **Raw SD** | 4.64 | | 4.52 | | 4.66 | | 4.22 | | 4.26 | | 5.87 | | 7.98 | | 6.57 | | 6.01 | | 3.70 | | 5.21 | | 4.41 | | 7.03 | | 4.33 | | 4.60 | | 3.97 | | **Raw SD** |
| **T: 90% Conf. int.** | 7 | | 7 | | 7 | | 7 | | 7 | | 5 | | 5 | | 5 | | 6 | | 7 | | 5 | | 7 | | 5 | | 6 | | 5 | | 8 | | **T: 90% Conf. int.** |

## Table A.15c SRP-A T Scores and Percentiles

| Raw score | Attitude to School T | Attitude to School %ile | Attitude to Teachers T | Attitude to Teachers %ile | Sensation Seeking T | Sensation Seeking %ile | Atypicality T | Atypicality %ile | Locus of Control T | Locus of Control %ile | Social Stress T | Social Stress %ile | Anxiety T | Anxiety %ile | Depression T | Depression %ile | Sense of Inadequacy T | Sense of Inadequacy %ile | Somatization T | Somatization %ile | Attention Problems T | Attention Problems %ile | Hyperactivity T | Hyperactivity %ile | Relations With Parents T | Relations With Parents %ile | Interpersonal Relations T | Interpersonal Relations %ile | Self-Esteem T | Self-Esteem %ile | Self-Reliance T | Self-Reliance %ile |
|---|---|---|---|---|---|---|---|---|---|---|---|---|---|---|---|---|---|---|---|---|---|---|---|---|---|---|---|---|---|---|---|---|
| 36 | — | — | — | — | — | — | — | — | — | — | — | — | 89 | 99 | — | — | — | — | — | — | — | — | — | — | — | — | — | — | — | — | — | — |
| 35 | — | — | — | — | — | — | — | — | — | — | — | — | 87 | 99 | — | — | — | — | — | — | — | — | — | — | — | — | — | — | — | — | — | — |
| 34 | — | — | — | — | — | — | — | — | — | — | — | — | 86 | 99 | — | — | — | — | — | — | — | — | — | — | — | — | — | — | — | — | — | — |
| 33 | — | — | — | — | — | — | — | — | — | — | — | — | 84 | 99 | — | — | — | — | — | — | — | — | — | — | — | — | — | — | — | — | — | — |
| 32 | — | — | — | — | — | — | — | — | — | — | — | — | 83 | 99 | — | — | — | — | — | — | — | — | — | — | 65 | 99 | — | — | — | — | — | — |
| 31 | — | — | — | — | — | — | — | — | — | — | 95 | 99 | 81 | 99 | 100 | 99 | 94 | 99 | — | — | — | — | — | — | 63 | 95 | — | — | — | — | — | — |
| 30 | — | — | — | — | — | — | — | — | — | — | 93 | 99 | 80 | 99 | 98 | 99 | 92 | 99 | — | — | — | — | — | — | 62 | 90 | — | — | — | — | — | — |
| 29 | — | — | — | — | — | — | 105 | 99 | — | — | 91 | 99 | 78 | 99 | 96 | 99 | 90 | 99 | — | — | — | — | — | — | 60 | 84 | — | — | — | — | — | — |
| 28 | — | — | — | — | — | — | 103 | 99 | — | — | 89 | 99 | 77 | 99 | 94 | 99 | 88 | 99 | — | — | — | — | — | — | 59 | 78 | — | — | — | — | — | — |
| 27 | — | — | — | — | — | — | 101 | 99 | — | — | 88 | 99 | 75 | 99 | 93 | 99 | 86 | 99 | — | — | — | — | — | — | 57 | 71 | — | — | — | — | — | — |
| 26 | — | — | — | — | 79 | 99 | 99 | 99 | — | — | 86 | 99 | 74 | 98 | 91 | 99 | 84 | 98 | — | — | — | — | — | — | 55 | 65 | — | — | — | — | 68 | 98 |
| 25 | — | — | 89 | 99 | 77 | 99 | 97 | 99 | — | — | 84 | 99 | 72 | 97 | 89 | 99 | 82 | 97 | — | — | — | — | — | — | 54 | 58 | — | — | — | — | 66 | 96 |
| 24 | — | — | 87 | 99 | 75 | 99 | 94 | 99 | — | — | 82 | 99 | 71 | 96 | 87 | 99 | 80 | 96 | — | — | — | — | 87 | 99 | 52 | 52 | 62 | 94 | — | — | 64 | 93 |
| 23 | — | — | 85 | 99 | 73 | 99 | 92 | 99 | — | — | 80 | 99 | 69 | 94 | 85 | 99 | 78 | 95 | — | — | — | — | 85 | 99 | 51 | 47 | 59 | 82 | — | — | 62 | 89 |
| 22 | 87 | 99 | 83 | 99 | 72 | 98 | 90 | 99 | — | — | 78 | 99 | 68 | 93 | 83 | 99 | 76 | 93 | — | — | — | — | 82 | 99 | 49 | 41 | 56 | 67 | — | — | 60 | 83 |
| 21 | 84 | 99 | 80 | 99 | 70 | 97 | 88 | 99 | — | — | 76 | 99 | 66 | 91 | 81 | 99 | 74 | 91 | — | — | 77 | 99 | 80 | 99 | 48 | 36 | 53 | 54 | — | — | 58 | 77 |
| 20 | 82 | 99 | 78 | 99 | 68 | 95 | 85 | 98 | 90 | 99 | 75 | 98 | 64 | 89 | 79 | 98 | 73 | 88 | — | — | 75 | 99 | 78 | 99 | 46 | 31 | 50 | 42 | — | — | 56 | 70 |
| 19 | 80 | 99 | 76 | 98 | 66 | 93 | 83 | 98 | 88 | 99 | 73 | 96 | 63 | 87 | 77 | 97 | 71 | 85 | — | — | 73 | 99 | 76 | 98 | 44 | 27 | 48 | 33 | — | — | 54 | 62 |
| 18 | 77 | 99 | 74 | 98 | 64 | 91 | 81 | 98 | 85 | 99 | 71 | 95 | 61 | 85 | 75 | 95 | 69 | 81 | — | — | 71 | 98 | 74 | 98 | 43 | 23 | 45 | 25 | 60 | 90 | 52 | 54 |
| 17 | 75 | 98 | 72 | 97 | 62 | 88 | 79 | 98 | 83 | 99 | 69 | 93 | 60 | 82 | 73 | 93 | 67 | 77 | 101 | 99 | 69 | 96 | 72 | 97 | 41 | 20 | 42 | 19 | 57 | 74 | 50 | 46 |
| 16 | 72 | 97 | 70 | 96 | 60 | 84 | 76 | 97 | 80 | 99 | 67 | 91 | 58 | 79 | 72 | 92 | 65 | 72 | 98 | 99 | 67 | 93 | 70 | 95 | 40 | 17 | 39 | 14 | 55 | 59 | 48 | 38 |
| 15 | 70 | 95 | 68 | 94 | 58 | 79 | 74 | 96 | 77 | 98 | 65 | 89 | 57 | 76 | 70 | 91 | 63 | 66 | 94 | 99 | 65 | 90 | 68 | 94 | 38 | 14 | 36 | 11 | 52 | 47 | 46 | 32 |
| 14 | 67 | 94 | 66 | 92 | 56 | 74 | 72 | 96 | 75 | 97 | 64 | 88 | 55 | 73 | 68 | 89 | 61 | 60 | 91 | 99 | 62 | 86 | 66 | 92 | 37 | 12 | 34 | 8 | 50 | 38 | 44 | 25 |
| 13 | 65 | 91 | 64 | 90 | 54 | 68 | 70 | 95 | 72 | 96 | 62 | 86 | 54 | 69 | 66 | 87 | 59 | 54 | 88 | 99 | 60 | 82 | 64 | 89 | 35 | 9 | 31 | 5 | 47 | 30 | 42 | 20 |
| 12 | 63 | 88 | 61 | 87 | 52 | 61 | 68 | 93 | 70 | 95 | 60 | 82 | 52 | 65 | 64 | 85 | 57 | 47 | 84 | 99 | 58 | 78 | 62 | 86 | 33 | 8 | 28 | 4 | 44 | 24 | 40 | 15 |
| 11 | 60 | 84 | 59 | 83 | 50 | 54 | 65 | 92 | 67 | 93 | 58 | 78 | 51 | 60 | 62 | 82 | 55 | 39 | 81 | 98 | 56 | 73 | 60 | 83 | 32 | 6 | 25 | 3 | 42 | 18 | 38 | 12 |
| 10 | 58 | 79 | 57 | 78 | 49 | 46 | 63 | 90 | 64 | 91 | 56 | 74 | 49 | 55 | 60 | 79 | 53 | 31 | 77 | 96 | 54 | 67 | 58 | 79 | 30 | 5 | 22 | 2 | 39 | 14 | 35 | 8 |
| 9 | 55 | 74 | 55 | 73 | 47 | 39 | 61 | 88 | 62 | 87 | 54 | 69 | 48 | 50 | 58 | 76 | 51 | 24 | 74 | 95 | 52 | 61 | 55 | 74 | 29 | 3 | 20 | 2 | 37 | 11 | 33 | 6 |
| 8 | 53 | 66 | 53 | 66 | 45 | 32 | 59 | 85 | 59 | 83 | 52 | 64 | 46 | 44 | 56 | 72 | 50 | 16 | 70 | 93 | 50 | 55 | 53 | 68 | 27 | 3 | 17 | 1 | 34 | 8 | 31 | 4 |
| 7 | 50 | 58 | 51 | 59 | 43 | 25 | 56 | 81 | 57 | 78 | 51 | 58 | 45 | 38 | 54 | 67 | 48 | 9 | 67 | 90 | 48 | 49 | 51 | 62 | 26 | 2 | 14 | 1 | 32 | 6 | 29 | 3 |
| 6 | 48 | 49 | 49 | 50 | 41 | 19 | 54 | 77 | 54 | 71 | 49 | 52 | 43 | 32 | 53 | 61 | 46 | 4 | 64 | 88 | 46 | 42 | 49 | 54 | 24 | 1 | 11 | 1 | 29 | 5 | 27 | 2 |
| 5 | 45 | 38 | 47 | 42 | 39 | 14 | 52 | 71 | 51 | 63 | 47 | 45 | 42 | 25 | 51 | 54 | 44 | 1 | 60 | 85 | 44 | 34 | 47 | 46 | 22 | 1 | 10 | 1 | 26 | 3 | 25 | 1 |
| 4 | 43 | 28 | 45 | 33 | 37 | 9 | 50 | 63 | 49 | 53 | 45 | 38 | 40 | 18 | 49 | 44 | 42 | 1 | 57 | 81 | 42 | 27 | 45 | 38 | 21 | 1 | 10 | 1 | 24 | 2 | 23 | 1 |
| 3 | 41 | 17 | 42 | 24 | 35 | 6 | 48 | 53 | 46 | 42 | 43 | 30 | 39 | 11 | 47 | 29 | 40 | 1 | 53 | 76 | 40 | 19 | 43 | 29 | 19 | 1 | 10 | 1 | 21 | 2 | 21 | 1 |
| 2 | 38 | 8 | 40 | 16 | 33 | 4 | 45 | 41 | 44 | 30 | 41 | 22 | 37 | 5 | 45 | 15 | 38 | 1 | 50 | 69 | 38 | 12 | 41 | 19 | 18 | 1 | 10 | 1 | 19 | 1 | 19 | 1 |
| 1 | 36 | 2 | 38 | 10 | 31 | 2 | 43 | 24 | 41 | 17 | 39 | 14 | 36 | 1 | 43 | 8 | 36 | 1 | 46 | 57 | 36 | 6 | 39 | 9 | 16 | 1 | 10 | 1 | 16 | 1 | 17 | 1 |
| 0 | 33 | 1 | 36 | 5 | 29 | 1 | 41 | 6 | 38 | 7 | 38 | 7 | 34 | 1 | 41 | 5 | 34 | 1 | 43 | 16 | 34 | 4 | 37 | 4 | 15 | 1 | 10 | 1 | 13 | 1 | 15 | 1 |
| **Raw mean** | 6.86 | | 6.59 | | 10.77 | | 4.11 | | 4.48 | | 6.71 | | 10.38 | | 4.68 | | 8.25 | | 2.05 | | 7.83 | | 6.37 | | 22.52 | | 19.84 | | 14.14 | | 17.13 | |
| **Raw SD** | 4.11 | | 4.74 | | 5.22 | | 4.49 | | 3.85 | | 5.40 | | 6.64 | | 5.25 | | 5.22 | | 2.92 | | 4.94 | | 4.82 | | 6.37 | | 3.56 | | 3.86 | | 4.91 | |
| **T:90% Conf. int.** | 8 | | 7 | | 6 | | 7 | | 8 | | 6 | | 6 | | 6 | | 7 | | 7 | | 6 | | 6 | | 5 | | 8 | | 7 | | 6 | |

# Table A.15d SRP-A Composite T Scores

| T score | School Problems Combined | School Problems Female | School Problems Male | Internalizing Problems Combined | Internalizing Problems Female | Internalizing Problems Male | Inattention/Hyperactivity Combined | Inattention/Hyperactivity Female | Inattention/Hyperactivity Male | Emotional Symptoms Combined | Emotional Symptoms Female | Emotional Symptoms Male | Personal Adjustment Combined | Personal Adjustment Female | Personal Adjustment Male | T score |
|---|---|---|---|---|---|---|---|---|---|---|---|---|---|---|---|---|
| 120 | — | — | — | — | — | — | — | — | — | — | — | — | — | — | — | 120 |
| 119 | — | — | — | — | — | — | — | — | — | — | — | — | — | — | — | 119 |
| 118 | — | — | — | — | — | — | — | — | — | — | — | — | — | — | — | 118 |
| 117 | — | — | — | — | — | — | — | — | — | — | — | — | — | — | — | 117 |
| 116 | — | — | — | — | — | — | — | — | — | — | — | — | — | — | — | 116 |
| 115 | — | — | — | — | — | — | — | — | — | — | — | — | — | — | — | 115 |
| 114 | — | — | — | — | — | — | — | — | — | — | — | — | — | — | — | 114 |
| 113 | — | — | — | — | — | — | — | — | — | — | — | — | — | — | — | 113 |
| 112 | — | — | — | — | — | — | — | — | — | — | — | — | — | — | — | 112 |
| 111 | — | — | — | — | — | — | — | — | — | — | — | — | — | — | — | 111 |
| 110 | — | — | — | — | — | — | — | — | — | — | — | — | — | — | — | 110 |
| 109 | — | — | — | — | — | — | — | — | — | — | — | — | — | — | — | 109 |
| 108 | — | — | — | — | — | 670–674 | — | — | — | — | — | — | — | — | — | 108 |
| 107 | — | — | — | — | — | 665–669 | — | — | — | — | — | — | — | — | — | 107 |
| 106 | — | — | — | — | — | — | — | — | — | — | — | — | — | — | — | 106 |
| 105 | — | — | — | — | — | 659–664 | — | — | — | — | — | — | — | — | — | 105 |
| 104 | — | — | — | — | — | 653–658 | — | — | — | — | — | 549–550 | — | — | — | 104 |
| 103 | — | — | — | — | — | 648–652 | — | — | — | — | — | 545–548 | — | — | — | 103 |
| 102 | — | — | — | — | — | 642–647 | — | — | — | — | — | 540–544 | — | — | — | 102 |
| 101 | — | — | — | 641–645 | — | 636–641 | — | — | — | — | — | 535–539 | — | — | — | 101 |
| 100 | — | — | — | 635–640 | — | 631–635 | — | — | — | — | — | 531–534 | — | — | — | 100 |
| 99 | — | 262 | — | 629–634 | — | 625–630 | — | — | — | 525–529 | — | 526–530 | — | — | — | 99 |
| 98 | 256–257 | 260–261 | — | 624–628 | — | 619–624 | — | — | — | 521–524 | — | 521–525 | — | — | — | 98 |
| 97 | 256–257 | 258–259 | 254–255 | 618–623 | 624–627 | 614–618 | — | — | — | 516–520 | — | 517–520 | — | — | — | 97 |
| 96 | 253–255 | 255–257 | 252–253 | 612–617 | 618–623 | 608–613 | — | — | — | — | — | 512–516 | — | — | — | 96 |
| 95 | 251–252 | 253–254 | 250–251 | 606–611 | 612–617 | 602–607 | — | — | — | 511–515 | — | 507–511 | — | — | — | 95 |
| 94 | 249–250 | 251–252 | 247–249 | 601–605 | 606–611 | 597–601 | — | — | — | 506–510 | 512–513 | 503–506 | — | — | — | 94 |
| 93 | 247–248 | 248–250 | 245–246 | 595–600 | 601–605 | 591–596 | — | — | — | 502–505 | 507–511 | 498–502 | — | — | — | 93 |
| 92 | 244–246 | 246–247 | 243–244 | 589–594 | 595–600 | 585–590 | — | — | — | 497–501 | 503–506 | 493–497 | — | — | — | 92 |
| 91 | 242–243 | 244–245 | 241–242 | 583–588 | 589–594 | 580–584 | — | — | — | 492–496 | 498–502 | 489–492 | — | — | — | 91 |
| 90 | 240–241 | 241–243 | 239–240 | 577–582 | 583–587 | 574–579 | — | — | — | 488–491 | 493–497 | 484–488 | — | — | — | 90 |
| 89 | 238–239 | 239–240 | 236–238 | 572–576 | 577–582 | 568–573 | — | — | — | 483–487 | 488–492 | 480–483 | — | — | — | 89 |
| 88 | 235–237 | 237–238 | 234–235 | 566–571 | 571–576 | 563–567 | — | — | — | 478–482 | 483–487 | 475–479 | — | — | — | 88 |
| 87 | 233–234 | 235–236 | 232–233 | 560–565 | 565–570 | 557–562 | — | — | — | 473–477 | 478–482 | 470–474 | — | — | — | 87 |
| 86 | 231–232 | 232–234 | 230–231 | 554–559 | 559–564 | 551–556 | — | — | — | 469–472 | 473–477 | 466–469 | — | — | — | 86 |
| 85 | 228–230 | 230–231 | 227–229 | 549–553 | 553–558 | 546–550 | 163–164 | 164–165 | 163–164 | 464–468 | 468–472 | 461–465 | — | — | — | 85 |
| 84 | 226–227 | 228–229 | 225–226 | 543–548 | 547–552 | 540–545 | 161–162 | 162–163 | 161–162 | 459–463 | 464–467 | 456–460 | — | — | — | 84 |
| 83 | 224–225 | 225–227 | 223–224 | 537–542 | 541–546 | 534–539 | 159–160 | 160–161 | 159–160 | 454–458 | 459–463 | 452–455 | — | — | — | 83 |
| 82 | 222–223 | 223–224 | 221–222 | 531–536 | 536–540 | 529–533 | 157–158 | 159 | 157–158 | 450–453 | 454–458 | 447–451 | — | — | — | 82 |
| 81 | 219–221 | 221–222 | 218–220 | 526–530 | 530–535 | 523–528 | 156 | 157–158 | 156 | 445–449 | 449–453 | 442–446 | — | — | — | 81 |
| 80 | 217–218 | 218–220 | 216–217 | 520–525 | 524–529 | 517–522 | 154–155 | 155–156 | 154–155 | 440–444 | 444–448 | 438–441 | — | — | — | 80 |
| 79 | 215–216 | 216–217 | 214–215 | 514–519 | 518–523 | 512–516 | 152–153 | 153–154 | 152–153 | 435–439 | 439–443 | 433–437 | — | — | — | 79 |
| 78 | 213–214 | 214–215 | 212–213 | 508–513 | 512–517 | 506–511 | 150–151 | 151–152 | 150–151 | 431–434 | 434–438 | 428–432 | — | — | — | 78 |
| 77 | 210–212 | 212–213 | 210–211 | 503–507 | 506–511 | 500–505 | 148–149 | 149–150 | 148–149 | 426–430 | 430–433 | 424–427 | — | — | — | 77 |
| 76 | 208–209 | 209–211 | 207–209 | 497–502 | 500–505 | 495–499 | 147 | 148 | 147 | 421–425 | 425–429 | 419–423 | — | — | — | 76 |
| 75 | 206–207 | 207–208 | 205–206 | 491–496 | 494–499 | 489–494 | 145–146 | 146–147 | 145–146 | 416–420 | 420–424 | 414–418 | — | — | — | 75 |
| 74 | 204–205 | 205–206 | 203–204 | 485–490 | 489–493 | 483–488 | 143–144 | 144–145 | 143–144 | 412–415 | 415–419 | 410–413 | — | — | — | 74 |
| 73 | 201–203 | 202–204 | 201–202 | 480–484 | 483–488 | 478–482 | 141–142 | 142–143 | 141–142 | 407–411 | 410–414 | 405–409 | — | — | — | 73 |
| 72 | 199–200 | 200–201 | 198–200 | 474–479 | 477–482 | 472–477 | 139–140 | 140–141 | 139–140 | 402–406 | 405–409 | 400–404 | — | — | — | 72 |
| 71 | 197–198 | 198–199 | 196–197 | 468–473 | 471–476 | 466–471 | 138 | 138–139 | 137–138 | 398–401 | 400–404 | 396–399 | — | — | — | 71 |
| 70 | 195–196 | 195–197 | 194–195 | 462–467 | 465–470 | 461–465 | 136–137 | 136–137 | 136 | 393–397 | 395–399 | 391–395 | — | — | — | 70 |
| 69 | 192–194 | 193–194 | 192–193 | 457–461 | 459–464 | 455–460 | 134–135 | 135 | 134–135 | 388–390 | 391–394 | 386–390 | — | — | — | 69 |
| 68 | 190–191 | 191–192 | 190–191 | 451–456 | 453–458 | 449–454 | 132–133 | 133–134 | 132–133 | 383–387 | 386–390 | 382–385 | — | — | — | 68 |
| 67 | 188–189 | 189–190 | 187–189 | 445–450 | 447–452 | 444–448 | 130–131 | 131–132 | 130–131 | 379–382 | 381–385 | 377–381 | 253 | 253 | 254–255 | 67 |
| 66 | 186–187 | 186–188 | 185–186 | 439–444 | 442–446 | 438–443 | 129 | 129–130 | 128–129 | 374–378 | 376–380 | 372–376 | 249–252 | 249–252 | 251–253 | 66 |

## Table A.15d SRP–A Composite T Scores (continued)

| T score | School Problems | | | Internalizing Problems | | | Inattention/Hyperactivity | | | Emotional Symptoms | | | Personal Adjustment | | | T score |
|---|---|---|---|---|---|---|---|---|---|---|---|---|---|---|---|---|
| | Combined | Female | Male | Combined | Female | Male | Combined | Female | Male | Combined | Female | Male | Combined | Female | Male | |
| 65 | 183–185 | 184–185 | 183–184 | 434–438 | 436–441 | 432–437 | 127–128 | 127–128 | 127 | 369–373 | 371–375 | 368–371 | 246–248 | 246–248 | 248–250 | 65 |
| 64 | 181–182 | 182–183 | 181–182 | 428–433 | 430–435 | 427–431 | 125–126 | 125–126 | 125–126 | 364–368 | 366–370 | 363–367 | 243–245 | 243–245 | 244–247 | 64 |
| 63 | 179–180 | 179–181 | 179–180 | 422–427 | 424–429 | 421–426 | 123–124 | 124 | 123–124 | 360–363 | 361–365 | 358–362 | 240–242 | 240–242 | 241–243 | 63 |
| 62 | 177–178 | 177–178 | 178–180 | 416–421 | 418–423 | 416–420 | 121–122 | 122–123 | 121–122 | 355–359 | 357–360 | 354–357 | 237–239 | 237–239 | 238–240 | 62 |
| 61 | 174–176 | 175–176 | 176–177 | 411–415 | 412–417 | 410–415 | 120 | 120–121 | 119–120 | 350–354 | 352–356 | 349–353 | 234–236 | 234–236 | 235–237 | 61 |
| 60 | 172–173 | 172–174 | 174–175 | 405–410 | 406–411 | 404–409 | 118–119 | 118–119 | 117–118 | 345–349 | 347–351 | 345–348 | 231–233 | 231–233 | 231–234 | 60 |
| 59 | 170–171 | 170–171 | 169–171 | 399–404 | 400–405 | 399–403 | 116–117 | 116–117 | 116 | 341–344 | 342–346 | 340–344 | 227–230 | 227–230 | 228–230 | 59 |
| 58 | 168–169 | 168–169 | 167–168 | 393–398 | 395–399 | 393–398 | 114–115 | 114–115 | 114–115 | 336–340 | 337–341 | 335–339 | 224–226 | 224–226 | 225–227 | 58 |
| 57 | 165–167 | 166–167 | 165–166 | 388–392 | 389–394 | 387–392 | 112–113 | 112–113 | 112–113 | 331–335 | 332–336 | 331–334 | 221–223 | 221–223 | 222–224 | 57 |
| 56 | 163–164 | 163–165 | 163–164 | 382–387 | 383–388 | 382–386 | 111 | 111 | 110–111 | 326–330 | 327–331 | 326–330 | 218–220 | 218–220 | 218–221 | 56 |
| 55 | 161–162 | 161–162 | 161–162 | 376–381 | 377–382 | 376–381 | 109–110 | 109–110 | 108–109 | 322–325 | 322–326 | 321–325 | 215–217 | 215–217 | 215–217 | 55 |
| 54 | 159–160 | 159–160 | 158–160 | 370–375 | 371–376 | 370–375 | 107–108 | 107–108 | 107 | 317–321 | 318–321 | 317–320 | 212–214 | 212–214 | 212–214 | 54 |
| 53 | 156–158 | 156–158 | 156–157 | 365–369 | 365–370 | 365–369 | 105–106 | 105–106 | 105–106 | 312–316 | 313–317 | 312–316 | 208–211 | 209–211 | 209–211 | 53 |
| 52 | 154–155 | 154–155 | 154–155 | 359–364 | 359–364 | 359–364 | 103–104 | 103–104 | 103–104 | 307–311 | 308–312 | 307–311 | 205–207 | 205–208 | 205–208 | 52 |
| 51 | 152–153 | 152–153 | 152–153 | 353–358 | 353–358 | 353–358 | 102 | 101–102 | 101–102 | 303–307 | 303–307 | 303–306 | 202–204 | 202–204 | 202–204 | 51 |
| 50 | 150–151 | 149–151 | 149–151 | 347–352 | 348–352 | 348–352 | 100–101 | 100 | 99–100 | 298–302 | 298–302 | 298–302 | 199–201 | 199–201 | 199–201 | 50 |
| 49 | 147–149 | 147–148 | 147–148 | 342–346 | 342–347 | 342–347 | 98–99 | 98–99 | 98 | 293–297 | 293–297 | 293–297 | 196–198 | 196–198 | 196–198 | 49 |
| 48 | 145–146 | 145–146 | 145–146 | 336–341 | 336–341 | 336–341 | 96–97 | 96–97 | 96–97 | 289–292 | 288–292 | 289–292 | 193–195 | 193–195 | 193–195 | 48 |
| 47 | 143–144 | 143–144 | 143–144 | 330–335 | 330–335 | 331–335 | 94–95 | 94–95 | 94–95 | 284–288 | 283–287 | 284–288 | 189–192 | 190–192 | 189–192 | 47 |
| 46 | 141–142 | 140–142 | 141–142 | 324–329 | 324–329 | 325–330 | 93 | 92–93 | 92–93 | 279–283 | 279–282 | 279–283 | 186–188 | 186–189 | 186–188 | 46 |
| 45 | 138–140 | 138–139 | 138–140 | 319–323 | 318–323 | 319–324 | 91–92 | 90–91 | 90–91 | 274–278 | 274–278 | 275–278 | 183–185 | 183–185 | 183–185 | 45 |
| 44 | 136–137 | 136–137 | 136–137 | 313–318 | 312–317 | 314–318 | 89–90 | 89 | 88–89 | 270–273 | 269–273 | 270–274 | 180–182 | 180–182 | 180–182 | 44 |
| 43 | 134–135 | 133–135 | 134–135 | 307–312 | 306–311 | 308–313 | 87–88 | 87–88 | 87 | 265–269 | 264–268 | 265–269 | 177–179 | 177–179 | 176–179 | 43 |
| 42 | 132–133 | 131–132 | 132–133 | 301–306 | 301–305 | 302–307 | 85–86 | 85–86 | 85–86 | 260–264 | 259–263 | 261–264 | 174–176 | 174–176 | 173–175 | 42 |
| 41 | 129–131 | 129–130 | 129–131 | 296–300 | 295–300 | 297–301 | 83–84 | 83–84 | 83–84 | 255–259 | 254–258 | 256–260 | 171–173 | 171–173 | 170–172 | 41 |
| 40 | 127–128 | 126–128 | 127–128 | 290–295 | 289–294 | 291–296 | 82 | 81–82 | 81–82 | 251–254 | 249–253 | 251–255 | 167–170 | 168–170 | 167–169 | 40 |
| 39 | 125–126 | 124–125 | 125–126 | 284–289 | 283–288 | 285–290 | 80–81 | 79–80 | 79–80 | 246–250 | 245–248 | 247–250 | 164–166 | 164–167 | 163–166 | 39 |
| 38 | 123–124 | 122–123 | 123–124 | 278–283 | 277–282 | 280–284 | 78–79 | 77–78 | 78 | 241–245 | 240–244 | 242–246 | 161–163 | 161–163 | 160–162 | 38 |
| 37 | 120–122 | 119–121 | 120–122 | 273–277 | 271–276 | 274–279 | 76–77 | 76 | 76–77 | 237–240 | 235–239 | 237–241 | 158–160 | 158–160 | 157–159 | 37 |
| 36 | 118–119 | 117–118 | 118–119 | 269–272 | 267–270 | 269–273 | 74–75 | 74–75 | 74–75 | 232–236 | 230–234 | 233–236 | 155–157 | 155–157 | 154–156 | 36 |
| 35 | 116–117 | 115–116 | 116–117 | — | — | — | 73 | 72–73 | 72–73 | 227–231 | 225–229 | 228–232 | 152–154 | 152–154 | 150–153 | 35 |
| 34 | 114–115 | 113–114 | 114–115 | — | — | — | 71–72 | 70–71 | 71 | 222–226 | 220–224 | 223–227 | 148–151 | 149–151 | 147–149 | 34 |
| 33 | 111–113 | 110–112 | 112–113 | — | — | — | — | — | — | 219–221 | 217–219 | 219–222 | 145–147 | 146–148 | 144–146 | 33 |
| 32 | 109–110 | 108–109 | 109–111 | — | — | — | — | — | — | — | — | — | 142–144 | 142–145 | 141–143 | 32 |
| 31 | 107–108 | 106–107 | 107–108 | — | — | — | — | — | — | — | — | — | 139–141 | 139–141 | 137–140 | 31 |
| 30 | 105–106 | 103–105 | 105–106 | — | — | — | — | — | — | — | — | — | 136–138 | 136–138 | 134–136 | 30 |
| 29 | 102–104 | — | 103–104 | — | — | — | — | — | — | — | — | — | 133–135 | 133–135 | 131–133 | 29 |
| 28 | — | — | 100–102 | — | — | — | — | — | — | — | — | — | 130–132 | 130–132 | 128–130 | 28 |
| 27 | — | — | 98–99 | — | — | — | — | — | — | — | — | — | 126–129 | 127–129 | 125–127 | 27 |
| 26 | — | — | — | — | — | — | — | — | — | — | — | — | 123–125 | 123–126 | 121–124 | 26 |
| 25 | — | — | — | — | — | — | — | — | — | — | — | — | 120–122 | 120–122 | 118–120 | 25 |
| 24 | — | — | — | — | — | — | — | — | — | — | — | — | 117–119 | 117–119 | 115–117 | 24 |
| 23 | — | — | — | — | — | — | — | — | — | — | — | — | 114–116 | 114–116 | 112–114 | 23 |
| 22 | — | — | — | — | — | — | — | — | — | — | — | — | 111–113 | 111–113 | 108–111 | 22 |
| 21 | — | — | — | — | — | — | — | — | — | — | — | — | 107–110 | 108–110 | 105–107 | 21 |
| 20 | — | — | — | — | — | — | — | — | — | — | — | — | 104–106 | 105–107 | 102–104 | 20 |
| 19 | — | — | — | — | — | — | — | — | — | — | — | — | 101–103 | 101–104 | 99–101 | 19 |
| 18 | — | — | — | — | — | — | — | — | — | — | — | — | 98–100 | 98–100 | 95–98 | 18 |
| 17 | — | — | — | — | — | — | — | — | — | — | — | — | 95–97 | 95–97 | 92–94 | 17 |
| 16 | — | — | — | — | — | — | — | — | — | — | — | — | 92–94 | 92–94 | 89–91 | 16 |
| 15 | — | — | — | — | — | — | — | — | — | — | — | — | 89–91 | 89–91 | 86–88 | 15 |
| 14 | — | — | — | — | — | — | — | — | — | — | — | — | 85–88 | 86–88 | 82–85 | 14 |
| 13 | — | — | — | — | — | — | — | — | — | — | — | — | 82–84 | 83–85 | 79–81 | 13 |
| 12 | — | — | — | — | — | — | — | — | — | — | — | — | 79–81 | 79–82 | 76–78 | 12 |
| 11 | — | — | — | — | — | — | — | — | — | — | — | — | 76–78 | 76–78 | 73–75 | 11 |
| 10 | — | — | — | — | — | — | — | — | — | — | — | — | 54–75 | 59–75 | 53–72 | 10 |
| T: 90% Conf. int. | 5 | 5 | 5 | 3 | 3 | 3 | 5 | 5 | 5 | 3 | 3 | 3 | 4 | 4 | 4 | T: 90% Conf. int. |

## Table A.15e  SRP–A Composite Percentiles

| %ile | School Problems Combined | School Problems Female | School Problems Male | Internalizing Problems Combined | Internalizing Problems Female | Internalizing Problems Male | Inattention/Hyperactivity Combined | Inattention/Hyperactivity Female | Inattention/Hyperactivity Male | Emotional Symptoms Combined | Emotional Symptoms Female | Emotional Symptoms Male | Personal Adjustment Combined | Personal Adjustment Female | Personal Adjustment Male | %ile |
|---|---|---|---|---|---|---|---|---|---|---|---|---|---|---|---|---|
| 99 | 205–257 | 203–262 | 207–255 | 511–645 | 516–627 | 503–674 | 145–164 | 147–165 | 144–164 | 433–529 | 440–513 | 423–550 | 248–253 | 249–253 | 248–255 | 99 |
| 98 | 199–204 | 198–202 | 201–206 | 493–510 | 499–515 | 488–502 | 141–144 | 143–146 | 140–143 | 418–432 | 425–439 | 411–422 | 246–247 | 247–248 | 246–247 | 98 |
| 97 | 195–198 | 195–197 | 196–200 | 481–492 | 486–498 | 476–487 | 138–140 | 140–142 | 137–139 | 407–417 | 414–424 | 401–410 | 244–245 | 245–246 | 245 | 97 |
| 96 | 192–194 | 192–194 | 193–195 | 470–480 | 476–485 | 467–475 | 136–137 | 137–139 | 135–136 | 398–406 | 405–413 | 394–400 | 243 | 243–244 | 244 | 96 |
| 95 | 190–191 | 190–191 | 190–192 | 462–469 | 467–475 | 459–466 | 134–135 | 135–136 | 133–134 | 391–397 | 397–404 | 387–393 | 242 | 242 | 243 | 95 |
| 94 | 187–189 | 188–189 | 188–189 | 454–461 | 459–466 | 452–458 | 132–133 | 133–134 | 131–132 | 385–390 | 390–396 | 382–386 | 241 | 241 | 241–242 | 94 |
| 93 | 185–186 | 186–187 | 185–187 | 447–453 | 452–458 | 446–451 | 130–131 | 131–132 | 129–130 | 379–384 | 384–389 | 377–381 | 239–240 | 240 | 240 | 93 |
| 92 | 184 | 185 | 183–184 | 441–446 | 446–451 | 440–445 | 128–129 | 129–130 | 128 | 374–378 | 379–383 | 373–376 | – | 239 | 239 | 92 |
| 91 | 182–183 | 183–184 | 182 | 436–440 | 440–445 | 435–439 | 127 | 128 | 127 | 370–373 | 374–378 | 369–372 | 238 | 238 | – | 91 |
| 90 | 181 | 182 | 180–181 | 430–435 | 435–439 | 430–434 | 126 | 126–127 | 125–126 | 365–369 | 369–373 | 365–368 | 237 | 237 | 238 | 90 |
| 89 | 179–180 | 180–181 | 179 | 426–429 | 430–434 | 426–429 | 124–125 | 125 | 124 | 362–364 | 365–368 | 361–364 | 236 | 236 | 237 | 89 |
| 88 | 178 | 179 | 177–178 | 421–425 | 425–429 | 422–425 | 123 | 124 | 123 | 358–361 | 361–364 | 358–360 | 235 | 235 | 236 | 88 |
| 87 | 177 | 178 | 176 | 417–420 | 421–424 | 418–421 | 122 | 123 | 122 | 355–357 | 357–360 | 355–357 | 234 | 234 | 235 | 87 |
| 86 | 175–176 | 177 | 175 | 413–416 | 417–420 | 414–417 | 121 | 122 | 121 | 351–354 | 354–356 | 352–354 | 233 | 233 | 234 | 86 |
| 85 | 174 | 175–176 | 173–174 | 409–412 | 413–416 | 411–413 | 120 | 120–121 | 120 | 348–350 | 351–353 | 349–351 | 232 | 232 | 233 | 85 |
| 84 | 173 | 174 | 172 | 406–408 | 409–412 | 407–410 | 119 | 119 | 119 | 346–347 | 347–350 | 347–348 | – | 231 | – | 84 |
| 83 | 172 | 173 | 171 | 402–405 | 405–408 | 404–406 | 118 | 118 | 118 | 343–345 | 345–346 | 344–346 | 231 | – | 232 | 83 |
| 82 | 171 | 172 | 170 | 399–401 | 402–404 | 401–403 | 117 | 117 | 117 | 340–342 | 342–344 | 342–343 | 230 | 230 | 231 | 82 |
| 81 | 170 | 171 | 169 | 396–398 | 399–401 | 398–400 | 116 | – | 116 | 338–339 | 339–341 | 339–341 | 229 | 229 | 230 | 81 |
| 80 | 169 | 170 | 168 | 393–395 | 395–398 | 395–397 | – | 116 | – | 335–337 | 336–338 | 337–338 | – | 228 | – | 80 |
| 79 | 168 | 169 | 167 | 390–392 | 392–394 | 393–394 | 115 | 115 | 115 | 333–334 | 334–335 | 335–336 | 228 | 227 | 229 | 79 |
| 78 | 167 | – | 166 | 388–389 | 390–391 | 390–392 | 114 | 114 | 114 | 331–332 | 331–333 | 333–334 | 227 | – | 228 | 78 |
| 77 | – | 168 | – | 385–387 | 387–389 | 388–389 | 113 | 113 | 113 | 329–330 | 329–330 | 331–332 | 226 | 226 | 227 | 77 |
| 76 | 166 | 167 | 165 | 382–384 | 384–386 | 385–387 | 112 | 112 | 112 | 327–328 | 327–328 | 329–330 | – | 225 | – | 76 |
| 75 | 165 | 166 | 164 | 380–381 | 381–383 | 383–384 | – | – | – | 325–326 | 325–326 | 327–328 | 225 | 224 | 226 | 75 |
| 74 | 164 | 165 | 163 | 378–379 | 379–380 | 380–382 | 111 | 111 | 111 | 323–324 | 323–324 | 325–326 | 224 | – | 225 | 74 |
| 73 | 163 | 164 | 162 | 375–377 | 376–378 | 378–379 | 110 | 110 | 110 | 321–322 | 321–322 | 323–324 | 223 | 223 | 224 | 73 |
| 72 | – | – | – | 373–374 | 374–375 | 376–377 | – | – | – | 319–320 | 319–320 | 321–322 | – | 222 | – | 72 |
| 71 | 162 | 163 | 161 | 371–372 | 372–373 | 374–375 | 109 | 109 | 109 | 318 | 317–318 | 320 | 222 | 221 | 223 | 71 |
| 70 | 161 | 162 | 160 | 369–370 | 369–371 | 372–373 | 108 | 108 | 108 | 316–317 | 315–316 | 318–319 | 221 | – | 222 | 70 |
| 69 | 160 | 161 | 159 | 367–368 | 367–368 | 370–371 | 107 | 107 | 107 | 314–315 | 313–314 | 316–317 | – | 220 | 221 | 69 |
| 68 | – | – | 158 | 365–366 | 365–366 | 368–369 | – | – | – | 313 | 312 | 315 | 220 | 219 | – | 68 |
| 67 | 159 | 160 | – | 363–364 | 363–364 | 366–367 | 106 | 106 | 106 | 311–312 | 310–311 | 313–314 | 219 | – | 220 | 67 |
| 66 | 158 | 159 | 157 | 361–362 | 361–362 | 364–365 | 105 | 105 | 105 | 309–310 | 308–309 | 312 | 218 | 218 | 219 | 66 |
| 65 | – | 158 | – | 359–360 | 359–360 | 362–363 | – | – | – | 308 | 307 | 310–311 | – | 217 | 218 | 65 |
| 64 | 157 | – | 156 | 357–358 | 357–358 | 360–361 | 104 | 104 | 104 | 307 | 305–306 | 309 | 217 | 216 | – | 64 |
| 63 | 156 | 157 | 155 | 355–356 | 355–356 | 358–359 | – | – | – | 305–306 | 304 | 307–308 | 216 | – | 217 | 63 |
| 62 | – | 156 | – | 353–354 | 353–354 | 357 | 103 | 103 | 103 | 304 | 302–303 | 306 | 215 | 215 | 216 | 62 |
| 61 | 155 | – | 154 | 352 | 352 | 355–356 | – | 102 | – | 302–303 | 301 | 305 | – | 214 | 215 | 61 |
| 60 | 154 | 155 | 153 | 350–351 | 350–351 | 353–354 | 102 | 101 | 102 | 301 | 299–300 | 303–304 | 214 | 213 | 214 | 60 |
| 59 | 153 | 154 | – | 348–349 | 348–349 | 352 | 101 | – | 101 | 300 | 298 | 302 | 213 | – | – | 59 |
| 58 | – | – | 152 | 347 | 347 | 350–351 | 100 | 100 | 100 | 298–299 | 296–297 | 301 | 212 | 212 | 213 | 58 |
| 57 | 152 | 153 | – | 345–346 | 345–346 | 348–349 | – | – | – | 297 | 295 | 299–300 | – | 211 | 212 | 57 |
| 56 | – | 152 | 151 | 344 | 343–344 | 347 | 99 | 99 | 99 | 296 | 294 | 298 | 211 | 210 | 211 | 56 |
| 55 | 151 | – | 150 | 342–343 | 342 | 345–346 | – | – | – | 295 | 293 | 297 | 210 | 209 | 210 | 55 |
| 54 | – | 151 | – | 341 | 340–341 | 344 | 98 | 98 | 98 | 293–294 | 291–292 | 295–296 | 209 | – | – | 54 |
| 53 | 150 | 150 | 149 | 339–340 | 339 | 342–343 | – | 97 | – | 292 | 290 | 294 | 208 | 208 | 209 | 53 |
| 52 | – | – | – | 338 | 337–338 | 341 | – | – | – | 291 | 289 | 293 | – | 207 | 208 | 52 |
| 51 | 149 | 149 | 148 | 336–337 | 336 | 339–340 | – | – | – | 290 | 288 | 292 | 207 | 206 | 207 | 51 |

## Table A.15e SRP–A Composite Percentiles (continued)

| %ile | School Problems Combined | School Problems Female | School Problems Male | Internalizing Problems Combined | Internalizing Problems Female | Internalizing Problems Male | Inattention/Hyperactivity Combined | Inattention/Hyperactivity Female | Inattention/Hyperactivity Male | Emotional Symptoms Combined | Emotional Symptoms Female | Emotional Symptoms Male | Personal Adjustment Combined | Personal Adjustment Female | Personal Adjustment Male | %ile |
|---|---|---|---|---|---|---|---|---|---|---|---|---|---|---|---|---|
| 50 | 148 | 148 | — | 335 | 334–335 | 338 | 97 | — | — | 289 | 287 | 291 | 206 | — | 206 | 50 |
| 49 | — | — | 147 | 334 | 333 | 336–337 | — | 96 | 97 | 288 | 285–286 | 289–290 | 205 | 205 | 205 | 49 |
| 48 | 147 | 147 | — | 332–333 | 331–332 | 335 | — | 95 | 96 | 286–287 | 284 | 288 | 204 | 204 | — | 48 |
| 47 | — | — | 146 | 331 | 330 | 334 | 96 | — | — | 285 | 283 | 287 | 203 | 203 | 204 | 47 |
| 46 | 146 | 146 | 145 | 330 | 329 | 332–333 | — | — | 95 | 284 | 282 | 286 | — | 202 | 203 | 46 |
| 45 | — | 145 | — | 328–329 | 327–328 | 331 | 95 | 94 | 95 | 283 | 281 | 285 | 202 | 201 | 202 | 45 |
| 44 | 145 | — | 144 | 327 | 326 | 330 | — | — | — | 282 | 280 | 284 | 201 | 200 | 201 | 44 |
| 43 | 144 | 144 | — | 326 | 325 | 328–329 | 94 | 93 | 94 | 281 | 279 | 283 | 200 | — | 200 | 43 |
| 42 | — | — | 143 | 324–325 | 324 | 327 | — | — | — | 280 | 278 | 282 | 199 | 199 | 199 | 42 |
| 41 | 143 | 143 | — | 323 | 322–323 | 326 | 93 | 92 | 93 | 279 | 277 | 280–281 | 198 | 198 | 198 | 41 |
| 40 | 142 | 142 | 142 | 322 | 321 | 324–325 | — | — | — | 278 | 276 | 279 | 197 | 197 | 197 | 40 |
| 39 | 142 | 141 | — | 321 | 320 | 323 | 92 | — | 92 | 277 | 275 | 278 | 196 | 196 | 196 | 39 |
| 38 | 141 | 141 | 141 | 320 | 319 | 322 | — | 91 | — | 276 | 274 | 277 | 195 | 195 | 195 | 38 |
| 37 | — | 140 | — | 318–319 | 318 | 321 | 91 | — | 91 | 275 | 273 | 276 | 194 | 194 | 194 | 37 |
| 36 | 140 | — | 140 | 317 | 316–317 | 319–320 | — | 90 | — | 274 | 272 | 275 | 193 | 193 | 193 | 36 |
| 35 | 139 | 139 | 139 | 316 | 315 | 318 | 90 | 89 | 90 | 273 | 271 | 274 | 192 | 192 | 192 | 35 |
| 34 | 139 | — | — | 315 | 314 | 317 | — | — | — | 272 | 270 | 273 | 191 | 191 | 191 | 34 |
| 33 | 138 | 138 | 138 | 314 | 313 | 316 | 89 | — | 89 | 271 | — | 272 | 190 | 190 | 190 | 33 |
| 32 | 138 | 137 | — | 313 | 312 | 314–315 | — | 88 | — | 270 | 269 | 271 | 189 | 189 | 189 | 32 |
| 31 | 137 | — | 137 | 312 | 311 | 313 | 88 | — | 88 | 269 | 268 | 270 | 188 | 188 | 188 | 31 |
| 30 | — | 136 | — | 310–311 | 310 | 312 | 88 | — | 88 | 268 | 267 | 269 | 187 | 187 | 186–187 | 30 |
| 29 | 136 | 135 | 136 | 309 | 309 | 311 | — | 87 | — | 267 | 266 | 268 | 186 | 186 | 185 | 29 |
| 28 | — | — | — | 308 | 308 | 310 | 87 | — | 87 | 266 | 265 | 267 | 184–185 | 185 | 184 | 28 |
| 27 | 135 | 134 | 135 | 307 | 306–307 | 308–309 | — | — | — | 265 | 264 | 266 | 183 | 183–184 | 183 | 27 |
| 26 | 134 | 133 | 134 | 306 | 305 | 307 | 86 | 86 | 86 | 264 | 263 | 265 | 182 | 182 | 181–182 | 26 |
| 25 | — | — | — | 305 | 304 | 306 | 86 | — | — | 263 | — | 264 | 181 | 181 | 180 | 25 |
| 24 | 133 | 132 | 133 | 304 | 303 | 305 | 85 | 85 | 85 | 262 | 262 | 263 | 179–180 | 180 | 179 | 24 |
| 23 | 132 | 131 | 132 | 303 | 302 | 304 | 84 | — | — | 261 | 261 | 262 | 178 | 178–179 | 177–178 | 23 |
| 22 | 131 | — | — | 302 | 301 | 303 | — | — | 84 | 260 | 260 | 261 | 177 | 177 | 176 | 22 |
| 21 | 130 | 130 | 131 | 301 | 300 | 301–302 | 84 | 84 | 84 | 259 | 259 | 260 | 175–176 | 176 | 174–175 | 21 |
| 20 | 130 | 129 | 130 | 299–300 | 299 | 300 | 83 | — | — | 258 | — | 258–259 | 174 | 174–175 | 173 | 20 |
| 19 | — | — | — | 298 | 298 | 299 | — | 83 | 83 | 257 | 258 | 257 | 172–173 | 173 | 171–172 | 19 |
| 18 | 129 | 128 | 129 | 297 | 297 | 298 | 82 | — | — | 256 | 257 | 256 | 170–171 | 171–172 | 169–170 | 18 |
| 17 | 128 | 127 | 128 | 296 | 296 | 297 | — | 82 | 82 | 255 | 256 | 255 | 169 | 169–170 | 168 | 17 |
| 16 | 127 | 126 | 127 | 295 | 295 | 295–296 | 81 | — | — | 254 | 255 | 254 | 167–168 | 168 | 166–167 | 16 |
| 15 | — | 125 | — | 294 | 294 | 294 | 80 | — | 81 | 253 | 254 | 253 | 165–166 | 166–167 | 164–165 | 15 |
| 14 | 126 | — | 126 | 293 | 293 | 293 | — | 81 | — | 252 | — | 252 | 163–164 | 164–165 | 162–163 | 14 |
| 13 | 125 | 124 | 125 | 292 | 292 | 292 | 79 | — | 80 | 251 | 253 | 251 | 161–162 | 162–163 | 160–161 | 13 |
| 12 | 124 | 123 | 124 | 291 | 291 | 290–291 | 78 | 80 | 79 | 250 | 252 | 250 | 159–160 | 160–161 | 158–159 | 12 |
| 11 | 123 | 122 | 123 | 289–290 | 290 | 289 | — | — | — | 249 | 251 | 248–249 | 157–158 | 158–159 | 155–157 | 11 |
| 10 | 122 | 121 | 122 | 288 | 289 | 288 | 78 | 79 | 78 | 248 | 250 | 247 | 154–156 | 155–157 | 153–154 | 10 |
| 9 | 121 | 120 | 121 | 287 | 288 | 286–287 | 77 | — | 77 | 247 | 249 | 246 | 152–153 | 153–154 | 150–152 | 9 |
| 8 | 120 | 119 | — | 286 | 287 | 285 | — | 78 | — | 245–246 | — | 244–245 | 149–151 | 150–152 | 147–149 | 8 |
| 7 | 119 | 118 | 119–120 | 285 | 286 | 283–284 | 76 | — | 76 | 244 | 248 | 243 | 146–148 | 146–149 | 144–146 | 7 |
| 6 | 118 | 117 | 118 | 283–284 | 285 | 282 | — | 77 | 75 | 243 | 247 | 242 | 142–145 | 143–145 | 140–143 | 6 |
| 5 | 116–117 | 115–116 | 117 | 282 | 283–284 | 280–281 | 75 | 76 | — | 241–242 | 246 | 240–241 | 138–141 | 139–142 | 136–139 | 5 |
| 4 | 115 | 114 | 115–116 | 280–281 | 282 | 278–279 | 74 | 75 | 74 | 239–240 | 245 | 238–239 | 133–137 | 134–138 | 132–135 | 4 |
| 3 | 113–114 | 112–113 | 113–114 | 278–279 | 281 | 276–277 | 73 | 74 | 73 | 237–238 | 243–244 | 236–237 | 127–132 | 128–133 | 126–131 | 3 |
| 2 | 110–112 | 109–111 | — | 276–277 | 279–280 | 274–275 | — | — | 72 | 235–236 | 242 | 233–235 | 119–126 | 119–127 | 118–125 | 2 |
| 1 | 102–109 | 103–108 | 98–112 | 269–275 | 267–278 | 269–273 | 71–72 | 70–73 | 71 | 219–236 | 217–241 | 219–232 | 54–118 | 59–118 | 53–117 | 1 |

## Table A.16a  SRP-COL T Scores and Percentiles

| Raw score | Atypicality T | Atypicality %ile | Locus of Control T | Locus of Control %ile | Social Stress T | Social Stress %ile | Anxiety T | Anxiety %ile | Depression T | Depression %ile | Sense of Inadequacy T | Sense of Inadequacy %ile | Somatization T | Somatization %ile | Attention Problems T | Attention Problems %ile | Hyperactivity T | Hyperactivity %ile | Sensation Seeking T | Sensation Seeking %ile | Alcohol Abuse T | Alcohol Abuse %ile | School Maladjustment T | School Maladjustment %ile | Relations With Parents T | Relations With Parents %ile | Interpersonal Relations T | Interpersonal Relations %ile | Self-Esteem T | Self-Esteem %ile | Self-Reliance T | Self-Reliance %ile | Raw score |
|---|---|---|---|---|---|---|---|---|---|---|---|---|---|---|---|---|---|---|---|---|---|---|---|---|---|---|---|---|---|---|---|---|---|
| 41 | — | — | — | — | — | — | — | — | — | — | — | — | — | — | — | — | — | — | — | — | 112 | 99 | — | — | — | — | — | — | — | — | — | — | 41 |
| 40 | — | — | — | — | — | — | — | — | — | — | — | — | — | — | — | — | — | — | — | — | 110 | 99 | — | — | — | — | — | — | — | — | — | — | 40 |
| 39 | — | — | — | — | — | — | — | — | — | — | — | — | — | — | — | — | — | — | — | — | 108 | 99 | — | — | — | — | — | — | — | — | — | — | 39 |
| 38 | — | — | — | — | — | — | — | — | — | — | — | — | — | — | — | — | — | — | — | — | 107 | 99 | — | — | — | — | — | — | — | — | — | — | 38 |
| 37 | — | — | — | — | — | — | — | — | — | — | — | — | — | — | — | — | — | — | — | — | 105 | 99 | — | — | — | — | — | — | — | — | — | — | 37 |
| 36 | — | — | — | — | — | — | 81 | 99 | — | — | — | — | — | — | — | — | — | — | — | — | 103 | 99 | — | — | — | — | — | — | — | — | — | — | 36 |
| 35 | — | — | — | — | — | — | 80 | 99 | — | — | — | — | — | — | — | — | — | — | — | — | 102 | 99 | — | — | — | — | — | — | — | — | — | — | 35 |
| 34 | — | — | — | — | — | — | 79 | 99 | — | — | — | — | — | — | — | — | — | — | — | — | 100 | 99 | — | — | — | — | — | — | — | — | — | — | 34 |
| 33 | — | — | — | — | — | — | 77 | 99 | — | — | — | — | — | — | — | — | — | — | — | — | 98 | 99 | — | — | — | — | — | — | — | — | — | — | 33 |
| 32 | — | — | — | — | — | — | 76 | 99 | — | — | — | — | — | — | — | — | — | — | — | — | 97 | 99 | — | — | 62 | 95 | — | — | — | — | — | — | 32 |
| 31 | — | — | — | — | — | — | 75 | 98 | 107 | 99 | — | — | — | — | — | — | — | — | — | — | 95 | 99 | — | — | 60 | 87 | — | — | — | — | — | — | 31 |
| 30 | — | — | — | — | — | — | 73 | 97 | 105 | 99 | — | — | — | — | — | — | — | — | 80 | 99 | 93 | 99 | — | — | 58 | 78 | — | — | — | — | — | — | 30 |
| 29 | 116 | 99 | — | — | 90 | 99 | 72 | 97 | 103 | 99 | 96 | 99 | — | — | — | — | — | — | 79 | 99 | 92 | 99 | — | — | 57 | 69 | — | — | — | — | — | — | 29 |
| 28 | 114 | 99 | — | — | 88 | 99 | 70 | 96 | 100 | 99 | 94 | 99 | — | — | — | — | — | — | 77 | 99 | 90 | 99 | 85 | 99 | 55 | 62 | — | — | — | — | — | — | 28 |
| 27 | 111 | 99 | — | — | 87 | 99 | 69 | 94 | 98 | 99 | 92 | 99 | — | — | — | — | — | — | 75 | 99 | 88 | 99 | 83 | 99 | 54 | 55 | — | — | — | — | — | — | 27 |
| 26 | 108 | 99 | — | — | 85 | 99 | 68 | 93 | 96 | 99 | 90 | 99 | — | — | — | — | — | — | 74 | 99 | 87 | 99 | 81 | 99 | 52 | 49 | — | — | — | — | — | — | 26 |
| 25 | 106 | 99 | — | — | 83 | 99 | 66 | 91 | 94 | 99 | 88 | 99 | — | — | — | — | — | — | 72 | 98 | 85 | 99 | 79 | 99 | 51 | 43 | — | — | — | — | — | — | 25 |
| 24 | 103 | 99 | — | — | 81 | 99 | 65 | 90 | 92 | 99 | 86 | 99 | — | — | 81 | 99 | — | — | 70 | 97 | 83 | 98 | 78 | 99 | 49 | 38 | — | — | — | — | — | — | 24 |
| 23 | 101 | 99 | 92 | 99 | 79 | 99 | 63 | 88 | 90 | 99 | 84 | 99 | — | — | 79 | 99 | — | — | 69 | 96 | 82 | 98 | 76 | 98 | 48 | 33 | 63 | 95 | — | — | 68 | 99 | 23 |
| 22 | 98 | 99 | 90 | 99 | 77 | 98 | 62 | 86 | 87 | 99 | 82 | 99 | — | — | 77 | 99 | — | — | 67 | 94 | 80 | 98 | 74 | 98 | 46 | 29 | 60 | 86 | — | — | 65 | 96 | 22 |
| 21 | 95 | 99 | 88 | 99 | 75 | 98 | 61 | 83 | 85 | 99 | 80 | 99 | — | — | 75 | 98 | 91 | 99 | 66 | 93 | 78 | 98 | 72 | 97 | 44 | 25 | 58 | 75 | — | — | 63 | 91 | 21 |
| 20 | 93 | 99 | 85 | 99 | 73 | 97 | 59 | 81 | 83 | 99 | 78 | 98 | — | — | 73 | 98 | 88 | 99 | 64 | 90 | 77 | 97 | 71 | 95 | 43 | 22 | 55 | 64 | — | — | 60 | 83 | 20 |
| 19 | 90 | 99 | 83 | 99 | 72 | 95 | 58 | 78 | 81 | 99 | 76 | 97 | — | — | 71 | 96 | 85 | 99 | 62 | 88 | 75 | 97 | 69 | 94 | 41 | 19 | 53 | 53 | — | — | 57 | 73 | 19 |
| 18 | 87 | 99 | 81 | 99 | 70 | 94 | 57 | 75 | 79 | 98 | 74 | 96 | — | — | 69 | 95 | 83 | 99 | 61 | 85 | 73 | 96 | 67 | 92 | 40 | 16 | 50 | 43 | 61 | 94 | 54 | 61 | 18 |
| 17 | 85 | 99 | 78 | 98 | 68 | 92 | 55 | 72 | 77 | 98 | 71 | 95 | 102 | 99 | 67 | 93 | 80 | 99 | 59 | 81 | 72 | 96 | 65 | 90 | 38 | 14 | 48 | 35 | 58 | 79 | 51 | 50 | 17 |
| 16 | 82 | 99 | 76 | 98 | 66 | 90 | 54 | 69 | 75 | 97 | 69 | 93 | 98 | 99 | 65 | 91 | 78 | 99 | 57 | 77 | 70 | 95 | 63 | 88 | 37 | 12 | 45 | 28 | 56 | 65 | 48 | 39 | 16 |
| 15 | 80 | 98 | 74 | 97 | 64 | 87 | 52 | 65 | 72 | 96 | 67 | 91 | 95 | 99 | 63 | 88 | 75 | 98 | 56 | 73 | 68 | 94 | 62 | 85 | 35 | 10 | 43 | 22 | 54 | 53 | 45 | 29 | 15 |
| 14 | 77 | 97 | 71 | 96 | 62 | 84 | 51 | 61 | 70 | 96 | 65 | 89 | 91 | 99 | 61 | 85 | 72 | 97 | 54 | 68 | 67 | 93 | 60 | 82 | 33 | 8 | 40 | 17 | 51 | 44 | 42 | 21 | 14 |
| 13 | 74 | 96 | 69 | 94 | 60 | 80 | 50 | 56 | 68 | 95 | 63 | 87 | 88 | 99 | 59 | 82 | 70 | 95 | 53 | 62 | 65 | 92 | 58 | 79 | 32 | 7 | 37 | 12 | 49 | 36 | 39 | 15 | 13 |
| 12 | 72 | 95 | 67 | 92 | 58 | 76 | 48 | 52 | 66 | 93 | 61 | 84 | 84 | 99 | 57 | 78 | 67 | 93 | 51 | 57 | 63 | 91 | 56 | 75 | 30 | 5 | 35 | 9 | 47 | 30 | 37 | 10 | 12 |
| 11 | 69 | 94 | 64 | 90 | 57 | 71 | 47 | 47 | 64 | 92 | 59 | 80 | 81 | 98 | 55 | 73 | 64 | 91 | 49 | 51 | 61 | 89 | 54 | 71 | 29 | 4 | 32 | 6 | 44 | 24 | 34 | 6 | 11 |
| 10 | 66 | 92 | 62 | 87 | 55 | 66 | 46 | 41 | 62 | 90 | 57 | 75 | 77 | 97 | 53 | 68 | 62 | 88 | 48 | 45 | 60 | 87 | 53 | 66 | 27 | 3 | 30 | 4 | 42 | 19 | 31 | 4 | 10 |
| 9 | 64 | 90 | 60 | 84 | 53 | 60 | 44 | 35 | 60 | 88 | 55 | 70 | 74 | 95 | 51 | 62 | 59 | 83 | 46 | 39 | 58 | 85 | 51 | 61 | 26 | 2 | 27 | 3 | 39 | 16 | 28 | 2 | 9 |
| 8 | 61 | 86 | 57 | 80 | 51 | 53 | 43 | 29 | 57 | 86 | 53 | 64 | 71 | 94 | 49 | 55 | 56 | 77 | 44 | 33 | 56 | 82 | 49 | 55 | 24 | 2 | 25 | 2 | 37 | 12 | 25 | 1 | 8 |
| 7 | 59 | 83 | 55 | 75 | 49 | 46 | 41 | 22 | 55 | 83 | 51 | 56 | 67 | 92 | 47 | 48 | 54 | 69 | 43 | 27 | 55 | 79 | 47 | 49 | 23 | 1 | 22 | 1 | 35 | 10 | 22 | 1 | 7 |
| 6 | 56 | 78 | 53 | 69 | 47 | 39 | 40 | 16 | 53 | 79 | 49 | 47 | 64 | 90 | 45 | 40 | 51 | 61 | 41 | 21 | 53 | 75 | 45 | 41 | 21 | 1 | 20 | 1 | 32 | 7 | 19 | 1 | 6 |
| 5 | 53 | 72 | 50 | 62 | 45 | 31 | 39 | 9 | 51 | 74 | 47 | 36 | 60 | 86 | 43 | 31 | 48 | 50 | 40 | 16 | 51 | 70 | 44 | 33 | 19 | 1 | 17 | 1 | 30 | 5 | 16 | 1 | 5 |
| 4 | 51 | 65 | 48 | 53 | 44 | 23 | 37 | 3 | 49 | 68 | 45 | 25 | 57 | 82 | 42 | 23 | 46 | 39 | 38 | 11 | 50 | 64 | 42 | 24 | 18 | 1 | 15 | 1 | 27 | 4 | 13 | 1 | 4 |
| 3 | 48 | 56 | 46 | 42 | 42 | 15 | 36 | 1 | 47 | 60 | 42 | 13 | 53 | 76 | 40 | 14 | 43 | 27 | 36 | 8 | 48 | 57 | 40 | 15 | 16 | 1 | 13 | 1 | 25 | 3 | 11 | 1 | 3 |
| 2 | 45 | 44 | 43 | 30 | 40 | 8 | 34 | 1 | 44 | 50 | 40 | 3 | 50 | 66 | 38 | 7 | 40 | 16 | 35 | 5 | 46 | 48 | 38 | 6 | 15 | 1 | 12 | 1 | 23 | 2 | 10 | 1 | 2 |
| 1 | 43 | 27 | 41 | 17 | 38 | 3 | 33 | 1 | 42 | 36 | 38 | 1 | 46 | 51 | 36 | 2 | 38 | 7 | 33 | 3 | 45 | 36 | 36 | 1 | 13 | 1 | 10 | 1 | 20 | 1 | 10 | 1 | 1 |
| 0 | 40 | 6 | 39 | 5 | 36 | 1 | 32 | 1 | 40 | 18 | 36 | 1 | 43 | 19 | 34 | 1 | 35 | 2 | 32 | 2 | 43 | 21 | 35 | 1 | 12 | 1 | 10 | 1 | 18 | 1 | 10 | 1 | 0 |
| **Raw mean** | 3.73 | | 4.82 | | 7.47 | | 13.25 | | 4.58 | | 6.63 | | 2.09 | | 8.30 | | 5.63 | | 11.39 | | 4.13 | | 8.55 | | 24.58 | | 16.97 | | 13.46 | | 16.66 | | **Raw mean** |
| **Raw SD** | 3.81 | | 4.28 | | 5.34 | | 7.24 | | 4.65 | | 4.83 | | 2.88 | | 5.07 | | 3.77 | | 6.16 | | 5.98 | | 5.58 | | 6.40 | | 3.96 | | 4.18 | | 3.46 | | **Raw SD** |
| **T: 90% Conf. int.** | 7 | | 7 | | 6 | | 5 | | 6 | | 6 | | 8 | | 6 | | 7 | | 6 | | 4 | | 7 | | 5 | | 7 | | 6 | | 8 | | **T: 90% Conf. int.** |

# Table A.16b SRP-COL T Scores and Percentiles

| Raw score | Self-Reliance T | Self-Reliance %ile | Self-Esteem T | Self-Esteem %ile | Interpersonal Relations T | Interpersonal Relations %ile | Relations With Parents T | Relations With Parents %ile | School Maladjustment T | School Maladjustment %ile | Alcohol Abuse T | Alcohol Abuse %ile | Sensation Seeking T | Sensation Seeking %ile | Hyperactivity T | Hyperactivity %ile | Attention Problems T | Attention Problems %ile | Somatization T | Somatization %ile | Sense of Inadequacy T | Sense of Inadequacy %ile | Depression T | Depression %ile | Anxiety T | Anxiety %ile | Social Stress T | Social Stress %ile | Locus of Control T | Locus of Control %ile | Atypicality T | Atypicality %ile | Raw score |
|---|---|---|---|---|---|---|---|---|---|---|---|---|---|---|---|---|---|---|---|---|---|---|---|---|---|---|---|---|---|---|---|---|---|
| 41 | — | — | — | — | — | — | — | — | — | — | 120 | 99 | — | — | — | — | — | — | — | — | — | — | — | — | — | — | — | — | — | — | — | — | 41 |
| 40 | — | — | — | — | — | — | — | — | — | — | 120 | 99 | — | — | — | — | — | — | — | — | — | — | — | — | — | — | — | — | — | — | — | — | 40 |
| 39 | — | — | — | — | — | — | — | — | — | — | 119 | 99 | — | — | — | — | — | — | — | — | — | — | — | — | — | — | — | — | — | — | — | — | 39 |
| 38 | — | — | — | — | — | — | — | — | — | — | 117 | 99 | — | — | — | — | — | — | — | — | — | — | — | — | — | — | — | — | — | — | — | — | 38 |
| 37 | — | — | — | — | — | — | — | — | — | — | 115 | 99 | — | — | — | — | — | — | — | — | — | — | — | — | — | — | — | — | — | — | — | — | 37 |
| 36 | — | — | — | — | — | — | — | — | — | — | 113 | 99 | — | — | — | — | — | — | — | — | — | — | — | — | — | — | — | — | — | — | — | — | 36 |
| 35 | — | — | — | — | — | — | — | — | — | — | 111 | 99 | — | — | — | — | — | — | — | — | — | — | — | — | 77 | 99 | — | — | — | — | — | — | 35 |
| 34 | — | — | — | — | — | — | — | — | — | — | 109 | 99 | — | — | — | — | — | — | — | — | — | — | — | — | 75 | 99 | — | — | — | — | — | — | 34 |
| 33 | — | — | — | — | — | — | — | — | — | — | 107 | 99 | — | — | — | — | — | — | — | — | — | — | — | — | 73 | 99 | — | — | — | — | — | — | 33 |
| 32 | — | — | — | — | — | — | 61 | 94 | — | — | 105 | 99 | — | — | — | — | — | — | — | — | — | — | 101 | 99 | 72 | 99 | — | — | — | — | — | — | 32 |
| 31 | — | — | — | — | — | — | 60 | 84 | — | — | 103 | 99 | — | — | — | — | — | — | — | — | — | — | 99 | 99 | 71 | 98 | — | — | — | — | — | — | 31 |
| 30 | — | — | — | — | — | — | 58 | 75 | — | — | 101 | 99 | — | — | — | — | — | — | — | — | — | — | 97 | 99 | 69 | 96 | — | — | — | — | — | — | 30 |
| 29 | — | — | — | — | — | — | 57 | 67 | — | — | 99 | 99 | — | — | — | — | — | — | — | — | 92 | 99 | 95 | 99 | 68 | 95 | 87 | 99 | — | — | 118 | 99 | 29 |
| 28 | — | — | — | — | — | — | 55 | 60 | — | — | 98 | 99 | 84 | 99 | — | — | — | — | — | — | 90 | 99 | 93 | 99 | 67 | 93 | 86 | 99 | — | — | 115 | 99 | 28 |
| 27 | — | — | — | — | — | — | 54 | 54 | 86 | 99 | 96 | 99 | 82 | 99 | — | — | — | — | — | — | 88 | 99 | 91 | 99 | 65 | 91 | 84 | 99 | — | — | 113 | 99 | 27 |
| 26 | — | — | — | — | — | — | 52 | 49 | 84 | 99 | 94 | 99 | 80 | 99 | — | — | — | — | — | — | 86 | 99 | 89 | 99 | 64 | 89 | 82 | 99 | — | — | 110 | 99 | 26 |
| 25 | — | — | — | — | — | — | 51 | 44 | 82 | 99 | 92 | 99 | 79 | 99 | — | — | — | — | — | — | 84 | 99 | 87 | 99 | 63 | 87 | 80 | 99 | — | — | 107 | 99 | 25 |
| 24 | 67 | 98 | — | — | — | — | 50 | 40 | 80 | 99 | 90 | 99 | 77 | 99 | — | — | 78 | 99 | — | — | 82 | 99 | 85 | 99 | 61 | 84 | 78 | 99 | — | — | 105 | 99 | 24 |
| 23 | 65 | 95 | — | — | — | — | 48 | 36 | 78 | 99 | 88 | 99 | 75 | 98 | — | — | 76 | 99 | — | — | 80 | 99 | 83 | 99 | 60 | 81 | 77 | 98 | 91 | 99 | 102 | 99 | 23 |
| 22 | 62 | 89 | — | — | 62 | 94 | 47 | 32 | 77 | 99 | 86 | 99 | 74 | 97 | — | — | 75 | 99 | — | — | 79 | 99 | 82 | 99 | 59 | 78 | 75 | 97 | 89 | 99 | 99 | 99 | 22 |
| 21 | 59 | 81 | — | — | 60 | 84 | 45 | 29 | 75 | 98 | 84 | 99 | 72 | 96 | 94 | 99 | 73 | 98 | — | — | 77 | 99 | 80 | 99 | 58 | 75 | 73 | 96 | 86 | 99 | 97 | 99 | 21 |
| 20 | 56 | 71 | — | — | 58 | 74 | 44 | 25 | 73 | 96 | 82 | 98 | 70 | 95 | 91 | 99 | 71 | 97 | — | — | 75 | 98 | 78 | 99 | 56 | 72 | 71 | 94 | 84 | 99 | 94 | 99 | 20 |
| 19 | 54 | 60 | — | — | 55 | 63 | 42 | 23 | 71 | 95 | 80 | 98 | 68 | 92 | 89 | 99 | 69 | 96 | — | — | 73 | 97 | 76 | 98 | 55 | 68 | 70 | 90 | 82 | 99 | 91 | 99 | 19 |
| 18 | 51 | 49 | 62 | 95 | 53 | 53 | 41 | 20 | 69 | 93 | 78 | 98 | 67 | 89 | 86 | 99 | 67 | 94 | — | — | 71 | 96 | 74 | 97 | 54 | 65 | 68 | 87 | 79 | 99 | 89 | 99 | 18 |
| 17 | 48 | 39 | 59 | 82 | 50 | 44 | 39 | 17 | 67 | 90 | 76 | 97 | 65 | 87 | 83 | 99 | 66 | 93 | 94 | 99 | 69 | 95 | 72 | 97 | 52 | 61 | 66 | 85 | 77 | 99 | 86 | 99 | 17 |
| 16 | 45 | 30 | 57 | 70 | 48 | 37 | 38 | 15 | 66 | 88 | 74 | 96 | 63 | 83 | 80 | 99 | 64 | 91 | 91 | 99 | 67 | 94 | 70 | 96 | 51 | 57 | 64 | 81 | 75 | 98 | 83 | 99 | 16 |
| 15 | 42 | 22 | 55 | 59 | 46 | 30 | 36 | 13 | 64 | 85 | 72 | 96 | 62 | 78 | 77 | 99 | 62 | 88 | 88 | 99 | 65 | 92 | 68 | 94 | 50 | 53 | 63 | 78 | 73 | 97 | 81 | 98 | 15 |
| 14 | 40 | 15 | 53 | 50 | 43 | 24 | 35 | 11 | 62 | 82 | 70 | 95 | 60 | 75 | 75 | 98 | 60 | 86 | 85 | 99 | 63 | 91 | 66 | 93 | 48 | 49 | 61 | 74 | 70 | 95 | 78 | 98 | 14 |
| 13 | 37 | 11 | 51 | 43 | 41 | 19 | 34 | 9 | 60 | 79 | 68 | 94 | 58 | 70 | 72 | 97 | 58 | 83 | 82 | 99 | 61 | 89 | 64 | 91 | 47 | 44 | 59 | 69 | 68 | 93 | 75 | 97 | 13 |
| 12 | 34 | 7 | 48 | 36 | 38 | 14 | 32 | 7 | 58 | 75 | 66 | 93 | 56 | 65 | 69 | 95 | 57 | 79 | 78 | 98 | 59 | 86 | 62 | 90 | 46 | 40 | 57 | 64 | 66 | 91 | 73 | 96 | 12 |
| 11 | 31 | 4 | 46 | 30 | 36 | 11 | 31 | 6 | 56 | 71 | 64 | 91 | 55 | 59 | 66 | 92 | 55 | 76 | 75 | 97 | 58 | 83 | 60 | 88 | 44 | 35 | 56 | 58 | 63 | 88 | 70 | 94 | 11 |
| 10 | 29 | 3 | 44 | 25 | 34 | 8 | 29 | 4 | 55 | 66 | 62 | 90 | 53 | 53 | 63 | 89 | 53 | 71 | 72 | 95 | 56 | 80 | 58 | 85 | 43 | 30 | 54 | 52 | 61 | 85 | 67 | 92 | 10 |
| 9 | 26 | 1 | 42 | 21 | 31 | 6 | 28 | 3 | 53 | 61 | 61 | 88 | 51 | 46 | 61 | 84 | 51 | 67 | 69 | 93 | 54 | 76 | 56 | 82 | 42 | 25 | 52 | 45 | 59 | 81 | 64 | 90 | 9 |
| 8 | 23 | 1 | 39 | 17 | 29 | 4 | 26 | 2 | 51 | 55 | 59 | 85 | 50 | 39 | 58 | 79 | 49 | 61 | 66 | 91 | 52 | 72 | 54 | 79 | 41 | 20 | 50 | 38 | 56 | 76 | 62 | 87 | 8 |
| 7 | 20 | 1 | 37 | 14 | 26 | 2 | 25 | 1 | 49 | 49 | 57 | 82 | 48 | 32 | 55 | 72 | 47 | 56 | 63 | 88 | 50 | 67 | 52 | 74 | 39 | 16 | 49 | 30 | 54 | 71 | 59 | 84 | 7 |
| 6 | 17 | 1 | 35 | 11 | 24 | 1 | 23 | 1 | 47 | 42 | 55 | 79 | 46 | 25 | 52 | 63 | 45 | 49 | 60 | 84 | 48 | 61 | 50 | 69 | 38 | 11 | 47 | 22 | 52 | 64 | 56 | 79 | 6 |
| 5 | 15 | 1 | 33 | 8 | 22 | 1 | 22 | 1 | 45 | 34 | 53 | 74 | 44 | 19 | 49 | 54 | 44 | 42 | 57 | 80 | 46 | 54 | 48 | 63 | 37 | 7 | 45 | 15 | 50 | 57 | 54 | 74 | 5 |
| 4 | 12 | 1 | 31 | 6 | 19 | 1 | 21 | 1 | 42 | 26 | 51 | 68 | 41 | 14 | 46 | 42 | 42 | 34 | 54 | 74 | 44 | 45 | 46 | 55 | 35 | 3 | 43 | 8 | 47 | 48 | 51 | 67 | 4 |
| 3 | 10 | 1 | 28 | 4 | 17 | 1 | 19 | 1 | 40 | 16 | 49 | 61 | 39 | 9 | 44 | 31 | 40 | 26 | 51 | 67 | 42 | 36 | 44 | 45 | 34 | 1 | 41 | 3 | 45 | 39 | 48 | 58 | 3 |
| 2 | 10 | 1 | 26 | 2 | 14 | 1 | 18 | 1 | 38 | 5 | 47 | 51 | 38 | 5 | 41 | 19 | 38 | 17 | 48 | 57 | 40 | 25 | 42 | 32 | 33 | 1 | 40 | 1 | 43 | 28 | 46 | 45 | 2 |
| 1 | 10 | 1 | 24 | 1 | 12 | 1 | 16 | 1 | 36 | 2 | 45 | 39 | 36 | 3 | 38 | 9 | 37 | 8 | 45 | 41 | 38 | 13 | 41 | 17 | 31 | 1 | 38 | 1 | 40 | 17 | 43 | 28 | 1 |
| 0 | 10 | 1 | 22 | 1 | 10 | 1 | 15 | 1 | 34 | 1 | 43 | 23 | 34 | 1 | 35 | 2 | 35 | 1 | 41 | 12 | 37 | 2 | 40 | 2 | 30 | 1 | 36 | 1 | 38 | 6 | 40 | 6 | 0 |
| **Raw mean** | 16.73 | | 12.76 | | 16.83 | | 24.32 | | 8.49 | | 3.61 | | 10.26 | | 5.26 | | 8.39 | | 2.77 | | 7.03 | | 5.12 | | 15.25 | | 7.85 | | 5.19 | | 3.60 | | **Raw mean** |
| **Raw SD** | 3.60 | | 4.52 | | 4.17 | | 6.89 | | 5.46 | | 5.13 | | 5.84 | | 3.56 | | 5.53 | | 3.24 | | 5.24 | | 5.04 | | 7.64 | | 5.67 | | 4.35 | | 3.73 | | **Raw SD** |
| **T:90% Conf. int.** | 7 | | 5 | | 7 | | 5 | | 7 | | 5 | | 6 | | 8 | | 5 | | 8 | | 6 | | 5 | | 5 | | 6 | | 8 | | 7 | | **T:90% Conf. int.** |

## Table A.16c SRP-COL T Scores and Percentiles

Each scale cell is shown as **T / %ile** (— indicates no value).

| Raw score | Self-Reliance | Self-Esteem | Interpersonal Relations | Relations With Parents | School Maladjustment | Alcohol Abuse | Sensation Seeking | Hyperactivity | Attention Problems | Somatization | Sense of Inadequacy | Depression | Anxiety | Social Stress | Locus of Control | Atypicality | Raw score |
|---|---|---|---|---|---|---|---|---|---|---|---|---|---|---|---|---|---|
| 41 | — | — | — | — | — | 104/99 | — | — | — | — | — | — | — | — | — | — | 41 |
| 40 | — | — | — | — | — | 103/99 | — | — | — | — | — | — | — | — | — | — | 40 |
| 39 | — | — | — | — | — | 101/99 | — | — | — | — | — | — | — | — | — | — | 39 |
| 38 | — | — | — | — | — | 100/99 | — | — | — | — | — | — | — | — | — | — | 38 |
| 37 | — | — | — | — | — | 98/99 | — | — | — | — | — | — | — | — | — | — | 37 |
| 36 | — | — | — | — | — | 97/99 | — | — | — | — | — | — | 90/99 | — | — | — | 36 |
| 35 | — | — | — | — | — | 95/99 | — | — | — | — | — | — | 88/99 | — | — | — | 35 |
| 34 | — | — | — | — | — | 94/99 | — | — | — | — | — | — | 87/99 | — | — | — | 34 |
| 33 | — | — | — | 62/95 | — | 92/99 | — | — | — | — | — | — | 85/99 | — | — | — | 33 |
| 32 | — | — | — | 60/89 | — | 91/99 | — | — | — | — | — | — | 83/99 | — | — | — | 32 |
| 31 | — | — | — | 59/80 | — | 89/99 | — | — | — | — | — | 115/99 | 82/99 | — | — | — | 31 |
| 30 | — | — | — | 57/72 | — | 88/99 | — | — | — | — | — | 112/99 | 80/99 | — | — | — | 30 |
| 29 | — | — | — | 55/63 | — | 86/99 | 78/99 | — | — | — | 102/99 | 110/99 | 78/98 | 94/99 | — | 115/99 | 29 |
| 28 | — | — | — | 54/55 | 84/99 | 85/99 | 76/99 | — | — | — | 100/99 | 107/99 | 77/98 | 92/99 | — | 112/99 | 28 |
| 27 | — | — | — | 52/48 | 82/99 | 83/98 | 75/99 | — | — | — | 98/99 | 105/99 | 75/97 | 90/99 | — | 110/99 | 27 |
| 26 | — | — | — | 50/42 | 80/99 | 82/98 | 73/98 | — | — | — | 95/99 | 103/99 | 74/97 | 88/99 | — | 107/99 | 26 |
| 25 | — | — | — | 49/36 | 79/99 | 80/98 | 71/98 | — | —/99 | — | 93/99 | 100/99 | 72/96 | 86/99 | — | 105/99 | 25 |
| 24 | — | — | — | 47/31 | 77/98 | 79/98 | 70/97 | — | 85/99 | — | 91/99 | 98/99 | 70/95 | 84/99 | 94/99 | 102/99 | 24 |
| 23 | 69/99 | — | 63/95 | 45/26 | 75/98 | 77/97 | 68/96 | — | 82/99 | — | 88/99 | 95/99 | 69/94 | 82/99 | 92/99 | 99/99 | 23 |
| 22 | 66/97 | — | 60/87 | 43/22 | 73/97 | 76/97 | 67/95 | — | 80/99 | — | 86/99 | 93/99 | 67/93 | 80/99 | 90/99 | 97/99 | 22 |
| 21 | 63/93 | — | 58/76 | 42/19 | 72/96 | 74/96 | 65/92 | 88/99 | 78/99 | — | 84/99 | 91/99 | 66/91 | 78/99 | 88/99 | 94/99 | 21 |
| 20 | 60/85 | — | 55/64 | 40/16 | 70/95 | 73/96 | 64/90 | 86/99 | 76/99 | — | 82/99 | 88/99 | 64/90 | 76/99 | 87/99 | 92/99 | 20 |
| 19 | 57/75 | — | 52/53 | 38/13 | 68/93 | 71/95 | 62/87 | 83/99 | 74/98 | — | 80/98 | 86/99 | 62/88 | 74/99 | 85/99 | 89/99 | 19 |
| 18 | 54/63 | 60/93 | 50/42 | 37/11 | 66/92 | 70/95 | 60/84 | 80/99 | 71/97 | — | 77/98 | 84/99 | 61/86 | 72/97 | 82/99 | 86/99 | 18 |
| 17 | 51/51 | 58/77 | 47/33 | 35/9 | 65/90 | 68/94 | 59/80 | 78/99 | 69/96 | 118/99 | 75/97 | 81/98 | 59/83 | 70/96 | 80/98 | 84/99 | 17 |
| 16 | 48/39 | 55/61 | 44/26 | 33/7 | 63/88 | 67/93 | 57/75 | 75/98 | 67/94 | 114/99 | 72/96 | 79/98 | 58/81 | 68/94 | 78/97 | 81/99 | 16 |
| 15 | 45/29 | 52/48 | 42/19 | 32/6 | 61/85 | 65/92 | 56/71 | 73/97 | 65/91 | 110/99 | 70/95 | 76/97 | 56/77 | 66/92 | 75/96 | 79/98 | 15 |
| 14 | 42/21 | 50/37 | 39/14 | 30/5 | 59/82 | 64/91 | 54/65 | 70/96 | 63/88 | 105/99 | 68/94 | 74/96 | 54/74 | 64/89 | 73/95 | 76/97 | 14 |
| 13 | 39/14 | 47/29 | 36/11 | 28/4 | 58/79 | 62/90 | 52/60 | 68/94 | 60/84 | 101/99 | 66/92 | 72/95 | 53/69 | 62/86 | 70/94 | 74/96 | 13 |
| 12 | 36/10 | 44/23 | 34/7 | 26/3 | 56/75 | 61/89 | 51/54 | 65/92 | 58/79 | 96/99 | 63/90 | 69/92 | 51/64 | 60/83 | 68/92 | 71/95 | 12 |
| 11 | 33/6 | 41/17 | 31/5 | 25/2 | 54/71 | 59/87 | 49/49 | 63/88 | 56/74 | 92/99 | 61/87 | 67/89 | 50/59 | 58/78 | 66/90 | 68/93 | 11 |
| 10 | 30/4 | 39/13 | 28/3 | 23/2 | 52/67 | 58/85 | 48/43 | 60/85 | 54/68 | 88/99 | 59/84 | 64/87 | 48/53 | 56/74 | 63/87 | 66/91 | 10 |
| 9 | 27/2 | 36/10 | 26/2 | 21/1 | 51/61 | 56/83 | 46/37 | 58/80 | 52/61 | 83/98 | 57/79 | 62/83 | 46/46 | 54/68 | 61/84 | 63/89 | 9 |
| 8 | 24/1 | 33/8 | 23/1 | 20/1 | 49/55 | 55/80 | 44/31 | 55/74 | 50/54 | 79/97 | 54/74 | 60/79 | 45/38 | 52/62 | 58/79 | 61/85 | 8 |
| 7 | 21/1 | 31/6 | 20/1 | 18/1 | 47/49 | 54/77 | 43/26 | 53/66 | 47/45 | 75/96 | 52/67 | 57/73 | 43/29 | 50/55 | 56/74 | 58/82 | 7 |
| 6 | 18/1 | 28/4 | 18/1 | 16/1 | 45/41 | 52/73 | 41/21 | 50/57 | 45/37 | 70/95 | 50/58 | 55/65 | 42/20 | 48/48 | 54/67 | 56/77 | 6 |
| 5 | 15/1 | 25/3 | 15/1 | 15/1 | 44/33 | 51/68 | 40/16 | 47/47 | 43/28 | 66/93 | 47/48 | 52/54 | 40/11 | 46/40 | 51/59 | 53/71 | 5 |
| 4 | 12/1 | 22/2 | 12/1 | 13/1 | 42/24 | 49/62 | 38/12 | 45/35 | 41/19 | 61/90 | 45/36 | 50/39 | 38/4 | 44/32 | 49/48 | 50/64 | 4 |
| 3 | 10/1 | 20/1 | 10/1 | 11/1 | 40/14 | 48/55 | 36/9 | 42/24 | 39/12 | 57/85 | 43/24 | 48/20 | 37/1 | 42/24 | 47/34 | 48/54 | 3 |
| 2 | 10/1 | 17/1 | 10/1 | 10/1 | 38/5 | 46/46 | 35/6 | 40/13 | 36/6 | 53/76 | 40/13 | 45/1 | 35/1 | 40/16 | 44/18 | 45/42 | 2 |
| 1 | 10/1 | 14/1 | 10/1 | 10/1 | 37/1 | 45/35 | 33/4 | 37/5 | 34/2 | 48/60 | 38/4 | 43/1 | 34/1 | 38/10 | 42/3 | 43/26 | 1 |
| 0 | 10/1 | 12/1 | 10/1 | 10/1 | 35/1 | 43/21 | 30/1 | 35/1 | 32/1 | 44/23 | 36/1 | 40/1 | 32/1 | 36/4 | 39/3 | 40/7 | 0 |
| **Raw mean** | 16.59 | 14.17 | 17.11 | 24.85 | 8.62 | 4.65 | 12.52 | 6.01 | 8.21 | 1.41 | 6.21 | 4.03 | 11.25 | 7.09 | 4.45 | 3.85 | **Raw mean** |
| **Raw SD** | 3.33 | 3.69 | 3.74 | 5.89 | 5.72 | 6.71 | 6.28 | 3.94 | 4.57 | 2.28 | 4.37 | 4.17 | 6.23 | 4.98 | 4.18 | 3.88 | **Raw SD** |
| **T: 90% Conf. int.** | 8 | 6 | 7 | 5 | 7 | 4 | 6 | 7 | 7 | 8 | 7 | 6 | 5 | 6 | 7 | 7 | **T: 90% Conf. int.** |

## Table A.16d SRP–COL Composite T Scores

| T score | Internalizing Problems Combined | Internalizing Problems Female | Internalizing Problems Male | Inattention/Hyperactivity Combined | Inattention/Hyperactivity Female | Inattention/Hyperactivity Male | Emotional Symptoms Combined | Emotional Symptoms Female | Emotional Symptoms Male | Personal Adjustment Combined | Personal Adjustment Female | Personal Adjustment Male | T score |
|---|---|---|---|---|---|---|---|---|---|---|---|---|---|
| 120 | — | — | — | — | — | — | — | — | — | — | — | — | 120 |
| 119 | — | — | — | — | — | — | — | — | — | — | — | — | 119 |
| 118 | — | — | — | — | — | — | — | — | — | — | — | — | 118 |
| 117 | — | — | — | — | — | — | — | — | — | — | — | — | 117 |
| 116 | — | — | 725–728 | — | — | — | — | — | — | — | — | — | 116 |
| 115 | — | — | 719–724 | — | — | — | — | — | — | — | — | — | 115 |
| 114 | — | — | 713–718 | — | — | — | — | — | — | — | — | — | 114 |
| 113 | — | — | 707–712 | — | — | — | — | — | — | — | — | — | 113 |
| 112 | — | — | 702–706 | — | — | — | — | — | — | — | — | — | 112 |
| 111 | — | — | 696–701 | — | — | — | — | — | — | — | — | — | 111 |
| 110 | 690–695 | — | 690–695 | — | — | — | — | — | — | — | — | — | 110 |
| 109 | 685–689 | — | 685–689 | — | — | — | — | — | — | — | — | — | 109 |
| 108 | 679–684 | — | 679–684 | — | — | — | — | — | — | — | — | — | 108 |
| 107 | 673–678 | — | 673–678 | — | — | — | — | — | 577–579 | — | — | — | 107 |
| 106 | 668–672 | — | 668–672 | — | — | — | — | — | 572–576 | — | — | — | 106 |
| 105 | 662–667 | — | 662–667 | — | — | — | — | — | 568–571 | — | — | — | 105 |
| 104 | 656–661 | 659–660 | 656–661 | — | — | — | — | — | 563–567 | — | — | — | 104 |
| 103 | 651–655 | 653–658 | 650–655 | — | — | — | — | — | 558–562 | — | — | — | 103 |
| 102 | 645–650 | 647–652 | 645–649 | — | — | — | — | — | 553–557 | — | — | — | 102 |
| 101 | 639–644 | 641–646 | 639–644 | — | — | — | — | — | 548–552 | — | — | — | 101 |
| 100 | 633–638 | 636–640 | 633–638 | — | — | — | 542–546 | — | 543–547 | — | — | — | 100 |
| 99 | 628–632 | 630–635 | 628–632 | — | — | — | 537–541 | — | 538–542 | — | — | — | 99 |
| 98 | 622–627 | 624–629 | 622–627 | — | — | — | 532–536 | — | 533–537 | — | — | — | 98 |
| 97 | 616–621 | 618–623 | 616–621 | — | — | — | 527–531 | — | 528–532 | — | — | — | 97 |
| 96 | 611–615 | 613–617 | 611–615 | — | — | — | 523–526 | 523–525 | 524–527 | — | — | — | 96 |
| 95 | 605–610 | 607–612 | 605–610 | — | — | — | 518–522 | 518–522 | 519–523 | — | — | — | 95 |
| 94 | 599–604 | 601–606 | 599–604 | — | — | — | 513–517 | 513–517 | 514–518 | — | — | — | 94 |
| 93 | 593–598 | 595–600 | 593–598 | — | — | — | 508–512 | 508–512 | 509–513 | — | — | — | 93 |
| 92 | 588–592 | 590–594 | 588–592 | — | — | — | 503–507 | 503–507 | 504–508 | — | — | — | 92 |
| 91 | 582–587 | 584–589 | 582–587 | — | — | — | 498–502 | 498–502 | 499–503 | — | — | — | 91 |
| 90 | 576–581 | 578–583 | 576–581 | 171–172 | — | 173 | 493–497 | 494–497 | 494–498 | — | — | — | 90 |
| 89 | 571–575 | 572–577 | 571–575 | 169–170 | 172 | 171–172 | 488–493 | 489–493 | 489–493 | — | — | — | 89 |
| 88 | 565–570 | 567–571 | 565–570 | 167–168 | 170–171 | 169–170 | 484–487 | 484–488 | 484–488 | — | — | — | 88 |
| 87 | 559–564 | 561–566 | 559–564 | 165–166 | 169 | 168 | 479–483 | 479–483 | 480–483 | — | — | — | 87 |
| 86 | 553–558 | 555–560 | 554–558 | 164 | 167–168 | 166–167 | 474–478 | 474–478 | 475–479 | — | — | — | 86 |
| 85 | 548–552 | 549–554 | 548–553 | 162–163 | 165–166 | 164–165 | 469–473 | 469–473 | 470–474 | — | — | — | 85 |
| 84 | 542–547 | 544–548 | 542–547 | 160–161 | 163–164 | 162–163 | 464–468 | 464–468 | 465–469 | — | — | — | 84 |
| 83 | 536–541 | 538–543 | 536–541 | 158–159 | 161–162 | 160–161 | 459–463 | 459–463 | 460–464 | — | — | — | 83 |
| 82 | 531–535 | 532–537 | 531–535 | 156–157 | 159–160 | 158–159 | 454–458 | 454–458 | 455–459 | — | — | — | 82 |
| 81 | 525–530 | 526–531 | 525–530 | 154–155 | 157–158 | 157 | 449–453 | 450–453 | 450–454 | — | — | — | 81 |
| 80 | 519–524 | 521–525 | 519–524 | 153 | 155–156 | 155–156 | 445–448 | 445–449 | 445–449 | — | — | — | 80 |
| 79 | 513–518 | 515–520 | 514–518 | 151–152 | 154 | 153–154 | 440–444 | 440–444 | 440–444 | — | — | — | 79 |
| 78 | 508–512 | 509–514 | 508–513 | 149–150 | 152–153 | 151–152 | 435–439 | 435–439 | 436–439 | — | — | — | 78 |
| 77 | 502–507 | 503–508 | 502–507 | 147–148 | 150–151 | 149–150 | 430–434 | 430–434 | 431–435 | — | — | — | 77 |
| 76 | 496–501 | 497–502 | 497–501 | 145–146 | 148–149 | 147–148 | 425–429 | 425–429 | 426–430 | — | — | — | 76 |
| 75 | 491–495 | 492–496 | 491–496 | 143–144 | 146–147 | 146 | 420–424 | 420–424 | 421–425 | — | — | — | 75 |
| 74 | 485–490 | 486–491 | 485–490 | 142 | 144–145 | 144–145 | 415–419 | 415–419 | 416–420 | — | — | — | 74 |
| 73 | 479–484 | 480–485 | 479–484 | 140–141 | 142–143 | 142–143 | 410–414 | 411–414 | 411–415 | — | — | — | 73 |
| 72 | 473–478 | 474–479 | 474–478 | 138–139 | 141 | 140–141 | 405–409 | 406–410 | 406–410 | — | — | — | 72 |
| 71 | 468–472 | 469–473 | 468–473 | 136–137 | 139–140 | 138–139 | 401–404 | 401–405 | 401–405 | — | — | — | 71 |
| 70 | 462–467 | 463–468 | 462–467 | 134–135 | 137–138 | 136–137 | 396–400 | 396–400 | 396–400 | — | — | — | 70 |
| 69 | 456–461 | 457–462 | 457–461 | 132–133 | 135–136 | 134–135 | 391–395 | 391–395 | 392–395 | — | — | — | 69 |
| 68 | 451–455 | 451–456 | 451–456 | 131 | 133–134 | 133 | 386–390 | 386–390 | 387–391 | — | — | 254 | 68 |
| 67 | 445–450 | 446–450 | 445–450 | 129–130 | 131–132 | 131–132 | 381–385 | 381–385 | 382–386 | 252–254 | 249–252 | 251–253 | 67 |
| 66 | 439–444 | 440–444 | 440–444 | 129–130 | 129–130 | 129–130 | 376–380 | 376–380 | 377–381 | 249–251 | — | 248–250 | 66 |

**Table A.16d** SRP–COL Composite *T* Scores (*continued*)

| T score | Internalizing Problems — Combined | Internalizing Problems — Female | Internalizing Problems — Male | Inattention/Hyperactivity — Combined | Inattention/Hyperactivity — Female | Inattention/Hyperactivity — Male | Emotional Symptoms — Combined | Emotional Symptoms — Female | Emotional Symptoms — Male | Personal Adjustment — Combined | Personal Adjustment — Female | Personal Adjustment — Male | T score |
|---|---|---|---|---|---|---|---|---|---|---|---|---|---|
| 65 | 433–438 | 434–439 | 434–439 | 127–128 | 128 | 127–128 | 371–375 | 371–375 | 372–376 | 246–248 | 246–248 | 245–247 | 65 |
| 64 | 428–432 | 428–433 | 428–433 | 125–126 | 126–127 | 125–126 | 366–370 | 367–370 | 367–371 | 243–245 | 243–245 | 242–244 | 64 |
| 63 | 422–427 | 423–427 | 422–427 | 123–124 | 124–125 | 123–124 | 362–365 | 362–366 | 362–366 | 240–242 | 240–242 | 239–241 | 63 |
| 62 | 416–421 | 417–422 | 417–422 | 121–122 | 122–123 | 122 | 357–361 | 357–361 | 357–361 | 237–239 | 237–239 | 236–238 | 62 |
| 61 | 411–415 | 411–416 | 411–416 | 120 | 120–121 | 120–121 | 352–356 | 352–356 | 352–356 | 234–236 | 234–236 | 232–235 | 61 |
| 60 | 405–410 | 405–410 | 405–410 | 118–119 | 118–119 | 118–119 | 347–351 | 347–351 | 348–351 | 230–233 | 230–233 | 229–231 | 60 |
| 59 | 399–404 | 400–404 | 400–404 | 116–117 | 116–117 | 116–117 | 342–346 | 342–346 | 343–347 | 227–229 | 227–229 | 226–228 | 59 |
| 58 | 394–398 | 394–399 | 394–399 | 114–115 | 114–115 | 114–115 | 337–341 | 337–341 | 338–342 | 224–226 | 224–226 | 223–225 | 58 |
| 57 | 388–393 | 388–393 | 388–393 | 112–113 | 113 | 112–113 | 332–336 | 332–336 | 333–337 | 221–223 | 221–223 | 220–222 | 57 |
| 56 | 382–387 | 382–387 | 383–387 | 110–111 | 111–112 | 111 | 327–331 | 328–331 | 328–332 | 218–220 | 218–220 | 217–219 | 56 |
| 55 | 376–381 | 377–381 | 377–382 | 109 | 109–110 | 109–110 | 323–326 | 323–327 | 323–327 | 215–217 | 215–217 | 214–216 | 55 |
| 54 | 371–376 | 371–376 | 371–376 | 107–108 | 107–108 | 107–108 | 318–322 | 318–322 | 318–322 | 212–214 | 212–214 | 211–213 | 54 |
| 53 | 365–370 | 365–370 | 365–370 | 105–106 | 105–106 | 105–106 | 313–317 | 313–317 | 313–317 | 208–211 | 208–211 | 208–210 | 53 |
| 52 | 359–364 | 359–364 | 360–364 | 103–104 | 103–104 | 103–104 | 308–312 | 308–312 | 308–312 | 205–207 | 205–207 | 205–207 | 52 |
| 51 | 354–358 | 354–358 | 354–359 | 101–102 | 101–102 | 101–102 | 303–307 | 303–307 | 304–307 | 202–204 | 202–204 | 202–204 | 51 |
| 50 | 348–353 | 348–353 | 348–353 | 99–100 | 100 | 100 | 298–302 | 298–302 | 299–303 | 199–201 | 199–201 | 199–201 | 50 |
| 49 | 342–347 | 342–347 | 343–347 | 98 | 98–99 | 98–99 | 293–297 | 293–297 | 294–298 | 196–198 | 196–198 | 196–198 | 49 |
| 48 | 336–341 | 336–341 | 337–342 | 96–97 | 96–97 | 96–97 | 288–292 | 288–292 | 289–293 | 193–195 | 193–195 | 192–195 | 48 |
| 47 | 331–335 | 331–335 | 331–336 | 94–95 | 94–95 | 94–95 | 284–287 | 284–287 | 284–288 | 190–192 | 189–192 | 189–191 | 47 |
| 46 | 325–330 | 325–330 | 326–330 | 92–93 | 92–93 | 92–93 | 279–283 | 279–283 | 279–283 | 187–189 | 186–188 | 186–188 | 46 |
| 45 | 319–324 | 319–324 | 320–325 | 90–91 | 90–91 | 90–91 | 274–278 | 274–278 | 274–278 | 183–186 | 183–185 | 183–185 | 45 |
| 44 | 314–318 | 313–318 | 314–319 | 88–89 | 88–89 | 89 | 269–273 | 269–273 | 269–273 | 180–182 | 180–182 | 180–182 | 44 |
| 43 | 308–313 | 308–312 | 308–313 | 87 | 87 | 87–88 | 264–268 | 264–268 | 264–268 | 177–179 | 177–179 | 177–179 | 43 |
| 42 | 302–307 | 302–307 | 303–307 | 85–86 | 85–86 | 85–86 | 259–263 | 259–263 | 260–263 | 174–176 | 174–176 | 174–176 | 42 |
| 41 | 296–301 | 296–301 | 297–302 | 83–84 | 83–84 | 83–84 | 254–258 | 254–258 | 255–259 | 171–173 | 171–173 | 171–173 | 41 |
| 40 | 291–295 | 290–295 | 291–296 | 81–82 | 81–82 | 81–82 | 249–253 | 249–253 | 250–254 | 168–170 | 167–170 | 168–170 | 40 |
| 39 | 285–290 | 284–289 | 286–290 | 79–80 | 79–80 | 79–80 | 244–248 | 244–248 | 245–249 | 165–167 | 164–166 | 165–167 | 39 |
| 38 | 279–284 | 279–283 | 280–285 | 77–78 | 77–78 | 78 | 240–244 | 240–243 | 240–244 | 161–164 | 161–163 | 162–164 | 38 |
| 37 | 274–278 | 273–278 | 274–279 | 76 | 75–76 | 76–77 | 235–239 | 235–239 | 235–239 | 158–160 | 158–160 | 159–161 | 37 |
| 36 | 268–273 | 267–272 | 269–273 | 74–75 | 74 | 74–75 | 230–234 | 230–234 | 230–234 | 155–157 | 155–157 | 156–158 | 36 |
| 35 | 266–267 | 262–266 | 267–268 | 72–73 | 72–73 | 72–73 | 225–229 | 225–229 | 225–229 | 152–154 | 152–154 | 152–155 | 35 |
| 34 | — | — | — | 70–71 | 70–71 | 70–71 | 220–224 | 220–224 | 220–224 | 149–151 | 149–151 | 149–151 | 34 |
| 33 | — | — | — | 69 | — | 68–69 | 215–219 | 215–219 | 216–219 | 146–148 | 145–148 | 146–148 | 33 |
| 32 | — | — | — | — | — | 67 | — | 214 | 215 | 143–145 | 142–144 | 143–145 | 32 |
| 31 | — | — | — | — | — | — | — | — | — | 140–142 | 139–141 | 140–142 | 31 |
| 30 | — | — | — | — | — | — | — | — | — | 136–139 | 136–138 | 137–139 | 30 |
| 29 | — | — | — | — | — | — | — | — | — | 133–135 | 133–135 | 134–136 | 29 |
| 28 | — | — | — | — | — | — | — | — | — | 130–132 | 130–132 | 131–133 | 28 |
| 27 | — | — | — | — | — | — | — | — | — | 127–129 | 126–129 | 128–130 | 27 |
| 26 | — | — | — | — | — | — | — | — | — | 124–126 | 123–125 | 125–127 | 26 |
| 25 | — | — | — | — | — | — | — | — | — | 121–123 | 120–122 | 122–124 | 25 |
| 24 | — | — | — | — | — | — | — | — | — | 118–120 | 117–119 | 119–121 | 24 |
| 23 | — | — | — | — | — | — | — | — | — | 114–117 | 114–116 | 116–118 | 23 |
| 22 | — | — | — | — | — | — | — | — | — | 111–113 | 111–113 | 112–115 | 22 |
| 21 | — | — | — | — | — | — | — | — | — | 108–110 | 108–110 | 109–111 | 21 |
| 20 | — | — | — | — | — | — | — | — | — | 105–107 | 104–107 | 106–108 | 20 |
| 19 | — | — | — | — | — | — | — | — | — | 102–104 | 101–103 | 103–105 | 19 |
| 18 | — | — | — | — | — | — | — | — | — | 99–101 | 98–100 | 100–102 | 18 |
| 17 | — | — | — | — | — | — | — | — | — | 96–98 | 95–97 | 97–99 | 17 |
| 16 | — | — | — | — | — | — | — | — | — | 93–95 | 92–94 | 94–96 | 16 |
| 15 | — | — | — | — | — | — | — | — | — | 89–92 | 89–91 | 91–93 | 15 |
| 14 | — | — | — | — | — | — | — | — | — | 86–88 | 85–88 | 88–90 | 14 |
| 13 | — | — | — | — | — | — | — | — | — | 83–85 | 82–84 | 85–87 | 13 |
| 12 | — | — | — | — | — | — | — | — | — | 80–82 | 79–81 | 82–84 | 12 |
| 11 | — | — | — | — | — | — | — | — | — | 77–79 | 76–78 | 79–81 | 11 |
| 10 | — | — | — | — | — | — | — | — | — | 50–76 | 57–75 | 42–78 | 10 |
| *T*: 90% Conf. int. | 3 | 3 | 3 | 5 | 5 | 5 | 3 | 3 | 3 | 4 | 4 | 4 | *T*: 90% Conf. int. |

**Table A.16e** SRP–COL Composite Percentiles

| %ile | Internalizing Problems | | | Inattention/Hyperactivity | | | Emotional Symptoms | | | Personal Adjustment | | | %ile |
|---|---|---|---|---|---|---|---|---|---|---|---|---|---|
| | Combined | Female | Male | Combined | Female | Male | Combined | Female | Male | Combined | Female | Male | |
| 99 | 517–684 | 501–660 | 530–728 | 149–172 | 149–172 | 149–173 | 436–546 | 427–525 | 444–579 | 252–254 | 252 | 251–254 | 99 |
| 98 | 497–516 | 488–500 | 502–529 | 144–148 | 145–148 | 143–148 | 421–435 | 416–426 | 425–443 | 249–251 | 249–251 | 248–250 | 98 |
| 97 | 482–496 | 478–487 | 484–501 | 140–143 | 141–144 | 139–142 | 411–420 | 407–415 | 412–424 | 247–248 | 247–248 | 246–247 | 97 |
| 96 | 471–481 | 470–477 | 470–483 | 137–139 | 139–140 | 136–138 | 402–410 | 400–406 | 402–411 | 246 | 246 | 244–245 | 96 |
| 95 | 462–470 | 462–469 | 459–469 | 135–136 | 136–138 | 134–135 | 395–401 | 394–399 | 394–401 | 244–245 | 244–245 | 243 | 95 |
| 94 | 453–461 | 456–461 | 450–458 | 132–134 | 134–135 | 131–133 | 388–394 | 388–393 | 387–393 | 243 | 243 | 242 | 94 |
| 93 | 446–452 | 450–455 | 442–449 | 130–131 | 132–133 | 129–130 | 383–387 | 383–387 | 381–386 | 241–242 | 242 | 240–241 | 93 |
| 92 | 440–445 | 444–449 | 435–441 | 129 | 130–131 | 128 | 377–382 | 379–382 | 375–380 | 240 | 241 | 239 | 92 |
| 91 | 434–439 | 439–443 | 429–434 | 127–128 | 129 | 126–127 | 373–376 | 374–378 | 370–374 | 239 | 239–240 | 238 | 91 |
| 90 | 429–433 | 434–438 | 423–428 | 125–126 | 127–128 | 125 | 369–372 | 370–373 | 366–369 | 238 | 238 | 237 | 90 |
| 89 | 424–428 | 430–433 | 418–422 | 124 | 126 | 123–124 | 365–368 | 367–369 | 362–365 | 237 | 237 | 236 | 89 |
| 88 | 419–423 | 426–429 | 414–417 | 123 | 124–125 | 122 | 361–364 | 363–366 | 358–361 | 236 | 236 | 235 | 88 |
| 87 | 415–418 | 422–425 | 410–413 | 122 | 123 | 121 | 357–360 | 360–362 | 355–357 | 235 | 235 | 234 | 87 |
| 86 | 411–414 | 418–421 | 406–409 | 120–121 | 122 | 120 | 354–356 | 357–359 | 351–354 | 234 | 234 | 233 | 86 |
| 85 | 407–410 | 414–417 | 402–405 | 119 | 121 | 119 | 351–353 | 354–356 | 348–350 | 233 | 233 | 232 | 85 |
| 84 | 404–406 | 411–413 | 399–401 | 118 | 120 | 118 | 348–350 | 351–353 | 346–347 | 232 | – | 231 | 84 |
| 83 | 400–403 | 407–410 | 395–398 | 117 | 118–119 | 117 | 345–347 | 348–350 | 343–345 | 231 | 232 | 230 | 83 |
| 82 | 397–399 | 404–406 | 392–394 | 116 | 117 | 116 | 343–344 | 345–347 | 340–342 | 230 | 231 | 229 | 82 |
| 81 | 394–396 | 401–403 | 389–391 | 115 | 116 | 115 | 340–342 | 343–344 | 338–339 | 229 | 230 | 228 | 81 |
| 80 | 391–393 | 398–400 | 387–388 | – | – | – | 337–339 | 340–342 | 335–337 | – | 229 | – | 80 |
| 79 | 388–390 | 395–397 | 384–386 | 114 | 115 | 114 | 335–336 | 338–339 | 333–334 | 228 | 228 | 227 | 79 |
| 78 | 385–387 | 392–394 | 381–383 | 113 | 114 | 113 | 333–334 | 336–337 | 331–332 | 227 | 227 | 226 | 78 |
| 77 | 383–384 | 390–391 | 379–380 | 112 | 113 | 112 | 331–332 | 334–335 | 329–330 | 226 | 226 | 225 | 77 |
| 76 | 380–382 | 387–389 | 377–378 | 111 | 112 | – | 329–330 | 331–333 | 327–328 | 225 | – | 224 | 76 |
| 75 | 378–379 | 385–386 | 375–376 | – | 111 | 111 | 326–328 | 329–330 | 325–326 | 224 | 225 | 223 | 75 |
| 74 | 376–377 | 382–384 | 372–374 | 110 | – | 110 | 324–325 | 327–328 | 323–324 | – | 224 | – | 74 |
| 73 | 373–375 | 380–381 | 370–371 | 109 | 110 | – | 323 | 325–326 | 321–322 | 223 | 223 | 222 | 73 |
| 72 | 371–372 | 377–379 | 368–369 | – | 109 | 109 | 321–322 | 323–324 | 319–320 | 222 | 222 | 221 | 72 |
| 71 | 369–370 | 375–376 | 366–367 | 108 | 108 | 108 | 319–320 | 321–322 | 318 | 221 | 221 | 220 | 71 |
| 70 | 367–368 | 373–374 | 365 | 107 | – | – | 317–318 | 320 | 316–317 | 220 | – | 219 | 70 |
| 69 | 365–366 | 371–372 | 363–364 | – | 107 | 107 | 315–316 | 318–319 | 314–315 | – | 220 | – | 69 |
| 68 | 363–364 | 368–370 | 361–362 | 106 | 106 | – | 314 | 316–317 | 313 | 219 | 219 | 218 | 68 |
| 67 | 361–362 | 366–367 | 359–360 | 105 | – | 106 | 312–313 | 314–315 | 311–312 | 218 | 218 | 217 | 67 |
| 66 | 359–360 | 364–365 | 358 | – | 105 | 105 | 310–311 | 313 | 310 | 217 | 217 | 216 | 66 |
| 65 | 358 | 362–363 | 356–357 | 104 | 104 | – | 309 | 311–312 | 308–309 | 216 | – | – | 65 |
| 64 | 356–357 | 360–361 | 355 | – | – | 104 | 307–308 | 309–310 | 307 | – | 216 | 215 | 64 |
| 63 | 354–355 | 358–359 | 353–354 | 103 | 103 | 103 | 306 | 308 | 305–306 | 215 | 215 | 214 | 63 |
| 62 | 352–353 | 357 | 352 | – | – | – | 304–305 | 306–307 | 304 | 214 | 214 | 213 | 62 |
| 61 | 351 | 355–356 | 350–351 | 102 | 102 | – | 303 | 305 | 303 | 213 | 213 | 212 | 61 |
| 60 | 349–350 | 353–354 | 349 | 101 | 101 | 102 | 301–302 | 303–304 | 301–302 | 212 | 212 | – | 60 |
| 59 | 348 | 351–352 | 347–348 | – | – | – | 300 | 302 | 300 | – | – | 211 | 59 |
| 58 | 346–347 | 349–350 | 346 | 100 | 100 | 101 | 299 | 300–301 | 299 | 211 | 211 | 210 | 58 |
| 57 | 345 | 348 | 345 | – | – | – | 297–298 | 299 | 297–298 | 210 | 210 | 209 | 57 |
| 56 | 343–344 | 346–347 | 343–344 | 99 | 99 | 100 | 296 | 297–298 | 296 | 209 | 209 | 208 | 56 |
| 55 | 342 | 344–345 | 342 | – | – | – | 295 | 296 | 295 | 208 | 208 | – | 55 |
| 54 | 340–341 | 343 | 341 | 98 | 98 | 99 | 293–294 | 295 | 294 | 207 | – | 207 | 54 |
| 53 | 339 | 341–342 | 340 | – | – | – | 292 | 293–294 | 293 | – | 207 | 206 | 53 |
| 52 | 338 | 340 | 338–339 | – | 97 | 98 | 291 | 292 | 292 | 206 | 206 | 205 | 52 |
| 51 | 336–337 | 338–339 | 337 | 97 | – | – | 290 | 291 | 290–291 | 205 | 205 | 204 | 51 |

## Table A.16e  SRP–COL Composite Percentiles (continued)

| %ile | Internalizing Problems | | | Inattention/Hyperactivity | | | Emotional Symptoms | | | Personal Adjustment | | | %ile |
|---|---|---|---|---|---|---|---|---|---|---|---|---|---|
| | Combined | Female | Male | Combined | Female | Male | Combined | Female | Male | Combined | Female | Male | |
| 50 | 335 | 337 | 336 | – | 96 | – | 289 | 289–290 | 289 | 204 | 204 | – | 50 |
| 49 | 334 | 335–336 | 335 | 96 | – | 97 | 287–288 | 288 | 288 | 203 | 203 | 203 | 49 |
| 48 | 332–333 | 334 | 334 | – | 95 | – | 286 | 287 | 287 | 202 | 202 | 202 | 48 |
| 47 | 331 | 332–333 | 333 | 95 | – | 96 | 285 | 286 | 286 | – | 201 | 201 | 47 |
| 46 | 330 | 331 | 331–332 | – | 94 | – | 284 | 284–285 | 285 | 201 | – | 200 | 46 |
| 45 | 329 | 329–330 | 330 | 94 | – | 95 | 283 | 283 | 284 | 200 | 200 | 199 | 45 |
| 44 | 327–328 | 328 | 329 | – | 93 | – | 282 | 282 | 283 | 199 | 199 | 198 | 44 |
| 43 | 326 | 327 | 328 | – | – | – | 281 | 281 | 282 | 198 | 198 | – | 43 |
| 42 | 325 | 325–326 | 327 | 93 | – | 94 | 280 | 280 | 281 | 197 | 197 | 197 | 42 |
| 41 | 324 | 324 | 326 | – | 92 | – | 278–279 | 278–279 | 280 | 196 | 196 | 196 | 41 |
| 40 | 323 | 323 | 325 | 92 | – | 93 | 277 | 277 | 279 | 195 | 195 | 195 | 40 |
| 39 | 322 | 321–322 | 324 | – | 91 | – | 276 | 276 | 278 | 194 | 194 | 194 | 39 |
| 38 | 320–321 | 320 | 323 | 91 | – | 92 | 275 | 275 | 277 | 193 | 193 | 193 | 38 |
| 37 | 319 | 319 | 322 | – | 90 | – | 274 | 274 | 276 | 192 | 192 | 192 | 37 |
| 36 | 318 | 317–318 | 321 | – | – | – | 273 | 273 | 275 | 191 | 191 | 191 | 36 |
| 35 | 317 | 316 | 320 | 90 | – | 91 | 272 | 272 | 274 | 190 | 190 | 190 | 35 |
| 34 | 316 | 315 | 319 | – | 89 | – | 271 | 271 | 273 | 189 | 189 | 189 | 34 |
| 33 | 315 | 314 | 318 | 89 | – | 90 | 270 | 270 | 272 | 188 | 188 | 188 | 33 |
| 32 | 314 | 313 | 317 | – | 88 | – | 269 | 268–269 | 271 | 187 | 187 | 187 | 32 |
| 31 | 313 | 311–312 | 316 | – | – | 89 | 268 | 267 | 270 | 186 | 186 | 186 | 31 |
| 30 | 312 | 310 | 315 | 88 | – | – | 267 | 266 | 269 | 185 | 185 | 185 | 30 |
| 29 | 311 | 309 | 314 | – | 87 | – | 266 | 265 | 268 | 184 | 184 | 184 | 29 |
| 28 | 310 | 308 | 313 | 87 | – | 88 | 265 | 264 | 267 | 183 | 183 | 183 | 28 |
| 27 | 309 | 307 | 312 | – | 86 | – | 264 | 263 | 266 | 182 | 181–182 | 182 | 27 |
| 26 | 308 | 305–306 | – | 86 | – | 87 | 263 | 262 | 265 | 181 | 180 | 181 | 26 |
| 25 | 307 | 304 | 311 | – | 85 | 86 | 262 | 261 | – | 179–180 | 179 | 179–180 | 25 |
| 24 | 306 | 303 | 310 | – | – | – | 261 | 260 | 264 | 178 | 178 | 178 | 24 |
| 23 | 305 | 302 | 309 | 85 | 84 | 85 | – | 259 | 263 | 177 | 176–177 | 177 | 23 |
| 22 | 304 | 301 | 308 | – | – | – | 260 | 258 | 262 | 176 | 175 | 176 | 22 |
| 21 | 303 | 300 | 307 | 84 | – | – | 259 | 257 | 261 | 174–175 | 174 | 174–175 | 21 |
| 20 | 302 | 299 | 306 | – | 83 | 84 | 258 | 256 | 260 | 173 | 172–173 | 173 | 20 |
| 19 | 301 | 298 | 305 | – | – | – | 257 | 255 | 259 | 171–172 | 171 | 172 | 19 |
| 18 | 300 | 296–297 | 304 | 83 | 82 | 83 | 256 | 254 | 258 | 170 | 169–170 | 170–171 | 18 |
| 17 | 299 | 295 | 303 | – | – | – | 255 | 253 | 257 | 168–169 | 168 | 169 | 17 |
| 16 | 298 | 294 | 302 | 82 | – | 82 | 254 | 252 | 256 | 167 | 166–167 | 167–168 | 16 |
| 15 | 297 | 293 | 301 | – | 81 | – | 253 | 251 | 255 | 165–166 | 165 | 165–166 | 15 |
| 14 | 296 | 292 | 300 | 81 | – | 81 | 252 | 250 | 254 | 163–164 | 163–164 | 164 | 14 |
| 13 | 294–295 | 291 | 299 | – | – | – | 251 | 249 | 253 | 162 | 161–162 | 162–163 | 13 |
| 12 | 293 | 290 | 298 | 80 | 80 | 80 | 250 | 248 | 252 | 160–161 | 159–160 | 160–161 | 12 |
| 11 | 292 | 288–289 | 297 | – | – | – | 249 | 247 | 251 | 158–159 | 157–158 | 158–159 | 11 |
| 10 | 291 | 287 | 296 | 79 | 79 | 79 | 247–248 | 246 | 249–250 | 155–157 | 155–156 | 156–157 | 10 |
| 9 | 290 | 286 | 294–295 | – | – | 78 | 246 | 244–245 | 248 | 153–154 | 153–154 | 153–155 | 9 |
| 8 | 289 | 285 | 293 | 78 | – | 77 | 245 | 243 | 247 | 150–152 | 150–152 | 151–152 | 8 |
| 7 | 288 | 284 | 292 | – | 78 | 72–73 | 244 | 242 | 246 | 148–149 | 147–149 | 148–150 | 7 |
| 6 | 286–287 | 282–283 | 291 | 77 | – | 71 | 243 | 241 | 244–245 | 144–147 | 144–146 | 145–147 | 6 |
| 5 | 285 | 281 | 289–290 | 76 | 77 | 75 | 241–242 | 239–240 | 243 | 141–143 | 141–143 | 142–144 | 5 |
| 4 | 283–284 | 279–280 | 288 | – | 76 | 74 | 240 | 238 | 241–242 | 137–140 | 137–140 | 137–141 | 4 |
| 3 | 282 | 278 | 286–287 | 75 | 75 | 72–73 | 238–239 | 236–237 | 239–240 | 131–136 | 132–136 | 132–136 | 3 |
| 2 | 280–281 | 276–277 | 283–285 | 74 | 75 | 71 | 236–237 | 234–235 | 237–238 | 124–130 | 126–131 | 125–131 | 2 |
| 1 | 266–279 | 262–275 | 267–282 | 69–73 | 70–74 | 67–70 | 215–235 | 214–233 | 215–236 | 50–123 | 57–125 | 42–124 | 1 |

# Appendix B

## Interpretive Tables

**Table B.1** Statistically Significant Differences Between *T* Scores on Clinical Composites

| | TRS | | | | | | PRS | |
|---|---|---|---|---|---|---|---|---|
| | Externalizing Problems vs. Internalizing Problems | | Externalizing Problems vs. School Problems | | Internalizing Problems vs. School Problems | | Externalizing Problems vs. Internalizing Problems | |
| Level | .05 | .01 | .05 | .01 | .05 | .01 | .05 | .01 |
| **Preschool** | | | | | | | | |
| Ages 2–3 | 8 | 11 | — | — | — | — | 8 | 11 |
| Ages 4–5 | 7 | 9 | — | — | — | — | 8 | 11 |
| Ages 2–5 | 8 | 10 | — | — | — | — | 8 | 11 |
| **Child** | | | | | | | | |
| Ages 6–7 | 8 | 10 | 7 | 8 | 8 | 10 | 7 | 9 |
| Ages 8–11 | 8 | 10 | 7 | 9 | 9 | 11 | 7 | 10 |
| Ages 6–11 | 8 | 10 | 7 | 9 | 8 | 10 | 7 | 9 |
| **Adolescent** | | | | | | | | |
| Ages 12–14 | 8 | 9 | 7 | 9 | 9 | 11 | 6 | 8 |
| Ages 15–18 | 7 | 8 | 6 | 8 | 7 | 9 | 6 | 7 |
| Ages 12–18 | 7 | 9 | 7 | 8 | 8 | 10 | 6 | 8 |

| | SRP | | | | | |
|---|---|---|---|---|---|---|
| | School Problems vs. Internalizing Problems | | School Problems vs. Inattention/Hyperactivity | | Internalizing Problems vs. Inattention/Hyperactivity | |
| Level | .05 | .01 | .05 | .01 | .05 | .01 |
| **Child** | | | | | | |
| Ages 8–11 | 10 | 12 | 11 | 14 | 10 | 12 |
| **Adolescent** | | | | | | |
| Ages 12–14 | 9 | 11 | 10 | 12 | 9 | 11 |
| Ages 15–18 | 9 | 11 | 10 | 12 | 8 | 10 |
| Ages 12–18 | 9 | 11 | 10 | 12 | 8 | 10 |
| **College** | | | | | | |
| Ages 18–25 | — | — | — | — | 7 | 9 |

**Table B.2** Frequencies of Differences Between Clinical Composites, for the General Norm Sample

| Form | Level | Composite | 25 | 15 | 10 | 5 | 2 | 1 |
|------|-------|-----------|----|----|----|---|---|---|
| | | | Frequency percentage (%) | | | | | |
| | | | Size of difference (regardless of direction) | | | | | |
| TRS | Preschool: Ages 2–5 | Externalizing Problems vs. Internalizing Problems | 11 | 14 | 17 | 22 | 27 | 30 |
| | Child: Ages 6–11 | Externalizing Problems vs. Internalizing Problems | 11 | 15 | 18 | 22 | 28 | 34 |
| | | Externalizing Problems vs. School Problems | 9 | 13 | 16 | 20 | 25 | 26 |
| | | Internalizing Problems vs. School Problems | 12 | 16 | 19 | 23 | 29 | 33 |
| | Adolescent: Ages 12–18 | Externalizing Problems vs. Internalizing Problems | 10 | 14 | 17 | 23 | 29 | 34 |
| | | Externalizing Problems vs. School Problems | 9 | 12 | 14 | 17 | 20 | 25 |
| | | Internalizing Problems vs. School Problems | 10 | 13 | 16 | 21 | 27 | 31 |
| PRS | Preschool: Ages 2–5 | Externalizing Problems vs. Internalizing Problems | 9 | 12 | 14 | 17 | 22 | 25 |
| | Child: Ages 6–11 | Externalizing Problems vs. Internalizing Problems | 10 | 14 | 16 | 20 | 28 | 31 |
| | Adolescent: Ages 12–18 | Externalizing Problems vs. Internalizing Problems | 7 | 10 | 12 | 14 | 18 | 22 |
| SRP | Child: Ages 8–11 | School Problems vs. Internalizing Problems | 10 | 13 | 15 | 18 | 28 | 32 |
| | | School Problems vs. Inattention/Hyperactivity | 9 | 12 | 15 | 18 | 22 | 28 |
| | | Internalizing Problems vs. Inattention/Hyperactivity | 9 | 12 | 14 | 18 | 23 | 25 |
| | Adolescent: Ages 12–18 | School Problems vs. Internalizing Problems | 10 | 13 | 15 | 19 | 23 | 28 |
| | | School Problems vs. Inattention/Hyperactivity | 10 | 14 | 16 | 19 | 24 | 27 |
| | | Internalizing Problems vs. Inattention/Hyperactivity | 9 | 12 | 15 | 20 | 26 | 29 |
| | College: Ages 18–25 | Internalizing Problems vs. Inattention/Hyperactivity | 9 | 13 | 15 | 21 | 26 | 29 |

# Table B.3 Mean *T* Scores Corresponding to Sums of *T* Scores

| Mean *T* | BSI or ESI | 3 scales | 4 scales | 5 scales | Mean *T* |
|---|---|---|---|---|---|
| 117 | — | — | — | — | 117 |
| 116 | — | — | — | — | 116 |
| 115 | — | — | — | — | 115 |
| 114 | — | — | — | — | 114 |
| 113 | — | — | — | — | 113 |
| 112 | 669–673 | — | — | — | 112 |
| 111 | 663–668 | — | — | — | 111 |
| 110 | 657–662 | — | — | — | 110 |
| 109 | 651–656 | — | — | — | 109 |
| 108 | 645–650 | — | — | — | 108 |
| 107 | 639–644 | — | — | — | 107 |
| 106 | 633–638 | — | — | — | 106 |
| 105 | 627–632 | — | — | — | 105 |
| 104 | 621–626 | — | — | — | 104 |
| 103 | 615–620 | — | — | — | 103 |
| 102 | 609–614 | — | — | — | 102 |
| 101 | 603–608 | — | — | — | 101 |
| 100 | 597–602 | — | — | — | 100 |
| 99 | 591–596 | — | — | — | 99 |
| 98 | 585–590 | — | — | — | 98 |
| 97 | 579–584 | — | — | — | 97 |
| 96 | 573–578 | — | — | — | 96 |
| 95 | 567–572 | — | — | — | 95 |
| 94 | 561–566 | — | — | — | 94 |
| 93 | 555–560 | — | — | — | 93 |
| 92 | 549–554 | — | — | — | 92 |
| 91 | 543–548 | — | — | — | 91 |
| 90 | 537–542 | — | — | — | 90 |
| 89 | 531–536 | — | — | — | 89 |
| 88 | 525–530 | — | — | — | 88 |
| 87 | 519–524 | — | — | — | 87 |
| 86 | 513–518 | — | — | — | 86 |
| 85 | 507–512 | — | — | — | 85 |
| 84 | 501–506 | — | — | — | 84 |
| 83 | 495–500 | — | — | — | 83 |
| 82 | 489–494 | — | — | — | 82 |
| 81 | 483–488 | — | — | — | 81 |
| 80 | 477–482 | — | — | 398–399 | 80 |
| 79 | 471–476 | — | — | 393–397 | 79 |
| 78 | 465–470 | — | — | 388–392 | 78 |
| 77 | 459–464 | — | 306–309 | 383–387 | 77 |
| 76 | 453–458 | — | 302–305 | 378–382 | 76 |
| 75 | 447–452 | 224–225 | 298–301 | 373–377 | 75 |
| 74 | 441–446 | 221–223 | 294–297 | 368–372 | 74 |
| 73 | 435–440 | 218–220 | 290–293 | 363–367 | 73 |
| 72 | 429–434 | 215–217 | 286–289 | 358–362 | 72 |
| 71 | 423–428 | 212–214 | 282–285 | 353–357 | 71 |
| 70 | 417–422 | 209–211 | 278–281 | 348–352 | 70 |
| 69 | 411–416 | 206–208 | 274–277 | 343–347 | 69 |
| 68 | 405–410 | 203–205 | 270–273 | 338–342 | 68 |
| 67 | 399–404 | 200–202 | 266–269 | 333–337 | 67 |
| 66 | 393–398 | 197–199 | 262–265 | 328–332 | 66 |
| 65 | 387–392 | 194–196 | 258–261 | 323–327 | 65 |
| 64 | 381–386 | 191–193 | 254–257 | 318–322 | 64 |
| 63 | 375–380 | 188–190 | 250–253 | 313–317 | 63 |
| 62 | 369–374 | 185–187 | 246–249 | 308–312 | 62 |
| 61 | 363–368 | 182–184 | 242–245 | 303–307 | 61 |
| 60 | 357–362 | 179–181 | 238–241 | 298–302 | 60 |
| 59 | 351–356 | 176–178 | 234–237 | 293–297 | 59 |
| 58 | 345–350 | 173–175 | 230–233 | 288–292 | 58 |
| 57 | 339–344 | 170–172 | 226–229 | 283–287 | 57 |
| 56 | 333–338 | 167–169 | 222–225 | 278–282 | 56 |
| 55 | 327–332 | 164–166 | 218–221 | 273–277 | 55 |
| 54 | 321–326 | 161–163 | 214–217 | 268–272 | 54 |
| 53 | 315–320 | 158–160 | 210–213 | 263–267 | 53 |
| 52 | 309–314 | 155–157 | 206–209 | 258–262 | 52 |
| 51 | 303–308 | 152–154 | 202–205 | 253–257 | 51 |
| 50 | 297–302 | 149–151 | 198–201 | 248–252 | 50 |
| 49 | 291–296 | 146–148 | 194–197 | 243–247 | 49 |
| 48 | 285–290 | 143–145 | 190–193 | 238–242 | 48 |
| 47 | 279–284 | 140–142 | 186–189 | 233–237 | 47 |
| 46 | 273–278 | 137–139 | 182–185 | 228–232 | 46 |
| 45 | 267–272 | 134–136 | 178–181 | 223–227 | 45 |
| 44 | 261–266 | 131–133 | 174–177 | 218–222 | 44 |
| 43 | 255–260 | 128–130 | 170–173 | 213–217 | 43 |
| 42 | 249–254 | 125–127 | 166–169 | 208–212 | 42 |
| 41 | 243–248 | 122–124 | 162–165 | 203–207 | 41 |
| 40 | 237–242 | 119–121 | 158–161 | 198–202 | 40 |
| 39 | 231–236 | 116–118 | 154–157 | 193–197 | 39 |
| 38 | 225–230 | 113–115 | 150–153 | 188–192 | 38 |
| 37 | 219–224 | 110–112 | 146–149 | 183–187 | 37 |
| 36 | 213–218 | 107–109 | 142–145 | 178–182 | 36 |
| 35 | 207–212 | 104–106 | 138–141 | 173–177 | 35 |
| 34 | 201–206 | 101–103 | 134–137 | 168–172 | 34 |
| 33 | 195–200 | 98–100 | 130–133 | 163–167 | 33 |
| 32 | 189–194 | 95–97 | 126–129 | 158–162 | 32 |
| 31 | 186–188 | 92–94 | 122–125 | 153–157 | 31 |
| 30 | — | 89–91 | 118–121 | 148–152 | 30 |
| 29 | — | 86–88 | 114–117 | 143–147 | 29 |
| 28 | — | 83–85 | 110–113 | 138–142 | 28 |
| 27 | — | 80–82 | 106–109 | 133–137 | 27 |
| 26 | — | 77–79 | 102–105 | 128–132 | 26 |
| 25 | — | 74–76 | 98–101 | 123–127 | 25 |
| 24 | — | 71–73 | 94–97 | 118–122 | 24 |
| 23 | — | — | 90–93 | 113–117 | 23 |
| 22 | — | — | 86–89 | 108–112 | 22 |
| 21 | — | — | 82–85 | 103–107 | 21 |
| 20 | — | — | 78–81 | 98–102 | 20 |
| 19 | — | — | 74–77 | 93–97 | 19 |
| 18 | — | — | 70–73 | 88–92 | 18 |
| 17 | — | — | 66–69 | 83–87 | 17 |
| 16 | — | — | 62–65 | 78–82 | 16 |
| 15 | — | — | 58–61 | 73–77 | 15 |
| 14 | — | — | 55–57 | 68–72 | 14 |
| 13 | — | — | — | 63–67 | 13 |
| 12 | — | — | — | 59–62 | 12 |
| 11 | — | — | — | — | 11 |
| 10 | — | — | — | — | 10 |

**Table B.4** TRS: Statistically Significant Differences Between Scale *T* Scores and the Mean *T* Score of the BSI or Adaptive Skills Composite

| Scale | Preschool | | | Child | | | Adolescent | | |
|---|---|---|---|---|---|---|---|---|---|
| | Ages 2–3 | Ages 4–5 | Total 2–5 | Ages 6–7 | Ages 8–11 | Total 6–11 | Ages 12–14 | Ages 15–18 | Total 12–18 |
| Comparisons with the mean BSI score | | | | | | | | | |
| Hyperactivity | 9 | 8 | 8 | 7 | 7 | 7 | 7 | 7 | 7 |
| Aggression | 9 | 8 | 8 | 8 | 8 | 8 | 8 | 8 | 8 |
| Conduct Problems | — | — | — | 10 | 10 | 10 | 10 | 9 | 9 |
| Anxiety | 14 | 13 | 14 | 12 | 12 | 12 | 12 | 10 | 11 |
| Depression | 11 | 9 | 10 | 10 | 9 | 10 | 10 | 9 | 9 |
| Somatization | 14 | 12 | 13 | 11 | 11 | 11 | 10 | 12 | 11 |
| Attention Problems | 9 | 7 | 8 | 7 | 7 | 7 | 7 | 7 | 7 |
| Learning Problems | — | — | — | 9 | 10 | 10 | 12 | 10 | 11 |
| Atypicality | 9 | 8 | 9 | 10 | 9 | 9 | 9 | 8 | 9 |
| Withdrawal | 11 | 10 | 11 | 11 | 8 | 9 | 9 | 8 | 9 |
| Comparisons with the mean Adaptive Skills score | | | | | | | | | |
| Adaptability | 7 | 6 | 7 | 7 | 7 | 7 | 7 | 6 | 6 |
| Social Skills | 6 | 6 | 6 | 6 | 6 | 6 | 6 | 5 | 6 |
| Leadership | — | — | — | 9 | 10 | 10 | 9 | 8 | 9 |
| Study Skills | — | — | — | 9 | 9 | 9 | 7 | 6 | 7 |
| Functional Communication | 7 | 7 | 7 | 7 | 7 | 7 | 7 | 6 | 7 |

**Table B.5** PRS: Statistically Significant Differences Between Scale *T* Scores and the Mean *T* Score of the BSI or Adaptive Skills Composite

| Scale | Preschool | | | Child | | | Adolescent | | |
|---|---|---|---|---|---|---|---|---|---|
| | Ages 2–3 | Ages 4–5 | Total 2–5 | Ages 6–7 | Ages 8–11 | Total 6–11 | Ages 12–14 | Ages 15–18 | Total 12–18 |
| Comparisons with the mean BSI score | | | | | | | | | |
| Hyperactivity | 11 | 8 | 10 | 9 | 10 | 9 | 9 | 9 | 9 |
| Aggression | 11 | 10 | 11 | 9 | 11 | 10 | 8 | 8 | 8 |
| Conduct Problems | — | — | — | 11 | 12 | 11 | 10 | 9 | 9 |
| Anxiety | 13 | 13 | 13 | 13 | 12 | 12 | 10 | 10 | 10 |
| Depression | 10 | 9 | 10 | 9 | 9 | 9 | 8 | 7 | 8 |
| Somatization | 12 | 12 | 12 | 12 | 12 | 12 | 11 | 10 | 10 |
| Attention Problems | 11 | 8 | 10 | 8 | 9 | 8 | 8 | 9 | 8 |
| Atypicality | 10 | 8 | 9 | 9 | 10 | 9 | 7 | 7 | 7 |
| Withdrawal | 11 | 9 | 10 | 10 | 10 | 10 | 9 | 9 | 9 |
| Comparisons with the mean Adaptive Skills score | | | | | | | | | |
| Adaptability | 9 | 8 | 9 | 8 | 9 | 8 | 7 | 8 | 7 |
| Social Skills | 8 | 8 | 8 | 7 | 7 | 7 | 7 | 7 | 7 |
| Leadership | — | — | — | 11 | 11 | 11 | 10 | 10 | 10 |
| Activities of Daily Living | 10 | 10 | 10 | 9 | 9 | 9 | 9 | 9 | 9 |
| Functional Communication | 9 | 8 | 8 | 8 | 8 | 8 | 7 | 8 | 8 |

**Table B.6** SRP: Statistically Significant Differences Between Scale *T* Scores and the Mean *T* Score of the ESI

| Scale | Child Ages 8–11 | Adolescent Ages 12–14 | Adolescent Ages 15–18 | Adolescent Total 12–18 | College Ages 18–25 |
|---|---|---|---|---|---|
| Attitude to School | 14 | 14 | 14 | 14 | — |
| Attitude to Teachers | 14 | 14 | 13 | 14 | — |
| Sensation Seeking | — | 14 | 13 | 13 | 12 |
| Atypicality | 13 | 14 | 13 | 13 | 14 |
| Locus of Control | 16 | 15 | 14 | 15 | 14 |
| Social Stress | 11 | 10 | 9 | 10 | 10 |
| Anxiety | 11 | 10 | 8 | 9 | 9 |
| Depression | 11 | 10 | 9 | 9 | 9 |
| Sense of Inadequacy | 13 | 11 | 11 | 11 | 10 |
| Somatization | — | 17 | 14 | 15 | 15 |
| Attention Problems | 14 | 13 | 11 | 12 | 12 |
| Hyperactivity | 14 | 14 | 13 | 13 | 14 |
| Alcohol Abuse | — | — | — | — | 10 |
| School Maladjustment | — | — | — | — | 13 |
| Relations With Parents | 12 | 11 | 11 | 11 | 11 |
| Interpersonal Relations | 14 | 14 | 13 | 14 | 14 |
| Self-Esteem | 12 | 11 | 10 | 11 | 9 |
| Self-Reliance | 13 | 11 | 11 | 11 | 12 |

**Table B.7** TRS: Frequencies of Differences Between Scale *T* Scores and the Mean *T* Score of the BSI or Adaptive Skills Composite

| Scale | Preschool: Ages 2–5 Frequency percentage (%) 25 | 15 | 10 | 5 | 2 | 1 | Child: Ages 6–11 Frequency percentage (%) 25 | 15 | 10 | 5 | 2 | 1 | Adolescent: Ages 12–18 Frequency percentage (%) 25 | 15 | 10 | 5 | 2 | 1 |
|---|---|---|---|---|---|---|---|---|---|---|---|---|---|---|---|---|---|---|
| **Comparisons with the mean BSI score - size of difference, regardless of direction** | | | | | | | | | | | | | | | | | | |
| Hyperactivity | 6 | 8 | 10 | 12 | 15 | 16 | 6 | 8 | 10 | 13 | 17 | 19 | 5 | 7 | 9 | 13 | 17 | 19 |
| Aggression | 5 | 7 | 9 | 12 | 16 | 19 | 6 | 9 | 10 | 13 | 17 | 22 | 5 | 8 | 10 | 14 | 17 | 19 |
| Conduct Problems | — | — | — | — | — | — | 6 | 9 | 11 | 13 | 16 | 19 | 6 | 8 | 11 | 15 | 19 | 22 |
| Anxiety | 9 | 13 | 15 | 18 | 21 | 25 | 10 | 13 | 16 | 20 | 28 | 30 | 9 | 12 | 14 | 18 | 21 | 25 |
| Depression | 7 | 8 | 10 | 12 | 16 | 19 | 5 | 8 | 10 | 14 | 17 | 20 | 5 | 7 | 8 | 11 | 15 | 21 |
| Somatization | 12 | 15 | 17 | 21 | 26 | 29 | 10 | 15 | 19 | 24 | 31 | 36 | 8 | 12 | 15 | 19 | 26 | 32 |
| Attention Problems | 7 | 9 | 10 | 13 | 17 | 19 | 6 | 8 | 10 | 13 | 15 | 17 | 6 | 8 | 10 | 12 | 16 | 19 |
| Learning Problems | — | — | — | — | — | — | 9 | 12 | 15 | 19 | 24 | 26 | 7 | 10 | 12 | 16 | 23 | 26 |
| Atypicality | 6 | 9 | 10 | 12 | 17 | 22 | 6 | 7 | 9 | 12 | 20 | 23 | 5 | 7 | 9 | 11 | 15 | 18 |
| Withdrawal | 7 | 10 | 12 | 15 | 21 | 25 | 7 | 10 | 12 | 14 | 19 | 25 | 7 | 10 | 12 | 14 | 24 | 28 |
| **Comparisons with the mean Adaptive Skills score - size of difference, regardless of direction** | | | | | | | | | | | | | | | | | | |
| Adaptability | 6 | 8 | 9 | 10 | 11 | 14 | 6 | 8 | 10 | 12 | 15 | 16 | 5 | 7 | 8 | 10 | 11 | 14 |
| Social Skills | 5 | 7 | 8 | 9 | 11 | 12 | 6 | 8 | 9 | 11 | 14 | 16 | 5 | 7 | 8 | 9 | 12 | 14 |
| Leadership | — | — | — | — | — | — | 4 | 5 | 6 | 7 | 8 | 9 | 4 | 5 | — | 7 | 8 | 10 |
| Study Skills | — | — | — | — | — | — | 6 | 7 | 8 | 10 | 11 | 12 | 5 | 7 | 8 | 10 | 12 | 13 |
| Functional Communication | 5 | 6 | 8 | 9 | 11 | 12 | 6 | 7 | 8 | 10 | 12 | 13 | 5 | 6 | 7 | 9 | 12 | 14 |

**Table B.8** PRS: Frequencies of Differences Between Scale *T* Scores and the Mean *T* Score of the BSI or Adaptive Skills Composite

| | Preschool: Ages 2–5 | | | | | | Child: Ages 6–11 | | | | | | Adolescent: Ages 12–18 | | | | | |
|---|---|---|---|---|---|---|---|---|---|---|---|---|---|---|---|---|---|---|
| | Frequency percentage (%) | | | | | | Frequency percentage (%) | | | | | | Frequency percentage (%) | | | | | |
| Scale | 25 | 15 | 10 | 5 | 2 | 1 | 25 | 15 | 10 | 5 | 2 | 1 | 25 | 15 | 10 | 5 | 2 | 1 |
| **Comparisons with the mean BSI score - size of difference, regardless of direction** | | | | | | | | | | | | | | | | | | |
| Hyperactivity | 6 | 8 | 9 | 11 | 14 | 16 | 7 | 8 | 10 | 13 | 15 | 17 | 5 | 6 | 8 | 9 | 12 | 16 |
| Aggression | 7 | 8 | 10 | 12 | 15 | 18 | 7 | 9 | 11 | 13 | 18 | 21 | 5 | 7 | 9 | 11 | 15 | 18 |
| Conduct Problems | — | — | — | — | — | — | 7 | 9 | 11 | 14 | 20 | 25 | 6 | 8 | 9 | 13 | 17 | 22 |
| Anxiety | 11 | 13 | 15 | 20 | 25 | 26 | 10 | 13 | 15 | 19 | 23 | 29 | 8 | 10 | 12 | 15 | 19 | 23 |
| Depression | 6 | 8 | 9 | 11 | 14 | 16 | 6 | 8 | 9 | 12 | 16 | 21 | 5 | 6 | 7 | 10 | 12 | 14 |
| Somatization | 9 | 12 | 14 | 17 | 22 | 24 | 11 | 14 | 17 | 19 | 25 | 29 | 9 | 11 | 13 | 16 | 20 | 23 |
| Attention Problems | 7 | 9 | 10 | 12 | 16 | 18 | 7 | 9 | 10 | 12 | 15 | 19 | 7 | 9 | 11 | 14 | 19 | 26 |
| Atypicality | 6 | 8 | 9 | 11 | 14 | 17 | 6 | 7 | 8 | 12 | 17 | 19 | 5 | 6 | 8 | 10 | 13 | 15 |
| Withdrawal | 9 | 12 | 14 | 17 | 22 | 24 | 8 | 11 | 13 | 17 | 21 | 27 | 7 | 10 | 11 | 14 | 17 | 20 |
| **Comparisons with the mean Adaptive Skills score - size of difference, regardless of direction** | | | | | | | | | | | | | | | | | | |
| Adaptability | 8 | 9 | 10 | 12 | 16 | 18 | 5 | 7 | 9 | 11 | 13 | 16 | 6 | 8 | 9 | 11 | 13 | 15 |
| Social Skills | 5 | 7 | 8 | 9 | 11 | 12 | 5 | 7 | 8 | 9 | 12 | 15 | 5 | 7 | 8 | 9 | 12 | 14 |
| Leadership | — | — | — | — | — | — | 5 | 6 | 7 | 8 | 10 | 13 | 5 | 6 | 7 | 9 | 11 | 12 |
| Activities of Daily Living | 8 | 10 | 12 | 15 | 19 | 21 | 6 | 8 | 9 | 11 | 14 | 15 | 6 | 7 | 9 | 11 | 13 | 15 |
| Functional Communication | 5 | 7 | 8 | 10 | 12 | 13 | 5 | 6 | 7 | 9 | 10 | 12 | 5 | 6 | 7 | 9 | 10 | 12 |

**Table B.9** SRP: Frequencies of Differences Between Scale *T* Scores and the Mean *T* Score of the ESI

| | Child: Ages 8–11 | | | | | | Adolescent: Ages 12–18 | | | | | | College: Ages 18–25 | | | | | |
|---|---|---|---|---|---|---|---|---|---|---|---|---|---|---|---|---|---|---|
| | Frequency percentage (%) | | | | | | Frequency percentage (%) | | | | | | Frequency percentage (%) | | | | | |
| Scale | 25 | 15 | 10 | 5 | 2 | 1 | 25 | 15 | 10 | 5 | 2 | 1 | 25 | 15 | 10 | 5 | 2 | 1 |
| **Comparisons with the mean ESI score - size of difference, regardless of direction** | | | | | | | | | | | | | | | | | | |
| Attitude to School | 10 | 13 | 16 | 18 | 28 | 29 | 9 | 11 | 14 | 17 | 22 | 24 | — | — | — | — | — | — |
| Attitude to Teachers | 9 | 12 | 14 | 19 | 23 | 29 | 9 | 12 | 15 | 18 | 23 | 28 | — | — | — | — | — | — |
| Sensation Seeking | — | — | — | — | — | — | 13 | 16 | 19 | 23 | 31 | 34 | 15 | 19 | 22 | 25 | 29 | 33 |
| Atypicality | 8 | 10 | 13 | 15 | 20 | 24 | 8 | 10 | 12 | 16 | 21 | 26 | 9 | 11 | 14 | 18 | 22 | 23 |
| Locus of Control | 7 | 10 | 11 | 14 | 17 | 21 | 7 | 10 | 12 | 16 | 20 | 22 | 7 | 9 | 10 | 13 | 15 | 19 |
| Social Stress | 6 | 7 | 8 | 11 | 13 | 15 | 6 | 8 | 9 | 11 | 14 | 16 | 5 | 7 | 8 | 10 | 11 | 13 |
| Anxiety | 7 | 9 | 11 | 13 | 16 | 19 | 7 | 9 | 11 | 14 | 16 | 18 | 7 | 8 | 10 | 13 | 16 | 18 |
| Depression | 5 | 7 | 8 | 11 | 14 | 15 | 5 | 6 | 7 | 10 | 12 | 14 | 4 | 6 | 7 | 9 | 15 | 20 |
| Sense of Inadequacy | 6 | 8 | 10 | 12 | 15 | 16 | 6 | 7 | 9 | 12 | 14 | 18 | 6 | 7 | 8 | 11 | 15 | 15 |
| Somatization | — | — | — | — | — | — | 8 | 11 | 13 | 18 | 24 | 29 | 9 | 13 | 16 | 21 | 25 | 29 |
| Attention Problems | 9 | 11 | 14 | 17 | 19 | 22 | 9 | 12 | 14 | 17 | 23 | 26 | 9 | 12 | 14 | 18 | 23 | 24 |
| Hyperactivity | 9 | 11 | 13 | 18 | 23 | 31 | 10 | 14 | 17 | 21 | 27 | 29 | 11 | 14 | 17 | 22 | 26 | 29 |
| Alcohol Abuse | — | — | — | — | — | — | — | — | — | — | — | — | 12 | 16 | 18 | 22 | 28 | 30 |
| School Maladjustment | — | — | — | — | — | — | — | — | — | — | — | — | 9 | 11 | 13 | 16 | 21 | 26 |
| Relations With Parents | 9 | 11 | 12 | 16 | 22 | 26 | 9 | 12 | 14 | 17 | 21 | 27 | 10 | 13 | 15 | 20 | 26 | 28 |
| Interpersonal Relations | 7 | 10 | 11 | 14 | 17 | 21 | 7 | 9 | 11 | 14 | 18 | 21 | 8 | 10 | 11 | 15 | 19 | 23 |
| Self-Esteem | 6 | 8 | 10 | 14 | 17 | 18 | 6 | 8 | 9 | 12 | 15 | 18 | 6 | 8 | 9 | 13 | 17 | 18 |
| Self-Reliance | 8 | 11 | 12 | 15 | 18 | 27 | 10 | 13 | 15 | 17 | 22 | 28 | 8 | 12 | 13 | 16 | 22 | 25 |

# Appendix C

## Item Lists

**Table C.1** BASC–3 TRS: Items Belonging to Each Scale

| Scale | Item numbers |
|---|---|
| Hyperactivity | 22, 34, 64, 77, 82, 86, 90, 97, 105 |
| Aggression | 24, 33, 46, 51, 55, 59, 61, 68, 92, 94 |
| Anxiety | 2, 19, 65, 69, 75, 84, 91, 95, 102 |
| Depression | 6, 14, 29, 41, 56, 74, 79, 87, 89 |
| Somatization | 9, 23, 28, 35, 39, 70, 76, 85, 88, 100 |
| Attention Problems | 1, 11, 17, 32, 38, 57, 80 |
| Atypicality | 8, 21, 45, 53, 73, 83, 96, 101 |
| Withdrawal | 18, 37, 47, 52, 63, 71, 103 |
| Adaptability | 3, 5, 36, 40, 43, 48, 98 |
| Social Skills | 7, 12, 26, 42, 66, 81 |
| Functional Communication | 4, 10, 15, 27, 49, 54, 60, 62, 99 |
| Anger Control | 6, 31, 51, 55, 61, 64, 72 |
| Bullying | 13, 43, 55, 77, 86, 92 |
| Developmental Social Disorders | 8, 15, 40, 52, 53, 58, 60, 63, 71, 73, 78, 83, 99, 101, 103, 104 |
| Emotional Self-Control | 6, 16, 19, 30, 51, 56, 64, 79, 87, 89, 94, 97, 98, 102 |
| Executive Functioning | 1, 11, 20, 27, 31, 34, 38, 51, 56, 60, 64, 79, 80, 86, 94, 97, 98 |
| Negative Emotionality | 6, 14, 44, 56, 74, 79, 94, 102 |
| Resiliency | 3, 5, 20, 25, 40, 56 |
| Clinical Probability Index | 11, 15, 21, 27, 38, 43, 52, 53, 60, 64, 78, 80, 83, 96 |
| Functional Impairment Index | 1, 4, 15, 38, 49, 51, 52, 60, 64, 78, 99 |
| Attentional Control Index | 1, 11, 17, 38, 80 |
| Behavioral Control Index | 34, 64, 86, 90, 97 |
| Emotional Control Index | 16, 30, 31, 51, 56, 72, 79, 94 |
| Overall Executive Functioning Index | 1, 11, 16, 17, 30, 31, 34, 38, 51, 56, 64, 72, 79, 80, 86, 90, 94, 97 |

TRS-P

**Table C.1** BASC–3 TRS: Items Belonging to Each Scale *(continued)*

| Scale | Item numbers |
|---|---|
| Hyperactivity | 4, 11, 30, 33, 40, 93, 103, 110, 126, 137, 154 |
| Aggression | 6, 10, 52, 61, 73, 82, 90, 111, 124, 138 |
| Conduct Problems | 23, 35, 43, 48, 70, 85, 121, 135, 149 |
| Anxiety | 8, 15, 26, 54, 68, 79, 83, 106, 112 |
| Depression | 12, 81, 91, 97, 114, 118, 133, 142, 146, 153, 156 |
| Somatization | 34, 56, 76, 80, 95, 105, 131, 134 |
| Attention Problems | 1, 14, 21, 53, 64, 88, 107, 152 |
| Learning Problems | 28, 44, 55, 72, 117, 120, 130, 147 |
| Atypicality | 9, 50, 63, 87, 125, 128, 132, 145, 151 |
| Withdrawal | 16, 37, 62, 96, 98, 115, 123, 144 |
| Adaptability | 3, 20, 24, 38, 42, 47, 59, 67, 69 |
| Social Skills | 5, 19, 31, 45, 104, 113, 116, 127, 141, 150 |
| Leadership | 25, 41, 49, 58, 86, 92, 102 |
| Study Skills | 7, 77, 94, 122, 129, 143, 148, 155 |
| Functional Communication | 2, 22, 32, 39, 60, 71, 74, 89, 119, 139 |
| Anger Control | 6, 61, 65, 75, 93, 111, 142 |
| Bullying | 35, 36, 48, 57, 61, 90, 109, 121, 124 |
| Developmental Social Disorders | 2, 16, 38, 50, 62, 63, 66, 71, 89, 100, 115, 127, 132, 136, 144 |
| Emotional Self-Control | 6, 15, 29, 51, 67, 69, 81, 91, 93, 111, 142, 154 |
| Executive Functioning | 1, 6, 14, 17, 18, 33, 39, 40, 51, 55, 58, 69, 86, 93, 103, 107, 108, 111, 122, 126, 142, 143, 148, 154 |
| Negative Emotionality | 6, 20, 46, 78, 91, 118, 133, 142 |
| Resiliency | 3, 17, 38, 39, 41, 42, 47, 49, 67, 84, 92, 101, 140 |
| ADHD Probability Index | 4, 6, 13, 14, 22, 25, 41, 53, 64, 70, 88, 91, 107, 111, 125, 135, 136, 139, 143, 148, 154 |
| EBD Probability Index | 10, 12, 23, 35, 52, 57, 61, 62, 70, 73, 85, 90, 91, 111, 118, 125, 133, 138, 139, 148, 154, 156 |
| Autism Probability Index | 5, 9, 45, 55, 58, 60, 62, 63, 86, 87, 91, 92, 100, 106, 108, 111, 119, 132, 141, 145, 151, 154 |
| Functional Impairment Index | 1, 2, 5, 15, 22, 23, 28, 32, 39, 45, 50, 53, 60, 62, 69, 71, 72, 78, 80, 81, 83, 86, 89, 91, 93, 94, 96, 98, 103, 105, 106, 111, 117, 120, 125, 126, 128, 130, 139, 143, 144, 146, 147, 155 |
| Problem-Solving Index | 17, 18, 39, 55, 58, 86, 108, 143, 148 |
| Attentional Control Index | 1, 14, 21, 53, 64, 88, 107, 152 |
| Behavioral Control Index | 30, 33, 40, 93, 103, 126, 154 |
| Emotional Control Index | 6, 29, 51, 69, 75, 111, 142 |
| Overall Executive Functioning Index | 1, 6, 14, 17, 18, 21, 29, 30, 33, 39, 40, 51, 53, 55, 58, 64, 69, 75, 86, 88, 93, 103, 107, 108, 111, 126, 142, 143, 148, 152, 154 |

TRS-C

**Table C.1** BASC–3 TRS: Items Belonging to Each Scale *(continued)*

| Scale | Item numbers |
|---|---|
| Hyperactivity | 4, 17, 32, 41, 89, 99, 108, 112, 123, 126, 140 |
| Aggression | 5, 11, 52, 61, 70, 77, 86, 110, 125, 141, 148 |
| Conduct Problems | 24, 34, 44, 60, 68, 113, 122, 137, 157, 160 |
| Anxiety | 10, 15, 22, 67, 74, 78, 103, 114, 151 |
| Depression | 8, 23, 56, 72, 87, 93, 116, 135, 138, 149, 153, 162 |
| Somatization | 33, 47, 54, 79, 120, 132, 145 |
| Attention Problems | 2, 14, 38, 53, 64, 96, 105, 124, 144, 161 |
| Learning Problems | 13, 48, 94, 111, 115, 118, 150, 155 |
| Atypicality | 12, 50, 63, 80, 82, 90, 129, 134, 136, 159 |
| Withdrawal | 3, 9, 62, 91, 95, 102, 127, 131 |
| Adaptability | 1, 20, 37, 43, 46, 57, 73, 119 |
| Social Skills | 6, 18, 25, 29, 45, 107, 128, 146, 158, 164 |
| Leadership | 28, 42, 49, 81, 88, 98, 154 |
| Study Skills | 7, 31, 58, 92, 100, 104, 121, 130, 147, 156, 165 |
| Functional Communication | 30, 36, 40, 59, 69, 85, 117, 142, 152 |
| Anger Control | 5, 8, 61, 65, 76, 89, 110 |
| Bullying | 34, 35, 55, 61, 86, 109, 125, 148, 157 |
| Developmental Social Disorders | 40, 50, 62, 63, 66, 69, 84, 85, 102, 119, 127, 131, 134, 139, 146 |
| Emotional Self-Control | 5, 8, 15, 26, 51, 72, 87, 89, 110, 123 |
| Executive Functioning | 2, 5, 8, 14, 16, 21, 36, 48, 51, 53, 58, 65, 71, 73, 81, 83, 89, 99, 105, 106, 110, 112, 123, 133, 144, 154, 156 |
| Negative Emotionality | 5, 8, 19, 23, 39, 46, 77, 87, 93 |
| Resiliency | 16, 28, 36, 37, 43, 49, 73, 75, 88, 97, 119, 143 |
| ADHD Probability Index | 4, 14, 32, 53, 92, 100, 104, 106, 117, 140 |
| EBD Probability Index | 19, 23, 35, 39, 43, 44, 46, 48, 51, 52, 55, 61, 65, 68, 80, 86, 93, 103, 110, 122, 123, 141, 147, 148, 157, 161 |
| Autism Probability Index | 10, 42, 66, 81, 82, 85, 88, 90, 102, 114, 127, 134, 136, 164 |
| Functional Impairment Index | 2, 3, 6, 15, 24, 30, 31, 36, 39, 40, 45, 50, 53, 56, 59, 62, 67, 69, 72, 78, 81, 85, 87, 89, 91, 94, 95, 99, 100, 103, 110, 111, 112, 117, 118, 120, 121, 129, 131, 142, 147, 150, 152, 155 |
| Problem-Solving Index | 16, 21, 48, 71, 81, 83, 106, 133, 154, 156 |
| Attentional Control Index | 2, 14, 38, 53, 64, 96, 105, 124, 144, 161 |
| Behavioral Control Index | 5, 17, 89, 99, 112, 123 |
| Emotional Control Index | 8, 26, 51, 65, 76, 110 |
| Overall Executive Functioning Index | 2, 5, 8, 14, 16, 17, 21, 26, 38, 48, 51, 53, 64, 65, 71, 76, 81, 83, 89, 96, 99, 105, 106, 110, 112, 123, 124, 133, 144, 154, 156, 161 |

TRS-A

**Table C.2** BASC–3 PRS: Items Belonging to Each Scale

| Scale | Item numbers |
|-------|--------------|
| Hyperactivity | 3, 13, 25, 36, 74, 102, 111, 117, 121, 133, 137 |
| Aggression | 9, 20, 43, 63, 84, 96, 99, 119 |
| Anxiety | 10, 21, 26, 37, 46, 60, 93, 104, 128, 129, 138 |
| Depression | 14, 23, 30, 35, 52, 71, 72, 80, 90, 98, 105 |
| Somatization | 6, 18, 24, 48, 56, 68, 87, 97, 106, 110, 122, 126, 132 |
| Attention Problems | 16, 28, 38, 59, 78, 92, 115 |
| Atypicality | 34, 41, 58, 76, 94, 101, 118, 127, 131, 135 |
| Withdrawal | 19, 31, 40, 75, 82, 86, 91, 108, 125, 130, 134, 136 |
| Adaptability | 1, 8, 17, 32, 42, 62, 79, 88, 116 |
| Social Skills | 2, 4, 11, 22, 53, 67, 100, 107, 123 |
| Activities of Daily Living | 15, 33, 39, 45, 47, 54, 57 |
| Functional Communication | 12, 51, 64, 66, 73, 81, 95, 103, 120, 124, 139 |
| Anger Control | 27, 35, 42, 63, 98, 99, 109, 111 |
| Bullying | 43, 49, 63, 71, 96 |
| Developmental Social Disorders | 17, 29, 31, 41, 50, 58, 66, 73, 88, 91, 113, 118, 120, 127, 131, 134, 139 |
| Emotional Self-Control | 10, 30, 35, 52, 80, 85, 98, 111, 133 |
| Executive Functioning | 2, 13, 16, 17, 25, 27, 28, 30, 35, 36, 38, 42, 52, 62, 73, 78, 81, 83, 92, 99, 111, 121, 133 |
| Negative Emotionality | 30, 52, 69, 90, 98, 99 |
| Resiliency | 7, 8, 17, 52, 75, 79, 83, 88, 100 |
| Clinical Probability Index | 2, 16, 17, 47, 52, 53, 78, 101, 111, 115, 117, 118, 120, 124, 130, 133 |
| Functional Impairment Index | 10, 11, 15, 16, 22, 25, 26, 28, 30, 35, 36, 40, 42, 47, 57, 66, 69, 73, 75, 80, 81, 82, 91, 100, 101, 111, 124, 130, 139 |
| Attentional Control Index | 16, 28, 38, 59, 78, 92, 115 |
| Behavioral Control Index | 13, 25, 36, 111, 121, 133 |
| Emotional Control Index | 27, 30, 35, 52, 85, 99, 109 |
| Overall Executive Functioning Index | 13, 16, 25, 27, 28, 30, 35, 36, 38, 52, 59, 78, 85, 92, 99, 109, 111, 115, 121, 133 |

PRS-P

**Table C.2** BASC–3 PRS: Items Belonging to Each Scale *(continued)*

| Scale | Item numbers |
|---|---|
| Hyperactivity | 24, 32, 42, 73, 93, 99, 114, 151, 159, 166, 172 |
| Aggression | 35, 41, 50, 59, 98, 106, 117, 121, 146 |
| Conduct Problems | 3, 7, 23, 43, 55, 68, 74, 141, 144, 164 |
| Anxiety | 9, 21, 31, 38, 54, 67, 84, 104, 107, 112, 128, 136, 147, 160 |
| Depression | 4, 34, 40, 45, 52, 60, 80, 100, 110, 116, 119, 124, 129 |
| Somatization | 6, 15, 20, 39, 49, 57, 63, 78, 105, 118, 132, 161 |
| Attention Problems | 1, 11, 28, 83, 91, 127, 175 |
| Atypicality | 12, 17, 58, 81, 88, 115, 122, 125, 145, 152, 157, 158, 167, 171 |
| Withdrawal | 48, 87, 96, 101, 111, 126, 156, 163, 170 |
| Adaptability | 47, 86, 92, 103, 130, 133, 135, 143 |
| Social Skills | 2, 14, 53, 77, 97, 113, 134, 137, 154, 174 |
| Leadership | 18, 29, 62, 120, 142, 155, 173 |
| Activities of Daily Living | 22, 27, 37, 46, 64, 66, 90, 149, 153 |
| Functional Communication | 5, 33, 56, 61, 69, 76, 85, 102, 109, 148, 165, 168 |
| Anger Control | 26, 35, 40, 41, 70, 73, 119, 121, 135 |
| Bullying | 35, 43, 50, 55, 59, 94, 106, 108, 117, 150 |
| Developmental Social Disorders | 5, 10, 30, 47, 53, 58, 76, 103, 111, 115, 125, 126, 139, 148, 152, 157, 165, 167, 170 |
| Emotional Self-Control | 4, 21, 34, 40, 44, 73, 119, 138, 147, 166 |
| Executive Functioning | 1, 11, 16, 24, 37, 44, 56, 71, 73, 91, 92, 95, 120, 121, 135, 142, 149, 159, 166, 175 |
| Negative Emotionality | 4, 25, 45, 52, 79, 110, 119, 121 |
| Resiliency | 8, 18, 56, 62, 92, 95, 103, 123, 169 |
| ADHD Probability Index | 7, 11, 24, 32, 83, 90, 91, 149, 151, 166, 175 |
| EBD Probability Index | 4, 18, 23, 35, 40, 43, 47, 52, 53, 55, 59, 60, 68, 74, 79, 87, 94, 98, 106, 117, 119, 121, 124, 134, 137, 138, 144, 150, 164, 172 |
| Autism Probability Index | 17, 30, 48, 81, 96, 111, 125, 126, 155, 158, 163, 168, 170 |
| Functional Impairment Index | 1, 4, 5, 7, 9, 11, 12, 15, 22, 24, 27, 33, 34, 38, 40, 43, 48, 56, 61, 64, 66, 69, 73, 76, 79, 81, 85, 87, 96, 100, 111, 122, 135, 137, 142, 147, 148, 149, 153, 163, 165, 168, 172, 174 |
| Problem-Solving Index | 16, 37, 56, 71, 95, 120, 142, 149 |
| Attentional Control Index | 1, 11, 28, 83, 91, 127, 175 |
| Behavioral Control Index | 24, 42, 73, 121, 159, 166 |
| Emotional Control Index | 44, 70, 135, 138 |
| Overall Executive Functioning Index | 1, 11, 16, 24, 28, 37, 42, 44, 56, 70, 71, 73, 83, 91, 95, 120, 121, 127, 135, 138, 142, 149, 159, 166, 175 |

PRS-C

**Table C.2** BASC–3 PRS: Items Belonging to Each Scale *(continued)*

| Scale | Item numbers |
|---|---|
| Hyperactivity | 10, 14, 23, 53, 107, 114, 130, 172 |
| Aggression | 28, 37, 55, 66, 69, 93, 103, 115, 146, 164 |
| Conduct Problems | 5, 22, 40, 52, 56, 61, 68, 76, 85, 98, 122, 138, 157, 162 |
| Anxiety | 4, 20, 32, 92, 99, 104, 120, 135, 141, 152, 153, 163, 166 |
| Depression | 3, 19, 35, 41, 50, 77, 89, 94, 102, 110, 117, 121, 140 |
| Somatization | 6, 18, 31, 42, 47, 58, 71, 88, 111, 154 |
| Attention Problems | 1, 9, 27, 43, 79, 87, 95, 119, 123 |
| Atypicality | 11, 25, 39, 84, 97, 108, 116, 139, 145, 150, 169 |
| Withdrawal | 33, 46, 83, 113, 127, 144, 149, 165 |
| Adaptability | 7, 54, 72, 82, 124, 129, 137, 156 |
| Social Skills | 2, 13, 51, 73, 91, 106, 128, 131, 147, 170 |
| Leadership | 17, 29, 57, 67, 132, 136, 148, 171 |
| Activities of Daily Living | 21, 36, 45, 60, 80, 86, 143, 151 |
| Functional Communication | 8, 34, 62, 70, 78, 81, 90, 101, 105, 133, 142, 158 |
| Anger Control | 26, 37, 41, 63, 66, 115, 130, 140 |
| Bullying | 28, 55, 66, 69, 85, 93, 100, 138, 146, 160, 167 |
| Developmental Social Disorders | 30, 33, 38, 51, 70, 81, 97, 108, 113, 124, 129, 142, 144, 145, 150, 156, 158, 159 |
| Emotional Self-Control | 3, 20, 32, 41, 44, 48, 53, 54, 89, 130, 140, 141 |
| Executive Functioning | 1, 9, 10, 14, 15, 27, 36, 53, 54, 64, 72, 75, 87, 107, 112, 115, 123, 130, 133, 136, 168, 173 |
| Negative Emotionality | 3, 16, 35, 50, 74, 76, 102, 115, 140 |
| Resiliency | 17, 54, 57, 67, 72, 109, 124, 126, 132, 133, 156, 161, 173 |
| ADHD Probability Index | 43, 67, 79, 87, 123, 124, 136, 143, 172 |
| EBD Probability Index | 2, 5, 13, 15, 26, 37, 41, 44, 53, 63, 66, 69, 85, 102, 115, 122, 128, 130, 164, 170 |
| Autism Probability Index | 25, 30, 38, 46, 51, 57, 70, 73, 81, 101, 108, 113, 124, 131, 144, 145, 165, 171 |
| Functional Impairment Index | 1, 3, 4, 5, 10, 21, 27, 32, 34, 36, 39, 41, 42, 46, 60, 62, 70, 74, 78, 80, 83, 85, 89, 90, 94, 105, 113, 116, 127, 130, 131, 133, 135, 136, 142, 143, 151, 158, 163, 165, 170 |
| Problem-Solving Index | 15, 36, 64, 75, 112, 133, 136, 168, 173 |
| Attentional Control Index | 1, 9, 27, 43, 79, 87, 95, 119, 123 |
| Behavioral Control Index | 10, 14, 53, 107, 115, 130, 172 |
| Emotional Control Index | 44, 48, 54, 63 |
| Overall Executive Functioning Index | 1, 9, 10, 14, 15, 27, 36, 43, 44, 48, 53, 54, 63, 64, 75, 79, 87, 95, 107, 112, 115, 119, 123, 130, 133, 136, 168, 172, 173 |

PRS-A

**Table C.3** BASC–3 SRP: Items Belonging to Each Scale

| | Scale | Item numbers |
|---|---|---|
| **SRP-C** | Attitude to School | 5, 16, 21, 70, 77, 98, 119, 131 |
| | Attitude to Teachers | 9, 47, 67, 80, 97, 110, 134 |
| | Atypicality | 13, 34, 46, 61, 69, 79, 88, 92, 102, 116 |
| | Locus of Control | 20, 31, 37, 42, 96, 111, 130, 133 |
| | Social Stress | 4, 44, 52, 59, 87, 99, 109, 112, 121 |
| | Anxiety | 27, 49, 65, 76, 83, 85, 91, 104, 118, 125, 136 |
| | Depression | 7, 14, 25, 38, 55, 62, 81, 94, 114, 129 |
| | Sense of Inadequacy | 8, 54, 63, 68, 78, 90, 108, 124 |
| | Attention Problems | 12, 28, 40, 53, 73, 103, 113, 122, 132 |
| | Hyperactivity | 1, 51, 71, 75, 86, 89, 106, 115 |
| | Relations With Parents | 45, 50, 56, 60, 74, 82, 105, 120, 135, 137 |
| | Interpersonal Relations | 10, 18, 35, 43, 57, 66, 95, 127 |
| | Self-Esteem | 3, 26, 33, 48, 84, 101, 123 |
| | Self-Reliance | 23, 58, 64, 72, 93, 117, 128 |
| | Functional Impairment Index | 1, 18, 20, 28, 40, 49, 51, 53, 54, 62, 66, 68, 86, 89, 93, 99, 103, 116, 119, 124 |
| **SRP-A** | Attitude to School | 5, 20, 87, 101, 107, 150, 162, 184 |
| | Attitude to Teachers | 6, 22, 64, 92, 130, 152, 159, 170, 175 |
| | Sensation Seeking | 31, 73, 81, 115, 127, 155, 172, 185, 188 |
| | Atypicality | 14, 68, 76, 91, 118, 125, 142, 156, 158, 164 |
| | Locus of Control | 12, 35, 41, 48, 102, 165, 180, 182 |
| | Social Stress | 4, 24, 80, 88, 108, 116, 123, 136, 144, 151, 178 |
| | Anxiety | 32, 44, 58, 65, 75, 83, 100, 121, 138, 146, 153, 161, 183 |
| | Depression | 25, 40, 46, 50, 55, 70, 96, 124, 134, 167, 173, 179 |
| | Sense of Inadequacy | 23, 36, 45, 53, 57, 60, 72, 77, 126, 135, 141, 147 |
| | Somatization | 11, 18, 43, 56, 62, 78, 111 |
| | Attention Problems | 9, 19, 34, 90, 95, 122, 148, 169 |
| | Hyperactivity | 67, 86, 97, 105, 117, 140, 176, 181 |
| | Relations With Parents | 1, 61, 66, 89, 103, 109, 137, 145, 157, 177, 187 |
| | Interpersonal Relations | 8, 29, 52, 74, 84, 93, 128, 163, 189 |
| | Self-Esteem | 3, 26, 37, 99, 110, 131, 168 |
| | Self-Reliance | 10, 63, 71, 85, 112, 120, 129, 133, 171 |
| | Anger Control | 68, 69, 75, 79, 116, 139, 165, 166, 174, 180 |
| | Ego Strength | 3, 27, 99, 128, 154, 163, 168, 177 |
| | Mania | 82, 94, 97, 114, 132, 149, 156, 158, 160, 181 |
| | Test Anxiety | 16, 28, 39, 72, 77, 104, 119, 143 |
| | Functional Impairment Index | 9, 11, 32, 34, 40, 46, 52, 56, 60, 63, 72, 74, 77, 90, 96, 97, 100, 108, 118, 119, 122, 126, 132, 138, 140, 156, 162, 171 |

**Table C.3** BASC–3 SRP: Items Belonging to Each Scale *(continued)*

| Scale | Item numbers |
|---|---|
| Atypicality | 15, 68, 73, 92, 104, 124, 134, 150, 165, 172 |
| Locus of Control | 4, 30, 37, 50, 83, 97, 137, 147, 169 |
| Social Stress | 3, 11, 31, 48, 84, 102, 113, 132, 159, 166, 190 |
| Anxiety | 14, 26, 40, 58, 62, 98, 119, 125, 136, 156, 160, 177, 183 |
| Depression | 6, 22, 34, 43, 49, 82, 96, 116, 141, 158, 167, 185 |
| Sense of Inadequacy | 27, 33, 42, 52, 66, 105, 122, 129, 155, 176, 180 |
| Somatization | 16, 24, 35, 53, 88, 106, 163 |
| Attention Problems | 9, 19, 38, 81, 115, 127, 148, 164, 187 |
| Hyperactivity | 67, 77, 90, 109, 146, 168, 179 |
| Sensation Seeking | 18, 39, 47, 70, 101, 112, 126, 143, 152, 171, 184 |
| Alcohol Abuse | 21, 65, 74, 79, 91, 94, 103, 118, 123, 130, 138, 144, 149, 192 |
| School Maladjustment | 2, 13, 28, 44, 51, 72, 89, 99, 110, 142, 170 |
| Relations With Parents | 20, 64, 69, 78, 87, 93, 111, 121, 133, 153, 178 |
| Interpersonal Relations | 8, 46, 71, 120, 128, 157, 173, 189 |
| Self-Esteem | 1, 7, 55, 60, 100, 174, 188 |
| Self-Reliance | 10, 61, 76, 107, 131, 161, 182, 191 |
| Anger Control | 59, 62, 63, 68, 135, 147, 162, 169, 175 |
| Ego Strength | 1, 29, 60, 87, 120, 140, 158, 188 |
| Mania | 75, 83, 95, 108, 109, 117, 124, 139, 151, 165, 168 |
| Test Anxiety | 23, 54, 66, 80, 85, 110, 114, 129 |

SRP-COL

# Index

## A

# B

# C

---

# D

# E

# F

development of  87
*F* Index  22, 42, 66
interpretation of  47, 60–62
*L* Index  67
multiple responses  *See* Unscorable responses
omitted  *See* Unscorable responses
standardized Amos loadings  88, 89, 139, 192
unscorable  *See* Unscorable responses
*V* Index  68

# L

LD  *See* Specific learning disorder
Leadership scale  51, 53, 57, 58
Learning Problems scale  41, 48, 50, 57
*L* Index  20, 22, 67, 68, 103, 104
    development of  20, 67
    interpretation of  22, 67
    items  67
    scoring  22
Locus of Control scale  74, 77, 82

# M

Male norms  *See* Norms, male
Mania scale  80, 81
Manifestation determination  9, 54
Minnesota Multiphasic Personality Inventory-2-Restructured Form (MMPI-2-RF)  260
Minnesota Multiphasic Personality Inventory-Adolescent (MMPI-A)  256
MMPI-A  *See* Minnesota Multiphasic Personality Inventory-Adolescent
MMPI-2-RF  *See* Minnesota Multiphasic Personality Inventory-2-Restructured Form
Modification index (MI)  88, 139, 192, 240
Multiple norms  *See* Norms, multiple

# N

Negative Emotionality scale  54, 55
Normative scores  16
Norms
    clinical  *See* Clinical norms
    female  17
    general  *See* General norms
    male  17
    multiple  19
Norm sample  106–112
    choice of  16–19
Norm tables  *See* Appendix A
    using  24

# O

Omitted items  *See* Unscorable responses

# P

# Q

# R